A HILLFORT THROUGH TIME

A hillfort through time: excavations at Rathgall, Co. Wicklow

Barry Raftery
and
Katharina Becker

Wordwell

First published in 2025
Wordwell Ltd
Unit 9, 78 Furze Road, Sandyford Industrial Estate, Dublin 18
www.wordwellbooks.com

Cover image—An Ráth Gheal, Rathgall Hillfort (Darren Doyle, Spéirview Ireland).
Frontispiece—Finds from Rathgall.

ISBN 978-1-913934-77-4

British Library Cataloguing-in-Publication Data.
A catalogue record for this book is available from the British Library.

Typeset in Ireland by Wordwell Ltd
Copy-editor: Emer Condit
Cover design and artwork: Wordwell Ltd
Printed by SprintBooks, Dublin

The publisher and authors would like to acknowledge the generous contributions made by:

University College Dublin
Ollscoil na hÉireann National University of Ireland
NMS National Monuments Service
UCC University College Cork, Ireland
Acadamh Ríoga na hÉireann Royal Irish Academy
Cill Mhantáin
OPW Office of Public Works
Comhairle Contae Cheatharlach Carlow County Council
Funded by An Chomhairle Oidhreachta The Heritage Council

CONTENTS

LIST OF FIGURES

CHAPTER 3

CHAPTER 6

CHAPTER 7

LIST OF TABLES

PREFACE

This publication presents the excavations at Rathgall, Rath East, Co. Wicklow, conducted by Barry Raftery, retired Professor of Celtic Archaeology at University College Dublin. Raftery published aspects of the site, primarily in the 1970s (Raftery 1970a; 1971b 1972a; 1972b; 1973a; 1973b; 1975; 1976; 2004; Raftery and Henderson 1987). The site was excavated under three licences: E84 covered the work on the summit of the hill and the cuttings extending southwards through the ramparts; E100 covered the excavation of the Z cuttings south of the enclosures; and E4394 covered the re-excavation of Raftery's cutting through Ramparts 2 and 3 in 2011, directed by Matt Seaver (Chapter 2, section 2.8) as part of the OPW's reinstatement work on the site.

Raftery was working on a comprehensive account of the site and led extensive phases of post-excavation analysis between the time of excavation and 2010, but fell ill and passed away before he could finalise the publication or integrate the results of the specialist analyses. The present volume aims to present his work and to integrate it with these new data, augmented and expanded in a final phase of post-excavation analysis conducted between 2010 and 2016. This included the finalisation and integration of site drawings and photographs. The photographic and, most importantly, finds archives were digitised, which opened up new possibilities for contextual and spatial analysis. In addition, some new data were generated which add greatly to our understanding of the site, including a series of new radiocarbon dates and their analysis and modelling. The re-excavation of parts of Raftery's Cutting X through Ramparts 2 and 3 and a geophysical survey of the site, both conducted in 2011, provide a context for the excavated remains.

Raftery had compiled a stratigraphic account of the site, which is here presented with editorial changes and comments, based on the interrogation of stratigraphic information contained in the drawings and photographic records. A strategic decision was made early in the process of work on this book to preserve the site director's voice, his thoughts and his recollections of the site as much as possible.

Where conflicts with new understandings of the site archive or its interpretation are noted, these are highlighted—variably flagged in editorial comments prefacing Raftery's text, in footnotes or by reference to other sections of the book. For ease of navigation, editorial comments that run alongside Raftery's narrative are presented in italics.

This approach respects the irreplaceable nature of the firsthand observation of the excavator while helping the reader to understand where new data and new understanding change the interpretation of the site, its features and sequence. The stratigraphic report in Chapter 2 should be read in close relation to its discussion in the following chapters.

The same approach is carried through into the chronology and discussion chapters, where Raftery's thinking about various issues is juxtaposed with the co-author's reinterpretation, allowing the reader to follow the different arguments and paths by which they were reached. This transparency allows Raftery's voice to be presented as authentically as possible, while at the same time presenting an alternative vision of the site that can incorporate new data and information that has come to light in the meantime.

An effort was made to present the finds and sample archive in a comprehensive manner so that the book can be used as a resource for further research on the site. Owing to the large number of recorded contexts and finds, however, some elements of this project are presented as digitally accessible appendices that can be accessed in the Digital Repository of Ireland (dri.ie). This includes the finds database, with its more than 10,000 entries, and allows, for example, the accessing of the full pottery catalogue (Chapter 3). Full versions of specialists' reports are also presented here. The finds archive is available for consultation in the National Museum of Ireland, and the paper and digital archive has been submitted to the National Monuments Service.

Katharina Becker

ACKNOWLEDGEMENTS

I would like to thank the many individuals and institutions who have made this publication possible. The commitment of many of the specialists to the project over the 50 years of its history reflects well not only on their loyalty but also on the person of Barry Raftery, whose own acknowledgements can be found on page 7. I am grateful both to them and to those who came on board later in the process, most of them giving their time and expertise freely.

Various stages of the preparation of the publication were over the years supported financially by the Royal Irish Academy, the Office of Public Works, the National Monuments Service, the Heritage Council, Wicklow County Council, the National University of Ireland publication fund, University College Dublin, University College Cork and Carlow County Council, importantly providing not only for the preparation of the publication but also of the archive for submission to the respective national holding institutions through the Archaeology Legacy Grant Scheme administered through the Standing Committee of the Royal Irish Academy, led by Joanna Brück in UCD and Conor McDermott, and receiving additional funding from the School of Archaeology in UCD. The open access publication was made possible by additional funding from Wicklow County Council. Significant contributions were made by Joanne Gaffrey, with her dedicated and meticulous work on the analysis, recording and organisation of the archive. Deirdre Kelly and Martha Revelle contributed to the preparation of the archives and artefacts as part of the recent work funded by the Royal Irish Academy and the School of Archaeology in UCD. Rob Sands integrated the old excavation grid with the GIS and produced the find plots. I also thank John Coles, Mary Cahill, Ian Armit, Stuart

Conor McHale, Barry Raftery and Nuala Raftery at the wedding of Susannah Kelly and Conor McHale.

Needham, Ian Ralston, Conor Newman, Julian Henderson, Andy Halpin, Anna Brindley, Jan Lanting, Ian Colquhoun, Jim Mallory, Emily Fioccoprile, Jo McKenzie, Paul Mullarkey, James Eogan, Roland Schwab, Adam Gwilt, Rose Cleary, Dirk Brandherm, Brendan O'Connor, Fionnuala Parnell, Tim Champion, Joanna Brück, Pete Marshall, William O'Brien, Nick Hogan, Giulia Gianella, M. Becker and Alison Sheridan, as well as the Discovery Programme—especially Anthony Corns and Rob Shaw—for providing their topographical survey model of the site. I thank the National Museum of Ireland for their support and for providing the image of the Milmorane bead. I am grateful to Matthew Seaver, Joanne Gaffrey, Niall Colfer, , Conor McDermott and Dr Rob Sands for their support of the 2011 excavation; to the Office of Public Works for on-site facilities; to Tommy Roche, Liam Lawlor and Mick Doyle of the OPW Kilkenny Depot for all their help on site; to Thomas Cummins; and to Maeve O'Callaghan, National Monuments Service, for overseeing the implementation of the Ministerial Consent. I thank the local community around Rathgall for their interest, and particularly Patrick Keogh, Rathwood, for his hospitality to the excavation team. The pollen work was funded by the Royal Irish Academy's Archaeological Research Fund 2006 and thanks are due to Willy Adam for assistance with fieldwork. Since 2015 my work on the project has been conducted under my employment in UCD and I am grateful to Professor William O'Brien for facilitating this.

The drawings are by Ursula Mattenberger, Conor McHale, Spark of Ink, Sara Nylund and Conor McDermott, and the artefact photography by John Sunderland, Albert Glaholm and David Jenning. I am grateful to the academic readers and referees John Coles, Ian Ralston, William O'Brien, Jim Mallory and Stuart Needham for their critical reviews and support. Sincere thanks to Emer Condit for her thorough copy-editing and to Nick Maxwell for layout, setting and his endless patience and constant support to Barry Raftery in bringing the publication to completion.

I am especially grateful to Conor McDermott, who contributed to and supported the project throughout its lifetime. He contributed to the production and editing of figures in his own time, the management of the project and related applications and budgets, and provided advice and moral support at every juncture, helping the project to overcome various hurdles. Without his generous and unfailing support in sharing his expertise and knowledge this book would not have appeared and it is testament not only to his collegiality but also to his friendship and loyalty to Barry Raftery.

I would particularly like to thank Gabriel Cooney for his support and guidance and for making this publication possible, as well as dedicated proofreading. I am grateful to Nuala Raftery for her confidence and support. Most of all, I would like to thank Barry Raftery for entrusting me with his excavation.

Katharina Becker

FOREWORD

It was a matter of great regret to the late Professor Barry Raftery that he had not been able, amongst a myriad of other commitments and responsibilities in and beyond UCD, to see his important field project at Rathgall to completion through its final publication. The present volume succeeds in conveying not only Barry's own research and thoughts on this important project but also the outcomes of further programmes of work—some of which are underscored by advances in methods that Barry could hardly have dreamt of as he began excavation at Rathgall in the late 1960s. There is here a happy and informative juxtaposition of Barry's own perspectives, reinterpretations of the record and additional results, including from geophysical survey of the neighbouring hillfort at Knockeen and from renewed selective examination of the enveloping works at Rathgall. Melded together, they furnish an excellent overview of what has been achieved at this key site to the considerable benefit, in particular, of later Irish prehistory. The book that you are holding is thus a testimony to the work not only of Barry and his team—in the field and subsequently—but also of a number of colleagues who have revisited, reassessed and extended elements of the remarkable discoveries which were initially unearthed at Rathgall some 50 years ago and promptly disseminated in *Antiquity*. These outcomes have been drawn together into the following substantial chapters, skilfully overseen by Dr Katharina Becker.

The investigation of Rathgall was and is a significant building block in the developing understanding of hillforts as a site category in Ireland, a field to which Barry Raftery made major contributions from the late 1960s. That period, and research extending over the succeeding decades, marked a new appreciation of these monuments, expertly summarised in the 1990s in Chapter 3 of *Pagan Celtic Ireland*. Barry had offered a series of general statements on the hillforts of Ireland from the outset of his career in the Department of Archaeology at University College Dublin, developing these initially through his UCD Master's dissertation and beginning in print with his 1972 paper arising from the Council for British Archaeology conference on *The Iron Age in the Irish Sea Province*; these provided key underpinnings of the wider settlement context to the Rathgall fieldwork. Something of the excitement of those days is apparent in the burgeoning numbers of hillforts known to (and classified by) Barry during these years—approaching 50 when the aforementioned paper appeared in 1972 and increasing by a further ten instances by the time that the substantial and appetite-whetting interim account on Rathgall was published as Chapter 16 in Dennis Harding's edited *Hillforts: later prehistoric earthworks in Britain and Ireland* in 1976. Since then, totals have continued to increase, to *c.* 125 in recent assessments: these numbers still include inland but not coastal promontory forts, thus remaining true to the classificatory scheme that Barry had developed and refined.

Rathgall remains the most substantially excavated hillfort in County Wicklow, which can now be more readily appreciated as Ireland's hillfort county *par excellence*, marked more particularly by its series of exceptionally large sites. There are more hillforts over 1ha in extent—or, indeed, over 5ha—per 100km^2 in Wicklow than in any other county in the island of Ireland. Perhaps the most surprising statistic garnered in the recent *Atlas of hillforts in Britain and Ireland* is that County Wicklow is the primary county within Britain and Ireland in terms of the total enclosed area within confirmed hillforts relative to the size of the county. Indeed, Wicklow outranks its nearest competitors—East Lothian and Gloucestershire—by at least 50%. Such numbers—albeit arbitrarily framed in terms of modern administrative subdivisions—serve to emphasise that the present volume is the definitive study of what is known to date about a major site in a very significant area for insular later prehistory as a whole, in Britain as in Ireland.

Barry's recourse to radiocarbon dating to fix Rathgall chronologically was pioneering and was from the outset set alongside the exceptional artefactual record from the site. The acquisition of many more determinations from secure contexts or particular classes of artefact and the application of Bayesian statistics to these mean that it is now clear that the zenith of the activities at Rathgall belongs late in the second millennium BC and lasted some two centuries. There was, however, recurrent recourse to the site, including at times within the Iron Age and in the early and high medieval periods. These, as well as the lesser surviving traces of its utilisation from earlier periods, are all proficiently summarised in the following pages.

As an excavation, Rathgall—like some contemporary fieldwork in Britain—was funded at the outset essentially as a job creation scheme for local unemployed labour. This was a regime very different from the commercial or applied—or, indeed, the well-funded research—projects of more recent decades, and the results achieved are all the more remarkable given the particularly heavy responsibilities that fell on the director and, to a lesser extent, the small numbers of professional assistants and students who could be accommodated on the project.

It is also plain, not least from the images included early in the volume, that Rathgall was a family affair, with Nuala and their daughters engaged on site (and Nuala too in record-keeping and in other ways). The present volume assuredly joins Barry's other great contributions to Ireland's archaeology, from his studies of La Tène material culture in the 1980s by way of his leadership of wetland investigations to *Pagan Celtic Ireland*—in sum, a remarkable legacy of which his family can be justifiably proud. Dr Katharina Becker and the contributors who have brought these important studies on the hillfort at Rathgall to fruition are to be applauded.

Ian Ralston
Abercromby Professor Emeritus of Archaeology, University of Edinburgh

1. THE SITE

1.1 INTRODUCTION

Barry Raftery

This text was written by Raftery in the 1990s. It summarises both the history of research on the site and the background to the undertaking of the excavation itself, revealing not only the research context but also the practical considerations that led to the choice of Rathgall for excavation.

The site of Rathgall, visible in the landscape as a trivallate hillfort, has produced extensive evidence for human activity from the Neolithic into the early modern period. In the Late Bronze Age, in particular, Rathgall was a site of intensive activity. The upstanding archaeological monument describes a large circular area with a maximum diameter of about 320m, enclosing 7.3ha (Figs 1.1a and 1.1b).

The site lies on the Wicklow side of the Wicklow/Carlow county boundary, some 5km east of the town of Tullow, Co. Carlow (Fig. 1.2). It sits on a low, rounded area of granite upland on the periphery of the Wicklow Mountains (see Mandal, this volume), at the southern edge and highest point of a south-west/north-east-running ridge, although its highest point is scarcely more than about 120m above sea level. The steepest slopes of the site of Rathgall itself are to the south, but even here the incline is modest. Elsewhere there are only gradual inclines from the summit; indeed, to the north and east the land is almost flat (Fig. 1.3).

Though rising to no great height, the fort nonetheless dominates the highest land mass in the region and commands a wide view in all directions (Fig. 1.4). The Wicklow Mountains to the north (Fig. 1.1b), the mountains of the Castlecomer Plateau to the west (Fig. 1.4) and the

Fig. 1.1a—Rathgall hillfort, looking east (Con Brogan, National Monuments Service).

Fig. 1.1b—Rathgall hillfort, looking north-east, with the Wicklow Mountains in the background (courtesy of Nick Hogan, UCC).

Fig. 1.2 (left)—Location map of Rathgall.

Blackstairs to the south are all clearly visible. In the immediate foreground, the countryside is undulating on all sides, for the most part grass today, with occasional areas of boggy land in the hollows. Slightly less than 2km away the substantial Derreen River winds south-westwards to the larger Slaney, an important axis of communication in the historic period, which flows, in ever-increasing volume, to the sea at Wexford.

Some 10km to the south-east a long, narrow valley, formed by the Derry River, the Derry Water and the Aughrim and Avoca rivers, stretches continuously through the granite from Clonegall on the Slaney, through Shillelagh, Tinaheely and Aughrim, to Arklow. While the Derry River is a tributary of the Slaney, the Derry Water, Aughrim and Avoca rivers discharge into the sea at Arklow. Thus the Rathgall region had ready access to the sea both to the east and to the south; indeed, the range of finds from the site demonstrates that Rathgall was embedded in far-reaching networks.

The visible monuments on the hill consist of a medieval stone cashel at the centre of three broadly concentric ramparts. Protected as a National Monument (No. 422, WI037-016), the site is open to the public.

For a site so imposing and, indeed, so accessible, the

Fig. 1.3—Looking south towards Rampart 1 (medieval cashel) from Rampart 2 (see Fig.1.15a) (Gabriel Cooney).

Fig. 1.4—Looking west across the medieval cashel (Katharina Becker).

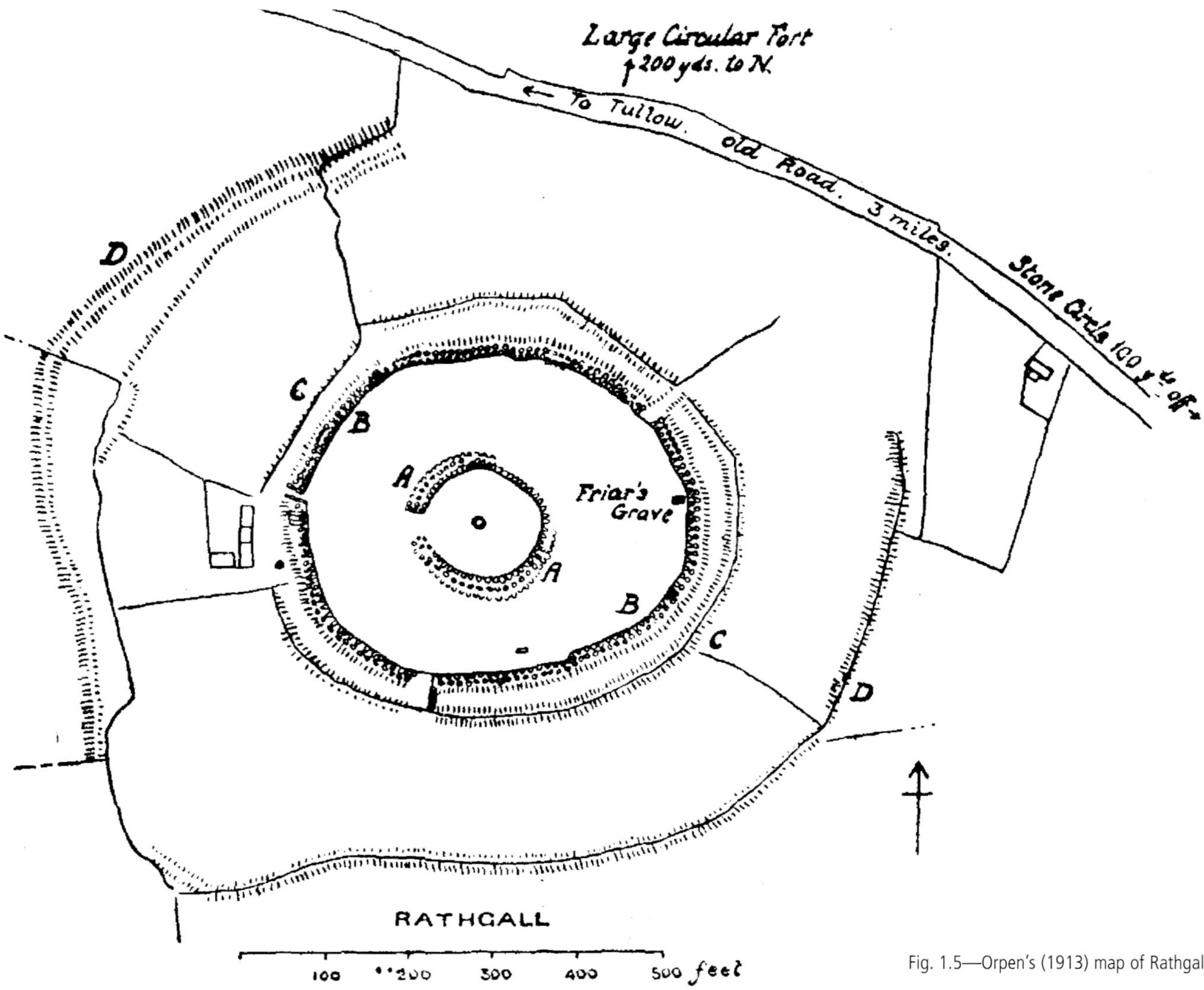

Fig. 1.5—Orpen's (1913) map of Rathgall.

apparent lack of interest in Rathgall by modern fieldworkers is surprising. O'Donovan in his Ordnance Survey Letters gives it no more than a passing mention, and that indefatigable fieldworker Westropp, in his magisterial survey of the forts of Ireland (1902), was similarly uninterested in the site, merely naming it in passing and providing a plan taken from the Ordnance Survey 6in. map. The first to provide a detailed description of the fort was Goddard Orpen (1911) (Fig. 1.5), whose work was impressively comprehensive and is still important today. In a second paper, Orpen (1913) considered Rathgall's possible status as one of the major Celtic royal sites of Leinster, but here his speculation was unbuttressed by any firm evidence. He did, however, argue convincingly that the name Rathgall was unlikely to be of any antiquity.

Orpen's interest in the site was not replicated by the scholars who followed him, in keeping with the general lack of interest in the Irish hillfort as a type. Macalister, in his many volumes on prehistoric Ireland, did not merely ignore Rathgall but also entirely ignored the hillfort as a phenomenon in the Irish landscape. Mahr (1937), too, in his major synthesis of Irish prehistory made no mention of hillforts. A few years later Ó Ríordáin, in the first book to deal wholly and in detail with Irish field monuments, while briefly considering the hillfort as a phenomenon of the Irish prehistoric landscape, had nothing to say about Rathgall (Ó Ríordáin 1942a), while in his *Prehistoric Ireland* Joseph Raftery (1951) made no mention of hillforts.

In the various subsequent editions of Ó Ríordáin's work the site was similarly ignored, although hillforts now merited some general consideration, and it was not until the final, updated version of the book, revised by de Valera, that hillforts were more seriously discussed and Rathgall itself was briefly considered (Ó Ríordáin 1979, 48). Earlier, in 1966, hillforts had received some attention and Rathgall was briefly described (Evans 1966, 214).

It was not until 1967 that Raftery, in his MA dissertation, provided the first overview of the Rathgall site. This was followed by extensive published overviews in 1969 and 1972. Work at Rathgall had, however, already commenced in 1969, ending in 1978 after an eight-year excavation campaign. Brief preliminary reports, and a number of more extensive discussions, were published. In the various monographs concerning themselves with prehistoric Ireland, Rathgall inevitably played an increasingly prominent role. Most recently, Waddell has provided a comprehensive overview of the available Rathgall evidence (2022, 247–9; 2010, 285–6; 1998, 270–2), although the absence of the full report has hampered the realisation in archaeological circles of its full significance. This will obviously be remedied by the publication of this volume.

In 1965 the writer had embarked on a two-year MA dissertation entitled 'Freestone Hill and the hillforts of Ireland'. The work was primarily concerned with the preparation of a full report of Gerhard Bersu's excavations of a hillfort known as Freestone Hill in County Kilkenny, which he had carried out in two seasons in 1948 and 1949. Apart from a preliminary report in a local journal (Bersu 1951), the important site remained unpublished. Along with the excavation report, the writer's dissertation contained a general consideration of Irish hillforts.

It was immediately apparent from the latter review that at the time our knowledge of the hillfort in Ireland was scant indeed, for up to then these sites had received no more than the most meagre of passing references in Irish archaeological literature. Only a handful of sites were known; moreover, no firm definition of what constituted a hillfort had ever been put forward. There was, however, a general assumption that Irish hillforts were an Iron Age phenomenon (a view to which, of course, the present writer then subscribed), following a wider assumption that hillforts in general outside the country dated from this period. Tacitly, too, when considered at all, the hillfort in Ireland was seen as indicative of intrusive peoples.

Thus, following publication of the Freestone Hill report (Raftery 1969) and the presentation in the same year, in Cardiff, of a paper outlining current knowledge on hillforts in Ireland (Raftery 1972), it was decided that the next logical step was to carry out excavations on a suitable hillfort site with a view to extending our meagre knowledge of these structures in Ireland.

In 1969, therefore, it was decided to commence excavations at a large and impressive hilltop site—Rathgall, Co. Wicklow. The excavation was driven by a number of obviously interrelated research questions which emerged logically from the writer's preliminary work on hillforts. It was hoped to shed light on the nature of a hillfort: was it a settlement, a place of refuge, a ritual enclosure or even an enclosure for animals, all of which had by then been postulated, at various times, in hillfort studies abroad? What could be learned about the material culture of those who used the site? What was its date and to what extent, if at all, could the hillfort be recognised as an index of foreign intrusion?

Rathgall was chosen with these research questions in mind for a number of fairly obvious reasons. First, by their nature, most hillforts occupy hilltop situations which are difficult of access, so that their excavation presents considerable logistical problems from the outset. Doubtless this had played a part in the virtual absence of hillfort investigations before 1948. Second, the choice of location of excavation trenches within large enclosures or along the ramparts, being largely arbitrary, could yield disappointing results which might not necessarily advance significantly our knowledge of the hillfort problem. Third, the problem of encountering reasonable stratigraphy on the lofty, windblown sites was at all times acute.

In view of these problems, Rathgall seemed particularly suitable. The site, though large and impressively constructed, straddled a ridge rather than encircling a hilltop and could be reached in minutes on foot from the modern road, formerly the main road from Tullow to Shillelagh. Indeed, apart from during particularly wet periods, motorised transport, including lorries and vans laden with equipment, could reach the hillfort centre without difficulty. There was also a good possibility, evident from the ploughing in adjoining fields, that some reasonable stratigraphy might be expected at the lower levels. Finally, the presence of a relatively small inner enclosure (which at the time was, rather uncritically, deemed to be an original feature) offered the possibility of pinpointing from the outset a focus of primary settlement. That this did in fact happen was coincidental, as this enclosure proved to be a construction far later than the period of the main prehistoric occupation of the site.

Besides these important practical considerations, three

Fig. 1.6 (top left)—Local workmen removing sod in Area 2.

Fig. 1.7 (middle left)—Sara Raftery on site, 1978.

Fig. 1.8—(bottom left) Nuala Raftery on site, 1971. Hut site in Cutting Z1:e/f, looking south.

Fig. 1.9 (above)—Barry Raftery on site using photographic tower, *c.* 1970.

papers by the historian Goddard Orpen early in the twentieth century (Orpen 1911; 1913; 1931) had put forward intriguing suggestions concerning the possible identification of the site as a major centre in early historic times. Rathgall was thus regarded as ideal for archaeological excavation, with the potential to shed light not only on the nature of the Irish hillfort but also on the wide range of problems concerning the later prehistoric and early historic periods in the country.

As was normal at the time, the excavation was carried out, and the funding provided, under what was then known as the 'Relief of Unemployment Scheme' and was administered by the Office of Public Works. The effect of this was that the excavation was entirely funded by the State but only on condition that men from the local labour exchange were employed. Strangely, women appear not to have been considered in this arrangement, at least not where archaeological excavation was concerned. Although not always rigidly adhered to, there was a proviso that four local men had to be employed for every one professional assistant or student. Needless to say, the latter received only the most meagre of subsistence expenses. The bulk of the money made available went to the locally recruited workforce. In order to engage any sort of adequate team of archaeological assistants, excessively large numbers of labourers would have to be taken on from the local labour exchange. Inevitably, therefore, the number of archaeologists helping at the site was limited.

The money made available was not primarily intended to assist in the quest for archaeological knowledge but to help alleviate local unemployment. In this regard the scheme is to be commended for the imaginative way in which it sought to combine the amelioration of rural unemployment with archaeological investigation. It should also be noted that the equipment required for the excavation—from six-inch nails, trowels and string to planks, tables and chairs, hut sites and everything else—was supplied by the then Board of Works. Indeed, it is fitting that the efficiency, helpfulness and generosity of the officials of the Board should be warmly acknowledged. This practice has, of course, long since ceased. Excavators are now entirely on their own in this regard.

Inevitably, the quality and diligence of the local workers varied greatly, and this became an increasing problem as the complexity of the excavation became apparent. In addition, the fact—today astonishing—that there was not a single full-time archaeologist accompanying the present writer in the course of the seven years of excavation added further to the difficulties of conducting a proper scientific investigation. The excavation director was thus under severe and continuing pressure to maintain the quality of the excavation. In this regard, it was fortunate that a hard core of excellent, reliable and thoroughly committed assistants worked on the site over several consecutive seasons. It is no exaggeration to state that without the contribution of these individuals the proper conduct of the excavation would have been impossible. It is thus appropriate to single out here in particular Dr Mark Clinton, Mr Eamonn P. Kelly, Mr Lawrence Walsh, Mr Luigi Rea and Ms Nuala Sproule (now Nuala Raftery). There were, in addition, many others whose contribution to the excavation was exceptional. Many of these have gone on to become professional archaeologists of considerable standing, while others have pursued other careers. To them all I offer my deepest thanks. For support of the work of the greater Rathgall project I am indebted to: John Coles, Bernard Wailes for facilitating early radiocarbon dates from the Smithsonian Museum, Leo Swan for aerial photography, Albert Glaholm, David Jennings, Anthony Corns, Ingelise Stuijts, R.M. Cleary, E. Byrnes, Mary Cahill, Mark Clinton, Luigi Rea, Eamonn P. Kelly, Laurence Walsh, Geraldine Stout, Matthew Stout, Jan Lanting, Anna Brindley, Susannah Kelly, Michael Kenny, Mark Gordon, Alva McGowan, Claire Cotter, Christina Haywood, Julian Henderson, Joyce Hickey and Penny Johnston. My sincere gratitude, too, to those whose names, after a gap of more than three decades, may have been inadvertently left out.

In the final preparation of this volume, a number of people deserve special thanks. These include Dr Christina Haywood and Susannah Kelly, who, where necessary, skilfully carried out repair and conservation of the artefacts; Mark Gordon, who worked on bringing the artefact catalogue to publication standard; Alva McGowan, who carried out extensive work on the plans and sections; and Sarah Nylund, who was responsible for the drawings of the glass beads. Nuala Raftery's original compilation of the site catalogue remains an outstanding contribution to the final publication of the excavation report. Above all, I am deeply indebted to Ursula Mattenberger, Department of Archaeology, UCD, whose skill and dedication—and, indeed, endless patience—in preparing the excavation drawings to publication standard made the successful completion of this volume possible.

For practical assistance over the years, the officers of the then Office of Public Works, both at Head Office in Dublin and in the field, are to be thanked for their courtesy and help. The National Museum of Ireland also assisted in many ways, not only during the course of the excavation but also up to the present day.

1.2 ARCHAEOLOGICAL LANDSCAPE

Barry Raftery and Katharina Becker

The number of visible monuments in the region of the fort is not large (Fig. 1.10). Among these are a handful of ringforts, including one that is 48m in diameter (see Grogan and Kilfeather 1997, 16, no. 86). Of considerable interest and importance is a large enclosure in the townland of Knockeen (Fig. 1.11) (*ibid.*, 420, no. 215). Now recognised as a bivallate fort, it sits on the northern end of the ridge, some 250m north of Rathgall, and may best be referred to as a hillfort. The inner enclosure, now partly damaged around the south-east and continuing to the north-north-west, is some 200m in diameter. In places it is of substantial construction, rising to a height of up to 1.5m. Traces of an original outer rampart, increasing the diameter of the site to some 300m, are recognisable in places in the field

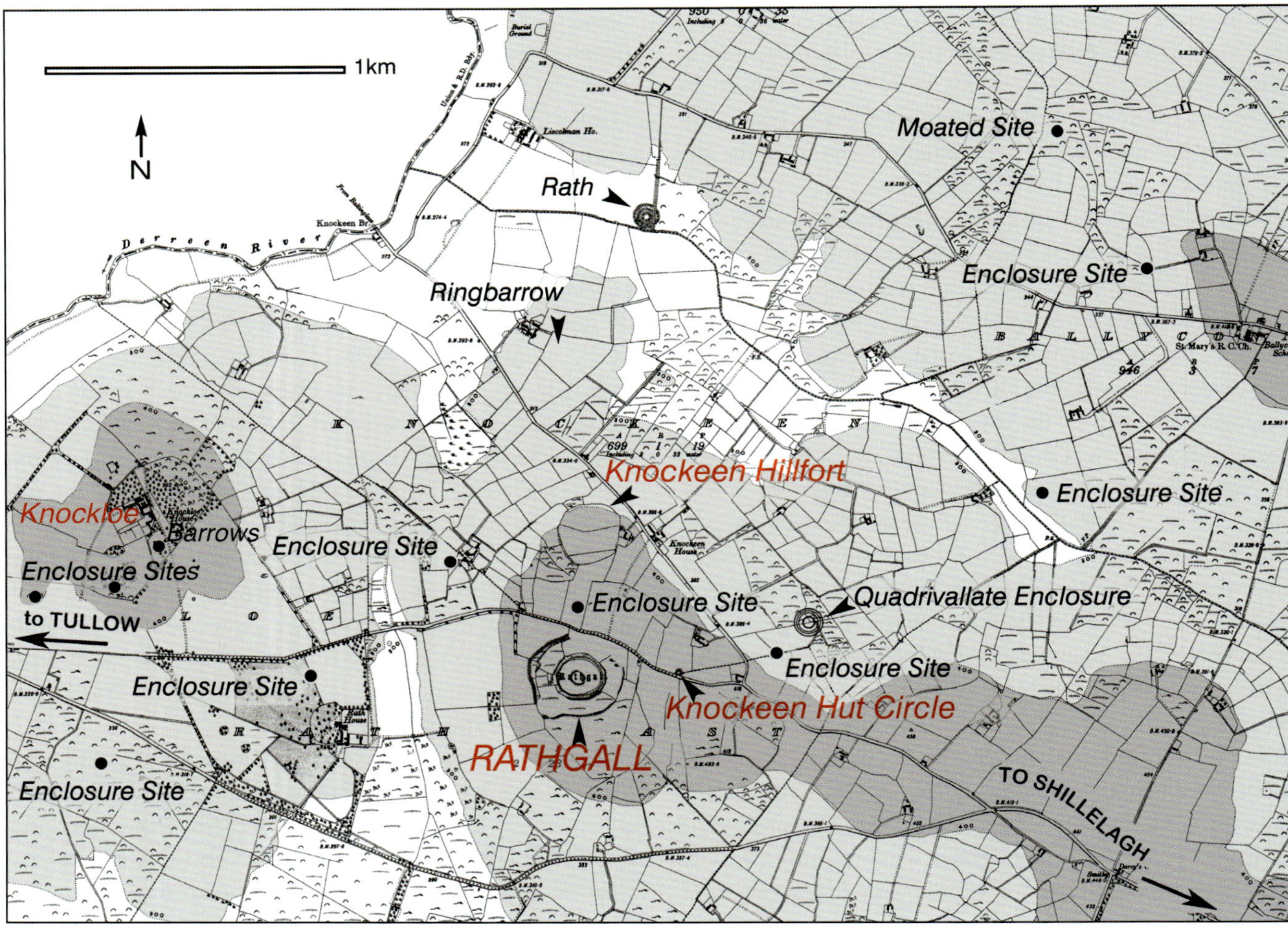

Fig. 1.10—Rathgall in its landscape.

boundaries. Two substantial fences, now destroyed, which originally radiated from the cairn have been described by Orpen (1911, 142) as possibly ancient. Without excavation, of course, there is no way of determining the veracity or otherwise of this suggestion. The cairn, now partly damaged, which is situated centrally within this enclosure may be considerably earlier than the Bronze Age features excavated on the hilltop (Grogan and Kilfeather 1997, 21, no. 121). It is subcircular in plan, having dimensions of 18.7m north–south and 10m east–west. Its height varies from 1.8m to 2.5m. The presence of what appear to be hut circles in the geophysical survey (see section 2.11) is interesting and it is intriguing to wonder whether this fort belongs to the same cultural horizon as Rathgall.

The small hut circle in Knockeen/Rath East (WI037-019; *ibid.*, 93, no. 608, fig. 4, pl. 3) is situated close to, and partly damaged by, the roadway some 150m east of Rathgall (Fig. 1.12a, b). It is marked by a circular bank with inner and outer stone revetments, which is 18m in diameter and about 1.5m wide. During surveying a coarse rim sherd (E100:104) and a fragmentary saddle quern (E100:130) were recovered on the surface. It may well be that these are broadly contemporary with Bronze Age Rathgall. These finds are important, for the site may thus be contemporary with the extensive activity uncovered to the south of the fort (see below), thus implying a widespread Bronze Age presence in the area surrounding Rathgall.

A number of other enclosures are located in the near vicinity, such as WI037-017, about 50m north of the site, visible as a crop mark 30m in diameter (Grogan and Kilfeather 1997). Two further enclosures are located to the east of the site and are also only visible as crop marks. WI037-020 is a bivallate enclosure about 30m in diameter, but enclosure WI037-021, discovered some years ago from

Fig. 1.11 (left)—Rathgall and Knockeen hillforts, looking north-west (Cambridge Unit).

Fig. 1.12a (above)—Knockeen hut circle (SMR: WI037-019----).

Fig. 1.12b (below)—Knockeen hut circle (SMR: WI037-019----), looking north-east (Leo Swan).

Fig. 1.13—Knockeen quadrivallate enclosure (WI037-021----), looking west (Leo Swan).

Fig. 1.14a (below)—Knockloe and Rathgall: Google Earth image.

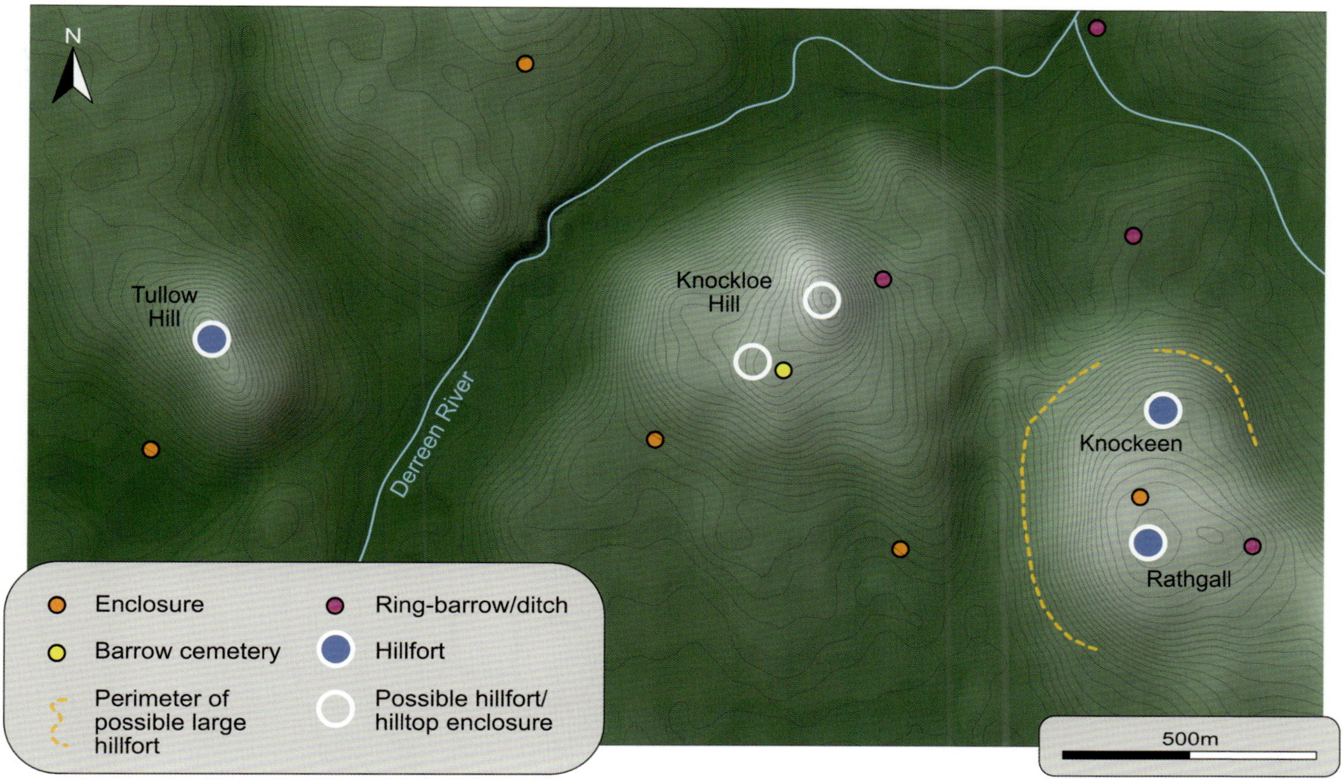

Fig. 1.14b—Knockloe, Knockeen and Rathgall (James O'Driscoll).

the air by the late Leo Swan in boggy land to the east of Rathgall, is especially interesting (*ibid.*, 608). This is now virtually invisible at ground level but from the air it can clearly be seen to consist of four concentric circular enclosures some 70m in overall diameter (Fig. 1.13). The outer three are fairly close together; the inner, which appears to be wider than the others, is somewhat further distant from them. This may well also be the remains of a Neolithic or Early Bronze Age monument of some sort, the character of which can only be established by excavation.

West of Rathgall are the ruins of Knockloe House. Immediately south of these a group of five possible barrows has been identified (WI037-29001 to 29005) (Fig. 1.14a, b). Their clustering in a field used for agricultural activity in recent memory has been cited as grounds for possible doubts about their antiquity and, indeed, their regular and clear shape raises suspicion. Immediately to the south-west of the cluster of barrows, a possible circular enclosure seems to be indicated on the satellite imagery of the area. It has a diameter of about 150m, is possibly enclosed by a ditch and has a small, central rise. On the historic maps of the area, vegetation in the form of gorse and 'brush wood' are indicated, and the feature may in fact be geological. At its northern boundary, a semicircular feature appears to intersect with it. The site is located on an elevation comparable to that of Rathgall at about OD 400–500m.

1.3 RATHGALL HILLFORT: THE VISIBLE REMAINS

Barry Raftery and Katharina Becker

The discussion of the upstanding monument begins with a detailed overview of the area before excavation (Fig. 1.15a). Four ramparts, for the most part concentric, enclose the hilltop, with discontinuous traces of a fifth enclosure recently recognised between Ramparts 3 and 4 after detailed topographical survey in the north-western and south-eastern areas. The maximum enclosed width of this enclosure is 310m and the total area enclosed is some 7.5ha (18 acres). The main defence is provided by Ramparts 2 and 3, which are separated from one another by between 8m and 12m. The innermost small stone Rampart 1 (the 'cashel') and the

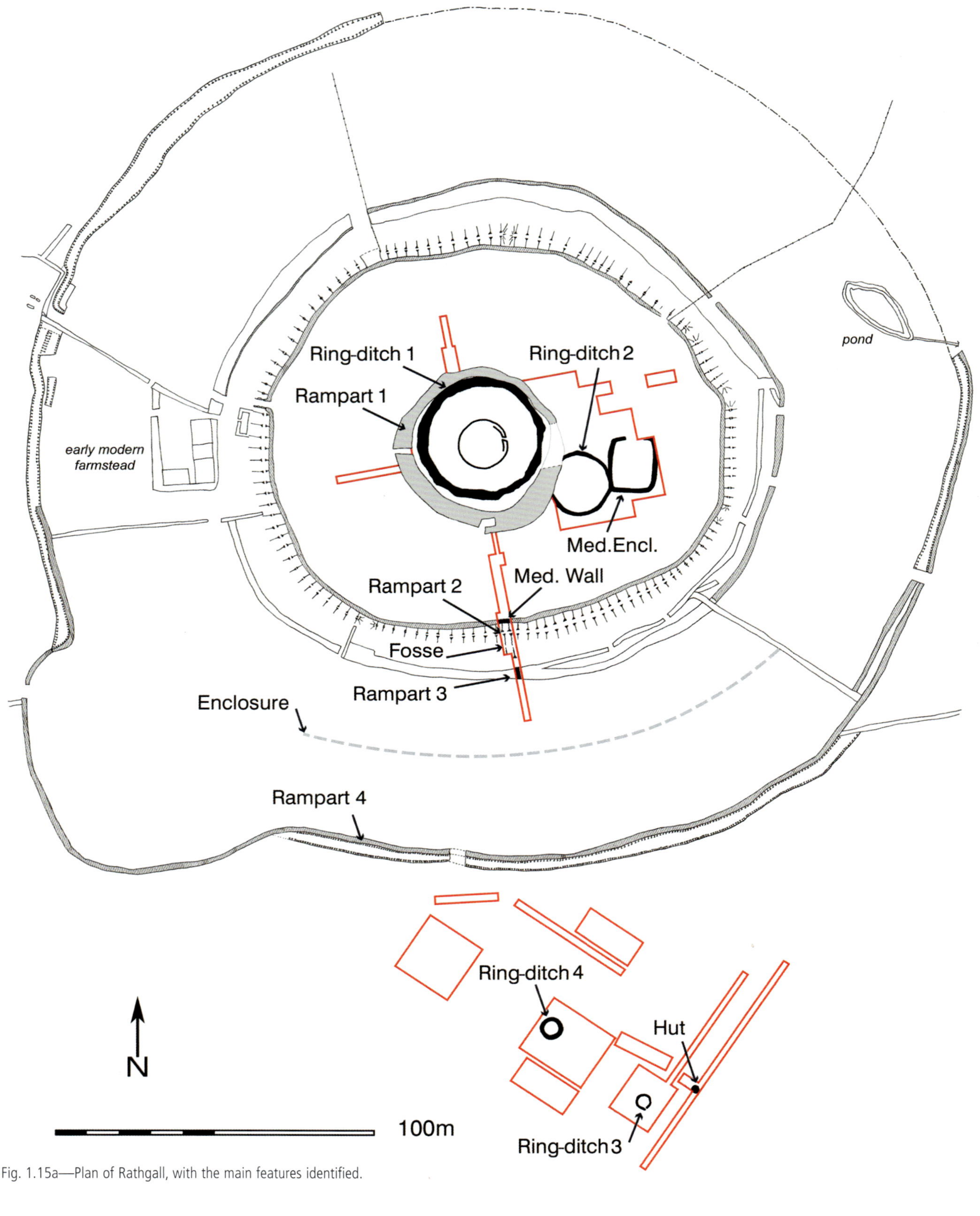

Fig. 1.15a—Plan of Rathgall, with the main features identified.

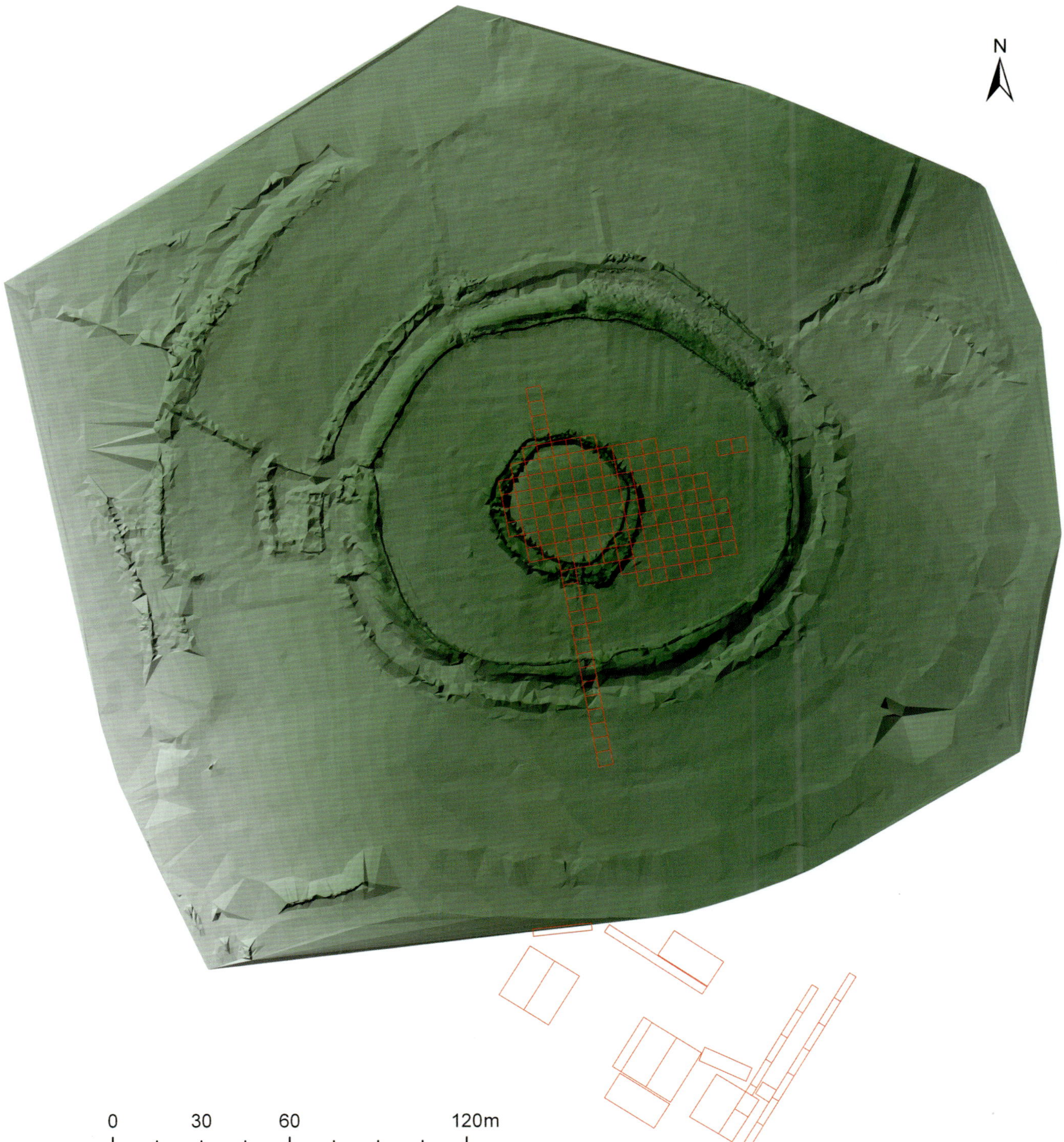

Fig. 1.15b—Topographical survey model of Rathgall (Discovery Programme, Anthony Corns/Rob Shaw; integration with the excavation grid by Rob Sands).

outer Rampart 4 are, however, significantly distant from the main central defence of Ramparts 2 and 3.

The outer rampart (Rampart 4) has been almost entirely removed in the north and north-east, where about 250m of its circumference have been levelled. The line of the original rampart here is, however, to a large extent visible as a slight rise in the field surface. It is said locally that the stones were removed (in 1888) for the construction of the impressive Rath House, some 800m to the west. The line of this rampart is somewhat irregular, for the most part roughly accommodating the rounded profile of the hill. For much of its circumference it is of decidedly flimsy construction, so that it is far from clear which portions are of ancient origin. In the south-west it displays a marked bulge, which appears to have no obvious defensive significance and is hardly dictated by topography. The geophysical imaging indicates that a large feature may be located in this area, providing a possible reason for the deviation in the course of the rampart.

Where it survives, the bank of Rampart 4 appears to be composed entirely of stones. In the north-east it is about 1m in height and slightly more than this in width, while to the east and south-east the width is as much as 3m in places, with a height of over 1m. Towards the west, where the rampart is considerably worn, the preserved height is at most 1m. In places some of the stones of the wall are of considerable size: in the east, for example, there is a boulder which is 1.8m long, 1.3m high and approximately 60cm thick. There are several other boulders of similar dimensions which may be original elements of the wall's construction. As already noted, however, it is not possible to determine which portions of the enclosure are ancient. A number of gaps occur in this rampart, notably in the east, but these do not appear to be original. In the west, however, almost opposite the main entrance in the main ramparts (see below), there is what might be a blocked-up original entrance, possibly even with hints of slab lining.

In this area, too, at distances varying from *c.* 10m to *c.* 25m from the outer bank, traces of what may be a separate rampart (not illustrated) can be recognised for a distance of about 200m along the north-west and west. At least in part this has been incorporated into a field boundary, so that its early date is not certain. It is of drystone construction, rising to no more than 1m above the interior. There is, however, a sharp drop in places to the exterior, where a scarp of up to 2m is discernible. Owing to extensive collapse and areas of heavy undergrowth its original width is unclear.

It was a matter of considerable surprise when, as already noted above, detailed survey of the site by the Discovery Programme in 2004 revealed the outline of a former enclosure between Ramparts 3 and 4 (Figs 1.15a and 1.15b) that was invisible at ground level. It could be traced for most of the southern circumference of the fort, apart from an area around the west and, to a lesser extent, in the east. It was some 25m outside Rampart 3.

A whole range of important questions are posed by this major discovery. The contrast between the substantial character of the main ramparts and the almost total obliteration of the new one is striking, indicating, surely, that the latter enclosure is significantly older than those which still survive. The presence of a Neolithic and Early Bronze Age occupation on the hill should thus be noted but, of course, only excavation at some point in the future can shed light on the date of this intriguing new discovery.

The main hillfort defences, Ramparts 2 and 3, are positioned 50–90m inside the outer rampart. These are, as noted above, 8–12m apart and it seemed clear, even before excavation, that they formed a single unitary line of defence. A more or less flat zone, averaging some 10m in width, occurred between the two. Subsequent excavation revealed this to be a silted-up ditch (see Chapter 2).

Rampart 3 (Fig. 1.16a) appears to be composed of an outer and inner facing with rubble in between. It was, for the most part, in a considerably denuded and collapsed state, and internally it was nowhere more than about 1m high. In general, however, its height was less than this. Where best preserved, a low retaining wall of sometimes substantial granite boulders was recognisable along its outer circumference. It was 2m wide for the most part, but at some points in the east and south its width seems to increase to almost 4m. Limited excavations in 1978 provided more detailed information on the nature of this wall (see Chapter 2).

Rampart 2 (Fig 1.16b–e) is the most substantial defensive construction at Rathgall. It was originally massive, essentially of rubble, faced on front and back by drystone walling of at times considerable size. Excavation showed it to be solidly built but demonstrating no very sophisticated construction. Its outer facing is collapsed in places but is best preserved in the north-west, where it towers externally as much as 5m above Rampart 3.

A well-preserved stone wall abuts the inner face of Rampart 2 for its entire circumference. This has a marked external batter and varies in width from about 3m at its base to 1m at the top. It is of rounded, moderately sized granite boulders and somewhat less than 2m in average height. For

Fig. 1.16a (left)—Rampart 3 viewed from top of Rampart 2, looking south-east.

Fig. 1.16b (below left)—Rampart 2 and northern face of western original entrance.

Fig. 1.16c (below right)—Looking east across the top of Rampart 2 in its southern extent, with the inner (secondary) stone facing projecting above the current height of the bank.

Fig. 1.16d (bottom left)—Blocked-up entrance through Rampart 2 in the south-east, looking west.

Fig. 1.16e (bottom right)—Blocked-up entrance through Rampart 2 in the south-east, looking east.

Fig. 1.17—Western main original entrance through Rampart 2, looking east.

most of its circumference its upper surface is roughly level with the top of the main rampart but in the south-east it is slightly lower, while in the north and north-west Rampart 2 is at least 50cm higher than the inner facing. Significantly, there is virtually no collapse from the latter, giving rise to the probability that it is of no great antiquity. Supporting this is its manifestly polygonal outline, as is the case with Rampart 1, which is clearly a late construction.

Originally there were at least four entrances through Rampart 2, already depicted by Orpen. In addition to the western entrance, its gap lined with large boulders, three further gaps through the rampart can be identified on the north, north-east and south-west. At least two of these were likewise lined with stones (those in the south-west and north-east), but it is unclear whether the north-western entrance that now constitutes the modern access to the site also had formerly been lined. It is notable, however, that all of them were sealed by the internal stone facing of Rampart 2 (e.g. Figs 1.16d, e). This may represent a later stage of modification, as clearly visible in the case of the south-western entrance (Fig. 1.16). Further breaks through the rampart are tentatively implied by dips in the rampart height on the north and east, although these may also be the result of recent erosion.

The fourth entrance through this rampart, in the west, is the only one that remains open, besides the modern entrance in the north-west which provides access to the site today. The western entrance is a simple gap some 2m wide, lined with substantial orthostatic slabs up to 1.8m in height (Fig. 1.17). These form a 6m-long entrance passage. A corresponding gap occurs in Rampart 3, situated at a slight angle to the entrance in Rampart 2.

Fig. 1.18a, b—Rampart 1 (stone cashel) at time of excavation, the western entrance.

Fig. 1.19—Area 1 within Rampart 1 (stone cashel) under excavation, looking south-west.

Fig. 1.20—'Chamber' in southern extent of Rampart 1, looking north-east.

Immediately adjacent to the entrance passage through Rampart 2 are the remains of a rectangular drystone structure abutting the rampart's outer face. It is 8m long and 3m wide, with a 1m-wide entrance gap in the west. The wall, which is of simple, drystone construction, survives to a maximum height of 1.4m and is about 60cm wide. This can hardly be other than the remains of the cottage complex which was surveyed in 1838 and engraved on the 6in. Ordnance Survey map of 1839. Orpen makes no mention of this. He does, however, refer to a 'chamber' at the site which was apparently the seat of an illicit poteen still. Just outside the corresponding gap in Rampart 3 the remains of an eighteenth-century farmyard are visible. A souterrain was dug into Rampart 2 in this area too, just to the south of the main western entrance.

The innermost enclosure, Rampart 1 or the cashel, is today a substantial polygonal construction of drystone masonry some 46m in greatest internal width (Figs 1.18–1.20). Its distance from Rampart 2 varies from 45m to 55m. The stones at the base of the wall are of considerable size, those higher up being progressively smaller. A rough facing on outer and inner sides is detectable, and where a portion of the wall was removed in the east in the course of the excavation an irregular filling of smaller stones was observed between. It is slightly battered on both sides. When the excavation commenced in 1969, substantial internal collapse had taken place in several places around its circumference. Besides the reinstatement of the part of Rampart 1 removed by the excavation campaigns presented in this volume, further work appears to have taken place between then and today.

Fig. 1.21—The entrance through Rampart 1 (stone cashel). Compare this to the condition visible in Fig. 1.18a, taken at the time of excavation, implying significant restoration work in recent decades.

Apart from the damaged areas, the wall has a fairly uniform height of about 1.5m above the interior. In thickness, however, it varies considerably. This is a reflection of two separate phases of construction, which became evident through aerial reconnaissance but were scarcely discernible at ground level. The primary enclosure, which survives around the north and east, was of modest dimensions, maintaining a consistent width of about 1.5m. Extending from the east around to the west, however, its thickness was increased from 4m to 7m, reaching its maximum dimensions in the south-east, where it contained a chamber of unknown date or function. Extending northwards from the entrance, however, it was decided, for whatever reason, to abandon the action of thickening the wall. Thus, from this point, the thickness of the secondary wall decreases sharply, almost hurriedly, joining with the original, slender wall at an awkward angle in the north-west (in Sqs 40 and Y1; see below).

The sole entrance through this rampart is in the west (Fig. 1.21). The wall here is just over 5m thick and the entrance takes the form of a simple passageway some 2.75m wide. It possesses no specific revetment. Its sides are formed simply by careful construction of the drystone walling, which at the time of the excavation had collapsed on either side of the entrance. Further collapse had also occurred at several points around the rampart's circumference.

Enclosed by Rampart 1 were the remains of an incomplete, more or less circular arrangement of moderately sized stones. This was 4.8m in average diameter. Within this circle there was a random scatter of stones similar in size to those of the ring. They were only in a single layer and were nowhere more than 15–20cm in height. In addition, it was clear that they rested directly on the modern surface. Orpen noted the presence of this structure more than a century ago and speculated as to its original purpose. It is likely that one of his suggestions—that it was a stand for a hayrick—is correct.

2. THE EXCAVATIONS

2.1 EXCAVATING RATHGALL

Barry Raftery

Excavations at Rathgall began on 30 June 1969 and continued for the following six years. No excavation took place in 1976 and 1977, but there was a final short season in August 1978. Apart from a narrow cutting outward through Rampart 3 to the south and extensive investigation further southwards, all the work took place within Rampart 3 (Fig. 2.1). The first season extended to the end of August, during which time the entire area within Rampart 1 (Fig. 2.2) was laid out in a 5m grid with north–south orientation. The principal aim, initially, was to carry out investigations in the innermost enclosure (Area 1), but it was also intended to conduct exploratory work in the area between Ramparts 1 and 2. Thus, extending outward from the base of Rampart 1, Cuttings X and Y were intended as the north/south-running trial trenches, while Cuttings A and B were to be the equivalent to the east and west. It was hoped that in due course, in a later campaign, a cutting might be made through Ramparts 2 and 3.

During the first season the north-eastern quadrant within Rampart 1 was excavated. In the following year, during August and September, the excavation was extended to the south-eastern quadrant. In addition, at a point in the east where the rampart had collapsed to its basal stones, the opportunity was taken to remove these and to extend the investigation to the exterior. This consisted initially of a short, 2m-wide trench to the east (B cuttings, part of Area 2; see Fig. 2.3), but such was the density of the archaeological levels encountered almost from the start that the cutting was expanded to the intended width of 5m and extended eastwards for a distance of 10m. In 1971 a small portion within the innermost enclosure in the south-east, unfinished in the previous year, was completed and the remaining western section of the inner enclosure was excavated. In the same year, too, trial-trenching took place on the slopes outside the fort to the south (Z cuttings—Outside Settlement and Outside Cemetery), and this was followed on a larger scale in the early spring of 1972, when official monies on a substantial scale unexpectedly became available on condition that all was

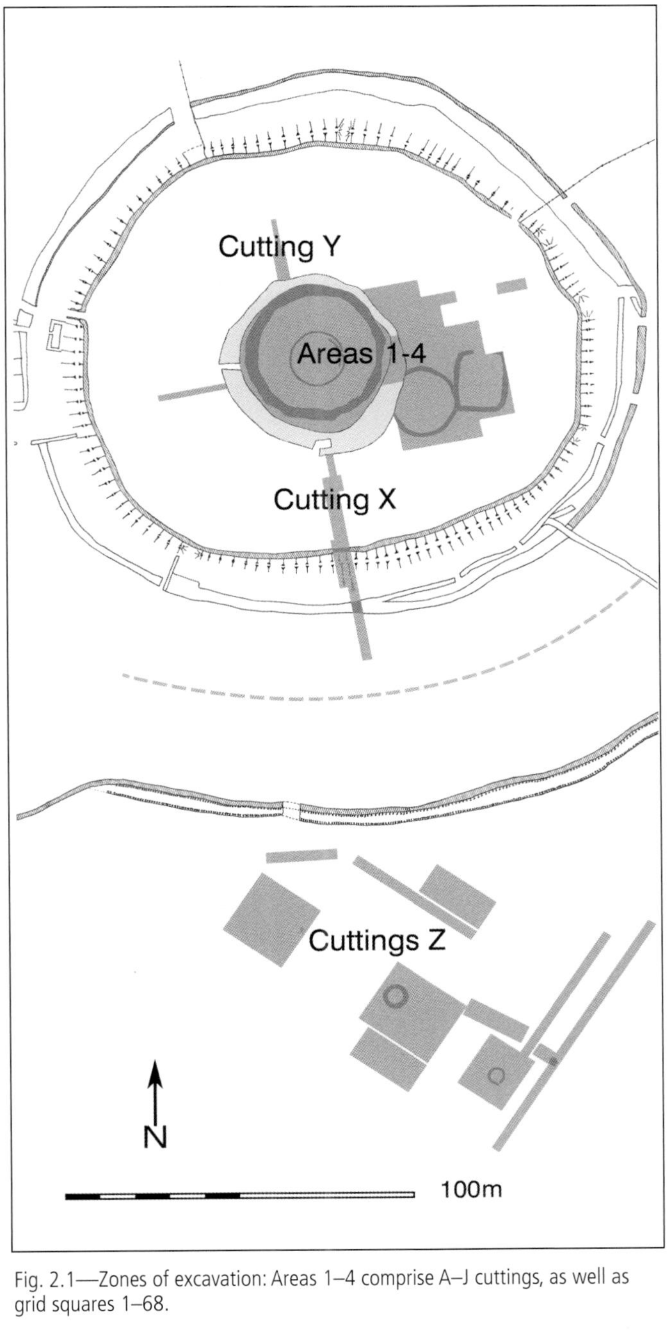

Fig. 2.1—Zones of excavation: Areas 1–4 comprise A–J cuttings, as well as grid squares 1–68.

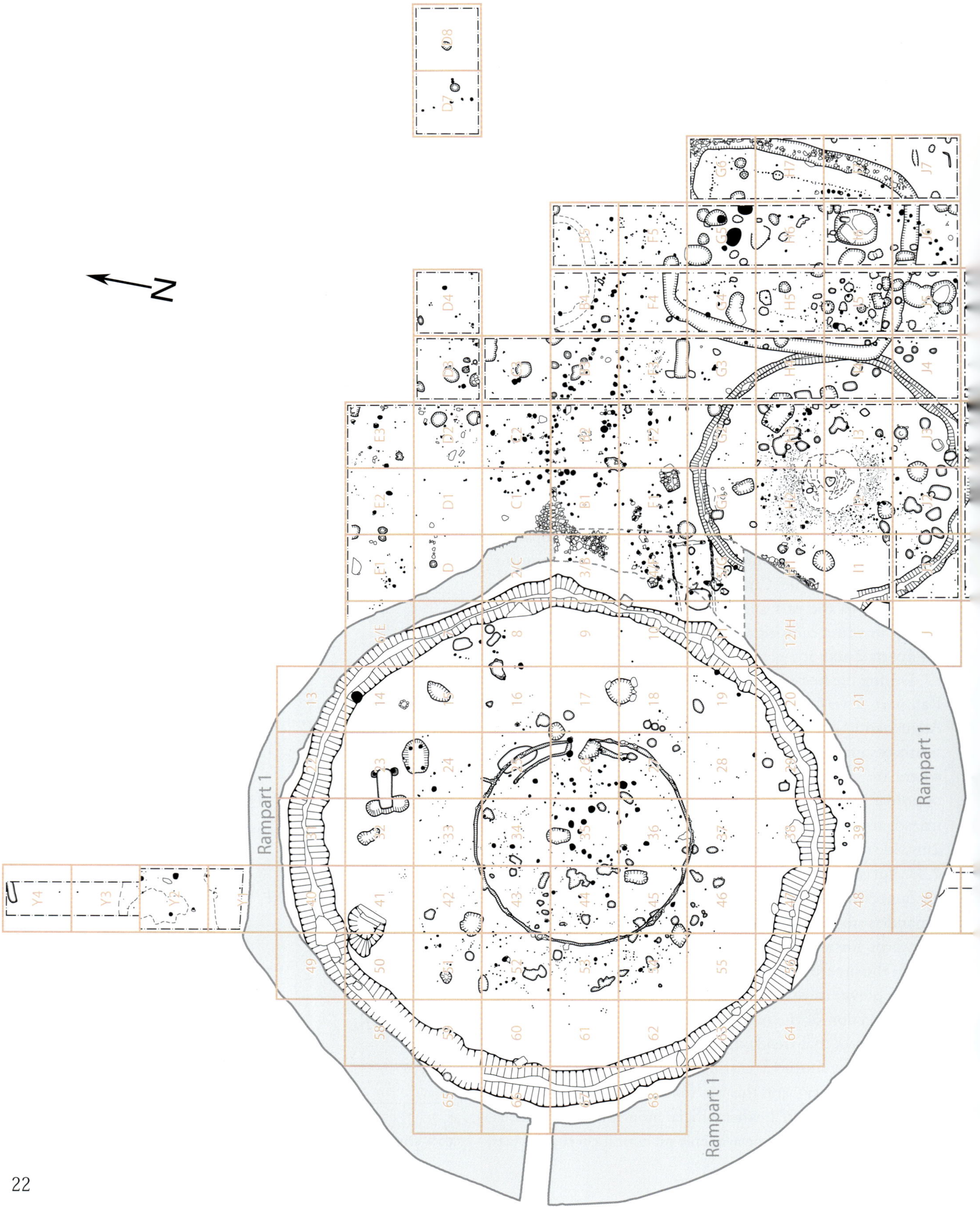
N
Rampart 1
Rampart 1
Rampart 1

spent before the end of the financial year. Later in the same year, extensive later Bronze Age activity, which had been revealed in 1970, was further investigated in the east (Areas 2–4), and Cuttings X–X4, immediately inside the second enclosure, and Y–Y4, immediately north of the inner enclosure, were also excavated.

In the 1973–5 and 1978 seasons the excavation outside Rampart 1 in the east was further extended and limited work was carried out in the south. In the course of the latter the cutting through Ramparts 2 and 3 was extended for a distance southward towards (but not as far as) Rampart 4, and the X cuttings, initially opened in 1972 immediately inside Rampart 2 in the south, were extended inward to the north as far as Rampart 1. The total area investigated within the hillfort during the eight seasons came to approximately 3,000 square metres. On the southern slopes a further 1,775 square metres were uncovered. Thus over the course of the excavation almost 5,000 square metres were excavated.

In drawing up a comprehensive and intelligible picture of what turned out to be a long sequence of activity at Rathgall, exceptional difficulties were created by the absence of proper stratigraphy over a very large percentage of the excavated area. In the inner enclosure, in particular, deep and systematic cultivation had taken place (including, it seems, the use of the spade as well as conventional ploughing) over a lengthy period. In this regard a range of early modern pottery, including seventeenth-century sherds, is interesting, as, indeed, was the discovery of two early bottle fragments of greenish glass (E84:5436) from deep in the fill of Pit 131 in Sq. 41/50 within the inner enclosure (below). In Orpen's time, however, the area within the fort, or at least within the inner enclosure, was pasture. Indeed, he refers to a bull in this area which occasioned some apprehension (Orpen 1911, 140)!

Directly under the sod, the site was everywhere covered by an undifferentiated layer of brown humus, varying in thickness from about 15cm to a maximum of about 30cm. This was the product of prolonged cultivation, which was clearly evident in the straight, shallow trenches that criss-crossed the site, showing up as shallow brown streaks in the yellow boulder clay. The humus layer was generally fine, not only as a result of agricultural activity but also through the actions of worms, which are well known as effective agents in breaking down soils. A surprising number of natural boulders, some of considerable size, projected from the natural yellow subsoil in the inner enclosure (see below).

The soil in the upper levels of the site was further disturbed by faunal activity, mainly that of rabbits. Rodent activity added to the excavation difficulties. The disturbance was most marked in the area of the inner enclosure and was considerably less evident outside. In this regard, the writer was informed by local farmers that the area of the inner enclosure had 'teemed with rabbits'. Their burrows, and the burrows of smaller creatures, were everywhere in the inner enclosure. A dead pygmy shrew was also found, and here and there the burrows of these tiny creatures could be seen as narrow dark streaks in the subsoil. With experience these became rapidly recognisable in the course of the excavation, and it was apparent from an early stage that features with a spongy brown filling were invariably of relatively recent date.

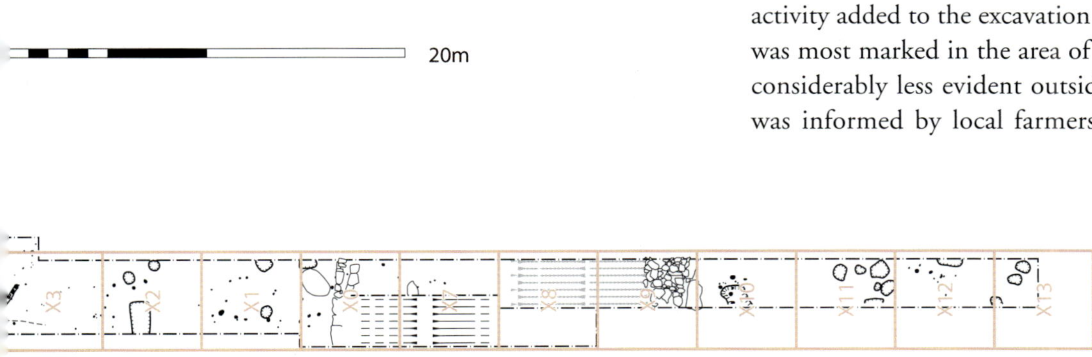

Fig. 2.2—The grid layout within the main area of excavation, enclosed by Rampart 3.

On the very first day of the 1969 excavation some seventeen sherds of coarse pottery were found within the inner stone enclosure during the initial desodding of the site. These occurred in the same levels as green-glazed wares, willow-pattern pottery, fragmentary clay pipes, horseshoe nails and other items of recent date. It was only where areas of grey or black showed up in the yellow subsoil, or where overlapping features showed up after the removal of the brown humus, that any stratigraphic interpretation could be attempted. As the excavation progressed, however, it became apparent that in the east, under and immediately outside Rampart 1, there were important areas of surviving stratigraphy.

A curious fact that emerged during the excavation was the proliferation of naturally occurring rocks, many of considerable size, which projected, often significantly, above the level of the yellow subsoil within the central enclosure. In places these were as much as 50cm above the modern surface and at times constituted an impediment to easy movement around the site. Outside the enclosure such stones were rare; indeed, for the most part they were entirely absent, notably in the area of intense occupation revealed in eastern Cuttings B–E (see below), although a significant concentration of such boulders could again be noted in Area 4, within the medieval enclosure.

The presence of these projecting rocks is puzzling. The removal of the ancient occupation layers here by modern agricultural activity has been particularly intense, so that the walking surface in antiquity would undoubtedly have been higher than the modern surface of the yellow subsoil. It is nonetheless difficult to envisage the larger boulders having ever been completely covered, so that it would seem that in this part of the site a fully level surface never existed. This obviously raises a question as to the extent to which normal domestic activity took place here.

2.1.1 Site recording
Katharina Becker

The site was divided into 5m grids, with an initial phase of

Fig. 2.3—The original grid peg of Square X9, found *in situ* in 2010 (lower right corner).

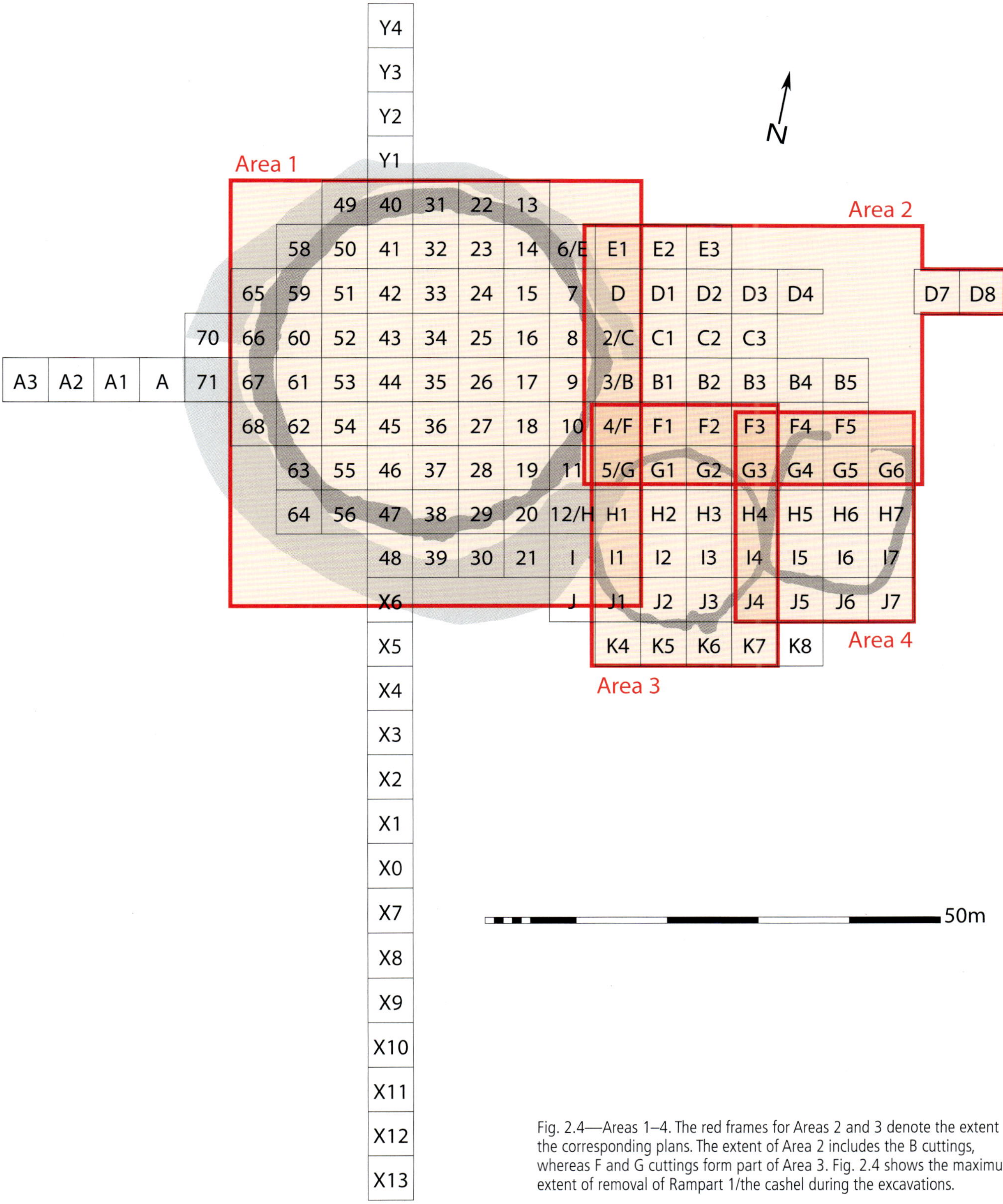

Fig. 2.4—Areas 1–4. The red frames for Areas 2 and 3 denote the extent of the corresponding plans. The extent of Area 2 includes the B cuttings, whereas F and G cuttings form part of Area 3. Fig. 2.4 shows the maximum extent of removal of Rampart 1/the cashel during the excavations.

recording of the cashel interior in 1m grid squares during the first season in 1969. In the following season, however, these were resolved into 5m grids. These grids—or cuttings, as Raftery calls them in the stratigraphic report—are numbered, and the reference point is the grid point in each square's south-western corner. Within the cashel, grid squares were numbered from 1 to 68. Additional cuttings opened in consecutive seasons were given prefixes: B–K in the east of the cashel; Y for the extension north of the cashel; and X for the extension south of the cashel. The latest campaigns focused on an area off the main summit of the hill to the south of the enclosure. This area was called the outer settlement and trenches were given the prefix O, followed by Roman numerals for the cutting numbers. For this publication the prefix O was replaced with Z, and Arabic instead of Roman cutting numbers were introduced.

The site grid had originally been laid out to magnetic north. In order to integrate the excavation grid into the GIS for the mapping of finds and correlation with the topographical and geophysical survey, the excavation grid was adjusted to the National Grid North. Reference points for this were the outline of Rampart 1 and a grid peg in Cutting X that had survived *in situ* since 1975 and became visible after the removal of vegetation in 2011 (Fig. 2.3).

For easier navigation of the site description, the excavation area within and east of Rampart 1 was subdivided into Areas 1–4 (Fig. 2.4). The area within the central enclosure was designated Area 1, and the area immediately east of this was divided into a northern section (Area 2) and southern sections (Areas 3 and 4). Other areas of test excavation in the north (Y cutting), south (X cutting) and west (A cutting)[1] will be described separately, as are the important excavations which took place outside the hillfort downslope to the south (Z cuttings, formerly O cuttings).

Further renumbering or renaming of features was avoided, except that the term 'fosse' was replaced with the term 'ring-ditch'. Terminologies were standardised throughout the text, but old nomenclature can still be found in the finds database—here, however, augmented by an 'interpreted context' field that indicates what the context was identified as in the post-excavation process, allowing these contexts to be related back to the stratigraphic report presented in this publication.

As outlined below, the site was excavated before the introduction of single-context recording. Raftery had, however, adopted a system that numbered cut features such as pits, post-holes, depressions, hearths, ring-ditches, ramparts and burials but did not differentiate between cuts or fills. Each of these categories is numbered, starting at 1. Depressions received the prefix D to differentiate them from other types of contexts with identical numbers. No context register survived in the archive, and stratigraphic information was drawn from site plans as well as the find logbooks.

2.2 AREA 1—INSIDE RAMPART 1

Barry Raftery

The stratigraphy in this area, defined by the medieval Rampart 1, the stone cashel, is probably the most disturbed within the excavated zones. In addition to cultivation, including ploughing, this disturbance included the creation of a haystack in the centre of the enclosed area, rabbit activity and, of course, the significant activity associated with the building of the cashel itself and later medieval and post-medieval activity, as evidenced by the pottery record (see Chapter 3).

As was clear from an early phase of excavation, the inner stone enclosure at Rathgall was late, almost certainly of medieval date, and extensive activity of later Bronze Age date emerged beneath it. Intensive ploughing activity, certainly from as early as the nineteenth century at least, resulted in large-scale destruction across the innermost enclosure, leaving the chronological phases difficult to establish. Initial excavation at the site extended for the most part within the inner enclosure, but increasingly, as will appear below, activity of at times extraordinary significance emerged, especially outside the stone enclosure in the east. The excavation exposed a shallow circular ditch (Fig. 2.5), within which a 15m bedding trench and a range of varied pits and post-holes occurred. Immediately outside the circular ditch, the remains of a very modest bank were exposed. The purpose of this primary enclosure is far from clear, but the central burial, with the gold ring and the human remains, argues strongly for the ritual intent of at least the phase of use represented by this deposit. It should be borne in mind, however, that ritual need be only one phase of activity on the site. Evidence of later activity emerged, in particular in the form of disturbance levels but also of possible Iron Age and medieval pits as well as a late Iron Age furnace, and a number of radiocarbon dates from various deposits and features within this area reflect both the predominantly Bronze Age and the later activity here.

The two principal prehistoric features discovered within the area of the inner stone wall were an annular ditch, Ring-ditch 1, which enclosed a circular structure with entrance to the east,

Table 2.1—Moulds from the north-west of Area 1 (inside Ring-ditch 1). Squares 51 and 52 constitute the focus of Raftery's Metalworking Zone 1.

Sq. no.	Find nos
43	E84:4876, 4897, 4908, 4954, 5616a–c
51	E84:5087a–c, 5102a–d, 5113, 5118a–c, 5141, 5153, 5167, 5168, 5169a–c, 5174, 5198, 5199a,b, 5215, 5216, 5237, 5239a–c, 5240, 5241, 5242a–d, 5244, 5245, 5246, 5247, 5248a,b, 5252, 5253a–d, 5261, 5262, 5263a,b, 5274, 5303a,b, 5540, 5547, 5548, 5553, 5612, 5613, 5618, 5717a,b, 5767, 5768a,b
52	E84:5011, 5012, 5013, 5014, 5056a–f, 5068, 5069, 5070, 5079, 5080a–m, 5090a–e, 5096a–i, 5100, 5101a–c, 5108, 5109, 5110, 5111, 5112, 5114, 5115a–h, 5129, 5130, 5131, 5132, 5133, 5134a–j, 5156, 5157, 5157.1, 5158, 5159, 5160, 5161, 5162, 5163, 5164, 5165a–j, 5183, 5184, 5185, 5186, 5187, 5188a–f, 5210, 5222, 5223, 5224, 5225, 5226a–e, 5555a–i, 5556, 5557, 5558, 5559, 5560, 5594, 5595a–h, 5597, 5598, 5599, 5602a–d, 5603, 5604, 5605, 5617a–h, 5621, 5622, 5623, 5641a–d, 5642a–f, 5655a–m, 5658, 5659, 5660, 5661, 5662
59	E84:5519a–c, 5693, 5699, 5719
60	E84:5449a,b, 5510, 5523a,b, 5536, 5538a,b, 5610, 5785
42/51	E84:5367a–e, 5669, 5670a,b
43/52	E84:5346, 5347, 5348, 5349, 5350a–l, 5357, 5358, 5359a,b, 5362a,b
51/59	E84:5579, 5587a–c
52/60	E84:5588, 5606

numerous post-holes, hollows, depressions and a total of 64 pits of various types (most of them Bronze Age but also some of possibly later date); an important series of sunken hearths were also brought to light here. In addition, there was considerable evidence of human activity in the form of surviving grey, brown, orange and black stains on the surface of the yellow subsoil. An important concentration of clay moulds was found, mainly concentrated in Sqs 51 and 52 (260 fragments, Metalworking Zone 1; Table 2.1), and numerous sherds of coarse pottery and other items of prehistoric (and later) date also came to light. Although, as stated above, the ancient stratigraphy within Rampart 1 had been largely destroyed, it was nonetheless possible to recognise in this zone a number of discrete phases of prehistoric activity.

2.2.1 The 15m structure

Following the removal of the upper humus in 1969, a circular structure showed up at an early stage of the excavation as a narrow arc of grey material in the yellow boulder clay (Figs 2.5, 2.6). The brown bands of recent agricultural activity that criss-crossed the area of this enclosure initially obscured the details, but its true character became clear as the excavation progressed.

This structure was complex (Fig. 2.7), consisting of an outer bedding trench and an incomplete arc of an inner bedding trench; this was a short distance from the outer trench[2] and extended from either side of the entrance (Figs 2.8 and 2.9). Substantial post-holes here indicate that pairs of sizeable gate posts must have existed on either side of the entrance gap (Fig. 2.10). Apart from a bulge in the south-west, the trench formed a fairly regular circle with an internal diameter of fractionally over 15m. The structure was not centrally located within the ditched enclosure (see below). To the north, east and west it was consistently 10–10.2m from the inner edge of the ring-ditch, but to the south its distance from the latter was nowhere more than 7.6m.

The bedding trench, as excavated, varied considerably in width and depth. On the east, on either side of the entrance, it was 20cm wide but little more than 10cm deep and the edges were not very sharply defined. For a distance of 60–70cm south of the entrance it was similarly shallow but then it began to deepen. Here, 1m beyond the gate post, it was 20cm deep and gradually expanded to a maximum width of 40cm while maintaining the same depth. On the south the ring-ditch assumed a more regular appearance, maintaining a regular width of 20cm and a depth of 20–25cm—and occasionally 30cm—with sharp edges, vertical sides and a flat bottom. A short length of apparent trenching in Sq. 25, extending from the main trench, is almost certainly a product of modern faunal activity.

Within the bedding trench, small packing stones occurred around much of its perimeter (Fig. 2.11). Except for a short stretch in the south-west where the stones were doubled, these always occurred only around the outer edge of the trench. Around its southern perimeter, apart from a few small gaps, packing stones extended in a continuous arc. The stones varied somewhat in size but were similar in shape, their flatter

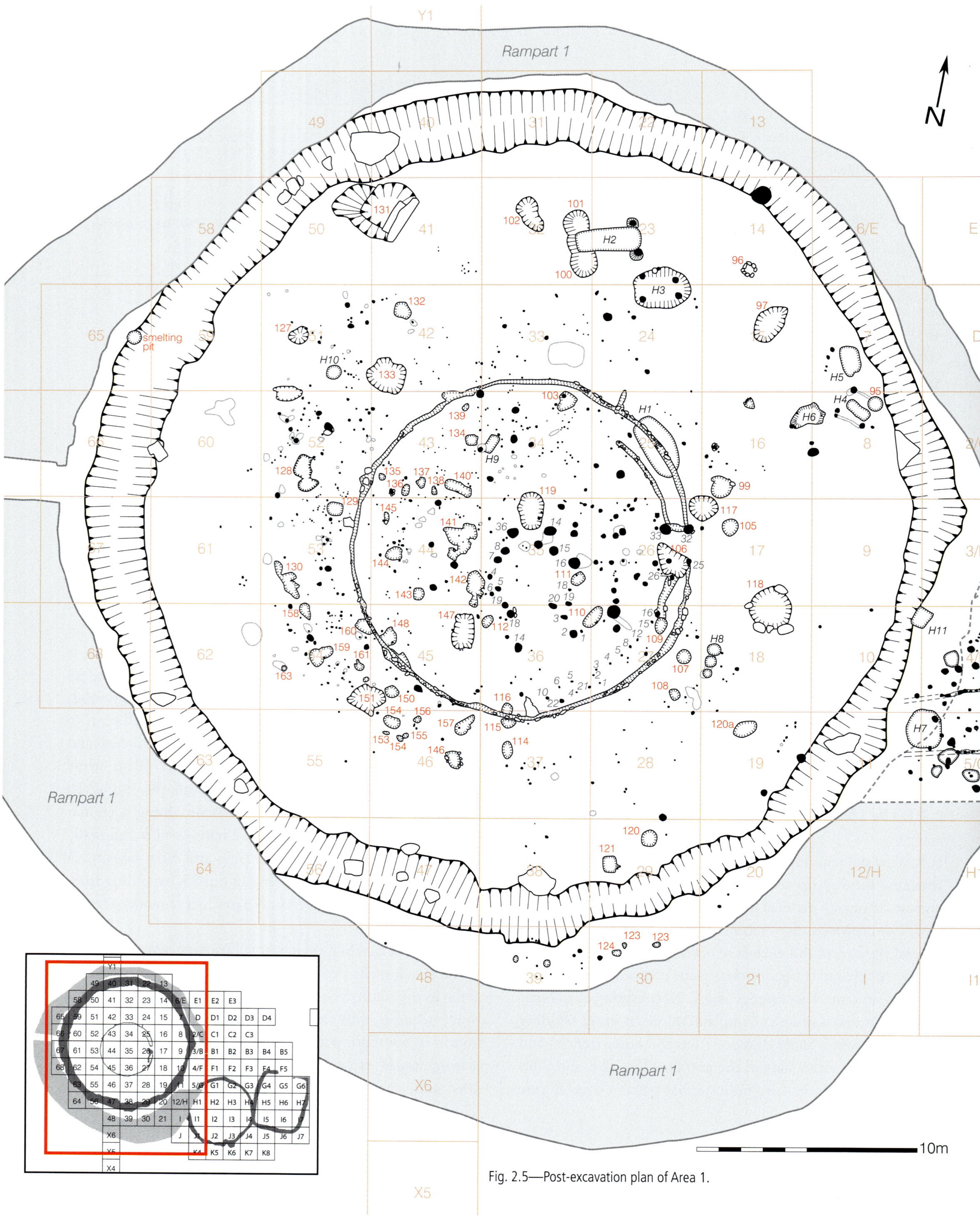

Fig. 2.5—Post-excavation plan of Area 1.

surfaces facing consistently inwards. They were placed closely together or, indeed, edge to edge on the base of the ring-ditch and projected 5–15cm above the present surface of the yellow subsoil. In the south-west, in Sq. 45, a triangular portion of a broken saddle quern (E84:5084) had been reused as a packing stone. On the north and west—covering about one third of its perimeter—there was a long stretch where packing stones were entirely absent. They were again present around the north-east but were absent on either side of the entrance gap.

The fill of the trench was, for the most part, a uniform grey but in some areas discontinuous patches of charcoal were visible. Here and there larger areas of charcoal were recognisable, and in some places the black patches appeared to be of vaguely D-shape with flat surfaces to the front. This allows, in all probability, for the former existence of a palisade of split roundwoods with flat surfaces to the exterior.[3]

The entrance gap, on the east, had been constructed with some care. Partially damaged by the digging of the later Pit 106, it was 2.2m wide. It was flanked by a pair of post-holes (nos 25 and 32), with diameters of 30cm and 53cm respectively and with surviving depths of 43cm and 50cm. Both had regular, vertical sides and flat bases, and some packing stones survived at the mouth of each. In the case of

Fig. 2.6 (left)—Bedding trench of the 15m structure during excavation, with packing stones *in situ*.

Fig. 2.7 (below)—The sections excavated through the bedding trench of the 15m structure and their locations.

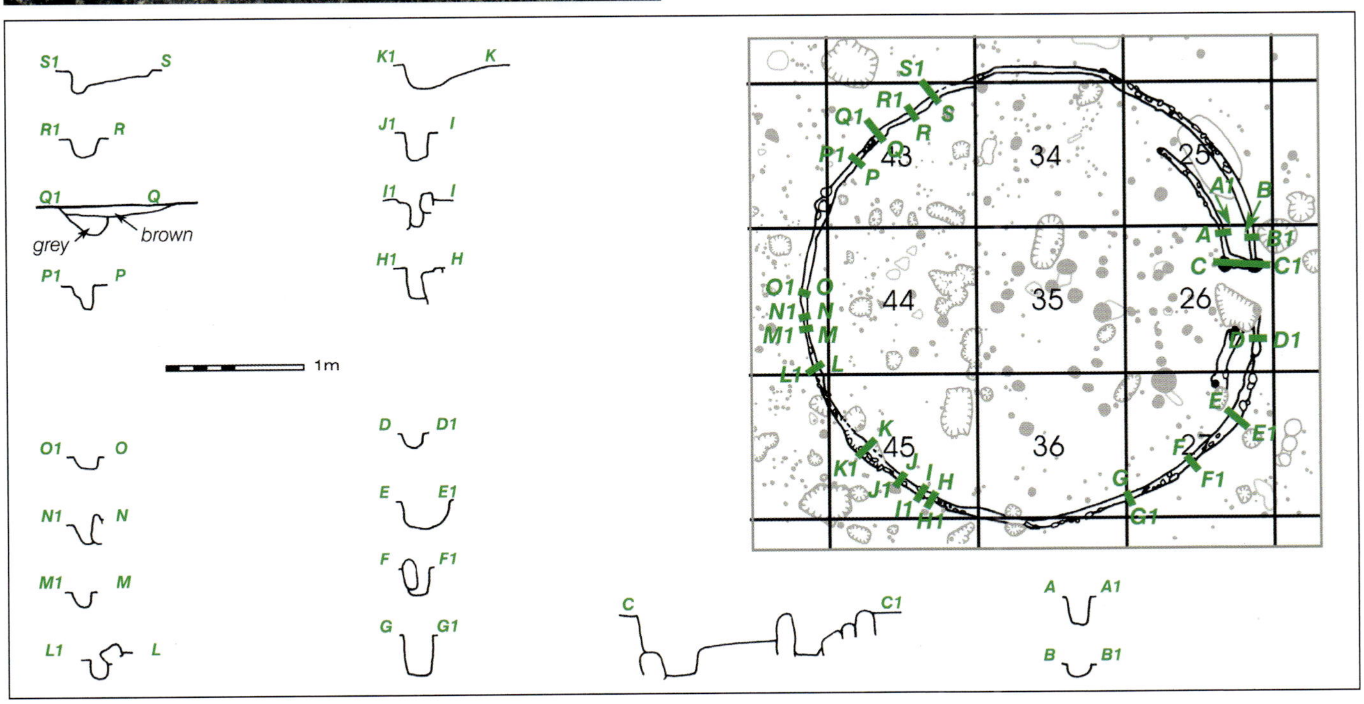

Opposite page.
Fig. 2.8 (top)—Inner and outer bedding trench after excavation, immediately north of the entrance to the 15m structure (Sq. 25, looking west).

Fig. 2.9 (bottom)—Bedding trench and arc of post-holes south of the entrance of the 15m structure after excavation (Sqs 26/27, looking east).

Fig. 2.10 (right)—Terminals of wall trenches with gate post-holes on either side of the entrance of the 15m structure (Sq. 26, looking north).

Fig. 2.11 (below)—Packing stones, positioned on the outer edge of the feature, were found around much of the perimeter of the bedding trench of the 15m structure (Sq. 15, looking south-west).

no. 32, the maximum internal distance between the packing stones was 33cm, thus giving an indication of the diameter of the original post (Fig. 2.12).

The inner bedding trench to the north of the entrance gap was similar to the outer. It had been carefully dug and maintained a constant 20cm in both width and depth. In contrast, however, it seems to have been dug with far less care to the south of the entrance, appearing more in the form of a series of elongated conjoined pits than as a continuous arc of trenching. In this zone its width varied from 30cm to as much as 50cm, and it was 20–30cm deep.

The terminal post-holes of the outer trench (nos 32 and 25) were apparently linked by straight, narrow trenches (Fig.

2.12) to a corresponding pair at the terminals of the inner trenches, which would originally have created a short passage 75cm in length. As in the case of the southern terminal of the outer trench, one of these post-holes had been largely destroyed, but traces of it remained in the base of Pit 106. The other post-hole (no. 33) was 50cm in diameter and 57cm deep. Some packing stones near its base suggest that the original post might have been about 25cm in diameter.

The fill of the inner trench was in each instance similar to the outer trench described above. The northern arc, which contained some packing stones, extended for about 4m, ending in a post-hole 20cm deep and 6cm in diameter. The corresponding southern arc of trenching, despite the damage earlier noted at its northern end, can hardly ever have extended for more than about 2m, ending in a substantial post-hole which was 28cm in diameter and 30cm deep (no. 16). Here Pit 109 partly cut across the trench. The southern arc, differing from the northern arc, continued as a curve of ten post-holes, 25–35cm apart on average (16–10). They were 20–25cm deep and 6–10cm in diameter, and all were filled with grey, silted material. This curve of post-holes ended abruptly after about 6.5m. All told, between the trench on the northern side of the entrance passage and the trench combined with the post-holes on the southern side, there was an inner arc which extended for about one third of the circumference of the outer bedding trench.

The bedding trench had been dug through Hearth 1 in Sq. 25 at a time when the latter was completely silted up (Figs 2.13 and 2.44; see below). The trench also cut through Pits 116, 148, 149 and 160. By contrast, the trench was itself cut by Pits 106 and 109. These overlaps thus indicate at least three phases of activity, though the length of time between them is uncertain.

Finds from the 15m structure

A relatively small number of artefacts were recovered from the 15m structure (Table 2.2). Most of these, including eighteen coarse potsherds (E84:1205, 1208–11, 3852–7) and a single, possible worked stone (E84:1207), came from the inner trench in Sq. 25 on the northern side of the entrance, while

Fig. 2.12—Northern terminal of the entrance feature of the 15m structure (Sq. 26, looking south).

Fig. 2.13—Hearth 1, cut by the bedding trench of the 15m structure, during excavation (Sq. 25, looking north).

Sq. 45 yielded seven coarse potsherds (E84:4845a–d, 4862, 5053, 5054) and the saddle quern fragment referred to earlier (E84:5084; see below). Three mould fragments (E84:5616a–c) were found in Sq. 43 in the fill of the inner bedding trench, while a single mould fragment (E84:2539) came from the exterior bedding trench in Sq. 26. Other finds from the 15m structure include coarse potsherds from the fill of the ring-ditch in Sqs 27 and 36/7. One green-glazed medieval potsherd (Dublin-type ware, E84:1206a) and four sherds of Leinster Cooking Ware (E84:1206b–e) came from among the stones along the edge of the bedding trench in Sq. 25, while an iron nail (E84:4847) and four sherds of Leinster Cooking Ware (E84:4846a–d) came from Sq. 45. These were obviously in a secondary position, like a number of other medieval finds which were described as having been found on or around the edge of the bedding trench.

A radiocarbon date (SUERC-42581) was recovered in 2012 from a sample that was labelled as 'from a charcoal patch (burnt

Table 2.2—Artefacts recovered from the 15m structure.

Context	Sq. no.	Find type	Find no.
Inner bedding trench	25	Coarse pottery	E84:1205, E84:1208–11, E84:3852–7
		Possible worked stone	E84:1207
Outer bedding trench	26	Mould fragment	E84:2539
	27	Coarse pottery	E84:2989
	36/37	Coarse pottery	E84:3958
	43	Mould fragment	E84:5616a–c
	45	Saddle quern fragment	E84:5084
		Coarse pottery	E84:4845a–d, E84:4862, E84:5053–4

post) in outer bedding trench'. The sample consisted of Corylus *and was of substantial size, and could conceivably represent part of a post (I. Stuijts, pers. comm.). This provided a date that calibrates to 760–420 cal. BC (Table 4.2).*

2.2.2 Ring-ditch 1

The following section describes Ring-ditch 1—formerly known as Fosse 1—and its fills. This holds a crucial position within the site's stratigraphy and chronological sequence, as it contained in some parts, particularly on its eastern side, deposits that derived from the immediately adjacent find-rich deposits in Area 2. Raftery saw the position of this material, low down in the ditch fill, as evidence for a Bronze Age date for the digging of the ditch (see below and Chapter 4, section 4.2). There are, however, some indications that deposition may have occurred later in the site's sequence, and both scenarios are discussed in detail in Chapter 4.

As noted earlier, the existence of Ring-ditch 1 came to light at a late stage in the 1969 excavations, resulting in a two-week extension of the work thanks to the generous provision of extra funding by the Office of Public Works. This feature manifested itself as a streak of fine grey material which showed up clearly in the natural yellow subsoil after the ubiquitous covering of brown humus had been removed (Fig. 2.14). At three points around its circumference, in the north-west, north-east and south-west, the silted-up ring-ditch was partly overlain by the wall of the inner enclosure, thus emphasising again the significant chronological distinction between these two features. In 1969 and in the two subsequent seasons the enclosure ditch was fully investigated.

Despite the hard, stony nature of the subsoil, the ditch had obviously been laid out with no little care, almost certainly from a central point, to provide a circle of considerable regularity. Its internal width was consistently 33.5m, apart from an east–west expansion where its width increased for a short distance to a maximum of 34.5m (Fig. 2.5). It was clearly the intention of the diggers to produce a regular, V-sectioned ditch, but this was achieved in only a few areas (Figs 2.15–2.19). In Sqs 31 and 40 (sections III and IV) the diggers had achieved smooth and regular sides, sloping evenly to a narrow base (Fig. 2.15). For the most part,

Fig. 2.14—Ring-ditch 1 inside Rampart 1 before excavation, after removal of topsoil (Sq. 20, looking north-east).

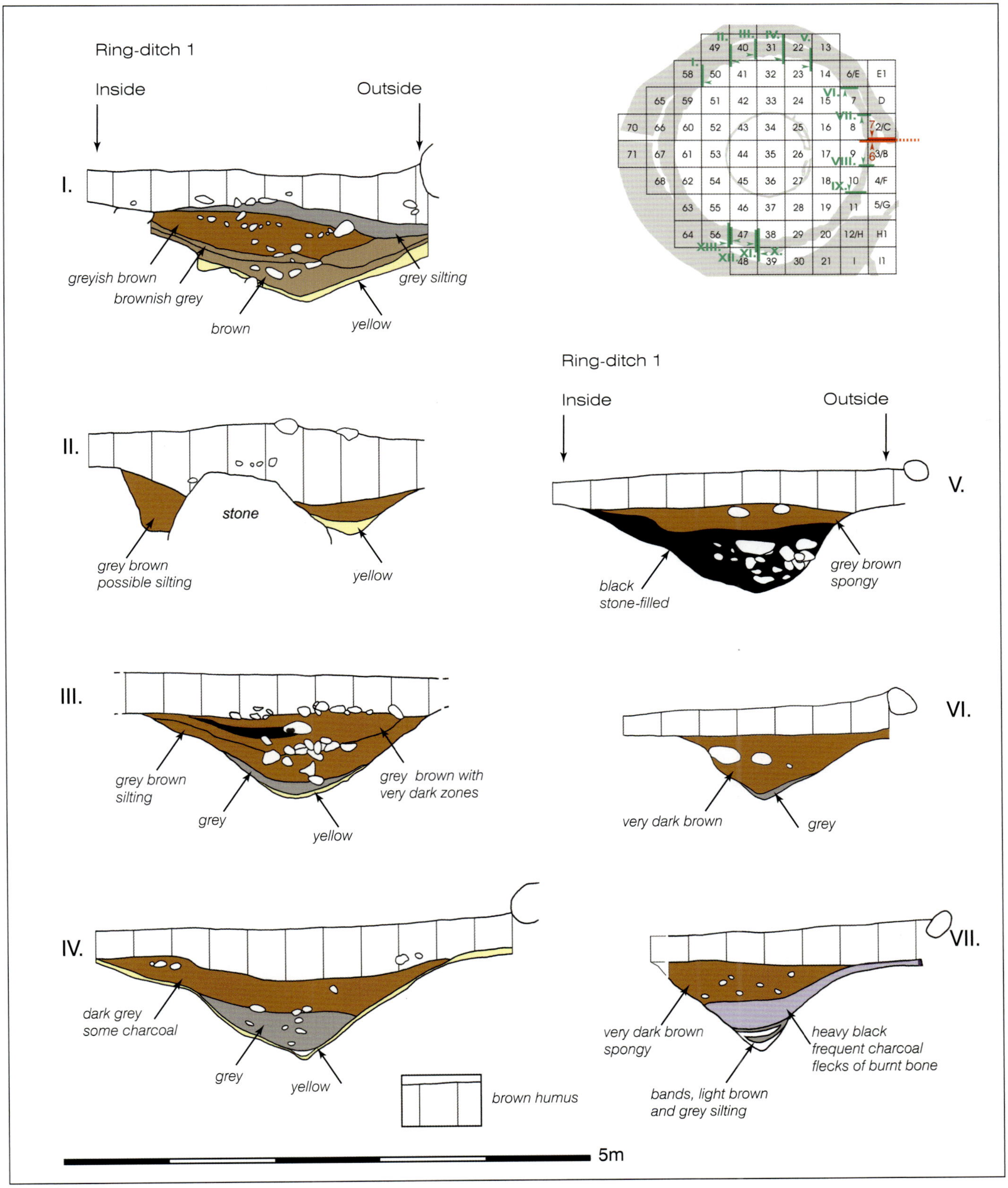

Fig. 2.15—Sections I–VII of Ring-ditch 1.

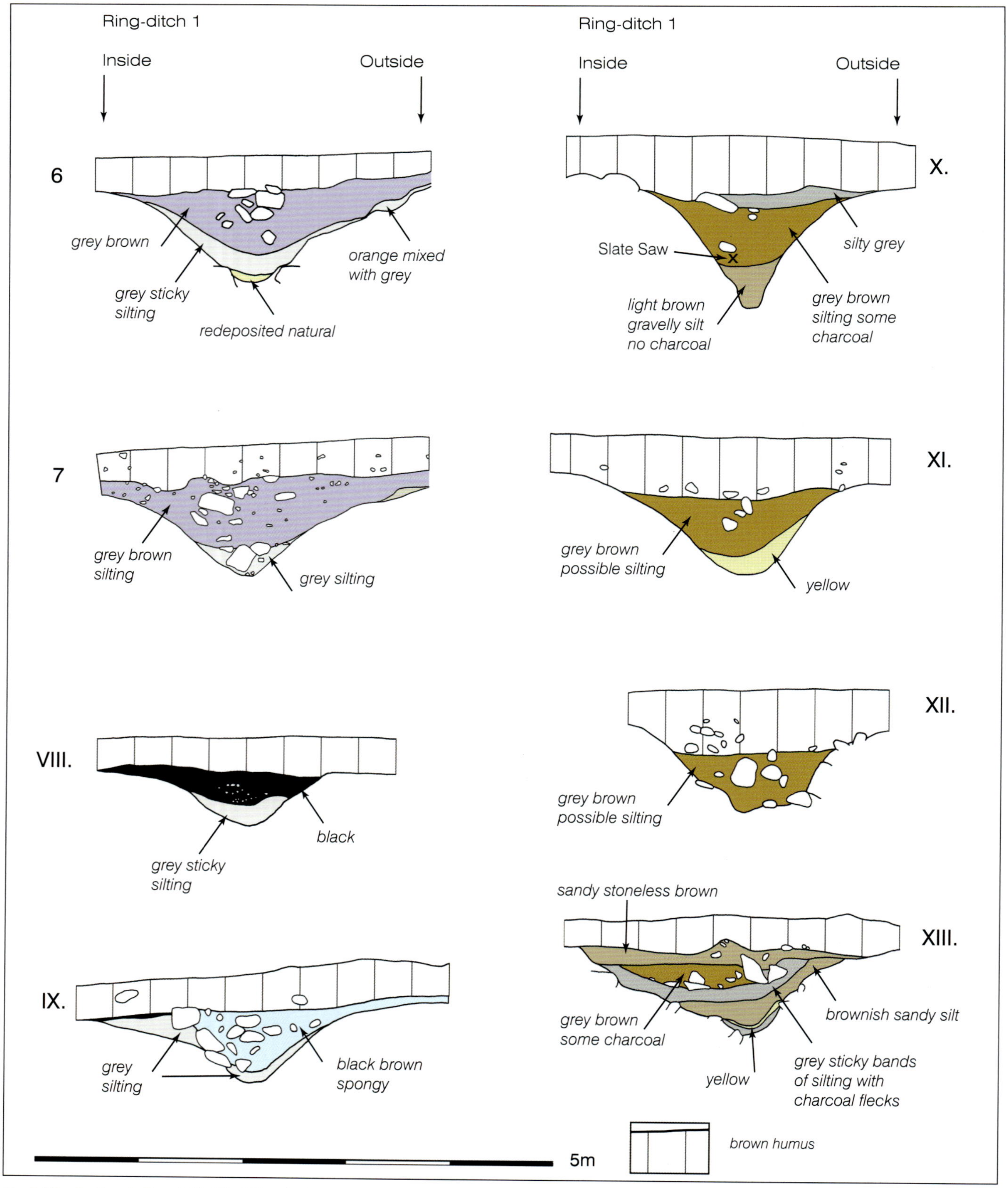

Fig. 2.16—Sections 6–7 and VIII–XIII of Ring-ditch 1.

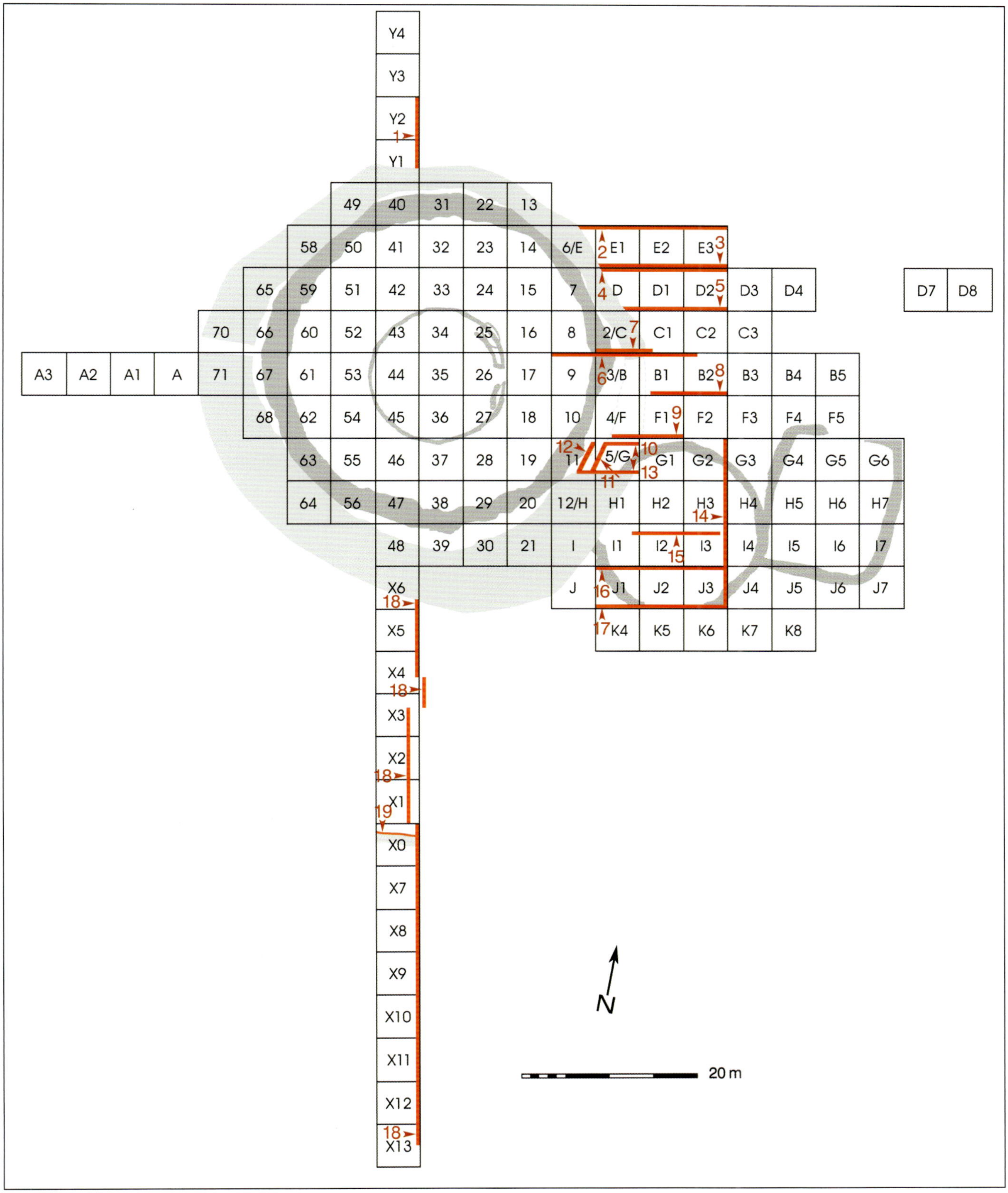

Fig. 2.17—Locations of long sections.

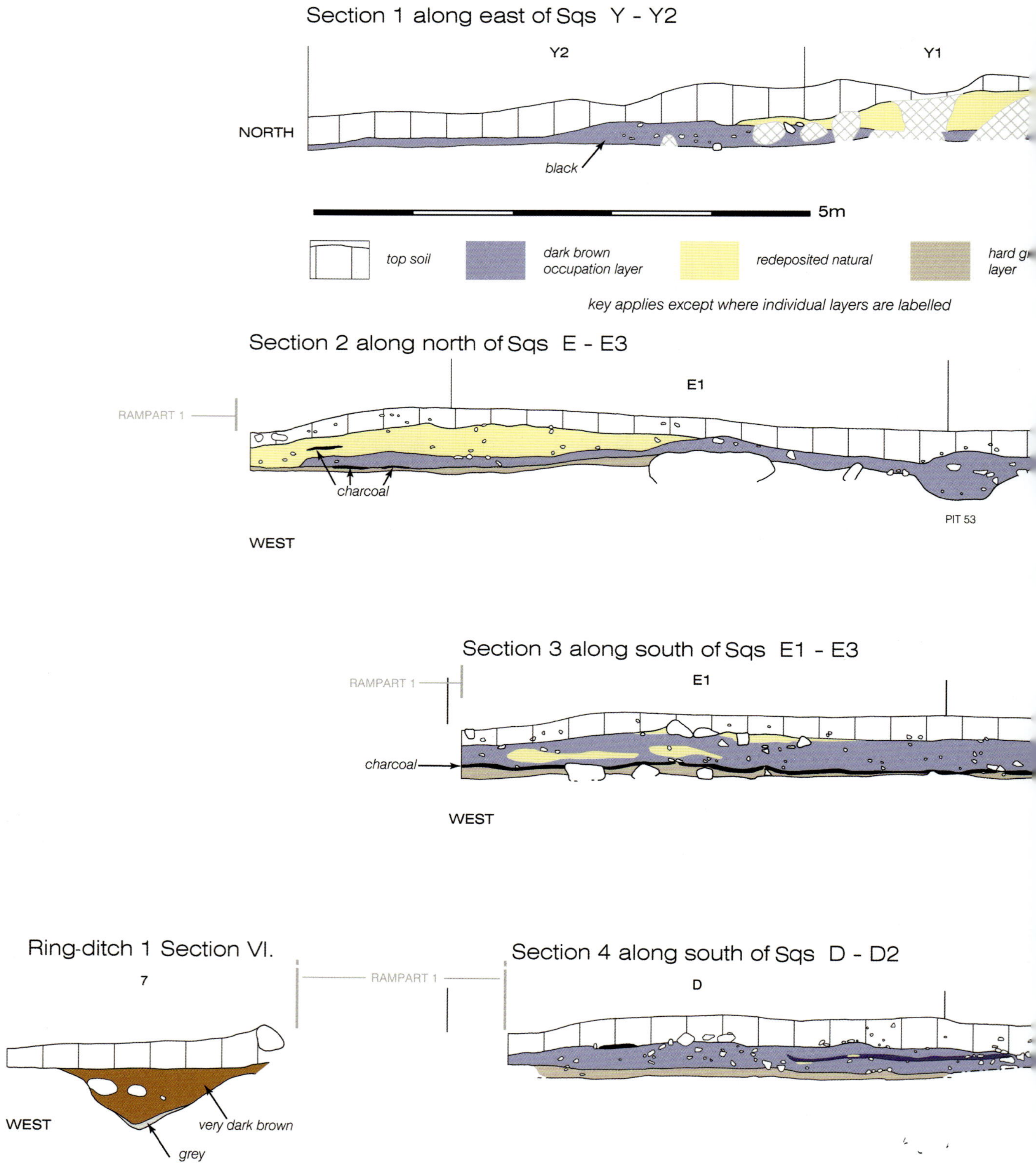

Section 1 along east of Sqs Y - Y2
Y2
Y1
NORTH
black
5m
top soil
dark brown occupation layer
redeposited natural
hard
layer
key applies except where individual layers are labelled
Section 2 along north of Sqs E - E3
RAMPART 1
E1
charcoal
PIT 53
WEST
Section 3 along south of Sqs E1 - E3
RAMPART 1
E1
charcoal
WEST
Ring-ditch 1 Section VI.
7
WEST
very dark brown
grey
RAMPART 1
Section 4 along south of Sqs D - D2
D

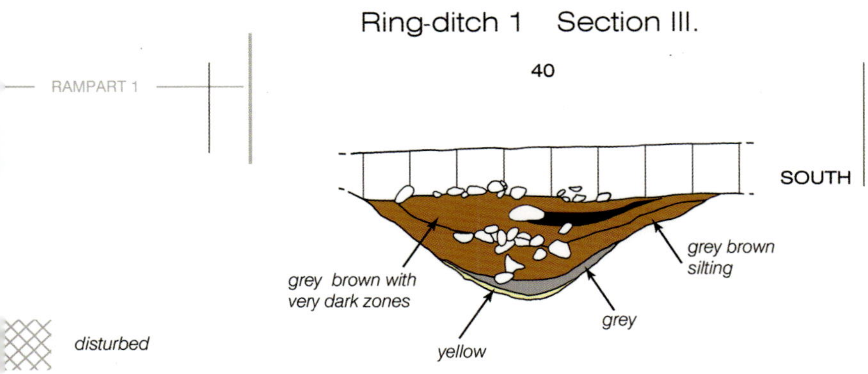

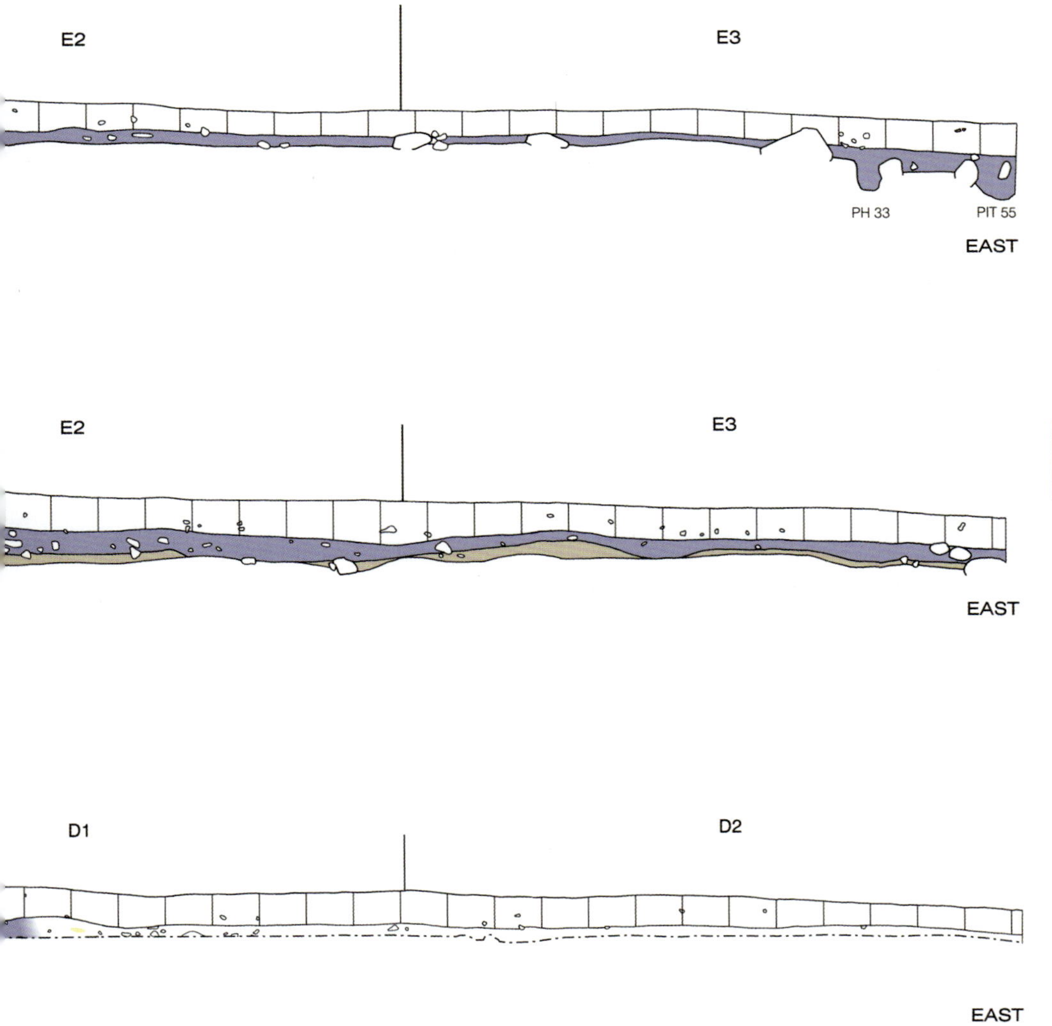

Fig. 2.18—(a) Long sections 1–4 and VI.

Ring-ditch 1 Section VII.

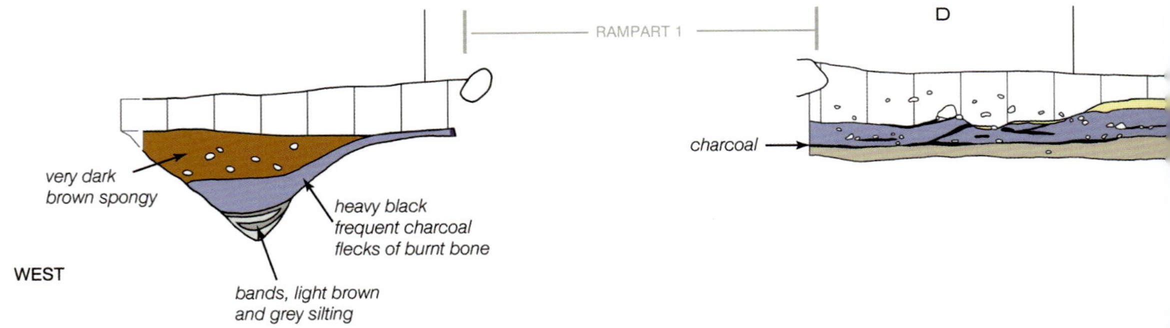

Section 7 along north of Sqs 2C - C1

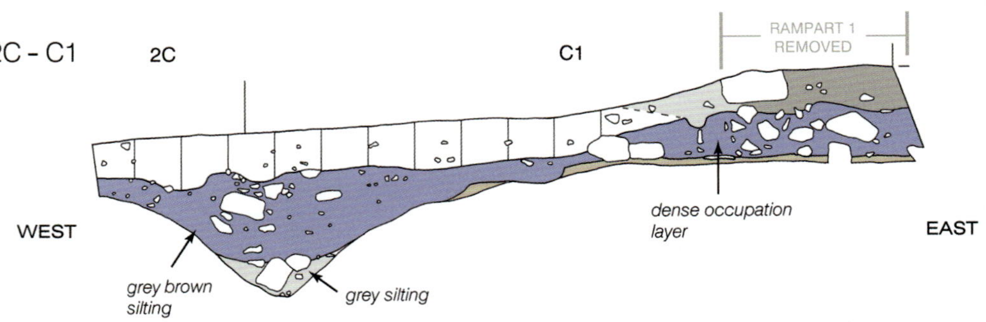

Ring-ditch 1

Section 6 along north of Sqs 9, 3B, B1,B2

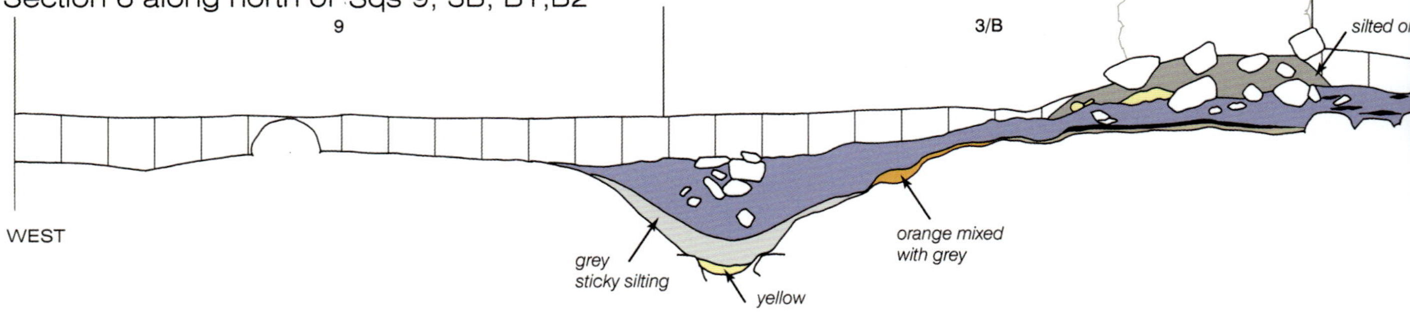

Ring-ditch 1

Ring-ditch 1 Section VIII.

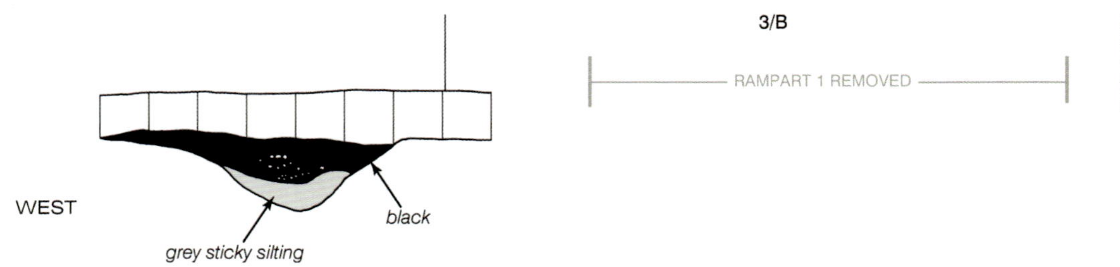

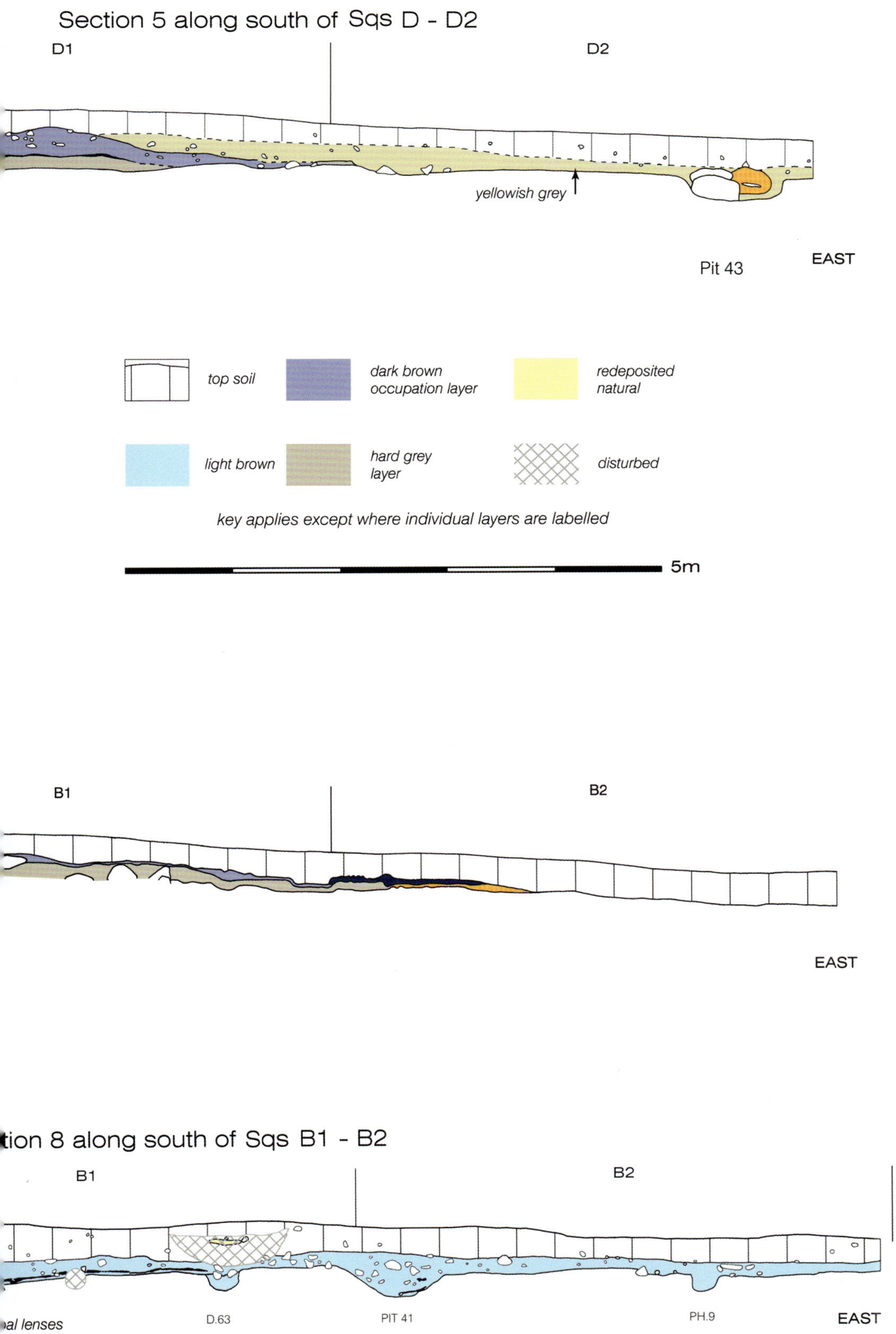

Fig. 2.18—(b) Long sections VII–VIII and 5–8.

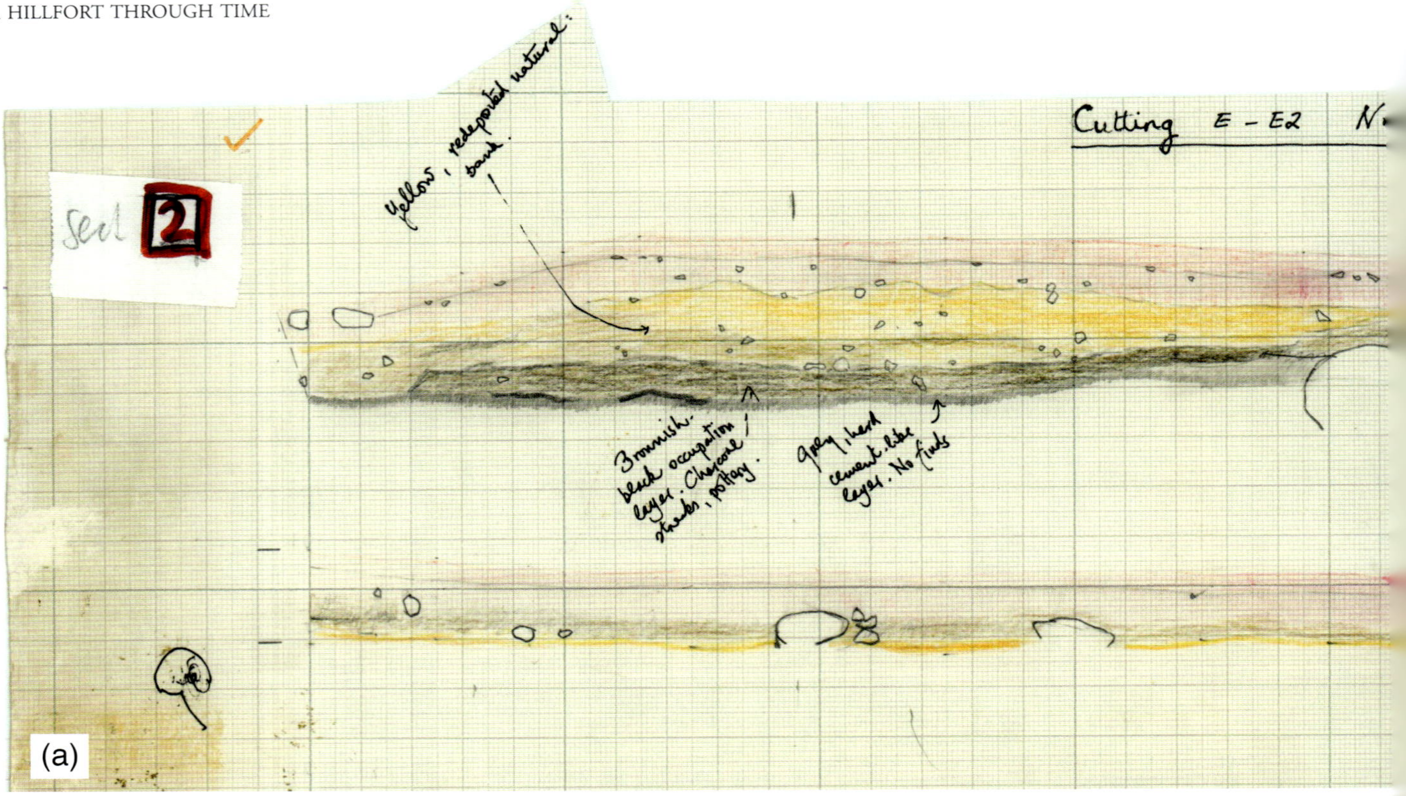
Cutting E – E2
yellow, redeposited natural sand.
Sect 2
Brownish-black occupation layer. Charcoal streaks, pottery.
Grey, hard cement-like layer. No finds
(a)

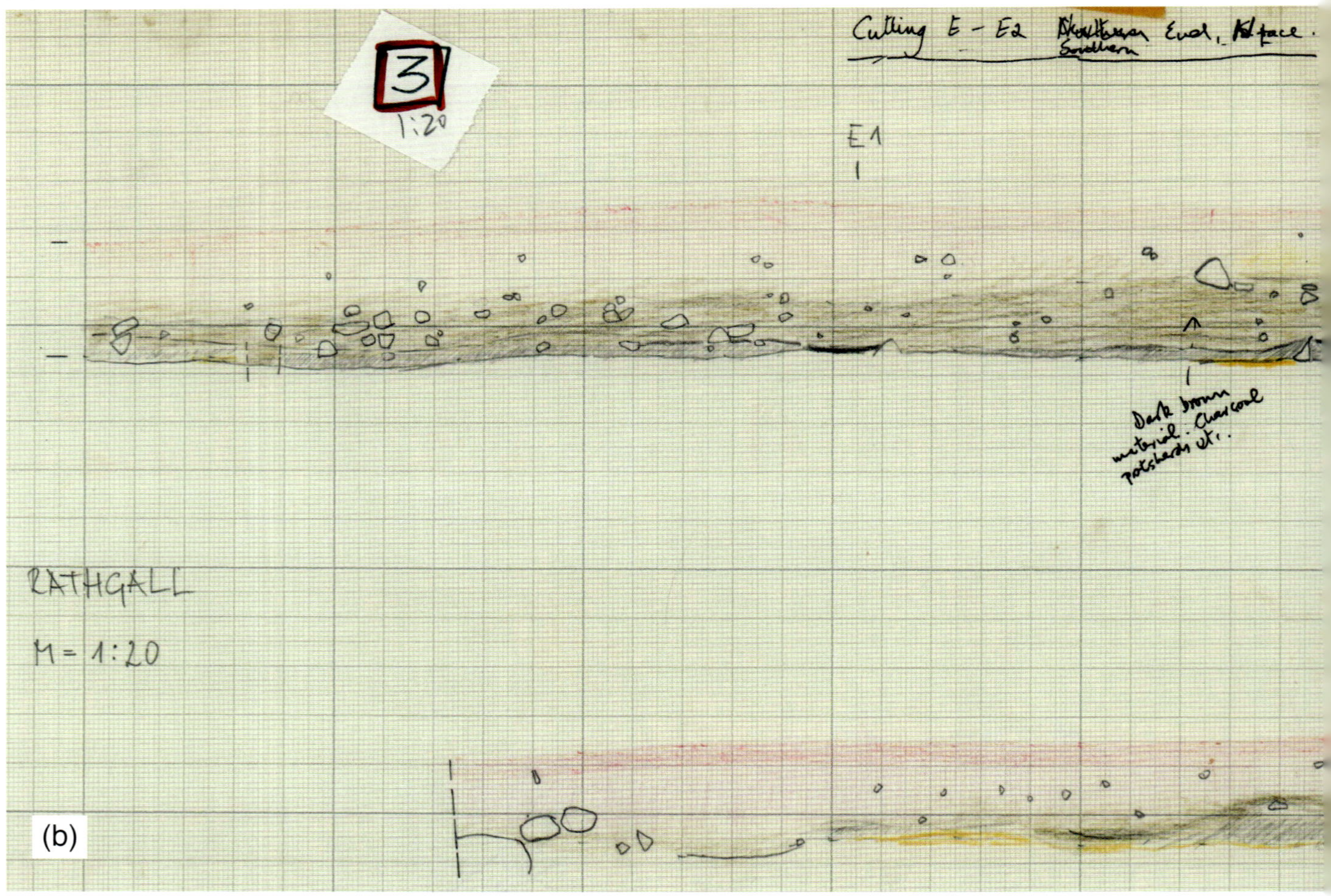
Cutting E – E2 Southern East face.
3
1:20
E1
Dark brown material. Charcoal potsherds etc.
RATHGALL
M = 1:20
(b)

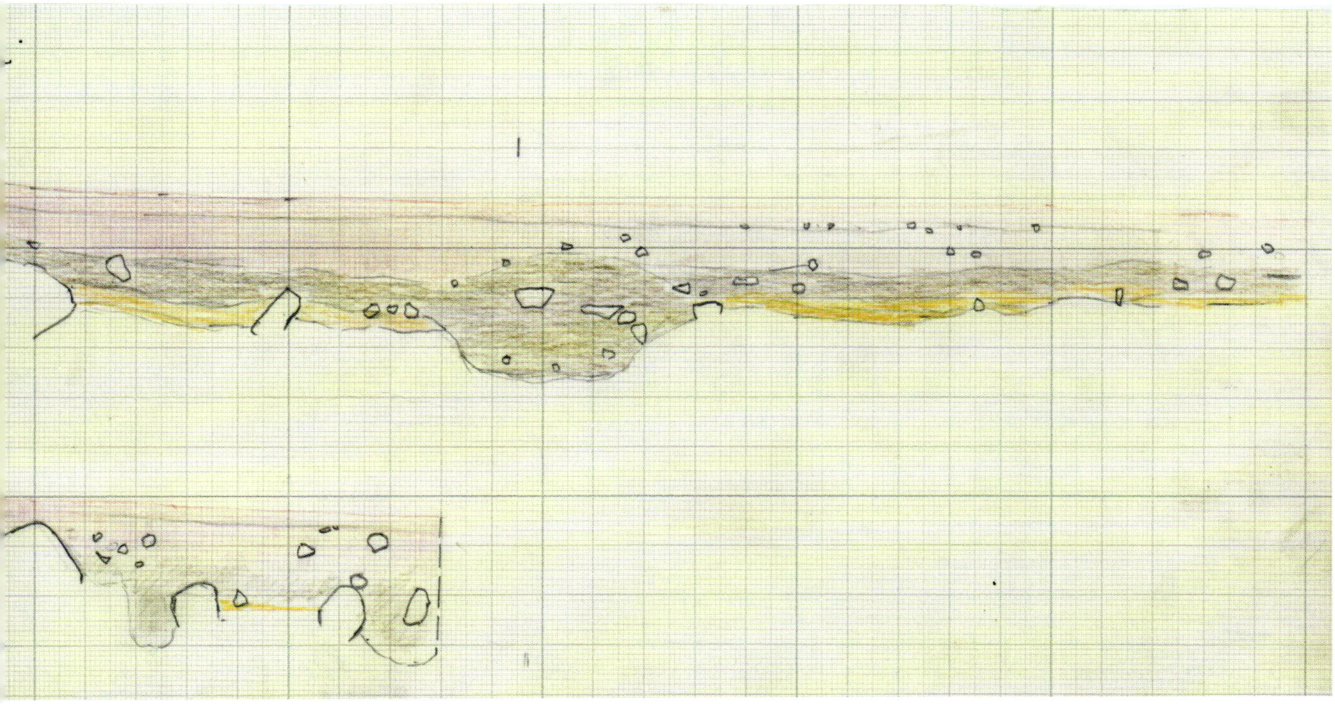

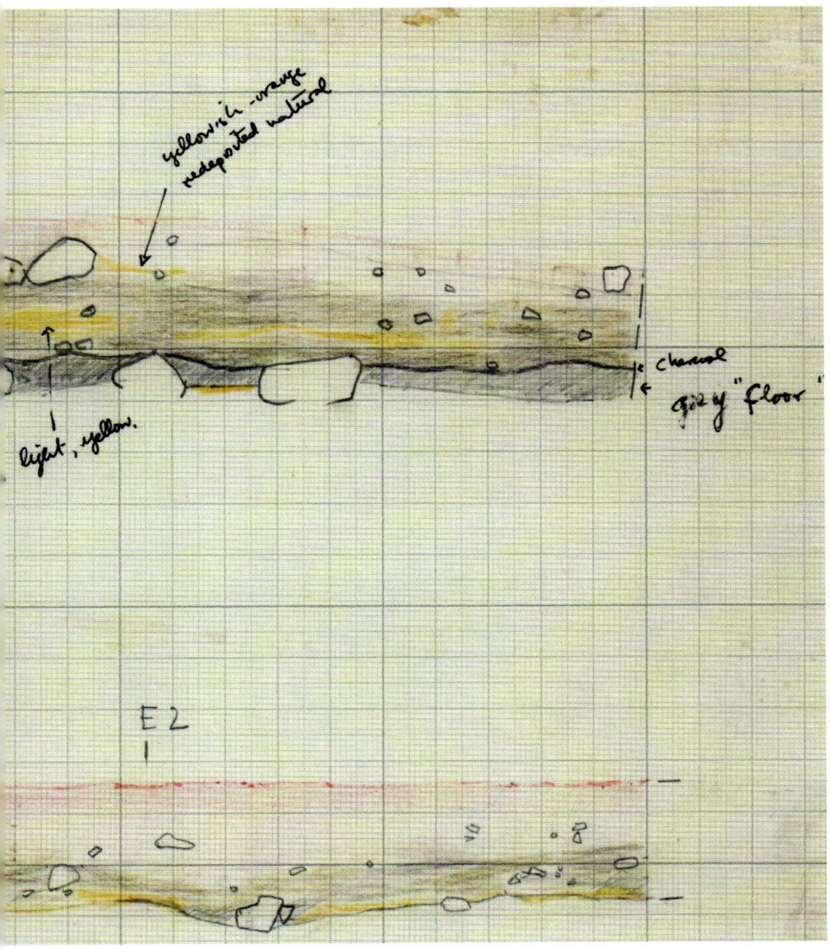

Fig. 2.19—(a) Original colour pencil drawing of long section 2. (b) Original colour pencil drawing of long section 3.

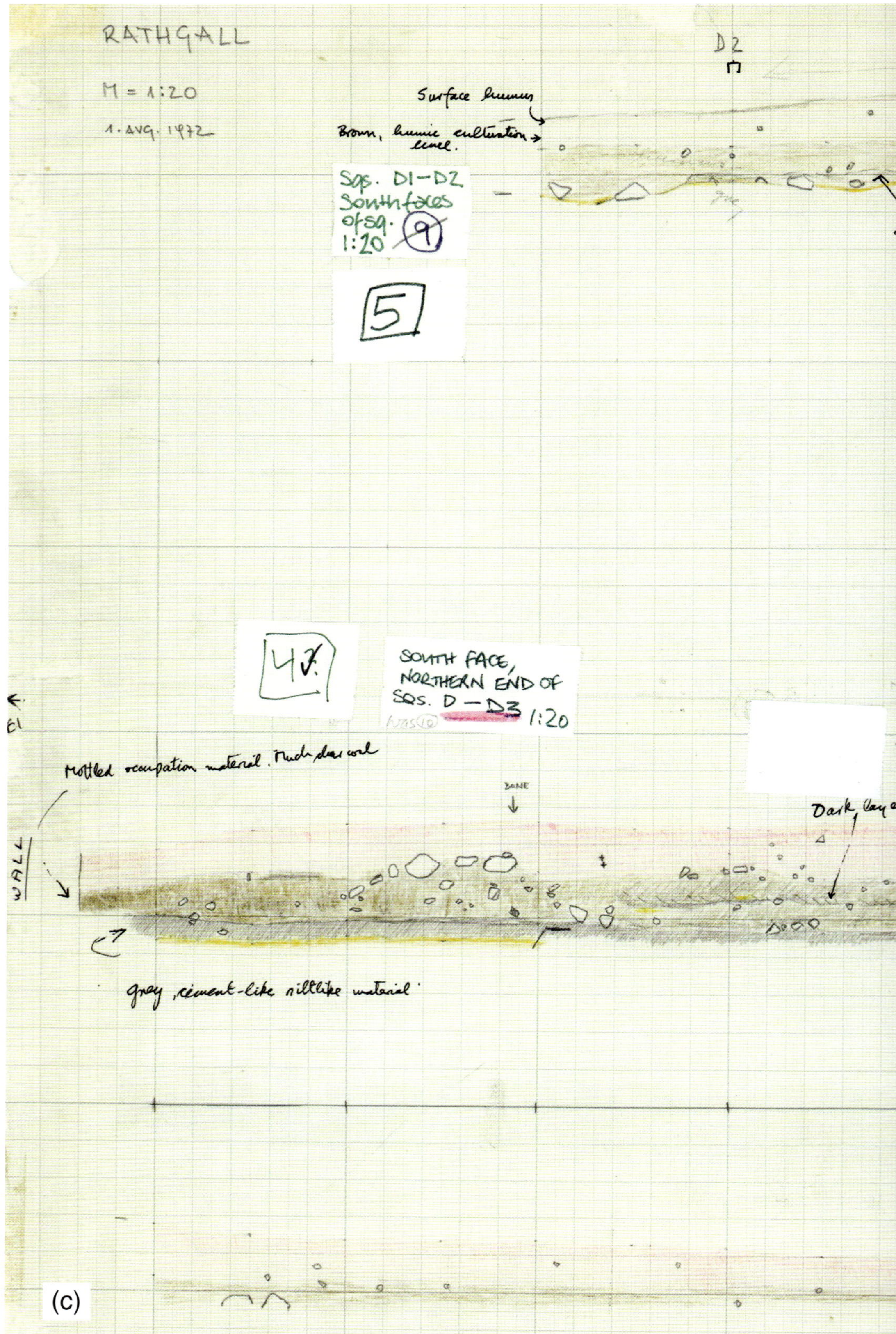

Fig. 2.19—(c) Original colour pencil drawing of long sections 5 and 4.

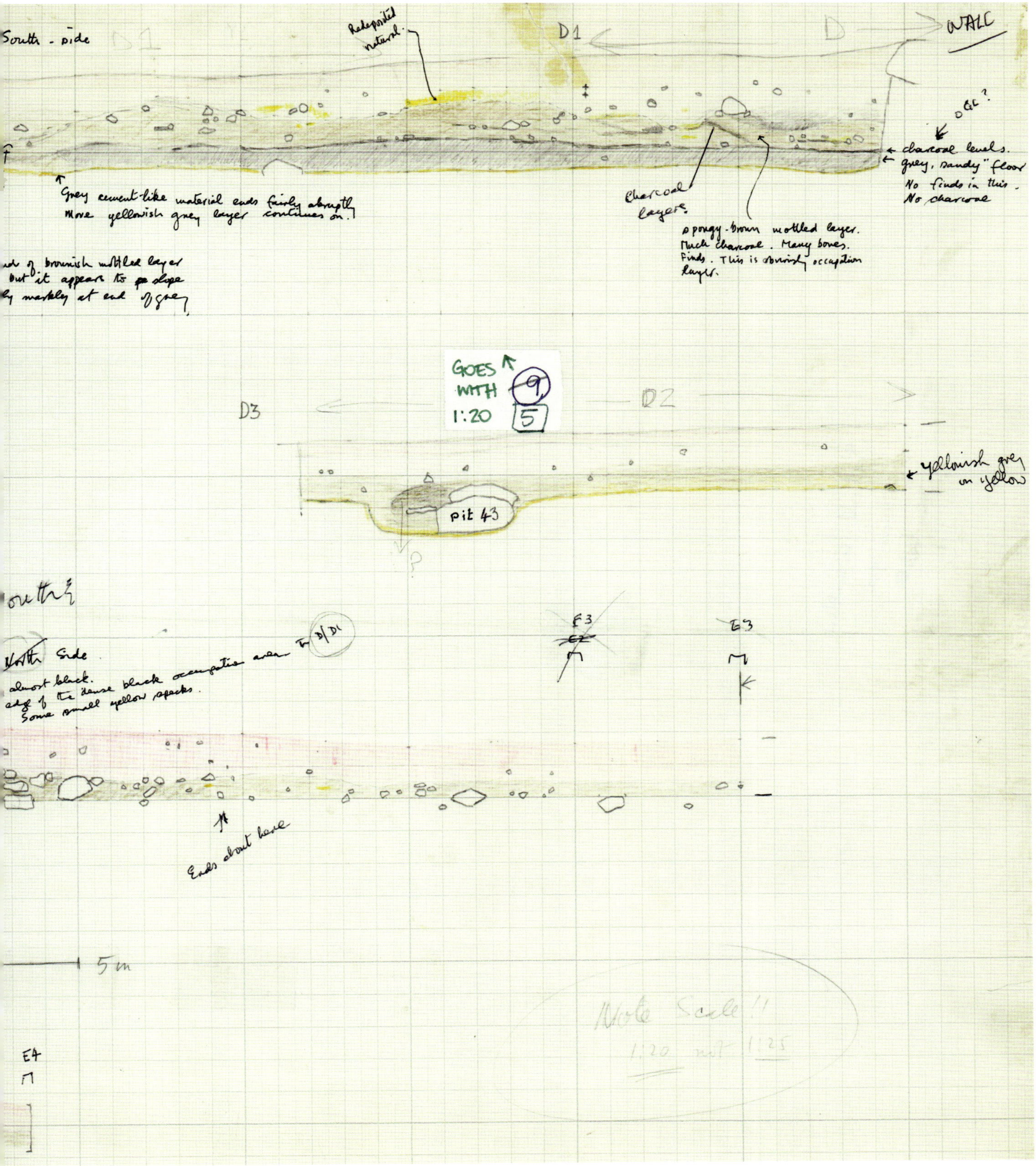
South - side
Redeposited natural.
D1
WALL
charcoal levels.
grey, sandy "floor
No finds in this.
No charcoal
Grey cement-like material ends fairly abruptly
More yellowish grey layer continues on.
Charcoal layers.
spongy-brown mottled layer.
Much charcoal. Many bones.
Finds. This is obviously occupation layer.
GOES WITH
9
1:20
5
D3
D2
yellowish grey on yellow
pit 43
North Side
almost black.
Some small yellow specks.
E3
Ends about here
5m
E4
Note Scale!!
1:20 not 1:25

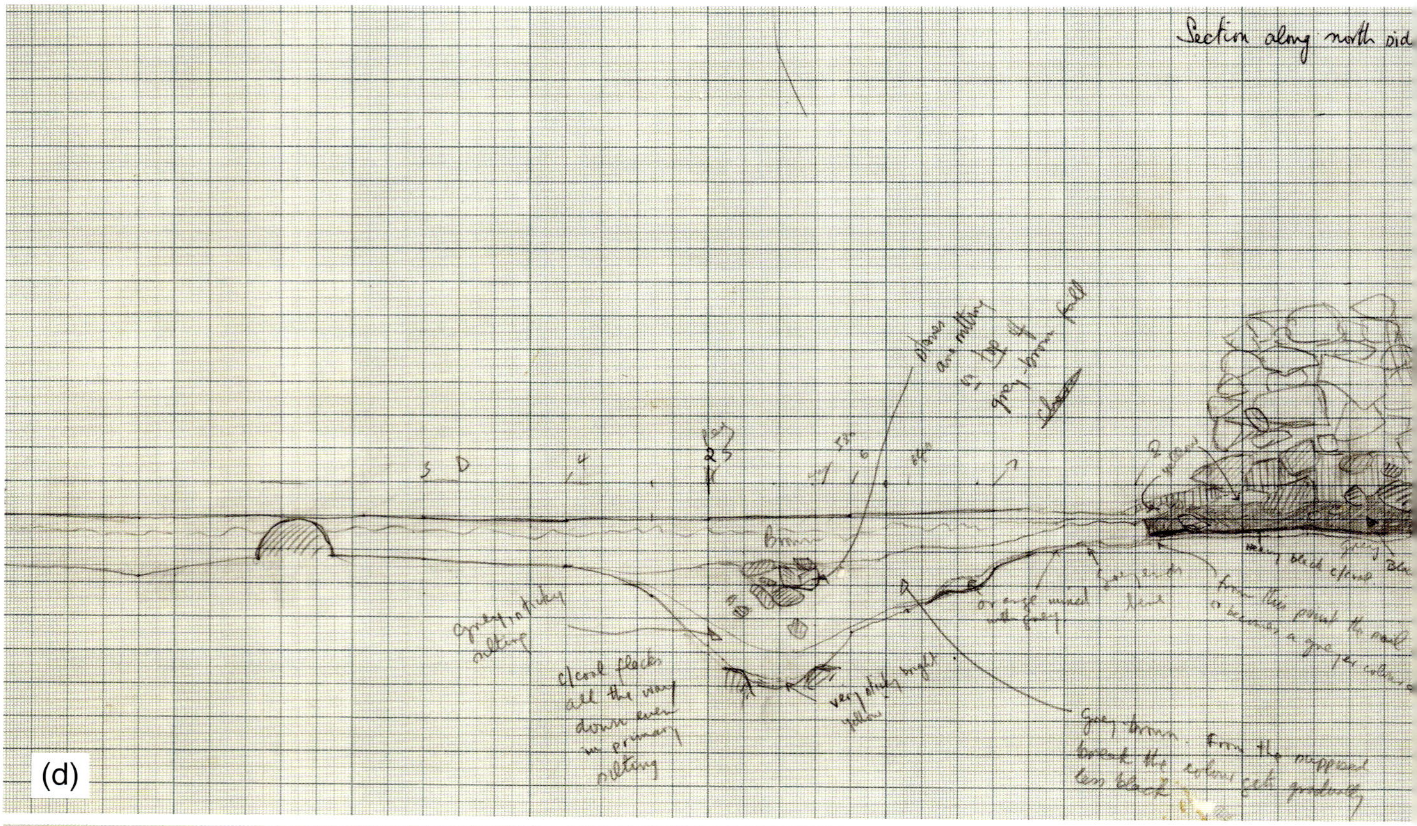
Section along north
Brown
c/coal flecks all the way down even in primary silting
(d)

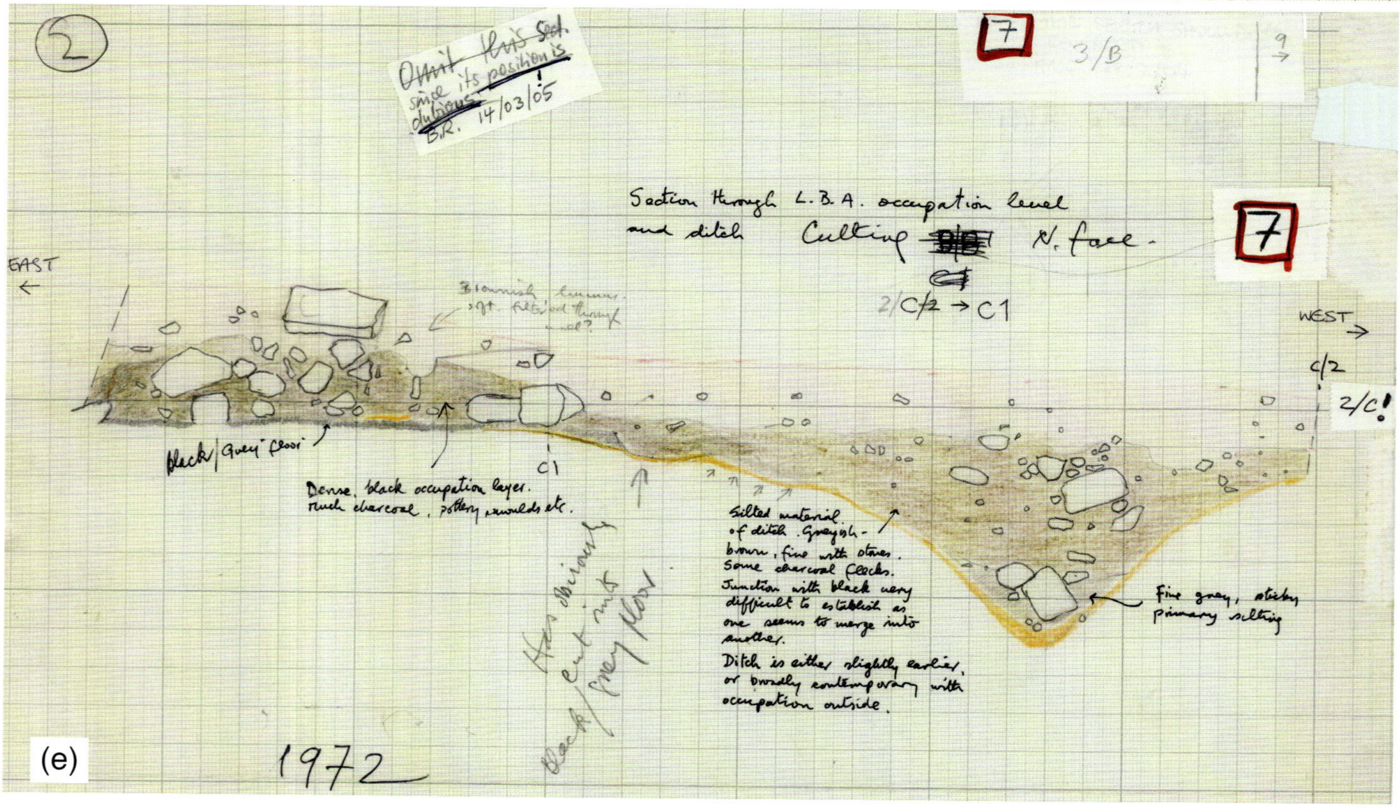
Omit this sect. since its position is dubious. B.R. 14/03/05
3/B
Section through L.B.A. occupation level and ditch Cutting N. face.
2/C/2 → C1
EAST
WEST
2/C!
black/grey floor
Dense, black occupation layer. Much charcoal, pottery, moulds etc.
C1
Silted material of ditch. Greyish-brown, fine with stones. Some charcoal flecks. Junction with black very difficult to establish as one seems to merge into another.
Ditch is either slightly earlier, or broadly contemporary with occupation outside.
Fine grey, sticky primary silting
1972
(e)

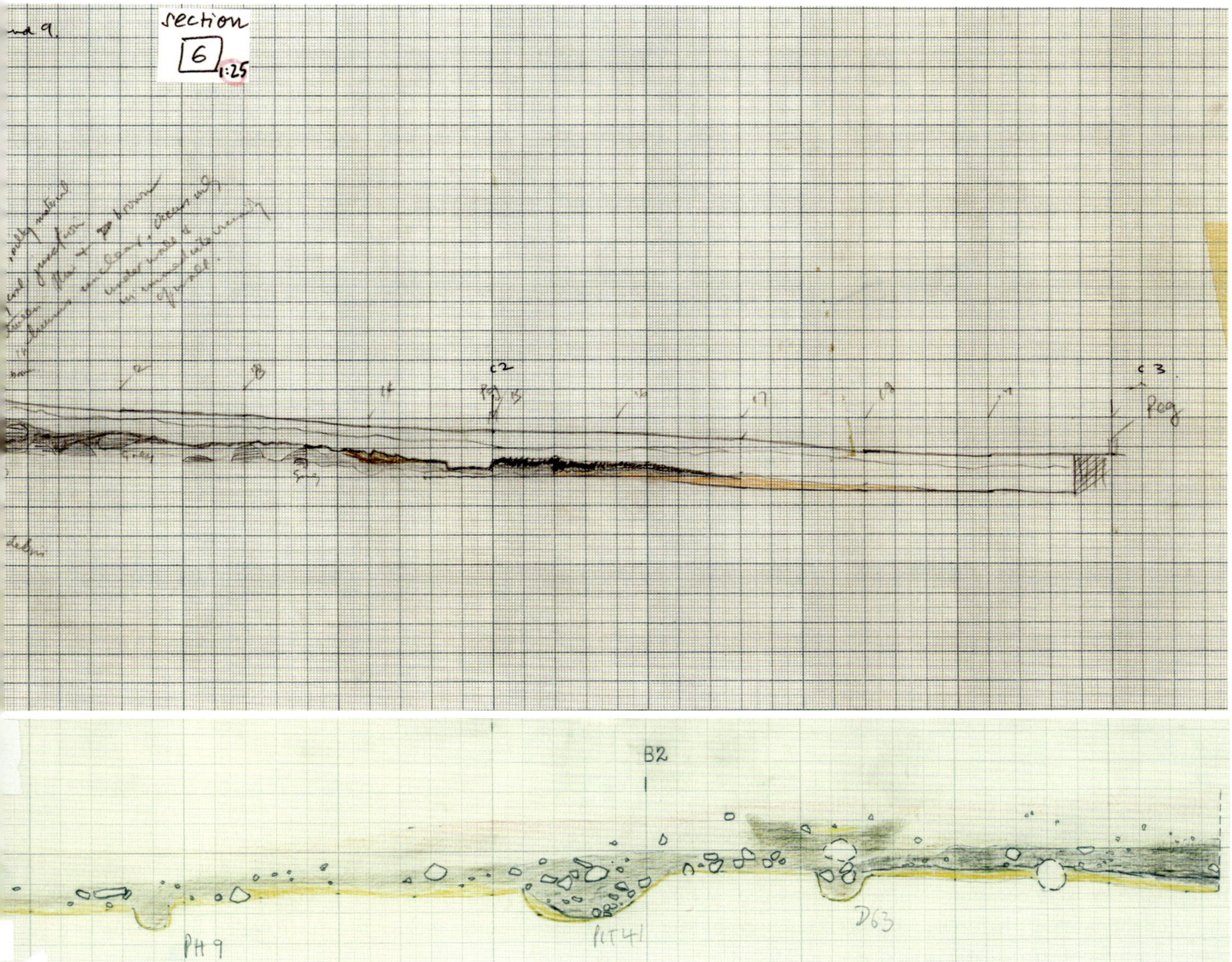

ig. 2.19—(d) Original olour pencil drawing of ong section 6. (e) riginal colour pencil rawing of long section . (f) Original colour encil drawing of long ection 8.

Fig. 2.20—A large boulder *in situ* in Ring-ditch 1 (Sqs 8/2/C, looking north).

however, because of the rocky and unyielding nature of the subsoil, the edges were jagged and irregular; moreover, through the presence in some places of large projecting boulders, they were occasionally unevenly stepped. While many of the boulders had obviously been removed by the diggers, others, of particularly large size, were left *in situ*.

This was particularly so in Sqs 8 (Fig. 2.20), 10/11 and 40, where in each case a large boulder almost completely filled the ditch.[4] Thus, from the beginning, it is clearly evident that defence was not a consideration in the digging of the ditch. Its purpose was to demarcate a circular zone and to separate this area from the exterior.

For most of its circumference the ditch averaged 2.5–3m in width at the top. On the east, however, for a stretch of about 10m, there was a noticeable constriction where, at its narrowest point, it was scarcely 1m wide (Fig. 2.5). In this area (Sq. 10) the ditch was filled by one of the very large boulders referred to above, to such an extent that it would have been simple, even for a child, to step across. The depth of the ditch below the upper surface of the boulder clay varied from *c.* 65cm to *c.* 85cm. Even if, as is probable, the ancient walking surface was somewhat higher than it appears today, the greatest depth of the ditch at any point would hardly have been significantly greater than as revealed by the modern excavation.

A curious feature in Sq. 38/9 was a deep, U-sectioned gully, filled with grey silting. It was 50–60cm wide and 45–50cm deep, and ran along the base of the ditch for a length of slightly over 1m before gradually disappearing (Figs 2.21 and 2.24). There does not appear to be any obvious explanation for this, but superficially it gives the impression of a palisade trench. This is unlikely to be the case, however, for nothing comparable occurs anywhere else around the circuit of the ditch and, indeed, the ditch is too substantial to have been planned as a palisade footing.

Around its circumference the fill of the ditch varied considerably. On the north-west, west and south-west this consisted for the most part of grey and grey-brown material, probably natural silting, mixed throughout with small and medium-sized stones. The sections drawn across the ditch in

Fig. 2.21 (above)—U-sectioned gully feature in Sq. 38/9, filled with grey silting (section X, looking west).

Fig. 2.22 (below)—Section III across Ring-ditch 1 in Sq. 40 (looking east).

Sq. 40 in the north (section III) (Figs 2.15 and 2.22) and Sq. 47 (sections X, XI and XII/XIII) in the south (Fig. 2.16) illustrate this uncomplicated filling. In addition, the paucity of artefacts from the ditch fill around its western circuit was noticeable (Table 2.3a). Indeed, the finds catalogue clearly shows that most of the finds in this sector came from material overlying the ditch—most, indeed, from disturbed ploughsoil. This is in keeping with the excavation evidence indicating scant occupation activity in this part of the site.

In Sq. 40 (section III) (Figs 2.15 and 2.22) three discrete layers were evident, with an upper darker grey which probably represents a final phase of vegetation growth. Noticeable concentrations of medium-sized stones were evident in both the second and third phases of its fill. The same could be recognised in Sqs 50 and 56 (sections I and XIII; Figs 2.15 and 2.16), where phases of natural soil development mixed with occasional flecks of charcoal occurred and there were also accumulations of pebbles and stones in the upper levels.

A radiocarbon date was obtained on a piece of Corylus *from the grey fill, which was noted to have derived from under stones in Sq. 56 (GrA-23341, 1290–960 cal. BC; Table 4.2). While Raftery does not mention it, section III in the north and sections X–XIII in the south seem to show an initial phase of silting, as observed for those in the east described below.*

In the context of the stone filling, Sq. 22 (section V) (Figs 2.15 and 2.23) was particularly informative. Here, along the base of the ditch on the east, there was a concentration of grey-black material mixed with small pebbles on the inner slope. At the same level, on the outer half of the ditch, there was a dense concentration of medium-sized stones piled

Fig. 2.23—Section V across Ring-ditch 1 in Sq. 22 (looking west).

directly, almost to its base, on the sloping side of the ditch. The position of this accumulation of stones and their outward, sloping angles imply deposition or collapse from the inside, and their position on the base of the ditch also indicates that this took place soon after the initial excavation of the ditch. All were eventually covered by a uniform accumulation of grey-brown soil. A small bronze ring came from the upper filling of the ditch here (E84:448) but otherwise, apart from 22 potsherds, a single mould fragment (E84:1275) and a piece of iron (E84:1290), there were few finds (Table 2.3a).

A layer of moderately sized stones occurred in Ring-ditch 1 around most of its circumference (Figs 2.25, 2.26), generally 10–20cm or less below the surface of the boulder clay. This layer was overlain by a layer of sticky grey-brown material, with subsequent silting and the development of a turf line. The stones were of medium size (with average dimensions varying from 5cm to 10cm), but occasionally some far larger ones occurred, as, for example, in Sq. 31, where two with dimensions of 50cm x 20cm x 30cm and 45cm x 25cm x 30cm were uncovered. In the latter square the stones occurred on—and apparently in—a dark, charcoal-filled layer and rested on the inner edge of the ditch. They were absent from the outer edge and had thus clearly fallen in or (though less likely) been thrown in from outside.

Raftery singles out Sq. 31, but it seems that this situation can be observed elsewhere. While there is no securely identifiable image of Sq. 31, a similar situation seems evident in Sqs 9/3 and 10 and F1 (Figs 2.25, 2.26 and 2.27). Charcoal from the upper levels in this area was dated to 896–371 cal. BC (D-135).

This layer of stones was a striking feature of the ditch fill. At times the stones were tightly packed together to form a layer resembling rough cobbling, as for example in Sqs 67, 62/8 (Fig. 2.28) and, especially, 20 (Fig. 2.29). On the north and in parts of the east it became sporadic and was at times entirely absent.

The level of this layer, near the top of the ditch, remained relatively constant, implying that the deposition of the stones was part of a single action. Oddly, however, in Sq. 38 the stone layer dipped gradually to the north, roughly from grid peg 29, sloping downwards almost to the ditch bottom. In contrast with the situation to the east, the stone layer here was completely covered by the grey silting which elsewhere filled much of the ditch. East of grid peg 29, however, the stone layer lay, as elsewhere, at a higher level in the ditch and was clearly on and in a black layer.

GrA-23350 and SUERC-42586 were derived from samples that were taken from black organic material, which seems to

Fig. 2.24– The possible U-sectioned gully at the base of Ring-ditch 1 (Sqs 38/39, looking south?).

Fig. 2.25—Section 6, Sqs 9/3 (looking north).

Fig. 2.26—'Cobbling' in Ring-ditch 1: (a) in Sq. 20, (b) in Sqs 58/59 and (c) in Sq. 10.

represent this black layer. The cobbling described here is not captured in section X, which is located at the western side of Sq. 38. A photograph of the section shows rocks on the inside of the slope within this square (Fig. 2.21).

It is impossible to envisage this layer of crude cobbling as having accumulated by accident. It is thus likely either that the stones were systematically deposited in the ditch as conventional filling, using stones gathered specifically for this purpose, or that they came from a dismantled structure. The possibility that there had once been a low wall around the inner (or, indeed, outer) edge of the ditch cannot be discounted, but the limited quantity of stones and their generally modest dimensions, as well as the discontinuous nature of the filling around the ditch, all serve to weaken this hypothesis. It seems more likely that the stones were part of a deliberate act of ditch-filling which was carried out in a single action using stones specifically gathered for the purpose. Clearly, too, the deposition of this stone layer took place in some areas when the ditch was already substantially filled, mainly with silting, around most of its circumference.

Fig. 2.27—Ring-ditch 1 in Sqs 3/9 during excavation, with stony fill on the inside slope of the ditch in front of section 6, looking north-west.

Fig. 2.28—'Cobbling' in Ring-ditch 1, Sq. 62 (looking north-west).

Fig. 2.29—'Cobbling' in Ring-ditch 1, Sq. 20 (looking north).

Around the eastern and north-eastern zone of the ditch the lower filling material was fundamentally different from that encountered elsewhere. The upper levels consisted of the same grey-brown material already described, with the stony layer covered by and embedded in this. The lower levels, however, were filled with a largely undifferentiated layer of dense black organic material, mixed with charcoal and containing many finds. This black layer, which filled the lower half of the ditch, mainly in Sqs 8/2 (Fig. 2.30) and 9/3 rested on a thick layer of primary silting. It was evident in the first season of excavation in 1969 that this zone was part of a continuous layer which emanated from under the wall of the inner enclosure, and the black layer clearly derived from activity immediately outside rather than inside the ditch (Fig. 2.31). This realisation led immediately in 1970 to the investigations outside Rampart 1 on the east and the removal of an initial 5m stretch of the inner stone enclosure, which exposed a continuous profile westwards along the northern face of Cutting 3/B through the ditch of the inner enclosure (section 6) (Figs 2.16, 2.31 and 2.32). This section is crucial in determining the relationship between the digging of the ditch (Ring-ditch 1) and the metalworking activity to its immediate east. Cuttings 8/2/C (sections 6, 7 and VII; Figs 2.19, 2.25, 2.33 and 2.34) and, especially, 9/3/B were filled with domestic and industrial detritus embedded in black organic material which lay on a layer of primary silting. The latter (sections 6 and 7), which from top to bottom contained a rich assemblage of archaeological material, rested directly on the inner, western, face of the ditch. On the base, and in the east, the black layer and the ditch face were separated by a layer of grey primary silting up to 5cm thick.

It was noticeable, however, that the material immediately under the wall differed somewhat in colour and texture from that in the ditch. Under the wall the layer was a dense black with numerous charcoal fragments, some of which were of considerable size. In the ditch, though filled with charcoal, the material was slightly less dense in colour and the charcoal consisted of smaller, more scattered fragments. The difference between the material under the wall and that filling the ditch was not, however, pronounced and it was only when the soil was moist that a hint of any differentiation arose; under most soil conditions it was impossible to establish any break between them. It was concluded, therefore, that the most likely explanation for the slight difference in texture between the two levels derived from the differing local environments, above and within the ditch, and the protection which the material outside the ditch had received from the later stone wall. In addition, over time there may have been a greater degree of water percolation (and perhaps worm activity) in the silted-up ditch, which would have further contributed to the marginally differing textures of the soil in the two zones. At any rate, it can be said that there was no clearly defined

Fig. 2.30—Ring-ditch 1, section VII (looking north).

Fig. 2.31—Ring-ditch 1, section 6 (looking north).

Fig. 2.32—Ring-ditch 1, section 6 (looking north).

Fig. 2.34—Ring-ditch 1, sections 6 to IX (looking north).

Fig. 2.33—Ring-ditch 1, sections VI and VII (looking north).

division between the material in the ditch and that above it along its eastern edge.

Both to the north and to the south of this dense occupation layer in 8/2/C and, especially, 9/3/B the situation was rather different. To the south in Sq. 10, for example, only a few mould fragments were found (Table 2.3a) and it was revealed that, following an initial phase of silting, stones had found their way in from inside the ditched enclosure, after which there were phases of gradual infilling and vegetation growth which formed an upper blackish layer (sections VIII and IX are on either side of Sq. 10; Fig. 2.16). *This description appears to relate to what is depicted in section VIII in terms of the vegetation growth and in section IX in terms of the stones.*[5] Similarly, in Sq. 7, while occupation material occurred, it was nowhere near as intensive as that in 8/2/C. Here, though a sizeable number of coarse potsherds, two glass beads and other items were found, only eight small, nondescript fragments of clay moulds, all worn, were brought to light in the upper fill.

Thus, as the external source of the ditch fill is not in question, it may be concluded with reasonable confidence that the ditch was open when the activity immediately outside it to the east in B/C was taking place. It may further be concluded that there was no great chronological distinction between the excavation of the ditch and the deposition in it of debris from outside.[6]

One or possibly two radiocarbon dates were obtained from deposits in Sq. 8 (SUERC-42585 and SI-1485), from samples of the black fill near the bottom of the ditch, which appear to represent the lowermost deposits above the initial layer of silting. Further up, at a depth of 25cm but still within the same black occupation deposits, a sample (GrN-27098) produced a calibrated date of 1280–1020 cal. BC in Sq. 2. A further date (SI-1484; for comments on Smithsonian dates please see Chapter 4) was taken on charcoal from 'black fill in lower portion' of the ditch, but as the grid square from which it originated is unclear it can only be presumed to also be from the redeposited occupation material in the eastern part of the ditch. While Raftery mentions above that occupation material occurred in Sq. 7, the samples obtained from this grid square are only described as from 'blackish organic material' 30–40cm below the ditch rim. The context was dated twice, as it initially produced a date of 760–450 cal. BC (GRN-27099, on Quercus *sp. branch wood), which was at the time considered to be too young, since it conflicted with the earlier Bronze Age dates. In the redating of these deposits a piece of hazel from the same sample produced an older date (GrA-23351, 1370–1040 cal. BC). The date SI-1483 appears to have been taken on a sample derived from the organic build-up in the ditch in Sq. 10, producing a determination of 430–50 cal. BC, whereas a second date from the same grid square agrees with the other Bronze Age dates at 1210–1010 cal. BC (SUERC-42580).*

The (yellow) bank

The ring-ditch may have been accompanied by a bank, possible evidence for which was exposed in Areas 1, 2 and 3. This was observed as a mound of sterile material, at times described as consisting of yellow redeposited natural (Fig. 2.35). The occurrence of this material is described in the accounts of the respective areas.

The first appearance of this material was in the E square (see below), where Raftery describes it as resting on occupation material of obvious Bronze Age date. Small deposits of apparent black occupation material were found on its surface, and material from one of these was radiocarbon-dated. Although no continuous profile was created to examine the relationship of this material with Ring-ditch 1 and no evidence for a bank was observed in those areas where Rampart 1 had been removed, Raftery nevertheless interpreted these yellow deposits as the remains of the former bank of Ring-ditch 1. The very straight edge formed by this deposit along the southern edge of the E1 square may raise suspicions that here the baulk line rather than the actual extent of this deposit is captured, but Raftery is unambiguous in his account. The presence of the sterile yellow deposit is beyond question and is also documented in the long sections of this area (Figs 2.18 and 2.19).

Another possible stretch of bank was documented in the form of a rather substantial deposit of soil in Cutting Y (see below) (Fig. 2.35), where it also rested on an apparent Bronze Age horizon.

Raftery noted a third deposit of redeposited natural which he interpreted as the remains of the former bank at the southern end of the rampart removal, in squares F/G. Here it underlies a layer of cobbling in brown soil which Raftery considered to be probably later and related to the rampart construction. There is, however, some ambiguity in Raftery's account of the stratigraphic relationship with Ring-ditch 2 in Area 3 (see section 2.4), which he describes as cutting through all layers except for the assumed medieval one. It is unclear whether the yellow redeposited material extended far enough to be cut by the ditch; the section taken at this point (section 13) seems to suggest that it did not.

The identification of these deposits as the remnants of the bank associated with the digging of Ring-ditch 1 has wider implications for the site's chronology (see Chapter 4, section 4.1). For the full discussion of these issues see Chapter 4, sections 4.2 and 4.4.

An alternative interpretation may be the introduction of natural soil onto the site, either as a raw material or to level the surface of the area in preparation for construction of the cashel. This, however, is entirely speculative and the actual date of the laying down of these deposits is unclear.

Finds from Ring-ditch 1

As already noted, the finds from the western sector of the ditch fill were nondescript. Notable, however, are a small number of scattered potsherds, and a Hiberno-Norse silver ingot (E84:5585; Fig. 3.30) from silting under the upper stone layer in Sq. 56, as well as a small, slab-like object of slate from Sq. 38 (E84:4706; Fig. 3.111), which was found well down in the ditch. There is a notable contrast between the density of finds in the east (1,229 finds) and in the west (199 finds, Sqs 47–40 inclusive) of the ditch fill. Coarse potsherds were of most frequent occurrence, but around the east and south significant concentrations of clay moulds (161 fragments in total) were also found. In this sector (Sqs 38–31) a minimum of 994 coarse pottery fragments and at least 161 of the overall 170 mould fragments from the entire ring-ditch were brought to light. In addition, among the more important items found were a saddle quern (E84:5500; Fig. 3.112), a small number of bronzes (E84:1355, 1463, 2200; Fig. 3.32), three glass beads (E84:1226, 1332, 1353; Fig. 3.14a) and one bracelet fragment of shale (E84:1383; Fig. 3.107) (Table 2.3a).

In Sq. 29 and the adjoining Sqs 19/20 a significant concentration of finds was also recovered, including a total of 188 coarse potsherds, 45 mould fragments and eleven water-rolled pebbles (Table 2.3a). Some fragmentary animal bones, all in a very poor state of preservation, were also present. Apart from some potsherds in the upper grey fill of these two squares, it was noticeable that most of the sherds, and virtually all the mould fragments, came from the black material among, and under, the layer of stones (the 'cobbling')

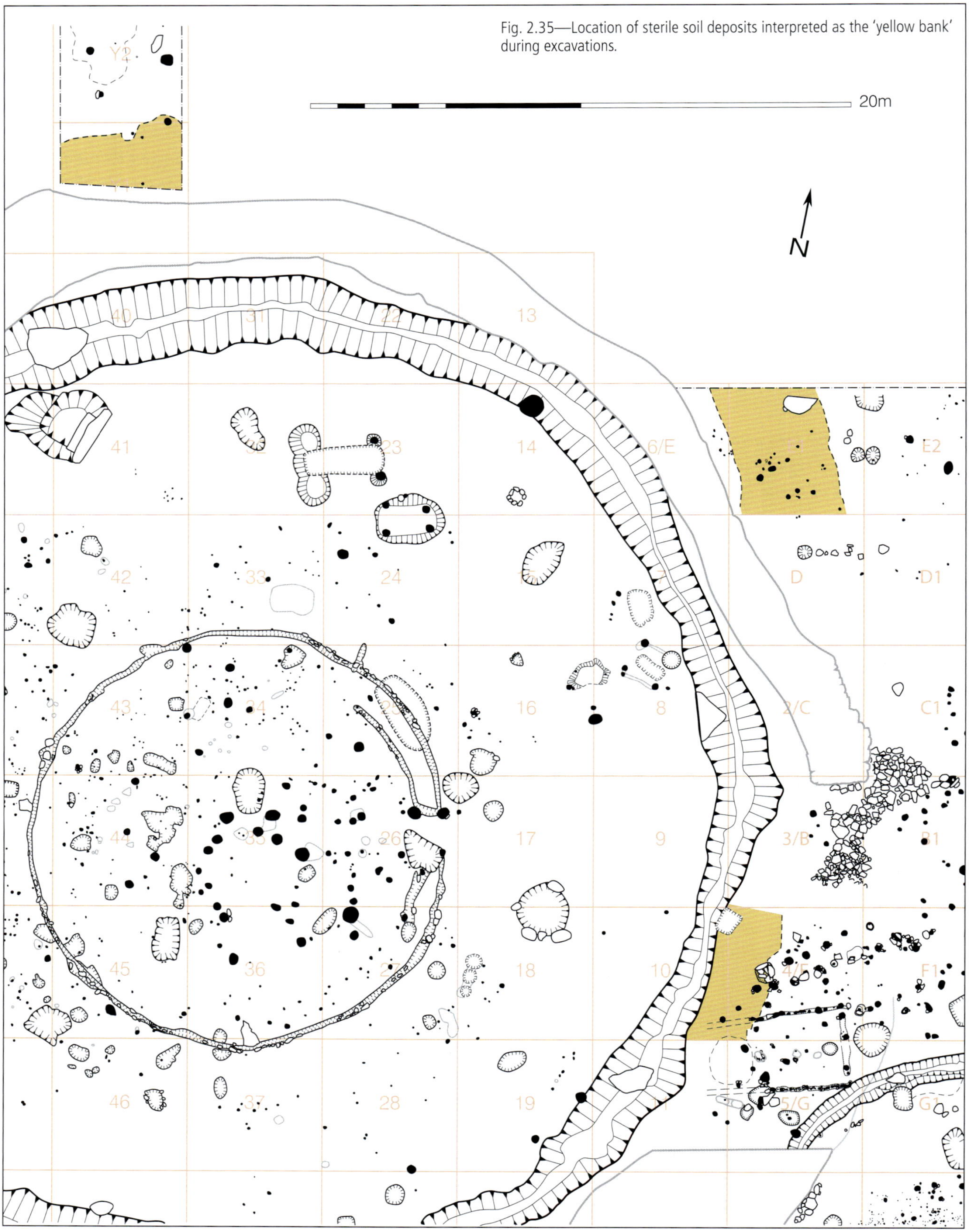

Fig. 2.35—Location of sterile soil deposits interpreted as the 'yellow bank' during excavations.

Table 2.3a—Finds from Ring-ditch 1.

Grid square	Fill description	Depth of objects (cm)	Object type	Find number
6	General undifferentiated black fill on eastern side (incl. black/brown)	20–55 below yellow	Coarse pottery	E84:1299, 1341, 1399, 1422, 1427, 1400
	Dark fill of ditch, upper levels	54	Coarse pottery	E84:1297
			Medieval pottery	E84:1298a
			Unidentified pottery (not found)	E84:1298b
	From black at/near base of ditch	50–55 below yellow	Coarse pottery	E84:1445, 1446, 1447, 1448*, 1449, 1450**, 1451
SECTION VI				
6/7	General undifferentiated black fill on eastern side (incl. black/brown)	30–50 below yellow	Iron	E84:1478
			Stone	E84:1479
			Coarse pottery	E84:1476a, 1476, 1477
			Moulds	E84:1475
	From black at/near base of ditch	50–55 below yellow	Mould	E84:1457.1
7	Upper levels of black fill of ditch (incl. brown/black, grey/black) along eastern half of ditch	Unspecified–40	Glass beads	E84:1226, 1332, 1353
			Coarse pottery	E84:1302, 1304a,b, 1306, 1308, 1334–1336, 1338, 1339.1, 1340a, 1340, 1347
			Mould	E84:1304c
			Stone	E84:1303, 1305, 1307, 1333, 1337, 1339
	General undifferentiated black fill on eastern side (incl. black/brown)	30–37 below yellow	Bronze	E84:1355
			Moulds	E84:1364a.1, 1366.1, 1364a,c,d, 1365, 1405
			Coarse pottery	E84:1348, 1357, 1358, 1359*, 1360, 1361, 1362, 1367, 1368, 1370, 1401, 1402, 1403, 1404
			Stone	E84:1363a–c
SECTION VII				
7/8	Base of ditch (incl. 'almost on')	Unspecified, 50–55 below yellow	Coarse pottery	E84:1481*, 1482, 1484
			Mould	E84:1483, 1484.1, 1485
8	General undifferentiated black fill on eastern side (incl. black/brown)	20–35 below yellow	Mould	E84:1309
	Black burnt material	40	Mould	E84:1309
			Coarse pottery	E84:1310, 1310.1, 1311, 1312, 1313, 1314
	From black at/near base of ditch	40–50 below yellow	Coarse pottery	E84:1429, 1430, 1431*, 1432.1, 1432, 1433, 1434, 1435, 1436, 1437, 1438, 1439, 1440, 1441
8/2	General undifferentiated black fill on eastern side (incl. black/brown)	40–50 below yellow	Mould	E84:1462
	From black at/near base of ditch	50–55 below yellow	Bronze	E84:1463
			Coarse pottery	E84:1452, 1452.1, 1453*, 1454, 1455, 1457a, 1457, 1458, 1459, 1460, 1461
			Mould	E84:1454.1
			Stone	E84:1456, 1467
	Base of ditch (incl. 'almost on')	50–55 below yellow	Coarse pottery	E84:1468
2	General undifferentiated black fill on eastern side (incl. black/brown)	Unspecified, 20–35 below yellow	Shale	E84:1383
			Mould	E84:1411.1
			Coarse pottery	E84:1411a,b, 1411, 1412, 1413, 1414–1419, 1420.1, 1420
			Stone	E84:1421, 1380
	From black at/near base of ditch	48–53 below yellow	Coarse pottery	E84:1442, 1443
			Mould	E84:1442a
			Saddle quern	E84:1428

Table 2.3a—Finds from Ring-ditch 1 (cont.).

Grid square	Fill description	Depth of objects (cm)	Object type	Find number
SECTIONS 6 and probably 7				
9	Upper fill/top fill of ditch (general)	Unspecified	Mould	E84:2262
			Stone & flint	E84:2263, 2264
	Upper levels of black fill of ditch (incl. brown/black, grey/black) along eastern half of ditch	15–20	Bronze	E84:2200
	General undifferentiated black fill on eastern side (incl. black/brown)	20–25	Moulds	E84:2315, 2316, 2319
			Stone	E84:4344, 4345
9/3	Among cobbling stones in upper levels	20 in ditch	Moulds	E84:2343–2367
			Coarse pottery	E84:2320–2339
	General undifferentiated black fill on eastern side (incl. black/brown)	Unspecified, 20–25 deep in ditch	Pottery	E84:2423, 2424, 2425
			Moulds	E84:2426, 2427, 2428, 2429, 2430, 2431, 2432, 2433, 2434, 2435, 2436, 2437
			Stone	E84:2438, 2439
	Grey silting in lower levels of ditch	Unspecified	Moulds	E84:2456–2479, 2491–2501, 2515–2518
			Coarse pottery	E84:2480–2490, 2512–2514
			Stone	E84:2502
3	Upper levels of black fill of ditch (incl. brown/black, grey/black) along eastern half of ditch	Unspecified	Moulds	E84:2276, 2277, 2278
			Coarse pottery	E84:2279
	Grey fill (incl. grey/brown, mauve)		Moulds	E84:2408, 2409, 2410
SECTION VIII				
10	General undifferentiated black fill on eastern side (incl. black/brown)	35–40	Coarse pottery	E84:2842, 2843, 2844, 2845, 2846, 4346, 4347, 4348, 4349
10/4	Black burnt material	40	Coarse pottery	E84:2752–2760
SECTION IX				
11	Upper levels of black fill of ditch (incl. brown/black, grey/black) along eastern half of ditch	20	Coarse pottery	E84:3287, 3288, 3289
	Dark fill of ditch, upper levels	Unspecified	Coarse pottery	E84:3378, 3379
			Stone (shale)	E84:3380
	Dark fill of ditch	Unspecified	Coarse pottery	E84:3432
11/12	General undifferentiated black fill on eastern side (incl. black/brown)	40	Coarse pottery	E84:5915
19/11	Base of ditch (incl. 'almost on')	Unspecified	Coarse pottery	E84:3783
	In lower fill of ditch (general)		Coarse pottery	E84:3788, 3789, 3790, 3791, 3792
			Stone	E84:3793
19/20	Dark fill of ditch	Unspecified	Coarse pottery	E84:5914a–k

NOTE TO TABLE 2.3a. Finds associated with Ring-ditch 1 are in this representation used to interrogate the stratigraphy of Ring-ditch 1. As the depths and context descriptions are those recorded for the objects in the finds register, they provide a rough representation of the depth and location of the respective fills of the ditch. Grid squares are indicated as recorded for each find. Lack of finds from particular contexts might lead to some contexts not featuring in this model.

Table 2.3a—Finds from Ring-ditch 1 (cont.).

Grid square	Fill description	Depth of objects (cm)	Object type	Find number
19	General undifferentiated black fill on eastern side (incl. black/brown)	20–30 below yellow	Coarse pottery	E84:3650–3667
			Moulds	E84:3668, 3669
	Black spongy fill	Unspecified, 20–25 deep in ditch	Coarse pottery	E84:4276–4286*, 4288*
			Mould	E84:4287
			Stone	E84:4289–4297
	Grey silting lower levels ??	Unspecified	Coarse pottery	E84:2476.1, 2477.1, 2478.1, 2479.1, 2480.1, 2481.1, 2482.1, 2483.1, 2484.1, 2485.1, 486.1
			Mould	E84:2487.1
20	Upper levels of black fill of ditch (incl. brown/black, grey/black) along eastern half of ditch	Unspecified	Mould	E84:4534
	General undifferentiated black fill on eastern side (incl. black/brown)	Unspecified, 50, 15–40 in ditch	Coarse pottery	E84:4517, 4899, 6048, 6049a–f, 4513, 4518, 4573
			Mould	E84:4514, 4515, 4516, 4900a,b, 6050
	Black fill of ditch among stones	Unspecified, 15–40	Coarse pottery	E84:4564, 4565a–c, 4573, 4574, 4584, 4591, 4592, 4599a–d, 4664a,b, 4681a–e
			Mould	E84:4563, 4613, 4682, 4683
	Grey fill (incl. grey/brown, mauve)	Unspecified	Coarse pottery	E84:5542a–c
	From black at/near base of ditch	Unspecified	Coarse pottery	E84:4760a,b
			Mould	E84:4761
			Stone	E84:4852, 4853
29	Dark fill of ditch, upper levels	Unspecified, 30	Coarse pottery	E84:4383, 4384, 4385, 4386, 4387, 4388, 4389, 4390, 4391, 4392, 4393, 4394, 4395, 4397, 4398, 4399, 4399.1, 4396, 4478
	Black fill of ditch among stones	Unspecified, 15–40	Coarse pottery	E84:4607a,b, 4622, 4623, 4674a–d
			Mould	E84:4675
	General undifferentiated black fill on eastern side (incl. black/brown)	Unspecified, 15–40 in ditch	Mould	E84:4851, 4542, 4543, 5107, 4735, 4779, 4778
			Coarse pottery	E84:4528, 4544, 5106, 4704a–d, 4733, 4734, 4701a–c, 4777a,b, 4774a,b, 4775, 4776
	Black spongy fill	Unspecified, 20–25 deep in ditch	Coarse pottery	E84:4247–4275
	Grey fill (incl. grey/brown, mauve)	Unspecified, 15–40 in ditch	Coarse pottery	E84:4545, 4557a–e, 4582, 4898, 4934a–k
			Mould	E84:4546, 4935a–j, 4936, 4937, 4938, 4939, 4940, 4941, 4942
	Deep part of ditch, black silting	55 in ditch	Mould	E84:4772, 4773
			Pottery	E84:4770a–c
38	Upper levels of black fill of ditch (incl. brown/black, grey/black) along eastern half of ditch	Unspecified	Coarse pottery	E84:4535a
	General undifferentiated black fill on eastern side (incl. black/brown)	Unspecified, 15–40 in ditch	Coarse pottery	E84:4969, 4970a–e
			Mould	E84:4971
	Grey fill (incl. grey/brown, mauve)	Unspecified, 20–80 in ditch	Coarse pottery	E84:4326, 4327, 4328, 4329, 4509a, 4510a, 4511, 4611, 4676a–g*, 4677, 4727a–g, 4728, 4769a–i
			Stone	E84:4612, 4706
	Gravelly fill	40–50 in ditch	Coarse pottery	E84:4700
39	Grey fill (incl. grey/brown, mauve)	Unspecified, 20–80 in ditch	Coarse pottery	E84:4590a–c, 4857

Table 2.3a—Finds from Ring-ditch 1 (cont.).

Grid square	Fill description	Depth of objects (cm)	Object type	Find number
SECTIONS X and XI				
47	Among cobbling stones in upper levels	Unspecified	Saddle quern	E84:5500
	Unspecified ditch fill	Unspecified, 50–65	Coarse pottery	E84:5197a–c, 5229a–c
	Grey fill (incl. grey/brown, mauve)	95–110	Coarse pottery	E84:5271, 5295a–e, 5296, 5297
			Stone	E84:5298
	Base of ditch (incl. 'almost on')	Unspecified, 50–55 below yellow	Coarse pottery	E84:5307, 5308, 5309a,b
SECTIONS XII and XIII				
56	Upper fill/top fill of ditch (general)	Unspecified	Coarse pottery	E84:5437, 5438*
	In grey fill under stones	Unspecified	Mould	E84:5584
			Stone	E84:5583
			Lead/silver	E84:5585
55	Grey fill (incl. grey/brown, mauve)	Unspecified, 20	Coarse pottery	E84:5625, 5626, 5627a–h, 5714a–k, 5715
63	Grey/brown, but possibly a different context as deposit is more mixed along WSW part of RD1	25 deep in ditch	Mould	E84:5805
		28	Coarse pottery	E84:5905
	Unspecified ditch fill	50	Coarse pottery	E84:5919
	Base of ditch (incl. 'almost on')	Unspecified, 50–55 below yellow	Coarse pottery	E84:6001a–p, 6002, 6003*, 6004
			Mould	E84:6005
68	Grey fill (incl. grey/brown, mauve)	Unspecified	Coarse pottery	E84:5981, 5982, 5983, 5984, 5985
	In mottled grey/black upper fill of ditch below large stone on edge of ditch	30–35	Coarse pottery	E84:5916a,b, 5917, 5918
	Unspecified ditch fill	Unspecified	Coarse pottery	E84:6039
67/68	Grey/brown, but possibly a different context as deposit is more mixed along WSW part of RD1	30	Coarse pottery	E84:5922a–h, 5923
67	Upper fill/top fill of ditch (general)	25–28	Moulds	E84:5878a,b
	Grey/brown, but possibly a different context as deposit is more mixed along WSW part of RD1	Unspecified, 28–35	Coarse pottery	E84:5903, 5967
			Unidentified pottery (not found)	E84:5913
			Leinster Cooking Ware	E84:5904
			Iron	E84:5906, 5907, 5908
			Stone	E84:5910
	Unspecified ditch fill	Unspecified	Stone	E84:6030
66	Grey/brown, but possibly a different context as deposit is more mixed along WSW part of RD1	Unspecified, 28–35	Beaker pottery	E84:5912a,b
			Middle Bronze Age pottery	E84:5854
			Coarse pottery	E84:5902, 6094
			Iron	E84:5901
65	Grey/brown, but possibly a different context as deposit is more mixed along WSW part of RD1	25–40	Mould	E84:5877
			Coarse pottery	E84:5890, 6149
			Leinster Cooking Ware	E84:6150
	Unspecified ditch fill	Unspecified, 50–65	Coarse pottery	E84:6043a–e

Table 2.3a—Finds from Ring-ditch 1 (cont.).

Grid square	Fill description	Depth of objects (cm)	Object type	Find number
59	Upper fill/top fill of ditch (general)	40	Mould	E84:5824
	Grey fill (incl. grey/brown, mauve)	Unspecified	Coarse pottery	E84:5944a–h
58	Grey fill (incl. grey/brown, mauve)	25 deep in ditch	Coarse pottery	E84:5797a–l, 5798, 5799
			Moulds	E84:5800a,b
58/59	Grey fill (incl. grey/brown, mauve)	Unspecified	Leinster Cooking Ware	E84:5863
SECTION I				
50	Upper fill/top fill of ditch (general)	Unspecified	Coarse pottery	E84:5475a–k, 5421a–d
			Mould	E84:5422
	In lower fill of ditch (general)	Unspecified	Coarse pottery	E84:5543, 5544, 5545a–g
49/50	Upper fill/top fill of ditch (general)	Unspecified	Coarse pottery	E84:5420a,b
49	Grey fill (incl. grey/brown, mauve)	Unspecified	Coarse pottery	E84:4600
SECTION II				
40	Grey fill (incl. grey/brown, mauve)	Unspecified, 35 deep in ditch	Coarse pottery	E84:5124a–d, 5208a–d, 5209
	Upper fill/top fill of ditch (general)	44	Stone	E84:5177
	Unspecified ditch fill	Unspecified, 50–65	Coarse pottery	E84:5193, 5255, 5256a–c
	Base of ditch (incl. 'almost on')	Unspecified, 50–55 below yellow	Coarse pottery	E84:5269a,b, 5270
41	Grey fill (incl. grey/brown, mauve)	Unspecified	Coarse pottery	E84:5327, 5328
SECTION III				
31	Grey fill (incl. grey/brown, mauve)	Unspecified, 53–75 deep in ditch	Coarse pottery	E84:1291, 4781
	Light brown fill	Unspecified	Coarse pottery	E84:1286
			Iron	E84:1287
	Unspecified ditch fill	Unspecified, 50–65	Coarse pottery	E84:1203, 1204
22/31	Upper levels of black fill of ditch (incl. brown/black, grey/black) along eastern half of ditch	Unspecified	Coarse pottery	E84:1343
SECTION IV				
22	Grey fill (incl. grey/brown, mauve)	Unspecified	Iron	E84:1290
	Upper fill/top fill of ditch (general)	Unspecified	Mould	E84:1275
	Unspecified ditch fill	Unspecified, 50–65	Coarse pottery	E84:1292, 1295
			Stone	E84:1344
SECTION V				
13	Upper levels of black fill of ditch (incl. brown/black, grey/black) along eastern half of ditch	Unspecified	Coarse pottery	E84:1345.1, 1346
14	General undifferentiated black fill on eastern side (incl. black/brown)	20–30 below yellow	Coarse pottery	E84:1397*, 1423, 1424, 1300, 1301, 1398
	Base of ditch (incl. 'almost on')	Unspecified, 50–55 below yellow	Coarse pottery	E84:1466

Table 2.3b—Finds from lower levels within Ring-ditch 1, including from the primary or basal levels of the ditch.

Sq. no.	Find type	Find nos
9/3*	Mould	E84:2456, E84:2457, E84:2458, E84:2459, E84:2460, E84:2461, E84:2462, E84:2463, E84:2464, E84:2465, E84:2466, E84:2467, E84:2468, E84:2469, E84:2470, E84:2471, E84:2472, E84:2473, E84:2474, E84:2475, E84:2476, E84:2477, E84:2478, E84:2479, E84:2491, E84:2492, E84:2493, E84:2494, E84:2495, E84:2496, E84:2497, E84:2498, E84:2499, E84:2500, E84:2501, E84:2515, E84:2516, E84:2517, E84:2518
	Coarse pottery	E84:2480, E84:2481, E84:2482, E84:2483, E84:2484, E84:2485, E84:2486, E84:2487, E84:2488, E84:2489, E84:2490, E84:2512, E84:2513, E84:2514
8/2	Coarse pottery	E84:1468
7/8**	Mould	E84:1483, E84:1484.1, E84:1485
	Coarse pottery	E84:1481, E84:1482a–k, E84:1482i, E84:1484
14	Coarse pottery	E84:1466
19	Coarse pottery	E84:2476.1, E84:2477.1, E84:2478.1, E84:2479.1, E84:2480.1, E84:2481.1, E84:2482.1, E84:2483.1, E84:2484.1, E84:2485.1, E84:2486.1
	Mould	E84:2487.1
19/11	Coarse pottery	E84:3783
38***	Coarse pottery	E84:4611, E84:4676a–g, E84:4677, E84:4727a–g, E84:4769a–l, E84:4728
	Stone: slate decorating tool?	E84:4706
39	Coarse pottery	E84:4590a–c, E84:4857
40	Coarse pottery	E84:5269a,b, E84:5270
47	Coarse pottery	E84:5307, E84:5308, E84:5309a,b
63	Coarse pottery	E84:6001a–p, E84:6002, E84:6003, E84:6004
	Mould	E84:6005

*All from grey silting in lower levels of ditch. **Almost on base of ditch under baulk. ***In grey/mauve silting in ditch near bottom. All other finds are described as coming from 'base' or 'at bottom of ditch'.

described above, and from the lower silting, where, indeed, moulds were particularly evident.

The ditch fill of Sqs 10 and 11 also yielded a small number of finds, mainly potsherds but including the fragment of a shale bracelet (E84:3380). All of these objects came from the upper black layer, apart from five coarse potsherds from the lower fill in Sq. 11/19. A saddle quern (E84:5926; Fig. 3.113) came from the upper fill of the ditch in Sq. 5[7] (Table 2.3a).

The principal concentration of finds in the ditch, however, came from Sqs 7, 8/2 and, most especially, 9/3. The artefacts occurred at various depths in the ditch (including a few from near the base) in the intense black fill which had accumulated rapidly from outside. Most of the finds consisted of coarse potsherds, which occurred, in varying quantities, at all levels. Square 9/3 was especially interesting, however, for, along with some 42 sherds of coarse pottery, it produced no fewer than 75 clay mould fragments. The latter came from three principal areas in the ditch fill: from the so-called 'cobbling' in the upper levels in the northern half of the ditch, from the dense black fill below this and from the lower silting. Moulds were otherwise rare in the ditch, apart from the small scatters mentioned earlier in the south-east.

Apart from the pottery and the moulds, several other items of interest were recovered from the black ditch fill in the eastern zone. From high in the fill, in Sq. 9, came a conical rivet of bronze (E84:2200; Figs 3.32 and 3.36). One complete and two fragmentary blue glass beads (E84:1226, 1332, 1353; Fig. 3.14a), a whetstone (E84:1333) and an indeterminate bronze fragment (E84:1355) were found in the black material in Sq. 7. A whetstone (E84:1380) came from the same layer in Sq. 2, along with a bracelet fragment of shale (E84:1383; Fig. 3.107) and a saddle quern (E84:1428). Some miscellaneous bronze fragments also came to light.

The occurrence of 29 naturally rounded water-rolled pebbles of differing colours, mainly concentrated in the black occupation fill of the ditch along its eastern extent, is interesting. These objects, which occurred in considerable quantities elsewhere (see below), are not native to the immediate locality and it must thus be assumed that they had been collected for a specific, though uncertain, purpose. A further concentration of crystals was noted within and close to the ditch (see Chapter 3, section 3.12).

As Raftery notes, there were particular concentrations of moulds within the ditch fill. While pottery occurs all around its perimeter, moulds occur in specific locations in the north-west, the south-east and the north-east. The north-western concentration corresponds possibly to Metalworking Zone 1, that in the north-east to metalworking in Area 2 (see section 2.3.1 below). These deposits appear to be distinct 'dumps' of material within the ditch fill.

2.2.3 Pits and post-holes in Area 1

In this section Raftery describes the various cut features uncovered in Area 1. In addition to the bedding trench that he recognised as the 15m structure, attempts were made to reconstruct the dense distribution of post-holes into a further structure. His opinion on how these features were to be interpreted had clearly changed from that expressed in earlier publications. A contrasting interpretation of the clustering of post-holes and pits around the 15m structure is discussed in Chapter 6; moreover, some of the post-holes (14, 36 and possibly a further example) around Pit 119 are suggested in Chapter 6 to have formed part of a feature complex as also pondered by Raftery in his discussion of this feature below.

Of the total of 64 features within Ring-ditch 1 which are designated as pits (Figs 2.36 and 2.37) a substantial number occurred within the 15m enclosure. Almost all of these showed up initially as areas of grey in the yellow subsoil. They were generally of the most ephemeral character; indeed, in many instances the distinction between 'pit' and 'depression' was decidedly arbitrary. Their shape varied somewhat but the majority were oval or circular, with rounded sides and flat or concave bases. Their depths averaged from 5cm to 50cm, with some up to 1m (Pit 131). They were mostly filled with grey silted material which occasionally contained flecks of charcoal. Pit 111 was filled with stones of moderate size, and Pit 115 was unique in having a black organic layer on its sides and base which underlay a sandy-grey soil containing occasional flecks of yellow (Fig. 2.36).

Some of these pits produced a few scraps of coarse pottery (Table 2.4). Pit 110 yielded half of a glass bead (E84:3000), and a second bead (E84:1591) came from ploughsoil in Sq. 36/27 (Fig. 3.14a), which also yielded two small, enigmatic glass fragments of uncertain date (E84:1502 and 1512).

Apart from the exceptional and important Pit 119, the only pit of any size was Pit 147 in Sq. 45, with almost vertical sides and a fairly regularly dug base. Its width was about 1.05m, its depth about the same. Its filling was a uniformly grey, silted material with occasional flecks of charcoal. It contained some cattle bone and eleven coarse potsherds (E84:5047a–k). Amorphous iron fragments (E84:5049 and 5048) were found sealed with the pottery within the pit fill. The exact date of this pit is unclear, but the iron fragments suggest a date in or after the Iron Age. A medieval date is likely for the very shallow Pit 142, which had a spongy brown filling (as opposed to the grey which was normal for all prehistoric features on the site); it did not yield any finds from its extent within the cut, but two sherds of Leinster Cooking Ware (E84:5051a, b) and a piece of iron (E84:5052), which are likely to date from the medieval period at the earliest, came from deposits overlying it.

In the zone between the 15m bedding trench and Ring-ditch 1 the excavation revealed a large number of post-holes, stake-holes and 38 pits (Fig. 2.5). There was no obvious order or plan discernible in these, and it seems likely that they represent developments over time which today, in the absence of any meaningful stratigraphy, remain largely indecipherable. It is interesting to note, however, that there is a decided clustering of such features around the immediate perimeter of the bedding trench in a rough band averaging 2–3m in width. Equally interesting is the fact that the zone between this and the enclosing Ring-ditch 1 is very largely devoid of features, with the notable exceptions of a number of large sunken hearths in the north-eastern sector (see below). It is also interesting to observe that the zone immediately outside the entrance to the 15m enclosure, extending as far as Ring-ditch 1, is largely devoid of pits and is entirely free of the post-holes which are otherwise numerous around the 15m structure. It might thus be suggested that the ordering of the pits and post-holes was focused on the latter. Among the few pits in the area outside the eastern entrance, Pit 118 was of particular importance (see below) (Fig. 2.38). A feature of a number of the pits was their highly irregular plan. In this regard, large pits such as Pit 97, Sq. 15 (2m by 1.25m), Pit 128, Sq. 52 (1.75m by 90cm), and Pit 130, Sq. 53 (2m by 60cm) (all are maximum dimensions), should be noted. *A Pit G, which may be the renumbered Pit 110, was dated and produced a Mesolithic radiocarbon date (SI-1481, 6600–6100 cal. BC).*

Pit 96, Sq. 14, was shallow and circular, 60cm in diameter and 15cm deep, and had carefully dug vertical sides and a flat, even base (Fig. 2.39). It was lined with eight equal-sized stones, which occurred 25cm above the base of the pit and gave every appearance of having been deliberately arranged. The filling was a uniform dark brown material. On the yellow soil of the pit, a single, straight streak of charcoal occurred

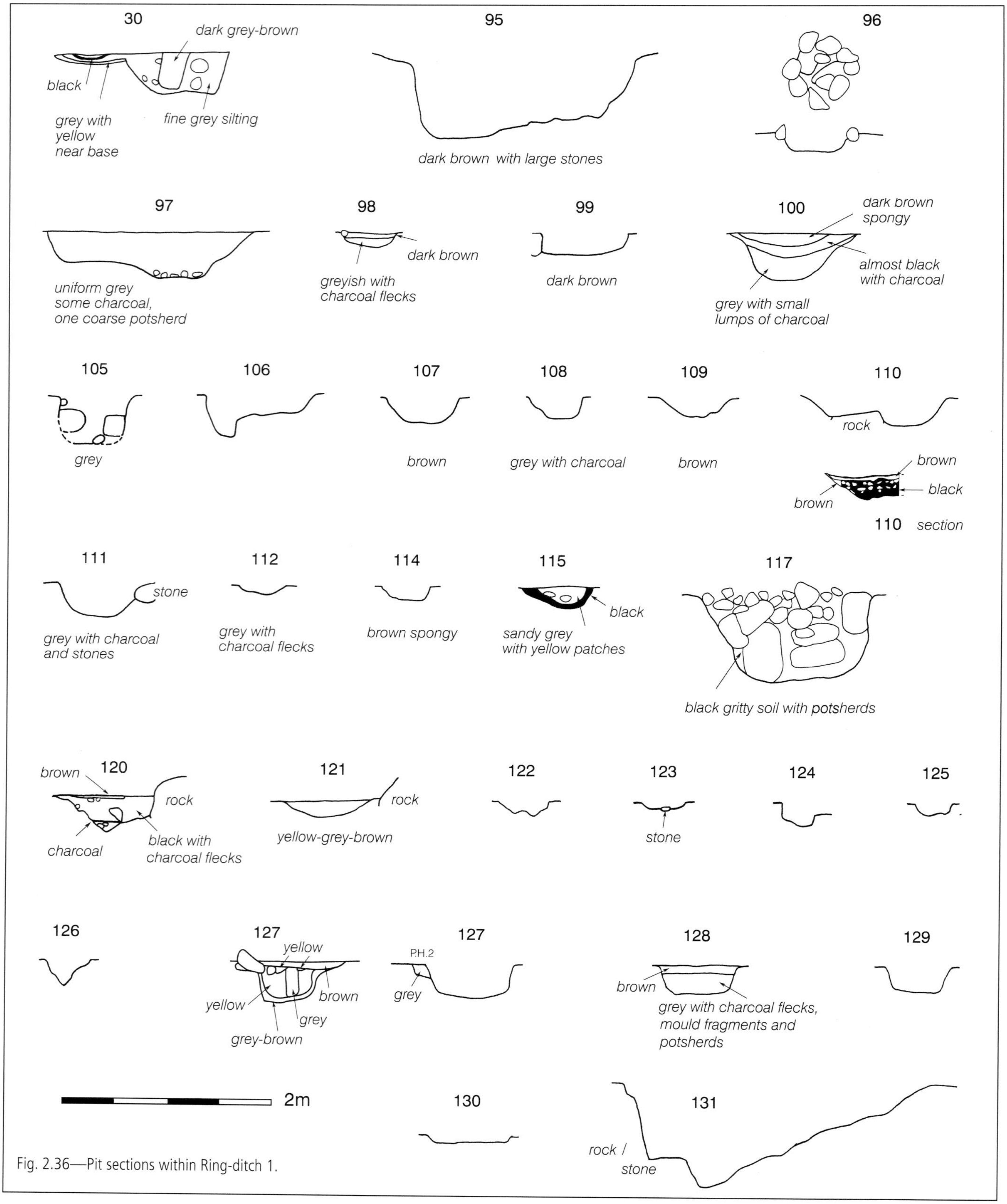

Fig. 2.36—Pit sections within Ring-ditch 1.

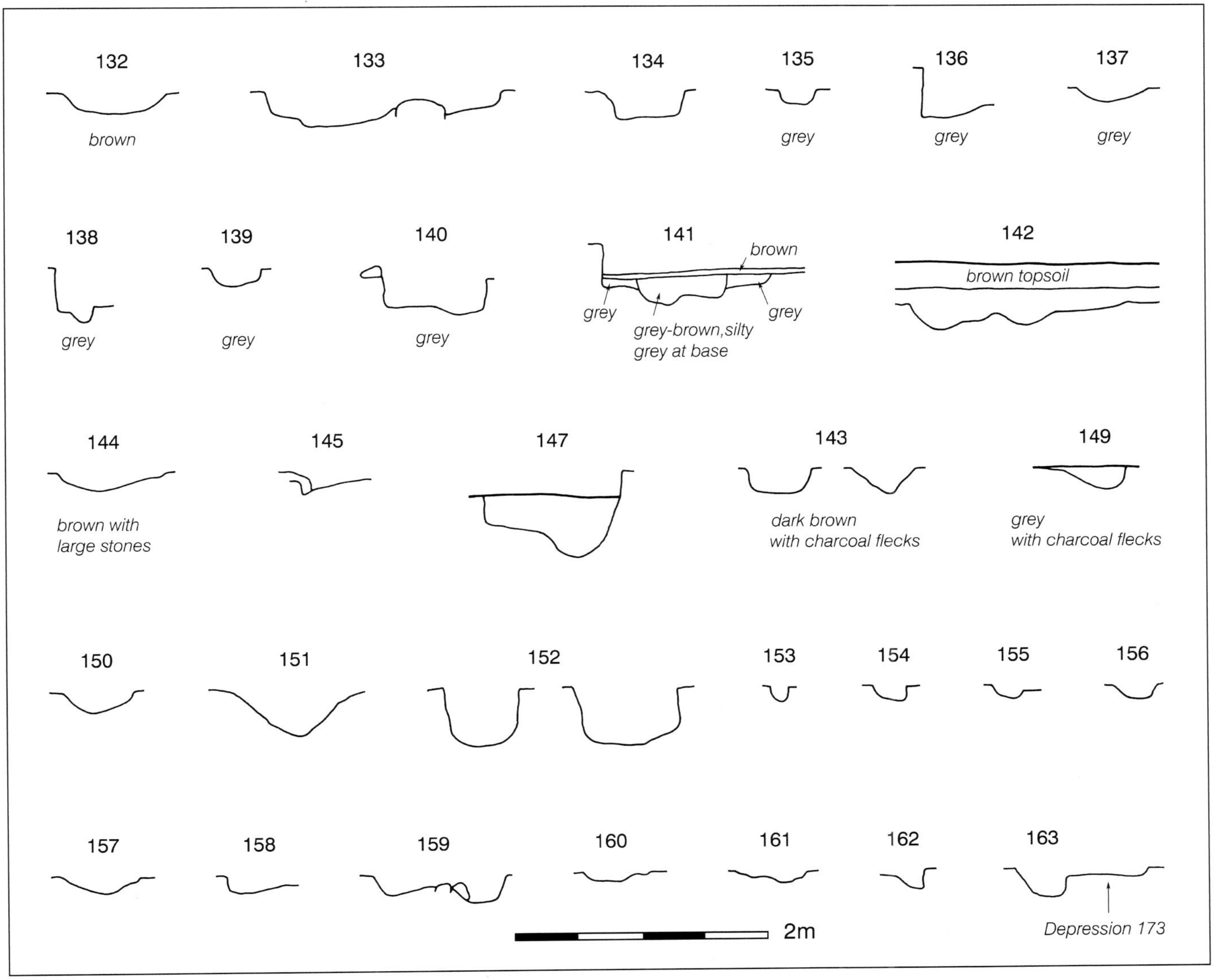

Fig. 2.37—Pit sections within Ring-ditch 1.

across most of its width. It is not possible to state whether this enigmatic item represents a burnt branch or some other burnt wooden feature, nor can it be established whether the burning came about deliberately or as the result of an accident. It should be noted in this regard, however, that no other traces of burning were observed on the base of the pit. *A sample (GrN-27100) from the fill of this pit produced a date of cal. AD 570–680.*

The majority of the pits on the site had an undifferentiated grey filling (though frequently containing charcoal flecks), but a number had been deliberately filled with medium-sized stones (e.g. Pits 95, 97, 111, 117, 144). In the case of Pit 97, the filling stones were of substantial size except for the base, where a rough layer of considerably smaller stones resembling cobbling occurred. All the stones were embedded in a uniform grey, silt-like material. In the case of Pit 117 (Sqs 26/17), the pit was packed from top to bottom with stones mixed with grey silting, but in this case the smaller stones were on the top. There can be no doubt that in such instances the pits had been deliberately filled with some care.

As already noted, many of the pits contained charcoal flecks (a feature common to pits in all parts of the excavation), which could be a product of smoke and soot drifting from fires across the site. There were examples, however, where the black organic layers, mixed with charcoal, are likely to have been a product of deliberate deposition and not simply of wind action. Examples are Pits 100, 110, 113[8] and especially

Pit 115, in which the black layer covered the sides and base of the cut. Pit 120 was notable, as it was completely filled with black organic material mixed with charcoal, with a particularly dense layer of the latter in its base where the section of the pit was decidedly pointed. *This pit produced a radiocarbon date of 820–550 cal. BC (GrA-23355).* Pit 110 was also completely filled with black organic material, heavily mixed with charcoal.

The large Pit 131, Sq. 50/41 in the north-west of the enclosure, stands apart from the others. It first came to light as a brown fill of earth and stones, the former immediately raising questions as to its antiquity since, virtually without exception, prehistoric pits proved to have been filled with grey or black material. The pit was large and irregular, with sides which were partly sloping and partly stepped, and a narrow base. Its maximum dimensions were about 2.75m by about 3m. It was up to 1m deep in the bedrock, but it is not clear whether it had been artificially created or was a natural fissure. At any rate, two fragments of eighteenth- or early nineteenth-century glass bottles in its base indicate with a high degree of probability that it is of relatively recent date.

Pit 118

Pit 118 (Fig. 2.38) was particularly interesting and was quite unlike any other pit discovered in the course of the Rathgall excavations. It was located 2.5m outside the 15m structure, lying slightly south of the entrance passage in that zone which, as noted above, was largely devoid of other features. This pit, like so many others, first became apparent during excavation through the exposure of a heavy concentration of medium-sized boulders, embedded in a matrix of greyish, silted material, which covered a roughly circular area about 2.5m across. The boulders filled the upper 60cm of what turned out to be a carefully dug pit. Excavation commenced in 1970 but it was not until the following year, after the boulders had been removed, that full investigation of the pit was completed.

The pit had been dug into the subsoil to a depth of 1.4m and had a regular, funnel-shaped section. At its mouth it was a flattened oval in shape, with maximum dimensions of 2.2m by 1.9m. It sloped steeply and regularly inwards for about 80cm, at which point its sides became almost regularly vertical, meeting the base more or less at right angles. The base itself was flat, with a slight incline from south to north, and here it had narrowed to dimensions of 90cm by 95cm.

The boulders which had first drawn attention to the pit obviously represented its final infilling after it was no longer in use. It seems, however, that the pit had already been abandoned some time before the deposition of the boulders, as the latter lay upon, and were embedded in, a thick layer of fine, sticky grey material, entirely devoid of any archaeological material.

The grey layer was approximately 1cm deep. It rested on, and was overlain by, a thin black organic level, averaging 2cm in thickness, which could be traced as a continuous covering of the sides and base of the pit. An earlier similar, though slightly thicker (3–4cm), black layer occurred underneath the first, also covering the sides and base of the pit. Between these two layers there was a thick fill of clean, yellow, redeposited natural subsoil, up to 10cm thick, and a similar, though somewhat thinner, yellow layer underlay the second organic pit lining.

The thin black layers were interpreted as the remains of wickerwork linings, and this was confirmed in the course of the excavation by the fortuitous survival of a tiny area of what appeared to be woven brushwood adhering to one side. Carbonisation obscured details, however (Fig. 2.38).

The lowest layer in the pit consisted of black, sticky material which rested directly on the sides and base, where a thin layer of loose yellow soil of natural origin occurred. It was up to 30cm thick at the bottom, its thickness decreasing gradually up the sides to a minimum of 8cm at the top.

Pit 118 (Sq. 17/18) yielded no fewer than 444 potsherds (Table 2.4), representing at least seventeen vessels (see Chapter 3). Virtually all of these came from the thick, black basal layer. The exceptions are three coarse potsherds (E84:6144a–c) which were found in the yellow basal fill immediately touching the black, and it is probable that they too came from the principal black deposit. The pit also produced one small clay mould fragment (E84:4488), two water-rolled pebbles (E84:4486, 4487) and the broken fragments of an almost complete clay crucible (E84:5934a–b, 5997a–c, 5998, 6054a–d) (Fig. 3.42). Significantly, matching pieces of the latter came from both upper and lower levels of the black fill, thus confirming the contemporaneity of all the objects recovered.

This pit had obviously been dug with care and clearly its funnel shape was not accidental. The black basal layer containing all the finds was far too thick to represent the remains of an organic lining so that it is difficult not to assume that it represents a primary filling. The way in which the thick layer evenly covered both sides and base suggests the possibility that a secondary pit, with double basketry lining and the yellow fill, had been dug into this.

Pit 118 was thus a complex creation. Its dimensions were

significant and it had initially been dug with very considerable care. This may have been for storage (grain being the most likely candidate), after which a phase of abandonment occurred, including the deposition of a sizeable quantity of pottery and other items. As noted above, a secondary phase of use followed, which involved the construction, with some care, of double basketry lining, perhaps also for grain. Following final abandonment, the pit was completely and deliberately filled in with stones, which became mixed with grey silting. Interestingly, not a single potsherd came from this upper fill.

Radiocarbon determinations (GrA-23344, GrA-23345, GrN-27104, GrN-27102, SUERC-42589, SUERC-43732) were obtained from samples within the fill of Pit 118 (Table 4.2).

Pit 119

Pit 119, described by Raftery below as a burial pit, ties in morphologically with the pyre pits found in the rest of the site (see Chapter 6; see also section 2.2.4). It is in more than one sense a central feature of the site, and Raftery published an extended discussion in 2004.

This pit, in Sqs 34/35, was one of the most interesting and important features uncovered on the site (Fig. 2.40). It first came to light as a thin band of black organic material, forming an incomplete, flattened-oval outline with dimensions of 1.85m by 1m, enclosing an area of clean, yellow soil. The black streak, generally 3–5cm in width, was partly damaged on the west by an area of rabbit disturbance. The pit, orientated more or less north–south, was positioned between post-holes 14 and 36. Projecting from the yellow soil was the tip of a boulder which appeared to be of substantial size.

With the removal of the yellow filling the character of the pit became clear. It was 33cm deep and had regular, almost vertical sides and a flat, carefully dug base. The boulder had been placed directly on top of a thick black basal layer which extended upwards on all sides to form a continuous, unbroken lining to the pit. It was thus evident that the black streak that had been initially visible on the surface was the upper edge of this black lining material. Excavation revealed that the latter had a maximum thickness of 8cm at the base, narrowing at the top, as noted above, to 3–5cm. The manner in which the black material coated the sides and base of the pit clearly indicated that it represented a former organic lining.

The boulder, of local granite, filled slightly less than half the pit (Fig. 2.40). It was flat-sided, and more or less rectangular in its plan and sections. Its regular proportions gave the clear impression of deliberate rather than random selection. It was 87cm long, 54cm wide and 37cm high. There was nothing whatever—not even the slightest hint of silting—between this stone and the black layer, and it was clearly evident that it had been placed directly on the black material probably immediately after the latter had been placed in position.

At the centre of the pit, sunk a few centimetres into the black material, a tiny penannular ring of presumed copper with gold foil covering was discovered (E84:6070; Fig. 3.1), along with a small quantity of burnt human bones which have been identified as those of an infant of uncertain sex. Osteological examination suggested that the remains represented only a portion of the burnt infant (Chapter 3.16), thus allowing for the possibility that this might be a token deposit rather than a formal burial. It should be borne in mind, however, that the small, soft bones of an immediately post-natal infant would not necessarily survive in their entirety in and after removal from the pyre, so that it cannot be ruled out that the remains in fact represent a formal burial (see also Chapter 6). *This burial could not be examined (see Table 3.47).*

There can be no doubt that the pit was specifically created for the deposition of the human remains and the ring. There are no indications that it had ever been used for any other purpose. The black material in the pit was not a burnt layer but must represent a decayed organic lining, most likely wickerwork of some sort. It is probable that the pit was carefully made and lined, the bones and the ring deposited, and the whole covered and sealed with the large boulder and the yellow soil, all in a single action. *The black material at the base of the pit yielded a radiocarbon determination of 1260–1040 cal. BC (GrN-27101).*

In the absence of any meaningful stratigraphy in this part of the site it is once more impossible to demonstrate a relationship between Pit 119 and any of the other features uncovered in the central enclosure. Judicious juggling of selected post-holes allows the recognition of a small oval of free-standing posts concentrated in the area south of the pit, which could be seen as representing some sort of mini-enclosure.[9] Such a feature might conceivably be related to whatever activities were associated with the deposition of the ring and the bones in the pit. Or perhaps it was only the two post-holes, PH 14 and PH 36, which were linked to the pit. These, as noted above, seem to be precisely positioned to flank the pit on the south, and they are amongst the most substantial post-holes of the group in this area. They were, respectively, 48cm and 42.5cm in width and 35cm and 25cm

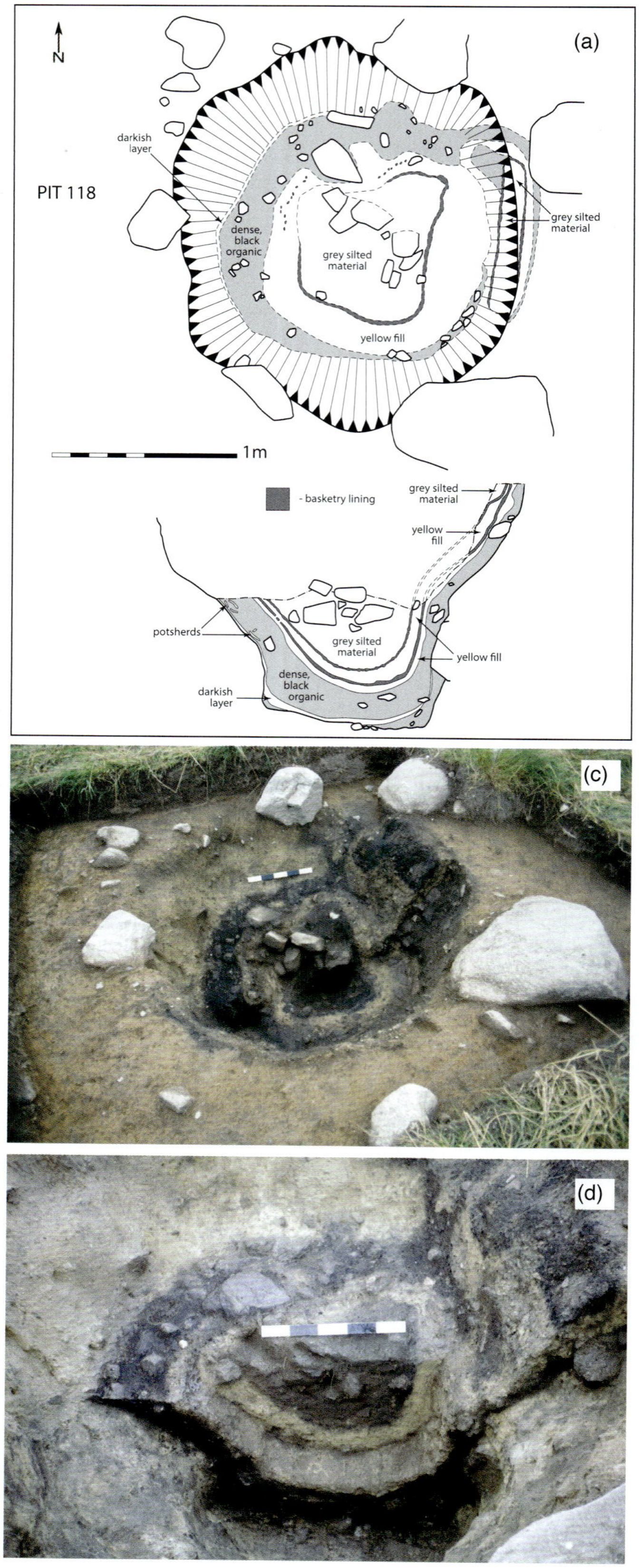

Fig. 2.38—(a) Plan and section of Pit 118. (b) Pit 118 before excavation (Sqs 17/18, looking south). (c) Pit 118 during excavation, with its upper part having been mostly removed (Sqs 17/18, looking north-east). (d) Section through lower part of Pit 118 (Sqs 17/18, looking north). (e) Carbonised possible basketry layer in Pit 118 (Sqs 17/18).[Continued overleaf]

Fig. 2.38 (cont.)— (f) Carbonised possible basketry layer in Pit 118 (Sqs 17/18). (g) Carbonised possible basketry layer in Pit 118 (Sqs 17/18). (h) Pit 118 after excavation (Sqs 17/18, looking south).

Fig. 2.39—Pit 96 with its stone fill and lining (Sq. 14, looking south).

in depth. A second pair of the larger posts, PH 15 and PH 8, along with the two just mentioned, might have formed some sort of funnel-shaped approach or façade to the burial pit.

There is a final point worth noting here. While Pit 119 is obviously situated off-centre within the 15m structure described above, even allowing for the unavoidably irregular edges of the surrounding ditch (Ring-ditch 1) it is, in fact, almost in the precise centre of this enclosure. This leaves little room for doubt that Ring-ditch 1 was deliberately dug to enclose Pit 119. Less clear, however, is the relationship between Ring-ditch 1 and the 15m construction *(but see discussion in Chapter 4, where a different chronological relationship is proposed).*

Finds from pits, post-holes and deposits enclosed by Ring-ditch 1

In the area between the 15m structure and the Ring-ditch 1 enclosure, occasional coarse potsherds found their way into the fill of some pits (nos 97, 102, 117, 120a, 121, 129, 130, 150 and 159) (see Table 2.4). In one of these, Pit 121 in Sq. 29, a large number of sherds were found in the dark filling material. Pit 130 in Sq. 53 contained a Middle Bronze Age sherd (E84:5418).

A complete saddle quern (E84:5925) was found upright in Pit 127 in Sq. 51 (Fig. 2.41). Three glass beads came from black occupation material in the immediate vicinity of Hearths 4, 5 and 6. An important item, a bronze bar toggle (E84:1374; Fig. 3.34), was found in disturbed soil in grid square 8, not far from the ditch in the vicinity of the same hearths (see below). Of the small number of nondescript depressions, only two (D158 and 170) contained a few (three) coarse potsherds, ten mould fragments and one flint chunk.

Scatters of clay mould fragments also occurred, occasionally in the silting of post-holes (e.g. PH 16, Sq. 42: E84:5669, 5670a–b) and in depressions (e.g. D158, Sq. 52, which yielded ten fragments: E84:5598, 5599, 5617a–h). Most important, however, was the significant concentration of mould fragments to the immediate north-west of the 15m

Fig. 2.40—(a) Plan and section of Pit 119 (Sqs 34/35). (b) Pit 119 during excavation, with the boulder still *in situ* and primary black fill showing (Sqs 34/35, looking south). (c) Pit 119 during excavation, with the boulder still *in situ* and primary black fill showing (Sqs 34/35, looking west). (d) Pit 119 and its primary black fill (Sqs 34/35, looking east). (e) Pit 119 after excavation (Sqs 34/35, looking east). (f) Pit 119 after excavation, detail of the cut (Sqs 34/35, looking north-east).

Fig. 2.41—Saddle quern E84:5925, found upright in Pit 127 (Sq. 51, looking north-east).

enclosure, centred on Sqs 51 and 52. The former, Sq. 51, yielded no fewer than 63 fragments, while 190 came from Sq. 52 (Table 2.1). These were heavily concentrated in the area between Hearth 10 (Sq. 51), which contained eighteen fragments, and Pit 128 (Sq. 52), which also yielded eighteen fragments. In addition, the latter produced 24 coarse potsherds (Metalworking Zone 1).

2.2.4 Hearths in Area 1

A number of features in all parts of the site were originally classified as hearths, but some of them have emerged in post-excavation work as likely pyres, e.g. Hearths 1–4 and Pit 119 in Area 1 (Fig. 2.42). While initially discussing them as hearths, Raftery considered their function to be unclear and explored a variety of explanations. The evidence for post settings in some of these very large hearths was suggested to be evidence for the hearths having been surrounded by screens or having been roofed. The association of moulds with some of them indicated a possible connection to metalworking (e.g. Raftery 1976, 343–4).

The substantial and at times layered charcoal deposits within these pits which Raftery discusses as remnants of organic lining are instead in Chapter 6 interpreted as the remains of pyre debris,

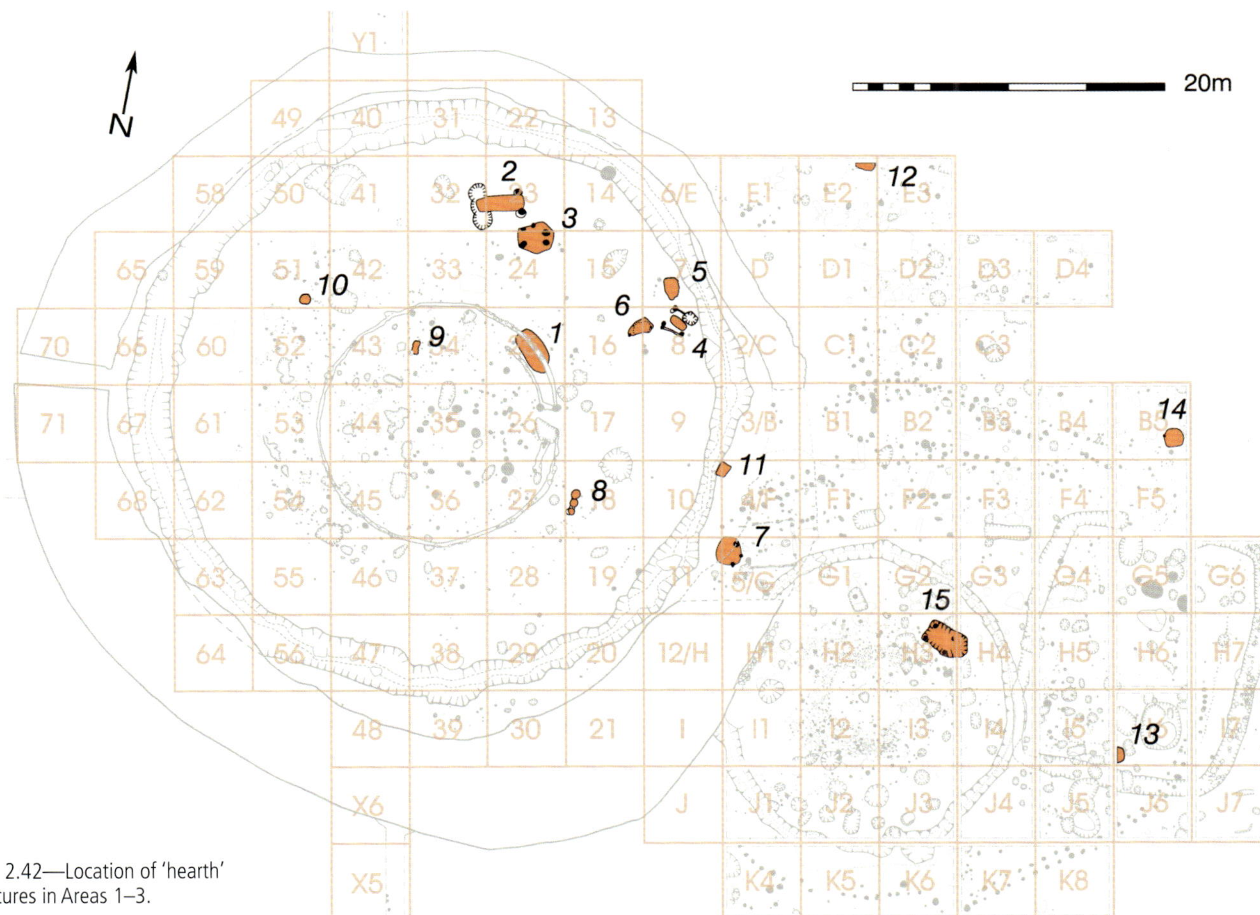

Fig. 2.42—Location of 'hearth' features in Areas 1–3.

Table 2.4—Artefacts recovered from pits in Area 1.

Feature no.	Sq. no.	Artefact type	Artefact no.
Pit 5	35	Mould fragment	E84:2510
Pit 13	15	Coarse pottery	E84:1325
Pit 15	32	Coarse pottery	E84:1372
Pit 110	36	Glass bead fragment	E84:3000
		Water-rolled pebble	E84:3169
Pit 117	17/26	Possible crucible fragment	E84:2449
		Mould fragment	E84:4140
		Coarse pottery	E84:2447; E84:2448; E84:2450; E84:4115–18; E84:4120–39
Pit 118	17/18	Crucible	E84:5934a,b; E84:5997a–c; E84:5998; E84:6054a–d
		Mould core fragment	E84:4488
		No ID	E84:5933
		Coarse pottery	E84:4484; E84:4485; E84:4489–96; E84:5927a,b; E84:5928–35; E84:5935.1; E84:5936; E84:5937; E84:5999a,c–i; E84:5999b,j,k; E84:6000; E84:6055–8; E84:6144a–c; E84:6152a–c; E84:6153–67; E84:6168a–e; E84:6169a–e; E84:6171–5; E84:6176a–d; E84:6177–85
		Unidentified	E84:6177a
		Water-rolled pebble	E84:4486; E84:4487
Pit 119	34/35	Gold small penannular ring	E84:6070
Pit 120A	19	Coarse pottery	E84:4036–41
Pit 121	29	Coarse pottery	E84:6022; E84:4819a–j; E84:4820–2; E84:5021; E84:6020–8
Pit 127	51	Saddle quern fragment	E84:5925
Pit 128	52	Mould fragment	E84:5655a–m; E84:5658–62
		Coarse pottery	E84:5654a–r; E84:5656; E84:5657; E84:5793; E84:5831a–c
Pit 129	53	Coarse pottery	E84:5170a–c
Pit 130	53	Middle Bronze Age pottery	E84:5418
Pit 131	41/50	Green glass, modern	E84:5436; E84:5868a–c
Pit 135	43	Coarse pottery	E84:5219; E84:5220; E84:5221a–c
Pit 143	44	Coarse pottery	E84:5020
Pit 147	45	Iron fragments	E84:5048; E84:5049
		Coarse pottery	E84:5047a–k
Pit 149	45	Coarse pottery	E84:5093
Pit 150	45	Coarse pottery	E84:5121a–d
Pit 152	46	Coarse pottery	E84:5120a,b
Pit 159	54	Coarse pottery	E84:5398; E84:5399a,b; E84:5400–2a,b; E84:5439a–w; E84:5440; E84:5442; E84:5444; E84:5470–1 (E84:5441 not located)
Pit 163	54	Iron fragment	E84:5415a–d
Pit 163?	54	Coarse pottery	E84:5414a–e

as, for example, underlined by the presence of such deposits within the post-holes—either representing burnt posts or post-holes filled with pyre debris after the extraction of the posts. Strikingly, Raftery refers to bones having been found in several of the hearths, adding to the possibility that more bone than is recorded in the sample records was actually found in these features.

These different interpretations have, of course, implications for the interpretation of the site, which will be explored more systematically later on. The reinterpretation of Pit 119 as the remains of a pyre pit has particularly far-reaching implications. Pit 119 had originally been considered a burial pit or funerary deposit (Raftery 2004), and its location, centred within the surrounding Ring-ditch 1, was taken to indicate the contemporaneity of both features, but the reinterpretation of the pit itself and the revision of the dating of Ring-ditch 1 remove the functional and chronological link between these two features (Chapter 4). While some of the hearths observed can be plausibly interpreted as likely pyre pits, others are not clearly identifiable as such and may instead be deposits of hearth material or small hearths.

The attribution of finds to hearths is not without complications. Raftery's textual account does not always tally with the finds records. This may be due to reinterpretation of hearths and their associated deposits after excavation. As some issues could not be resolved, conflicts are pointed out in the text below. One of the ambiguous aspects is, for example, the attribution of materials to hearths with additional spatial information such as 'SW', suggesting that these finds were found in deposits adjacent to the actual hearth cut. These are not included in the tables presented here but may have been considered by Raftery to have formed part of the actual feature.

A number of large hearths, each with evidence for considerable burning, came to light in the course of the excavation (Figs 2.42 and 2.43). The more important of these were concentrated in the north-eastern section of the Ring-ditch 1 enclosure. The largest, Hearth 1, has already been noted above, as it clearly pre-dated the 15m structure. The chronological relationship of the others, however, is by no means as clear. It is thus difficult to determine their relationship to Hearth 1, to each other or to other features on the site. Nevertheless, their heavy concentration in the north-eastern quadrant of the enclosure is important, and they may well be related to features of an early phase of activity on the site. The term 'hearth' is used here for convenience to describe these structures, but the extent to which the term is appropriate in individual examples is not entirely clear. While Hearths 11–17 will be described in the relevant sections of the areas where they occur, the overall group is discussed here.

Hearth 1

This hearth (Figs 2.42–2.44), located in Sq. 25, was oriented north-west/south-east. It first appeared in the yellow subsoil as a more or less oval area of black, charred material covering an area 3.15m long by 1.45m wide. Excavation revealed it to have been dug with some care, with generally vertical sides which met the flat base at a gently rounded angle. The pit was consistently 45cm deep. Two vertical greyish stains, as well as some faint horizontal greyish and blackish streaks, occurred on the sides. It is not clear whether these are accidental staining or the remains of some sort of wicker lining, such as occurred in Pit 118. The latter possibility does not, however, seem likely in this instance.

On the base of the pit, and extending slightly up the sides, was a layer of carefully laid cobbles composed of stones of relatively small size (lengths averaging 10–15cm). At one point the cobbling was absent, and here there was a concentration of powdered granite with a yellow mix and charcoal lumps. This is likely to represent a zone where the stones of the cobbled lining had disintegrated, probably owing to intense heat. Lying directly on the cobbles was a layer of black, heavily burnt material, 5–8cm thick. This was mixed with numerous tiny splinters of calcined animal[10] bone, most of which disintegrated when removed.

This material was covered by a brownish layer, about 10cm thick at the centre, mixed with ashes and powdered granite which had the consistency of sand. Above this was a layer of yellow redeposited natural soil, 8cm in maximum thickness. A zone of cobbling, which in this instance was about 75cm in width and composed of stones somewhat smaller than those lower down, lay on the yellow layer. The latter, as underneath, was covered by heavy black burning, followed, in turn, by a yellow layer and further burning, similar to that present in other hearths.

Despite the seeming complexity of the layering, it seems that the stratigraphy of this hearth has been satisfactorily resolved. Three phases of use can be recognised. Each of the lower two consisted of a layer of fine cobbles followed by intensive burning, and these were separated from one another by a layer of fine yellow soil. The third phase is represented by a further layer of yellow soil, similar to that already described, separating phase two from phase three. Cobbles appear to have been absent here. The uppermost layer, lying on the yellow, again consisted of heavy black burning similar to that encountered in the lower levels. The bedding trench of the 15m structure, as already noted above, cut through the upper layers of this hearth, which by this time was completely filled.

In places, some recent disturbance of Hearth 1 had occurred, resulting in the presence of occasional medieval and later sherds in upper levels (see Table 2.5). More relevant, however, are the 29 coarse potsherds, 23 of which, along with three water-rolled pebbles, came from the lowest level. The remaining potsherds came from the upper black levels (Table 2.5).

The finds records (Table 2.5) contradict this, with some of the medieval sherds being assigned to lower levels, while some of those that Raftery mentions as having been found in lower levels

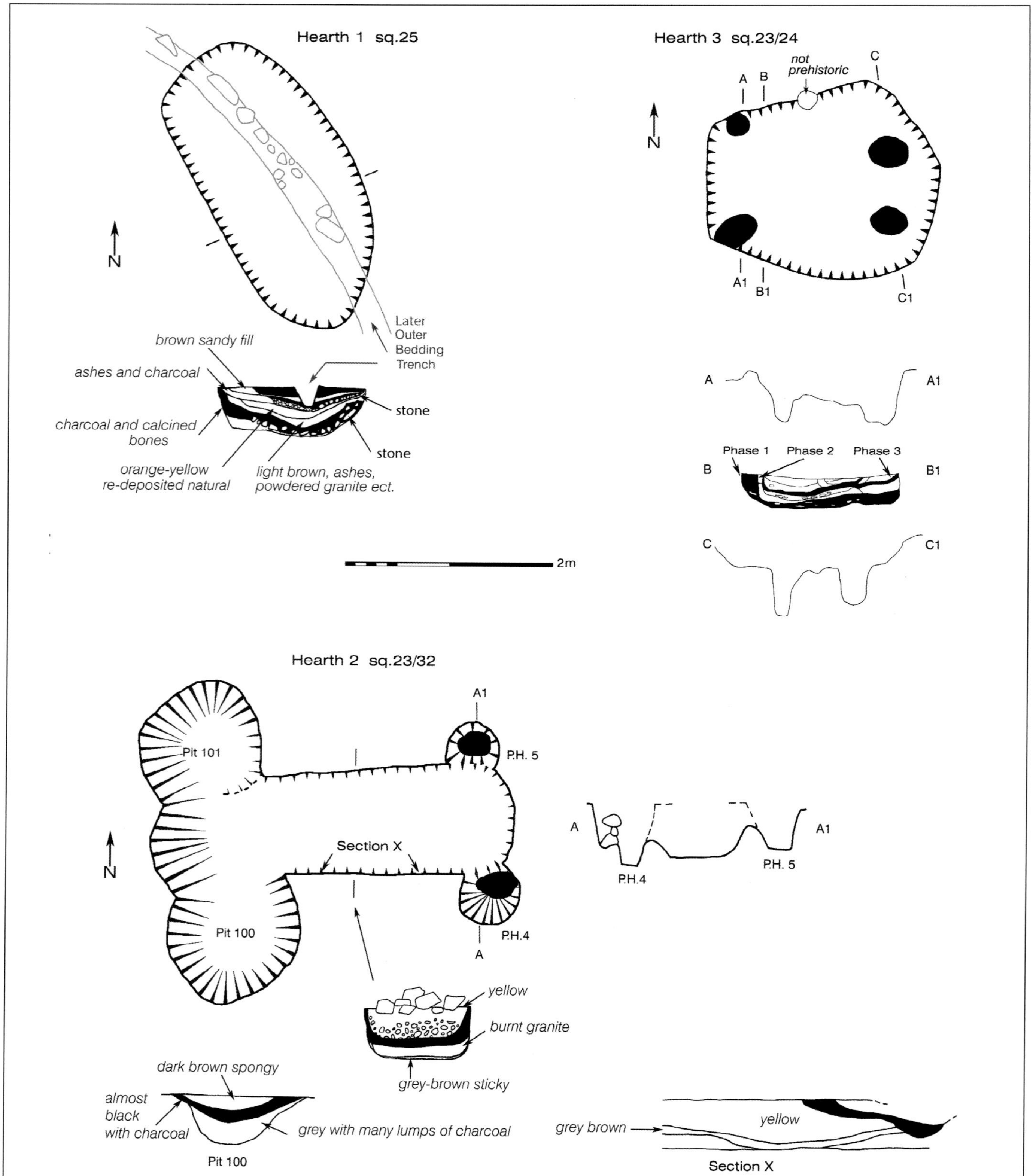

Fig. 2.43—(a) Plans and sections of Hearths 1–7.

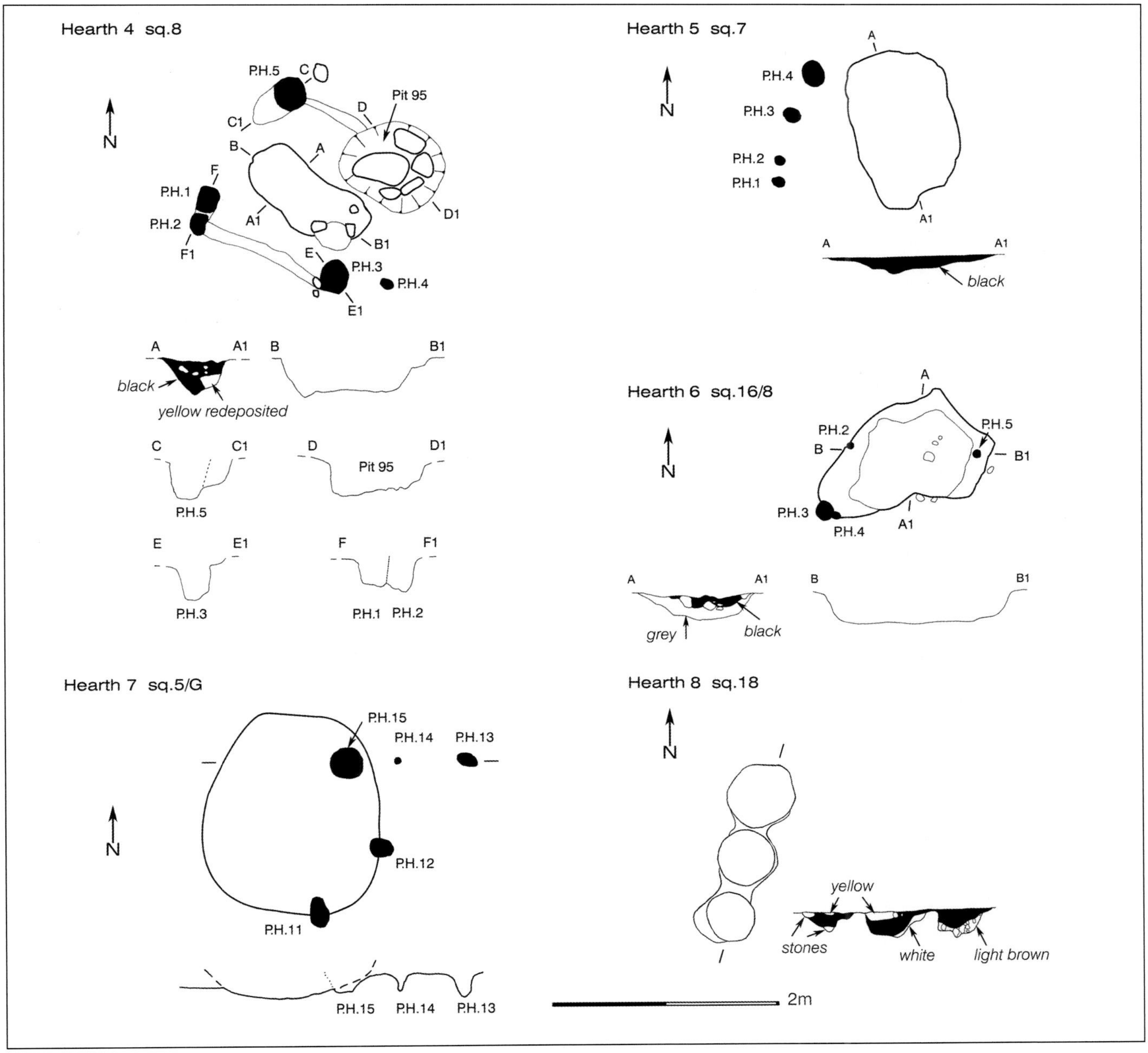

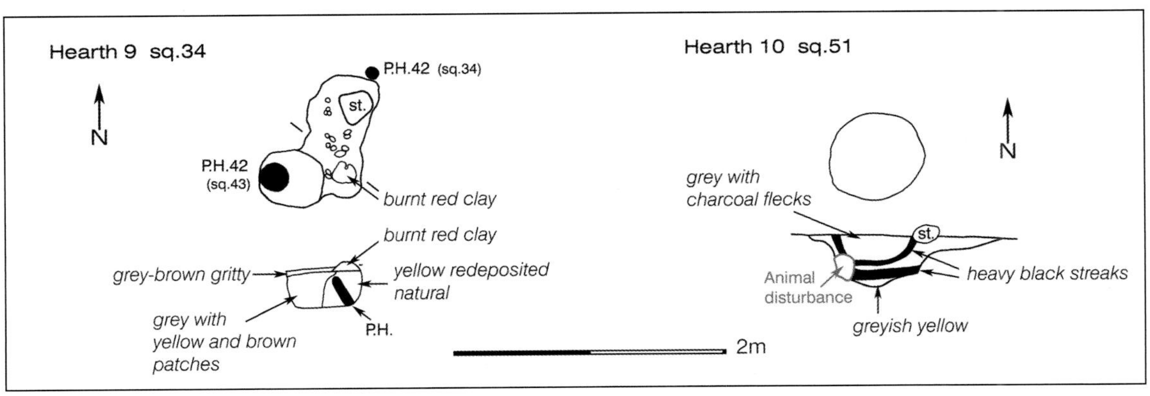

Fig. 2.43 (cont.)—(b) (above) Plans and sections of Hearths 4–8. (c) (left) Plans and sections of Hearths 9–10.

Fig. 2.44—(a) Hearth 1 after excavation (Sq. 25, looking north-east). (b and c) Hearth 1 during excavation, with successive layers of infilling visible (Sq. 25, looking north-east).

appear and in fact to have come from unspecified contexts. It is not clear what Raftery's description of these find associations is based on; this is particularly problematic in the case of medieval pottery sherds 678 and 680, which Raftery attributes to an upper level, and the piece of iron 679. These finds may be the result of the strong medieval disturbance that could also be noted in the 15m structure in this area. A radiocarbon date of 1360–820 cal. BC was obtained from charcoal from the second phase of the hearth (D-134).

Hearth 2

This hearth (Figs 2.43 and 2.45), which had been dug in a fairly exact east–west alignment, was situated about 6.6m (7.5m) north-west of Hearth 1, occurring for the most part in Sq. 23. When first exposed, it appeared in the yellow subsoil as a concentration of stones and rocks, some of quite substantial dimensions, embedded in a matrix of greyish-yellow silt. Although the basic elements of this feature are straightforward, there were some details which are not entirely clear.

The hearth proper consisted of a regularly dug rectangular pit with fairly sharp angles, a regular vertical profile and a carefully dug flat base. Its dimensions were 2.85m by 95cm and its depth was a constant 40cm. Unlike Hearth 1, it seems to have had only a single phase of use. This phase, lying on a very thin, sticky grey layer, was represented by a basal zone of scorched, powdered granite. Upon this was a thick layer of heavily burnt black material which, at the centre, reached a maximum thickness of about 8cm. This sloped upwards around the sides, revealing itself on the surface as a thin line (as was precisely the case with Pit 119) which formed the outline of the hearth (Fig. 2.45). On the surface, the pit was completely filled with a layer of relatively small, tightly packed stones averaging about 20cm in thickness. This was gently concave in long section, with stones projecting from its upper filling at each end. In the centre, where it was some 15cm below the upper level of the pit filling, the stony layer was covered by yellow, redeposited natural soil. All was finally covered by a layer of fairly large stones.

There was a circular pit at each corner (Fig. 2.45). The two at the eastern end were clearly recognisable as post-pits of substantial size. That at the south-east (PH 4) was oval in shape at the top, with dimensions of 60cm by 55cm. Excavation revealed a layer of packing stones, so that the post-hole proper could be estimated as having had a diameter of 35cm, tapering gently to a flat base, where its diameter was 15–17cm. It was 60cm deep. The second post-hole, in the north-east (PH 5), was oval at the top with dimensions of 50cm by 40cm. Its base, which was flat and regularly circular, was 20cm in diameter. In depth it was slightly shallower than PH 4. Both post-holes were filled with a black organic substance mixed with charcoal (Fig. 2.45). The two post-holes were deeper than the hearth and in each instance there was a rounded lip, about 25cm high, between the floor of the pit and the post-holes.

On the surface at the western end of the hearth a zone of tightly packed stones and black burnt material occurred, extending on either side of the hearth for 1–1.25m. The two thin black organic lines which defined the long edges of the pit cut sharply across this black zone. This black area proved, on excavation, to mark two subcircular pits which flanked the western corners of the hearth. The first (Pit 100), at the south-western corner, had steeply sloping sides and a diameter varying from 1.2m at the top to 75cm at the base. The latter, which was perfectly flat, was on exactly the same level as the base of the hearth. Pit 101, at the north-western corner of the hearth, had similarly sloping sides, its diameter varying from 1.1m to a basal diameter of 75cm. The base of this pit, which was also perfectly flat, was 10cm deeper than the base of the hearth.

Fig. 2.45—(a) Hearth 2 before excavation (Sqs 23/32, looking south-west). (b) Hearth 2 after excavation (Sqs 23/32, looking north). (c) Hearth 2 central pit with primary fill partially removed (Sqs 23/32, looking west).

Both pits were packed with medium-sized stones, and in each there was a thick, grey layer with some charcoal on the bottom, upon which there was a black charcoal-filled deposit up to 10cm thick. A darker brown layer overlay this, and over all there was a spread of black burnt material.

It is difficult to explain the various components of this rather curious feature. The main portion can be taken to have been a hearth comparable to Hearth 1. The basal layer of powdered granite represents the granite cobbling, transformed to powder by the heat of the overlying fires. The stones and the yellow soil of the upper packing are difficult to interpret. The nature of the layering seems too careful and systematic to be seen as simple infilling. Only the uppermost stones give the appearance of casual deposition.

The corner features are similarly enigmatic. All, however, appear to have been contemporary with the hearth. The two post-holes at the eastern end (nos 4 and 5) cut into the corners of the hearth and appear to have been dug at the same time as the hearth. They clearly held two vertical posts of substantial proportions.

At the western end of the hearth, the two very large circular pits, nos 100 and 101, are, if anything, even more enigmatic. It does appear, however, that there was no significant interval between the digging of the various elements, as is emphasised by the exactly level bases of the hearth and Pit 100. As the thin black organic lining of the hearth appears to cut across the pits, it may be that it was dug when the latter were already completed.

The nature and purpose of this structure are unclear. There can be little doubt that the main central section was a sunken hearth similar to the others found in its immediate vicinity. The corner elements are not, however, as easily explained. The two large post-holes at the eastern end could have been supports for a roof of some sort, if similar supports occurred at the opposite end. At the western end, however, the two large pits hardly qualify as matching supports, but it is not impossible that posts had been driven into the pits to provide western roof supports, although it must be admitted that no evidence of such post-holes was noted during excavation.[11]

Six fragments of coarse pottery (as well as a possible worked stone, E84:1473) came from this hearth. Three of these came from among the upper stones in the northern and north-western part of the hearth. The rest were found in the black charcoal layer. One sherd of medieval pottery (E84:390, Leinster Cooking Ware) is considered intrusive[12] (Table 2.5).

Two radiocarbon dates were derived from this hearth. One came from a corner deposit in Pit 100 (D-133, 1290–797 cal. BC). A second sample is described as being from this hearth also, but from exactly which context it was derived is unclear (SI-1476, 790–400 cal. BC).

Hearth 3

This hearth (Figs 2.42 and 2.43) was about 1.5m south-east of Hearth 2, straddling Sqs 23/4, and was oriented more or less east–west. It first became apparent as a subrectangular area, mottled brown in colour, which consisted of charcoal, ashes, sandy material and occasional patches of yellow soil (Fig. 2.46). One of the long sides was regularly straight; the other (the southern) had been damaged by secondary digging. The two ends were gently rounded. Its maximum dimensions were 2.25m by 1.95cm. Around its eastern, northern and western edges the mottled zone was clearly outlined by a thin streak of somewhat lighter brown which averaged about 3cm in width. The brown streak could not be recognised around the south owing to the later disturbance.

Two triangular areas of redeposited yellow subsoil, each bounded on the exterior by a thin line of black organic material, enclosed the central zone along the northern and southern sides. These streaks were about 1.3m apart in the west and 1.5m or so apart in the east. The northernmost extended from the north-western corner of the dark zone just described, not parallel to the latter but splaying out from it in a north-easterly direction. It was possible to trace it as an independent entity for about 1.5m, at which point it bent sharply inwards towards the central zone for a distance of about 20cm, to end about 20cm distant from the latter. It was between 4cm and 10cm in width. The other black streak, extending from the south-western corner in a south-easterly direction, appeared to be discontinuous but this was a product of later disturbance. Its preserved length was no more than 90cm and it was never more than 3cm in width. As with the northernmost streak, its maximum distance from the central zone was 40cm. At the eastern and western ends, any continuations of these black bands were difficult to recognise. It was possible to detect the black streak in the west, immediately outside the light brown streak referred to earlier. In the east there was a more irregular spread of black at the end of the hearth, but the original presence of the black streak here is not in question.

Detailed examination of the contents of this hearth indicates that there were certainly two and possibly three phases of use. The lowest layer, which lay directly on the base of the pit, consisted of a thick deposit of charcoal and ashes mixed with small deposits of yellow soil and some very small stones. Its thickness varied from 25cm to 30cm (Figs 2.43 and 2.46).

Fig. 2.46—(a) Hearth 3 before excavation (Sqs 23/24, looking south). (b) Hearth 3 section with layering of charcoal and soil (Sqs 23/24, looking east). (c) Vitrification around post-holes of Hearth 3 (Sqs 23/24, looking north). (d) Hearth 3 after excavation, with post-holes showing (Sqs 23/24, looking north).

The layers above this appear to represent a narrower, more regularly rectangular hearth, which showed on the surface between the triangular zones of redeposited natural soil. It looks as if a smaller basket had been inserted into the larger hearth, after the latter was no longer in use, and the sides filled with yellow soil. The basket, which was recognisable on the surface as a thin brown band surrounding the central concentration of burnt material, was about 1.05m wide. Above it was a grey sandy layer with yellow flecks, some 6–8cm thick, a black zone of charcoal averaging 5cm in thickness, a sandy-brown layer mixed with charcoal flecks and an upper layer of ashes, sand and charcoal. The hearth had been dug into on the south, probably subsequent to its second period of use, cutting away some of the upper layers (including the enclosing streaks of brown and black) but not the basal black.

When all the layers had been removed, the original sunken hearth was revealed as having been regularly dug with steep sides and a smooth flat base 38cm below the surface. It was more or less a flattened oval in plan, though it was somewhat narrower in the west than in the east. Its maximum dimensions were 2.4m long by 1.82m wide.

In the base of the pit four post-holes were revealed, each of which had originally held a vertical post (Figs 2.43 and 2.46). They formed a rectangle with dimensions of about 1.3m by about 80cm. A fifth, shallower post-hole, set slightly off-centre on the north-west, had a brown humus fill and is certainly not prehistoric.

Running anticlockwise from the north-west, the post-holes may be described as follows.

Post-hole 1 was almost perfectly circular, with a diameter of 25cm and a depth of 30cm. It was filled with dark brown material mixed with fragments of charcoal. Post-hole 2 was oval, with dimensions at the mouth of 40cm by 25cm. It was 20cm deep and its filling was the same as that of post-hole 1. Post-hole 3 was rectangular with rounded corners. Its upper dimensions were 30cm by 20cm and it was 40cm deep. It was entirely filled with charcoal. Post-hole 4 was oval at the top, where its dimensions were 40cm by 30cm. It was 50cm deep. It was filled with charcoal but in this instance the remains of the actual post could be recognised as a circular brownish fill in the black. The post was 20cm in diameter and it confirmed the assumption that the posts which originally stood in the post-holes had been vertical.

Eight coarse potsherds came from this hearth, all from the black material in the eastern area. They are likely to belong to phase 1 but it cannot be certain that some do not come from phase 2. There are no indications, however, of any significant time-lag between the two phases, so that all the sherds may be regarded as essentially contemporary. A hone (E84:64)[13] and the remains of two crucibles (E84:1586, 1590; Fig. 3.42) also came from the black layer. In addition, part of the shank of a bronze pin (E84:53; Fig. 3.35) was found, though this is not necessarily prehistoric, as one piece of iron (E84:1254) also found its way into this layer (Table 2.5).

A radiocarbon date of 1308–1016 cal. BC was derived from possibly this hearth or material around it (GrN-27097).

Hearth 4

This hearth (Fig. 2.47) was 8.5m south-east of Hearth 3 in Sq. 8 and was close to the inner edge of Ring-ditch 1, which had clearly been cut across it (Figs 2.42, 2.43 and 2.47). Hearths 5 and 6 lay immediately to its north-west and west but it cannot be demonstrated that the three features are contemporary (Fig. 2.48). Nevertheless, there is a degree of probability that they are not far removed from one another in time.

Following the removal of the upper humus, the hearth appeared in the yellow subsoil as a curious complex of pits and post-holes enclosing a central, irregularly oval area of blackish-brown material from which a number of smallish stones protruded. The central area was about 1m in length and 50–60cm wide. It was enclosed on all sides by a zone of light yellowish-grey material which was noticeably lighter in colour than the surrounding darker yellow boulder clay. This in turn was flanked, on both the north-east and the south-west, by a pair of thin greyish-brown streaks which ran parallel to one another and were 1.35m apart. That in the south-west was the more clearly defined of the two. It consisted of a band about 10cm wide and 1.1m long, ending in the south-east in an area of black material which was clearly a post-hole. The second band, on the opposite side of the dark central area, was less clearly defined but nonetheless visible as a thin grey band 80cm long and 10cm wide. A circular black area at its north-western end was obviously a post-hole. At its other extremity there was a circular area of grey (which turned out to be Pit 95) filled with stones of moderate size.

Excavation confirmed the assumption that the central zone was a pit with more or less straight sides and rounded ends. It was 1.18m long and averaged 46cm in width. Apart from a few depressions, its base was generally flat. Its sides, for the most part, sloped sharply to a maximum depth of 30cm. The filling material was entirely uniform, consisting of black organic material mixed with charcoal and a few small stones and patches of redeposited yellow subsoil.

Fig. 2.47—Hearth 4 before excavation (Sq. 8, looking north-west).

The post-holes had all been dug vertically and were of substantial size. In each instance they were situated at the end of one of the grey streaks. Running anticlockwise from the south-west, they may be described as follows (Fig. 2.43).

Post-hole 1 was about 35cm in diameter at the mouth, narrowing to 20cm at its flat base. Along one part, in the south-west, there was a stepped expansion 24cm deep, but it reached a maximum depth of 36cm. It was filled throughout with blackish-brown material and contained three mould fragments (E84:2377–9). Post-hole 2 appeared to be doubled. On the surface it formed an elongated patch of black, burnt material but when excavated there were two interlocking post-holes, 26cm and 23cm in their respective diameters. That at the end of the grey streak was, at 31cm, the deeper of the two; the other was about 23cm in depth. Both were filled with grey material. Post-hole 3 was 30cm in diameter at the mouth, narrowing to a basal diameter of about 22cm. It was 30cm deep and its fill was a mixture of black organic material with some charcoal.

At the fourth corner there was a pit rather than a post-hole. Pit 95, with maximum dimensions of 85cm by 95cm, was not quite circular. It had near-vertical sides and had been dug to a depth of 25–28cm. Its fill was a fine, uniform, brownish-grey material from which five moderately sized stones protruded. Four defined the edge of the pit and appeared to form a semicircle. The fifth, which was the largest, lay within the arc formed by the other four. The four stones around the sides were in a near-upright position, while the larger one could have fallen forward from an originally upright stance. Excavation revealed that the stones rested almost, but not quite, on the base of the pit and were embedded in the grey filling material. It is thus possible that these stones had been deliberately placed to outline the sides of the pit.

The two grey-brown streaks were no more than about 5–12cm deep. They might represent slot-trenches, supporting some sort of modest lateral walling, or are perhaps linked in some way to a roofed structure.

Pit 95 yielded a sherd of possible Leinster Cooking Ware (E84:2302), coarseware (E84:2369) and a mould fragment (E84:2370), as well as one sherd of Beaker pottery (E84:2004), 49 sherds of coarse pottery,[14] eight mould fragments and one fragment of an iron horse-bit (E84:2009) at a high and probably disturbed level (Table 2.5). Post-holes in the north-east and south-west corners of the hearth also produced mould fragments.

Hearth 5

This hearth (Figs 2.42, 2.43 and 2.48) was situated in Sq. 7, 1.5m to the north of Hearth 4. In contrast to the hearths just described, it was an uncomplicated structure. It was irregularly oval, with maximum dimensions of 1.44m by 90cm, and extremely shallow, the sides sloping gradually (and somewhat irregularly) to a maximum depth at the centre of no more than 15cm. Apart from a few areas of dark brown, the hearth contained a generally undifferentiated fill of black burnt material, including a considerable amount of charcoal, sometimes in quite large lumps. A scatter of relatively small burnt stones occurred throughout.

Immediately outside the hearth, extending in a south-westerly direction from its north-west corner, was a line of four post-holes spaced 15–20cm apart (Fig. 2.43). The largest of these, which was 20cm in diameter, was that closest to the hearth, and from this their sizes tapered noticeably to the southernmost post-hole, which was 10cm in diameter. All four of these post-holes are recorded in the site archive as having been filled with charcoal, but their depth appears not to have been recorded.

The hearth contained eighteen coarse potsherds, one unidentified sherd and six clay mould fragments. Two sherds of medieval pottery came from the upper levels and are considered later disturbance[15] (Table 2.5).

Hearth 6

This example (Figs 2.42, 2.43 and 2.49), less than 1m west of Hearth 4 in Sqs 8/16, was little different from that just described. It was roughly pear-shaped in outline, with maximum dimensions of about 1.6m by 95cm, and for the most part had a regularly flat base and near-vertical sides. Its maximum depth was 20cm. The main upper fill consisted of a dense black material, 8cm in maximum depth, with patches of dark brown, charcoal and stones mixed throughout. An

Fig. 2.48—Hearths 4, 5 and 6 after excavation (Sqs 8/16, looking west).

Fig. 2.49—Hearth 6 after excavation (Sqs 8/16, looking north-east).

occasional pocket of yellow soil also occurred. This layer, which reached the surface on the north, east and west, lay on a thick, sticky greyish deposit which was devoid of stones. The black material, however, extended virtually to the southern edge of the pit. The few post-holes in the hearth are later features.

This hearth yielded a considerable number of finds, including well over 100 potsherds, seven mould fragments, three crucible fragments and two water-rolled pebbles (Table 2.5). Most of these objects came from the black, stony layer, but at least fourteen came from the grey level near the base. Three medieval/post-medieval potsherds (E84:902, 2113 and 2274) are considered intrusive.[16]

Radiocarbon dates of 1230–1030 cal. BC (SUERC-42588) and 1220–1020 cal. BC (SUERC-43325) were obtained on carbonised residue from pottery sherds from within Hearth 6.

Hearth 8

Hearth 8 (Figs 2.42, 2.43b and 2.50) was a somewhat enigmatic feature. It first appeared on the surface in Sq. 18 as three conjoined circular areas of black, mixed with occasional patches of yellow soil. Upon investigation it emerged that this consisted of three closely spaced circular pits (A, B and C) grouped in linear formation. They were aligned roughly north-east/south-west, and from the northern to the southern ends there was a slight but noticeable gradation in their diameters. Thus, from north to south, their respective dimensions were (A) 55cm by 70cm, (B) 50cm by 60cm (50cm on Fig. 2.43) and (C) 40cm by 38cm. The pits had been dug with some care. They had vertical or gradually inward-sloping sides, and concave or, in places, almost V-shaped bases. In total, the pits extended over a combined length of 1.7m. Each pit was separated from the next by a narrow baulk of earth, 5–15cm wide. The average depths of the three pits (from north to south) were 25cm, 23cm and 18cm.

The relationship of the pits to each other is not clear but, as noted above, all three were revealed as a common spread of black material, which gave every indication of representing a single phase of deposition. Most of Pit B extended directly into Pit A, and in the case of the latter the black lay on top of a dark brown stony layer covered by a lighter brown soil. This was in places mixed with the remains of a yellow layer.

Fig. 2.50—(a) Hearth 8 before excavation (Sq. 18, looking south). (b) Hearth 8 after excavation (Sq. 18, looking south).

Hearth 9

This hearth (Fig. 2.43) occurred in Sq. 34 within the area enclosed by the 15m structure. It was irregularly rectangular in outline, with maximum dimensions of 90cm in length, 45cm in width and 30cm in depth. The pit was, for the most part, filled with grey silting and yellow, redeposited natural soil, but in its upper levels there was a considerable amount of burnt red clay and gritty, grey-brown, ashy material, indicating that burning had taken place.

Hearth 10

This feature (Fig. 2.43) lay to the north-west of the 15m structure, and about 4m distant from it, in Sq. 51. It was a small, regularly oval pit with dimensions of about 75cm by 70cm. Its sides sloped downwards to an even, rounded base. It was 38cm deep. In this pit were two black organic layers. The first, which was 7cm thick, lay on the base. The second, separated from the first by a layer of greyish material, covered the sides and base and was only 3–4cm thick. The uppermost fill was a deposit of greyish material containing numerous charcoal flecks.

This pit, presumed to be a hearth of some sort, contained nineteen mould fragments as well as nine coarse potsherds. Most of the moulds came from the upper black layer, or from the greyish material which covered it. Three further mould fragments and one potsherd came from the lowest level. In addition, a sizeable number of mould fragments were scattered in the immediate vicinity of the hearth, particularly to the south in Sq. 52 and in D158 to the west. The moulds were thus clearly concentrated on Hearth 10 (Table 2.5).

A radiocarbon date of 920–410 cal. BC (SI-1478) was obtained on the burnt fill of this hearth, suggesting that this feature and the associated moulds may possibly belong to the later phase of Bronze Age activity (see Chapter 4). However, Smithsonian dates have to be considered as problematic (see Chapter 4).

Discussion

At least fifteen possible hearths were identified within the main excavation area, as well as an example outside the main rampart to the south (see below). In addition, while not represented as a formal cut, the concentrations of charcoal in the B/C and C/D cuttings (see section 2.3 below) may represent hearths. The nine hearths described here were defined by clearly identified cuts which showed evidence for burning, although in some cases this may reflect the deposition of burnt materials within a pit cut. Exceptional are the hearths with rather complex sequences of burning episodes, such as Hearths 1, 2, 3. In the case of Hearths 2 and 3, these are also separated by layers of cobbling. The exact purpose of some of the larger examples, however, is at times enigmatic.

The main concentration of hearths (and related structures) was found within the central enclosure, concentrated particularly in the north-eastern zone. Here the six large and, for the most part, impressive examples occurred, as well as a lesser, but important, seventh example somewhat to the west of the others.

The relationship of the hearths to one another is not in every instance completely clear but the probability that they overlap chronologically is arguable. The first point to bear in mind is the certainty that Hearth 1 is an early feature, clearly pre-dating the central 15m enclosure. The fill of the hearth pit indicates phases of heavy burning. The presence of coarse potsherds as well as some animal bones, along with the absence of clay mould fragments, leaves little room to doubt that here are the remains of a hearth.

Of the six other central hearths considered here, three seem to have held substantial upright timbers of some form. Particularly impressive in this regard is Hearth 3, which differs from Hearth 4 in several details. In the first instance, Hearth 4 is considerably smaller than Hearth 3 and, rather than having sharp sides and a flat base, as in the case of Hearth 3, its sides slope sharply inwards to the centre. More significant is the fact that the substantial post-holes, linked in three instances by narrow, straight grooves, occur a distance outside, rather than within, the hearth, as in Hearth 3. A large circular pit in the fourth corner appears to be later. The matter is not certain, but it may be that here a roofed feature similar to that obviously recognisable in Hearth 3 existed before the substantial pit was dug.

The fills of Hearths 3 and 2 were far more complex than is the case with Hearth 4, where a single dense layer of burnt material was present. In the case of the former (Hearths 3 and 2), black burnt layers were present, mixed with areas of cracked and splintered stones which had resulted from heavy burning. The original use of these hearths remains a matter of some uncertainty, allowing the possibility that here the burning was deliberate, possibly to create charcoal for use in casting. Or should we accept a more conventional view that here was a reused fireplace? The matter remains open for further consideration. The scraps of pottery and the few mould fragments from these hearths, at any rate, are likely to have gradually found their way over time into the pits.

The other large hearths in this area—Hearths 5 and 6—are relatively shallow, with gently sloping sides and base and with evidence of heavy burning. The uncomplicated character of their fill suggests again a single phase of burning. The purpose of these zones of heavily burnt material remains uncertain. In each case a few clay mould fragments were present, as well as some coarse potsherds. The latter need have no significance,

Table 2.5—Finds from hearths in Areas 1–3.

Hearth 1, Sq. 25

Context	Depth (cm)	Find type	Find no.
Dark black	20	Coarse pottery	E84:621
		Medieval pottery	E84:681
		Post-medieval pottery	E84:682
In black area at base of medium-sized stone, SE	25	Coarse pottery	E84:721a,b, 722
Dark black burnt patch in yellow, SE	28	Coarse pottery	E84:677
		Medieval pottery	E84:678, 680
		Iron	E84:679
Unspecified		Middle Bronze Age pottery	E84:1247
		Coarse pottery	E84:1249, 1262, 1263, 1264, 1265, 1266, 1267
		Water-rolled pebble	E84:1268
		Post-medieval pottery	E84:1269

Hearth 2, Sqs 23/32

Context	Depth (cm)	Find type	Find no.
Dark burnt patch beside stones near middle of square	38–40	Iron fragment	E84:341
In black burnt area under stones, W	25–30	Coarse pottery	E84:389
		Medieval pottery	E84:390
Black charcoal level		Coarse pottery	E84:1471, 1472, 1474

Hearth 3, Sqs 23/24

Context	Depth (cm)	Find type	Find no.
Unspecified		Coarse pottery	E84:1252, 1253, 1588
		Iron fragment	E84:1254
		Crucible fragments	E84:1586, 1590

Hearth 4, Sq. 8

Context	Depth (cm)	Find type	Find no.
Upper level	40–45	Coarse pottery	E84:1964
		Mould fragments	E84:1961, 1962, 1963
Black, heavily burnt area, E	27	Coarse pottery	E84:841
In black burnt area, near middle of square	30	Coarse pottery	E84:824
In Hearth 4, N	35	Coarse pottery	E84:1296
Unspecified		Beaker pottery	E84:2004
	20–40	Coarse pottery	E84:1998, 1999, 2000, 2001, 2002, 2003, 2006, 2007, 2035, 2037, 2235, 2236, 2237, 2238, 2239, 2240, 2241, 2242, 2243, 2244, 2245, 2295, 2368, 2371, 2372, 2373, 2374, 2375, 2376
	40	Mould fragments	E84:1863a,b, 2005, 2246, 2301
	15	Iron possible horse-bit	E84:2009
Post-hole in NE corner of Hearth 4		Mould fragments	E84:2280, 2281, 2282, 2282.1, 2283.1, 2283, 2284.1, 2284, 2285, 2285.1, 2286, 2286.1, 2287.1
			E84:2287
			E84:2288
			E84:2288.2
			E84:2289
			E84:2289.1
			E84:2290
			E84:2290.1
			E84:2291
			E84:2291.1
Post-hole in SW corner of Hearth 4		Mould fragments	E84:2377, 2378, 2379
Black burnt area, N. Possibly Hearth 4	28	Coarse pottery	E84:843–5

Table 2.5 (cont.)—Finds from hearths in Areas 1–3.

Hearth 5, Sq. 7

Context	Depth (cm)	Find type	Find no.
SW. Very dark material, in parts almost black	21	Coarse pottery	E84:805
Very dark material, in parts almost black	21	Medieval pottery	E84:806, 810
		Coarse pottery	E84:809
Dark brown, in parts almost black. Heavy occupation in this area. S. Hearth 5	21	Coarse pottery	E84:811a–c
Dark brown, in parts almost black. Heavy occupation in this area. W. Hearth 5	21	Coarse pottery	E84:812
Black (burnt?) area, SW	27	Coarse pottery	E84:848
Black, among stones, SW	28	Coarse pottery	E84:849a,b
Unspecified	10–40	Coarse pottery	E84:1951, 1991, 1992, 1993, 1994, 1996, 1997, 2221
	40–45	Mould fragments	E84:1946, 1947, 1948, 1949, 1950, 1988
Hearth 5, S	21	Coarse pottery	E84:808

Hearth 6, Sqs 8/16

Context	Depth (cm)	Find type	Find no.
Black area, NW	30–35	Coarse pottery	E84:900, 901a–e, 903d–l, 925a,b, 940, 941, 942, 1214, 1215, 1216, 1217a–c, 1219
		Medieval pottery	E84:902
		Mould fragments	E84:903a–c
Unspecified	33–35	Coarse pottery	E84:1406, 1407, 1408, 1409, 2085, 2086, 2087, 2088, 2089, 2090, 2091, 2092, 2093, 2094, 2095, 2096, 2097, 2098, 2099, 2100, 2101, 2102, 2103, 2104, 2105, 2106, 2107, 2108, 2109, 2111, 2112, 2125, 2129, 2130, 2131, 2132, 2133, 2134, 2135, 2136, 2137, 2138, 2265, 2266, 2267, 2268, 2269, 2270, 2271, 2272, 2273, 2275, 2341, 2342
		Medieval/post-medieval pottery	E84:2113, 2274
		Crucible fragments	E84:1752a–f, 1753, 1754
		Mould fragments	E84:1406.1, 1410a,b, 2114
		Water-rolled pebbles	E84:2139, 2140
Grey level at bottom		Coarse pottery	E84:2115, 2116, 2117, 2118, 2119, 2120, 2121, 2122, 2123, 2124, 2126, 2127, 2128
Black (burnt) patch NE	20–26	Coarse pottery	E84:625, 629, 630
In black burnt material on edge of hard grey area, NE		Coarse pottery	E84:1322, 1323, 1323.1
Black charcoal fill		Coarse pottery	E84:2141, 2142, 2143, 2144, 2145, 2146, 2147, 2148, 2149, 2150, 2151, 2152, 2153
In black charred area, N	26	Coarse pottery	E84:831, 833
Dark brown, NW	30	Mould fragment	E84:899

Table 2.5 (cont.)—Finds from hearths in Areas 1–3.

Hearth 10, Sq. 51			
Context	**Depth (cm)**	**Find type**	**Find no.**
Hearth 10, context unspecified	15–30	Coarse pottery	E84:5243a–h, 5779
		Mould fragments	E84:5118a–c, 5167, 5168, 5169a–c, 5215, 5244, 5245, 5246, 5247, 5248a,b, 5261, 5547, 5767, 5768a,b

Hearth 11, Sq. 3 (misidentified in the finds logbook as Hearth 12)			
Context	**Depth (cm)**	**Find type**	**Find no.**
Hearth 12 under wall		Coarse pottery	E84:1651

Hearth 13, Sq. I6			
Context	**Depth (cm)**	**Find type**	**Find no.**
Unspecified fill		Coarse pottery	E84:9185

Hearth 14, Sq. B5			
Context	**Depth (cm)**	**Find type**	**Find no.**
Black burnt material	30	Coarse pottery	E84:9107, 9226
		Mould fragment	E84:9227

Hearth 15 (Pit 9), Sq. H3		
Context	**Object type**	**Find no.**
On or in black fill of hearth's 'black lining'	Crucible fragment	E84:8394
	Mould fragment	E84:8359
	Coarse pottery	E84:8360 E84:8362 E84:8395 E84:8406
From section strip: in grey fill of NE post-hole of Pit 9 = Hearth 15 (four-poster pit)	Crucible fragment	E84:8462

though the presence of almost 100 potsherds in Hearth 6 is worth noting.

Hearth 2, unlike those considered above, is especially complex, and the detailed structure, already described, is difficult to interpret. The overlapping phases of black, burnt material, medium-sized stones and powdered granite are indicative of a complex sequence which seems scarcely likely to represent a simple hearth construction. The substantial post-holes at one end closely resemble those already referred to above in Hearths 3 and 4, where they were presumably for roof supports. At the other end, however, rather than post-holes there were two sizeable pits, Pits 100 and 101, which are difficult to regard as further roof supports. Detailed examination of this feature strongly suggests that this is a single construction, leaving its original purpose uncertain. Perhaps bronze-working played some part in the use of this structure but the matter remains entirely open.

Most of the other structures here referred to as hearths are, in the main, of less impressive dimensions than those already discussed, and they generally appear to have been simple and unelaborate, usually no more than a few centimetres in depth. The enigmatic triple-unit structure, Hearth 8, remains unclear, however, while Hearth 10, smaller and less complex, has been referred to above as a possible hearth. The 28 mould fragments within the pit, and the almost 100 from its immediate vicinity, lend support to this, even though the pit itself is shallow and without any obvious features.

2.2.5 The iron-working hearth

In Area 1, large amounts of slag (see Chapter 10) scattered across the disturbed contexts focused on a pit which came to light in 1969 at the eastern edge of Sq. 65, about 1m in from Rampart 1 and cut into the silted-up ditch (Figs 2.5, 2.51 and 2.52). It had been partly disturbed by recent cultivation activities and was first recognised as an area of charcoal mixed with a scatter of irregular lumps of iron slag spread over an area measuring about 2m north–south by about 75cm east–west. Some smaller deposits of charcoal occurred outside the main black zone, notably on the north and south-west. Immediately

Opposite page
Fig. 2.51 (top)—Pre- and post-excavation plans and section of iron-working hearth.

Fig. 2.52 (below)—(a) The iron-working hearth before excavation (Sqs 65/59, looking north-east). (b) The iron-working hearth after excavation (Sqs 65/59, looking north-east).

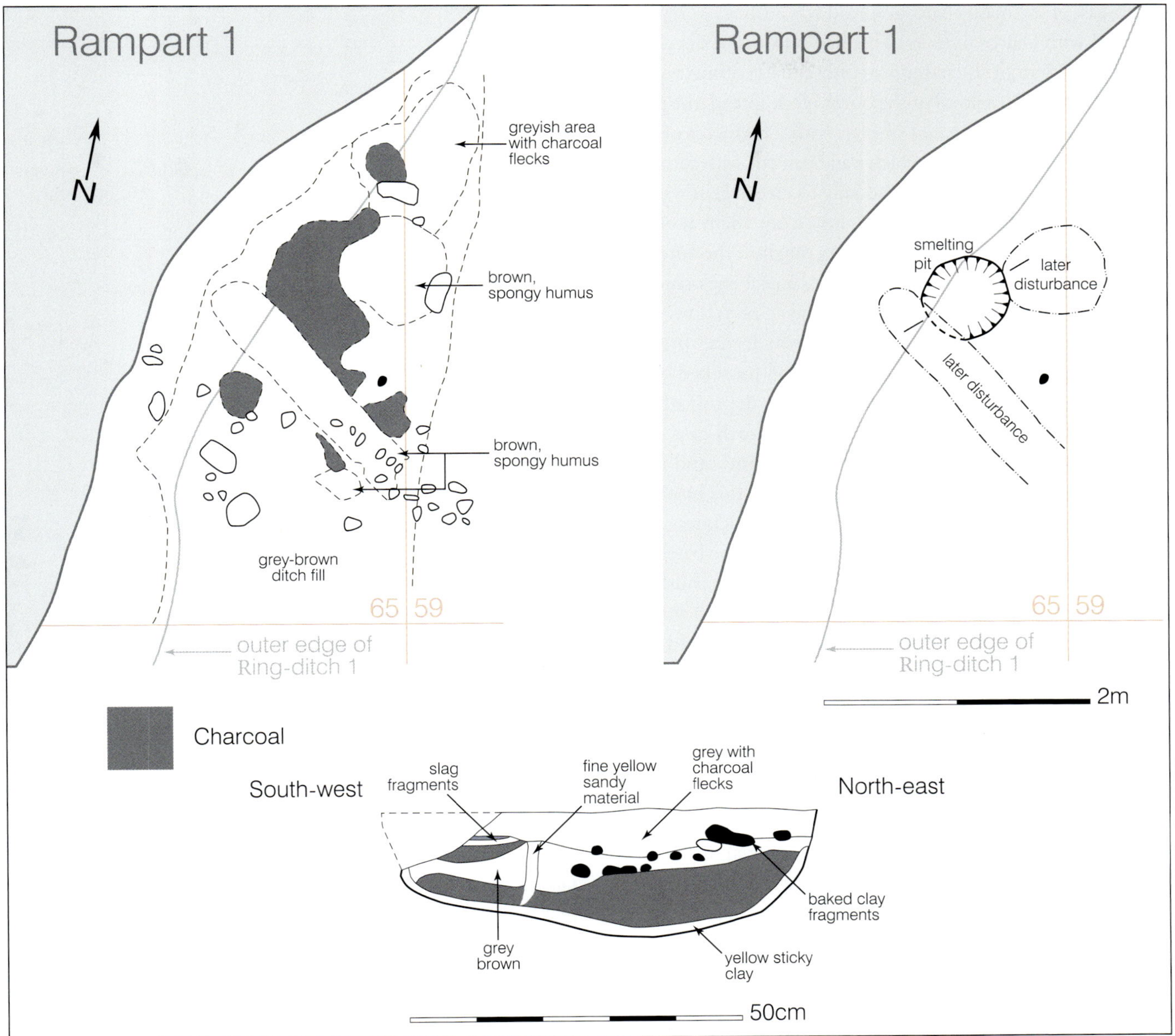
Rampart 1
N
greyish area
with charcoal
flecks
brown,
spongy humus
brown,
spongy humus
grey-brown
ditch fill
65
59
outer edge of
Ring-ditch 1
Rampart 1
N
smelting
pit
later
disturbance
later disturbance
65
59
outer edge of
Ring-ditch 1
2m
Charcoal
South-west
slag
fragments
fine yellow
sandy
material
grey with
charcoal
flecks
North-east
baked clay
fragments
grey
brown
yellow sticky
clay
50cm

(a)
(b)

north-east of the main charcoal spread was an area of grey burnt material with charcoal flecks. This had maximum dimensions of roughly 25cm by 40cm but was only a few centimetres thick.

Following the removal of the burnt black spread, the pit was revealed as regularly circular in plan with a diameter of about 62cm (Fig. 2.52). Its sides, which had been cut with some care, were almost vertical, curving gradually to meet a gently sloping base. The depth of the pit varied slightly, from 18cm at one end to about 14cm at the other. It had been dug into the outer edge of the completely silted-up ditch of the central enclosure.

At the base of the pit was a thin layer of yellow, sticky material, no more than 1cm thick, which was probably nothing more than a natural deposit of loosened yellow subsoil. Directly on this lay a thick, dense deposit of black charcoal. This was most substantial in the north-east, where it was up to 8cm thick, while around the south and south-west its thickness decreased to 4cm. Covering this black layer was a spread of grey-brown material whose thickness varied from about 3cm around the north-east (where the black layer was thickest) to a maximum of about 8cm in the south-west (where the black layer was thinnest). Both on and in the grey-brown layer were small, amorphous lumps of bright red baked clay. It was noticeable that the clay lumps only occurred over about two thirds of the pit, ending at the point where the basal charcoal deposit thinned and where the thickness of the covering grey-brown layer correspondingly increased. About 20cm from the pit's south-western end was what seemed to be a thin, vertical stake-pipe, 2cm in diameter, filled with fine yellow soil, perhaps as a result of the withdrawal of the stake.

To the immediate south of this feature, directly on the greyish-brown material, lay a roughly circular deposit of iron slag. This had been partly cut away by a modern plough trench but survived to a diameter of 11cm. Charcoal adhered to both its upper and lower surfaces. The final upper filling of the pit, 5–8cm thick, consisted of greyish material with charcoal intermixed.

Samples of the iron slag from this feature were analysed (see Chapter 3, section 3.10) and indicated that smithing, rather than smelting, took place here and in a small hearth construction. A crucible fragment identified within the slag sample examined by Rehren was used for bronze-casting, suggesting that bronze-casting may have taken place alongside the iron-smithing (see Chapter 3, section 3.10).

Radiocarbon dating of charcoal from the pit placed the smelting activity in the second quarter of the first millennium cal. AD (GrN-27103, cal. AD 270–540; SI-1480, cal. AD 230–540).

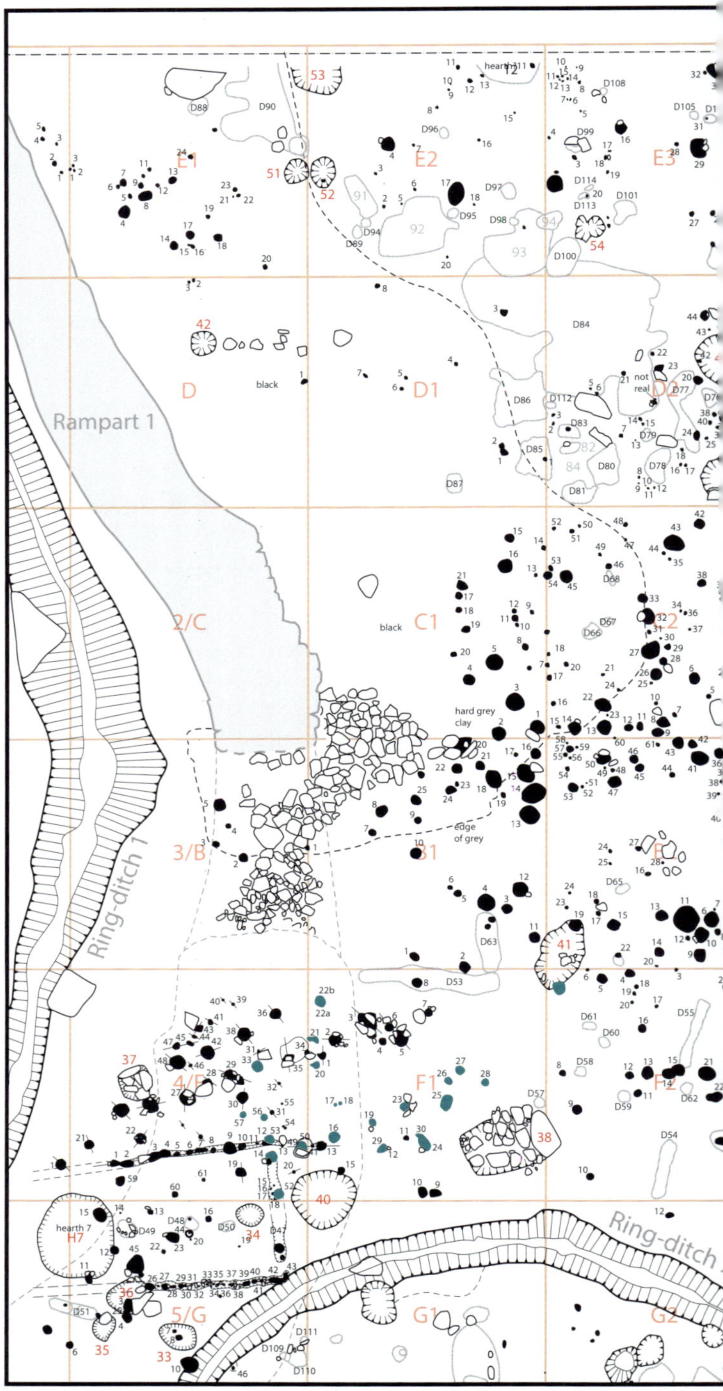

2.3 INSIDE RAMPART 2—AREA 2

Barry Raftery

The following section describes the archaeology revealed in Area 2 (Figs 2.3 and 2.53). The character of the archaeology in this zone differs strongly from that encountered inside Rampart 1, as

Fig. 2.53—Plan of Area 2.

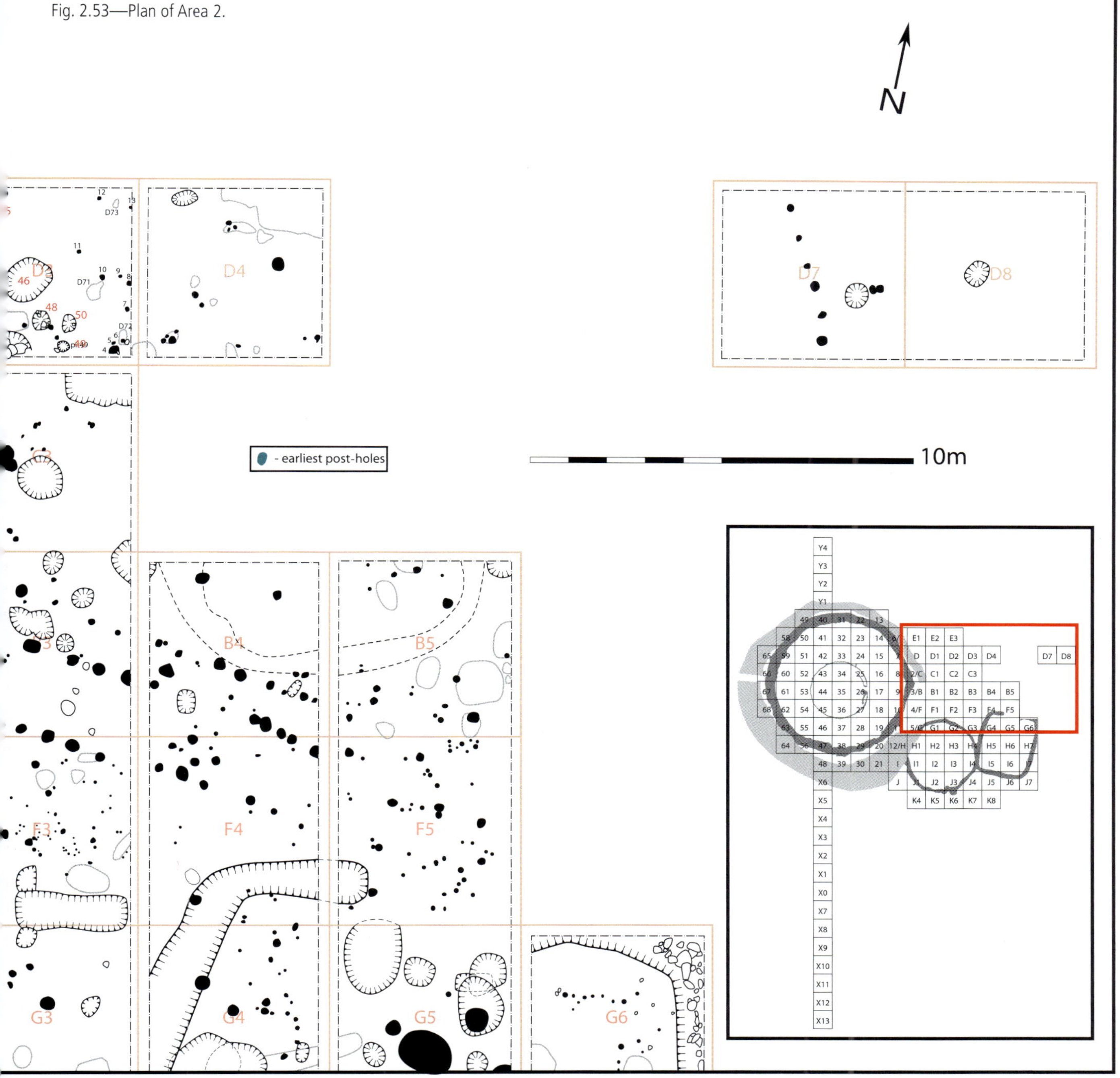

here, in Area 2, areas of stratified deposits appear to have survived the truncation and disturbance of the site.

While no direct stratigraphic link exists between Area 2 deposits and features and those in the northern Y and southern X or the D2/3 cuttings, their character, finds associations and radiocarbon dates suggest their broad contemporaneity—notwithstanding, of course, that the majority of cut features must remain undated. Nevertheless, while of overall broadly similar character, no stratigraphy survives in these areas, and the find-rich deposits appear to be limited to the western part of Area 2.

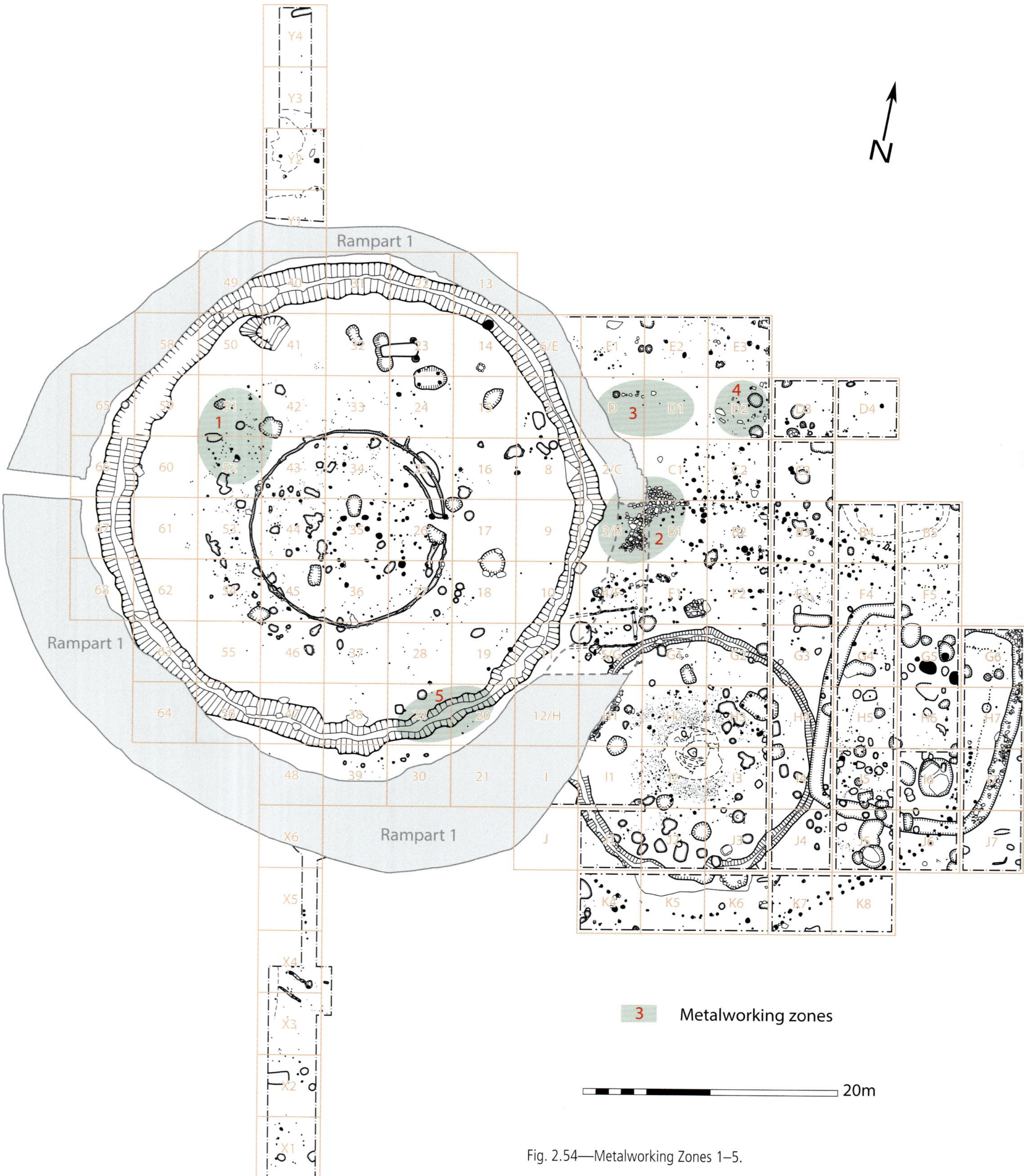

Fig. 2.54—Metalworking Zones 1–5.

As was noted earlier, 5m of the inner stone wall, where there had been significant recent disturbance, were removed in 1970 in order to trace the origin of the material found in previous seasons deposited in Ring-ditch 1. Preliminary investigation under and outside the wall, in Cutting B, was later doubled to include Cutting C. It was apparent from the outset that intensive Bronze Age activity, including bronze-casting on a significant scale, had occurred in this zone. Thus, after the completion of the excavations in the inner enclosure in 1971, a major phase of investigation immediately east of Ring-ditch 1 was begun in 1972. In the course of this campaign some 17m of the inner stone enclosure were removed, opening some 85m^2. Cuttings were opened northwards as far as E and south of the initial B/C investigations as far as Cutting K (Areas 3 and 4, see below), significantly extending the area under investigation. Smaller trial excavations were also carried out, in 1974 north of the inner stone enclosure in Cutting Y, and in 1972 and later in 1978 in Cutting X. Some very limited investigations took place outside the inner enclosure on the west but this proved almost entirely sterile (Cutting A).

Most of the activity excavated was clearly of Late Bronze Age date, as was indicated both by the associated material and by the relevant radiocarbon dates. As the campaign progressed, it was possible to isolate a series of phases of activity, but in spatial terms only two broad zones could be recognised. These were a northern zone (Area 2) where domestic and industrial activity had taken place on a scale of extraordinary intensity, and a southern zone where fewer finds occurred, metalworking evidence was largely absent and, above all, where significant burial activity occurred (Areas 3 and 4, see below).

Initially, a narrow, exploratory trench, 5m long and 2.5m wide, was opened where the stones of the inner wall had been virtually removed. It became obvious, however, almost from the very first day that such a limited investigation was inadequate in view of the emerging wealth of archaeological material and the increasing complexity of the stratigraphy. This cutting was therefore extended to the standard excavation width of 5m and to a length of 10m. As it had been laid out before the removal of the inner wall (an action, indeed, which had not been initially intended), it overlapped with grid square 3 inside the stone enclosure. Thus with the removal of the wall it became referred to as Cutting 3/B. Over time, the excavation was extended into what is now known as Areas 2 and 3.

Fig. 2.55—Post-holes bounding the deposits across Cuttings B and C, looking west.

2.3.1 Area of industrial activity (Area 2)

The overview plan of this area (Fig. 2.53) predominantly represents cut features revealed after the removal of topsoil and other deposits. In Area 2, Raftery's area of industrial activity, these deposits were rich in charcoal and finds. They extended from the southern edge of the B cuttings northwards into the D cuttings, where they filled hollows or depressions, but were not recorded in the E cuttings, where cut features dominated. In the E cuttings the cut features were overlain by the remains of a possible bank (the yellow bank in E). The finds-rich deposits were the only surviving area of vertical stratigraphy on the site. They were focused on Raftery's Metalworking Zones 2–4 (Fig. 2.54) and were bounded at their southern edge by a 'line of post-holes' (see below) (Fig. 2.55). It is these deposits that create the stratigraphic link with Ring-ditch 1, discussed below and in Chapter 4. The occurrence of redeposited natural soil in Cuttings Y and E is discussed as evidence for a possible bank of Ring-ditch 1 (see also p. 55) and hence contributes

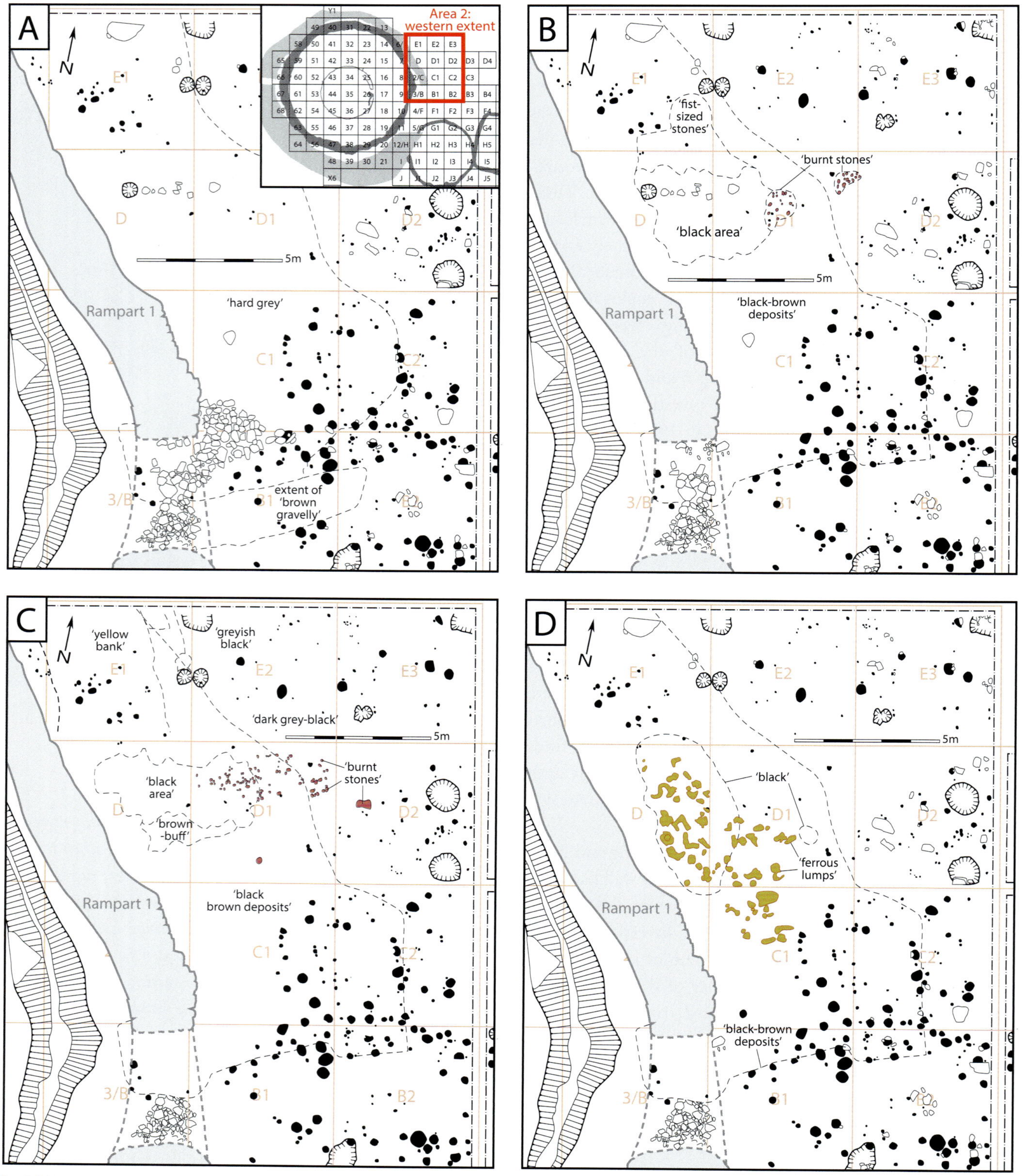

Fig. 2.56—Deposits in Area 2.

to the debate about the chronological relationship of Areas 1 and 2 (see Chapter 4, sections 4.2 and 4.3). Further remains of this possible bank of Ring-ditch 1 were revealed in the F/G cutting in Area 3 and are discussed there.

The stratigraphy in the area between Metalworking Zones 2 and 3 in the B–E cuttings is represented in a simplified way in Fig. 2.56. The documentation of these deposits was limited, but their broad extents and sequence were established based on sketches by Raftery in the archive, his descriptive account below and the long sections which cross this area. The information from these records was cross-referenced with the context descriptions of the finds from this area. The finds, divided up by the different contexts to which they are allocated, are listed below (Tables 2.6–2.8). The level of disturbance as evidenced in the finds associations, as well as the association of datable finds and radiocarbon dates, is discussed in Chapter 4, sections 4.3 and 4.5. Overlying the natural was a grey, sterile layer of leaching, the so-called 'hard grey' or 'grey floor' (Fig. 2.56, A). Its extent appears to match in the main that of the black-brown deposits (Fig. 2.56, B), whereas in the adjacent grid squares, including those in which the find-filled depressions of Metalworking Zone 4 were located, no such horizon of leaching was recorded. At a later point in the report Raftery mentions grey deposits under which or through which post-holes were observed in the area around Ring-ditch 2. These appear to be comparable to those observed here in the west of Area 2, but it is unclear to exactly which post-holes he is referring; they may be those delineating the metalworking activity along the south of grid squares C1–C2. At this level, a concentration of black and brown material, including burnt stones, began to show in Sqs D/D1 and extending into E1, which at its next level of documentation (Fig. 2.56, C) became more focused, with an increased quantity of burnt stones. The extent of the grey floor, the black-brown material and the concentration within it are also recognisable in the long section transecting this area. The uppermost level (Fig. 2.56, D) contained the so-called ferrous lumps and appears to have been severely disturbed, as evidenced by the frequent admixture of medieval and other artefacts; the lower level also appears to have been affected by disturbance, as suggested by the medieval amber bead 4246 within low levels in C1.

It is unclear what these different deposits represent, whether they were in their primary position and whether the later disturbance also included redeposition (such as through levelling) that may, for example, have led to the spreading of some of the primary Bronze Age deposits into the areas to the north and east, filling 'depressions' (see also Chapter 3, section 3.9). The origin in the Late Bronze Age of the material that made up the bulk of these occupation deposits is, however, unambiguous, as indicated by the ubiquitous material culture and a series of radiocarbon dates derived from it.

In addition to the radiocarbon dates listed in the text below, a further date of 1300–1060 cal. BC (GrA-23346) was obtained from deposits in Sq. E2 from beside the deposits that are suggested to be the yellow bank. A date of 1250–1030 cal. BC (GrN-27108) was obtained from a suspected wooden feature in Sq. D. It is unclear what this feature may have been; no description or photographic records could be correlated to this date.

The initial excavation in Cutting B, followed by further investigations in 1972 in C, D and E, revealed evidence of Bronze Age domestic and industrial activity (Fig. 2.53). This extended northwards from a post-hole alignment in B–B2 (see below) along the north of these grid squares to include C/C1 and D/D1 in a broad, irregular zone, roughly 12m by 12m, immediately outside, and in part under, the inner (and obviously later) Rampart 1.

Within this zone of occupation there were three main areas of human activity, dominated especially by

Fig. 2.57—Metalworking Zone 2 (Sq. 3/B, looking south).

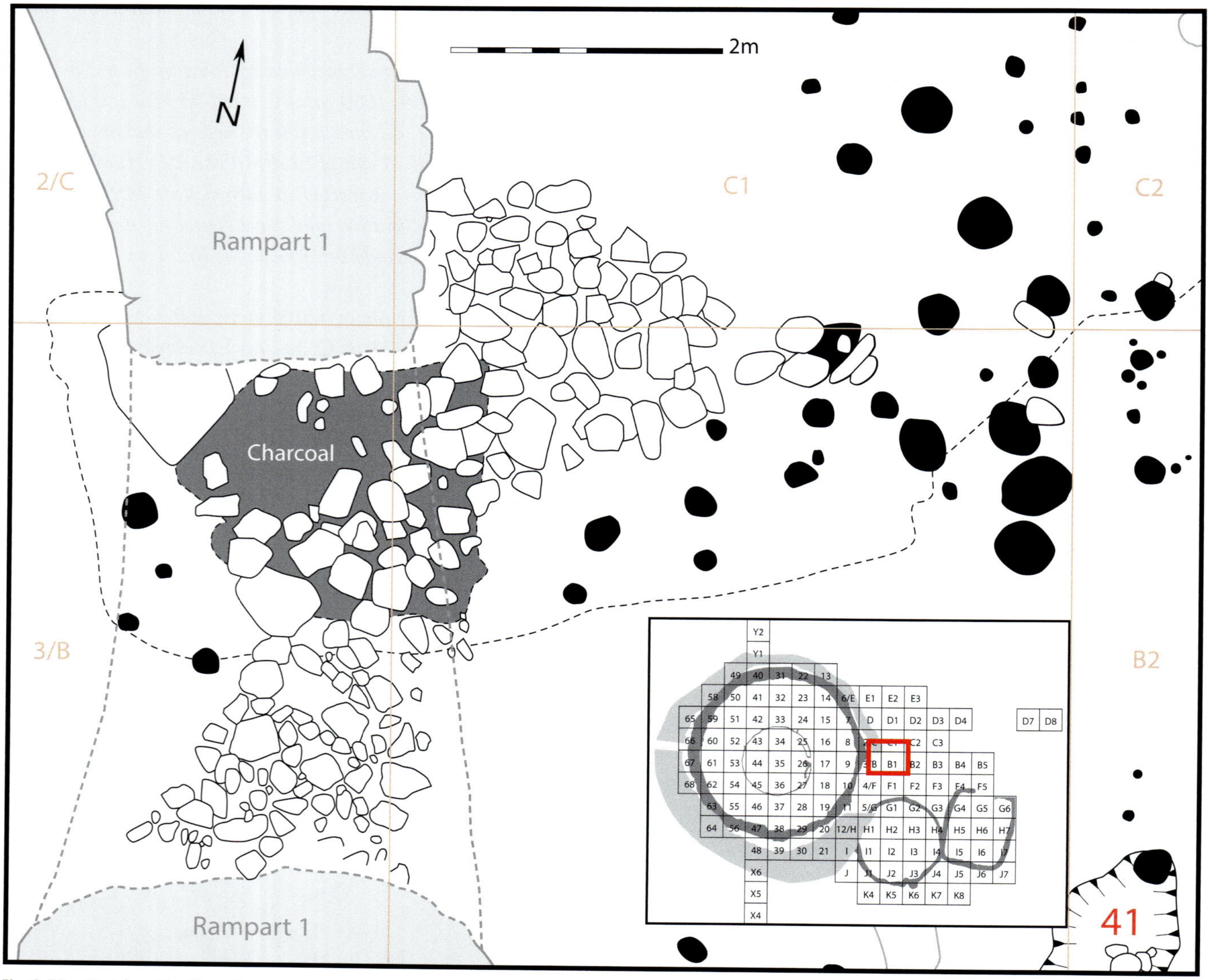

Fig. 2.58—Metalworking Zone 2.

concentrations of mould fragments (Fig. 2.54). The first of these was Metalworking Zone 2, which was initially discovered in 1970 in the northern section of B/B1 and which extended into central and southern areas of C. The second zone in this area, which included extensive evidence for domestic as well as bronze-working activity (Zone 3), was largely concentrated in D and in the adjoining part of D1 but partly extended into E. The third significant area here was centred on D2 and contained a further concentration of mould fragments (Zone 4) as well as material of non-industrial character. In contrast to Zones 2 and 3, this focus of activity—which, at least spatially, is certainly separate from Zone 3—is difficult to associate with an identifiable

Fig. 2.59—Cobbling associated with Metalworking Zone 2 (Sqs C1/B1/B, looking west).

occupation level but consisted rather of a scatter of large, irregular pits and conjoined depressions which extended across the cutting and northwards into E3. Such pits and depressions were otherwise virtually absent in the area under discussion. A small scatter of moulds in D3, to the immediate east of Zone 4, may emanate from the Zone 4 activity.

The cobbling—Metalworking Zone 2 (Cutting 3B/C1)

Following the removal of Rampart 1 in 3/B and the zone of brown, humic soil underneath, a black layer was revealed which rested on an area of flat stones, extending north–south across the width of the cutting (Fig. 2.57).

This black layer, which was bounded by post-holes on the south, extended for a distance of 2–3m northward and north-eastward into C. It was most pronounced under the wall (where it reached a maximum thickness of 20cm), gradually thinning before it finally ran out after about 2m in C2. When the black layer in C1 had been removed down to the grey, a small, regularly rectangular area of particularly dense black material mixed with charcoal showed up in the western part of this zone (Figs 2.58 and 2.59). Mould fragments and potsherds were heavily concentrated in a subrectangular area extending northwards from the line of post-holes on the northern side of B1 for about 2.5m into C1 (Table 2.6). It was clear that the heaviest concentration was focused on the circular space in the cobbling in the northern zone of B and in the western part of C1. In 3/B (as noted above) there was a particular concentration of mould fragments, but it was interesting that on the actual cobbling there were very few objects. In stark contrast to the density of finds in B and the adjoining C1, it was noteworthy that overall B1 was virtually devoid of finds.

The stones on which the black layer rested, which lay directly on the sterile grey layer, provided a fairly level surface and may reasonably be regarded as cobbling. They continued northwards, partly covered by the wall, for at least 1m into Sq. C1, and from there they extended eastwards for a distance of about 2.5m.

The width of the cobbling was 1.7m where the stones emerged from under the wall in the south. In this area they were of no great size, most having length/width dimensions in the order of 25cm or less. Towards the centre of the cutting the cobbled area narrowed to a width of about 1.5m. From there, continuing to the northern baulk and under Rampart 1, the area of stones widened to 2.75m and was covered by the above-mentioned deposit of black organic material, up to 20cm thick. On the north, a thin deposit of yellow, redeposited natural soil, roughly oval in shape and with dimensions of *c.* 1.6m by *c.* 30cm, lay on this black material, more or less parallel to the northern baulk.

The cobbles, which had been covered by the black material, were laid closely together with some care and had obviously been chosen for their relatively flat surfaces. There can be little doubt that they were intended to form a zone of paving and that they were directly related to the intensive metalworking activity in this zone. It was noticeable, however, that the stones in the southern area (those not covered by the black layer) were smaller and more irregularly shaped than those forming the clearly recognisable cobbling to the north. It was just as evident that these stones had not been laid down with the same care as the obvious cobbling; indeed, in places it seemed that they had been piled on one another somewhat randomly rather than constituting a single, carefully laid surface. It is thus open to question whether they were part of the original cobbling.

Following the removal of the black layer covering the cobbles, it emerged that on the immediate northern edge of the cutting, roughly corresponding to the yellow patch noted above, there was a subrectangular zone with dimensions of some 1.25m by 75cm, and about 20cm deep, where the stones were entirely absent. This was clearly a deliberate hollow left in the paving. It was completely filled, to a depth of nearly 20cm, with dense black material, including much charcoal, which had spilled out across the stones. A significant concentration of clay mould fragments came from this hollow and a small number came from the surrounding black spread, so there can be no doubt that this was an important focus of metalworking activity (Table 2.6). This concentration of black material, extending across B1/C1 and encircled by carefully arranged and specially selected stones,[17] differed from all the other comparable structures on the site.

The zone of activity described above in Cuttings B/C had no very clear boundary along the north. In this area the black merged gradually into a very dark brown organic zone, which became increasingly more pronounced to the north. The difference became emphatically clear, however, roughly along the junction between Cuttings C and D, where the area of densest human occupation uncovered anywhere on the site was discovered (Metalworking Zone 3, see below).

A date of 1210–1010 cal. BC (GrN-27115) was obtained on burnt material from the section strip between Sqs B1 and C1. The 'black layer under the wall' in grid square 3/4 that produced many finds and a radiocarbon date of 1230–970 cal. BC (GrN-27105) possibly represents the same deposit of material.

Table 2.6—Artefacts recovered from Metalworking Zone 2 and adjacent C cuttings.

Finds from around and on the 'cobbling' in Area 2 (depth 30cm)		
Sq. no.	**Find type**	**Find no.**
B1	Moulds	E84:1628a,b, 1629, 1630, 1631, 1652
B1/C1	Moulds	E84:4088, 4089, 4090, 4091
	Coarse pottery	E84:4085, 4086
	Early Neolithic pottery	E84:4087
B/C	Glass bead	E84:8217
3/B	Coarse pottery	E84:3433, 3434
3	Coarse pottery	E84:1674, 1888, 1940
	Early Neolithic pottery	E84:1939
	Beaker pottery	E84:1642
	Medieval pottery	E84:1675
	Pottery (unidentified)	E84:1643, 1676
	Iron	E84:1644, 1692, 1890
	Flint	E84:3141
	Glass and clay pipe	E84: 1645, 1677
C1	Moulds	E84:4350–78, 4381
	Clay	E84:4382
	Coarse pottery	E84:4379, 4380

Finds from black deposits in Cutting B/C (under and outside wall) (depths 15–30cm)		
Sq. no.	**Find type**	**Find no.**
B1	Moulds	E84:1783, 1812–19, 1826, 1835a,b, 1866–8, 1875–80, 1881a,b, 1882, 1910–12, 2075, 2401, 2957–62, 8060–2
	Coarse pottery (30)	E84:1756, 1757, 1913, 1914, 1974, 2963, 2964, 2965, 8057, 8076
	Unidentified pottery	E84:1758
	Medieval pottery	E84:8058, 8059 (unknown depth)
	Glass beads	E84:8049, 8052, 1965
	Shale bracelet	E84:8053
C1	Moulds (170)	E84:2800, 2828–32, 2878, 2879, 3140, 3522a–h, 3523–6, 3605–9, 3628–33, 3694, 3712–19, 3760–76, 3833–5, 3947–56, 4004–6, 4203, 4212, 4468–70
	Coarse pottery (310)	E84:2761, 2763–7, 2769, 2798, 2799, 2816–27, 2833, 2863–74, 2877, 3130–9, 3351, 3491–521, 3587–604, 3634–48, 3692, 3693, 3696–711, 3720, 3735–59, 3801–32, 3858, 3921–46, 3981–99, 4169–82, 4189–202, 4207–11, 4449–66, 4481, 7892
	Medieval/post-medieval pottery	E84:2768, 2770, 2771 (at 15–20cm), 2875, 2876 (at 30cm)
	Unidentified pottery (not found)	E84:2762, 3998
	Glass beads	E84:4244, 7956
	Gold	E84:8000
	Amber	E84:4246
	Stone	E84:3527, 3610–12, 3649, 3695, 3721, 3777–9, 3836–9, 3957, 4007–10, 4183, 4204, 4205, 4206, 4213, 4471, 4472, 4482
B/C	Moulds	E84:8096–107, 8112, 8114, 8206
	Coarse pottery (27)	E84:8082, 8084, 8086, 8203a,b, 8204, 8205, 8207, 8220
	Stone	E84:8142, 8218
B1/C1	Moulds	E84:4000–3, 4050–2, 8102, 8108–11, 8113, 8115–19, 8229–31
	Crucible	E84:8094.1, E84:8094
	Coarse pottery	E84:4047–9, 8081, 8083, 8085, 8087–9, 8091–3, 8120–4
	Unidentified pottery (not found)	E84:8095

Table 2.6 (cont.)—Artefacts recovered from Metalworking Zone 2 and adjacent C cuttings.

Finds from Area 1 but associated with Area 2, Metalworking Zone 2 (i.e. black material under and inside wall) (depth 15–38cm)		
Sq. no.	**Find type**	**Find no.**
2	Coarse pottery	E84:1086–8, 1089a–c, 1090, 1091a–c, 1096a–d, 1097, 1098, 1099, 1100, 1101, 1102a,b, 1137a–d, 1138, 1221, 1318, 1320
	Mould fragment	E84:1320a
	Water-rolled pebble	E84:1321
3	Coarse pottery	E84:2228
3/4	Coarse pottery	E84:6105a–m, 6106
	Mould fragments	E84:6095, 6107
4	Coarse pottery	E84:2253, 2317, 2390, 2391, 2393, 2533, 2534
	Mould fragment	E84:2255
	Flint	E84:2392, 2538
	Medieval pottery	E84:2254, 2318, 2532, 2535, 2536
	Iron fragment	E84:2076, 2537

Table 2.7—Finds from deposits in Area 2 that comprise Metalworking Zones 3 and 4 (focused on Cuttings D/D1 and D2), as well as those from the wider extension of these deposits into the E cuttings. The finds are listed stratigraphically, based on context description and depth indications.

Finds from 'black "lumpy ferrous" material', Sqs D–D2 (depth 15–32cm); medieval and later finds found at max. depth of 24cm, except in Sq. D2, where they are found at a depth of up to 30cm		
Sq. no.	**Find type**	**Find no.**
D	Coarse pottery (132)	E84:6290a–c, 6293, 6297a–l, 6298, 6329a–h, 6334a–f, 6347a–k, 6349a–f, 6379a–n, 6380, 6381, 6382, 6393a–l, 6394, 6395, 6406–10, 6446a–p, 6447–52, 6461a,b
	Leinster Cooking Ware	E84:6296
	Unidentified pottery (not found)	E84:6453
	Clay pipe	E84:6295
	Stone	E84:6294, 6383, 6412a,b
	Gold bead	E84:6384
	Glass beads	E84:6300, 6333
	Bronze	E84:6299
	Moulds (20)	E84:6291a,b, 6292, 6335, 6348a,b, 6350, 6363a,b, 6396, 6411a–d, 6454a,b, 6459, 6460a–c
D1	Coarse pottery (47)	E84:6289, 6343a–c, 6344, 6351, 6373, 6374a–h, 6376, 6377, 6386a–l, 6388, 6439a–o, 6440–4
	Medieval/post-medieval pottery	E84:6330, 6331, 6352
	Moulds	E84:6345, 6364, 6375, 6387
	Crucible	E84:6445
	Glass	E84:6378 (22–24cm)
	Iron	E84:6332
D2	Coarse pottery	E84:6389, 6391, 6455
	MBA pottery	E84:6457
	Medieval pottery	E84:6456
	Moulds	E84:6392
	Crucible	E84:6390

Finds from 'immediately below lumpy material' (i.e. 'thick black charcoal layer') (depth 27–65cm)		
Sq. no.	**Find type**	**Find no.**
D	Coarse pottery (200)	E84:6518–28, 6534, 6539a–s, 6540, 6565, 6566, 6567
	Moulds (9)	E84:6529, 6530, 6531, 6532, 6533a,b, 6541, 6568a,b
	Stone	E84:6535–7, 6542, 6571a–c
D/D1	Coarse pottery (81)	E84:7588–97, 7599, 7601
	Early Neolithic pottery	E84:7600
	Moulds (14)	E84:7602–9, 7610a–e, 7611
	Crucible	E84:7598
	Stone	E84:7612a,b, 7613, 7614
	Glass bead	E84:6700
D1	Coarse pottery (20)	E84:6503a–e, 6575a–c, 6576, 6578a–g, 6580, 6581, 6582
	Moulds	E84:6504, 6563a,b, 6564, 6577, 6579a,b
	Glass beads	E84:6562
	Shale	E84:6561a,b

Finds from 'brown ashy material (under black)' (depth 35–65cm)		
Sq. no.	**Find type**	**Find no.**
D/D1	Coarse pottery (111)	E84:7286, 7288, 7289, 7290, 7549–54, 7561, 7562, 7568, 7577, 7628, 7629, 7630
	MBA pottery	E84:7287
	Moulds (26)	E84:7543, 7545–8, 7555, 7556, 7558, 7559, 7569a–d, 7576, 7631, 7632, 7633, 7634, 7635, 7636, 7637, 7638a–c
	Crucible	E84:7544, 7560
	Glass beads	E84:7627
	Stone	E84:7291, 7563a–d, 7564, 7565, 7566, 7567, 7570
D2	Coarse pottery	E84:7148a,b
	Moulds	E84:7149, 7150, 7151, 7152

Finds from under wall adjacent to Metalworking Zone 3		
Sq. no.	**Find type**	**Find no.**
D	Coarse pottery	E84:7960a–d
	Glass beads	E84:7578, 7579, 7580
	Stone	E84:7961

Table 2.7 (cont.)—Finds from deposits in Area 2 that comprise Metalworking Zones 3 and 4 (focused on Cuttings D/D1 and D2), as well as those from the wider extension of these deposits into the E cuttings. The finds are listed stratigraphically, based on context description and depth indications.

Finds from general black charcoal/habitation deposits (specific contexts not identifiable from descriptions in finds logbooks but these are possibly the same black deposits that are presented above), Zone 3 (depth 27–60cm)

Sq. no.	Find type	
D/D1	Coarse pottery (1294)	E84:6681–4, 6688–92, 6694–6, 6718, 6722, 6730–5, 6739–41, 6747–55, 6758–61, 6768–70, 6773–6, 6807, 6808, 6813–17, 6823, 6831–4, 6908, 6910, 6912, 6914, 6915, 7040, 7041, 7044, 7091, 7132–5, 7137–40, 7169, 7174, 7176–82, 7211–14, 7311a,b, 7312, 7313, 7339a–j, 7340, 7343, 7351–5, 7421, 7423, 7424, 7425, 7437–9, 7458–9, 7462–5, 7468
	MBA domestic urn-type	E84:7164
	Unidentified (not found)	E84:7422
	Moulds (121)	E84:6685, 6686, 6687a–f, 6693a–e, 6720a,b, 6736, 6737a,b, 6742–4, 6745a–c, 6762, 6771, 6809–11, 6818–21, 6822a–e, 6836, 6909, 6911, 6913, 6993, 7033–9, 7042a–f, 7043, 7092, 7136, 7141a–d, 7142–5, 7146a–c, 7165–8, 7170a–g, 7172, 7173, 7183, 7209, 7215a,b, 7216–19, 7314, 7315, 7341, 7342, 7356, 7357, 7358, 7359, 7360.1, 7360–5, 7366a,b, 7426–8, 7429a–d, 7440, 7441, 7461a–c
	Crucible	E84:7175, 7442
	Bronzes	E84:6767a–c
	Iron	E84:7430 (40–60cm)
	Glass bead	E84:7466
	Stone (45)	E84:6717a–c, 6719a–d, 6721, 6738, 6746a–c, 6763a,b, 6772, 6812, 6849, 6916, 6917, 6951, 7093, 7094a–d, 7153, 7154, 7171a–f, 7220, 7249, 7361a, 7361a–d, 7443, 7460
D	Coarse pottery (10)	E84:6489a–h, 6490, 7457
	Bronze	E84:7250
	Stone	E84:6796
D1	Moulds	E84:6795a–c
	Flint	E84:6756

Finds from 'lowest levels of black' in Metalworking Zone 3, Area 2 (depths 40–60cm)

Sq. no.	Find type	Find no.
D/D1	Coarse pottery (274)	E84:7264, 7265, 7267, 7268, 7274, 7285, 7469, 7478–83, 7485, 7486, 7487a–m, 7488, 7489, 7497a–h, 7525–7, 7530, 7531, 7533–9
	Unidentified pottery (not found)	E84:7484
	Moulds (34)	E84:7233, 7235, 7269–73, 7275–9, 7280a–d, 7470a,b, 7471–6, 7492–6, 7528, 7529, 7540, 7541, 7542
	Crucibles	E84:7266, 7477
	Amber	E84:7507
	Shale	E84:7532
	Stone	E84:7281, 7282, 7283, 7284, 7490a,b, 7491

All finds from Sq. D2 (incl. topsoil from immediately below sod; also includes D84 finds (see below)), Zone 4, Area 2 (depths 10–40cm). Medieval and later finds found at max. depth of 30cm. Finds from lumpy material, which may or may not be Zone 4, have been included here also. See p.97, bottom left.

Sq. no.	Find type	Find no.
D2	Coarse pottery (116)	E84:6250a–e, 6261, 6262, 6264a–c, 6278, 6313a–c, 6322a–c, 6325, 6340a,b, 6346a–d, 6389, 6391, 6455, 6492a–e, 6505, 6506a,b, 6554a–e, 6555a,b, 6569, 6594a–e, 6595, 6643, 6711a,b, 6781a–d, 6803, 6845, 6856, 6918a–f, 6935a,b, 6938, 7061a–g, 7062, 7148a,b, 7325, 7328, 7367, 7695.1, 7696, 7722, 7793b, 7894, 7895, 7896, 7897, 7898, 7916a–d, 7917, 8029
	Medieval/post-medieval pottery/clay pipe	E84:6208, 6251, 6252, 6263, 6323, 6324, 6353, 6414a,b, 6456, 6793a–d, 6496
	Middle Bronze Age pottery	E84:6457, 7793a,c
	Moulds (102)	E84:6253, 6265a,b, 6365, 6366, 6392, 6413a,b, 6494, 6497, 6498, 6499, 6556a,b, 6596a–c, 6712, 6729, 6802, 6919, 6936, 6937, 7063, 7064, 7149, 7150, 7151, 7152, 7257a–d, 7258, 7326a–c, 7327, 7368, 7369, 7693, 7694, 7695, 7723, 7724, 7792, 7899, 7900–15, 8028
	Crucibles	E84:6314, 6390
	Glass beads	E84:6666, 6680, 7788
	Bronzes	E84:6458, 6924, 7697, 7786
	Iron	E84:6209, 6266, 6267a,b, 6493, 6597
	Stone	E84:6216, 6495, 6547, 6557, 6570, 6598, 6613, 7065, 7066, 7918a,b
	Bone (object?)	E84:6254

All finds from Sq. E2 (incl. topsoil), Area 2 (depth 10–40cm); medieval and later finds not found below a depth of 26cm

Sq. no.	Find type	Find no.
E2	Coarse pottery (87)	E84:6215, 6230, 6239, 6269, 6326a,b, 6327, 6430, 6500.1a–m, 6558, 6559, 6585a,b, 6648, 6652, 6662, 6664a,b, 6679, 6801, 6805a–g, 6824a–e, 6847a–c, 6954a,b, 6955, 6957, 6966, 6967, 7015, 7016, 7188, 7189, 7191a–l, 7193, 7195a–f, 7262, 7296, 7305a–f, 7306, 7764a–c
	Medieval/post-medieval pottery/clay pipe	E84:6229, 6237, 6248, 6249, 6317, 6342, 6429b, 6560, 6631, 6500
	Middle Bronze Age pottery	E84:6419, 6429a, 6477, 6586, 6650, 6651, 7158, 7196
	Moulds (16)	E84:6649, 6671, 6672, 6673, 6848, 6899a–c, 7017, 7147, 7192, 7307, 7639, 7765a,b, 7766
	Bronze	E84:7185
	Iron	E84:6268, 6316, 6328, 6341, 6431, 6587a–d, 6806, 6826
	Stone	E84:6255, 6270, 7194, 7197

Table 2.7 (cont.)—Finds from deposits in Area 2 that comprise Metalworking Zones 3 and 4 (focused on Cuttings D/D1 and D2), as well as those from the wider extension of these deposits into the E cuttings. The finds are listed stratigraphically, based on context description and depth indications.

All finds from Sq. E3 (incl. topsoil, excl. pits and depressions) (depth 12–25cm); mix of finds from all levels to a depth of 25cm

Sq. no.	Find type	Find no.
E3	Coarse pottery	E84:6315, 6354, 6401a,b, 6402, 6403, 6481, 6507a,b, 6632a–f, 6640.1, 6645, 6701a–c, 6830a–c, 7581a,b, 7640a–c, 7654
	Medieval/post-medieval pottery	E84:6228, 6321, 6355, 6356, 6483, 6644a,b
	Unidentified (not found)	E84:6482, 6646
	Moulds	E84:6702, 7582, 7585, 7757
	Iron	E84:6227, 6633, 6634, 6790
	Stone	E84:6647

All finds from Sq. D3 (incl. topsoil); all finds come from just below sod to max. depth of 30cm

Sq. no.	Find type	Find no.
D3	Coarse pottery	E84:6850, 6851, 6860a–d, 6861a–d, 6868d, 6877, 6879a,b, 6943, 6982a–g, 7004a–c, 7028a,b, 7079a–c, 7084, 7114a–c, 7123a–e, 7125, 7126, 7127, 7203a–f, 7259a,b,d, 7399a–c, 7400, 7411a–e, 7412, 7413, 7417a–h, 7418, 7431, 7432, 7517, 7759, *7885, **7886
	Medieval/post-medieval pottery/clay pipe	E84:5853.1, 6839, 6840a,b, 6854, 6867, 6868a–c, 6869, 6870, 6873a,b, 6874, 6875, 6878a,b 6880a–c, 6932a,f, 6934, 6942, 6983a–k, 7001a–f, 7002, 7003, 7026, 7027a–d, 7029, 7080a–d, 7085, 7116a,b, 7124a–d, 7200, 7201, 7202a–f, 7259c, 7261, 7297a,b, 7398a–f, 7401, 7402, 7403, 7433
	Bronze	E84:6923
	Gold wire	E84:6950 (found at a depth of 10–15cm)
	Moulds	E84:6883, 6963, 6985, 6986, 7082, 7129, 7204a,b, 7260, 7297.1, 7414, 7434a,b
	Iron	E84:6841, 6852, 6862, 6863, 6864, 6865, 6866a,b, 6881, 6882, 6944, 6964, 6965, 6987, 6988, 6989a,b, 7030, 7031, 7086, 7117a,b, 7130, 7205, 7415, 7515, 7516
	Stone	E84:6842, 6855, 6945, 6946, 6984, 7081, 7083, 7118, 7131, 7398g, 7416

*Finds from depression 113. **Finds from depression 69.

Finds from Area 2, Depressions 84 and 93 (depths 27–35cm)

Sq. no.	Pit no.	Find type	Find no.
D2	D84	Coarse pottery (23) Moulds (40) Stone Mercury-gilded bronze object Bronze fragments	E84:6555a,b, 7894, 7895, 7896, 7897, 7898, 7916a–d, 7917 E84:6556a,b, 7899–915 E84:6557, 7918a,b E84:6458 (found at a depth of 27–30cm) E84:7786
E2	D93	Coarse pottery Moulds	E84:7262, 7764a–c E84:7765a,b, 7766
E3	D107	Coarse pottery	E84:7758

Besides the large quantities of moulds and pottery, a significant number of other objects came to light in the dense black occupation material (Table 2.6). These included five glass beads (E84:1965, 4244, 7956, 8049, 8217, 8052), a socketed bronze gouge (E84:3300; Fig. 3.32), a small penannular ring of presumed copper with gold foil cover (E84:8000; Fig. 3.1) and a fragment of a shale bracelet (E84:8053; Fig. 3.107). Perhaps most interesting, however, was a small, narrow, triangular fragment of sheet bronze from brown soil in Sq. B2[18] (E84:863; Fig. 3.35). Although unstratified and found at a high level in the humus, it is likely that this is waste from bronze-working that was, in all probability, contemporary with the metal production undoubtedly taking place in the immediate vicinity.

The line of post-holes

A series of post-holes of substantial size, all showing up initially in the grey subsoil as circular patches of burnt black material, were uncovered in 1970 in Cutting B1 (Figs 2.53 and 2.55). They extended diagonally in a north-north-east/south-south-west direction along the northern edge of the cutting, and it was possible to recognise a line which corresponded to a large extent with the edge of the most obviously regular cobbled area (the 'cobbling'). Most especially, they clearly formed a southern boundary to the thick zone of black material described above, and also, to a very large extent, to the greyish layer of presumed leaching which lay beneath (Fig. 2.55).

The post-holes ran in a regular straight line as far as the eastern end of B1, at which point they were doubled, the line being staggered here to continue in an easterly direction outside the initial line, finally disappearing into the baulk in B2. In the narrow triangular area between these post-holes and the section strip, mainly in B2 (before excavation in Cutting C/C1 had commenced), a number of other post-holes occurred. Most importantly, it was in this narrow, triangular area of black, between the post-holes and the baulk, that all the moulds and the related material first came to light. Significantly, no moulds occurred to the south of the line of posts, and the quantity of pottery and other finds there was very greatly reduced.

It was believed after the first season of investigation that the narrow triangular zone of posts in Sq. B–B2 constituted the side of a rectangular building (Raftery 1971; 1976), but subsequent excavations in Cuttings C, D and E failed to confirm the existence of such a structure. An enigmatic arrangement of moderately sized post-holes in Cuttings

Fig. 2.60—'Ferrous lumps' in Metalworking Zone 3 (Sqs D/D1, (a) looking east and (b) looking south-east).

C1/C2 provide the only significant concentration of post-holes anywhere north of the B/B1 cuttings, but these do not represent any obvious construction.

The line of post-holes discussed above ended at the zone of cobbling. There were certainly no post-holes *under* the cobbling, and there was no indication that the line continued beyond it to the west or that it turned northwards to flank the ditch. The precise nature of these post-holes is not easy to establish. They seem too large and too far apart to represent the sails of a wattle wall, so that a barrier of horizontal timbers, possibly even planking, may have occurred, attached to spaced uprights.

The band of post-holes which, as noted above, formed the southern boundary of the Zone 2 metalworking area also, to a very large extent, bounded the underlying sterile grey zone (Fig. 2.56, A and D). In the C cuttings, however, the grey zone seemed to disappear across the centre of C2, and it is interesting to note that some of the larger post-holes uncovered in this zone (PHs 14, 22, 27, 32 and 33) seemed to correspond roughly to the eastern edge of the grey zone. Northwards, the grey basal layer extended as far east as D1 and E1 but became increasingly patchy in D2 and E3.

Alternatively, aside from the possibility that the line or scatter of posts along the south of B1 and C1/C2 bounds the Area 2 deposits, it is also conceivable that some of these posts belong to the circular post alignment or stockade in Areas 2–4, discussed below (see section 2.4.5).

Metalworking Zone 3 (D–D1/E1)

The first indication of the exceptional nature of Cutting D was the discovery, immediately under the covering humus, of a zone of irregularly shaped lumps of hard, reddish-brown material resembling iron slag (Fig. 2.60). Embedded in these lumps were numerous small pieces of charcoal, so they were clearly not a product of leaching or of any other natural agency. The lumps, as well as being circular and oval, included examples that were pear-shaped, D-shaped, sausage-shaped, banana-shaped and irregularly S-shaped. The smallest of these were the circular and oval lumps with greatest dimensions of 12–25cm. The larger ones averaged 40–60cm in maximum length and 15–25cm in thickness.

These lumps, which appeared when the ploughsoil was removed, lay directly on and in the upper levels of the occupation surface. They extended diagonally across the square in a north-west/south-east band that varied roughly in width from about 1.5m to about 3m. They were most densely concentrated in the western part of D1 and in the northern part of D2, but were also more widely dispersed in the northern area of C1. They were about 1.5–2m distant from the wall of the inner enclosure and were found nowhere else on the site. A very large number of artefacts occurred among these lumps, the majority, inevitably, consisting of sherds of coarse pottery (Table 2.7). A particularly important find, however, and unique on the site, was a hollow bead of gold (E84:6384; Fig. 3.6). *A radiocarbon date of 1210–1010 cal. BC (GrN-27106) was obtained on material from this deposit in Sq. D.*

Following the removal of the lumps, it emerged that from the inner stone wall (Rampart 1) eastwards, almost to the eastern end of D2, the thick, dark brown occupation layer noted above became especially pronounced in the central area of the square (Fig. 2.61). Within this zone an irregularly shaped area of particularly dense black organic material occurred, measuring about 2.5m from east to west and with a maximum width from north to south of about 3m. Towards

Fig. 2.61—Black occupation layer and burnt stones in Metalworking Zone 3 (Sqs D/D1/E1, looking north).

Fig. 2.62—Black occupation layer and burnt stones in Metalworking Zone 3 (Sqs D/D1/E1, looking north).

Rampart 1 it reached a maximum thickness of some 25cm. Its northern boundary more or less corresponded to the northern boundary of the area of lumps. To the south, however, the lumps continued beyond the black zone for a distance of 1–1.5m, extending almost as far as Cutting C. They were absent over the eastern part of the black zone.

In this black zone there were extensive pockets of ashy material and numerous lumps of charcoal, as well as tiny splinters of animal bone consisting most frequently of the brittle outer casings of cattle teeth. The latter, because of the acidic conditions, rarely had any internal elements preserved, causing the surviving pieces to disintegrate significantly when lifting was attempted. It was also noticeable that in the north-eastern part of the black zone there was an area of roughly fist-sized stones, all of which had been subjected to burning. This zone was about 2.5m in length and continued eastwards beyond the black for another 2.5m (Figs 2.56, 2.61 and 2.62).

The range and variety of artefacts contained in the black layer were truly spectacular. Sherds of coarse pottery were, as elsewhere, ubiquitous, but the sizeable concentration of the Zone 3 clay mould fragments, numbering almost 300 pieces, was striking. Occasional bronzes occurred, including a fine chain-link fragment (E84:6299) and what appears to be a fragmentary axe blade (E84:7250; Fig. 3.32). Glass beads and bracelets of shale were found, while the more mundane aspects of life were represented by stone objects, three rubbing stones (E84:6537, 6721 and 7284; Fig. 3.117), whetstones and polishing stones of various types. One of the most spectacular and beautiful finds recovered anywhere in the course of the excavations was an elegantly made pendant of gold and glass (E84:6700; Fig. 3.3) which came from this black zone in D1 (Table 2.7). An item of considerable interest was a small mass of carbonised, crushed cereal grains, which Professor G.F. Mitchell brought to Trinity College Dublin for study. He was able to isolate this from material that he recovered in the black layer in C1, and concluded that 'the mass must represent either a loaf, or porridge, or brewers' grains; the first possibility is perhaps the most likely' (Mitchell 1976, 155). It is a matter of regret that no further examination of this object was carried out and that it was subsequently lost in Trinity College.

Two radiocarbon dates—GrN-27109, 1220–990 cal. BC, and GrN-27110, 1380–1120 cal. BC—were obtained from the heavily charcoal-filled black layer in D/D1. A further charcoal-rich sample (GrN-2711, 1200–930 cal. BC) was taken from ashy brown material immediately south of the black concentration in D/D1. This 'ashy brown' material may be related to the material that is traceable in the finds records as being located under the black finds-rich layer, overlying the grey (see also Chapter 4, section 4.3).

Metalworking Zone 4

At the eastern end of the same cutting, and covering almost all of D2, at a distance of 1.25–1.5m east of the dense occupation zone described above, there was an extended area of irregular hollows, pits and depressions (Figs 2.53 and 2.63). Such features were completely absent to the south in C, but they continued, though less densely, to the north-east and east into E.

All these depressions were shallow and, for the most part, nondescript. Most were small and irregular in plan, and they were generally no more than 10cm to a maximum of about 25cm in depth. A few contained thin layers of black, organic material (e.g. nos 91–5) but they were usually filled with grey silting. It was thus uncertain in most instances whether the hollows here designated as 'depressions' were of natural or

Fig. 2.63—Depressions in D2 before excavation—Metalworking Zone 4 (Sq. D2, looking west).

Fig. 2.64—Mercury-gilded mount E84:6458 (photo: John Sunderland).

artificial origin. Some contained pieces of charcoal and tiny splinters of bone, while a few, such as D82 and D107, contained a single coarse potsherd. The spread of such finds need have no great significance, the items probably having come to their final resting-places by means of natural agencies. (*Raftery seems to suggest redeposition as the origin of these finds.*)

Important, however, is the largest of these features, D84, which consisted of an irregular series of conjoined hollows in the north-west of D2, extending into the north of D1 and into the south of E3, covering an area of roughly 4m by 3m (Fig. 2.53). The hollows were uneven and irregular, and their depths varied from 10cm to about 30cm. Their fill throughout was a mixture of mottled grey-brown and black silty soil containing numerous charcoal flecks.

This series of depressions yielded a significant body of material, scattered randomly throughout the hollows in the grey-brown material (Table 2.7). The finds inevitably included numerous coarse potsherds, but present were some 101 mould fragments, part of a glass bead, some bronze fragments of various types and two chips of flint or chert. Of greatest potential importance, however, is the mercury-gilded bronze mount (E84:6458; Figs 2.64, 3.2 and 3.8) that came from the north of D2 in very dark brown material, 27–30cm deep, within the zone of the D84 hollows. Four further coarse potsherds (E84:7262, E84:7764a–c) and three mould fragments (E84:7765a–b, E84:7766) came from the hollow area designated D93, which, located along the southern edge of E2, may legitimately be regarded as part of D84.

Depression(s) 84/93 (Fig. 2.53) formed the focus of a wider spread of mould fragments scattered across D2, with a handful occurring in neighbouring E3 as well as a few further east in D3. This discrete concentration of moulds might, as is here suggested, be regarded as Metalworking Zone 4. The absence of any of the associated black, burnt material that was present in Zones 1, 2 and 3 should, however, be noted (see below), so that the matter is far from certain.

Apart from the possible Hearth 12 in Sq. E2, fourteen pits of fairly nondescript character occurred in the D and E cuttings. With the single exception of Pit 42 in Sq. D, it was noticeable that all were located to the north and east of the main occupation area described above, which, along with C and C1, was regularly flat and was completely devoid of any features.

The three largest of these pits, nos 43, 44 and 46, which were 1m, 1.55m and 1.25m in diameter respectively, were all surprisingly shallow, with maximum depths of no more than 20–30cm (Figs 2.53 and 2.69). Pits 43 and 44 were filled with

Table 2.8—Artefacts recovered from pits in Area 2.

Sq. no.	Pit no.	Find type	Find number
B3	201	Coarse pottery	E84:9082, 9147
	202		E84:9155
B3/B5	204	Shale bracelet	E84:9129
		Coarse pottery	E84:9110
		Bone object, unknown type	E84:9134
C3	209	Hone	E84:9163
		Flint	E84:9164
F3	90	Coarse pottery	E84:8584
E1	51	Coarse pottery	E84:6674a–c, 6797a,c, 6798, 6799, 7055a,b
E1/E2	53	Coarse pottery	E84:7716a–d, 7719
		Mould	E84:7717, 7718
E3	54	Coarse pottery	E84:7643
		Mould	E84:7644
		Flint	E84:7646
	55	Coarse pottery	E84:7652
		MBA domestic urn-type pottery	E84:7653
B2	41	Coarse pottery	E84:2621–2
F1/F2	38	Coarse pottery	E84:7655a,b, 7656, 7709, 7710

grey silt and were devoid of finds. Pit 46, similarly without finds, had been carefully and deliberately filled in with stones of moderate size. All the other pits in the area were similarly shallow and, with a few exceptions (such as nos 47, 52, 53 and 54, which had layers of black organic material), were filled exclusively with grey silt. Some had flecks of charcoal and small fragments of animal bone (e.g. nos 42 and 52). Four pits, nos 52–55, contained sherds of coarse pottery, while in Pits 54 and 55 several fragments of coarse Late and Middle Bronze Age pottery occurred (E84:7643, 7653) (Table 2.8). Two pits, nos 42 and 54 (in which Neolithic sherds were found), contained clay mould fragments, and the latter also yielded a single flint chip and a collection of possibly human bones.[19] Two of the nondescript hollows, nos 107 and 113, each contained a single potsherd.

Besides the pits and hollows, a small number of post-holes were also brought to light along the length of the E cuttings. Almost inevitably, no convincing arrangement or pattern could be deduced. Moreover, none was of any significant size, so that they are unlikely to have been of any great importance.

In the south of Cutting B a series of post-holes came to light which, prior to their full investigation, appeared to mirror those along the northern edge of the cutting. Like the former, these also appeared as burnt black circular patches in the yellow subsoil. They were fewer in number and less regularly aligned than those on the northern side of the cutting but they did run roughly parallel with them. Their purpose, however, was not clear, nor was their relationship, if any, to the northern line of post-holes.

An interesting detail in this area was the presence of a thin layer of very hard gravel forming a narrow, irregular-sided zone along the centre of B1 between the two post-hole zones described above (Fig. 2.56). It extended westwards as far as the cobbled zone and, though it was not observed beyond the latter, it appears to have been more or less focused on the narrowest and shallowest part of the ditched enclosure in Sqs 9/10. A striking feature of the finds distribution in this gravel area is the extreme paucity of artefacts; indeed, there are some indications that this zone was bounded along the south by an arc of post-holes. This should, of course, be considered with caution, as the stratigraphy is especially poor here, but it is nonetheless tempting to speculate on the possibility that an approach way once existed, leading further west. Here there is considerable uncertainty owing once more to extensive agricultural activity. It may well be, however, that the bank-and-ditch feature referred to above was by now redundant, encouraging us once more to think of the 15m enclosure as the feature to which the narrow zone may have led. At any rate, the area to the south of this suggested approach was different in every way from that in the northern sector.

The deposits in the E cuttings appear similar in nature to those in Cuttings B–D to the south-east. They contain finds but do not show the same density of charcoal and artefacts as those deposits that Raftery defined as his metalworking zones (above). Overlying these deposits was apparently redeposited natural, which Raftery interpreted as part of the yellow bank of Ring-ditch 1. It is, however, difficult to correlate descriptions, drawings and photographic records of this area, and features described cannot always be identified. It is not possible to determine the exact stratigraphic relationship of the features under the bank and the deposits in the neighbouring squares. Radiocarbon dates from these deposits suggest a general contemporaneity (see Chapter 4, section 4.4).

The most important feature in the E cuttings was a low, gently rounded bank of yellow soil that extended across the width of E1, covering almost the entire square. It reached a maximum width of 4m and was about 30cm in height at the centre, tapering gradually and evenly to the sides. Its western edge partly extended under the recent stone wall. On the upper surface of the bank some small scatters of fist-sized stones occurred, and there was also a series of shallow, charcoal-filled depressions, some of which contained coarse potsherds. A sample for radiocarbon dating was taken from black material overlying the bank in E1 (GrN-27113, 1300–1060 cal. BC).

The bank terminated, somewhat abruptly, at the extreme northern end of D, but it may have been cut away to make space for the major activity extending southwards from there. Indeed, the bank did not appear again until Cutting G, after a blank stretch of some 17.5m. It was evident that here in the north (in E) it sealed an area of clearly early scattered occupation material, including the nondescript sprinkling of small stake-holes and a small amount of earlier pottery. The rich zone of the D/D1 complex was part of the wider occupation in the B–D area which post-dated the erection of the enclosing bank, the circular ditch inside it and whatever features could be regarded as contemporary.

2.3.2 Cutting Y

Limited excavation in March 1974 consisted of a narrow trial trench in Cutting Y immediately outside Rampart 1 on the north (Figs 2.3, 2.65, 2.66 and 2.67). Here the low, narrow yellow bank, already investigated along the east, could be seen around the immediate edge of Rampart 1 on the north. As with Cuttings D7 and D8, the purpose of the investigation was to determine the nature and extent of any occupation in this area well away from the zone of intense activity in the east, and also to compare the construction of the bank with that already examined in Cuttings E1 and G (see above). Extending from the base of the rampart, an initial 5m-wide cutting some 7.5m in length was opened. This was subsequently extended for a further 2m to the north at a reduced width of 2.5m. Despite its limited extent, the cutting yielded important information.

A layer of brown humus some 20cm in maximum thickness sealed the yellow material of the bank. The latter was preserved as a low mound that covered the entire width of the cutting, continuing, as noted above, in the unexcavated areas both eastwards and to the west. In the excavated section it maintained a uniform height of 50cm. The visible width of the bank varied from 1.5m in the east to almost 2.5m in the west. To the north it sloped evenly downwards to the ancient surface. Since at least half of this bank lay under the wall, neither its maximum original height nor its width can be determined with precision. The stone wall at this point is 2.5m wide, however, and, since no trace of the bank was discernible in the zone immediately inside the latter, the maximum possible width of the bank at this point is about 5m. Furthermore, as the section of the same bank in Cutting E1 is some 3.75m wide and about 50cm high, it may be taken as probable that the bank segment in Cutting Y1 was of broadly similar dimensions (see above).

The yellow soil of the bank, which had been considerably interfered with by rabbit activity, was clean and sterile and completely unmixed with any other soil type. It was almost totally devoid of stones. A single find—a small, finely cast blade fragment of bronze (E84:8717; Fig. 3.35)—came from this material. It was found in the yellow soil, 28cm below the upper surface of the bank, and most probably derives from pre-bank occupation.

The bank lay directly on a layer of black organic material with a uniform thickness of 10–12cm. This layer extended northwards across the cutting for about 9.8m, gradually decreasing in thickness in this direction before giving way to the natural subsoil. In and on this layer were scatters of small stones, which contrasted with the virtually stone-free character of the covering yellow bank. Lying on this blackish material in the centre of Y2, and extending for a short distance into Y3, was an irregularly shaped area of greyish-brown soil with maximum dimensions of *c.* 4.75m by *c.* 2.5m. A scatter of sizeable lumps of baked clay was found in the black layer (see Cummins, this volume). *A sample from the black layer in Y2 produced a radiocarbon date of 1230–1020 cal. BC (GrN-27117).*

Several nondescript pits and some post-holes occurred, all associated with this pre-rampart phase. Most were filled with dark grey silted material, but in a few cases the filling was black. The scattered post-holes do not suggest any obvious pattern but it is interesting to note that, apart from what was designated as PH 12 in Y1 (not labelled on Fig. 2.65), all of them skirt the dark brown area referred to above. It may therefore be significant that PH 12, which before examination appeared a typical example, proved upon excavation to be a very ephemeral feature.

The three largest and deepest post-holes in Y1 (4, 10 and 13) appear to form an arc around the dark brown area and are roughly equidistant from one another. Post-hole 4 contained coarse potsherds (E84:8748, 9) and there were animal bones in nos 10 and 13. Depression 195, close to PH 10, also contained potsherds (E84:8745–7).

Once more, as might be expected, the finds from the Y cuttings consisted overwhelmingly of coarse potsherds. A total of 396 fragments were found and their density and distribution are of interest. Square Y1 yielded 37 sherds, all in the black

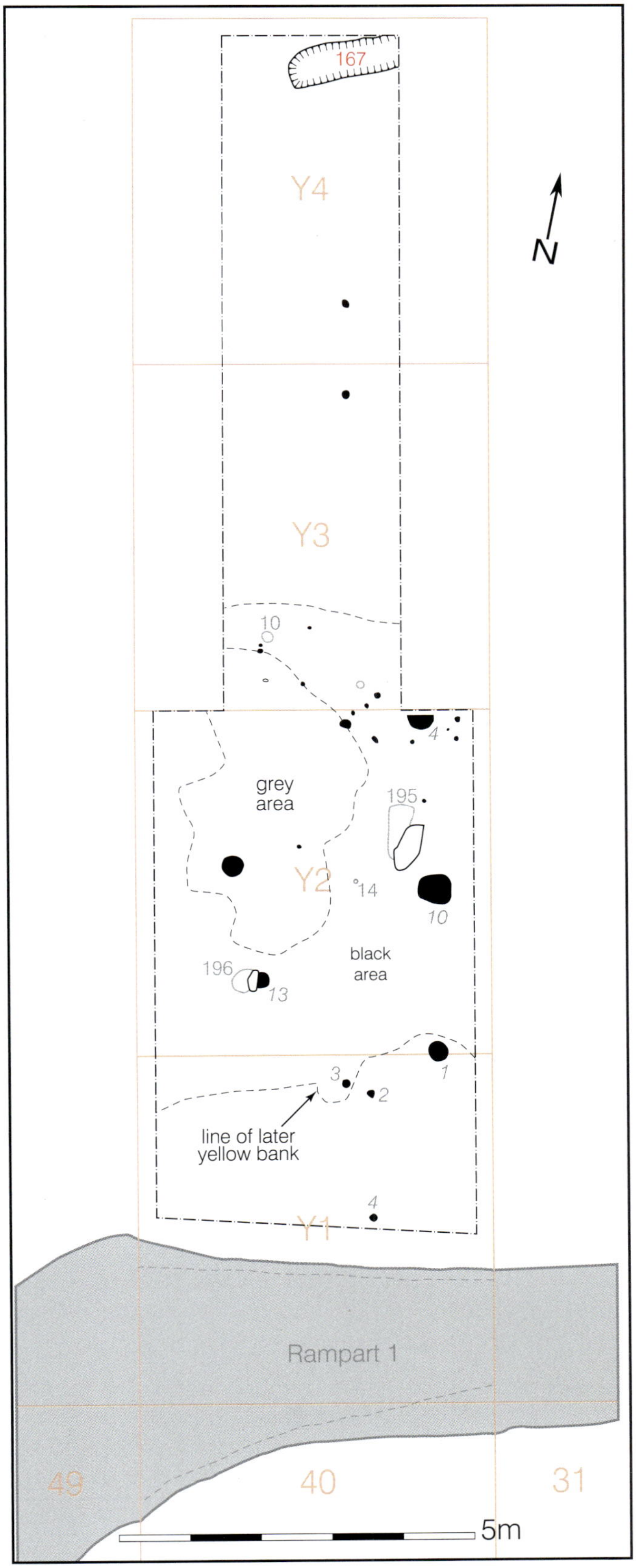

Fig. 2.65 (left)—Plan of the Y cuttings.

Fig. 2.66 (top)—Y cutting section, looking south.

Fig. 2.67 (above)— Possible bank material in Cuttings Y1/Y2, looking south.

material under the bank. Y3 yielded eight and Y4 produced ten. The rest, no fewer than 341 fragments, came from Y2. Where these came from a recognisable context (as opposed to the covering brown humus), they were invariably from the black burnt layer, with a few from the thin grey-brownish material that rested directly on the black.

Four glass beads came from Y2, three from the black layer (E84:8614, 8687 (Fig. 3.14b) and 8716) and the fourth from the upper humus (E84:8600; Fig. 3.14b). Two further glass beads came from under the bank in Y1 (E84:8733, 8735; Fig. 3.13), and they clearly derived from the base of the black or from the sticky grey layer[20] that underlay it.

As noted above, it is difficult not to assume that the bronze blade fragment referred to above, which was found in the yellow material of the bank, came from the same layer as the pottery and the beads. In Y4 the only relevant feature was Pit 167, which yielded two coarse potsherds (E84:8713) and seven clay mould fragments (E84:8714, 8734; Fig. 3.76). In the same square the fragment of a shale bracelet (E84:8657; Fig. 3.107) came to light in the brown humus, almost on the yellow subsoil. Several scattered mould fragments were also found.

2.3.3 The flattened-oval feature in B4/B5

In Sqs B4/B5 approximately half of a curious flattened-oval feature was uncovered (Fig. 2.68). The zone uncovered was first revealed as an area of black organic material, mixed with smallish stones, enclosed by a band of lighter, brownish-black soil. The exposed section of this feature had dimensions of 9.25m by 3.25m, indicating an approximate original width of about 6.5m. The outer band of lighter material merged gradually with the black zone which it enclosed, so that its precise width can only be roughly assessed. Nonetheless, this was on average around 60–75cm, increasing to a maximum of around 1.25m in the north-western sector of B4. The black area was 10–12cm thick and, as it merged with the peripheral brown, the latter gradually decreased in thickness before its final disappearance. In places there was a thin layer of yellowish-grey, silt-like soil which was never more than 5cm thick, and there were several depressions in the black which resembled shallow pits but were in all probability natural hollows in the underlying surface.

The finds from this area consisted of a concentration of coarse potsherds, numbering about 94 fragments (E84:9062, 9063, 9065–7, 9088, 9117, 9120–8, 9166), three mould fragments (E84:9119, 9118) and three water-rolled pebbles (E84:9029, 9064, 9116). Most of these came from the dark/black material, with only a small handful found in the enclosing brownish band.[21]

The nature of this feature is unclear. It is tempting to regard it as representing the site of a structure of some sort, but this suggestion is inevitably weakened by the absence of any post-holes in the area. Nonetheless, the size, the discrete concentration of black occupation material and the precise flattened-oval shape of the enclosing band of brown are all in keeping with this hypothesis. The significant scatter of domestic pottery in the black material, contrasting with the limited quantity of this material in the brown enclosing band, may also be significant. The absence of a hearth within the area of the structure should, however, be noted, though such, of course, could be present in the unexcavated area.

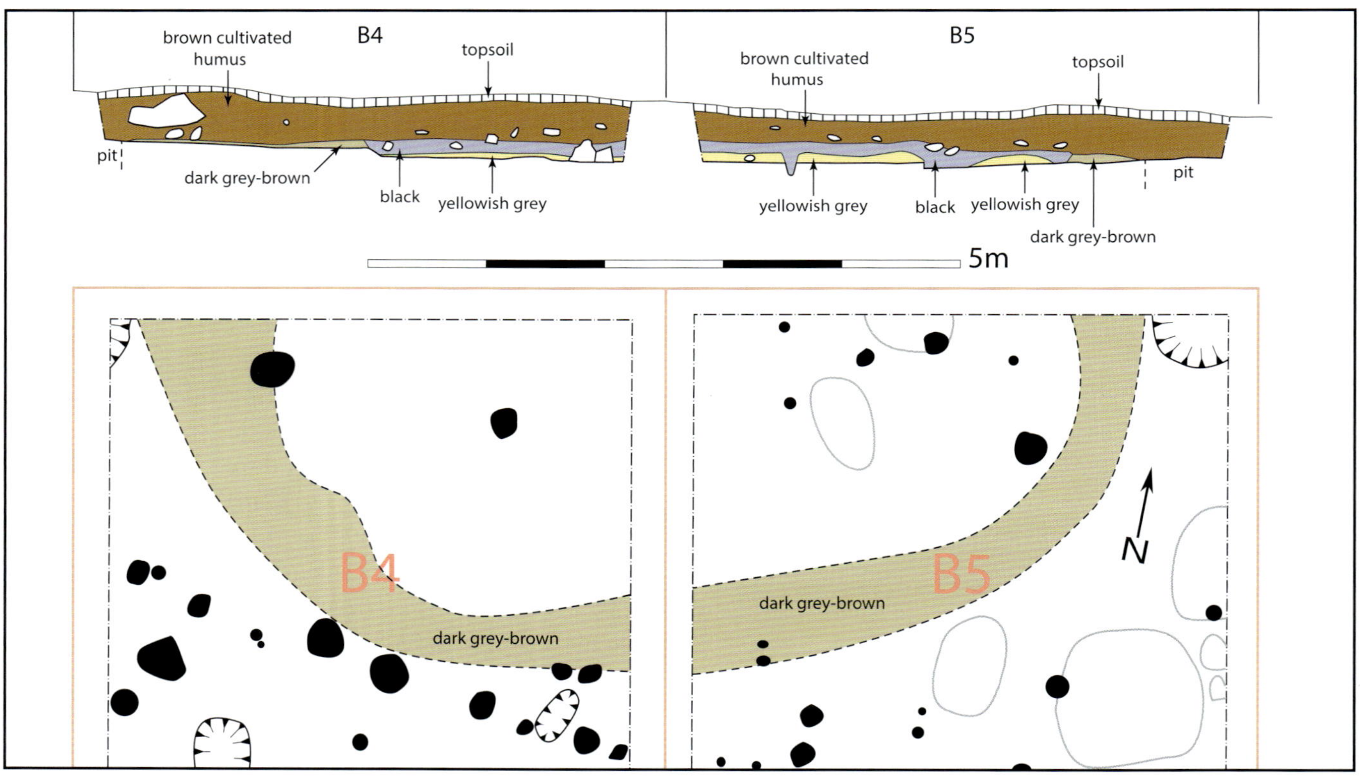

Fig. 2.68—Plan and section of the flattened-oval feature in B4/B5.

2.3.4 Pits in Area 2

A lesser concentration of fifteen generally nondescript pits occurred in Sqs B3, C3, D2 and D3 and E (Figs 2.5, 2.53 and 2.69). These were all shallow (the difference between these and the so-called 'depressions' was in many instances arbitrary), being generally 15–25cm deep. In almost every instance the filling material was grey silt, which usually showed up in the course of excavation as circular grey patches in the yellow subsoil. Only two (Pits 41 in Sq. F1/B2 and 53 in E1/2) had black organic layers. Pit 46, with dimensions of 1.25m by 1.1m, was pear-shaped and completely (and, it would seem, deliberately) filled with stones, some of modest size, which were embedded in basal grey silt. It was no more than 25cm deep, however, with gently sloping sides and a flat base.

Pit 47 cut into a short, straight, shallow trench. Pit 52 in Sq. E2 was almost completely filled with greyish silt. Lying across its surface (but not specifically in the pit) was a shallow area of black, containing charcoal and a few animal bones. The impression here was that this was scattered material randomly trodden into the surface.

Five of the pits of this group contained artefacts. All had sherds of coarse pottery (the greatest number was twelve sherds in Pit 51) and one (Pit 54) contained a single rim sherd (E84:7643), two clay mould fragments (E84:7644, 7645) and a flint flake (E84:7646). Pit 55 contained two sherds of pottery, one coarse (E84:7652) and one from a domestic cordoned urn (E84:7653). Pit 53 contained five coarse potsherds (E84:7716a–d, 7719) and two mould fragments (E84:7717, 7718). With the exception of Pit 55, in which the finds were from the greyish fill, the objects found were invariably from the black or darkish-brown organic material (Table 2.8).

2.3.5 Hearths in Area 2

Possible Hearth 11

This consisted of a small, shallow, rectangular area of burnt material situated mainly in Sq. 10, with a slight extension into Sq. 4/F (Fig. 2.42[22]). It lay on the immediate outer edge of the main ditch, which seems to have cut across it slightly. It was 1m long, 75cm wide and no more than a few centimetres deep. It consisted of a thin spread of burnt black material, on the surface rather than in the depression, and produced no finds.

Hearth 12

About half of this feature (Figs 2.42 and 2.70), which occurred in the north-east corner of Sq. E2, was excavated. It consisted of nothing more than a zone of reddish, burnt soil on the surface, indicative of intensive burning. No pit had been dug. Sufficient remained to show that it was originally sub-oval in form, with dimensions of about 1.4m by 1.6m. A number of post-holes occurred in its immediate vicinity, and one penetrated it close to the northern section strip. There are no indications, however, that these had anything to do with the burnt area. No finds came from this feature.

Hearth 14

This feature (Figs 2.42 and 2.70) occurred in the south-east corner of Sq. B5. It was a flattened oval in shape, with internal dimensions of 1.3m by 1.2m. The pit was on average 54cm deep, but where a large boulder projected from its base in the south its depth decreased to some 35cm. On its base the pit was filled almost to the level of the boulder with a layer of mottled yellowish-grey material which was, for the most part, 15–20cm thick. A layer of medium-sized stones, up to 20cm deep in the deepest part of the pit, lay on this layer. On top of these stones lay a thick, undifferentiated layer of black burnt material. It contained charcoal fragments and mixed in with these were eleven coarse potsherds (E84:9107, 9226) and five clay mould fragments (E84:9227) (Table 2.5). Burnt animal bones were also present.

2.3.6 Cutting A

Cutting A,[23] 2.5m wide and 20m long, was excavated westwards from the base of Rampart 1 (Fig. 2.3). Its purpose was to determine whether in the west, too, there was evidence for human activity contemporary with that encountered elsewhere on the site, and on a comparable scale of intensity. Uniquely, however, apart from a few shallow, nondescript pits filled with grey silt, no other features were found. Few artefacts came to light in the western zone, among these two coarse potsherds in the grey fill of Pit 6 (E84:9609a, b) and, in the same square in the topsoil, a clay mould fragment (E84:9630), a bronze scrap and a coarse potsherd (E84:9631) were found. This suggests the absence of any significant human activity in the zone approaching the western entrance to the main enclosure.

(The attribution of finds to these squares is not unambiguous, owing to the renumbering explained in note 23, resulting in finds from A squares having possibly been found in this or the later B cuttings. The squares are labelled A–A3 on the plan in Fig. 2.3, which — it is assumed — should be read as A1–A4.)

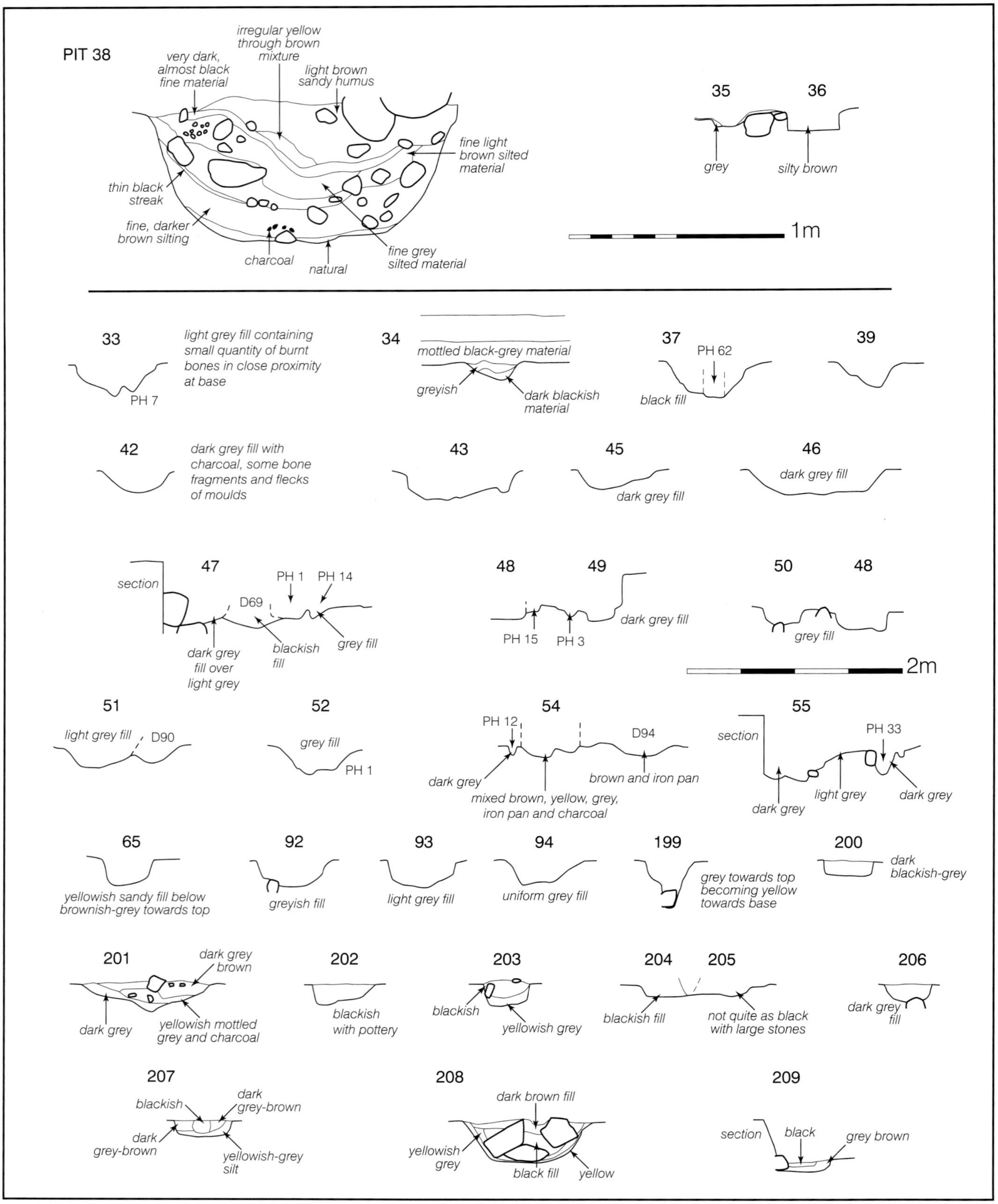
PIT 38
very dark, almost black fine material
irregular yellow through brown mixture
light brown sandy humus
fine light brown silted material
thin black streak
fine, darker brown silting
charcoal
natural
fine grey silted material
35
36
grey
silty brown
1m
33
light grey fill containing small quantity of burnt bones in close proximity at base
PH 7
34
mottled black-grey material
greyish
dark blackish material
37
PH 62
black fill
39
42
dark grey fill with charcoal, some bone fragments and flecks of moulds
43
45
dark grey fill
46
dark grey fill
47
section
D69
PH 1
PH 14
dark grey fill over light grey
blackish fill
grey fill
48
49
PH 15
PH 3
dark grey fill
50
48
grey fill
2m
51
light grey fill
D90
52
grey fill
PH 1
54
PH 12
D94
dark grey
mixed brown, yellow, grey, iron pan and charcoal
brown and iron pan
55
section
PH 33
dark grey
light grey
dark grey
65
yellowish sandy fill below brownish-grey towards top
92
greyish fill
93
light grey fill
94
uniform grey fill
199
grey towards top becoming yellow towards base
200
dark blackish-grey
201
dark grey brown
dark grey
yellowish mottled grey and charcoal
202
blackish with pottery
203
blackish
yellowish grey
204
205
blackish fill
not quite as black with large stones
206
dark grey fill
207
blackish
dark grey-brown
dark grey-brown
yellowish-grey silt
208
dark brown fill
yellowish grey
black fill
yellow
209
section
black
grey brown

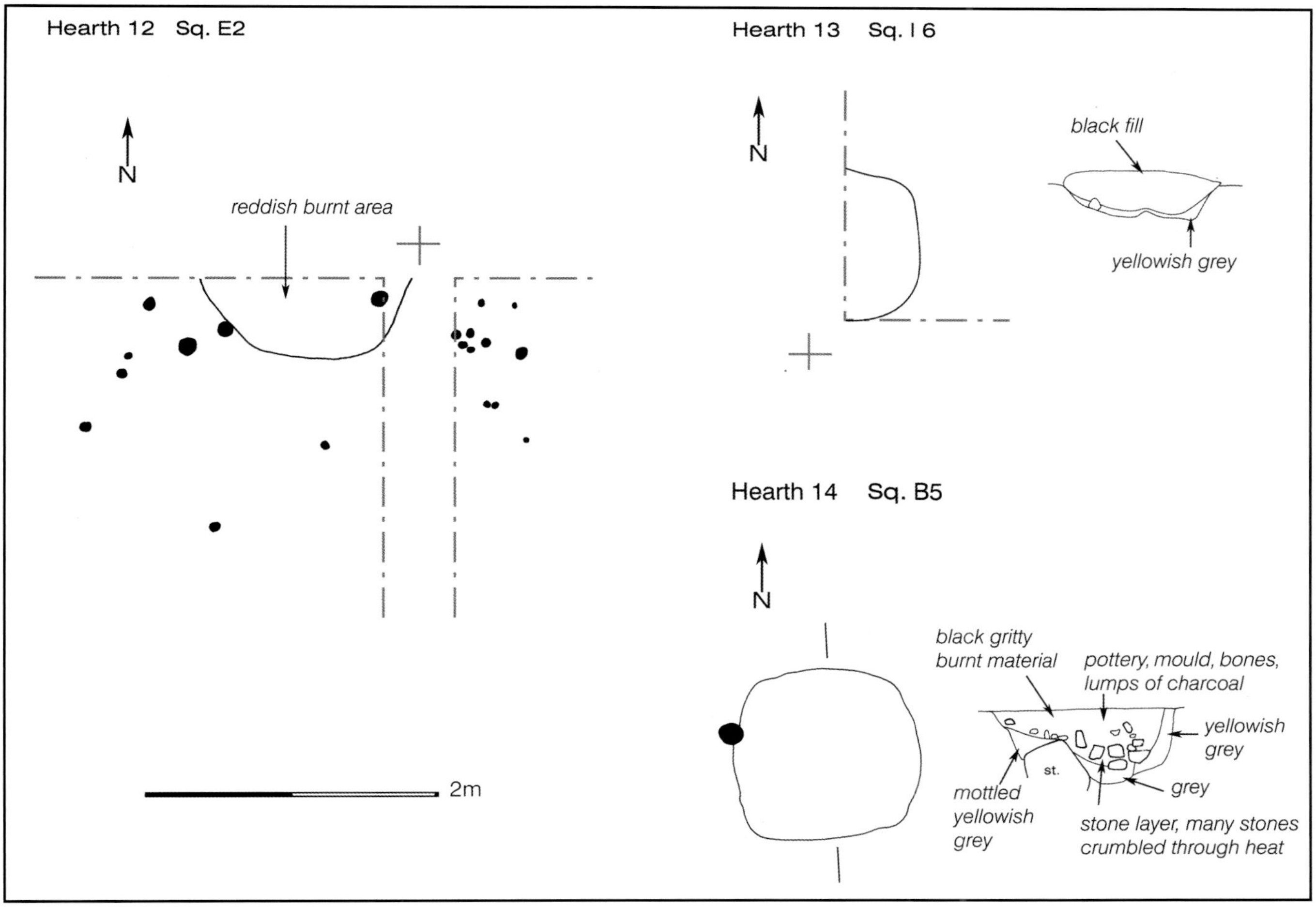

Opposite page:
Fig. 2.69—Pit sections, Area 2.

Fig. 2.70 (above)—Plans and sections of Hearths 12 and 14.

2.4 AREA 3
Barry Raftery

The finds-rich deposits observed in Area 2 only extended to the southern end of the C cuttings in general, only in their western extent extending into B and B1. From Sq. B southwards, dark, less finds-rich soils dominated. These are depicted in the section drawings as dark brown, rather homogeneous deposits, interspersed with charcoal layers. In the following paragraph Raftery describes the stratigraphic relationship of the cut features observed in the F and G cuttings to the hard grey soil that was also observed underlying the deposits in the north. In both instances it is safe to assume that a layer of leaching thus manifested itself. He also outlines the deposits under the cashel wall after its removal in 4/F and 5/G and their possible interrelationship with Ring-ditch 2, which was also uncovered in Area 3 (see section 2.4.3), as well as a rectangular structure (see 2.4.2).

2.4.1 Deposits in Cuttings F and G (Figs 2.71–2.81)

In this area (Cuttings F/G) the removal of the sod revealed a fairly level zone characterised for the most part by extensive patches of grey material, probably the remains of the old turf line, interspersed with areas of the natural yellow subsoil (where, presumably, the grey had been removed at some time in antiquity). The thickness of the grey layer varied from 2cm to 5cm. Almost all the excavated features showed up in this grey layer, including the post-holes, which were readily recognisable as circular patches of brown, grey-brown or black material. Given the complete sterility of the grey layer, it came as some

Fig. 2.71—View across the collapse of the cashel wall before the removal of walling in the course of excavation, facing west.

Fig. 2.72—Cobbling exposed under the cashel wall in Cutting B and extending under the still-extant cashel in Cutting F (looking south).

Fig. 2.73—Cobbling and the underlying mound—the possible prehistoric bank—exposed after the removal of the cashel in Cuttings F and G (looking south).

Fig. 2.74—Area inside Rampart 1 (Sq. B), looking outside to the east (Sq. B1).

surprise that in some areas, after the final removal of this layer, post-holes—some of substantial size—were brought to light (Fig. 2.53[24]). These were mainly concentrated in Sq. F1 but some also occurred in the eastern part of F. As all the recognisable Bronze Age features, without exception, had been dug into, rather than under, the grey layer, it seems that these post-holes, sealed by the latter, pre-date this phase of activity on the site, perhaps by some considerable time.

Clearly, not all can be taken as contemporary, but apart from those beneath the grey level—an obviously early group—it is all but impossible to order them stratigraphically or, indeed, chronologically. Moreover, they varied considerably in size: some, for example, were less than 10cm in depth, while others were more than 30cm deep (see below).

As already noted above, in the course of the excavation some 17m of the wall of the inner stone enclosure were removed to examine the nature of the prehistoric levels underneath (Fig. 2.71), which had been protected from modern ploughing activities. This yielded important stratigraphical information and added considerably to the elucidation of the site stratigraphy. Nonetheless, the situation in this western part of the F/G zone remains, in some details, problematic.

Following the removal of the walling in Cuttings F and G, a low mound of greyish-brown material appeared, on which rested a layer of stones of varying sizes (Figs 2.72, 2.73 and 2.74). This mound extended across the width of the cutting along its length but no formal structural features could be recognised. It was noticeable, however, that for much of its exposed length there was a greater concentration of larger stones along the centre and the western areas of the mound, while to the east, extending across the lower slope of the underlying mound, the stones were considerably smaller and more scattered. Towards the north the stones became similarly small and increasingly scattered before eventually, after an exposed length of some 10m, they finally disappeared in the northern part of Cutting F. It seems evident that the final removal of this layer of cobbling here was a deliberate act, probably to create clear space for the later activity. Where the stones were largest, in the south-west, they averaged 1–2m in length/width, but there was one that was particularly large, measuring almost 3m in length.

The brownish layer on and in which these stones rested *(labelled 'cobbling' on section drawing 13)* (Fig. 2.75) seemed comparable with the modern humus cover which, as already noted, was found in all areas. The layer in question, however, was darker than the obviously recent humus and was spongier in texture. It contained charcoal flecks and not a single find, but it clearly covered all the lower layers, which were unquestionably prehistoric (see below). In Cutting 5/G it was particularly evident that this stony layer was the only one not cut by Ring-ditch 2 (section 13). Significantly, too, it was evident that Ring-ditch 2 also cut across the south-east corner of the small, rectangular, post-slot structure in Cutting G (see below). This upper layer of stones is thus clearly later than all the other phases of activity exposed in this zone. The fact that it lies in a brown, spongy layer, completely devoid of any material, strongly hints that it is of relatively recent date and could represent part of the foundation of the medieval cashel. It must remain possible, nonetheless, that further excavation at some time in the future might indicate that it is a late prehistoric level.

Underneath this layer of cobbling was a substantial body of yellow, redeposited natural soil, up to 25cm thick (visible on sections 11/10, 12 and possibly 13) (Figs 2.75, 2.76, 2.78 and 2.79). The yellow material, clearly comparable to that encountered in E1 and Y1, formed a low bank, 3.6m in maximum width, which extended northwards across Cutting G and into the southern part of Cutting F, where its thickness decreased to some 10cm before it disappeared after a short distance. This layer was virtually stoneless and was again archaeologically sterile, as was the case with the comparable yellow layer in Cutting Y (apart from the single bronze blade from Sq. Y1, E84:8717; Fig. 3.35) and also, to a very large extent, in Cutting E. There can thus be no doubt that this layer represents the remains of the yellow earthen bank thrown up from the digging of Ring-ditch 1. The lack of bank material south of F may be explained by its later removal (but see Chapter 4).

Sealed by the low yellow bank was a layer, 15–25cm in maximum thickness, that consisted of dark brown organic material interspersed with black zones of varying density. The latter, which contained large amounts of charcoal, showed in section as thin, wavy, mostly discontinuous streaks, generally 2–4cm thick. This dark layer, which lay directly on the grey subsoil, was the only one that formed a continuous surface under the stone wall and the only one that could be traced northwards for about 4m, approximately as far as the southern post-holes in B. Along this stretch, however, it became increasingly patchy, with extensive zones of basal grey material exposed. Elsewhere it had been completely removed by recent agricultural activity. A few stones, some of moderately large size, lay on the grey subsoil in the eastern and northern areas of F.

A significant point to note is the scarcity of finds in these lower, dark layers in Cuttings F and G. All that came to light

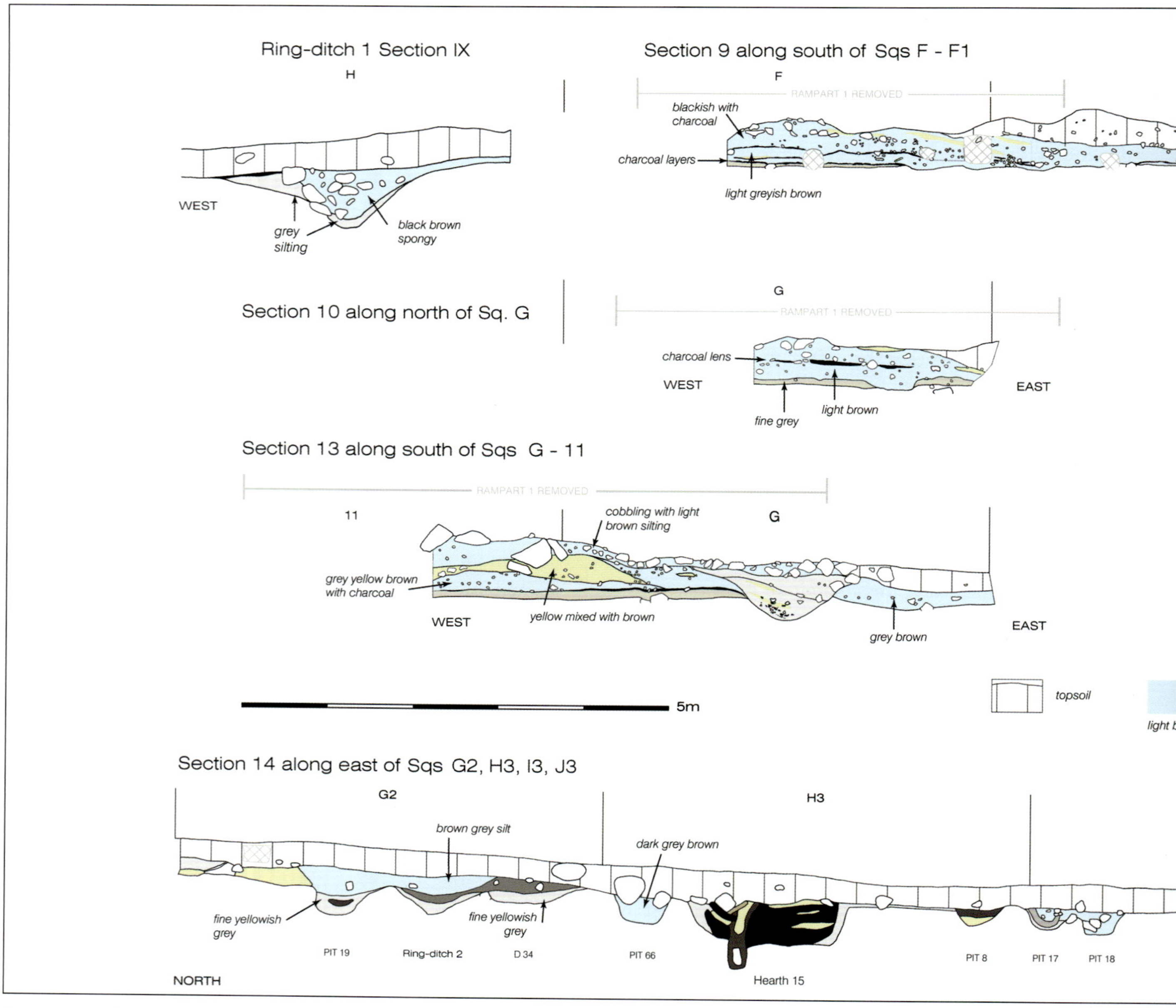

here were a few random scraps of pottery, none of which were likely to be in a primary context.[25] This was in striking contrast to the situation in C/C1 and the immediately adjoining areas of B/B1, where, as already noted, finds were prolific. It must thus be concluded that no significant occupation activity occurred in F/G and the dark sterile material preserved under the wall in this area cannot be seen as evidence of such. It seems most likely, therefore, that this material represents the remains of an old sod layer, elsewhere removed but here preserved under the stone wall.

A small number of pits and post-holes, none of any obvious significance, occurred in this area under the wall. Pit 35 (which, like Pit 36, contained dark brown humus) had been cut into the basal grey layer, and the thin black zone mentioned above lay within this. Pit 36, however, had been cut through both the black layer and the underlying grey layer, as well as through a small deposit of yellow soil which at this point lay on the black layer. Post-hole 45 cut through the grey subsoil but the black covering material had spread across it, although there appears to have been localised subsidence here which could have caused the black layer to sag into the post-hole.

Along the immediate outer edge of the cashel, mainly in Sq. G and possibly extending slightly into Sq. H, was a narrow, irregular band of small to medium-sized stones some 10–20cm

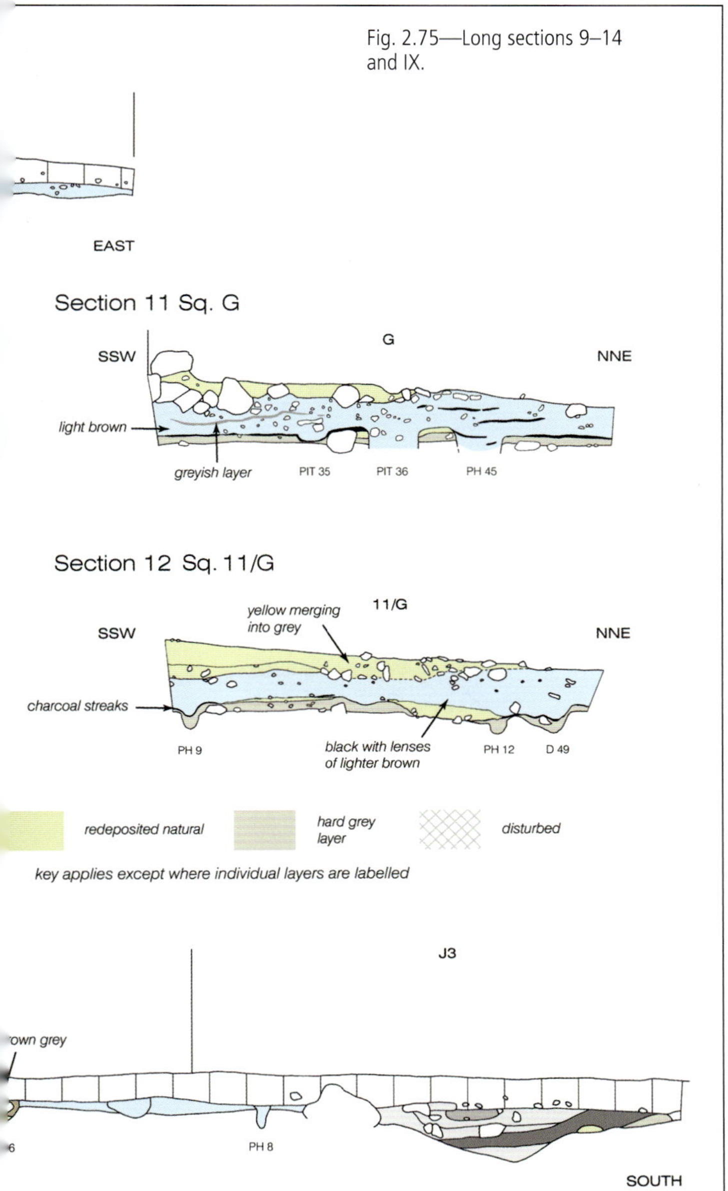

Fig. 2.75—Long sections 9–14 and IX.

Fig. 2.76—Long section 12, looking west.

Fig. 2.77—Long section 11, looking west.

in width. These had been thrown down along this narrow band in no real order. Whether these stones were part of the later stone enclosure or represent the remains of an earlier feature covered by the wall is unclear. Similarly, it is completely unclear whether these stones continue under the later stone wall. It is, at any rate, clear that this stone feature cuts across the early ditch enclosure, and it is not impossible that this is a late feature, as has been suggested in Cutting F.

A radiocarbon date of 1191–925 cal. BC (GrN-27107) was obtained from brown material in Sq. F2.

The dark layer is characterised here by Raftery and in the sections as interspersed with large numbers of charcoal streaks but is finally interpreted as the remains of an old sod layer. Raftery notes that only very few scraps of pottery were found in the basal layers underlying the yellow natural in the make-up of the 'bank'.

The finds records mention a small selection of prehistoric finds that were retrieved after the removal of the wall. Their contexts are described as 'in black area among stones' or in black gritty area of black 'bank', presumably referring to the raised bank-like appearance of the area of the cashel wall after removal and thus redeposited. The finding of Leinster Cooking Ware and a penny from 1948 among the same 'cobbling' underpins Raftery's interpretation of this upper layer as recent.

Raftery identifies the yellow deposits that are visible in some of the sections in this area as the bank associated with Ring-ditch 1. The fact that this is cut by Ring-ditch 2 is seen as dating this deposit, adding to its credibility as being a prehistoric bank of Ring-ditch 1. Section 13 is not, however, unambiguous in its depiction of this

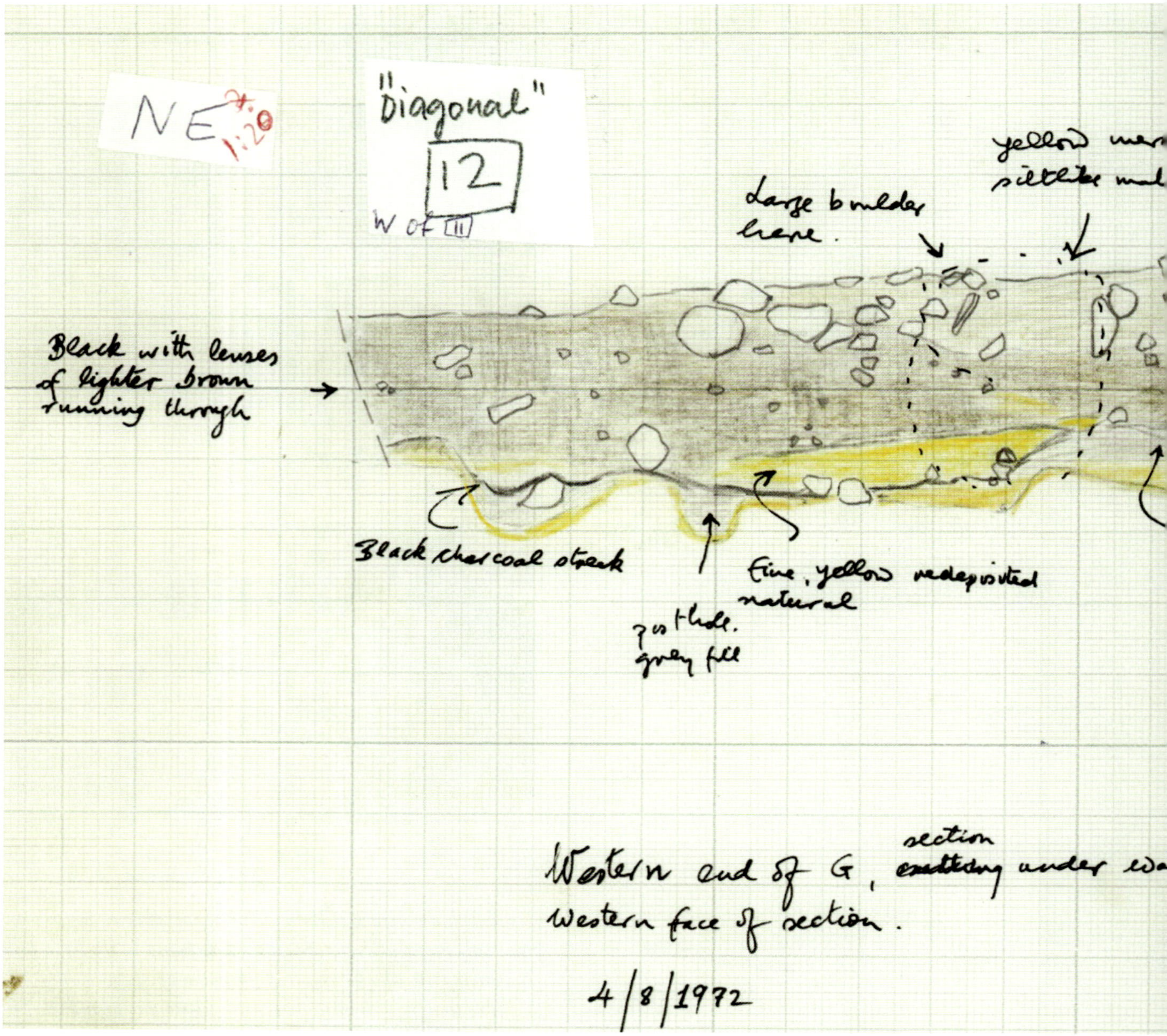

intersection. While Ring-ditch 2 clearly cuts the grey layer (Fig. 2.80) and the overlying brown deposits, the extent of the 'yellow' is not entirely clear.

2.4.2 The rectangular structure and Hearth 7

Traces of this feature (Fig. 2.82) began to appear in Cutting F when the upper layers had been removed. Mottled zones, yellow, brownish and greyish in colour, were revealed, but extensive concentrations of black were present in the area covered by the bank and immediately to its east. These zones extended to the north across the full width of the cutting, giving way in Cutting B to grey, sandy material. Particularly noticeable was a regular, narrow streak of dense black material, about 20cm wide, which extended eastwards from the larger zone of black for a distance of about 1.4m. Further investigation here, involving the removal of most of the black covering material, revealed that the black streak was in fact the upper spread of a narrow, fairly straight trench which could be traced for about 2.1m before it was again lost in a wider zone of black to the west. At the eastern end of this narrow streak, and in line with it, were several patches of charcoal, while immediately to the

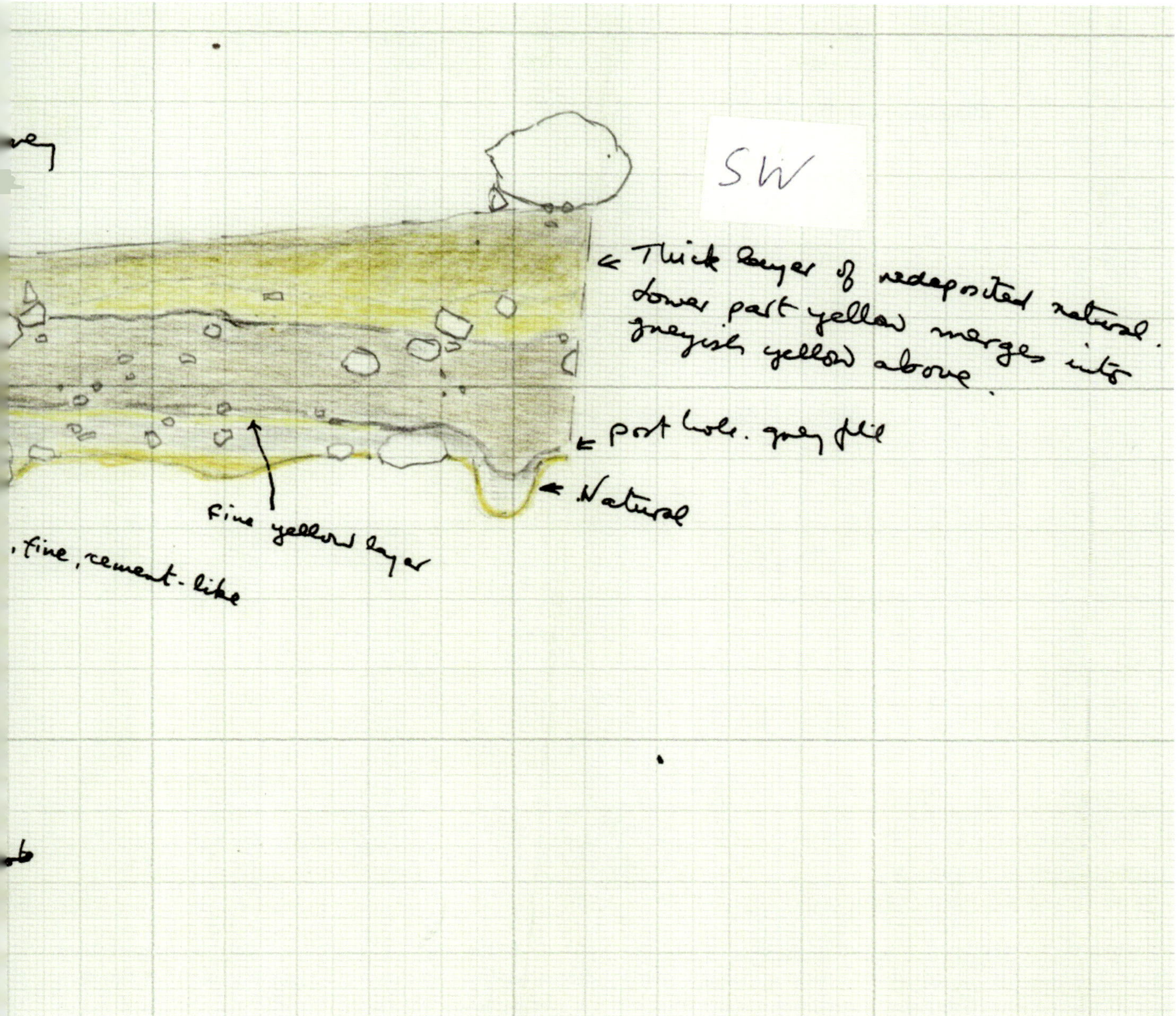

Fig. 2.78 —Original pencil drawing of long section 12.

south, disappearing into the section strip, several further areas of the same material occurred.

When finally exposed, the black streak was revealed as a line, about 3.5m in length, of twelve small stake-holes set in a narrow slot, with a thirteenth some 15cm beyond the twelfth and in line with it at its eastern end (Figs 2.83 and 2.84). These stake-holes or post-holes were of modest dimensions, averaging 8–10cm in diameter and 10–12cm in depth. PH 9 was more substantial, however, being about 25cm wide and 20cm deep. Small packing stones were present in several of the post-holes, all of which were otherwise completely filled with charcoal.

In the adjacent Cutting G there was no zone of black like that encountered in the western zone of Cutting F. Instead, there was a mottled greyish surface with very occasional patches of charcoal. In this grey material there was a line of eighteen stake-holes in a narrow slot, generally about 15cm wide, which was similar to that in Cutting F and on average 2.6m distant from it. It was virtually parallel to the first line described and could be traced for about 2.75m. At its western end, however, it was truncated by Pit 36. Like those in Cutting F, the stake-

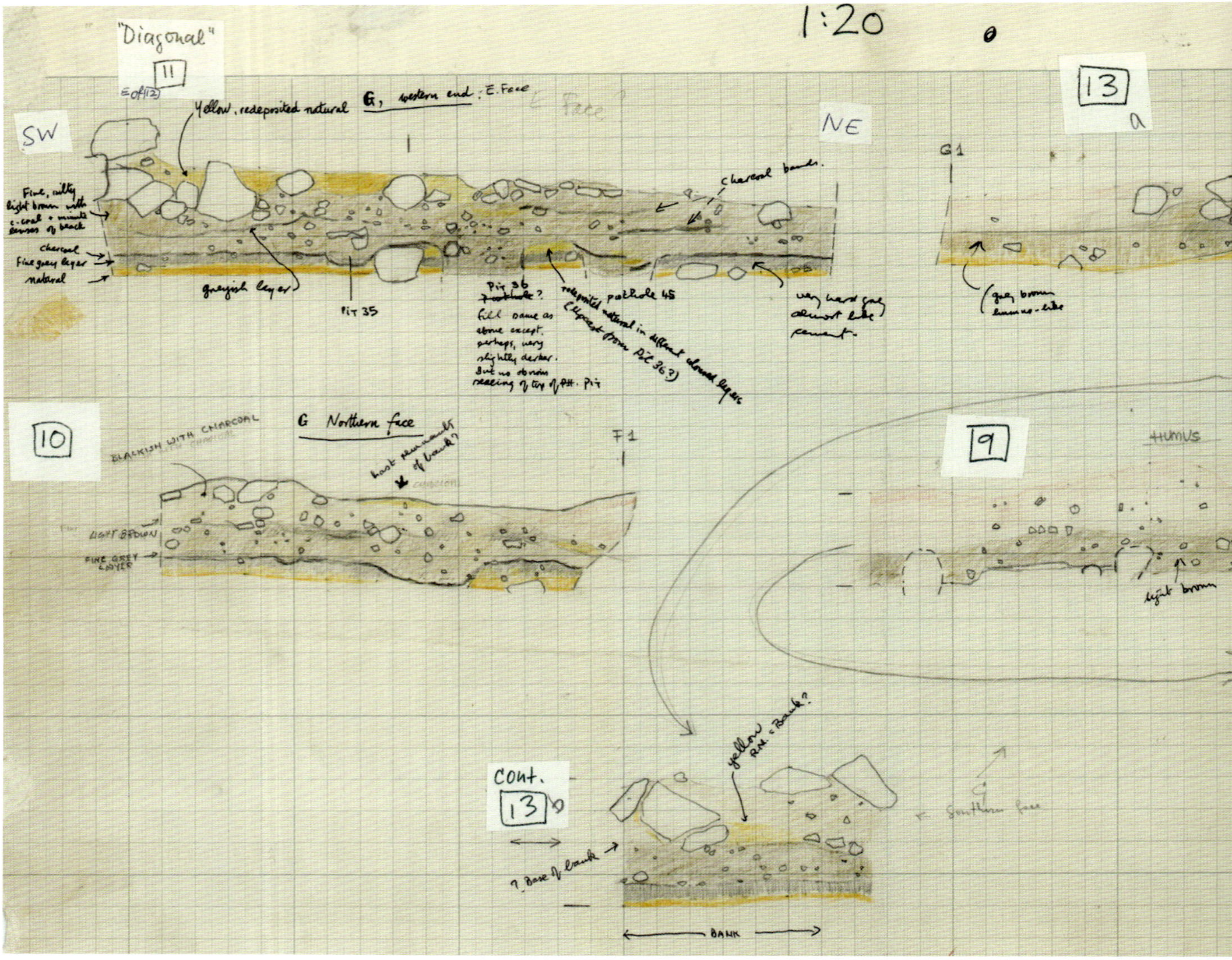

holes were of modest proportions, none being more than 12cm deep. Similarly, as noted above, packing stones were occasionally present. Otherwise, apart from a short stretch about 50cm in length in the east, this slot, too, was completely filled with charcoal.

The short eastern portion devoid of charcoal is important. Here the upper portion of the slot was filled with grey, silted material, beneath which the base of a post-hole occurred. This was precisely the point where the burial enclosure (Ring-ditch 2) overlapped with the slot. The material filling the upper portion of PH 42/43 was actually the silt that filled Ring-ditch 2 (see section 2.4.3, Fig. 2.85), indicating that the latter had been dug across the stake-hole and was thus later than the possible rectangular structure.[26]

It seems likely that these two lines of stakes may have been linked in the east by a shallow, roughly parallel-sided depression, D47, which was 20–25cm wide and 10–12cm deep on average. It was filled with a greyish-brown material and at its northern and southern ends a number of very insignificant stake-holes occurred. In the centre, for a distance of almost 1m, there were no stake-holes. The matter here, however, is uncertain.

At the western end of this 'structure' there were several post-holes, but these did not indicate an obvious closing feature. A large shallow pit (Hearth 7; Fig. 2.86), a flattened oval in shape, with dimensions of 1.62m by 1.8m but no more than about 7cm deep, occurred slightly off-centre a short distance outside the slot zone. This hearth was completely filled with black, carbonised material. There was no silting, which suggested that the black material had accumulated rapidly. This hearth, like

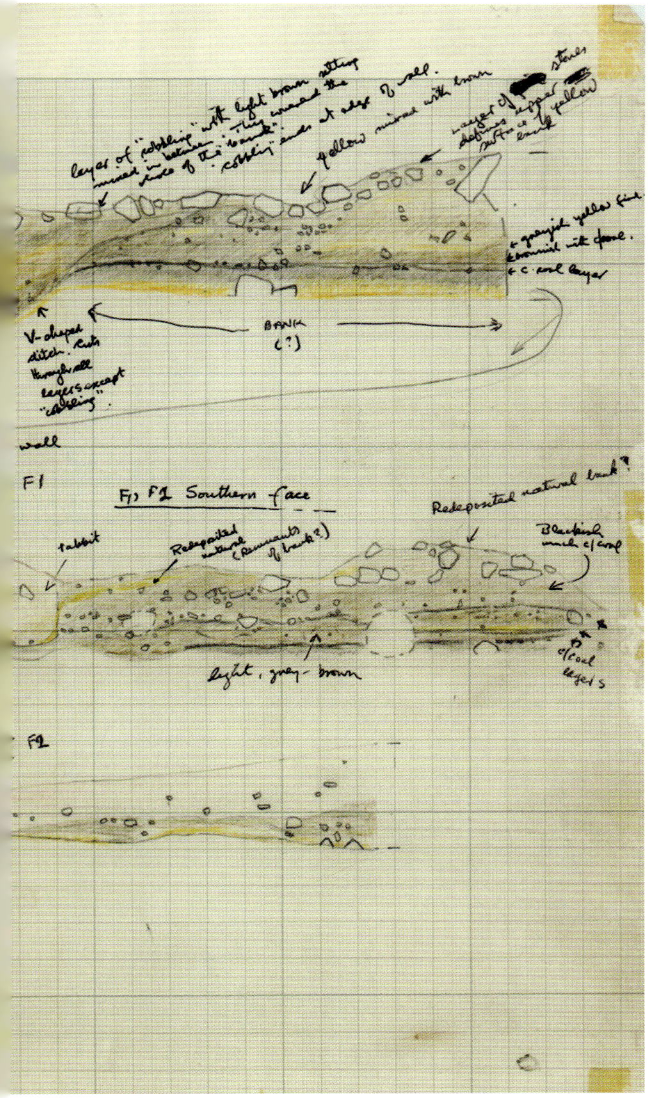

Fig. 2.79 (above)—Original pencil drawings of long sections 9–14.

Fig. 2.80—Grey floor under a thin horizon of black occupation material.

Fig. 2.81—Primary stone-rich layer under the Rampart 1 wall: primary construction level in Sq. H1 (looking west).

the two post-slots, underlay the principal black layer referred to above, and so these features might be related.

This post-slot feature is earlier than Ring-ditch 2. Clay mould fragments were found in the eastern end of the southern slot. The moulds could thus relate to the ditch and not necessarily to the post-slots, but it should not be forgotten that not a single mould fragment came from the ditch fill, so it is perhaps more likely that the moulds in question belong to a phase pre-dating the burial ditch.

This structure is enigmatic, reminiscent of a closely similar, though smaller, structure unearthed to the south-west in Sq. X4. The latter consisted of a pair of parallel post-slots forming a small enclosure which was definitely open at each end. This strengthens the possibility that the structure in F4 was similarly open-ended. It may be that in each instance some sort of flimsy construction with parallel walls open at the ends had once existed. They could well have been of wickerwork. Any roofing feature that might have been present would have been equally flimsy and light, for the uprights which once stood in the narrow trenches could not have supported any significant weight. The probable Hearth 7 situated at the western end of the structure in G/F may have had a similar function to the latter.

A radiocarbon date of 1373–1044 cal. BC (GrA-23347) was obtained on a sample of Corylus *(S72:115) from a bedding trench of the subrectangular structure in Sq. G.*

Hearth 7

This was a shallow, oval pit in Sqs 5/G and 11, with dimensions of 1.8m by 1.62m. It had regularly curving sides, a gently convex base (Figs 2.43b and 2.86) and a maximum depth of

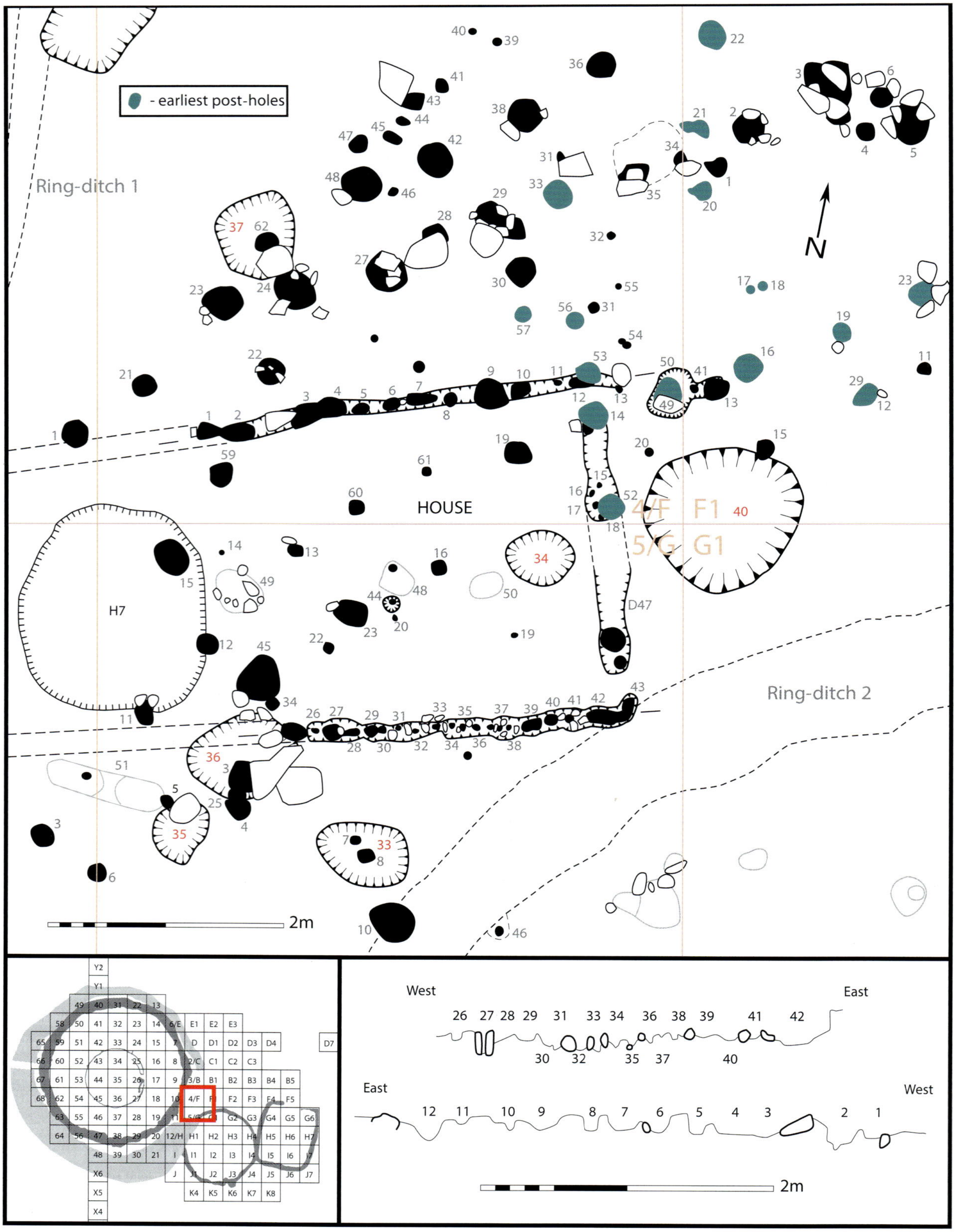

Fig. 2.82—Plan and sections of rectangular structure in 5/G and 4/F.

Fig. 2.83—Rectangular structure in Sqs 5/G and 4/F (looking south), with Hearth 7 to its west.

Fig. 2.85—Rectangular structure in Sqs 5/G and 4/F being cut by Ring-ditch 2 (looking west), after excavation.

Fig. 2.84—The (northern) slot-trench of the rectangular structure in 5/G and 4/F.

Fig. 2.86—Hearth 7 before excavation in Sqs 11 and 5/G (looking south-east).

no more than about 7cm. The filling material was a black spongy substance with considerable concentrations of charcoal. This feature contained a single coarse potsherd, which was retrieved from the black extent of the hearth in the baulk. The hearth was cut by later post-holes. Clear evidence of burning was visible in the subsoil.

A radiocarbon date of 785–408 cal. BC (SI-147) is associated with Hearth 7.

2.4.3 The burial complex: Ring-ditch 2

Raftery published the discovery of this part of the site in 1973. This area comprises not only the central pyre area within the cluster of stake-holes but also Hearth 15, which is reinterpreted in Chapter 6 as a further pyre feature. This adds to the multiphase character of the burial activity in this area, which is also implied by the presence of multiple burials described by Raftery below. It is striking that a pit feature, 90, with two adjoining features, 86/89, in F3 recalls the morphology of other possible pyre hearths in Area 1; it is not, however, mentioned in the records as a hearth feature (see p. 145). Various features containing charcoal-rich 'linings' and evidence for small amounts of human bone in the area enclosed by Ring-ditch 2 are interpreted in Chapter 6 as evidence for the deposition of pyre contents. The plan for Area 2, at the intersection of cuttings H3 and H4 and I3/I4 in particular, as well as in the south, between the J and K squares, shows some disjoints that could not be resolved in the post-excavation process, e.g. Fig. 2.87. Three pits in the area contained medieval pottery, otherwise the zone appears to be comprised mainly of Bronze Age features.

Ring-ditch 2, which enclosed a number of burials and related features and deposits (Figs 2.87, 2.88), closely resembled Ring-ditch 1 in the inner stone enclosure and consisted of a regular, circular enclosure, 18.2m in diameter. Nowhere around its circumference did it depart by more than a few centimetres from this, leaving little room to doubt that it had been carefully laid out (as was probably also the case for Ring-ditch 1), presumably using a string of some sort stretched from a central post. Although a small segment covered by the inner stone wall in the west was not excavated, it may be taken as virtually certain that there had never been an entrance gap, as had obviously also been the case with Ring-ditch 1.

Ring-ditch 2 had been dug with considerable care and clearly every effort was made to maintain a neat and regular V-sectioned profile (Figs 2.89–2.92). Once more, however, as was the case with Ring-ditch 1, the hard and rocky nature of the subsoil made this extremely difficult in places. Nonetheless, despite the occasional projecting stones and the rather jagged nature of the ditch sides around some of its circumference (especially in the south-west; Fig. 2.91), the diggers succeeded to a large extent—indeed, to a greater extent than in the case of Ring-ditch 1—in achieving a regular profile. The sides were thus relatively smooth, maintaining a fairly consistent angle of about 45°, leading to a narrow, at times almost pointed, base, though in other parts more gently rounded.

The ditch was occasionally as little as 60cm in maximum width at its top but for most of its circumference it was 1.1–1.2m wide on average. It was deepest in the north-west, where its base was some 86cm below the modern humus. It was otherwise generally 60cm or less in depth, being shallowest at two points in the north and east, where it was no more than 25–26cm below the surface.

Around most of its circumference the ditch fill was relatively uncomplicated, and the indications are that, once dug, the ditch was allowed to silt up gradually over a number of years without recutting. Apart from some thin lenses of yellow, redeposited natural soil, the fill consisted in the main of layers of greyish silted material. Charcoal flecks and areas of black, burnt material were here and there present, being especially concentrated in the upper levels in H4. Stones of moderate size occurred sporadically, particularly in J1 and, to a lesser extent, in J2, where they lay on the primary silting. These stones may have been deliberately thrown in but scarcely represent any sort of systematic filling operation, as might have been the case in parts of Ring-ditch 1. Two pits, 19 and 25, in Sqs G2 and G1, had been cut into the edge of the ditch when silting was well advanced (Fig. 2.87).

The long section in Sqs G/G1 (Fig. 2.75, section 13) indicated unambiguously that here the ditch cut through all the levels of certainly prehistoric date, including the bank of redeposited yellow subsoil which itself clearly lay on top of all the main Bronze Age levels (but see above).

The ditch was not prolific in finds (Table 2.9). A scatter of coarse potsherds occurred mainly in the grey silt. No more than seventeen of these came from deep down in the primary silting (E84:7404, 8379, 8381–3, 8464, 8479, 8480a–d); the rest were randomly scattered in silt higher up. Of the total number of potsherds, the great majority were concentrated on the eastern side of the ditch in H4, I4 and J4. These are the cuttings more or less adjacent to the concentration of pits in J5 and I5 in Area 4 which are described below. More important finds are a decorated glass bead (E84:8675; Fig. 3.13), found 15–20cm deep in the upper grey silt of the ring-ditch in I4,[27] and two amber beads (E84:8526, 8527; Figs 3.9 and 3.10), found close together in J4 in the upper grey fill. A few scattered flint flakes also occurred but not a single mould fragment was recovered.[28]

A radiocarbon date of 1386–1059 cal. BC (GrN-27112) was obtained on hazel from a bulk sample from the ditch fill in G2.

Haphazard scatters of greyish and blackish material were encountered within the burial enclosure, and the ground level was bumpy and uneven over much of the interior. It seems, however, that some effort had been made to remove as many of the projecting natural boulders as possible. This had not been complete, however, and in places some remained.[29] It would appear that less attention was paid to the removal of the stones around the immediate inner edge of the ditch than in the central zone, which was stoneless and regularly flat. This was where the primary burial occurred and where the

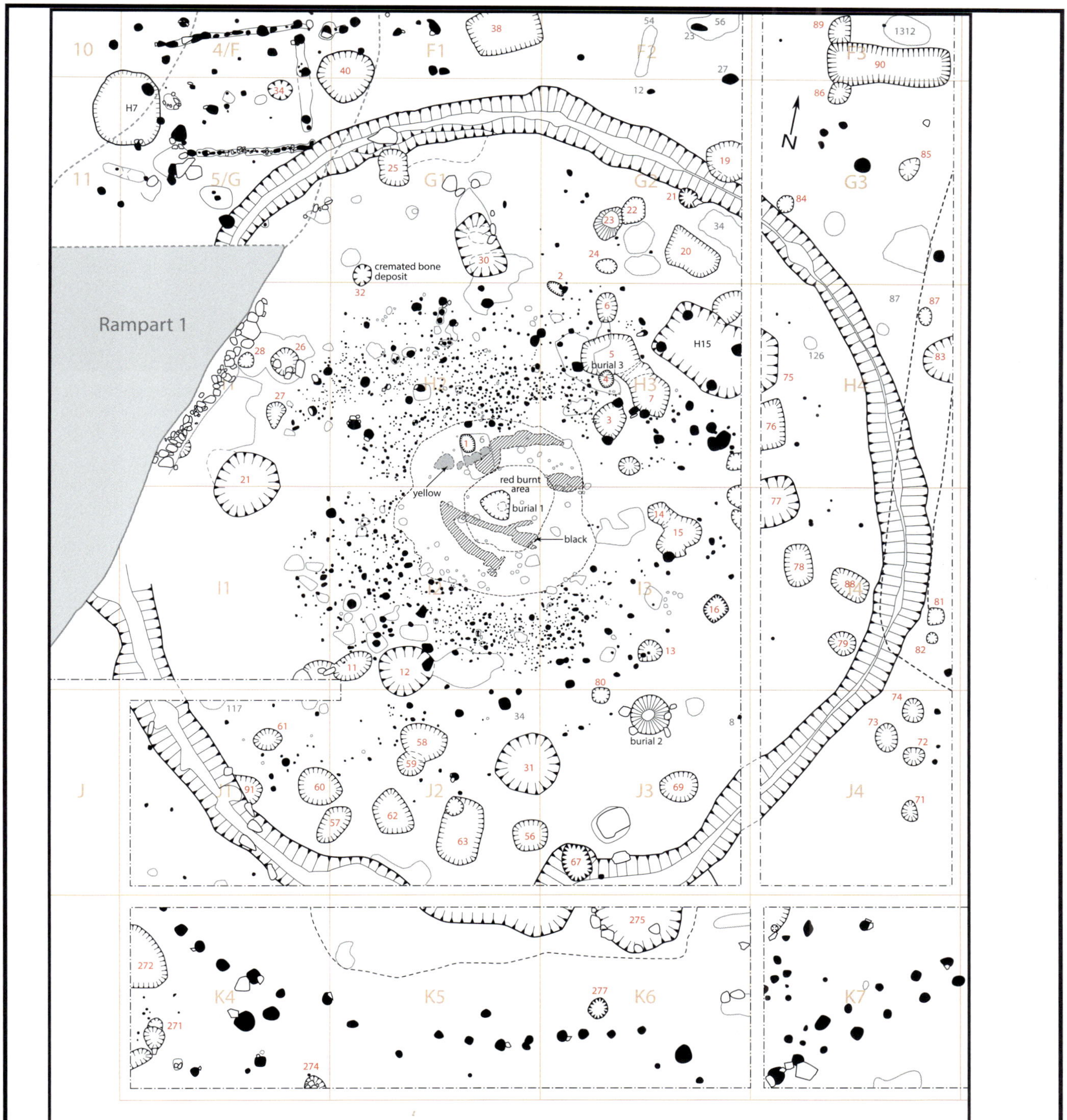

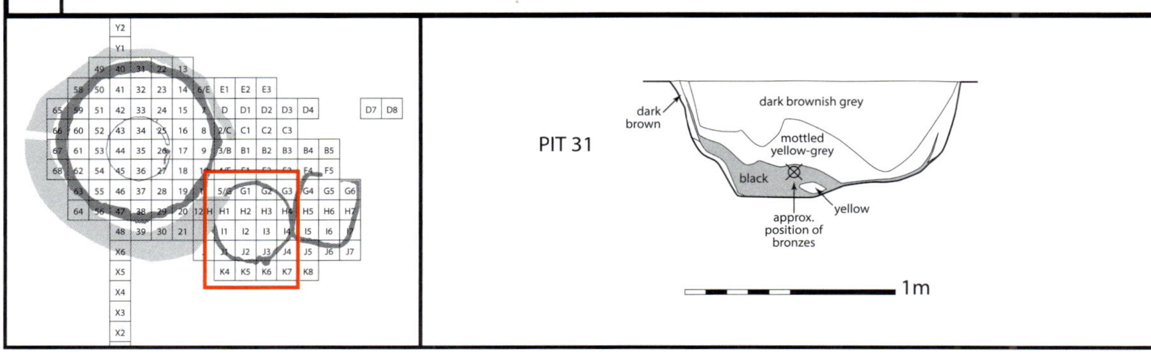

Fig. 2.87—
Plan of Area 3.

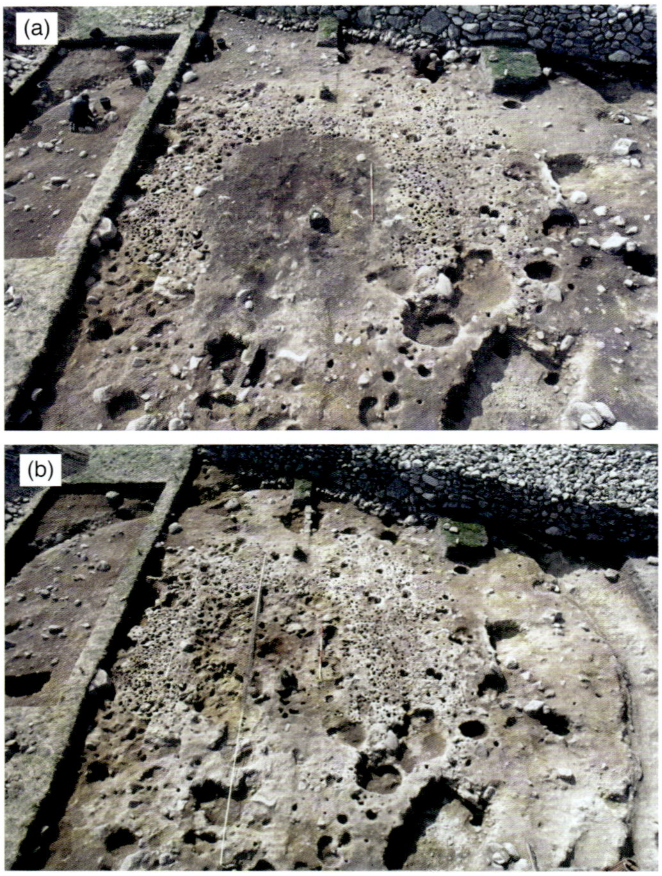

Fig. 2.88—Features enclosed by Ring-ditch 2: (a) mid-excavation view of Sqs H1, H2, H3, I1, I2 and I3 (looking west); (b) post-excavation view of Sqs H1, H2, H3, I1, I2 and I3 (looking west); (c) detail of features in Sqs H2 and H3 (looking south-west).

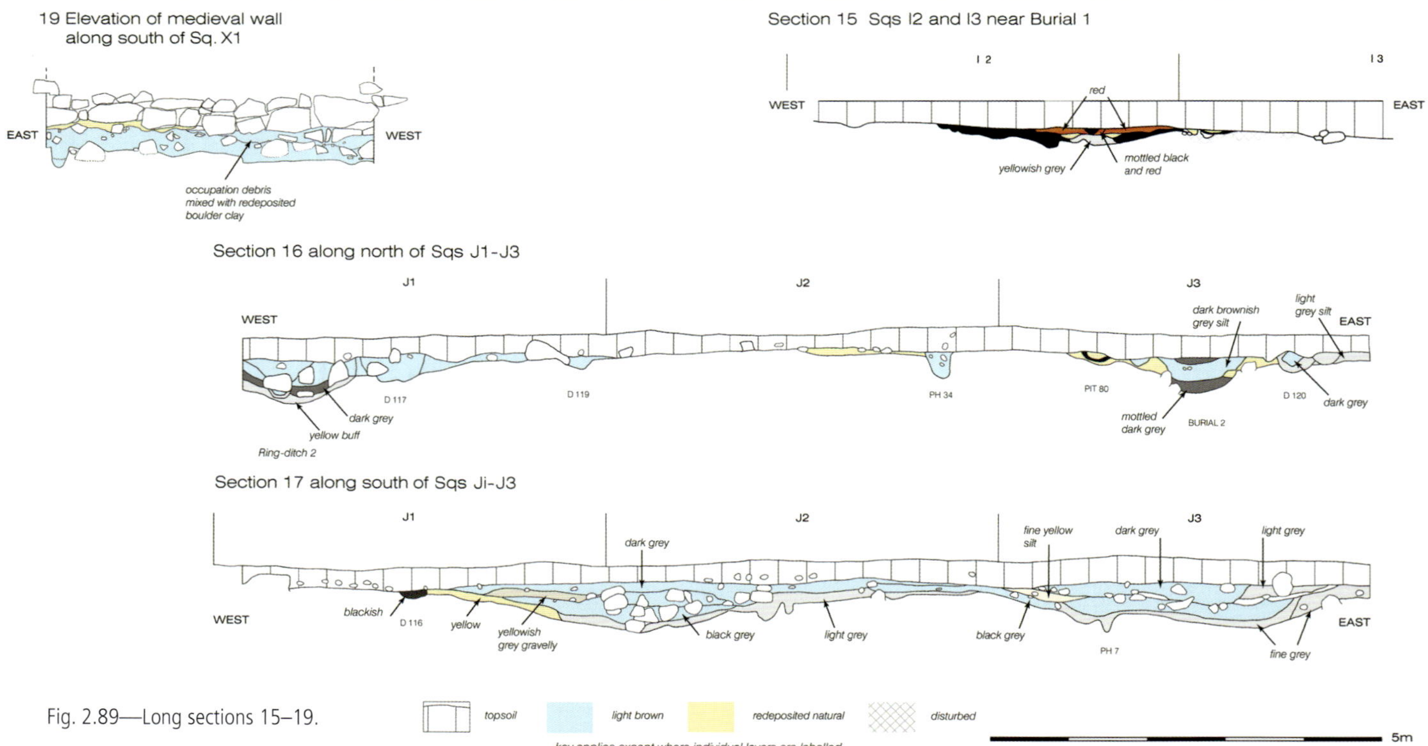

Fig. 2.89—Long sections 15–19.

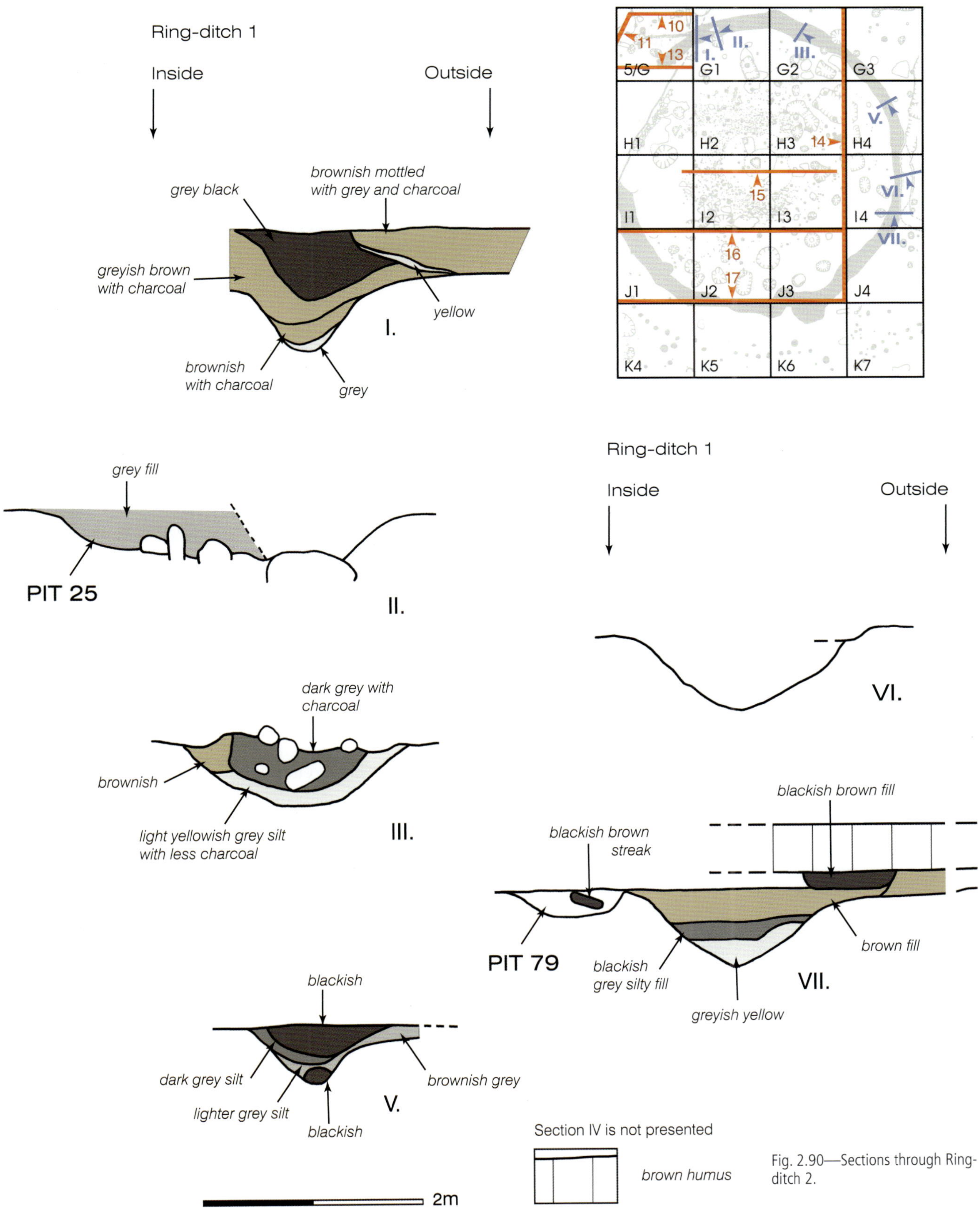

Fig. 2.90—Sections through Ring-ditch 2.

Fig. 2.91—South-western extent of Ring-ditch 2 after excavation (Sqs I1 and J1, looking north-west).

Fig. 2.92—Ring-ditch 2 in Sqs G3/H4/I4/J4 after the removal of the overlying medieval trench and excavation of the ring-ditch (looking north).

cremation itself had probably been carried out (see below, but see also Chapter 6). In places scatters of redeposited natural soil were encountered (doubtless upcast from the excavation of the ditch), suggesting that an attempt was made to level the surface in preparation for the burial activities.

Burial 1

In the centre of the enclosure was a roughly circular area of red, heavily burnt soil (Figs 2.87 and 2.88), and centrally placed within this was a pit containing what was undoubtedly the primary burial (Figs 2.93 and 2.94). When initially exposed, it was subtriangular or pear-shaped, with maximum dimensions of about 75cm across. The rim sloped gently inwards at the top but the pit proper had sides which were for the most part vertical. The pit cut was a flattened oval in form, with greatest dimensions of 50cm by 60cm. At the base it measured 35cm by 28cm. A layer of natural yellow subsoil, 6–8cm thick, had been laid down to level the floor of the pit. A flat slab of stone, 6–7cm thick, was placed on this layer, exactly filling the base of the pit.

Surrounding the slab, and in places partly overlapping it, was a ring of twelve irregularly shaped, fist-sized stones. While most touched each other, in a few cases they were up to 4cm apart. They varied from 5cm to 10cm in length, with heights/widths generally of 3–5cm. The pit, in all its details, had a close parallel in one uncovered in Sq. Z3, immediately outside the hillfort on the south (see section 2.9.4 below).

A deposit of burnt bones, mixed with fine reddish soil, had been placed on the slab, neatly arranged in a small oval heap 10cm high, with a maximum basal width of 25cm. The bones were not centrally placed but were at the south-eastern end of the pit, partly resting against one of the stones of the enclosing ring. Thus they covered an area of no more than about 20% of the pit's base. The cremation was that of a

Table 2.9—Artefacts recovered from the ditch of Ring-ditch 2.

Sq. no.	Artefact type	In upper ditch fill	In lower ditch fill	Depth in ditch unknown
G1	Coarse pottery			E84:9463
G2	Coarse pottery		E84:7404	E84:7366a
	Flint			E84:7511
H4	Coarse pottery	E84:8465, 8466, 8467, 8468, 8578, 8579, 8580, 8581, 8582, 8662, 8663, 8664	E84:8464	E84:8623
	Clay (possible moulds?)	E84:8583		
I2	Coarse pottery		E84:8379	
I4	Coarse pottery	E84:8545, 8546, 8547, 8548, 8676		
	Flint	E84:8553		
	Glass beads	E84:8675		
J2	Coarse pottery		E84:8381, 8382, 8383	E84:8388
J3	Coarse pottery	E84:8447, 8486a–c	E84:8479, 8480a–d, 8481a–c	
J4	Middle Bronze Age pottery	E84:8609		
	Coarse pottery	E84:8488a–j, 8489, 8521, 8522, 8532, 8533, 8534, 8535, 8536, 8538, 8539, 8540, 8541, 8542, 8555, 8556, 8557, 8561, 8561.1, 8562, 8563, 8564, 8565, 8608, 8624, 8625, 8626, 8627		
	Medieval pottery*	E84:8626a		
	Flint	E84:8523, 8524, 8543, 8544a–c, 8558, 8610	E84:8611	
	Amber	E84:8526, 8527		
K4	Coarse pottery			E84:9603a–c
K5	Coarse pottery			E84:9604a–b
	Flint			E84:9605
	Stone	E84:9567		
K6	Coarse pottery			E84:9544
	Glass bead			E84:9545

*Leinster Cooking Ware from upper grey fill in Sq. J4 is considered intrusive.

mature adult male (see Chapter 3, section 3.16).

After deposition of the bones, the pit had been refilled, mostly with the fire-reddened soil, which had doubtless been extracted in the course of the pit's initial excavation. There was also an admixture of blackened, burnt material and a few small deposits of natural yellow subsoil. The burnt material filling the pit had evidently been scraped from its immediate vicinity as the pit had been dug, slightly off-centre, into a roughly circular zone of heavily burnt red soil. This was about 2m in diameter and flecks of charcoal and occasional tiny fragments of human bones were present. The soil had in places been reddened to a depth of 5–8cm, suggesting a pyre fire of some intensity.

Immediately south of the burial pit, lying directly on the red burnt surface, was a broad, black sooty streak extending discontinuously in a north-west/south-east direction (Figs 2.87 and 2.86). There was a similar zone of the same sort of sooty material to the south-west of this. At its southern end the latter was about 50cm distant from the first streak, but the two blackened areas gradually converged until they finally met in the north-west. There were similar zones of heavily burned black material outside the central reddened area to the north, and a similar, smaller area occurred on the east. It is possible that these burnt areas represent the remains of the funeral pyre.

Cremated bone from the central Burial 1 was radiocarbon-dated to 1207–1002 cal. BC (SUERC-42578), and charcoal from the surrounding pyre in G/G1 was dated to 1264–1045 cal. BC (GrN-27114). Human bone and animal bone were identified in this pyre spread (S74:30, Table 3.47), as well as a fragment of a bronze object (E84:8407).

The intensely fire-reddened centre was in turn surrounded

Fig. 2.93—Burial 1 during and after excavation (Sq. I2, looking north-east).

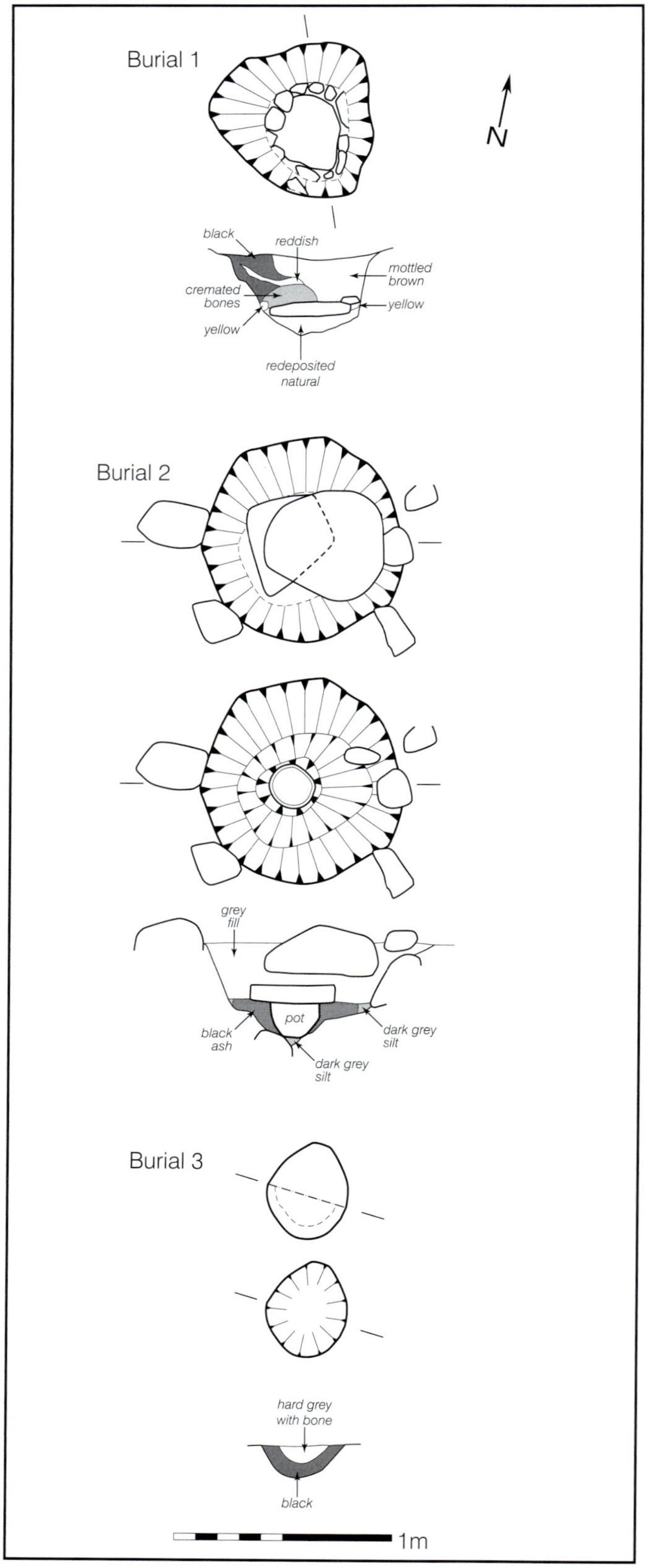

Fig. 2.94—Plans and sections of Burials 1, 2 and 3 within Ring-ditch 2.

by a zone of lesser burning, 1–1.5m wide. This comprised areas of black, sooty material (as noted above) and some patches of reddening, although the latter was not in any way comparable with the intense redness of the central area. A few nondescript stake-holes were encountered here after removal of the burnt material but these obviously pre-dated the burial.

The burial pit was thus centrally situated within a flat, roughly circular area, approximately 4m by 4.5m in diameter. It is possible that this was the site of the funeral pyre, with the burial located in the very spot where the final obsequies had been enacted.

This area was enclosed by a curious, enigmatic feature for which there is no ready explanation (Figs 2.87, 2.88 and 2.95). It consisted of a broad zone of stake-holes, for the most part densely packed. These formed a roughly horseshoe-shaped arrangement which was largely open to the east, where a 3m-wide stretch was virtually devoid of stake-holes. The area of the stake-holes was somewhat irregular in width. For the most part this measured 1.5–2.5m, but in the west there

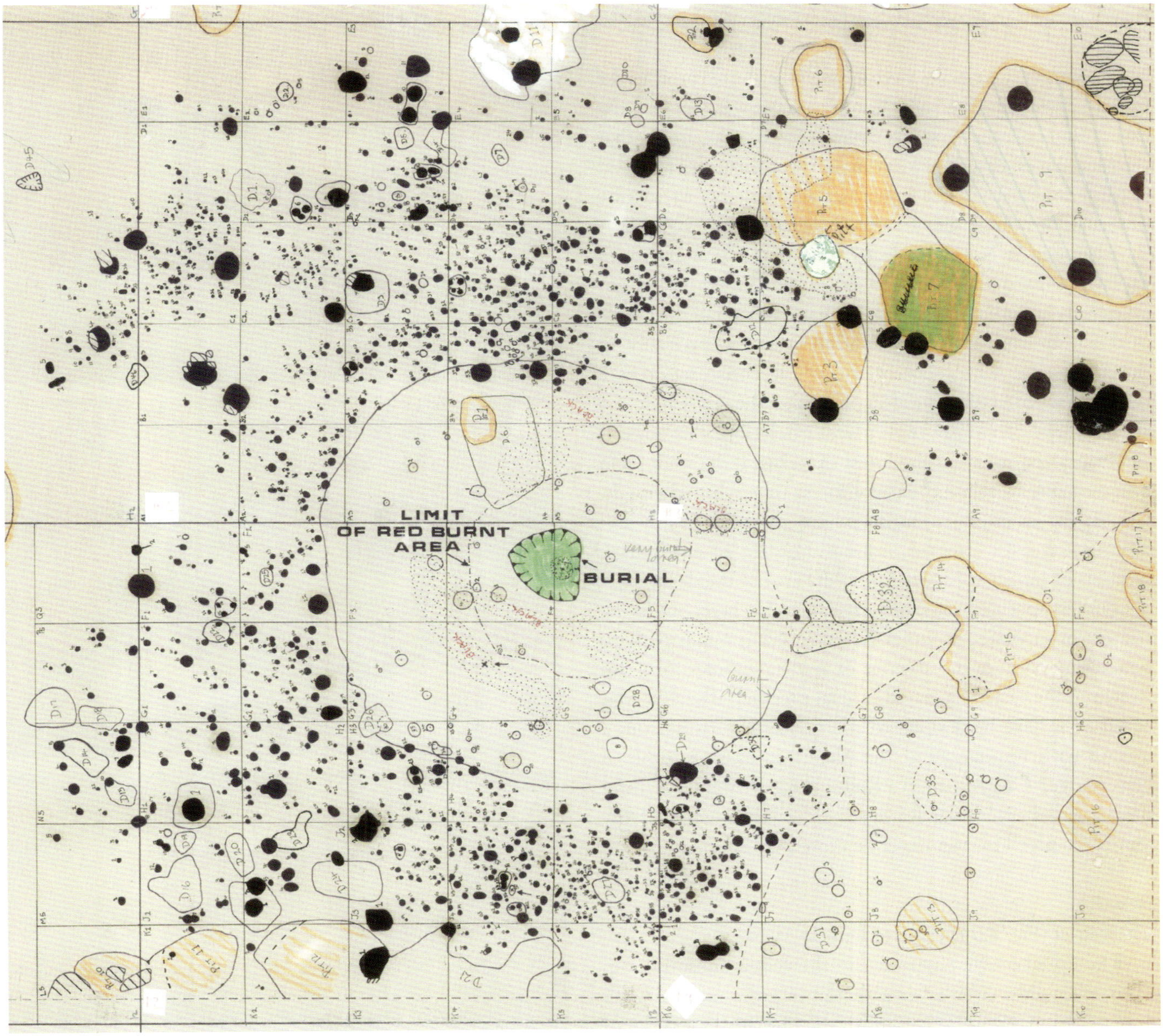

Fig. 2.95—Interim working plan of the stake-holes within the centre of Ring-ditch 2 (Sqs H1, H2, H3, I1, I2 and I3).

was a short length where it was scarcely 1m wide.

No fewer than 1,501 tightly packed stake-holes were brought to light, often separated from one another by no more than a few centimetres. Most were 3–5cm in diameter but a small number reached diameters of up to 12cm. Depths varied from a few centimetres to 15cm in a small number of examples. They were almost universally filled with a fine grey silt-like material, leaving uncertainty as to whether the original stakes had rotted *in situ* or had been physically removed.

The purpose of this curious arrangement is wholly mysterious. Although the holes were closely spaced, no overlapping was observed. This may well indicate that most, if not all, were in existence at the same time. In this regard, however, the varying dimensions and depths of the stake-holes (presumably indicating that the uprights projected to varying heights) remain puzzling. While not impossible, it is difficult to envisage them as representing the erection over time of successive constructions. The holes were all vertical-sided, so that if they were, indeed, contemporary it must be envisaged that a dense forest of upright stakes once surrounded the burial area.

The larger stake-holes were loosely distributed around the burial area within the stake 'forest' but, as was so often the case at Rathgall, there was no obvious pattern. Assuming that the stake-holes, or a significant majority of them, are regarded as contemporary, the question arises as to whether a structure of secular or non-secular activity is represented.

Although it is axiomatic to state that our inability to explain a particular archaeological phenomenon is not necessarily an indication of non-secular character, it does seem in this instance that the explanation lies, most probably, in the latter area. The focus of the whole construction is a burial—not merely a burial deposit, but the site where the actual burial ceremony took place. Encircling this zone—surely a sacred zone—is the forest of stakes. It does not seem unreasonable to relate the stake forest to the burial rituals. Could, for example, mourners have inserted freshly cut saplings into the ground around the area of the burial, symbols of transient life enclosing the area of the dead?

Endless speculation is, of course, possible here, but in the context of suggested complex burial rituals it might perhaps be relevant to note the absence of any stake-holes for a 3m stretch in the east. The sacred funeral precinct, if such it was, could thus have been open to the rays of the rising sun, a feature with resonances at the Neolithic passage tomb of Newgrange, Co. Meath (O'Kelly 1982). Might we infer similar ritual activity at Rathgall, although on a decidedly humbler scale? This can never be more than speculation.

Burial 2

This burial (Fig. 2.94) came to light in 1974.

The burial pit first appeared in the yellow subsoil in Sq. J3 as a roughly circular area of sandy grey material with dimensions of 97cm by 1.06m. In the immediate vicinity of this grey area there were several stones of natural origin, as well as two which clearly were not. These were embedded in the grey soil, projecting slightly above the surface. The larger of the two stones, when removed, proved to be flat-bottomed with rounded ends and a slightly gabled top. Its maximum width was 52cm and it was 22cm in greatest thickness. It lay slightly off-centre in the eastern part of the pit and had been carefully placed on its flat surface.

The removal of this boulder revealed the upper portion of a pit with sides sloping very slightly inwards. It was completely filled with the same grey material that was first exposed on the surface. A single sherd of coarse pottery was recovered from this grey fill, near the edge of the pit (E84:8478). A flat slab of elongated lozenge shape was revealed 5cm further down. Its greatest dimensions were 42cm by 53cm and it was 9cm thick. All its surfaces were regularly flat. When it first appeared, this slab was embedded in the grey filling material, as was the larger stone which had lain above it.

Fig. 2.96—(a) Burial 2 during excavation, (b) with vessel E84:8484 *in situ*, and (c) filled with pyre remains (Sq. J3, looking north).

Fig. 2.97—Ceramic vessel E84:8484 from Burial 2 (photo: John Sunderland).

Fig. 2.98—(a) Burial 3 before excavation, appearing as a black ring (Sq. H3, looking north-east). (b) Burial 3 after removal of secondary fill and sectioned (Sq. H3, looking north).

Upon removal of the slab, the slightly crushed circular rim of a pottery vessel was revealed (E84:8484; Fig. 2.96). It had been placed upright in a flat-bottomed, circular pit dug into the base of the larger pit. The former, 30cm in diameter and 15cm deep, had been carefully dug to mirror closely the size and shape of the pot. The base of the pit, which was somewhat uneven, had been levelled with a filling of grey silt-like material, on which the vessel stood.

The pot (Fig. 2.97), which was 15cm in height, projected slightly above the level of the basal pit. It was packed to the brim with black material consisting, for the most part, of charcoal and burnt bones. Black, burnt material, containing tiny flecks of burnt human bone, was also packed around it, again to the level of the rim, so that the outer and inner packing provided a continuous level surface. There can thus be little doubt that the packing material had been scraped up from the funeral pyre. The slab, which had been placed directly on the rim, rested also on this black material, and when it was lifted the outline of the vessel was clearly evident as a circular black stain on its underside.

The bones from the vessel represented the well-burnt remains of a female of indeterminate age (section 3.16).[30] *The bones provided a date of 1050–845 cal. BC (GrA-22304).*

Burial 3

This feature (Figs 2.94 and 2.98) appeared in Sq. H3 in what was initially termed Pit 4 (cut into Pit 5). It was oval in shape, with an evenly concave base. Its dimensions were 32cm by 37cm and it had a maximum depth of 13cm. A uniform layer of black organic material, with a maximum thickness of 3cm, covered the sides and base. On this lay a layer of hard grey material which contained burnt bones. The latter have been identified as adult human but appeared not to represent the complete remains of a cremated individual. It is thus by no means certain that this was a formal burial. A single sherd of coarse pottery (E84:8463) was recovered from grey silting approximately 5cm above the sealing stone for the burial.[31]

Two radiocarbon dates were obtained on charcoal samples from the pit, one on Quercus, *1515–1396 cal. BC (GrN-27118), and the other on* Corylus, *1313–1017 cal. BC (GrA-23353).*

Pit 32

Post-excavation analysis identified a further, although minute, deposit of human bone in the fill of Pit 32 in Sq. G1/H2 (see section 3.16).

Pits within the Ring-ditch 2 enclosure

Within the area enclosed by Ring-ditch 2, apart from the many post- and stake-holes referred to above, there were a considerable number of pits of varying types, as well as a number of shallow depressions. Many of the latter are probably natural hollows in the ground surface which, over time, filled with the detritus of occupation (Table 2.10), but some are likely to have been artificially created.

The precise chronological relationships between the various pits and depressions, and between them and the ditch, are in general difficult to establish with any great degree of certainty. It is noteworthy, however, that almost all the pits and depressions, especially the former, were situated in the band between the ditch and the central zone of stake-holes discussed above. Similarly, it is striking that these only rarely overlapped and that outside Ring-ditch 2, apart from a concentration in the east, there were very few pits.

A total of 84 pits were excavated within the zone created by Ring-ditch 2 (Figs 2.87 and 2.99). Of these, Pit 31 was exceptional and is discussed separately below. The rest of the pits varied considerably in dimensions but were generally 20–40cm deep.

In general, the pits were filled with varied layers of redeposited natural soil, darkish occupation material or grey silt which sometimes contained charcoal and animal bones, some also containing finds (Table 2.10). Stones were present in the filling of some pits, but this was uncommon and, apart from Pit 46[32] and especially Pit 25, there were no indications of any systematic infilling. The pits appear in general to have been filled over time through natural agencies. A few yielded scraps of coarse pottery. Pit 87, situated a short distance outside the ditched enclosure on the east in H4, stood apart from the rest, as it contained no less than 50 coarse potsherds.

A small group of pits contained clay mould fragments.[33] Pit 7 in H3 contained two coarse potsherds and one nondescript clay mould fragment (E84:8386, 8387). Even more important was Pit 20 in G2. This was an irregular oval, 1.25m by 75cm, with a maximum depth of about 20cm, which contained 22 clay mould fragments and fragments of crucible 2 (E84:6901, 6902, 7309; Fig. 3.42). Among the larger pits, Pit 6 in H3 was subcircular in plan, 75cm in diameter and about 28cm deep. It was filled with grey silt which contained one rim sherd and one mould fragment. Pit 21 in G2 and Pit 23 also contained mould fragments (note that there is also a Pit 21 in 11/I1). It may be significant that these pits were located immediately adjacent to Hearth 15, which also contained mould fragments (see below), and further moulds were found in a depression in the area and a single fragment on the central pyre area.

Outside this cluster, only a small group of pits in K4 and K6 contained mould fragments. Pit 272 contained a larger number of coarse pottery and mould fragments, and Pit 241 in K6 (not on plan) also contained a mould fragment and a pottery sherd.

Several of the pits possessed what appeared, in each instance, to be a lining of black organic material (e.g. nos 1, 5, 7, 15, 17, 25, 58[34]), and three of these (nos 5, 7, 15) had regularly flat bases and steep, carefully dug sides.

Pit 5 had dimensions of 1.07m by 87cm. Its sides were carefully dug, sloping slightly inwards to a circular, flat base some 75cm in diameter. It was 28–30cm deep. Apart from an area of yellowish, redeposited natural material in the south-west, the pit had a substantial lining of black organic material which was 12.5cm thick on the base and 5–7cm thick around the sides. The upper portion of this pit was filled with brownish-grey material, some of which was fine, the rest coarser. Several small stones were present in the upper and lower layers. This pit had been dug into Pit 7.

Pit 58

Pit 58, immediately west of Pit 31 and Burial 2, first showed up as an oval of grey material with traces of black organic matter at the edges. Following excavation, it emerged as a carefully dug pit, with dimensions at the mouth of 88cm by 1.12cm. It was more or less funnel-shaped, 1.22–1.25m in depth, narrowing to a flat, roughly circular base which was about 75cm in diameter. It had an upper layer of sterile, brownish-grey silted material which, in its lower levels, contained streaks of light yellow natural soil. This lay on a thick organic layer of spongy blackish-brown material which extended around the sides and upwards to the rim of the pit. It was noticeable that this layer contained more stones than elsewhere, though they were by no means prolific and were relatively small. It was 15cm above the base and was 25cm in greatest thickness. Layers of grey silt mixed with patches of yellow soil in its lowest levels occurred in the base. The pit only yielded a single find, a potsherd (E84:8417), which occurred in the upper grey silt. This sherd belonged to a group that could not be unambiguously identified but may be of medieval date.

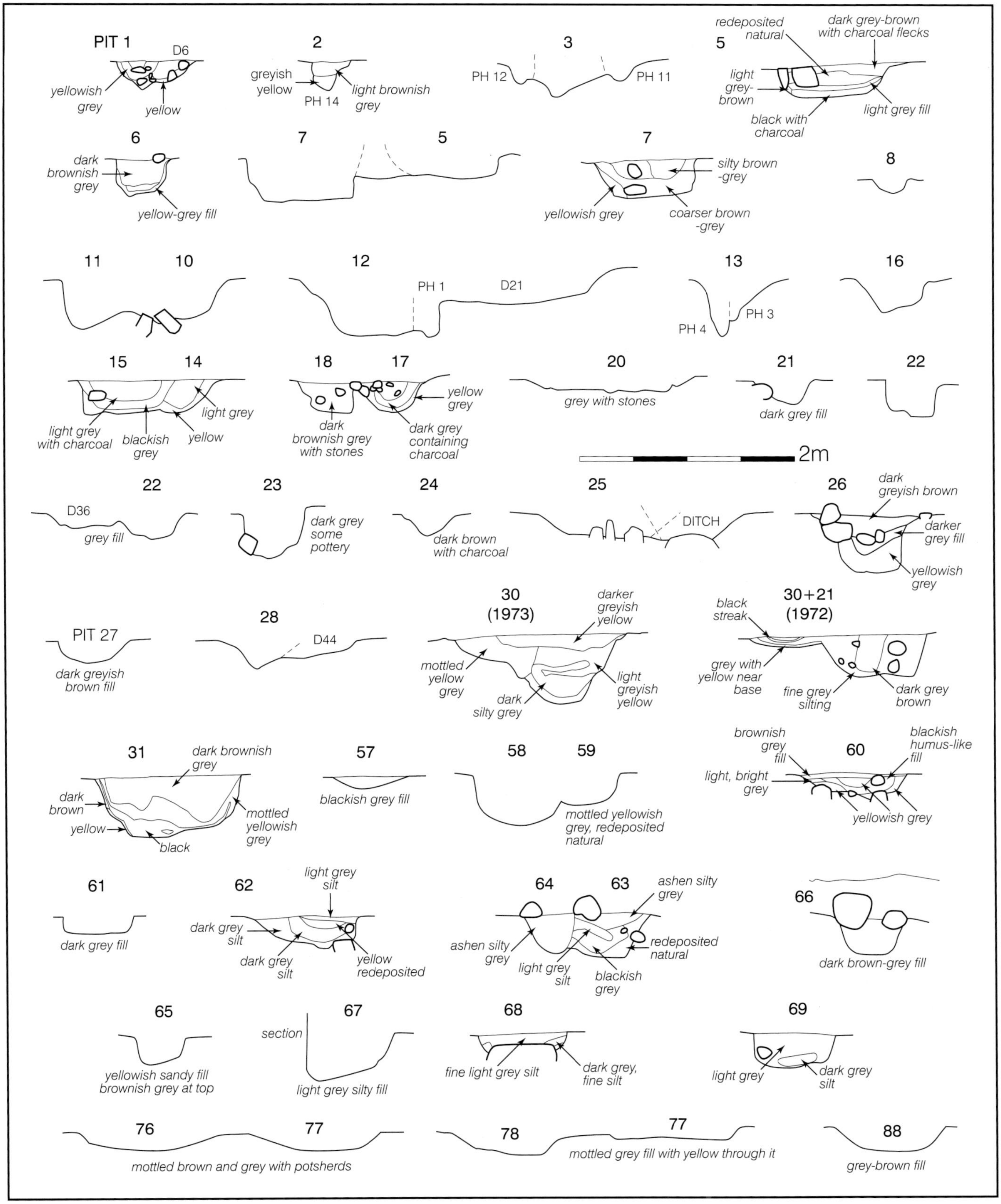

Fig. 2.99—Sections of pits in the area enclosed by Ring-ditch 2.

Pit 25

Pit 25 in Sq. G1 had been dug into the side of Ring-ditch 2, on the interior, when the latter was already well silted. A radiocarbon date of cal. AD 590–880 (SI-1479) was obtained on its black lining.

Bronze hoard (Pit 31)

This pit (Figs 2.87, 2.99 and 2.100), which straddled Sqs J2 and J3, was situated in the southern part of the burial enclosure, south-west of Burial 2. It appeared initially as a regularly circular area of greyish material, 1.37m in diameter. In places around its perimeter a narrow band of darker material was discernible. In this were a number of small stones and pebbles, some of which projected slightly above the surface. Upon excavation, the pit was revealed as having carefully dug sides which sloped gently inwards to a flat, two-tier base. It was for the most part some 40cm deep, but in one area this increased by up to 15cm.

The filling of this pit was uncomplicated. A fine, dark, brownish-grey material occurred in the upper half, merging unevenly with a more mottled, yellowish-grey material lower

Fig. 2.100—(a) Pit 31, which contained the bronze hoard, before excavation (Sqs J2/J3). (b) Pit 31, sectioned (Sqs J2/J3).

Fig. 2.101—Spearhead E84:8345 from Pit 31 (photo: John Sunderland).

Fig. 2.102—Sword blade fragment E84:8346 from Pit 31 (photo: John Sunderland).

Fig. 2.103—Chisel E84:8344 from Pit 31 (photo: John Sunderland).

down. The sides and base were covered with a black organic material in which occasional pebbles and small patches of yellow soil occurred. This layer, which decreased slightly in thickness towards the top, had a maximum depth of about 18cm and was thickest where the pit was deepest.

At the centre of the pit, approximately 40cm deep in the mottled yellowish-grey material, three bronze objects were found, all lying within a few centimetres of each other and at the same level. These consisted of a spearhead (E84:8345; Figs 3.31 and 2.101), a fragment of a sword blade (E84:8346; Figs 3.31 and 2.102) and a small chisel (E84:8344; Figs 3.31 and 2.103; Table 2.10). No trace of any organic container in which these objects might have been buried was found, nor was there any indication of a prepared hollow in the fill of the pit.

It seems implausible to regard these three objects as having been lost or, indeed, as representing no more than discarded rubbish. Bronze was a valuable commodity which could be recycled with relative ease. Deliberate deposition, either for practical reasons or with ritual intent, must therefore be seen as the likely explanation for the presence of these objects together in a pit. The bronzes could have been hidden as valued personal equipment or with a view to recycling (or, indeed, both). The cut blade fragment could very likely have been intended for smelting. In addition, the chisel has clearly been used for fine tooling which, in all probability, was on metal (see Chapter 3, section 3.6) rather than on wood. It seems, therefore, that, while a ritual context is not impossible, at a site with so much evidence for bronze-working it is perhaps most plausible that these bronzes had been deposited with a view to recovery and reuse in the context of metalworking. A single sherd of Bronze Age coarseware (E84:8390) was included in the upper grey fill of the pit.

Hearth 15

Evidence for the existence of this feature (originally labelled Pit 9; Figs 2.42, 2.104 and 2.105) emerged at an early phase of the excavation when the covering brown humus in Sq. H3 had been removed. It showed up initially as a roughly oval area of greyish-black material, approximately 2.2m by 1.8m, which extended into Sq. H3 for a distance of some 1.6m. Upon further excavation it became evident that the blackish zone covered two separate pits, nos 9 and 20,[35] but it was evident that these two pits were contemporary. The presence of numerous clay mould fragments as well as coarse potsherds in Pit 20 is thus of relevance in discussing the function of Hearth 15.

After the removal of the black covering layer, what came to be Pit 9 emerged as an oval zone of greyish material within which there was a noticeable concentration of moderately sized stones. Along one edge traces of black organic material were discernible. Upon excavation it was revealed to be rectangular in shape with regularly rounded corners. It had maximum dimensions of 1.5m by 2.4m. Its sides, which were nearly vertical, had been dug with considerable care. It had an almost perfectly level base with a consistent depth of 55cm.

The upper layer of the pit consisted of a silty, grey-brown material which contained a number of stones and small boulders, some of which projected above the surface of the pit filling. This layer, representing the final infilling after the abandonment of the pit, was generally about 20cm thick, apart from one area where its depth was almost 30cm.

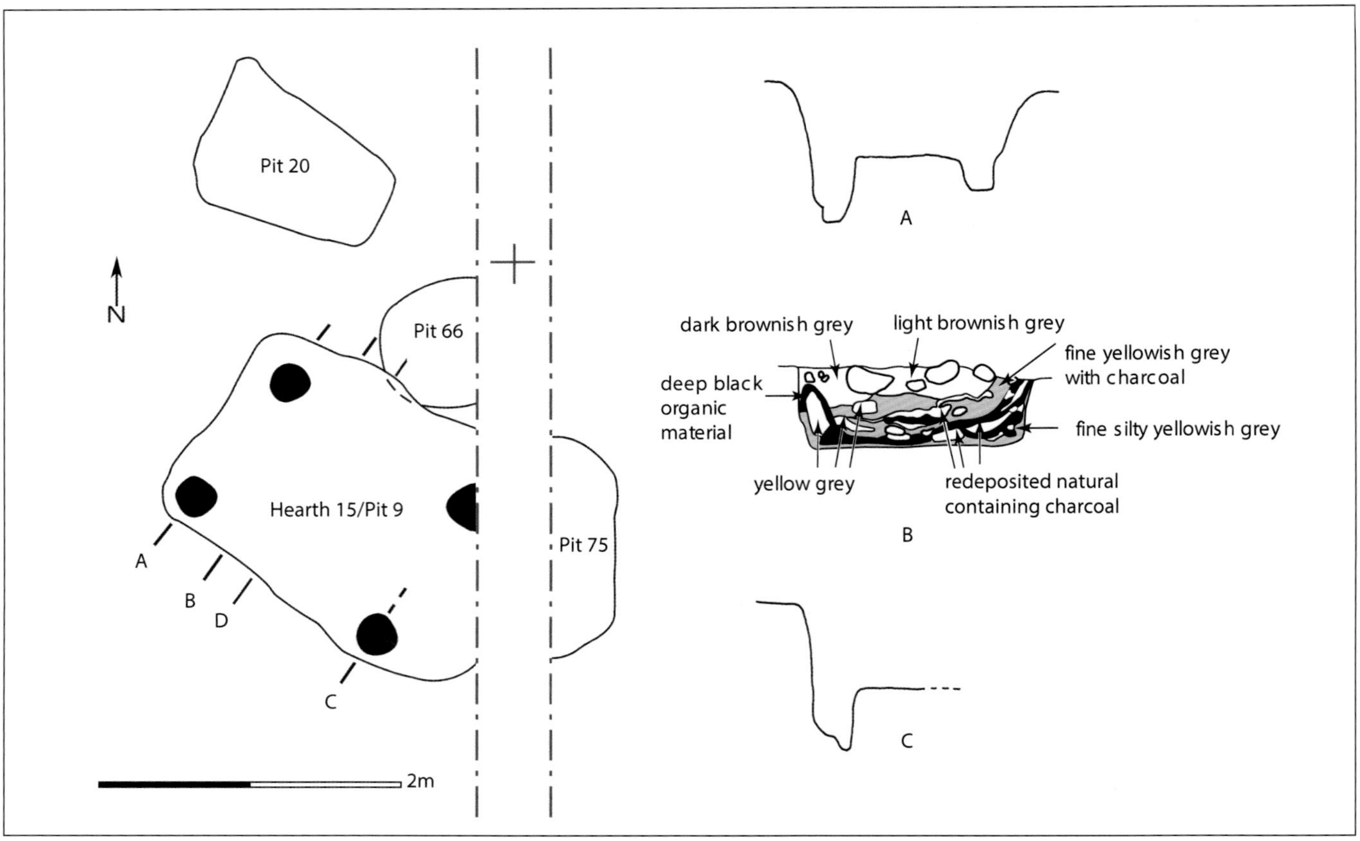

Fig. 2.104—Plan and section of Hearth 15.

The lower levels consisted of a series of layers of yellowish, redeposited natural soil mixed with charcoal fragments. Interspersed with these yellow layers were discontinuous layers of black organic material. The lowest level, however, unlike the other levels, entirely covered the base and sides of the pit almost to the lip. It consisted of a thick, black organic layer, generally 10–12cm thick but reaching a thickness of almost 25cm in the north-west.

When the lowest layer of black material had been removed, four circular post-holes, each 25cm in diameter, were discovered, one in each corner of the pit. In the north-west they had been inserted tightly into the rounded corners, while in the south-east they were a short distance in from the corners. The post-holes, on the long axis of the pit, were 1.2–1.3m distant from one another, while transversely they were 75cm apart. All were vertical and had flat bottoms. The two along the south-western side were 42cm and 44cm deep respectively, while that in the north-east, with a depth of only 22cm, was considerably shallower.

The fourth post-hole, which showed in the baulk in the south-east corner, was the most informative. From this it was evident that the insertion of the posts and the creation of the lower organic lining were contemporary actions. Over time, a second and in places a third black layer accumulated, each separated from the other by a sterile layer of yellow, redeposited natural soil. There are no indications that the posts were ever removed and thus the brownish material filling each post-hole probably represents the rotted stumps.

The post showing in the baulk section (Fig. 2.105e) seems to have lasted longer than the other three. It appears that its stump survived to a higher level than the others and its post-pipe survived almost to the top of the pit through the yellow sealing layer, thus indicating a surviving post-hole depth here of almost 75cm. Finally, the upper layers of the pit, with all the posts decayed, were filled with brownish organic material and with grey silt, along with stones of small and medium size.

This post-hole, as outlined by Raftery above, demonstrates the contemporaneity of the burning activity and the post-holes. In contrast to the other post-holes, however, it also shows that posts were replaced, contary to Raftery's interpretation above. It is impossible to tell whether the original post burned in situ *or was removed, as the charcoal may have subsided into a post void after*

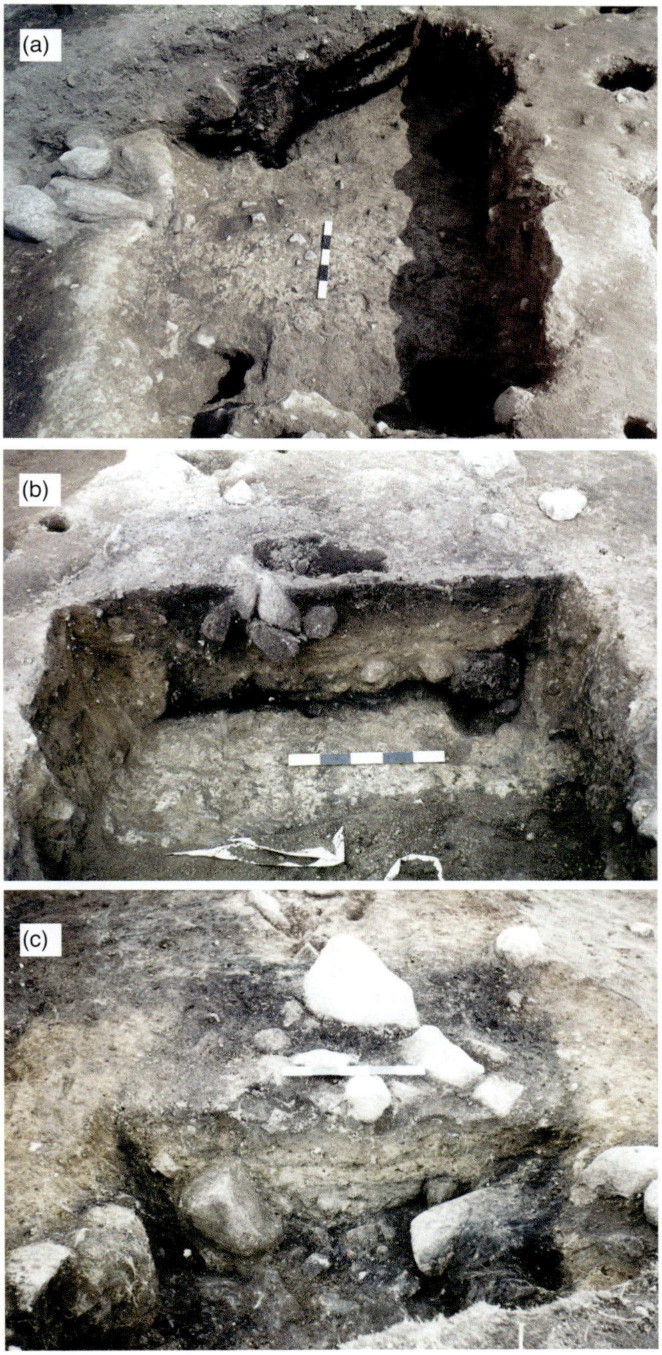

Fig. 2.105—(a) Hearth 15 after excavation, looking east, and showing section in baulk (Sqs H3/H4). (b) Hearth 15, section B, showing vitrification on pit base, charcoal fill and post-holes (Sqs H3/H4, looking north-west). (c) Hearth 15, section D, showing stone-rich layers (Sqs H3/H4, looking north-west). (d) Hearth 15, with post-holes emptied and baulk section showing (Sqs H3/H4, looking north). (e) Section of Hearth 15 with post-hole excavated in the baulk profile (Sqs H3/H4, looking east).

its removal, but it is clear that a second post was inserted when the layers of charcoal were already in situ. *The fact that the secondary post was placed in exactly the same location as the first would suggest reuse of the feature, i.e. episodic use of these pyre hearths as discussed in Chapter 6.*

The lower blackish fill of this pit contained six coarse potsherds, two mould fragments and fragments of a crucible. One of the mould fragments occurred in the upper greyish fill (Table 2.10). This must have filtered down from above after the post had rotted.

2.4.4 The post circle

The zone of intensive industrial activity discussed above in Area 2 was, as already described, bounded by a series of post-holes, to an extent linear, which extended more or less diagonally in a north-easterly direction, in the cobbled zone, in B and B1. It is difficult not to regard this line of post-holes as representing a demarcation feature of some sort which formed the southern boundary to the industrial/occupational complex.[36] As regards the latter, it was striking that there were no pits or post-holes south of this demarcation line. In

Table 2.10—Artefacts recovered from pit features in Area 3.

Feature	Sq. no.	Artefact type	Artefact no.
Pit 3	K7	Glass bead fragment	E84:9372
Pit 7	H3	Coarse pottery	E84:8386
		Mould fragment	E84:8387
Pit 9 = Hearth 15	H3	Mould fragment	E84:8359, 8462
		Crucible fragment	E84:8394
		Coarse pottery	E84:8395, 8360, 8362, 8406
Pit 10	I1	Coarse pottery	E84:8384, 8389
Pit 11	I2	Coarse pottery	E84:8393
Pit 19	G2	Coarse pottery	E84:7506
Pit 20	G2	Crucible fragment	E84:6901, 6902, 6905, 7155, 7156, 7157, 7309
		Mould fragment	E84:6903, 6904, 6940, 7331a–b, 7221, 7330a–b, 7332, 7333, 7334, 7335, 7337a–e
		Mould fragment	E84:6906
		Coarse pottery	E84:6907, 6939, 6981, 7329a–g, 7336, 7338
Pit 21	K6	Mould fragment	E84:9594
Pit 23	G2	Coarse pottery	E84:7520a–e, 7521, 7522, 7523
		Mould fragment	E84:7524
Pit 26	H1	Coarse pottery	E84:8405
Pit 31	J3	Chisel, bronze	E84:8344
		Coarse pottery	E84:8390
		Socketed spearhead, bronze	E84:8345
		Sword fragment, bronze	E84:8346
Pit 32	G1	Disc, stone	E84:8404
Pit 56	J3/J2	Coarse pottery	E84:8419a–b
Pit 57	J2	Coarse pottery	E84:8410a–b, 8411
	J1/J2	Saddle quern	E84:8477
Pit 58	J2	Medieval pottery	E84:8417
Pit 65	H3	Bipolar core	E84:8487
Pit 73	J4	Coarse pottery	E84:8644
Pit 75	H4	Coarse pottery	E84:8638, 8640, 8641, 8655, 8637, 8639
Pit 76	H4	Leinster Cooking Ware	E84:8656
Pit 87	H4	Coarse pottery	E84:8678, 8679, 8707
Pit 88	I4	Coarse pottery	E84:8715
Pit 241	K6	Coarse pottery	E84:9622
		Mould fragment	E84:9623
Pit 271	K4	Coarse pottery	E84:9516, 9517, 9524a–e, 9539, 9540, 9541, 9542
		Hone	E84:9518
Pit 272	K4	Coarse pottery	E84:9553a–b, 9556, 9558, 9560, 9583.1, 9597, 9598, 9613, 9632, 9635, 9638, 9639, 9559, 9557, 9633, 9637, 9554, 9634, 9636
		Regular flake debitage	E84:9561
		Mould fragment	E84:9583
		Mould fragment	E84:9599
		Natural stone	E84:9600
Pit 273	K6	Coarse pottery	E84:9618, 9619, 9620
Pit 275	K6	Coarse pottery	E84:9614, 9615
		Dublin-type coarseware	E84:9616

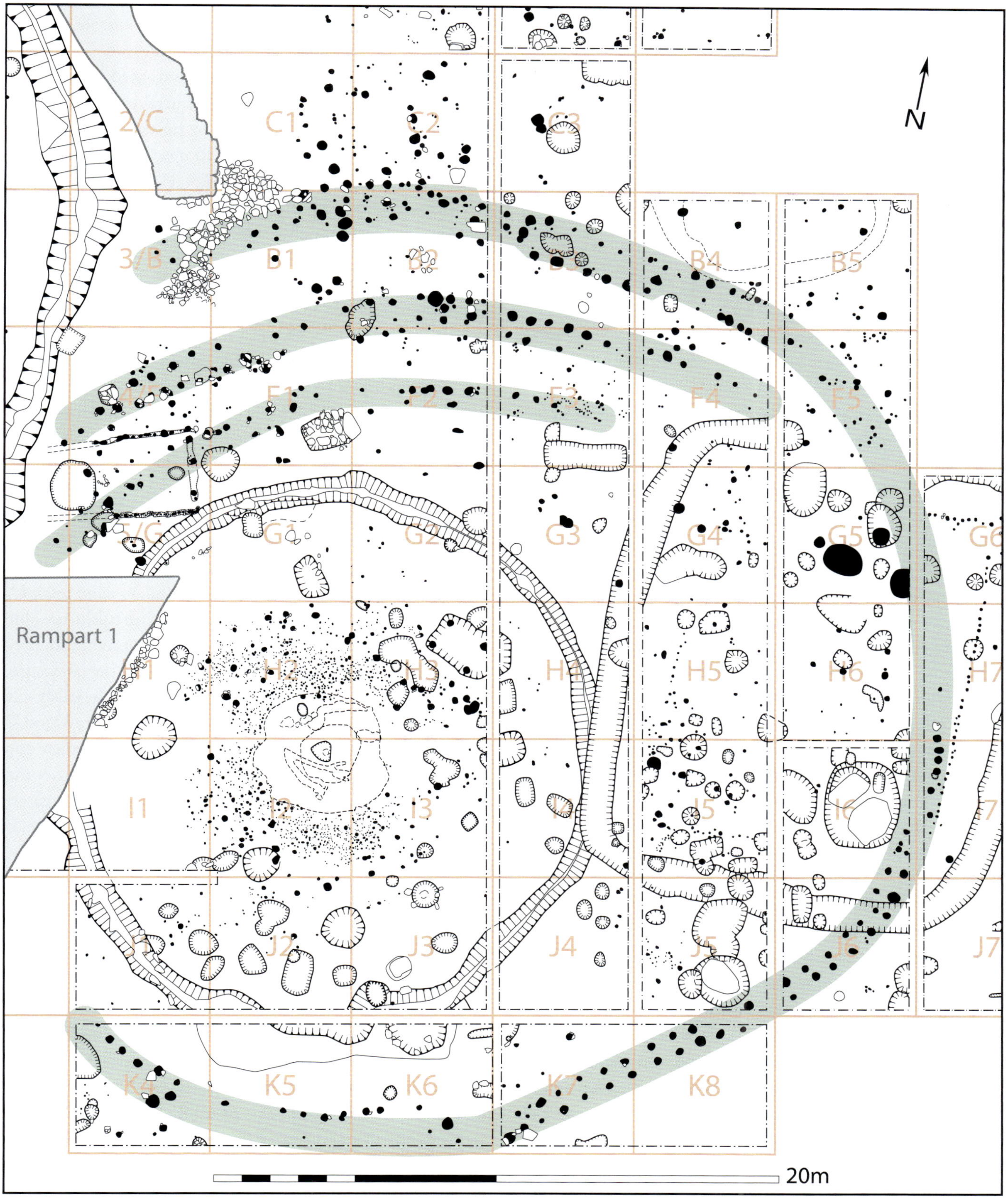

Fig. 2.106—Possible groupings of post alignments in Area 2.

Fig. 2.107—Double post row in Sqs K7 and K8, looking south.

contrast, however, there were large numbers of post-holes, some of impressive size, scattered across the east of the metalworking complex, but these are unlikely to belong to a single phase—a matter which is once more rendered exceptionally difficult by the particularly poor stratigraphy in this zone.

Of the many post-holes (excluding those under the grey layer referred to above) there is a hint that some, at least, were orientated on the burial enclosure (Fig. 2.106). The arcs they form are not consistently concentric with the latter, however, apart from a short stretch on the south, and to a lesser extent on the north-west. Here they were consistently at a 3–5m distance from Ring ditch 2. In contrast, on the north-east, east and south-east the post-holes diverged significantly from the curve of Ring-ditch 2, reaching a distance from it of up to 11m. Interestingly, however, and perhaps significantly, it was here that the greatest concentration of pits in this area occurred, within the zone enclosed by the possible stockade (section 2.6).

The post-hole arrangements are tantalisingly incomplete and it is difficult to isolate patterns with any great confidence, and, in fact, to separate them in B from the general cluster of post-holes that here may obliterate the line. It is strikingly noticeable that the post rows encircling Ring-ditch 2 are in places doubled (Fig. 2.107). This is evident in Sq. F, and possibly also in the eastern part of F2 and in the western area of F3, but it is especially noteworthy in an extended arc on the east and south, extending from I7 to K7. Here a curve of regularly paired post-holes occurred which was comparable with the small arc of doubled posts in Sq. F. From the south-west corner of K7 these posts extended in a line as far as the south-west corner of J6, at which point they gradually curved north-eastwards, coming to an end, as far as can be determined, in the north-west corner of I7.

In the K4–K6 zone post-holes continued in a single, somewhat irregular line around the burial complex. In the south-east corner of K6 the line of posts seemed to turn slightly to the south-east, possibly to meet the more regular double row to the south-east in K7. Hypothetically these features are deliberate, and a gap between the two lines, 75cm wide and flanked on either side by a post-hole slightly larger than elsewhere, may have been an original entrance feature. The post-holes in the south-west, however, were shallower and less pronounced than those forming the paired group in the south-east so that this must remain uncertain.

Between the end of the double posts in I7 and the end of the row of posts in F4 there was a space of about 15m where post-holes were absent. This is the area where the entrance to the medieval enclosure occurred (section 2.5, below), so it could be that earlier post-holes had been obliterated by medieval activity.

Centrally within this gap, however, and situated along an imaginary arc linking the post-hole lines that end in F4 and I7, were two substantial post-holes, PH 1 (1.12m in diameter) and PH 8 (63cm in diameter) (*not labelled on plan; probably refers to the large post-holes in G5*), 1.08m apart. Is it possible that these represent some sort of entrance feature? If so, they must indicate a stratigraphically early date for the enclosure, a date earlier than the burial ditch which very obviously cut into the grey layer under which these post-holes were found.[37]

It should be noted, however, that in the east, where the suggested post-hole enclosure diverges considerably from the ring-ditch, the space between the two contained the greatest concentration of pits, contrasting with the virtual absence of pits of any significance elsewhere in the excavated area here. The matter is complex, but it seems more likely that Ring-ditch 2, the suggested post ring and the pit concentration between the two in the east are all broadly contemporary. It is nonetheless strange that there should have been regularly spaced double posts in some sections (notably in the south-east) and single posts—or, indeed, no posts—in other sections. The irregular—or perhaps roughly hexagonal—nature of the enclosing post ring is also strange and is scarcely typical of prehistoric enclosures elsewhere.

An interesting alternative possibility is that the posts, arcing gently through F4 to F, formed the southern side of an approach to the central enclosure, with the posts discussed earlier, which formed the southern boundary to the metalworking complex in B/C, representing the northern side

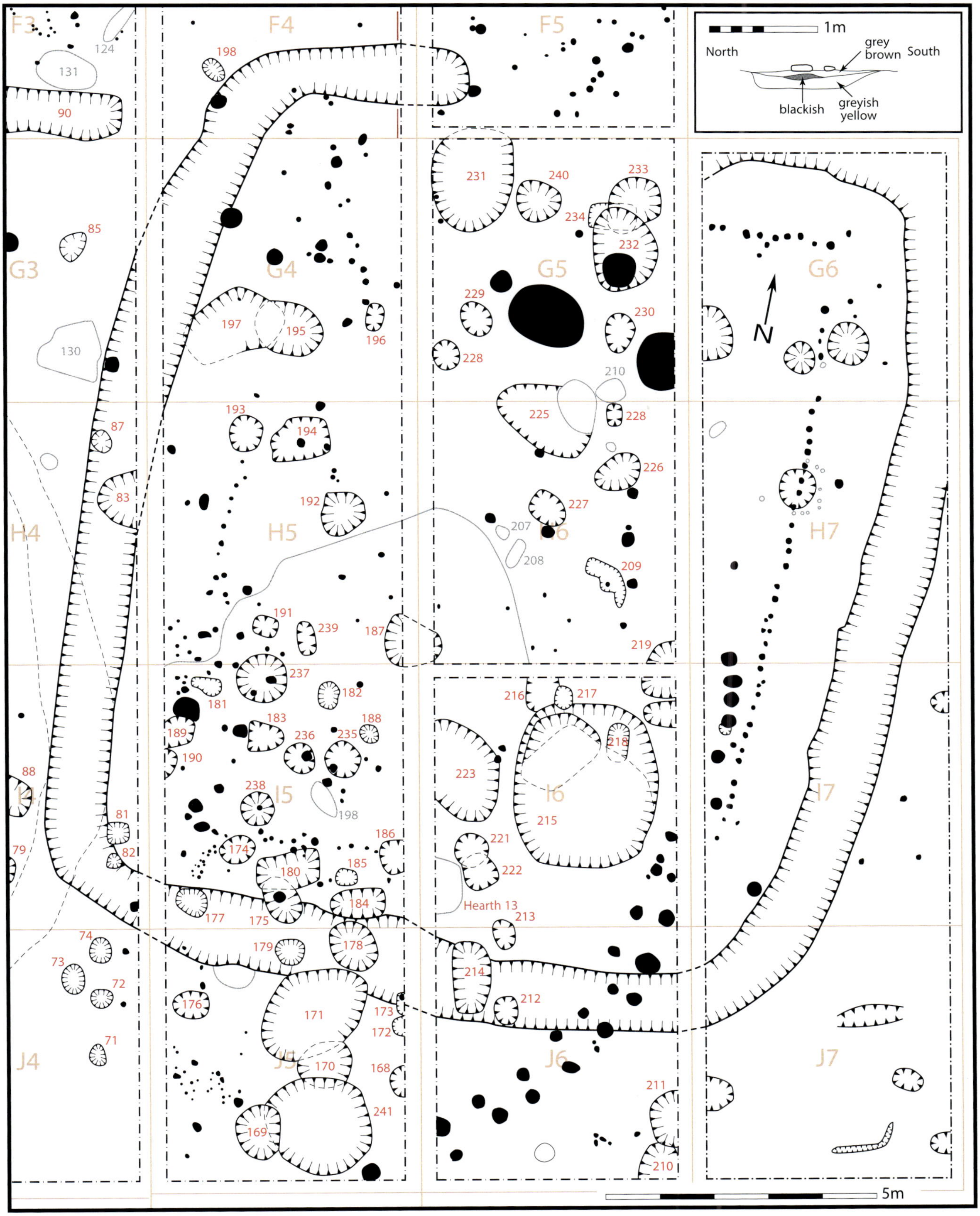

Fig. 2.108—The medieval house in Area 4.

of such an approach. In F4 and B3 the two suggested lines of posts were in fact more or less parallel and about 2m apart and, as mentioned above, pits were rare in this zone. To the west of this the 'corridor' thus formed gradually increased in width from 2m to 4m as it approached the ditch to the inner enclosure. A possible problem with this hypothesis is that the cobbling in Sq. 3/B–B1, which is undoubtedly associated with the metalworking activity, appeared to extend across most of the square and thus across this hypothetical approach to Ring-ditch 1.

See Chapter 3, section 3.9, for a discussion of the metalworking deposits in this area. It is important to note that there appears to be more than one post row, suggesting potentially a sequence of enclosures. As noted above, the conflict of a hypothetical completed circle with Ring-ditch 1 is also potentially indicative of their chronological relationship.

Fig. 2.110—The enclosure trench before excavation in Sqs J6–I6 (looking north).

Fig. 2.111—The eastern side of the medieval house, looking south (Sqs G6, H7, I7 and J7).

2.5 AREA 4: THE MEDIEVAL ENCLOSED HOUSE
Caroline Sandes

To the east of the cashel and the Late Bronze Age burial complex a rectilinear trench was uncovered (Figs 2.108 and 2.109). It enclosed an area with internal dimensions of 15.63m by 12.88m, with the long axis running north–south. The trench had rounded corners and a flat base, and its width varied from 88cm to 1.25m. It was approximately 9cm deep, though it may have been at least double this originally, as the extensive ploughing that occurred on the hilltop would have reduced it considerably. The filling of the trench was a grey silt with some stones, and in some areas a clear stone infill (Fig. 2.110). A gap forming the entrance in the north side was 3.75m wide, though it may originally have been narrower. In the eastern side of the

Fig. 2.109—Enclosure trench of medieval house in Area 4, Sqs G4/F4 (looking north).

Fig. 2.112—The north-western corner of the enclosure trench and cluster of stake-holes in G4 and F4 (looking north-east).

trench were stones that averaged approximately 20cm in diameter. It is possible that this was a drainage trench, but there are some marked similarities between it and the foundation trenches of the medieval houses excavated at Lough Gur, Co. Limerick (Cleary 1982; 1983). Within this rectilinear enclosure at Rathgall, roughly parallel to the trench, was a row of stake-holes (Figs 2.110–2.112), with a break at the south-east corner and opposite the entrance. The stake-holes were 6–12cm in diameter and *c.* 1.25m from the internal edge of the trench. The dimensions of the maximum space enclosed by this feature were 12.75m by 9.88m. There was no evidence for a hearth, but this may have been destroyed by the later cultivation of the site. About twenty sherds of medieval pottery came from the trench.

This brief account and the accompanying illustrations are the only record of the medieval house that was uncovered in the east of the site. It was attempted to date the structure, but the radiocarbon dating of a sample from the bedding trench failed (UB-2349).

2.6 PITS IN AREAS 3 AND 4 OUTSIDE OF RING-DITCH 2

Barry Raftery

The following descriptions, along with their plan and section drawings, constitute the primary records of pits in Areas 3 and 4 outside Ring-ditch 2. Where pits discussed by Raftery could not be identified on drawings, this is noted.

Based on their distribution within the perimeter of the post alignment, Raftery suggests a Bronze Age date for most pits in Areas 3 and 4, despite their main concentration being in the zone of the medieval house in Area 4. The lack of medieval finds from these contexts supports this notion, with only Pits 188 and 176 and Hearth 13 in Sq. I5 and a second pit in G6[38] having produced a sherd of what is likely to be Leinster Cooking Ware. The concentration of medieval wares is otherwise, without exception, derived from topsoil contexts or the bedding trench of the medieval house (see section 2.5, above).

It is striking that those pits which Raftery singles out as having been filled with a primary deposit of charcoal-rich material are clustered in and immediately around I5, with one additional example in each of H5, I6 and J5. These deposits may be related to the burial activity as discussed below (Chapter 6), and their clustering immediately outside Ring-ditch 2 is striking. The size of some of the boulders deposited in some of these pits—in particular Pit 215—raises the question, however, of whether these should not be seen as having been deposited here after the medieval occupation of the area had ended. As is clearly visible in some site photographs, while some significant depth of material was removed, it is difficult to imagine that this amounted to deposits that would have covered the enormous size of the boulders.

2.6.1 Pits east of the burial enclosure

Outside the burial enclosure described above (Ring-ditch 2) many pits and post-holes of varying types came to light (Figs 2.113 and 2.114). It may obviously be assumed that not all these features are contemporary (though many, in fact, are likely to be), so that their original arrangement is difficult to determine. Within the mass of post-holes, a roughly hexagonal arrangement—in places doubled—might be isolated surrounding the burial precinct (*see 'the post alignment', above*). This enclosure, if such it was, diverged considerably in the east from Ring-ditch 2, leaving a space of about 10m between the two. While it is undated, it is notable, however, that pits were concentrated to the east and south-east of Ring-ditch 2 in the space bounded by the stockade. The only other pits of any note outside the enclosure occurred to the north of the ring-ditch, but there they were far fewer in number and were noticeably more scattered. Although most of the pits occurred within the zone defined by the rectangular medieval enclosure (see above), it is assumed that this is coincidental and that most, if not all, are of prehistoric date.

The pits (Table 2.11) varied considerably in their size and in the nature of their filling material. Most, however, were circular or ovoid in shape. Most frequently (as elsewhere), pits were first revealed during excavation as grey stains in the yellow subsoil, from which stones of varying sizes, and in varying numbers, sometimes projected. Occasionally the pits appeared as patches of darker soil or, less often, of black organic material. In plan these patches were usually regularly circular or oval. In the course of the excavation, as distinct from those features designated as pits, those referred to as 'hollows' also occurred in some numbers. The latter were shallow depressions of varying outline deemed to have been of natural origin. Of course, it may be that some of the very small pits were similarly of entirely natural origin or were nothing more than filled-in hollows left after the extraction of stones. Nevertheless, there were, in fact, pits of quite modest size which overlapped one another and were thus certainly of artificial origin.

A total of 78 pits came to light in the area here under consideration. Most were of modest dimensions, less than 1m

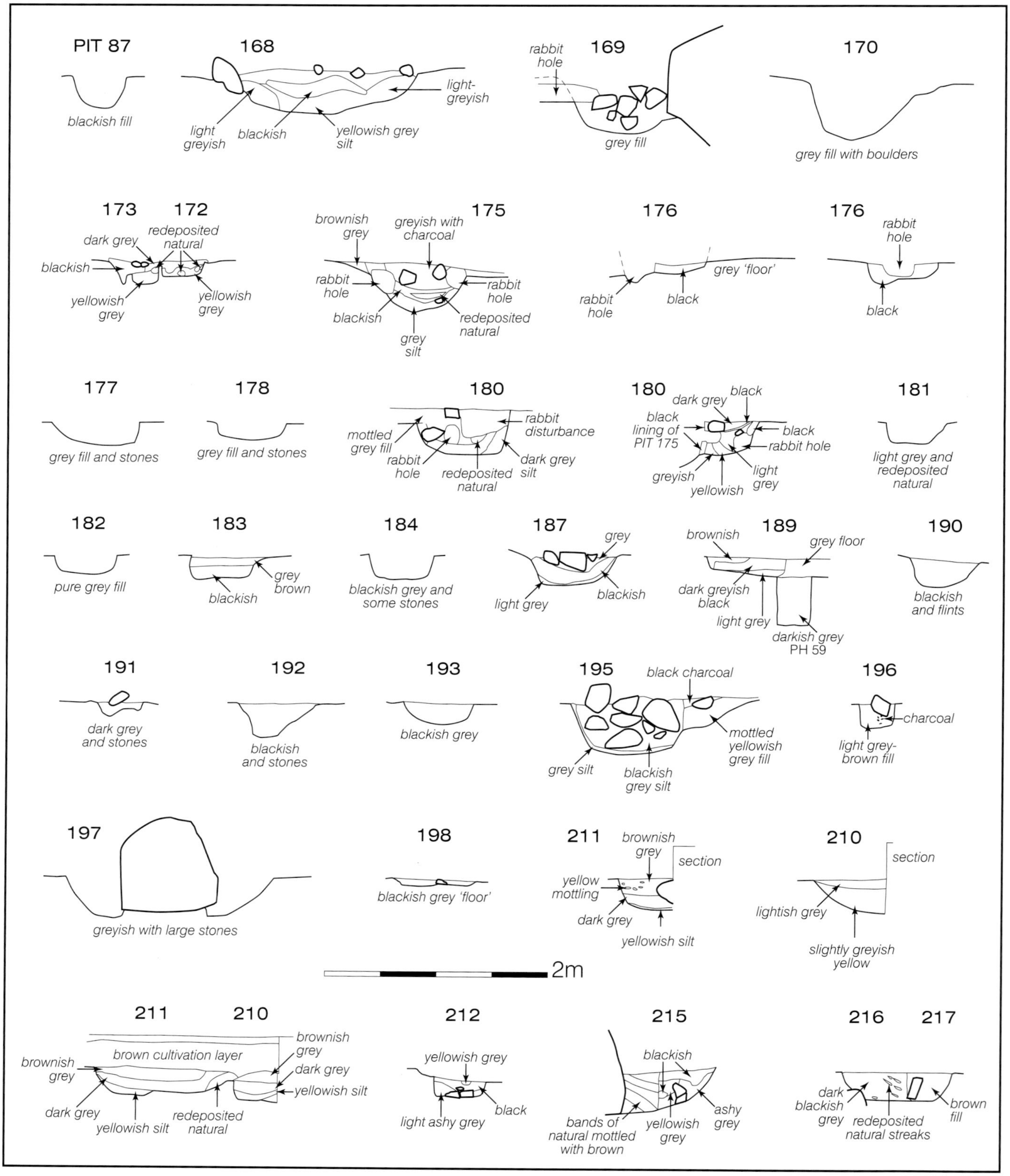

Fig. 2.113—Sections of pits in Area 4.

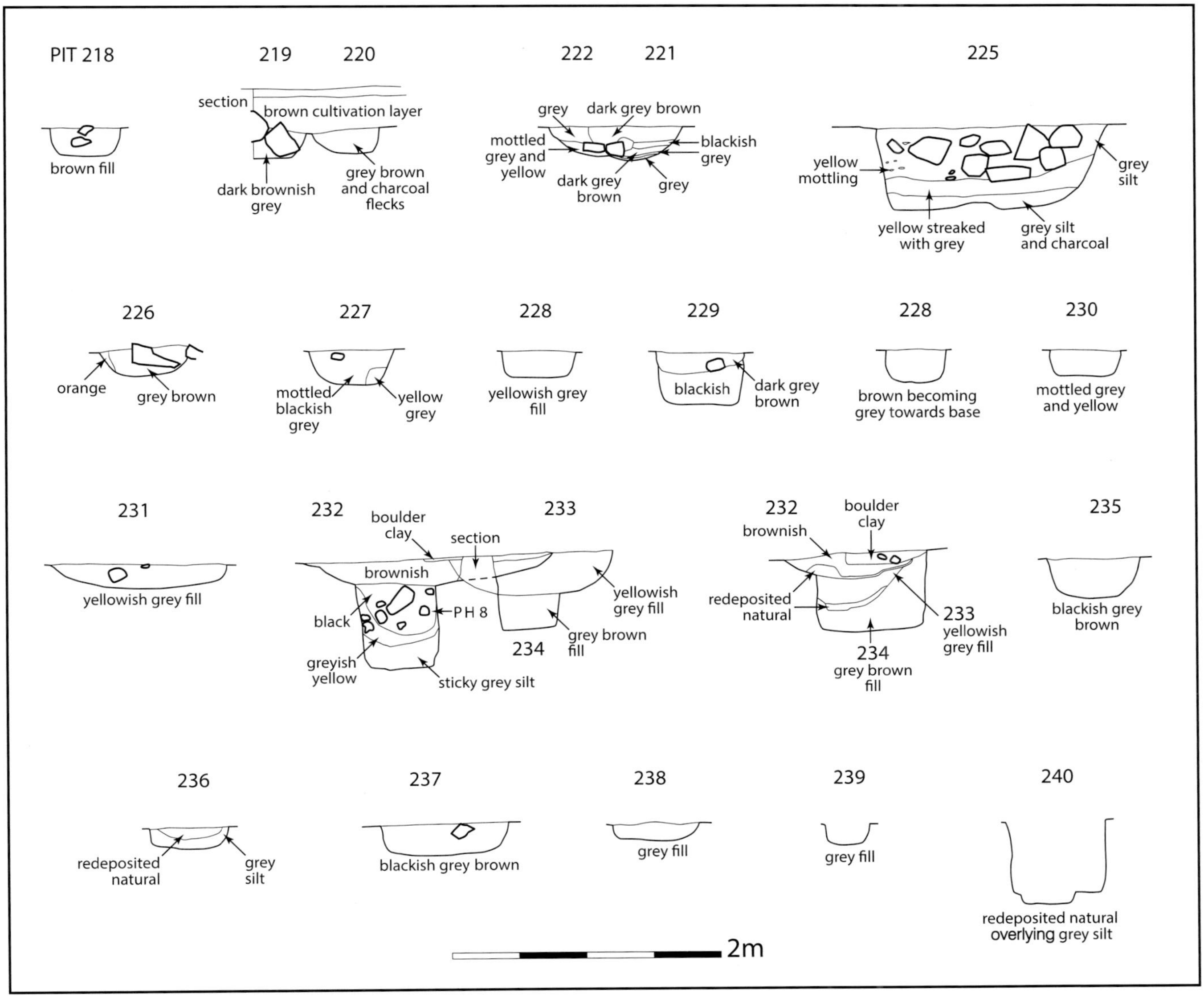

Fig. 2.114—Sections of pits in Area 4.

in diameter, with some as little as half of this. The larger pits were, with a few important exceptions, on average 1–1.2m wide. The largest, Pit 215 (I6), was 3m in diameter, and several others—231 (G5), 171 (J5), 241 (J5) and 223 (I6)—measured more than 1.5m and up to 2m (Figs 2.108 and 2.114).

In general, the pits had regularly sloping sides and most frequently had been dug with considerable care to form bases which were either regularly flat or gently concave. Some pits with more rounded profiles occurred, and there were a number with wholly irregular cross-sections. The smallest pits were the shallowest, on occasion as little as 25cm deep—e.g. Pits 182, 183 (I5) and 193 (H5) (Figs 2.108, 2.113 and 2.114). In general, however, pits averaged 20–40cm in depth, with a very small number exceeding this.

While most of the pits, as stated above, had grey silting in their upper levels, the nature of their lower layers varied considerably, suggesting that they did not always have a common function. One pit referred to above, Pit 231 (G5), was one of the larger pits in this zone but was otherwise nondescript, apart from the discovery of three decorated Neolithic potsherds (E84:9224a,b, E84:9225) in its filling. The possibility that the pit is early cannot thus be discounted, but a Bronze Age date, with the potsherds representing a secondary intrusion deriving from early fragments scattered in the vicinity, is perhaps the most likely.

Fig. 2.115 (left)— Pits in Sq. J5, looking north.

Fig. 2.116 (above)—Pit 215 in Sq. I6, (a) before and (b) after excavation (looking east).

In many instances pits revealed a consistent fill of fine grey material down to the base, indicating that rapid silting had taken place—e.g. nos 175, 177 (I5), 178 (J5), 183 (I5) (Fig. 2.114), 238 (I5) and 239 (H5) (Fig. 2.115). In other examples, significant quantities of stones, often of quite substantial size, filled or partly filled the pit. In such instances there can be little doubt that the stones had been placed as deliberate filling. This was particularly noticeable in some of the larger pits, such as 169 (J5), 171 (J5; *no section*), 195 (G4), 208, 209 (*neither 208 nor 209 is identified on plan; no sections; probably renumbered*) and 225 (G5/I6) (Figs 2.114 and 2.116), and in such cases the filling had clearly been carried out systematically and with care.

In this regard, the very large boulders in Pits 215 (I6; Fig. 2.116) and 223 (I6; *no section*), and to a lesser extent in Pit 197 (G4; Fig. 2.113, after removal of stone), demonstrate the not-inconsiderable care and effort which had been taken in their filling. The rocks in Pit 208 (*not illustrated*) had been thrown in directly on top of the primary silting, and dark brown occupation material, including splinters of animal bone, had obviously been thrown in with the stones. In Pit 215 (I6), however, the very large boulder present had been rolled into the pit after it had been open and in use for some time. The boulder thus rested on a 5cm-thick layer of burnt black, gritty material. Redeposited natural soil was packed in around this boulder, along with several smaller stones. A small, shallow depression in this pit, filled with black organic material, 40cm in diameter and 10cm deep, had been dug into the upper surface of the yellow filling material in the south. It probably represents reuse, on a more modest scale, after a phase of primary infilling.

As in the case of Pit 223 (I6), there were other examples in which a black, organic layer (often containing potsherds and other items) lay directly on the base. There were also pits where a black layer occurred in the upper levels, with silting and traces of redeposited natural soil below.

The subrectangular shape of Pit 90 (Sq. F3/G3; Fig. 2.87) set it apart from the other pits. It had fairly regular, more or

Feature	Sq. no.	Artefact type	Artefact no.
Pit 168	J5	Coarse pottery	E84:8957, 8958, 8959
Pit 169	J5	Natural stone	E84:8949
		Bipolar core	E84:8950
Pit 171	J5	Coarse pottery	E84:8947, 8948, 8972
Pit 174	I5	Coarse pottery	E84:8955, 8956, 9006, 9007, 9008, 9027
Pit 176	J5	Unidentified bronze object	E84:8914
		Coarse pottery	E84:8932, 8933, 8934, 8936.1, 8936
		Leinster Cooking Ware	E84:8935
		Middle Bronze Age pottery	E84:8937
		Regular flake debitage	E84:8971
Pit 180	I5	Coarse pottery	E84:8980
		Irregular flake debitage	E84:9044e, 9061
		Regular flake debitage	E84:9044d,f,g
		Convex scraper	E84:9044a–c
Pit 182	I5	Coarse pottery	E84:9014
Pit 186	I5	Coarse pottery	E84:9198
		Convex scraper	E84:9199
Pit 187	H5	Coarse pottery	E84:9046
Pit 188	I5	Leinster Cooking Ware	E84:9026
		Regular flake debitage	E84:9039
		Coarse pottery	E84:9040, 9041, 9045, 9060
Pit 190	I5	Regular flake debitage	E84:9019a,c
		Indeterminate flint fragment	E84:9019b
Pit 192	H5	Convex scraper	E84:9036e
		Regular flake debitage	E84:9036j
		Indeterminate retouched fragment	E84:9036a
		Irregular flake debitage	E84:9036h
		Convex scraper	E84:9036b–d,g
		Edge-retouched flake	E84:9036f
Pit 195	G4	Coarse pottery	E84:9087
Pit 196	G4	Irregular flake debitage	E84:9086
Pit 213	I6/J6	Coarse pottery	E84:9189
		Regular flake debitage	E84:9190
Pit 214	J6	Coarse pottery	E84:9182, 9186
Pit 215	I6	Complete crucible	E84:9000
		Coarse pottery	E84:9188, 9201, 9149, 9150, 9208
		Glass bead	E84:9183
		Irregular flake debitage	E84:9200
		Flint	E84:9207, 9208
Pit 216	I6	Coarse pottery	E84:9209
Pit 219	I6	Coarse pottery	E84:9206
Pit 225	H6	Coarse pottery	E84:9233
Pit 227	H6	Coarse pottery	E84:9232
Pit 231	G5	Middle Neolithic bipartite bowl	E84:9224a–b, 9225
Pit 237	I5	Coarse pottery	E84:9239
Pit 269	G6	Coarse pottery	E84:9511, 9512, 9513
		Bipolar core	E84:9514
Hearth 13	I6	Coarse pottery	E84:9185
	J5	Perforated stone object	E84:8944
	G6	Leinster Cooking Ware	E84:9430

Table 2.11 (left)—Artefacts recovered from pit features in Area 4.

less vertical sides, averaging 50cm in depth, and a base which for the most part was flat. Its fill was not unusual, with at least four phases of regular silting clearly recognisable in its western portion. Low down in its eastern section, however, a deposit of blackish, organic material occurred, above which and below which silted material occurred. Concentrations of medium-sized stones were present in the uppermost levels of the pit, embedded in, and lying on, the silting of the final phase. The stones were particularly concentrated at the western end, where they lay deeper in the pit fill and, in their upper levels, continued in a spread over the adjacent Pit 89. Among these stones six coarse potsherds were found. Pit 89, considerably smaller than Pit 90, was filled completely with grey silted material and had obviously been dug before Pit 90, as it was fully silted when the latter came to be dug. Pit 86, on the opposite side of Pit 90, was also filled with grey silt and was either contemporary with the latter or, more likely, later.

Obviously, not all the pits uncovered had been dug at the same time, and some were already silted up or had been filled in before others were dug. Similarly, several phases of activity are occasionally recognisable in a single pit—for example, in Pits 215 and 223 (both I6). The former, as noted above, was one of the largest of the pits excavated and had been carefully dug, with regular, inward-sloping sides and a flat base. Three levels were recognisable in the filling material. The remains of a basal layer of primary silting partially survived, a portion having been apparently removed along the lower zone to accommodate a thick black organic layer, which in turn was partly cut into, and covered by, what is now a thick zone of sterile yellowish-brown soil. This had been deliberately filled with a series of large rocks, including a huge boulder that lay on, and was surrounded by, the yellowish fill. There were no finds in either the grey silt or the yellow material that filled most of the pit. In the surviving black organic layer, however, important finds occurred, including twelve coarse potsherds, three pieces of flint, one blue glass bead (E84:9183) and, most strikingly, a beautifully made miniature clay crucible (E84:9000; Fig. 3.43).

The poor stratigraphy over much of this area of the site generally made it difficult to establish with any degree of confidence the relative chronological sequence of activities represented by the pits. Furthermore, the spread in the vicinity of Neolithic pottery and flints, as well as the evidence of much later medieval activity (see below), call for caution in the interpretation of the dating of these cut features. Nevertheless, the later Bronze Age dating of most of the pits appears likely. There were instances where pits—sometimes three or even four—overlapped, indicating the intensity of the Bronze Age settlement on the hilltop. The length of time that elapsed between the digging and final silting of individual pits and the excavation into them of secondary examples remains uncertain in most instances. Clearly, however, changes were constantly taking place over a considerable period.

Thirty pits contained fragments of coarseware, generally either single sherds or with a few fragments (Tables 2.10 and 2.11). The occasional Neolithic items that sometimes occurred with the later material are likely to be in secondary contexts. One pit (176) contained a small bronze object of uncertain character (E84:8914) along with thirteen coarse potsherds in the greyish upper material. Lower down, in the black organic layer of the same pit, there was a flint flake. Another pit in B3 (204) yielded a shale bracelet fragment (E84:9129), a single potsherd (E84:9110) and a polished bone fragment (E84:9134[39]).

It is difficult to see any of these artefacts as deliberate depositions. The tiny crucible E84:9000 from Pit 215 (Fig 3.43), however, is most intriguing in this regard, especially as it was undamaged and, presumably, still usable when it came to be buried. Obviously, an object as small as this could be mislaid and lost, but this remains uncertain. Here, at least, it must be accepted that deliberate burial, for whatever reason, is not impossible. On the whole, however, the items found are likely to have been discarded or lost.

Pit 195 was first revealed as an oval grey area, 1m by 1.25m, with a number of large stones projecting from the surface. It was 55cm deep, with vertical sides and a very gently concave base. Apart from a thin lens of silt in the bottom, it was completely filled with large stones embedded in a matrix of black organic material. As noted above, some of these stones were visible before the pit was excavated. The only find from this pit, a coarse potsherd (E84:9087), came from the grey silt.

Pit 196 (Fig. 2.113) was a small oval pit with maximum horizontal dimensions of 50cm by 30cm. It was 20cm deep and had regular vertical sides and an almost flat base. It was filled with greyish-brown material containing significant concentrations of charcoal and a single flint flake (E84:9086).

Pit 197 was irregularly oval, with maximum dimensions of 1.9m by 1.25m. It had regular, sloping sides and a rounded base, and had a maximum depth of 46cm. The original fill of this pit consisted of large boulders, some lying virtually on the base, mixed with zones of blackish and greyish soil mixed in among the stones. It had been dug into by Pit 195 on the east.

Pit 194 was a flattened oval in shape, with dimensions of 1m by 75cm. It had steeply sloping sides and a rounded base and was 28–30cm deep. In the lower levels there were thin layers of greyish silt, with some black patches, and a layer of black, organic material at the top.

Viewing these pits as a group, it must therefore be admitted that their original purpose is not, in most instances, readily apparent. They varied considerably in size, shape and depth, as well as in the nature of the material with which they were filled. Some were small, nondescript depressions containing nothing more than grey silt. A significant number of others had a black organic layer and, in the great majority of these, any finds present came from on or in this layer. Sometimes several phases of use could be recognised, and pits were not infrequently dug across one another. Finds, as noted, were almost invariably items broken and discarded.

2.6.2 Pits north of the burial enclosure

In the area north of Ring-ditch 2 there were only three pits. Two of these, Pits 40 (Sqs 4/F/5G/G1/F1) and 41 (no location), were shallow and insignificant (*no sections*). Pit 40 (Fig. 2.87) was flat-bottomed with sloping sides and was hardly more than 12cm deep. It was filled with an organic, blackish material throughout. Pit 41 (Fig. 2.53), into which PH 19 had been dug, was of similar character; two coarse potsherds came from its upper fill (E84:2621, 2622).

The fill of the third pit, Pit 38 (Sq. F1), was more complex (*no section*). It was oval (1.45m by 1.15m) with near-vertical sides and a gently concave base and was 65cm deep. In the base of the pit was a thick layer of fine, dark brown material which, in its lowest levels, contained a few lumps of charcoal. Some small stones were scattered in this layer. In one area of the pit there was a thin black streak, 10cm or less in thickness, which may represent a short-lived phase of vegetation growth. On top of this, and extending somewhat beyond it, was a layer of fine brown soil containing a few stones, some of which were relatively large. Above this layer was a thick deposit of fine grey material with some charcoal but containing far fewer stones than any of the other layers. This was sealed by a very dark, almost black layer of fine material, up to 6cm thick, which contained eleven coarse potsherds (E84:7709). The upper sealing material consisted of stones, mostly medium-sized (apart from one with maximum dimensions of 1.1m x 25cm x 30cm), mixed with light brown sandy humus, with patches of yellow soil throughout. Here five coarse potsherds were found in the lowest levels (E84:7655a–b, 7656, 7710) (Table 2.8).

Possible Hearth 13
This feature (Fig. 2.42) occurred in the south-western corner of Sq. I6. Only half was uncovered but it was clearly subcircular in plan with a diameter of approximately 1m. It was on average 30cm deep and its sides sloped steeply to a roughly flat base. A layer of yellowish-grey silt lay on the base and was in turn covered by an undifferentiated layer of blackish organic material which contained no stones. Two coarse potsherds came from this dark material (E84:9185), as well as a stone object and a sherd of medieval pottery.

2.7 THE X CUTTINGS
Barry Raftery

In 1972 an exploratory trench was opened between Ramparts 1 and 2 on the south (Fig. 2.117). The cutting (X0–X4), which extended northwards from the base of Rampart 2, was 18.5m long and 5m wide, with a short eastward extension at its northern end. This investigation yielded considerable evidence of human activity—again, for the most part, of Bronze Age date (Table 2.12). In 1978, the final year of excavation at Rathgall, the cutting was extended southwards through Ramparts 2 and 3 (see below), continuing further downslope for 18.5m to end in Sq. X13 (Fig. 2.118). At the same time, the northern end of the 1972 cutting, though reduced to a width of 1.25m, was extended northwards to Cutting X6, thus providing a continuous section, just under 64m in length, southwards from there as far as Cutting X13 in the south.

In these cuttings heavy modern cultivation had once again obliterated the early levels, and it was only when the covering humus had been removed down to the yellow boulder clay that evidence for prehistoric occupation came to light. This was present in varying forms along the entire length of the area opened, demonstrating once more the extraordinary extent of Bronze Age activity on the hilltop.

In X4, for example, in the northern part of the cutting, an extensive area of black organic material yielded 33 coarse potsherds. Denser and more extensive was the black zone in X5, which extended right across the cutting. Even though the investigated area was no more than 1.25m wide, it produced

Fig. 2.117—View from Rampart 3, looking north along the length of Cutting X up to Rampart 1 (Sqs X7, X8 and X9).

no fewer than 362 potsherds, mostly prehistoric. It also contained a glass bead fragment (E84:9588) and, perhaps most importantly, a possible mould gate (E84:9493). A complete glass bead was found in the same square in light brown soil (E84:9400; Fig. 3.14).

Scattered post-holes came to light in the yellow subsoil and there were shallow, irregular depressions throughout the cutting (notably in Sqs X1 and X2), all of which were filled with grey silt, occasionally mixed with charcoal. There appears to have been a greater concentration of larger post-holes in the south, most especially in Sqs X and X1, though again no coherent pattern could be recognised. Further north, in the later extension in Sqs X5 and X6 along the western edge of the cutting, a short line of five post-holes was indicated, all with a fine grey fill. The post-holes were graded in depth from each end to the centre, where, at 30cm, the deepest hole occurred.

In the X cuttings there were only three pits of any note. Pit

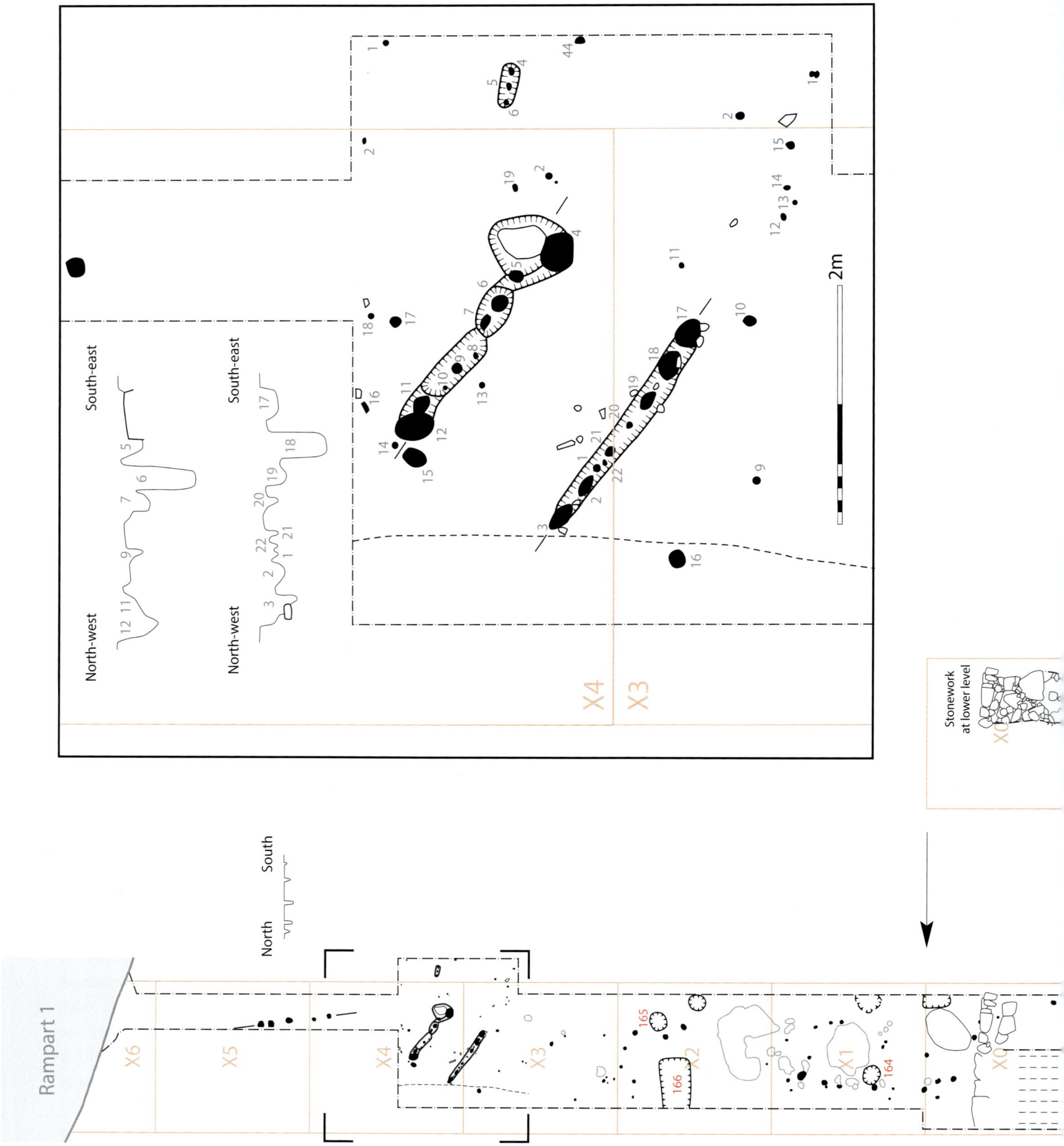

North-west
South-east
2m
X4
X3
Stonework at lower level
X0
North
South
Rampart 1
X6
X5
X2
X1

Fig. 2.118—Plan of Cuttings X0–X13.

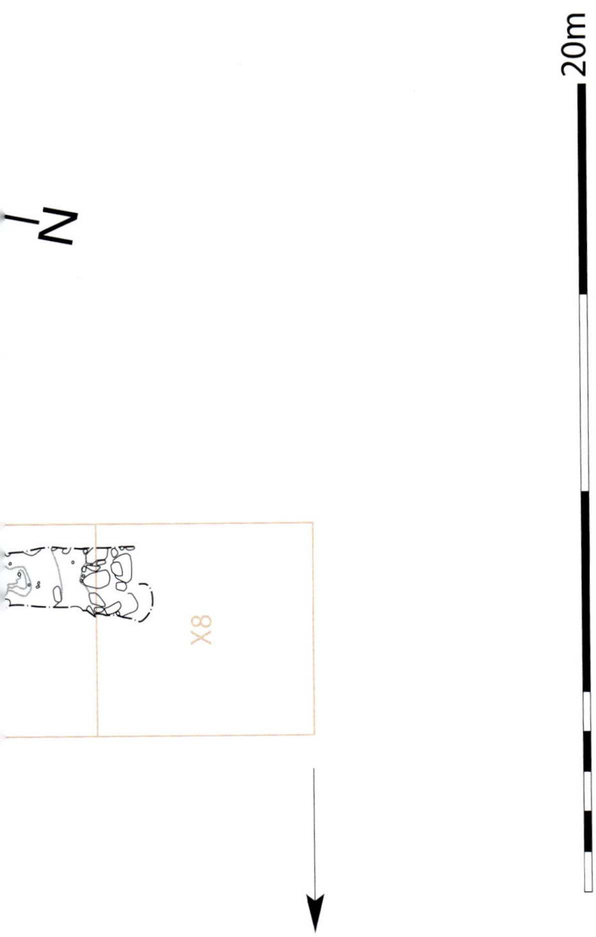

165 in Sq. X2 (Fig. 2.118) was subcircular with a rounded base; it was some 50cm in diameter and 37cm deep. It was filled with a uniform grey, silt-like material. Pit 164 (Fig. 2.119) was similar in size and shape. In this case, however, there was a thin layer of grey silt on its base, overlying which was a layer of black organic material. This not only covered the base but also the sides in a manner reminiscent of the pits earlier considered which are likely to have had an organic lining of some sort. It was 12cm thick at the centre, tapering in thickness upwards along the sides, and contained splinters of animal bone. The upper portion of the pit was filled with grey-brown silt.

Pit 166 in Sq. X2 (Figs 2.118 and 2.120) was rectangular in plan, orientated east–west, and was the largest and most carefully dug pit uncovered in this area. It had straight sides and carefully rounded corners. In width it expanded slightly from 1m in the east to 1.05m in the west. Though it was not fully visible in the latter area, its exposed length of 1.5m was probably only slightly less than its complete length. It maintained a regular depth of some 42cm below the natural subsoil.

When first exposed after the removal of the brown humus, the outline of Pit 166 manifested itself as a thin band of black organic material, 2–4cm in width, which enclosed layers of yellow and brown soil. The excavated section showed that there was a thin basal layer of fine, primary silting, 2–3cm thick, which was covered by a sterile greyish-brown level with pockets of yellow. It was *c.* 5cm thick at the base of the pit but increased to as much as 15cm in thickness along the sides. On top of this was the black level noted above, which formed a complete layer covering sides and base to a maximum thickness of 5–6cm, tapering slightly to the top. It was, in fact, the top of this layer that originally provided the outline of the pit on the surface. The black layer was covered by a dark, brownish fill, 15cm in maximum depth, which in turn was overlain by a deposit of yellow redeposited soil (Fig. 2.120).

Following the removal of the filling material of the pit, it was a matter of some surprise to discover in its base, in the

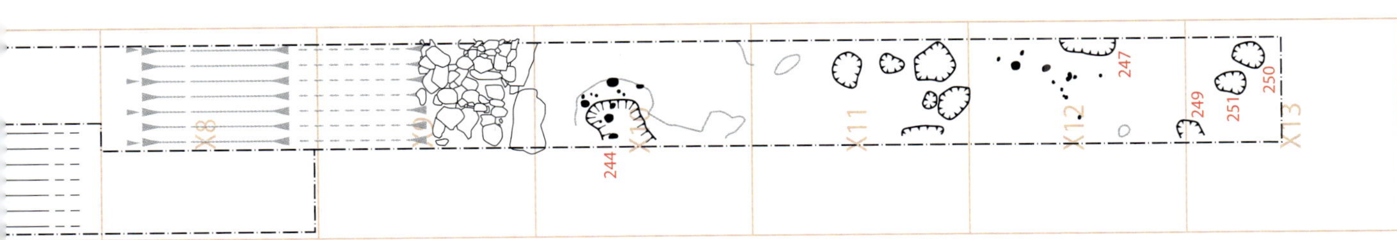

Fig. 2.119—Pit 164 in Sq. X1 sectioned (looking south-west).

eastern half, the flattened-oval outline of a second, smaller pit, marked by a thin line of black organic material. This had maximum dimensions of 88cm by 68cm. When investigated, it was shown to be a mere 8–10cm in maximum depth. It transpired that this feature consisted of a thin basal layer of black, with a few grey patches and a fine covering of yellow soil which left the edges of the black exposed around its perimeter, as was the case with the main pit. This 'pit within a pit' is puzzling, but the only logical explanation that comes to mind is that the larger pit was later than the smaller one and was cut across the latter, thus removing all but its lowest level.

No fewer than 84 sherds of coarse pottery came from this pit (E84:8246–60), all but one (E84:8260) from the black level of the main feature. A single sherd was found in the yellow material covering the basal 'mini-pit' (possibly E84:8262). In a small patch of grey in the base of the latter a few tiny fragments of probable cattle bone were found (Table 2.16).

Radiocarbon dates of 1270–990 cal. BC (GrA-23349) and 1460–1240 cal. BC (GrN-27116) were obtained from the black fill of this pit.

A number of further pits were scattered throughout the cuttings (Fig. 2.118).

Fig. 2.120—Pit 166 in Sq. X2 before and during excavation, (a) looking north, (b) looking east and (c) looking north.

2.7.1 The rectangular structure

One of the most interesting features uncovered in the X cuttings was a curious pair of short, narrow, roughly parallel post-hole slots in X3/X4 (Figs 2.118, 2.121 and 2.122). They resembled each other closely in length and were orientated north-west/south-east. The southern example, Slot 1, was 1.9m in length; the northern Slot 2 was 5cm shorter than this. The two were 1.2m apart for most of their length. At the south-eastern end, because of the large size of PH 4, the measured distance between them was 1m, but it seems clear that the intention was to lay out the two trenches exactly

Fig. 2.121—Rectangular structure in Sqs X3/X4 before excavation (looking south-east).

Fig. 2.122—Rectangular structure in Sqs X3/X4 after excavation (looking south-east).

parallel to one another (Fig. 2.118).

Slot 2 consisted of nine post- or stake-holes, set roughly 10–20cm apart, in a narrow slot, 22–25cm wide. Its base, which was somewhat irregular, meandered slightly from a straight line. At its eastern end there was a shallow, circular depression containing a small stone, at the side of which was PH 4. At its western end there were two further post-holes (14 and 15) which were not set in the trench but which, from their position, appear likely to belong to the same feature.

The post-holes averaged 10–12cm in depth, the only exception being PH 6, which was 60cm deep with a maximum width of 30cm. Post-holes 4 and 12, at the eastern and western ends respectively, were also more substantial than the others, though they appear not to have been as carefully dug, or as deep, as PH 6. Traces of charcoal occurred in all the post-holes, but this was particularly evident in PH 12 and, more especially, in PH 4, which, as noted above, also contained splinters of burnt bone.

Slot 1 resembled Slot 2 but was more regularly dug as a single, parallel-sided feature, 20cm wide. It contained nine post-holes, which were set somewhat closer together than in the case of Slot 2 and, apart from PH 18 (and, to a lesser extent, PH 3 at the western end), their depths were similar to the majority of those in Slot 1. PH 3 was 30cm deep, tapering to a thin point, but PH 18, 55cm deep and almost 25cm in diameter, closely resembled PH 6 in Slot 2. All the post-holes contained black organic material and charcoal in the lower levels, covered by grey silt at the top.

This structure closely resembles that in Cuttings F/G (section 2.4.1 above), although the latter is more than twice the length of that described here. The similarities are such, however, that it seems probable that these two features (notwithstanding their differing sizes) served a common purpose, although this remains as yet obscure. It seems likely that the parallel walls were of wickerwork, although the post-holes are, in each instance, rather closer together than would be normal for the typical sails used for wattle walling. The open ends (which almost certainly existed in the structure in X3/X4, and probably also in the case of the larger example in F/G) would seem to preclude their use as animal pens. The possibility might be considered that light roofing once existed, and in this context the structures could, perhaps, have been some sort of drying racks. For the moment, however, these two structures remain enigmatic.

2.7.2 Rampart construction

When a brief examination of Ramparts 2 and 3 was carried out in 1978, it occasioned some surprise that a deep, carefully dug, V-sectioned ditch was found between them. Neither here nor, indeed, elsewhere around the defensive circumference had there been any surface indication that such a ditch existed. Similarly surprising was the discovery, during the recent survey of the site (section 2.11, below), of traces of a former, incomplete enclosure, uncertain both in its dating and its original purpose, between the third and fourth ramparts.

Around the inner perimeter of the main rampart (Rampart 2) was, as noted above, the well-preserved stone wall (see Chapter 1, section 1.4) which is clearly visible today. It rested on a layer of undifferentiated brown humus and had

Fig. 2.123—Section through Rampart 2 in Sqs X0/X7 (looking south).

been built up against, and on top of, the obviously earlier construction. The space between this facing and the earlier rampart was filled with tightly packed stones, which provided a solid construction some 1.5m in maximum thickness.

When exposed in the course of the excavation, the height of the early rampart in most areas was 1.5m, but it could be observed to be considerably higher than this in some areas, most especially around the north. Its basal width was around 7m and its maximum thickness was some 2.5m.

Though only a small section of the rampart was examined, a number of details of potential significance emerged. First, it was evident that built up against the recent inner stone enclosure in the north there was a thick zone of yellow soil, largely without stones, which directly covered the core of the stone-built rampart (Figs 2.123 and 2.124). This layer gradually thinned out upwards, becoming extremely sparse at the summit of the rampart, with the stone construction predominant. To the north of this, stones of the rampart are present in some quantity but are not as closely packed as in the main core area of the rampart. The critical question is, therefore, whether the rampart represents one or two phases of early activity.[40]

It is possible that the thick yellow layer on the north represents a secondary, earthen extension of an original, purely stone rampart. Against this, however, is the fact that there was no clear division between the yellow layer and the stones of the rampart proper; indeed, in places it seemed that the yellow and the stones had clearly merged. Nevertheless, the yellow layer extended directly northwards to the inner stone face (where it was partly covered by stones of the recent construction), strongly suggesting that this was an individual construction separate from the principal stone construction of the main rampart. It is thus possible that an overwhelmingly rubble rampart had been extended northwards using yellow soil. The fact, however, that there is no clearly recognisable division between the rubble core of the rampart and the covering yellow layer leaves this matter open. If we do indeed have two phases here, it can only be concluded that the interval between them was not excessive.

On the old ground surface, a short distance outside the recent inner face, three large boulders formed a rough line along the length of the rampart in the excavated zone. One of these inclined somewhat to the outside. About 2m inside these there was a single boulder and a number of lesser boulders, which might have formed a line roughly parallel to the first. The area between contained stones and rocks, some of considerable size. It is possible that this might represent the preserved base of an original rampart construction. These stones were covered by the yellow layer of the bank, which was in turn covered by the recent wall. It is possible, therefore, that the original face had collapsed, the material of the rampart had poured out over the fallen stones and the later (medieval?) builders had used the collapsed stones to construct the secondary wall which stands today.

An interesting detail here was the presence of a clearly unweathered rim sherd of coarse pottery (E84:9629) lying directly against the outer face of one of the possible revetment stones which inclined slightly to the exterior. This sherd lay directly on the yellow basal material of the rampart and its position suggests that there was no appreciable interval between its deposition and the collapse of the stone against it.

Immediately outside the rampart (Rampart 2) to the south was the ditch, which had been dug with very considerable care to a V-shaped section (Fig. 2.124). Its depth below the prehistoric surface was about 2m, while its base was 3.5m below the surviving summit of the rampart. Any projecting rocks which might have existed had been removed, so that the sides sloped evenly downwards at angles of about 45º to a narrow, carefully and regularly created base. It was completely filled with rubble, most of which presumably came from the collapsed bank. Grey silt, which covered each face, lay directly on the base of the ditch below this rubble. On the northern face the silted layer was as much as 50cm in thickness, while on the opposite, southern face it was no more than 12–15cm thick.

On the north, near the top of the ditch, a very large

boulder, embedded in the lower silt, lay directly against the inner ditch face. Extending downwards from this boulder, almost to the base of the ditch, there was a line of stones of medium size (Fig. 2.124). On the opposing face of the ditch there were two boulders, both with fairly regular, flat surfaces, which lay directly on the outer silted layer and which also extended almost to the base of the ditch. One of these boulders, which sloped outwards from the ditch bottom, was particularly large. It was 2m long and some 75cm in maximum width, but this decreased significantly to a narrow base no more than 20cm across. The other boulder, of somewhat smaller dimensions, had a slight inward slope. All the collapsed rubble from the bank was packed on top of the larger boulder. The smaller boulder lay higher up in the ditch fill and appeared to be part of the general inward collapse.

There can be little doubt that the rubble filling the ditch represents collapse from Rampart 2. The large boulder lying on the silt at the top of the inner ditch face seems likely to be a collapsed facing stone which slid downwards before the mass of the core material poured across it. The large boulders on the opposite face of the ditch are not so easily explained. The largest of them bears the entire weight of the rampart collapse, which lies directly on it. One explanation for this might be that the boulder was originally part of the outer revetment of the main rampart and collapsed forward into the ditch as the rampart collapsed. This is to an extent feasible, but the fact that the narrowest end of the boulder lies deepest in the ditch would, in this instance, be problematic. Had the boulder been originally in an upright position with the narrow end at the top, it would have required a somersault to finish up with its narrow end at the bottom. This is difficult to envisage. A forward collapse of the revetment into the ditch as part of a general collapse (scarcely avoidable if the facing falls away) could not possibly allow a boulder of this size—or, indeed, any revetment boulder—to perform a somersault. It therefore seems more likely, accepting this large boulder to have been part of the outer revetment of the main rampart, that it had either lain horizontally or had in fact originally stood with its narrower end at the bottom.

There is the alternative possibility that the large boulder was an *inner* revetment stone of the outer rampart (Rampart 3) and that it fell downwards into the ditch, which would more logically explain its position. Supporting this possibility are the markedly different thicknesses of the opposing layers of primary silting on the two ditch faces. The boulder in question, as noted above, lay on a silted layer no more than 2cm thick, while the silt on the opposing ditch face was at least four times as thick. This could be taken to indicate that the large boulder lying on the southern slope of the ditch collapsed first, that silting continued for a while, building up to a greater thickness in the ditch base, before the inner rampart collapsed, covering the thicker silted layer and bringing the rubble of the inner rampart onto the large boulder.

Inevitably, there are problems with this interpretation, too. The distance of the boulder in question from the denuded third rampart was rather more than 3m and the ground slopes fairly gently from that rampart to the ditch. Could the boulder have tumbled that far into the ditch? It should also be noted that there was no concentration of stones between the large boulder under discussion in the ditch and what remained of Rampart 3. A rampart collapse on a scale that would have carried the large boulder a distance of 3m along a gentle slope into the bottom of the ditch should have left a trail of stones in its wake.

The matter cannot, therefore, be satisfactorily resolved, illustrating the often-enigmatic way in which evidence is presented from limited excavation cuttings. Only through more extended investigation of the rampart is there a possibility of shedding light on the present difficulty. It seems most likely, however, notwithstanding the interpretative difficulties noted above, that somehow the massive boulder in question was originally part of the main, inner rampart. It is, at any rate, clearly evident from the sizes of the various boulders uncovered that the twin ramparts formed a defensive obstacle of no small significance.

The outer of the two main ramparts (Rampart 3) is now heavily denuded but it seems never to have been as imposing as was the inner defence. This third rampart was built solely of stones and cannot have been more than about 2.5–2.75m wide. It survived in the excavation cutting for a maximum height of about 75cm (Figs 2.124 and 2.125), consisting for the most part of no more than a single course of medium-sized rocks. Along its inner face there were several large stones lying on the slope of the ditch, which was here rather more gentle than elsewhere, and it is likely that they came from an original inner revetment (*but see above*). The base of the outer face was, however, preserved. This comprised three contiguous stones with fairly flat outer and inner surfaces, set in a regular line. The largest was about 1m long and they were 60–70cm high.

Despite uncertainty in some details, it is evident that the construction of the rampart, whether a product of one or two phases of construction, was not technically complex. It

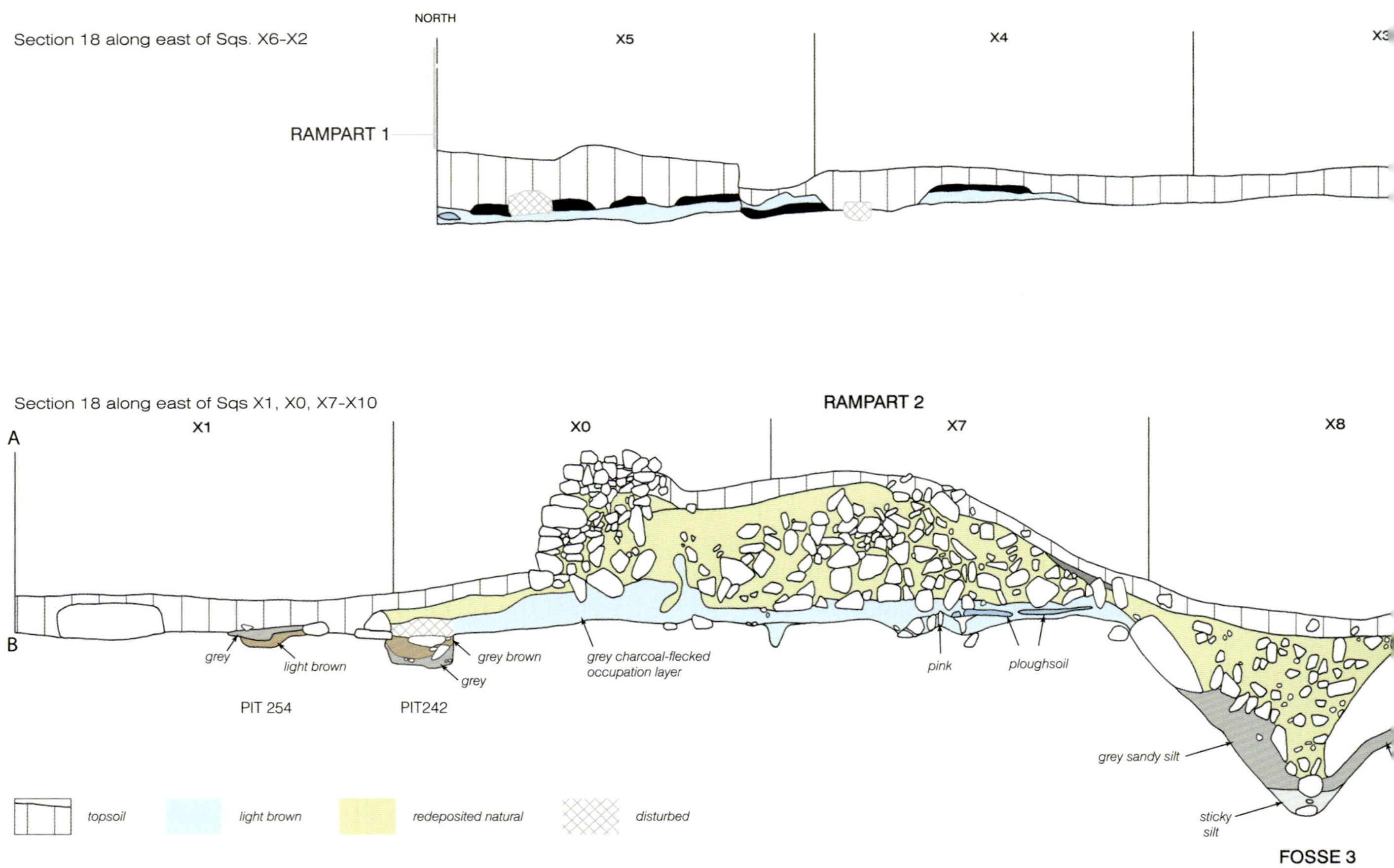

Fig. 2.125—Post-excavation view of the rampart cutting, looking north towards Rampart 3 and Rampart 2 (behind) (Sqs X9–X11).

involved considerable time and effort nonetheless. The original height of either rampart is difficult to determine but there is no doubt that, when complete, a formidable barrier was offered. If even a single metre was added to the surviving height of the inner defence it would, including the ditch, have been a minimum of 4.5m in height. It could well have been more than this. A vertical outer face of even this height would have been imposing and impressive. The contemporaneity of the two ramparts is not entirely certain but both rest on the same grey layer and there is nothing in the uncomplicated stratigraphy to suggest that they were not part of the same defensive construction.

In sharp contrast to the situation almost everywhere else during the excavation, not a single artefact came from

Fig. 2.124—Long sections through Sqs X6–X2 and Sqs X1, X0, X7–X10.

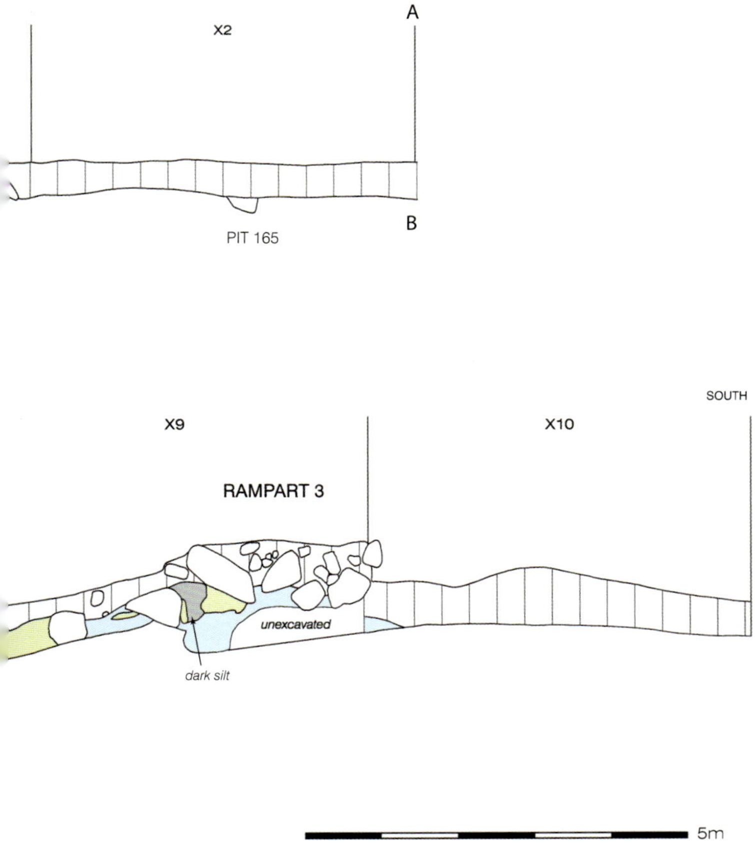

anywhere in the ditch.

Besides one Bronze Age date (1370–910 cal. BC; UB-2348), radiocarbon determinations obtained from various samples throughout the ditch fill produced a later Iron Age date (170 cal. BC–AD 560; UB-2345) and a number of early medieval dates (see also section 2.8 and Chapter 4).

2.7.3 Pre-hillfort activity

The excavation revealed a substantial phase of pre-hillfort activity immediately below Rampart 2 (Figs 2.124 and 2.126). This consisted of a thick grey layer, with a regularly flat surface, which averaged 20–25cm in depth. Occasional stones from above had penetrated this layer but these were clearly secondary. Small subcircular and irregularly shaped patches of yellow soil were present, and there were larger patches of a lighter, creamy-grey material which in places penetrated the fine grey layer to average depths of 5–10cm, but occasionally even deeper than this.

These zones were certainly not pits in any conventional sense. They appear to be material which became mixed with the grey by chance or was trodden into it from above. There was one particular zone of this creamy material which, in section, was mottled and discontinuous. This patch did, however, penetrate almost as far as the natural yellow subsoil. The grey layer underlay both ramparts and was cut away by the intervening ditch. It was scarcely encountered elsewhere in the course of the excavation, apart from some possibly comparable material represented by greyish zones that were revealed further north in the vicinity of the inner stone rampart.

The lower levels of Ramparts 2 and 3 appeared to rest directly on the grey soil, thus implying that there were no stratigraphical indications of any significant time-lag between their erection and the underlying human activity clearly represented by the grey layer. As already noted above, there were, unfortunately, no finds from the body of the rampart or from the ditch fill. The mottled grey layer underneath, however, produced some 63 scattered sherds of coarse pottery and at least thirteen worn clay mould fragments of varying sizes, a few no more than tiny crumbs. Virtually all these finds came from the upper 5cm of the grey layer. They were thinly scattered along the length of the cutting, but there was a slight concentration in the southern section. Of the finds, 50 potsherds and at least eleven mould fragments (together with several small crumbs) came from under the bank in Sq. X7. Thirteen sherds and a single mould fragment were found in X, while in X8 the only find was a single mould fragment (Table 2.12).

The grey material was examined in 1975 by Professor G.F. Mitchell of Trinity College, Dublin. In a preliminary assessment, he expressed the view that it was in fact prehistoric ploughsoil. This conclusion was based on the finely comminuted quality of the soil, which suggested cultivation over a considerable period. He also noted the almost complete absence of stones, which, in his view, suggested deliberate clearance.

The interval between the use of the above layer and the disposal of the artefacts found in it is critical. In the last analysis, this cannot be established with certainty and more extensive excavation is required to shed light on this very

Fig. 2.126—Pre-rampart activity shown at the base of the section through Rampart 2 in Sqs X0/X7 (looking north).

important question. The material from the grey layer could thus be significantly early. There seems, however, to be a degree of probability that the ploughsoil, the artefacts derived from it and the construction of the hillfort defences all belong to phases of Bronze Age activity on the site which are not significantly separated from one another.

Two radiocarbon dates obtained at the time (2100–1480 cal. BC, UB-2343; and 2630–1820 cal. BC, UB-2344) are complemented by those from the same deposits obtained in the 2011 campaign (see Chapter 2, section 2.8, and Chapter 4, section 4.4).

2.7.4 Cuttings X10–13

As noted above, a 2.5m-wide trench extended the X cuttings southwards beyond the hillfort defences for a distance of 17.5m (Fig. 2.118). This, though modest in extent, uncovered pits, post-holes and zones of black habitation material, as well as a sizeable quantity of artefacts, which indicate the wide spread of occupation in this area. The extent of such activity appears, however, to have been less intense than that exposed in the cuttings north of the ramparts, where a noticeably larger concentration of features came to light. The artefacts recovered indicate that, once more, this occupation belonged almost entirely to the later Bronze Age, although the chert barbed and tanged projectile fragment from ploughsoil in Sq. X11 (E84:9300; Fig. 3.100) could well indicate the former presence in the vicinity of some earlier Bronze Age activity. There are no indications, however, that the latter was of any significant duration.

The principal surviving zone of occupation was in Sq. X11, where there was a spread of black organic material in the western section of the cutting. This was a thin layer (*this may be Pit 244*) containing considerable quantities of charcoal and splinters of burnt bone, coarseware sherds and a single glass bead (E84:9321; Fig. 3.14b), as well as a post-medieval sherd, suggesting a late date for the deposition of this feature.

The pits uncovered were for the most part nondescript. They were generally subcircular or oval in shape, with maximum widths varying from about 75cm to about 1.2m and average depths of 15–25cm. Most were filled with layers of grey silt and flecks of charcoal were frequent, noticeably in Pits 247 and 249, both in Sq. X12. None contained any elaborate stratigraphy.

The only pit of note was Pit 243/4 in Sq. X10,[41] which, projecting from the western baulk, was only partly excavated. It had been dug into a wider hollow and appears to have been more or less a flattened oval in shape, with a width of almost 1m. It was exposed for a maximum length of 1.5m and must originally have been at least 50cm longer. It had been dug with care to create a flat bottom and regularly vertical sides.

Table 2.12—Artefacts recovered from X cuttings.

Finds from below Rampart 2 (grey (mottled) layer)			
Sq. no.	**Find type**		
X	Coarse pottery	E84:9267, 9268, 9316, 9522	
	Moulds	E84:9523	
X7	Coarse pottery	E84:9428, 9431, 9445, 9446, 9448, 9449a–o, 9449, 9459a–d, 9460, 9502a–n, 9503, 9504, 9505, 9509, 9527, 9562a,b, 9565, 9566	
	Moulds	E84:9317a–c, 9370a,b, 9429, 9447, 9450a–d, 9506	
X8	Moulds	E84:9586	
Finds from pits in the X cuttings			
Sq. no.	**Pit no.**	**Find type**	
X2	Pit 166	Coarse pottery	E84:8246, 8247, 8248, 8249, 8250, 8251, 8252a,b, 8253, *8254, 8255, 8256, 8257, 8258, 8259, 8260, 8262
X0	Pit 242	Beaker pottery	E84:9296, 9359
		Coarse pottery	E84:9269, 9270, 9295, 9296, 9357a–h, 9358, 9472, 9525a–f, 9547a–o, 9548, 9549, 9550, 9551, 9552
X11	Pit 243	Coarse pottery	E84:9305, 9306, 9309, 9311, 9313, 9318, 9319a–f, 9346a–g
		Moulds	E84:9307, 9308, 9310, 9312, 9320, 9347, 9348, 9349
X11	Pit 244	Coarse pottery	E84:9304, 9322a–k, 9324a–h, 9325
		Moulds	E84:9302, 9303
		Glass bead	*E84:9321
		Flint	E84:9323a,b
		Medieval pottery	**E84:9326
X11	Pit 246	Coarse pottery	E84:9396
X12	Pit 247	Coarse pottery	E84:9335, 9364, 9440
		Middle Neolithic pottery	E84:9441
		Coarse pottery	E84:9442, 9443, 9444a–c
X12	Pit 248	Coarse pottery	E84:9433a,b
X13	Pit 250	Coarse pottery	E84:9336
		Shale bracelet	E84:9337
X11	Pit 252	Coarse pottery	E84:9351a,b
		Stone spindle-whorl	E84:9352
X11	Pit 253	Coarse pottery	E84:9373, 9374a–g, 9375, 9526a,b
		Mould	E84:9376
X1	Pit 254	Coarse pottery	E84:9353a–g, 9354, 9355, 9376.1, 9377, 9377.1, 9378, 9379, 9494a–f
		Flint	E84:9495

* Context description unclear—may not be this feature. **Should be 'Identified in the log book as a mould fragment'.

The fill consisted of a series of fine layers of grey silt and yellow soil, 5–10cm in maximum thickness, which had filtered in from the sides. A flat-bottomed post-hole, 62–65cm in depth and with a maximum width of 20cm, cut through all the layers into the base of the pit. The lower part of this post-hole was filled with yellow material, while above, to a depth of some 40cm, a darkish grey zone with mixed areas of charcoal occurred. A number of smallish, flat-sided stones lay on one another along the edge of the grey material and must represent packing stones which helped to secure an original post.

Several other post-holes of similar character occurred close by, having also been inserted into the fill of the pit. Four of these formed a roughly straight line, but the significance of this cannot be determined in such a narrow cutting. They do show, however, that the features uncovered here do not represent a single phase of activity. A concentration of post-holes in Sq. X12, all shallower than those referred to above, are even less informative.

All the pits contained varying amounts of coarse pottery in their silt. In one (Pit 250) there was a single sherd but otherwise the quantity was larger. Pits 242 (not labelled on Fig. 2.18) and 243/4 (both with 47 sherds) had the largest amounts. A single mould fragment came from Pit 253 (not labelled on Fig. 2.118) in Sq. X11 and ten mould fragments were found in the grey material in Pit 243/4. A single sherd of Middle Bronze Age pottery (E84:9309) also came from Pit 243. The only other pit finds of any significance were a shale bracelet fragment from Pit 250 in Sq. X13 (E84:9337; Fig. 3.107) and a stone spindle-whorl fragment (E84:9352; Fig. 3.110) from Pit 252 in Sq. X11 (Table 2.12) (not labelled on plan).

2.8 NEW EVIDENCE FOR DATING THE CONSTRUCTION SEQUENCE OF RAMPART 2 AND DITCH 2 AT RATHGALL HILLFORT: FIELDWORK AT CUTTING X, 2011

Matthew Seaver and Joanne Gaffrey, with contributions from Lorna O'Donnell and Meriel McClatchie

2.8.1 Introduction

In August 2011 a team from the School of Archaeology, University College Dublin, set out to record and re-evaluate part of the excavation trench known as Cutting X, the only one to examine Rampart 2, Ditch 2 and Rampart 3 at Rathgall hillfort (Fig. 2.127).[42] The trench was to be backfilled as part of Office of Public Works plans to improve access to the monument. All rubble and soil that had accumulated since 1978 was removed and the east-facing section was heavily cleaned. The trench was recorded in plan and the section face drawn. New soil samples were taken from the basal fills to provide new radiocarbon dates, and Kubiëna tin samples were taken from underneath Rampart 2 to aid any future soil analysis. The results of the assessment provided new, tighter dates for the deposits underlying Rampart 2 and surprising dating for the ditch, which has knock-on consequences for the construction of Rampart 2. Here discussion of the questions posed by the original fieldwork and the results of the 2011 investigation will be presented, and the implications of these for the dating of the enclosures considered.

2.8.2 The 2011 fieldwork

The original fieldwork in Cutting X examined Rampart 2 and Ditch 2 and discovered an underlying grey soil deposit, pits and post-holes, along with a range of Bronze Age artefacts (section 2.7 above), but left significant questions regarding the sequence of construction and dating. The radiocarbon-dated samples obtained from underneath the bank in 1978 had high standard deviations and, while broadly Bronze Age, did not narrow down the chronology for the formation of deposits pre-dating the rampart (see Chapter 4, section 4.4, for the complete list and discussion of radiocarbon dating). The radiocarbon dates for the ditch were all taken from diffuse charcoal from the upper 1m of the backfill and ranged from the Bronze Age to the medieval period. An analysis of the artefact distribution showed that the deposits beneath the ramparts contained Bronze Age mould fragments and potsherds. While the original excavation assigned artefacts to general 10m grid squares, Raftery notes that these artefacts were concentrated in the mottled area to the north of the cutting under Rampart 2. No artefacts were found within the ditch or in the deposits running up to Rampart 3 during the original excavations, despite the occurrence of extensive features and artefacts to the south (outside) of this rampart.

The 2011 fieldwork closely studied the east-facing section of Ramparts 2 and 3, which measured 7.5m in width and 1.5m in height (Figs 2.128 and 2.129). The re-examination identified the pre-bank deposits noted by Raftery and at least four stages of rampart construction:

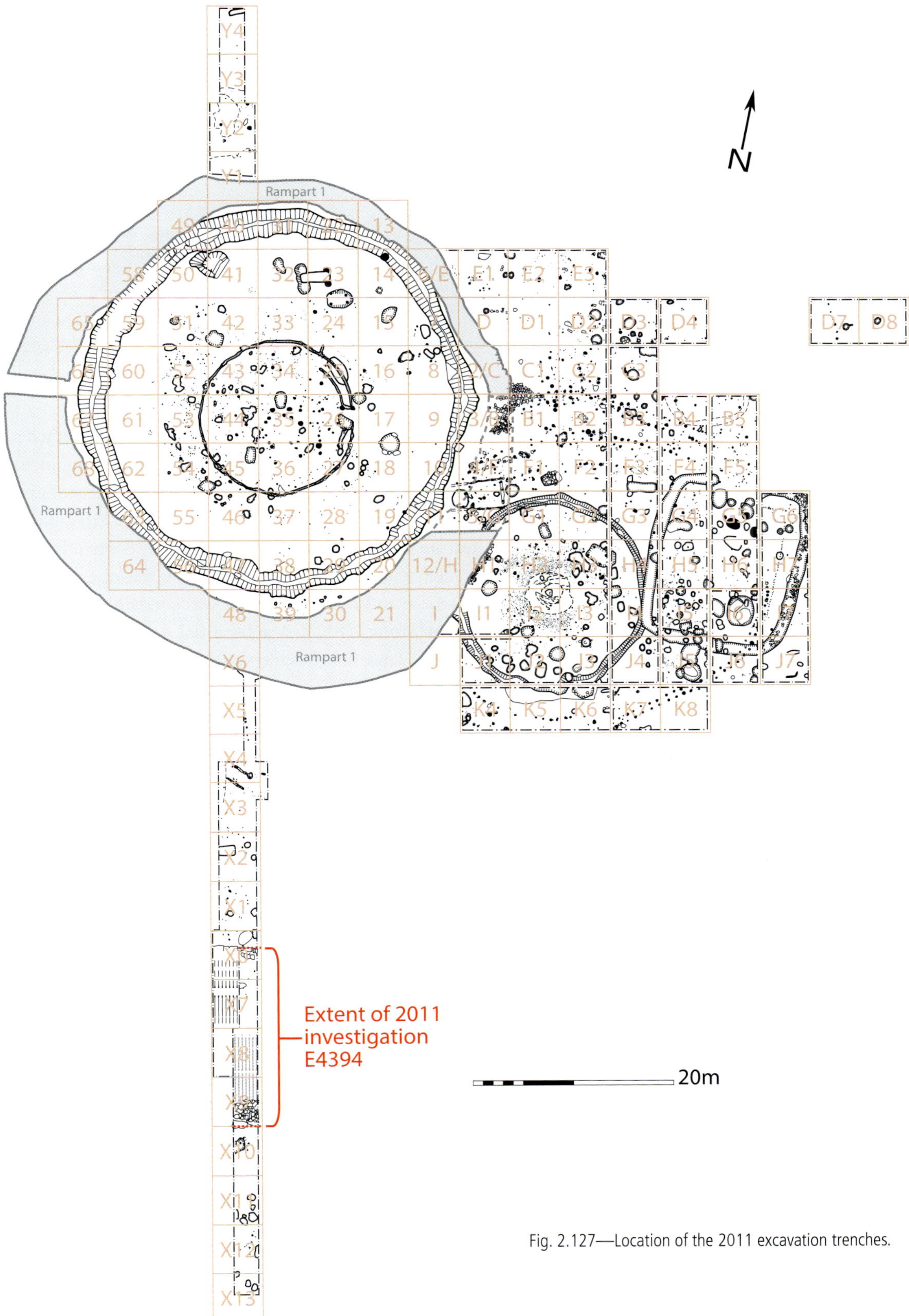

Fig. 2.127—Location of the 2011 excavation trenches.

Fig. 2.128—Composite image of the east-facing section of Cutting X after cleaning in 2011, showing corresponding grid marks from 1978.

- large stone blocks at northern end (F19);
- yellow sandy rampart with infrequent stones at northern end (F10);
- yellow sandy soil and frequent stones in rampart to the south (F16);
- stone revetment on inner face of rampart (F20).

The earliest feature identified was a very large stone slab (at least 1.2m east–west by 0.5m in width) at the northern end of the cutting underneath Rampart 2, which was overlain by a second, similar-sized stone and several boulders (F19). It was set into the yellow sandy natural soil (F12/13). Two archaeological features, a shallow pit with a concave base, 0.5m wide by 0.15m deep (F14), and the base of a stake-hole, 0.08m wide and 0.05m deep (F15), were uncovered to the south of these large stones, both of which appear to have been part of the 1978 excavations. The relationship of these features to the overlying deposits was not originally recorded, although the 1978 section drawing suggests that they were cut through the deposits underlying the rampart. The large basal stone of F19 was abutted to the south by orange silty deposits containing mottled grey blocks similar in colour and consistency to the 'grey' deposit further south, indicating that it had been disturbed by the rampart construction (F18). The earliest deposit to the south of F18 was reddish-brown silty sand containing occasional charcoal flecks (F3); it was 0.06–1m thick and was overlain by a thin deposit of iron pan followed by soft grey silty sand, 0.12–0.17m thick, which contained occasional charcoal flecks (F1). This could be a grey podzol deposit or a relict ploughsoil deposit, which would need to be tested through analysis of thin sections (T. Cummins, pers. comm.). At the northern end of the trench, an earthen rampart of yellow soil with sparse stones (F16), which contained distinct blocks of weathered grey soil, overlay the large stones F19 and the deposit F18; it was 1.1m in width and 1.2m in height. This feature was recognised by Raftery in 1978 when he noted that an area with significantly fewer stones was noted in plan at the northern end of the trench. It was overlain by a very clear tip line of stones (F17). A substantial bank of yellow clay with frequent large field boulders and roughly quarried granite stone was subsequently thrown up, covering the bank (F10). The final stage in the construction of the rampart was the addition of a stone revetment, 1.6m wide and 1.2m high (F20), on its northern inner edge.

The ditch was V-shaped in section and measured 3.8m in width by 2.5m in depth; it was re-examined immediately south of the rampart, where it cut through deposits F1 and F3 (F21). The ditch had a gentle break of slope on its northern side and a narrow concave base. It had been cut through the yellow sandy natural boulder clay, which, from an inspection of the ditch edges, contained very few stones. The basal fill of the ditch was grey-brown silty clay with sparse flecks of charcoal and occasional stones, up to 0.1m thick (F8). On the northern side this was overlain by a deposit of soft orange-brown silty sand (F6), also 0.1m in thickness, which contained sparse charcoal flecks and no stones. On the northern side of the edge of the ditch overlying this deposit there was a very large rectangular granite block (1.2m by 0.4m) which had slipped into the ditch fill and otherwise lay against the natural edge of the ditch, suggesting that this happened at an early stage. The grey deposit (F1) that underlay the rampart ended on the northern side of this stone. On the southern side a similar deposit, 0.12m thick (F7), sat

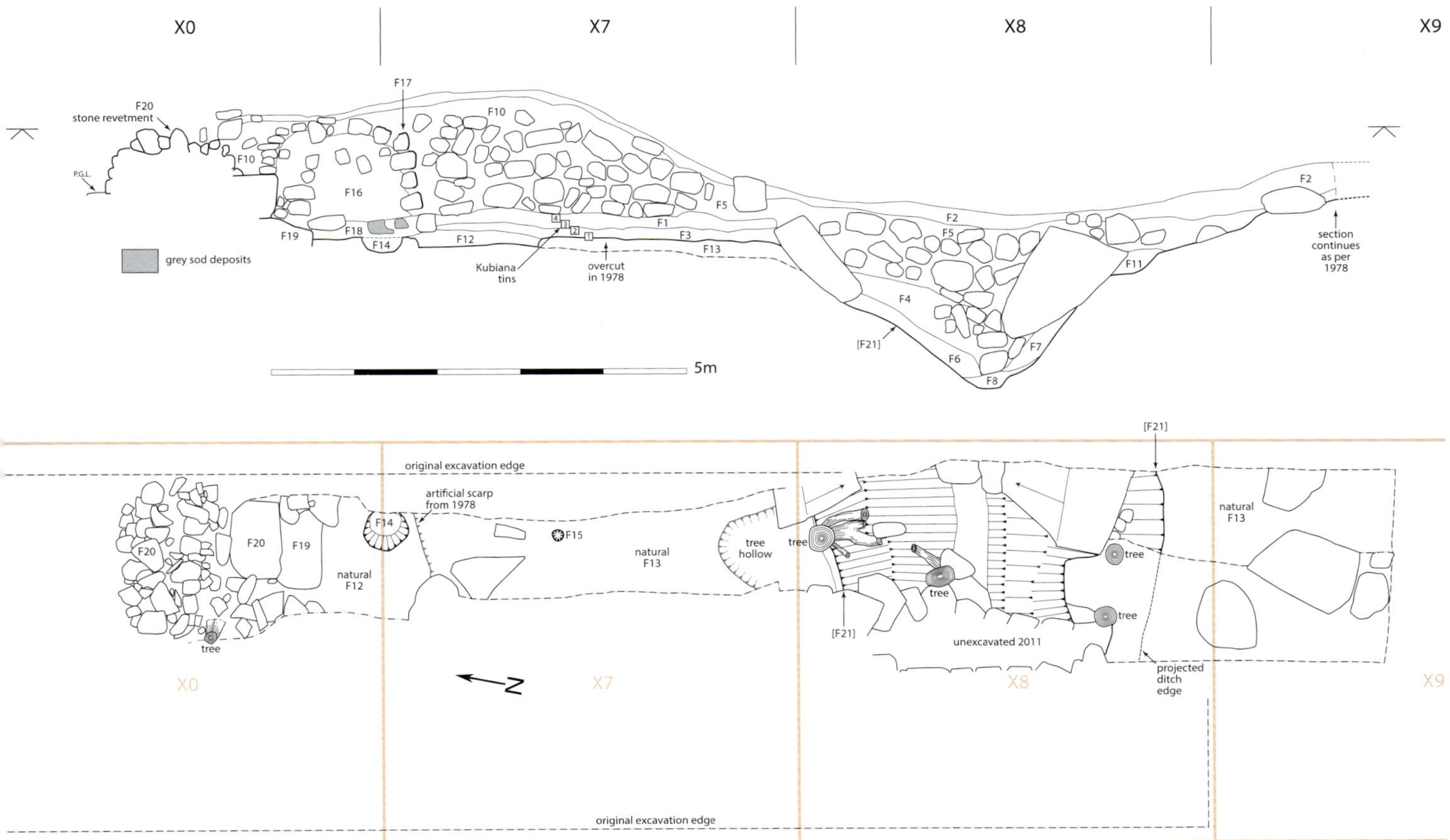

Fig. 2.129—Section and plan from 2011 excavation in Sqs X0, X7, X8 and X9.

on the edge of the ditch. F6 was overlain by a deposit of soft orange-brown silty sand with far more frequent stones, particularly towards the centre of the ditch (F4). These stones had clearly collapsed from the rampart. A very large triangular granite block (1.6m by 0.8m) overlay F7 and F4 on the southern side of the ditch. This is likely to have fallen from Rampart 3 and is similar in size and shape to some of the very large orthostatic stones present within this boundary. It had a flat base at one end, which may have allowed it to stand upright. On the southern edge a shallow pocket of clean reddish sandy silt, up to 0.14m thick (F11), underlay this stone. This preceded the upper fill of the ditch, which was yellow silty sand up to 1m deep, with frequent granite stones which are likely to have collapsed from Rampart 2 (F5). This material contained sparse charcoal flecks and was overlain by a thin layer of humus (F2).

No artefacts were recovered during the 2011 clean-up, excavation and reinstatement, and no animal bone was recovered from the ditch—the latter likely to be a consequence of acidic soil conditions and consistent with the original excavations. While charcoal remains indicate a range of activity in the environs of the ditch while it was open, there was almost no evidence for charred plant remains.

Radiocarbon dating, stratigraphy and the implications

Charcoal samples from within both deposits underlying Rampart 2 were tightly dated to the Middle Bronze Age, complementing the artefact remains and suggesting that they accumulated during occupation pre-dating the construction of the rampart (Table 2.13). The charcoal, although on the basis of a relatively small number of samples, indicated a somewhat different profile of species beneath the rampart than within the ditch (see O'Donnell, below).

The basal fills of the ditch were heavily sampled once a clean section face had been obtained. Four AMS radiocarbon dates were produced from short-lived charcoal species and a single charred plant seed (see McClatchie, Appendix 1, and O'Donnell, Appendix 2, below). These produced dates from the Mesolithic and the Middle Bronze Age and, significantly, two closely placed dates within the seventh century AD (see also Chapter 4, section 4.4, for a discussion of the dates). These were from basal fills on either side of the ditch (Table 2.13), indicating that the ditch began to silt up in the early medieval period and cannot have been dug much before that date. There were no clear indications that this ditch was a recut of a prehistoric predecessor. While further sections across the enclosing ditch at other points around its circumference would be desirable to confirm this finding, the weight of evidence points to this conclusion. If this is the case, what are the implications for the construction of Rampart 2?

The huge quantity of soil that would have been obtained from the excavation of the ditch must have been used to construct Rampart 2, at least in part. This may explain the very mixed range of original radiocarbon dates obtained from the upper fill of the ditch, which was at least in part likely to have been derived from a collapsed part of the rampart. There were very few stones in the excavated sides of the ditch and the large quantity of these used in the rampart construction must have come from somewhere else. The combination of rounded boulders and more rectangular fragments which had the appearance of being split suggests that it could have resulted from construction waste. There were clearly earlier phases to the construction of Rampart 2, with the earliest comprising the large stones at the northern end. These are similar to those used to construct Rampart 3. The difficulty is that Rampart 3 itself is undated and appeared from the 1978 excavations to be constructed within or overlying a grey soil horizon similar to that underlying Rampart 2. Therefore comparing the construction sequence of both ramparts does not help to date the earliest phases of Rampart 2.

2.8.3 Conclusion

The fieldwork at Rathgall in 2011 provided new secure and close dates for the Bronze Age activity that pre-dated Rampart 2. It identified four stages in the construction of that rampart. Significant questions remain about the dating of these phases, but secure dates helped to put the original radiocarbon dates from the ditch into context.

While a great deal more investigation is clearly needed to determine the character of early medieval Rathgall, it would seem possible that, like Dún Aonghasa, it was significantly modified in the seventh century AD on account of its perceived significance in the past (Cotter 2012; see Chapter 7).

APPENDIX 1: ANALYSIS OF NON-WOOD PLANT MACRO-REMAINS

Meriel McClatchie

Methodology

A possible charred seed from F7, Sample 10, was presented for analysis. Identification was carried out using a stereo-microscope, with magnifications ranging from x6.3 to x50. The seed was identified by comparison with reference material in McClatchie's collection of modern diaspores.

Material recorded

One charred seed of *Vicia/Lathyrus* sp. (vetches/pea).

Comments

The extracted seed is suitable for AMS ^{14}C dating. Species of the vetch/pea genera can be found growing in a variety of environments, including grassy and woody places. Species of the vetch and (wild) pea genera are often considered to have been utilised in foods, whether for humans or animals, particularly during the historic period.

APPENDIX 2: WOOD CHARCOAL ANALYSIS

Lorna O'Donnell

Introduction

Eight soil samples from excavations at Rathgall were submitted for charcoal analysis (Seaver 2012). Charcoal or carbonised wood is one of the most frequently found ecofacts on Irish archaeological sites. It can be used for radiocarbon dating, reconstruction of woodland flora and interpretation of fuel selection patterns.

Methodology

Processing

Soil samples were processed by means of mechanical flotation tanks. This involved the agitation of the soil sample in a water-filled tank lined with a 1mm nylon mesh, releasing the lighter environmental material (flot) such as seeds and charcoal from the soil matrix. This lighter fraction was collected in a sieve of 300μm mesh size. Once dry, the retent was sorted using a stack of sieves with mesh sizes of 4mm, 2mm and 1mm. Charcoal larger than 2mm in size was sorted out of the retent and the flot; all seeds were extracted and any finds (bone, pottery, flint and other such archaeological material) were also sorted from the retent. All material

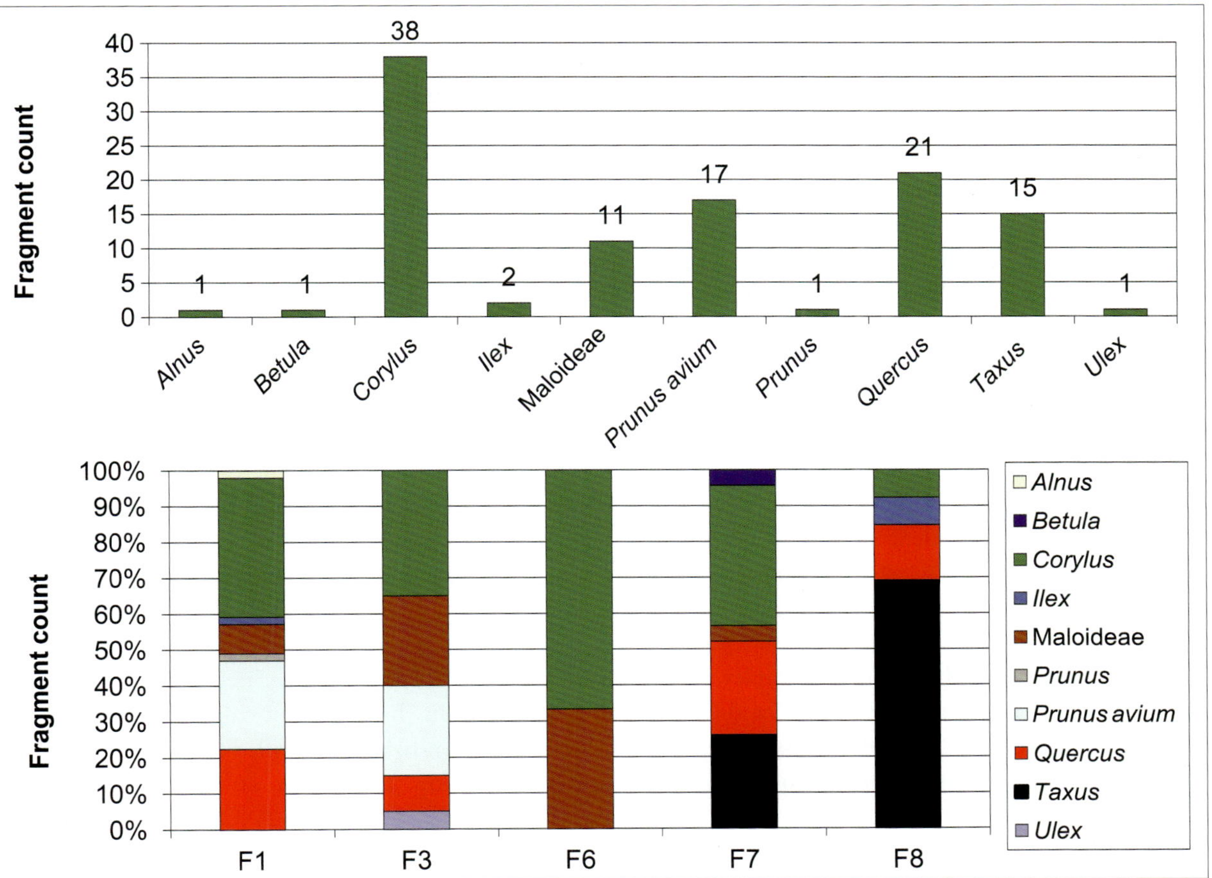

Fig. 2.130—Charcoal from the 2011 excavations by species.

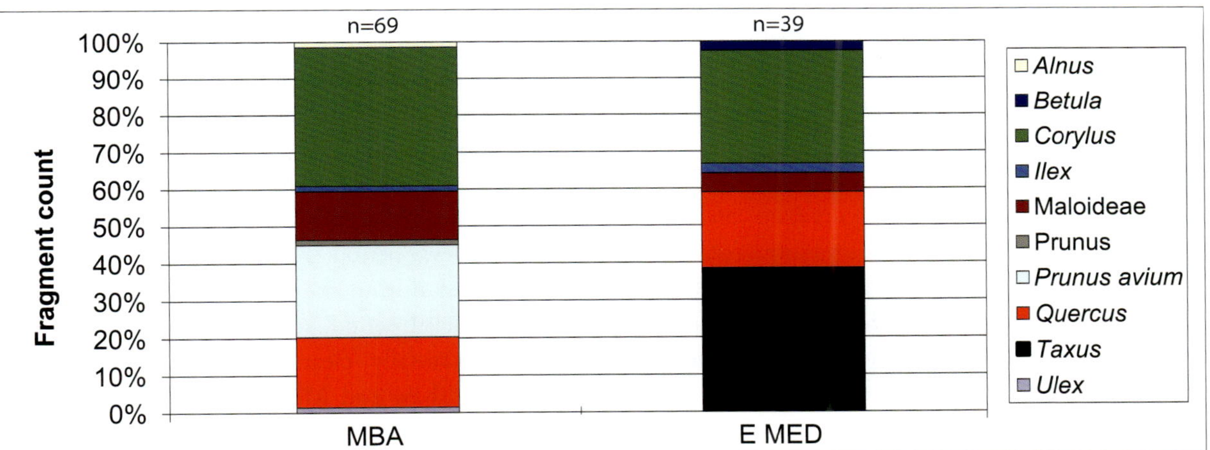

Fig. 2.131—Charcoal from the 2011 excavations by period.

retrieved from residue-sorting was recorded.

Charcoal identification

Each piece of charcoal was examined and orientated first under low magnification (10x–40x). They were then broken to reveal their transverse, tangential and longitudinal surfaces. Pieces were mounted in plasticine and examined under a metallurgical microscope with dark ground light and magnifications generally of 20x and 40x.

Each taxon or species will have its own particular anatomical characteristics, and these are identified by comparison with keys (Schweingruber 1978; Hather 2000; Wheeler *et al.* 1989) and a reference collection supplied by the National Botanical Gardens of Ireland, Glasnevin.

Details of charcoal recording
The general age group of each taxon per sample was recorded, and the growth rates were classified as slow, medium, fast or mixed. Ring curvature of the pieces was also noted—for example, weakly curved annual rings suggest the use of trunks or larger branches, while strongly curved annual rings indicate the burning of smaller branches or trees (Fig. 2.131). Tyloses in vessels in species such as oak can denote the presence of heartwood. These occur when adjacent parenchyma cells penetrate the vessel walls (via the pitting), effectively blocking the vessels (Gale 2003, 37). Insect infestation is usually denoted by round holes, considered to be caused by burrowing insects. Their presence normally suggests the use of decayed degraded wood, which may have been gathered from the woodland floor or may have been stockpiled. Short-lived twigs with strongly curved annual rings were selected for radiocarbon dating.

Results
Charcoal was examined from eight samples from Rathgall, derived from five features (F1, F3, F6, F7 and F8). Overall the level of charcoal is low; only 108 fragments were identifiable. Ten wood taxa were recorded, which is quite diverse, given the low number of fragments present in the samples. Hazel (*Corylus avellana*) and oak (*Quercus* sp.) are the two most common taxa. Alder (*Alnus* sp.), birch (*Betula* sp.), holly (*Ilex aquifolium*), pomaceous fruitwood (Maloideae), wild/bird cherry (*Prunus avium/padus*), *Prunus* sp., yew (*Taxus baccata*) and gorse (*Ulex* sp.) were also recorded (Fig. 2.130; Tables 2.13–2.15). Short-lived species with strongly curved annual rings indicating twigs or small branches were separated for AMS radiocarbon dating (Table 2.14).

Examination of the ring curvature on the charcoal fragments revealed that trees in a variety of stages of growth were burnt at Rathgall. Both larger branches and smaller twigs of the most commonly identified tree, hazel, were burnt. This is indicated by the presence of both weakly and strongly curved annual rings within the fragments. Annual rings within the oak fragments are almost all (with the exception of S9, F7) weakly curved, indicating that large branches were burnt. The presence of tyloses in three cases (S5, S11 and S12) suggests that some of this oak represents burnt heartwood. Annual ring counts overall are low in the charcoal fragments, ranging from two (oak, S10, and holly, S12) to twelve (hazel, S7).

Growth is medium in most cases, which indicates that fairly average conditions for tree growth existed around the Rathgall area. There are some exceptions to this; fast growth was noted in *Prunus* from S7 and holly from S12. In contrast, the oak in S11 is slow-grown, suggesting that optimal conditions for growth were not present. Alternatively, the tree may have suffered trauma which inhibited growth. The presence of tyloses within this slow-grown oak sample, while possibly indicating heartwood, may also suggest repair to the tree after damage.

Some temporal change is noted (Fig. 2.131). Oak, pomaceous fruitwood, holly and hazel were identified from both the Middle Bronze Age and early medieval periods, indicating their continuity in the landscape over approximately 2,000 years. No Prunoideae trees (including *Prunus avium/padus* and *Prunus*) were recorded from the early medieval deposits, whereas they accounted for 25% of the Middle Bronze Age contexts. Yew was important in the early medieval period (28% of the identifications) but was not identified in the prehistoric contexts.

Comparative material
The main trees identified from the Middle Bronze Age deposits (hazel, cherry, oak and pomaceous fruitwood) have frequently been identified from other Bronze Age sites in the Wicklow area, such as at Charlesland (03E0146) and Ballynagran (06E0552) (O'Donnell 2004a; 2006). Regional studies indicate that these trees were also common in other areas of Leinster and Munster during the Bronze Age (O'Donnell 2007; 2011). During this period in Ireland's woodland history, clearances that began during the Neolithic period had opened up the forest canopy, allowing many scrub trees such as cherry, blackthorn, pomaceous fruitwoods and hazel to flourish.

Pollen data from Wicklow indicate that hazel was important during the Middle Bronze Age and the early medieval period. The level of oak, however, is considerably higher during the Middle Bronze Age than in the early medieval period, suggesting that oak woodlands had been substantially cleared during the later use of Rathgall (Bradshaw and McGee 1987, 223). It is likely that Irish woodlands had been depleted by the early medieval period. O'Sullivan (1998a) notes that various sources of evidence indicate that the early medieval Irish landscape had only occasional small woods, hedgerows and scrubby woodland embedded within a highly managed agricultural landscape. Certainly there is lower species diversity in the samples dating from the early medieval period, although this could easily be a product of the low number of fragments identified. Holly, hazel and birch also grew during the medieval period at Charlesland, Co. Wicklow (04E0774), but not yew and

Table 2.13—Results of charcoal analyses.

Sample	Feature	Flot weight (g)	Identification	Common name	Frag. count	Weight (g)	Size (mm)	Growth	Ring count
5	1	0.23	*Corylus avellana* L.	Hazel	6	0.1	4–5	Medium	7–9
5	1	0.23	*Ilex aquifolium* L.	Holly	1	0.03	3	Medium	4
5	1	0.23	Maloideae L./Miller	Pomaceous fruitwood	4	0.05	2–4	Medium	3–4
5	1	0.23	*Prunus avium/padus* L.	Pomaceous fruitwood	8	0.23	5–6	Medium	4–5
5	1	0.23	*Quercus* L. Liebl	Oak	5	0.16	4–5	Medium	4–5
6	3	0.18	*Corylus avellana* L.	Hazel	7	0.17	6–7	Medium	5–6
6	3	0.18	Maloideae L./Miller	Pomaceous fruitwood	5	0.37	3–5	Medium	4–8
6	3	0.18	*Prunus avium/padus* L.	Wild/bird cherry	5	0.15	3–5	Medium	4–5
6	3	0.18	*Quercus* L. Liebl	Oak	2	0.02	4	Medium	4
6	3	0.18	*Ulex* L.	Gorse	1	0.62	12	Medium	15
7	1	0.45	*Alnus glutinosa* L. Gärtner	Alder	1	0.05	5	Medium	6
7	1	0.45	*Corylus avellana* L.	Hazel	2	0.06	4–5	Medium	10–12
7	1	0.45	*Prunus avium/padus* L.	Wild/bird cherry	1	0.04	3	Medium	4
7	1	0.45	*Prunus* sp.		1	0.08	7	Fast	3
7	1	0.45	*Quercus* L. Liebl	Oak	1	0.02	3	Medium	4
8	6	0.24	*Corylus avellana* L	Hazel	2	0.1	7–8	Medium	4–5
8	6	0.24	Maloideae L./Miller	Pomaceous fruitwood	1	0.02	3	Medium	3
9	7	0.24	*Corylus avellana* L.	Hazel	4	0.25	5–8	Medium	6–8
9	7	0.24	*Quercus* L. Liebl	Oak	2	0.05	4	Medium	5–6
9	7	0.24	*Taxus baccata* L.	Yew	6	0.46	5–16	Medium	6–10
10	7	0.18	*Betula* Ehrh.L.	Birch	1	0.01	3	Medium	3
10	7	0.18	*Corylus avellana* L.	Hazel	5	0.11	6–8	Medium	9–10
10	7	0.18	Maloideae L./Miller	Pomaceous fruitwood	1	0.02	3	Medium	5
10	7	0.18	*Quercus* L. Liebl	Oak	4	0.04	3–4	Medium	2–10
11	1	0.19	*Corylus avellana* L.	Hazel	11	0.21	3–4	Medium	5–6
11	1	0.19	*Prunus avium/padus* L.	Wild/bird cherry	3	0.11	4–5	Medium	6–8
11	1	0.19	*Quercus* L. Liebl	Oak	5	0.12	4–5	Slow	9–10
12	8	0.32	*Corylus avellana* L.	Hazel	1	0.03	4	Medium	3
12	8	0.32	*Ilex aquifolium* L.	Holly	1	0.25	5	Fast	2
12	8	0.32	*Quercus* L. Liebl	Oak	2	0.04	3	Medium	4
12	8	0.32	*Taxus baccata* L.	Yew	9	0.23	3–4	Medium	3–5

Table 2.14—Radiocarbon dates obtained from 2011 fieldwork within Ditch 2.

Sample no.	Feature	Lab code	Charred material	%C13	BP	2-sigma calibration
E4394:S12:F8	Primary ditch fill	UBA-19277	Hazel	-23.8	1388±29	cal. AD 606–672
E4394:S8:F6	Primary ditch fill	UBA-19281	Hazel	-25.2	3339±33	1731–1527 cal. BC
E4394:S9:F7	Primary ditch fill	UBA-19282	Hazel	-25.1	1387±24	cal. AD 613–668
E4394:S10:F7	Primary ditch fill	UBA-19283	Vetch	-25.9	7265±34	6219–6060 cal. BC
Sample no.	**Feature**	**Lab code**	**Dated charcoal**	**%C13**	**BP**	**2-sigma calibration**
E4394:S5:F1	Grey deposit	UBA-19279	Wild/bird cherry	-18.3	3054±27	1408–1261 cal. BC
E4394:S6:F3	Reddish silt under F1	UBA-19280	Hazel	-25.6	3018±26	1386–1133 cal. BC
E4394:S11:F1	Grey deposit	UBA-19278	Hazel	-27.3	3072±28	1413–1268 cal. BC

Table 2.15—Charcoal selected for AMS ^{14}C dating.

Sample	Feature	Identification	Fragment count	Weight (g)	Size (mm)	Growth	Ring count
5	1	*Prunus avium/padus* (wild/bird cherry)	1	0.06	6	Medium	5
6	3	*Corylus avellana* (hazel)	1	0.08	6	Medium	6
7	1	No suitable material for AMS ^{14}C dating					
8	6	*Corylus avellana* (hazel)	1	0.08	8	Medium	5
9	7	*Corylus avellana* (hazel)	1	0.14	5	Medium	8
10	7	Maloideae (pomaceous fruitwood)	1	0.02	3	Medium	5
11	1	*Corylus avellana* (hazel)	1	0.03	4	Medium	6
12	8	*Corylus avellana* (hazel)	1	0.03	4	Medium	3

pomaceous fruitwood, in contrast to Rathgall (O'Donnell 2004b). By the early medieval period Irish woodlands were recognised as a valuable resource. According to the Brehon Laws, trees were separated into four classifications, depending on the economic value of the wood: 'nobles of the wood', 'commoners of the wood', 'lower divisions of the wood' and 'bushes of the wood'. Trees like oak, holly and hazel were considered 'nobles of the wood', while the lowest classification (bushes of the wood) included bracken, bog myrtle and gorse or furze. Fines were imposed on people caught cutting branches or cutting at the base of the trees. These fines varied according to the classification of the tree and included heifers and sheep (Kelly 1976). The importance placed on woodlands in these periods shows that they may have been a diminishing feature in the Irish countryside.

The new radiocarbon dates from this phase of excavation of Rathgall indicate that the ditch began to silt up *c.* cal. AD 606–668. It is interesting to note that this is approximately 100 years after the AD 536 narrow-ring event, a time when oak trees in Ireland demonstrated more than six years of extremely narrow ring growth. It is recorded in timbers from Ireland, Europe, eastern Asia and the western United States, suggesting a force that was strong enough to inhibit growth across much of the northern hemisphere. This correlates with environmental disaster in the written record, for example the mention of 'famine' and 'failure of bread' in AD 536 and AD 537 in the Annals of Ulster (Hall 2011, 116). Some of the oak trees in particular from Rathgall, which may have been more than 100 years old when felled, could have been growing when this narrow-ring event occurred.

Summary

Charcoal was analysed from eight samples from five features at Rathgall. Ten wood taxa were identified, the most common of which are oak and hazel. Twigs, branches and larger trunks were burnt on the site. A mosaic of different woodlands probably grew close to the site and were utilised for fuel.

2.9 EXTERNAL ACTIVITY SOUTH OF THE RAMPARTS (Z CUTTINGS)

Barry Raftery

Documentation of this area is limited and some things remain unclear. For example, earlier versions of a plan of the Z2 cutting (OII) indicate that its numbering started with O2:3. The last of the six cuttings was accordingly numbered O2:8. The numbering of the finds, however, attributes finds from the ring-ditch to O2:7 and O2:6, i.e. Z2:f and g, suggesting that the numbering on the earlier plan is incorrect. No original plan was available in the archive and the area plans for the ring-ditch do not indicate grid numbers. Furthermore, some features attributed to Z2:g appear to be located in Z2:f.

In a large, trapezoidal field immediately downslope from the outermost hillfort rampart on the south, some curious, regularly circular concentrations of fern growth were visible in a series of aerial photographs taken by Norman and St Joseph in 1969 (Figs 1.15a, 2.132). From the beginning of the excavations at Rathgall in 1969 these had been a subject of some discussion, and so the availability of limited funding in September 1971, following the main season's excavation within the central hillfort enclosure, permitted four weeks of trial-trenching through the areas where the fern circles occurred.

The investigations demonstrated unequivocally that the fern growth was a product of natural forces unrelated to human activity. Completely by accident, however, important evidence of Bronze Age activity was brought to light. It was thus a matter of great good fortune that in the early spring of 1972 official monies, which for accounting reasons had to be disposed of before the end of the financial year (then 5 April), unexpectedly became available. This enabled further, extensive excavation to take place in the same general area from the last week in February to the end of March of that year. The conditions were miserably inclement, frequently involving early morning delays until the ground had thawed sufficiently

Fig. 2.132—Aerial photograph of Rathgall and Knockeen (background), looking north, showing fern circles in the area south of Rampart 4 (Norman and St Joseph).

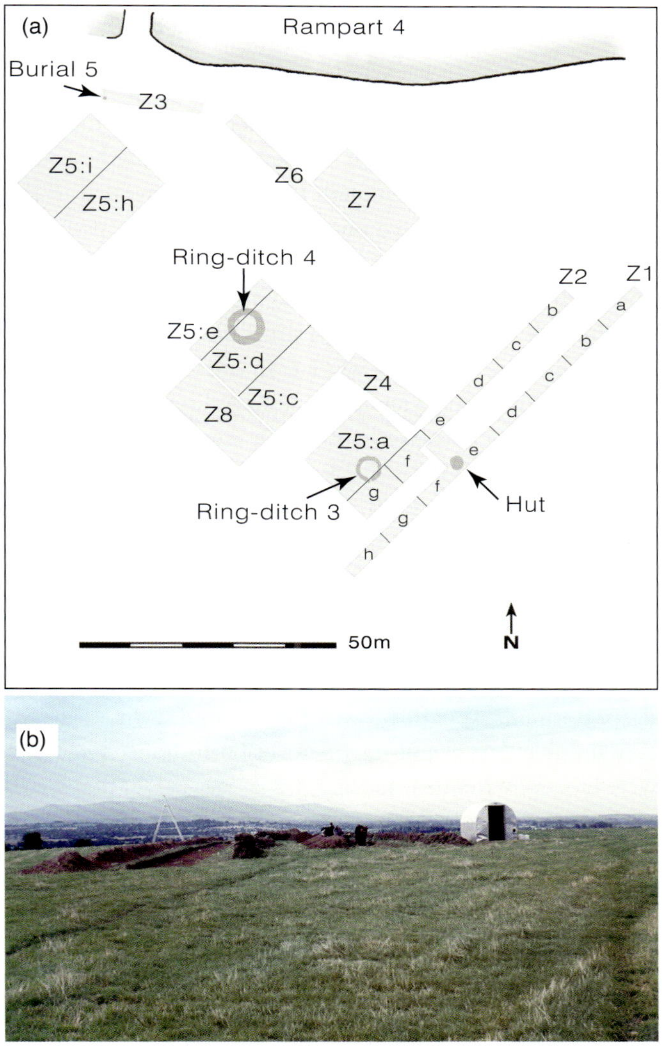

Fig. 2.133—(a) Plan of Z cuttings. (b) View along the excavations of Cuttings Z1 and Z2 outside Rampart 4, looking south-west.

to enable work to begin.

In the first season (1971) two long, narrow north–south trenches (Z1 and Z2; Fig. 2.133), with minor extensions, were excavated close to, and parallel to, one another through the area of the vegetation rings. Each of these trenches was 2.5m wide and they were respectively 60m and 80m in length. A further area of investigation, Cutting Z3, a narrow trench 20m long and 2.5m wide, was dug outside one of the presumed entrance gaps in Rampart 4 and about 10m distant from it. A total of just over 400m^2 was uncovered. In the second season (1972), as a sizeable workforce of local labourers was employed, it was possible to extend the excavated area westwards in large 20m by 20m squares, as well as opening a number of other cuttings, mainly to the north-west of the initial cuttings Z1 and Z2, in the zone approaching the outer rampart. In the course of these two seasons a total area of 1,736.25m^2 was investigated.

The two seasons of excavation yielded considerable evidence of prehistoric activity. This included two circular ditched enclosures, a hut site, a possible burial pit and a range of pits and post-holes. In addition, a number of artefacts, including mould fragments, were discovered (see below). While the total number of finds was tiny compared with the volume of finds from within the fort (there were 202 catalogue entries, representing 208 objects,[43] from the area outside), they were nonetheless of considerable interest and importance. With a few exceptions of Neolithic, Early Bronze Age and early medieval date, all belonged to the Bronze Age, and the activity on the southern slopes thus overlapped culturally, and probably chronologically, with that revealed uphill to the north. It should be stressed, however, that deep ploughing had been even more intensive in this area than elsewhere, so that no trace of the original prehistoric levels was found.

2.9.1 The hut site—Cutting Z1

Cutting Z1 was the first of two main cuttings opened across the vegetation rings in 1971. Its 80m length was divided into 10m segments (Z1:a–Z1:h). Along its entire length, a well-defined series of recent plough furrows was revealed in the yellow subsoil, all oriented north-east/south-west. Apart from two small pits in Sq. Z1:d and a small scatter of coarse potsherds in the ploughsoil, the only significant indication of a prehistoric presence over the entire 80m was the remains of a small hut site in Sqs Z1:e/Z1:f. In order to excavate this fully, the cutting was extended for a short distance to the west. The finding of two fragments of Beaker pottery indicates earlier activity in Z1 (E100:13a–b).

The pits (nos 1 and 2) were situated closely together in the south of Cutting Z1:d near its western face (Figs 2.154 and 2.155). They were subcircular in plan, with maximum diameters of 70cm and 30cm respectively. Pit 1 (the larger) was about 25cm deep, with steep sides and a flat base. Pit 2 had sharply sloping sides and a rounded base. It was 10–12cm deep. Both pits were filled with a black, humus-like material containing charcoal and fragments of burnt bone. The latter were especially frequent in Pit 1.

Indications of more intensive occupation activity began to emerge some 10–12m south of these pits. In the southern part of Z1:e, as well as in Z1:f and g, three fragments of coarse pottery were found, and small flecks of charcoal appeared scattered in the lower levels of the covering brown humus. It rapidly became apparent that these features were associated with the small hut site.

The latter first appeared as irregular patches of greyish and greyish-brown soil within which an irregularly circular outline could in part be recognised. Around the east, the latter was formed by a band of grey which developed into an amorphous expansion on the west. Close to the grey band on the east, an irregularly C-shaped area of grey showed up in the subsoil, and it was noticeable that on the south there were two irregular expansions near each other in the grey arc and that they were joined by a narrower straight band of the same material.

Excavation confirmed, as had been instantly suspected, that this was indeed the remains of a small hut (Figs 2.134 and 2.135). The grey band was in fact the grey fill of a narrow, carefully dug trench, which can only have been intended originally to support a series of upright timbers. The fill was a very fine, silty grey material containing a considerable quantity of carbonised wood, generally in small fragments.

Fig. 2.134—Hut feature in Cutting Z1:e–f (looking south-east).

The trench formed a regular hexagonal outline with straight sides and rounded angles. It had internal dimensions varying from 2.25m to 2.5m and had for the most part been carefully dug to a U-shaped cross-section. Its depth, in general, was 20–25cm, but on the south-east this decreased to as little as 15cm, while on the north, for a short stretch, it was no more than 10cm deep. Such irregularity is doubtless related to—but not, perhaps, entirely explained by—the extensive removal of the original prehistoric levels and these cannot be regarded as original depths.

The curious pair of closely spaced expansions on the circumference of the bedding trench on the south-west appeared, on excavation, to be an interesting entrance feature (Fig. 2.136). In this zone there was a marked flattening of the bedding trench to a narrow, straight groove, creating an entrance gap. On either side of this gap the trench, at 25cm, was at its deepest, and it emerged that the two expansions in the grey band were in fact two substantial post-holes filled with the same silted material as the post slot. The post-holes were 55cm apart, and in each case there are suggestions that the timbers which had once stood in them had been secured in place by packing stones.

The south-western post-hole, 25cm wide and 30cm deep, was the most substantial of the two. Three small stones set around the edge of the hole at roughly regular intervals appear to have been inserted deliberately, thus indicating that the original upright was about 20cm in diameter. The opposing post-hole was some 35cm deep but its width was fractionally less than 15cm. A fairly sizeable stone wedged into the bedding trench immediately adjacent to this post-hole may have served as a packing stone.

It thus appears that the south-western post-hole was the

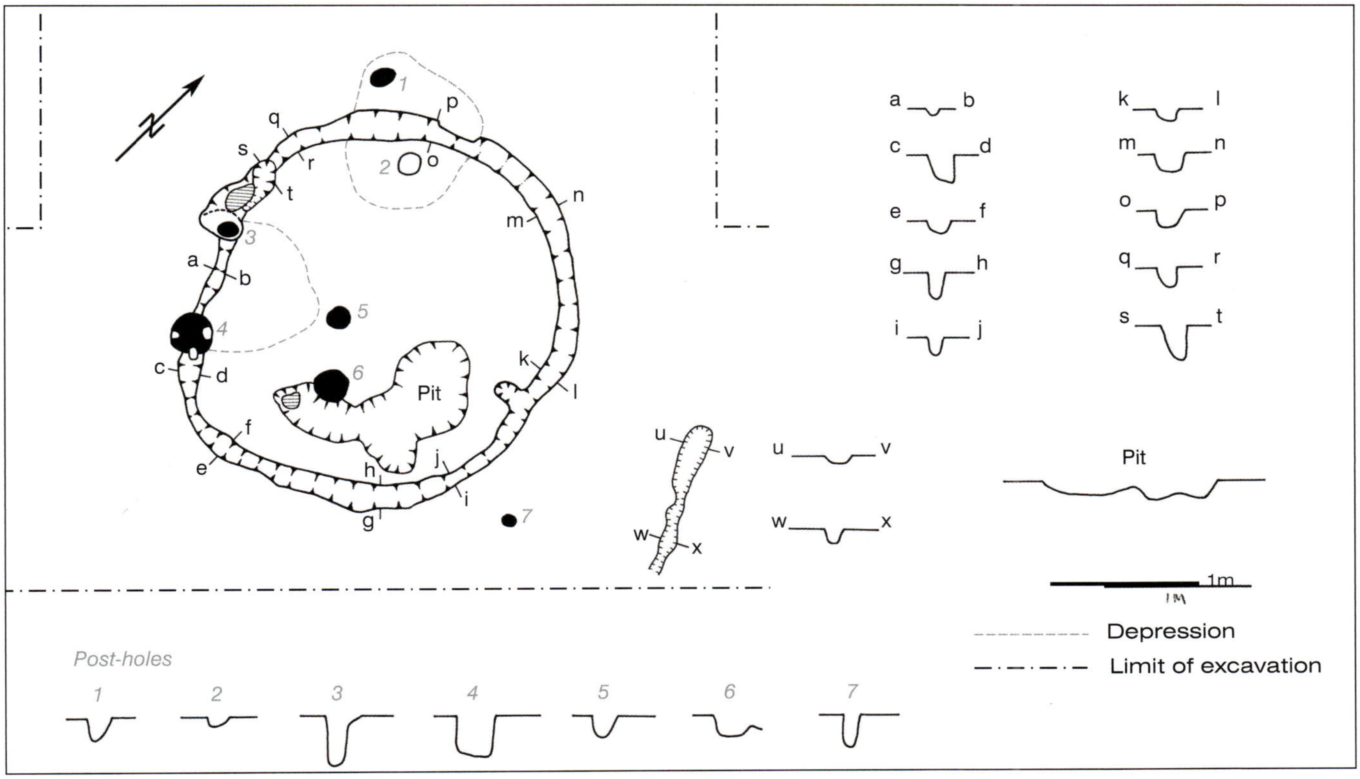

Fig. 2.135—Hut 1 and associated features, plans and sections.

Fig. 2.136—Entrance posts and threshold of Hut 1 in Cutting Z1:e–f (looking south-east).

more important of the two and, if it is taken that the entrance gap was closed by a door of some sort, it is on this side that the door probably hung. The suggestion that a door once existed is supported by the presence of the narrow, shallow groove linking the two post-holes. This sloped slightly to the west. Its width varied from 6cm to 10cm and it maintained a constant depth of no more than about 5cm. There can be little doubt that the groove originally held a wooden threshold of some sort against which a doorway of organic material (wood, leather or heavy textile) presumably closed.

Immediately inside the door, extending inwards for a distance of about 75cm, an irregular area of grey-brown material occurred. This was hard-packed but was nowhere more than 1cm thick. It could represent trampling in the vicinity of the entrance. Somewhat off-centre there was a post-hole (PH 5), 15cm in width and depth, with a second post-hole of similar dimensions a short distance west of this (PH 6). The latter cut into an irregular pit—possibly even two conjoined pits—with a maximum length of about 1.25m and a width varying from 25cm to 65cm. It had an irregular base and was 12–15cm deep. The fill of this feature (grey-brown with flecks of charcoal) was similar to that which occurred in the vicinity of the entrance. There were no discernible layers.

In the north-western part of the interior a roughly oval area, slightly over 1m long and slightly under 1m wide, extended across the bedding trench. This layer, which consisted of undifferentiated grey-brown material, thus post-dated the abandonment of the house. It did, however, overlie PH 1, which is thus likely to have been contemporary with the house construction. On the east, a short distance outside the bedding trench, another post-hole (PH 7) was discovered (again possibly contemporary with the hut), and about 1m east of this a shallow, irregular-sided groove (perhaps a drain?) ran diagonally into the baulk in a south-westerly direction. It was 5–15cm in width and 5–10cm in depth. Its sides were fairly steep and its fill consisted of the same undifferentiated grey material that was present in all the other features.

The absence of a hearth or, indeed, of any trace of burning within the hut raises questions concerning the function of the tiny structure. It might be deemed too small to have fulfilled the function of a secular dwelling, but it should not be forgotten that any occupation layers that might have existed could have been removed by agricultural activities. Nevertheless, in view of the curious ring-ditches found in its vicinity, it is entirely possible that this structure—small but built with considerable care—served a purpose other than domestic habitation.

Finds from this area were few, consisting of the small amount of scattered coarse pottery referred to above and four further potsherds which came from the grey fill of the bedding trench (E100:4, 5a–b, 6).

2.9.2 Ring-ditch 3 (Cutting Z2/Z5:a)

Cutting Z2 (Fig. 2.133), the second cutting opened in 1971, proved to be archaeologically sterile apart from its south, where part of a small, penannular-ditched enclosure (Ring-ditch 3) was discovered, along with a series of pits and post-holes, many of substantial size. This prompted a small extension of the cutting by 2.5m to the south-west and 1m to the east. It was decided that the full investigation of this curious feature was desirable, so in 1972 the cutting was further enlarged by opening part of the immediately adjoining Z5:a. In total, an area of 20m by 10m was excavated.

Over the course of the two years of excavation an important body of finds came to light associated with this complex. These included clay mould fragments and coarse potsherds, some of them retrieved from the features forming and associated with Ring-ditch 3. A whetstone (E100:35) was found in the brown covering layer (topsoil), which also contained coarseware sherds, mould fragments and a barbed arrowhead (E100:31; Fig. 3.101).

The complex of features spread over an area measuring approximately 22m by 25m, with a few post-holes and scattered pits occurring beyond this zone (Z2:c–d). Ring-ditch 3 was the focus of the complex (Figs 2.137–2.139). It consisted of a penannular circular trench with a maximum internal diameter of 3.85m. An entrance gap occurred on the south; it was 80–85cm wide and the ditch terminals were carefully rounded. The ditch maintained a fairly consistent width of 1.2–1.5m, apart from at two points where bulges occurred on its inner edge on the south-east, possibly where rocks had been removed. On the north-east a large, natural boulder completely filled the ditch. No attempt had been made to remove it and thus it seems clear that the ditch was little more than a symbolic enclosure with no practical function, a feature already observed in the case of Ring-ditch 1 on the hilltop.

Notwithstanding the presence of the boulder, the ring-ditch had been dug with considerable care. Around most of its circumference the sides sloped steeply to a base which was, for the most part, regularly flat (Fig. 2.140), although in places it narrowed somewhat to a more V-shaped profile (Fig. 2.138). Its fill, completely devoid of stones, was surprisingly uniform. Apart from some dark brown humic material on the inner face in some areas (Fig. 2.141), this was a fine, uniformly grey silted material that seems to have accumulated quite rapidly. The fill of the ditch yielded some finds of coarse pottery, a mould fragment (E100:77) and a slate fragment with perforation (E100:78).

The surface of the area enclosed by the ditch was level and, apart from a few patches of black organic material near the centre, modern cultivation had completely removed all trace of prehistoric levels. The intensity of the cultivation here, as elsewhere on the slopes, had been far greater than almost anywhere upslope within the hillfort.

A curious concentration of post-holes and stake-holes, no fewer than 86 in number, were uncovered within the ditched enclosure. A small number of shallow, insignificant depressions were also present, as well as two pits (Pits 4 and 14) (Figs 2.137, 2.138 and 2.142). Pit 4, roughly D-shaped in form, had been cut by the penannular ditch. It was located at the north-eastern edge of the enclosure and had maximum dimensions of *c.* 1.3m by *c.* 1m. Its sides were fairly steep at the top but gradually curved inwards to a concave base. Its greatest depth was 23cm and it contained a single fill of fine, grey, sandy material, almost completely without stones, which yielded two sherds of coarse pottery.

Pit 14, near the entrance to the enclosure, was irregularly

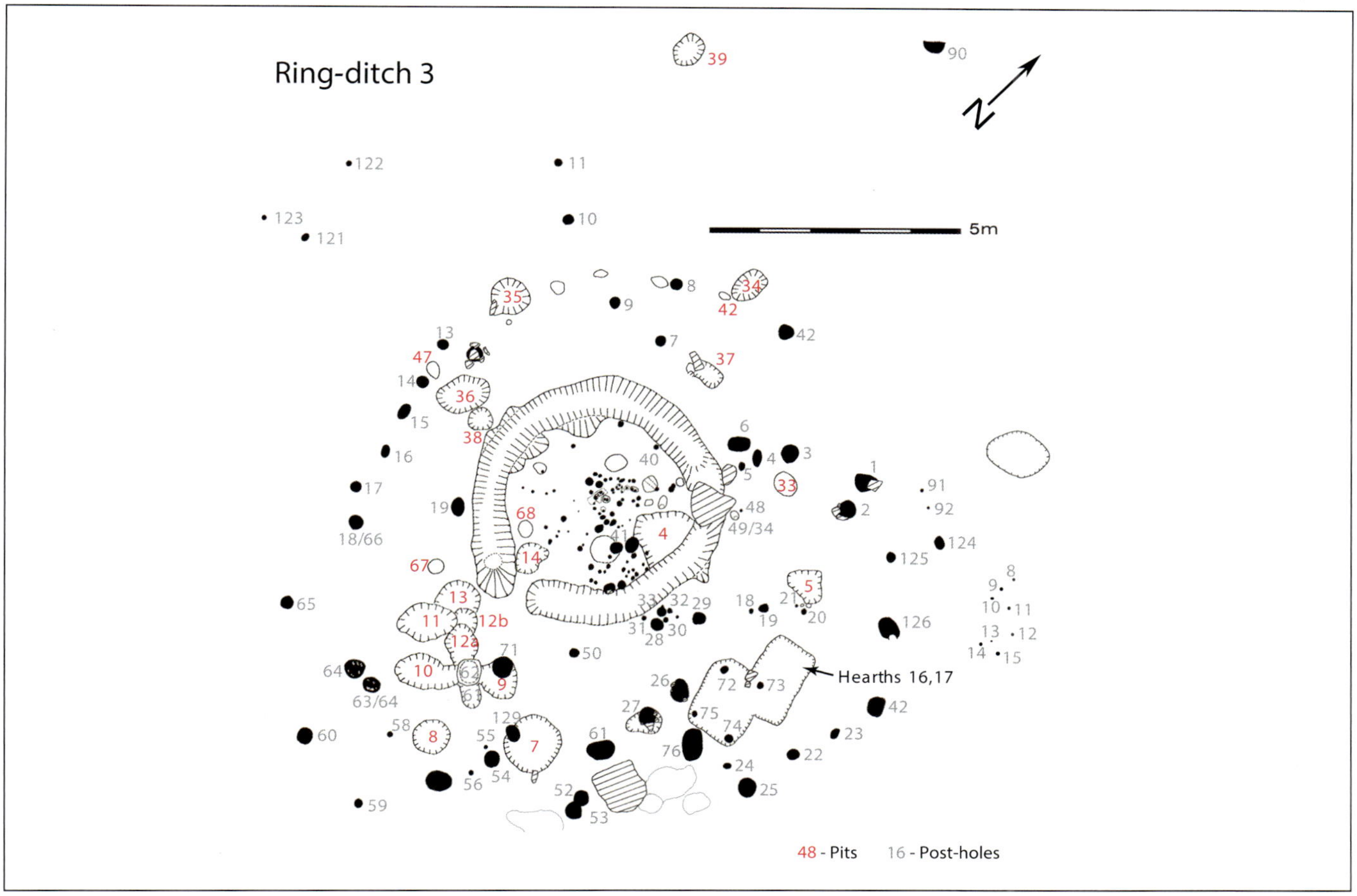

Fig. 2.137—Plan of Ring-ditch 3 and associated features in Cuttings Z2:g and Z5:a.

oval in shape, with maximum dimensions of *c.* 65cm by *c.* 50cm. It was 50cm deep and its sides sloped almost vertically to a gently rounded base. The pit was completely stone-free. In the upper 15cm or so the fill consisted of an undifferentiated grey sandy material, while below this the colour gradually became fawn, with redeposited natural in its lowest levels. There were no finds from this pit and it was completely devoid of any charcoal.

In the south-eastern part of the enclosure there was a shallow, circular depression, 55cm in diameter and 6cm deep. It was filled with a layer of dark brown organic material containing numerous tiny flecks of charcoal but no finds.

As was so often the case at Rathgall, the absence of stratification and the obvious multi-period character of the site made it exceedingly difficult to recognise any coherent pattern in the proliferation of post-holes, which varied considerably in diameter and depth. Virtually all were filled with grey silt. In PH 41, however, traces of rotted wood survived. This post-hole was 20cm in diameter and 15cm deep, with a slightly rounded base. The remains were those of a post 10–12cm in diameter with a slightly tapering tip. It survived as a fill of packed charcoal, which towards its base was a denser black than it was above. Around the lower charcoal, yellow natural soil mixed with flecks of charcoal had been packed. This had been inserted into a post-hole 30cm in diameter. It was noteworthy that this post-hole had been dug into Pit 4, which had itself been cut through by Ring-ditch 3. The post-hole and ditch were thus evidently later than Pit 4. Otherwise, only PH 64[44] calls for comment. This was 32cm in depth, one of the deepest post-holes encountered within the penannular enclosure. It contained a loose, flat, upright stone in the base, perhaps an original packing stone. The post-holes otherwise were filled with grey silt. The largest were of substantial size, being as much as 40cm deep and with widths of up to 35cm. Others which could still be regarded as post-holes were 10–12cm in depth and width, but those

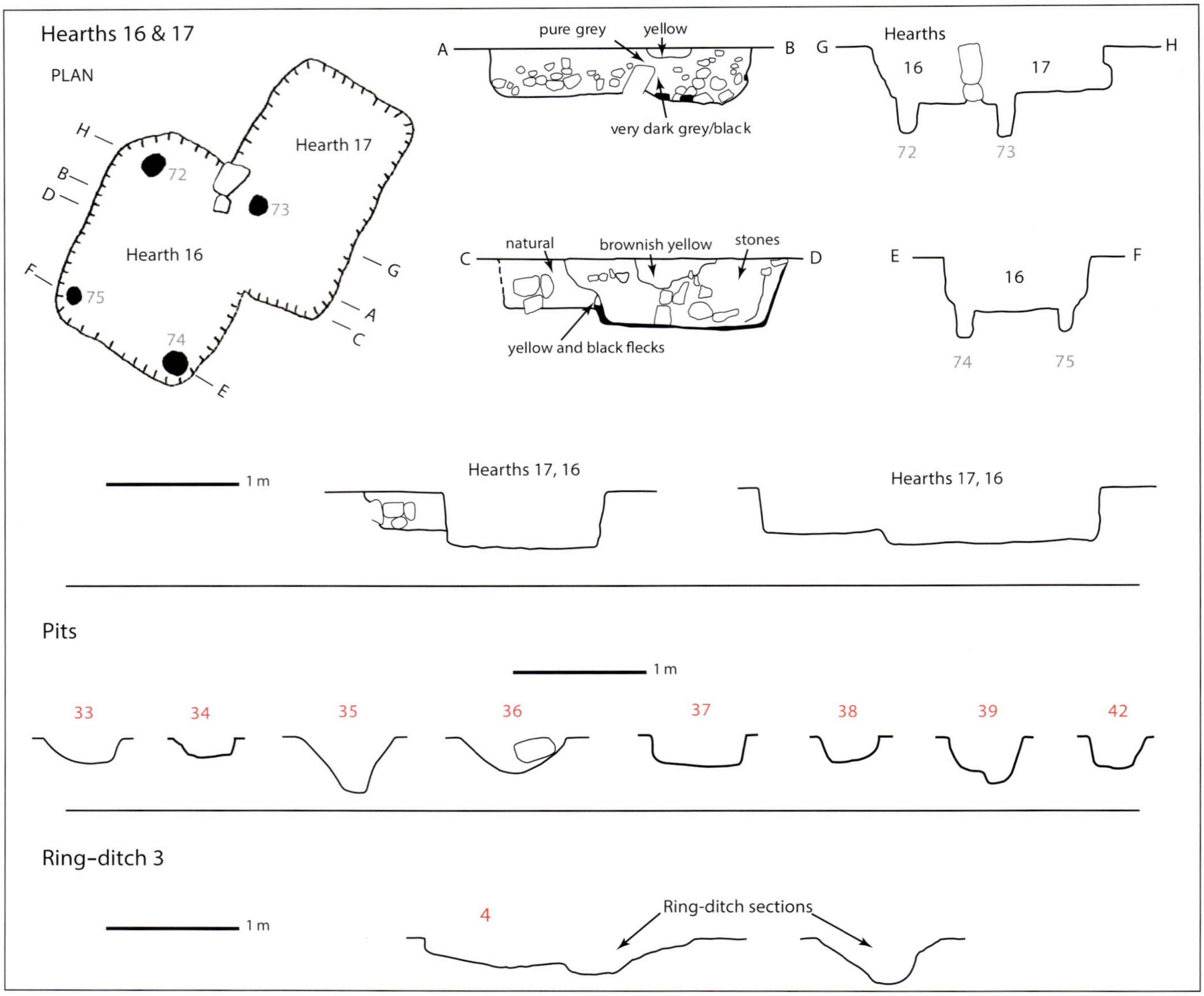

Fig. 2.138—Plan of Hearths 16 and 17 and sections of associated pits, post-holes and Ring-ditch 3 in Cuttings Z2:g and Z5:a.

that were 2–4cm in diameter can only be seen as stake-holes.

These features were concentrated in the centre and in the south-eastern quadrant of this tiny enclosure. A depression that cut across the eastern part of the enclosure was clearly secondary, and it is possible that it might have removed some post-holes belonging to the original phase of activity. Some post-holes may pre-date the digging of the ditch. For example, the edges of PH 48 and PH 49 appear to have been damaged by the latter. A small concentration of post-holes immediately outside the ditch (PHs 28–33) might similarly represent activity pre-dating the digging of the small ditched enclosure.

The discrete concentration of post-holes slightly off-centre within this small enclosure seems likely to represent activity contemporary with, and associated with, the latter feature, but it is difficult to recognise any order in this superficially disorganised jumble. Nevertheless, it may be possible to isolate a tiny circular arrangement, approximately 1m in diameter, possibly with a narrow entrance gap on the east. It is not impossible that the ditched enclosure was of a non-secular nature and that the suggested post arrangement might, for example, represent a small shrine or a platform of some sort for a raised structure of votive character.

Fig. 2.139—Ring-ditch 3 and associated features after excavation (Cuttings Z2:g and Z5:a, looking south-east).

Fig. 2.140—Gap and south-eastern terminal of Ring-ditch 3 (Cuttings Z2:g and Z5:a, looking north-east).

Pits and post-holes outside Ring-ditch 3

As noted earlier, a number of post-holes and pits occurred outside this small circular enclosure. Most of the pits were concentrated around the south, outside the entrance to the enclosure. To the north and west only a scattered handful occurred, and these were smaller than those around the entrance. The post-holes, too, though more or less encircling the ditched enclosure, were rather more numerous around the east, where most of the pits were concentrated.

Pits 5, 7 and 8 were fairly nondescript. The first, a small pit no more than 25cm deep, had a stoneless fill of grey silt and was devoid of finds. Pit 7, with dimensions of 1.15m by 1.05m, was larger and very slightly deeper than Pit 5. It also had a fill of grey, stoneless, silted material but contained 28 coarse potsherds. Pit 8 was somewhat smaller but had been carefully cut, with vertical sides and a regular, flat base. In its grey silted fill there were four coarse potsherds. The upper brown fill of Pit 8 contained three coarse potsherds, and a fourth came from the grey layer lower down.[45]

A complex of five conjoined pits, nos 9–13, along with a number of unclearly established post-holes, occurred immediately outside the entrance to the penannular enclosure. They were irregular in shape and varied in depth from about 5cm to 10cm. In every case the fill consisted of grey-brown silty material with no charcoal. The pits appear to cluster around Pit 62, and the way in which they overlap with one another indicates that they are not all directly contemporary. They did, however, give the impression of a fairly continuous phase of digging, suggesting that together they belong to a single, extended period of activity.

Finds from this zone were few and, in general,

Fig. 2.141—Excavated cross-section of Ring-ditch 3 south of Pit 4 (Cutting Z2:g, looking north).

Fig. 2.142—Interior of Ring-ditch 3 with associated stake- and post-holes and Pit 4 before excavation (right) (Cutting Z5:a, looking north-west).

unelaborate. One interesting artefact, however, was the fragmentary, finely made arrowhead (or lancehead) of black chert earlier referred to (E100:31; Fig. 3.101), which came from the brown ploughsoil in Sq. Z2:f.

Pit 7 was filled with a grey sandy fill which contained coarse potsherds. Besides Pits 5, 7 and 8, other pits also produced limited quantities of pottery. Twenty sherds came from the grey fill of Pit 9, 22 sherds and four clay mould fragments from Pit 11, and seven potsherds from the shallow part of Pit 12a. One mould fragment (E100:64; Figs 3.54 and 3.55) was found in a depression in Sq. Z2:g, and a single coarse potsherd was found in the upper grey fill of PH 53.

North-west, west and south-west of the ditch, eight simple scattered pits occurred. These varied from 38cm to about 75cm in maximum diameter and were generally shallow, being 25cm or less in depth. Only one, Pit 35, with a depth of 43cm, exceeded this (Fig. 2.138). Profiles varied somewhat, bases tending to be flattish, with sides more or less vertical or sloping slightly inwards. The sides of Pit 35, the deepest example, sloped sharply inwards to a narrow, flat base. In every instance the pits were filled with grey silt. None contained pottery or any other artefacts. Two pits of similar type (Pits 39 and 40,[46] not on plan) occurred on the north, isolated from the others and some 7m distant from the ditch.

About 5.5m north-east of the enclosure was a shallow, oval pit (*this could not be identified on plan*) with approximate dimensions of 1m by 1.25m. It showed on the surface as an area of black, ashy material clearly indicating intense burning. Investigation revealed that it had been carefully dug, with gently sloping sides and a flat base, yet it was no more than 10–12cm deep. The black layer had a maximum thickness of 8cm and overlay a thin layer of red ashy material which covered the entire base of the pit. Underneath this was a very slight layer of mixed yellowish and greyish material, doubtless created by the original digging of the pit.

It is evident that a phase of intense burning took place in this pit, pointing to a possible function as a hearth of some sort. Its shallowness differentiates it from the so-called hearths uncovered within the main enclosure on the hilltop to the north, but it clearly had no organic lining as was observed on several of the latter pits. Its isolated position north-east of the enclosure and the surrounding post-holes leaves the question of its purpose open, but it should not be forgotten that the area further to the east of this possible hearth was not excavated. Thus, since it is entirely unlikely that the two largely random seasons of excavation in this area revealed all the evidence for prehistoric activity here, it is difficult to comment on the purpose of such scattered features.

As well as the various types of pits described above, a series of post-holes occurred around the perimeter of the ditch, some of which were of substantial proportions. They were generally 2–4m distant from the ditch. As has so frequently been the case in the course of the Rathgall excavations, no obvious patterning could be discerned, although they did appear to be focused on the enclosure and may form a loose enclosure or fence. It was particularly noticeable that the largest and deepest of the post-holes were clustered around the east (where the entrance occurs). One, PH 71, had been dug into Pit 9. The latter was one of the clusters immediately outside the entrance to the penannular enclosure, and the post-hole had clearly been inserted into the pit after it had silted up.

Hearths 16 and 17

Hearths 16 and 17 in Z2:g were of considerable interest (Figs 2.137, 2.138, 2.143 and 2.144). They were situated some 2m south of Ring-ditch 4 and about 4m south-east of the Ring-ditch 4 entrance gap. Each had been carefully and regularly dug, and it was quite clear that Hearth 16/Pit 3b was the earlier of the two and that Hearth 17/Pit 3a had been dug into its north-eastern corner.

The fill of the hearth consisted to a very large extent of stones, the smallest fist-sized but many significantly larger. They were tightly packed in places and gave every impression of having been carefully and deliberately deposited (Fig. 2.144). Many displayed evidence of intense burning. Heat-blackened stones and stones that were cracked and brittle were frequent. One of the packing stones was a discarded quern-stone (E100:29; Fig. 3.112). The upper 10–12cm of the pit

Fig. 2.143—Hearth 17 (right) after excavation and Hearth 16 (left) during excavation with the lower dark fills *in situ* (Cutting Z2:f/g, looking west).

Fig. 2.144—Hearth 16 (top) after excavation and Hearth 17 (above) during excavation with the fills in section (Cutting Z2:f/g, looking south-east).

were filled with a grey-brown organic material intermixed with small charcoal flecks and splinters of animal bone. This material had worked its way down through the stones, filling all the interstices between individual examples. *It is unclear whether any of the bone was identified as animal bone. A cremated bone sample in the archive (E100:35; Table 3.47) was not identifiable.*

After the filling of the pit, a small oval depression seems to have been dug into the fill and, strangely, was then almost immediately backfilled with undifferentiated yellow soil. Its dimensions were approximately 45cm by 30cm and it reached a maximum depth of 18cm. Its purpose is entirely speculative, but it was cut through by Hearth 17/Pit 3a (below) soon after it had been filled.

Hearth 16/Pit 3b had maximum dimensions of 1.52m by 1.2m. Its sides had been dug with considerable care and were almost vertical. The base was regularly flat and met with the sides in a near-right angle. The depth of the pit below the surface of the yellow subsoil was a consistent 44cm. A thin, continuous layer of black organic material, consisting almost entirely of carbonised wood, covered the sides and base of the pit (Fig. 2.145). Its thickness averaged 2–4cm; in some areas this increased slightly, but never to more than about 5cm. This black lining had been removed in the north-east corner by the digging of Hearth 17/Pit 3a and in this area it became patchy and discontinuous.

On the base of the pit there was a circular post-hole in each corner (PHs 72–75; Fig. 2.146), each of which penetrated the black lining. It cannot now be stated with certainty whether they had been hammered through the latter or whether the lining (wattle?) had been woven around them. The latter possibility, considering the two similar hearth features within the hillfort, is, however, the most likely (but

Fig. 2.145—Hearths 16 (left) and 17 (right) after excavation, with the post-holes in the corners of Hearth 17 exposed before excavation (Cutting Z2:f/g, looking east).

Fig. 2.146—Hearths 16 (left) and 17 (right) after excavation, with the post-holes in the corners of Hearth 17 excavated (Cutting Z2:f/g, looking east).

see Chapter 8, section 8.2). The post-holes were all 12–15cm in diameter and penetrated the base of the pit to a depth of 15–20cm. All were filled with black spongy material similar to that forming the pit lining.

Six coarse potsherds came from Hearth 16/Pit 3b, from the grey material among the stones. From the same layer in the pit came four clay mould fragments (E100:27 and 47) and a flint flake (E100:45). The fragmentary saddle quern (E100:29; Fig. 3.112) has been referred to above.

Hearth 17/Pit 3a was in broad outline similar to that just described, with near-vertical sides and a flat base. It, too, was rectangular in shape with rounded corners, but at a number of points there was a slight overhang at the top, which may, however, be no more than the result of pressure over time from above. With a length of 1.65m it was slightly longer than Hearth 16/Pit 3b, but it was only 1.05m wide and 37cm deep. It cut into the north-eastern corner of the earlier Hearth 16/Pit 3b but had a precisely similar orientation.

There was no organic lining in Hearth 17/Pit 3a, nor were there any post-holes present. Interestingly, the only attempt at any sort of basal lining occurred where the two pits overlapped. It seems possible that the material filling Hearth 16/Pit 3b formed an unsuitable or unstable edge to the corner of Hearth 17/Pit 3a. This would have necessitated an attempt to define and bolster the edge of the secondary pit, which was carried out by means of at least two sizeable, flat-surfaced stones, carefully placed in the relevant space, on their long edges, one on top of the other. Another large slab found lying flat on the base of the pit immediately adjacent to its original line may once also have been a third upright support for the side of Hearth 17/ Pit 3a.

The fill of this pit resembled that of Hearth 16/Pit 3b. In the main, it was packed from top to bottom with stones of dimensions similar to those earlier described and which had also suffered heavily from heat. They were embedded in, and intermixed with, an organic soil similar to that in Pit 3b but somewhat greyer in colour. Some charcoal fragments were scattered throughout this fill, and in the same greyish material were eleven coarse potsherds and three clay mould fragments.

A roughly trapezoidal zone of hard grey soil, covering an area of about 1.15m by 2.25m, extended westwards from the conjoined hearths, almost as far as the penannular ditch (Ring-ditch 3) in the west and as far as Pit 5 in the north. It was nowhere more than 1–2cm thick. It is possible that this represents the remains of a trodden floor, perhaps associated with the two hearths (*or possible vitrification of the soil*).

2.9.3 Ring-ditch 4 (Cuttings Z5:c/Z5:d/Z5:e)

A square measuring 20m by 20m (comprising Z5:c, Z5:d and Z5:e) was opened 10m west of Cutting Z5 (Fig. 2.133). The discovery of a portion of a ring-ditch in the western end of Z5:d (Figs 2.147 and 2.148) led to the extension of the cutting for a further 5m into Z5:e to facilitate its full investigation.

Following the removal of the covering humus, the ditch first appeared as a regularly circular band, generally around 4m wide, of stones embedded in a greyish, silt-like material (Fig. 2.149). The stones projected above this, at times by as much as 20cm, and were closely packed together for the entire circumference of the circle. The size of the stones varied somewhat, though none could be described as boulders. The largest had dimensions of around 60–65cm, but many were much smaller than this.

These stones represented the upper layer of the ring-ditch, which had clearly been deliberately filled in. Following their removal and the excavation of the layers below them, the nature of the ring-ditch became clear. It had been carefully dug to an almost perfect circle, which must have been set out from a central point. Its external diameter varied only slightly, from about 7.1m to about 7.25m, and the width of the ditch at the top thus ranged from about 1.17m to about 1.4m. Considerable effort had been made to ensure that, despite the rocky nature of the subsoil, the sides of the ditch were regular and even, sloping regularly inwards to a flat or gently concave base which was always about 30cm wide (Fig. 2.150).

Medium-sized rocks of natural character had been left projecting from the outer face in a few places, but in no instance were these as large or as prominent as that projecting into Ring-ditch 3 (see above). For most of its circumference the depth of the ditch ranged from 70cm to 80cm. For a short distance on the north-west and west the ditch was as little as 40cm deep.

The stratigraphy of the ditch was uncomplicated, and the overriding impression is that it silted up over a relatively short time, as seems to have been the case with Ring-ditch 3. When this process was almost complete, the top of the silting was, as noted above, carefully filled with stones. The principal filling material consisted of layers of fine greyish and brownish soil, occasionally filled with charcoal flecks. The only exception to this was the east-facing section in Z5:d, where there was a thick deposit of black peaty material in the southern zone of the ditch near the top which appears to have partly overlain, and itself been partly overlain by, deposits of grey silt.

Twenty-eight coarse potsherds and twelve clay mould fragments came from the lower ditch, in every case below the upper stone filling or among the stones.[47] A bipolar flint core (E100:174; Fig. 3.101), a possible saddle quern fragment (E100:195) and a fragment of a quern-stone (E100:202) were also found. Most of the finds were concentrated in the southern sector and were virtually absent elsewhere. *A sample of carbonised matter from a sherd from the upper levels of the grey fill was dated to 1000–830 cal. BC (SUERC-42587).*

Within this circular enclosure the surface sloped gently to the east. The only features that occurred were three shallow hollows filled with grey silt and a line of three closely spaced post-holes at the approximate centre of the enclosure. The post-holes (nos 1, 7, 8) were 30cm apart and their diameters ranged from 22cm to 25cm. The central post-hole was the largest. It was 45cm deep, narrowing from the top to a rounded base 8cm in diameter. It was filled with a yellowish, silt-like material which contained some charcoal flecks and a

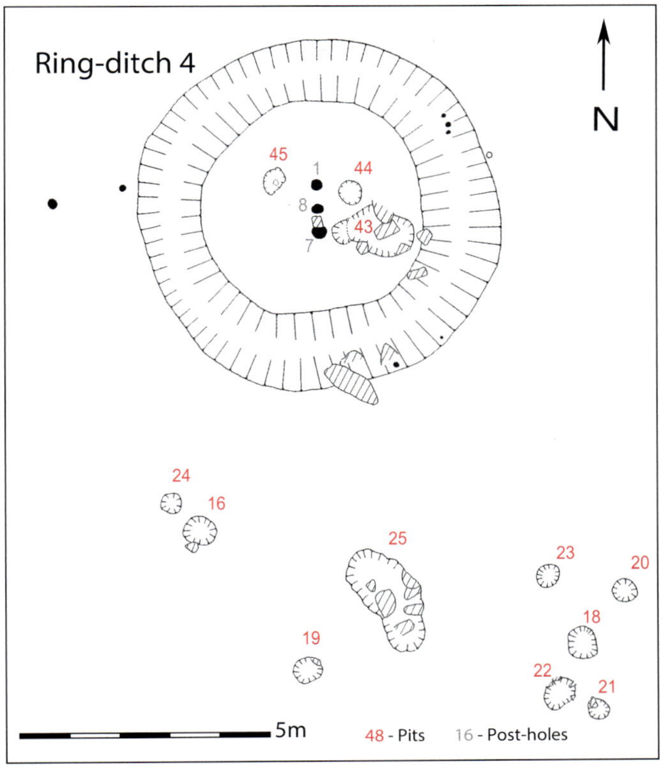

Fig. 2.147 (left)—Plan of Ring-ditch 4.

Fig. 2.148 (below)—Sections excavated through Ring-ditch 4.

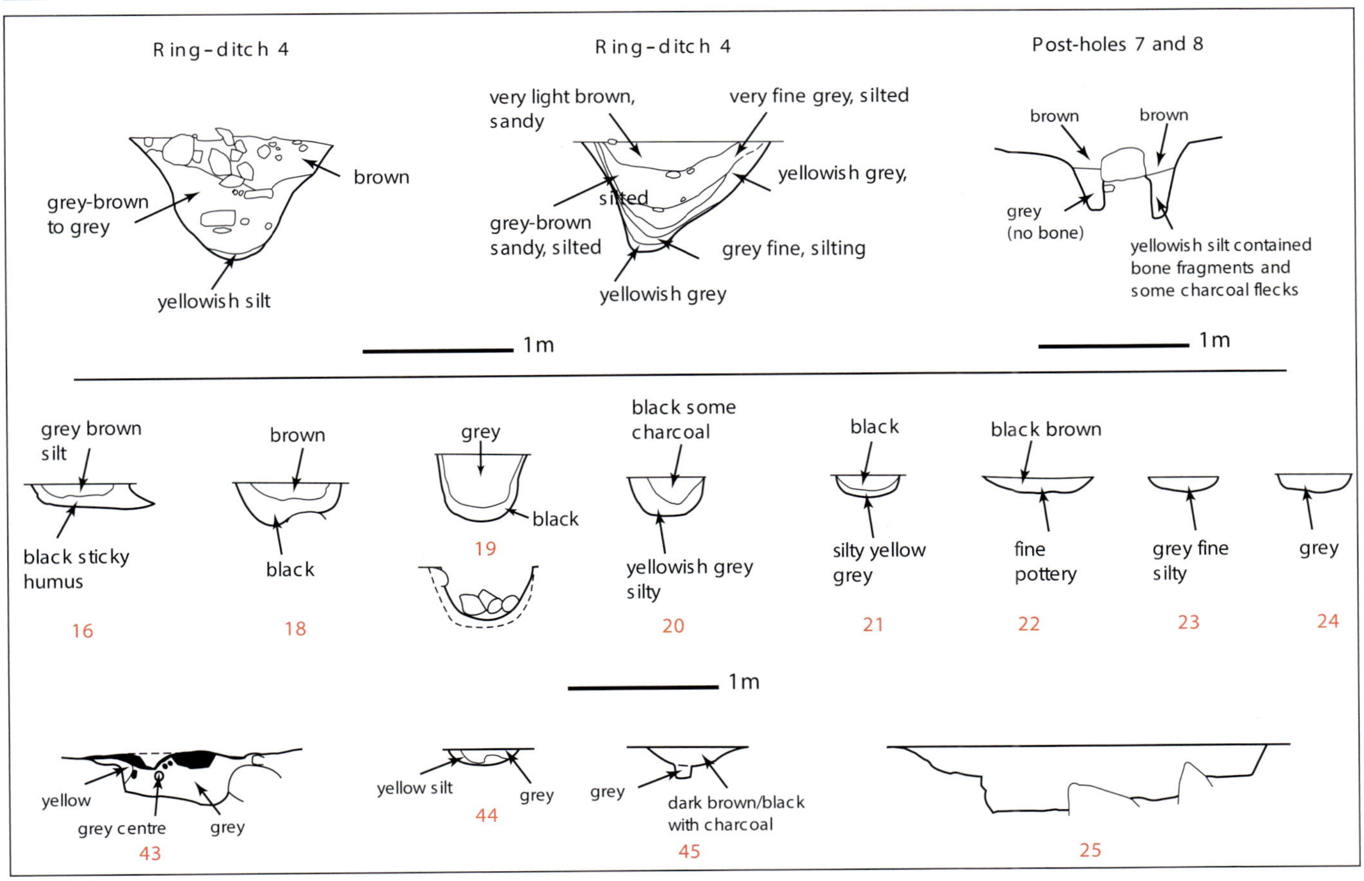

Fig. 2.149—Ring-ditch 4 before excavation.

small number of cremated bone fragments. *These proved to be human and yielded a radiocarbon age determination of 1220–980 cal. BC (GrA-26533).* A natural rock some 30cm wide, with flat sides and a rectangular cross-section, occurred between Post-holes 7 and 8. The latter was 28cm deep and its basal diameter was 28cm. Its fill was a uniform grey silt with no bones or charcoal. Post-hole 3 contained the fragment of a stone axe.

Three pits (Pits 43–5) occurred within the annular ditch. Two of these (Pits 44 and 45) were small and irregularly oval, with maximum diameters of just under 50cm and with depths of 22cm and 12cm respectively. In Pit 44 an irregular black organic layer overlay a lower greyish-yellow silt. Pit 45 was filled with a uniform mix of dark brown to black material mixed with charcoal. Three coarse potsherds and a mould fragment were found in the black layer of Pit 44.

The larger of the three pits, Pit 43, occurred near the eastern edge of the ditch. It was an irregular oval in shape, with greatest dimensions of about 1.5m by about 1m. It had near-vertical sides and a maximum depth of 38cm, and its base was more or less flat. The lower fill was, for the most part, a fairly uniform grey, with some patches of yellow, which was sealed by an upper black organic layer. The latter had a maximum thickness of about 12cm at the centre, tapering to as little as 2cm or 3cm towards the edges of the pit. The upper black material contained five coarse potsherds and three clay mould fragments. The pit also produced some burnt bone.[48]

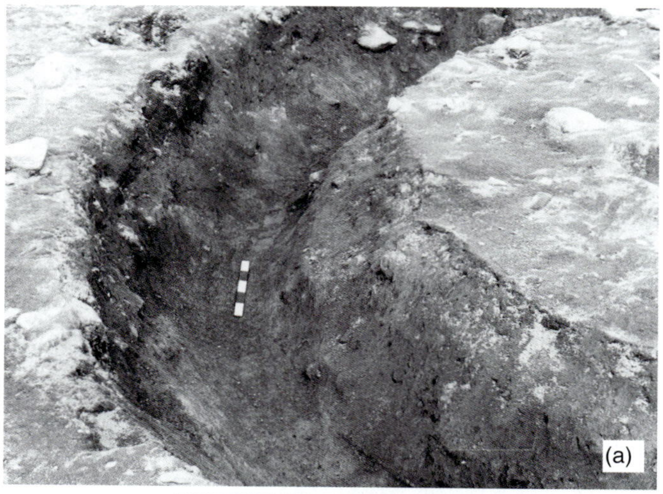

Fig. 2.150—Ring-ditch 4 in Cutting Z5:e/d after excavation: (a) north side of ditch, looking east; (b) overview, looking south-east.

There were nine pits outside the ditched enclosure (Fig. 2.147). All were located to the south of the ditch, their distance from the latter varying from about 2.75m to about 5m. Five were clustered together towards the east and the rest scattered to the west of these. With the exception of Pit 25 these pits were circular to oval in outline, none with diameters greater than 62cm and several with diameters less than 40cm. All were gently concave in section (Fig. 2.148) and five of the nine were surprisingly shallow, being a mere 10–12cm deep (nos 16 and 21–24). Pit 19, at 45cm, was the only one of any respectable depth. In three instances (Pits 16, 18 and 19) the remains of a black organic lining, 5–6cm thick, formed a continuous layer on sides and base. All three were filled with a sterile grey-brown layer, and the base of Pit 19 was filled with an irregular layer of small stones. The other pits were in general filled with greyish or yellowish-grey silt, with a blackish organic layer in the upper level in two instances.

Several of these pits contained artefacts. In and on the black lining material of Pit 16 no fewer than 38 coarse potsherds were found (including an almost complete base) along with a flint blade. *In addition, a substantial portion of a cremation burial was found in this pit (see Buckley, this volume), which was radiocarbon-dated to 1200–970 cal. BC (SUERC-42579). Pit 19 also produced a minute quantity of cremated human bone.*

Pit 17[49] yielded a flint scraper (E100:128; Fig. 3.101) and three clay mould fragments (E100:127.1, 129), while Pit 22 contained sherds of Early Neolithic carinated pottery (Vessels 16–18) as well as a sherd of Bronze Age coarseware.

Pit 25 was considerably larger than any of the others in this cutting. Owing to naturally projecting stones it was irregularly oval in outline, with maximum dimensions of 2.4cm by about 1.8cm. On the south-west, natural stones projected in places from the base so that here the depth of the pit was 20cm or less. At the northern end, however, it was as much as 30cm deep. It was entirely filled with grey silt, but near the southern end an almost square zone of brownish, sandy material lay on, and in, a layer of bright orange burnt material in the grey fill.

This burnt patch, approximately 55cm by 50cm, had straight, regular sides, and in places a thin streak of black burnt material lined its edges (Fig. 2.151). Upon investigation it emerged that the black layer formed what appeared to be a sort of container, within which was the burnt orange soil. On the surface it formed an almost perfect square. Its sides, where they survived, were steeply sloping at the top, in places being almost vertical, for a depth of about 10cm. The base of this

Fig. 2.151—Rectangular feature in fill of Pit 25 before excavation (Cutting Z5:d, looking south).

'container', however, was markedly concave, reaching a depth of 18–20cm at the centre. There were patches of charcoal in the red burnt material but it yielded no finds.

It is difficult to interpret this feature. There seems no doubt that this was a deliberately created container of some sort, and its regularity at the top suggests that it could have been a box or casket, placed in, or sunk into, the grey silt. The base of the enclosing layer was, however, concave and irregular, though it is of course possible that a once-flat bottom had subsided over time. It was completely filled with the heavily burnt soil, which was absent outside. It is noteworthy that there were only a few patches of charcoal mixed in with the red material, so it seems that the intense heat necessary to create such a heavily burnt red layer can hardly have taken place *in situ*. The impression, therefore, is that burning, for whatever purpose, had taken place, and the

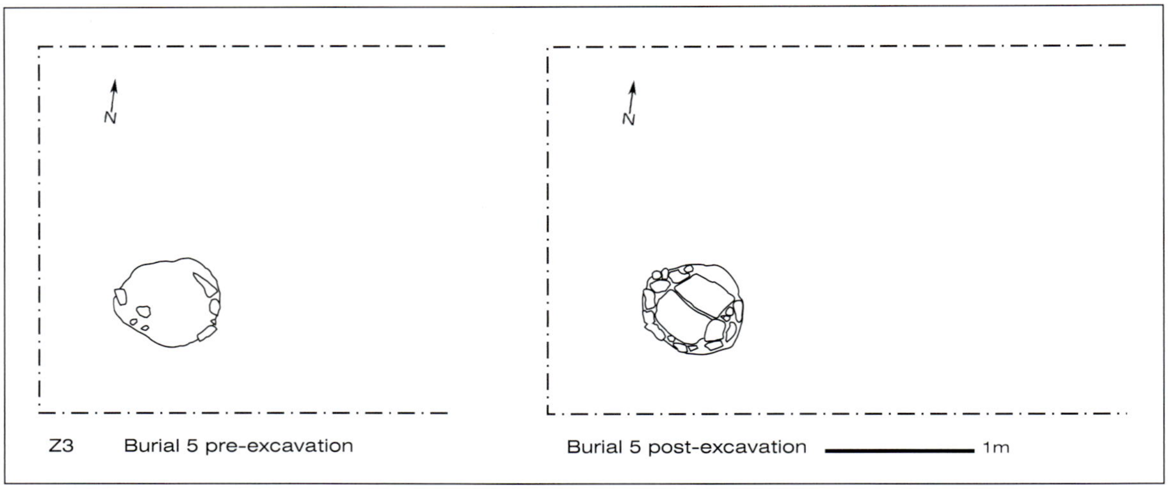

Fig. 2.152—Pre- and post-excavation plans of Burial 5.

burnt soil was gathered and placed in a small container, which may have been a box, and buried in the silted fill of Pit 25.

A piece of waste bronze (E100:175) was found in a small post-hole immediately outside the ring-ditch on the west.

2.9.4 Burial pit in Cutting Z3

Z3 was the narrow trench, 20m by 2.5m, which was extended a short distance outside one of the possible southern entrances through the outer rampart. A few small areas of charcoal were exposed, but the feature of most significance was a small, more or less circular pit (Figs 2.152 and 2.153) at the extreme western end of the cutting. It was sealed by a brown cultivation layer that emerged initially as a roughly circular area of charcoal-flecked, greyish-brown material, 60cm in diameter, with several small stones projecting around its eastern edge. Excavation revealed that the pit had been carefully dug to a depth of some 20cm, with a flat base and regular, almost vertical sides. The base of the pit had been lined with two flat slabs of stone, each about 35cm in length and some 5cm thick. These two slabs did not completely cover the base, and a few small additional stones had been placed beside them to provide a continuous flat surface. The southern and western perimeter of the pit was lined with a series of small stones with flat surfaces on inside and outside, each one having obviously been deliberately selected.

This pit had clearly been created with considerable care. It is unfortunate that it had suffered cultivation disturbance, which had removed some of the small encircling stones around the north and north-east. The small depressions left by these were, however, readily apparent. The resemblance between this pit and the stone-lined pit (Burial 1) that contained the central cremation within the Ring-ditch 2 enclosure on the hilltop is striking. A number of tiny slivers of burnt bone were found within the grey fill but these could not be identified with any confidence. They are, however, most likely to be human remains. It is thus probable that this feature is a disturbed cremation burial of later Bronze Age date, like Burial 1.

Fig. 2.153—Burial 5 after excavation (Cutting Z3, looking north-east).

The few finds from Cutting Z3 were all from the disturbed ploughsoil. Apart from a weathered potsherd of indeterminate character, two stone artefacts were found. The first is the fragment of a possible rubbing stone (E100:30), while the second is a carefully made, polished stone artefact which may be a reused axehead with a ground blade (E100:24).

2.9.5 Cuttings Z4, Z6–Z9

Plans survive only for Cuttings Z5:h and Z7, as well as sections of pits and post-holes in Z7.

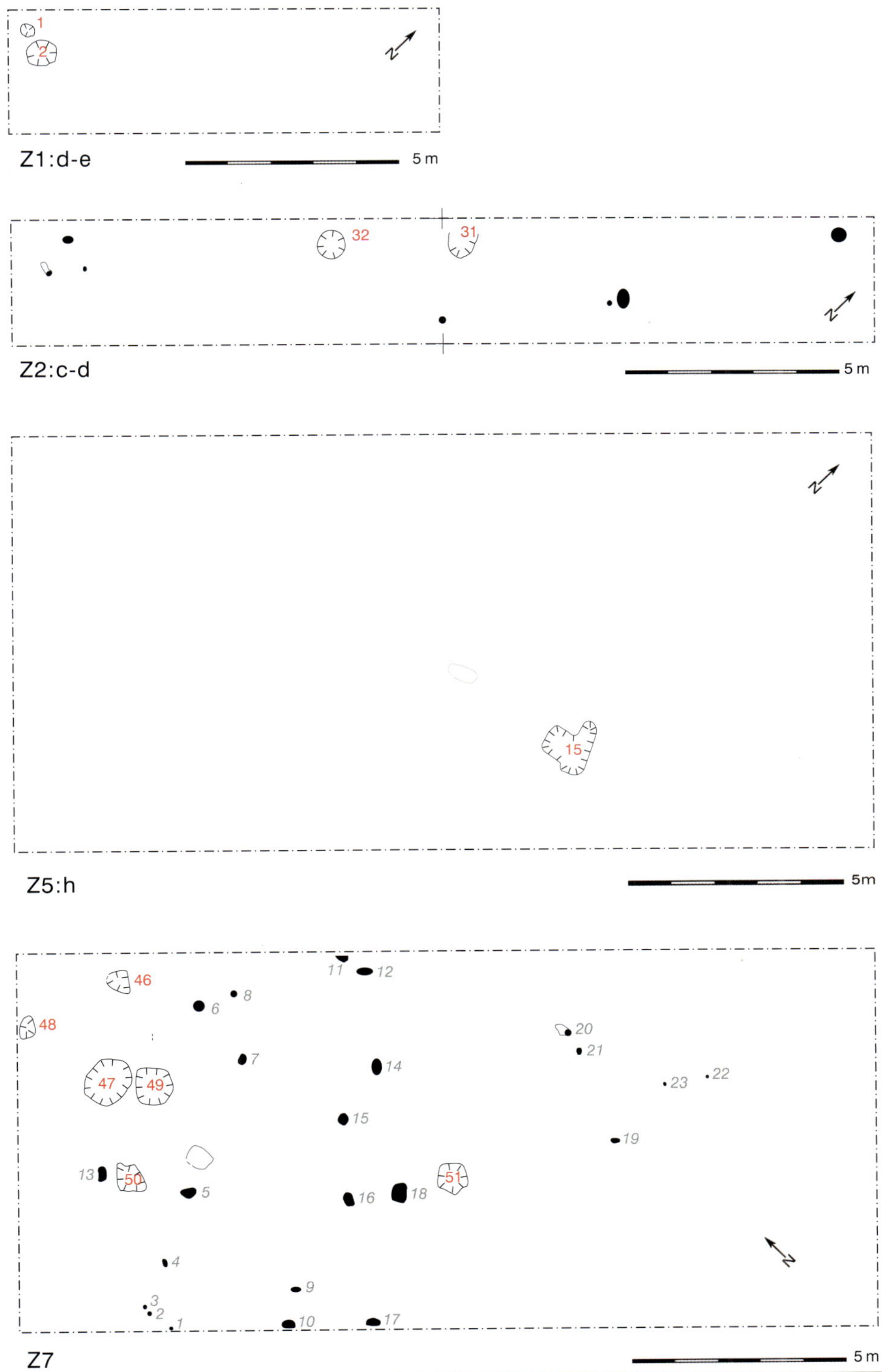

Fig. 2.154—Plan of Cuttings Z1, Z2, Z5:h and Z7.

Cutting Z4

This cutting, with dimensions of 17.5m by 5m, was excavated immediately to the west of Z2:e. It proved to be archaeologically sterile, apart from a small, shallow pit (Pit 6) at its north-eastern end. The pit appeared as a small area of charcoal with patches of red burnt soil around it. It was roughly oval, approximately 50cm by 40cm, with steep sides and a rounded base. Its greatest depth was 23cm. It emerged on excavation that the upper layer of burning was no more than 10cm deep and that this rested on a sterile layer of grey sandy material.

Cutting Z6

This cutting was 40m long and 2.5m wide. Scattered along it were five small, nondescript pits or depressions (nos 26–30). These were mainly oval in form and 50cm or less in diameter. They were less than 20cm deep and were filled with grey silted material, occasionally with flecks of charcoal. One (Pit 28) contained seven coarse potsherds. A number of small, uneven hollows and depressions were also revealed in this area, all filled with grey silt and occasional flecks of charcoal. One very shallow depression contained a flint flake. The cutting otherwise yielded five scattered potsherds, one of which (E100:134) was a decorated example from a Middle Neolithic globular bowl.

Cutting Z7

This cutting, measuring 20m by 10m, was parallel to, and immediately to the north-east of, Cutting Z6 (Figs 2.154 and 2.155). Six small, nondescript pits occurred in its northern section, and there was also a seemingly random scatter of post-holes of varying size. The pits were small and insignificant, mostly oval in outline, 12–25cm deep and with dimensions varying from about 60cm to about 1.1m. In every case they were devoid of charcoal and were completely filled with undifferentiated grey silt. None contained any artefacts. The post-holes, too, were invariably filled with grey material. Post-holes 6 and 7, the only ones of any substance, reached depths of 25cm. The rest were shallower than this, occasionally considerably so. The only finds from the cutting were two coarse potsherds, both from the covering brown humus.

Cutting Z8

This cutting, immediately south-east of Cuttings Z5:c and d, had dimensions of 20m by 10m. It proved to be archaeologically sterile, with the possible exception of part of a perforated stone object (E100:150; Fig. 3.109), which came from the brown ploughsoil immediately under the sod.

Cutting Z5:h/i

This cutting covered 400m² and was situated some 30m north-west of Z5:d. Apart from a small number of scattered artefacts, including a glass bead (E100:93; Fig. 3.14a) and a fragmentary saddle quern (E100:97; Fig. 3.116), it produced no more than a single pit, Pit 15, and a small patch of greyish-black material in the south-west corner of Z5:h.

The latter, a flattened oval in form with dimensions of about 75cm by 35cm, was a depression, probably natural, which was shallowly concave in section with a maximum depth of 10cm. It was filled with greyish-black material mixed with some small charcoal flecks and yielded seven coarse potsherds.

Pit 15, about 2m south-east of the depression, was

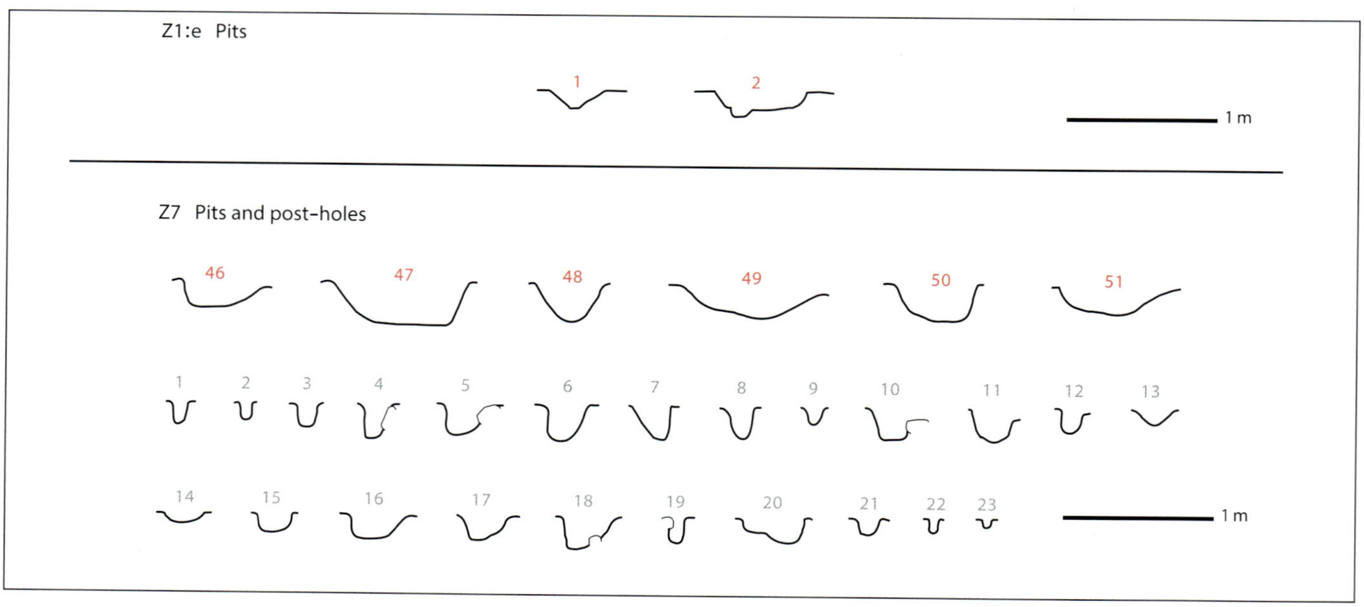

Fig. 2.155—Pit sections in Cuttings Z1 and Z7.

originally rectangular in plan, with rounded corners which had been irregularly extended at its eastern end to a maximum width of about 1.35m. The original pit measured 1.1m by 75cm and, although it was no more than 15cm deep at most, it had been carefully dug, with a flat base and smooth, almost vertical sides. It was filled with a layer of black, spongy material, mixed with numerous charcoal flecks. This black material contained 82 coarse potsherds, which were largely concentrated in the western area of the pit where the extension occurred.

2.9.6 Discussion

The most obvious questions raised by the exposed activity in the south (Fig. 2.156) concern, the nature of the various features recovered and their relationship to the complex activity within the hillfort. More specifically, the key question is the extent to which the various enclosures revealed represent ritual rather than ordinary settlement activity. Certainly, a quantity of normal occupation debris came to light, both within the various excavated features and scattered randomly in the area outside. Similarly, it is evident that the spread of material is not necessarily contemporary with the varied features exposed; some may be earlier or later. This material, however, included standard potsherds of normal Late Bronze Age form, some clay mould fragments, a single glass bead, three (and possibly four) fragmentary quern-stones, occasional bits of flint and a variety of other worked stones of varying types, including a polishing stone. There can be little doubt that normal settlement activity is represented by these varied artefacts. This is especially so in the case of the mould fragments, which must indicate bronze-casting somewhere in the vicinity. Indeed, the single large clay mould fragment

Fig. 2.156—The excavations in the outside (Z) cuttings (Leo Swan).

(almost certainly part of a sword casting) with traces of a longitudinal hollow, originally for the creation of a strengthening rod, is especially striking in this regard. Metalworking thus undoubtedly took place somewhere in the vicinity, although the precise area of activity is as yet unknown. Uncertainty remains regarding the extent to which this scattered material is directly related to the various enclosures revealed.

Apart from a few scattered items of possibly early date, all the structures discovered belong to the later Bronze Age. The very small quantity of material discovered over a wide area of excavation outside the fort to the south, in sharp contrast with the situation inside the enclosure, may well be indicative of a relatively short period of activity in this zone.

It must be admitted that there can be no certainty concerning the purpose of the strange structures revealed on the hilltop, although everything about them seems to point to ritual use. Ring-ditch 4, which had central posts, was a complete circle, with no entrance and no internal features, and a very small quantity of scattered items, as discussed above, which need have had no direct link with the enclosure. As was the case with the structure on the hilltop (Ring-ditch 2), the encircling ditch was complete. Obviously, there were differences, as Ring-ditch 4 was considerably smaller than the Ring-ditch 2 enclosure and lacked a formal burial. Everything about this construction, however, points almost certainly to ritual use. Indeed, the burnt human bones found in the central post-hole in Ring-ditch 4, as well as the possibly associated Pit 16 immediately outside the ring-ditch, seem to confirm the ritual significance of this structure.

Ring-ditch 3 is somewhat smaller than Ring-ditch 4 and, unlike the latter, contains an entrance gap. Its purpose is quite uncertain and a secular purpose of some sort cannot be rejected. Nevertheless, the curious arrangement of post-holes in the centre of the enclosure and the very limited indications of activity on the site seem to suggest ritual rather than secular use. The precise, closely spaced posts that once stood within the enclosure are intriguing and, though some overlapping of structures is evident, the meaning of this in the wider use of the main construction remains to be established. In addition, an enclosing fence line and the two overlapping hearths should be noted.

As well as the three constructional features considered above, a range of pits, post-holes, hollows, the possible remains of a damaged burial pit, and a pair of large and very interesting sunken hearths were exposed in the course of the excavation. Some of the pits, as noted, were of considerable proportions, in both diameter and depth, but no obvious purpose can be put forward for these. To an extent, some extend in lines around the main pits, but in truth there is no obvious arrangement and it might be wondered whether there are others remaining below ground in areas as yet unexcavated. There is more to be considered, including the peculiar rectangular construction of burnt material, possible timber, that occurred in Sq. Z5:c. The function of the hut in Z1 is unclear, but may well be related to the funerary activity in this area.

This whole area, broadly overlapping with the hilltop activity, indicates the wider extent of activity at Rathgall. It is very likely that the activity revealed in the excavations does not comprise the total area of contemporary activity in this area. Moreover, it appears that geophysical survey in the area to the south of the excavated zone may hint at the presence of at least one and possibly more small circular structures comparable to Ring-ditch 4 (see section 2.11).

2.10 RATHGALL HILLFORT—THE GEOPHYSICAL SURVEY

Ian Elliott

2.10.1 Introduction

In spring 2012, a detailed fluxgate gradiometer survey was conducted across the State-held landholding at Rathgall hillfort. This was the first extensive geophysical survey conducted in the environs of this important heritage site.

The bulk of the Rathgall site is presently under close-cropped grass or pasture. A number of upstanding stone walls and embanked field fences, other than those comprising the monumental remains, traverse the site. In addition, some 60m to the west of the central stone enclosure are the remains of an early modern farmstead, and its surroundings and a small field immediately to its north were heavily overgrown with weeds and thistles. Some 140m to the north-east, between Rampart 3 and (the location of) Rampart 4, is a low-lying pond. A narrow annular strip between Ramparts 2 and 3 was restricted and quite overgrown, and its uneven surface precluded it from being surveyed.

Avoiding upstanding features and other obvious areas of overgrowth and disturbance, the site was conveniently subdivided into eight separate survey areas between the existing field boundaries (Fig. 2.157). Overall, the site measured *c.* 600m north–south and 400m west–east, and the survey areas identified totalled some 17.5ha.

The site presented no significant survey problems, but we expected to encounter traces of metallic litter and other detritus and disturbance associated with the long-term occupation and reuse of the land over many centuries.

2.10.2 Solid geology and soils

The solid geology of the Rathgall area is Acid Intrusive volcanic, consisting of Carlow Granite (Houghton 1979, 14–15). Bedrock is not generally exposed at the site, although there appear to be numerous granite erratics present and there has been extensive use of granite boulders and smaller stones in the upstanding structures and boundaries across the site. Instead, the site is covered by boulder clay, which is the result of glacier action during the last glaciation.

The soil encountered at Rathgall is likely to be acid brown earth, of coarse texture, derived from a parent material of mostly granite or rhyolite glacial tills (National Soil Survey 1980).

Granite, being an igneous rock, has generally an inherent enhanced magnetism but, unless ferrous minerals are present in abundance, its magnetic susceptibility is considerably lower than that of other igneous rocks such as basalt or porphyry (Telford *et al.* 1990, 71ff). In any case, the relatively homogeneous tills overlying the base rock typically have a masking effect, and archaeological features excavated into this overburden or the underlying rock *should* still produce anomalous responses that are detectable by magnetic survey instrumentation (Clark 1996, 92ff).

2.10.3 Survey methodology

From the viewpoint of archaeological investigation, the majority of the Rathgall site is a blank canvas and therefore a relatively rapid, detailed and comprehensive survey was required, to identify not only additional monumental features but also zones of activity and archaeological potential that might attract further investigation in the future.

Paired Geoscan Research FM36 and FM256 fluxgate gradiometers, mounted on a CF6 frame and operating in dual mode, were employed in the present survey. A fluxgate gradiometer is effective in detecting even weak anomalies to a depth of more than 1m and is thus well suited to ground conditions on the island of Ireland, where the topsoil layer rarely seems to exceed 50cm.

A Topcon Differential GPS system was used to establish a grid of survey pegs across the site at each survey area. The Topcon equipment is relatively compact and lightweight in use and, interacting with every satellite system available, usually has uninterrupted coverage, except where tree cover is significant. The user-friendly interface lends itself to the setting out of surveys in a regular grid pattern on any convenient orientation. Data were plotted using AutoCadLT 2004 software.

In advance of the proposed fieldwork, UCD School of Archaeology had established a semi-permanent survey framework across the site, tied into National Grid co-ordinates. Short wooden stakes hammered into the ground acted as fixed reference points of known location.

Utilising these fixed survey stations, the DGPS was used to establish the 20m x 20m geophysical survey panels, or 'grids', with the corners being marked by plastic survey pegs. The grids covered all accessible areas of the site (Fig. 2.157).

The detailed fluxgate gradiometer survey was conducted over all areas (exclusive of any parts of the land covered by extant buildings, roadways, ditches, etc.) along successive 20m traverses, spaced 2m apart, with readings of the localised magnetic field gradient recorded to the nearest tenth of a nanotesla (nT) at 25cm intervals along each traverse. The effective survey resolution was 0.25m x 1m, which is the widely accepted standard for detailed archaeological survey (David 2008, 22).

A total of 13.76ha were surveyed by fluxgate gradiometer, which equates to 344 grids, each 20m x 20m in area. With 1,600 readings per grid, a total of 550,400 individual soundings of the earth's magnetic field were recorded during the seven days of survey.

2.10.4 Data-processing

The data plots were generated as bitmap images, were subsequently converted in MS Paint to jpeg format, and were cropped and assembled using Adobe Photoshop and Illustrator (Figs 2.157 and 2.158). The processed data are displayed as edge-matched, linear greyscale plots. The magnetic data plots are clipped to ±3nT, relative to a background datum of 0nT (representing the undisturbed earth's magnetic field of *c.* 48,000nT).

In general the Rathgall data were of good quality, with some inevitable grid-edge discontinuities arising from the survey methodology in sometimes uneven or overgrown areas.

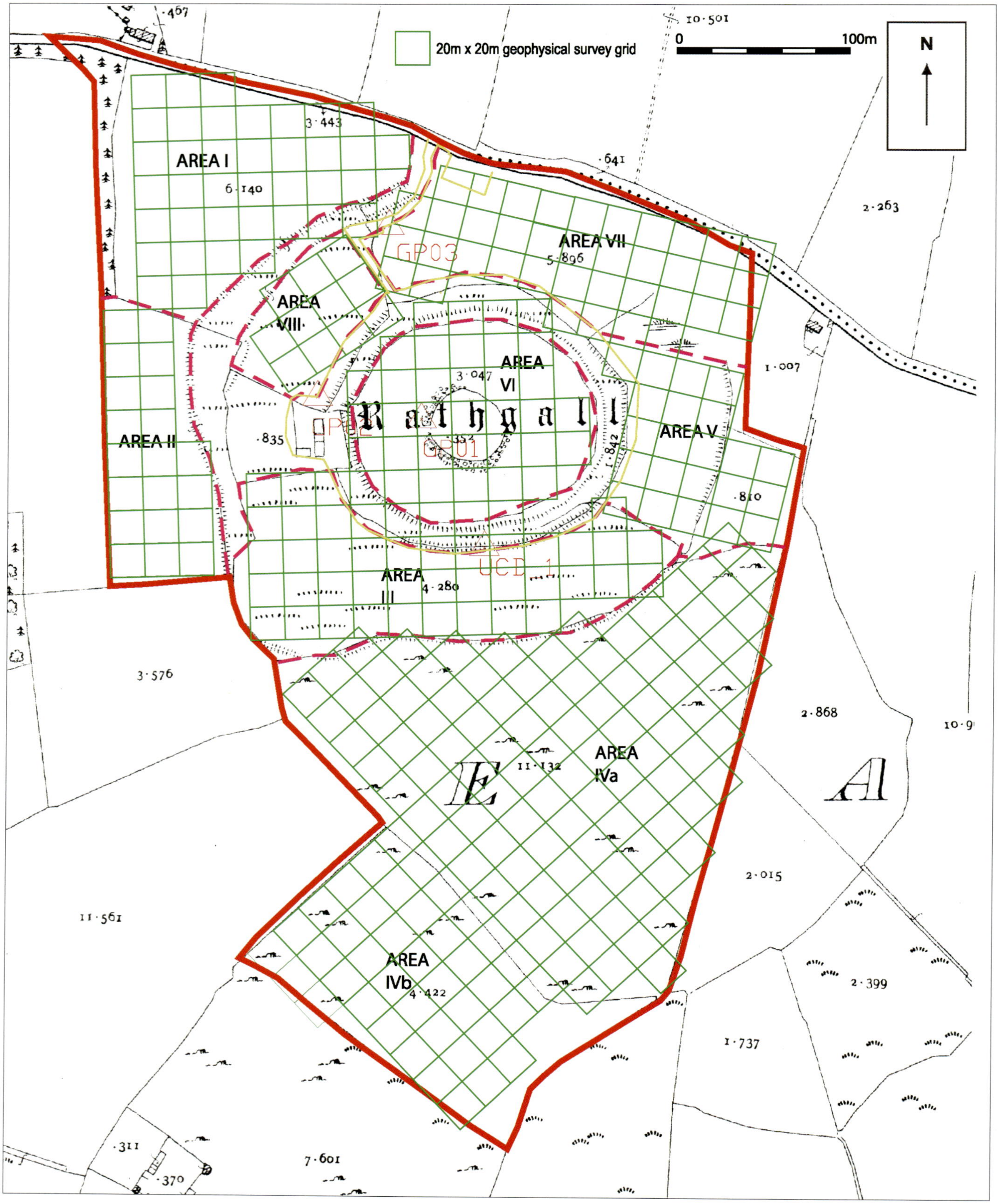

Fig. 2.157—Layout of geophysical 20m grids in Areas I, II, III, IVa, IVb, V, VI, VII and VIII over an OS 25in. map extract.

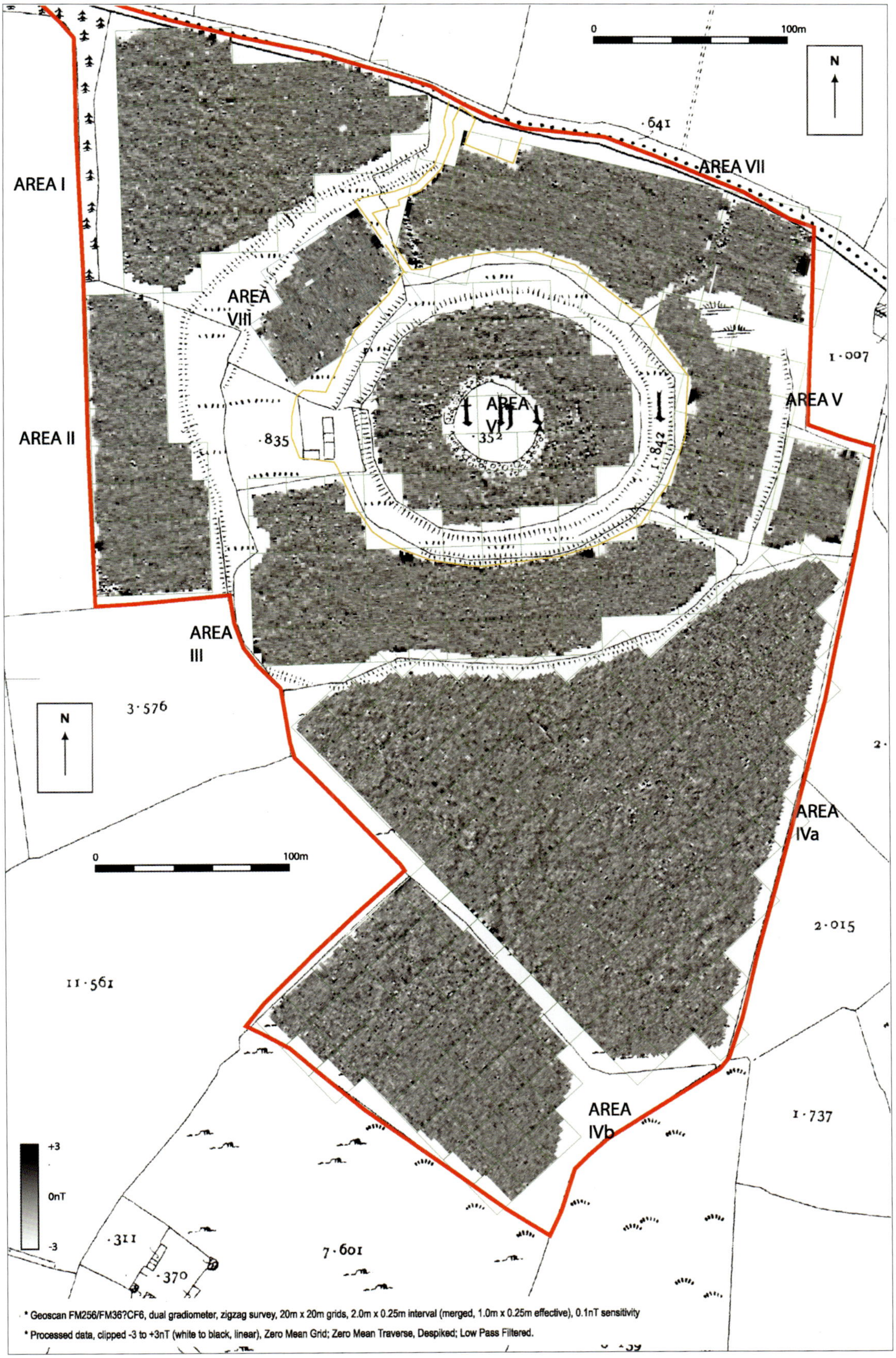

Fig. 2.158—Processed fluxgate gradiometer survey results.

These do not detract unduly from the broader picture represented by the bulk of the data. The site also yielded widely dispersed ferrous interference, fairly typical artefacts of agricultural activity over prolonged periods of occupation. Widespread weaker interference may derive from the inclusion of granite fragments in the soil or from weaker anthropogenic sources but, again, stronger, more readily identifiable anomalies contrast sufficiently with the background for probable archaeologically significant features to be identified.

Grid data were initially balanced by the application of the Zero Mean Traverse function (correcting for internal drift, or other inter-traverse inconsistencies, within a grid) and the Zero Mean Grid function to inter-balance grids or blocks of grids. Subsequent processing included the application of the Despike function, the result of which is to reduce somewhat the dominance of strong ferrous signals that might mask weaker archaeological anomalies. Further reduction of noise was derived from the application of the Low Pass Filter function, which smooths the data by the elimination of relatively rapidly varying magnetic responses.

Because the fluxgate gradiometer, by its design, effectively behaves as a high pass filter device, the effect of broader (slowly varying) magnetic variation, including the geological effect of underlying strata of igneous bedrock, is effectively reduced.

2.10.5 Results and interpretation

In the processed data set (Figs 2.158–2.160), anomalous features contrasting with the background surrounding data have been identified, taking into account relative strengths, morphology and data treatment history, and drawing inferences from experience and knowledge of local geological, topographical, historical, archaeological, agricultural and modern interference conditions.

In general the site displays a relatively low-intensity magnetic background noise level of a couple of nanoTesla. Against this, it is possible to identify even weak anomalies up to 3–5nT, which is the range of values associated with archaeological features such as pits and trenches, while stronger anomalies, such as those generated by hearths (15–30nT), intensive burning (40–60nT) or ferrous material (70nT+), are readily detectable.

Area I

A few weak extended but disjointed linear anomalies indicate possible field drains, but there is a great deal of magnetic disturbance in the western half of the area, and agricultural activity that has ploughed out earlier structures could readily generate such features. A broader extended anomaly, running south-east/north-west, is reminiscent of a former ditch-like field boundary.

Area II

Noise levels in Area II are generally more suppressed than in parts of Area I, and weak extended curvilinear anomalies *c.* 30–40m in diameter are identified, along with some linear features in the northern part of the field, possibly indicating former enclosures, though there is insufficient evidence of a significant ditch. The strong magnetic disturbance in the extreme south-western corner of this field indicates intense burning, or probable ferrous debris.

Area III

This area, lying between Ramparts 4 and 3, extends upslope to embrace the southern flanks of the main hillfort site. A number of extended linear and curvilinear anomalies, representing excavated trench-like features, are evident, including a long, curving ditch running circumferentially midway between the two identified ramparts; this had also been identified in the topographical survey of the site. Centrally within the zone between this ditch and Rampart 3 lies an extended area of nondescript but heightened magnetic disturbance. A circular zone of similarly elevated disturbance lies to the south-west. An area of noise, possibly indicating habitation debris, lies to the north.

Area IV

This extensive area covers two fields lying to the south and south-east of the hillfort. Area IVa, to the north, is relatively flat and displays widespread possible structural features, with spreads of burnt material. The ground falls away to the south-west into Area IVb. The survey data indicate that the density of features reduces in this area, but some linear extended features, of the same general characteristics as in Area IVa, may even extend through the modern field boundary that subdivides the areas.

Area V

Area V extends across two fields effectively divided by the outer Rampart 4. These areas appear relatively magnetically quiet, although a few discrete features—including ferrous debris and, more significantly, a couple of small curvilinear

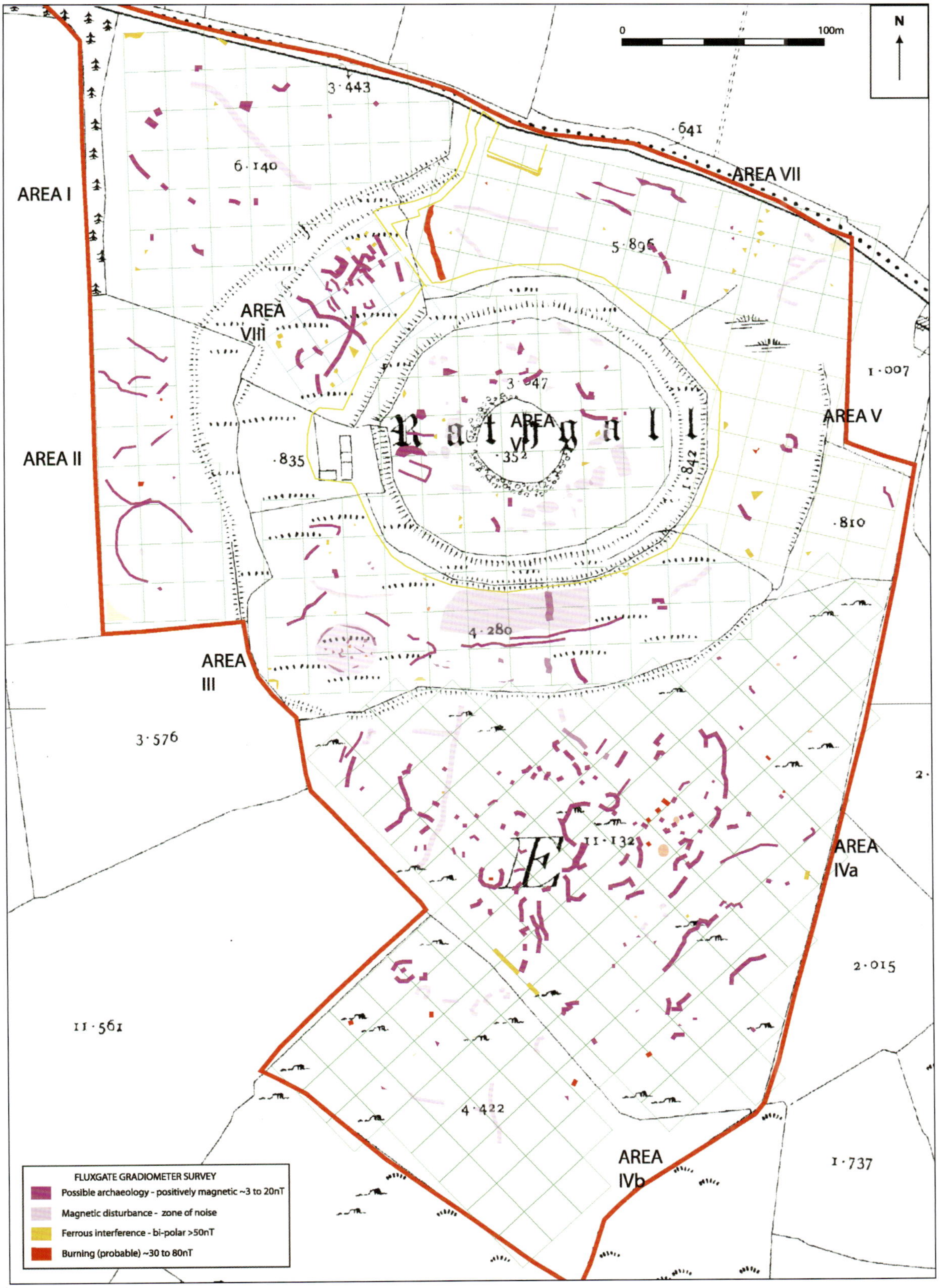

Fig. 2.159—Interpreted fluxgate gradiometer survey results.

anomalies—have been identified.

Area VI

Area VI encompasses the area within Rampart 2, excluding that within the cashel, and indicates widespread disturbance, especially to the east of the central enclosure—the zone of Raftery's excavation. Possible structural remains are present throughout the area, which was otherwise magnetically noisy, as might be expected in this focal area of the site.

Area VII

A number of weak extended curvilinear features are evident in this northern area of the site. An earlier cinder trackway might be indicated by the extended high-intensity linear anomaly at the western end of the area. In the eastern part of the area, one or more linear features may indicate the presence of drains emptying into the pond area that lies between Areas VII and V.

Area VIII

This area, lying relatively close to the modern roadway and adjacent to the farm building, shows evidence for extensive magnetic disturbance in the form of ferrous debris and extended linear features indicating probable structural remains and field boundaries.

2.10.6 Discussion

In general there is a somewhat elevated level of background noise of a couple of nanoTesla across the site. Most of the anomalies detected are weak, with poorer edge definition than might be hoped for. The latter is indicative of low haematite (iron mineral) concentrations in the parent soils at the site, as might be expected in granite-derived drift, while the noise may also derive from the presence of scattered granite, as well as ferrous debris and other disturbance in the topsoil. In general, excavated features such as ditches/fosses and pits that encroach into the subsoil layer are revealed in survey data as anomalies with enhanced magnetic signals, owing to the concentration within of anthropogenic materials, deposits of enhanced-susceptibility topsoil, ash and even magnetotactic bacteria.

Topographically, Area I is a relatively elevated portion of the site and, while it falls away to the west, one could nevertheless expect that it might have been a focus of activity in the past. The disturbed ground here may well indicate the survival of archaeological deposits and features. None of the linear features appear to respect the modern field boundaries, suggesting activity in an earlier era.

Area II appears to present some evidence for structural remains, although, with the exception of one or two strong bipolar anomalies, which may be unrelated debris, internal detail is virtually non-existent. Thus enclosures are more likely than actual buildings. The anomalies are, in any case, weak and ephemeral. The ground here slopes down relatively steeply from east to west and might not have been the ideal location for a substantial building.

Area III includes several features of probable archaeological significance, including an enclosing element. Whether it is a feature that is contemporary with the prehistoric structures at the site or a much later boundary that respected the upstanding structures is not possible to determine. An area of general disturbance within this boundary lies in close proximity to the southern sector of Rampart 3 and the hillfort structure and associated archaeology within. Such magnetic disturbance may indicate a habitation site or other zone of intensive activity. It is also notable that this was an area where archaeological excavation has been conducted, and the southernmost extent of the X cuttings through Ramparts 2 and 3 can be identified. The geophysics data indicate a linear area of disturbance close to, and on a slightly different alignment to, the recorded trench (Fig. 2.160), but it seems quite likely that they are one and the same. A circular zone of heightened magnetic activity, measuring approximately 30m across, lies some 100m to the west and is centrally aligned within the unusual bulbous eccentricity in the alignment of Rampart 4, a feature for which there is no known explanation. There is some indication of intensive magnetic disturbance within this circular zone, possibly indicating burning or a hearth location, and this is possibly the strongest candidate for a circular building.

The intensive magnetic disturbance in Area IV strongly suggests the presence of an extended spread of structural remains. The phase of exploratory excavation conducted at the site extended into this area (Z cuttings), revealing a number of features, including circular ditches and huts. Our present survey indicates that many more such features may be present. At least one possible circular feature indicated in the survey may coincide with the location of one of the excavated ring-ditches if the excavation areas were to be transposed some metres to the east. This may be due to divergence between the recording of the original excavation grid and the modern GPS-based survey. Given the noise present on the site, however, and the weakness of most detected anomalies, the evidence is not conclusive.

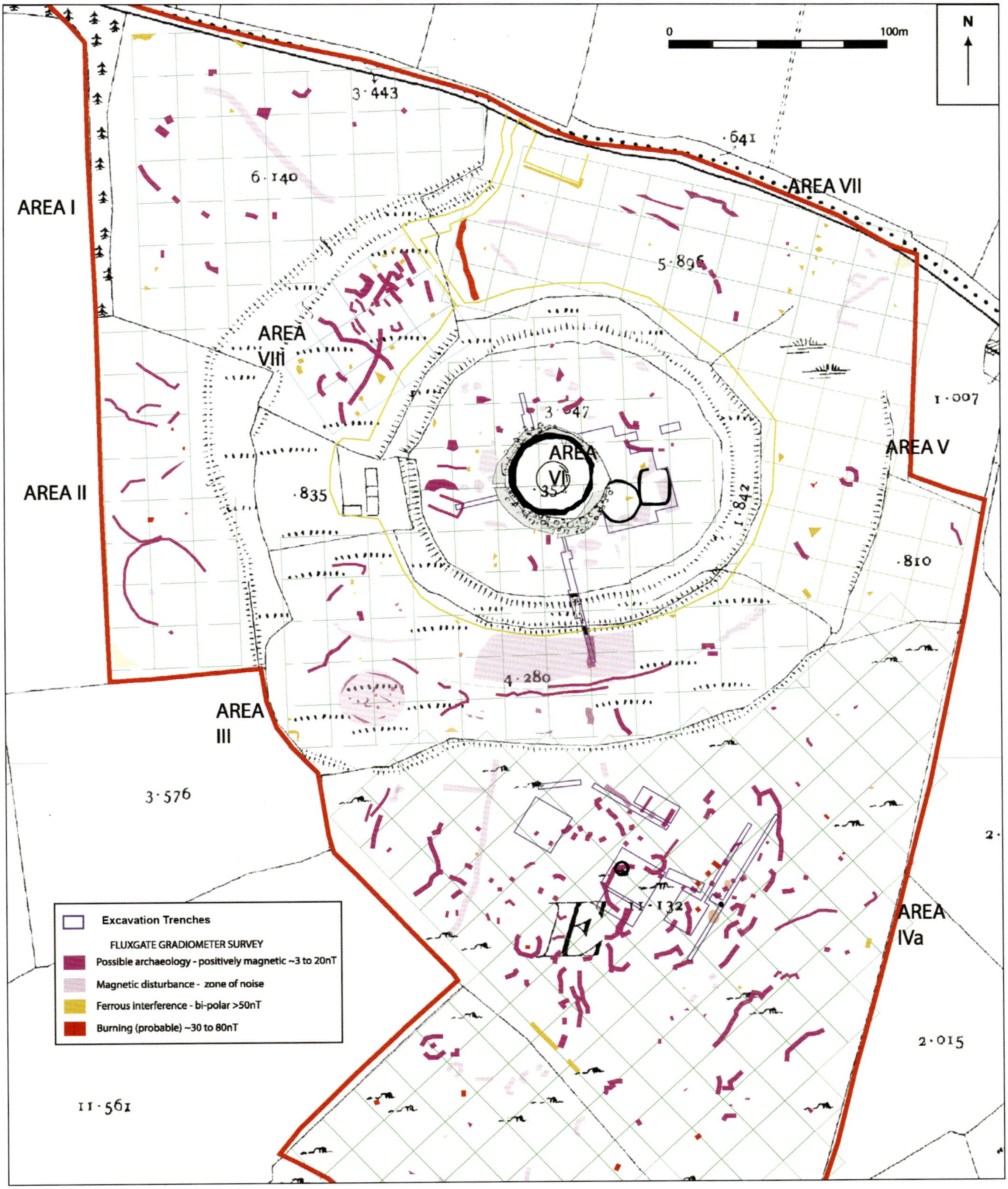

Fig. 2.160—Comparison of interpreted geophysical survey results with archaeological excavation trenches.

Importantly, though, it is clear that this area of the site was once a focus of extensive habitation activity. Note that archaeological backfilled excavation trenches, owing to their generally relatively short existence many years earlier and their subsequent backfilling with original material, rarely show up with any distinction in subsequent fluxgate gradiometer surveys, and this appears to be the case here also.

Area V may also reveal evidence for at least one circular hut-like feature, and some widespread magnetic disturbance may confirm the presence of habitation deposits, however limited.

Excavations revealed that Area VI, at the heart of the complex, has been a focus of activity for more than 2,000 years, and this is surely reflected in the heightened magnetic noise detected in the present survey. It was further possible to define some discrete areas of intense magnetic activity to the east of Rampart 1, and these may well coincide with the extensive archaeologically excavated area. As the area within Rampart 1 had previously been completely excavated and was found to be covered by deep grass growth at the time of the present geophysical survey, it was decided not to include it in the survey. Outside this enclosure, especially to the west, the extensive spread of linear anomalies may indicate the presence of further huts and other structures.

Area VII, lying to the north of the site, includes a number of linear features indicating former boundaries, and it would appear from their relative alignments that at least one of these features probably confirms that Rampart 4 extended across this area prior to presumed agricultural improvements and road-making activities in recent centuries. Concerning the latter, there appears to be evidence within the western boundary of this area for an earlier access roadway to the site, the intensely enhanced magnetic signal indicating the possible presence of a once-heated material such as cinders.

Within Area VIII there is extensive evidence for probable former structural remains. Given the location of the adjacent farmstead, there may well be similar or earlier remains present in this area also.

2.10.7 Conclusions

Previous intensive archaeological investigation at Rathgall effectively embraced an area totalling an estimated 5,600m^2. The present survey has increased the investigated area 25-fold to 137,600m^2, revealing in the process a wealth of potential archaeological material. The results appear to confirm that widespread habitation and related activities could have occurred almost anywhere within the area defined by Rampart 4, the outermost identified enclosure at the site. It is also evident, however, that considerable archaeological remains exist well outside this rampart to the south of the recorded monument. This appears to confirm the results of the excavations conducted more than four decades ago, and considerably extends the archaeological knowledge base in this area.

2.11 GEOPHYSICAL SURVEY AT KNOCKEEN HILLFORT, CO. WICKLOW

James O'Driscoll

Approximately 250m to the north of Rathgall, another large hillfort in the townland of Knockeen (WI037-018) (Fig. 1.10) is positioned overlooking the flat plains to the north. Knockeen hillfort is recorded as a large, univallate site measuring *c.* 203m north–south by 196m east–west, occupying an area of 3.14ha. The site has been levelled at the north and east, although the defences at the south and west remain in good condition. Knockeen was depicted in both editions of the Ordnance Survey maps, indicating that destruction of the bank was undertaken after 1906. Where the bank is visible it consists of earth and stone, and in places there seems to be an intermix of yellow clay. It measures approximately 1.5m in height and up to 6m in width. There is no obvious ditch visible on the surface. There are a number of breaks in the bank. One of these, a 4m-wide gap at the south, could be an original entrance, and it is interesting to note that this is aligned on Rathgall hillfort. A possible second enclosing element has been noted in aerial and satellite imagery approximately 50m from the hillfort. This is depicted as a field boundary at the south-west in the second-edition Ordnance Survey maps. These maps also depict a possible counterscarp bank less than 10m from the inner enclosing elements. A large cairn at the highest point of the interior (WI037-018001) measures 19m by 10m and is approximately 2.5m high. Field stones have been added at its eastern and western sides; these are easily recognisable, as the main cairn is mostly covered in earth and smaller stones. There is no visible surface evidence for contemporary occupation of the hillfort.

Geophysical survey (Licence No. 14R0008) was undertaken at the site in order to clarify the presence of possible additional enclosing features, as well as to identify any internal activity. It also formed part of a comparative study for a Ph.D thesis focusing on the spectacular group of nine large hillforts in the Baltinglass region 18km to the north of Rathgall and Knockeen (O'Driscoll 2016). The extent of the survey incorporates as much of the interior of Knockeen hillfort as it was possible to survey, as well as some of the inner enclosing elements and a section of the possible outer defences at the south-west. In total, an area of 5.8ha was surveyed, using magnetic gradiometry at 0.125m sample and 0.5m traverse intervals. A Bartington 601 gradiometer was used for this survey, with data de-stripped, edge-matched and filtered in Geoplot 4. The same geology and pedology encountered at Rathgall were present at Knockeen, allowing for a good contrast between the background geological responses and those of potential archaeological origin.

2.11.1 Geophysical survey results

Hillfort defences and related features

There were a number of areas that it was not possible to survey. **G1** represents areas that comprised fodder for cattle, as well as zones that were waterlogged (Figs 2.161 and 2.162). Considering the good quality of the agricultural lands in the area, it is not surprising to detect agricultural features such as levelled field walls and ridge-and-furrow marks. An excellent example of such ridge and furrow abuts the enclosure elements at the north (**G2**). **G3a–G3g** consist of a number of relict field boundaries that are mainly visible within the interior of the hillfort, but can also be seen abutting the defences at the north-western side. It is notable that this group of levelled field walls has two different orientations, north-west/south-east and east/west, and therefore probably comprises two separate field systems. A strong band of alternating high/low magnetism extends from the inner face of the enclosing elements at the south-west (**G3h**). This is unlikely to represent an ancient feature associated with the defences; rather the response is indicative of a buried wire from a disused wire fence.

At the north, north-west and south-west, the gradiometry survey detected the remains of the levelled portion of the hillfort bank (**G4**). This is apparent in the results as a faint positive magnetic feature that follows the projected circuit of the defences until it turns sharply at the north-west. This sharp turn is depicted in both editions of the Ordnance Survey maps. The anomaly is approximately 6–8m wide and this is broadly representative of the width of the extant bank at the south.

Approximately 10m outside of **G4**, **G5** represents a similar band of positive magnetic readings. It is concentric with the latter feature and measures approximately 9m in maximum width. It is positioned as the edge of a steep fall in topography which probably marks the edge of the inner bank and therefore may represent another, unrecorded, bank or counterscarp. Such a feature was partially depicted in the second-edition Ordnance Survey maps, at the south-western side of the defences. It appears as the partial remains of a field boundary and was placed approximately 10m from the inner hillfort bank. This is partially visible in the geophysical survey results at the south-west. Considering that there is no steep scarp or other notable topographical feature, it could be suggested that a ditch was positioned between **G4** and **G5**. The evidence suggests that **G5** would have surrounded the entire circuit of the hillfort.

Ranging from 40m to 55m from the inner enclosing elements, a faint band of negative magnetic readings may represent the remains of an outer enclosure (**G6**). This corresponds with a curving boundary visible on the second-edition Ordnance Survey maps and some aerial photographs. The faintness of the response means that it is difficult to identify in the results and could not be traced beyond the survey area, but if we project the circuit of the feature it would surround a total area of approximately 6.22ha. **G7** represents an area of increased magnetic activity that obscures **G6**.

A number of linear responses (**G8a–G8c**) joining the internal and external enclosing elements likely represent levelled radial banks used to divide the area in between the enclosing elements. Such radial banks have been noted at other hillforts, such as Clashanimud, Co. Cork. Interestingly, **G8c** does not extend beyond the projected circuit of the possible outer enclosing element **G6**, supporting the interpretation that this feature originally extended around the entire circuit of the hillfort.

Hillfort interior and habitation features

There are approximately 28 circular anomalies, most of which are within the interior of the inner enclosure of Knockeen (**G10–G37**), and these will be discussed below, working from north to south. They may represent hut structures associated with the occupation of the hillfort. It must be stressed, however, that many of the geophysical responses are faint, ephemeral features, and therefore their interpretation must be regarded as tentative.

At the eastern side of the interior, **G9** represents an area of increased magnetic activity and could indicate an area

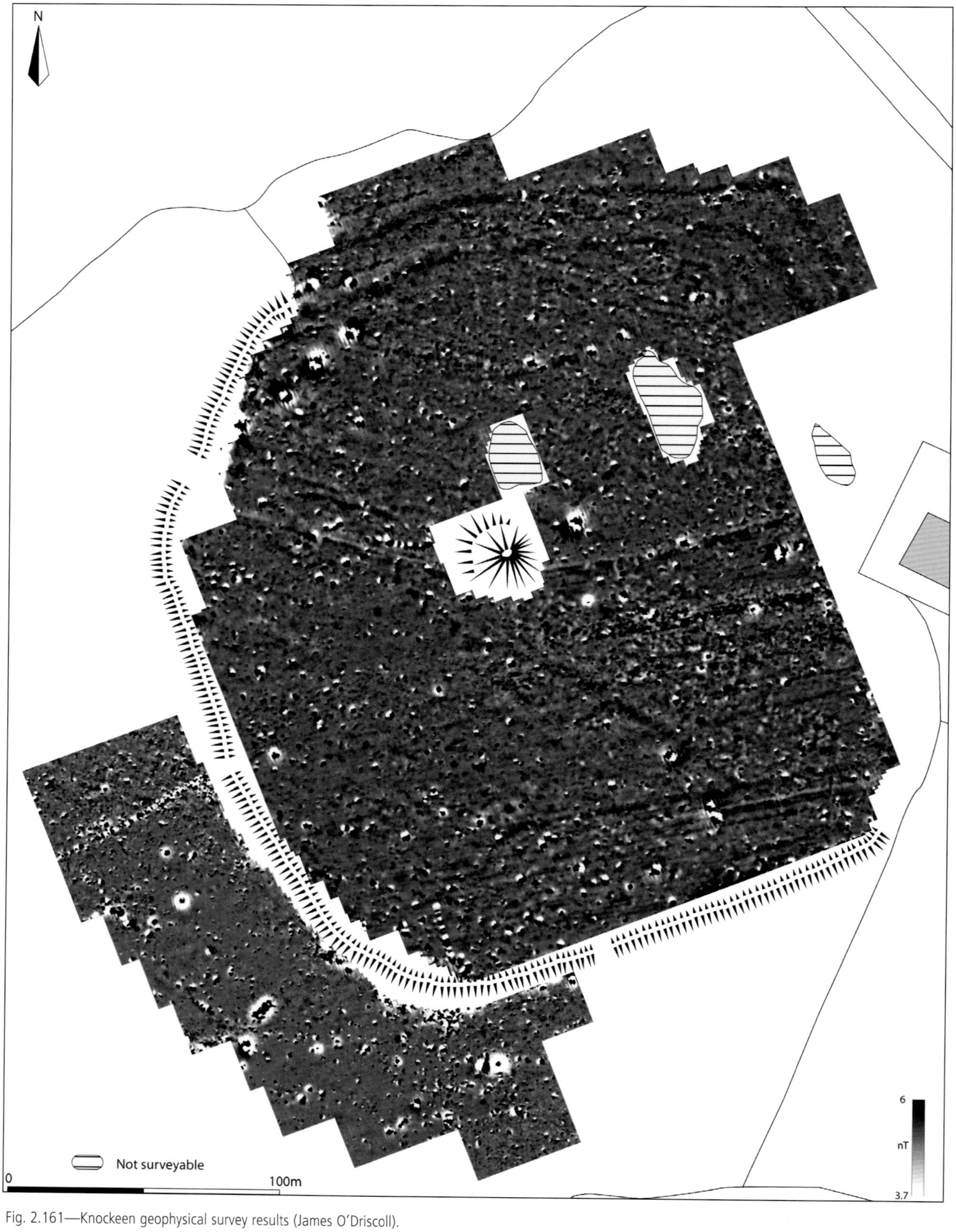

Fig. 2.161—Knockeen geophysical survey results (James O'Driscoll).

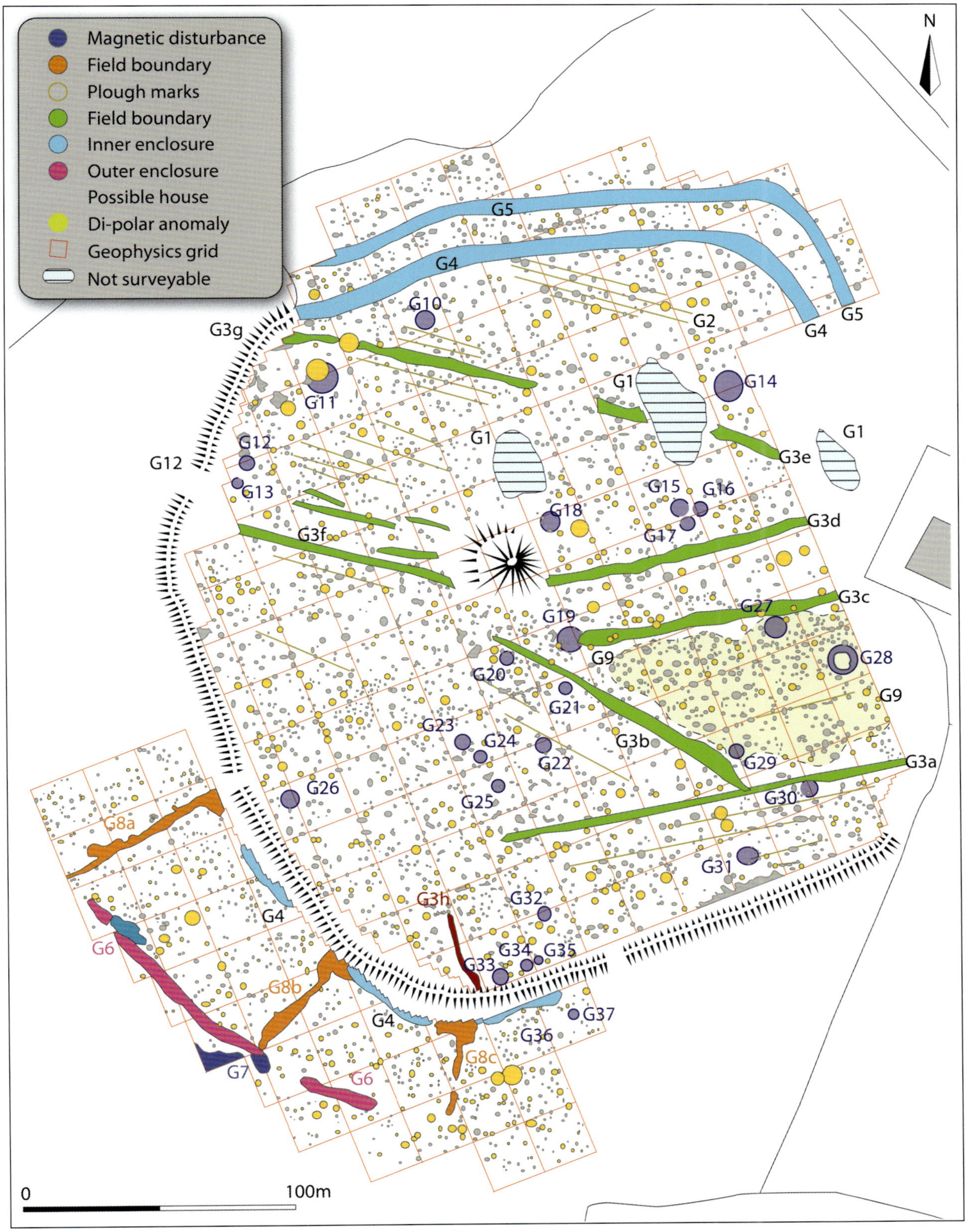

Fig. 2.162—Knockeen geophysical survey interpretation (James O'Driscoll).

where craft manufacture took place. Without excavation, however, it is difficult to substantiate this interpretation and **G9** could equally be a more modern feature.

G10 comprises a band of positive magnetic anomalies approximately 6.5m in diameter. At its northern side, two strong positive pit-like features could represent a possible entrance. The interior of the band defining the potential structure is characterised by a distinct uniform set of readings that could possible indicate an introduced floor layer.

G11 is one of the more convincing hut structures. It comprises a circular setting of pit-like features that are connected by smaller and fainter readings. This could represent a setting of structural posts linked together by a shallow trench that acted as a setting for a wattle wall. The possible structure measures approximately 11m in diameter and is obscured on its north-western side by a large dipolar anomaly.

G12 and **G13** are positioned at the north-western edge of the interior close to the bank of the inner enclosure. Both of these features are visible on the ground as low circular, grass-covered bands. These correspond to responses in the geophysical results. **G12** consists of a circular setting of pit-like features approximately 5m in diameter. **G13** consists of a circular band of positive magnetics measuring 3.5m in diameter. At its northern edge, two strong pit-like features may represent an entrance.

A large, circular setting of pit-like features (**G14**) is positioned at the north-eastern side of the interior. It measures approximately 10m in diameter and may represent a hut structure.

There is a group of three possible structures to the north-east of centre. Here anomalies are characterised by narrow bands of negative magnetic readings, with faint positive anomalies abutting the inner face of the latter readings (**G15**, **G16** and **G17**). This could be interpreted as hut structures with stone footings.

G18 comprises a circular setting of positive pit-like features approximately 7m in diameter, immediately to the east of the central cairn.

A circular band of negative magnetic readings with an internal set of positive pit-like features abutting the interior face of the latter readings could represent a possible hut structure (**G19**). A central positive magnetic anomaly could be associated with a central structural timber or a central hearth.

A subcircular setting of pit-like features positioned to the south of the central cairn could represent a potential hut structure (**G20**) approximately 5m in diameter.

Thirty metres to the south-east of **G20**, a circular setting of pit-like features measures approximately 5m in diameter (**G21**). The interior is characterised by negative readings which could indicate an introduced floor layer. A faint circular setting of pit-like features (**G22**) 30m south of **G21** could also represent a possible hut structure approximately 5m in diameter.

A circular setting of pit-like anomalies (**G23**) measuring 5m in diameter may represent a hut structure, although this particular feature is quite faint. Fifteen metres to the south-east, a circular setting of pit-like features measuring 4m in diameter (**G24**) could represent a potential structure.

A faint circular setting of pit-like anomalies 20m south (**G25**) may represent a hut structure. This measures approximately 4m in diameter and has a central positive magnetic feature that could represent a hearth.

At the south-west of the interior, a circular setting of pit-like features (**G26**) measuring 5m in diameter may represent a structure. The feature also has a central positive set of readings that could indicate a hearth.

A subcircular setting of pit-like features (**G27**) within the area of increased magnetic activity at the south-east of the hillfort interior measures approximately 7m in diameter and could represent a potential hut structure.

At the south-eastern edge of the area of increased magnetism, a circular band of negative magnetic readings surrounds an area of slightly higher readings (**G28**). This has a total diameter of 12m. Although it could represent a possible hut structure, the broad negative bands defining the feature are approximately 3m wide. The feature could therefore also represent a barrow monument, the negative band of readings corresponding with the now-levelled earthen banks.

A subcircular setting of pit-like features approximately 5m in diameter is positioned in the south-eastern corner of the hillfort (**G29**).

G30 represents a subcircular setting of pit-like features surrounding an area of negative readings. When projected, the feature has an approximate diameter of 6m.

The anomaly **G31** comprises an elliptical setting of pit-like features that measures 7m east–west by 5m north–south. It also has a central positive magnetic anomaly that could represent a hearth.

There is a group of four potential structures near the southern edge of the hillfort interior (**G32**, **G33**, **G34** and

G35). All four comprise circular settings of pit-like features. **G32** measures approximately 5m in diameter and surrounds a central area of uniform low magnetic gradient. **G33** measures 5m in diameter and has a central positive anomaly that could represent a hearth. **G34** measures approximately 4m in diameter and abuts **G35**, which is positioned immediately to the east and measures approximately 3m in diameter.

There are two possible hut structures, **G36** and **G37**, outside the hillfort interior, located between the inner and outer enclosing elements near the possible original entrance at the south. They comprise a conjoined pair of circular anomalies that consist of settings of pit-like features measuring 7m (**G36**) and 4m (**G37**) in diameter.

2.11.2 Discussion of results

The geophysical survey at Knockeen revealed a number of ephemeral anomalies consisting of circular areas of uniformly 'quiet' magnetism, some of which are surrounded by a series of pit-like features that might represent post-holes. It is tempting to suggest that these are hut structures and that the juxtaposition of Knockeen and Rathgall represents the residence of an élite and the prestige-goods craftsmen under their patronage, with a larger domestic habitation site. Unfortunately, the geophysical evidence is too ambiguous to state this with any degree of certainty, and excavation is needed for clarification. The potential concentration of hut structures at Knockeen is, however, significant.

The settlement record of Bronze Age Ireland consists almost exclusively of individual, isolated farmsteads scattered throughout the island (Ginn 2013; 2016), a picture which is broadly reflected in other settings across Britain (Musson 1970; Drewett 1979; Ashmore 2001; Brück 2002) and north-west Europe more generally (Brück and Fokkens 2013, 91; Chytrácek 2007; Kristiansen 2018). The evidence for settlements at Irish hillforts has not, however, been integrated into the broader narrative of this contemporary settlement pattern (although see O'Driscoll, forthcoming).

While there are hillforts that show little or no evidence for any type of activity other than the building of the hillfort itself, such as Clashanimud, Co. Cork (O'Brien and O'Driscoll 2017), and Rahally, Co. Galway (Mullins 2008), 31 Irish hillforts show surface evidence for settlement activity, though only nine of these sites have more than ten visible structures within their interiors. With further excavation and survey, more extensive settlements are likely to be discovered, as indicated by the investigations at Dún Aonghasa, where no structures were visible on the surface before excavation revealed ten houses (Cotter 2012, I, 262–72). Survey at Knocknashee, Co. Sligo, identified over 50 structures within the hillfort (Brandherm *et al.* 2018), while up to 26 structures have been recorded at the inland promontory hillfort of Caherconree, Co. Kerry (O'Driscoll 2019a; 2019b). Even larger settlements have been identified at Brusselstown Ring (607 possible structures), Knockdhu, Co. Antrim (167 possible structures), and Freestone Hill, Co. Kilkenny (91 possible structures) (O'Driscoll, forthcoming), for example, which, along with the seemingly unenclosed Bronze Age hilltop settlements of Mullaghfarna, Co. Sligo (150 possible structures), and Turlough Hill, Co. Clare (140 possible structures) (Bergh 2015), and the low-lying 'village' at Corrstown (73 possible structures) (Ginn and Rathbone 2011; Ginn 2013; Rathbone 2013), highlight that dense and complex settlements existed in Bronze Age Ireland (for a detailed discussion see O'Driscoll, forthcoming). The potential settlement within Knockeen hillfort is therefore not an isolated example.

Systematic study of the larger settlements reveals evidence for hierarchical organisation, with distinct differentiation in construction styles and internal clustering (O'Driscoll, forthcoming). This may reflect the nature of the settlements themselves, which probably comprised a number of different kin groups that built and settled (either permanently or intermittently) the hillforts, with each group using architecture and house distribution as a means of displaying and retaining distinct group identity within an amalgamated settlement. In this regard, there seems to have been more importance placed on the household than on communal cohesion, though Lock (2011, 355) suggests that we should not underestimate the importance of participation in communal work and the social relationships that this can create, viewing the act of constructing a hillfort as a means of creating 'a peaceful and harmonious life within small scale agricultural communities'.

Unfortunately, the recorded settlement at Knockeen is too small to permit any inferences regarding its dynamics and structure. The lack of evidence for domestic settlement within Rathgall, however, seems to contrast with the potential density of settlement at Knockeen. Indeed, Condit (1998, 19) has noted a similar contrast in terms of the morphological layout of Rathgall and Knockeen and other 'pairs' of hillforts in Ireland. He argues that there is a ritual element to the juxtaposition of 'paired' or closely sited hillforts and suggests that these groups may have been built by a single community, with one site being differentiated by a particular morphological layout and acting as a ritual centre. He cites Knockadigeen and Ballincurra hillforts, both in County Tipperary, as an example, noting that the former is a widely spaced bivallate fort and the latter is a univallate example with a central cairn. Ahenny and Curraghadobbin also follow this model, the former being univallate and the latter bivallate with a central cairn. Similarly, a pair of hillforts in southern Offaly, Ballymacmurragh and Cumber Lower, sit on opposing hilltops, with the former consisting of two closely spaced banks and ditches and the latter of two widely spaced enclosing elements and a central cairn.

This juxtaposition could also be interpreted as separate communities competing for the control of a strategic location. Brown (2009, 203), for example, suggested that the Iron Age hillforts of Barbury Castle and Liddington Castle in Wiltshire, England, are strategically placed on opposite hills at the northern end of the River Og valley to control the direct route into Wiltshire from the north. There is an important difference, however, between examples like these, which are positioned on opposing hilltops, and sites such as Rathgall and Knockeen, which are located in close proximity on the same hill or ridge. Condit (1998, 19) and Armit (2007, 35) have both noted that such a close spatial relationship would not make sense if the sites were populated by independent rival communities.

In this regard, the geophysical results at Knockeen are particularly important. They revealed the probable presence of a second enclosing element—a bank and ditch—55m from the inner enclosure. The survey also revealed that the inner defences are more substantial and included an additional counterscarp bank. The results show the morphological similarities between Knockeen and Rathgall, both of which can now be described as widely spaced multivallate hillforts. Furthermore, an area of increased magnetic disturbance on the eastern side of the interior at Knockeen could suggest the remains of some kind of industrial activity, although this remains a speculative interpretation without excavation evidence.

Both Arkush (2011, 156–61) and Ralston (2006, 33–4) suggest that dense settlement patterns and groups of sites with common architectural features may represent areas where several communities interacted in a peaceful manner as part of an alliance network. Cunliffe (1991, 537–8) and Williams and Mytum (1998, 144) argue that groups of Iron Age hillforts in Britain could represent the archaeological manifestation of the Celtic system of partible inheritance, a system which split the belongings of a father equally between his sons (Brown 2009, 225–6), but how applicable such models are to Bronze Age Ireland is unclear.

A primary issue with the above models is the assumption, without comprehensive radiocarbon dating, that these 'pairs' and groups are contemporary. Although it is clear that the juxtaposition is deliberate, their construction and occupation could have been sequential. On the North Island of New Zealand, some Pā (large areas enclosed by earthworks similar in form and dimension to hillforts) were abandoned after the burial of a chief and new Pā were constructed close by, sometimes within a few hundred metres of the former (Armit 2007). The ritual nature of the abandonment might explain why the builders of the later fort did not take advantage of the pre-existing defences (*ibid.*, 35).

The ongoing investigation of a large cluster of nine hilltop forts in the Baltinglass region of County Wicklow, just 18km to the north of Rathgall, reveals that the group comprises a palimpsest of sites dating from the Early Neolithic to the Bronze Age, with historical evidence suggesting that some of them were reused in the Late Iron Age and the early medieval period (O'Driscoll 2016; O'Brien and O'Driscoll 2017; O'Driscoll and Gleeson, forthcoming). Within the group, however, a number of sites were broadly contemporary, such as Sruhaun, Rathnagree and potentially Tinoran (Middle/Late Bronze Age), or Rathcoran, Spinans Hill 1 and Hughstown (Early Neolithic). This protracted period of fort construction highlights the need for comprehensive and secure dating information in order to accurately contextualise these hillfort groups.

Links with the past were important as a way of legitimating power, status and claims to the land. This is a recurring facet of élite power found throughout Europe during the prehistoric and early medieval periods. We see a pattern of reuse, with Iron Age hillforts positioned within Early Neolithic causewayed enclosures (such as Maiden Castle, Dorset) or early medieval ringforts positioned within Late Bronze Age hillforts (Rathgall or Tinoran, Co. Wicklow). Some Bronze Age hillforts were built on hills where there were older burial mounds, an explicit referencing of the past tied to the creation of identity and the legitimisation of power through visible links with the past and reoccupation of a much older site (Knockeen, for example). Similarly, the deliberate positioning of some late prehistoric barrows in relation to each other demonstrates a marked concern with the past and the creation of ancestral history and lineage in the Irish Bronze Age (Cooney 2009, 378). Thomas (2007, 261) comments that in many traditional societies the knowledge of descent, genealogy, alliance and inheritance is an important form of power. Bradley (1987, 14–15) noted similar evidence in early medieval Britain and argued that the selective appropriation of older prehistoric monuments was a way to create fictitious genealogies, which were important in order to promote or protect the interests of a social élite and to protect those institutions from challenge. A similar situation could be posited for earlier societies, with the deliberate construction of a Bronze Age hillfort in close proximity to another fort, such as at Knockeen and Rathgall, representing a means of referencing an older centre of power in order to legitimate the authority of a new élite.

Without secure dating information from Knockeen, it is difficult to contextualise its relationship with the nearby Rathgall. Nevertheless, the above represents a series of possible interpretations which, at the very least, highlight the potential functional and/or symbolic links that may have existed between the two sites, depending on their contemporaneity.

NOTES

1 This is the small test cutting in the west of the cashel, originally named the B cutting. As the A cutting in the east was extended and integrated into the overall grid in Areas 2–4, the B cutting was apparently renamed the A cutting.

2 In the recording of finds and samples, *bedding trench* can refer in Area 1 to either Ring-ditch 1 or the bedding trench of the 15m structure. It appears that in most cases the following applies: outer bedding trench = Ring-ditch 1 or the bedding trench of the 15m structure; inner or interior bedding trench = 15m structure bedding trench. Exterior and interior bedding trench: it appears that this is to reflect the two lines of bedding trench in Sqs 25–28. A problem is the fact that the bedding trench (once called interior bedding trench) is twice mentioned as located in Sq. 18, a good 1m or so east of the actual bedding trench. In the case of E84:3435, this is complicated by the fact that the context is described as cutting into Hearth 8. This is indeed located in grid square 18, but a good 1m away. The fact that the find located here is of iron may suggest that the situation describes an earlier, disturbed level of excavation, where features had a greater extent than in the final plan of the emptied-out feature cuts.

3 These are the 'posts', a sample of which was dated; see Chapter 4.

4 It is, however, unclear whether the ditch was completely bottomed out in these instances. Considering the photographs, it may appear possible that some of these large boulders are part of the later infill.

5 Also in adjacent Sq. 11 no mould fragments were recorded but only coarseware pottery.

6 But see Chapter 4, sections 4.3 and 4.4. While there indeed may not have been a great chronological interval between the digging of the ditch and the deposition of the Bronze Age material in it, the possibility that this took place at a later stage than originally envisaged is discussed in Chapter 4.

7 The find came from what was probably the uppermost fill of the ditch, which most likely extended into Sq. 5.

8 Not on plan.

9 See Raftery 1970a for the discussion of these posts as possibly representing a building. See also discussion in Chapter 6 for the possibility of a further post-hole to mirror post-holes 14 and 36 at the northern end of the pit.

10 It is not clear what the identification of animal bone is based on, as it appears likely that the small fragments would not have allowed identification.

11 It is conceivable that these pits represent dug-out posts.

12 This was recorded as having been found in the black burnt area under stones. It was verified by the pottery specialist to be Leinster Cooking Ware. This problem can currently not be resolved unless there was some unrecognised disturbance that would have caused this fragment to be integrated into the lower fill. A recording error cannot be excluded either.

13 There is some ambiguity here regarding the association of finds with the hearth. Hone E84:64 was attributed by Raftery to the hearth; the finds records, however, state that it was 'associated with the hearth, in dark occupation layer', an attribution frequently mentioned in the finds records. Notes by Raftery in a logbook suggest that he may have considered the deposits around the cut of the hearth as being directly related to it: 'all 1969 find from dark occupation level outside hearth is hearth phase 1'. This may find support in a section of Hearth 3 (Fig. 4.1), in which he annotated materials around the hearth as Hearth 3. On the other hand, further finds that were logged as having been found 'in association with hearth 3' were not included in his list of finds from Hearth 3, e.g. E84:51, 52a–d, 59, 63, 80 or iron fragment E84:60. This may mean that the attribution of the above-mentioned ambiguous finds is based on a reassessment of the stratigraphy.

14 And an unlocated sherd, E84:844.

15 Though they are recorded as having been found at a depth of 21cm, relative to the depth of the hearth.

16 Though they are recorded as having been found at a depth of up to 35cm.

17 This is not entirely clear from the photographic evidence.

18 This is recorded as having come from Cutting A, which was renamed Cutting B.

19 This appears to be based on the mix-up between Pit 54 and Pit 4 in the post-excavation process. See comment in Table 3.47 for sample S73:14.

20 This can be assumed to be a layer of leaching, which, however, is not mentioned elsewhere.

21 The finds records do not allow the identification of these items.

22 There is no drawing of this hearth in the archive.

23 Note that the initial cutting outside the wall break in the east of the

cashel was initially called Cutting A but was renamed Cutting B in following seasons when a larger area was opened in this zone.

[24] This finds support in the list of finds attributed to the grey hard floor in F2: E84:6949, E84:7095a–h, E84:7096, E84:7097, E84:7504, E84:7575, E84:7586a–d, E84:7587, E84:7738, E84:7760a–b, E84:7871, E84:7875, E84:7958a–b, E84:7959.

[25] The finds records for Sqs F and G list a number of finds associated with black deposits. These include about twenty prehistoric mould and pottery fragments. While difficult to assess, this suggests a horizon containing prehistoric material, disturbed in the area of the cashel. See also discussion in Chapter 4, section 4.3.

[26] Section I across the ring-ditch (see below) appears to show, in contrast, a cut into the filled-in ditch, which, however, is located beside the intersection with the rectangular structure.

[27] A further glass bead, E84:9545, has no precise context information.

[28] E84:8583 could not be located and may be a sherd or mould fragment.

[29] It is interesting to note that neither the drawing of section 13 nor the corresponding Fig. 2.83 show the existence of the 'grey floor' in the interior of the ring-ditch, providing further evidence for the clearing of the interior of Ring-ditch 2.

[30] See Chapter 3, section 3.16: Erskine's original assessment also identified bones of an infant, but this could not be demonstrated in the reanalysis.

[31] The comment about the stone sealing this burial suggests that this may be a mix-up with Burial 2. No other record of Burial 3 suggests that it was closed with a stone.

[32] This could not be identified on plan.

[33] Pit 42 was noted by Raftery as having contained mould fragments, but these cannot be identified.

[34] This is not always recorded in the post-excavation section drawings and in the case of Pit 1 does not tally with the labelling of fills.

[35] This is the only record of Pits 9 and 20 in G2 having been covered by one deposit.

[36] The initial preliminary reports (Raftery 1970a; 1971a), based on the initial, 5m-wide B–B2 cutting, referred to the probable existence of a rectangular building, based on the line of post-holes referred to above, which bounded the metalworking along the northern edge of B/B1. As noted above, further excavation gave little support to this hypothesis and no buildings could be convincingly recognised.

[37] It is unclear whether Raftery here refers only to the two large post-holes in G5 or all post-holes here discussed as representing an enclosure. The consideration of post-holes that had been identified under the grey as part of the enclosure is in any case in conflict with Raftery's previous statements, in which he explicitly excludes the post-holes that were found under the grey layer from the group forming the concentric arrangements around Ring-ditch 2. In addition, the post-holes that were highlighted in annotated plans as having been found under the grey layer are restricted in the main to those that are not the ones discussed here as part of the post enclosure.

[38] The finds records locate this sherd to Pit 27 in G6. According to the pit concordance records, however, Pit 27 was located in H7.

[39] This could not be located and it is unclear whether it is an artefact.

[40] Please compare to the observations of the bank make-up in the 2011 excavations (section 2.8).

[41] Note that these are listed in the database as X11 but appear on plans in X10.

[42] All work was conducted under Ministerial Consent E4394 from the Department of Arts, Heritage and the Gaeltacht and the National Museum of Ireland.

[43] 202 finds numbers issued, 208 objects in database, with thirteen void entries.

[44] A Post-hole 64 is on Fig 2.137 located outside the structure, south-west of its entrance.

[45] All four sherds from Pit 8 are from grey silt, according to finds records.

[46] Not identified on plan.

[47] See discussion of these black linings in Chapter 6.

[48] A cremated bone sample from this context could not be identified to species (Table 3.47).

[49] Not on plan.

3. MATERIAL REMAINS

Barry Raftery and Katharina Becker

Over the seven years of excavation at Rathgall the site yielded a quite extraordinary quantity of items. In the excavation catalogue slightly over 10,000 find numbers have been allocated to individual objects or groups of objects. These are the primary record of the continued human presence at the site from the Neolithic to the modern era, but the great majority appear to belong to the Late Bronze Age. Among these, coarseware pottery is particularly frequent, with probably approximately 14,600 sherds, assigned 5,138 find numbers, as well as a single complete vessel. Other material includes objects of gold, bronze, glass, amber, shale and stone, as well as a large number of mould fragments. A number of clay crucibles are also represented, both from the Bronze Age and from later periods. In addition, the site produced a small quantity of late Iron Age and early medieval bronzes, a Viking silver ingot and a significant body of late medieval pottery, as well as two contemporary silver coins.

Some of the contexts that contained artefacts have been hopelessly disturbed and disrupted over the last few centuries. Besides the extensive ploughing activity, an enormous amount of disturbance was caused by rabbits, which, appear to have occupied the area of the Rathgall fort in their hundreds, if not thousands. The preservation of the later prehistoric strata in the central area of the site would also have been affected by the early medieval activity, not only but particularly associated with the construction of the stone cashel.

The artefacts play a special role within the Rathgall excavation archive, as their attribution to specific contexts and their recorded depths often contributed to the elucidation of stratigraphic issues, and in particular shed light on the often-significant levels of disturbance of the site (see Chapter 4, section 4.2). To allow future interrogation of the artefacts archive, the database has been made available in the online repository (www.dri.ie), in addition to the catalogues presented here in textual and tabular form.

3.1 GOLD AND AMBER

Barry Raftery and Katharina Becker

The wealth and importance of Bronze Age Rathgall are emphasised by the discovery of six items either completely or partially of gold. Apart, of course, from the many gold hoards in Ireland, no prehistoric site in the country has ever produced a comparable range of objects of this metal. All but one came from the eastern zone of intense occupation, in the thick black layers in Cuttings C and D in Area 2, the exception being the penannular ring (E84:6070; Fig. 3.1) which was found in Pit 119 in Sq. 34/35 in Area 1.

The association of the gold artefacts with contexts dated to the Late Bronze Age phase of activity seems unambiguous, and the various radiocarbon dates and the mass of material derived from these occupation layers speak to their Bronze Age background. Disturbances can, however, be identified owing to the presence of typologically later materials; while such are not present in the depression in which the mercury-gilt mount was found, unaccounted-for disturbance has to be considered a possible explanation for the presence of this object that is as yet without parallels both typologically and technologically (see section 3.2 below).

3.1.1 Penannular rings

The two small penannular rings (E84:6070 and 8000; Figs 3.1 and 3.2)—formerly, and somewhat unfortunately, called 'ring money' (Varndell 2001) or 'hair-rings'—are a well-known component of the Irish Bronze Age (Eogan 1964; 1994; 1997; Taylor 1980; Northover 2000; Raftery 2004; Becker *et al.* 2020). They are found in Ireland and in various parts of Britain, as well as in western France, Belgium and the Netherlands (e.g. Becker *et al.* 2020; Billand and Talon 2007; O'Connor 1980; Warmenbol 1999; 2017). They are small penannular rings, at times made of solid gold but often also of a base metal core covered with gold foil, like the examples from Rathgall. They are closely related to a range of ring ornaments of the Late Bronze Age to which a

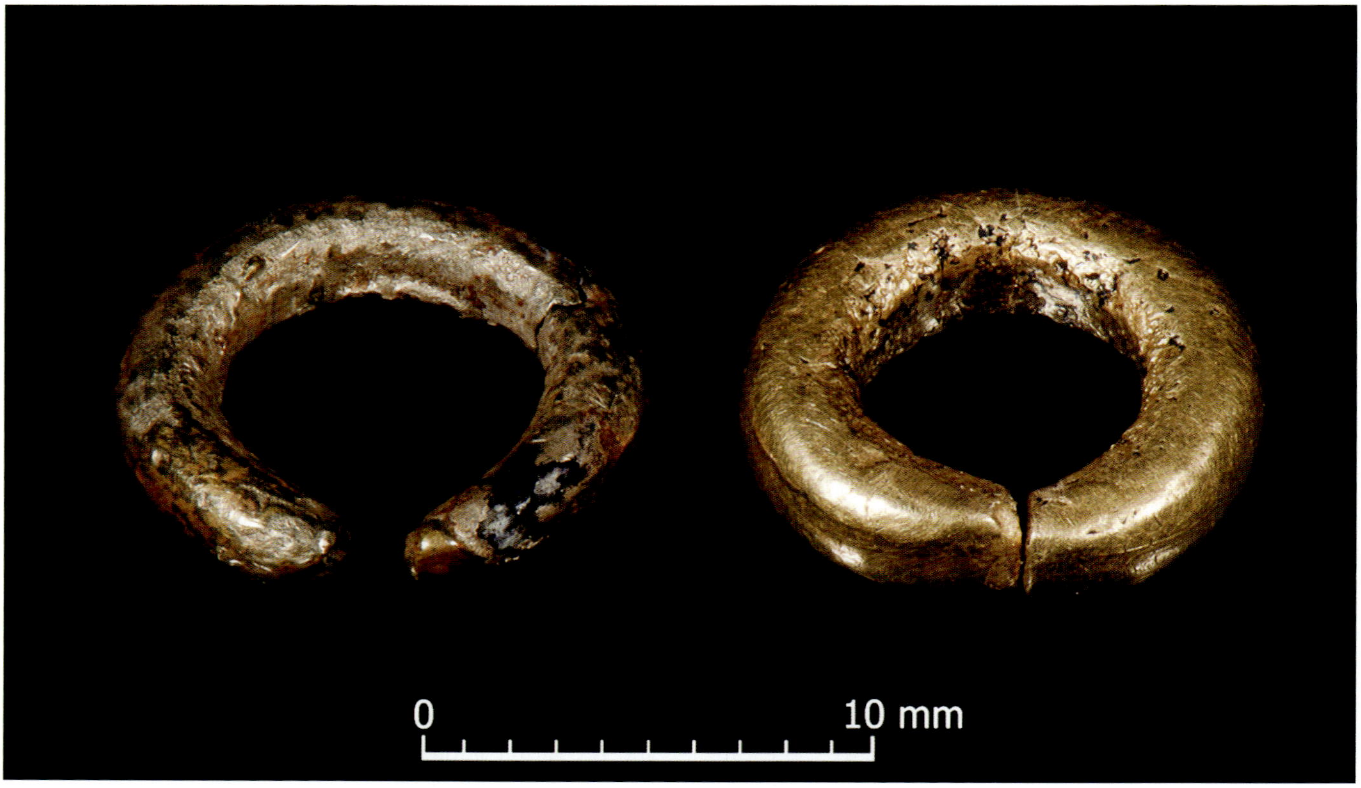

Fig. 3.1—Gold penannular rings E84:8000 and 6070 (photo: John Sunderland).

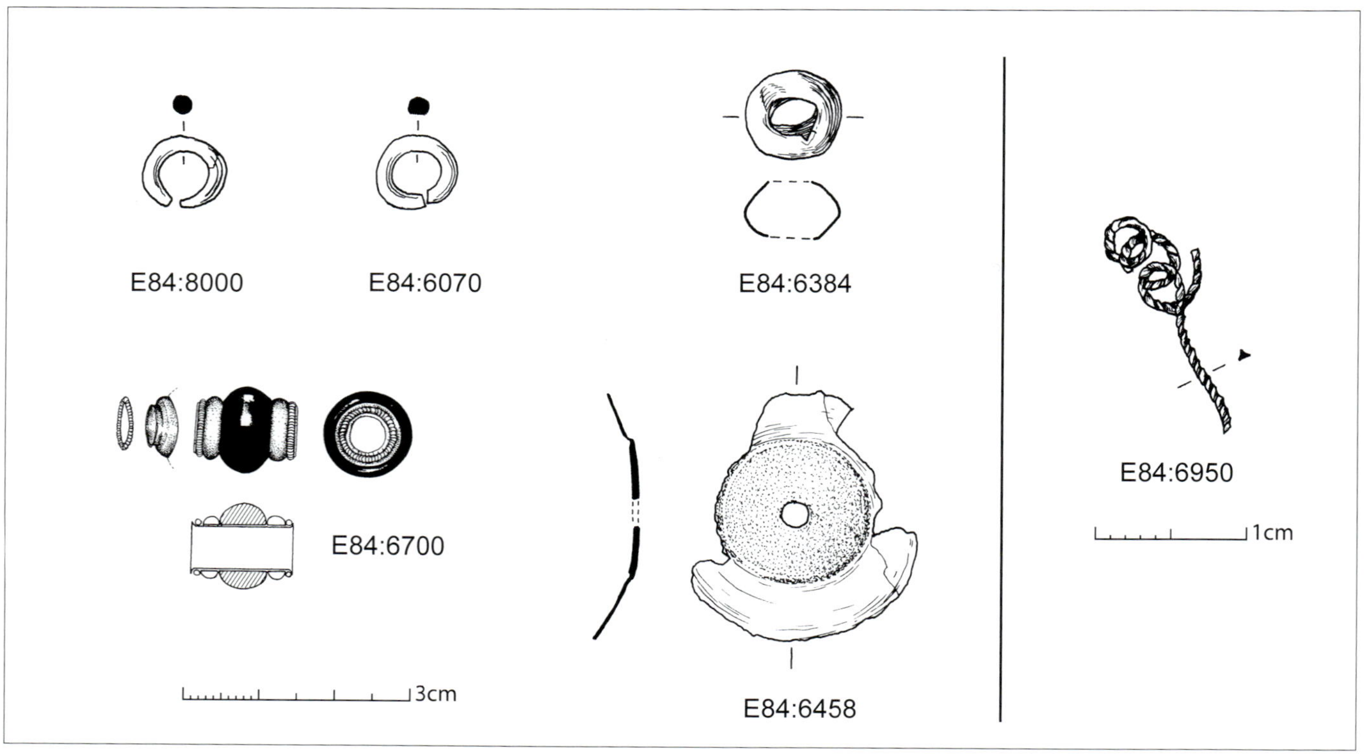

Fig. 3.2—Gold and gold composite artefacts (scale 1:1).

confusing variety of terminologies have been applied (e.g. Meeks *et al.* 2008). The form to which the Rathgall examples belong is the most numerous one that also appears to stand chronologically early within the corpus of Late Bronze Age gold ring ornaments.

Few Irish examples are provenanced, and information on their find context is available for even fewer. Examples have been found in an occupation layer in a roundhouse at Ballypriorbeg, Co. Antrim (Suddaby 2003, 87–9), in burnt mounds at Killeens, Co. Cork (Brindley *et al.* 1990, 26–7), and Rathmore, Co. Wicklow (McLoughlin 2001), as a secondary deposit in a portal tomb at Killaclohane 2, Co. Kerry (Becker 2021), and as a residual find in the fill of one of the ditches of the early medieval enclosure at the Hill of Ward, Co. Meath (Steve Davis, pers. comm.).

Based on the occurrence of related forms of thick penannular rings in Dowris-phase hoards and in the Scottish Balmashanner hoard, the Irish material had been grouped with Late Bronze Age artefacts (Eogan 1994; 1997), but an earlier, possibly even Middle Bronze Age, emergence of the type had been discussed by Northover (2000, 302) and Eogan (1964, 285).

Both rings from Rathgall came from contexts that were radiocarbon-dated. The more secure of the two deposits was dated to 1260–1040 cal. BC (GrN-27101) using charcoal from the lining of burial or pyre pit 119 (Raftery 2004; see Chapter 2, section 2.2.3). The second ring (E84:8000; Figs 3.1 and 3.2) was found in the occupation layer in Sq. C1 in Area 2. Charcoal samples from this area were dated to 1260–

Fig. 3.3—Gold-mounted bead E84:6700.

970 cal. BC, 1300–1000 cal. BC and 1260–970 cal. BC respectively (see Chapter 4, section 4.4). While there seems to be a broad consistency in the make-up of this very rich zone, the precise nature of the deposits in which the second of the two Rathgall penannular rings was found in C1 is entirely uncertain. The same black area that produced this ring contained, among other things, three glass beads (E84:4244, 7956, 8079; Figs 3.13, 3.14a and 3.14b), a lignite/jet bracelet (E84:3867), a slender bronze socketed gouge (E84:3300; Fig. 3.32),[1] inevitably a large quantity of coarse pottery, many clay mould fragments and other items. Unlike the first of the rings, this example appears not to have been in any deliberately placed context. Rather it appears, like so much else from the site, to have been either hidden or—perhaps more likely—lost. Or was there some deliberate destruction at the site whereby widespread damage was caused? The matter is utterly unclear, especially in view of the enormous body of material from the zone which yielded the rings and so much else.

The deposits that contained a hair-ring made of a base metal at Ballypriorbeg, Co. Antrim (Dunne 2003), were dated to 1373–1019 cal. BC (Church 2003). There are six other dates from the site, none of which post-dates 1000 BC. The context of a hair-ring in a burnt mound at Killeens, Co. Cork (beneath the trough), was radiocarbon-dated to 1500–1290 BC on oak (GrN-11438; 3115±35 BP; Brindley *et al.* 1990, 26–7).

On the Continent the situation is comparable, with radiocarbon dates placing the rings in the range of *c.* 1300–1000 BC (e.g. Billand and Talon 2007, 349) and pointing to the existence of these forms in phases prior to the Dowris phase from 900 BC (Becker *et al.* 2020; Raftery 2004), though the later existence of these types is indicated by the Balmanshanner, Angus, hoard (Coles 1959–60, 91, 98, nos 24–6; Eogan 1994, 141, pl. 14), as well as the association of the Covesea Sculptor's Cave rings (Becker *et al.* 2020) and a ring from the County Limerick hoard (Eogan 1983, 105–6, fig. 57D, no. 4). In Ireland, the chemical composition of the gold component of a number of analysed hair-rings may support an early date within this broad date range. Warner (2004, 79) regarded them on the basis of their composition as belonging to the same horizon as Middle Bronze Age four-flanged torcs.

Context and function

Most of the Irish examples have been found as single finds, with the exception of the aforementioned examples. The association of the rings with a burial context at Rathgall is thus unusual within an Irish context, but is rather characteristic for patterns of association elsewhere, with rings particularly in France and Belgium often found individually in cremation burials (cf. Billand and Talon 2007). The important collections of hair-rings found at the Sculptor's Cave, Covesea, Scotland (Becker *et al.* 2020), and the nine (or ten) examples, along with a range of other extraordinary gold items, from an underground river at Han-sur-Lesse, Prov. Namur (Warmenbol 1999; 2004), have been seen as representing some deep ritual importance. In this regard Warmenbol wrote in eloquent terms:

> 'The cave or the river gives access to another world, where the dead reside and Death rules. Where the two worlds meet, deposits were made, the objects going through the shimmering water-surface, to the same effect as little Alice climbing through the shining looking-glass. There is another world beyond, beyond that which the mirror shows, a world where a "vorpal sword" is needed' (Warmenbol 2004, 219).

The fact that human remains were found in this place as well as in the Sculptor's Cave underlines—while reflecting a different depositional history in these instances—the direct connection of these penannular rings with the human body, as evidenced by the various burial associations. Their frequent association with burial contexts suggests that it is indeed in the personal sphere that these items belong.

In Ireland, deposition in the natural landscape dominates, as the characteristic feature of the deposition of metalwork in this period in general. The finding of one of the Rathgall examples in Pit 119 underlines its association with burial rituals in this country, too. The fact that these items are usually found singly in burials on the Continent—only one deposited at a time—speaks against their use as hair decoration or earrings. It appears possible that these are septum rings (Becker *et al.* 2020).

Origins

While it is today generally held that these Irish gold rings are of Irish manufacture, it has nonetheless been pointed out on more than one occasion that uncannily similar gold rings are known from the Egyptian–Palestinian area, where they are seen as wig-rings. Hawkes (1961, 468) and Hartmann (1970, 29) considered this possibility, but there has been general scepticism on this matter (cf. Taylor 1980, 65; Eogan

1997, 308–10; Raftery 2004, 88–9). The close connection with France, Belgium and, of course, Britain creates a more relevant and meaningful context, illustrating and underlining the links between these regions in this early phase of the Late Bronze Age.

3.1.2 The composite pendant—the gold-mounted bead

A third object of gold from Rathgall (E84:6700; Fig. 3.3) is a spectacular piece, both technically and aesthetically. It came from the centre of the black occupation layer, 40cm deep in Sq. D/D1, and, as has already been noted, was found in this layer with a very large collection of material, including numerous moulds and potsherds. As is evident from the detailed description (p. 209), this is a masterpiece in the manufacture of fine jewellery. In particular, the minute, tightly twisted wire skilfully attached to each mount attached to either end of a glass bead displays gold-working of exquisite quality. Aesthetically, the rich green colour of the bead is a perfect foil for the glittering gold.

Once more a key question is whether this object is a local creation or an import. A stylistically and technologically comparable object was found, along with a second, undecorated, amber bead, in a bog at Milmorane, Co. Cork (Fig. 3.4) (Mitchell 1948; 1951; O'Kelly 1989, 186). Surprisingly, despite the exceptional quality of this bead, the Milmorane find has never been fully published, though photographs of the object have appeared in several exhibition catalogues (e.g. *Ausstellung* 1981, 42, no. 43). It is particularly interesting that, according to the finder's report, a splinter of a glass bead accompanied the other objects. Unfortunately, however, nothing survives of this (Cahill 2009, 96).

Fig. 3.4—The Milmorane bead (courtesy of the National Museum of Ireland). © National Museum of Ireland.

The Milmorane object consists of a large amber bead mounted on a gold tube in a similar manner to the Rathgall pendant. The perforation at each end is funnel-shaped, and four loops of twisted gold wire have been fitted within the gap left between the gold tube and the amber. These inserts, with a twisted wire, are somewhat more elaborate than those of the Rathgall object. Other differences are that the Milmorane cylinder does not protrude and that there are no additional rings, but the principle of manufacture is comparable.

These two fine objects thus share important technical and aesthetic details. It is to be assumed that each was intended for suspension and to be worn, most probably, as a neck ornament. The Rathgall object might have been the centrepiece of a bead necklace. Indeed, though entirely speculative, it is possible that the many plain glass beads found in the eastern zone of dense activity at the site, in the vicinity of the gold and glass pendant, formed part of a single necklace with the latter as a spectacular centrepiece.

The key question, once again, is whether the Cork ornament is of native manufacture. Obviously, the amber is imported and, as noted below, a Continental origin for the glass from Rathgall has also been suggested (see section 3.4). The fact that two such technically similar objects should be found at a distance from one another in this country, and each with a centrepiece of differing character, lends some support to the hypothesis of local manufacture. In his analysis of the prehistoric Irish gold, Hartmann (1971, 28) included Milmorane in his MC/PC group, which, he states, makes up about half of all prehistoric Irish gold (he numbered 247 pieces). This group of gold belongs overwhelmingly to what Eogan, more than 40 years ago, referred to as the Dowris phase, lending support to the suggestion that the Milmorane bead—though using imported amber—could have been made in Ireland.

3.1.3 The biconical bead

A biconical gold bead (E84:6384; Figs 3.2 and 3.5) was found in the brownish-black material, among the 'ferrous' lumps (Chapter 2, section 2.3.1), of Area 2 in Sq. D, lying on the dense black occupation layer. Though seemingly simple in appearance, the bead was in fact made with no

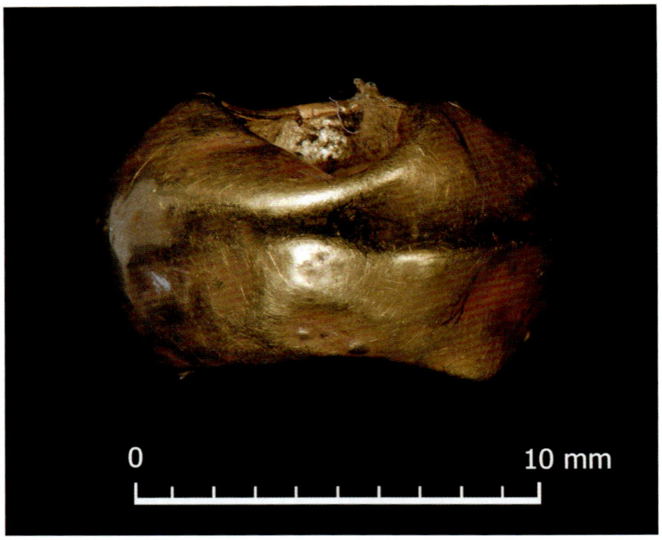

Fig. 3.5—Gold biconical bead E84:6384 (photo: John Sunderland).

little skill. It is now strongly deformed but originally was of biconical shape, with a gentle curved outline.

Comparable objects of gold have come from French hoards such as those from Cazevielle (Hérault), Laure (Aude) and Narbonne (Aude) (Briard *et al.* 1982–3), but the finds from Burton in Wales are particularly important (Gwilt *et al.* 2007; 2009). This hoard contained four gold biconical beads and a flange-twisted torc, as well as a transitional palstave and a trunnion chisel. These can be dated to the Penard phase on typological grounds. Biconical beads were also found in the Beer Hackett, Dorset, hoard and are considered typical for the Beer Hackett–Taunton phase (e.g. Eogan 1967, 134, 145–7; 1994, 41, fig. 20), the suggested chronological parameters of which broadly range between 1400 BC and 1275 BC, though the possible later, i.e. Penard phase, date of the associated twisted ornaments has also been discussed (Roberts 2007; Gwilt *et al.* 2007). The three or four biconical beads from the Burton hoard closely resemble the Rathgall example. They were made from small, thin sheets, as in the case of the Rathgall object, and detailed examination has indicated that two cores were welded together to form the biconical cylinder. It is possible that the Rathgall bead was made in the same way. Traces of a possible joint are visible on its inside.

Within Ireland a number of such biconical gold beads have been found but have no provenance (Armstrong 1933, 90–1, pl. XIV, 242–3). A necklace consisting of biconical gold beads and amber beads was found at Cruttenclogh, Co. Kilkenny; these, however, are decorated. Ten biconical gold beads were found in a bog near Malin, Co. Donegal, and, importantly, these were found with twisted gold wire fragments (Cahill 2009, 96) comparable to that found at Rathgall (below). Here, as in Rathgall, it is conceivable that beads and wire once formed part of a necklace. At Rathgall, however, the wire and bead were not found in direct association. Not of gold but of tin and decorated with ribs was a biconical bead found in a *fulacht fiadh* at Sonnagh, Co. Mayo. While not directly associated with a sample that produced a radiocarbon date of 1401–1294 cal. BC (Kerrigan and Gillespie 2010, 82–91), this seems in broad agreement with the dates for the gold beads. A biconical bead of bone was found in a pit at Knockadoon, Lough Gur (Cleary *et al.* 2003, fig. 18.1766), in a pit within a house thought to date from the later part of the Middle Bronze Age. A necklace consisting of 25 ceramic biconical beads (8.26mm by 7.84mm by 6.62mm) was found in a cremation burial (pit 50) at Burtown Little, Co. Kildare (Grogan and Roche 2010b), from which the cremated bones of an adult female provided a radiocarbon date of 1890–1630 cal. BC (2σ) (SUERC-25369) (Moloney 2010, 8). This find and Early Bronze Age finds from Tomfarney, Co. Wexford, and from Ireland (Sikora and Reilly 2011, 601, fig. 3.236) demonstrate the existence of ceramic beads of this shape in the earlier part of the Bronze Age.

The later existence of biconical beads as such is also indicated, however: Cahill and Mullarkey (2010) drew attention to biconical beads from Flag Fen (Pryor 2001, 291, 302, 306–8) which would allow for a later date; similarly, the association of one biconical bead with the Late Bronze Age hoard from Adabrock (Anderson 1911) on the Isle of Lewis, Scotland, suggests that the type may have had a long currency.

3.1.4 The gold wire fragment

The tiny length of twisted gold wire (E84:6950; Figs 3.2, 3.6), though unstratified, came from Sq. D3 amid a large concentration of pottery and clay mould fragments at a depth of 10–15cm in brown humus (Table 2.7). Though tiny, under magnification it is clear that, yet again, this is a remarkable object, most particularly in the delicate twisting of the wire. Surprisingly, however, the method of attaching the small rings to the wire is somewhat crude, although this is evident only under magnification. The wire, one of exceptional fineness, was obviously joined through the ring to something else, whether to another length of wire or to

Fig. 3.6—Gold wire E84:6950 (photo: John Sunderland).

some very fine object of gold. This cannot be established, and it is quite impossible to imagine the nature of the original object of which this is a tiny fragment. Cahill (2009, 96) suggests that this is a collection of a goldsmith's stock or leftover scraps, and, indeed, it appears likely that these are scraps of wire that were used for the manufacture of another item, the scrap kept together in this informal but safe arrangement. Twisted gold ornaments are typical of the Middle Bronze Age tradition and, increasingly, the use of twisted gold wire has also been evidenced, such as in the Burton hoard, Wrexham (see above), the Poulton, Gloucestershire, hoard (Art Fund, https://www.artfund.org/supporting-museums/art-weve-helped-buy/artwork/9842/poulton-hoard; accessed 12.4.22) and from the seabed at Salcombe, Devon (British Museum online collection 2010,8032.4; Stuart Needham, pers. comm.). Most if not all of these are of Penard date, suggesting a date for a horizon of twisted gold ornaments in the later part of the Middle Bronze Age.

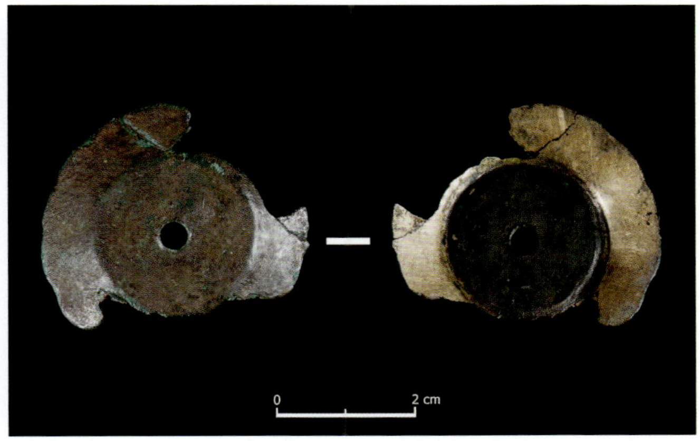

Fig. 3.7—Mercury-gilded mount E84:6458 (photo: John Sunderland).

3.1.5 The gilded mount

The sixth object containing gold from Rathgall is enigmatic: a perforated, circular, mercury-gilded mount (E84:6458; Figs 3.2 and 3.7), discovered in Sq. D2. It was found 27–30cm below the surface in the fill of a large, irregular depression extending in a series of shallow, linked hollows across the north-eastern half of Sq. D2 and for a short distance into the adjoining areas of D1 to the west and E3 to the north.

The precise form of this object when complete is unclear, as, indeed, is its original function. Two things are, however, evident. First, the central perforation indicates that it was riveted to something. Second, the fact that the gilding only occurs around the inner, sloping edge of the object, and is entirely absent from the flat, central section (and always was), indicates that something, perhaps a decorative mount of some sort, had originally been riveted on this area of the object. Thus we may envisage an elaborate decorative creation, consisting of a central feature such as a shaped amber stud and a golden surround, intended perhaps as an artificial flower of very considerable delicacy. The use of such a disc to form a covering for the pommel of, for example, a sword or dagger is conceivable, although no parallels are forthcoming.

The mount is not, as is to be expected for the Bronze Age, covered with gold sheet. Rather it is gilded, and the examination of the object by the British Museum (see section 3.2) indicates mercury gilding.

The earliest widely accepted dating for mercury gilding is in the fourth or third century BC in China (Lins and Oddy 1975, 369), but in western Europe the conventional date for its earliest use is in the Iron Age (Giumlia-Mair 2020, 6). All these dates are thus significantly later than the date of the horizon from which the gilded mount from Rathgall may have come.

Up until recently, an object with mercury gilding, a so-called *Vollgriffschwert* (a Late Bronze Age form of sword with solidly cast hilt) from an uncertain find-spot but possibly (though not certainly) from the River Niers near Oedt, Ldkr. Kempen-Krefeld in Germany (Loewe 1971, 234–6), was believed to be conceivably of a similarly early date to—or even a slightly earlier date than—the Rathgall mount. The object was studied in great detail by Driehaus some 40 years ago, and his extended and meticulously detailed account of his findings (Driehaus 1968) left him in no doubt that the sword and the mercury gilding were of genuinely prehistoric manufacture. While the 7% quicksilver present in the gold underlines that it is genuine mercury gilding (Anheuser 1999, 15), it now appears that the sword itself is a modern fake. XRF revealed that the blade is of a Bronze Age alloy but that the hilt is of a gun-metal alloy (Cu-Zn-Sn-Pb), which was unknown during the Bronze Age. This and other indicators suggest that it is a pastiche of different metals and technologies, some of which have only been known since the nineteenth century (Schwab *et al.* 2010; Joachim and Willer 2013).

Owing to a lack of contextual security and good parallels, it is currently impossible to say whether the mount from Rathgall is indeed prehistoric. In a draft of this discussion about the context of the mount Raftery wrote: 'These hollows filled over time with natural silting and with various types of domestic rubbish along with a range of discarded artefacts, including, inevitably, numerous coarse potsherds as well as a number of glass beads and some clay mould fragments. It is within the zone of these depressions, in the north-west area of D2, that the gilded mount was found. In this area the few medieval potsherds present occurred mixed in with iron fragments, broken clay pipes and some pottery of very recent date.' The analysis of the heavily corroded bronze base of the mount suggests that it is made of tin bronze—in agreement with but not conclusive for a prehistoric context but also for an early medieval date. The possibility of its being the mount, for example, for the decoration of a shrine should be considered.

3.1.6 Gold catalogue

E84:6070: Small penannular ring of base metal with gold foil overlay. The core is probably copper but this has not, as yet, been scientifically demonstrated. The ring is an almost exact circle and maintains a constant thickness. Owing to an almost imperceptible flattening around the interior, it is very slightly D-shaped in section. Its ends are almost touching. Its surface is of gold foil of exceptional thinness. Numerous minute, haphazard scratches are present all around the outer circumference, and tiny, irregular zones of wear are evident in some areas. No junction of the gold cover, either externally or internally, is evident.

Ext. diam.: 1.1cm by 1.5cm. Int. diam.: 5.5mm. T: 2.5mm.

Sq. 34/35, in black charcoal fill of Pit 119 within Ring-ditch 1: 'Near centre, under boulder, associated with tiny chips of cremated human bones. About 5cm deep in black material, probably originally on surface.'

E84:6384: Hollow biconical gold bead, dented on both faces. In the interior, a straight, vertical junction from top to bottom appears to be present.

Diam.: 1.3cm. H: 6.5mm. Original diam. of perforation: 7.5mm. T of gold: less than 1mm.

Sq. D, in dark brown/black material in zone of 'ferrous' lumpy material, 24–28cm below surface.

E84:6458: Perforated mount of tin bronze with a small quantity of lead. Circular, with central perforation, and shallowly splayed around its outer circumference. There is now damage around the edge in two areas. The perforation is precisely circular and superficially resembles that made by a twist drill. Examination in the British Museum Research Laboratory, however, using a high-powered microscope (see section 3.2), has shown that it was made with a punch. A slight lip around its outer edge suggests that it was punched from the inside. Dividing the sloping outer zone and the central area there is a very fine incised line which could have been cut into the bronze using a delicately pointed compass. The outer edge is very slightly irregular, but this is likely to be secondary wear. The gilding occurs on the inner face of the sloping band. It is separated from the perforated central area by the fine, enclosing line, apart from three spots where minuscule flecks of gold occur immediately inside and a single fleck, of similarly minute dimensions, which occurs on the immediately inner face of the circular groove. The gilding is complete and regular where it survives, but under high magnification extremely fine scratches are detectable extending irregularly around and across the gilded surface. On the scanning electron microscope in the British Museum the gilding was shown to be uniformly 3μm thick, sitting directly on the corroded bronze. On the plain outer surface it is difficult, owing to patina, to determine whether the splaying around the outer circumference was cast or hammered. It seems most likely, however, that it was finely hammered.

Diam.: 3.25cm. Diam. of central area: 1.9cm. Diam. of central perforation: 3mm. T: 0.5–1mm. W of gilded zone: 8mm.

Sq. D2, in darkish material, in northern section of square, in depression D84.

E84:6700: Pendant, consisting of a glass bead centrally mounted on a gold cylinder. The bead is a dark translucent green in colour and is regularly shaped. At one point there is a tiny circular perforation, presumably in some way a product of the glass manufacture. Through the bead a fine gold cylinder has been inserted, and mounted on this, on either side of the bead, are two gold rings, forming two gold collars flanking the central glass bead. These rings, which are identical in size and shape, appear to be D-shaped in section but are in fact delicately flattened around both their inner and outer circumferences. This ensures, in each instance, a perfect junction with the glass bead and with a tiny ring of coiled gold wire fitted on each end of the tube to secure them in position. The wire, though no more than 7.5mm in external diameter, possesses in each instance no fewer than 58 tight twists of D-sectioned hammered wire. The twisted rings, finally, are tightly secured in place by the minute out-turning of the gold tube. This has been achieved with great skill, as each end of the tube is perfectly regular. Under magnification tiny nicks, some of incredible fineness, are visible, which mark, and secure in place, the out-turned and overlapping edge of the gold cylinder on top of the gold wire coil. These are not identical in form, some being simple incisions and others being subtriangular. Where the twisted wire is missing at one end, these nicks appear to be present also around the outer edge of the tubed flange. This seems to imply the use of a pincers-like instrument of awesome fineness. At roughly corresponding points on each face these zones appear to be worn for a distance of 3–4mm. This may result from the suspension of the pendant, presumably on a necklace of some sort. No junction is visible in the gold, either within the tube or on the convex bands surrounding the beads. Similarly—a detail of possibly even greater skill—no point of junction is readily apparent on the tiny twisted gold rings. On the surviving example there is a very slight opening between the twists and it is possible that the join was here.

L: 2.25cm. Diam. of bead: 2.05cm. Int. diam. of tube: 5.5mm. Diam. of gold rings: 8.5mm. W of gold rings: 2.5mm. Ext. diam. of twisted rings: 7.5mm. T of twisted wire rings: less than 0.5mm. T of wire itself: less than 0.1mm.

Sq. D/D1, in thick, black charcoal, 40cm below surface.

E84:6950: Twisted gold wire with two tiny rings attached. The wire, of exceptional fineness and triangular cross-section, has been expertly worked into an even and regular twist. One end is bent back into an irregular loop, through which a tiny gold ring of twisted wire is threaded. The thickness and the twist of this ring are virtually identical with those of the wire. Its ends have been cut flat and are only a fraction of a millimetre apart. This ring is looped through a second ring, which is even smaller than the first and is, in this instance, annular. Fine, skilfully produced twisting occurs on one face, while on the other the surface of the gold is virtually flat apart from slight hints here and there of former twisting, reflecting damage by heat during the soldering of its two ends.

Estimated L of wire: 18mm. T of wire: 0.7–0.9mm. Int. diam. of penannular ring: 2mm. Int. diam. of annular ring: 1.5mm. Ext. diam. of rings: 3.5mm and 4.3mm.

Sq. D3, in upper brown humus, 10–15cm deep.

E84:8000: Small penannular ring of base metal with gold foil overlay, now in two parts. The core is badly corroded and crumbly. It is greenish in colour and probably copper. The gold foil cover, which in a few places is slightly damaged, is of consistent thickness (less than 1mm) and is regularly smooth, apart from some very fine depressions which are only visible under high magnification. These tiny imperfections may, however, be secondary wear. To the naked eye the ring appears to be circular in section, but under high magnification it can be seen that the inner face is very slightly flat, giving a faintly D-shaped section to the object. The ends of the ring are fractionally under 2mm apart, and at each end its thickness narrows fractionally. Here, under magnification, it appears that the surface of the gold cover curves evenly from the exterior to the interior. This seems a product of the process of applying the gold to the core. Even under high magnification, however, no division in the foil cover is detectable, so that the means by which the latter was applied to the core is not clear.

Ext. diam.: 1.1cm. Int. diam.: 6.5mm. T: 2.5mm.

Sq. C1, in dense black occupation layer in north-west, almost under inner stone enclosure.

3.1.7 Amber

Amber occurs frequently in the Irish Late Bronze Age (see MacWhite 1944a; Briggs 1997; Eogan 1999), almost invariably in the form of beads, which, in some instances, have been found in considerable numbers in hoards, often associated with items of bronze. The quantity of amber from Rathgall is limited, consisting of three beads and several small fragments. Two beads (E84:8526 and E84:8527) are of a typical spherical shape represented in great variety within the Bronze Age record (Figs 3.8–3.10).

Amber objects, which are relatively common in the later phases of the Irish Bronze Age, are conventionally held to be imports. Their ultimate source is most frequently regarded as being in the north European area, either southern Denmark or northern Germany, where substantial deposits of Baltic amber are found, although local occurrence of washed-up amber and local deposits of Baltic amber in Ireland have also been evidenced (Briggs 1997). Quite substantial finds of amber occur along the east coast in Britain, but their use in prehistory is a controversial topic (cf. Briggs 1997; Beck and Shennan 1991). The question of the origin of the Irish amber will not be resolved without a systematic analytical programme, addressing local deposits and objects.

While one of the beads (E84:4246; see p. 211; Fig. 3.11) and a fragment (E84:7507), possibly from a bracelet or larger bead, come from the C1/D1 concentrations, two of them (E84:8526 and 8527; Figs 3.8–3.10) were found in the upper fill of Ring-ditch 2 in J4. The filling of the ditch shows little evidence of phasing, strongly suggesting rapid burial, perhaps immediately after the central burial activity was complete. While the finds from its fill may derive from the burial activity, they may also be residual from earlier phases of activity.

E84:7507: Fragment, broken at each end. A tiny, gently curving, circular-sectioned fragment which has clearly been carefully cut and polished. There is thickening from one end to the other. Too little survives to determine its original character. It might possibly be the remains of a small bracelet or bead.

L: 11mm. W: 7.3mm. T: 6mm.

Sq. D/D1, lowest levels of black habitation area.

E84:7234: Several tiny, broken fragments of amber, too small to indicate any features.

D/D1, in brown material, south of black area.

Fig. 3.8—Amber bead E84:8526 (photo: John Sunderland).

Fig. 3.9—Amber bead E84:8527 (photo: John Sunderland).

E84:8526: Complete bead with a regularly circular shape, tapering slightly in thickness and with slight damage along one face. Central, slightly tapered perforation with regular edges. Flat area immediately around each edge, roughly 11mm in diameter. Some recent damage on one edge. One face considerably scored, possibly in recent times. Dark reddish-brown in colour.

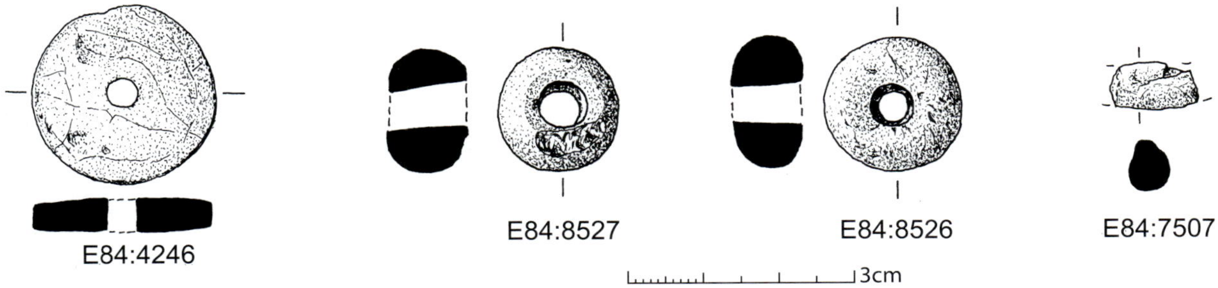

Fig. 3.10—Amber beads (scale 1:1).

Diam.: 18.7mm. T: 9.7mm. Diam. of perforation: 5.4mm.

J4, upper grey fill of Ring-ditch 2, 5cm from E84:8527.

E84:8527: Amber bead, with small amount of damage on one face. Closely similar to that described above but irregular and somewhat thinner in outline. Vertical thickness somewhat greater. Flat area immediately around each edge, roughly 10mm in diameter. Asymmetrical cross-section. Dark reddish-brown in colour.

Diam.: 16.8mm. T: 10.9mm. Diam. of perforation: 6mm.

J4, upper grey fill of Ring-ditch 2, 5cm from E84:8526.

3.1.8 The Hiberno-Norse bead

Matt Seaver and Paula Harvey

E84:4246: A single amber bead likely to be of early medieval date was found at Rathgall. While small amber studs were present in earlier objects such as the eighth-century Tara Brooch, the size and shape of the bead from Rathgall suggest a Hiberno-Norse origin. Polished disc beads with cylindrical perforations are known from excavations in Hiberno-Norse Dublin from tenth-century contexts where amber-working workshops are known (Harvey, forthcoming). Apart from urban Hiberno-Norse sites, amber beads have been found in at least eleven other settlement sites from the period, among which Lagore yielded by far the most, with sixteen beads (Doyle 2015, 98). Few of these are disc-shaped. Recent excavations are adding to the total, with work at Caherconnell, a large cashel site, revealing an amber stud of tenth-century date which is likely have Scandinavian links (Comber 2019, 52, fig. 63). A disc-shaped bead, albeit smaller, of ninth- to tenth-century date and of Hiberno-Norse association was found overlying cremations at Cloghermore Cave (Connolly *et al.* 2005, 192–3). While the bead from Rathgall has not been analysed at an elemental level, it is likely to be of Baltic origin in common with those examined from Anglo-Scandinavian York (Panter 2000, 2649–74).

Fig. 3.11—Amber disc bead E84:4246 (photo: John Sunderland).

E84:4246: Amber disc. Complete, perforated, circular in plan and almost oval in section, with flattened ends. Very regular in shape. Edge of disc smooth and consistent in thickness all the way around. Disc thickens consistently towards virtually central cylindrical perforation. Polished surface, with small amount of damage on both faces. Brownish-red in colour.

Diam.: 24.5mm. T: 5.9mm. Diam. of perforation: 3.4mm.

C1, in black occupation layer, almost in grey 'floor'.

3.2 THE RATHGALL MERCURY-GILDED MOUNT

P.T. Craddock and N.D. Meeks

The scientific examination and qualitative X-ray fluorescence surface analysis at the British Museum (Lab. File 4542) of a number of items from the Rathgall excavations included the small gilt mount E84:6458 (Fig. 3.7). The bronze is totally corroded; the copper has been preferentially leached out, leaving a tin-rich corrosion product which was identified by X-ray diffraction as containing both cassiterite (SnO_2) and romarchite (SnO). This is rather unusual, but has been encountered elsewhere (Tylecote 1978). Analysis showed that the mount is of tin bronze with a little lead and that the gilding was of gold with a little silver, but also contained mercury (Table 3.1). A possible example of mercury gilding from a Bronze Age context immediately raised interest and further investigation was undertaken. To this end, a small sample was detached and examined by scanning electron microscopy. This showed the gilding to be in a uniform layer, approximately 3μm thick, sitting directly on the corroded bronze surface (Fig. 3.12), and micro-analysis confirmed the presence of mercury. There can be no doubt that this is a mercury-gilded artefact that has become corroded during prolonged burial.

The technique is not intrinsically difficult. Finely divided gold is ground up with mercury to form an amalgam, sometimes referred to as 'butter of gold', which gives some idea of the consistency of the mixture. The copper or copper-alloy surface to be gilt must be carefully cleaned, especially to remove all traces of grease, and the amalgam is applied with a stiff brush. The piece is then heated to above the boiling-point of mercury (356°C) and most of the mercury is driven off, leaving a gilded surface with a small but persistent trace of mercury. The piece would then be burnished to produce a lustrous golden-coloured surface.

To carry out mercury gilding the craftsmen must have had access to the necessary materials. The gold, of course, presents no problem; the Wicklow Mountains are believed to have been one of the main sources of gold in the Late Bronze Age (Taylor 1980), but the mercury could be considered to be more problematic. Mercury does, however, occur in Ireland and was actually produced commercially in the 1970s as a by-product of copper production at the Gortdrum mine, about 5km north of Tipperary Town (Williams and McArdie 1978). The deposit is of copper sulphides, mainly chalcopyrite and tennantite, in a country rock of limestone and outcrops at surface. Indeed, the mineralisation was visible in the face of a small undated stone quarry, although with no apparent attempt to work the vein itself. The tennantite was found to be rich in mercury, both as the sulphide cinnabar and as metallic mercury in solid solution in the tennantite. In this form it would be easy to release from the mineral. There are, in fact, records of metallic mercury being found in nineteenth-century Ireland. When railway cuttings were being dug in the south-west of the country, 'liquid silver', identified as mercury, was encountered running from the rocks on at least one occasion (John Jackson, pers. comm.). Thus the raw materials were potentially available, but is there any evidence for the use of mercury gilding in the Bronze Age of the British Isles? To this the answer has to be no. Gold foil-covered objects were quite common in the Late Bronze Age (Taylor 1980), including on the two hair-rings from the site (see above), but mercury gilding is not present (Northover and Anheuser 2000). The major study of penannular gold rings from the British Isles (Meeks *et al.* 2008) revealed a range of quite sophisticated and well-executed gilding techniques but with no trace of mercury. The earliest examples of the technique from the British Isles are currently some pieces from the Iron Age Snettisham gold torcs, dated to the first century BC (Northover in Oddy 1993; Northover and Anheuser 2000).

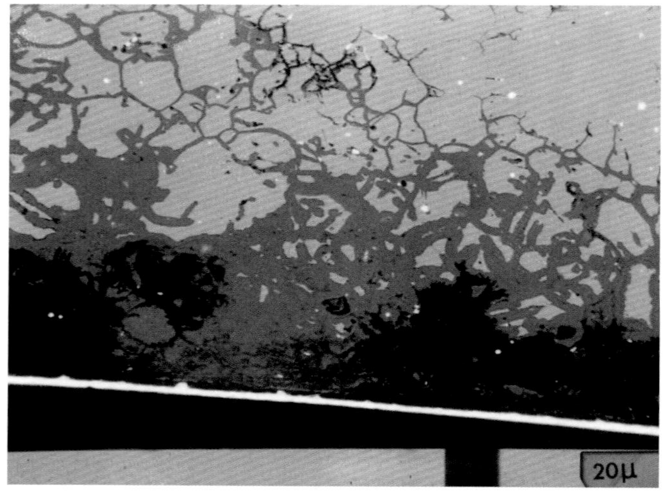

Fig. 3.12—SEM image of the mercury-gilt mount E84:6458.

Elsewhere there are a number of early examples (Oddy 1993), the earliest being a bronze sword with a mercury-gilded hilt of Bronze Age date, found in the River Niers near Oedt in North Rhine Westphalia (Driehaus 1968). This piece has always been somewhat suspect, admittedly to some extent because of the mercury gilding. More recent scientific

Table 3.1—SEM/XRF analysis of the mercury-gilded mount E84:6458.

	SN	CU
Au3 (bronze sampled at the back of the disc)*	5.30%	94.7
Au2 (bronze exposed below gilding)	Same spectrum as Au3—not quantified	
Au1 (gilded area)	CU, AU, HG, AS , tr SN ZN—not quantified	
*Au3: Also traces (not quantified) of Fe (iron), As (arsenic) and Pb (lead).		

investigation has established that the gilded hilt of a leaded gun-metal alloy is likely to be modern and is certainly a relatively recent addition to the blade, which may well itself be ancient (Schwab *et al.* 2010). Recent work on metalwork from the Iberian Peninsula has shown that mercury gilding was practised, albeit on a limited scale, from the Iron Age in the later first millennium BC (Perea *et al.* 2008; Martinón-Torres and Ladra 2011), and other examples are also known from the later Spanish Iron Age (Tait 1976). Elsewhere, mercury gilding is attested in China (Lins and Oddy 1975; Jett and Chase 2000) and in Greece (Craddock 1977), both from the mid-first millennium BC.

It might be thought that the composition of the underlying copper might give an indication of date. Brass, the alloy of copper and zinc, began to replace bronze, the alloy of copper and tin, over much of Europe and the Mediterranean from the beginning of our era. In Ireland, however, bronze continued as the predominant alloy through most of the first millennium AD, right up until the arrival of the Vikings (Craddock *et al.* 2001; Craddock 2001).

Overall, mercury gilding is certainly attested in Europe from the late first millennium BC but not from the second. Furthermore, the absence of the technique on any other gilded Bronze Age metalwork from the British Isles is surely significant. Thus, although the Bronze Age smiths certainly had the technical capability and could well have had access to the necessary materials, on balance it would seem that the mount is likely to be intrusive.

3.3 THE COMPOSITION OF THE GOLD ORNAMENTS FROM RATHGALL

Richard Warner and Paul Mullarkey

The gold objects from Rathgall were analysed by automated energy-dispersive X-ray fluorescence spectroscopy (XRF or EDX) in the National Museum of Ireland (NMI) in 2002–3.[2] In all cases the whole objects were placed in the chamber; no samples were removed and no cleaning was undertaken. The area irradiated was quite small (about 0.7mm across) and could be selected visually, and up to three readings were taken (at different points) on each object (Table 3.2). This non-invasive technique measures only the surface layer, and some authors have claimed that significant changes in the distribution or concentration of the relevant major constituents (silver, gold and copper) might occur through differential solution after deposition (Hook and Needham 1989).

It must be mentioned that small values for tin are not measurable by simple in-air XRF in the presence of high levels of gold and silver. This is a matter of particular regret in the case of late Middle Bronze Age and Late Bronze Age objects, where tin is the most important discriminator between the various alloys and object groups (Warner 2004).

It will be noted that only two of the six artefacts are made of gold alone, the other four being composites of more than one material. An attempt was made, with the composite objects, to analyse only the gold portion, but it will be seen that in two cases it was not possible to distinguish the copper in the gold from that in the base-metal core.

Penannular ring **6070** (Fig. 3.1) consists of foil on a base-metal core. Visual inspection indicated that the core is copper or a copper alloy. The small amount of copper recorded in all the analyses of this object (0.2%) indicates that the analytical results, including the copper, relate only to the gold foil.

Penannular ring **8000** consists of a gold-foil-covered base metal. The analysis shows very variable copper levels of between 10% and 33% and it is certain that the X-ray beam was partly irradiating the base-metal core to give us a mixed result, representing both gold surface and core material. The gold programme to which the XRF machine was set can give very unreliable results if metals other than silver and gold are present in large amounts. The high copper reading *appeared* to indicate that the core was copper or a copper alloy.

Bead **6700** consists of gold and glass.

Mount **6458** is gilded base metal. The single analysis of the gold surface showed very high copper, but, as explained with regard to **8000** (above), this is likely to be spurious. The core appears to be bronze, and no copper value can be reliably estimated for the gold itself.

The hollow *bead* **6384** and the *looped wire* **6950** are of gold only and the results reflect this.

Table 3.2—Gold artefact analyses.

Object number E84:	Type	Materials	Object number	Detail	Analysis number	Au %total	Ag %total	Cu %total
6070	Penannular ring	Gold foil on base metal*	263		495	97.4	2.5	0.15
					496	97.2	2.7	0.15
					497	97.1	2.7	0.2
					Mean	**97.2**	**2.6**	**0.2**
6384	Hollow bead	Gold	308		822	84.7	13.4	1.9
					823	83	14.4	2.6
					Mean	**83.8**	**13.9**	**2.2**
6458	Phalera or mount	Gold on base metal*	312		834	46.2	1.1	52.7
6700	Composite bead	Glass & gold*	310	Collar	829	83.3	13.8	2.9
					830	84.3	13.2	2.5
				Coil	831	82.6	14.4	3
					Mean	**83.4**	**13.8**	**2.8**
6950	Twisted wire with rings	Gold	311	Ring 1	832	81.6	13.9	4.5
				Ring 2	833	81.5	15.2	3.3
					Mean	**81.5**	**14.6**	**3.9**
8000	Penannular ring	Gold on base metal*	309	Large fragment	824	58.2	7.9	33.9
					825	74.3	15.3	10.4

To sum up: in the cases of artefacts **6070**, **6384**, **6700** and **6950** the gold alone was analysed and the copper measured was in the gold alloy. In the cases of **8000** and **6458**, however, the base-metal core of the object has caused spurious values to be recorded and the true level of the copper in the gold is therefore unknown.

A few comments on variability are necessary. The three analyses for **6070** are extremely close and indicate a very homogeneous metal. The same goes for **6700**. As for **6384** and **6950**, the variations in the two measures of each are not significant. The extreme variations in the composite object **8000** are due to the variable effect of the underlying core material as the probe was relocated.

3.4 GLASS

3.4.1 Prehistoric glass beads

Barry Raftery, Katharina Becker and Joanne Gaffrey

One of the most remarkable aspects of the Rathgall excavations is the surprisingly large number of glass beads that came to light (Figs 3.13, 3.14a and 3.14b). Besides a medieval bead (see below) and the group of 88 Bronze Age beads (Raftery and Henderson 1987; Henderson 1988a; 1988b; 1989b)[3] discussed below, a group of four beads of tubular shape stand out (E84:2511, E84:7842, E84:7843, E84:7921) (Figs 3.13, 3.27 and 3.29). Blue in colour, in shape they closely resemble Roman cylinder beads (Tempelmann-Maczyńska 1985, 38–9, Tafel 3; Guido 1978, fig. 37, pl. IVa). These, a rather simple form, appear to have a long duration, dating from the first half of the first millennium AD (Tempelmann-Maczyńska 1985, 2, 38–9), but do not appear in pre-Roman times in Britain (*ibid.*, 94–5). Bead fragment E84:7842 could conceivably be part of a segmented bead. They all derived from disturbed topsoil contexts. A small purple bead (E84:7067) was also found in disturbed deposits in Sq. D4, and two tiny ring-beads, E84:7466 and 7627 (Fig. 3.14a), similarly stand out from the rest of the corpus. E84:7627 was found at a depth of 20cm in brown material; E84:7466 was found at a depth of 40–60cm in black occupation material, and may also be part of the Bronze Age corpus. A dark blue bead, E84:7979 (Fig.

3.14b) is of likely later date too, based on colour and opacity.

The remaining beads date from the Bronze Age, based on morphology, chemical composition and association, with 52 from certain or probable Bronze Age contexts (see Table 3.3). The distribution of the beads on the site is focused on B/C and D/Dl, indicating that they are closely associated with the concentration of metalworking activity revealed in these zones.

The Bronze Age beads

The beads are for the most part of various shades of blue or greenish-blue, most of them consisting of opaque glass. Some indigo blue ones appear more translucent and are of likely later date: 1965, 7979. A few specimens, darker in colour, tend more towards purple. They are small and fairly consistent in size, with their external diameters varying from 6mm to 13.5mm. The perforations vary considerably in diameter from 1.9mm to 6mm, and larger in a few instances. In cross-section they are invariably irregularly D-shaped and vary in thickness from 1.3mm to 13.8mm. Some have a more barrel-shaped profile owing to their higher ratio of thickness to overall diameter (e.g. E84:9315, 7444, 7788, 8375), whereas most are of a flattened spherical shape in section.

The great majority of the beads are plain, annular specimens (e.g. Figs 3.13 and 3.14a). The exceptional bead E84:6700 (Fig. 3.3), one of these plain annular beads mounted with skill and complexity on a tube of fine sheet gold, has been described above (section 3.1).

Altogether, sixteen beads or bead fragments are decorated. These are eye beads of round to subtriangular shape, with the eye decoration consisting of sets of 1–3 concentric circles of pale turquoise to white glass marvered into the surface at each of the three corners. Some examples are only very slightly angular in cross-section, others round to barrel-shaped, e.g. E84:9315. One of the eye beads, E84:3670 (Figs 3.13 and 3.21), is a fragmentary example, subtriangular in form but slightly larger than the other subtriangular beads. Its base colour is of a darker blue than the rest, and the decoration of the two surviving corners consists of a single ring of pale turquoise glass enclosing a reddish-brown centre.

Some of the beads consist of a clay core with a shell-like layer of opaque glass. The first example, less than half of which remains, is oval in section and considerably larger than the others (E84:779; Figs 3.13 and 3.15). Given that its internal diameter (the distance between the edge of the perforation and the external edge of the bead) is 7mm and the diameter of the perforation is about 5mm, the bead may originally have been some 19mm in diameter and measured 13.9mm in thickness. It is a deep indigo in colour. E84:7467 (Fig. 3.13) is very similar, as it would also have been comparatively large originally, measuring 7.3mm in internal diameter and 13.8mm in thickness. Both consist of a clay core covered by a skin of turquoise glass. Similarly, clay seems to be adhering to the inside of a small bead fragment, E84:8052 (Fig. 3.13), and a further five fragments of glass appear to be the outer shell of such beads (E84:6538, 6562, 838, 1569; Figs 3.16–3.18[4]).

The contexts of the beads

The distribution of the beads within the excavated area is with few exceptions focused on Areas 2 and 3 and around the eastern perimeter of Ring-ditch 1 adjacent to Area 2 (Fig. 3.19; cf. also fig. 1 in Raftery and Henderson 1987).

By far the greatest concentration occurred in Area 2, particularly the D/D1 focus and the area immediately adjacent to it, the black material in the section strip towards E1. In these squares no fewer than sixteen beads were recovered in the black occupation layer or from just below it (decorated (Fig. 3.13): E84:6562, 7000 (Fig. 3.20), 7580, 8215, 8216; undecorated (Fig. 3.14a): E84:6300 (Fig. 3.22), 6333, 7184, 7190, 7300, 7466, 7578, 7579, 7627, 7679; gold-mounted: E84:6700 (Fig. 3.1)). Two of the beads came from among the enigmatic 'lumps' and the remainder from the deposits underneath them.

To the south of these, in B1/C1, the Zone 2 metalworking focus, a further six came to light (E84:8052 (Fig. 3.13), 1965 (Fig. 3.22), 4244 (Fig. 3.14a), 7956, 8049, 8217 (Fig. 3.14b)), including some from the extent of the black layer under the cashel wall. In D2, within the Metalworking Zone 4 mould focus, three beads were found, at least two of which were from D84 (E84:6666, 6680, 7788;[5] Fig. 3.14b), the depression that yielded the enigmatic gilded bronze mount (E84:6458; Figs 3.2 and 3.8).

It was also in Area 2 that most of the decorated beads were found. Nine were found in the intensive B–E zone of activity (E84:6562 (Fig. 3.14a), 6700 (Fig. 3.3*)*, 7000 (Fig. 3.20), 7580, 8052, 8077, 8079, 8215, 8216 (Fig. 3.14a)), three of which came from the D/D1 area (E84:6562, 7000, 7580) and two from the E1 section strip (E84:8215, 8216 (Fig. 3.14a)) (cf. Raftery and Henderson 1987, fig. 1).

To the south and east of these major concentrations, beads were more dispersed. Three scattered examples came from the lower levels, including the basal black layer under

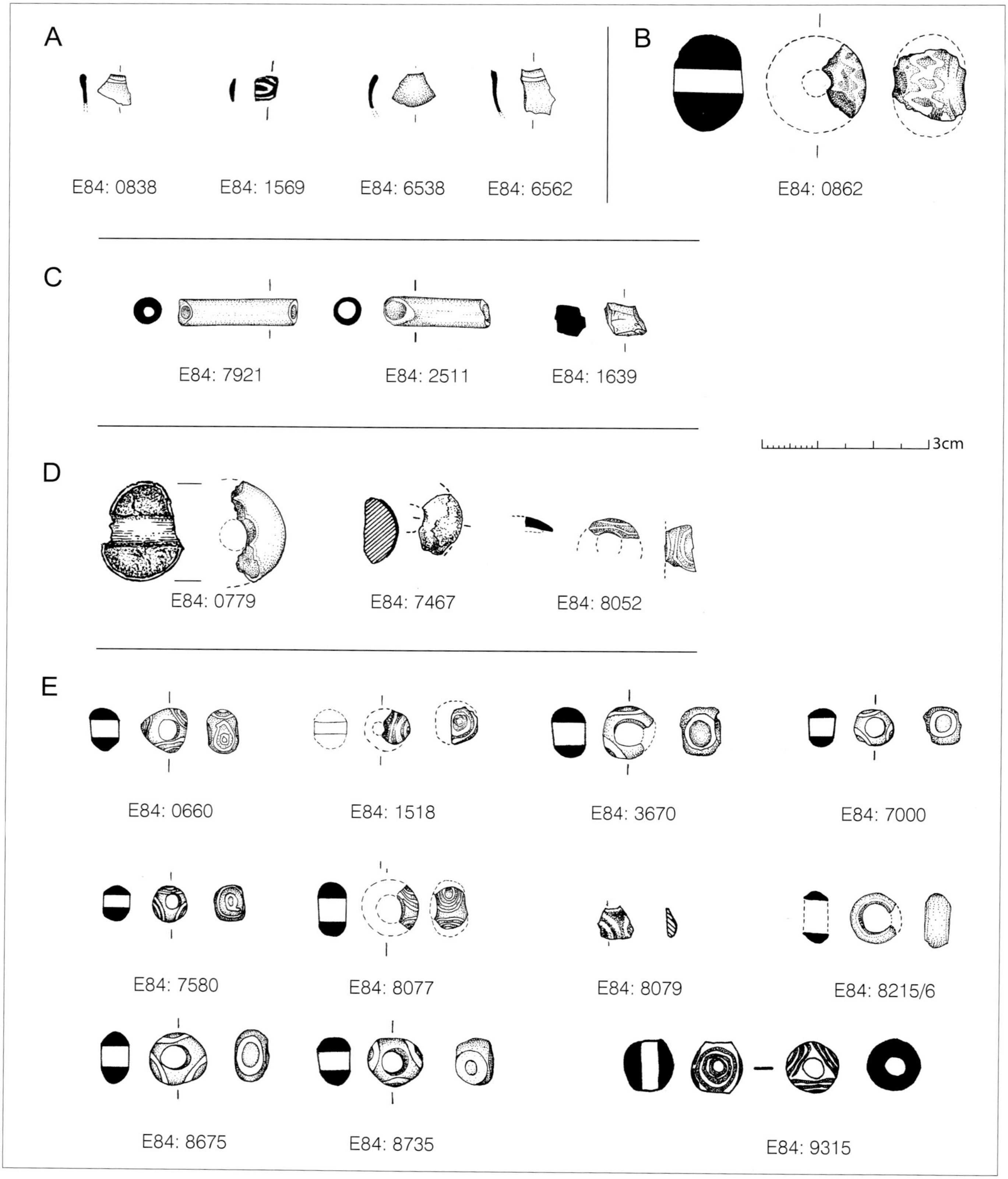

Fig. 3.13—Decorated glass beads, glass beads with clay cores, glass shell fragments, tubular beads and medieval bead E84:0862.

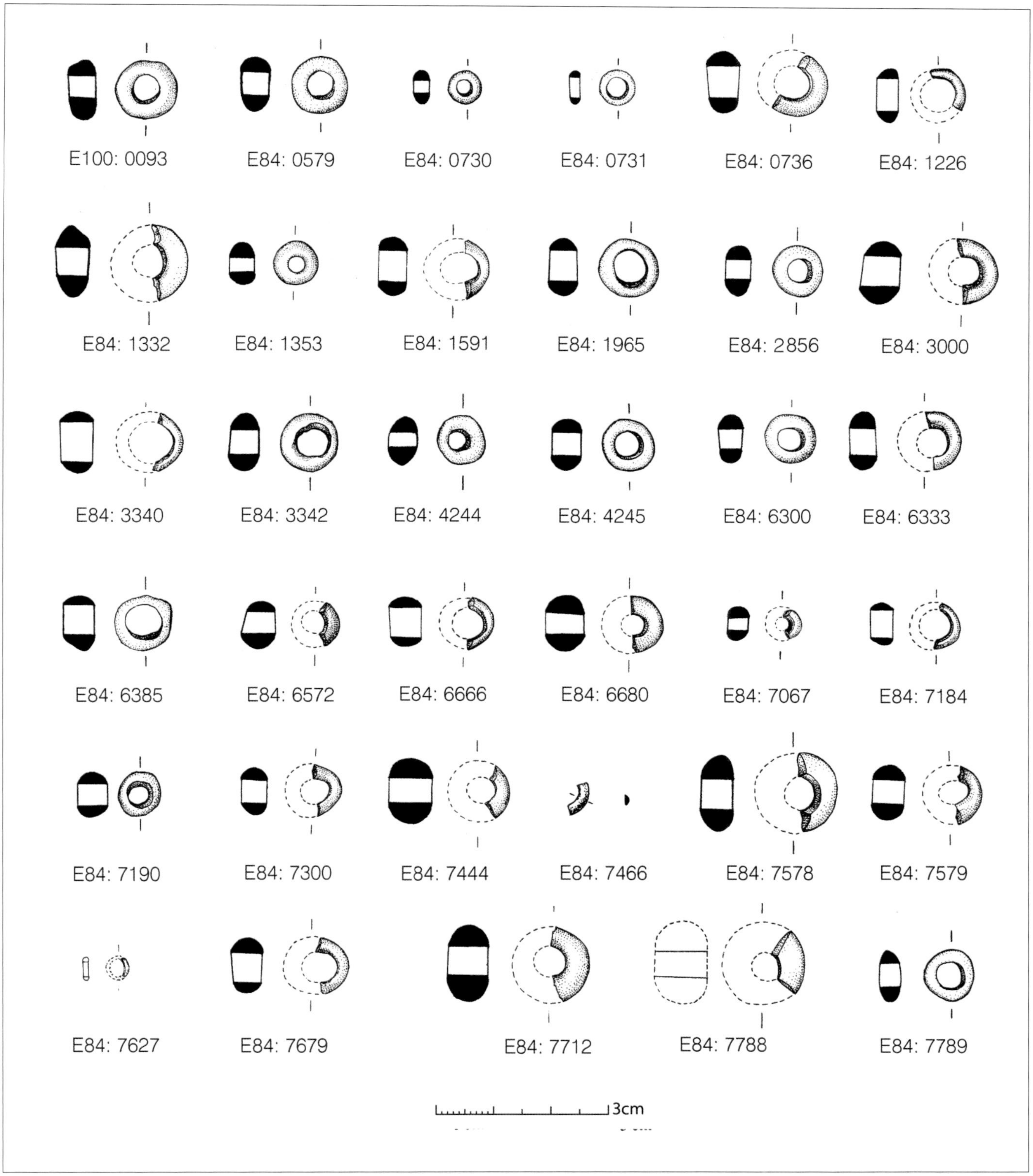

Fig. 3.14a—Undecorated glass beads (E100 and E84, numerical order 579–7789; scale 1:1).

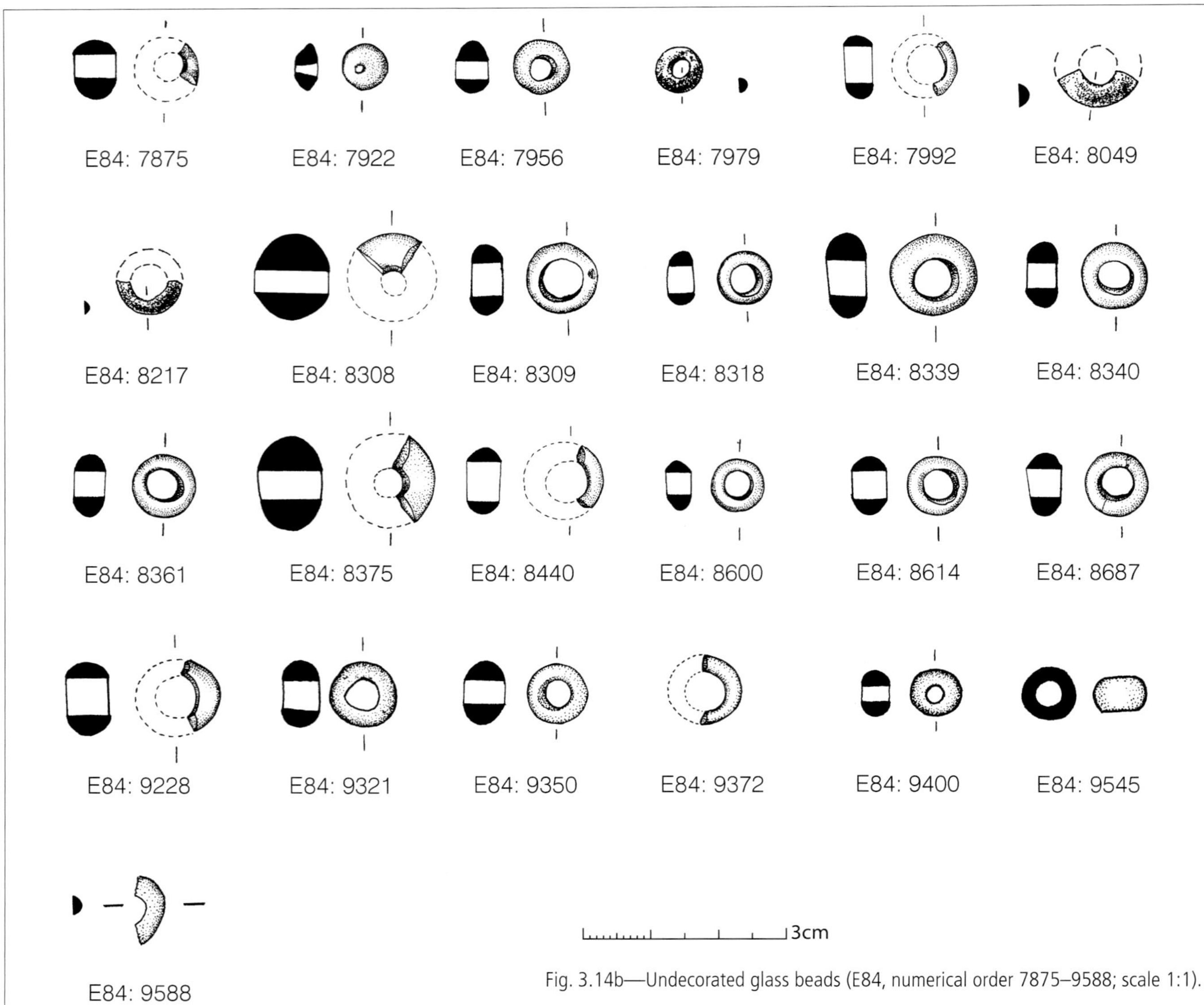

Fig. 3.14b—Undecorated glass beads (E84, numerical order 7875–9588; scale 1:1).

the cashel wall in F/F1 (E84:6538, Fig. 3.13, 7712, Fig. 3.14a, and 7875, Fig. 3.13), a further three from the black deposits within its fill in this area in Sq. 7 (E84:1353, 1226, 1332; Fig. 3.14a) and further examples from disturbed layers just inside the eastern edge of Ring-ditch 1. Finally, of note was a concentration of four beads in Y2 (E84:8600, 8614, 8687 (Fig. 3.14b), 8716) in the zone of black occupation and brown material. Where the black was sealed by the yellow bank in the adjoining Y1, two further beads came to light (E84:8733 (not illustrated), 8735; Figs 3.13 and 3.23).

Within Ring-ditch 2 (Sqs I2, I4, J3) eight dispersed examples occurred (E84:8308, 8309, 8318, 8339, 8340, 8361, 8375 (Fig. 3.14b), 8675 (Figs 3.13 and 3.24)). None of these came from any meaningful context, with the exception of E84:8675, which came from the upper ditch fill or silting.[6] Outside this zone isolated beads occurred, including two from among the potsherds and mould fragments in D4 (E84:7067, 7444; Fig. 3.14a) and one each in B5 (E84:9228; Fig. 3.14b) and D7 (E84:7362a; not illustrated).

Bead E84:3000 (Fig. 3.14a) was associated with a coarse potsherd and a water-rolled pebble from the fill of Pit 110 in Sq. 36. A single bead (E84:9372; Fig. 3.14b) was found in the upper fill of Pit 3 in K7, and one example (E84:9183; not illustrated) also came from the fill of Pit 215 in I6, along with a mini-crucible (E84:9000; Fig. 3.43) and a coarse potsherd (E84:9149).

On the southern slopes outside the hillfort only a single

glass bead was recovered (E100:93; Fig. 3.14a). This was found in Z5:h in disturbed brown soil, under a stone, at a depth of 25–30cm, almost on the yellow subsoil. It was of the same type as those found on the hilltop.

It is strikingly obvious that the bead distribution is focused on the area of intense industrial activity on the east. The three beads from the ditch fill in the east, in Sq. 7, came from the upper black fill, which is thought to derive from Area 2 activity (E84:1226, 1332, 1353; Fig. 3.14a). A further but smaller number of beads came from other parts of Ring-ditch 1.

Context and significance

Rathgall has produced one of the largest concentrations of true glass beads from an individual site in Bronze Age Europe. Its 88 beads are, however, surpassed by the large number of beads (180) from Hauterive-Champréveyres, Switzerland, and by the largest concentration (2,651 beads) from Frattesina, Italy (Angelini *et al.* 2009, 330). In fact, the number of beads found at Rathgall could easily represent a single necklace. Nevertheless, they demonstrate how Rathgall was tied into international trade networks. In typological terms, a wide range of forms has been documented on Late Bronze Age sites, ranging from plain annular rings, *Pfahlbautönnchen*, to eye beads with concentric ring decoration, at times applied to the corners of triangular/subtriangular beads, such as also found at Rathgall (cf. Dobiat 1987; Haevernick 1978; Bellintani and Stefan 2009).

While glass beads have been found in Europe from the Early Bronze Age onwards, examination of the earliest glass beads in Egypt, Iran, Mesopotamia and other regions of the Near East has established that in these areas the standard glass composition in the Middle and Late Bronze Age was high magnesium (HMG; Henderson 1988a, 440; Varberg *et al.* 2016). Glass beads became increasingly more common across Europe from the end of the second millennium BC onwards; the examined European glass objects show the same composition and were either imports or locally worked from imported HMG glass. It is noteworthy, however, that beads of glass are relatively rare in the Urnfield cemeteries; when they occur, with a few notable exceptions, the great majority of graves contain only a small number of beads, very often no more than a single example. Indeed, Neuburg (1949, 50) points to an early Palestinian rabbinical text which indicates that beads were—literally—worth their weight in gold. The late second millennium BC saw the emergence of locally produced glass alongside beads made of imported HMG glass before becoming the material for the production of beads from the twelfth–tenth centuries BC. This mixed-alkali glass with low magnesium and high potassium oxide levels—LMHK glass (Henderson 1988a, 439–40; 1988b)—has been identified on about 30 sites across Europe (cf. Venclová *et al.* 2011 for a recent list of sites). Regional studies of glass, for example in Bohemia (Venclová *et al.* 2011), northern Italy (Towle 2002; Angelini *et al.* 2004; 2005; 2009; Henderson *et al.* 2015), Switzerland (e.g. Henderson 1993), Middle Europe (Mildner *et al.* 2014) and France (e.g. Cherel and Gratuze 2018), have started to reveal the complexities of both the typological and the compositional profiles and their role in provenancing. Traditionally, Frattesina on the River Po, in particular, has been seen as a production centre for this first true European glass. Frattesina was securely dated to between 1200 and 1000 BC (Bietti Sestieri *et al.* 2015), while Hauterive-Champréveyres, which also produced a significant number of glass beads (Henderson 1993), yielded oaks that provided a narrow *terminus ante quem* of between 1060 and 1049 BC. While Rathgall has been cited as an example of LMHK glass in the latest Bronze Age in many publications, the revised dating of the Bronze Age phase of the site to between 1200 and 1000 BC in fact puts it in the same broad horizon as these other sites (Chapter 4, section 4.4).

Beads E84:660, 3670, 7580 and 8735 from Rathgall were analysed by X-ray fluorescence (Raftery and Henderson 1987; Henderson 1987, table 1; 1988a) and shown to consist of LMHK glass. Seven beads were included in a later analysis with electron probe micro-analysis (Henderson 1988b). These are not presented with find numbers and it is thus impossible to correlate analytical results with beads. All were found to consist of LMHK glass, apart from one decorated example (E84: unknown) which has inlaid circles of LMG (low-magnesium soda-lime glass) glass (*ibid.*, 81, sample 7). This natron glass becomes the main type of glass in use from about 800 BC onwards (Henderson 2013, 92–3; Hartmann *et al.* 1997), but recently early occurrences of LMG glasses have been considered the result of experimental raw material combinations (Mildner *et al.* 2014, 102).

Besides the beads from Rathgall, a group of beads from Lough Gur (Grogan and Eogan 1987, 364, 365, fig. 22, 385; Henderson 1987) and from Freestone Hill (Raftery 1969; Henderson 1988a, 442) could also be shown to be of LMHK glass. Circle K (site E252) at Lough Gur yielded no fewer than 33 specimens of translucent blue-green glass, including five with inlaid circle motifs comparable to those

Table 3.3—Glass beads recovered at Rathgall (square and context).

Sq. no.	Context description	Find no.
3	In brown soil	E84:1569
7	South; in dark brown immediately under sod	E84:660
	South-west; in darkish brown	E84:730
	In black upper fill of Ring-ditch 1	E84:1226, 1332, 1353
8	South-east; in darkish brown	E84:731
	In dark brown near middle of square, between and associated with Hearths 4–6	E84:779
	In dark brown, just beside black, heavily burnt area of Hearth 6	E84:838
9	Middle; second layer under sod	E84:1518
10	In brown spongy layer under section strip	E84:4245
11	First layer under sod	E84:2511
16	On yellow	E84:579
19	In dark brown soil, almost on yellow, centre	E84:2856
	In brown soil	E84:3340
30	In brown soil	E84:3342
35	In dark brown soil	E84:1591
36	In brown area in north-east (Pit 110)	E84:3000
39/30	At junction of 39 and 30; in dark brown fill amongst stones projecting from underneath wall	E84:3670
63/64	In material overlying ditch or may have been washed out of section strip by rain	E84:5795
A3	North of 'bank', just beyond its edge	E84:862
B/C	Among cobbles, in black, in section strip under wall	E84:8217
B/F	In brown in section strip	E84:8077
B1	North-west corner of square; in circular black area immediately east of cobbling and immediately south of stone ring; the burnt area under mottled black level in grey	E84:1965
	Under wall in lowest layers of black	E84:8049
	In black under wall	E84:8052
B5	In brown fill of Depression 200	E84:9228
C1	In black occupation material almost on grey floor	E84:4244
	In south-west of square, in black	E84:7956
C1/D1	On grey floor with charcoal flecks in section strip	E84:8079
D	In dark brown, with black patches among amorphous ferrous lumps	E84:6300, 6333
	In black material going under wall	E84:7578, 7579, 7580
D/D1	In thick black charcoal area	E84:6700
	In black material	E84:7466
	In brown ashy material under black	E84:7627
D1	In black charcoal area, lumpy occupation material having been removed	E84:6562
	In greyish-brown material immediately north of black charcoal habitation area	E84:7000
	In brown, under black charcoal habitation area	E84:7184
	On edge of black in north of square	E84:7190
	In brown smudgy area under bank	E84:7300
D2	In dark brown near large stone in west of square	E84:6666
	In dark brown	E84:6680
	In west of square, in dark brown-filled depression	E84:7788
D4	In brown	E84:7067
	South-east of square in greyish-yellow	E84:7444
D7/D8	In brown	E84:7362a
D8	In south-east corner of square, grey area	E84:7467
E1	In black; section strip	E84:7679, 8215, 8216
F	In grey against south section	E84:7875
F1	In dark brown area under wall	E84:6538
	Curved black area among charcoal and thick black material	E84:7712
F2	In brown	E84:6385
F2/G2	In section strip	E84:7979, 7992
F5	In brown humus	E84:9240
G2	In brown	E84:6572
G3	In brown humus, almost on grey, at east end of square	E84:8440
G5	In brown at north end of square	E84:9144
G7	In brown	E84:9350

Table 3.3 (cont.)—Glass beads recovered at Rathgall (square and context).

Sq. no.	Context description	Find no.
H	In brown immediately under cobbling under wall	E84:7789
	In brown	E84:7842, 7843, 7921, 7922
I2	In brown, almost on yellow, in centre of square	E84:8308, 8309
	In grey area on yellow: section strip between I2 and H2	E84:8318
	In shallow brown depression near south section strip, at edge of area of stake-holes	E84:8375
I4	In grey upper fill of ditch, 15–20cm down, under stone; certainly in ditch silting; eastern edge of ditch	E84:8675
I6	Pit 215; black area immediately east of large boulder in south-east corner of square	E84:9183
J3	In brown humus	E84:8339, 8340, 8361
K6	In north-west corner of square, in black/grey area; outer edge of Ring-ditch 2	E84:9545
K7	In north-west corner, in grey-brown	E84:9315
	In upper black fill of Pit 3, in south-west corner of square	E84:9372
Z5:d	In brown soil under stone, almost on yellow	E100:93
X11	In centre of square, mixed with charcoal, bones, redeposited soil	E84:9321
X5	Light brownish material	E84:9400
	In black layer in northern central part of square	E84:9588
Y1	In south-east of square close to wall, in grey sticky material, 62cm below upper surface of yellow	E84:8733
	In north-west corner, in basal grey material, under yellow bank and black occupation layer	E84:8735
Y2	In brown humus	E84:8600
	In black burnt area at western edge of (originally 2.5m) cutting	E84:8614, 8687
	In north-east corner of square, almost at base of black layer	E84:8716
Unknown	Unknown	E84:736

from Rathgall, that were unfortunately without archaeological context, most having been found in the sod (topsoil) or at a high level in the north-eastern quadrant (Grogan and Eogan 1987, 364). While earlier Neolithic pottery was also found on the site, the association of the glass with bronze artefacts and mould fragments and pottery of Late Bronze Age forms seems likely (Cleary 2018, 167). The five analysed specimens from Circle K could be shown to be of LMHK composition (Henderson 1987). Circle J (site E251) produced two beads from disturbed contexts that are likely to be of Late Bronze Age date. An enclosure at Knockadoon Hill, Lough Gur (site E549) (Cleary *et al.* 2003, 133–4), also produced two beads that are very likely of Late Bronze Age date, based on their shape and colour and their association in F2, a context dated to the Late Bronze Age. Site C (Ó Ríordáin 1954) also produced nine glass beads of greenish-blue glass. Of these, eight were found in the gravel layer and one beneath with both Beaker and Class II, i.e. Late Bronze Age, pottery (*ibid.*, 355, fig. 26), as well as bronze artefacts, including a socketed axehead and more. The presence of this material in a site that appears to have been primarily of Neolithic and Beaker date is attributed to later pit-digging (Cleary 2018, 178).

The clustering of the bead finds throughout the Lough Gur landscape is striking, and a possible—if unlikely—context for this might be the bronze- and gold-working that was taking place on some sites, such as settlement enclosure 'Circle K' (but see below).

A small bead from a later Bronze Age burial mound at Dunbeg, Co. Down, may be Bronze Age in date (Mogey *et al.* 1956; Henderson 1989b, 24), as may one from Mullaghmore that was described by Mogey (1949) as a 'small blue' bead. The Freestone Hill beads, though not securely stratified, can be seen, in the light of recent research (Raftery 1995, 150–1), as belonging to a later Bronze Age horizon which is represented, above all else, by Late Bronze Age coarseware pottery. One bead from Dún Aonghasa on the Aran Islands appears to have a comparable compositional profile but has not been examined with suitable analytical methods (FitzGerald and Warner 2012, 101). For a long time the single bead from All Cannings Cross, Wiltshire (Henderson 1988a, 442–3), was the only evidence for LMHK glass from Britain. Recent identifications and finds have added a group of beads from a burial at Stotfold, Bedfordshire (Paynter 2014), and a single bead each from the Sculptor's Cave, Covesea (Hunter and Davis 2020), and from Thwing, East Yorkshire (Terry Manby, pers. comm.). However, the substantial number of LMHK glass beads from at least three sites in Ireland may suggest a direct link between Ireland and parts of the Continent that have produced examples of this glass, namely France, Belgium, Germany, Switzerland and Italy.

The blue to turquoise colouring of the Rathgall beads,

characteristic of the bulk of the early European glass, comes from copper, likely derived from bronze scrap (cf. Henderson 2013, 188; 1988a, 438) or copper oxide (e.g. Hartmann *et al.* 1997), and the ratio of copper to tin has been shown to be comparable (Cherel and Gratuze 2018, 351). While red glass, as also found on one of the Rathgall beads (E84:3670; Figs 3.13 and 3.21), has been argued to be the result of the addition of reduced copper, possibly achieved by the reheating of blue beads at low temperatures, recent analyses of a bead from Trémargat, France, with a red eye closely comparable to that from Ireland, demonstrated a high iron content and, indeed, haematite appears to have been used. The high iron values of the bead from Rathgall (8.6%) may suggest that this could be the case here also (Cherel and Gratuze 2018). Moreover, beads consisting of a clay core with a glass cover such as those found at Rathgall find parallels in France: three beads with a clay core from the Paris basin and the island of Ouessant (*ibid.,* p. 355).

Glass-working at Rathgall?

The earliest glass in Ireland appears to be of Late Bronze Age date, with Rathgall and the other sites that have produced LMHK glass beads thus representing an important new development. Given the scarcity of LMHK beads from Britain, it appears possible that the background for the appearance of this material lies on the European mainland. Hartmann *et al.* (1997, 555), in view of the mixed-alkali glass-making site at Frattesina, suggested that 'it might be possible that all mixed-alkali glasses from Ireland, Switzerland and central Germany were produced at this site'. Brill (1992, 21) went further, stating that 'there is little doubt in our minds that the Frattesina and Rathgall beads (although differing in appearance) represent a single glass-making technology. They were almost certainly made in factories that were connected by links that will some day emerge to define that specific technology … The technological link implies a cultural link of some sort.' Indeed, Frattesina has for a long time been seen as the only production site, supplying LMHK glass to a wide range of sites. The extent of glass analysis across Europe is far from comprehensive, however, and further analysis may modify this picture. Indeed, recent research has started to explore the possibility of glass-making at other sites in northern Italy and Switzerland (Angelini *et al.* 2009; Towle 2002, 229), primarily based on the different regional typologies represented in the spectrum of LMHK beads, even if glass from France is still seen as the result of trade with northern Italy (Cherel and Gratuze 2018). Henderson, for example, pointed to greater similarities in the ratio of calcium oxide and magnesia between Rathgall and Mariconda, Italy, than between Rathgall and Frattesina (Henderson 2013, 199), and a higher soda content than most samples within the range from Frattesina (*ibid.*, 193–4), while recent isotopic studies have indicated the existence of two distinct production centres within a small dataset studied from northern Italy (Henderson *et al.* 2015).

Green and turquoise-coloured annular ring-beads similar to those found at Rathgall and consisting of LMHK glass were found all over the distribution of LMHK beads, including at Frattesina (cf. Angelini *et al.* 2009, fig. 1b; Bellintani and Stefan 2009). Eye beads were also found at, for example, Frattesina and Hauterive, although with slightly different morphologies and decorative patterns than at Rathgall. Beads at Frattesina are of globular or round shape and with either three or four eyes, but with the eyes consisting invariably of one ring only. These (few) beads have stratified eyes, whereas the decoration of the glass beads at Rathgall is marvered (inlaid into the glass).

Another factor that should also be borne in mind is the interesting possibility of native Irish manufacture, perhaps using imported Italian glass. The early export of Egyptian raw glass has been demonstrated by the discoveries in the sunken fourteenth-century BC wreck near Ulu Burun in Turkey (Cunliffe 2001, 261), so that such a hypothesis is by no means implausible. In this context Henderson has pondered whether the cracking of the beads with clay core may have possibly been due to flaws in the production process, which would suggest their production locally (Henderson 1988a, 442). This is an appealing idea, particularly considering the apparent association with metalworking on the site—as also found at the only clearly evidenced glass production site north of the Alps, Frattesina, and at more tentative candidates such as Hauterive-Champréveyres and Aubervilliers, France (Melin *et al.* 2017; Melin 2016), or, indeed, Lough Gur. The fact, however, that similar clay-cored beads have been found in Brittany also opens up the possibility that such unusual beads were imported into Ireland. A small fragment of blue glass, E84:1639 (Fig. 3.26), that may be related to the production process has not been analysed.

If local production should, indeed, be invoked, it is perhaps best to envisage the importation of raw glass from which the beads were made. This would also find support in the fact that the composition of the beads from the site is very homogeneous (Henderson 1988b, 89). Nevertheless, in our current limited state of knowledge, the balance of probability suggests that it was the beads themselves which were brought to the country. A workshop origin in the Swiss–north Italian area is intriguing, but their route to Ireland, if such was the case, need not have been direct, and the route via France to the west (Cherel and Gratuze 2018) would seem plausible.

While it may be possible that some of the beads from Rathgall represent local experimentation, it cannot be doubted that both their raw material and their morphology can be clearly traced to the European mainland. Thus, more so than any other body of material from the site, they are of fundamental importance in an evaluation of Rathgall's cultural affinities. In particular, the rarity of LMHK glass in Britain, in contrast to the significant assemblages from three Irish sites, shines a particular light on this possibly direct connection.

3.4.2 Glass beads and miscellaneous glass catalogue

Barry Raftery, Katharina Becker and Joanne Gaffrey

Unless otherwise stated, the beads are of blue to turquoise glass.

Decorated beads

E84:660: Complete, subtriangular bead (Figs 3.13 (E) and 3.25). Convexity of one side slightly more pronounced than that of the other two. Roughly central cylindrical perforation, with somewhat irregular edges. Decoration consists of a pair of irregular concentric circles of pale turquoise glass marvered into each of the three corners.

Diam.: 8mm. T: 6.1mm. Diam. of perforation: 4.2mm.

Sq. 7, south, in dark brown material immediately under sod.

E84:838: Small fragment of eggshell-thin glass (Figs 3.13 (A) and 3.16). Original form unclear. Decoration consists of thin arc of pale turquoise glass running concentric with the one original, slightly curved, edge.

T: 6mm. Int. diam.: 1mm.

Sq. 8, in dark brown material, just beside black, heavily burnt area of Hearth 6.

E84:1518: Fragment, originally subtriangular in shape. Approximately one quarter remains (Fig. 3.13 (E)). Slightly tapering perforation. Asymmetrical cross-section. Decoration consists of the remains of three regularly concentric rings of pale turquoise glass.

T: 5.5mm. Int. diam.: 2.4mm.

Sq. 9, middle, second layer under sod.

E84:1569: Small fragment (Fig. 3.13 (A)), original shape unclear. Decoration consists of two irregular concentric ovals of pale turquoise glass.

T: 4.3mm. Int. diam.: 1mm.

Sq. 3, in brown soil.

E84:3670: More than three quarters survive, indicating an original subtriangular shape (Figs 3.13 (E) and 3.21). Roughly central, slightly tapering perforation. Cross-section more or less symmetrical. Decoration consists of two-colour 'eye' motifs on both surviving corners. Each 'eye' consists of an opaque reddish-brown spot of glass around which pale, opaque turquoise glass has been trailed onto the surface of the bead and marvered into position. In one case the ring covers a portion of the red glass. A tiny amount of pale turquoise glass survives on either side of the break, confirming that this missing corner was also decorated.

Diam.: 10.2mm. T: 6.7mm. Diam. of perforation: 6.3mm.

Sq. 39/30, at junction of 39 and 30, in dark brown fill amongst stones projecting from underneath wall.

E84:6562: Small fragment, original form unclear (Figs 3.13 (A), 3.16 and 3.17). Decoration consists of a thin arc of pale turquoise glass running concentric with the one original curved edge.

T: 8mm. Int. diam.: 0.9mm.

Sq. D1, in black charcoal zone, immediately below 'lumpy' occupation material.

E84:7000: Complete bead, roughly circular but surface unevenly faceted (Figs 3.13 (E) and 3.20). Thickness irregular. Cylindrical perforation more or less central. Subtriangular? Surface of glass at centre of one decorative ring tapers to sharp point. Decoration consists of three irregular rings of pale turquoise glass.

Diam.: 7.4mm. T: 6.3mm. Diam. of perforation: 4.3mm.

Sq. D1? In greyish-brown material immediately north of black charcoal habitation area.

E84:8052: Small fragment; less than a quarter remains (Fig. 3.13 (D)). It may originally have been barrel-shaped in cross-section. Decoration consists of two surviving segments of ornament, each consisting of a pair of concentric rings of pale turquoise glass. Substance resembling baked clay adheres to inner surface.

T: 6mm. Int. diam.: 2.2mm.

Sq. B1, in black under wall.

E84:8079: Fragment; original shape unclear (Fig. 3.13 (E)). Decoration consists of the remains of two concentric rings of pale turquoise glass and part of a second similar motif, which appears to have extended around one edge of the broken edge.

T: 5.9mm. Int. diam.: 2mm.

Sq. C1/D1, on grey floor with charcoal flecks in section strip.

E84:8215/6: Two separately numbered fragments of one bead; approximately three quarters surviving (Fig. 3.13 (E)). Decoration consists of a ring of pale turquoise glass defining edges of perforation. Roughly central cylindrical perforation.

Diam.: 9.2mm. T: 4.7mm. Diam. of perforation: 5.5mm.

Sq. E1, in black section strip.

E84:8675: Complete bead (Figs 3.13 (E) and 3.24). Circular, splaying slightly in thickness. Cylindrical perforation with irregular edges. Asymmetrical cross-section. Considerable variation in thickness of internal diameter. Decoration consists of three irregular ovals which are light grey in colour.

Diam.: 10.1mm. T: 6.1mm. Diam. of perforation: 5.9mm.

Sq. I4, in grey upper fill of ditch, 15–20cm down, under stone. Certainly in ditch silting, eastern edge of ditch.

E84:8735: Complete bead, subtriangular in shape (Figs 3.13 (E) and 3.23). Central cylindrical perforation. Decoration consists of a regular oval ring of pale turquoise glass marvered into the surface of each of the three corners.

Diam.: 9.5mm. T: 6.1mm. Diam. of perforation: 5mm.

Sq. Y1, in north-west corner, in basal grey material, under yellow bank and black occupation layer.

E84:9315: Complete bead (Fig. 3.13 (E)). Subtriangular with barrel-shaped cross-section. Central cylindrical perforation, one edge of which protrudes slightly. Decoration consists of three sets each of three concentric rings of pale turquoise glass marvered into each of the three sides. The outer circle of each set converges at the corners of the bead with that of the other two.

Diam.: 9.9mm. T: 9.7mm. Diam. of perforation: 4.3mm.

Sq. K7, in north-west corner, in grey-brown.

E84:7580: Bead. Could not be located in the archive but is depicted in Fig. 3.13 (E).

Sq. D, black layer continuing under the wall.

E84:8077: Blue glass bead fragment with pale blue concentric ring decoration. Not found but illustrated in Fig. 3.13 (E).

Sq. B/F, in brown material in section strip.

Miscellaneous

E84:1639: Portion of blue glass, roughly cylindrical in shape, with a subcircular cross-section and rough, uneven surface (Figs 3.13 (C) and 3.26). Both ends are at an angle to the long axis and parallel to one another.

Diam.: 6mm. L: 6.8mm.

Sq. 17, middle of square near large stone.

Undecorated beads

E100:93: Complete bead, circular (Fig. 3.14a). Cylindrical perforation, virtually central, with irregular edges. Small circular depression at one point on exterior surface.

Diam.: 10.6mm. T: 5mm. Diam. of perforation: 4.9mm.

Sq. Z5:h, in brown soil under stone, almost on yellow.

E84:579: Complete bead, circular (Figs 3.14a and 3.22). Undulates in thickness. Cylindrical perforation. Cross-section and internal diameter vary in width. Fault in glass at one point where small circular depression occurs.

Diam.: 10mm. T: 5.4mm. Diam. of perforation: 5mm.

Sq. 15, down to yellow.

E84:730: Complete bead, circular (Figs 3.14a and 3.28). Central cylindrical perforation with one irregular edge.

Diam.: 5.3mm. T: 3mm. Diam. of perforation: 2.5mm.

Sq. 7, south-west, in darkish brown material.

E84:731: Complete bead, circular (Figs 3.14a and 3.28). Central cylindrical perforation with one damaged and one slightly stretched edge.

Diam.: 6mm. T: 2.1mm. Diam. of perforation: 3.5mm.

Sq. 8, south-east, in darkish brown material.

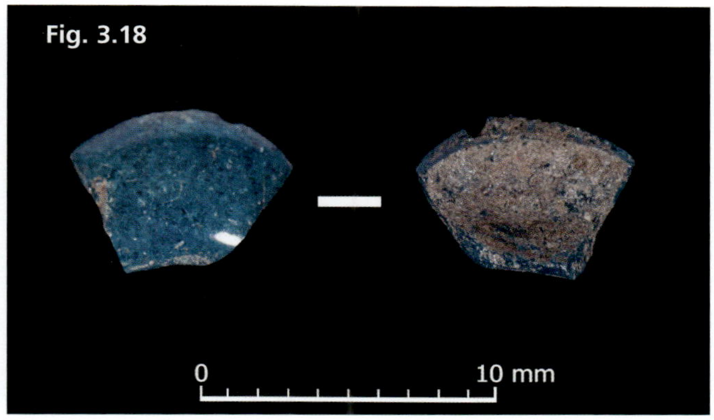

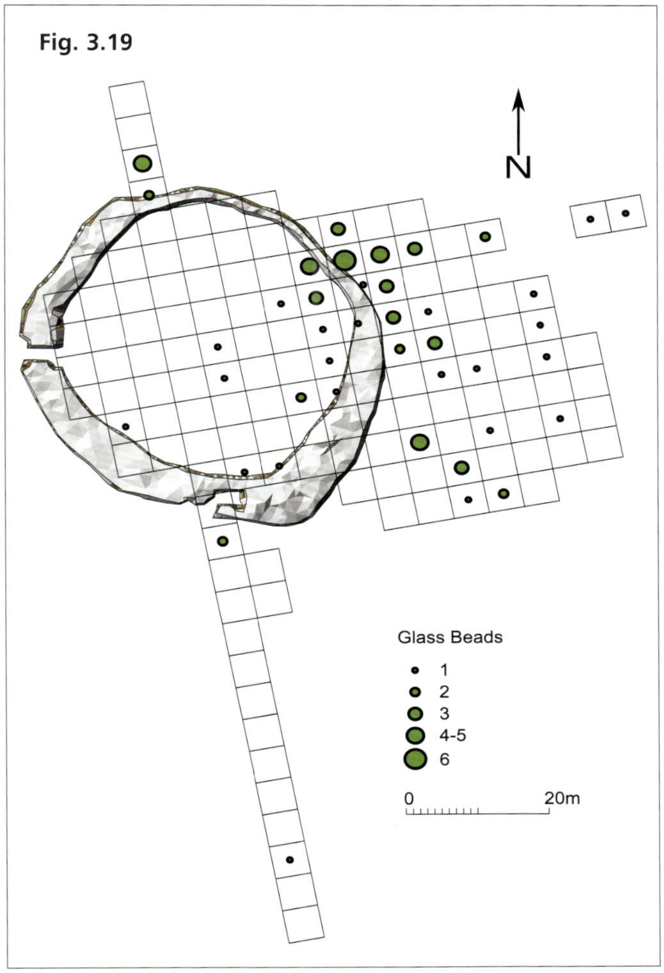

Fig. 3.15—Large bead with clay core E84:779 (photo: John Sunderland).

Fig. 3.16—Glass shell fragments E84:838, 1569, 6538 and 6562 (photo: John Sunderland).

Fig. 3.17—Glass shell fragment E84:6562 (photo: John Sunderland).

Fig. 3.18—Glass shell fragment E84:6538 (photo: John Sunderland).

Fig. 3.19—Distribution map of glass beads.

E84:779: Fragment, originally circular; less than half remains (Fig. 3.13 (D)). Consists of thin layer of glass around clay core. Undulates in thickness owing to protrusion of glass from both edges of perforation. Virtually central cylindrical perforation with one particularly damaged edge.

T: 13.9mm. Int. diam.: 7mm.

Sq. 8, in dark brown material near middle of square, between and associated with Hearths 4–6.

E84:1226: Fragment, originally circular (Fig. 3.14a). Tapers considerably in thickness from one broken end to the other. Cylindrical perforation with irregular edges. Internal diameter somewhat irregular.

T: 4mm. Int. diam.: 1.9mm.

Sq. 7, north of square, in black upper fill of ditch.

E84:1332: Fragment; less than half remains (Fig. 3.14a). Tapers very slightly in thickness. Curve of external surface tapers sharply at one point, forming a short, rounded ridge. Roughly central cylindrical perforation.

T: 6.2mm. Int. diam.: 4mm.

Sq. 7, south-east of square, in black upper fill of ditch.

E84:1353: Complete bead, circular, with central cylindrical perforation (Fig. 3.14a).

Diam.: 7.5mm. T: 4.5mm. Diam. of perforation: 3mm.

Sq. 7, north of square, in upper black fill of ditch.

E84:1591: Approximately half remains (Fig. 3.14a). Originally circular. Thickness curves slightly to one broken end. Almost central cylindrical perforation. Slight variety in internal dimension.

T: 4.8mm. Int. diam.: 2.6mm.

Sq. 35, in dark brown soil.

E84:1965: Complete bead, dark blue, with cylindrical perforation and asymmetrical cross-section (Figs 3.14a and 3.22).

Diam.: 10.4mm. T: 5.1mm. Diam. of perforation: 6.2mm.

Sq. B1, north-west corner, in circular black area immediately east of cobbling and immediately south of stone ring; the burnt area under mottled black level in grey.

E84:2856: Complete subcircular bead; opaque (Fig. 3.14a). Cylindrical perforation with irregular, damaged edges. Asymmetrical cross-section.

Diam.: 9mm. T: 4.9mm. Diam. of perforation: 4mm.

Sq. 19, in dark brown soil, almost on yellow, centre.

E84:3000: Half survives (Fig. 3.14a). Tapers in thickness from one broken end to the other. Virtually central cylindrical perforation with very slight variation in internal dimension.

Diam.: 11.1mm. T: 6.8mm. Diam. of perforation: 5.8mm.

Sq. 36, in brown area in north-east (Pit 110).

E84:3340: Less than half survives (Fig. 3.14a). Originally circular in shape. Thickness tapers slightly from one broken end to the other. Roughly central cylindrical perforation, of which one edge is slightly damaged.

T: 5.9mm. Int. diam.: 2mm.

Sq. 19, in brown soil.

E84:3342: Complete bead (Fig. 3.14a). Thickness varies slightly. Asymmetrical cross-section; slight variation in internal diameter. Cylindrical perforation with one particularly irregular edge. Small area of discolouration on external surface.

Diam.: 10.3mm. T: 5.5mm. Diam. of perforation: 5.7mm.

Sq. 30, in brown soil.

E84:4244: Complete bead, circular, varying somewhat in thickness (Fig. 3.14a). Cylindrical perforation with irregular, stretched and damaged edges. Asymmetrical cross-section. Variation in internal diameter.

Diam.: 8.7mm. T: 5.8mm. Diam. of perforation: 3.2mm.

Sq. C1, in black occupation material almost on grey floor.

E84:4245: Complete bead, circular, with cylindrical perforation and asymmetrical cross-section (Figs 3.14a and 3.22). Thickness of internal diameter varies.

Diam.: 9.7mm. T: 5.6mm. Diam. of perforation: 4.4mm.

Sq. 10, brown spongy layer under section strip.

E84:5795: Fragment, approximately a quarter of a bead. Tapers slightly in thickness towards one broken end.

T: 4mm. Int. diam.: 1.9mm.

Sq. 63/64, in material overlying ditch, or may have been washed out of section strip by rain.

E84:6300: Complete bead, circular, tapering in thickness from one side to the other (Figs 3.14a and 3.22). Off-centre cylindrical perforation with damaged edges.

Diam.: 8.9mm. T: 4.9mm. Diam. of perforation: 4.3mm.

Sq. D, in dark brown material with black patches, among amorphous ferrous lumps.

E84:6333: Incomplete bead, approximately half remains (Fig. 3.14a). Cylindrical perforation. Asymmetrical cross-section. Internal diameter wider at one broken end than at the other.

Diam.: 10mm. T: 4.6mm. Diam. of perforation: 5mm.

Sq. D, in dark brown material, among black patches and amorphous ferrous material.

E84:6385: Complete bead (Fig. 3.14a). Not quite circular, as edge tapers gently in one place to rounded point, thus slightly distorting the circular shape. Central cylindrical perforation.

Diam.: 10.5mm. T: 5.9mm. Diam. of perforation: 6.2mm.

Sq. F2, in brown material.

E84:6538: Small portion of bead, original form unclear (Fig. 3.13 (A)). Glossy surface.

T: 5.7mm. Int. diam.: 1mm.

Sq. F1, in dark brown area under wall.

E84:6572: Small fragment of bead; approximately a quarter remains (Fig. 3.14a). Tapers slightly in thickness and in the width of the perforation.

T: 5.4mm. Int. diam.: 2.4mm.

Sq. G2, in brown material.

E84:6666: Fragment of bead, tapering in thickness from one broken end to the other (Fig. 3.14a). Cylindrical perforation. Asymmetrical cross-section. Slight variation in internal diameter.

Diam.: 8.5mm. T: 5.8mm. Diam. of perforation: 5mm.

Sq. D2, in dark brown material near large stone in west of square.

E84:6680: Fragment of bead; slightly more than half remains (Fig. 3.14a). Originally circular. Perforation more or less central.

Diam.: 9.9mm. T: 6.8mm. Diam. of perforation: 3.4mm.

Sq. D2, in dark brown material.

E84:7067: Fragment of bead; less than half remains (Fig. 3.14a). Purple. Original perforation more or less central. Notably regular internal diameter. Slight protrusion from one edge of perforation.

T: 4.3mm. Int. diam.: 2.2mm. Diam. of perforation: 2mm.

Sq. D4, in brown material.

E84:7184: Fragment of bead; less than half remains (Fig. 3.14a). Virtually central cylindrical perforation. Slight variation in internal diameter.

T: 4.9mm. Int. diam.: 1.2mm.

Sq. D1, in brown material under black charcoal habitation area.

E84:7190: Complete bead, circular in shape, with slight variation in thickness (Fig. 3.14a). Central cylindrical perforation with one damaged end.

Diam.: 7.6mm. T: 5.9mm. Diam. of perforation: 3.9mm.

Sq. D1, on edge of black material in north of square.

E84:7300: Fragment of bead (Fig. 3.14a). Original shape may have been subcircular but is not clear. Cylindrical perforation. Symmetrical cross-section, though internal diameter thicker in centre.

T: 4.2mm. Int. diam.: 2.2mm. Diam. of perforation: 4.3mm.

Sq. D1, in brown smudgy area under bank.

E84:7362: Fragment of bead, somewhat more than half remaining. Cylindrical perforation. Asymmetrical cross-section; internal diameter thicker at one broken end than the other. Otherwise regular.

Diam.: 11.2mm. T: 5.4mm. Diam. of perforation: 5.9mm.

Sq. D7/D8, in brown material.

E84:7444: Fragment of bead, less than half remaining (Fig. 3.14a). Almost barrel-shaped cross-section. Cylindrical perforation; internal diameter thicker at one broken end than the other.

T: 7.9mm. Int. diam.: 3.1mm.

Sq. D4, south-east, in greyish-yellow material.

E84:7466: Small portion of bead, less than a quarter remaining (Fig. 3.14a). Tapers slightly in thickness. Cylindrical perforation. Asymmetrical cross-section.

T: 4.1mm. Int. diam.: 2mm.

Sq. D/D1, in black material.

E84:7467: Fragment of bead, less than half remaining (Fig. 3.13 (D)). Originally barrel-shaped in section. Consists of clay core covered by very thin 'skin' of glass which is missing in places, exposing the clay core. Almost central perforation which appears to taper slightly.

T: 13.8mm. Int. diam.: 7.3mm.

Sq. D8, in south-east corner, grey area.

E84:7578: Fragment of bead, slightly less than half remaining (Fig. 3.14a). Cylindrical perforation. Asymmetrical cross-section. Internal diameter wider at one end than the other.

Diam.: 13.5mm. T: 6mm. Diam. of perforation: 6.3mm.

Sq. D, in black material going under wall.

E84:7579: Fragment of bead, less than half remaining (Fig. 3.14a). One side of the otherwise cylindrical perforation tapers slightly. Asymmetrical cross-section. Internal diameter varies.

T: 5.5mm. Int. diam.: 3mm.

Sq. D, in black material going under wall.

E84:7627: Tiny fragment of bead, originally circular (Fig. 3.14a). Sharp protrusion in centre of one face. Apparently central cylindrical perforation. No obvious variation in internal diameter.

T: 1.3mm. Int. diam.: 0.8mm.

Sq. D/D1, in brown ashy material under black.

E84:7679: Fragment of bead, half remaining (Fig. 3.14a). Tapers in thickness from one broken end to the other. Cylindrical perforation. Asymmetrical cross-section. Internal diameter varies.

Diam.: 9mm. T: 5.6mm. Diam. of perforation: 5.2mm.

Sq. E1, in black material in section strip.

E84:7712: Fragment of bead, originally circular, with less than half remaining (Fig. 3.14a). Slightly tapering perforation with one damaged and one very regular edge. Asymmetrical cross-section. Internal diameter varies. Surface glossy.

T: 6.8mm. Int. diam.: 4.4mm.

Sq. F1, in curved black area among charcoal and thick black material.

E84:7788: Fragment of bead, approximately a quarter remaining (Fig. 3.14a). Barrel-shaped section. Complete perforation probably central. Slight variation in surviving internal diameter.

T: 9.7mm. Int. diam.: 4.5mm.

Sq. D2, in west of square, in dark brown filling of depression.

E84:7789: Complete bead, subtriangular in shape (Figs 3.14b and 3.22). Thickness varies. Central cylindrical perforation with extremely regular edges.

Diam.: 8.7mm. T: 3.7mm. Diam. of perforation: 5mm.

Sq. H, in brown material immediately under cobbling under wall.

E84:7875: Portion of bead, less than a quarter remaining (Fig. 3.14b). Probably circular originally. Conical perforation.

T: 7mm. Int. diam.: 3.1mm.

Sq. F, in grey material against southern section.

E84:7922: Complete bead (Figs 3.14b and 3.28). Circular, with one face almost flat, the other conical. Conical perforation, wider on flat side. Asymmetrical cross-section. Dark blue in colour.

Diam.: 6.6mm. T: 3.5mm. Diam. of perforation: 1.9mm.

Sq. H, in brown material.

E84:7979: Complete bead (Figs 3.14b and 3.28). Circular shape with slightly pronounced convexity at one point. This is particularly evident on one face where a slight protrusion has been produced either by paring or breaking, resulting in varied thickness. Cylindrical perforation with irregular, damaged edges. Asymmetrical cross-section.

Diam.: 7.5mm. T: 4.5mm. Diam. of perforation: 3.9mm.

Sq. F2/G2, in section strip.

E84:7992: Portion of bead, originally circular, less than half remaining (Fig. 3.14b). Virtually central cylindrical perforation. Internal diameter even and regular.

T: 4.1mm. Int. diam.: 1.9mm.

Sq. F2/G2, in section strip.

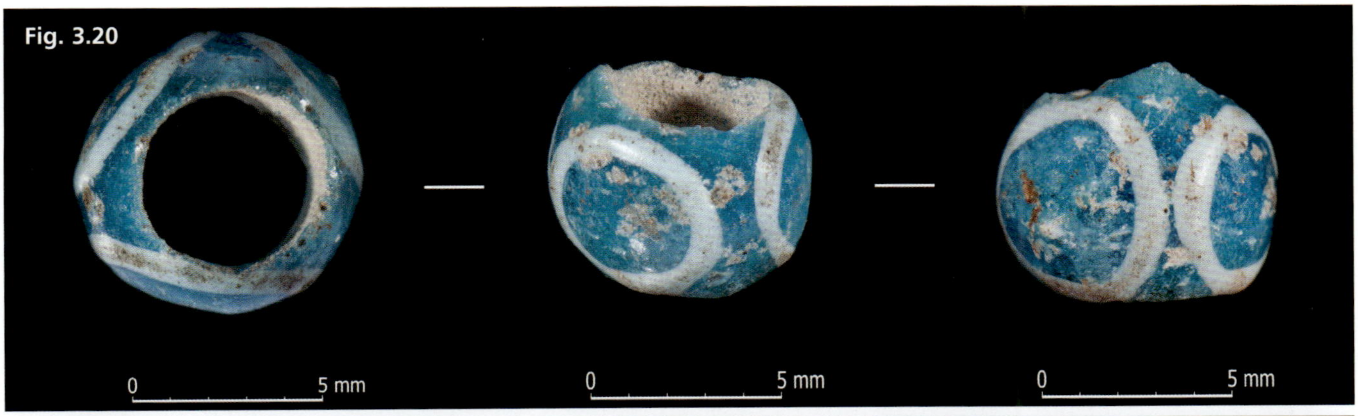

Fig. 3.20—Glass bead E84:7000 (photo: John Sunderland).

Fig. 3.21—Glass bead E84:3670 (photo: John Sunderland).

Fig. 3.22—Glass beads: top row (L–R): E84:8339, 4245, 579, 7789; bottom row (L–R): E84:6300, 1965, 8309 (photo: John Sunderland).

Fig. 3.23—Glass bead E84:8735 (photo: John Sunderland).

E84:8049: Fragment of bead, originally circular, less than half remaining (Fig. 3.14b). Almost barrel-shaped in cross-section. Virtually central cylindrical perforation. Small circular depression at one point on external surface.

T: 7.9mm. Int. diam.: 3.5mm.

Sq. B1, under wall in lowest layers of black material.

E84:8217: Fragment of bead, originally circular; half survives (Fig. 3.14b). Roughly central cylindrical perforation. Surface glossy.

Diam.: 10mm. T: 5mm. Diam. of perforation: 6mm.

Sq. B/C, among cobbles in black material in section strip under wall.

E84:8308: Fragment of bead, originally circular; less than a quarter survives (Fig. 3.14b). Barrel-shaped in section. Asymmetrical perforation, one wall of which curves slightly. Some variation in internal diameter.

T: 10.9mm. Int. diam.: 5.3mm.

Sq. I2, in brown material, almost on yellow layer, in centre of square.

E84:8309: Complete bead, circular in shape (Figs 3.14b and 3.22). Thickness varies. Small circular depression at one point on external surface. Cylindrical perforation with slightly damaged edges. Asymmetrical cross-section. Variation in internal diameter.

Diam.: 10.6mm. T: 5.8mm. Diam. of perforation: 6.3mm.

Sq. I2, in brown material, almost on yellow layer, in centre of square.

E84:8318: Complete bead, circular in shape (Fig. 3.14b). Thickness varies slightly. Roughly central cylindrical perforation with irregular edges, from one of which is a slight protrusion.

Diam.: 8.3mm. T: 4.1mm. Diam. of perforation: 4mm.

Sq. I2, in grey area on yellow layer in section strip between I2 and H2.

E84:8339: Complete bead, opaque in colour (Figs 3.14b and 3.22). Subcircular shape, slight irregularity along external edge. Roughly central cylindrical perforation with minor damage on one edge.

Diam.: 12.6mm. T: 6.4mm. Diam. of perforation: 6mm.

Sq. J3, in extreme north-east corner, in brown humus.

E84:8340: Complete bead, circular in shape (Fig. 3.14b). Roughly central cylindrical perforation with one slightly damaged edge.

Diam.: 10mm. T: 5mm. Diam. of perforation: 5mm.

Sq. J3, 18cm deep in brown humus near north-east corner of square.

E84:8361: Complete bead, circular, with slight variation in thickness (Fig. 3.14b). Roughly central cylindrical perforation, one edge of which is slightly stretched. Some damage on other edge.

Diam.: 9.2mm. T: 5mm. Diam. of perforation: 4.8mm.

Sq. J3, in south-east of square, in brown material, almost in yellow layer, 25cm deep.

E84:8375: Fragment of bead, opaque in colour and originally circular in shape, but less than half remains (Fig. 3.14b). Central cylindrical perforation. Slight depression surrounds one edge of perforation.

T: 10.3mm. Int. diam.: 5mm.

Sq. I2, in shallow brown depression near southern section strip, at edge of area of stake-holes.

E84:8440: Fragment of bead, originally circular, less than half surviving (Fig. 3.14b). Tapers very slightly in thickness towards one broken end. Cylindrical perforation, probably central.

T: 5.3mm. Int. diam.: 2.1mm.

Sq. G3, in brown humus, almost on grey layer, at eastern end of square.

E84:8600: Complete bead, circular in shape (Fig. 3.14b). Roughly central cylindrical perforation with slight protrusion from one edge.

Diam.: 7.8mm. T: 4mm. Diam. of perforation: 4.6mm.

Sq. Y2, in brown humus.

E84:8614: Complete bead, circular in shape, splaying slightly in thickness (Fig. 3.14b). Cylindrical perforation, one edge of which is slightly stretched. Asymmetrical cross-section. Internal diameter somewhat varied.

Diam.: 8.8mm. T: 6mm. Diam. of perforation: 4.8mm.

Sq. Y2, in black burnt area at western edge of (originally 2.5m) cutting.

E84:8687: Complete bead, circular in shape, splaying slightly in thickness (Fig. 3.14b). Cylindrical perforation

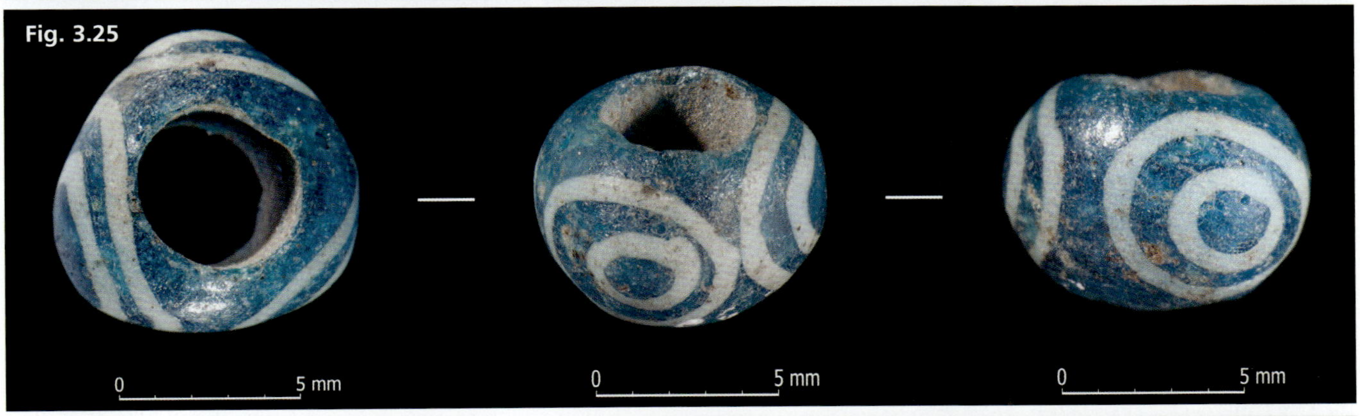

Fig. 3.24—Glass bead E84:8675 (photo: John Sunderland).

Fig. 3.25—Glass bead E84:660 (photo: John Sunderland).

Fig. 3.26—Glass fragment E84:1639 (photo: John Sunderland).

Fig. 3.27—Glass tubular bead fragments E84:2511, 7843 and 7842 (photo: John Sunderland).

Fig. 3.28—Glass beads E84:730, 731, 7922, 7979 (photo: John Sunderland).

Fig. 3.29—Glass tubular bead fragment E84:7842 (photo: John Sunderland).

with irregular edges. Asymmetrical cross-section. Internal diameter varies slightly.

Diam.: 9.6mm. T: 6.9mm. Diam. of perforation: 4.9mm.

Sq. Y2, in black burnt material at western edge of section strip. Two halves, 5cm apart.

E84:8716: Complete bead, circular in shape. Central cylindrical perforation, from one edge of which is a slight protrusion.

Diam.: 8.8mm. T: 6mm. Diam. of perforation: 4.3mm.

Sq. Y2, in north-east corner, almost at base of black layer.

E84:8733: Complete bead. Thickness splayed. Cylindrical perforation. Asymmetrical cross-section.

Diam.: 9.3mm. T: 5.5mm. Diam. of perforation: 4.8mm.

Sq. Y1, in south-east of square close to wall, in grey sticky material, 62cm below upper surface of yellow bank.

E84:9144: Complete bead, circular in shape, with cylindrical perforation and asymmetrical cross-section.

Diam.: 9.4mm. T: 4.9mm. Diam. of perforation: 5mm.

Sq. G6, at eastern end, in brown material.

E84:9183: Complete bead, circular in shape. Cylindrical perforation with irregular edges. Asymmetrical cross-section.

Diam.: 9mm. T: 5mm. Diam. of perforation: 5mm.

Sq. I6, Pit 215, in black area immediately east of large boulder in south-east corner of square.

E84:9228: Fragment of bead, originally circular (Fig. 3.14b); less than half remains. Cylindrical perforation. Asymmetrical cross-section. Variation in internal diameter.

T: 7mm. Int. diam.: 3.4mm.

Sq. B5, in brown fill of Depression 200.

E84:9240: Complete bead, circular in shape. Undulates in thickness. Cylindrical perforation with irregular edges, one of which is stretched out slightly. Asymmetrical cross-section. Internal diameter varies.

Diam.: 10.5mm. T: 6.4mm. Diam. of perforation: 6.1mm.

Sq. F5, in brown humus.

E84:9321: Complete bead, circular in shape (Fig. 3.14b); splays slightly in thickness. Stretched along one edge of perforation. Slightly tapering perforation with irregular edges. Asymmetrical cross-section.

Diam.: 10.2mm. T: 6mm. Diam. of perforation: 5.5mm.

Sq. X11, in centre of square, mixed with charcoal, bones and redeposited soil.

E84:9350: Complete bead, circular in shape (Fig. 3.14b). Central cylindrical perforation with irregular edges.

Diam.: 9mm. T: 6.2mm. Diam. of perforation: 4.1mm.

Sq. G7, in brown material.

E84:9372: Fragment of bead, half remaining (Fig. 3.14b). Cylindrical perforation with irregular edges. Asymmetrical cross-section. Internal diameter thicker at one broken end than at the other.

T: 5.2mm. Int. diam.: 2.3mm. Diam. of perforation: 6mm.

Sq. K7, in upper black fill of Pit 3, in south-west corner of square.

E84:9400: Complete bead, circular, with central cylindrical perforation (Fig. 3.14b). Notably regular in overall dimensions.

Diam.: 7.6mm. T: 4.8mm. Diam. of perforation: 2.7mm.

Sq. X5, in light brown material.

E84:9545: Complete bead, circular, undulating somewhat in thickness (Fig. 3.14b). Cylindrical perforation with one slightly stretched edge. Asymmetrical cross-section.

Diam.: 8.5mm. T: 5.7mm. Diam. of perforation: 5mm.

Sq. K6, in north-west corner of square, in black/grey area, outer edge of Ditch 2.

E84:9588: Fragment of bead, originally circular (Fig. 3.14b); less than half remains. Cylindrical perforation. Slightly asymmetrical cross-section. Internal dimension increases from one broken end to the other. Number of depressions along the exterior surface, as well as some discolouration.

T: 6.5mm. Int. diam.: 3.2mm.

Sq. X5, in black layer in northern central part of square.

Other beads

E84:736. Not located; no finds records. Illustrated in 3.14a, but may be misnumbered.

E84:2511: Complete turquoise glass bead (Figs 3.13 (C) and 3.27), cylindrical in shape. Both ends oblique to the long axis, one more acutely than the other. Central cylindrical perforation.

Diam.: 5mm. Diam. of perforation: 2.5mm. L: 18.4mm.

Sq. 11, first layer under sod.

E84:7842: Fragment (?) of green glass bead, cylindrical in shape (Fig. 3.29). Parallel striations along length as a result of glass production. Oval, off-centre perforation, 2.9mm in width and 2.1mm in depth. Deep groove at one end, parallel to broken end and 1.2mm distant from it.

Diam.: 7.4mm. Int. diam.: 2.4mm. L: 8.2mm.

Sq. H, in brown material.

E84:7843: Fragment (?) of blue glass bead, cylindrical in shape (Fig. 3.27). Subcircular, off-centre perforation.

Diam.: 5.2mm. Int. diam.: 1.9mm. Diam. of perforation: 2.2mm. L: 13mm.

Sq. H, in brown material.

E84:7921: Complete blue glass bead, circular in cross-section (Fig. 3.13 (C)). Both ends slightly oblique to the long axis. Central cylindrical perforation.

Diam.: 4.8mm. Diam. of perforation: 2mm. L: 21mm.

Sq. H, in brown material.

3.4.3 Early medieval glass bead

Margaret Mannion and Matthew Seaver

The polychrome glass bead (E84:0862; Fig. 3.13 (B)) found at Rathgall is of early medieval date. The red opaque core with yellow and white inlay can be paralleled in beads from cemeteries of the Merovingian period on the Lower Rhine such as Type 35.16 (Siegmund 1995, 46), with red beads common throughout the fifth to eighth centuries. A closer parallel comes from another examination of Alemannic–Frankish beads from a cemetery at Pleidelsheim in Baden-Württemberg, Koch Group 20: red body with decoration in either opaque yellow or white, simple trail or crossing waves, SD 6 (AD 555–580) and SD 7 (AD 580–600) phases (Koch 2001, 359–60). Opaque red beads with white and/or yellow crossed waves and sometimes dots are found in the Merovingian cemetery at Pandhof (Find 10128) in Maastricht and date from AD 530–680 (Kars 2011, 324, 344). Frankish beads of this type are also held by the Metropolitan Museum of Art—for example, the bead from Niederbreisig, Germany, 17.193.19 (https://www.metmuseum.org/).

Beads of this colour scheme can also be found in Anglo-Saxon contexts in England, such as the fifth- to seventh-century cemetery at Cliffs End, Kent (McKinley *et al.* 2015). Brugmann (2004) includes examples from Anglo-Saxon cemeteries in her synthesis of glass beads at Mill Hill (Grave 59) and Morning Thorpe (Grave 216).

SEM-EDS analysis of red glass opaque beads from Anglo-Saxon and Merovingian graves has shown that they were created using the by-products of iron- and copper-smelting (Peake and Freestone 2012). It is unclear whether the beads found in England were imported from north-western Europe or were produced in both areas.

Imported red beads are known from Irish excavated contexts, including a biconical example at Lagore which has a red body and a white wave decoration with blue collar (Mannion 2013, 65). The closest parallel to the Rathgall bead may be a red bead with an ordered pattern of yellow trails found at Garranes, Co. Cork (Ó Ríordaín 1942b, 116, fig. 14.270 and pl. 5). We can suggest on this basis that the Rathgall bead was imported from Anglo-Saxon England or Frankish areas of Europe and is likely to be sixth- to seventh-century in date.

E84:0862: Portion of red paste or enamel bead (Fig. 3.13 (B)). Originally circular in shape; only a quarter remains. Barrel-shaped in cross-section. Decoration consists of a band of lozenges of coloured paste, each one rendered half in yellow and half in white. White paste inlaid with tiny pieces of quartz. Yellow paste may also be inlaid with tiny pieces of yellow stone. The red paste of the bead appears to have been mixed with a black pigment, as black striations appear throughout. Apparently central irregularly tapered perforation. Some damage on exterior surface near one edge of perforation.

T: 12.4mm. Int. diam: 6.3mm. L: 12.9mm.

Sq. A3, north of 'bank', just beyond its edge.

3.5 SILVER INGOT

John Sheehan

A silver ingot (E84:5585; Fig. 3.30) was found in the fill of Ring-ditch 1 in Sq. 56. This may be described as a small, oblong ingot, of oval cross-section, with rounded ends. It features smooth hollow pitting on one surface. It is 2.04cm long, 0.86cm wide and 0.58cm thick. There is a nick on one edge. It weighs 5.61g. Standard Viking-age silver ingots normally take oblong, bar-shaped form, are usually trapezoidal or oval to D-shaped in section, and most often feature rounded terminals. They form a significant element of silver hoards throughout the Viking world, and functioned primarily as a simple means of storing bullion. They occur, either complete or in hack-silver form, in at least half of the 80 recorded hoards of ninth- or tenth-century date from Ireland that contain non-numismatic material (Sheehan 2014, 196). Sixteen of these finds are 'mixed hoards' also containing coins, and thus their deposition dates may be determined. All of these are of tenth-century date, though the large number of ingots and ingot-derived hack-silver in the Cuerdale, Lancashire, hoard, which was deposited *c.* AD 905–10 and originated in large part in Hiberno-Scandinavian Dublin (Graham-Campbell 1987, 332–6; Sheehan 2011, 95), as well as the dominance of ingots in the assemblage of Viking-age silver from the *longphort* at Woodstown, Co. Waterford (Sheehan 2014, 196–200), serve to illustrate that ingots must also have been in circulation in Ireland during the second half of the ninth century. In short, the overall evidence indicates that ingots were more common in later ninth-century Ireland than is indicated by the evidence of the coin-dated hoards alone, and that they formed a regular element of Ireland's tenth-century hoards.

Viking-age ingots were manufactured by casting, when molten silver was poured into moulds, and they vary greatly in size. The largest collection in Britain and Ireland is contained in the Cuerdale hoard, from which around 180 complete examples survive. These range in length from 0.5cm to 12cm, with the smaller examples, those below 2cm in length, usually classified as 'bean-shaped' ingots or 'droplets' (Kruse and Graham-Campbell 2011, 75). The distinction between the latter types and small standard ingots is somewhat arbitrary. Their production, however, was the result of less deliberate procedures than those utilised for standard cast ingots, as has been suggested by the results of ingot-casting experiments which demonstrated that such droplets/bean-shaped ingots are formed when insufficient silver is poured into a mould

Fig. 3.30—Silver ingot E84:5585.

(Kruse *et al.* 1988, 90–1). Almost 50 ingots of this type have been identified in the Cuerdale hoard and the type also occurs in three tenth-century mixed hoards in Ireland, indicating that this type of material was circulating in Ireland and the Irish Sea area throughout the later ninth and tenth centuries (Sheehan 2014, 206). In the Cuerdale find some of the larger examples may belong to the lower range of standard cast ingots (Kruse and Graham-Campbell 2011, 74). The Rathgall ingot, measuring just over 2cm in length, lies within the range of overlap between the types, though it is classified here as a small cast ingot.

The results of X-ray fluorescence (XRF) analysis demonstrate that the Rathgall ingot has a silver content of 93.46%, the remainder being mainly composed of gold (2.45%), lead (1.64%) and copper (0.8%). These results are in keeping with the findings of a series of XRF analyses that have been carried out on Viking-age silver objects of this type from Britain (Kruse and Tate 1995; Graham-Campbell 2011, *passim*), which indicate that the majority have a silver content of over 90%. All of the ingots in the Cuerdale hoard, for instance, have a silver content of more than 90%, and when this is combined with their gold and lead contents the majority are greater than 95% 'silver' (Graham-Campbell 2011, 82, 192, table 1). This is also the case with the Rathgall ingot. Its silver profile does not correspond directly with that of the Islamic coins which are a feature of some Viking-age hoards in the Irish Sea area. Most of these coins are composed of a distinctive alloy, with very high levels of silver (97–98%), relatively high bismuth (0.2–0.4%), an absence of zinc and very low gold (0–0.2%). The silver utilised for the production of the Rathgall ingot is quite different from this and corresponds with the profile found in the majority of Viking-age silver objects in the Irish Sea area, which was generally derived from a number of different sources, including Anglo-Saxon coinages, in admixtures of coins and hacked bullion (Kruse 1993, 191–3).

Diminutive ingots of the type represented at Rathgall are of fairly uncommon occurrence. In Ireland examples are represented in three hoards—Ballywillin, Co. Longford, Ladestown, Co. Westmeath, and a small find provenanced only to 'Irish midlands'. In the first two of these finds droplets or 'bean-shaped' ingots also occur, a reminder that there is a degree of overlap between small ingots and these types. The 'Irish midlands' hoard is a small, unpublished find comprising only a diminutive ingot, 2.75cm in length, and a fragment of a much larger one. The Ladestown find derives from a probable crannog, known as Rushy Island, on the north-western shore of Lough Ennell. It consists of twelve items, including some ingots and hack-silver, and includes a diminutive ingot, 2.5cm in length, along with two fragments of coins; one of the latter has been identified as an example of the First Hand type of Aethelraed II, indicating a *terminus post quem* date of AD 985 for the deposition (Graham-Campbell and Sheehan 2009, 84). While this hoard suggests that this type of diminutive ingot was current during the closing decades of the tenth century, the third find, from Ballywillin, indicates that it was also in circulation during the opening decades of that century.

The Ballywillin hoard was found on a crannog in Lough Kinale, a site which has also produced important ecclesiastical finds of early medieval date (Kelly 2006; Fredengren *et al.* 2010). The hoard, which is coinless, consists of five ingots and 33 pieces of hack-silver (Graham-Campbell and Sheehan 2009, 84–5, fig. 6). Two of the ingots are of bean-shaped type, while two are diminutive standard cast ingots, 1.94cm and 2.5cm in length. Much of the hack-silver derives from ingots, while brooches and brooch-pins, a plaited arm-ring and sheet scrap are also represented, with the brooch fragments deriving from penannular brooches of both the 'ball' and bossed types. The latter fragments are of particular interest because they derive from a brooch that is clearly related to those that form subgroup F in Johansen's classification (1973, 105, 109–12; Graham-Campbell 1975, 45–6). These are considered to be of Hiberno-Scandinavian rather than Irish manufacture and, like the ball-type brooches, are of importance in testifying to contact and interaction between the Hiberno-Scandinavian and Irish silver-working traditions. The brooch hack-silver serves to place the Ballywillin hoard within the group of finds represented by Dysart Island no. 4, Co. Westmeath (Ryan *et al.* 1984, 339–61), and related Hiberno-Scandinavian finds in Britain, especially from Cuerdale and Goldsborough, deposited *c.* AD 905–10 and *c.* AD 925 respectively, suggesting that the Ballywillin find may be assigned to the early tenth century.

Viking-age ingots functioned as convenient ways of storing bullion. It is not surprising, therefore, that the practice of 'nicking' their edges developed as a simple method for testing silver quality during economic transactions. Interestingly, there is a nick on one of the edges of the Rathgall ingot, suggesting, perhaps, that it was used at some stage to top up the weight of silver that was changing hands in a commercial transaction. The other recorded examples of diminutive ingots from Ireland do not display this feature, though it is commonly found on examples of standard size. It occurs on at least one example of a diminutive ingot, 2.1cm in length, in the Cuerdale hoard (Graham-Campbell 2011, 184, no. 1:129).

The Rathgall ingot is not unusual in terms of its find context, as the discovery of Viking-age silver objects on early medieval settlement sites, such as ringforts, crannogs and ecclesiastical sites, is not uncommon (Sheehan 1998, 173–5). It is more unusual, however, in terms of its geographical context in south Leinster, for this is a region that has produced very few Viking-age silver hoards or single finds of gold or silver of Scandinavian character. The exception, of course, is the massive twisted gold arm-ring from Rathedan, Co. Carlow, which, at 380g, is the largest Viking-age gold ornament from Ireland (Bøe 1940, 101, fig. 68).

3.6 BRONZE ARTEFACTS

Most of the bronze artefacts came from the D/D1 focus in Area 2 (Metalworking Zone 3). Several came from the fill of Ring-ditch 1 and, as has been noted above, three bronzes were found in a hoard in Pit 31 inside Ring-ditch 2. A number of unstratified items of bronze were also found. A group of Bronze Age artefacts as well as a small group of Iron Age, medieval and post-medieval artefacts were identified on typological grounds. In other cases the dating remains unclear. The results of XRF analysis reveal largely heavily corroded items not suitable for compositional analysis (Table 3.4). Only a small group produced significant results. Among these, only the composition of the chemically stripped possible axe blade fragment E84:7250 would agree with a Bronze Age date. The values for the other items suggest later (Iron Age or medieval) dates.

3.6.1 Later prehistoric bronze artefacts
Barry Raftery and Katharina Becker

Bronze hoard, Pit 31: spearhead, sword blade fragment and chisel

Pit 31, straddling Sqs J2/J3 within Ring-ditch 2, produced three bronzes—a spearhead, a section of a sword blade and a small chisel. As has already been discussed, the items, when found, were spread in the pit fill over an area of 5–10cm and it is reasonable to view them as having originally constituted a hoard.

Although the blade of the spearhead was partly corroded, it is clear that it was complete when buried (E84:8345; Figs 2.101 and 3.31). It had a circular socket and hollow blade. Originally it was of leaf-shaped form, with curved base and markedly concave sides. On each face of the socket there is an irregularly circular rivet hole, which was obviously used to rivet the spearhead to the wooden haft. The spearhead is of a small shape and has a short socket, which strongly tapers and shows parallels with some Blackmoor examples of the Ewart Park phase (S. Needham, pers. comm.).

The short sword blade fragment E84:8346 (Figs 2.102 and 3.31) had been clearly and deliberately cut at each end. Although not enough survives to establish the type with certainty, it could belong to Eogan's Class 4, the typical swords of his Dowris phase of the Irish later Bronze Age (Eogan 1965; 1964; Waddell 1998).

Perhaps most interesting and unusual is the small chisel (E84:8344; Figs 2.103 and 3.31). Close examination indicates that the blunt end has been subjected to a series of fine hammer blows, and that the wear evident on the cutting edge is more severe along one end than along the other. The fine

Table 3.4—XRF results: the analytical measurements obtained by X-ray fluorescence.

Copper-alloy and silver objects that were in reasonable condition to allow a quantitative assessment of their alloy components											
Object. no.	Artefact	Copper	Tin	Lead	Zinc	Silver	Gold	Arsenic	Antimony	Iron	No. analyses	Context
E84:863	Strip	98	0	0.2	0.1	0.2	0	0.3	0	0.5	2	Sq . A3
E84:2010	Ingot	79	18	1.3	0.2	0.2	0	0	0.1	0.2	1	Sq. 36, light brown
E84:5703	Ring	0.2	45	55	0.3	0	0.1	0	0	0.2	2	Sq .67
E84:5585	Ingot	0.6	0	1.5	0	94	1.9	0	0	0.2	2	Sq. 52, RD1, lower fill
E84:5836	Sheet	63	17	11	2.6	0.6	0	1.8	1.3	0.9	2	Sq. 61, almost on yellow
E84:7250	Axe blade fragment	87	10	0.6	0	0.2	0	0.3	0.6	0.1	2	BA—Sq. D, black charcoal

Copper-alloy artefacts examined with XRF but which turned out to be too corroded to provide meaningful results beyond the presence and absence of alloy components												
Object. no.	Artefact	Copper	Tin	Lead	Zinc	Silver	Gold	Arsenic	Antimony	Iron	No. analyses	Context
E84:53	Metal bar, likely scrap metal	35	60	0.6	0	0.6	<0.020	1.5	0.2	0.6	1	Sq. 24, edge of dark area
E100:175	Waste bronze or scrap?	46	50	0.8	0	0.2	<0.020	0.6	0.2	0.3	1	BA? Sq. Z5:e, edge of PH
E84:448	Ring	44	51	0.7	0.1	0.7	<0.020	0	<0.05	2.6	1	Sq. 22, top of ditch fill
E84:460	Ingot fragment, bar-shaped, oval section	32	52	11	0	1.6	0	0.9	2.2	0.5	2	Sq.16, light brown
E84:552	Scrap	21	56	19	0.1	0.1	0	0.8	0.3	2.2	1	Sq. 25, light brown
E84:1016	Brooch fragment, post-medieval?	32	61	4	0	0.2	<0.020	0.1	<0.05	1.7	1	Sq. 14, dark brown near wall
E84:1151	Tweezers?, poss. medieval, or belt fitting	24	63	12	0	0.6	0.1	0.3	<0.05	0.3	1	Disturbed zone
E84:1152	Stud, decorated	47	50	0.3	0	0.1	<0.02	0.1	<0.05	1.5	2	Disturbed zone
E84:1374	Bar toggle, Hallstatt type	28	54	15	0.1	0.2	0	1.6	0.3	0.5	2	Sq. 8, on yellow subsoil
E84:1463	Fragment	11	46.4	41	0	0.1	0	0.2	<0.05	0.8	1	BA: RD1, black fill, Sq. 8/2, base
E84:1517	Waste metal	43	37	18	0	0.3	<0.02	1	0.4	0.2	1	Sq. 35
E84:2200	Rivet—possible Bronze Age cauldron rivet	22	59	9	0.1	3.4	0	1.4	3.1	1.6	1	Black fill, upper levels of ditch, Sq. 15, 20cm
E84:2384	Stud, decorated	38	55	2	0.1	0	<0.02	0.1	<0.05	3.3	2	Sq. 8
E84:3300	Gouge	32	59	6	0	0.4	<0.02	0.3	0.4	2	1	C2, 'beside stone'
E84:3350	Disc	41	53	0.9	0	2.6	0	0.1	<0.05	1.4	2	Sq. 28, on orange
E84:4914	Fragment, possibly of pin	28	52	14	0.5	0.6	0	0.3	0.1	3.9	1	Sq. 54, first layer under sod
E84:6299	Chain-link?	26	46	18	1.2	1.4	<0.02	2.9	1.5	2.9	1	In dark brown with black patches among amorphous ferrous lumps, Sq. D, 15–19cm
E84:6923	Pin?	16	66	12	0.1	1	0	0.4	0.1	3.9	1	In brown, D3
E84:7185	Chisel fragment?	14	56	11	0	6.1	0	3.5	4.9	3.2	2	In brown outside 'black bank' in E2
E84:8080	Graver?	26	58	10	0.1	1	<0.02	0.7	1.1	2.9	1	E1
E84:8342	Pin shaft fragment	38	43	14	0.7	0.6	0	0.6	0.7	1.7	1	Sq. J4, in brown humus immediately under sod
E84:8363	Medieval stick-pin	27	52	12	1.7	0.6	<0.02	0.4	1.2	4.5	1	Sq. J4

A number of copper-alloy artefacts were not examined as they were too corrroded: E84:236; 1164, 1351, 1355, 4732, 1788, 5258, 6087, 6767a–c, 6924, 7060, 7697, 7728, 7786, 8407, 8912, 8914, 9543.

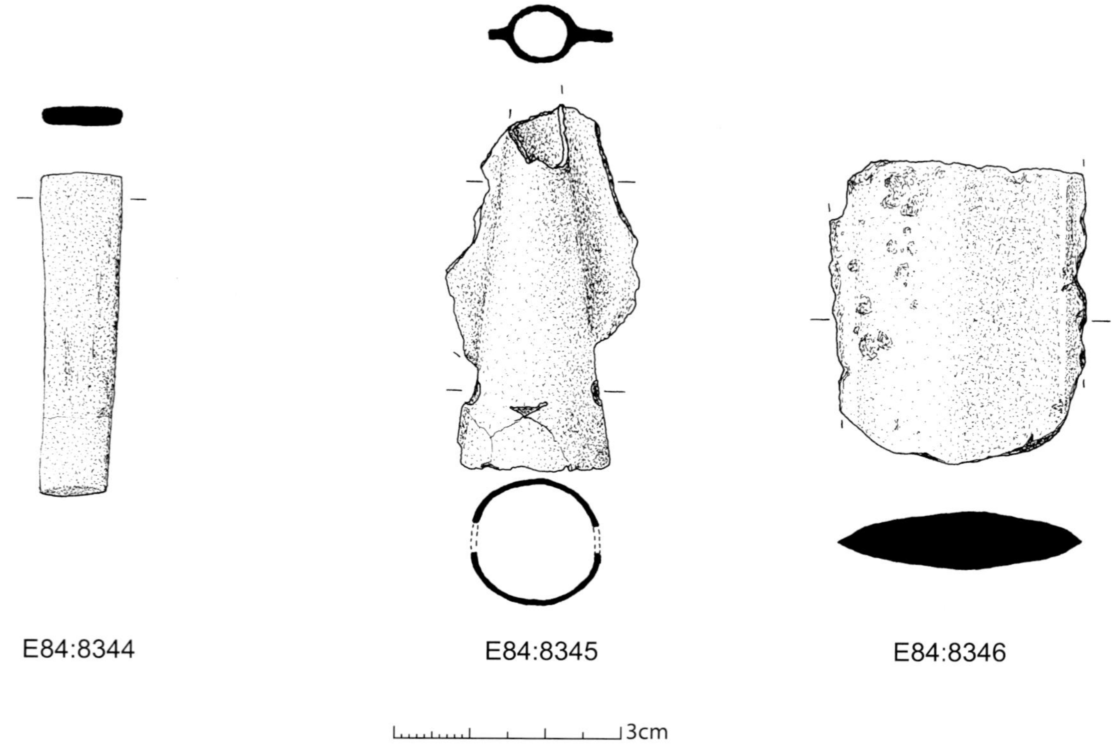

Fig. 3.31—Bronze hoard E84:8344, 8345, 8346 (scale 1:1).

striations across the blade, and at right angles to it, clearly indicate deliberate sharpening. The blade has a very fine, double facet on one side, apparently indicating secondary sharpening or use in this area. The object may be seen as a small, hand-held graving tool. If this interpretation is correct, the object represents the first such tool from Ireland and illustrates once more the extent of the fine metalworking that was being carried out at later Bronze Age Rathgall.

There are several possible explanations for the presence of these three objects together in a pit. Since bronze at the site could be readily melted down and reused, it seems that deliberate discarding can be ruled out. The three items were therefore either buried for safe keeping and later collection or were intended for some ritual or symbolic purpose. The latter might be deemed the more likely scenario. An interesting avenue of speculation thus opens up. Is it possible, for example, that the three items in the hoard, representing fighting (blade fragment), hunting (spearhead) and metalworking (chisel), had a very specific meaning?

E84:8344: Very fine chisel, possible graving tool (Figs 2.103 and 3.31). Shape almost rectangular but there is a very slight decrease in width from butt end to blade. Each face gently convex with sharp angles and regular, flat sides. Butt flat but slightly birred along each edge, which is a result of probable hammering. Considerable wear on blade, which is gently convex with fine facets on cutting edge. Very fine parallel striations on one edge seem to suggest secondary filing, probably intended for sharpening. Flattened facet on each edge, indicating that cutting was concentrated in corners.

L: 445cm. W: 11mm to 9.5mm at blade. T: 3.5mm to 2mm.

Sq. J3, upper grey fill of Pit 31.

E84:8345: Incomplete socketed spearhead (Figs 2.101 and 3.31). Broken at tip and along one edge. Originally leaf-shaped blade, with curved base and gently concave sides. Line of blade continues on each side as slightly raised casting seam to open edge of socket. This line interrupted on each side by irregularly circular rivet hole. Hollow circular socket and hollow blade.

Socket: 2.1cm x 2.15cm (ext. diam.). W of blade: 2.85cm. Diam. of socket at broken tip: 0.08cm. T of bronze at socket: 0.015cm.

Sq. J3, upper grey fill of Pit 31.

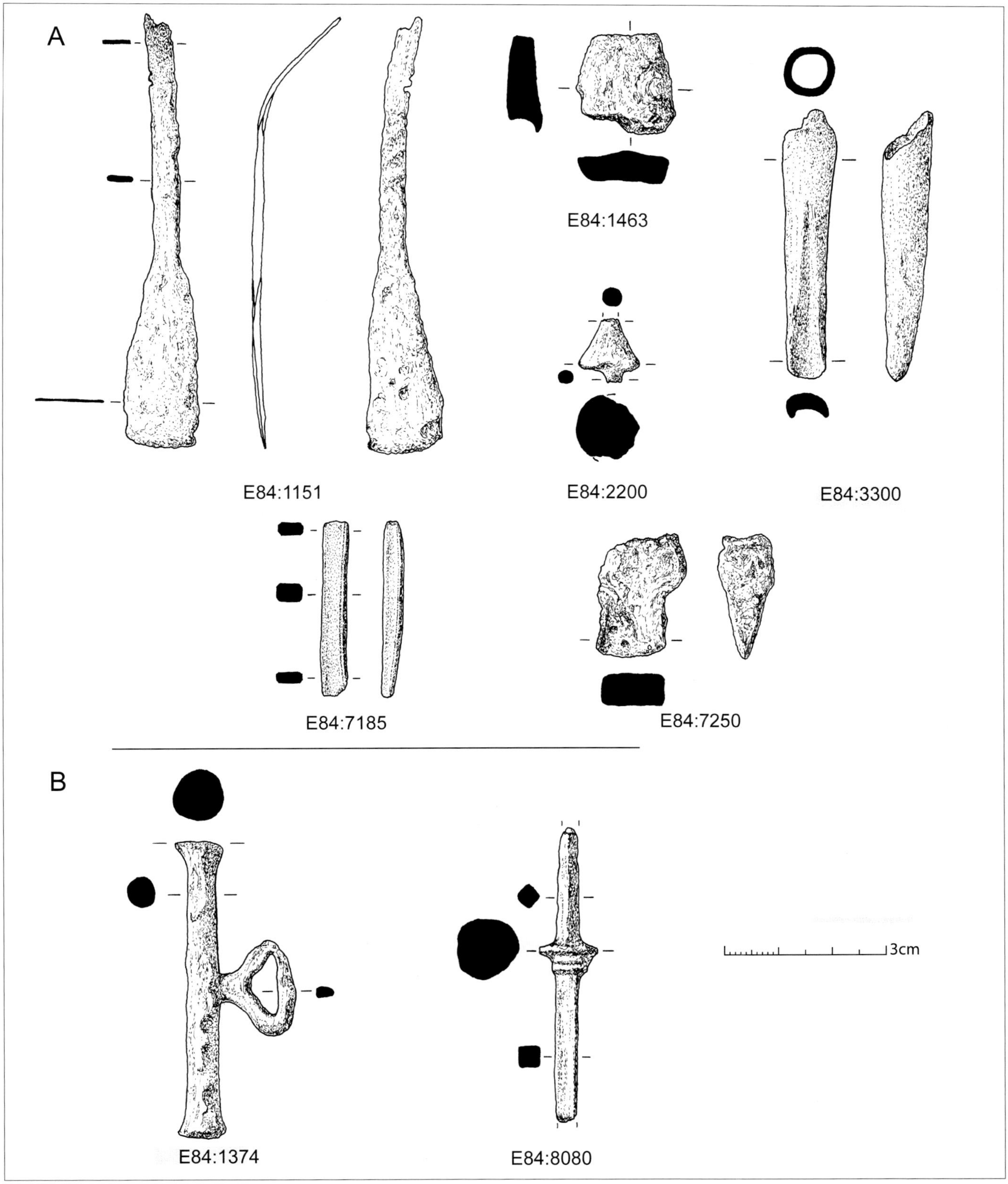

Fig. 3.32—Bronze artefacts (scale 1:1).

E84:8346: Fragment of sword blade (Figs 2.102 and 3.31). Regular, lozenge-shaped section with rounded mid-rib. Edges damaged. Traces of slightly concave bevel along each edge. This is 5cm wide along one edge (probably near original width) and only 3.5cm wide on the other edge, where damage is more extensive. This bevel has been cast with the blade. The edges, which are roughly parallel to one another, appear to have been deliberately broken and may in fact have been cut.

L: 4.1cm. W: 3.4cm at one end, 3cm at the other. Max. T: 0.08cm.

Sq. J3, upper grey fill of Pit 31.

Socketed gouge and possible tanged chisel

A bronze socketed gouge (E84:3300; Figs 3.32 and 3.34) came from the black layer in Sq. C2.[7] The object is of considerable delicacy and was clearly intended for very fine work. It is entirely different in size and form from all the known Irish bronze gouges, which, without exception, are larger, heavier implements with splaying, convex blades (MacWhite 1944b). These implements were intended for relatively heavy chiselling on a scale quite distinct from the exquisitely fine tooling for which the Rathgall specimen must have been used. It is, of course, normally assumed that the typical Irish gouges were associated with woodworking, but the delicate Rathgall object might have served a purpose different from that of the larger, heavier examples. The possibility that it was associated with fine metalworking of some sort, perhaps even gold-working, cannot be dismissed. It is unique in Ireland and foreign manufacture is not impossible. In this regard, at any rate, among other bronze gouges from the Yattendon hoard in Berkshire there is one which is reminiscent of the Rathgall specimen (Burgess *et al.* 1972, fig. 18:50). Socketed gouges form part of the Dowris phase in Ireland, but also have earlier, Wilburton phase associations in Britain (e.g. O'Connor 1980, 137, 175).

Another bronze artefact (E84:8080; Figs 3.32 and 3.33) came from E1, in the section strip in its south, directly adjacent to the D/D1 focus. It was in the disturbed brown material but was low down, and clearly came from the occupation levels in this area. Originally a tanged object of some sort, it had unfortunately snapped and only the junction of the tang and its functional end survive, joined by an expanded collar. Its original form is thus unclear, but it is tempting to see it as the remains of a cutting implement, perhaps with curving, expanded blade, a well-known type which is generally regarded as having been for cutting leather[8] (Burgess *et al.* 1972, figs 14:46 and 18:43, 4; Roth 1974; Eogan 1983). The dating of this type is unclear, especially in view of the classic, tanged bronze chisel, closely similarly to those referred to above, that came unquestionably from the Hallstatt C Staple Howe settlement horizon (Brewster 1963, 113, fig. 61:5). Indeed, collared tools such as the tanged and collared chisels are evidenced as early as the Penard phase in Britain (Needham 2017, fig. 8).

E84:3300: Fragment of socketed gouge (Figs 3.32 and 3.34). Tapered cylinder in shape, narrowing to a transverse

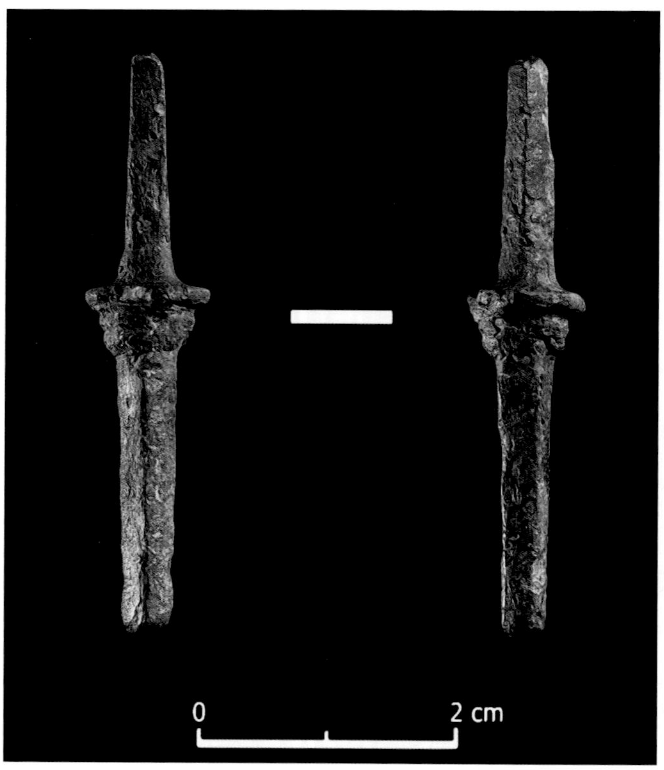

Fig. 3.33—Bronze tanged object E84:8080 (photo: John Sunderland).

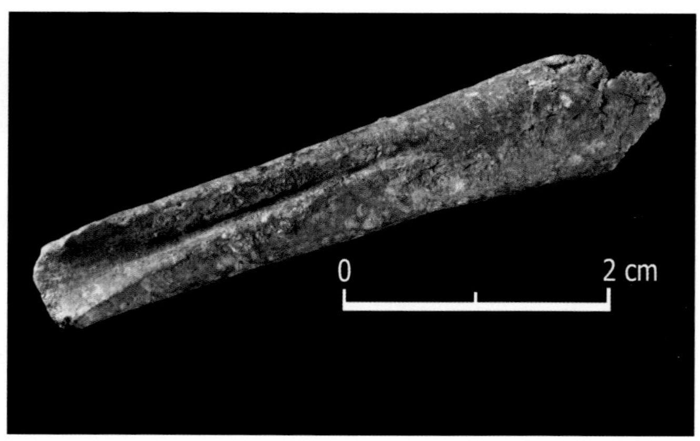

Fig. 3.34—Bronze gouge E84:3300.

edge at the working end. This edge is semicircular in section and thus the gouge is not a complete cylinder at the working end. However, the distance between the two longitudinal edges of the incomplete cylinder narrows towards the centre of the gouge, until it is complete. Irregular oblique break at wider circular end. Undecorated.

Dimensions: 5.05cm x 0.78cm x 0.3cm.

Sq. C2, beside stone in middle of square.

E84:8080: Tanged implement (Figs 3.32 and 3.33). Subtriangular plate, from one side of which a tang protrudes. A working end protrudes from another side. Two ridges decorate the working end, which is square in section but at a different angle to the tang. Both working end and tang taper slightly. The former appears to be broken at the end, possibly in antiquity; quite corroded.

Dimensions: 5.54cm x 1.13cm x 0.51cm.

Sq. E1, on southern face of section strip.

Fragments

Other artefacts were found in deposits that are considered to be of Bronze Age date. These include a small, fragmentary piece of bronze from deep in Sq. D, in the black charcoal area; it may be the bladed end of a chisel (E84:7250; Fig. 3.32) but over-cleaning of the object some years ago leaves this now uncertain.

E84:8717: Fragment of narrow bladed implement (Fig. 3.36). Extensive corrosion and over-cleaning have obscured finer details. Thin, regularly oval section, tapering sharply towards edges. It seems to have had straight sides, which appear to narrow gradually to point. At wider end, at one edge, there are the remains of what might once have been a rivet hole. On the opposite edge there may be the remains of a second rivet hole but this is far more uncertain. Between these two features the edge of the object is roughly curved but again it is uncertain whether this is an original feature. At the narrower end, on one face, there is a particularly pronounced shallow, circular depression, 4mm in diameter. It is unclear whether this is an original feature. Object tapers from 1.8cm at its widest to 0.4cm at the very tip.

Dimensions: 8.58cm x 1.8cm x 0.33cm.

Sq. Y1, at centre of square at southern end, immediately in front of (later) wall, in yellow material of bank, 28cm below upper surface of bank and 50cm above greyish-black layer.

3.6.2 Early Iron Age

Barry Raftery and Katharina Becker

Bar toggle

A bar toggle (E84:1374; Figs 3.32 and 3.35) was also found in 1969, in disturbed soil in the section strip of Sqs 8/16, not far from Ring-ditch 1. It was close to the eastern industrial/habitation area and was found immediately adjacent to Hearth 6, one of the three large hearths concentrated in the eastern part of the Ring-ditch 1 enclosure. As discussed elsewhere (Raftery 1975; 1997b), the object is clearly a north European type (Baudou 1960, 89–90, maps 9 and 10), and numerous examples of varying form occur in that area, notably in southern Denmark and northern Germany. They are most frequently found in graves. Two main forms occur: those which are gently curved and those which, like the Irish examples, are straight. The curved examples, of which large numbers have been found in Jutland, belong to Montelius IV; those which are straight, apart from an occasional possible Montelius IV context (*ibid.*, 90), date from Montelius V. In absolute terms, the Montelius IV material dates from about 1150 cal. BC onwards, while Montelius V corresponds to Hallstatt B3, with a later currency into the early Hallstatt C (Gerloff 2007, table 13.2).

The Rathgall specimen resembles some of those from

Fig. 3.35—Bronze toggle E84:1374 (photo: John Sunderland).

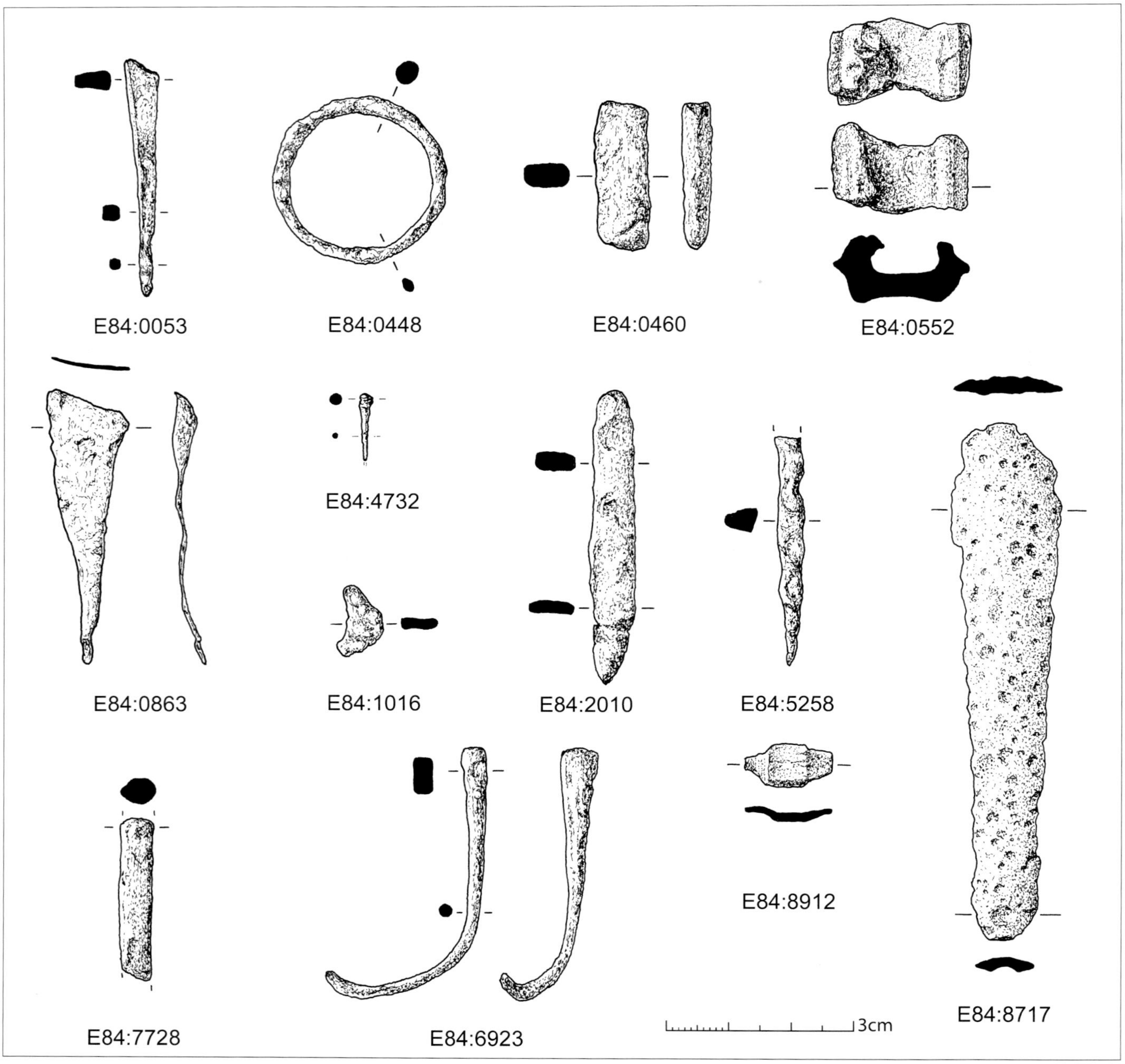

Fig. 3.36—Bronze artefacts (scale 1:1).

northern Europe and, lacking any real comparisons in Britain, it seems reasonable to assume, as does Waddell (1998, 270), that the object is most likely to be an import from that area. As the writer has noted elsewhere (Raftery 1975; 1997b), the only relevant comparisons from Ireland are the two somewhat smaller examples from a Bronze Age phase of settlement on the hilltop site of Navan Fort, Co. Armagh, another site of importance during the later Bronze Age or earliest Iron Age. In the graves of northern Europe these objects are most frequently associated with personal items, and they are often looped on bronze rings, suggesting that they may have been commonly worn on the person. It is not impossible that they served as dress-fasteners, in the manner of comparable objects of plastic or bone today. At any rate, they are not to be confused with the superficially comparable *Ringknebel* from Urnfield contexts in central and western Europe, which, unlike the objects here under discussion, appear to have been most often associated with horse harness. There are no indications that the northern European examples under discussion here had any equine significance.

It is unfortunate that the Rathgall toggle was unstratified. Nevertheless, its location in the immediate vicinity of the three large hearths, and only a short distance west of the zone of intense Bronze Age activity, allows for the strong possibility that it derives from the latter horizon.

E84:1374: Bar toggle (Figs 3.32 and 3.35). Solid, single-piece casting. Consists of straight rod, circular in section, with gradually expanding ends. Extremities flat. Projecting loop at centre, subtriangular in shape, with rounded corners. Lozenge-shaped section.

L: 55.5mm. Diam.: 6.5mm. Diam. at ends: 105mm. T of loop: 3mm. Projection of loop: 155mm. Max. int. W: 10mm.

Sq. 8, in baulk, on yellow subsoil close to western edge of ditch.

Conical rivet

A conical rivet (E84:2200; Figs 3.32 and 3.37) came from the black burnt layer high up in Ring-ditch 1 in Sq. 9, directly adjacent to the Zone 2 metalworking. Rivets are common on bronzes of the later phases of the European Bronze Age. In Ireland, too, they are known not only in bronze, e.g. on shields (Coles 1962) and horns (Coles 1963), but also on items of gold, such as gorgets (e.g. Hartmann 1970, Taf. 22, 23; Eogan 1994, pl. IV, fig. 185). The Rathgall rivet, of course, is quite different from the latter and may well have come from a cauldron, indicating the former existence or repair of such an object on the site.

In a wider context, Irish Bronze Age cauldrons have been subjected to considerable study for more than half a century (Hawkes and Smith 1957; Leeds 1930), and it has become evident that Ireland was an important centre of manufacture of these splendid objects, especially those referred to as Atlantic B cauldrons. Exports and influences from the country are detectable northwards as far as Scandinavia, southwards to Iberia and eastwards to Britain and France. Hawkes and Smith (1957) suggested that the floruit of cauldron manufacture in Ireland was between the eighth and sixth centuries BC (cf. also Eogan 1964). More recently, however, Gerloff (2010) has argued for a considerably earlier date, and cauldron manufacture in Ireland is now seen as commencing perhaps as early as the late second millennium

Fig. 3.37—Bronze rivet E84:2200 (photo: John Sunderland).

BC. Conical rivets comparable to the Rathgall example are found on cauldrons of class B1 and are in fact identified as one of the main distinguishing characteristics of this class by Leeds (1930) (Gerloff 2010, 128). Gerloff's B0 vessels also have conical rivets, although these are less 'spiky' than those of B1 (*ibid.*). Gerloff subdivided B1 cauldrons into types Llyn Fawr, Ballyshannnon and Lisdromturk. By virtue of their parallels to Llyn Fawr, the Ballyshannon and Lisdromturk types are datable to Hallstatt C, i.e. the eighth or seventh century BC (*ibid.*, 149, 155, 157).

E84:2200: Fragment of conical rivet (Figs 3.32 and 3.37). Subcircular in plan, concave in section. Short, off-centre cylindrical projection from base. Tip of cone is broken and most of circular edge is damaged. Where undamaged, slight lip visible around bottom of base. Undecorated.

Dimensions: 1.24cm x 1.11cm.

Sq. 9, in black fill of upper levels of Ring-ditch 1, burnt material.

Later Iron Age bronze objects

Three bronze objects of later Iron Age date were identified from the site. A decorated strap-tag (E84:1153; Fig. 3.38) was found in Sq. 7, unfortunately in an area of recent brown humus which, moreover, had been heavily disturbed by rabbit activity. It was, however, of a type well known in the early centuries AD (Raftery 1970b; see below). Two domed bronze studs, each decorated with a concave-sided triangle, were also found. The first (E84:1152) was found close to the strap-tag and in the same disturbed layer. The second (E84:2384) was recovered in the following year (1970), once more unclearly stratified, in Sq. 8, about 8m south of the other two bronzes. There can be little doubt that all three of these artefacts came from the same belt. A near identical stud was found in Eastern Scotland (Hunter 2006, 154, fig. 18c).

The decorated tag is now damaged but the original design is visible (described below). The object is considerably worn but faint traces of tinned bronze are recognisable on both faces.

Raftery compared this object to the strap-ends (*Riemenzungen*) as discussed by Raddatz in 1957 in his discussion of the objects from the Thorsberg bog find in northern Germany. In particular, he drew attention to those of group J and within this group JII, where a broadly trapezoidal binding plate with two or three rivets had a ring-shaped functional end. However, the closely comparable 'spoon-shaped' versions of the type, which likewise have a trapezoidal binding plate but a solid and concave spoon-shaped end, may also have echoes of the Rathgall piece, especially if decorated like some of the pieces from Illerup (Ilkjaer 1993, fig. 35). Importantly, as observed by Raftery (1970b), the decoration and the execution of the Rathgall piece with its 'filled' circular end represents a reinterpretation of the type, and as such may not be derived from either.

In recent years, the study of these objects has revealed their complex cultural and functional context. While strap-ends of Raddatz's type O with round cross-section have at Illerup, Denmark, another depositional site in a bog, comparable to that of Thorsberg, been shown to form part of horse gear, those of group JIII (Ilkjaer 1993) may be part of personal belt sets (*ibid.,* 189) and such of JII part of sword belts, but also on occasion of horse gear (cf. Ilkjaer 1993, 173–206). Recent review of the dating of the JII form (Blankenfeldt 2015, 152) suggests their dating to the Roman Imperial period into the third century AD.

Today seen as part of the belt decoration of Germanic sword belts or personal belts, both when found in the Barbaricum (outside the boundaries of the Roman Empire) and, less frequently, on Roman military sites (Matešić 2017, 349), the finding of this object reflects connectivity between Ireland and the Continent during the Roman Imperial period, and possibly, as suggested by Raftery in 1970, the wearing of a belt or decoration of a horse harness with an item modelled on a Continental type.

The two buttons or mounts, also likely to have decorated a belt or other leather item such as a horse harness, were not found in association with the strap-tag but would stylistically agree with a broadly contemporary late Iron Age date.

The strap-tag was thus an item of some value, and it may be taken that the wearer, possessing Roman-style belt fittings, was of some substance.

E84:1152: Bronze stud (Fig. 3.38). Cast. Circular in plan, dome-shaped in cross-section. Rectangular tang projects from underside, broken at end. Decorated; band around edge of circumference and three relief segments on surface creating a triangle with convex sides. The concave-sided triangle is a simple motif, widespread both geographically and in time. It is, however, especially common in the Roman period.

Dimensions: 2.41cm x 1.51cm.

Sq. 6, dark brown occupation with charcoal flecks in west of square.

E84:1153: Decorated, cast-bronze strap-tag (Fig. 3.38). Traces of tinning on front. Damaged in places, especially along sides and at decorated end, where section of ornament missing. Functional section consists of two parallel mounting-plates with openwork decoration on one face. Small, circular perforation originally at each corner, obviously intended for rivets to secure strap in position, but only one of these survives. Sides gently convex, narrowest at junction with circular end. Decoration consists of an incised openwork triskele, the touching crescentic ends of two complete arms slightly expanded. From open edge of mount an incised curved line curves around the triskele, extending outwards to join with circular end. At this point, at each edge, two incised arcs, open to edges of mount, clearly give the impression of spiral ends to the curved lines. End of mount consists of a circle enclosing three touching, openwork circles. In one instance, and probably originally in all three, one circle loops across the other. Sunken triangular depression in space between three circles. Rear of tag flat and without elaboration apart from triangular depression between the three circles.

L: 4.6cm. Max. W: 2.3mm. T of binding plates: *c.* 1mm. Distance between plates: 2–3mm. Diam. of surviving rivet hole: 1.5mm.

Sq. 7, disturbed zone—rabbit burrows.

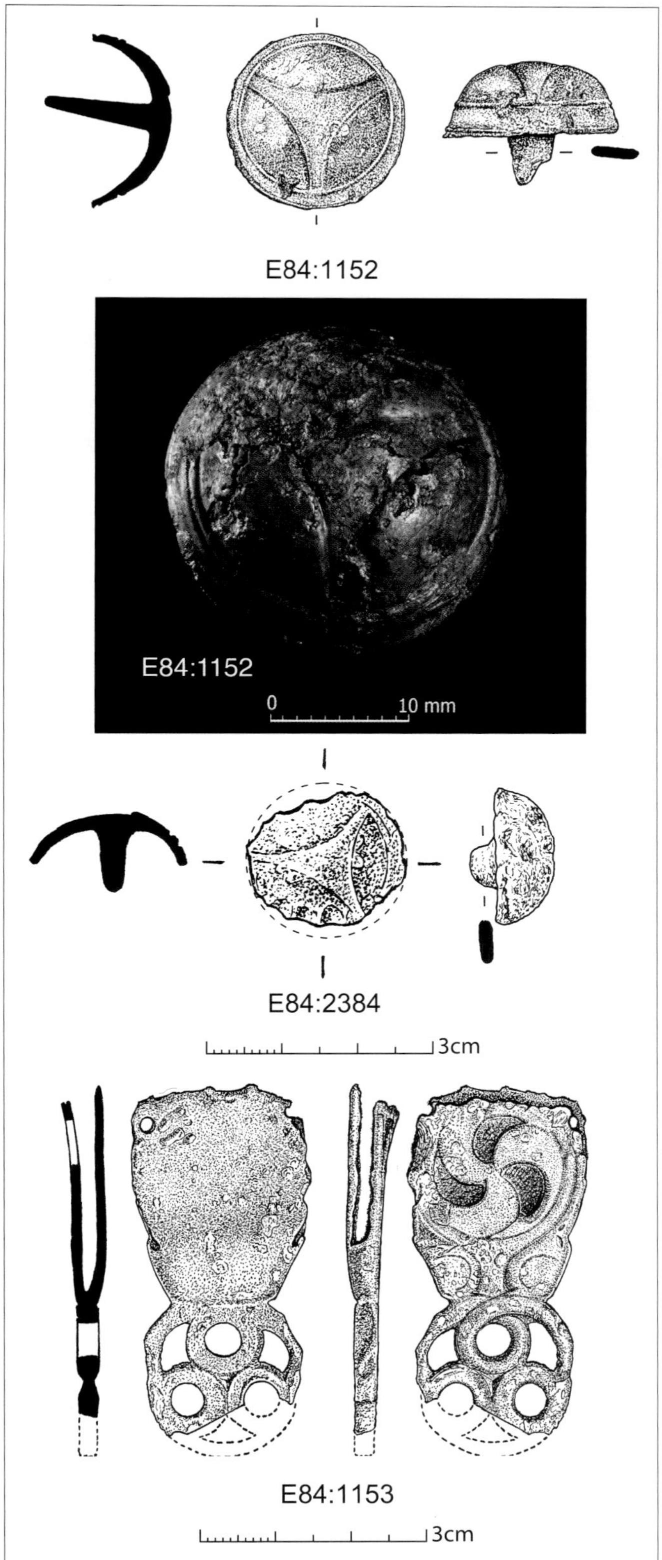

Fig. 3.38—Iron Age bronzes E84:1152 (top and inset photograph), 2384, 1153 (scale 1:1) (photo: John Sunderland).

E84:2384: Circular stud (Fig. 3.38). Domed section. Underside hollow, with a projecting oval tang. Decoration, as on E84:1152, consists of three raised arcs which join to create a concave-sided triangle. As a result of heavy corrosion, the object is far less well preserved than E84:1152.

T: 10.9mm. Diam.: 19.9mm.

Sq. 8, in small, dark brown hollow in grey base, 1m south of Hearth 6, at western edge of square.

Undated bronze objects

Annular bronze ring

An annular bronze ring (E84:448; Fig. 3.36) was found in the first season of excavation (1969)—the first possibly prehistoric item to be found on the site. It came from Sq. 22 in the grey upper silt of Ring-ditch 1.[10] Annular bronze rings are not a diagnostic type, and the dating of this ring is unclear.

E84:448: Bronze ring, irregular in section; roughly subcircular (Fig. 3.36). Very thick for almost half of its circumference, gradually narrowing to a point directly opposite the centre of the thickest section. Possibly decorated with undulating facets along the outer surface, though this may be the result of damage and heavy corrosion.

W: 0.4cm. T: 0.39cm. Diam.: 2.82cm.

Sq. 22, in dark brown material (the first appearance of the ditch), in south-west of square.

Bronze ingots and possible metalworking waste

As noted at the outset, a number of items of bronze came from the dense occupation material in Zones C to E outside Ring-ditch 1 in the east. These included a small, broken, figure-of-eight-shaped loop of uncertain purpose (E84:6299) and what appear to be the remains of a small bronze ingot (E84:2010) (Fig. 3.36) from Sq. 36 inside Ring-ditch 1. If the latter interpretation is correct, these are important elements of the metalworking industry which was evidently being carried out with some intensity on the site. Similarly, the small fragment of thin sheet bronze (E84:863; Fig. 3.36), unfortunately an unstratified object from Cutting A3, is likely a waste product of bronze-working.

Sheet fragment/tweezers

Another fragment of thin sheet bronze, also from disturbed layers in Sq. 6 (E84:1151; Figs 3.32 and 3.39), is somewhat enigmatic, as it is not entirely certain that this is, in fact, an artefact. It consists of a thin, parallel-sided length of bronze, terminating at one end in a gradually widening section with a regular, straight end. The narrow section bends gently to the other end, which is broken. The first suggestion is that this is the remains of a slender pair of tweezers. Such are known, in varying forms, during the later Bronze Age (e.g. Crannog 61, Lough Gara, Co. Sligo). However, though the narrow section is straight and regular, as might be expected of tweezers, the wider end exhibits a measure of irregularity which is not readily in keeping with its use as tweezers. The question of its purpose must thus remain uncertain.

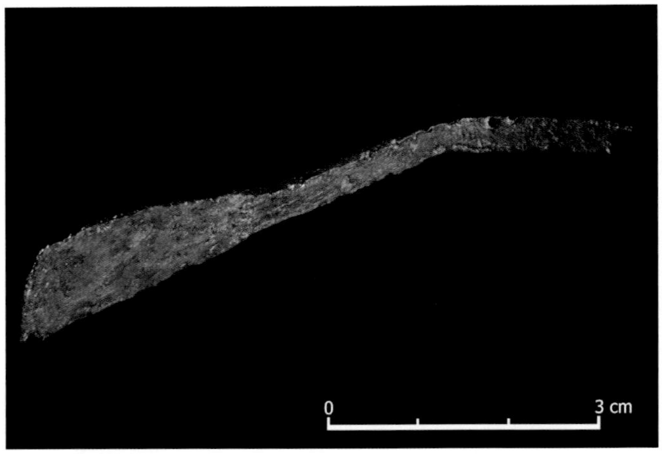

Fig. 3.39—Bronze object E84:1151 (photo: John Sunderland).

E84:1151: Fragment of tongs/tweezers? In plan, splayed tip tapers to a narrow strip which curves sharply in section towards the broken end (Figs 3.32 and 3.39). In section, thickest along the middle, between the splayed tip and the broken narrower end. Along the edges of this thickest section, on the external side, run two parallel lines of decoration, one along each edge. The remains of one line can be seen on the splayed tip on the same side, but this end is heavily corroded; the original edges are mostly not visible. The broken narrower end is also very corroded, and no decoration is visible.

Dimensions: 8.13cm x 1.39cm x 0.1cm.

Sq. 6, east, disturbed zone (mainly rabbit burrows).

E84:6924: Small bronze fragments. Irregularly shaped flakes.

Dimensions: 0.95cm x 0.43cm x 0.1cm.

Sq. D2, in brown material, below black area.

E84:7185: Fragment of chisel? Rectangular in plan and cross-section (Fig. 3.32). Tapers in longitudinal section towards one end, resulting in chisel shape. Bevelled longitudinal edges. Damaged at tapered end, broken at the other. Undecorated.

Dimensions: 3.37cm x 0.5cm x 0.41cm.

Sq. E2, in brown material outside black 'bank'.

E84:7250: Bronze object (Fig. 3.32). Small object, body roughly square in section with a blade-shaped expansion. Heavily corroded. Apparently undecorated.

Dimensions: 2.16cm x 1.6cm x 1.02cm.

Sq. D, in black charcoal area.

E84:7786: Small fragments of bronze.

Dimensions: 0.1cm.

Sq. D2, in dark brown fill of Depression 84, in west of square.

E84:8407: Fragment of object, cylindrical in shape, one end broken obliquely. Heavily corroded.

Dimensions: 0.56cm x 0.37cm.

Sq. I2, in black area immediately to the south of burial pit.

E84:1164: Tiny fragments of irregular shape, possibly originally of sheet bronze.

Dimensions: 0.3cm x 0.2cm x 0.1cm.

Sq. 6, east, in dark brown occupation material flecked with charcoal near wall.

E84:1355: Small bronze fragment. Irregular shape in plan and roughly subrectangular in cross-section.

Dimensions: 0.85cm x 0.8cm x 0.38cm.

Sq. 7, south, black fill of Ring-ditch 1.

E84:1463: Bronze fragment (Fig. 3.32). Subtrapezoidal in plan, subrectangular in section. Rough, uneven surface. Particularly oxidised at one point.

Dimensions: 1.89cm x 1.78cm x 0.86cm.

Sq. 8/2, bottom of black fill of Ring-ditch 1.

E84:53: Fragment of pin (Fig. 3.32)? Tapering rectangle in longitudinal section. Trapezoidal cross-section. In longitudinal section, two long sides curve towards tapered end.

Ridges visible along edges of longitudinal sides, where less corroded. Broken at wide end. Apparently undecorated.

Dimensions: 3.99cm x 0.54cm x 0.33cm.

Sq. 24, just at edge of dark area *c.* 1.55m from southern baulk and *c.* 25cm from eastern baulk.

E84:236: Fragmented pin? Shaft remains. Cylindrical in shape with circular cross-section. Undecorated.

Dimensions: 1.3cm x 0.38cm.

Sq. 15, south, in light brown material.

E84:460: Fragment of object (Fig. 3.36). Subrectangular in plan, oval in section. Heavily corroded, but apparently broken at one end and complete at the other. Possible rivet in complete end. Undecorated.

Dimensions: 2.4cm x 0.9cm x 0.5cm.

Sq. 16, west, in light brown material.

E84:552: Fragment of bronze object (Fig. 3.36). Broken along both longitudinal edges. Irregular, roughly subrectangular in plan. Rough, angular C-shape in section. Narrow transverse projections at either end (casting seams?). Ends of 'C' project from one face, both broken at end. Two convex ridges run the length of the longitudinal sides of opposite face. Some quartz and mica fragments embedded in parts of surface.

Dimensions: 2.23cm x 1.55cm x 0.48cm.

Sq. 25, in light brown material near middle of square.

E84:863: Bronze strip, triangular in plan (Fig. 3.36). Metal is gently curved, creased at the narrower end. Apparently undecorated.

Dimensions: 4.59cm x 0.05cm.

Sq. A3, north, in light brown material.

E84:1016: Fragment of bronze object (Fig. 3.36). Subtriangular in plan, with rounded corners and a concave base. Rough, flattened oval in section. Heavily corroded. Apparently undecorated.

Dimensions: 1.28cm x 0.54cm x 0.38cm.

Sq. 14, in dark brown material near wall.

E84:1788: Fragment of bar. Subrectangular in plan. Subrectangular to square in section. Corroded surface. Broken at both ends.

Dimensions: 1.75cm x 0.36cm x 0.4cm.

Sq. 3, in dark brown soil in west of square.

E84:2010: Ingot? Oblong in shape; subrectangular, tapering to a point at one end (Fig. 3.36). Subrectangular in section. Heavily corroded. Apparently undecorated.

Dimensions: 4.84cm x 0.8cm x 0.46cm.

Sq. 36, in light brown soil.

E84:3350: Disc. Rectangular in cross-section. Notably regular in dimension, but heavily corroded. No apparent decoration.

Dimensions: 1.22cm x 0.4cm.

Sq. 28, on orange material.

E84:4732: Fragment of pin? Roughly circular head (Fig. 3.36). Heavily corroded; apparently undecorated.

Dimensions: 1.31cm x 0.28cm x 0.1cm.

Sq. 44, in brown material.

E84:4914: Heavily corroded fragment of pin. Details unclear. More-or-less circular ring-shaped head; varies somewhat in width and is subrectangular in section. Straight, broken shaft, irregularly triangular to oval in section, expands considerably in thickness where it joins the ring. Owing to the corrosion the nature of this expansion is unclear.

L: 3.3cm. W of pin: 4mm. Max. diam. of ring: 1.4cm.

Sq. 54, in first layer under sod.

E84:5258: Fragment of bronze pin; shaft remains (Fig. 3.36). Tapers in thickness from 4.8mm to 1.3mm. Subtriangular in cross-section. Heavily corroded.

Dimensions: 3.83cm x 0.48cm.

Sq. 44, under baulk.

E84:6087: Fragment of sheet bronze, subcircular in plan. Irregular, damaged edge. Quite corroded. Apparently undecorated.

Dimensions: 1.33cm x 1.08cm x 0.09cm.

Sq. 34/35, in brown level, section strip.

E84:6299: Fragment of chain-link? Distorted U-shaped bar, rectangular in cross-section, with concave, almost touching sides and splayed broken ends. Possibly formed complete unit originally. Some damage at complete end. Undecorated.

Dimensions: 1.83cm x 0.76cm x 0.29cm.

Sq. D, in dark brown material with black patches among amorphous ferrous lumps.

E84:6767a–c: Three very small bronze fragments. One

cylindrical, the others irregular.

Dimensions: 1.34cm x 0.61cm x 0.44cm.

Sq. D/D1, on black charcoal area.

E84:6923: Hooked pin (Fig. 3.36). Flat head with rectangular cross-section. Shaft circular in cross-section. Curves and tapers to a point. At head, shaft widens and thickens. Undecorated.

Dimensions: 4.71cm x 0.24cm.

Sq. D3, in brown material.

E84:7697: Bronze fragment, roughly ovoid in longitudinal plan. Subtriangular in section, with a convex base.

Dimensions: 0.56cm x 0.13cm x 0.19cm.

Sq. D2, east, almost on yellow layer.

E84:7728: Fragment of cylindrical bronze object (Fig. 3.36). Heavily corroded. Broken at both ends. Undecorated.

Dimensions: 2.71cm x 0.53cm.

Sq. H2, in brown material.

E84:8912: Fragment of object (Fig. 3.36). Central raised square with two trapezoidal 'wings'. In section it has a very slight S-bend. Opposite side to raised area is a square depression. Heavily corroded.

Dimensions: 1.4cm x 0.72cm x 0.2cm.

Sq. J5, in black gritty material on yellow at north-east.

E84:8914: Bronze fragment, roughly L-shaped in plan. Subrectangular in section. Interior of 'L' quite smooth, with cracking visible on surface. Exterior highly irregular and rough.

Dimensions: 0.82cm x 0.4cm x 0.39cm.

Sq. J5, in grey charcoal matter of Pit 176 in north-west corner of square.

3.6.3 The stick-pins
Matthew Seaver

An almost complete stick-pin and a further decorated stick-pin shaft fragment were uncovered during excavations at Rathgall (Figs 3.40 and 3.41). They were found close to the remains of a rectangular medieval house. The most intact pin is comparable to O'Rahilly's conical-headed class of pin, which is dated to *c.* 1100–1260. This typology was devised using a contextual analysis of pins from the Dublin city excavations and further enhanced by Scully's analysis of objects from the Waterford city excavations (O'Rahilly 1998; Scully 1997). The Waterford pins were generally between 500mm and 750mm in length, which accords well with the Rathgall example. The decoration on the Rathgall pin (E84:8363) has parallels with the thirteen decorated Waterford pins, where motifs on shanks included zigzags, chevrons and oblique stabbing. The Waterford pins were thought to be handmade, as none were of the same dimensions. A second broken shank from Rathgall (E84:8342) was decorated in a similar way and is of the same date. These pins were used as dress-fasteners and occasionally as shroud-pins on a range of urban and rural sites up to the mid-fourteenth century.

E84:8363: Bronze pin (Fig. 3.41). Head and most of shaft remain. Cylindrical shaft, changing to a rectangular cross-section three quarters of the way along its length. Head is subconical. The base of the cone is slightly undercut, with a distance of 0.9mm between the base of the cone and the body of the shaft. Decoration on head consists of raised spiralling lines from the tip of the cone to the base. Whole shaft is decorated with linear zigzag and wave-like decoration identical to that on the shaft of another bronze pin (E84:8342).

Dimensions: 6.32cm x 0.2cm x 0.19cm.

Sq. J4, in brown humus immediately under sod in south-west corner of square.

E84:8342: Fragmented pin (Fig. 3.40). Cylindrical. Decoration consists of four incised lengthwise lines, alternating equally between a zigzag and a wave-like motif. Shallowly engraved and quite rough, though very fine and difficult to see. Surface of the pin is glossy (burnished?) and very slightly faceted. Broken at both ends.

Dimensions: 4.05cm x 0.29cm.

Sq. J2, in south-east corner of square in brown humus.

3.6.4 Medieval and post-medieval copper alloys
Matthew Seaver

The cast copper-alloy objects of later date are dominated by personal dress items such as cast copper-alloy livery buttons and buckles from belts, shoes and other costume items. Belt buckle E84:1130 is likely to be of post-eighteenth-century date, as such buckles have separate drilled holes for a vertical separate spindle (Whitehead 1996, 96). The most distinctive

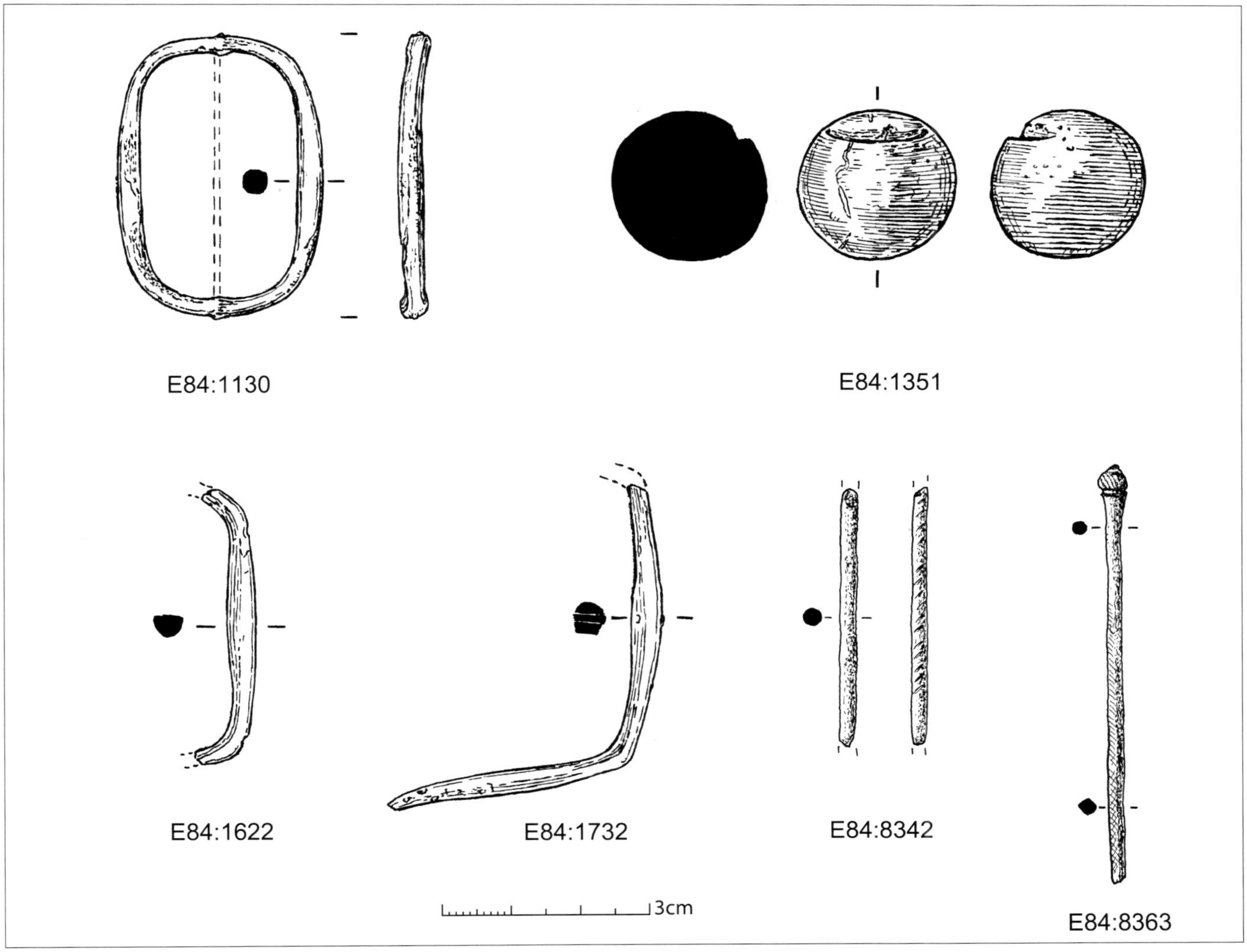

Fig. 3.40—Medieval and post-medieval bronzes E84:1130, 1351, 1622, 1732, 8342, 8362 (scale 1:1).

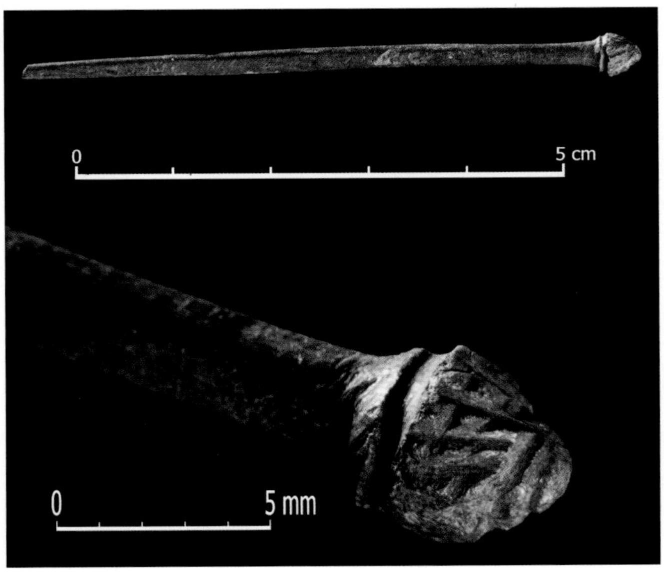

Fig. 3.41 (left)—Bronze pin E84:8363, with detail of the head (photo: John Sunderland).

of the livery buttons is an example from A.E Jones, Cork Hill, Dublin, which is likely to date from the early nineteenth century.

E84:1130: Belt buckle (Fig. 3.40). Subrectangular in plan and square in cross-section. Increases in thickness towards middle of shorter sides, where possible remains of rivets are visible. Also increases in thickness along longer sides, thus corners are narrowest. Not heavily corroded. Undecorated.

Dimensions: 4.12cm x 3cm x 0.33cm.

Sq. 2, north-west, in light brown material.

E84:1351: Later nineteenth–twentieth-century Codd bottle stopper (Fig. 3.40).
On yellow just outside ditch, north.

E84:1622: Fragment of belt buckle (Fig. 3.40). One longitudinal side and adjoining corners remain. Roughly oval in section, but one face slightly faceted, with a central ridge running the length of the fragment. Opposite face quite flat with well-defined edges. Widens and thickens toward centre. Broken at both ends. Undecorated.
Dimensions: 4.05cm x 0.43cm x 0.33cm.
Sq. 9, in dark brown soil.

E84:1732: Fragment of belt buckle (Fig. 3.40). Two perpendicular sides survive. Section varies from almost circular through subtriangular to D-shaped. Thickness and width expand towards one end, where bar begins to curve. At thickest point, there are the possible remains of one rivet on each side. Apparently undecorated.
Dimensions: 7.59cm x 4.3cm x 0.45cm.
Sq. 3, just outside 'silted' area near wall footing.

E84:5702: Button. Circular in shape. Slightly convex, with five-feather decoration at the centre of the upper surface, surrounded by a continuous line 0.8mm from the edge of the button. An oval-shaped loop projects from the centre of the interior, concave side, surrounded by an inscription which reads 'JON– & SONS CORK YHILL DUBLIN'.
Sq. 67, first layer under sod, in brown material.

E84:5830: Post-medieval button.
Sq. 66, in brown material.

E84:7060: Fragment of pin. Cylindrical in shape, with circular cross-section and corroded remains of head at one end. Broken at other end. Undecorated.
Dimensions: 2.1cm x 0.3cm.
Sq. D7, in brown material.

E84:8809: Fragment of belt buckle? Flattened rectangle in section. Angular C-shape in plan, with one arm considerably shorter than the other, both broken at the ends. One corner slightly narrower than the other. Some damage along exterior side of longer arm. Undecorated.
Dimensions: 1.52cm x 0.24cm x 0.19cm.
Sq. F4, centre, in brown humus immediately below sod.

E100:175: Waste bronze.
Sq. Z5:e, at edge of small charcoal-filled post-hole immediately to west of stone ring.

E84:5836: Fragment of sheet bronze.
Sq. 61, almost on yellow layer, among stones.

E84:1517: Waste bronze?
Sq. 35, north-east, first layer under sod.

E84:4167: Bronze button.
From unknown context. Dump.

E84:4547: Bronze button.
Sq. 30, in brown material.

E84:5257: Bronze button.
Sq. 51, in brown material on yellow layer.

E84:5316: 'Albert' chain.
Sq. 60, in brown material, second layer under sod.

E84:7790: Bronze button.
Sq. H, in brown material.

E84:9254: Bronze button.
Sq. K8, in brown material at eastern end.

E84:9543: Bronze rod, circular cross-section.
L: 64mm. Diam. 5mm.
Sq. K5, in shallow brown depression on yellow layer.

3.7 THE CRUCIBLES

Justine Bayley, Thilo Rehren, Katharina Becker, Paul Mullarkey and Barry Raftery

3.7.1 Crucible types

The crucible fragments fall into two broad groups: thick-walled fragments consisting of fairly strongly tempered grey-brown ceramics, and thinner-walled fragments of more heavily tempered material with a more irregular external surface.

The first group represents thick-walled crucibles of characteristic Bronze Age pointed-oval (half-pear-shaped) form with base thicknesses of more than 20mm and rim thicknesses of over 10mm (Figs 3.42 and 3.43; Table 3.5). Considering what appear to have been phases of metalworking of some considerable intensity, it is perhaps surprising that the number of crucible fragments from the site is so limited, though British Bronze Age sites with large quantities of clay moulds similarly have few crucibles, e.g. Springfield Lyons, where there were 22 fragments of crucibles but nearly 1,000 mould fragments (Needham and Bridgford 2013, 51). The three almost complete vessels, crucibles 1, 2 and 4, and the substantially represented crucible 3, as well as several fragments of further crucibles, were found widely distributed over the site. Crucible 1 was found in Pit 118 in Area 1, crucible 2 has a strong association with Pit 20 in G2, Area 3, in the interior of Ring-ditch 2, and crucible 4 was found in Pit 215 in the eastern part of Area 3. The latter and crucible 1 survived complete, if fragmented, making it likely that they were in their primary depositional context. In contrast, fragments of what appears to be crucible 3 were found in both Hearths 3 and 6. These have been suggested to represent pyre pits and the deposition of the metalworking-related material within these features may be secondary, as implied also by the moulds and pottery from these contexts. A number of fragments show no clear joins but appear to possibly represent one crucible (2) and derive from contexts within Ring-ditch 2. Fragments from a crucible similar to crucible 2, however, showing no potential joins, were found in the deposits in Area 2.

As discussed in section 3.9, the complete crucible 1 in the basal layer of Pit 118 and crucible 4 in Pit 215 may be deliberate deposits, given their spatially as well as contextually separate deposition from the moulds. Besides the large number of pottery sherds, representing eighteen vessels, only one possible mould fragment was found in Pit 118. Pit 215 contained flints, pottery and glass beads besides the crucible fragments, but no mould fragments.

Crucible 1, the most complete surviving crucible within the Bronze Age group, has an almost flat base, a depth of about 25mm and outer dimensions of about 80mm by 100mm (Figs 3.42 and 3.44). Crucible 2, of similar size, may have had a similar flat base, while crucible 3, possibly even larger than the other two, appears to have been more rounded. The shapes of their rims also vary. While the walls of crucible 1 taper towards the top and finish in a round, slightly irregular thinner rim, those of crucible 2 are in areas flat, and those of the well-finished crucible 3 are bevelled to the inside.

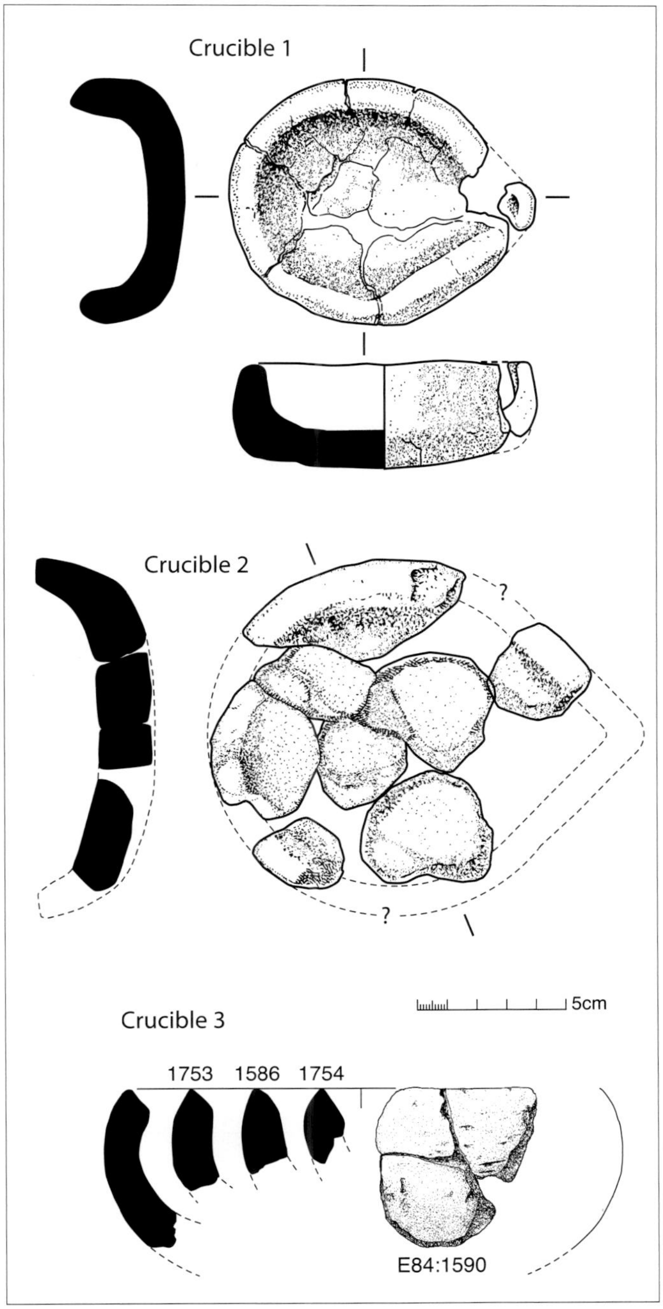

Fig. 3.42—Crucibles 1–3.

On its own within the assemblage stands crucible 4 (Fig. 3.43 and 3.44), which is small and shallow, atypical for Bronze Age crucibles. Nevertheless, it shares with crucibles 1–3 its pointed oval shape, the result of the pouring lip drawn outwards to project beyond the oval-to-round outline. It is 56mm long and 44mm wide. The edges of the shallow dish have been turned up to form an irregular rim.

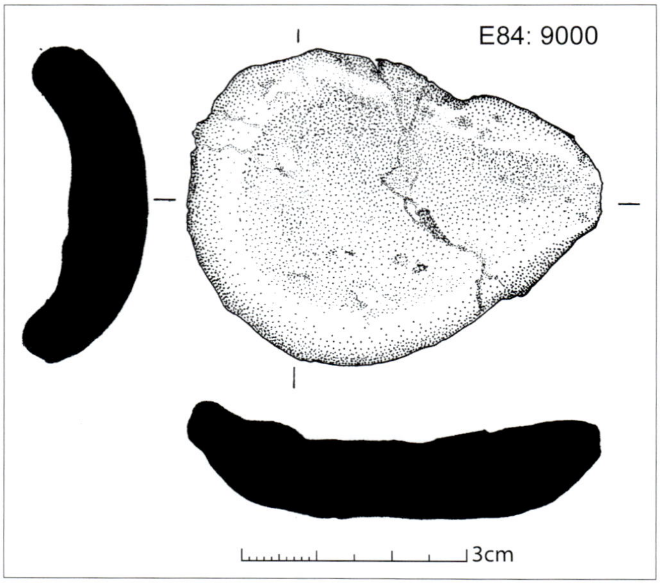

Fig. 3.43—Crucible 4 (scale 1:1).

Fig. 3.44—Crucibles 4 and 1, before identification of additional fragments of crucible 1 (photo: John Sunderland).

The tapering end of the crucible is shaped to form a spout with a slightly raised rim. The maximum depth of the small dish is 9mm.

Slag deposits adhere to the insides of three of the four crucibles. The unstratified crucible fragment 709 shows evidence for relining, also trapping some corroded bronze.

These open crucibles would have been heated from above, being reduced-fired inside but showing oxidation of their outer surfaces. The exception is crucible 4, which is reduced-fired both outside and inside.

Some of the other fragments (Table 3.5, Probable Bronze Age crucibles) represent other metallurgical ceramics which are relatively thick-walled at up to 14mm, but either represent objects with very small openings (in the case of E84:8094 about 28mm) or come from the pointed end of a Bronze Age crucible where the apparent diameter is much reduced. Other virtually straight rim fragments would come from parts of the crucibles that are less curved than average. Their primary distribution is in Area 2.

The second group of crucible fragments are from thin-walled vessels; most are rims, none of which join. They appear to represent several small, straight-sided vessels, typically 5mm thick at the rim and less than 10mm at the base. Most substantial are the fragments shown in Figs 3.47 and 3.47, with an estimated original diameter of about 40mm. The finish is rather irregular and the thickness of the rim can vary significantly on the same fragment. Except for the flat rim on fragment E84:7442, all rims are rounded. Some of these sherds are uniformly reduced-fired but others show varying degrees of oxidation, which suggests either that they were not used for melting metal or that they had ended up back in a fire after their metallurgical use had finished.

Fig. 3.45—E84:1271A and 7266, possible parting vessel fragments (scale 1:1).

3.7.2 Comparanda

Crucibles 1, 2 and 3 belong to Tylecote's (1986) Type J1. These are represented on several other sites in Ireland (cf. O'Carroll 2012b; Ó Faoláin 2004) and, interestingly, the shape of such a pointed-oval crucible is preserved by the Cooga bronze ingot (Ó Faoláin 2004, 23). Most of these crucibles have round bases like crucibles 2 and 3 from Rathgall. While both rounded and flat rims have been observed in Britain (e.g. Needham 1980), crucibles 2 and 3 from Rathgall are the only examples with flat or bevelled areas on their rims so far known from Ireland. The only example in the Rathgall assemblage with a round rim, crucible 1, has a flat bottom, which is unusual within the corpus in Britain and Ireland, the exception being a single fragment from Mucking (cf. Bond 1988, 22).

Crucible 4 is without parallels within Bronze Age assemblages but resembles an early medieval cupel(?) from Christchurch Place in Dublin (Fig. 3.46). While such a basic form of vessel may have been in use in different ways at different periods, this parallel is important in relation to the analytical results for this vessel.

In his survey of Late Bronze Age casting-related material in Ireland Ó Faoláin (2004) discussed a crucible group B represented at Lough Eskragh, Co. Tyrone, and Johnstown, Co. Wicklow, which have walls of either thinning or constant thickness towards the base. We consider a Late Bronze Age date unproven and instead interpret the group of small, thin-walled vessels that may have been round or triangular (Table 3.5) as more likely to be early medieval. While there is a small degree of doubt about the dating of these vessels (see below), on the basis of size and shape they are best compared with early medieval crucibles and related vessels with round or triangular shapes (cf. Tylecote 1986, fig. 50; Comber 2004). Among these a group seems to have been subject to reducing conditions, while others are oxidised, some with white residues on their inner surfaces (see below), and on the basis of XRF data seem to potentially have had a range of metallurgical uses.

Fig. 3.46—Cupel from Christchurch Place, Dublin (E122:433) (photo: Justine Bayley).

3.7.3 The XRF analysis of the crucibles

The XRF analyses were undertaken in an attempt to identify the metal alloys that were melted in the crucibles. They were carried out at various times over the last decade at the National Museum of Ireland by Paul Mullarkey, using a Spectro Midex EDXRF (energy-dispersive X-ray fluorescence) spectrometer with a molybdenum anode X-ray tube. The diameter of the tube collimator and measurement spot size is 0.7mm, and the distance from the sample surface varies from 2mm to 5mm. The operating conditions for the X-ray tube were 45kV and 0.6mA at normal air pressure. Sample counting time was 180 seconds. The principal elements sought were copper, tin, lead, zinc, silver, gold, arsenic, antimony, iron and mercury. All results were normalised to 100% and standards for copper, silver and lead alloys were routinely analysed to determine the accuracy of the measurements. Typical errors for these analyses are about ±1–2% for the major alloy components, about ±5–10% for the minor components and ±10–50% for the remaining elements at levels below 1%.

The artefacts were analysed within the sample chamber, and the measurement spot, which is indicated by a laser, was viewed on an adjacent monitor screen, thus allowing for accurate positioning of the analysis sites. Where possible, at least three sites were selected on each artefact or component. There was no sample preparation, such as polishing or abrasion of the surface, as it would have resulted in unacceptable damage. Results were affected by the surface conditions of the object, such as curvature, indentations, pitting and the presence of contaminants, surface dirt and corrosion products.

3.7.4 Discussion of XRF results

The data (Tables 3.6 and 3.7) represent only those elements included in the quantification programme of the instrument used, which were then normalised to add up to 100wt%. When interpreting these data one needs to bear in mind that the analysed material was predominantly ceramic, which typically consists of silica, alumina, lime and other light metal oxides not analysed for here; these typically add up to around 95wt% of all material present in ceramics. Of the ceramic material, only the iron oxide is included in the analysed elements and reported in the tables as elemental (metallic) iron. The iron oxide content of clay can vary widely. Analyses of crucibles from Tara, however, have yielded 2–4wt% iron oxide (Crew and Rehren 2002, 89); it is reasonable to assume that the Rathgall crucibles have a similar composition, and that the total iron content reported in Tables 3.6 and 3.7 does not represent more than about 5wt% of the entire ceramic as analysed. The weight percentage data for each element in the tables are therefore an estimated 20–30 times too high, owing to the automatic re-normalisation of the data, regardless of their actual concentration in the sample. Bearing this in mind, we can identify the dominant iron content in Tables 3.6 and 3.7 as part of the ceramic rather than the actual crucible charge and focus only on the non-ferrous metals. The iron content has been retained in the tables as a reminder of the rather low absolute concentrations of non-ferrous elements on which our subsequent interpretation is based.

Another important consideration is the fact that we are not looking at data from actual alloy remains but at the burnt (oxidised) part of the original metal charge, which then reacted with the vitrified ceramic on the inside of the crucibles. This burning of copper alloys during melting and casting affects different elements in the alloy differently, as has been pointed out for British material by Dungworth (2000) and then experimentally demonstrated by Kearns *et al.* (2010). The latter, in particular, has shown (on moulds, but the principle is identical for crucibles) that zinc values are highly enriched in the vitrified surface of the ceramic, followed by lead and then tin—and that copper leaves the least traces when casting copper alloys. Thus even relatively high zinc and lead concentrations on the crucible surface do not necessarily indicate the processing of brass or leaded copper alloys (Kearns *et al.* 2010).

An additional challenge is to separate natural trace levels of zinc and other metals in the clay from those contributed by the charge; in particular, zinc can be naturally high in the environment. Unfortunately, no analyses are available of unused crucible fragments or their outer surfaces to act as proxies for the natural zinc levels; we may assume, however, that the analysis of fragment E84:8094, with 99wt% iron reported, is close to the natural composition of the ceramic (Table 3.6). Similarly, the two analyses of fragment E84:7266, with 84wt% and 87wt% iron respectively, potentially reflect mostly the underlying ceramic material rather than the composition of its metal-rich vitrified surface (Table 3.7). In contrast, those analyses where the reported iron content falls below *c.* 85wt% are more likely to have a higher non-ferrous metal content in the analysed material, most likely reflecting the alloy content of the vitrified surface and hence that of the crucible charge. Thus the lower the reported iron content, the more likely it is that the non-ferrous metal detected is due to metallurgical activity.

Overall, the data in Tables 3.6 and 3.7 are significantly distorted relative to the original alloy charge, through the different behaviour of the various metals present and their post-burial corrosion, and through the instrument-inherent quantification and normalisation processes. Accordingly, any interpretation of the information can only be qualitative, despite its numerical presentation, and needs to take into account the effects of these factors. Having said this, we believe that the following statements can be made regarding the four thick-walled crucibles.

Crucible 1 (Fig. 3.42) is represented by two analyses of a single fragment (E84:6054a). Both have very low readings for everything except iron (nominally 83wt% and 79wt%), indicating that the actual alloy charge component is very low, and the geological background most likely contributes to the values in Table 3.6. The evidence for the original alloy composition is therefore very weak; at best, one can speculate that it could have been a low-tin bronze.

Crucible 2 (Fig. 3.42) is represented by three fragments (E84:7309, 6902 and 6901a), for which we have four separate analyses. Their iron content lies consistently between 64wt% and 70wt%, indicating that the non-ferrous metals are forming a more significant proportion at all analysed spots. The main non-ferrous metals detected are tin and lead, with average nominal values of 11wt% and 7wt% respectively. Zinc is virtually absent, while copper is recorded as an average of 2wt%. Bearing in mind the preferential oxidation of lead over tin and of tin over copper, we can be relatively certain in saying that this crucible was used for melting a normal tin bronze with low levels of lead; the zinc is most likely environmental or just a reflection of trace element levels in the alloy.

Crucible 3 (Fig. 3.42) is also thought to be represented by three analysed fragments (E84:1590, 1752 and 1753), for which we have six separate analyses. One of these has a very high nominal iron content of 83wt% (most likely representing the ceramic matrix rather than the metallurgical charge) and is therefore not considered further. The remaining five analyses have between 45wt% and 55wt% nominal iron, indicating a very good representation of non-ferrous metals in these analyses. Among these, lead dominates with more than 22wt% on average, followed by *c.* 12wt% tin and 6wt% copper; zinc is again present below 1wt% nominal concentration, thought to be within the geological background levels for this element. Based on Dungworth 2000 and Kearns *et al.* 2010, we can say that this crucible was likely to have been used for melting a normal tin bronze with relatively low levels of lead.

Crucible 4 (Fig. 3.43) is nearly complete (E84:9000) and there are four analyses, which are dominated by lead—nominally over 85wt% lead, suggesting that the crucible was used to melt lead metal. The only other process that would produce a vitrified ceramic surface dominated by lead is cupellation (refining) of precious metals, but no precious metals were detected and there is no central depression in the vitrified surface, normally present in cupels. There is also no other evidence from Britain and Ireland for cupellation in the Bronze Age.

Fragment E84:709 stands out from the other analysed pieces through its very low nominal iron content and very high levels of copper, tin, lead and antimony (the latter not included in Table 3.6 but reported as nearly 3wt%). This composition is typical of dross, a particular type of metal-casting waste comprising mostly mixed metal oxides which form on the surface of the liquid metal during casting and often adheres to the crucible surface; its composition is consistent with the inferred low-lead tin bronze of crucibles 2 and 3. Such dross layers can detach from the crucible during burial, as appears to have happened here, and are easily recognised and hence recovered during excavation owing to their bright green copper-corrosion colours.

Some other ceramics are thought likely to be early medieval rather than Bronze Age on the basis of their form. The interpretation of the XRF data from these thin-walled vessels (Table 3.7) is more complex because a far wider range of metallurgical processes are known to have been employed by this time. In addition to metal-melting, which was demonstrably practised at Rathgall in the Bronze Age, there is the possibility that one or more refining processes for precious metals were carried out in later periods.

In an attempt to resolve the use to which the thin-walled vessels were put, they were examined by XRF. Most of the sherds that were analysed had more than one spectrum recorded, usually with rather different results (Table 3.7). This variability is not unexpected, as the distribution of metal traces on the sherds is unlikely to be uniform and several different areas will have been analysed.

Some of these sherds may be parts of metal-melting crucibles, as they appear to have been heated under reducing conditions (Table 3.5, Early medieval crucibles; Fig. 3.47). The XRF analyses of E84:7447, 6390 and 7598 suggest that tin bronze was being melted, with 7447 also having some lead and zinc present, which is not unusual for medieval copper alloys (e.g. Bayley 1991; 1992, 127–33). Considering the experimental evidence in Kearns *et al.* 2010, the zinc content in the original alloy is still likely very low, and just exaggerated in the data owing to its chemical behaviour and tendency to be strongly enriched in the vitrified surface. Most Irish copper-alloy objects that pre-date the arrival of the Vikings are tin bronzes (Craddock *et al.* 2001, 121–2).

The original XRF analyses also included data for arsenic, antimony, silver, gold and mercury. Owing to their mainly very low concentrations (in addition to the other factors mentioned above), however, it was decided to include only the silver data in Tables 3.6 and 3.7, which report silver concentrations of between one third of 1% and about 1%. Only two vessels have significantly higher values, E84:7477 (Fig. 3.47) and 1271a (Fig. 3.45), potentially representing the presence of elevated silver on these fragments. The constant appearance of silver in almost all other analyses most likely indicates that this is a background phenomenon, resulting from how the material has formed (i.e. as vitrified ceramic) and then been analysed (see above), although the use of copper smelted from argentiferous ores or recycled copper alloys contaminated with a minor amount of silver cannot be ruled out.

Both E84:7477 (Fig. 3.47) and 1271a (Fig. 3.45) belong to a group of fragments that represent small, thin-walled vessels that appear to have oxidised-fired inner surfaces, and thus are unlikely to have been used as metal-melting crucibles (Table 3.5). The elevated silver values for 7477 (probably the same vessel as fragments 6445 and 2449) and 1271a, as well as the bleached appearance and pink/purple colouration of the inner surface of 1271a and 7266 (Fig.

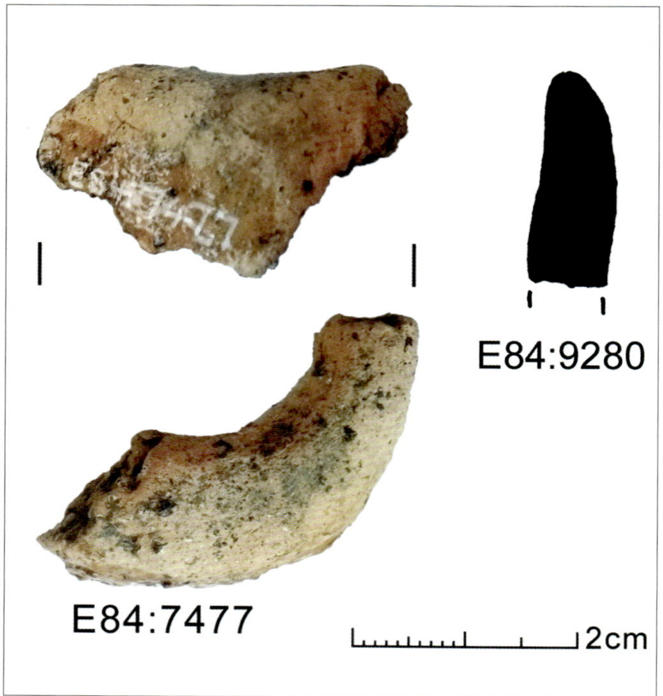

Fig. 3.47—Possible parting vessel fragment E84:7477 and crucible E84:9280.

Fig. 3.48—First-century Roman parting vessel from Chichester. Note that the orange-red fabric has a partly bleached inner surface with a pink-purplish colouration (photo: © Historic England).

3.45), which may be from the same vessel, could be indicative of their use as parting vessels. Parting involves heating thin sheets of gold/silver alloy surrounded by a 'cement' of powdered ceramic and common salt in a lidded vessel (Bayley 1991; 2008). The salt reacts with the silver, separating it from the gold, but also reacts with iron in the ceramic fabric of the vessel, imparting a characteristic bleached appearance with a pink or purplish surface layer of redeposited iron oxides (Fig. 3.48). A similar colour (quite different from the orangey reds of oxidised-fired ceramics) can also be seen in crucibles used to melt zinc-containing alloys (Tim Young, pers. comm.), though no significant amounts of zinc were detected in these crucibles. E84:7560 may also belong to this group. Arguing against the potential identification as parting vessels are the low and inconsistent levels of silver detected.

The final group of thin-walled vessels (Table 3.5, Function unclear) are unlikely to be crucible fragments as they are oxidised-fired, though none have been analysed. They could be unused crucibles, but equally could represent small-sized round vessels with a non-metallurgical function (E84:7442, 1273, 8131, 7544).

3.7.5 Discussion of the crucibles

The crucible assemblage from Rathgall represents one of the largest prehistoric collections of such artefacts from Ireland, comparable only to Dún Aonghasa, where three crucibles of similar forms were found. While three large crucibles from Rathgall are of characteristic Bronze Age form, the small crucible (E84:9000) is currently without parallels. While it was found in association with diagnostic later prehistoric pottery in a boulder-sealed pit, the location of this pit in the area of the early medieval house raises questions about the possibility of this association being secondary. If accepted as prehistoric, the identification of lead-rich residues found within the small crucible poses further questions.

As the XRF of the surface deposits of the three large crucibles demonstrates, they were used for the melting of tin bronze and can be seen as standing in a direct functional relationship to the large corpus of moulds found at Rathgall. While clearly fitting into Tylecote's (1986) general typology of crucibles (his Type J1), a great degree of variation in cross-section and rim shape can be observed between these crucibles, and even within the same object. Typically for prehistoric crucibles in general, these are handmade, rough vessels which were possibly made by the metalworker rather than by a specialised potter (but see discussion of pottery production on site in section 3.11). In contrast to the moulds, the crucibles from Rathgall are roughly tempered and thick-walled to meet technical requirements, but not made from specifically selected (potentially refractory) clay. As demonstrated by the evidence for relining of some of the crucibles at Rathgall, found on other sites also (Mecking and Walter 2004), crucibles were sometimes curated and reused, possibly explaining the low numbers of crucibles against the

Table 3.5—Catalogue of crucibles.

Find no.	Crucible no.	Square	Context	Illustration	Colour of ceramic	Notes
Bronze Age crucibles						
5934a–b		17/18	Pit 118		Reduced	
5997a–c		17/18	Pit 118	Figs 3.42, 3.44	Reduced	
5998	Crucible 1	17/18	Pit 118		Reduced	
6054a		17/18	Pit 118		Reduced	
6054b–d		17/18	Pit 118		Cream	
7309		G2	Pit 20			
6905		G2	Pit 20			
6901		G2	Pit 20			
6902		G2	Pit 20			
7157	Crucible 2 (tentative)	G2	Pit 20	Fig. 3.42		
6757		G2	No info.			
8394						
7155		H3	Pyre Hearth 15			
7156						
7639		E2				
7902		D2	Depr. 84			
7344	Comparable to crucible 2, but no joins and found in Areas 2 and 1	E1/E2				
7155		D/D1				
5995		52/53	In section strip			
1590		23/24	Hearth 3			
1586		23/24	Hearth 3			
1753	Crucible 3	8/16	Hearth 6	Fig. 3.42		
1752a–f		8/16	Hearth 6			
1754		8/16	Hearth 6			
9000	Crucible 4	I6	Pit 215	Figs 3.43. 3.44	Grey	
709	Crucible lining	7				
Probable Bronze Age crucible fragments or related materials						
175						
6314	Bronze waste	D2				
7623		E1/E2			Pinkish-buff	Partly vitrified
7175		D/D1			Grey, one buff surface	Rim
6913.1		D/D1			Orange-brown	Rim
1735		26			Brown	Rim
8094		B/C			Reduced, orange-buff surface	Rim, very coarse, ?relined
8094.1		B/C			Pinkish-red	Rim
5712		66			Grey/orangey-pink	? Base of crucible
Early medieval crucibles						
9280		K7		Fig. 3.47	Dark grey	Rim
7447		D8			Grey	Rim, red glassy outside
7598		D/D1			Red/cream-buff surface	Rim
800		8			Grey, buff surface	Rim
7346		D/D1			Grey	Rim
6390		D2			Pinkish-red/cream-buff	White residue inside
Early medieval vessels, some possibly used for parting						
2449		17	Pit 117		Pinkish-white	? Joins 7477
1271a		15		Fig. 3.45	Grey, pink/red inner surface	
7266		D1/D2		Fig. 3.45	Grey, pink inside with white surface	
7560		D/D1			Oxidised	Rim, ? cf. 1271a/7266
7477		D/D1		Fig. 3.47	Orange/brown all through	? Same vessel as 6445
6445		D1/D2			Orange/red	Rim
Function unclear						
1273		22			Oxidised	? Rim
7442		D/D1			Oxidised	Rim, ? vitrification
8131		B1/C1			Reduced, oxidised surface	Rim
7544		D/D1			White	Rim

Table 3.6—Analytical results for coarse, thick-walled crucibles and related materials.

Crucible no.	Find no.	Context	Copper %	Tin %	Lead %	Zinc %	Silver %	Iron %	Interpretation
1	6054a	Pit 118	0.3	0.9	1	1.6	1.4	83	Low-tin bronze?
	6054a		2.8	1.6	2	1.4	1	79	
2	7309	Pit 20	0.9	13.8	7	0.2	1	66	Tin bronze (with minor lead)
	6902		4.2	6.6	8	0.2	0.6	70	
	6901a		1.1	17.2	6	0.2	0.9	64	
	6901a		1.3	7.8	7	0.2	0.8	69	
3	1590	Hearth 3	12	20	8	0.5	0.4	48	Tin bronze (with minor lead)
	1590		6.5	7.8	28	0.8	0.4	46	
	1590		6.5	7.8	28	0.8	0.4	46	
	1590*		7.3	20.5	14	0.7	0.8	44	
	1752	Hearth 6	1.1	1.2	1.2	1.5	0.9	83	
	1752		0.5	6	29	1	0.9	55	
	1753		4.7	16.4	19	0.5	0.6	50	
4	9000*	Pit 215	0.3	0.1	85	0.2	0.1	12	Lead
	9000*		0.1	0.1	89	0.1	0.1	9.8	
	9000*		0.2	0.1	96	0	0	3.7	
	9000*		0.3	0.1	99	0.1	0	0.6	
Crucible fragment?	8094	B1/C1	0.2	0.9	0.5	1.6	0.3	99	No metallurgical use
Dross	709	Sq. 7	56	12.2	26	0.1	0.9	0.2	Fragment of lining with Cu alloy
Dross	709		11.6	35	48	0.1	1	0.7	
Waste metal	175*		45	50.9	1	<0.01	0.3	1	Tin bronze

*Re-analysed in 2020.

large number of casting episodes represented in the mould corpus from Rathgall. The apparent largely differential treatment of the crucibles in deposition (see above) likewise points to this, with crucibles often not discarded with moulds but deposited separately.

The second group of small and thin-walled vessels found at Rathgall were fragmentary, but some had also been used for melting tin bronze. The remainder were more problematic, with some showing no evidence of any metallurgical use while others may have had a function in precious metalworking, possibly as parting vessels. While some of them are clearly from disturbed contexts and thus likely to derive from later periods of activity, some of them came from the lower levels of the occupation materials, e.g. the charcoal-rich deposits that contained large numbers of Bronze Age moulds in Area 2. This suggests either unrecognised disturbances to quite a depth or the use of small and thin-walled crucibles or vessels, otherwise unknown from the Bronze Age in Britain and Ireland, alongside the larger Tylecote J1 forms. Both those vessels identified as possible parting vessels, as well as crucible 4, may have been used for precious metalworking, though the XRF data for this are not strong. Typologically they find parallels in the early medieval period, and their ambiguous contexts at Rathgall are suggestive of disturbance or redeposition in the medieval period. This scenario may be considered a possibility for crucible 4, as although it was found together with ceramic sherds, a Late Bronze Age glass bead and some flints, it was within the interior of the medieval house—and no parallels for this vessel form are known from the Insular Bronze Age.

A further crucible is represented in the assemblage of the Iron Age iron-working hearth, p. 298.

3.8 CLAY CASTING MOULDS

Barry Raftery, Katharina Becker and Joanne Gaffrey

One of the striking aspects of Rathgall is the large number of clay mould fragments recovered in the course of the excavation: 1,100 lots of moulds, which in some cases consist of several fragments, were assigned find numbers. The vast majority of fragments came to light within the principal hillfort defences (i.e. in the area within Rampart 2), and a further 40 fragments were found in the area of Bronze Age activity outside the fort in the south. Concentrations of moulds within Rampart 2, the 'metalworking zones' (Fig. 3.49), may represent the actual locations of metalworking activities, but disturbance by later activity is also a clear factor in the distribution of the material, reflected in a high degree of fragmentation. The distribution of the mould fragments that are thought to belong to mould units is to an

Table 3.7—Analytical results for thin-walled crucibles and vessels.

Find no	Copper	Tin	Lead	Zinc	Silver	Iron	Notes and interpretation
7598	7.1	1.9	1.4	1.9	0.5	78	Tin bronze melting
7447	4.6	38.0	16.8	7.2	0.1	30	Tin bronze melting
7447	5.0	18.4	9.9	1.3	1.3	53	Tin bronze melting
7447*							No significant metal traces
7477	0.1	6.5	0.3	1.1	4.2	60	?
7477*	0.2	0.4	0.8	1.5	2.2	>80	1 of 4 new analyses detected silver
7266	1.8	2.0	0.7	0.7	0.7	84	?
7266	1.8	1.5	0.7	0.8	0.6	87	?
7266*							No significant metal traces
1271a	3.3	3.2	1.6	1.0	1.9	75	?
1271a*	3.8	0.9	2..4	1.1	1.1	80	?
1271a*	1.5	4.6	1.8	0.6	6.7	55	?
6390	12.0	2.2	0.6	0.5	0.7	75	Tin bronze melting

Note: Most of the crucbles were analysed in 2016. Those finds marked * were re-analysed in 2020.

extent the result of prehistoric activity, as well as later disturbance processes—both factors difficult to untangle (see section 3.9).

3.8.1 Casting technology

The assemblage consists of fragments of bivalve clay moulds, as characteristic of the later part of the Bronze Age and evidenced on a number of sites in Ireland (e.g. Ó Faoláin 2004; Coghlan and Raftery 1961; Collins 1970). The complex method of metalworking in the later Bronze Age in Ireland has been described in detail by Ó Faoláin (2004), who discussed the processes of clay preparation, mould fabrication, drying and firing, mould preheating, pouring position and pouring. As he noted, copper and tin (generally seen as from Cornwall in south-west England, though Brittany is, of course, a possibility) were of primary importance. Local charcoal, selected clays (not all of which were, of necessity, immediately local), specialist tools and the equipment to ensure and maintain the required heat (around 1100°/1200°C) for melting the ores and to finish off the fresh castings were all required. Bellows were needed, but no tuyères were recognised in the corpus of ceramics. Edged tools—whether weapons such as swords, or tools such as axes—were in need of sharpening, but apart from the small chisel (E84:8344; Fig. 3.31), perhaps the small, socketed gouge (E84:3300; Fig. 3.39) and two polishing or burnishing stones from the outer settlement, which may also have been used in the processing of precious metal, no metalworking tools have been recognised on the site. It seems clear that the creation of a single bronze artefact was a meticulous, complex and time-consuming process requiring a properly organised workshop, a series of specialist tools and an extensive range of raw materials. While it is impossible to speculate about the duration or frequency of the casting activity on the site, many episodes are indicated by the large number of moulds and the range of objects.

The mould assemblage from Rathgall gives us glimpses of these various steps of production. The matrices, where well preserved, are grey or white-grey, a result of the reducing environment created by the casting process. The colour of the mould fabrics varied considerably, ranging from grey and buff to orange, reflecting variability in the conditions of their firing and the casting process. So, for example, mould fragments found concentrated in Sqs 51 and 52 (Metalworking Zone 1) differed from those elsewhere, as they were for the most part a bright brick or orange colour, reflective of different firing conditions.

Clay casting moulds such as those at Rathgall consist of an inner bivalve mould and an outer wrap. The valves were made of fine clay that was formed around a wooden template

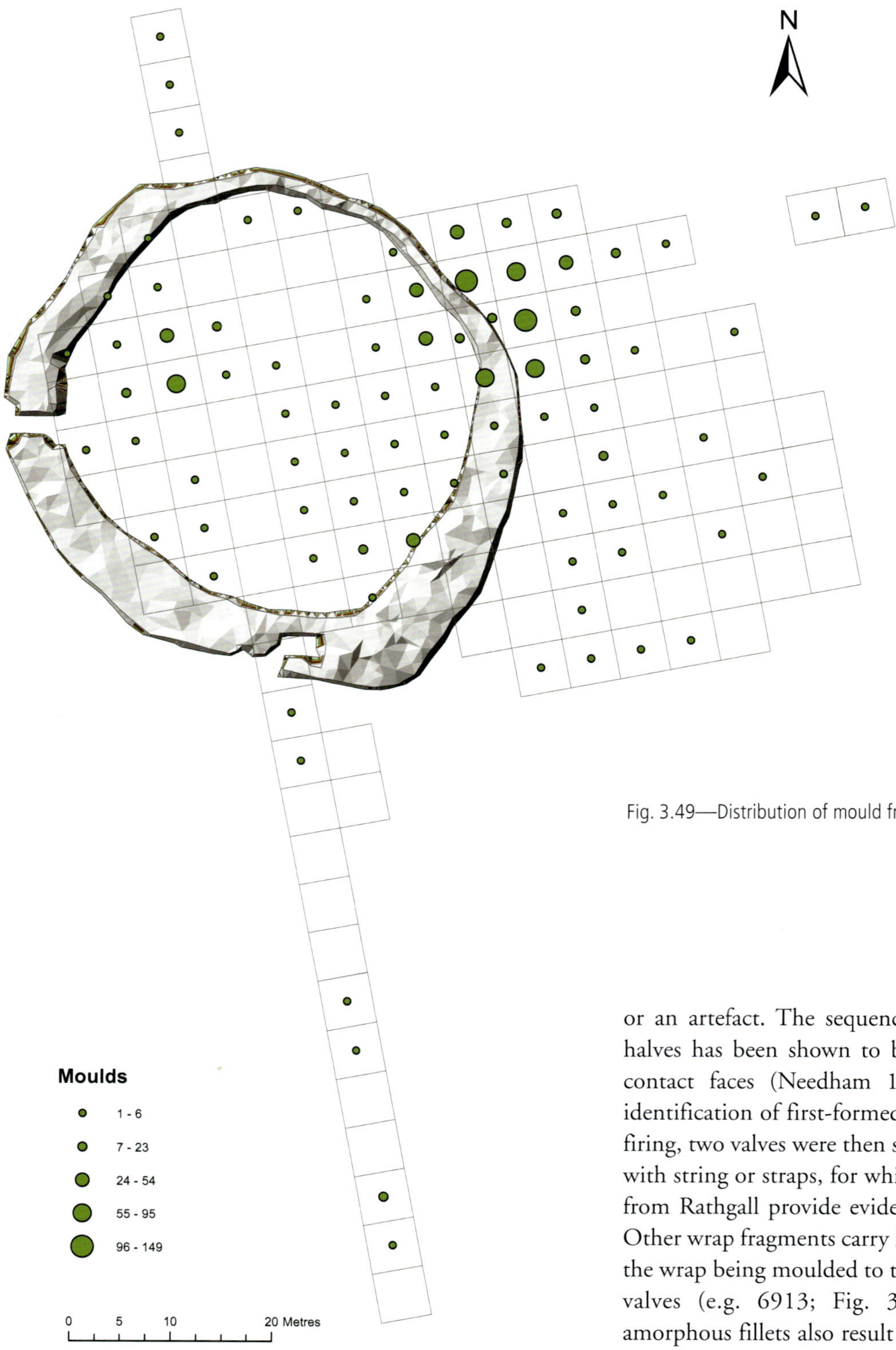

Fig. 3.49—Distribution of mould fragments.

or an artefact. The sequence of the creation of these two halves has been shown to be reflected in the angle of the contact faces (Needham 1980), allowing the occasional identification of first-formed or second-formed valves. After firing, two valves were then secured to each other by binding with string or straps, for which a number of wrap fragments from Rathgall provide evidence (e.g. E100:063; Fig. 3.50). Other wrap fragments carry intervalve ridges that result from the wrap being moulded to the outside of the join of the two valves (e.g. 6913; Fig. 3.50). Occasionally occurring amorphous fillets also result from the moulding of the wrap onto the inner valves. The wraps are, as a general characteristic, made of clay of a coarser texture, achieved in Rathgall by being tempered with ground granite.

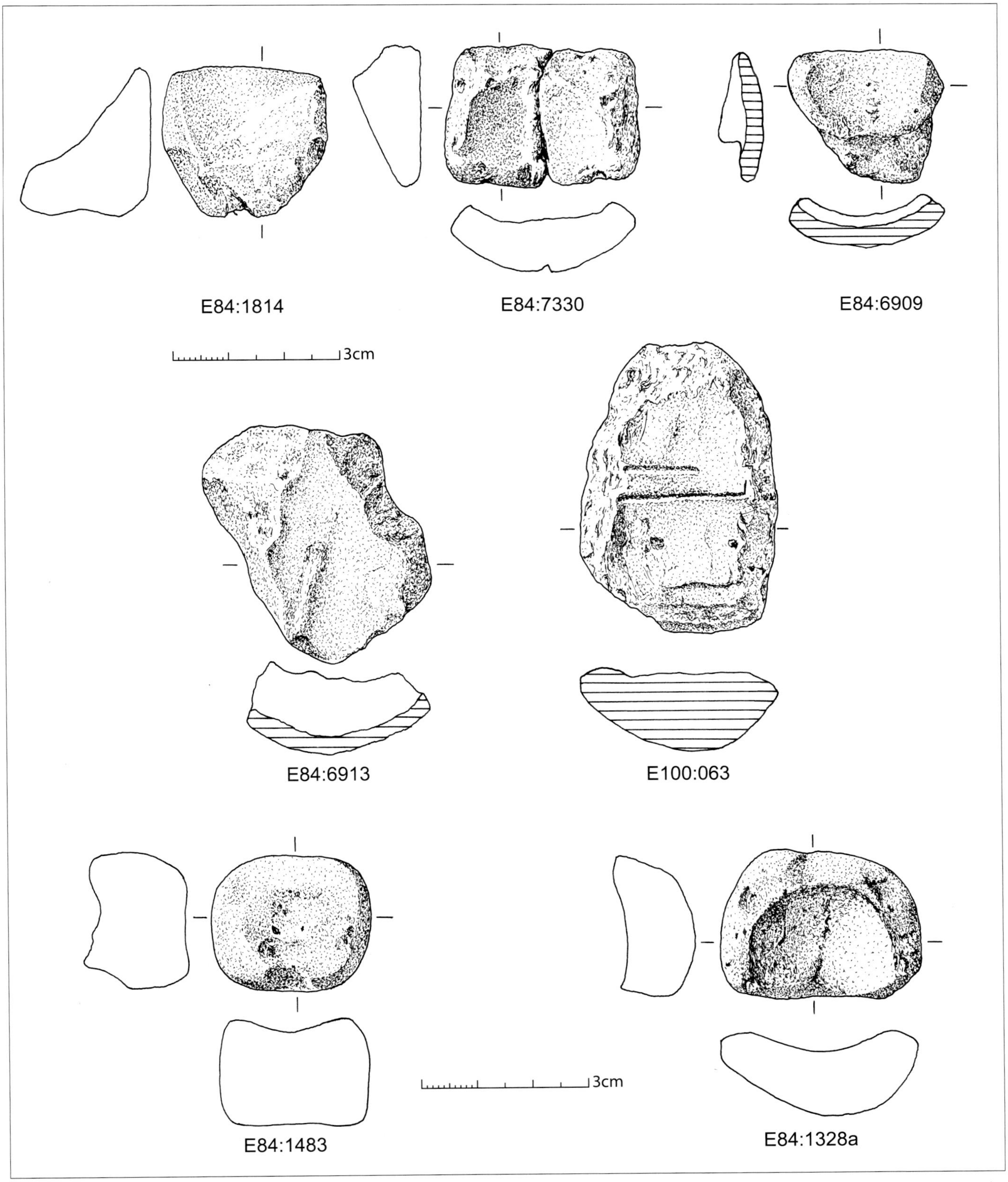

Fig. 3.50—Pouring gate fragments (E84:1814, 7330, 6909), intervalve ridge (E84:6913), binding marks (E100:063) and casting cores (E84:1483, 1328a) (scale 1:1).

The two-piece but univalve pin moulds represent a variation of this technique, as the mould for the shank is formed by piercing an existing pin through a clay core before impressing the underside of the pin into the top of the mould (Fig. 3.80). A separate cap provides the matrix for the top of the pin head. These two elements were then held in place by an outer wrap. This is the standard technique observed elsewhere (e.g. at Aubervilliers; Melin 2016), though bivalve clay moulds for pin shanks are thought to have been found at Dún Aonghasa (O'Carroll 2012a, 8.19, 8.24–25) and Navan Fort (Waterman 1997). At Rathgall there is a possibility that more than one pin mould may have been joined by an outer wrap found on pin mould B (E84:5107) and fragment E84:7102, perhaps indicating the casting of several pins in one casting episode, as evidenced on moulds found in a contemporary context at Aubervilliers, Seine-Saint-Denis, France (Mélin 2016), and Cladh Hallam, Outer Hebrides, Scotland (T. Cowie, pers. comm.)—a practice that can be traced into the Iron Age, with several brooches at Bibracte (Beck *et al.* 1982–3), for example, being cast in a comparable arrangement.

Fig. 3.51—Mould gate fragments.

A very large fragment of a sword or, less likely, a spearhead mould (E100:64; Figs 3.53 and 3.55) was discovered downslope to the south of the site. The object had broken along its length, revealing a void that provides clear evidence for the former presence of a longitudinally inserted strengthening rod. Such have been demonstrated elsewhere in Ireland, particularly on sword moulds, including examples from Lough Eskragh, Co. Tyrone, Whitepark Bay, Co. Antrim (Collins 1970, 34–6), and Boho, Co. Fermanagh (Hodges 1954, 62–4; Coghlan and Raftery 1961; Tylecote 1987, 89), among others. A large fragment of such a mould was found at Rush, Co. Meath, in a deposit of burnt mound material. The phasing of the site provides a *terminus post quem* of 975–955 cal. BC for the mould fragment (Emmet Byrne, pers. comm.). While a number of moulds at Rathgall were probably for the casting of large blades or swords, E100:64 is the only example with evidence for the use of such a strengthening feature and it may be pertinent that this was found outside the main focus of casting activity. A number of gates, allowing for the molten metal to be poured into the mould, have been identified within the assemblage (Table 3.8; Figs 3.50–3.51). Both integrated (e.g. E84:3760) and separately fashioned gates are evidenced at Rathgall. The use of the latter is implied by the flat shape of some mould tops, for example E84:7221 or 8706 (Fig. 3.51) and 7492. Fragment 7221 appears to be a part of an integrated gate, as indicated by the contact face present on the fragment, but a seat for a separate actual gate also appears to be provided at its top.

For the casting of socketed implements, clay cores were carefully positioned within the mould to create the void of the socket. A minimum of nineteen cores for the casting of socketed objects have been identified within the assemblage (Table 3.9; Figs 3.50 and 3.52). A number of these (e.g. E84:4350, 1462, 4778, 6903, 9347 (not illustrated)) have vertical seams on either narrow end which may be the result of their having been fashioned in core moulds of, for

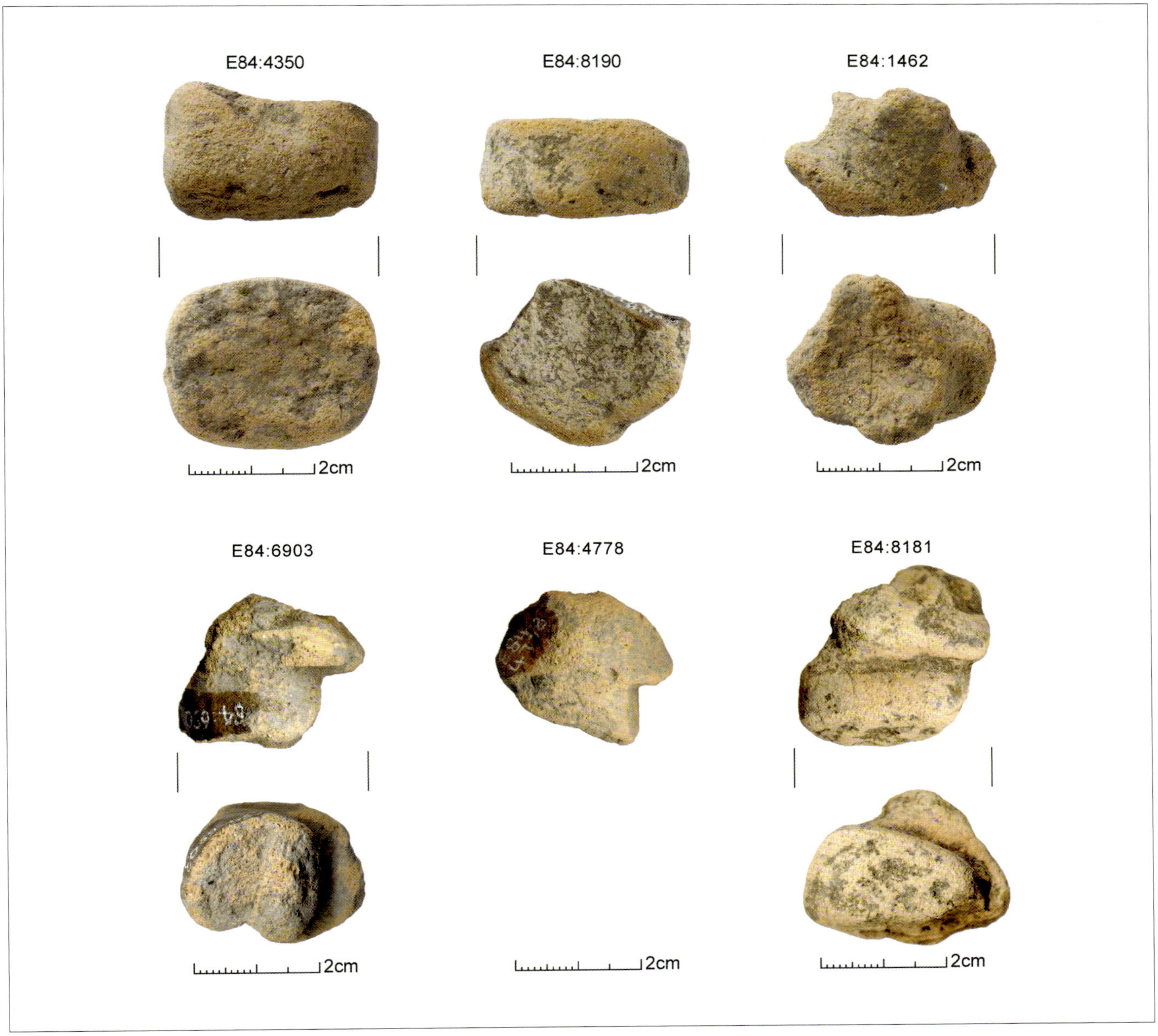

Fig. 3.52—Core fragments.

example, wood or bronze. Some fragments also retain part of the material that would have been positioned on top of the gate to seat the core (cf. E84:4778, 6903, 8181 (Fig. 3.52), 9347).

The cores are mostly for the casting of subcircular to oval sockets or apertures and are mostly straight-sided; only one possible core with a lateral expansion appears to represent the casting of a shouldered object (E84:1462). The cores of subcircular shape and with an estimated diameter of about 3cm are likely to have been for the casting of socketed axes (e.g. E84:4350). The surviving flat side of one of the cores (E84:4778) suggests the casting of an implement of rectangular cross-section, such as, for example, a hammer like that known from the Bishopsland hoard (Eogan 1983, no. 16, 16–38). Other, small-sized core fragments may have been for the casting of chisels or gouges or hammers. While most core fragments represent only short portions of a formerly longer core, two flat and circular clay discs

(E84:8190, 8189; Fig. 3.52) are double concave, apparently catering for the casting of a circular shallow void. Small core fragments for the casting of tongue-shaped chapes, which are also represented by their valves, are discussed below.

Different means of rivet-hole provision can be observed within the assemblage on a possible tool hafting plate, a possible sword haft and a possible sickle or knife haft. Knife haft E84:3606 shows impressions within its matrix into which presumably charcoal or wooden placeholders were inserted to provide for the creation of the rivet hole in the casting process. A placeholder made of fired clay seems to have been integrated into the actual matrix in the case of E84:3606, where an abraded circular feature is still noticeably raised above the matrix (Fig. 3.58). In contrast, small ring-shaped depressions, stamped into the matrix of the little straps or plaques (Fig. 3.81), appear to provide for the casting of a small, circular depression in the surface of the object that would mark the location of the small rivet holes, which could be perforated or drilled through after casting (e.g. E84:7884, 3425). The casting of these little tabs themselves may suggest that sheet metalworking was also taking place at Rathgall.

3.8.2 The objects cast at Rathgall

The range of objects cast at Rathgall includes weapons, tools and personal ornaments, as well as what may have been sheet-metal vessels. The mould fragments vary in size, ranging from little more than amorphous crumbs of baked clay to sizeable pieces where the nature of the original object cast can be deduced with some confidence. The quite wide range of artefact types that can be identified add significantly to our knowledge of Late Bronze Age material culture by providing evidence for object forms that did not survive in the artefact record.

In addition to the more recognisable fragments discussed or listed below, the full database of mould fragments with

Table 3.8—Mould gate fragments recovered at Rathgall.

Sq. no.	Artefact no.	Feature/context no.	Figure
9	2316	Black fill of Ring-ditch 1	
	2319	Black fill of Ring-ditch 1	
20	6112	In black area under wall collapse	
52	5069	In brown material	
G2	7330	Pit 20	Fig. 3.50
	7332		
	7335		
	7221		Fig. 3.51
B1	1814	In dark occupation layer—very black, N	Fig. 3.50
B5	9227a	In black burnt material of Hearth 14	
B/C	8114	In black under wall, lower levels	
C1	3947	In dark black occupation layer, SW	
	3950	In dark black occupation layer, SW	
	3834	In dark brown/black occupation layer, SW	
	3714	In black occupation layer, SW	
	3760	In dark black occupation layer	Fig. 3.51
	2980	In dark brown soil, NW	
	4356	Extreme SW in black occupation level among cobblestones	
D/D1	7043	In black charcoal-filled habitation area	
	6909	In black charcoal area	Fig. 3.50
	6993	In black charcoal habitation area	
	7492	In black material, lowest levels	
E2	7147	In dark brown, lumpy material	
Y3	8706	In grey patch on yellow at northern end of cutting	Fig. 3.51

Table 3.9—Casting cores.

E84:	Context	Notes	Dimensions of original core as measured or estimated	Fig.
8190	E1, in section strip	flat, irregular circular, double concave	central thickness of 2mm, diameter est. 25mm	3.52
4350	C1, extreme SW in black occupation level among cobblestones	possible core fragment	29mm x 22mm or 25.5 x 32.5, max. surviving height 20mm	3.52
1462	8/2, black fill of Ring-ditch 1	irregular, longitudinal ridge, concave profile and expanding	height 8mm	3.52
1483	7/8 almost on base of Ring-ditch 1 under baulk	subrectangular/oval in plan	24 x 28mm, 20mm thickness	3.50
4778	29, shallow part of Ring-ditch 1, in black fill	fragment of core of rectangular or subrectangular cross-section, top with seat for valve; intervalve ridge		3.52
6903	G2, black area with stones in SE, Pit 20?	subcircular/heart-shaped, intervalve ridge, top with seat for valves	>24mm diameter	3.52
8181	E1, in section strip	oval/subrectangular, top with seat for valves	c. 27 x 20mm	3.52
9347	X11, Pit 243	subcircular, excess material on top providing seat for valves, intervalve ridge	c. 22 x 19m	
3772	C1, in dark black occupation material, SW	round plan, conical section, dished top		
1721	B1, near cobbling and Hearth 7	possible core, circular plan with probably regular shape, possible fabric impression	c. 40mm	
8189	E1, in section strip	possible core fragment		
9303	X11, Pit 244, close to Pit 243	core fragment with seat for top of valves		
9521	K5	possible core fragment		
6904	G2, black area with stones in SE, Pit 20?	possible core fragment		
2493	9/3, in grey silting in lower levels of Ring-ditch 1	possible core fragment		
4217	20, in dark brown over ditch	possible core fragment		
4488	17/18, in sticky grey semicircle around the bottom edge of Pit 118	possible core fragment		
6428	F1, in brown	possible core fragment		
1328a	7/8, from brown, in baulk	possible core fragment		3.50

individual fragment descriptions forms part of the archive. The vast majority of the moulds were found in the E84 excavation and in these cases the 'E84:' prefix has been omitted from the find numbers in the catalogue below. Those objects from the E100 excavation will retain their prefix.

Bladed implements

A number of moulds appear to have been for the casting of blades of lozenge or lenticular cross-section of various widths, suggesting the presence of swords or knives/rapiers (Fig. 3.53; Tables 3.10 and 3.11). The impression that some of the narrow blades represent rapiers, in contrast to some of the wider ones representing swords, is possibly corroborated by the evidence for a possible hafting plate.

Such a possible rapier is represented by mould fragment 2283 (Fig. 3.54), which has a very narrow (24mm narrowing to 16mm) lozenge-shaped cross-section (Fig. 3.54). Similarly lozenge-sectioned blades are represented in blades B and C (Table 3.10). These fragments, while unlikely to be from the same object, were found primarily in the D cuttings and eastern Ring-ditch 1 fill (Sqs 7, 8 and 22). It is possible that the slightly more substantial blade B and that represented by

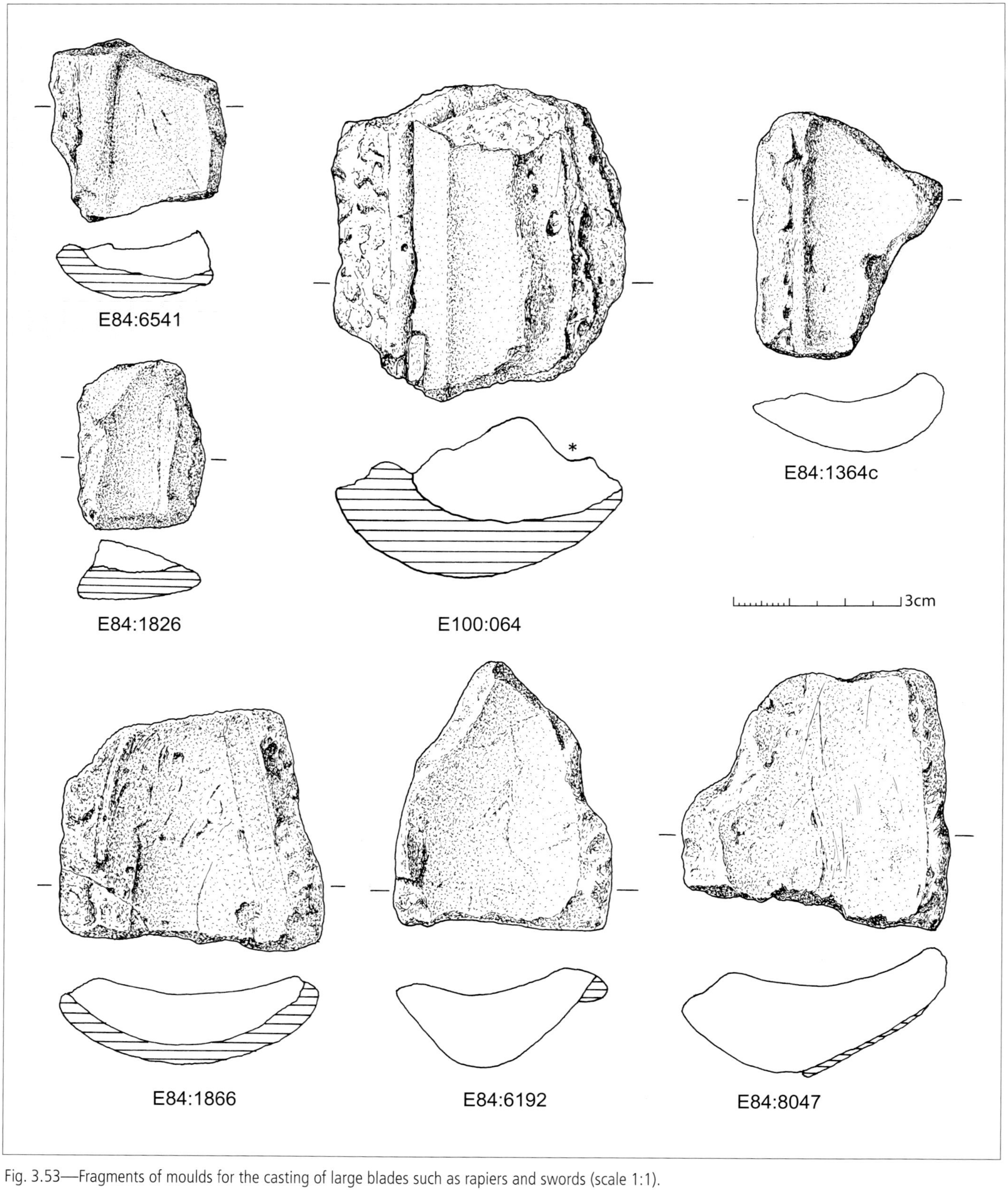

Fig. 3.53—Fragments of moulds for the casting of large blades such as rapiers and swords (scale 1:1).

fragment E100:64 (Figs 3.53 and 3.55) may have been for the casting of early Ballintober-type swords, as these can also have lozenge-shaped cross-sections (Eogan 1965, Class 1; Burgess and Colquhoun 1988, nos 50–57). Two fragments, E84:2434 and 2315 (Fig. 3.56), may indicate the casting of a very narrow and thin blade; fragment 1364c (Fig. 3.53), while representing a thicker blade of lenticular section, also seems to have been for the casting of a very narrow blade. Rapiers of Group IV have flattened or rounded cross-sections, while lozenge-shaped sections are found on those of Group II (Burgess 1968a, fig. 1; Burgess and Gerloff 1981). One matrix has provision for a rivet hole at a substantial distance from the outer edge of a very thin hafting plate. This could conceivably be the hafting plate of a rapier (cf. Raftery 2004, 88) (Fig. 3.58), although the mould may also be understood as representing part of the shoulder of a sword, examples of which at times show a similar curvature (e.g. Wilburton swords; Burgess 1968a, fig. 9.1–4). Neither of these possibilities are entirely convincing, and perhaps the unique example of the Taplow spearhead with its mock rivets—one of a small group of Irish and British rapier-shaped spearheads (Davis 2015) and dated to the Penard phase (Needham *et al.* 1997, 87, DoB 14)—may offer a better explanation.

Fig. 3.54—Possible rapier mould fragment E84:2283 (scale 1:1).

Fig. 3.55—Possible sword mould fragment E100:64 (photo: John Sunderland).

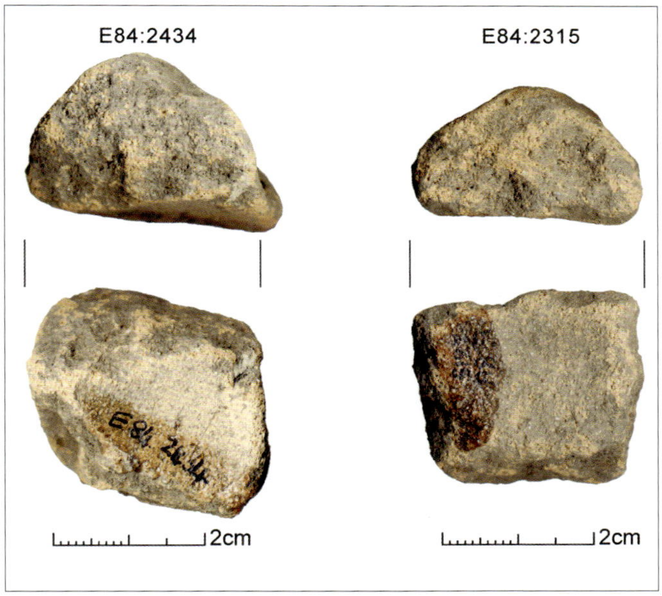

Fig. 3.56—Possible rapier blade mould fragments (scale 1:1).

Three other groups of mould fragments appear to represent wider blades of lenticular section that could represent swords (Table 3.10). Mould groups F–H are flat to concave and represent blade widths ranging from 21mm to about 40mm. The largest group of mould fragments (sword blade H) exhibits a great degree of variation in cross-sections and a maximum width of about 50mm and may represent a leaf-shaped sword. The notion that this relatively large group of fragments represents one mould is supported by the focus of their distribution in Sqs B1 and C1, with one fragment in

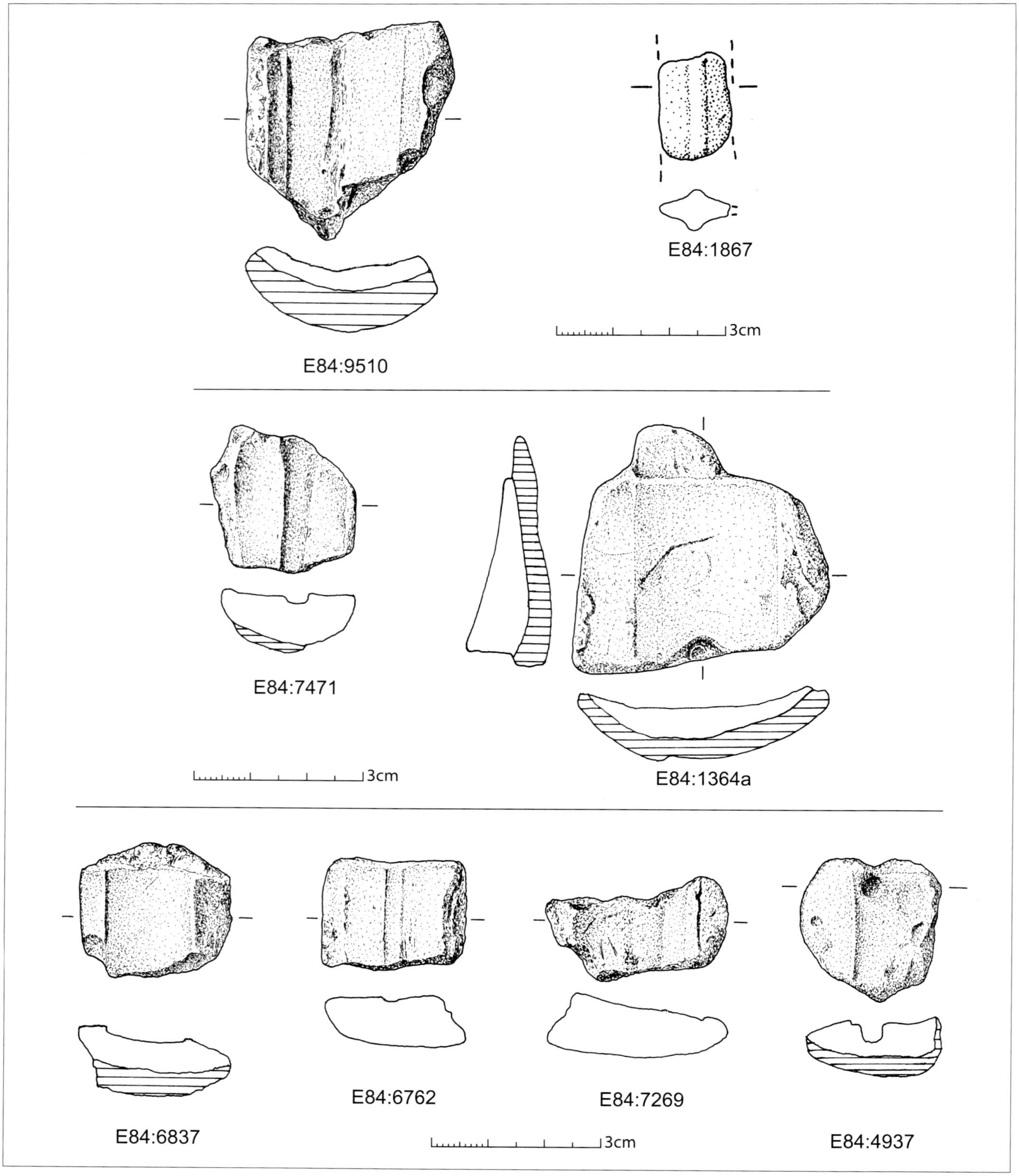

Fig. 3.57—Mould fragments: possible chape (9510), chape core (1867), possible sickle blade (7471), sickle haft (1364a), knife blades (6837, 6762, 7269) and possible knife haft (4937) (scale 1:1).

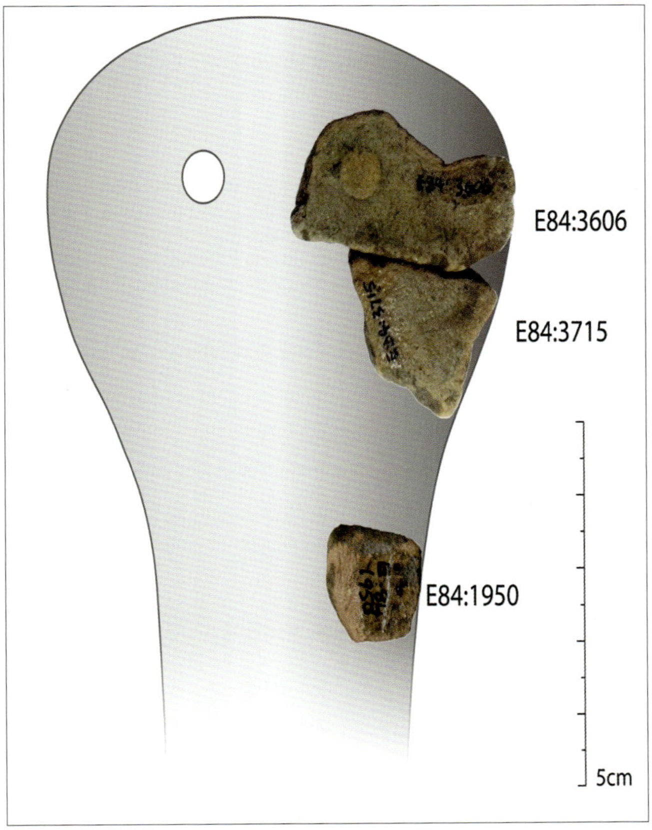

Fig. 3.58—Possible hafting plate mould fragments and indication of location on schematic of object type (scale 1:1).

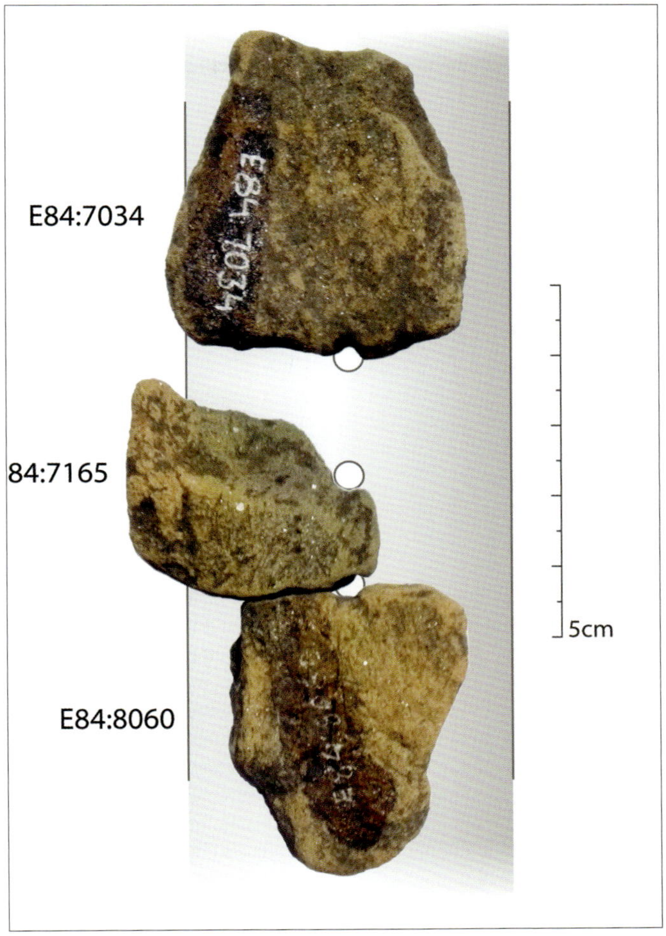

Fig. 3.59—Possible hafting plate mould fragments and indication of location on schematic of object type (scale 1:1).

the fill of the adjacent ditch in Sq. 8.

A second hafting plate is represented within the range of moulds from the site (Table 3.11): three fragments represent a wide, possibly parallel-sided and probably rather flat hilt, with three rivet holes arranged centrally at distances of about 11mm (Fig. 3.59). This is an object for which it is difficult to find parallels. While hafting plates of wide and parallel-sided shape are found on early swords of Ballintober form, rivet holes on those are arranged in pairs. Central positioning of rivet holes in sets of two or three can be found on the early flange-hilted swords of Eogan's Class 2, but a flange is demonstrably not present on the example from Rathgall, with its flat matrix. It is conceivable that this sword—as far as its handle shape can be deduced from the heavily abraded mould—may stand at the transition of both forms, but the fragmentary nature of the object makes certainty impossible.

Early flange-hilted swords (Classes 2 and 3) emerge in Britain in the Wilburton phase. While not known from associations in Ireland, Group IV rapiers, characteristic of the Penard phase in Britain, were suggested by Eogan to still be in use during this phase (Herity and Eogan 1977, 183) as spearheads with protected openings (see below), part of the British Wallington/Penard phase (Burgess and Gerloff 1981, 108; Needham 2017).

Chapes

A group of moulds for the casting of tongue-shaped chapes, as well as the corresponding cores, were found on the site (Table 3.12). While no direct fits exist within the group, some tentative links have been identified between a number of fragments, suggesting the presence of more than three valves and indicating that at least two chapes had been cast here on site (Figs 3.60–3.64). The discrete clustering of the valve groups in two locations—Metalworking Zone 2 and around Sq. 52—support this. The core fragments (Figs 3.64 and 3.57) are loosely distributed through Sqs B, C, D and E, with a fragment from the grey silt at the bottom of the ring-ditch in Sq. 9/3B.

Table 3.10—Bladed implement moulds recovered at Rathgall.

Artefact type	Blade no.	Fragment nos	Context
Flat to lozenge-shaped blade sections	A	E84:2283	Post-holes in NE corner of hearth
	B	E84:7270	Sq. D/D1 in lowest levels of black charcoal area
	C	E84:6541; 1222; 1275	Sq. D in black charcoal area (6541); Sq. 7 in sandy colourec (1222); Sq. 22, upper level of Ring-ditch 1 (1275) A small group of non-joining fragments, likely to represent the same mould for the casting of a blade with flat lozenge section.
	D	E100:64	Sq. Z2:g, in grey fill of Depression III, near large boulder
	E	E84:2434, 2315	Sq. 9, black fill of Ring-ditch 1
Lenticular-sectioned blades	F	E84:1364c	Sq. 7, black/brown fill of Ring-ditch 1
	G	E84:1866; 2359	Sq. B1, black layer immediately outside wall (1866); Sq. 9/3 cobbling in N of upper fill of Ring-ditch 1 (2359)
	H	This is a large group of sword mould fragments which may all be part of the same or very similar moulds. They are for the casting of a lenticular blade. The make-up of the mould itself is distinct, with a very thick inner valve and relatively thin wrap. The cross-sections represented in the fragments vary from flat lentoid to deeply dished and widths also vary, with large fragments such as 1863 having a maximum width of 53mm and 2277 representing the blade near its tip. While fragments 1863a and 1863b as well as 1813, 2829 and 3607 join, the rest of the fragments are considered part of the same mould based on the characteristic make-up of the mould. The tight spatial clustering of these fragments in the B1 and C1 square is encouraging.	
		E84:6192	B1, sandy soil immediately under wall
		E84:4057	
		E84:2277	3, grey-black upper fill of Ring-ditch 1 in NE corner in extrer W of square
		E84:8047	B1, under wall
		E84:1813	B1, in dark occupation layer, very black
		E84:2829	C1, from brown, almost black, soil, SW near wall
		E84:3607	C1, in dark brown/black occupation layer, SW
		E84:1630	B1, dark brown soil surrounding and covering stone paving area of removed wall
		E84:3523	C1, dark black occupation layer, SW
		E84:1863a,b	8, Hearth 4
		E84:1813	B1, in dark occupation layer, very black
		E84:3607	C1, in dark brown/black occupation layer, SW
		E84:2378	8, post-hole in SW corner of Hearth 4
		E84:2377	9, post-hole in SW corner of Hearth 4
	Blade I	E84:7166	D/D1, in black charcoal habitation area
		E84:1908	35, among stones
		E84:7144	D/D1, in black charcoal habitation area
		E84:7167	D/D1, in black charcoal habitation area
	Blade J (possible)	E84:8180 and 7233	E1 and D/D1, lowest levels of black
	Other sword blade mould fragments	1826	B1
		275a	15
		1629	B1
		6123	20/21
		1876	B1
		3523	C1

es	Figure
nge-shaped blade with a thickness of 10mm and a width of 24mm (max.), tapering to a thickness of 8mm and width of 16mm over the nt length of 39mm. Width represents half the width of the blade.	Fig. 3.54
nge- or sub-lozenge-sectioned blade, more than 7mm thick, with straight edge.	
	Fig. 3.53
e clay mould, fractured along its length; tubular hollow for the splint visible. For the casting of a lozenge-sectioned sword or—less likely—aight-edged spearhead blade.	Figs 3.53, 3.55
very narrow blade.	Fig. 3.56
cular-sectioned blade with convex outline and an estimated width of 25mm and thickness of 8mm.	Fig. 3.53
e tip and part of lenticular-sectioned blade. Width of matrix tapers from 28mm to 23mm over a length of 45mm.	Fig. 3.53
	Fig. 3.53
	Fig. 3.53
	Fig. 3.53

Table 3.10 (cont.)—Bladed implement moulds recovered at Rathgall.

Artefact type	Blade no.	Fragment nos	Context	Notes	Figure
Other sword blade mould fragments (cont.)		3523	C1		
		6663	F1		
		1829	B2		
		2957	B1		
		4051	B1/C1		
Possible sword mould fragments		1769	B1		
		3294	C1		
		3526	C1		
		4002	B1/C1		
		7038	D/D1		
		1628	B1		
		2359	9/3		
		4089	C1/B1		
		7585	E3		
		7358	D		
		6671	E2		
		1309	8		
		899	8, Hearth 6		
		6387	D1		
		7231	D/D1		
		6686	D/D1		
		6699	E1		
		1457a	9/3		
		2510	35, Pit 5		
		4353	C1		
		8073	C1		

Table 3.11—Hafting plates.

Artefact type	Artefact no.	Context	Note
Hafting plate 1	3606	Sq. C1, in dark brown/black occupation layer, SW	The matrix is flat with a slight lip at one edge, representing a very narrow contact face. This is for the casting of a very thin, blade-like object. At one end there is within the grey matrix the orange remains of an abraded provision for a rivet hole 7mm wide, suggesting that this was the very flat haft of an object. Assuming that this was centrally placed (double?), this would mean that the haft was 4.4cm wide. Fig. 3.58.
	3715	Sq. C1, in black occupation layer, SW	
	1950	Sq. 7, possible hearth (Hearth 5)	
Hafting plate 2	8060	Sq. B1, in black under wall—upper levels	Fig. 3.59
	7165	Sq. D/D1, in black charcoal habitation area	
	7034	Sq. D/D1, in black, charcoal-filled habitation area	

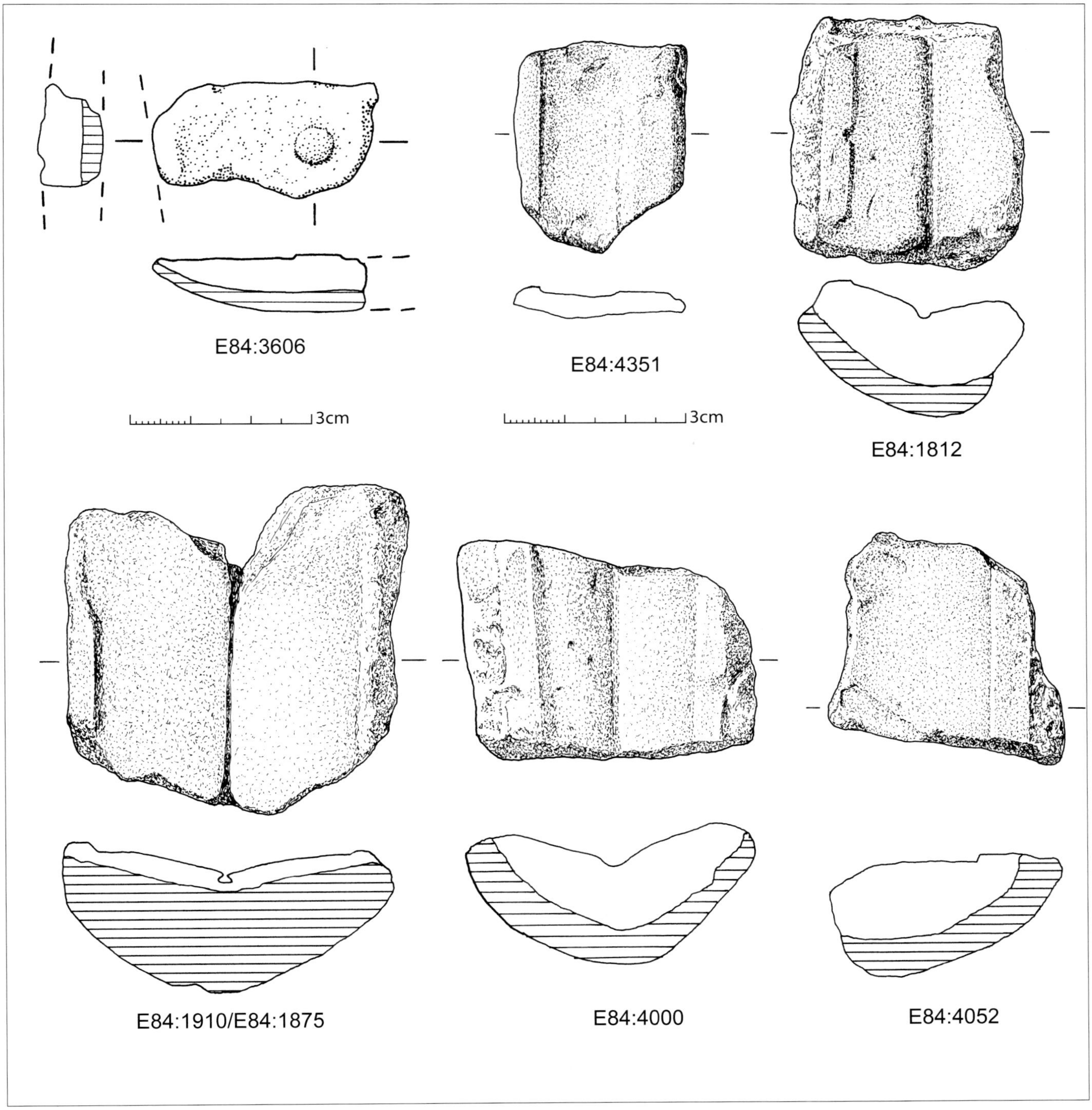

Fig. 3.60—Mould fragments representing possible hafting plate (3606) and sword chape fragments (4351, 1812, 1910/1875, 4000, 4052) (scale 1:1).

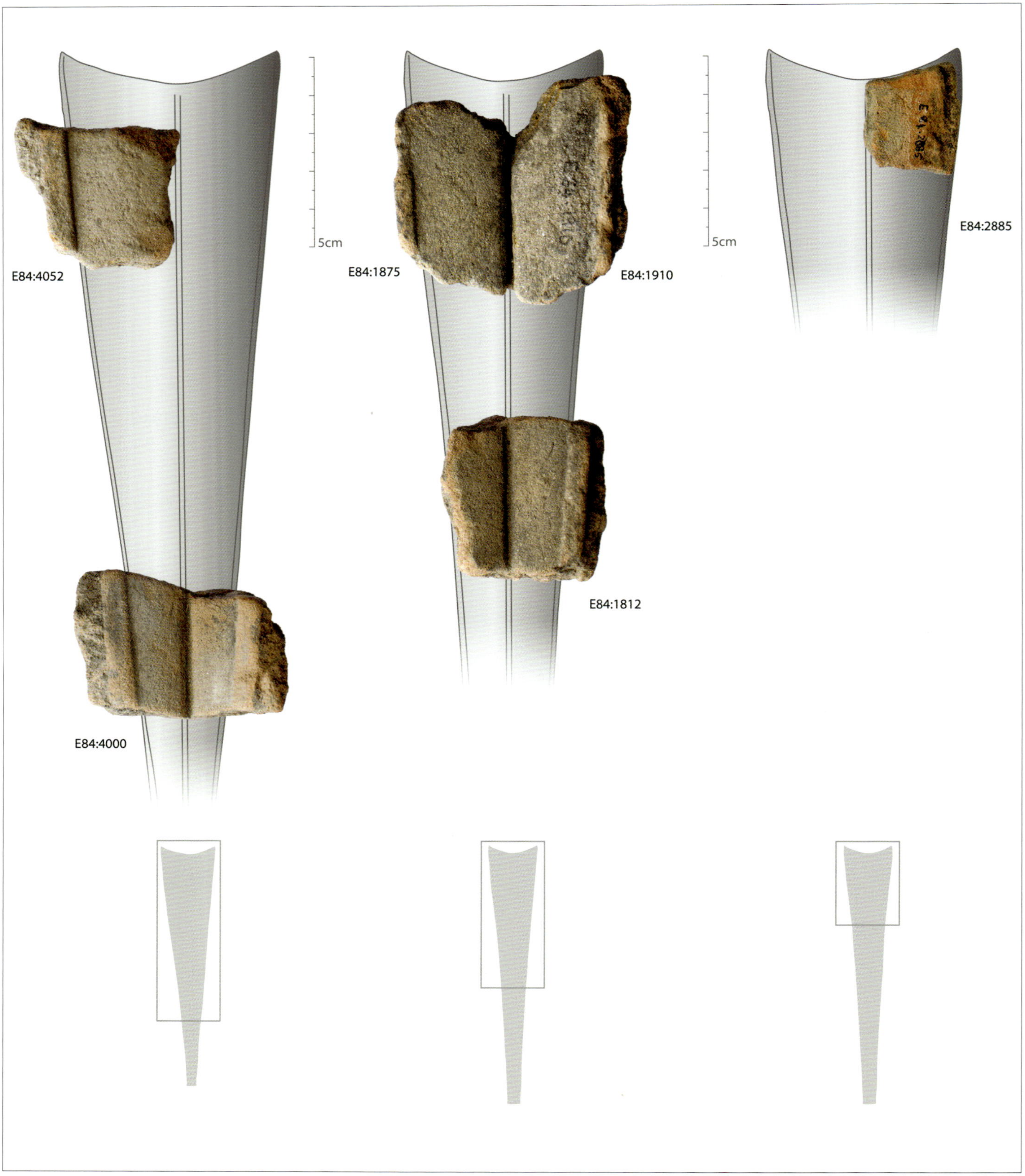

Fig. 3.61—Chape mould fragments and indication of location on schematic of object type.

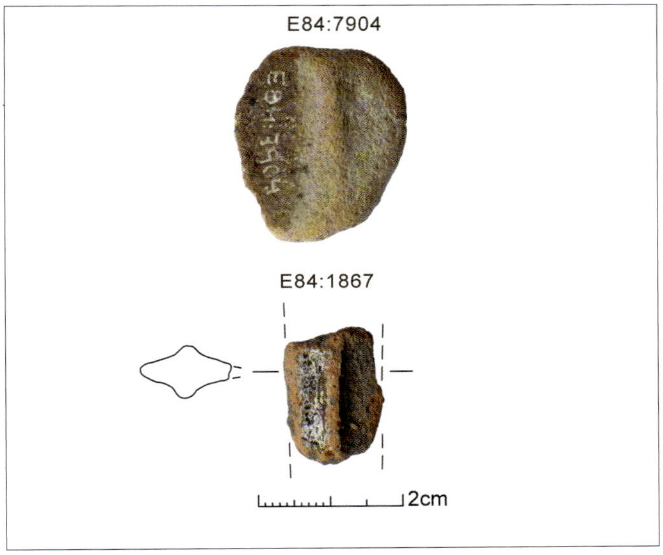

Fig. 3.62 (above left)—Chape moulds 9510 and 5357 (scale 1:1).

Fig. 3.63 (above)—Chape mould fragments 1910 and 1875.

Fig. 3.64 (left)—Chape core fragments 7904 and 1867 (scale 1:1).

Only one fragment (2885) appears to represent the proximal end of the chape and it indicates that this had a slight curvature (Fig. 3.61). This may suggest a late position within the sequence of chape development, confirming its Roscommon/Wilburton phase date (Needham 2017, fig. 16; Burgess 2012, fig. 3), which is also supported by the pronounced ribs found on many of the fragments. Extrapolating from the largest fragments constituting valves 1 and 2, a width of 3.5cm and a length of around 15cm would appear to be a realistic estimate of the dimensions of the finished object.

Prior to this find from Rathgall, the only secure example of a lozenge-sectioned chape from Ireland came from the County Roscommon hoard (Eogan 1965, 169). A mould fragment comparable to those identified here as possibly for the casting of tongue-shaped chapes was found at Ballylegan, Co. Tipperary (Becker 2009), where it was thought to be for the casting of a knife. It was originally thought that the Rathgall examples were for the casting of spearheads (cf. Becker 2010), but spearheads of lozenge-shaped cross-section are rare and tend not to have a raised midrib, and do not offer good parallels for the objects cast in this group of moulds.

Spearheads

A minimum of three spearheads can be identified within the corpus (Table 3.13). Spearhead mould A (Figs 3.65 and 3.68) represents a small spearhead with protected openings and a shallow midrib. A fragment of a gate with runnel and the end of a socket are likely to form part of the same mould. These fragments were found in Sqs 7/8/16, including the fill of Hearth 6, with the possibly related socket fragment from K4 in the black layer of Pit 272. A number of fragments of spearhead B (Figs 3.66 and 3.68) were found close to and associated with Hearth 10 in Metalworking Zone 1. Here, however, were also found the tips of two spearhead mould valves that do not seem to constitute matches for spearhead B, having no contact faces and being of larger size (5100 and 5540). In contrast, the fragments comprising spearhead B have a clearly defined narrow contact face. This very well-preserved mould was for the casting of a spearhead with a deep midrib and a possible peg hole created by two angled cuts on fragment 5109. These may have been expanded to

Table 3.12—Chape moulds recovered at Rathgall.

Artefact type	Fragments	Context	Figure
Mould 1, chape valve 1	1875/1910	Sq. B1, from black area immediately outside wall (from which most of the moulds from this area came)	Figs 3.60, 3.61, 3.62
	4351	Sq. C1, extreme SW in black occupation level among cobblestones	Figs 3.60, 3.61
	1812	Sq. B1, in very black occupation layer in N of square	Fig. 3.60
	2885	Sq. C1, in dark brown soil near wall, SW	Fig. 3.61
Mould 1, chape valve 2	4000	Sq. B1/C1, in black occupation area	Fig. 3.60, 3.61
	4052	B1/C1, in black occupation area, in Baulk W	
Possible parts of mould 1	4735	Sq. 29, in black fill of Ring-ditch 1, W	
	6532	Sq. D, in thick black charcoal area; lumpy habitation layer removed, SE	
	8116	Sq. B1/C1, in black under wall, lower levels	
	8117	Sq. B1/C1, in black under wall, lower levels	
	1947	Sq. 7, Hearth 5	
	4381	Sq. C1, extreme SW, in black occupation level among cobblestones	
	6531	Sq. D2, in thick black charcoal area; lumpy habitation layer removed, SE	
	3835b	Sq. C1, in dark brown/black occupation layer, SW	
	8192	Sq. E1, in section strip	
	1631	Sq. B1, dark brown soil surrounding and covering stone 'paving' in area of removed wall; found close to hearth	
	3522b	Sq. C1, dark black occupation area, SW	
	6350	Sq. D, in dark brown with black patches among amorphous ferrous lumps	
	6411a	Sq. D, in black, among lumpy areas	
	7272	Sq. D/D1, in lowest levels of black charcoal area	
	2800	Sq. C1, dark brown, almost black soil	
	1822	Sq. B2, in dark soil	
Possible mould 3	5357	Sq. 43/52, in section strip	Fig. 3.62
	5157	Sq. 52, in brown, yellow beginning to show	
	5108	Sq. 52, in brown, hearth just showing (Hearth 10)	
	5598	Sq. 51, depression in extreme NW corner (D158)	
	5210	Sq. 52, almost on yellow; near stones S of hearth in Sq. 51	
	5556	Sq. 52, in brown, almost on yellow, among E post-holes	
	4908	Sq. 52, in brown	
	5056a	Sq. 52, in brown	
	5244	Sq. 51, in Hearth 10	
	5261	Sq. 51, in Hearth 10	
Other possible chape mould	9510	Sq. K6, brown, almost on yellow N	Fig. 3.62
Chape cores	7904	Sq. D2, in grey depression on yellow (D84)	Fig. 3.64
	1867	Sq. B1, black area immediately outside wall	Fig. 3.64
	7757	Sq. E3, in black area	
	3835a	Sq. C1, in dark brown/black occupation layer, SW	
	2501	Sq. 9/3, from grey silt in lower levels of Ring-ditch 1	
	7905	Sq. D2, in grey depression on yellow (D84)	
	7223	Sq. D/D1, in brown on edge of black	

Table 3.13—Spearhead moulds recovered at Rathgall.

Artefact type	Artefact no.	Context	Remarks
Spearhead A (protected loop)	1410a	Sq. 8/16, Hearth 6, in baulk	Figs 3.65, 3.68
	1485a	Sq. 7/8, almost on base of Ring-ditch 1 under baulk	Figs 3.65, 3.68
	9583	Sq. K4, in black layer, Pit 272	Figs 3.65, 3.68
	1485b,c	Sq. 7/8, almost on base of Ring-ditch 1 under baulk	
	1410b	Sq. 8/16, Hearth 6 in baulk ?	
Spearhead B	5547	Sq. 51, from Hearth 10	Figs 3.66, 3.68
	5109	Sq. 52, in brown, Hearth 10 just showing	Figs 3.68, 3.66, 3.68
	5252	Sq. 51, in brown, almost on yellow	
	5167	Sq. 51, Hearth 10	
	5160	Sq. 52, in brown, yellow beginning to show	Probably complementary valve to 5252 & 5540
	5222	Sq. 52, in brown, N	
	5785	Sq. 60, almost on yellow	
	5111	Sq. 52, in brown	Possibly fragment of socket, Fig. 3.66
	5110	Sq. 52, in brown	
	5198?	Sq. 51, about 60cm N of hearth in brown	Possibly same spearhead
	5767	Sq. 51, about 60cm N of hearth in brown	Possibly same spearhead
	5241, 5129, 5012, 5168	Other possible fragments from hearth in Sq. 52 with flat matrix remain that may possibly be from this object	
	5100	In brown	Blade near tip, possibly spearhead B
	5540	Sq. 51, near centre of square	Possibly tip of spearhead
Spearhead C	6726	Sq. D1, in brown on edge of charcoal area	Fig. 3.67
	8101	Sq. B/C, in black under wall, lower levels	Fig. 3.67
Possibly spearhead C	8100	Sq. B/C, in black under wall, lower levels	
	3605, 3524	Sq. C1, dark black occupation layer, SW	Two joining fragments
Spearhead D	6596a	Sq. D2, in brownish/black	
	7170b	Sq. D/D1, in black charcoal habitation area	
	8179	Sq. E1, in section strip	
	6685	Sq. D/D1, in black charcoal area	
	6809	Sq. D/D1, in black charcoal area	
Possible spearhead fragments	8139, 8206		
	7967	Sq. D, in mottled material in N section strip	

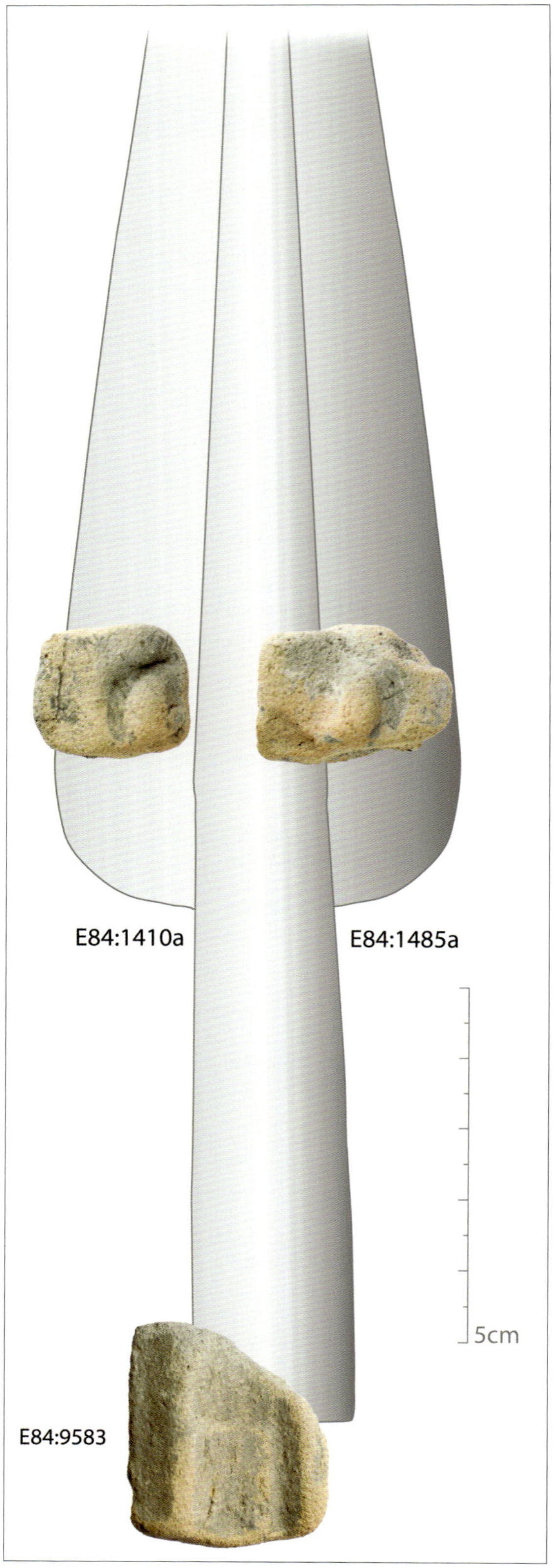

Fig. 3.65—Spearhead A mould fragments and indication of location on schematic of object type (scale 1:1).

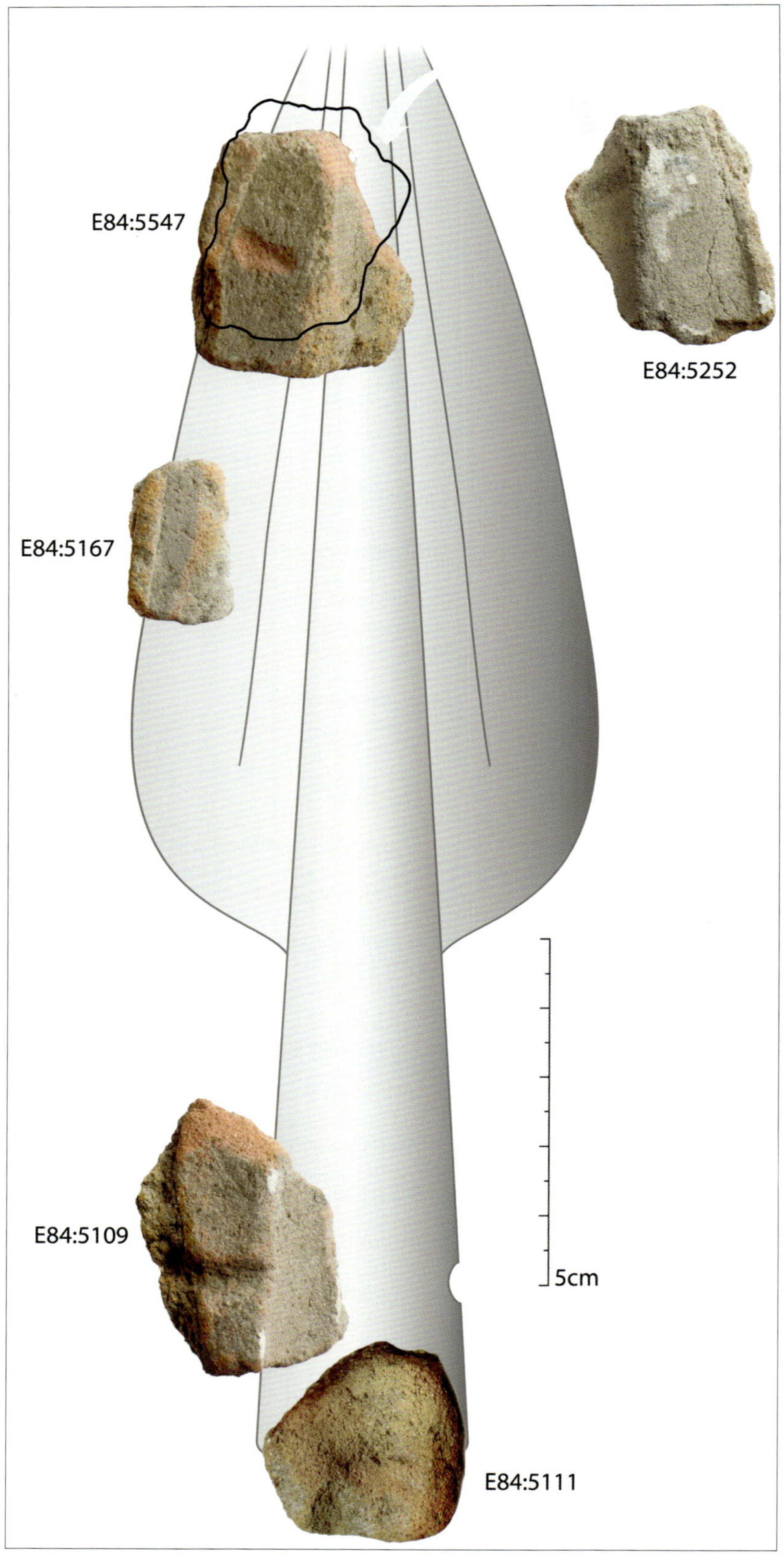

Fig. 3.66—Spearhead B mould fragments and indication of location on schematic of object type (scale 1:1).

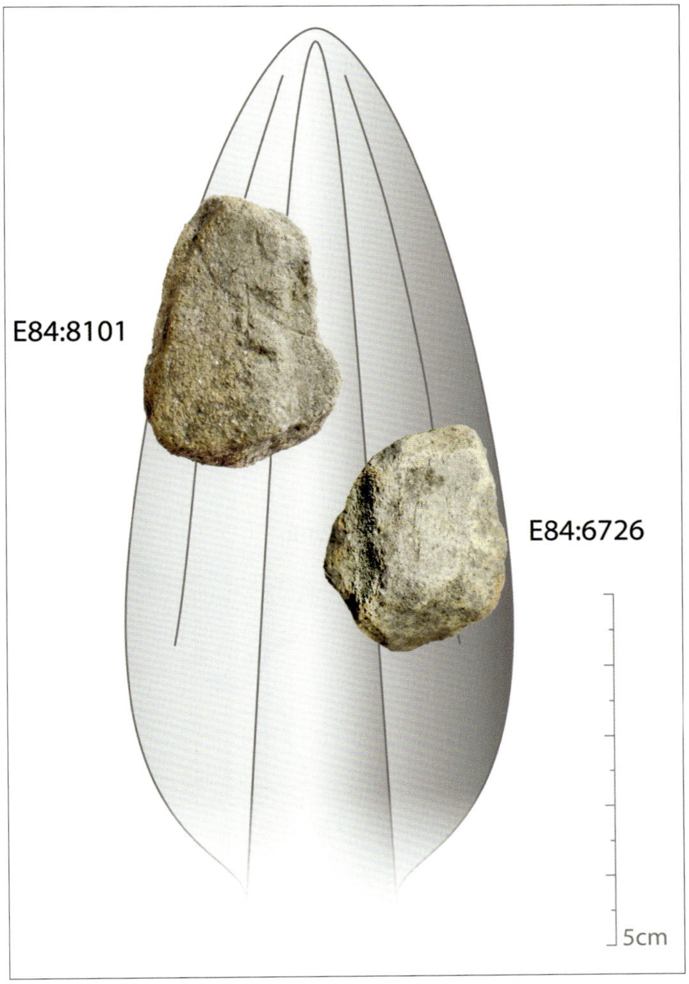

Fig. 3.67—Spearhead C mould fragments and indication of location on schematic of object type (scale 1:1).

Fig. 3.68 (right)—Fragments of moulds for the casting of spearheads (scale 1:1).

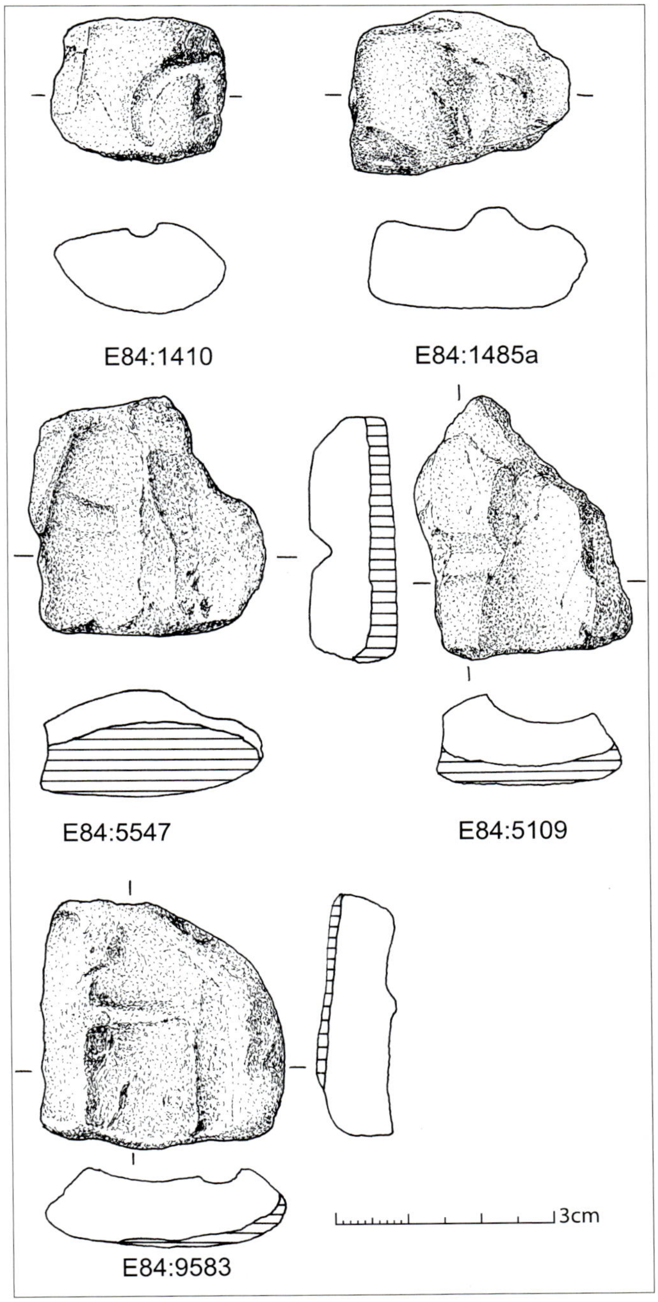

circular form after casting. It is unlikely that this cut represents a vent, as vents have not been observed on any clay moulds in Ireland. The blade has a gently rounded outline throughout. Two fragments from Sqs B/C and D1 appear to represent a third distinct mould, C, with a similar rounded blade (Fig. 3.67). In this concentration, a number of further possible spearhead fragments were found that cannot be confidently assigned to one particular unit.

The spearheads represented by the moulds here appear to be small to medium-sized. While relatively little can be deduced regarding their blade shape, they appear to be leaf-shaped in outline, with a pronounced midrib in some cases. The presence of a protected loop on spearhead A is notable. Protected-loop or protected-opening spearheads have not been found in hoards in Ireland, nor have they appeared on other moulds in Ireland. A typo-chronological position in the sequence between side-looped spears and lunate spears may be assumed (Ramsey 1989, 83). The British evidence indicates a date in the Penard and Wallington phase (Needham *et al.* 1997, 87). This, combined with their low frequency (Ramsey counted about 40 pieces in 1995), indicates a short lifespan towards the end of the Middle Bronze Age. This is also

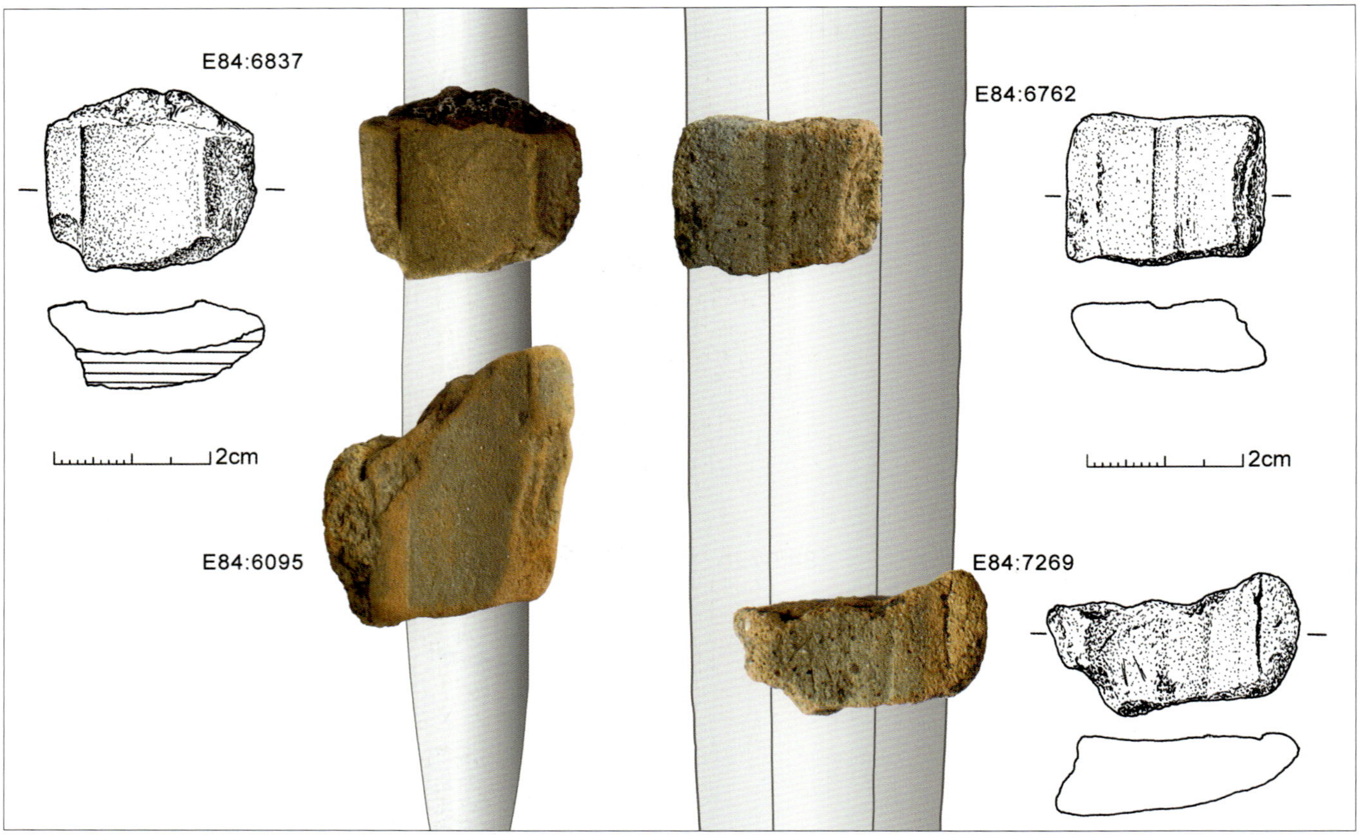

Fig. 3.69—Mould fragments representing knife blades A and B and indication of location on schematic of object type (scale 1:1).

supported by a fifteenth–thirteenth-century BC radiocarbon date for wood from a protected-loop spearhead from Cloghore, Co. Donegal (Brindley 2001, 154). They seem to be succeeded in the Wilburton phase by lunate-opening spearheads (Needham *et al.* 1997, 90), although, depending on the absolute dating of the Wallington phase, a later date for this form in northern Britain appears possible (Burgess and Gerloff 1981) (but see Chapter 6).

The dating of the use of pegs is not entirely clear; the earliest examples appear at the end of the Middle Bronze Age, and they are definitely represented in the Roscommon phase (Irish Class 3 swords have been found in the Youghal, Co. Cork, hoard together with two plain leaf-shaped spearheads with peg holes; Eogan 1983). In Britain spearheads with peg holes are known from Wilburton and Blackmoor (e.g. Coles 1959–60; Burgess 1968b) and from Middle Bronze Age Penard phase assemblages (e.g. Burgess 1968b, 34, note 6). An early date for a pegged spearhead was also obtained from a radiocarbon-dated example (1420–1100 cal. BC; Needham *et al.* 1997, 87), supporting the typo-chronological dating. In Ireland early examples of pegged spearheads—although of Middle Bronze Age morphology—could be dated to 1370–1051 BC, while smaller versions, similar to the Rathgall example, could possibly date from 1000 BC onwards (Becker 2013a).

Knives and daggers

Fragments of the moulds for two small knife or dagger blades are represented in the assemblage (Table 3.14), as well as a fragment of a mould for the casting of what may be the haft of a small blade. While knife mould A seems to represent a blade with a lenticular section, mould B seems to provide for a thin flat blade with a slight rib (Figs 3.69 and 3.57). While knife mould A seems to resemble classic Late Bronze Age socketed knives of type Thorndon or Dungiven, as described by Hodges (1956, 38), the object cast in mould B would more closely resemble a dagger or dirk—or, indeed, may represent the blade of a socketed knife of type Kells, which is triangular with a decorative line (Hodges 1956, 38, 36, fig. 4). The haft fragment 4937 (Fig. 3.57) listed below would appear to be too small for the hafting of a dagger but may be for a small knife. A further number of mould fragments

Table 3.14—Knife and dagger moulds recovered at Rathgall.

Artefact	Artefact no.	Context	Figure
Knife A	E84:6095	Sq. 3/4, under collapse of wall in black layer	Fig. 3.69
	E84:6837	Sq. G, in greyish-black material among 'cobbling' on yellow after removal of large stones of 'bank'	Figs 3.69, 3.57
Knife B	E84:7269	Sq. D1, in lowest levels of black charcoal area	Figs 3.69, 3.57
	E84:6762	Sq. D/D1, in black charcoal area	Figs 3.69, 3.57
	E84:6743	Sq. D/D1, in black charcoal area	
	E84:8007	Sq. C1, in brownish material in NW	
	E84:7426	Sq. D/D1, in black habitation material	
Hafting plate	E84:4937	Sq. 29, in grey fill of Ring-ditch 1, W	Fig. 3.57
Other small blades	E84:6142, 2363, 2287, 5976, 9370, 2286, 4938, 5108		

appear to have been for the casting of blades of a variety of sizes and cross-sections but are undiagnostic.

Sickles

A number of fragments may represent moulds for sickles (Table 3.15). Fragment 7900 (Fig. 3.70) is from a mould for an asymmetric, curved blade with a midrib and appears to represent the end of the blade directly above its haft. Fragment 1364a probably represents a sickle with a tang of flat oval cross-section (Figs 3.57 and 3.70). The end of the socket is clearly delineated by a step that represents the slightly expanding and deepening body of the sickle blade, apparently in line with the socket rather than at a right angle, as would be typical for most Late Bronze Age sickles. This arrangement of haft to blade can be paralleled on some socketed sickles, such as W.10 (Wilde 1861, fig. 406, 527), Athlone, Co. Westmeath (Waddell 2010, fig. 7.33.3), or from the Thames at Sion (Fox 1939). The (minimum) thickness of 7mm indicated by the matrix depth would seem too shallow to cater for the casting of a socket, and the expansion rather than the contraction of the blade in relation to the socket would also speak against this possibility. Tanged sickles are unusual but not unknown in the Late Bronze Age, and the best parallel for the example from Rathgall is the sickle from Ballygowan, Co. Kilkenny, with a perforated tang of lozenge-shaped cross-section, set in line with the blade (Eogan 1983, no. 93). The possibility that valve 1364a represents a knife socket was considered. While most

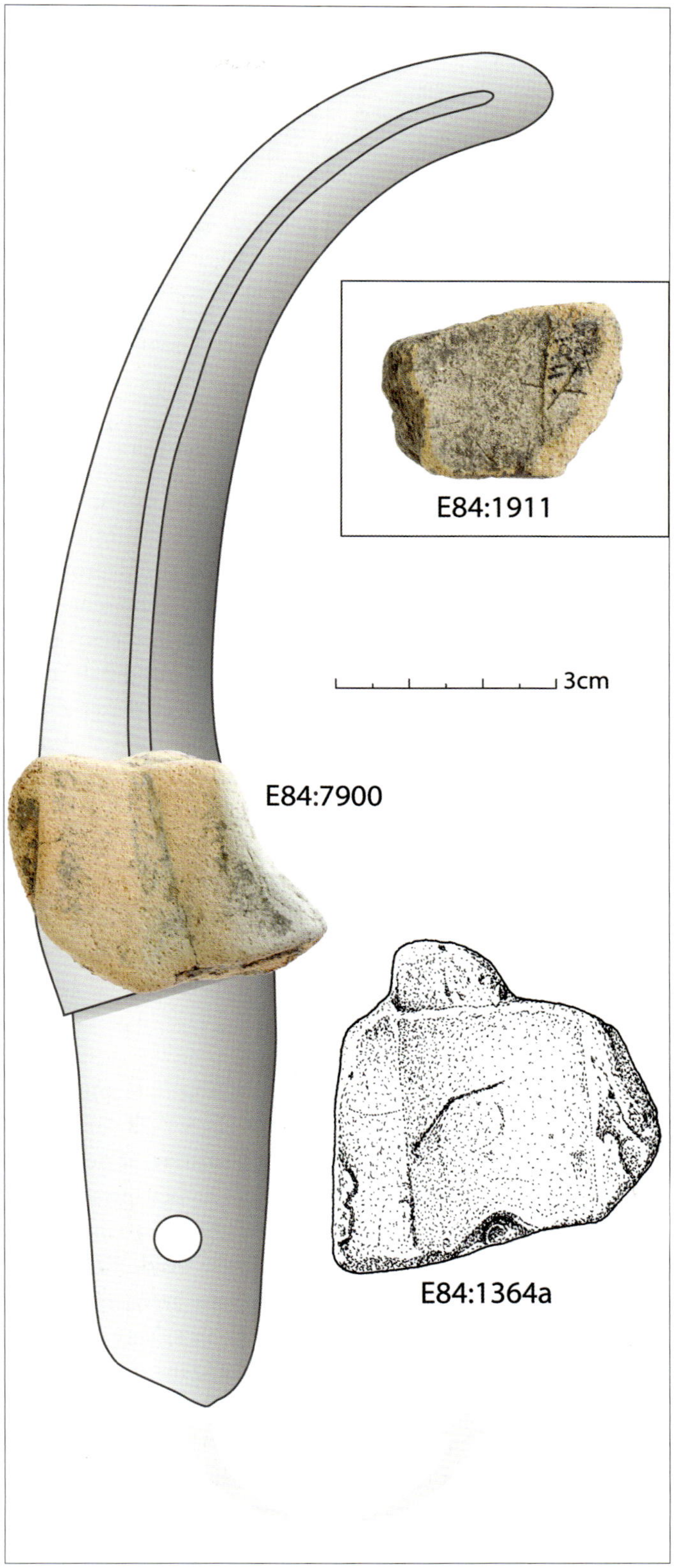

Fig. 3.70—Possible sickle mould fragments and indication of location on schematic of object type (scale 1:1).

Table 3.15—Sickle moulds recovered at Rathgall.

Artefact	Artefact no.	Context	Notes	Figure
Sickle A	7900	Sq. D2, in grey depression on yellow (D84)		Fig. 3.70
	7149	Sq. D2, in light, ashy brown almost on yellow	Too abraded to show any definite joins, but texture, colour and shape very similar to the other fragments.	
	7792	Sq. D2, in grey on yellow	Too abraded to show any definite joins, but texture, colour and shape very similar to the other fragments.	
	1364a	Sq. 7, black/brown fill of Ring-ditch 1, E		Fig. 3.70
Possible sickle fragments	7471	Sq. D/D1, in black material, lowest levels		Fig. 3.57
	1911	Sq. B1, black area immediately outside wall (from which most of the moulds from this area came)		Fig. 3.70

socketed knives have substantial sockets, the example from the Derryhale, Co. Armagh, hoard (*ibid.*, no. 44, fig. 22) has a rather flat, subrectangular socket, which could provide a comparison with the shape of the object represented by mould fragment 1364a. On balance, however, it seems more likely that this is for the casting of a broad tanged haft, most likely for a sickle. Owing to the similarity in material and firing, it is possible that both fragments are from the same mould, as may be two other, much-abraded fragments, also from D2 and the fill of Ring-ditch 1 in Sq. 7.

A small fragment (1911) of a mould for a thin, blade-like object with a slightly curved outer side may be for the casting of a sickle blade (Fig. 3.70). Fragment 7471 (Fig. 3.57) may similarly represent the matrix for the casting of a sickle blade owing to the asymmetric position of its midrib.

Axes and palstaves

Different forms of axehead were cast at Rathgall, ranging from palstaves to bag-shaped socketed axes (Figs 3.71 and 3.72; Table 3.16). The casting of at least one palstave, if not more, is indicated by three mould fragments. The best preserved of these (3722; Figs 3.71 and 3.73) was discovered in a thin scatter of occupation material immediately inside Ring-ditch 1 in Sq. 20. It is a large fragment that seems to have been for the casting of a palstave with very low flanges. Very likely the complementary valve is represented by fragment 4613 (Fig. 3.74), which was found among stones within the black fill of Ring-ditch 1 in Sq. 20, and by a further heavily damaged fragment, 3767, found in Sq. C1 in the black occupation layer. The close proximity of these fragments further supports the argument that they formed one mould, although its surviving portion is not substantial enough to allow its exact typological identification. The latest Irish palstaves of Ramsey's Derryfadda variant, which can be considered as parallel to the British transitional palstave series of the Penard phase (Ramsey 1989, 180), are found in the hoards from Bishopsland, Co. Kildare, and Derryfadda Lower, Co. Mayo. In Britain, late palstaves occur in Wilburton assemblages (Needham 2017, e.g. 145–50; Burgess 1968b, 9, 36, fig. 9:11). A fragment possibly for the casting of a flattish axe body may be affiliated with this axe form (7548; Fig. 3.71).

Socketed, bag-shaped axes are also represented (8622.1 and 7903; Fig. 3.71). Two large pieces of valves for the casting of such objects appear to represent complementary parts of the same mould. These are for the casting of an axe some 6.5cm in length that appears to have been rather flat and possibly oval in cross-section. There are no other diagnostic features. The earliest bag-shaped socketed axe in Ireland of Eogan's Class 2 was found in the County Roscommon hoard (Eogan 2000, 30–1), and it is possible that the mould was for the casting of an axe of this type, although they have a long chronological currency throughout the Late Bronze Age.

A zone of fine parallel ridges—at least two—is found on the neck of a likely axe mould (7317; Fig. 3.75). The decorative zone is at the same level as the loop. Such ridge and groove decoration is commonly found on socketed axes of Class 3, usually above the loop (e.g. Eogan 2000, 31, pls 7–9). These axes have a rectangular cross-section. They are not found in association in Ireland but their absence from Dowris hoards suggested to Eogan an earlier date, as do their parallels to British Wallington/Wilburton axes of type Fulford and Highfield. Their distribution in Ireland is north of a line between Wicklow and Roscommon (*ibid.*, 37).

Fragments of two valves (Fig. 3.76), likely to have formed one mould, in Sq. D are difficult to interpret. While resembling in some aspects the body of a bag-shaped axe, the

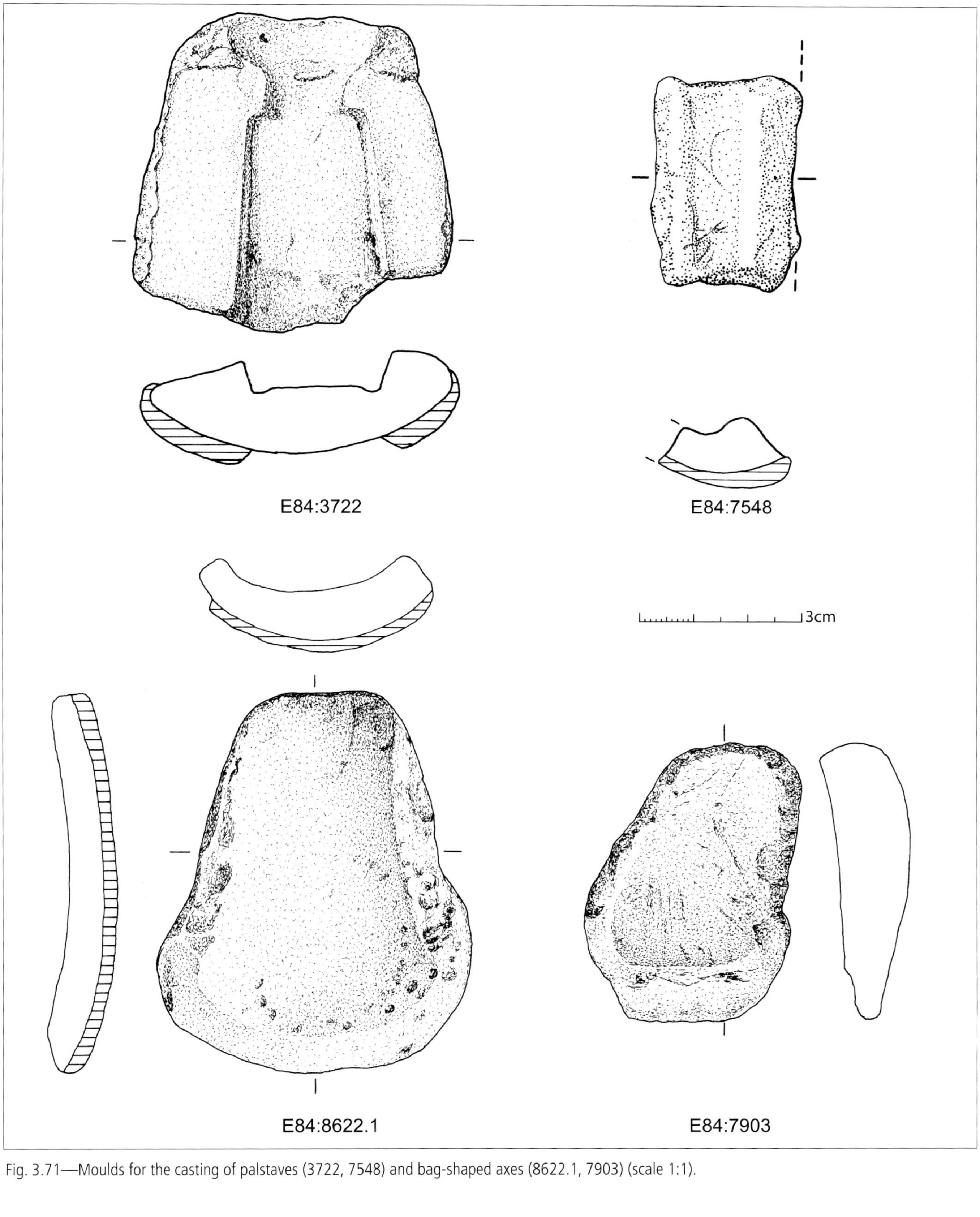

Fig. 3.71—Moulds for the casting of palstaves (3722, 7548) and bag-shaped axes (8622.1, 7903) (scale 1:1).

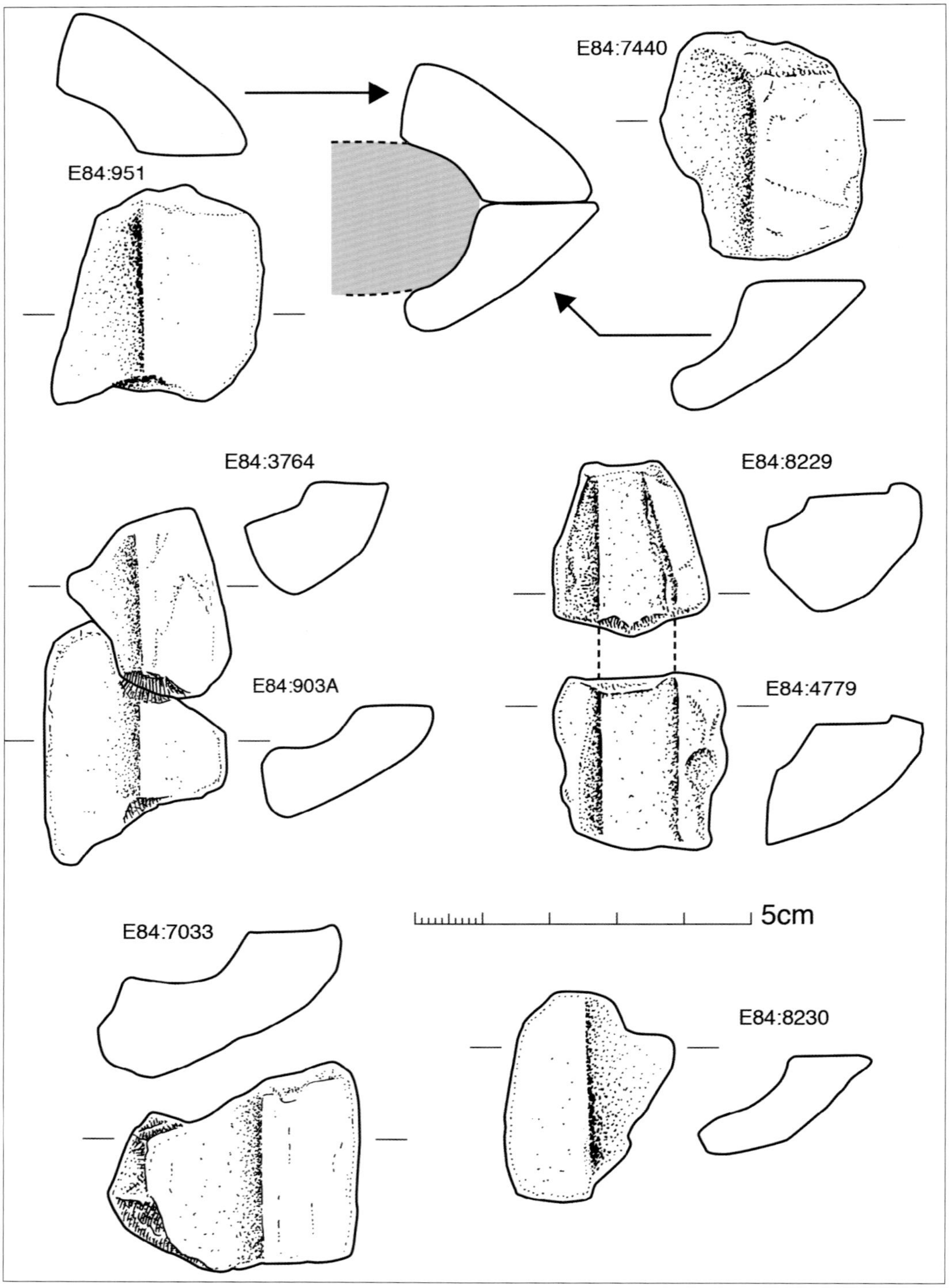

Fig. 3.72—Moulds for the casting of axes (scale 1:1).

object cast would have tapered in thickness towards both the hypothetical blade and the opposite end, and thus could not have had a socket.

Several further fragments (Fig. 3.72) are characterised by a wide contact face with a concave matrix stepped off it at right angles. Although the relatively large number of similar fragments were clustered in the D squares, no direct matches could be made, with the exception of fragments 3764 and 903A, which are of a different thickness and fabric. These two fragments appear to represent the body of an axe close to its cutting edge.

A small fragment of a mould (7276; not illustrated)

Table 3.16—Axe and palstave moulds recovered at Rathgall.

Artefact type	Artefact no.	Context	Notes	Figure
Palstave	3722	Sq. B1, black area immediately outside wall from which most of the moulds from this area came		Figs 3.71, 3.73
	4613	Sq. 20, in black fill of Ring-ditch 1 among stones	This is very likely the complementary valve for fragment 3722 above.	
	3767	Sq. C1, in dark black occupation layer, SW		
Possible palstave	7548	Sq. D/D1, in brown ashy material under black		Fig. 3.71
Socketed axe	8622.1	Sq. H4, in small, black-filled depression (D126) within Ring-ditch 2 enclosure, 1m inside ditch at W end of square		Fig. 3.71
	7903	Sq. D2, in grey depression on yellow (D84)	Possibly a complementary piece to 8622.1, but heavily abraded.	Fig. 3.71
Socketed axe with ridge moulding	7317	Sq. E1, black area immediately outside 'bank' in E1, extreme S part of cutting		Fig. 3.75
	7319	Sq. E1, black area immediately outside 'bank' in E1 in extreme S part of cutting	Very abraded.	
Axes with sub-hexagonal body	7033	Sq. D/D1, in black charcoal-filled habitation area		Fig. 3.72
	903a	Sq. 8, black area, NW, Hearth 6		Fig. 3.72
	3764	Sq. C1, in dark black occupation layer, SW		Fig. 3.72
	8230	Sq. B1/C1, in section strip, in black		Fig. 3.72
	8229	Sq. B1/C1, in section strip, in black		Fig. 3.72
	7440	Sq. D/D1, in black habitation area		Fig. 3.72
	951	Sq. 7, dark brown within semicircle of stone		Fig. 3.72
	4779	Sq. 29, in shallow part of ditch in black fill, W	Very wide contact face and steep transition to body of object cast. Same valve as 8229.	Fig. 3.72
	7966	Sq. D, in mottled material in N section strip	Complementary valve to 6529	Fig. 3.76
	6529	Sq. D, in thick black charcoal area; lumpy habitation refuse removed; SE	Complementary valve to 7966	Fig. 3.76
	3763	Sq. C1, in dark black occupation layer, SW		
Possible axe mould fragments	7276	Sq. D/D1, in lowest levels of black charcoal area		
	8065	Sq. F2/B2, in section strip, in grey layer, almost on yellow		
	5246	Sq. 51, in hearth in S of square		
	2498	Sq. 9/3, in grey silt in lower levels of Ring-ditch 1		
	1944	Sq. B1, near 'cobbling' in SW of square		
	7209	Sq. D/D1, in black charcoal habitation area		
	3085	Sq. C1, in brown soil, S		
	2558	Sq. 19, in light brown soil, SE		
	3896	Sq. 20, N, in dark brown, almost on orange		
	7475	Sq. D/D1		
	7639	Sq. E2, SW corner, near section in dark material almost on yellow		
	6984	Sq. D1, in brown, centre		
	6783	Sq. D1, on yellow area		
	6498	Sq. D2, in dark brown, centre		
	7143Sq.	D/D1, in black charcoal habitation area		
	7142.	Sq. D1, on yellow area		
	6782	Sq. D1, on yellow area		
	6919	Sq. D2, in brown		
Similar forms	6670	Sq. D1, in dark charcoal area		
	1366.1a	Sq. 7, in black fill of Ring-ditch 1, in E, 30–35cm deep		
	2558	Sq. 19, in light brown soil, SE		
	7555	Sq. D/D1, in brown ashy material under black		
	6848	Sq. E2, black area		

Fig. 3.73—Palstave mould fragment 3722 (scale 1:1).

Fig. 3.74—Palstave mould fragment 4613 (scale 1:1).

Fig. 3.75—Fragment 7317 of mould for the casting of an axe with ribbing and a loop (scale 1:1).

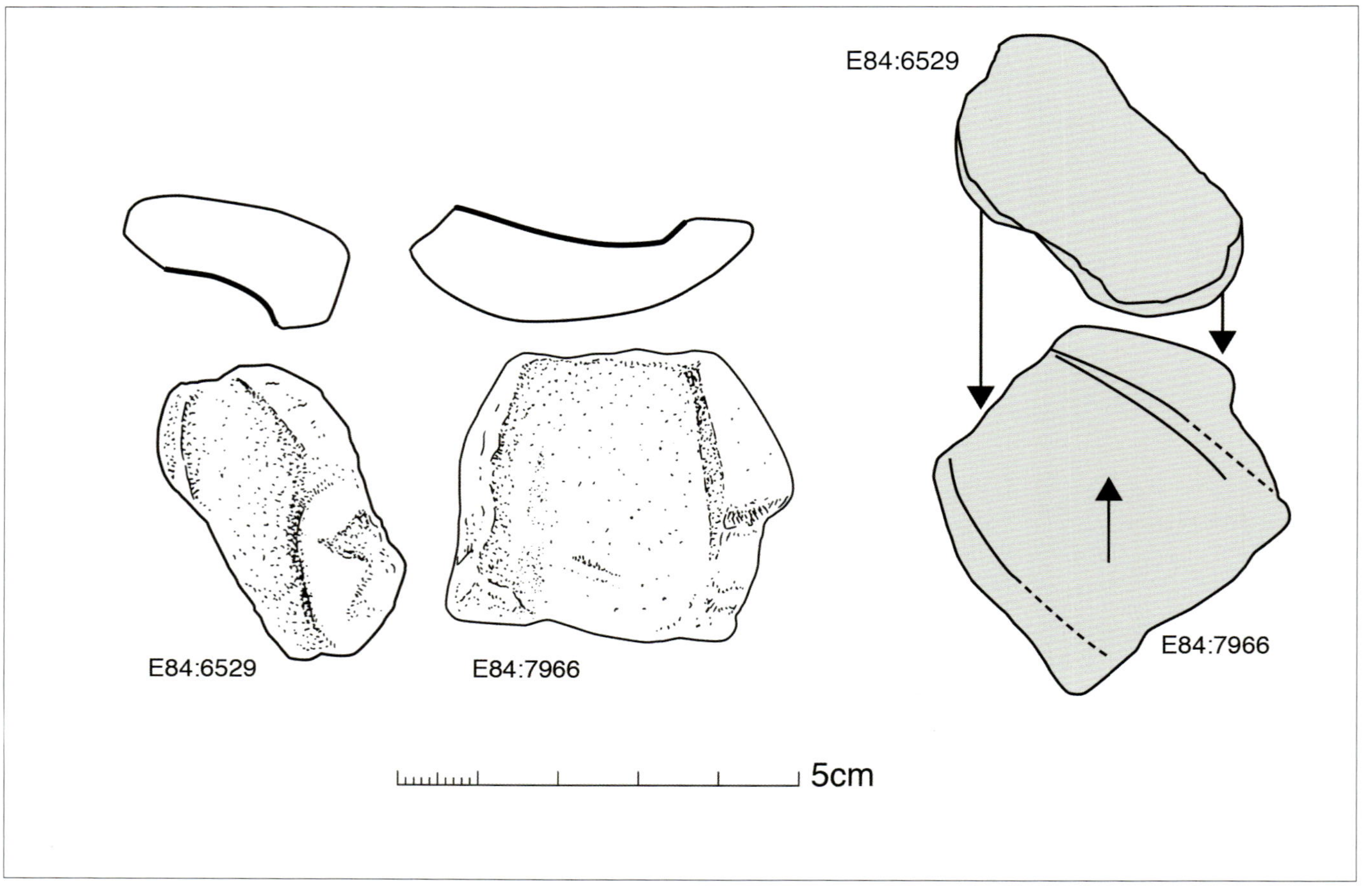

Fig. 3.76—Possible axe mould (scale 1:1).

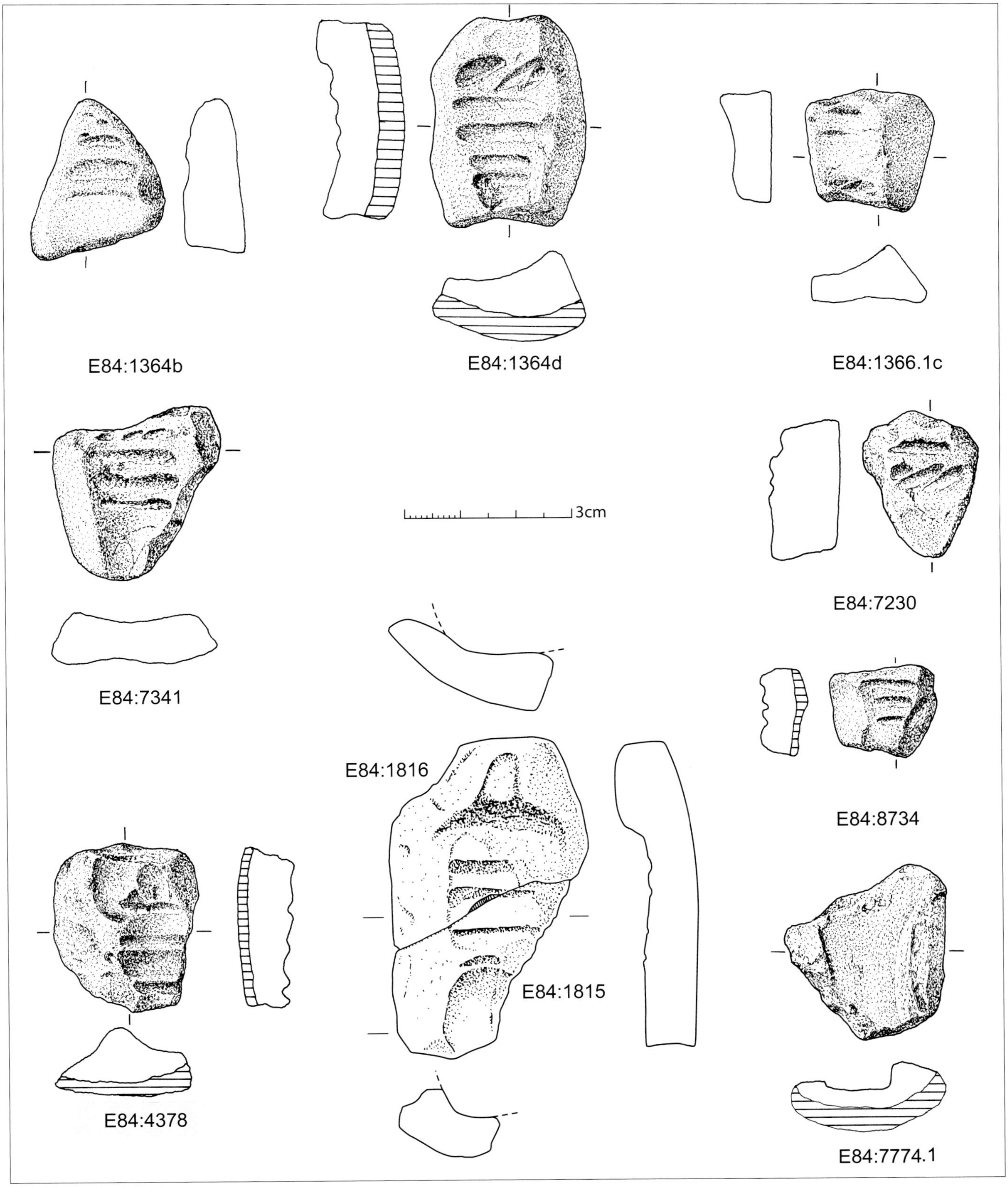

Fig. 3.77—Moulds for the casting of decorated sockets of small tools and possible tool mould fragment 7774.1 (scale 1:1).

providing for the casting of a narrow rib, as found, for example, on axes of Class 7, may have been for the casting of an axe, although it may also have formed part of a mould for a different object.

Decorated sockets

There are ten portions of moulds for the casting of probably three small sockets with rope moulding and ribbing (Figs 3.77 and 3.78; Table 3.17). Sockets A and B appear to have been decorated with a combination of ribs and rope moulding, whereas socket C was decorated only with a series of ribs. The sockets cast in these moulds appear to have had a small diameter, with socket C (E84:4378) having a diameter of about 2cm. Rope or cord moulding has been applied for the decoration of socketed tools and axes in Ireland since the Bishopsland phase, the tools and axe in that hoard being examples. Rope moulding continues to be used for the decoration of axes in the Wallington and Wilburton phases (see above and Needham 1990, 265) and is not a very common feature of later Dowris phase axes in Ireland, last appearing on Eogan's Class 4 axes, which are datable to the early Dowris phase (cf. Eogan 2000). Decoration with ribs and/or rope moulding as found on socket A and with ribs as on sockets B and C is also found on axes but is not evidenced among the range of tools known from the Irish Bronze Age, which are dominated by those dating from the Dowris phase,

Table 3.17—Moulds of decorated sockets recovered at Rathgall.

Artefact	Fragment no.	Context	Notes	Figure
Decorated socket A	1364b	Sq. 7, black/brown fill of Ring-ditch 1, E		Fig. 3.77
	1364d	Sq. 7, black/brown fill of Ring-ditch 1		Fig. 3.77
	7230	Sq. D/D1, in brown on edge of black		Fig. 3.77
	1366.1c	Sq. 7, in black fill of Ring-ditch 1 in E, 30–35cm deep		Fig. 3.77
	7341	Sq. D/D1, in black habitation material		
Socket C	4378			Fig. 3.77
	1815/1816	Sq. B1, dark occupation layer in N of square		Fig. 3.77
	3608	Sq. C1, in dark brown/black occupation layer, SW	Small fragment that may form part of the same mould.	
Socket B	8734	Sq. Y4, in black fill of shallow trench at N end of square, pit		Fig. 3.77
	7899	Sq. D2, in grey depression on yellow (D84)	Possibly from the same mould as 8734.	
Possible rope moulding	7217	Sq. D/D1, in black charcoal habitation area	Small, worn mould fragment. Very slight possibility that two oblique depressions near the suggested rounded edge might represent the remains of rope moulding. Max. L: 2.3cm. Max. T: 9mm.	

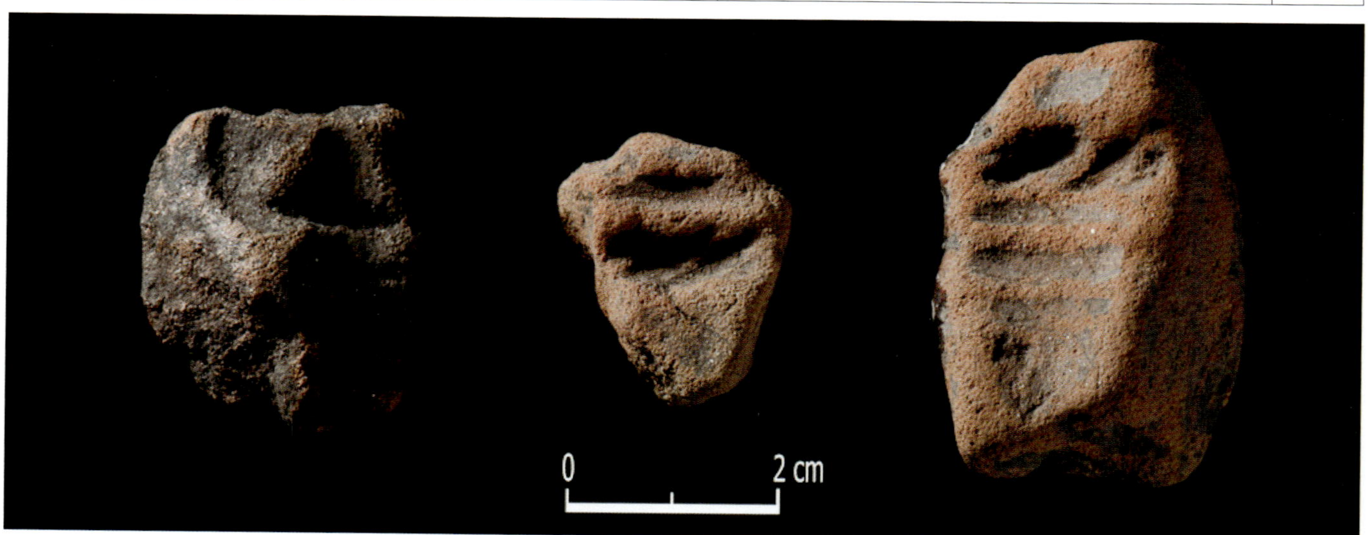

Fig. 3.78—Moulds for the casting of decorated sockets E84:4378, 7230, 1364d (photo: John Sunderland).

with its hoard associations (cf. Eogan 2000). The presence of a loop on socket C suggests that this example represents a mould for the casting of a small socketed axe or hammer.

Chisels or other small tools

A number of valves represent tools such as chisels and punches (Table 3.18). Mould fragment 8096 is a second-made valve with the remains of a matrix for the casting of the blunt end (minimum width 1.1cm) of an object with chamfering like a punch (Fig. 3.79). Other moulds may have been for the casting of chisels that could have been used in a variety of crafts, although 7774.1 may also have been for the casting of a small tool handle and 5240 may have been for the casting of a small socket with a collar. Other fragments represent moulds for the casting of a bar or possible chisel blanks of subrectangular section (e.g. 580, 6906, 2437, 5112).

Further fragments of moulds for the casting of small axes or the tapered sockets or bodies of small tools are listed in Table 3.19. These are characterised by a concave matrix stepping off a contact face, suggesting the casting of a small tubular shape.

Fig. 3.79—Mould for the casting of the end of a tool such as a punch or chisel (scale 1:1).

Table 3.18—Moulds for chisels and other tools recovered at Rathgall.

Artefact type	Fragment no.	Context	Notes	Figure
Punch	8096	Sq. B/C, in black under wall, lower levels		Fig. 3.79
Chisels, possible	7774.1	Sq. H3, context unknown		
	6497	Sq. D2, in dark brown, centre		
	2498	Sq. 9/3, in grey silting in lower levels of Ring-ditch 1	Possibly part of same mould as 7774.1	
Collared shaft?	5240	Sq. 51, in brown, on yellow		
Chisels/bars	5805	Sq. 63, in grey fill of Ring-ditch 1, 45cm below sod, 25cm below ditch edge		
	6906	Sq. G2, black area with stones in SE, Pit 20		
	2437	Sq. 9/3, black fill of Ring-ditch 1		
	5112	Sq. 52, in brown, hearth just showing (Hearth 10)		
	6536,a,b	Sq. D1, in black charcoal area, lumpy occupation material having been removed		
	9594	Sq. K6, Pit 21		

Pins and studs

At least four moulds for the casting of small disc-headed pins can be identified on the site (Fig. 3.80; Table 3.20). Pin A has a disc-shaped head 8.5mm in diameter, with a 2.5mm-wide boss in its centre. Pin B appears to have a large and strongly raised central boss, 7.5mm in diameter and standing 1.5mm proud of the head, which only had a diameter of 14mm. Pin C is comparable to pins A and D and appears to have had a simple domed head of subrectangular outline and minute size.

The embossed small disc heads represent disc-headed pins. These, like sunflower pins, have a central stud and can

Table 3.19—Small axe/socket moulds recovered at Rathgall.

Artefact type	Fragment no.	Context
Small axes or sockets	903B	Sq. 8, Hearth 6
	2497	Sq. 9/3, in grey silt in lower levels of Ring-ditch 1
	4514	Sq. 20, in dark black fill of Ring-ditch 1
	4563	Sq. 20, in black fill of Ring-ditch 1, among stones
	5422	Sq. 50, in upper fill of Ring-ditch 1, NE
	5604	Sq. 52, in L-shaped hollow in NW
	7644	Sq. E3, Pit 54
	3609	Sq. C1, in dark brown/black occupation layer, SW
	5612	Sq. 51, in brown, on yellow, N

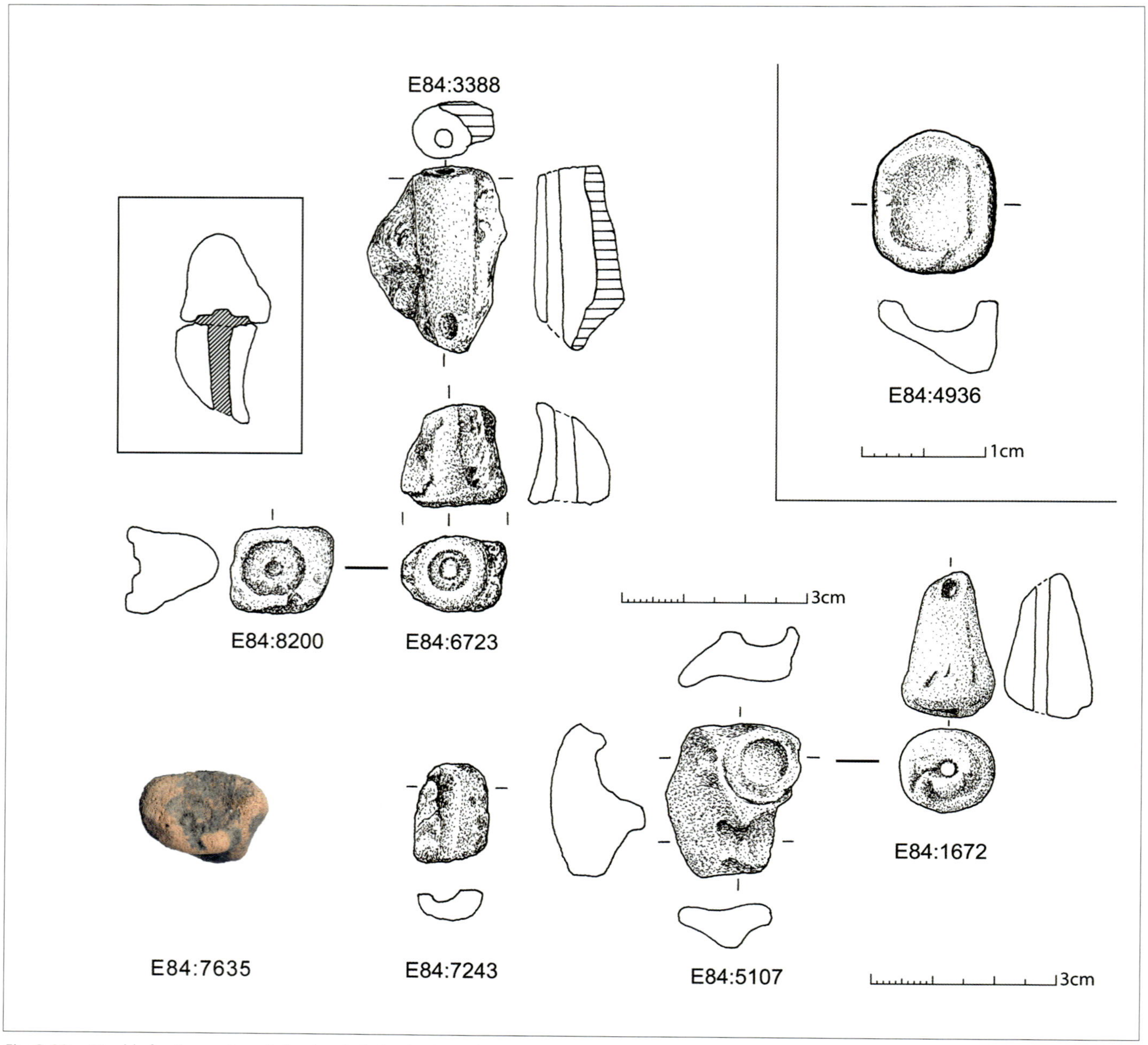

Fig. 3.80—Moulds for the casting of disc-headed pins (scale 1:1).

occur in a variety of sizes, with or without decoration (Eogan 1974, 79–82). Eogan noted that the known disc-headed pins had diameters of 12–52mm but that over half of them had a diameter of between 20mm and 30mm (*ibid.*, 79). The Rathgall examples seem to sit at the lowest end of this range, at 8.5mm and 15mm.

Disc-headed pins are demonstrated by associations in hoards to have been in use in the Dowris phase (e.g. Newport, Co. Mayo; Eogan 1983, no. 110), but an earlier date was also considered possible on the basis of some tentative associations with basal looped and other spearheads, as well as Montelius IV associations of pins of this type in Scandinavia (Eogan 1974, 95–6). In his discussion of an example of a sunflower pin from Haughey's Fort with a small head, resembling that of small disc-headed pins with a flange, Brandherm (2014, 60–1, figs 1 and 2) drew attention to Atlantic parallels for disc-headed pins. This pin's context at Haughey's Fort—the initial infilling of

Table 3.20—Pin moulds (Fig. 3.80)

Artefact	Fragment no.	Context	Notes
Pin A	8200	Sq. E1, in section strip	Cap piece with matrix for top of a disc-headed pin with a convex surface (8.5mm in diameter), with central depression to form a tiny boss, 2.5mm in diameter, in the centre. About 1mm high. Fig. 3.80.
	6723	Sq. 7, in black charcoal area	Top of shank piece with impression of underside of circular disc head, about 7–8mm in diameter, from which a circular perforation leads to a circular shank about 3.3mm in diameter. A very narrow (2mm) contact face surrounding the head is only marginally raised. The overall surviving depth of matrix is 15.5mm. Fig. 3.80.
	3388	Sq. C1, dark brown, SW	Cylinder for casting pin shank. Possibly part of the same pin. Fig. 3.80.
Pin B	1672	Sq. 26, in lightish brown soil	Represented is the top of the pin shank, including an almost completely weathered matrix for the underside of a circular pin head. The maximum possible diameter of the circular pin head to be cast on top of this is 15.5mm. Fig. 3.80.
	5107	Sq. 29, in black fill of Ring-ditch 1 at shallow end	Cap piece with matrix for top of circular head of a pin. The diameter of the head may be 14mm, with a central large boss, 7.5mm in diameter and standing 1.5mm proud of the plate of the pin. The inner valve is surrounded by an usually large fragment of outer wrap, with a further small convex impression possibly suggesting the former presence of a further matrix for a pin head. Fig. 3.80.
Pin C	7635	Sq. D/D1, in brown ashy material under black	Heavily abraded possible cap piece with matrix for circular head of a pin. The diameter of the head may be 14mm, with a central large boss, 7.5mm in diameter and standing 1.5mm proud of the plate of the pin. The inner valve is surrounded by an usually large fragment of outer wrap, similar to 5107. Fig. 3.80.
Pin D	4936	Sq. 29, in grey fill of Ring-ditch 1	Possible cap piece for casting of pin head. Fig. 3.80.
Other pin moulds	7901	Sq. D2, in grey depression on yellow (D84)	Possible pin shank with integrated gate.
	4940	Sq. 29, in grey fill of Ring-ditch 1	Possible pin shank tip, 1.5–2.5mm thick.
	7243	Sq. D/D1, in brown area	Possible pin shank, *c.* 4mm thick. Fig. 3.80.
	7915	Sq. D2, in grey depression on yellow (D84)	Possible pin shank, tiny.
	2496	Sq. 9/3, in grey silt in lower levels of Ring-ditch 1	Possible pin shank, tiny.
	5584	Sq. 56, in grey fill of ditch under stones	Possible pin shank tip, tiny.

the innermost ditch, dated to between 1150 and 1050 BC (e.g. Mallory and Baban 2014, 13–14)—supports the early date for similar pins from Rathgall. At Dún Aonghasa, sunflower and likely disc-headed pins—with and without central stud and closely resembling those from Rathgall—were found (see especially O'Carroll 2012a, pins 5 and 6, fig. 8.21, 36–9).

Bracelets and other ornaments

A group of fragments represent a mould for the casting of a flat object with longitudinal fine ribbing such as a ribbed bracelet (Figs 3.81 and 3.82; Table 3.21). The grooves are 1–2mm apart and are about 2mm wide. Two of the fragments (7493 and 6742) have a slight lip around their outer edge, suggesting that they are fragments of a second-made valve. Fragment 7327 has very abraded sides. The largest fragments suggest a width of *c.* 20mm for the original object cast. Fragment 7327 would appear to represent a narrower valve and may be from another mould; alternatively, it may suggest that the object tapered along its length. The great degree of degradation of some of the fragments makes it difficult to judge this, however.

The fragments that can be confidently assigned to this type are found in Sqs C1, D/D1 and D2 within the main metalworking zones. Fragments 5800a (not illustrated) and 5800b were found in an upper layer of the ditch in Sq. 58, in the north-western part of Ring-ditch 1. Ribbed bronze bracelets are known from the Middle Bronze Age Ornament Horizon of southern Britain (e.g. O'Connor *et al.* 2017; Roberts 2007) and are closely paralleled by French examples, such as, for example, the finds of similarly relatively narrow ribbed bracelets among those at Aizenay (Lourdaux and Gomez de Soto 1998, figs 4 and 6), dating from the later stages of the Middle Bronze Age. A broadly similar, if not exactly comparable, ribbed strip with ring and hook terminals possibly representing a bracelet was part of the St Andrews, Scotland, hoard (Cowie *et al.* 1991, 57, pl. 10). Based on radiocarbon dates (Trevor Cowie and Brendan O'Connor, pers. comm.) as well as on the associated objects, the assemblage was dated to the Ewart Park/St Andrews

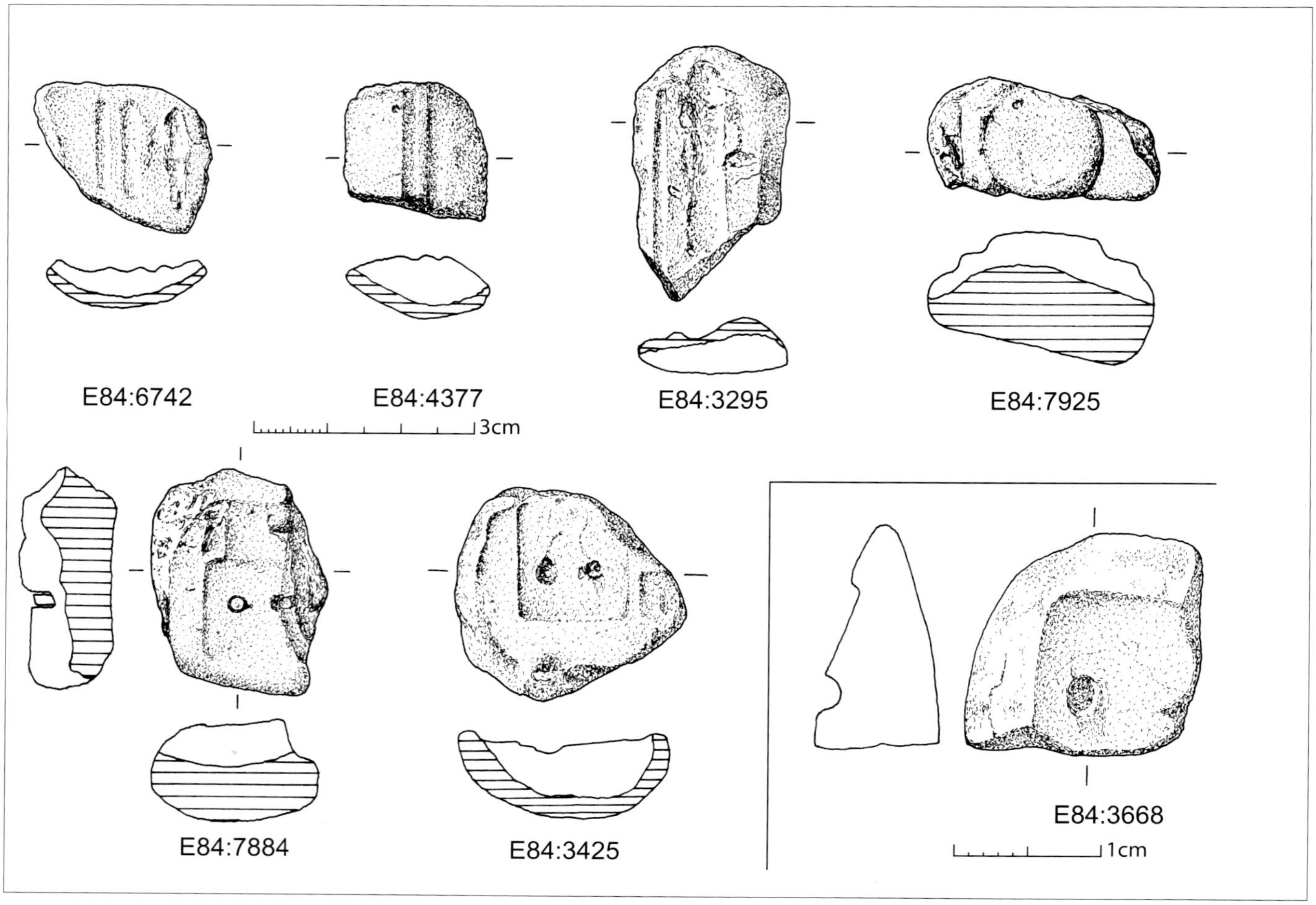

Fig. 3.81—Moulds for the casting of ribbed bracelets (6742, 4377, 3295), a possible mount (7925) and tabs (7884, 3425, 3668) (scale 1:1).

phase of the Scottish Late Bronze Age. In Ireland, the closest parallel is the ribbed bracelet fragment that formed part of the Bishopsland hoard (Eogan 1983, no. 16.14); this, however, is much narrower than the object in question at Rathgall. Wide ribbed bracelets are also known in gold from Ireland, although these are much wider.

The casting of a flat and simple strip or band is implied by fragment 4090 (Fig. 3.82).

A flat disc appears to have been cast in one or more moulds represented by fragments 8115 (Fig. 3.82) and 7380. The discs cast would have had a diameter of between 3.5cm and 5cm. Raftery noted a concentric circular pattern on 8115, although this can no longer be identified. The objects cast may have been heads for sunflower pins or other circular discs. A very tentative parallel are the phalerae of the Island or Wilburton hoards (O'Connor 1980, fig. 46 A, fig. 48, no. 23). A very similar casting mould fragment forms part of the

Table 3.21—Moulds for bracelets and other ornaments.

Artefact type	Artefact no.	Context
Bracelet A	6742	Sq. D/D1, in black charcoal area
	7327	Sq. D2, on yellow
	7493	Sq. D/D1, in black material, lowest levels
	1877	Sq. B1, black area immediately outside wall
	7360	Sq. D/D1, in black habitation area
	5800a,b	Sq. 58, in grey fill of Ring-ditch 1, E, 25cm below top of ditch
Bracelet B	4377	Sq. C1, extreme SW, in black occupation level among cobblesto
	3295	Sq. C1, in brown fill of curved bedding trench in W immediately under wall
Band	4090	Sq. B1/C1, in black occupation material in and over stones in ba
Disc	8115	Sq. B1/C1, in black under wall, lower levels
	7380	Sq. E1, in black material outside wall
Mount	7925	Sq. E/E1, in black under yellow in 'bank', S
Tab 1	3668	Sq. 19, in black fill of Ring-ditch 1, SE
Tab 2	7884	Sq. H(1?), in brown
	3425	Sq. 27, PH 28

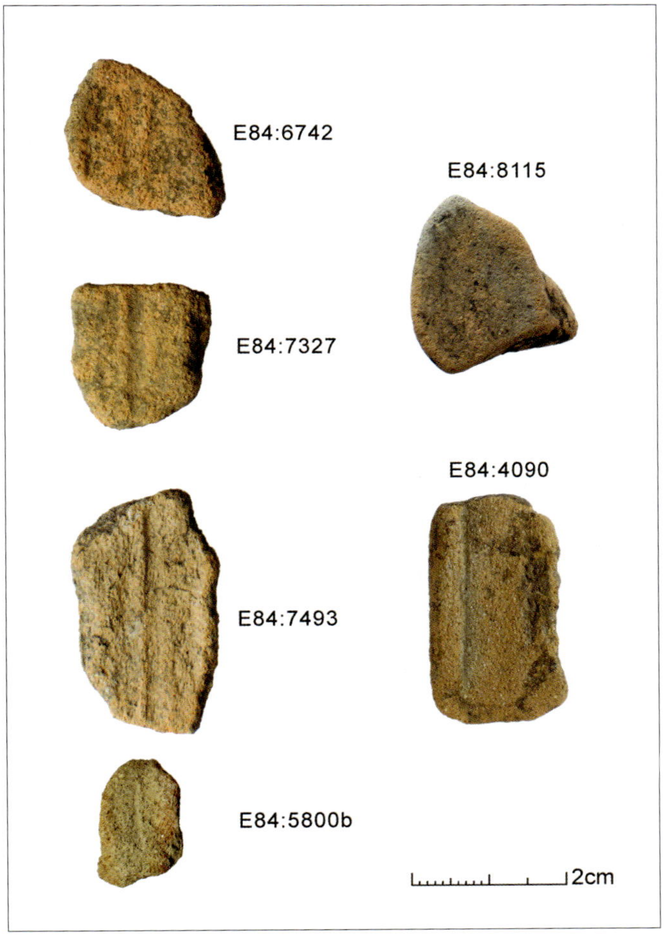

Fig. 3.82—Moulds for the casting of a ribbed bracelet (on the left), a disc (8115) and a band or flat bracelet (4090) (scale 1:1).

assemblage from Aubervilliers (Melin 2016).

Here also a mould for the casting of a disc with deeper circular grooves is represented, offering the closest parallel for the object cast in mould 7925 (Fig. 3.81). The matrix of this mount consists of a central raised disc, 17.5mm in diameter, flanked by a recessed circular surround. On one side the surround is set at an approximately parallel angle to the central disc, but on the opposing side it slopes downward by approximately 30 degrees. This asymmetry is difficult to interpret as the intended shape of an object to be cast and it may be a failed mould.

Straps/tabs

Valve fragments 3668, 7884 and 3425 appear to be for the casting of tabs with a flat, slightly lenticular cross-section (Figs 3.81 and 3.83; Table 3.21). The three extant fragments suggest that at least two of these objects were cast here, but it is also conceivable that the object had two opposing rivet holes at each end. The presence of the little clay dowels in each perforation suggests that these were not meant to be filled with metal but would create dimples in the surface of the cast, to be perforated in the finishing process. These are in principle comparable to the lateral tabs of the base plates used in the construction of buckets (e.g. Gerloff 2010). These, however, are larger than the examples from Rathgall

Notes	Figure
	Figs 3.81, 3.82
Possibly the same as A, but the mould is of different thickness.	Fig. 3.81
	Fig. 3.81
	Fig. 3.82
Circular flat object such as a disc. The diameter of the object cast would have been about 3.5cm. Raftery noted a concentric pattern that can no longer be identified.	Fig. 3.82
A large flat disc with a diameter of about 50mm.	
The matrix has a central raised disc, 17.5mm in diameter, flanked by flatter surfaces; however, the surface on one side is approximately horizontal to the central disc, whereas the other slopes downward by approx. 30 degrees. Presumably for casting an ornamental piece with a large circular depression or perforation. Diameter of central area on disc is apparently 19mm.	Fig. 3.81
	Fig. 3.81
Rectangular matrix, 14mm across, with two rivet-like objects in two perforations located centrally and 3mm apart. The matrix is broken off at one end, suggesting that the object cast would have been longer than the surviving 16mm. The thickness of the object cast would have been greatest (about 1.5mm) near the rivet holes. Both moulds may represent part of the same or a very similar object.	Fig. 3.81
	Fig. 3.83

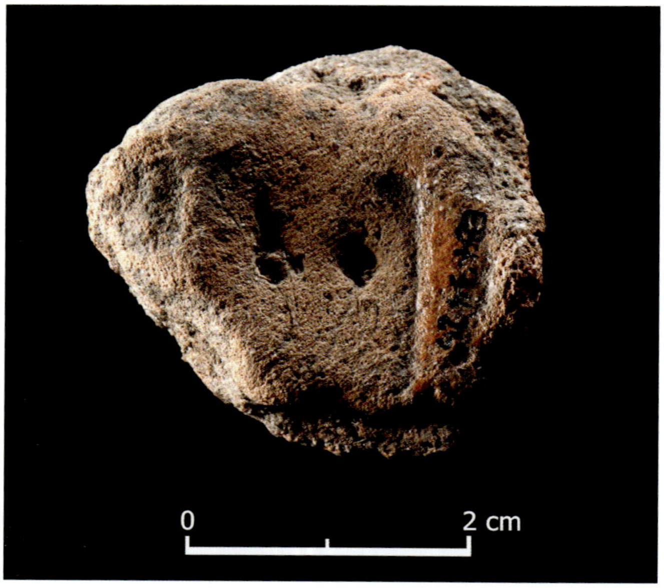

Fig. 3.83—Tab mould fragment E84:3425 (photo: John Sunderland).

and only carry one rivet hole each. It is possible that the Rathgall examples were for smaller objects composed of sheet metal.

3.9 BRONZE AGE METALWORKING AT RATHGALL

Katharina Becker

Metalworking is one of the main aspects of activity at Bronze Age Rathgall. Crucibles and moulds constitute the bulk of the evidence for this and suggest activity at significant levels. A number of metal items possibly associated with this phase of metalworking activity came to light. These included a probable bronze-casting jet[11] and a small, triangular strip of thin sheet bronze found in Cutting D (E84:0863; Fig. 3.36). This is likely to be a piece left over from cutting a bronze sheet during the manufacturing process—the date of which, however, is unclear. As has already been discussed, the small, fine-bladed chisel (E84:8344) found with two other bronzes (E84:8345, 8346) in Pit 31 might well have been used for fine metalworking (Figs 3.31 and 2.101–103), but it may also represent a woodworking tool. E84:8096 (Fig. 3.79) may be a preform for a chisel-like tool, and as such may also indicate metalworking on site.

The most substantial body of evidence for metalworking in the Bronze Age consists of the moulds. The distribution and contexts of these across the site may in principle inform us about areas of activity, which may in turn throw light on how the process of metalworking was organised on the site. The distribution of the mould fragments is, however, influenced by processes of disposal, deposition, deterioration and later disturbance. The differentiation between primary deposits and redeposited materials and an understanding of the taphonomic processes at play are thus of relevance in relation to questions about the character, extent and organisation of the metalworking, as well as the site's phasing.

Moulds have a wide distribution across the site and represent a probably much higher number of casting episodes than is implied by the number of identified objects (section 3.8 above). The highly fragmentary and often abraded nature of the mould fragments—broken by use and, as debris, often exposed to the elements and to further site activity—contributes to the difficulties in understanding their use and later history. Nevertheless, some observations about primary deposition and later redeposition can be made.

The deposits and the contexts from which they derive suggest two major zones of primary deposition. The disturbed but substantial deposits of prehistoric material in Area 2 produced a large number of these moulds, and the composition of these deposits—charcoal-rich and including a variety of other apparently discarded materials, such as pottery—suggests that this is a zone in which these were deposited over a period of time onto the ground surface rather than into cut features. The lack of the 'protective embrace of cut features—pits and ditches—which most often allow the survival of clay refractory debris in a recognisable state, providing of course that they reach that context fairly quickly' (e.g. Needham 1980; Needham and Bridgford 2013, 68–74), that has to be surmised for many of these fragments explains the degree of fragmentation and abrasion on many. It is, in fact, informative that many of the mould fragments that were apparently simply discarded across such a vast area as Area 2, not protected in cut features, were still in good condition. Given the evidence for disturbance of the area in medieval times, possibly in association with the construction of the stone cashel on top of these deposits, this is especially striking, and it appears likely that the substantive nature of the deposits themselves protected the moulds. As noted by Roche (section 3.11 below), the pottery from these deposits is also in good condition. The distinct end of the distribution of these materials at the southern end of Area 2, broadly along the post-hole alignments between Areas 2 and 3, may suggest that this acted as a revetment of sorts.

A close association of deposits of moulds with the possible metalworking Hearth 10 (Fig. 2.42) is represented in Metalworking Zone 1 in Sqs 51 and 52, with a small spread as far as Ring-ditch 1 to the west and eastwards into Sq. 43. Unfortunately, there was no real stratigraphy in this area and almost all the fragments were thus in the disturbed brown soil horizon. This spread may be related to metalworking activity associated with Hearth 10, which itself contained a number of mould fragments, none of which show any links with the other metalworking zones in Area 2. The fragments from Hearth 10 also stand out from the wider assemblage by being highly oxidised. One of the objects cast here is a spearhead that has an apparent wide midrib and peg hole—spearhead B, fragments of which were also found in adjacent squares. A possible further fragment of spearhead B in the fill of Ring-ditch 1 in Sq. 38, at a considerable distance, may be due to a misattribution of this fragment to the mould unit or may otherwise represent a wide spread of fragments from this location. Some possible chape fragments were also found in Hearth 10, among other, not clearly identifiable mould fragments.

A focus of mould deposition was the area of cobbling in the B and C squares (Metalworking Zone 2). Raftery considered this to be an area of primary deposition in the context of metalworking at this location, possibly focused on a charcoal concentration within the cobbling that may represent a hearth feature (Fig. 2.54).

3.9.1 Metalworking materials from Area 2

Of contrasting morphology are the four-poster hearths, which may, as explored in Chapter 6, be possible pyre pits, though Raftery also considered a function in the realm of metalworking. One mould fragment was found in a primary, charcoal-rich phase of Hearth 3 in Area 1, and fragments of both crucibles and moulds were contained in Hearth 15 in Area 3—the mould from its black fill, another mould fragment from the fill of one of the post-holes, and the crucible fragment on the lower black lining of the hearth. The small number of mould fragments and their integration into the feature appear most likely to indicate residuality. A larger number of mould fragments are attributed to Hearth 4 in Area 1. One of its four corner posts (Pit 95) was apparently dug out; the pit was then filled with a soil deposit containing the mould fragments and was topped with stones. The hearth appears to have had two parallel slots on either side of the central pit and in this it differs from the other pyre features. While it is conceivable that it is a very large hearth within a small building, this appears unlikely given the large size of the pit. At least three objects are represented among the 33 mould fragments from Hearth 4, and further fragments that are attributed to the hearth without detailed context information may also be derived from this (secondary) context. In other areas moulds were found in cut features, which may or may not represent prehistoric activity themselves (e.g. Pits 128 and 95 in Area 1, and Pits 53 and 54 in the E cuttings). Small quantities of mould fragments in a number of contexts, such as three in Sq. 43 in the fill of the circular bedding trench (E84:5616a–c), are probably residual inclusions. While the irregular pits Hearths 5 and 6 do not show the distinct four-poster arrangement, they likewise may be pyre pits rather than metalworking hearths.

The identification of links between the moulds in the different metalworking zones in Areas 2 and 1 adds further evidence that is particularly relevant to the question of the relationship between the metalworking and the digging of Ring-ditch 1—a topic that constitutes one of the main relative chronological issues (see Chapter 4, sections 4.2–4.5), as well as the actual processes of metalworking within the areas described.

Raftery had defined three mould concentrations in Area 2 (Metalworking Zones 2–4; Fig. 2.54), which he saw as further areas of primary deposition. The relationship between Metalworking Zones 2 and 3 is of crucial importance for understanding the make-up of the deposits in Area 2 and the question of whether they represent different activity zones generated at different times. In both areas the metalworking residues are associated with the thick, black, charcoal-rich material that Raftery named the 'occupation deposits' in the 'area of industrial activity', as well as with vast amounts of pottery, glass beads and other finds. A number of moulds show links across Metalworking Zones 2–4. Chape 1 and the chape cores, in particular, have a distribution across the B, C and E squares. Similarly, knife mould B was found in both D/D1 and C1, and the possible bracelet mould A in B1/D/D1/D2. If one does not want to invoke large-scale disturbance that would lead to lateral disposal of mould fragments across 5m, these observations would suggest disposal processes across this wider area that do not indicate a fundamental temporal difference in generation of these deposits.

Some mould units extend from deposits in Area 2 across

Ring-ditch 1 into Area 1. A possible fragment of chape mould 1 (4735) was found in the fill of Ring-ditch 1 in the dump of casting material in Sq. 29 and another one in Hearth 5, Sq. 7 (1947). Links between Metalworking Zones 2/3 (in this instance Sq. C1) and Hearth 7 are also implied by the finding of fragments of the same hafting plate 1 and of fragments constituting pin mould A in E1, C1 and Sq. 7.

This suggests the spreading of these items across this zone before the existence of Ring-ditch 1, indicating that there was no temporal difference or physical obstructions that would have created different patterns of dispersal from Metalworking Zones 2 and 3 (see Chapter 4). Furthermore, this dispersal took place early enough for the moulds to be integrated into the hearth features, which appear to be of Bronze Age date themselves. This suggests, therefore, that in the Bronze Age the moulds had already been fragmented and dispersed across this wider area. Importantly, this must also have taken place before the digging of Ring-ditch 1.

This contradicts Raftery's assumption that the ring-ditch had been dug before the accumulation of Metalworking Zone 3, with its bank keeping the moulds in this area from slipping into the ditch. In contrast, material adjacent to the B and C squares (Metalworking Zone 2) was thought to have moved into the ditch after it had been dug. This was based on the impression that there were no moulds in the fill of Ring-ditch 1 beside the D squares. This can now be shown to be incorrect, with the ring-ditch fill in Sqs 9/3/8/2 having produced 86 mould fragments and that in Sqs 7 and 7/8 yielding eleven.

Some further links are created by fragments of moulds found in Ring-ditch 1: this includes one of the chape core fragments in primary silt in Sq. 9/3, directly adjacent to Metalworking Zone 2, and a fragment of sickle A in the black-brown fill of Ring-ditch 1 in Sq. 7. Several fragments of decorated tool socket A were found in the ditch fill in Sq. 7 and two others in Sq. D1. Importantly also, spearhead A, which is *not* represented in the eastern deposits but is represented by two fragments in Hearth 6 in Sq. 8/16, is also found in the ring-ditch fill in Sq. 7/8, almost on its base.

The presence of mould fragments in basal or basal silting layers is especially important, as is the heavily abraded nature of most fragments from this layer, which suggests that the moulds were lying around on the site, exposed to the elements, and entered the adjacent ditch through processes of silting, from inside and outside..

Some mould links may furthermore suggest that certain mould fragments found within Ring-ditch 2 in Area 3 originated from the metalworking activity in Area 2: knife A was represented in Sqs 3/4 and in G; socketed axe mould fragment 7093 was found in D2, while possibly complementary part 8622.1 was found in H4. While a less secure connection than that offered by knife A, in combination these findings are suggestive of the material in Area 3 deriving from Area 2.

We may suggest that these different patterns observed in the area enclosed by Ring-ditch 1 and those in its fill represent two phases of mould dispersal—one before or contemporary with the creation of the hearths and before the digging of the ditch, and the other one at the time the ditch was silting up—and moulds entering the ditch apparently from both the inside and the outside. The quantitative difference in the respective parts of the ditch fill may in that instance also be paralleled with those in other parts of the site—for example, the apparent dump of material that constitutes Metalworking Zone 5, with areas adjacent to it.

The position of Hearth 4 with its moulds directly adjacent to Ring-ditch 1 is striking and may lend yet further support to the hypothesised timing of the digging of the ring-ditch after the metalworking phase. While no record of actual physical overlap is present in the site archive to support Raftery's statement that '… hearth 3 [*sic*] in Sq. 8 was close to the inner edge of Ring-ditch 1 which had clearly been cut across it', the proximity in itself is indeed suggestive of the temporal relationship that Raftery clearly asserts.

Considering the mould units represented in Metalworking Zone 5, it appears possible that the material there may derive from the Metalworking Zones 2/3. Fragments of the palstave mould were found in B1 and Sq. 20, directly adjacent to Sq. 29. The chape 1 fragment mentioned above (4735) and two fragments of the mould suggested to comprise pin mould B found in Sq. 26, in the fill of Ring-ditch 1 in Sq. 29 and in D1 lend further support to this. Given the wide spread of mould fragments across the site, the repetitive nature of these far-reaching links is striking, and among them also the possible fragment of bracelet A in Sq. 58 should be mentioned as an exception.

3.9.2 Organisation of metalworking and activity areas

Crucibles provide a complementary form of metalworking evidence. These were reused on multiple occasions, as indicated by their characteristic relining, which is evidenced at Rathgall as at many other sites (see section 3.7). Unlike moulds, they are unlikely to shatter routinely during use; in fact, the relining and reuse may suggest not only a number of consecutive casting episodes but also the retaining of the items over longer periods of time.

This difference between crucibles and moulds is also reflected in their respective distribution across the site. Unlike the moulds, with few exceptions crucibles are found in cut features. Two moulds and a crucible fragment were recovered from Hearth 15 and Pit 20, situated close together in Sqs H3/4 and G2. Pit 20 in G2 produced two sherds which may or may not have formerly represented part of the same crucible. This pit is a striking deposit and one of the substantial mould deposits outside Area 2, having contained five fragments of coarse pottery as well as three crucible fragments and sixteen mould fragments.

Within Area 4, strikingly, the small, complete crucible 4 was found in Pit 215, which also produced a glass bead, some coarse pottery and flint debitage in a black layer, sealed with a large boulder. It should, however, be noted that, in spite of the association with prehistoric finds, the possibility that this unusual crucible is of medieval date cannot be excluded. The location of the pit in the area of the medieval house may support this, and the association of prehistoric artefacts with medieval pottery—as, for example, in the case of Pit 76 in H3 and apparently Pit 244 in X11—calls for caution in interpreting all cut features as primary Bronze Age deposits.

Crucible 1 was deposited almost complete, if broken, in the basal deposit of Pit 118 in Area 1, and substantive fragments of crucible 3 were found in pyre Hearth 3 as well as possibly in pyre Hearth 6, which also contained substantial amounts of pottery and some mould fragments. It is also notable that the cut features containing moulds and crucible fragments—both the pyre hearths and other pits—are found exclusively outside Area 2.

In contrast, within Area 2, despite the majority of mould fragments originating from here, only a small group of rather dispersed crucible fragments were found in Metalworking Zones 2 and 3 (see Table 3.5). It may be possible to suggest that Area 2 was reserved for the disposal of the remains of the metalworking activity derived from the adjacent hearths, such as that possibly represented in the hollow in Metalworking Zone 2. The fact that these deposits also include vast amounts of pottery, metalwork and glass beads reflects that this may have been taking place as part of complex processes of deposition (see Chapter 6). It seems possible to suggest that Metalworking Zone 2 represents an actual zone of metalworking, with disposal towards the north and forming Metalworking Zones 3 and 4.

It appears possible that, as suggested by Raftery, a metalworking hearth is represented in the charcoal-filled hollow or hearth in his Metalworking Zone 2. Hearth 7, which unfortunately was only dated with a problematic Smithsonian date, is located adjacent to a rectangular structure in F/G (Figs 2.42–2.82). It is tempting to see this as a workshop structure. Rectangular structures are associated with metalworking in Irish prehistory, particularly in the Iron Age (e.g. at Tara; Crew and Rehren 2002). The possibility of a rectangular structure having been associated with the metalworking activity at Haughey's Fort has also been discussed (Brandherm 2014). Hearth 7, however, has produced no metalworking evidence.

3.10 IRON SLAG ANALYSIS

Thilo Rehren

3.10.1 Introduction

This report covers the visual assessment and instrumental analysis by optical microscopy and X-ray fluorescence (XRF) analysis of some twelve slag sample lots from Rathgall, Co. Wicklow (E84). These derive from the iron-working hearth (samples 5876, 5924, 5979 and 6019) in Sq. 65, the fill of which is described as 'containing black material and burnt clay fragments', and adjacent Sqs 67 (5867), 66 (5865) and 59 (5514). No context is recorded for sample 5945. The lots of samples are identified here by finds numbers that were voided in the finds catalogue, while for the year 1971 a sample register was kept. The main questions to be addressed were whether the samples are really metallurgical slag; if so, whether they derived from smelting or smithing; and whether any other metallurgical activities can be identified from this material. Two samples of charcoal were dated to the third–sixth centuries AD (see pp 461 and 471).

3.10.2 Macroscopic assessment

The assemblage comprises eight individual finds numbers; some of these represent single fragments of finds, while the majority are lots of up to twenty individual pieces. The general appearance of the samples is dark brown and rusty, with a high degree of porosity and maximum dimensions of about 8cm; most are much smaller, not exceeding about 4–5cm. The morphology of the slags ranges from plano-convex, near-circular pieces 8cm in diameter and with a maximum thickness of 3cm to small, non-diagnostic fragments. Very few pieces show impressions of fuel fragments ('negative charcoal') or signs of dripping and running; clear flow features are absent. The first impression is of heavily corroded and rather 'rusty' material, ranging in colour and apparent density from fused hearth ceramic to proper slag. The total amount of material does not exceed a few kilograms, indicating either a rather small-scale operation or a low recovery and retention rate, or both. Sample 6019/S71:82 contained iron slag fragments as well as a crucible fragment.

3.10.3 Crucible fragment 6019/S71:82

The crucible fragment was semi-quantitatively analysed by XRF on its concave interior and its convex exterior. This means that the sample was not prepared in the same way as the others but was simply placed in the XRF instrument as provided and analysed. This enabled the separate analysis of the opposite surfaces of the object without changing its physical integrity but compromised the accuracy of the resulting data; hence no table is provided here but just an assessment. The composition was found to be that of a typical ceramic, with 50–60wt% silica, around 15wt% alumina, just under 10wt% iron oxide, and a low percentage of lime, potash and soda, as well as phosphorus oxide. The interior of this fragment contained about 0.1% of copper oxide and about 0.5% of zinc oxide, together with about 0.05% each of lead oxide and tin oxide. These levels are 10–100 times higher than those on the exterior and those of the slag samples, and clearly represent evidence for the working of a copper-based alloy in this crucible fragment, although it is impossible to deduce the nature of the alloy worked from the ratio of metal oxides present.

3.10.4 XRF analyses

The execution of XRF analyses, using a Spectro Xlab 2000 Pro with polarised primary beam, multiple targets and energy-dispersive spectrometer, was aimed at identifying both main and trace element compositions. A total of eight samples were selected which appeared to be not too corroded and which were sufficiently large to allow the preparation of about 8g of powdered material. About 10g were cut off the samples with a diamond-coated circular saw, cleaned and then crushed, milled and pressed into pellets, with a low-density wax as a binder. The analyses were performed using a dedicated calibration method for iron-rich materials (Veldhuijzen 2003). All sample preparation and XRF analyses were carried out by Alexander Veldhuijzen at the Wolfson Archaeological Science Laboratories at the UCL Institute of Archaeology, and his help is gratefully acknowledged. Full results are provided in Table 3.22 but, given the inevitable degree of corrosion even within larger samples (see below), these must be interpreted with much caution. The results span a range of compositions which is dominated by silica and iron oxide, typically with less than 5% of alumina, and even less calcium oxide, phosphorus oxide, potash and soda. Only a sample of vitrified hearth lining (5924r) has more silica than iron oxide, and another sample (5982) appears to be a mixture of slag and hearth lining on account of its similarity in manganese, calcium and magnesium oxides to sample 5924r.

The proper slag samples range from *c.* 75wt% to 45wt% iron oxide and from 15wt% to 30wt% silica. The twofold increase in silica goes together with a threefold rise in alumina, lime, magnesia and potash. Interestingly, manganese oxide appears to be negatively correlated with iron oxide, i.e. it increases as iron oxide decreases. The level of phosphorus is generally high and increases with decreasing iron oxide. The most significant (though as yet unexplained) increase is seen for barium oxide, which increases about sixfold with silica. The trace element pattern is also consistent with iron metallurgy; levels of copper are typically at or below 100ppm (= 0.01%), with zinc, lead and tin even lower.

When comparing these values to iron slags from elsewhere, the low content of manganese oxide (*c.* 0.5wt%) and the high phosphorus oxide level of more than 2wt% are remarkable; the relatively low alumina content is also of interest. Expressed as the ratio of Al_2O_3 to SiO_2, it falls in the region of 1:5 to 1:7, compared to many smelting slags from Europe with typical ratios of 1:3 to 1:4.

Non-ferrous metalworking of any kind can now be safely excluded for the slag samples, and the identification of iron metallurgy confirmed. A distinction between smithing and smelting, however, is difficult to make on the basis of these data alone. The chemistry of smelting slag is typically dominated by the ore composition and further modified by absorbed furnace wall material and fuel ash; bog ore often, though not always, contains considerable amounts of alumina, phosphorus and manganese in addition to silica, and hence these oxides appear high in smelting slag. Smithing slag, in contrast, consists of smelting slag trapped in the smithed iron, plus fuel ash and molten hearth material, plus burnt iron from the worked metal, and any fluxes such as quartz sand which may have been added in the process. As a number of materials contribute to both types of slag, there is inevitably a chemical continuum, which can only be resolved by a larger comparative study, including known ore samples, smelting slag and local clay. However, very low levels of alumina, manganese and titania are often characteristic of smithing slag, which is dominated by a higher proportion of burnt iron and typical fuel ash and flux components (silica, lime, alkalis).

3.10.5 Optical microscopy

A total of eleven samples were selected for preparation of polished blocks for metallographic analysis. Five of these overlapped with existing XRF pellets; the others were selected to broaden the coverage of the material. Sample preparation was carried out in accordance with standard procedures at the UCL Institute of Archaeology, resulting in a polished surface suitable for reflected light microscopy and SEM analysis. No SEM investigation was undertaken, however, as this was deemed unnecessary for this investigation. All samples show extensive evidence for porosity and are heavily corroded. Even the best-preserved ones have an estimated one quarter of their material directly affected by corrosion, making the XRF data accordingly less representative of the original composition of the samples, and severely influenced by the burial conditions.

Sample E84:5982PB (PB indicates polished block) is a typical piece of fused and melted ceramic material, incorporating residual quartz particles, charcoal dust and a few iron-rich areas in a predominantly glassy matrix. The glassy nature of much of the matrix indicates a high degree of fuel ash contribution, while the few areas rich in iron oxide provide the link to iron metallurgy. This structure and composition are here interpreted as hearth lining fluxed by fuel ash, consistent with a smithing activity. The eponymous XRF sample is from a different fragment, which is of a more typical slag composition, although it stands out by its disproportionately high silica content relative to the minor oxides (Table 3.22).

Sample EA84:5945PB is a highly corroded porous slag, consisting of long, thin fayalite crystals and badly corroded wuestite and / or metallic iron particles in a glassy matrix. A

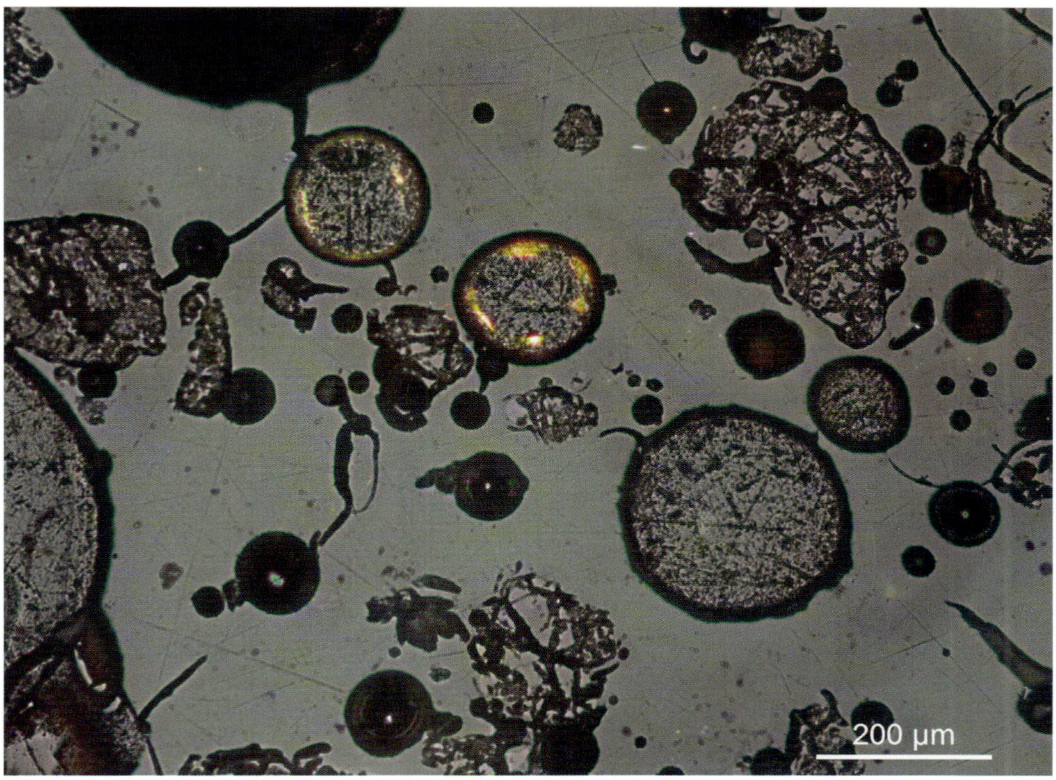

Fig. 3.84—Micrograph of sample 5982, showing a mostly glassy groundmass with isolated quartz grains (top right, centre bottom, centre) and circular porosity (black or filled with resin, grey). Width of image *c.* 1.2mm.

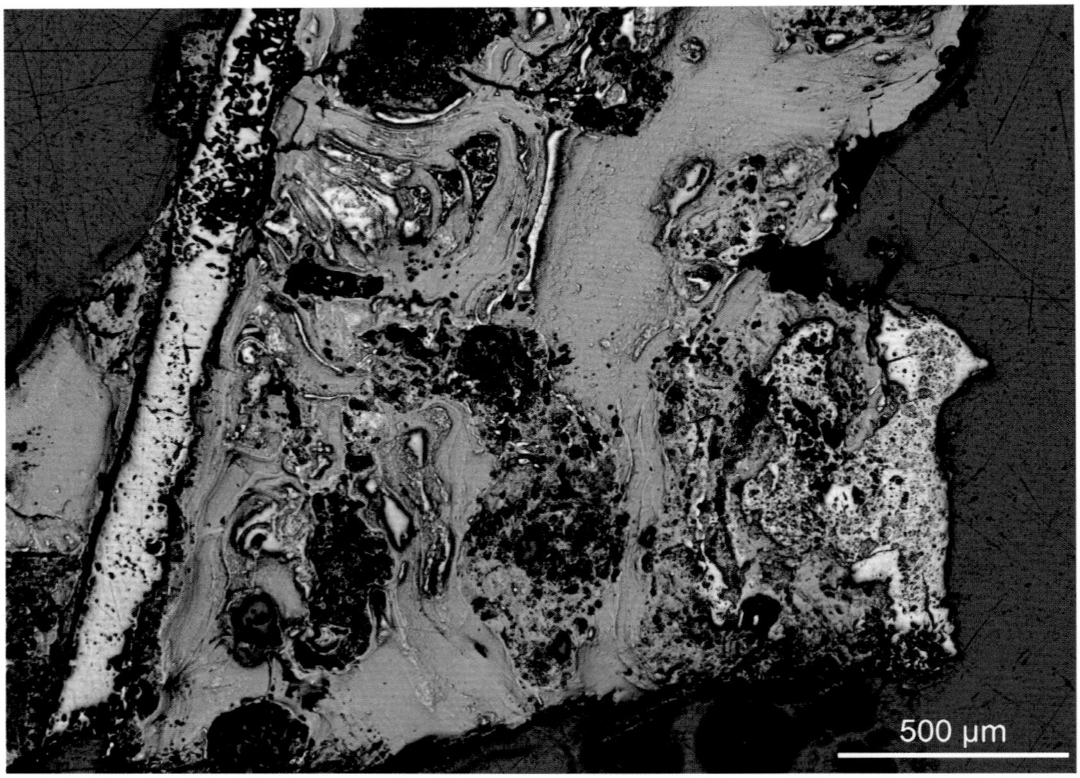

Fig. 3.85—Micrograph of sample 6019PB, showing a piece of hammer-scale (thin angular particle, left) in a groundmass of iron hydroxides (main part of image).

few quartz grains are embedded in the matrix, and large quantities of secondary iron hydroxides are present. While the mineralogy is consistent with either smelting or smithing slag, the porosity is more indicative of smithing. The related XRF sample is particularly low in alumina (ratio to silica 1:8), further supporting the argument for smithing.

EA84:5843PB is an extremely wuestite-rich slag, porous and rich in charcoal inclusions. The matrix between the wuestite agglomerates is fayalitic glassy but only preserved in a few residual core areas; otherwise it is completely corroded. The adhering soil material, cemented to the slag piece by iron hydroxides, is also rich in charcoal dust, indicating a workshop floor environment.

EA84:5694PB is the most corroded sample. As far as one can make out, it used to be a fayalitic slag with charcoal inclusions, little wuestite and a scatter of kalsilitic structures. A few specks of metallic iron have survived. The occurrence of kalsilitic structures is not restricted to smithing but is more often found there than in smelting slags. These structures form when a relatively high content of alkali oxides, in particular potash, is present, resulting in the formation of either a second, immiscible, liquid rich in potash and alumina in the main iron silicate slag melt, or the crystallisation of kalsilite-related phases ($KAlSiO_4$) when the crystallisation of fayalite from the main slag melt changes the composition of the diminishing melt phase towards the alumina–potash end of the system.

EA84:6019PB (Fig. 3.85) is from the same bag that yielded the crucible fragment, which did not contain much material that was visibly identified as slag. This particular piece proved to be a major lump of iron hydroxides (rust) with one large piece and several smaller pieces of hammer-scale shown in Fig. 3.85 embedded in it, along with charcoal dust and other particles. This is strong evidence for the presence in this material of fragments of a smithy floor, soil contaminated with charcoal and hammer-scale and consolidated by iron rust.

EA84:5514aPB is a fragment of quickly cooled fayalitic slag with a large amount of glassy matrix and some wuestite. The typical porous structure has advanced the corrosion, as in all the other samples, attacking first the glassy matrix and then the fayalite and wuestite at almost equal rates. The material and structure are non-diagnostic and could be from either smelting or smithing slag. The chemical composition is also not diagnostic; the alumina/silica ratio of 1:6 and the manganese oxide level (less than 0.5wt%) are generally low but typical of the range encountered in this material here so far, as is the high content of phosphorus oxide of more than 2wt%.

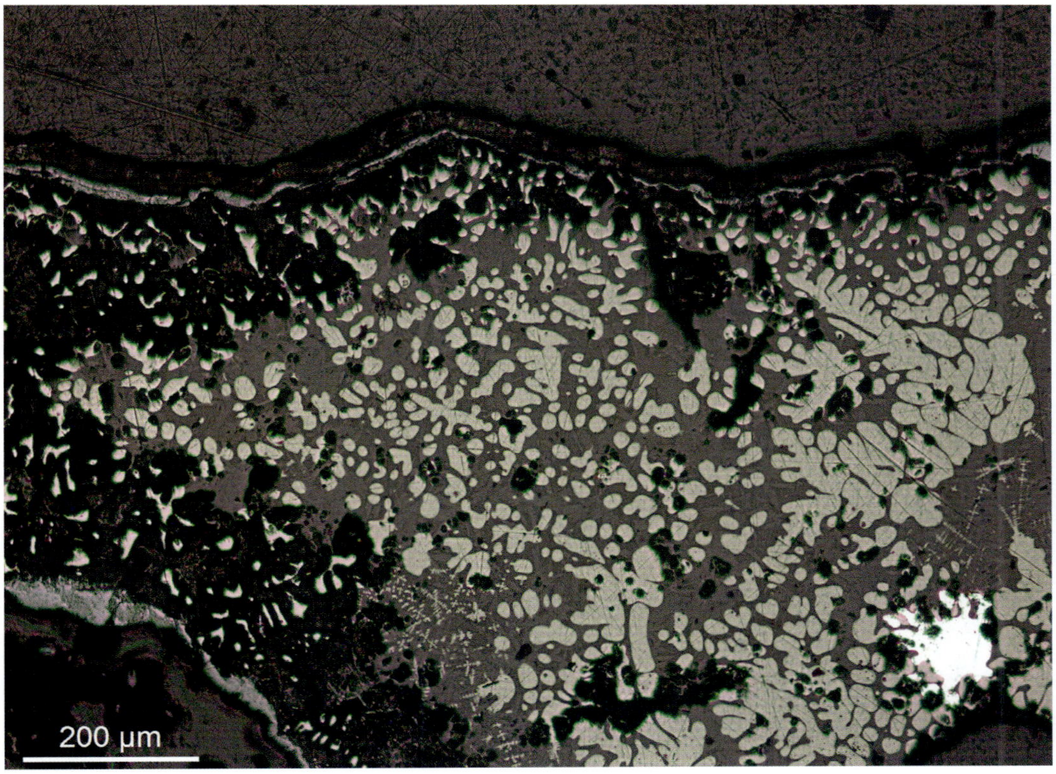

Fig. 3.86—Micrograph of sample 5514c, showing a silica-rich groundmass (mid-grey) with a high level of wuestite (light grey, rounded particles). Note the advanced corrosion of the slag, particularly in the left part of the image (dark parts of slag particle, with preferential leaching of the silicate matrix), and the particle of metallic iron (bright) in the lower right corner. The upper dark grey part of the image shows the resin in which the sample is embedded. Width of image c. 1.2mm.

EA84:5514bPB is very similar to the above sample but also contains considerable amounts of kalsilite-like structures, as well as areas almost free of wuestite but containing fragments of hammer-scale, next to a splash of metallic iron and charcoal. The shape and size of fayalite crystals varies abruptly across the sample; such heterogeneity in structure and composition is more often found in smithing slag than in smelting slag. The associated XRF analysis stands out with a particularly high level of P205 of over 3wt%; otherwise it is within the expected norm.

EA84:5514cPB is again very similar to the previous two samples but in addition shows massive aggregates of dense wuestite in a glassy fayalitic matrix. Again, there are several large splashes of metallic iron and a marked heterogeneity in structure and composition (Fig. 3.86). Some of the wuestite aggregates give the impression of dissolving in the silicate matrix and may well represent former hammer-scale particles. The XRF analysis of this sample is extremely iron-rich, with an alumina/silica ratio of 1:9. Both structure and composition are more in line with smithing than smelting slag.

EA84:5979aPB is completely corroded wuestite slag with a few splashes of metallic iron. Charcoal particles are present, while the already low original amount of silicate matrix is almost completely corroded. The adhering soil, consolidated by iron hydroxide, contains several hammer-scale particles, again strongly indicating smithing.

EA84:5979bPB is a fayalitic slag with a high proportion of glass in the matrix; in some areas kalsilitic structures are widespread. Several neatly defined wuestite aggregates resemble former hammer-scale particles, which appear to be dissolving in the silicate melt. The associated XRF analysis is characterised by an unusually high content of manganese oxide, of around 1%; otherwise it is within the normal range. All features except the high manganese level are indicative of smithing rather than smelting slag (Fig. 3.87).

EA84:5876PB is microscopically very similar to the previous sample.

3.10.6 Interpretation

The macroscopic, chemical and microscopic evidence points both individually and in combination very clearly to smithing as the main, probably exclusive, activity responsible for the formation of this material. Non-ferrous metallurgy can safely be ruled out for all the slag, although the presence of a small crucible fragment does demonstrate the former presence of some copper-based metallurgy within the workshop. A similar co-appearance of smithing and copper-

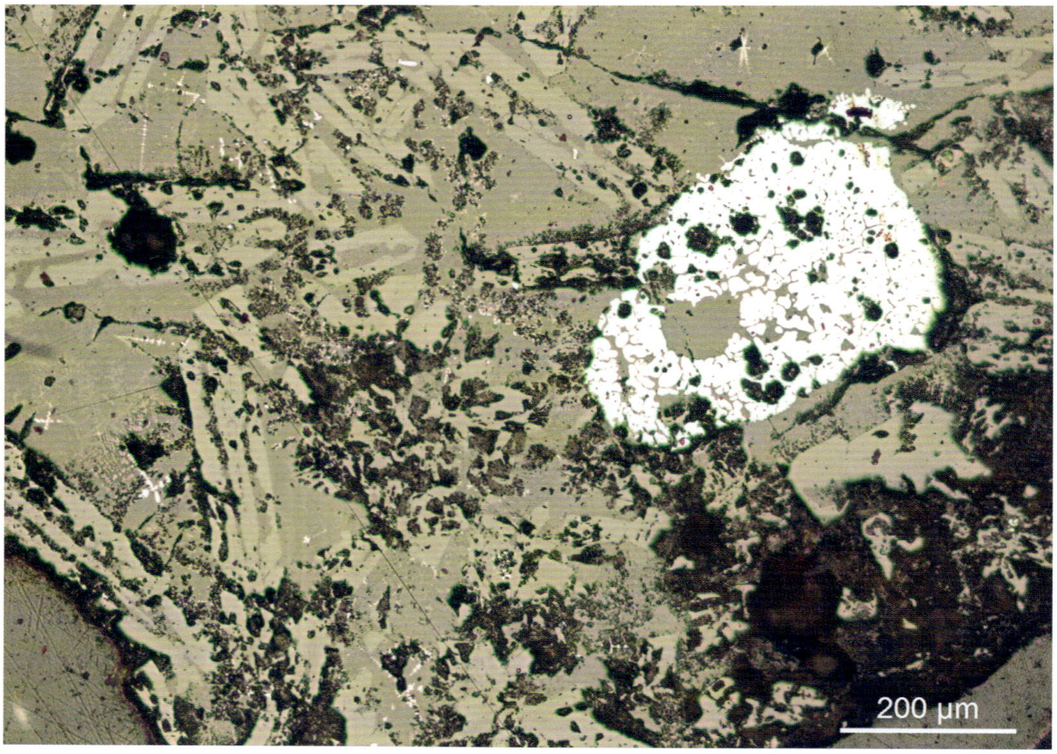

Fig. 3.87—Micrograph of sample 5979b, showing a mostly glassy groundmass (mid-grey) with elongated crystals of fayalite (light grey), areas rich in kalsilite (dark grey, angular, centre) and a wuestite lump (bright, centre), possibly a former hammer-scale fragment. Width of image *c*. 1.2mm.

Table 3.22—Results of XRF analyses of slag materials recovered at Rathgall. Data in wt% for the first ten rows, and in ppm for the remaining 6 rows (in italics).

	5514c	5924g	5945	5514a	5514b	5979b	5982	5924r	6019 inside	6019 outside
	Slag	Slag	Slag	Slag	Slag	Slag	Slag/hearth	Hearth lining	Crucible	Crucible
FeO	78.2	69.2	69.6	64.3	60.7	45.8	52.3	30.2	8.9	8.6
MnO	0.4	0.3	0.3	0.4	0.6	1	0.2	0.3	0.2	0.6
TiO_2	0.1	0.1	0.1	0.2	0.1	0.2	0.2	0.2	0.4	0.2
SiO_2	13.5	18.5	21	22.5	24.3	30.6	35.9	53.6	53.4	58.8
Al_2O_3	1.5	3.9	2.9	3.8	4	4.6	5	4.7	19	15.3
CaO	1.6	2.4	1.4	3	3.1	6.3	0.9	2	3.4	4.4
MgO	0.8	0.8	0.8	1	1.3	2.2	0.5	0.6	0.2	2
K_2O	0.6	1.3	0.8	1.8	2.1	2.8	1.9	2.2	4.3	6.3
Na_2O	0.6	1.1	0.5	0.7	0.6	1	1.2	1.2	1.9	3.3
P_2O_5	2.4	2.5	2.3	2.4	3.2	5.3	2.1	4.9	9.6	3.5
BaO	*120*	*250*	*250*	*350*	*420*	*890*	*130*	*410*	*130*	*610*
ZrO_2	*55*	*50*	*70*	*110*	*80*	*110*	*110*	*95*	*75*	*130*
CuO	*400*	*50*	*130*	*40*	*80*	*55*	*55*	*80*	*1850*	*310*
ZnO	*15*	*15*	*10*	*20*	*15*	*25*	*15*	*15*	*7300*	*80*
PbO	*20*	*20*	*20*	*15*	*15*	*10*	*10*	*5*	*635*	*25*
SnO_2	*20*	–	*5*	*5*	*5*	*20*	–	–	*570*	*30*

alloy casting was found at Tara (Crew and Rehren 2002) and is a common feature of later prehistoric metalworking. Within the possible spectrum of ferrous metallurgy, the macroscopic assessment already suggested that most of this material is from smithing, as indicated by its porous nature and in particular by the typical plano-convex shape of the better-preserved fragments. This shape, often labelled PCB (plano-convex bottom) or SHB (smithing hearth bottom), is typical of smithing, although some PCBs are known to have formed in smelting furnaces. The most convincing evidence for smithing comes from the cumulative microscopic evidence; the frequent occurrence of hammer-scale, the heterogeneity in structures and compositions in the micro-scale, the apparent continuum to vitrified hearth material and the frequent incorporation of charcoal particles all strongly suggest that these slags formed in a smithy rather than in a smelting furnace. The chemical composition is either neutral as far as the issue of smithing versus smelting is concerned, or more similar in some features to smithing slag than smelting slag. The high degree of corrosion has frustrated some of the analytical attempts; in particular, the XRF results are probably severely compromised. This could have affected, for instance, the level of phosphorus oxide found; this component is known to be easily concentrated from circulating groundwater to form either iron phosphate or to be absorbed by the glassy phase. The former is the main source for elevated phosphorus levels in waterlogged situations, as shown *par excellence* in medieval Novgorod, where blue iron phosphate is the dominant iron corrosion phase; the latter is well known, for instance from ceramic studies (Freestone *et al.* 1985). The selective corrosion of the silicate phases (glass first, but also fayalite) over the iron and iron oxide is obvious from the microscopic investigation; this will have had a major impact on the apparent iron oxide levels of the studied slag samples, and no more detailed discussion can therefore be made regarding this material. Given, however, that the overall evidence strongly points to smithing rather than smelting, and that phase diagram (and other equilibrium-based) interpretations are often rather meaningless with such material, this is probably not a great loss. For related reasons, no attempt was made to study individual phases by SEM; this would have not created any additional useful or relevant information. The quantity of slag suggests a small-scale operation.

Slag has often been called indestructible in the archaeological record; this is based primarily on the experience with archaeometallurgy in the deserts and semi-arid regions of the Near East, which dominated early archaeometallurgical research. More recently, however, an investigation of early medieval copper-smelting remains from Ross Island, Co. Cork, has found a similarly severe corrosion of the slag material (Meyerdirks *et al.* 2005). The surprisingly bad state of preservation of the material from Rathgall is therefore probably not specific to this site but more likely a reflection of the generally different environmental conditions prevailing in much of north-west Europe compared to the Near East. The co-existence of ferrous and non-ferrous metalworking on early Irish sites has been demonstrated, e.g. at Tara, Co. Meath (Crew and Rehren 2002).

3.11 POTTERY

A large assemblage of *c.* 5,300 sherds of prehistoric pottery, representing a minimum of 448 vessels, was found during the excavations. It includes a minimum of 22 Early Neolithic carinated bowls and 'cups', five Middle Neolithic globular bowls, ten Beaker vessels, 30 Middle Bronze Age vessels and 378 Late Bronze Age coarse vessels. A Neolithic stone globular bowl is also discussed below.

3.11.1 Prehistoric pottery
Helen Roche

The excavations at Rathgall produced an exceptional pottery assemblage, not only in the quantity of vessels represented but also in the range of vessel forms, demonstrating that the site was in at least episodic use from the Early Neolithic to the Late Bronze Age. The pottery was found in all excavated areas, in both sealed archaeological deposits and disturbed and topsoil contexts, and the bulk of the material represented Late Bronze Age vessels. In general the pottery was well preserved, with evidence for minor weathering visible on a large number of sherds, generally shown by an erosion of the outer surface and the exposure of inclusions. This report presents a general discussion of the assemblage; detailed descriptions of vessels and individual sherds are accessible in the site archive. Where in the rest of the volume individual sherds are referenced by their find number, this can be found in the pottery report in the archive or on the finds database (www.dri.e).

3.11.2 Early Neolithic assemblage

Helen Roche

Carinated bowls and 'cups'

This is a small assemblage consisting of 27 sherds, mainly rim sherds, derived from a minimum of 22 vessels (Table 3.23). Of these, Vessels 1–18 represent Early Neolithic carinated bowls (3, 5–6, 8–9, 11, 15–17) (Fig. 3.88a) and three small cups (Vessels 20–21, 23). Sherds representing seven carinated bowls were found within Area 1, widely dispersed in Sqs 3, 20, 29, 34, 43, 51 and 54. Eight carinated vessels were identified in Areas 2 and 3 in Sqs C1, D/D1, C1/B1, F2, G2/F2, H1, H5 and K8, and three vessels in the fill of Pit 22 in the Z cuttings (Z5:d). The three 'cups' were found in a relatively confined part of Area 2 in Sqs C1/B1, D1 and D/D1.

The generally hard, compact fabric of the Early Neolithic pottery is dark orange-brown-black to orange in colour, with the outer face darker and generally smooth but with inclusions occasionally protruding. The temper consists of crushed quartzite (2–5.2mm) and more finely crushed mica, which is frequently visible on the surface. The surfaces have also been carefully smoothed over with a wash or slurry of fine clay applied with the fingers.

Fourteen out-turned pointed rims (Vessels 1–5, 7–13, 16, 17) and three out-turned rounded rims (Vessels 6, 14, 15) (Fig. 3.88a) were identified. The surviving shoulder sherds are gently angled or moulded (Fig. 3.88a, 16). This form represents the earliest type of Neolithic pottery (Case 1961: 'Dunmurry–Ballymarlagh styles'; Sheridan 1995: 'classic' carinated bowls). This vessel type consists of a hemispherical bowl with a distinct shoulder or carination, a straight or curved neck, and a simple, often slightly out-turned, pointed or rounded rim. Vessels of this type in Ireland usually have deep bowls with a neck to bowl height ratio of *c.* 1:2, although the ratio ranges from 1:1 to 1:4. They also have neutral or open profiles, i.e. where the neck diameter is equal to or less than that of the rim. Cups (Vessels 20, 21, 23) have been found sporadically throughout the country in association with carinated bowls.

The three cups are similar in fabric to the carinated bowls described above. They are generally small and casually executed with a shallow profile (Fig. 3.88a, 20–21). They tend to have simple rounded or pointed upright rims but are occasionally slightly in-turned. The fabric often has a sandy texture and tends to be thoroughly fired, owing principally to the small size of the vessels. Rather than being coil-built, these small cups were simply pinched into shape. They are generally smaller than the carinated bowls, ranging in size from *c.* 5cm to 9cm in maximum external diameter.

Table 3.23—Carinated bowls and 'cups' recovered at Rathgall.

Carinated vessels	Wall thickness (mm)	Sq. no.	Context details	Depth (cm)	Carinated vessels & 'cups'	Wall thickness (mm)	Sqs between Ramparts 1 & 2 & outside Rampart 4	Context details	Depth (cm)
1	5.9	3	Dark brown near cobbling	30	8	6.9	C1	Brown burnt material	30
2	9.6	20	Immediately under sod	10	10	6.2	D/D1	Brown ashy under black	50–60
3	8.1	29	?	?	9	7.9	C1/B1	Section strip	
4	5.9	51	Brown	18–25	11	8.9	F2	Immediately under sod	10
5	9.2	54	Brown	20–25	14	6.8	G2/F2	Brown	–
6	7.8	34	Brown almost on yellow	20–22	12	5.1	H1	Brown	–
7	8.9	43	Brown	15	15	8.9	H5	Brown almost on yellow	30
					13	8.9	K8	Brown	10–15
					16–18	6.4, 5.9	Z5:a	Pit 22	
					20	6.8	D/D1	Under black/brown	50–65
					21	6	C1/B1	Black	–
					23	7.1	D1	Brown	15–19

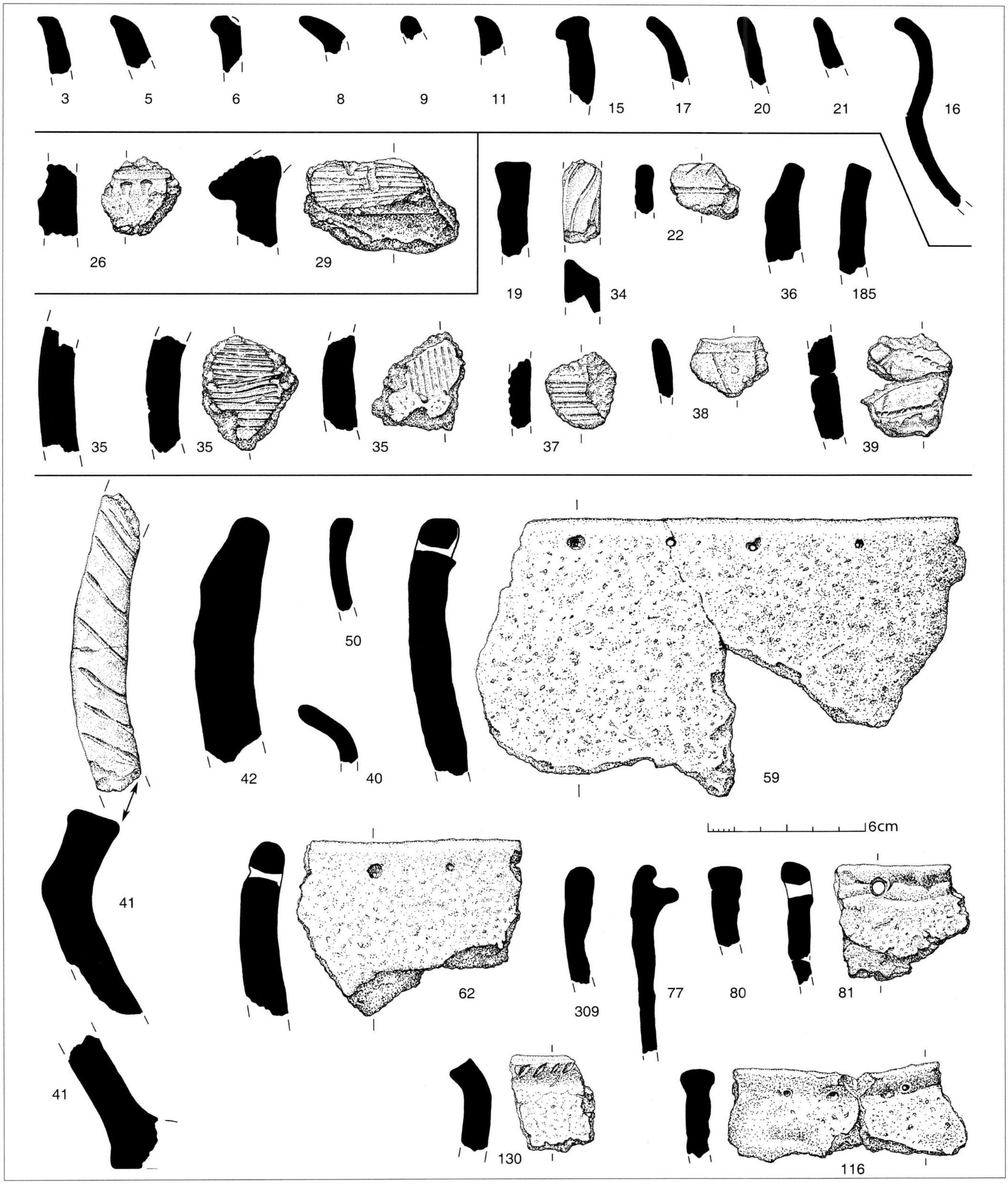

Fig. 3.88—(a) Early Neolithic pottery, Middle Neolithic pottery, Middle Bronze Age pottery and Late Bronze Age coarseware (scale 1:2).

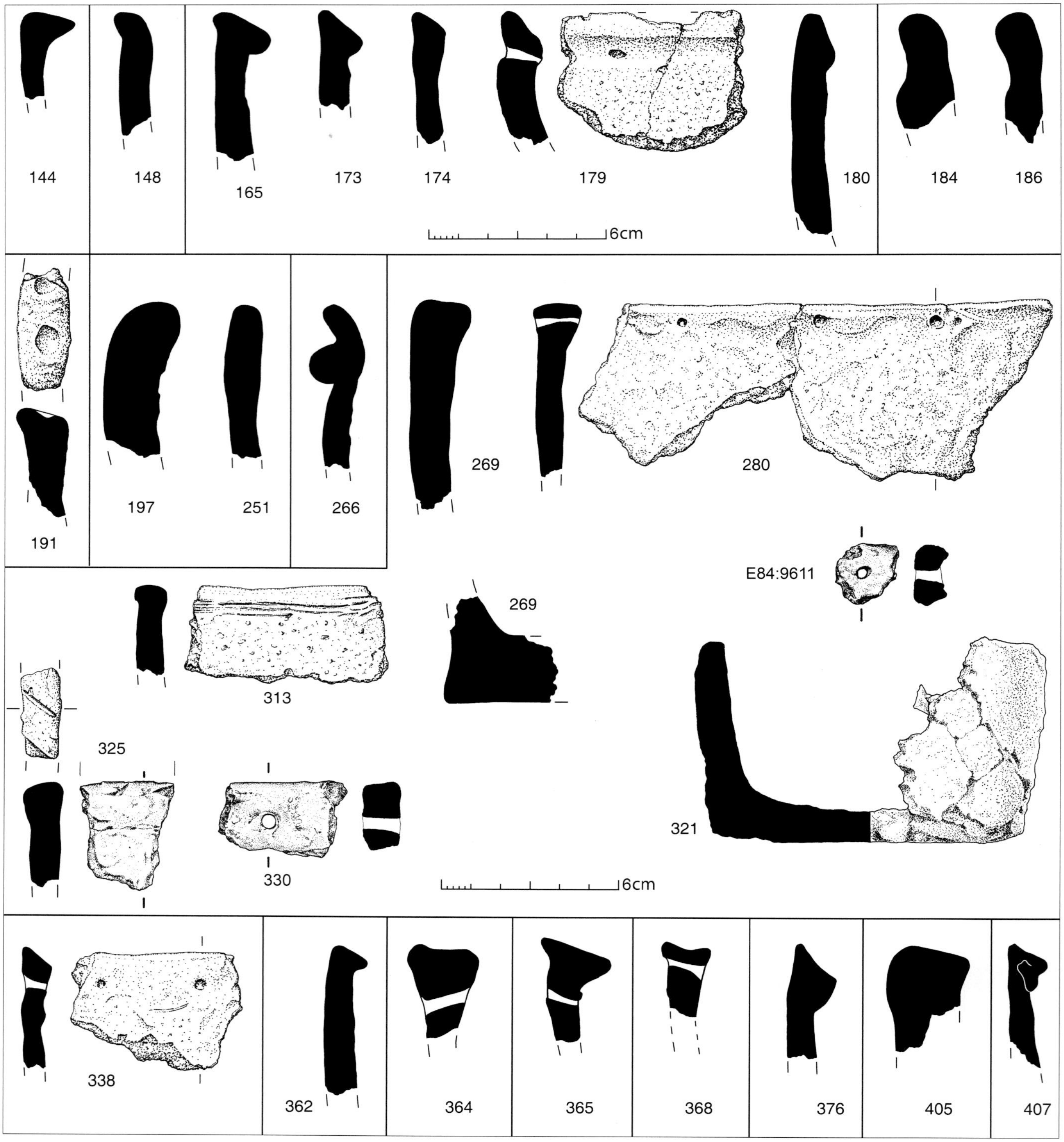

Fig. 3.88—(b) Middle and Late Bronze Age coarseware.

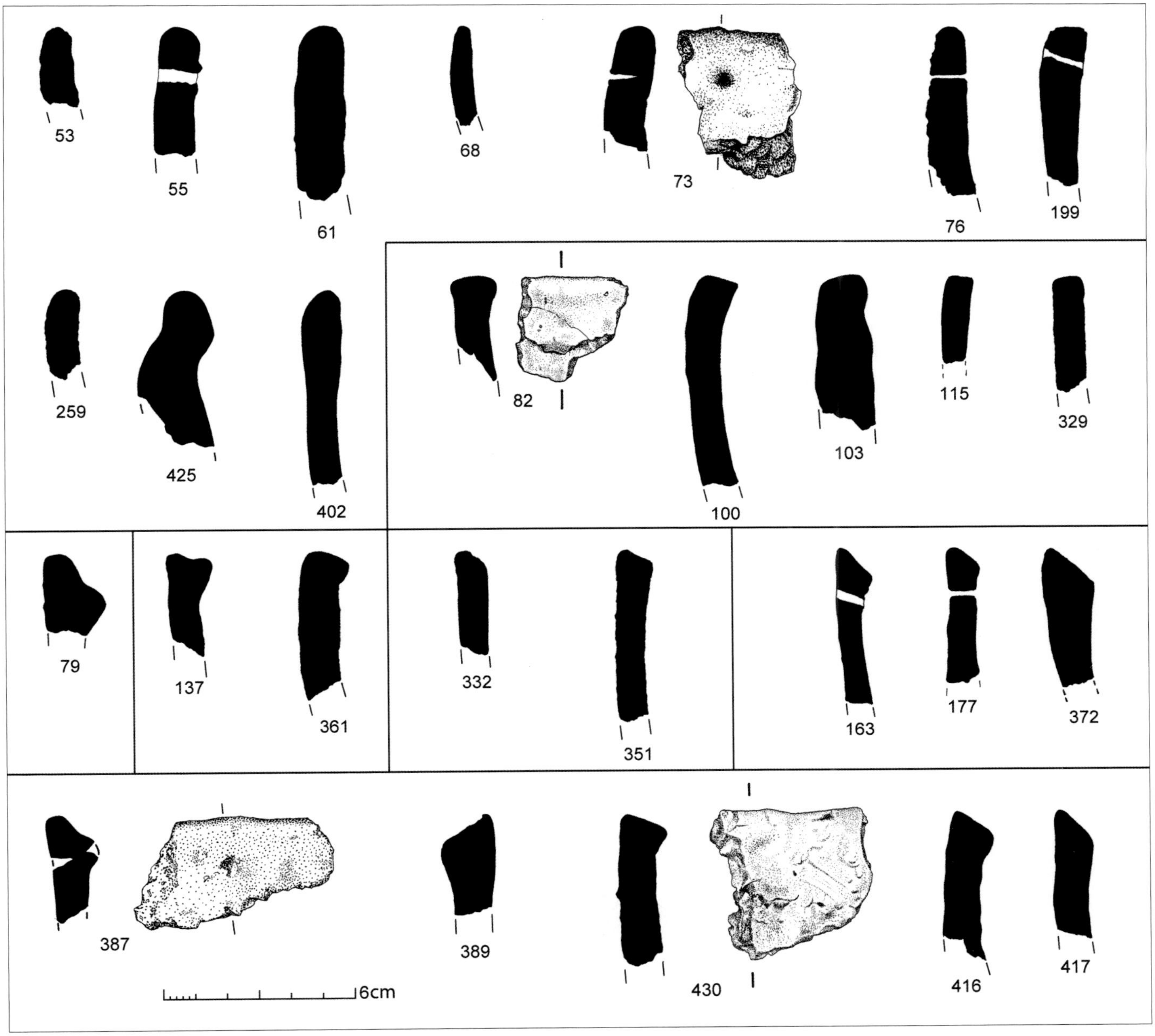

Fig. 3.88—(c) Late Bronze Age coarseware.

Discussion

The Rathgall bowls have a wide variety of parallels on other Neolithic domestic sites, including those with characteristic Early Neolithic rectangular houses, and in funerary contexts in portal and court tombs (Herity 1982). Closely comparable material has been found to the north of this region in south County Dublin at Kilgobbin and Beaverstown (Grogan 2004a; 2004b), and in house sites at Corbally, Co. Kildare ('Silliot Hill'; Purcell 1998; 1999). Similar pottery has also been found further afield in the earliest Neolithic phase at Knowth (Eogan and Roche 1997) and at Newtown, Co. Meath (Gowen and Halpin 1992), as well as at Coolfore and Richardstown, Co. Louth (Ó Drisceoil 2003; Byrnes 1999), and in the north of the country at Ballyharry and Lyles Hill, Co. Antrim (Moore 2004, 144; Evans 1953). In the south-west examples were found at Lough Gur, Co. Limerick, at Circles J, K, L, Site 10 and Site C (Grogan and Eogan 1987; Ó Ríordáin 1954).

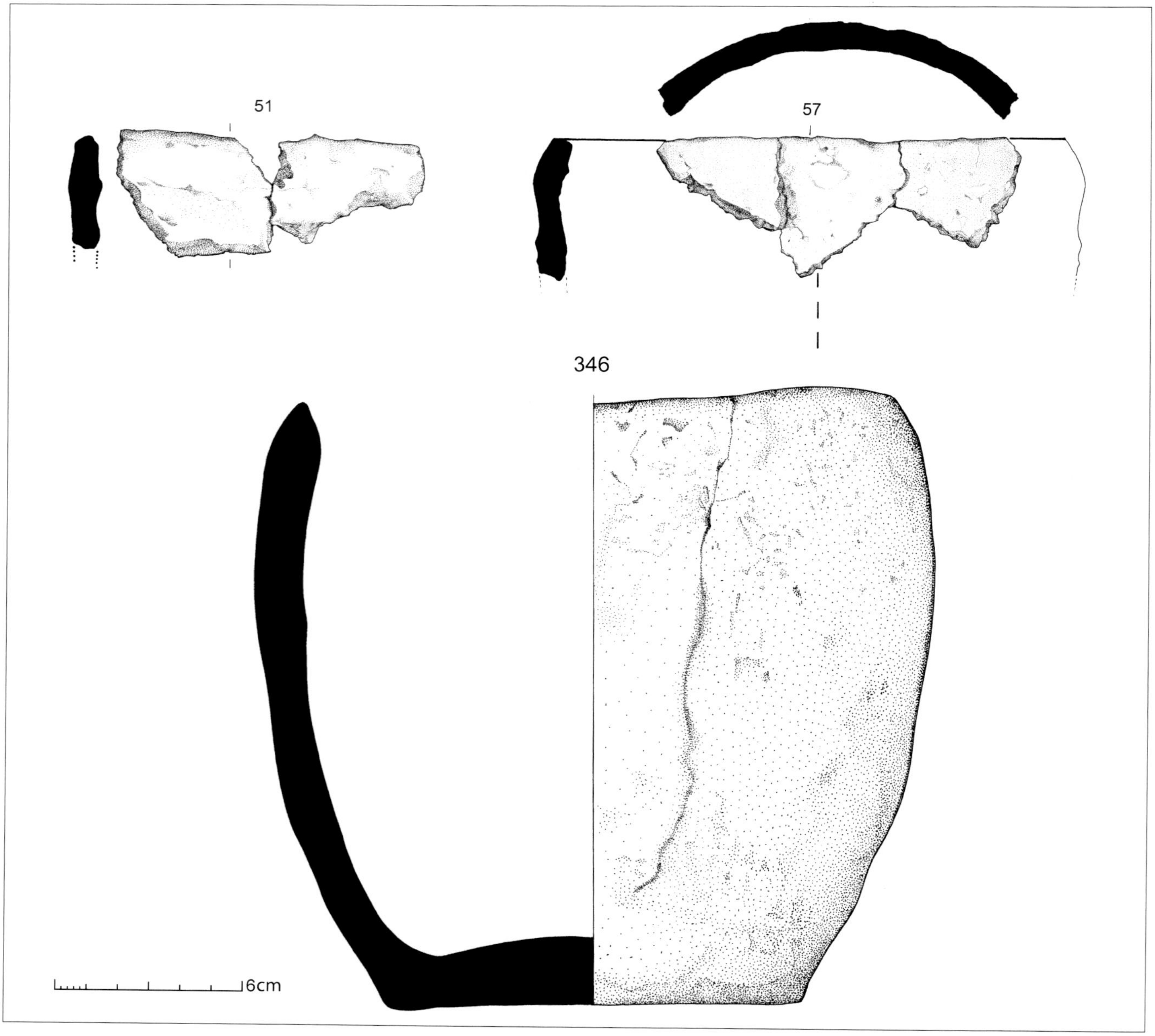

Fig. 3.88—(d) Late Bronze Age coarseware, including Vessel 346 from Burial 2.

Small cups were initially recognised by Ó Ríordáin (1951, fig. 9.3; 1954, 327, 328–30, fig. 13) at Lough Gur and were subsequently described from other sites on the Knockadoon peninsula (Grogan and Eogan 1987), with especially well-known examples coming from Site C and Circle K (Ó Ríordáin 1954, 327, fig. 15; Grogan and Eogan 1987, 370, fig. 32: 2514–18). While some fine cups, similar to those from Rathgall, occur especially in the north-east, those from Lough Gur are squat with relatively thick lower bodies.

The context at Rathgall appears to represent limited domestic or funerary activity belonging to the beginning of the Neolithic in this region, *c.* 3800–3600 BC (Sheridan 2010b). The dispersal of the sherds throughout the site suggests small-scale activity that was disturbed during later phases of occupation. Although the assemblage is small, it is an important contribution to the archaeological record of this period, as finds of this type of pottery were rare in this region until recently.

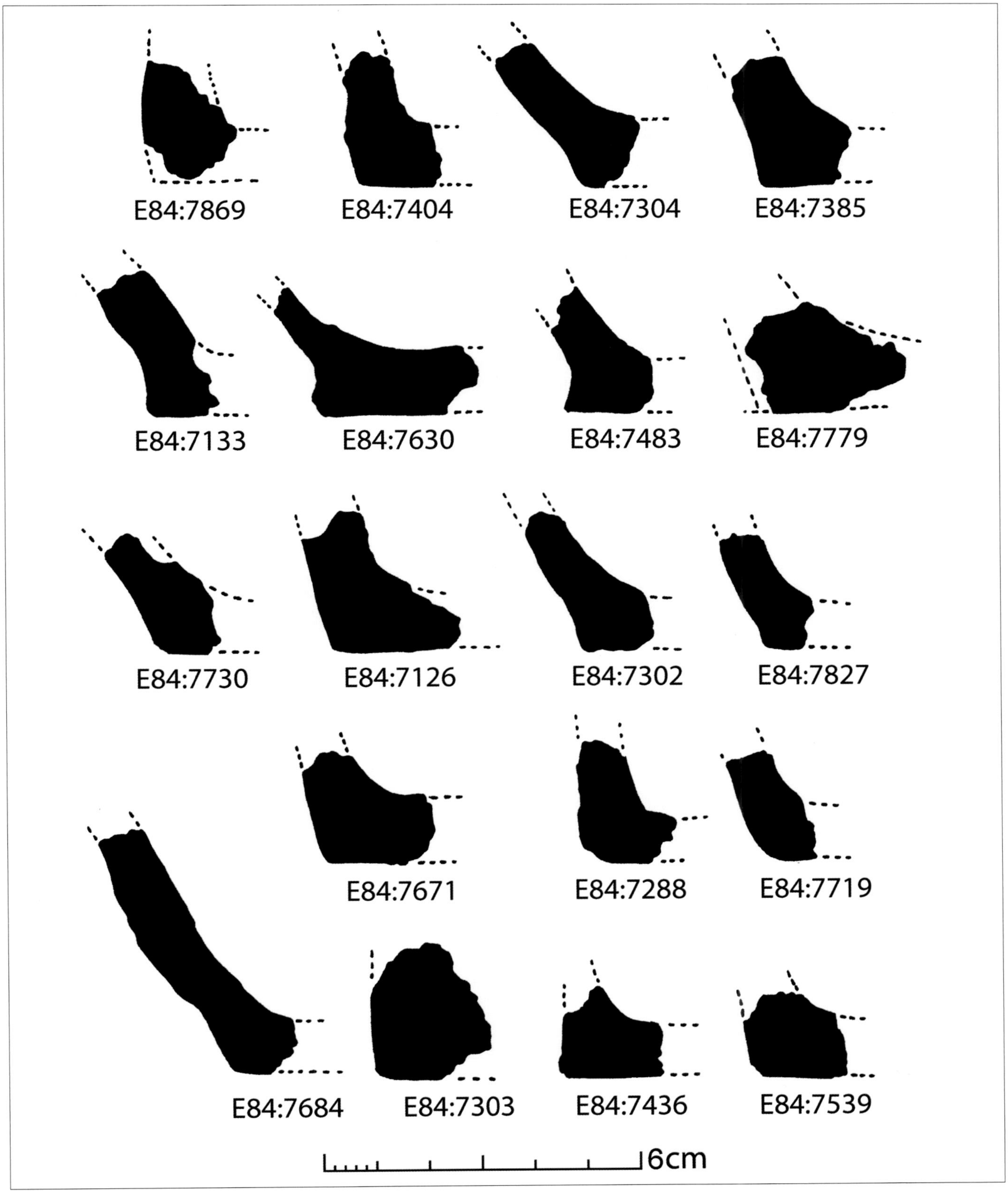

Fig. 3.88—(e) Late Bronze Age coarseware base angle sections.

3.11.3 Middle Neolithic assemblage

Helen Roche

Five vessels of Middle Neolithic shape (3600–3000 BC) were recognised (Table 3.24): a bipartite bowl (Vessel 24) and four globular bowls (Vessels 26, 29; Fig. 3.88a). The sherds were dispersed through Areas 1–3 and the Z cuttings (Fig. 3.89). Bipartite bowls are a feature of the Middle Neolithic period, most commonly associated with Linkardstown-type tombs such as Ballintruer More, Co. Wicklow, and Drimnagh, Co. Dublin, and are well dated in these contexts to *c.* 3550–3450 BC (Brindley and Lanting 1989–90; Sheridan 1995, 18). These vessels have come from other funerary sites, such as the portal tomb at Ballykeel, Co. Armagh (Collins 1965), and court tombs at Annaghmare (Waterman 1965), Co. Armagh, and Ballynamona Lower, Co. Waterford (Powell 1938). The sherds representing Vessel 24 indicate a well-executed, highly decorated, horizontal-rimmed bipartite bowl, similar in form to the bowl from the single burials at Baunogenasraid, Co. Carlow (Raftery 1974), and Jerpoint West, Co. Kilkenny (Ryan 1973). This type of bowl was categorised as Style 1A Necked Vessels by Herity (1982, 269–70) and as Drimnagh Style Bowls by Brindley and Lanting (1989–90, 1).

The heavy club rim with channelled decoration (Vessel 29; Fig. 3.88a) is typical of the Dundrum bowls of the group of Sandhills ware defined by Case (1961, 189) and categorised as Broad-Rimmed Vessels by Herity (1982, 273–5). Such vessels, although not unknown from funerary contexts, e.g. the vessel associated with the individual burial at Linkardstown, Co. Carlow (J. Raftery 1944; Herity 1982, fig. 18), are more commonly found in habitation contexts. Similar vessels to the example from Rathgall are known from Lambay Island and Dalkey Island, Co. Dublin, Townleyhall II, Co. Meath, and the Dundrum Sandhills sites, Co. Down (Herity 1982, fig. 72, no. 6; fig. 62, nos 1–2; fig. 66, nos 1–2; fig. 68, nos 1–6). Although little survives of Vessel 26 (Fig. 3.88a), the cavetto neck and decoration can be compared to a broad-rimmed vessel from Townleyhall II (Herity 1982, fig. 73, no. 8). Little can be said concerning the body sherd representing Vessel 27 other than that the curvature of the sherd and its decorative motifs are consistent with those of Middle Neolithic globular bowls.

Globular stone vessel

Stone vessel 25 (Fig. 3.96), represented by three rim sherds (E84:3840, 1715 and 5236) and two body sherds (E84:4142 and 1927), is unusual not only in that it is made from sandstone (Steve Mandal, pers. comm.) but also in the high-quality carving of the faceted rim. Although little of the body survives, it can be seen that a cavetto neck was present and the body slopes out in a similar way to ceramic globular bowls. There is also visible evidence that the body was decorated. It is difficult to date such a bowl but it is suggested here that it is a stone version of a Middle Neolithic globular bowl. The shape of the rim is not unlike that of a bowl from the court tomb at Bavan, Co. Donegal, described as having a heavy faceted rim with similarly positioned decoration with impressed strokes (Herity 1982, 334, fig. 50, no. 3). Few stone bowls have been recorded from prehistoric contexts in Ireland, one example being a flat-based vessel that appears to have come from Knowth, Co.

Table 3.24—Middle Neolithic vessel assemblage recovered at Rathgall.

Vessels	Wall thickness (mm)	Decoration	Squares	Context details	Depth (cm)
24 (bipartite bowl)	6-8.4	Closely spaced concentric rows of incised lines and ladder patterns on exterior surface of rim. Below shoulder are two raised vertical ribs, between which are vertical incised lines. Base has basket-weave pattern.	G5	Pit 231	-
25 (stone bowl)	11.8	Short scores on the exterior and interior circumference of rim and external surface.	27, 35, 51 (& C1)	Brown near yellow; under sod; brown/black material	25–30; 12; 27–30
26	13.8	Shallow horizontal groove, below which is a horizontal row of bone impressions.	F2	In brown just above yellow	35
27	12.1	Deep circular impressions.	E1	Black under yellow 'bank'	35
28	10.1	Row of circular bone impressions on the exterior surface.	X	Pit 247	–
29	14.9	Concentric channels.	OV:1	Brown just above yellow	–

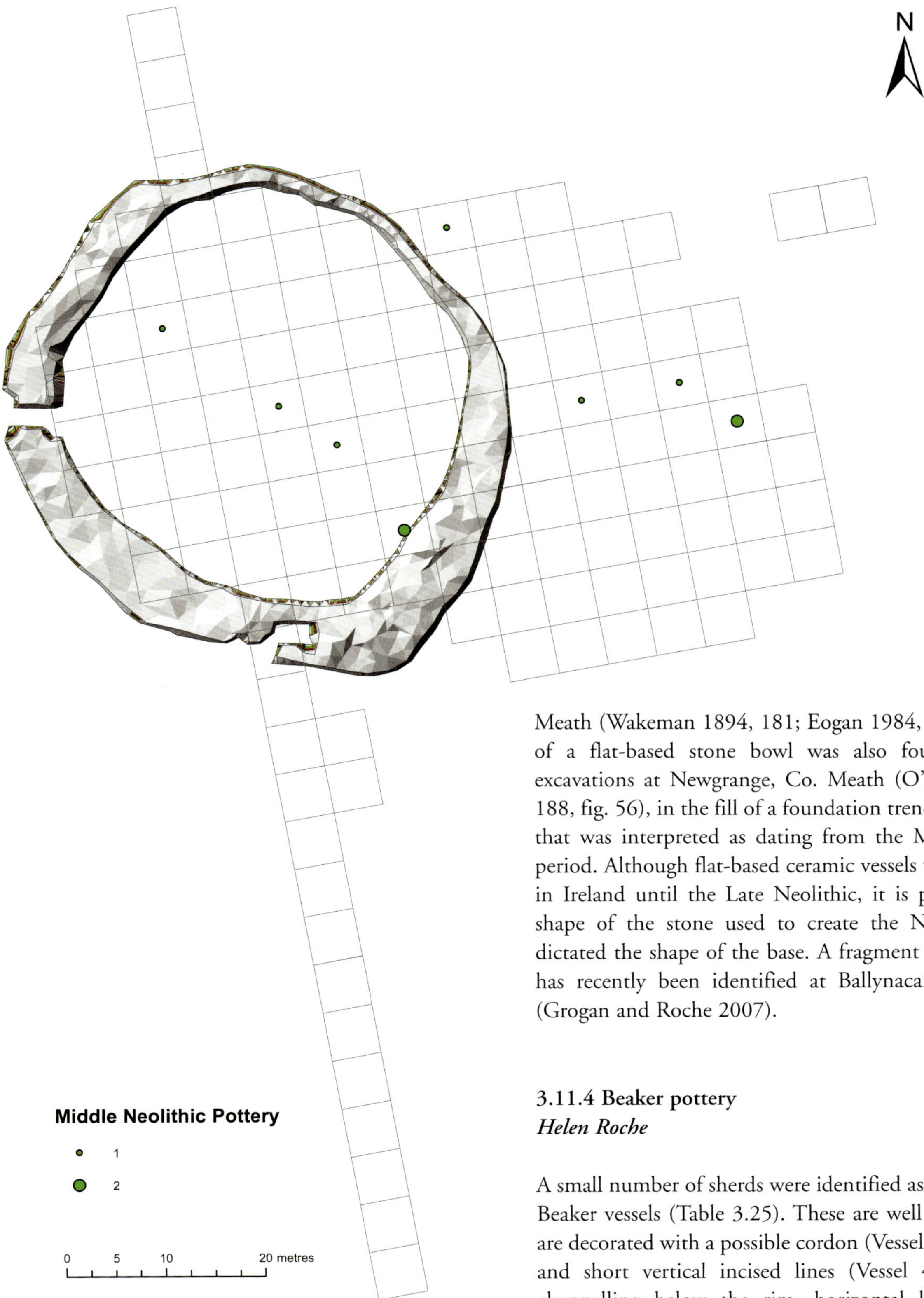

Fig. 3.89—Plot of Middle Neolithic pottery.

Meath (Wakeman 1894, 181; Eogan 1984, 168). A portion of a flat-based stone bowl was also found during the excavations at Newgrange, Co. Meath (O'Kelly 1982, 76, 188, fig. 56), in the fill of a foundation trench of a small hut that was interpreted as dating from the Middle Neolithic period. Although flat-based ceramic vessels were not current in Ireland until the Late Neolithic, it is possible that the shape of the stone used to create the Newgrange vessel dictated the shape of the base. A fragment of a stone vessel has recently been identified at Ballynacarriga, Co. Cork (Grogan and Roche 2007).

3.11.4 Beaker pottery
Helen Roche

A small number of sherds were identified as representing ten Beaker vessels (Table 3.25). These are well made and some are decorated with a possible cordon (Vessel 435), horizontal and short vertical incised lines (Vessel 438), horizontal channelling below the rim, horizontal lines and lattice patterns (Vessel 431) and comb motif impressions (Vessel 432). These sherds were found primarily in Areas 1–3, with

Table 3.25—Beaker pottery recovered at Rathgall.

Vessel no.	Wall thickness (mm)	Vessel description	Square	Context details
431	6.5–8.7	Flat rim, shallow horizontal groove on exterior below rim. Impressed horizontal lines and irregular diagonal line in a rough lattice pattern.	45, 66, 2	Sq. 45: yellow starting to show in brown, depth 18–22cm. Sq. 66: grey upper fill of Ring-ditch 1, depth 30–35cm. Sq. 2: dark brown, depth 25cm.
432	7.3	Horizontal lines of comb motif impressions.	62	In brown, yellow showing, depth 25–28cm.
433	4.6		7	Dark brown, depth 15–20cm.
434	4.6–6.4		3, 14, 30	Sq. 3: near cobbling, depth 20cm. Sq. 14: light brown, depth 20cm. Sq. 30: brown soil, depth 20cm.
435	6.5–7.7	Possible cordon below rim.	F2, C1	Sq. F2: in brown, depth 25–28cm. Sq. C1: dark brown, depth 23–25cm.
436	6.2–8.1		B4, J3/I3, A5, I3	Sq. B4: brown humus immediately below sod, depth 30cm. Sq. J3/I3: brown humus, almost on yellow, depth 30cm. Sq. A5: dark brown, depth 20cm. Sq. I3: on yellow, depth 40cm.
437	4.9–7.5		D7, I5	Sq. D7: brown soil, depth 20–25cm. Sq. I5: brown humus immediately below sod, depth 30cm.
438	5.4–8.6	Horizontal and short vertical incised lines.	G4, D4, G2, G3, J2	Sq. G4: mottled grey-brown on yellow, depth 25cm. Sq. D4: in brown, black patches showing, depth 20–22cm. Sq. G2: in brown, depth 16–18cm. Sq. G3: brown, almost on yellow, depth 30–40cm. Sq. J2: brown, almost on yellow.
439	6.9–4.7		X	Black fill of Pit 242.
440	7.5–8.1		Z1:c	In brown soil.

two individual sherds from the X cuttings and the outside settlement. Residue on Vessels 438, 431 and 434 and sooting on Vessel 440 indicates their use in cooking. A single out-turned rim fragment, E84:2004, was recorded as having been associated with Hearth 4.

3.11.5 Middle Bronze Age assemblage
Helen Roche

A small but important assemblage represents 30 Middle Bronze Age vessels (Table 3.26). The sherds were found scattered widely across the site, focused on Areas 1–3 (Fig. 3.90). The fabric is in the main compact, ranging in thickness from 5.3mm to 13.8mm. The colour varies from orange to brown and black, with the interior surfaces often showing traces of carbonised residues, indicating that they were used at some stage for cooking. The exterior surfaces are generally smooth, with occasionally protruding temper consisting of crushed quartzite generally up to 4.6mm long. The surfaces show evidence that they were carefully smoothed over, probably at the time of manufacture, with a wash or slurry of fine clay applied with the fingers.

For the most part, each vessel is represented by a single rim sherd, making it difficult to give a positive identification of vessel shape. The form of the rims and the surviving curvature of the body sherds suggest that all the vessels were tub-, bucket- or barrel-shaped, most likely with flat bases, while decorative motifs suggest an ancestry in the preceding cordoned urn tradition. The Rathgall vessels can be regarded as a form of decorated domestic urn, a type which has increasingly been recognised in Ireland (cf. Grogan 2004a; 2004b; 2004c; 2004d; Grogan and Roche 2010a). The decorative motifs on these vessels vary; some examples are poorly executed but others, for example on Vessels 35 and 37 (Fig. 3.88a: 35, 37), achieve a high standard. Decoration ranges from fingernail impressions, incised triangles and zigzags, zones of scoring, grooves and cord impressions, forming patterns of rows and lines, to the cordon decoration on Vessels 33, 36 and 181. Such vessels seem to represent the last vestige of pronounced decoration and were probably in use for a relatively short period of prehistory, somewhere around 1400–1300 BC, before decoration became a rarity on ceramic vessels during the Late Bronze Age (but see discussion in Chapter 6). Similar low cordons are present on vessels from Lyles Hill, Co. Antrim (Evans 1953, fig. 17:81, 83, 84).

Vessels 32, 38 (Fig. 3.88a) and 39 (Fig. 3.88a) are similar in form, representing small, thin-walled vessels with similar poorly incised and cord decoration on the area just below the rim. Small quantities of comparable pottery can be identified on some of the Lough Gur sites: almost identical sherds were

Table 3.26—Middle Bronze Age vessel assemblage recovered at Rathgall.

Vessels	Wall thickness (mm)	Decoration	Squares	Context details
19	12.3	Rilling	F1	In rabbit burrow and immediately under sod: depth 10cm
22	7.9	Oblique scoring on rim top and horizontal incised line on exterior	D/D1	Light mottled ashy brown, south of 'bank', depth 40–60cm
30	13.8		19/20	Brown
31	8.9	Row of deep fingernail impressions or scores	25	Hearth
32	6.9	Three perforations 7.8mm below rim, fine incised lines, probably forming triangles or zigzags	27	Light brown
33	8.1–9.1	Cordon and oblique incised lines creating triangular motifs	44, 66	Sq. 44: upper fill of ditch; Sq. 66: near yellow with trenches, post-holes and circular structure showing
34	13.4	Oblique scoring on area of bevel	D/D1	Black charcoal-rich
35	11–12.9	Shallow, well-executed grooves, forming a basket-weave motif	D2, D4, E1, E2, E3	Dark brown; brown just above yellow; black; Pit 55
36	12.9	Raised cordon 12.7mm below rim	D7	Post-hole 4
37	8.1	Horizontal grooves	F5	Brown
38	5.3	Horizontal line of fine twisted cord impressions below rim; below are opposing oblique fine twisted cord impressions, possibly forming triangles	H2	Brown humus
39	10.9–11.4	Horizontal and oblique rows of twisted cord impressions	K4	Post-hole 1
125	8.8	Horizontal incised line	K5	In ring-ditch
152	12.5	A shallow horizontal constriction or groove is present 13.9mm below the rim	2	Black fill of Ring-ditch 1, depth 48–53cm
179	14.9	A constriction or channel is present 11.4mm below the rim; three perforations, two in section, are present 12.5mm below the rim and within the constriction	54	Grey fill of Pit 159
181	13.8–17.7	A raised cordon is present on the exterior surface	2, 8/2	Sq. 2: dark brown soil, depth 25–38cm; Sq. 8/2: black fill of Ring-ditch 1, depth 50–55cm below yellow
185	10.1	Rilled surface	F2	Hard, greyish material, over yellow, depth 30–35cm
186	8.1–8.8	Three perforations are present, one in section, 7.4mm below the rim; a horizontal constriction is present 9mm below the rim	7	Upper levels of black fill of Ring-ditch 1, depth 30–35cm
263	13.1	A shallow groove is present 12.5mm below the rim		Sq. Y2, brown humus, depth 25cm
265	7.4–11.6	Faint evidence for decoration in the form of an irregularly applied horizontal incised line	43, 65, 66	Sq. 43: almost on yellow, depth 30–35cm; Sq. 65: no context detail, depth 25–28cm; Sq. 66: immediately under sod, under stones, depth 10cm
268	7.2		X3	Brown soil, depth 20cm
313	9.8	Three horizontal rows of irregularly spaced incised lines are present on the exterior surface immediately below the rim	I5	Brown humus immediately below sod, depth 30cm
318	18.9	A shallow channel is present 17.4mm below the rim; a row of faint circular impressions is present on the surface of the rim	J4	Brown humus, depth 10–15cm
408	12.9		Z2g	Grey fill of Pit 7
427	9.7–10.4		F2	Brown material, yellow patches, depth 21–22cm
441	8.8–10.1		59, C2, 53	Sq. 59: brown soil, depth 18–22cm; Sq. C2: brown soil; Sq. 53: grey fill of Pit 130
442	5.9–6.5		16, D2	Sq. 16: no context details; Sq. D2: grey on yellow, depth 35cm
443	6.8–9.4		E/E1, J3/I3, J5	Sq. E/E1: brown/black material, depth 40–60cm; Sq. J3/I3: brown material; Sq. J5: grey charcoal matter in Pit 176
444	5.6		J4	Upper grey fill of Ring-ditch 2
445	5.5		K7	Brown, almost on yellow

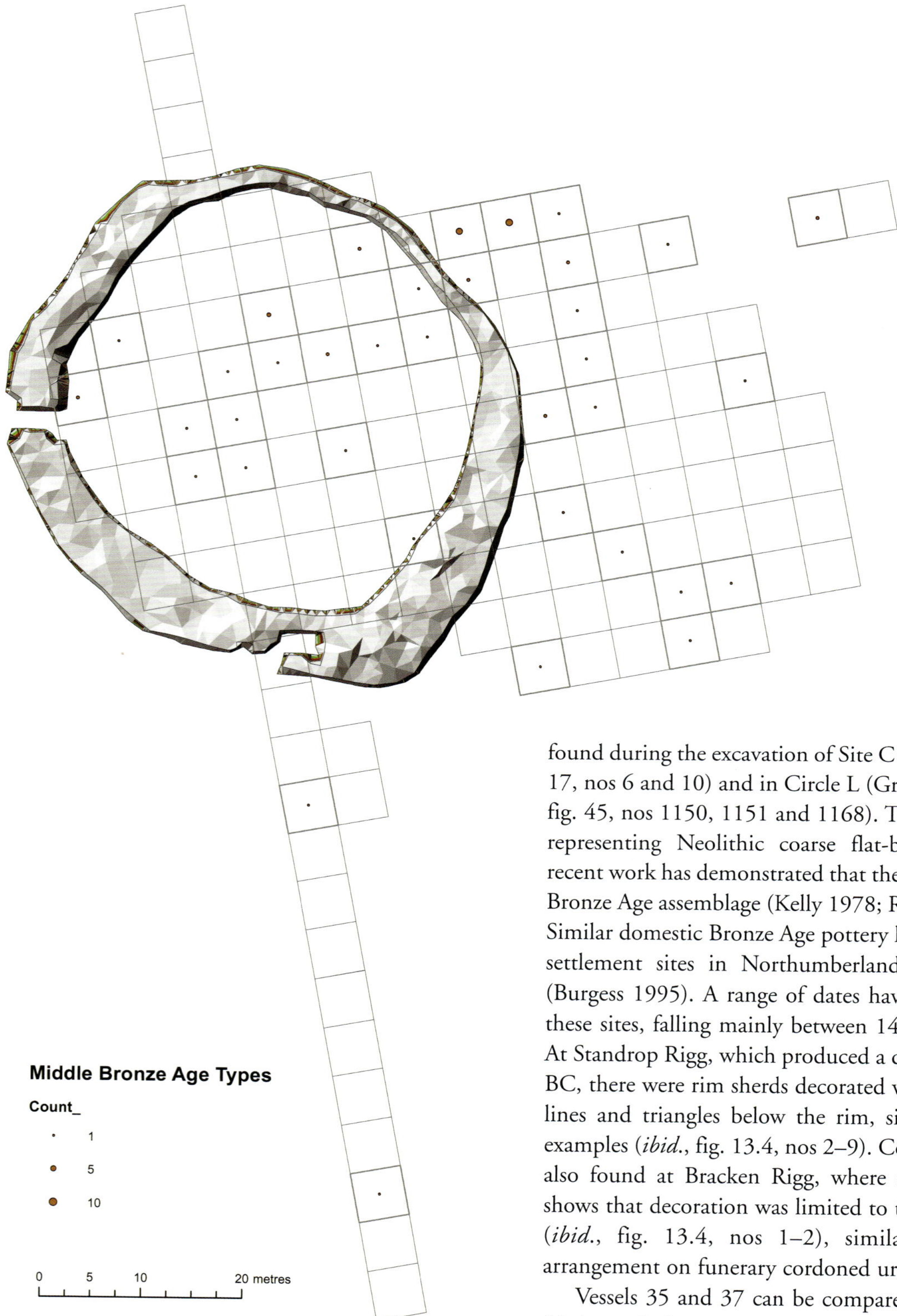

Fig. 3.90—Plot of Middle Bronze Age forms.

found during the excavation of Site C (Ó Ríordáin 1954, fig. 17, nos 6 and 10) and in Circle L (Grogan and Eogan 1987, fig. 45, nos 1150, 1151 and 1168). These were identified as representing Neolithic coarse flat-based ware but more recent work has demonstrated that they are in fact part of the Bronze Age assemblage (Kelly 1978; Roche 2004c, 112–13). Similar domestic Bronze Age pottery has also been found on settlement sites in Northumberland in northern Britain (Burgess 1995). A range of dates have been obtained from these sites, falling mainly between 1400 and 1010 cal. BC. At Standrop Rigg, which produced a date of 1390–1130 cal. BC, there were rim sherds decorated with incised horizontal lines and triangles below the rim, similar to the Rathgall examples (*ibid.*, fig. 13.4, nos 2–9). Comparable vessels were also found at Bracken Rigg, where a reconstructed vessel shows that decoration was limited to the area below the rim (*ibid.*, fig. 13.4, nos 1–2), similar to the decorative arrangement on funerary cordoned urns.

Vessels 35 and 37 can be compared to sherds of similar fabric and decorative motifs, although comb-impressed, found at Knowth in post-tomb domestic contexts. At the time of publication they were incorporated into the Beaker assemblage (Eogan 1984, 259, fig. 89, nos 1399–1404) and were later published as Grooved Ware, a misinterpretation by this author (Eogan and Roche 1997, 204, fig. 44, V51). A re-evaluation of this pottery as a result of the identification of similar pottery at Rathgall and the presence of a Middle Bronze Age date (1500–1264 cal. BC) in the area of the Knowth pottery demonstrates that it is part of the Middle Bronze Age repertoire of pottery forms.

Decoration on Vessels 22 (Fig. 3.88a), 33 and 34 (Fig. 3.88a), with oblique scoring on the area of the bevel, differs from the above examples and resembles that occasionally found on Late Bronze Age coarseware. The oblique scoring on the exterior surface just below the rim of an otherwise undecorated pot found in the settlement site at Black Law, Northumberland (Burgess 1995, fig. 13.3), demonstrates the existence of this motif in the Middle Bronze Age. The relatively thin-walled body sherds of Vessel 34 also share fabric characteristics with the Middle Bronze Age assemblage and are not dissimilar to the fabric of the preceding cordoned urns. Perforations were noted on Vessels 32, 186 and 179 (Fig. 3.88b). Other uncommon features present on the Rathgall vessels are horizontal grooves, channels or incised lines just below the rim of Vessels 22, 37, 125, 152, 179, 263, 265, 313 and 318. Two vessels have a rilled surface (Vessels 19 (Fig. 3.88a) and 185).

3.11.6 Late Bronze Age pottery assemblage
Helen Roche

Over 12,000 sherds (*c.* 98.42kg), representing at least 378 mainly flat-based barrel-shaped or straight-sided Late Bronze Age vessels dating from *c.* 1200–800 BC, were identified from Rathgall. The bulk of the assemblage was derived from Areas 1–3, but also from the Y cuttings and the outside settlement (Fig. 3.91). Especially large numbers came from Pit 118 (Sqs 17/18) and Sqs D/D1, E/E1 and C1 in Area 2. The sherds in the build-up of soil here, which reached a depth of up to 0.4m, were weathered but often large fragments, suggesting dumped material that was not trampled into the ground.

The pottery from Rathgall forms the largest Late Bronze Age assemblage found in Ireland to date. In addition, it includes the greatest variety of rim forms found on any one site, as well as forms not yet identified elsewhere—for example, an almost complete cereal-dish-sized vessel (Vessel 321; Figs 3.88b and 3.92), a vessel with an applied cordon (Vessel 266; Fig. 3.93), and Vessels 77 (Fig. 3.88a), 79 (Fig. 3.88c) and 78 with internal bevels that probably functioned as a lid seating. Owing to the large number of sherds, it was difficult to assign body sherds and fragments to specific vessels with any certainty. It was therefore decided that only distinct rims and body sherds that actually joined or clearly formed part of the same pot would be used to identify individual vessels. The large numbers of sherds and fragments not assigned to individual vessels were catalogued according to fabric thickness: (a) fine (*c.* 6–10mm thick), (b) medium (*c.* 10–14mm) and (c) coarse (*c.* 14–21.2mm); the majority had thicknesses of up to 14mm. As vessels may thicken considerably from rim to base, the measurements should be used as a guide rather than a strict parameter. The catalogue containing detailed descriptions of unassigned sherds can be found in the site archive.

Fabric details and vessel construction

Regardless of wall thickness, the fabric throughout is coarse and gritty, with generally uneven surfaces where inclusions protrude; these consist mainly of locally available crushed granite and quartzite. The vessels are largely fired to create orange-buff exterior and interior surfaces with darker cores. The outer faces of most of the vessels were finished by wetting the hand or fingertips and rubbing them over the surface—an action that formed a thin wet paste or 'slurry' which helped to smooth the vessel and to mask the inclusions otherwise visible on the surface. In fact, a fingerprint is present on the interior surface of Vessel 251, just below the rim. Although coarse in nature with large pieces of temper, many examples (e.g. Vessels 44, 52, 78 and 105) are well executed, with a hard compact matrix and smoothed exterior surfaces. Vessels 73, 184, 191 and 192, although thick-walled (up to 16.3mm), are exceptionally well executed with consistently sized temper, creating an almost stone-like smoothness on the exterior surface. A significant number of vessels are unusually thin-walled (6–10mm) for Late Bronze Age pottery. Surprisingly, however, these examples are largely of poor quality, with a brittle, friable fabric matrix and carelessly finished exterior surfaces. A number of poor-quality vessels of coarse crumbly fabric and containing large inclusions—for example Vessels 50, 72, 91, 107, 142, 214 and 315—also formed part of the assemblage. Various degrees of weathering are present on the majority of the sherds and in general the break edges are worn and show evidence of abrasion, which suggests that a number of the sherds were exposed to open weather

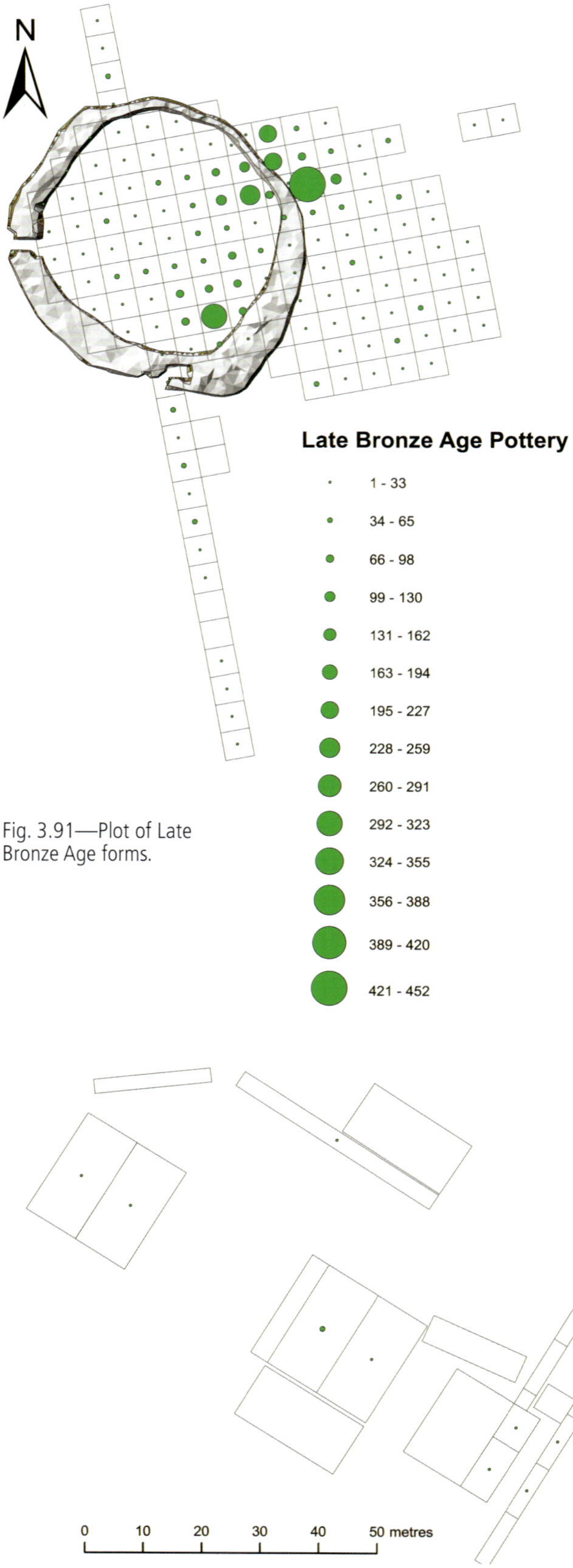

Fig. 3.91—Plot of Late Bronze Age forms.

Fig. 3.92—Vessel 321 (E84:8517) (photo: John Sunderland).

conditions and surface disturbance for a length of time.

With the exception of one—the exceptionally small Vessel 321, which appears to have been pinched into shape—all vessels were coil-built, as is evident from horizontal coil breaks present on sherds from Vessel 350.

Vessel forms

The majority of the sherds represent barrel-shaped or straight-sided vessels with simple angular base junctions (Fig. 3.88e) or sometimes with a slight foot, and with a broad range of rim forms. The nearly complete urn from Burial 2 within Ring-ditch 2 (Vessel 346; Fig. 3.88d) is also barrel-shaped, with a flat, inward-sloping rim and a gently footed base. Rim diameters range between 10cm and 30cm, vessel height between 6.8cm and 20cm, and base diameters between 9.2cm and 12.5cm. Eleven vessels have short necks (Vessels 40–1) and barrel-shaped bodies (Vessels 182–4, 187–92). Comparable vessels are known from the lakeshore sites at Ballinderry 2, Co. Offaly, and Knocknalappa, Co. Clare, from the crannog at Moynagh Lough, Co. Meath, and from Mooghaun, Co. Clare (Hencken 1942, fig. 2; Grogan *et al.* 1999, fig. 6; Bradley 2004, fig. 13.4; Grogan 2005a, fig. 1:V4).

The profiles of Vessels 114, 254 and 244 (not illustrated) expand outwardly below the rim and are similar to vessels

Table 3.27—Recorded rim fabric types from vessels within Area 1.

Rim forms	Vessel nos, fine fabric (c. 6–10mm thick)	Vessel nos, medium fabric (c. 10–14mm thick)	Vessel nos, coarse fabric (c. 14–18.6mm thick)
Constricted neck	40		41
Rounded rims	64, 65, 68, 69, 74	43–58, 76	59, 61, 62, 73
Rounded with internal ledge	77	78, 79	
Rounded with rounded external expansion	80		
Rounded with rounded external and interior expansions	81		
Flat rims	82, 86, 88, 99, 105, 114–17 127, 128	83–5, 87, 89, 90, 92–5, 97, 98, 100–2, 104, 106, 108–13, 118, 119, 121, 122, 124, 126, 129, 419	91, 96, 103, 107, 120, 123 and 42: 19.3–23.2
Flat out-turned	130		
Flat inward-sloping	131		
Flat with rounded inward expansion	132, 140, 142–4	134–9, 141, 145, 146	
Flat, outwardly expanded		147–9, 363	
Flat with external and interior expansions	150	151	
Bevelled rims	154, 155, 162–4, 167, 172, 176, 177, 422	153, 156–9, 165, 166, 168–71, 173–5, 178, 180, 423, 421,	160, 161
Vessel without rim		181	

Table 3.28—Rim types and vessel numbers from Areas 2 and 3 and others between Ramparts 1 and 2.

Rim forms	Vessel nos, fine fabric (c. 6–10mm thick)	Vessel nos, medium fabric (c. 10–14mm thick)	Vessel nos, coarse fabric (c. 14–20.8mm thick)
Constricted-necked vessels	187	182, 188–92	183–4
Rounded rims	193, 200, 201, 208, 211, 212, 216, 217, 221, 223, 227, 231, 232, 243, 245, 247, 249, 251, 252, 255, 258, 261, 264, 424	195, 196, 198, 199, 202–7, 209, 210, 214, 215, 218–20, 222, 224–6, 228–30, 233–8, 240, 241, 246, 248, 250, 253, 257, 259, 260, 262	194, 197, 213, 239, 242, 244, 254, 256, 425
Rounded with internal ledge			
Rounded, out-turned	266		
Flat rims	270, 275, 277, 280, 285–7, 293, 299, 302, 306, 312, 315, 322, 325, 327, 331	267, 269, 271–3, 276, 278, 279, 281–4, 288–92, 296–8, 300, 301, 303–5, 307–9, 311, 314, 316, 317, 319, 321, 323, 324, 326, 328–30	274, 294, 295, 310, 318, 320, 426
Flat, inward-sloping	332, 336, 338–41, 347, 351	333–5, 337, 342–6, 348–50	
Flat, outward-sloping		352–4	
Flat with rounded inward expansion	360	133, 355–9, 361	
Flat with pointed inward expansion	362		
Flat, outwardly expanded		364	
Flat with external and internal expansions	365, 366	367	
Flat with central channel		368	
Bevelled rims	369, 371, 374, 375, 378, 379, 384, 388, 392, 394, 395, 400	370, 372, 373, 376, 377, 380–3, 385–7, 389–91, 393, 396–9, 401	

Table 3.29—Rim types and vessel numbers from area outside Rampart 4.

Rim forms	Vessel nos, fine fabric (c. 6–10mm thick)	Vessel nos, medium fabric (c. 10–14mm thick)	Vessel nos, coarse fabric (c. 14–21.2mm thick)
Rounded rims		402	
Flat rims		403, 404, 406	405
Flat, inward-sloping	407	411	
Flat, outwardly expanded		412	
Bevelled rims	413–15, 418	416, 417, 430	
(Also included in this category but not assigned to individual vessels are 24 rim fragments, six base-angle sherds, 100 body sherds, 151 fragments and 70 crumbs.)			

from Priestsnewtown, Co. Wicklow, Knockaholet, Co. Antrim, and Lough Gur Circle P, Co. Limerick (Grogan and Roche 2006; Henry 1934; Grogan and Eogan 1987, pl. 23), all of which appear to represent burials. Similar vessels also came from a domestic site at Lough Eskragh, Co. Tyrone (Collins and Seaby 1960). The small, straight-sided bowl (Vessel 321; Fig. 3.92) is unusual, as it is almost complete and also unique in Ireland, but similar forms may be represented in fragmented assemblages from other sites.

Vessel 42 (Fig. 3.88a) is an unusually fashioned vessel, unlike any other pot on the site or from elsewhere in the country, and is represented by a large sherd from an in-turned rim (E84:5327; Sq. 41) and a body sherd (E84:5950; Sq. 67). It is up to 23.2cm thick and has a heavy, almost stone-like matrix. Because of the density of the fabric, it is perhaps more likely to have been used for storing liquids, despite the presence of carbonised residue.

Rim forms identified in the Rathgall assemblage fall into three main types: (a) simple rounded rims, (b) simple flat rims and (c) bevelled rims. There are also variations of these forms. The rim forms at Rathgall are typical of vessels found on Late Bronze Age domestic and funerary sites in Ireland. What distinguishes the Rathgall assemblage, however, are the several variations of the simple rounded and flat rims that occur, representing inward and outward expansions and sloping surfaces (cf. Tables 3.27–3.29). With the exception of rims with an internal ledge, all these rim forms can be paralleled on other Late Bronze Age sites in Ireland, although Rathgall is unique in having all these forms in use.

Perforations and decorative features

As is characteristic of Late Bronze Age assemblages throughout the island, the only surface alterations or additions to the vessels are perforations, dots and slashes. Vessels 309 and 343 and two unassigned sherds (nos 9590a and 9601a) have corrugated surfaces. Their fabric is similar to the rest of the Late Bronze Age assemblage, but they could possibly date from the later part of the Middle Bronze Age. Similar pottery has been found at Site C, Lough Gur, Co. Limerick (Ó Ríordáin 1954, fig. 17:1).

Fig. 3.93—Vessel 266 (E84:7777) (photo: John Sunderland).

Vessel 266 is a unique example of a vessel with an applied cordon (Fig. 3.93). This is D-shaped in cross-section and attached to the exterior surface. A row of perforations is present below the rims of 98 Late Bronze Age vessels; although found on various rim types (see Tables 3.30 and 3.31), these are most frequent on simple rounded and flat and bevelled rims. In all examples the perforations had been fashioned before firing. Although it is possible that these represent a purely decorative feature, it is also likely that they had a practical function. They may have provided ventilation in lidded vessels for stored dried goods, such as cereals, fruit or nuts, to prevent the growth of mould, the perforations being small enough to prevent the intrusion of large insects. Several of these vessels show evidence for use in cooking, with charred residues actually within the perforations, possibly indicating that the perforations facilitated the emission of steam from the pot while cooking, thus diminishing the possibility of heat damage to the pot. It seems improbable that perforations were used to attach a fabric or skin lid to the vessel, as in most cases they were too

Table 3.30—Vessels with perforations and other decorative features from Area 1.

Vessel	Rim forms	Wall thickness (mm)	Perforations below rim (distance in mm below rim)	Decorative & other features (measurements in mm below rim)	Squares	Context details	Depth (cm)	Figure
41	Constricted necks	16.3–17		Oblique slashes surface of rim	31	Grey fill of ditch		
43	Rounded rims	9.5–11.1	One: 10.5		2	Black near wall		
47		13.3	Two: 7		7	Light brown		
55		12.5–14.7	Four: 12–15.4		6, 14, 22	Light & dark brown & ditch fill		
56		10.7–11.5	Six: 7.1–7.7		15	Light brown; dark brown; brown in yellow	12–15; 22–3; 30	
58		12	One: 8		17	Dark patch	20	
59		14.1–15.1	Eight: 8.6		17/18	Pit 118	–	
60		10.3–11.2	Two: 7.8		17/18	Pit 118	–	
61		10.6–20.6	One: 7.4		17/18	Pit 118	–	
62		15.3–17.3	Four: 11.2		17/18	Pit 118	–	Fig. 3.88
63		9.3–12.8	Two: 14.2		24	Under baulk	–	
70		10.7	One: 12.5		36	Dark brown	25–30	
71		10.1	Two: 10.6		36/37	Outer bedding trench	–	
73		12.2–16.3	Two: 14.2–14.5	Impressed dot: 16.8	52, 53, 54	Brown; under sod	15–18; 10–12	Fig. 3.88
76		14.3	Two: 13.3		62	Brown	20–25	Fig. 3.88
79	Rounded with internal ledge	13.9	One: 21.7		44/45	Section strip	–	
81	Rounded with rounded ext. & int. expansions	8.8	One: 8		29	Grey ditch fill	30	Fig. 3.88
85	Flat rims	12.2		Dot on interior: 12.5	7	Dark brown	40	
42		19.3–23.2		Deep groove: 36.5mm on surface below rim	41, 67	Upper grey fill of Ring-ditch 1, under sod over 'cobbling'		
86		8.1–8.8	Three: 7.4	Horizontal low groove: 9	7	Black/brown ditch fill	30–35	
90		10.1	One: 12.7		8	Ditch base	40–50	
93		11.5	Two: 9.2		34	Light brown	25	
95		10.7–11.9	One: 4.7		7, 7/6, 15	Yellow among stones; black ditch fill	30	
97		10.1	Three: 9.8		16	Black burning in dark brown	20	
99		9–9.5	Three: 10.5		17/18	Pit 118	–	
101		10.2	Two: 3.8		17/18	Pit 118	–	
104		11.3–13.1		Incised line on body sherd	17/18	Pit 118	–	
108		11.7	One: 7.1		24	Yellow surface	27–29	
113		9.1–13.7	One: 6.3		28, 27/28, 37	Yellow surface	30	
114		8.5	One: 16.4		29	Inner edge of ditch	30	
115		8.5	Three: 10		29	Ditch upper fill	30	
116	'T'-shaped	8.1	Four: 8.8		29	Pit 121	–	Fig. 3.88
121		11.1	One: 8.9		45	Brown	15–18	
126		9.9–12.5	One: 9.2		62, 65, 67/68	Base of brown; brown/grey ditch fill; brown under wall	25–28; 30; 10–15	
419		11–11.5			16	Light brown, NE	15–16	
130	Flat out-turned	9.9		Oblique slashes on exterior below rim	25	Hearth 1	–	

Table 3.30 (cont.)—Vessels with perforations and other decorative features from Area 1.

Vessel	Rim forms	Wall thickness (mm)	Perforations below rim (distance in mm below rim)	Decorative & other features (measurements in mm below rim)	Squares	Context details	Depth (cm)	Figure
134	Flat with internal lip	9.7–11.8	One: 6.7		6	Near ditch base	55	
136	Flat with inward expansion	9.8–10.9	One: 13.3		8	Dark brown/black; ditch base	25–35	
139		11.1		Impressed dot: 17.5	17/18	Pit 118	–	
142		7.3–7.5	One: 7.3		26,17/ 26,29	Almost on yellow; Pit 117; black ditch fill	35; 20–25	
149	Flat outward expansion	10.2	One: 16.7		43	Brown/yellow	25–30	
363		10		Dot on external surface: 7.1	61	Brown	20–25	
150	Flat with ext. & int. expansions	8.2	One: 5.7		7	Dark brown	30	
153	Bevelled rims	10.7	One: 5		7, 8	Black; near ditch base	21–30; 40–50	
154		6.9–7.7	Two: 12.4		7	Black, near wall; black ditch fill	35; 30–37	
156		10	One: 15.5		8	?	?	
157		12.1–13.3	One: 14		8	Light brown	20–24	
161		14.1	One: 14.9		14/23	Baulk	–	
163		6.7	One: 12.6		17/18	Pit 118	–	Fig. 3.88
166		10.3–11.7	Three: 10.9–12.9		27, 28, 44, 45/36	Light brown & yellow; Pit 143	20–25	
169		10.2–11.1	Two: 13.4		27, 44	Dark brown; brown	30; 25–30	
172		8.5–10.7	Three: 10.4		28, 29, 37	Brown; black ditch fill	15–25; 20–25	
173		10.9–11.5	Three: 6.8		33, 37, 45, 45/36	Black & Pit 149; brown	25; 15–20	
175		10.7–12.7	Two: 11.7		40	Ditch fill	50	
177		9.7	One: 12.1		54	Pit 159	–	
178		13.5		Impressed dot: 4.8	54	Pit 159	–	
421		12.3			14, in dark brown, almost black fill of Ring-ditch 1, E	25 below yellow		
422		10.8			29, Ring-ditch 1	35 in ditch fill		
423		8.5–14.3			29, Pit 121			
448		10.5–3.1		Footed base	18, Pit 118			

small and too close together to easily facilitate the attachment of a lid with a fibre or sinew string; furthermore, the perforations have no evidence for wear or rubbing, which would have been caused by the constant or occasional pulling of string. It is even less plausible that these facilitated suspension, as the sheer weight of most Late Bronze Age coarse vessels (up to 8,000g for an empty pot) would probably result in breakage. The vertical perforation through the bevel of Vessel 376 may possibly also relate to such considerations.

Impressed dots were present on the exterior surface and just below the rim of thirteen vessels. Usually there is just one dot (Vessels 73, 139, 351, 359, 363, 178, 209, 327), but three were identified on Vessel 273 and two on Vessels 169

Fig. 3.94—Vessel 130 (E84:1262) (photo: John Sunderland).

and 389, while one occurred on the interior surface of Vessels 85 and 352. As no complete rims were present, it is not possible to say whether the dots continued around the circumference of the rim. Seven vessels are unusual in having decorated rim surfaces (Tables 3.30 and 3.31). Vessels 41 (Fig. 3.88a), 133 and 325 (Fig. 3.88b) are decorated with oblique slashes; the rim surface of Vessel 191 (Fig. 3.88b) is decorated with impressed circular impressions, and fingernail impressions are present on the rim of Vessel 274, while two impressed dots are found on the rim of Vessel 359. Vessel 130 (Fig. 3.94) is decorated with slashes on the exterior surface just below the rim. Other uncommon features present on the Rathgall vessels are horizontal grooves or channels just below the rim of Vessels 42 (Fig. 3.88a) and 86 and an incised line on Vessel 104.

Comparative assemblages

Rathgall is one of a small group of major Late Bronze Age sites in Ireland, and its pottery assemblage is an important addition to our understanding of prehistory in Ireland. Although the prolonged Late Bronze Age activity on the site provides an extraordinary richness of features and artefacts, the Early and Middle Neolithic, Beaker period and Middle Bronze Age phases (but see discussion in Chapter 5) are important in showing episodic use of this site for over 3,000 years. Late Bronze Age pottery similar to that from Rathgall has a wide distribution throughout the country, coming from a broad variety of sites, both domestic and funerary. It is also now datable to *c.* 1200–800 BC, with radiocarbon dates from key assemblages at Haughey's Fort, Co. Armagh (Mallory 1995), Mooghaun South, Co. Clare (Grogan 2005a; 2005b), Dún Aonghasa (Cleary 2012), Corrstown (Conway *et al.* 2004–5) and the settlement and funerary sites at Lough Gur, Co. Limerick (Grogan and Eogan 1978; Ó Ríordáin 1954), besides Rathgall itself.

Until recently relatively few Late Bronze Age pottery assemblages had been recorded in this region of Leinster, with known sites comprising an enclosure at Johnstown South and a burial at Carrig, the secondary reuse of the wedge tomb chamber at Moylisha (all in County Wicklow), in settlement contexts at Dalkey Island, Co. Dublin (Fitzpatrick 1998; Grogan 1990; Ó h-Iceadha 1946, fig. 2; Liversage 1967–8), and at the hillfort at Freestone Hill, Co. Kilkenny (Raftery 1969, 86–96). In the past few years small domestic assemblages have been identified in north Wicklow, including Ballynabarny (Gahan 2004), Charlesland, Greystones (Grogan 2004c), Rathmore (McLoughlin 2004) and a funerary site at Priestsnewtown (Grogan and Roche 2006). Further north in County Dublin, Late Bronze Age pottery has been found on sites at Kilgobbin (Grogan 2004a), Beaverstown (Grogan 2004b), Cherrywood/Laughanstown (O'Donovan 1998), Flemington (Byrnes 2004), Skidoo (Dehaene 2004; Roche 2004a), Lusk (Roche 2004b), and Darcytown 1 and 2 (Grogan and Roche 2008a; 2008c; 2007b), as well as at Lismullin (Grogan and Roche 2009a), Co. Meath, and the reassessment of the pottery at the enclosure at Lugg, Co. Dublin (Kilbride-Jones 1950; Roche and Eogan 2007).

The decoration of the pots at Rathgall can also be paralleled. Perforations below the rim of Late Bronze Age vessels are known from other sites, with a noticeable concentration in the northern part of the country, but not in the same quantity as found at Rathgall. The closest sites that produced parallels are Freestone Hill, Co. Kilkenny (Raftery 1969, fig. 32), and Ward Upper, Site 6, Co. Dublin (Roche and Grogan 2005). Further south-west, examples were found at Site C, Circles J and K at Lough Gur (Ó Ríordáin 1954, fig. 17, 19:2, 4, 12, 22; Grogan and Eogan 1987, figs

Table 3.31—Vessels with perforations and other decorative features from area between Ramparts 1 and 2.

Rim forms	Vessel	Wall thickness (mm)	Perforations below rim (measurements in mm below rim)	Decorative & other features (measurements in mm below rim)	Squares	Context details	Depth (cm)	Figure
Constricted necks	191	12.5		Circular impressions on rim surface	I4	Brown	25	
Rounded rims	196	12.5	Two: 8.8		B1/C1	Black under wall	–	
	199	10.6	Two: 9.6		C1	Black	25–30	Fig. 3.88
	206	10.4–11.9	Two: 7.5		D/D1	Black	40–60	
	207	11.7–13	Four: 9.3		D, D/D1	Black; under black/brown; charcoal patches	40–60; 50–65; 29–32	
	209	11.1–12.3	Five: 4.6–7.9	Impressed dot: 10.3mm	D, D1, D/D1	Black; black charcoal; dark brown/black	40–60; 30; 22–24	
	210	11.8	One: 7.7		D/D1	Black	40–60	
	214	10.1	One: 3.5		E1	Brown/black patches	16–18	
	218	11.3	One: 6.7		E1	Black	30	
	219	12.3	One: 4.7		E1	Black	30–40	
	223	8.6	One: 3.8		E1	Black areas on 'bank'	–	
	225	14	Two: 9.1		E1	Black under yellow	35	
	226	13.8	One: 11.6		E1	Black under yellow	35	
	227	7.6–9.2	Two: 5.5		E1	Section strip		
	234	10.6	One: 11.6		E/E1	Brown/black	40–60	
	235	13.4	Two: 6.8–9.8		E1, E/E1	Brown/black	40–60	
	238	11.2	One: 11.8		E3	Brown	15	
	240	11.3	One: 10.3		F2	Brown	23–27	
	247	8.3	One: 11.7		I3	Brown	15–20	
	251	9.9		Fingerprint on interior below rim	J3	Lower brown almost on natural	30	
	252	9.3	One: 11.4		J6	Black	30	
	256	13.9–15.2	Three: 7.6–9.8		X1ext.	Brown	15–25	
	257	12.2	One: 21.2		X1/2	Pit 247		
	262	11.1	Two: 10.4		X11	Pit 243		
	424	9.6–10.4			B5	Black area in NW of square immediately below sod	30	
	425	19.9			G4/B5	In mottled grey-brown almost on yellow, E extension of initial cutting; in black area in SE corner of square; Hearth 14	25	
		1						
Rounded, out-turned	266	8.6–9.3		Applied cordon: 14.3	X1, X3, D/D1	Brown; black (one cordon)	15–25; 40–60	
Flat rims	273	10.4		Three dots	C1	?	?	
	274	15		Row of fingernail impressions on rim surface	C2	Dark brown	30	
	275	8.5	One: 10.7		D	Black	24–28	
	276	12.4	Two: 13		D1	Yellow 'floor'	36	
	278	10.8	One: 8.5		D/D1	Black charcoal area	33–38	
	280	8.8–9.6	Five: 3		D/D1	Black charcoal area; black lowest level	33–38 & 40–60; 50–60	Fig. 3.88

Table 3.31 (cont.)—Vessels with perforations and other decorative features from area between Ramparts 1 and 2.

Rim forms	Vessel	Wall thickness (mm)	Perforations below rim (measurements in mm below rim)	Decorative & other features (measurements in mm below rim)	Squares	Context details	Depth (cm)	Figure
Flat	283	11.4	One: 12.5		D/D1	Black charcoal area	40	
	285	8.8	Two: 12.4		D/D1	Black among stones	30–35	
	287	8.7	One: 9.5		D/D1	Black charcoal area	40–60	
	293	8.2	One: 4.7		D3	Almost on yellow	25–30	
	296	10.4–10.5	Three: 11.9		D4	Black area; brown under sod; brown	25–30; 15; 20–23	
	307	12.1	One: 11.4		E2	Almost on yellow	35	
	308	11.9	One: 10.2		E3	Pit 54	–	
	314	12.4	One: 8.8		I5	Brown humus	30	
	322	9.6	Two: 10.9		J4	Grey fill of ditch	50	
	325	9.9		Oblique slashes on rim surface	K, K4, K6	Black, Pit 272; black, Pit 273	—	
	327	9.5		Impressed dot on exterior	X1ext.	Brown	25	
	330	11.1	One: 12.7		X7	Grey under bank	–	
	426	17.6–19.8			B2	Pit 41		
	428	9.8–12.3			F1/F2	Lowest levels of Pit 38	30	
Flat, inward-sloping	333	11.2	One: 12.5		C1	Dark brown/black	15–20	
	335	11–11.15	Two: 11		D, D/D1	Dark brown; black	29–32; 40–60; 50–60	
	338	6.8	Two: 10.3		E1	Brown	16–18	Fig. 3.88
	342	10.6	One: 11.5		E3	Dark brown	14–15	
	351	8.1	Two: just below rim		X5	Black burnt material close to stones under wall		
Flat, outward-sloping	352	10.5		Dot on interior surface: 4.5	B5	Brown humus	30	
Flat, outward expansion	364	11.6	One: 17.9		X11	Pit 253	–	
	429	8.7			D	Black habitation area	40–60	
	359	10.8		Two dots on rim top	G	Black layer		
Flat, inward expansion	133	10.5		Oblique slashes on rim surface	K4	Black, Pit 272	–	
Flat with ext. & int. expansions	365	9.5–9.6	Three: 15		C1	Black	25–30	
Flat with central channel	368	10.3	One: 5.1		D/D1	Black charcoal area	33–38	Fig. 3.88
Bevelled rims	373	10	One: 13.2		C1	Black	25–35	
	375	6.2–6.6	Three: 10.9		D	Black charcoal area	29–35	
	377	12.8–13.8	Seven: 15.8		D, D/D1	Dark brown/black charcoal area	15–16/40 up to 60	Fig. 3.97
	382	13.9	One: 14.8		E/E1	Brown under yellow	30–35	
	385	10.7	One: 12.8		G2	Pit 23	–	
	387	11	One: 12.7		H6	Brown humus	30	
	389	12.9		Two dots: 12.9	I4, I5	Grey-filled depression	–30	
	392	9.9	One: 8.7		X1ext.	Brown	25	
	394	7.2	Two: 14.9		X3	Brown	20–25	
	397	10.6	One: 9		Y2	Black	35–40	
	399	12.4	One: 15.5		Y2	?	?	
	400	8.8	One: 14.1		Y2	Black	30–40	
	401	13.8	One: 14.9		Y2	?	?	
	430	10–11.7			X5	In black near wall		Fig. 3.88

7, 16 and 27: V9, V11, 1872, 1987, 441), and in funerary and settlement contexts at Kilbane, Co. Limerick (Grogan and Roche 2008b). The remaining examples come from the northern part of the country, at Navan Fort, Co. Armagh (McCorry 1997, figs 34:5 and 36:4), Lyles Hill and Ballintoy, Co. Antrim (Evans 1953, fig. 26: 24; NMI Files), Site A, Mullaghmore, and the Dundrum sandhills, Site 7, Co. Down (Mogey *et al.* 1956, fig. 4; Collins 1959, fig. 6: 5–8), and Magheragallan, Co. Donegal (NMI Files).

Impressed dots near the rim were present on vessels from Circle J, Lough Gur, Co. Limerick (Grogan and Eogan 1987, fig. 6:V4), and Navan Fort, Co. Armagh (McCorry 1997, fig. 36:5).

Decorated rims are not common on Late Bronze Age vessels, but impressed circular and stabbed impressions are present on the rim surfaces of vessels from Lyles Hill, Co. Antrim, and Navan Fort, Co. Armagh (Evans 1953, fig. 17:77; McCorry 1997, fig. 36: 1–3). Vessel 130 (Fig. 3.94) from Rathgall is decorated with slashes on the exterior surface just below the rim, similar to an example from Navan Fort (McCorry 1997, fig. 35:6).

The use of coarseware bucket-shaped urns in a burial context as in the ring-ditch at Rathgall also finds parallels on other sites. Towards the end of the Middle Bronze Age (*c.* 1600–1100 BC) the use of special funerary vessels was replaced in burial contexts by that of domestic pots (Grogan and Roche 2010a). As part of this process of change, the placement of vessels in upright positions in pits becomes a feature of the record. A wide variety of Late Bronze Age burials have now been identified and, in general, these belong to three general types: cremations contained in intact upright or inverted domestic pots, similar to Burial 2 at Rathgall; cremations accompanied by sherds of pottery, similar to Burial 3 at Rathgall; and unaccompanied cremations. While many burials are in isolated and unmarked pits, flat cremation pit cemeteries and cemeteries enclosed within ring-ditches or enclosures are also represented. Other monuments utilised for funerary ritual include megalithic tombs, stone circles and boulder burials. A ring-ditch intruding on the foundations of a Neolithic house at Tankardstown South, Co. Limerick, contained two upright coarse vessels, one set inside the other in a pit and both containing cremations (Gowen and Tarbett 1988). The ring-barrow at Mullaghmore, Co. Down (Mogey *et al.* 1956), contained a central cremation, representing at least four individuals, associated with coarse pottery. The burial complex at Kilbane, Castletroy, Co. Limerick, included a ring-ditch in Area 1 (Grogan and Roche 2008b), and several

Fig. 3.95—Vessel 269 (E84:9082) (photo: John Sunderland).

Fig. 3.96—Vessel 25 (E84:3840) (photo: John Sunderland).

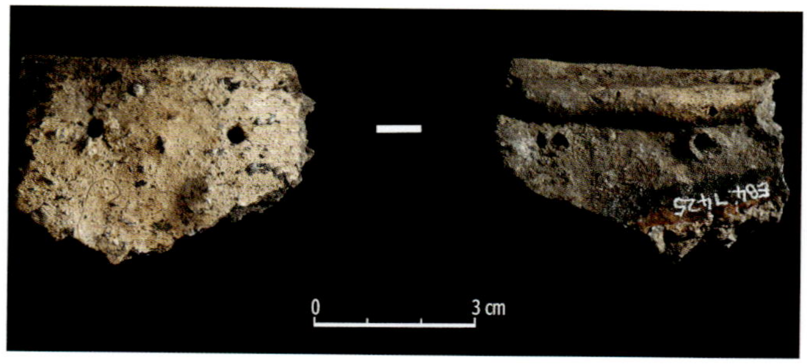

Fig. 3.97— Vessel 377 (E84:7425) (photo: John Sunderland).

cremation burials occurred in both upright and inverted coarse domestic vessels beside the ring-ditch.

The majority of the vessels display clear evidence, in the form of internal and external sooting or blackening, for prolonged domestic use. Fire-staining on a number of vessels clearly indicates the use of lids during cooking and, although neither ceramic nor stone lids were identified during the excavation, it is likely that wooden lids were used, which of course would not have survived. A band of dark grey/black staining occurs on the outer surface of Vessels 92, 108, 123, 131, 146, 219, 222, 288, 230, 235, 236, 269 (Fig. 3.95), 295

Table 3.32—Vessels with defined black staining on the rim surface.

Staining pattern	Vessel no.	Rim type	Wall thickness
Staining on outer surface	92	Flat	11.9mm
	97	Flat	10.1mm
	122	Flat	9.7–10.6mm
	123	Flat	18.6mm
	131	Flat, inward-sloping	9mm
	146	Flat, inward-sloping	11.5mm
	251	Rounded	9.9mm
	295	Flat	15.1mm
	296	Flat	10.4–10.5mm
	309	Flat	12.3mm
	310	Flat	17.5mm
	349	Flat, inward-sloping	10.1mm
	367	Flat, with int. & ext. expansion	11.7mm
	376	Bevelled	9.8–10.9mm
	398	Bevelled	11.3mm
	401	Bevelled	13.8mm
Staining on inner surface	95	Flat	10.7–11.9mm
	98	Flat	10.1–10.6mm
	136	Flat	9.8–10.9mm
	147	Flat	11.2mm
	188	Rounded with constriction	10.5–14.2mm
	189	Rounded with constriction	12.4mm
	228	Rounded	12.4–13.2mm
	249	Rounded	8.8mm
	253	Rounded	10.3mm
	253	Rounded	10.3mm
	282	Flat	12.2–13mm
	305	Flat	10.7mm
	311	Flat	10.7–11.1mm
	341	Flat, inward-sloping	8.1–8.2mm
	352	Flat, outward-sloping	10.5mm
	403	Flat	13.5mm
	366	Flat, sharply in-turned rim	9.5–10mm
Staining on centre of rim surface	402	Rounded rim	11mm
	403	Flat rim	12.3–14.4mm
	404		13.3–14.6mm
	405		21.2mm
	406		12.4mm
	407		8.6mm
	409		12.8mm
	410		11.2–12.5mm
	411		13.6–14.3mm
	412		10.1mm
	413	Internally bevelled	9.8mm
	414		8.9mm
	415		7.9mm
	416		11.4mm
	417		10.6mm
	418		8.2mm

and 303 and extends to between 30–50mm beneath the rim; it can be suggested that such staining may be the result of steam escaping from under a lid during the use of the pot for cooking. This type of staining was also present on similarly dated vessels from funerary contexts at Priestsnewtown, Greystones, Co. Wicklow, and Kilbane, Co. Limerick (Grogan and Roche 2008b; 2004). Interesting staining was also identified on the surface of several Rathgall rims in the form of a sharp black demarcation on either the inner or the outer area of the rim surface, and on one example the staining is present on the centre of rim surface (see Table 3.32). Where the staining is present on the outer surface, it may possibly be the result of prolonged use of a lid that did not extend to the outer rim edge or a poorly fitted lid that allowed the steam to escape. A better-fitted lid, where steam did not escape and instead circulated around the inner surface, might explain staining on the interior rim surface. The dark staining around the centre of the flat rim of Vessel 366 may also be the result of a snugly fitted lid from which a certain amount of steam escaped but was mostly contained beneath the lid; in this instance the unusually wide rim may also have been a contributing factor. While it may be that flat or bevelled rims would have been more suitable for securing a lid—and, indeed, a small majority were flat-rimmed—a variety of rims with staining were identified, including rounded and flat inward-sloping rims.

3.11.7 The medieval pottery

Caroline Sandes with Clare McCutcheon

Introduction

The medieval occupation at Rathgall is represented by the evidence of a house, medieval pottery, and coins of Edward I (1272–1307) and Edward III (1327–77). Prior to excavation the site had been subjected to extensive cultivation. As a result, many of the upper layers of the archaeological stratigraphy were badly disturbed or destroyed. Most of the pottery was found in disturbed contexts across the site and had suffered from weathering.

The material was examined initially for a master's degree thesis (Sandes 1993). Owing to the lapse in time between this study and the proposed publication, it was felt appropriate to revisit the material, particularly in the light of work on large medieval pottery assemblages in the wider Dublin (McCutcheon 2000; 2006) and Kilkenny areas (cf. McCutcheon 2007).

Methodology

A total of 1,240 medieval sherds and 67 sherds of post-medieval ware formed the assemblage for the original study (Sandes 1993). Over the intervening years, the pottery had been stored in open boxes, along with prehistoric pottery and other small finds, in drawers in the National Museum of Ireland and the School of Archaeology, UCD. After an extensive search of drawers and boxes, a further 649 sherds of medieval and 238 sherds of post-medieval pottery were recovered. Following some reassembly, this was reduced to 1,841 medieval sherds. In comparing the catalogue with the database, another 29 sherds were entered, sight unseen. These form a group originally listed as Type 5, and it is probable that another 38 undecorated body sherds, listed without finds numbers and not included in the current total, may be located with this group. The majority of the medieval pottery (83%) consists of small sherds of Leinster Cooking Ware (see table below). The post-medieval pottery was correspondingly reduced to 178 sherds.

The material was identified visually and the number of sherds in each fabric type listed, with the objective minimum number of vessels (MNV) and the more subjective minimum vessels represented (MVR). Accurate minimum numbers of vessels can only be given in the case of jugs, for example, where the rim/handle junction is present, although several other vessels may be represented in the assemblage. The probable form of the vessels and the date range of the distribution of this material in Ireland are also included.

The initial analysis of the glazed ware identified several locally made fabric types with some subdivisions, in addition to a small quantity of imported ware (Sandes 1993). The original splitting of sherds into six groups and subgroups (Types 1–4, 5A, 5B, 6A and 6B) has been retained, but all have now been lumped into three broad categories of hand-built, wheel-thrown and fineware, as the reanalysis of the material suggests that all of the glazed ware may be identified as locally made, in a broad tradition of Anglo-Norman pottery made in Ireland during the thirteenth century (McCutcheon 2006). The sherds originally identified as imported have more in common with a group of material identified at Kells Priory as 'Kells type G' (McCutcheon 2007). This is very similar in appearance to Bristol Redcliffe ware and was identified as such originally. Experience with quantities of Redcliffe ware at Waterford (Gahan and McCutcheon 1997, 301–3) and Cork (McCutcheon 2003, 206–7), however, where it is

Medieval pottery

Fabric type	Sherds	MNV	MVR	Form	Date
Leinster Cooking Ware	1,547	–	20	Cooking pots, storage jars	L12th–M14th
Wicklow-type coarseware	72	–	4	Jugs	M13th–E14th
Wicklow-type ware	244	–	2	Jugs	13th–14th
Wicklow-type fineware	7	–	1	Jug	L13th–14th
Total	1,870	–	27		

quite plentiful, confirms that this material is very similar to but not the same as Bristol Redcliffe. Thin-sectioning could only confirm that the fabric was not inconsistent with the underlying clay in Kells (McCorry 2007), but of course the clays of south-east Ireland and south-west England are not dissimilar. No imported wares were recovered in Rathgall, but this is not unusual on an inland site with access to the production of Anglo-Norman pottery of the period. At Kells Priory, Kilkenny, a large Anglo-Norman foundation with access to the river trade with Kilkenny, Waterford and New Ross, only 6% of an assemblage of over 7,700 medieval sherds was imported (McCutcheon 2007), while at Carrickmines Castle the quantity was less than 1% (McCutcheon 2012).

Leinster Cooking Ware

This amounted to 1,547 sherds, 83% of the total medieval pottery assemblage. The result was a minimum number of between eighteen and twenty vessels.

All the pottery is handmade and was probably coil-built. Blackening and soot deposits are present on most sherds, and some are decorated with incised lines. Like the glazed wares, they have suffered severely from weathering and exposure. This poses serious problems when attempting to sort the pottery into groups. It can, however, be distinguished by thickness and, to an extent, by coarseness. The rims can be divided into three types: thumb-frilled or pinched (nos 225–47A and 756–77); plain or undifferentiated (nos 248–56 and 778–804A); and flat overhanging or slightly rolled over (nos 257–87 and 805–27A).

The thickness of the sherds varies considerably, from 3–6mm (Type 1A) to 7–11mm (Type 1B). The fabric itself varies from leathery and smooth to a rough surface. It was fired to an orange-red to dark brown colour with a grey core. Some of the sherds were reduced to a grey-buff colour with a grey core. The rims vary in diameter, and the majority are horizontal with upright necks. They all seem to have come from shouldered vessels. Bases are usually sand-marked—the result of the vessel being worked on and/or left to dry, before firing, on a bed of sand—and some have a slight concavity at the junction of the base (nos 290 and 855). Most of the sherds have broken off at this point, so it is difficult to tell how pronounced this was or how much the bases sagged in most cases. The estimated base diameters range from 150mm to 260mm. Most are blackened or have black deposits on the interior, suggesting use as cooking pots. The thickness of the sherds is of the same range as the walls of the pots, but they tend to get a little thicker at the junction of base and wall.

Type 1A: There are 63 rim sherds, of which 24 are thumb-frilled or pinched, nine plain or undifferentiated, and 31 flat overhanging or rolled over. Their estimated diameters vary from 110mm to 280mm, and they tend to be thicker than the body and base sherds, being between 5mm and 10mm thick. One sherd (no. 288) consists of one third of the base angle and lower half of the wall of a cooking pot. This pot appears to have been relatively straight-sided, and the rim evidence suggests that it would have had a rounded shoulder with an upright neck. A small number (3.5%) of the sherds are decorated. This decoration mostly occurs in the form of finely incised lines that average about 1mm in width and are between 5mm and 18mm apart. On rim sherds 230 and 257 there are faint incised lines starting at the top of the shoulder. On the former there are two lines that form a loop shape, after which the lines appear to have continued down the pot. This, and the evidence from some of the other decorated sherds, would suggest that the decoration occurs on the shoulders of the vessels (nos 403 and 406) and that these lines were vertical. On one sherd (no. 257) the lines run diagonally along the base of the neck–top of the shoulder. One sherd (no. 419) has a narrow, 'bow'-shaped applied strip, and parallel to this are two very finely incised lines 8mm apart. Dublin, Ferns Castle, Wexford town, Kells Priory and Jerpointchurch produced similar pottery with similar decoration (Ó Floinn 1988, 331). At Kells Priory, Co. Kilkenny, a body sherd of Leinster Cooking Ware (E110:17012) has three incised lines between 7mm and 15mm apart. The sherd appears to be from the shoulder of a vessel and the lines run horizontally. This decoration is similar to that on several sherds (nos 403–18) from Rathgall. The vast majority of the sherds are blackened by fire.

Type 1B: There are 77 rim sherds, of which 22 are thumb-frilled or pinched, 28 plain or undifferentiated, and 27 flat and overhanging or slightly rolled over. These have estimated diameters that vary from 120mm to 340mm, and they are slightly larger than the group described above. Some of these sherds are also decorated. Diagonally incised lines occur on the shoulder of two rim sherds (nos 757 and 758). On one sherd (no. 949) there is a shallow, horizontal incised line, and one (no. 948) has a plain, narrow incised strip running along one edge of the sherd but it is broken off at this point. One rim sherd (no. 779) has a perforation just below the rim. Perforations are seen in pottery, both glazed and unglazed, from Wood Quay in Dublin, Knowth, Co. Meath, and Rathmullan, Co. Down. The Rathmullan sherd came from a post-thirteenth-century phase, and it was suggested that the perforation was for suspending the pot over the fire (Lynn 1981–2, 130–1, 148). The combination of the weight of a full pot, the heat of a fire and the inevitable knocking about while stirring the stew, however, must make this unlikely. One must also ask the obvious question: suspended from what? Is there evidence of a metal fixture over a hearth or perhaps slung from the roof? Where is the wear and/or damage around the neck of the pot? In addition, many later medieval illustrations show ceramic pots within metal pots placed over an open fire. At Wood Quay the perforations were not in a straight line and may represent an attempt to repair a broken vessel. A recent find of a lead plug in Leinster Cooking Ware at Carrickmines Castle shows that even the lowliest vessel was deemed worthy of repair (McCutcheon 2012). Several such repairs are also known from other sites in Ireland and England, and in Waterford an undecorated wooden bowl was repaired with metal staples (Hurley and McCutcheon 1997, fig. 16:2.9).

The large number of sherds that were blackened and the large estimated rim diameters of some of the vessels imply that the Leinster Cooking Ware from Rathgall represents cooking pots and perhaps storage jars. Although some of the estimated rim diameters were small, i.e. between 110mm and 150mm, there were no sherds of spouts or handles, and from this it can be deduced that there were no jugs or skillets represented in the material. Furthermore, there is a lack of the characteristically thick sherds that are associated with platters, so it would appear that they were not represented either.

Vessel rims are the most distinctive elements of a cooking pottery assemblage. Parallels are generally found on most sites, for example at Ferns Castle, Co. Wexford, and Kilferagh, Co. Kilkenny. The most distinctive of the rim forms from Rathgall is the thumb-frilled or pinched type. This form is common to Leinster Cooking Ware from south Leinster, though not from north Leinster, and is recorded from a variety of sites, such as Ballyloughan Castle, Co. Carlow (de Paor 1962), Kells Priory, Co. Kilkenny (Ó Floinn 1988, 344; McCutcheon 2007), a hut site in Kilmacanoge South, Co. Wicklow (Lucas 1970, 166), and urban sites such as Wexford (Ó Floinn 1988, 346).

At Kilferagh, Co. Kilkenny, the pottery included squat cooking pots with everted rims, some of which had pinched decoration and are similar to those found at Rathgall, for instance no. 228. The site was dated to the late thirteenth–early fourteenth century (Hurley 1987a, 96). Similar rim types were recorded from Jerpointchurch, Co. Kilkenny, and Ferns Castle, Co. Wexford. Most of the pottery at the latter site was stratified in late thirteenth–early fourteenth-century contexts (Sweetman 1979).

Excavations at Ballyloughan Castle, Co. Carlow, produced a small amount of Leinster Cooking Ware (de Paor 1962, 2). The rims were uneven, flat or bevelled outwards and usually frilled. The latter rim forms were virtually identical to some of those from Rathgall (i.e. nos 226 and 227). The striking similarities between them suggest that they were receiving this particular pottery from the same source or potter. Ballyloughan Castle is about 20km from Rathgall. It has been estimated that local glazed wares had a radius of distribution of *c.* 15km from their point of manufacture (Ó Floinn 1988, 341), but with cooking wares this was presumably less. The site of production, then, may have been somewhere between Ballyloughan and Rathgall.

Blackcastle, Co. Kildare, was a settlement site dated to the thirteenth–early fourteenth century. The cooking ware had rims that were thick (7–16mm) and heavy compared to the walls and had mostly pinched decoration. Rim diameters varied from 150mm to 300mm, probably representing forms ranging from small pots and skillets to large pots and storage vessels. The top-heavy rims and necks suggest that they were of low, squat pots (Hurley 1987b). Top-heavy rims and necks are a feature of some of the Rathgall unglazed wares (nos 759 and 757), which may suggest that they too were from low, squat pots.

The plain or undifferentiated type of rim is not as common as the frilled ones discussed above, nor can they be as easily paralleled. One rim sherd from Kilferagh (Hurley 1987a, 95) is somewhat similar to one at Rathgall (no. 250). There is also a rim sherd from Lough Gur of local thirteenth–fourteenth-century ware (Cleary 1982, 93) which is similar to a rim from Rathgall (no. 248). One rim sherd (no. 778) is from a flat, undifferentiated rim but it has been slightly impressed with a stick or finger, which has given the neck a faintly rippled appearance. This is not a very common feature, and it is possible that it was unintentional—for instance, a secondary result of forming the rim.

This rim type is best compared with that of Souterrain Ware, for example at Rathmullan, where two similar rim sherds came from early Anglo-Norman levels (Lynn 1981–2, 122). Souterrain Ware, however, tends to be straight-sided, whereas Leinster Cooking Ware pots are generally shouldered.

The most common rim form found on the Leinster Cooking Ware from Rathgall is the flat, overhanging or rolled-over rim type. This is also the rim form found most widely on other sites, for example at Kilferagh, Co. Kilkenny (Hurley 1987a, 94), Ferns Castle (Sweetman 1979, 233) and Ardnehue, Co. Carlow. The last site was described as a 'kitchen midden' and identified as a possible Gaelic site (Malcolmson 1864–6, 119; Ó Floinn 1988, 333, 325). This rim form can be compared with that of the unglazed cooking pottery at Downpatrick (Pollock and Waterman 1963, 95), and also with that from Shop Street, Drogheda (Sweetman 1984, 185). One sherd (no. 808) is from a flat rim with an estimated diameter of 22cm and has notches at intervals along the internal edge. These would appear to have been made with a small stick or a fingernail. Dalkey Island produced some everted rims of cooking ware which had fingertip or stab-marks along the lip (Waterman 1967–8, 190). There is a large, globular cooking pot from Rathmullan, Co. Down, also with a diameter of *c.* 220mm. The rim is bevelled outwards, and the upper edge is decorated with a continuous row of notches, *c.* 10mm apart and made by pressing in an object with an edge angle of *c.* 90° (Lynn 1981–2, 130–1).

Decoration on the bodies of Leinster Cooking Ware is rare, but where it does occur, on 22 sherds, it is in the form of finely incised lines. Two sherds have applied strips, one of which is 'bow'-shaped, probably impressed with a finger, and there are also two finely incised lines parallel to the strip. Applied strips are unusual for Leinster Cooking Ware but are a feature of Everted Rim Ware, and these are often thumb-impressed.

It is possible that differences in fabric and rim form point to different sources for the pottery. As with the glazed wares, however, it is always possible that several potters were drawing clay from slightly different areas. This is based on the close similarity between some of the Leinster Cooking Ware at Rathgall, principally that with frilled rims, and that from Ballyloughan Castle. Leinster Cooking Ware has been found from the middle of the twelfth century in Waterford (Gahan and McCutcheon 1997) and continued until *c.* 1400 and possibly beyond (Ó Floinn 1988, 336).

This assemblage at Rathgall represents vessels ranging from small cooking pots to large storage jars. Rim forms differ and they are all shouldered vessels. Base diameters range from 150mm to 260mm and fall within the range of the rim diameters. This suggests that a base was of a diameter similar to or smaller than that of the rim. Therefore the sherds from Rathgall would appear to derive from relatively short and squat shouldered pots with upright necks and horizontal rims. The squatter form of vessel is recorded from Kilferagh, Co. Kilkenny, and Blackcastle, Co. Kildare; the former produced something similar to Ham Green Ware, but otherwise neither of these sites produced this ware and both date from the late thirteenth/early fourteenth century (Hurley 1987a, 103; 1987b, 93), later than the now-accepted date for Ham Green Ware. The more globular form was recorded from Jerpointchurch. The dating of the pottery from this settlement was based on its association with the Ham Green Ware recovered from the site. It is probable, however, in the light of the redating of Ham Green Ware (Ponsford 1991; Nicholson and Hillam 1987), that this site may date from the first half of the thirteenth century. It is therefore possible that the globular cooking vessel may represent an earlier form than the squatter vessel.

Wicklow-type wares

There are 323 sherds of glazed wares, representing 17% of the total assemblage. With few exceptions, they have suffered extensively from weathering and exposure. This has been so severe as to make identification or classification into specific types or groups problematic. They are now loosely divided into three groups based on visual inspection, but all fall within the parameters of a tradition of locally made ware in Ireland. Coarsewares are those glazed wares that have a relatively coarse fabric and are hand-built; finewares are wheel-thrown in a fine clean clay; all others fall between in a clean but not fine clay and are wheel-thrown. As noted above, the groups of similar sherds have been retained below, along with the original discussion of other locally made glazed wares in the area.

The designation of a ware as a type is recommended practice in pottery studies and indicates that a ware has been consistently found in a particular area while evidence for a production centre or kiln has not yet been discovered (Blake and Davey 1983). As the general terms 'London-type' (Pearce *et al.* 1985), 'Dublin-type wares' (McCutcheon 2000) and 'Kilkenny-type wares' (McCutcheon 2007) have been adopted to describe wares that share general traditions and clay sources from large assemblages, the term 'Wicklow-type ware' may be used in the broadest sense here. Similar pottery has come from sites throughout the region. At Kilferagh, Co. Kilkenny, some green-glazed pottery of pink-buff fabric with a grey core was recorded. It was thin, of a smooth paste with some quartz/quartzite inclusions. Decoration included applied vertical strips and thumb-impressed rosettes (Hurley 1987a, 93). Similar material has also come from Kells Priory, Co. Kilkenny (McCutcheon 2007), and Dublin (McCutcheon 2000). At Ballyloughan Castle, Co. Carlow, some sherds of fine, hard, terracotta-coloured ware with a pale green glaze, an applied vertical strip and rilling were recovered from a pit dated to the fourteenth century (de Paor 1962, 9). Group B from Ferns Castle, Co. Wexford (Sweetman 1979, 229), and the local glazed ware from the settlement of Jerpointchurch, Co. Kilkenny (Foley 1989, 115), are also of similar fabric and decoration, but tend to be finer than that at Rathgall. Group H from Blackcastle, Co. Kildare, is of pink-buff fabric with no obvious tempering agent and mottled green glaze, but it is also finer than the ware recovered at Rathgall. Further research may show that the Rathgall material could have been produced in Kilkenny, based on similar material recovered from the Highhays kiln there (Ó Drisceoil *et al.* 2022).

The first group (49 sherds) have a wheel-thrown fine fabric, hard-fired to an orange-red or pink-buff colour with a grey core, and glazed in green ranging in shade from pale to mottled brown. The fabric contains a small quantity of micaceous inclusions and quartz. These are generally very small, not exceeding 2mm in diameter. The fabric is very typical of a wide area on the east coast from Dublin to Wexford, as the underlying clay is derived from the granite of the Wicklow Mountains.

This group represents at least three jugs, based on rim differences. One sherd (no. 59) consists of two thirds of a rim and the top third of a strap handle. It has an estimated diameter of 110mm. There is no spout but from the point of breakage it would appear that it once had a bridge spout. There are small pierced holes along the top of the rim at irregular intervals. Just below the rim is a very slight ridge, and the neck has small applied bosses. The handle has two deeply incised vertical grooves. Two other rim sherds have thumb-impressed decoration under the rim, and body decoration consists of applied strips that are a dark grey colour.

The ware is glazed in green that varies in shade, and decoration includes plain applied strips that are brown under the glaze, thumb-impressed decoration around the neck and applied bosses. Spouts are either simple pulled ones or bridge, and handles are of strap type with deep incised or slashed decoration. As already noted, it is similar to the standard local glazed ware found throughout Anglo-Norman Ireland in the thirteenth century.

A further 64 sherds can be divided into two subgroups, 36 sherds of Type A and 28 sherds of Type B. The fabric of Type A is fine but soft, with only a few mica inclusions. The fabric colour ranges from orange to an orange-brown or orange-pink, and the glaze from a yellow-green to a yellow-brown. The fabric of Type B tends to be a little coarser with more inclusions, which are up to 4mm in diameter. The fabric colour is similar, except darker in some cases, and the glaze ranges from a yellow-green to a brown-green. Rim diameters suggest that Type 5A includes sherds from jugs while Type 5B sherds, originally described as cooking pots, are most likely to represent storage jars, some of which may have been put to the side of a fire.

There is a flat rim sherd (no. 103) of Type A ware with an external ridge just below the rim and an estimated diameter of 100mm, and part of a strap handle with a diagonally incised central line. Type B ware has a rim form that is flat but slightly rolled over, and one (no. 139) has an estimated diameter of 200mm. A base-angle sherd of Type B ware (no. 142) is thumb-frilled. Some sherds of Type A ware have traces of incised or combed line decoration (e.g. no. 114).

The rim form of Type A ware is typical of that seen on jugs throughout the country, for instance from the Downpatrick kiln (Pollock and Waterman 1963), Knowth, Co. Meath, Clough Castle, Co. Down (Waterman 1954, 131), Trim Castle, Co. Meath (Sweetman 1978, 167), and Jerpointchurch, Co. Kilkenny (Foley 1989, 116). From Jerpointchurch there was also a sherd with similar 'decoration in the form of bands of horizontal rilling, usually in the area of the shoulder, which were formed using a fingernail' (*ibid.*, 119).

Ferns Castle, Co. Wexford, produced some local glazed ware similar to that of Type A. Group A consisted of vessels of a very crude, open, gritty oxidised fabric. Two of these, however, were finer and thinner-walled than the rest in this group. These two jugs both had elaborate applied decoration and brown glaze and were from layers dating from the late thirteenth–early fourteenth century (Sweetman 1979, 226, figs 4:2 and 4:3).

Glazed storage jars, in a shape very similar to cooking jars, are not as common as either unglazed cooking ware or glazed jugs. Dalkey Island produced some sherds of two small, wheel-turned vessels. They were of hard brown or reddish-brown clay with everted rims and traces of external glaze (Waterman 1967–8, 190). Group C from Blackcastle, Co. Kildare, was probable cooking ware of similar fabric to that from Rathgall. The fabric was bright orange with quartz/quartzite inclusions, and no traces of any glaze owing to weathering (Hurley 1987b, 104). The glazed cooking pots from Clough Castle, Co. Down, date mostly from the first half of the thirteenth century, though there are some known from the second half of that century. The former are of brownish-buff and grey fabric but with white inclusions, and olive-green or brown glaze (Waterman 1954, 128). Carrickfergus Castle produced some cooking ware of buff or reddish-brown fabric with a grey core and tempered with fine grits and mica flecks, and small drops of yellowish-brown glaze externally (Waterman 1952, 113), but these may have been accidental splashes.

Similar vessels are also recorded from Trim Castle, Co. Meath (Sweetman 1978, 168), and King John's Castle, Limerick (Sweetman 1980, 211), but in a reduced fabric. Glazed cooking pottery is recorded from sites in Britain, for instance from York; Brandsbury-type ware includes some glazed cooking ware and has a date range of *c.* 1250–1350, and Early York glazed ware dates from the later twelfth and early thirteenth centuries (Brooks 1987, 152–3). Glazed cooking ware is also known from some more southerly kilns. Wheel-thrown cooking pots of Minety-type from north Wiltshire often have green glaze on the top and inside the rim and date from the mid-thirteenth to the late fourteenth century. Where glaze occurs on Redcliffe cooking pots it is internal and dates generally from the mid-thirteenth to the late fifteenth century (Good and Russet 1987, 37). Many glazed cooking pots, however, may be more usefully identified as glazed storage jars, some of which have been set into the side of the fire, exactly as glazed jugs would have been.

Type A and B ware is yellow- or brown-green-glazed ware of fine, orange-brown fabric, though the fabric of the cooking pots is slightly coarser and has more mica inclusions. There is similar material from Ferns Castle, but more importantly from Blackcastle, Co. Kildare, and it is possible that this group came from a kiln in Carlow, as Blackcastle is about 6km from Carlow.

The third group, representing at least two vessels, is characterised by soft, uniform orange fabric with a grey core. It is also subdivided based on fabric thickness. Twenty-nine sherds are in a ware that is quite thick and open, has a small quantity of red grit inclusions along with mica, and has the remains of a pale yellow-green glaze. Thirty-one sherds are in a thinner ware and have a powdery or gritty texture. Most of the sherds of the first group make up part of a globular jug (no. 166). It had a thumbed basal angle, though not at regular intervals. The sand-marked base was rather uneven, so the thumbing probably served to steady the jug. A bridge spout (no. 167) is of identical fabric and has thumb impressions around it. The base had an estimated diameter of 230mm and the rim 120mm. There are no rim sherds in the second group but the base sherds suggest that they were also thumb-frilled, and there is a shoulder sherd (no. 195) with thumb or finger impressions along it. As noted above, it is possible that some of the Highhays production may have supplied Rathgall and other areas. There is a hill near the town known as Croker's Hill, and in the town itself there is a street known as Crocker Street, a name generally synonymous with 'earthenware potter' (Le Patourel 1968). Excavations in Kilkenny during the 1990s have produced a sizeable assemblage of locally made ware which is very similar in many ways to that found in Dublin, with three divisions of hand-built coarseware, wheel-thrown ware and wheel-thrown fineware (McCutcheon 2000). Group A from Ferns Castle, Co. Wexford, is of crude, open gritty fabric tempered with quartz, mica and pebble, and often oxidised (Sweetman 1979, 226). This is not unlike Kilkenny-type ware, nor are the jug forms that are ascribed to this group at Ferns Castle. One example of the latter has thumb-impressed decoration on the spout and base and a simple rim. It is glazed in a dark mottled green. The fabric is very similar to that from Rathgall, and the thumbing around the spout is almost identical in pattern, though both spout and pattern are slightly larger. There is another jug of this group from Ferns Castle with a heavily thumbed spout, and most of the jugs of this group have thumbed bases. The pottery from Ferns Castle was dated to the late thirteenth–early fourteenth century (*ibid.*, 228). Thumbing around the spout is not a common feature but may be influenced by contemporary Chester-type ware.

Kilkenny-type ware is of soft, orange fabric with some mica, quartz and red grit inclusions, and has a pale yellow-green glaze. Decoration occurs in the form of thumb impressions along the base angle and around the spout. Outside of the immediate south Leinster region, Group D from Blackcastle, Co. Kildare, is similar in fabric to Kilkenny ware. There are six sherds of orange-red fabric with large inclusions of quartz/quartzite and external splashes of olive green glaze. This included one thumb-frilled base sherd (Hurley 1987a, 104). Other than this, however, there is little to compare in terms of fabric with Kilkenny ware outside the region.

The glazed pottery from Rathgall can be compared with the various local pottery groups throughout the country in terms of some features and decorative forms such as rim form, thumb-frilled decoration under the rim, strap-handle form and decoration, applied strips and thumbed bases. The local glazed wares support this to an extent, as the local variations and the material itself point to well-established pottery production.

3.11.8 The post-medieval wares
Caroline Sandes with Clare McCutcheon

Introduction

The principal types of post-medieval pottery at Rathgall are black-glazed wares and glazed red earthenwares. These include handled vessels, storage jars and dishes. Although pottery was being used for a far greater number of different vessel types, there is less distinction between the products of different kilns. This is further emphasised by local copying of originally imported material. This is particularly seen in the case of slipware. Slipware of similar type is recorded from a number of sites, and in some cases it may be of local manufacture. There appear, however, to be at least three different sources for it outside of Ireland: Devon, Bristol and Staffordshire. There is also greater continuity of wares; both black- and brown-glazed wares continue in use right through the post-medieval period.

Post-medieval pottery

Fabric	Sherds	MNV	MVR	Form	Date
Portuguese redware	1	–	1	Costrel	17th
Black-glazed ware	44	–	4	Pancheon, three jars	L17th–19th
Glazed red earthenware	33	–	4	Cup/jug. 2 dishes, counter	L17th–19th
GRE: slip-trailed	22	–	1	Dish	L17th–18th
Bristol/Staffordshire slipware	1	–	1	Cup?	18th
Creamware	1	–	1	Plate	18th
Pearlware	35	–	4	Eggcup, lid, plate, preserve jar	19th–E20th
Shell-edged ware	1	–	1	Bowl?	19th
Transfer-printed ware	12	–	5	Saucer, two plates, bowl, jug	19th
Painted pearlware	24	–	5	Saucer, four cups	19th–E20th
Banded ware	3	–	1	Mug/jar?	19th
Stoneware	1	–	1	Jar	19th–E20th
Total	178	–	29		

The collection at Rathgall dates from the end of the seventeenth century–beginning of the eighteenth century. It is possible that Rathgall was used as a temporary camp at this time, perhaps for the practice of transhumance or booleying. No. 1237 was recovered from the brown fill of the curved bedding trench immediately under the wall of Rampart 1, which suggests that it is post-medieval or later in date.

It can be concluded that the post-medieval pottery points to Rathgall's being either occupied temporarily or used as a folly sometime in the late seventeenth–eighteenth century.

The post-medieval wares came from the same disturbed contexts as the medieval pottery, and in some cases were mixed with them.

Portuguese redware

'Merida-type ware is a misnomer for Portuguese coarsewares of characteristic brick-red fabric with quartz and mica inclusions, which were probably manufactured in the High Alentejo, an area extending inland from Lisbon and to the east' (Gutiérrez 2007, 64; Newstead 2013). Costrels were traded from here from the thirteenth century to the present day (Hurst *et al.* 1986, 69). The fabric is fine, sandy and micaceous, normally unglazed but occasionally burnished. Medieval pieces tend to be rougher and brown, while the sixteenth- and seventeenth-century fabric is harder, finer and usually red-brown to red (*ibid.*). It is difficult to tell these apart, but the practice in recent pottery reports has been to place this ware within the late medieval assemblage (cf. McCutcheon 2003, 224).

Black-glazed ware

Black glazing results from the addition of iron to lead glaze on the red earthenware fabrics. The fabric is often highly fired to a near-stoneware purple, although other varieties have a white marbled appearance. The fabric of the black-glazed wares made in Ireland appears to be a less highly fired red earthenware (Meenan 1997, 349).

There are at least two vessels represented by four sherds, and these include a dish and a smaller vessel. The former has an estimated rim diameter of 320mm, and the latter 190mm. The lower part of one vessel was partly reconstructed and had an estimated base diameter of 150mm. The vessels had internal black glaze, and in one case an external matt brown glaze as well.

Eighteen sherds, including two different strap handles with central ridges, represent two vessels. No. 1265 had shallow grooves in the central ridge and on either side of it, and no. 1266 had incised decoration on either side of the central ridge. There is a rim with an estimated diameter of 19cm, and sherds from a base with an estimated diameter of 11cm.

Black ware is common and turns up on most post-medieval sites. It originated in the Buckley potteries, or other kilns, in the Chester area (Lynch 1984, 302). The black ware from Charlotte's Quay, Limerick, represents storage vessels and smaller and finer cups or jars. The latter are of brown-buff to grey fabric, while the storage jars are reddish-brown with cream streaks (*ibid.*). Type 3C from Rathgall has similar streaks; it is possible that this, too, came from storage vessels, and therefore the other black ware at Rathgall perhaps came from smaller jars and other such vessels. The black ware at Charlotte's Quay dated from the late eighteenth century (*ibid.*, 312). Black ware with streaks of yellow clay in it was also found in an early eighteenth-century context at Dunbar Street, Belfast. The glaze is uniformly black, but often containing white specks, and covers the entire vessel except for the underside of the base. The commonest vessel form is a vertical-sided bowl with a heavy rim, rectangular in cross-section. There are also two handled vessels, an open bowl or pancheon, at least one smaller, finer bowl and an open dish. This ware may have come from Staffordshire (NcNeill and Baillie 1988, 363). Black ware of seventeenth-century date also came from Dooneendermotmore Fort, Co. Cork (O'Kelly 1952–3, 47).

Black ware also has a long span of use: for instance, at Shop Street, Drogheda, it occurred in the earliest post-medieval layers, which dated from the first half of the seventeenth century, and continued until the first half of the eighteenth century (Sweetman 1984, 186). Black ware of both types of fabric seen at Charlotte's Quay also came from Inns Quay, Dublin, where it was dated to the late seventeenth–eighteenth century (McMahon 1988, 296, 312). Black ware is recorded from Ferns Castle, Co. Wexford, where it dates from the eighteenth century (Sweetman 1979, 234), and from Dunboy Castle, Co. Cork, where it dates from the seventeenth century (Gowen 1978, 45).

Glazed red earthenware

This ware is also relatively fine, though thick. It is fired to an orange-brown colour and has internal and external glaze. There are at least four vessels represented by sixteen sherds, including two dishes and a handled vessel such as a jug or a cup. One vessel, no. 1237, was partly reconstructed and had an estimated rim diameter of 320mm. No. 1238 is a sherd from a rim with an estimated diameter of 27cm. Estimated base diameters are between 140mm and 200mm.

Drumlummin, Co. Tipperary, the site of a post-medieval house, produced some pottery similar to the brownware at Rathgall. The pottery from the former was of local Irish origin and dates from the mid- to late seventeenth century (Cleary 1987, 127). Some large dishes with rim diameters of between 30cm and 40cm were of sandy-textured paste with some mica and quartz inclusions. The rims were out-turned and in some cases had a lid seating, and were knife-trimmed to form a bevel. The glaze fired brown or dark green internally but with some evidence of external glaze. The jug and cup sherds were of similar fabric and glaze. The former had a strap handle (*ibid.*, 129, 131). In the main the pottery from this site was of earthenware vessels for domestic use; there were practically no imports, and the assemblage provides a good range of native domestic wares (*ibid.*, 139). Similar brownware came from King John's Castle, Limerick, and dates from the third quarter of the seventeenth century (Sweetman 1980, 212–13).

Brownware also turned up at Inns Quay, Dublin, and included several different vessel types, such as dishes, bowls, cooking pots, storage vessels and a chamber-pot. Although some of this ware may have come from the Liverpool or Chester area, some of it may have been local (McMahon 1988, 297). There were some brownwares recorded from Dunbar Street, Belfast. These were probably local and dated from the early eighteenth century. The fabric is open-textured with a few inclusions. It is a red or orange colour, sometimes with a grey core. The vessels are glazed only in parts, both internally and externally, in a thick, glossy brown glaze, which is green over reduced parts. Rims are everted, varying from rolled-over to rather angular forms. The vessels include large and small bowls, for storage and table use respectively, and a handle suggests a pipkin (McNeill and Baillie 1988, 361). Brownware of local manufacture was also recorded from the promontory fort of Dooneendermotmore, Co. Cork, and dated to the late sixteenth–early seventeenth century (O'Kelly 1952–3, 48).

Brownware comprised a variety of vessel forms and was the standard domestic ware. It was, for the most part, of local manufacture. The brownware at Rathgall would appear to fall into this category and probably dates from the end of the seventeenth century.

Glazed red earthenware: slip-trailed

There are twenty sherds of this ware, representing one dish. The fabric is fine and orange-brown throughout, though there are some mica inclusions. The brown glaze is internal, and there is trailed linear yellow slip decoration. The dish has an estimated rim diameter of 32cm and a base diameter of 17cm. It is about 11.5cm high.

Trailed slip was a common method of decoration on post-medieval pottery. Slip consists of potter's clay mixed with water to form a semi-liquid state. When it was used for decorative purposes, it was either washed over the surface of the vessel, thus providing a contrasting colour to that of the body of the vessel, or it was trailed. Trailed slip decoration was achieved by pouring the slip through a quill or from a spouted 'slip-cup' or 'quill-box'. The flow from the latter was controlled by placing a finger over an air-hole in the vessel (Savage and Newman 1985, 265, 296). Pottery with this kind of decoration is often referred to as 'slipware'.

Slipware very similar to that from Rathgall came from Ferns Castle, Co. Wexford. This material was of south-western English type, though some of it which contained small amounts of mica may be local copies. There were about 29 plates or shallow dishes represented, glazed in buff, light or dark brown or green, with either line or dot decoration of yellow trailed slip. The post-medieval pottery came from undatable contexts, but that from the fill of the fosse was given a *terminus post quem* of 1760 by a halfpenny of George II (Sweetman 1979, 234–6).

Inns Quay, Dublin, produced some 27 sherds of similar material from south-west England, representing thirteen dishes or platters. They were glazed on the interior in orange, brown or green-brown, and had wavy line or line and dot decoration on the rim, and dots and linear decoration on the base. This material, like the rest of the post-medieval pottery, dated from the late seventeenth–eighteenth century (McMahon 1988, 297, 312).

From these two examples it would appear that this material dates from the late seventeenth–eighteenth century. It is possible that this slipware from south-west England could have come from Devon. The two main pottery-producing centres in north Devon during post-medieval times were Barnstable and Bideford. North Devon is known mostly for its sgraffito ware, but it also produced trailed slipware. From the beginning of the seventeenth century pottery from this area was coming into Ireland in considerable quantities, and the south-east of the country became a major market for north Devon pottery. In 1683, for example, New Ross and Waterford imported 1,225 dozen earthenware vessels from north Devon. Wexford, too, imported varying quantities, ranging from ten dozen in 1682 to 430 dozen in 1701 (Grant 1983, 106). The port of New Ross, however, would have been the principal port for the region in which Rathgall is situated. New Ross is on the tideway of the River Barrow, only fifteen miles from Waterford, and so was well placed for trading further inland (*ibid.*, 110).

Slipware was recovered from the early eighteenth-century site of Dunbar Street, Belfast. There were two imported subgroups from either Bristol or Staffordshire and a third, local group. The latter was of a red fabric, or grey when reduced, and was decorated by trailing white slip or trailing brown slip onto a white under-slip. These sherds were from plates or dishes (McNeill and Baillie 1988, 360).

Slipware is represented at Rathgall by one dish. It dates from the late seventeenth–eighteenth century and is possibly from one of the kilns of north Devon. The presence of mica in the fabric suggests, however, that its origin is more likely to be local.

Bristol/Staffordshire slipware

This ware was made in both the Bristol and Staffordshire areas in the late seventeenth and eighteenth centuries (Jennings 1981, 104). Bristol's close connections with Ireland might lead one to suppose that the slipwares came from there, but the overwhelming majority of later seventeenth- and eighteenth-century pottery was imported from Staffordshire.

Creamware

In the 1760s, cream-coloured earthenware with a creamy glaze was developed by Josiah Wedgwood to combat the overwhelming influx of blue and white Chinese porcelain. Instead, it only succeeded in putting tin-glazed earthenwares out of business, and creamware became known as English faïence on the Continent.

Pearlware

Wedgwood's development of creamware was further refined as pearlware, with a harder-fired clay and a blue rather than green tinge in the collected glaze (Savage and Newman 1985, 216). This formed the basis for many decorative forms of the later eighteenth and nineteenth centuries, such as shell-edged, mochaware, transfer-printed and banded wares.

Shell-edged ware

This term describes 'a moulded border decoration on the scalloped rim of certain plates, principally of pearlware, but first used on Bow porcelain and creamware' (*ibid.*, 262).

Transfer-printed ware

Transfer-printing is commonly associated with the so-called 'willow pattern', but the variety of patterns is wide, with landscapes (particularly English and Italianate) very popular, as well as many varieties of Chinese style or chinoiserie. While the principal colour used is a deep blue, decoration also comes in red, grey, brown, purple, green and black. The decoration consists of the application of a coloured tissue paper design.

Painted pearlware
Rather than transfer-printing, these pearlware plates and cups were decorated with freehand painting, often rather crudely drawn.

Stoneware
The term is used here to cover all English stonewares, made of a clay and fusible stone which can be fired to partial vitrification, not then requiring a glaze to make it impervious to liquids (*ibid*., 275).

3.12 CHIPPED STONE
Graeme Warren

3.12.1 Introduction

This report discusses an assemblage of 299 flaked stone artefacts from Rathgall. A further 21 pieces were identified as natural. Bipolar working is common, and a limited range of retouched forms are present. Most of the assemblage is likely to be Early–Middle Neolithic in date, although the possibility of a significant Bronze Age component cannot be excluded.

3.12.2 Distribution

Given the significant area excavated and the size of some of the other artefactual assemblages, the quantity of worked flint is quite low. Collection standards for flint during the excavation appear to have been acceptable, with small and irregular material being reasonably well represented. The comparatively small assemblage size is an important consideration in characterising this assemblage overall. Lithics were recovered from 78 squares at Rathgall, with six having no reliable spatial information (see Fig. 3.98). Thirty-nine squares contained only one artefact. Only sixteen squares contained more than five artefacts and only eight over ten artefacts. The most from any square was 48 from I5. Taken at a broad level, the largest concentrations of artefacts came from the south-east of the site. This area sees particular concentrations of bipolar working and a notable group of often fragmented convex scrapers (see below).

Ring-ditch 1 itself was associated with a very low number of artefacts, with most squares in this area having only one find, and some having two. Of the 32 artefacts from this area only one was of chert. Of the 31 flint finds, only two were burnt, 21 were abraded and one was lightly patinated. Eleven were broken and twenty were edge-damaged. This is a higher proportion of breakage and abrasion and a lower proportion of burning than in the assemblage elsewhere, which *may* imply greater residuality. No convex scrapers were recovered from this area and only one concave scraper. Seven natural rock crystals were recovered from Rathgall, six from within Ring-ditch 1 and one from immediately outside it (Fig. 3.99). These include single and multiple crystals ranging in length from 24mm to 8mm (13.3±5.7mm, 5.3±2.9mm, 4.4±2.7mm). The significance of their deposition in this area is not immediately apparent but the pattern is very strong.

Ring-ditch 2 also yielded few artefacts, especially from the very centre of the enclosure.

The two chert barbed and tanged arrowheads were recovered from peripheral areas of the site (X11, Z2:9; E84:9300, Fig. 3.104, and E100:31, Fig. 3.105). Specific associations between lithics and other dated artefacts are outlined below.

3.12.3 Raw materials

The assemblage is dominated strongly by flint, with a handful of chert and a single quartz flake (Table 3.33). These other materials are found across Areas 1 and 2 and in more peripheral areas. The main concentration of lithics in the south-east of the site is of flint, mainly from a pebble source; indeed, many pieces are clearly from a beach pebble source. The nearest beaches are over 30km away as the crow flies, and this would not be the most likely route to have travelled. Small amounts of flint are also known in glacial deposits in the south-east of Ireland but are poorly understood. There is clear evidence (see below) that in many cases unmodified pebbles were being brought to Rathgall and reduced on site. Other flint artefacts may have been imported as finished pieces. A small number of artefacts seem likely to have been manufactured on Ulster White Limestone Flint (often identified as 'Antrim' flint) but this was not a significant component of the assemblage. The flint is varied in colour and quality, and the presence of rare examples of an unusual pink flint is notable.

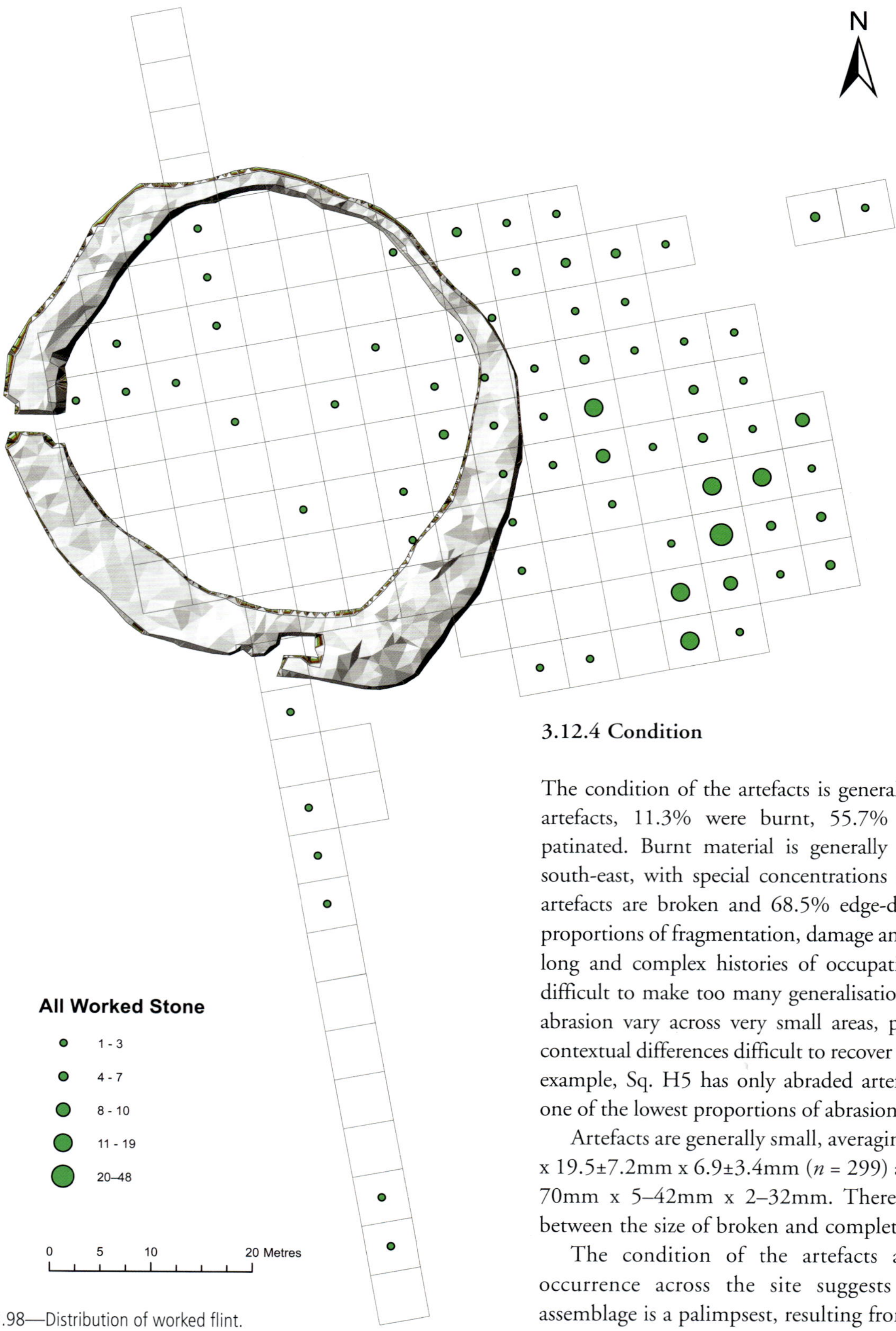

Fig. 3.98—Distribution of worked flint.

3.12.4 Condition

The condition of the artefacts is generally poor. Of the flint artefacts, 11.3% were burnt, 55.7% abraded and 3.4% patinated. Burnt material is generally concentrated to the south-east, with special concentrations in I5/H5; 40.8% of artefacts are broken and 68.5% edge-damaged. These high proportions of fragmentation, damage and abrasion reflect the long and complex histories of occupation of the site. It is difficult to make too many generalisations, as proportions of abrasion vary across very small areas, presumably reflecting contextual differences difficult to recover from the archive. For example, Sq. H5 has only abraded artefacts, whereas I5 has one of the lowest proportions of abrasion on site (Table 3.34).

Artefacts are generally small, averaging only 25.4±9.4mm x 19.5±7.2mm x 6.9±3.4mm (n = 299) and ranging from 8–70mm x 5–42mm x 2–32mm. There is little distinction between the size of broken and complete artefacts overall.

The condition of the artefacts and their scattered occurrence across the site suggests strongly that the assemblage is a palimpsest, resulting from many centuries of activity and disturbance.

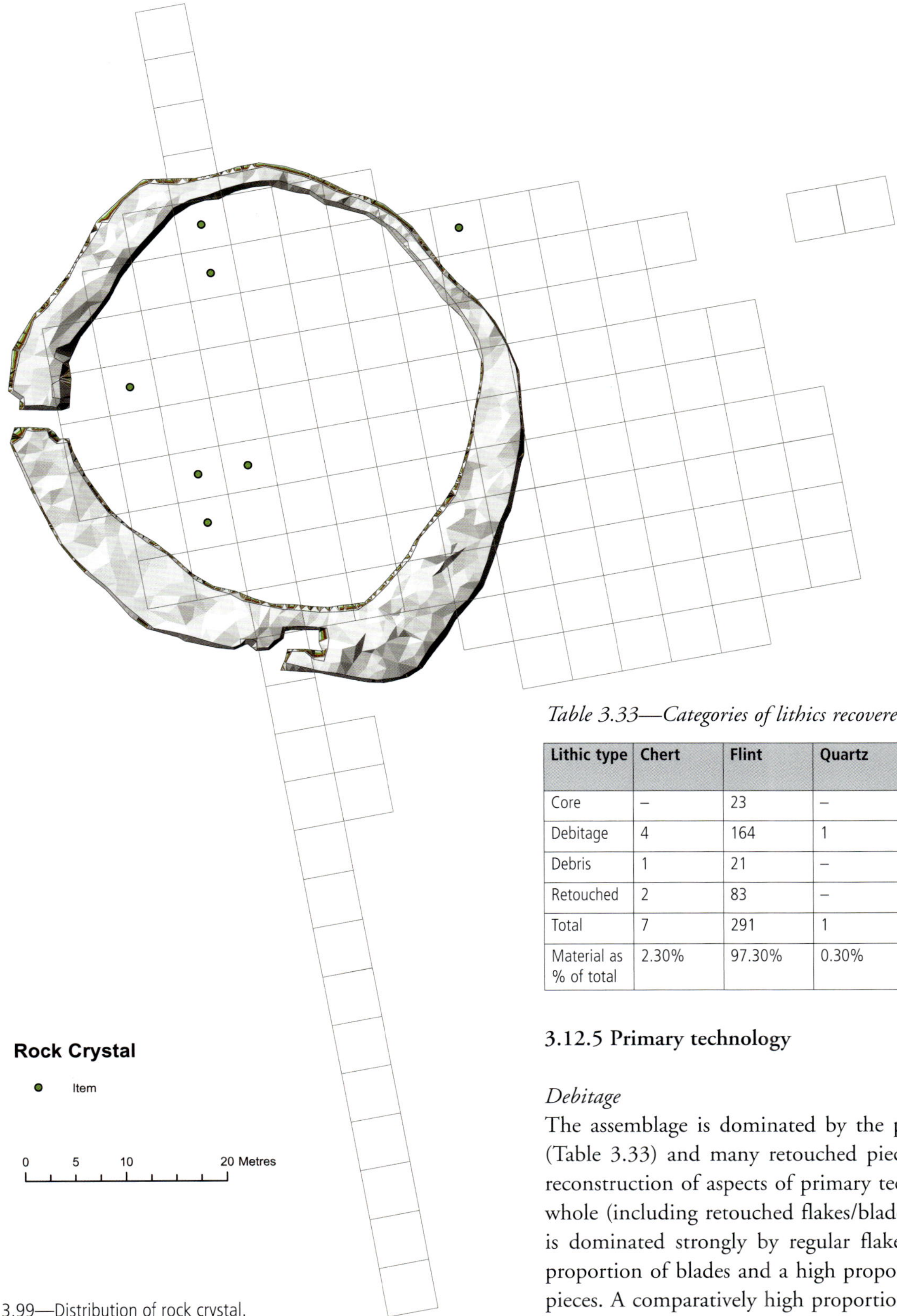

Fig. 3.99—Distribution of rock crystal.

Table 3.33—Categories of lithics recovered from Rathgall.

Lithic type	Chert	Flint	Quartz	Total	As % of total
Core	–	23	–	23	7.70%
Debitage	4	164	1	168	56.20%
Debris	1	21	–	22	7.40%
Retouched	2	83	–	86	28.80%
Total	7	291	1	299	–
Material as % of total	2.30%	97.30%	0.30%	–	

3.12.5 Primary technology

Debitage

The assemblage is dominated by the products of debitage (Table 3.33) and many retouched pieces allow for further reconstruction of aspects of primary technology. Taken as a whole (including retouched flakes/blades etc.), the debitage is dominated strongly by regular flakes, with a negligible proportion of blades and a high proportion of fragmentary pieces. A comparatively high proportion of all materials are cortical (64.8%; see Table 3.35), with primary debitage well

Table 3.34—Results of the lithic assemblage analyses by square.

Abraded	D7	F2	F4	G2	G4	G6	H5	H6	I5	I6	I7	J4	J5	K7	Z5:d
No	0	8	4	5	3	7	0	10	29	3	4	7	5	4	0
Yes	5	8	1	3	4	5	11	11	19	3	3	5	5	11	5
No (%)	0.00%	50.00%	80.00%	62.50%	42.90%	58.30%	0.00%	47.60%	60.40%	50.00%	57.10%	58.30%	50.00%	26.70%	0.00%
Yes (%)	100.00%	50.00%	20.00%	37.50%	57.10%	41.70%	100.00%	52.40%	39.60%	50.00%	42.90%	41.70%	50.00%	73.30%	100.00%

Table 3.35—Analysis of cortex proportions on debitage products at Rathgall

Debitage type	Primary	Secondary	Tertiary	Total
Indeterminate fragment	7	9	22	38
Flake (regular)	11	86	47	144
Flake (irregular)	12	14	10	36
Blade		4	3	7
Flake (indeterminate)	5	10	4	19
Total	35	123	86	244
	14.30%	50.40%	35.20%	

Table 3.36—Analysis of platform type for debitage products at Rathgall

Debitage type	Collapsed	Cortical	Dihedral	Faceted	Linear	Plain	Total
Indeterminate fragment		3				3	6
Flake (regular)	15	40	5	3	4	34	101
Flake (irregular)	7	19			1	7	34
Blade	3				1	1	5
Flake (indeterminate)	3	5					8
Total	28	67	5	3	6	45	154
Platform type as % total	18.20%	43.50%	3.20%	1.90%	3.90%	29.20 %	

represented, and a very high proportion of platforms are cortical or collapsed (Table 3.36), both resulting from the early stages of reduction of pebbles. More elaborate platform preparation is very rare. A comparatively small proportion of flakes could be definitively identified as bipolar (6.6%), but only 44.3% were definitely platform flakes (*n* = 244). Bipolar working is most likely associated with the high numbers of cortical and collapsed platforms. Most debitage is small (Fig. 3.102).

Retouch is rare on bipolar debitage (see below for discussion of bipolar reworking of retouched objects) and retouched debitage is on average larger (30.9±8.2mm x 24.5±6.1mm x 8.1±3mm, *n* = 33) than non-retouched (25.1±10.3mm x 18.8±7.5mm x 6.6±3.4mm, *n* = 94) (data controlled for breakage). There is no meaningful distinction between retouched and non-retouched in terms of platform types.

Cores

Quantifying the presence of cores in the Rathgall assemblage is complicated slightly by the elaborate 'reworking' of convex scrapers. Nine 'bipolar cores' are scrapers that have been reworked. A single platform core was present, recovered from Sq. F2 (E84:7106; Fig. 3.101). This was abandoned with a large amount of raw material remaining, possibly because of problems with step fractures.

Bipolar cores are predominantly worked from two ends only, rather than four (E84:6255, E84:6994, E84:7449a, E84:8989, E84:9464a, E84:9470a, E100:174) (Figs 3.100, 3.101, 3.103–3.105). Excluding reworked scrapers, they are generally small, 28.9±3.1mm x 19±4.9mm x 8.4±2.5mm (*n* = 18, controlled for breakage), with many reworked scrapers of broadly the same size range. Bipolar cores are often non-cortical.

Discussion

Taken altogether, these data demonstrate a range of approaches to working flint at Rathgall. Flint is not available at the site and must have been imported. Most of the flint appears to have come from pebble sources, and at times these pebbles are quite large. Whilst the possibility of some *remanié* and other till flint in the lowlands cannot be excluded (Woodman *et al.* 2006), the most likely source for these pebbles are the beaches of the Irish Sea, a distance as the crow flies of over 30km. It is somewhat surprising that there is strong evidence for the early stages of working this material, as efficiency might have suggested that this would take place nearer the source. Similar patterns of flint exploitation in the uplands are demonstrated in a Later Neolithic context at Piperstown, Co. Dublin (Rice 2006), although Piperstown is only *c.* 10km from likely beach sources.

Bipolar working is frequent on site, but many of the retouched objects were made through platform reduction routines. There is some possible evidence for the reworking of these objects, but in general it appears that many of these may have been brought to the site in their finished form. This mixture of curated platform technologies and on-site bipolar reduction is common in Irish prehistoric lithic assemblages. Bipolar working is present in Ireland from the earliest Neolithic through into the Bronze Age, and changes over time in the nature of bipolar working are not well understood (see e.g. Sternke 2010; 2011; Woodman *et al.* 2006).

3.12.6 Secondary technology

A total of 86 retouched artefacts were recovered from Rathgall (Table 3.37). This is a very high proportion and may partly reflect collection biases, but is also likely to indicate something of the character of activity on site. Two large chert barbed and tanged arrowheads were found on the peripheries of the site but otherwise all the retouched objects are of flint.

Projectile points

Two large barbed and tanged arrowheads of black chert are present. E100:0031 (Fig. 3.105) is a basal fragment with a very clear central tang. Both barbs are truncated but are unlikely to have been extensive. E84:9300 (Fig. 3.104) has short barbs, one truncated by a break. The retouch is invasive and parallel and has created a lightly serrated edge. Both artefacts are similar to 'Ballyclare' arrowheads (Green 1980), although they do not meet the strict metric definitions. Woodman *et al.* (2006, 138) argue that the larger forms of barbed and tanged arrowheads had developed by 1700 BC, with no evidence of longevity of use beyond the Early Bronze Age. The use of large non-flint materials at this time is attested at Ballyarnet, Co. Londonderry, where two large chert arrowheads were dated to 1800–1500 BC (Ó Néill *et al.* 2002; Ó Néill 2004). Although it may initially seem surprising that chert was used for large, formal retouched artefacts, Woodman and Scannell (1993, 54) note that chert was frequently used for larger leaf-shaped arrowheads in the Lough Gur assemblages but that this pattern is not at all clear in barbed and tanged forms. They also argue that the larger barbed and tanged forms 'were produced at a limited number of locations and then were disseminated using the exchange systems which had been established through the distribution of metalwork' (*ibid.*). In some areas, chert may provide the only suitable raw material for the production of large blanks.

Table 3.37—Secondary technology: analyses of retouched artefacts recovered at Rathgall.

Class	Subclass	*N*	Notes
Awl	-	1	+ 1 possible
Butt-trimmed form?	Distally trimmed	1	
Flake/blade	Edge-retouched	17	+ 1 possible
Indet. retouched fragment	—	11	
Indet. retouched piece/unclass.	—	1	
Invasively retouched form	—	2	
Projectile	Barbed and tanged	2	
Scraper	Concave	13	
Scraper?	Concave	2	+ 1 possible
Scraper	Convex	30	
Scraper?	Convex	6	
Total		**86**	

Butt-trimmed form, possible

This is a large flake, possibly on UWL Flint, with two areas of retouch (E84:4637; Fig. 3.100). At the proximal left a light concave area is defined by short retouch and truncated by a break. At the distal left a small area is marked with irregular retouch which may possibly be edge damage. The overall form of the flake is somewhat leaf-like, yet this is unlikely to be a true 'butt-trimmed form' because of the lightness of the trimming and the overall character of the object. This artefact should not be considered as anything beyond highly equivocal evidence for Mesolithic activity on site.

Scraper, concave

A total of thirteen certain, two probable and one possible concave scrapers were recovered (E84:5593 (Fig. 3.100), E84:7104a, E84:7105, E84:7738, E84:8528, E84:8622 (Fig. 3.101), E84:9089b (Fig. 3.103)). Three are double concave scrapers, all forming notable triangular forms with very shallow concavities (E84:8622, Fig. 3.101; E84:9089b, Fig. 3.103). One may strictly be best classified as a triple concave scraper with two concurrent concavities. Many single-concavity scrapers are fragmentary and often have inverse retouch across a broad edge of the flake. No hollow scrapers *sensu stricto* were identified. Hollow and concave scrapers are not uncommon in upland assemblages and date from the Neolithic in general (Woodman *et al.* 2006).

Scrapers, convex

The dominant artefact class consists of convex scrapers, of

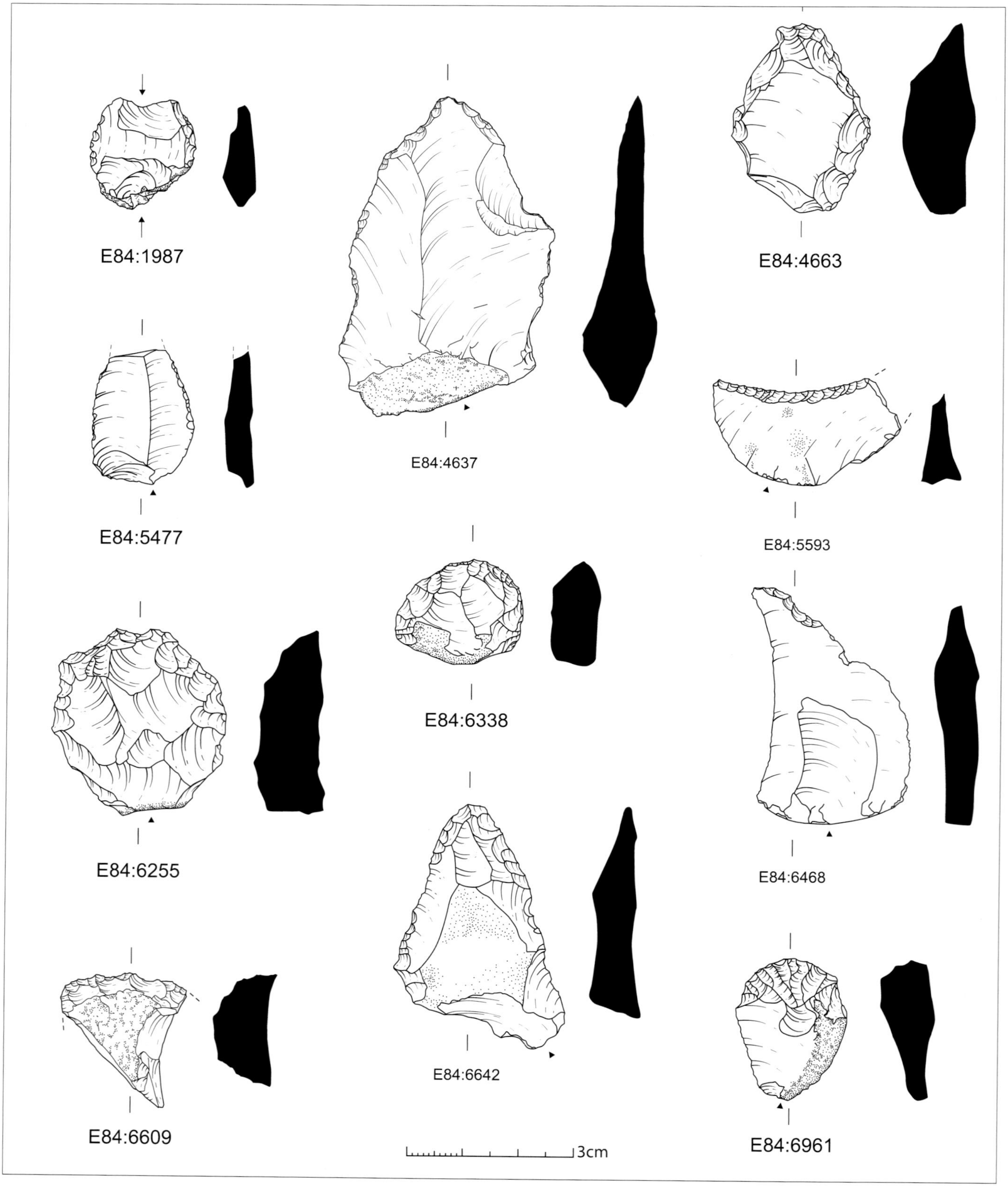

Fig. 3.100—Worked flint (scale 1:1) sorted numerically.

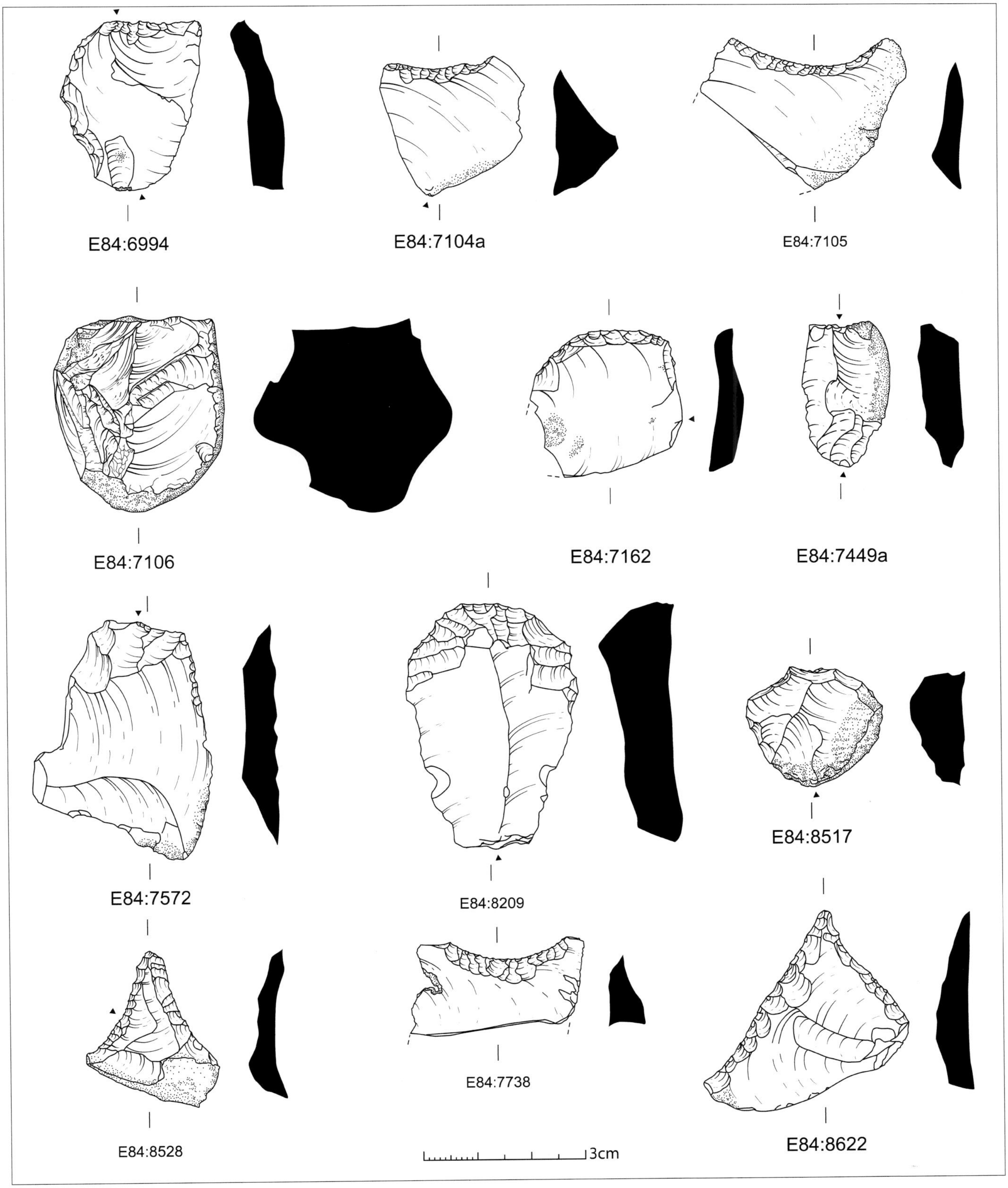

Fig. 3.101—Worked flint (scale 1:1).

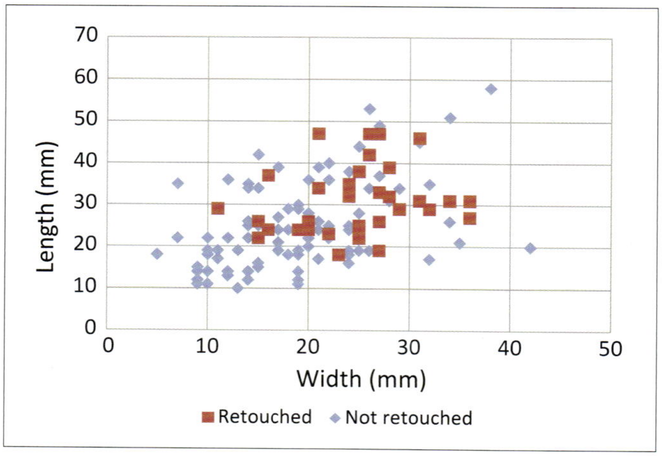

Fig. 3.102—Size of debitage (in mm), controlled for breakage.

which 30 definite and six probable examples, or fragments thereof, have been identified (E84:1987, E84:4663 (possible), E84:6255, E84:6338, E84:6609, E84:6961 (Fig. 3.100), E84:7162, E84:8209, E84:8517 (Fig. 3.101), E84:8760, E84:9018a, E84:9036c, E84:9036d, E84:9036e (Fig. 3.103), E84:9098, E84:9191e, E84:9202, E84:9216a, E84:9330, E84:9451, E84:9500 (Fig. 3.104), E100:128 (Fig. 3.105)). Many of these scrapers have been fragmented (see below for discussion) and some indeterminate retouched fragments may also have derived from scrapers. They are concentrated in the south-east of the site, especially in I5 and H5. Scraper typology is very ambiguous: most of the types here are short convex end/side scrapers, some rather round in form. Few fall into the category of disc scrapers *sensu* Woodman *et al.* 2006, which are required to be 20mm in maximum dimension (Fig. 3.106). Chronologically these forms are hard to date precisely. Woodman *et al.* (2006, 161) discuss 'small, rather more dome-shaped scraper(s) where retouch can continue around the periphery and on occasions extend across the surface' as being 'securely associated' with Beaker assemblages. Some of the Rathgall examples (e.g. E100:128) may approach these forms, but it is difficult to be certain.

One of the most interesting features of the Rathgall assemblage is the fragmentation of convex scrapers. In a number of instances scrapers have been broken, seemingly intentionally, with a firm blow. These artefacts present some analytical challenges and many are somewhat ambiguous. I am grateful to Sol Mallía-Guest and Emmett O'Keeffe for comment. A number of 'modalities' of fragmentation can be identified.

On several artefacts a bipolar blow was struck perpendicular to the main axis of the object (Fig. 3.100; E84:1987, E84:6255; see also E84:9179h, E84:9413). These blows in places truncate the working edge but do not wholly remove it. It is possible that this is associated with hafting, and close parallels are present at the early Neolithic house site of Corbally, Co. Kildare (Mallía-Guest 2011). On some examples a bipolar blow has been struck along the long axis of the artefact (E84:9199 (possible), E84:9036g), while others appear to have been 'quartered' along both axes, sometimes in association with a bipolar blow (Fig. 3.100; E84:6609) and sometimes not (E84:9044c). In a very small number of cases, the reworking of a retouched object through bipolar techniques produces a blank that then receives peripheral retouch. Here some degree of recycling might be proposed (E84:8998b). Other examples seem to have used bipolar blows to remove the lower surface (original ventral of the flake), seemingly as a rejuvenation strategy and sometimes associated with heavy wear to the new edges. There are other examples where a blow to the ventral has removed a substantial area of the working edge. Sometimes this may be rejuvenation (E84:2222, slightly abraded edge) and at other times not (E84:9037, which is clearly not rejuvenation). There are also thermal fragments (E84:9036) and more indeterminate fragments. It is important to emphasise that these artefacts do not represent the technical sequences described by Sternke (2011), where retouch is used to provide a platform for bipolar reduction. The Rathgall examples are formal retouched tools, in some cases clearly heavily utilised.

It is difficult to interpret these data, which are broadly paralleled on numerous Neolithic sites, for example Corbally (Mallía-Guest 2011), various north Mayo sites (Driscoll 2011) and Eagle's Nest, Lambay Island (GW, pers. obs.), and these parallels are generally Early/Middle Neolithic rather than Later Neolithic. It is likely that multiple strategies in the past require untangling here, and we require more information on the use-life of artefacts, hafting, rejuvenation and how they finish their active lives. Some of the Rathgall artefacts appear to have been recycled, but it is important to note that this is not part of a broad tendency to recycle all materials—concave scrapers, for example, are not used in this way. Some may have been rejuvenated, but it is tempting with some of the fragmentation to see it as a form of decommissioning. The reasonably close spatial association of these artefacts may support this argument.

It is also important to note the possibility that some of this activity may be much later in date. Broken scrapers were

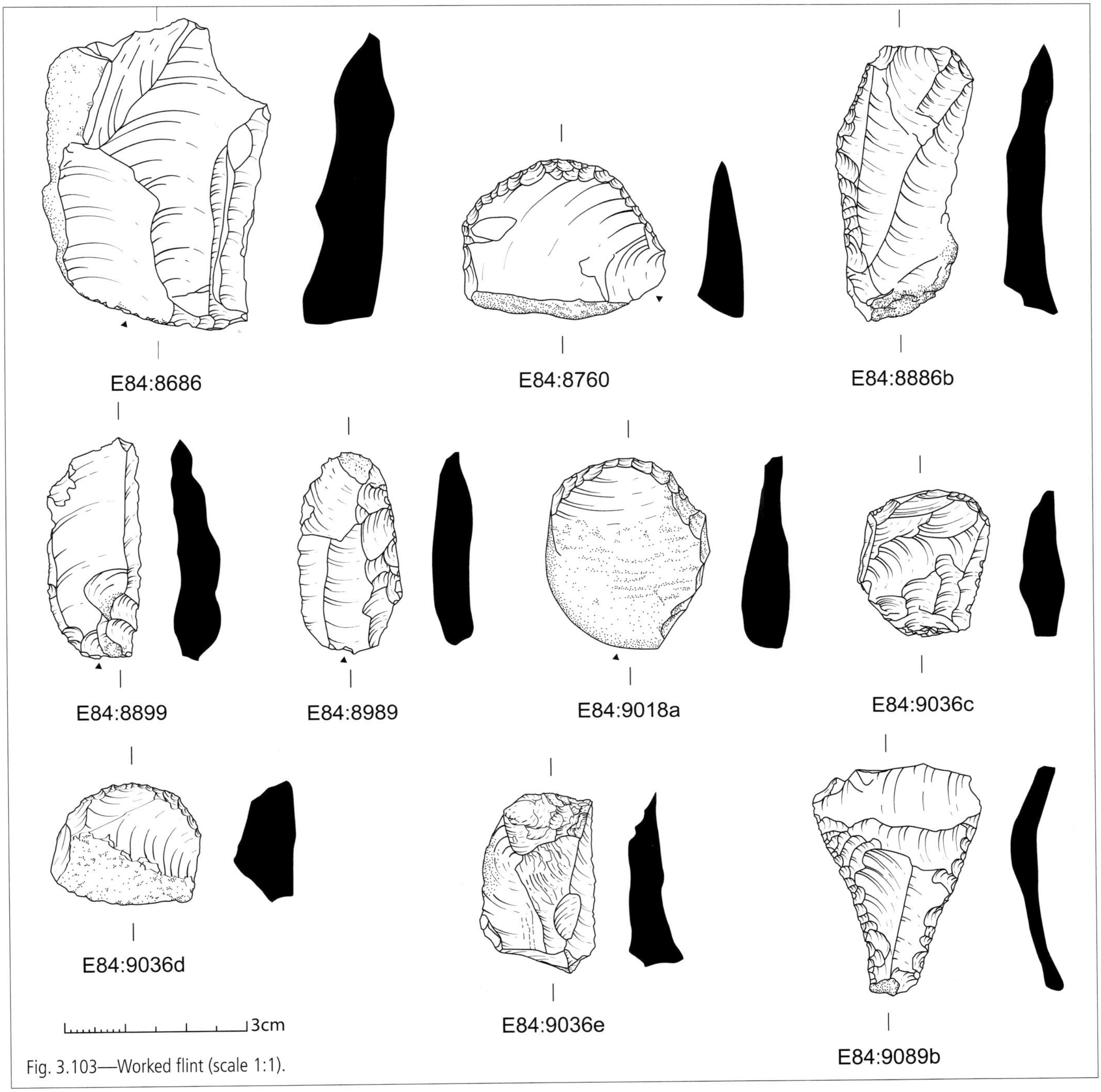

Fig. 3.103—Worked flint (scale 1:1).

sometimes found with later prehistoric ceramics, notably in three pits: Pit 180 included one complete and two broken convex scrapers in association with Middle–Late Bronze Age ceramics. Pit 186 contained one fragmented scraper (E84:9199) and some coarseware. As argued below, however, using associations with ceramics to date the lithics at Rathgall is problematic.

The general spatial association of many of these fragmented artefacts with the medieval house might imply that these fractures and breakages resulted from the recycling of materials in the historic period, as has been argued at Clogher, Co. Tyrone, for example (R. Warner, pers. comm.). The nature of post-Bronze Age lithic technology in Ireland is rather ambiguous (see Warren and Little 2017; Woodman *et al.* 2006, 100). Harper (1973–4, 39) reviewed lithics from early medieval contexts, arguing for 'a remarkably strong case

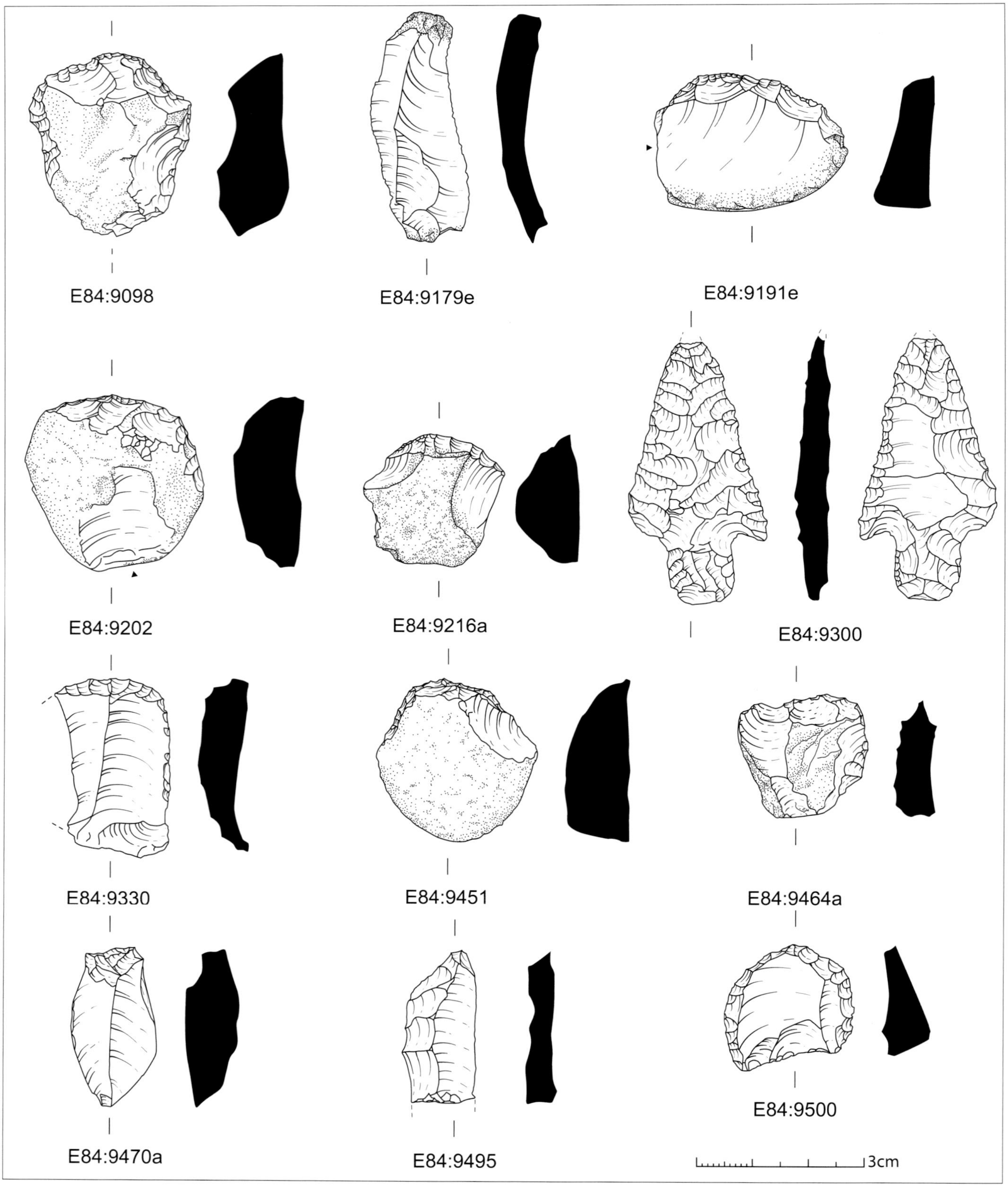

Fig. 3.104—Worked flint (scale 1:1).

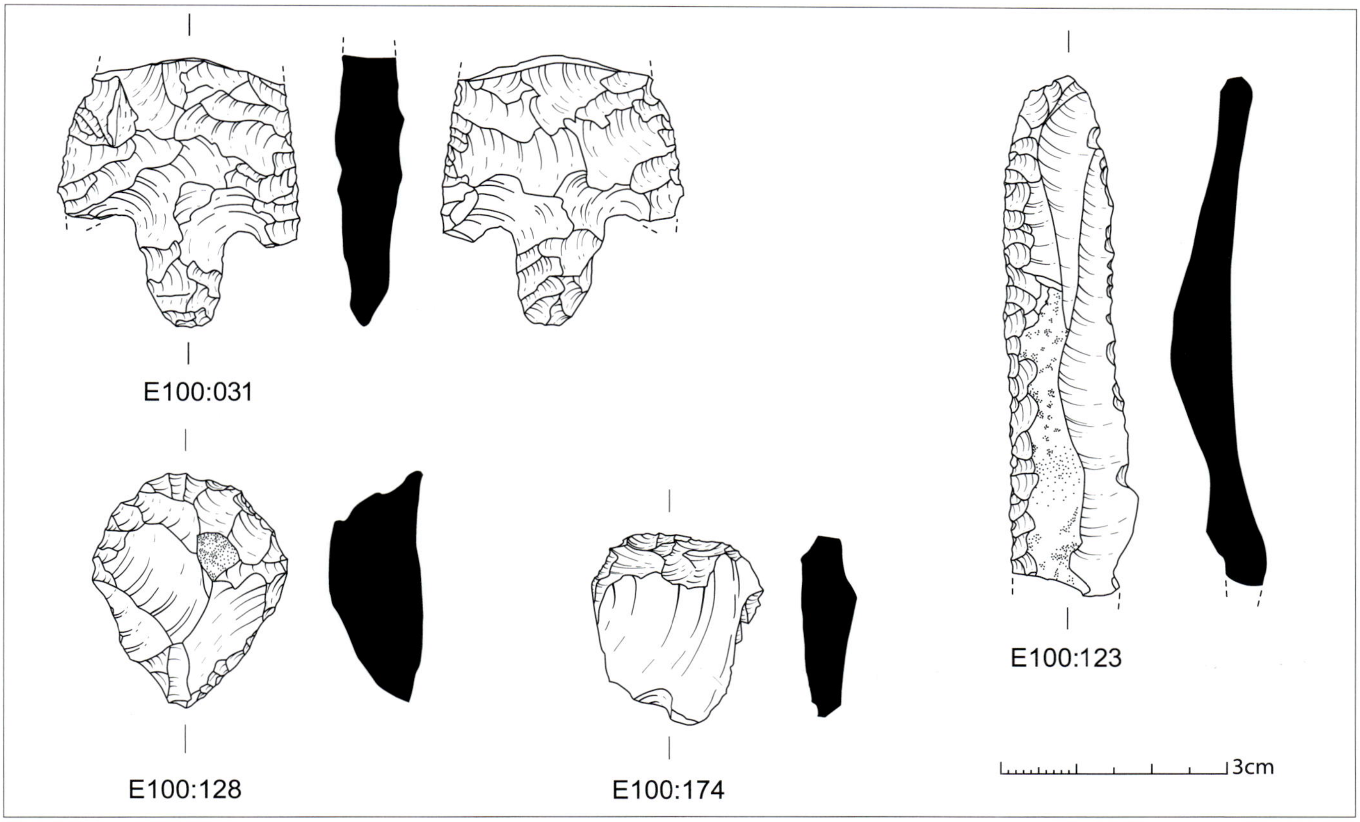

Fig. 3.105—Worked flint (scale 1:1).

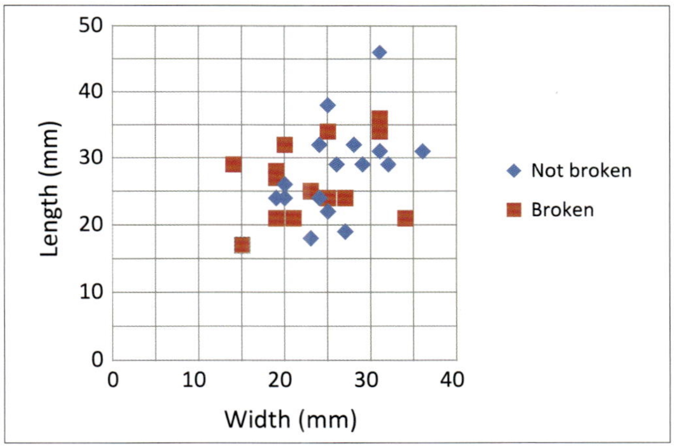

Fig. 3.106—Size of convex scrapers.

for viewing a limited range of flint work as common and contemporary elements in the artifact assemblage of the early medieval period'; since that time a number of medieval or early medieval sites in Ireland have returned lithic materials (see O'Sullivan *et al.* 2008) but the nature of historic stoneworking badly needs further research. Woodman *et al.* (2006) argue that, after the Early Christian period, lithic artefacts are restricted to strike-a-lights, gun flints and plough pebbles. Accepting that little by way of a broader interpretative framework exists for post-prehistoric lithic technology, the shattered scrapers from Rathgall seem most likely to be prehistoric, and probably Neolithic, in date. As noted above, close Neolithic parallels can be identified for many of the practices described. Becker (pers. comm.) has also raised the possibility that the medieval house disturbed earlier activity.

Awl

An awl and a possible awl are likely to be of later prehistoric date (E84:9272g, E84:7745.1).

Edge-retouched

These seventeen (and one possible) artefacts have small areas of mainly peripheral edge retouch but do not form a clear morphological class (E84:5477, E84:6468 (Fig. 3.100), E84:6994, E84:7572 (Fig. 3.101), E84:8886b, E84:8899 (Fig. 3.103)). They are not chronologically distinctive. In two cases these artefacts are on reworked scrapers. There are two invasively retouched pieces. In one instance this provides a backing for an opposed edge (E84:8989, Fig. 3.103; E100:123, Fig. 3.105).

Two similar retouched blades show semi-invasive blunting retouch to one side and very minor modification, possibly light serrations, mixed with edge damage on the other. E100:0123 (Fig. 3.105) is the largest at 71mm in length and is a blade with semi-invasive, semi-parallel scalar retouch on all of the right-hand lateral, while the left lateral has a very short retouch/serration. E84:8886b (Fig. 3.103) is shorter but comparable in overall form. Finely retouched blades of this kind are most likely to be Neolithic in date.

3.12.7 Chronology

Accurately assessing the chronological range represented by this palimpsest assemblage is difficult and the small size of the assemblage must be stressed. In Ireland in general only a comparatively small number of lithics are sharply diagnostic of particular periods, and our understandings of change over time in routines of production are still somewhat coarse-grained, especially in terms of possible regional variation. In an assemblage dominated by bipolar routines and convex scrapers, the assemblage might contain considerable time depth that we cannot easily differentiate. Bronze Age working, for example, makes extensive use of bipolar technologies and a range of short convex scrapers (Woodman *et al.* 2006). A degree of residuality, however, can be demonstrated. Table 3.38 shows formal retouched artefacts from 'dated' contexts and clearly demonstrates that a significant number of concave scrapers have been recovered from Middle/Late Bronze Age contexts. These artefacts are not likely to have been manufactured at that time and are best considered residual. There is therefore no strong evidence that the convex scrapers found in association with Middle Bronze Age ceramics are Bronze Age in date, as they are equally likely to have been redeposited. Some pits, for example Pit 180, seem to have contained only small convex disc scrapers characteristic of the Bronze Age; these examples may well be in good association with the Bronze Age ceramics from the same pit but such exclusive associations are rare. For many pieces we cannot demonstrate that they are Bronze Age and the more parsimonious interpretation is that they are redeposited.

Many of the techniques utilised and artefacts produced can be paralleled in Early and Middle Neolithic assemblages in Ireland (see above for discussion). This includes the concave and convex scrapers, edge-retouched blades and the broad technological systems utilised. Early and Middle Neolithic ceramics are present in low numbers in the ceramic assemblage, and it is interesting to note that one of the concentrations of this material in the area immediately north of Ring-ditch 2 (e.g. Sq. F2) includes the main concentration of concave scrapers on site. There is no clear correlation between the concentration of convex scrapers in the I5 area and Neolithic ceramics. There is no compelling evidence for Mesolithic or Later Neolithic activity, and the general paucity of large flakes and blades should be noted.

The site demonstrates links with the wider landscape, most notably in the importation of some finished artefacts and raw materials. The importation of pebbles from some distance to hilltop locations is paralleled at Piperstown, Co. Dublin (Rice 2006), albeit in a later Neolithic/early Bronze Age context. Stone was worked on the hilltop at Rathgall, and one assumes that a range of tasks were carried out with concave scrapers

Table 3.38—Analysis of formal retouched artefacts from 'dated' contexts at Rathgall.

Find no.	Name (1)	Name (2)	Context	Date
E100:110	Blade	Edge-retouched	In black, bone-filled layer of Pit 16	^{14}C and artefacts: Bronxe Age (BA)
E84:2054	Scraper	Concave	Outside 'cobbling' in W of square	Likely in occupation deposit; BA
E84:8524	Scraper	Concave	In upper grey fill of ditch near W end of section strip J4	BA, fill of Ring-ditch 2
E84:8686	Indet. retouched fragment	—	In dark brown fill of Depression 128	With many BA moulds and pottery
E84:9044a	Scraper	Convex	In black layer, Pit M = Pit 180	With BA pottery
E84:9044b	Scraper	Convex	In black layer, Pit M = Pit 180	With BA pottery
E84:9044c	Scraper	Convex	In black layer, Pit M = Pit 180	With BA pottery
E84:9089b	Scraper	Concave	In fill at base of rectangular trench (medieval)	Medieval enclosure trench
E84:9098	Scraper	Convex	In fill at base of rectangular trench (medieval)	Medieval enclosure trench
E84:9199	Scraper?	Convex	Pit 186	With BA coarseware
E84:9293	Flake	Edge-retouched	(Pit 78:3) Pit 244	With BA pottery and moulds
E84:9605	Flake	Edge-retouched	Ring-ditch K5	BA, fill of Ring-ditch 2

and other retouched tools. It is interesting to note that concave scrapers are often, although not exclusively, associated with upland locations (see Bergh 2009; Burenhult 1984; Woodman *et al.* 1991–2).

Beaker ceramics are present in the pottery assemblage but generally in low numbers and spread across large areas of the site. Some of the scraper forms in the lithic assemblage may be Beaker in date but, given the lack of spatial detail, it is not possible to point to any meaningful spatial associations.

The two large chert arrowheads indicate Early Bronze Age activity, probably after 1700 cal. BC. As these objects are rather peripheral to the rest of the assemblage, it is not clear that this represents an extensive phase of stoneworking on site, but the deposition of these two objects does indicate activity at Rathgall at this time.

3.12.8 Conclusion

The small assemblage from Rathgall is a palimpsest and many of the artefacts are abraded and edge-damaged, reflecting many years of occupation. It was mainly recovered at low densities across the site, with a significant concentration in the south-east in association with a medieval structure which may have disturbed earlier activity. All of the objects were imported onto the site—either as finished artefacts or, more surprisingly, as pebbles, some of which at least were carried from the coast. Bipolar and platform routines were used, with compelling evidence for the former taking place on site. Regular flakes, often small, were the key outcome of these technical sequences. Retouched forms are comparatively common, albeit limited in diversity, with convex and concave scrapers dominating. Much of the assemblage would be coherent with an Early or Middle Neolithic date, although aspects certainly relate to later occupation in the Bronze Age. Given the degree of residuality, as well as the nature of the archive, it is difficult to assess to what degree different aspects of the assemblage relate to different chronological periods.

3.13 GROUND STONE OBJECTS

Barry Raftery

This discussion of the stone implements from Rathgall and its accompanying catalogue is complemented by the full inventory of such finds in the finds database.

3.13.1 The shale bangles from Rathgall

Fraser Hunter

Character of the assemblage

The Rathgall excavations produced thirteen fragments of bangles in oil shale and similar dark organic-rich materials. They show diversity of form and size, and also in their production stage: three are unfinished, six broke in use, and a further four broken fragments show attempts at repair.

The unfinished bangles indicate local availability of source material, or at least access to blocks of raw material or part-finished items through exchange networks. The absence of working debris need not be significant, as this is often overlooked on excavations, but the absence of early-stage blanks and rough-outs might suggest the importation of part-finished rough-outs (such as 7532) for on-site finishing (Fig. 3.107). The asymmetrical or slightly angular internal sections of two bangles suggest that they may have been made by removing a central core, but the evidence is not strong enough for certainty and technical details of the production process are not clear.

The finished items show notable diversity of size and form. The sections vary from simple D-forms (the commonest type in prehistory), to fattened D, tall, narrow D, pear-like and subrectangular. There is a notable preponderance of fine circular sections (four examples), which are not common on other sites. The range of internal diameters, from 45mm to 80mm, suggests that both male and female ornaments are represented (cf. Hunter 2016, fig. 4; female bangles are predominantly *c.* 55–65mm and male *c.* 70–80mm in internal diameter, though the distributions overlap).

Four of the bangles show attempts to reuse them after breakage, with trimming and squaring of irregular ends, and holes drilled for repair or reuse as pendants. Interestingly, three of these are made of materials other than the dominant grey shale, suggesting that more exotic or unusual material was preferentially valued and repaired.

Four broad material types can be identified from visual inspection (using the criteria established by Davis 1993). Most are a laminar grey shale (sometimes heavily spalled); all the unfinished bangles are of this material. Two fragments (1383, 8657) are a dark, compact material, perhaps a canneloid shale, while there are single finds of a dark laminar shale (8054) and a compact grey material, darker than the norm (9466) (Fig. 3.107).

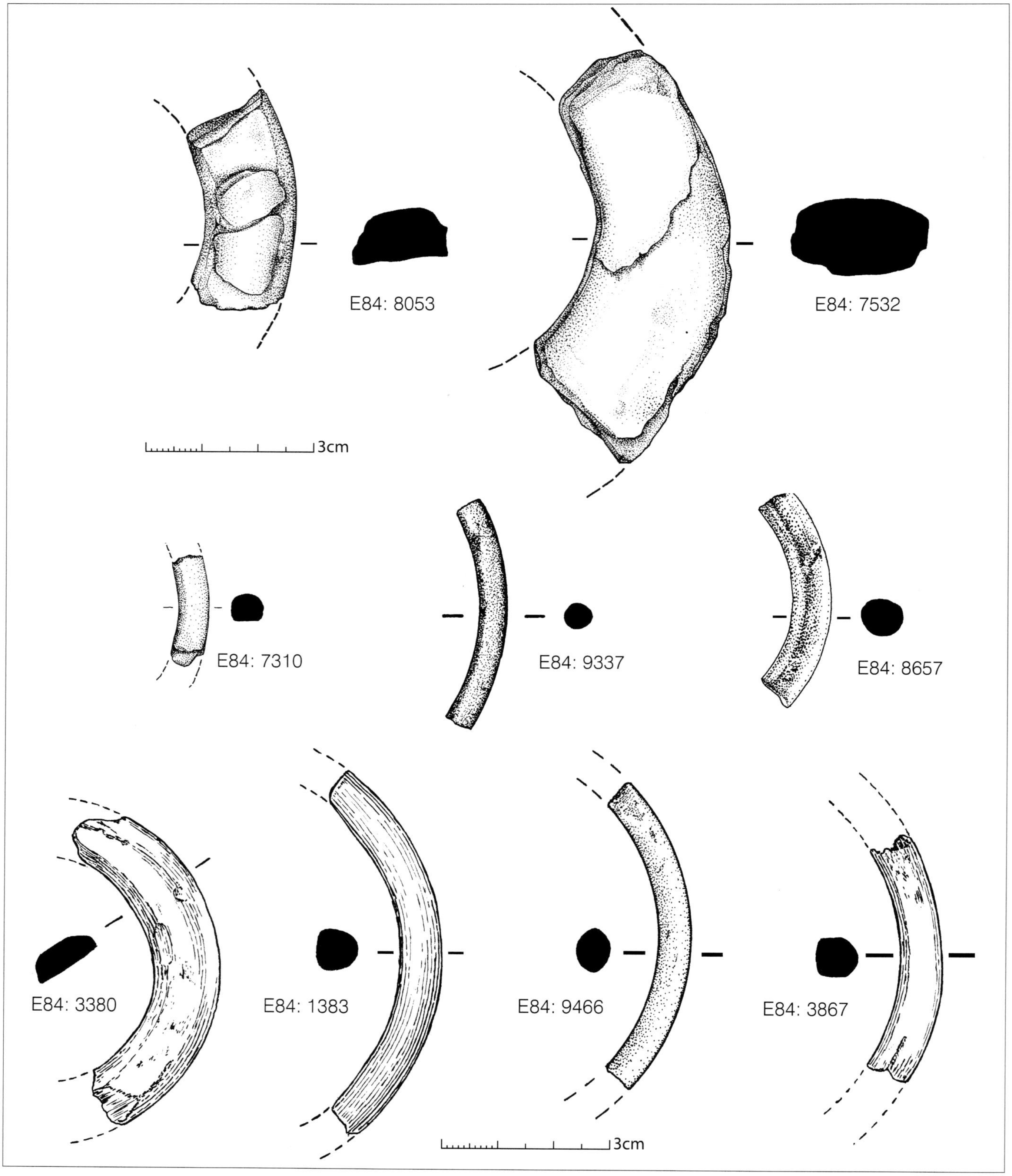

Fig. 3.107—Bracelets of shale (scale 1:1).

Comparisons (with Katharina Becker)

Bangles of black, organic-rich stone are a long-lived type, used intermittently in Ireland and Britain from the late Neolithic/Beaker period to the Norse period (e.g. Beaker period examples from Lough Gur; Norse ones from Woodstown, Co. Waterford; Ó Ríordáin 1954, 354, fig. 26, nos 1–2; Grogan and Eogan 1987, fig. 7, no. 1514, fig. 22, nos 3136–40—others from Lough Gur are insecurely stratified; Hunter and Sheridan 2014), with a particular concentration in the early medieval period (e.g. Edwards 1990, 96; Kerr *et al.* 2013, 32). Fortunately, contextual evidence suggests that the Rathgall ones are most likely to be Late Bronze Age in date (*c.* 1200–1000 BC). This is a time when such bangles were popular in both Ireland and Britain. Discussion here will focus on the Irish evidence. Such bangles (and other jewellery in the same materials) are known from ten certain or probable Late Bronze Age sites (Table 3.39). Sadly, most are not published in sufficient detail to allow comparison with the Rathgall finds: few are illustrated; descriptions use inconsistent terminology and often fail to report key dimensions (such as the internal diameter, which is key to defining what size of hand could wear it); and material identifications are also highly variable. Nonetheless, broad patterns can be noted which confirm the observations from Rathgall. Hencken (1942, 15) noted that the range of diameters at Ballinderry suggested that they were both male and female ornaments, in contrast to the smaller (female) bangles typical of the early medieval period. The few published images (from Ballinderry, Lough Eskragh and Haughey's Fort) show a notable diversity of section, as seen also at Rathgall, with specific parallels for some Rathgall forms (e.g. circular sections at Lough Eskragh and Ballinderry no. 99; the extended D section of 1383 is paralleled by Ballinderry no. 227). Frequent evidence for repair or reuse (often in the form of a perforation at one end) indicates that these were valued items. Less easily paralleled is the production evidence from Rathgall, though without an experienced eye this can be hard to spot. Nonetheless, it hints at differences between producer sites (such as Rathgall) and consumer sites.

The geological source of the material has seen no detailed study. Lignite and cannel coal sources in northern Ireland are mapped in Hunter 2008, fig. 1, but a wider overview is lacking. An organic shale is known from the local area (McConnell and Phillcox 1994; Stephen Mandal, pers. comm.), however, and the presence of manufacturing debris suggests that the grey shale comes from local sources. Others may be more exotic, but their locations cannot yet be specified.

Summary

Bangles of black stone were worn by both men and women at Rathgall. They were manufactured in a grey shale on site, perhaps from imported perforated rough-outs, as only the

Table 3.39—Late Bronze Age finds of oil shale and related materials from Ireland.

Location	County	Site type	Bangle	Repaired	Other	Notes	Reference
Adamstown 2	Waterford	Industrial?	1 (D-sectioned)			Cannel coal (XRF/X-ray)	Hunter, F. & Sheridan, A. 2009. Appendix 11
Ballinderry 2	Offaly	Crannog	6 (triangular, lentoid and extended D sections)				Hencken 1942, 13–15
Berrilstown 1	Meath	Uncertain	1 (no details)			Date not certain	Rathbone 2006
Haggardstown site 13	Louth	Enclosure	1 (fat D section)	Groove near one end suggests repair or reuse		Probably lignite (visual inspection)	Information from excavator (find 06E0485:86:1)
Haughey's Fort	Armagh	Hillfort	2 (one incomplete, one oval section, perforation at end)	Yes, perforation			Mallory 1991a, fig. 16.7
Killymoon	Tyrone	Industrial	1 (form not stated)				Hurl *et al.* 1995, 50, no. 10412
Knocknalappa	Clare	Crannog	1 (form not stated)				Raftery 1942
Lough Eskragh	Tyrone	Crannog	1 (circular section)			Jet (petrological identification)	Williams 1978, 8, fig. 7 A 1
Moynagh Lough	Meath	Crannog	5 (circular and oval sections recorded)	Ends cut on one, suggesting repair	5 beads, 2 rings	1 decorated bangle	Bradley 2004, 97
Rathgall	Wicklow	Hillfort	13 (various sections)	Yes	Includes manufacturing evidence	Shale, canneloid shale (visual inspection)	This report

later stages of production are represented. Other raw materials (other oil shale and canneloid shale) may have come from further afield, and these more exotic items were more likely to be repaired or reused. They are part of a broader Late Bronze Age tradition in Ireland, though the manufacturing evidence is rare and suggests that this may have been a particular role at the site. More generally, the evidence provides an important well-dated assemblage of bangle types in use in the Late Bronze Age which can form a basis for further studies in Ireland and Britain.

3.13.2 Catalogue of shale bracelets

Unfinished bangles

E84:3380: Adhering surface dirt obscures details, but this seems to be a fragment spalled from an unfinished bangle. The interior is quite circular in plan and rounded in profile; the exterior is near-vertical, rounding into the top face, which is flat with occasional facets, implying that it was in the course of being finished. L: 56mm. W: 12mm. H: 4.5mm. Internal diam.: 45–50mm (35% survives). Probably an oil shale, given its grey colour and laminar nature. Sq. 11 (Fig. 3.107).

E84:7310: Unfinished bangle fragment, spalled into two parts. Near-circular section with natural flattened faces; knife facets on interior and exterior edges. Shale (grey, laminar). L: 21mm. W: 5.3–5.7mm. H: 5.3–5.5mm. Internal diam.: 55–60mm (10% survives). Sq. E1 (Fig. 3107).

E84:7532: Unfinished perforated rough-out, subrectangular in section with exterior and interior rounded, the faces flat with abrasion scars. Oil shale (grey and laminar). L: 71mm. W: 21.5–27mm. H: 13.5mm. Internal diam.: min. 55–60mm (27% survives). Sq. D/D1 (Fig. 3.107).

Finished bangles, broken in use

E84:6561a,b: Two fragments (once joining but now worn) of a fine circular-sectioned bangle, with faint circumferential and occasional transverse tool marks. Shale (grey, laminar). Total L: 42mm. W: 5.2–5.5mm. H: 5.4–5.5mm. Internal diam.: *c.* 75–80mm (17%). Sq. D1.

E84:7381: Fine circular-sectioned bangle fragment, rather eroded. Does not appear to be part of 6561, as it is rather smaller. Oil shale (grey, laminar). L: 25.8mm. W: 4.8–5.2mm. H: 4.3–4.7mm. Internal diam.: 70–75mm (11% survives). Sq. E.

E84:8054: Fine circular-sectioned bangle, well finished, with no tool marks and little polish. Oil shale (dark, laminar, slightly grainy texture). L: 20mm. W: 5.5mm. H: 5.5mm. Internal diam.: uncertain owing to size; only 6% survives. Sq. B1.

E84:9129: Tall, thin, D-sectioned bangle in two joining parts; interior flat; surfaces worn but seem well finished. Shale (grey, laminar, mineral inclusions). L: 62.5mm. W: 4.8–5.4mm. H: 10.2–11.4mm. Internal diam.: 50–55mm (52% survives). Sq. B3.

E84:8053: Bangle fragment with broad subrectangular section, the flat surviving face curving into the rounded edges. Spalled just below section midpoint. Not very highly polished, but no residual tool marks to indicate that it was unfinished. Oil shale (grey, spalling). L: 40mm. W: 16.5mm. H: 10mm. Internal diam.: 55–60mm (17% survives). Sq. B1 (Fig. 3.107).

E84:9337: Fine circular-sectioned bangle fragment, well finished, with no visible tool marks apart from the odd circumferential scratch; polished to a medium lustre. Some use damage. Shale (grey, laminar). L: 41.5mm. W: 5.1–5.2mm. H: 4.7–4.9mm. Internal diam.: 75–80mm (17% survives). Sq. X13 (Fig. 3.107).

Bangle fragments with evidence of repair or reuse

E84:1383: Bangle with fat D section, the interior slightly rounded with circumferential and some angled abrasion; exterior very well finished, with some wear scratches. Attempts to repair or reuse it are indicated by four transverse knife cuts near one broken end; the end has been snapped to square it at the outermost surviving mark, suggesting that these were marking-out lines. Canneloid shale or shale (compact, almost black, conchoidal fracture, hint of laminar structure). L: 64mm. W: 7.4–7.8mm. H: 7–7.4mm. Internal diam.: 70–75mm (30% survives) (Fig. 3.107).

E84:3867: D-sectioned bangle, interior slightly rounded; surface worn and splitting, no visible tool marks. Attempts at reuse, with a notch cut into one end and a slight channel on top (their purpose unclear). Shale (grey, laminar). L: 44.8mm. W: 7.3–8mm. H: 7.3–7.5mm. Internal diam.: 75–80mm (16% survives). Sq. C1 (Fig. 3.107).

E84:8657: D-sectioned bangle fragment; the asymmetrically rounded inner edge suggests that it was made by removing a central core. Interior shows abrasion; exterior smoothed and polished to a high lustre. Conchoidal fracture where both ends are snapped almost square; one was slightly abraded to square it off. The faces at this end were flattened by abrasion and an incipient hollow in this face indicates an attempt to perforate it for repair. Faint scratches define a working limit towards the other end, where a similar attempt to drill a hole ended in failure, as part of the surface spalled off and the drill jumped across the surface, leaving an irregular groove. Cannel coal or canneloid shale (dark, compact, conchoidal fracture). L: 39mm. W: 6.9–7.3mm. H: 6.5–7.1mm. Internal diam.: 45–50mm (23% survives). Sq. Y4 (Fig. 3.107).

E84:9466: Well-made bangle with squashed pyriform section, pointed to the interior (the section perhaps suggesting manufacture by the removal of a core). Slight facet along one face; interior has extensive circumferential and angled abrasion scratches; exterior well finished to a medium polish, with extensive signs of wear. Attempts to reuse or repair are attested by a knife-cut circumferential groove near one end to mark where the end should be trimmed; it was probably abandoned owing to spalling. Oil shale (grey, laminar, compact). L: 56mm. W: 6mm. H: 8.5mm. Internal diam.: 70–75mm (25% survives). Sq. I7 (Fig. 3.107).

3.13.3 Miscellaneous stone artefacts

Hammerstones

Hammerstones are found in a variety of contexts, both in the central zone of the site and in the Z cuttings. Most of these derived from secondary contexts, with only E84:7565 found in a context associated with the main concentration of metalworking materials in Sqs D–D1, and 7692 and 8681 also from contexts of possible Bronze Age date.

Hones, whetstones/burnishing stones

Whetstones, scattered across the excavation zone, were most frequent; 39 specimens may be considered as either certainly or possibly belonging to this category. The majority of these, however, fall into the doubtful category because of the uncertain nature of the wear upon them, and Mandal (section 3.14) considers only seventeen of them to fall within this category. Thus, excluding those which are superficially doubtful or which come from disturbed ploughsoil, few examples remain.

An especially interesting fragment (E100:161; Figs 3.108 and 3.118) was carefully worked to a square shape with rectangular cross-section and an exceptional smoothness on all surfaces. It is regarded by Mandal (see section 3.14) as an original stone axehead which had been extensively repolished and reused as a whetstone/polishing stone of some sort. It is made from a banded, fine-grained green tuff, which Mandal suggests as having been imported into Ireland. It was extensively worked on all sides to create an almost square polishing stone or whetstone of some sort, with smooth, faceted edges.

This object raises many questions. Had it originally been an axehead, the effort involved in its reworking would have been extensive. Might one wonder whether a broken axehead, some two or three thousand years old, was picked up by a Bronze Age occupant of the site, who laboriously ground the fragment to shape? It is a quite exceptional piece, beautifully green in colour and almost sensuously smooth to the touch. Undoubtedly the stone was specially chosen. If it was created as an axehead it would, when complete, have been an object of considerable beauty, reminiscent, perhaps, of the superbly fashioned axeheads of the Neolithic such as the magnificent green jadeite specimens of Britain and Ireland, which are generally seen as of non-secular significance (Waddell 1998, 49). In such a context, its refashioning—especially if this indeed took place in the Bronze Age—prompts intriguing questions concerning the use and importance of the object. The quality of the stone is not otherwise paralleled on the site, and the question arises as to whether this item was of special significance. Its location in the fill of a post-hole might also be significant, though this could equally, of course, be entirely accidental.

The smooth surfaces, including the faceted sides, suggest that it was used either as a small anvil/cushion stone or, as its small size suggests, as a polishing or burnishing stone or hammer for metalworking. It was found on the southern slope outside the fort, at a depth of 35cm in the grey silt almost on the base of Post-hole 3, Sq. Z5:a. This post-hole was one of a small group of large, deep examples which encircled the Ring-ditch 3 complex at a distance of about 1.5m from Ring-ditch 4 (see Chapter 2, section 2.9.2).

Object E100:24 probably had a similar function and may also be a reused axehead, with its broken end taking the shape of a flat, carefully polished surface instead of a blade. This object was also found in the outer zone, in the west of Cutting Z3, near Burial 5.

Similar objects of stone occur in a number of hoards in France along with implements associated with bronze-working. The hoard known as La Petite Laugère at Génelard (Saône-et-Loire), for example, contained a shaped stone closely similar to that from Rathgall, in association with a small bronze anvil and other items, all clearly related to metalworking (Thevenot 1998; see Armbruster 2001, 12–13, Abb. 4). A date in Hallstatt A1 was clear, a dating entirely in keeping with Bronze Age activity at Rathgall. This

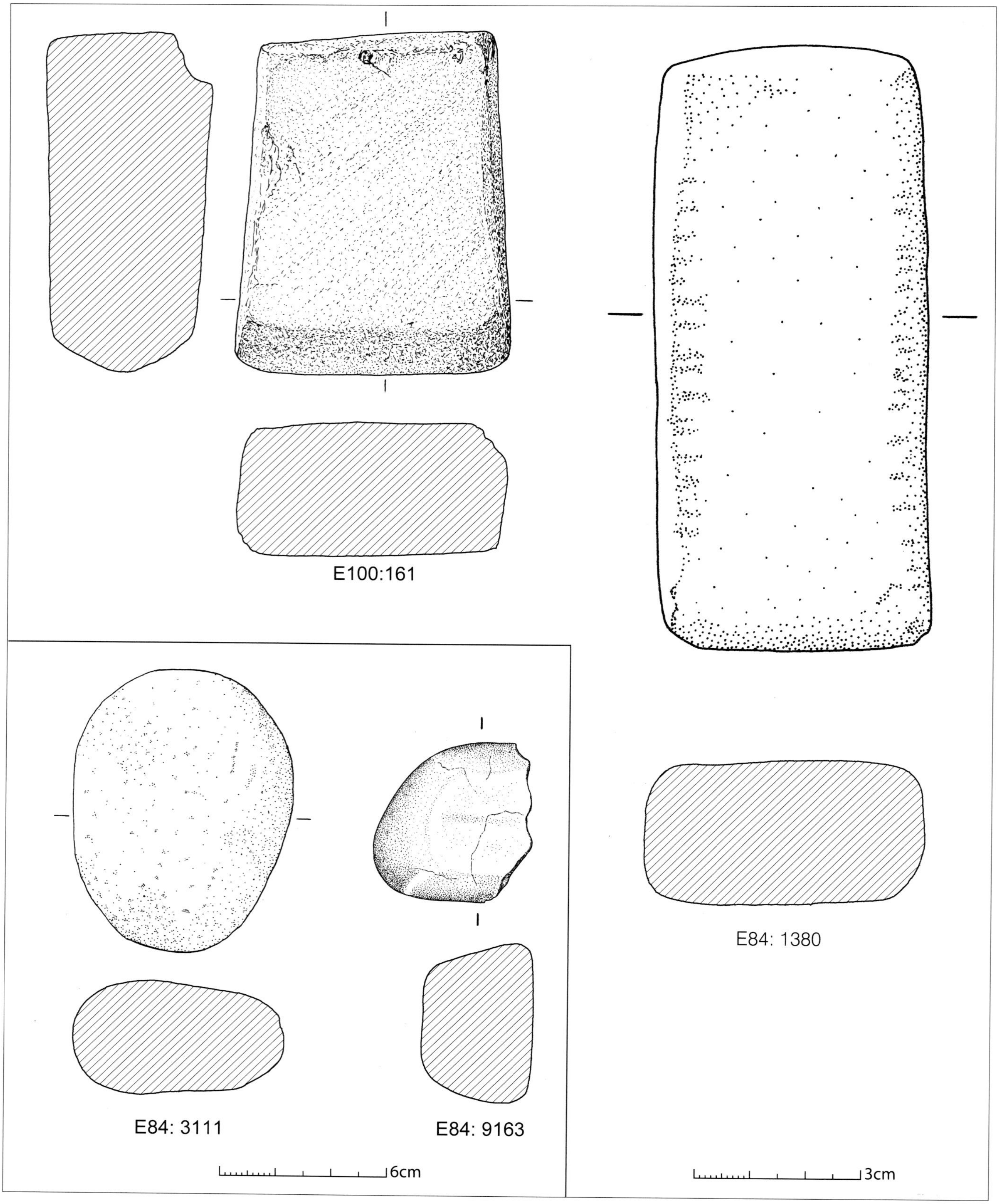

Fig. 3.108—Burnishers, hammerstones and hones (scale 1:1; scale of E84:3111 and 9163 1:2).

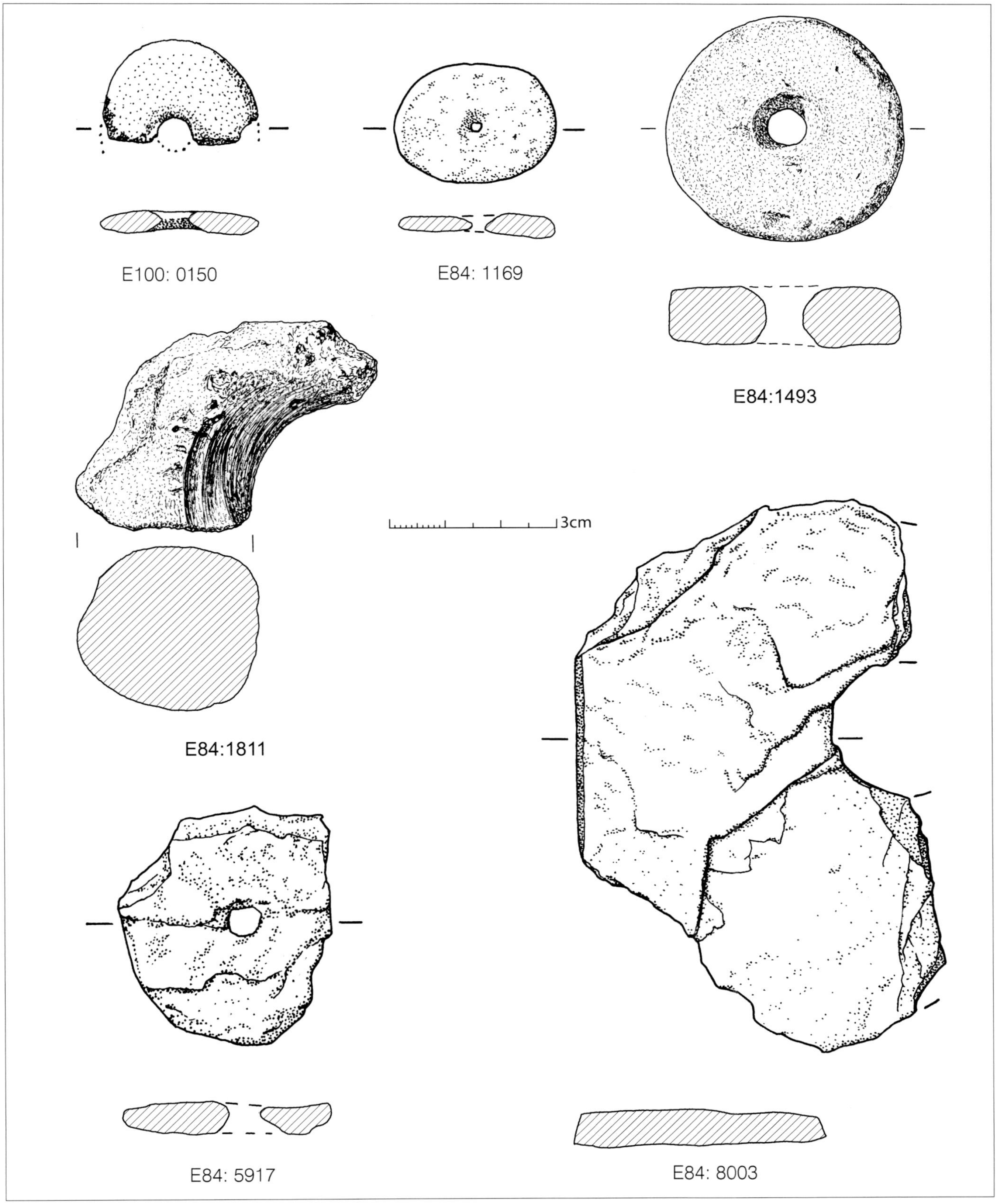

Fig. 3.109—Spindle-whorls and perforated stones (scale 1:1).

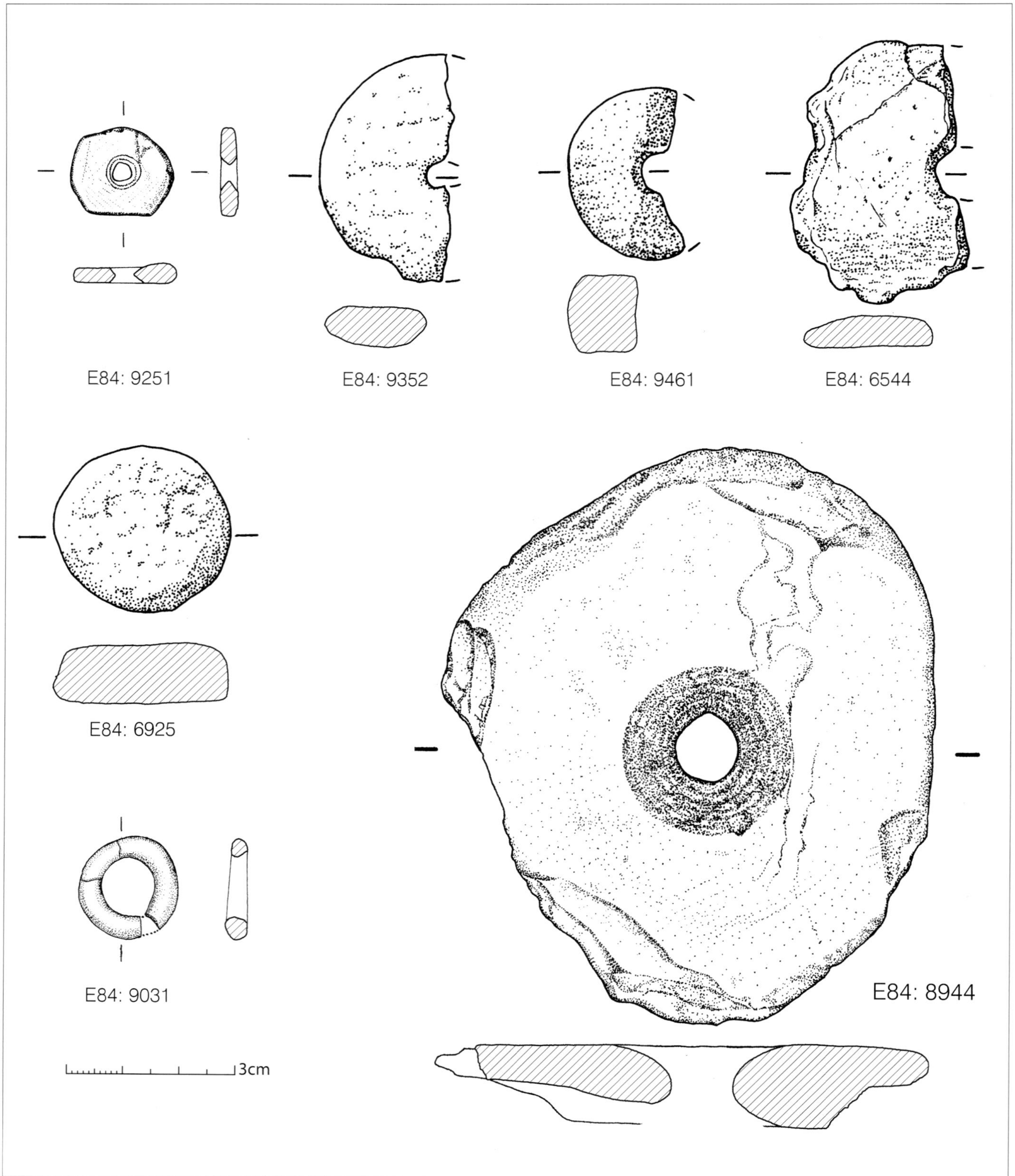

Fig. 3.110—Spindle-whorls/perforated stones/discs and miscellaneous objects (scale 1:1).

stone and similar forms are interpreted as tools used in bronze- or gold-working (cf. Freudenberg 2009; Armbruster 2001; 2010). While the larger of the Rathgall objects, E100:161, may have functioned as a rather small cushion stone or anvil, it may also have been used as a burnishing or polishing tool. The surface on the axe fragment E100:24 suggests that it was used as a hammer in metalworking (S. Mandal, pers. comm.). Hone E84:1380 could conceivably also have had a function within the realms of metalworking (Fig. 3.108).

Other stone artefacts

Other items from the site include a variety of perforated stones, some possibly worked stone balls and a number of possible spindle-whorls. A small stone ring of fine-grained red sandstone (E84:9031) is a particularly well-made object, possibly intended as a finger-ring. It came from Sq. C3, but unfortunately in disturbed humus. Little can be said about these stones, which are generally of the crudest kind, with little effort made at shaping. They are, for the most part, casually collected items which were no doubt used to sharpen a metal edge or the tip of a bronze pin. Following use, most are likely to have been discarded.

A broken fragment of what was once a carefully fashioned, perforated stone object, carefully polished around its inner face (E84:1811; Fig. 3.109), could have been a ring.

The heavy, black occupation zone in D/D1 produced a significant number of stone items. These included pebbles from the black deposits and the ashy material below it, as well as from the ditch. A white pebble, worn flat on one surface, resembles a modern gaming-piece (E84:2685). It was found some 30cm below the modern surface, almost on the yellow subsoil.

A number of perforated stones or discs may have functioned as spindle-whorls (Figs 3.112–117). It is notable that none of them come from clearly identifiable prehistoric contexts and it may be assumed that they belong to the medieval phase of use of the site.

Serrated slate blade

A small number of worked slate objects of unclear function were found. These included a very thin, saw-like artefact (E84:4706; Fig. 3.111), which came from Ring-ditch 1 in Sq. 38, at a depth of 80–90cm in greyish silt. Rather than having been a cutting implement, it might perhaps have been used for decorating pottery, for example, or leather, and it appears not to have been longer than it now is.

Fig. 3.111—Slate object with serrated edge E84:4706 (photo: John Sunderland).

Pebbles and crystals

The large number of small, water-rolled pebbles is interesting. No fewer than 293 of these, the majority black, came to light. They were thinly spread across the site but it was noticeable that far and away the greatest concentrations came from C1, which yielded 49 examples, and D/D1/D2, which produced 74. No indication of any wear is evident on these stones, nor can anything be said about their possible origin, so that again their purpose—if, indeed, they had any—is entirely speculative. A concentration of crystals in and beside the fill of Ring-ditch 1 has been noted (see section 3.12.2).

3.13.4 Quern-stones (Figs 3.112–117)

Agricultural activity is most extensively represented in the archaeological remains by quern-stones, as well as by possible stone rubbers. These were found scattered in various areas of the site, a few possibly in primary contexts but most in secondary situations, several seemingly having been abandoned and reused. Their dating is problematic, owing to the generally undiagnostic nature of forms. In all, no fewer than nineteen complete or fragmentary saddle querns were recovered or identified on site, as well as possible rotary quern fragments, some of which may possibly also be jamb stones. It is noticeable that, while a few had been worked to shape with some care, most of the quern-stones were of the simplest, most rudimentary form, possessing little more than a single flat, or gently concave, functional surface. Not one example discovered compares in any way with the finer of the Neolithic specimens.

Quite a few of the quern-stones were broken and six of them had been reused by the builders of the later enclosure (five possible quern fragments among the stones of Rampart 1, two in the inner face of Rampart 2). Two further quern-stones were surface finds lying between the inner and the second ramparts. Three came from the fill of Ring-ditch 1 (E84:5500 and E84:5926; E84:1428). Two of these were found in the upper levels of the ditch in Sqs 5 and 47, while 1428 was found in an upright position in black occupation material near the bottom of the ditch in Sq. 2. The triangular fragment of a quern-stone (E84:5084) had been reused as a packing stone in the central palisade (15m structure) in Sq. 45, and two others came from Pits 57 and 127. A single complete quern-stone was found in the black occupation area in Sq. D, immediately after the removal of the 'lumps'.[12] Two, in B4 (8880) and in X1 outside Rampart 3 (8233), were without clear context. A final fragmentary example was picked up on the surface within the small Knockeen hut circle in the course of surveying activities.

In the area outside the hillfort to the south, four quern-stones and a number of worked stones that may have been quern-stones came to light. The first of these (E100:29 and 62) came from Hearth 16 Pit 3B in Sq. Z2:f. Two further examples in Z5 came from the brown ploughsoil (E100:103 and 97) and the fourth fragmentary example was found in Ring-ditch 5 among the upper filling stones (E100:195), from where E100:30 may also originate, as it is attributed in the finds records to the 'stone circle', which appears to be the initial identification of the stone fill of the ring-ditch. Some of the possible quern-stones (E100:102, 97, 138) came from this area, too. While saddle quern fragment E100:202 came from the fill of Ring-ditch 4, the attribution of fragment E100:38 appears less certain.

The distribution of the querns provides strong support for the view that agriculture was widespread during the occupation at Rathgall. It is possible that some querns could belong to the much earlier phase of Neolithic activity on the site but, in the absence of much stratigraphical information or other means of dating, this is speculative and a Bronze Age date is equally possible—and even likely in the case of the examples from the occupation area and the fill of Ring-ditch 1. Later rotary querns are also represented, and a number of possible rotary quern fragments may be rough-outs for the production of such objects or jamb stones.

These stone artefacts were presumably used for grinding plant produce of some sort, probably generally grain, but this was not necessarily the case in every instance. Material from the forest, such as hazelnuts and acorns, might have been ground on these objects. The lack of grain from the soil samples may be due to issues of preservation.

The reuse of fragmentary quern-stones is, of course, entirely logical but it is nonetheless interesting to ponder on the processes by which these stones were broken. How, for example, did the fragment in Sq. 45 come to be smashed into a small, triangular fragment? Was it deliberately broken to provide a packing stone? Even the more common form of breakage, consisting of the creation of half-stones, is unclear. Again, it is possible to wonder whether it is the result of deliberate breakage. This, however, would have been a tiresome, seemingly entirely unnecessary process, which would surely have left marks on the surviving fragments—marks that are entirely absent. Heat cracking could be postulated but, again, no traces of heat were observed on any of the fragments. Or was there a deeper reason, perhaps even the deliberate breaking of these objects? Might it be postulated that here is a relationship with the production of life-supporting sustenance? Such, of course, is pure speculation. It does remain curious, however, how large stones, fashioned into quern-stones, sometimes at least with considerable care, came to be broken and deliberately deposited.

3.13.5 Worked stone catalogue

(Stone objects listed in the database but not in the catalogue here are considered natural pieces of stone showing no signs of modification.)

Hones/whetstones and rubbing stones

E84:1380: Hone (Fig. 3.108). Rectangular in plan, rectangular in section; thicker at one end than the other. Polished surface. Rounded but well-defined edges, worn through use. Large number of very light striations diagonally across both faces. The longitudinal edges are particularly polished. Transverse sides also demonstrate signs of wear, particularly at thinner end. All four longitudinal edges are heavily worn, with many short grooves running perpendicular to the edges, most heavily toward the centre of each edge. The transverse edges at each end are also worn, but differently; there are striations along and perpendicular to each transverse edge, but they are much shallower and narrower, most visible under magnification. The stone is slightly cracked at the thicker end, on the transverse side. Dark grey in colour.

L: 112mm. W: 51mm. T: 28.1mm.

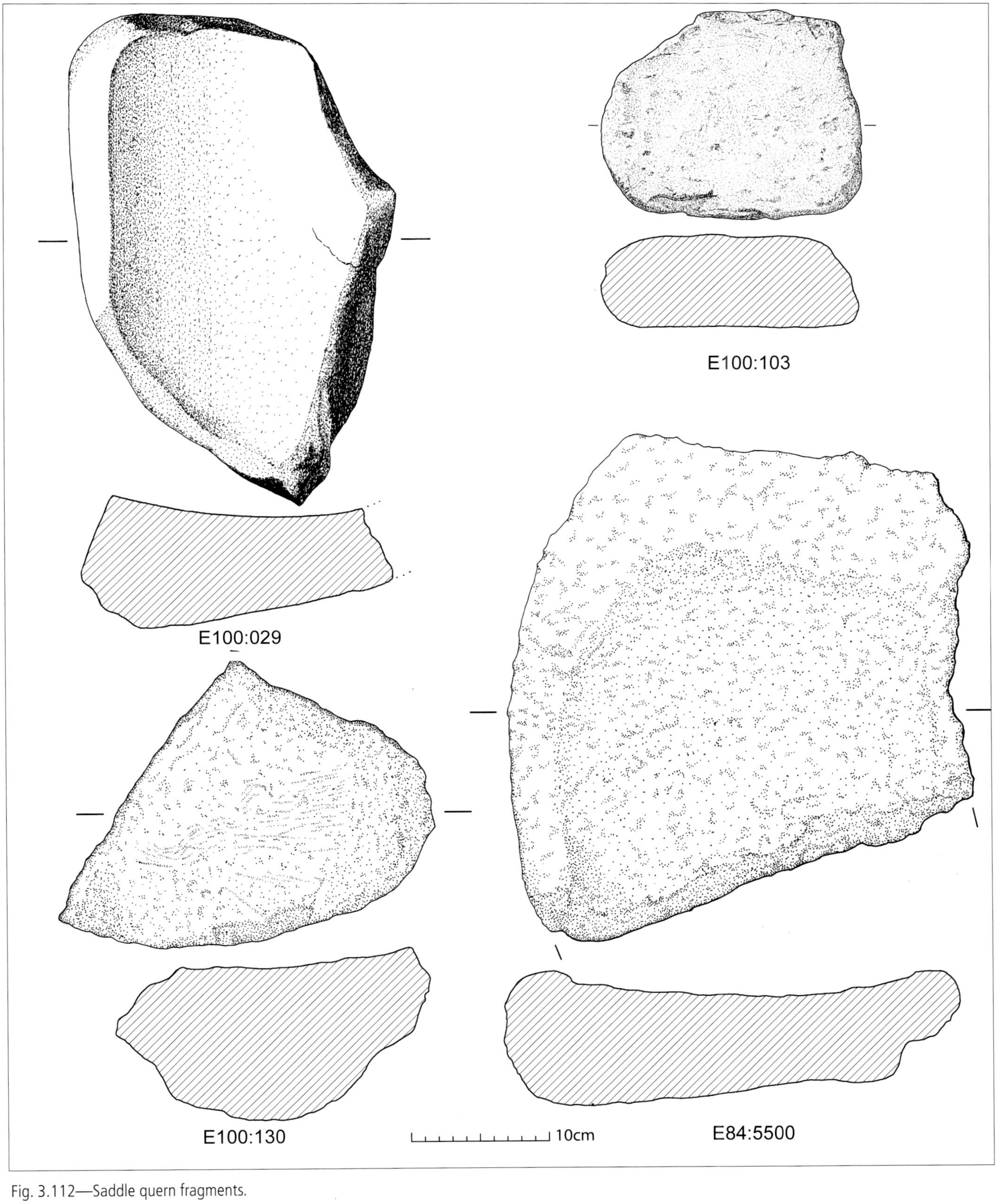

Fig. 3.112—Saddle quern fragments.

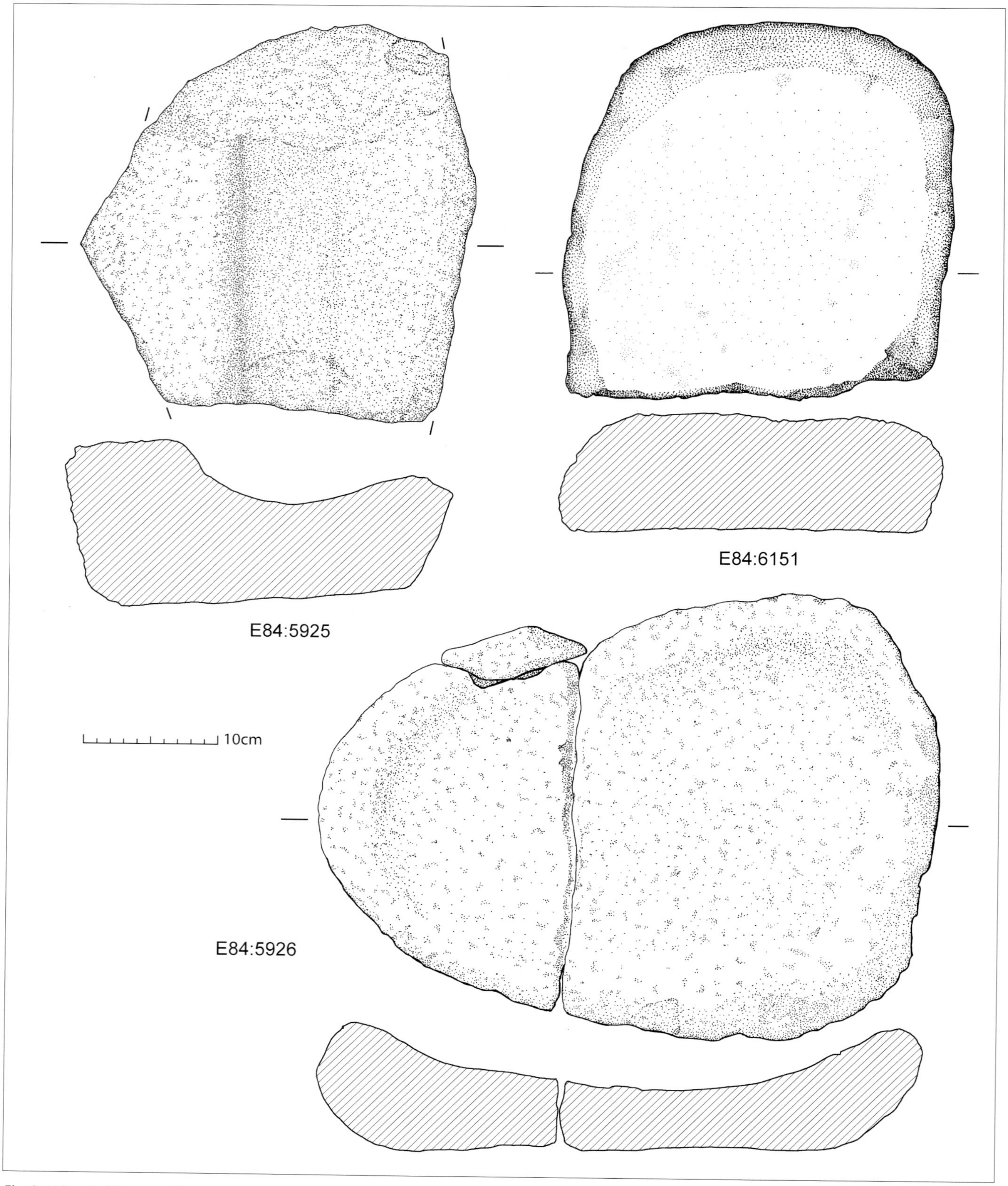

Fig. 3.113—Saddle quern fragments.

Sq. 2, in black fill of ditch (Ring-ditch 1).

E84: 6177.1. Rubbing stone. No further info.

E84:9163: Fragment of possible hone (Fig. 3.108). Roughly D-shaped in plan, trapezoidal in section. Polished surface. All sides and edges worn, except where broken. Light grey in colour.

L: 54.4mm. W: 59.2mm. T: 46mm.

Sq. C3, Pit 209.

E84:6537: Rubbing stone fragment (Fig. 3.117). Suboval in plan, dome-shaped in section. The flatter face is the worked surface, though it is slightly convex. Piece missing from one end. Considerable working along both longitudinal edges of the worked face, where the stone is polished in places from use. Also short grooves perpendicular to edge possibly visible along both longitudinal edges. Opposite face unworked, irregular, rough and convex.

L: 225mm. W: 188mm. T: 70mm.

Sq. D, in thick black charcoal area, after 'lumpy' habitation refuse removed.

E84:6551: Rubbing stone (Fig. 3.117). A quadrant in plan, dome-shaped in section. Flatter face is worked; very smooth; almost polished in places. Worked right to one original edge. Other two edges are the straight perpendicular edges and appear to be broken. Opposite face rough but regular and convex.

L: 221.3mm. W: 169mm. T: 65mm.

In wall at south-east of central structure.

E84:7284: Rubbing stone fragment or possible jamb stone (Fig. 3.117). Leaf-shaped in plan, subrectangular in section. Worked face very smooth, mostly polished. Worked right to original edge, where this remains. Polished area is around edge; very centre of worked face smooth but not polished. Opposite face rough and irregular, with concavity in centre, roughly 45mm in diameter, possibly natural.

L: 234mm. W: 140mm. T: 54mm.

Sq. D/D1, no information on label.

Hammerstones

E100:98: Hammerstone. Oval in plan and section. Smooth faces; one particularly polished. Edge of stone straight and possibly pitted all the way round. Mid-brownish-grey.

L: 54mm. W: 48.1mm. T: 29.8mm.

Sq. Z:5e, in brown humus level.

E84:1516: Hammerstone. Object not found.

E84:3111: Hammerstone (Fig. 3.108). Oval in plan, flattened oval in section. Polished surface. Rounded edges. Large areas of pitting at both ends. Dark pinkish-grey in colour.

L: 105mm. W: 77.5mm. T: 42mm.

Sq. 27, in dark brown.

E84:4168: Hammerstone. Subtriangular in plan, flattened oval in section. Smooth, almost polished surface. Rounded edges. Broken across transverse section with a rough, uneven face and sharp irregular edges. The other end is smooth, broad and rounded. One face is a little flatter than the other, one slightly more convex. Small circular area of pinkish patination on the edge of the rounded end, where there is also some possible pitting. Along one longitudinal edge there is also some subtle scoring, the grooves perpendicular to the edge. Also pinkish patination along this edge. Light grey in colour with areas of a pinkish hue on the surface and in the broken cross-section.

L: 84.9mm. W: 81mm. T: 46.4mm.

Sq. D, in dump; no context.

E84:4242: Fragment of possible hammerstone. Roughly dome-shaped in plan, dome-shaped in section. Smooth surface. Rounded edges except where the stone is broken across its transverse section. On the edge of the rounded end there is some pitting. Light grey in colour.

L: 59.9mm. W: 56mm. T: 32.9mm.

Sq. 29, in dark brown over ditch (Ring-ditch 1).

E84:6197: Fragment of hammerstone, oval in plan and section. Polished surface with rounded edges. One face is flatter than the more convex opposite face. Rough along the edges, particularly at either end, where the stone is also damaged; one flake has been removed from one end and a number from the other. The rough longitudinal edges may be the result of use, like the damage at either end. Mid-grey in colour.

L: 94.2mm. W: 69.5mm. T: 41.9mm.

'Chamber in Wall' (of Rampart 1).

E84:7565: Hammerstone. Subcircular in plan, flattened oval in section. Smooth surface on both faces. Rough, rounded edges. In the centre of one face there is a polished area. There

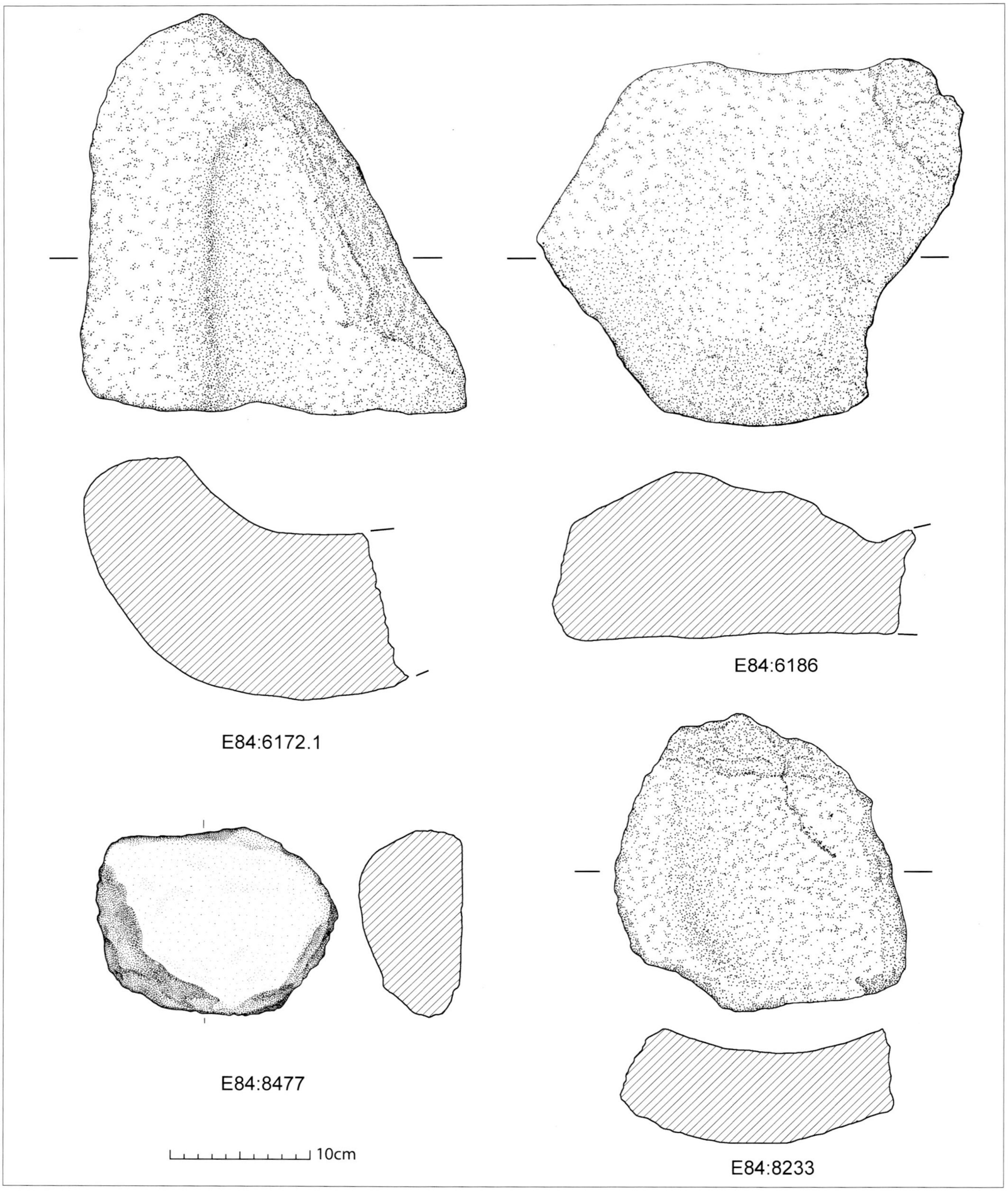

Fig. 3.114—Saddle quern fragments.

is also a corresponding area of use on the other face, not quite polished but smoother than the rest of the surface, which occurs in a concavity most likely caused by use. Some roughness of the edge is due to damage, which may be pitting. Three-quarters of the way across the width of one of the faces the stone begins to taper sharply, creating one slightly more sharply tapered side. Light grey in colour, with some brownish patination on one face.

L: 88.1mm. W: 80mm. T: 25mm.

Sq. D/D1, in ashy brown material under black.

E84:7692: Possible hammerstone, worked. Oval in plan, flattened oval in section. Polished surface. Rounded edges. Some possible pitting on the edge of one rounded end. Small number of grooves with erratic orientation on both faces. Both types of working possibly the result of use as a hone and a hammerstone. Also a small amount of possible working along both longitudinal edges. Mid-grey in colour.

L: 62.2mm. W: 39.4mm. T: 11.2mm.

Sq. E1, in black under bank.

E84:8681: Possible hammerstone. Almost spherical; circular in plan and oval in section. Smooth surface. Light grey in colour.

T: 40.5mm. Diam.: 61mm.

Sq. Y2, in black, burnt material along northern extension of square.

E84:8898: Fragment of possible hammerstone. Semi-ovoid in plan (broken transversely). Tapered oval in section (egg-shaped). Rough surface. Rounded edges. Pitting on original end, and possibly along whole edge. One face possibly smoothed. Mid-grey in colour.

L: 62.1mm. W: 49mm. T: 36.9mm.

Sq. G4, in brown humus.

Spindle-whorls and perforated stones/slate

E100:150: Perforated stone object (Fig. 3.109). D-shaped in plan, flattened oval in section. Rough surface. Hourglass-shaped perforation. Mid-grey in colour.

T: 5.9mm. Diam.: 27.3mm. Diam. of perforation: 5.8mm.

Sq. Z8, in brown under sod.

E84:188: Spindle-whorl. Roughly circular in plan, flattened oval in section. Rough surface. Tapered, off-centre perforation. Some recent scoring across one face. Damaged along part of edge and on one face. Mid-grey in colour.

T: 15.5mm. Diam.: 53mm. Diam. of perforation: 12mm.

Sq. 33, at north-east corner of square in brown patch on yellow.

E84:1027: Stone disc, possible worked object. Naturally disc-shaped stone but possibly roughly worked.

Sq. 2/8, baulk.

E84:1169: Perforated stone disc (Fig. 3.109). Oval in plan, flattened oval in section. Hourglass perforation in centre of disc, 6mm in maximum diameter, narrowing to 2mm in middle. Made by boring from both sides, probably with a metal drill, otherwise stone would split easily. Under magnification, lines are visible along inside of perforation, presumably made by the drill. Tapers in thickness. Smooth surface and rounded edges. Grey in colour.

L: 29mm. W: 22mm. T: 5mm. Diam. of perforation: 6mm.

Sq. 2, in dark brown.

E84:1470: Perforated stone object. Square in plan, subrectangular in section. Rough surface. Very wide hourglass perforation. Asymmetrical cross-section. Light grey in colour.

L: 39.5mm. W: 29mm. T: 17.9mm. Diam. of perforation: 16.9mm.

No context, dump.

E84:1493: Spindle-whorl (Fig. 3.109). Circular in plan, rectangular in section. Smoothed surface. Hourglass perforation. Slightly damaged on one face. Mid-grey in colour.

T: 11mm. Diam.: 42.1mm. Diam. of perforation: 12.4mm.

Sq. 9, under sod in north centre of square.

E84:1811: Perforated worked stone, C-shaped in plan (Fig. 3.109). One end is almost circular in section, while the other is very damaged and irregular. Both faces are quite rough. The side on the exterior is very rough, as it appears to be quite damaged. The interior side, inside the curve, is polished, with some striations visible running the length of the interior curve, where it may have been worked. The working may be the result of boring, suggesting that this object may be a fragment of a perforated stone disc or stone ring. It is mid-grey in colour.

L: 61mm. W: 27mm. T: 32.1mm.

Sq. 9, in dark brown.

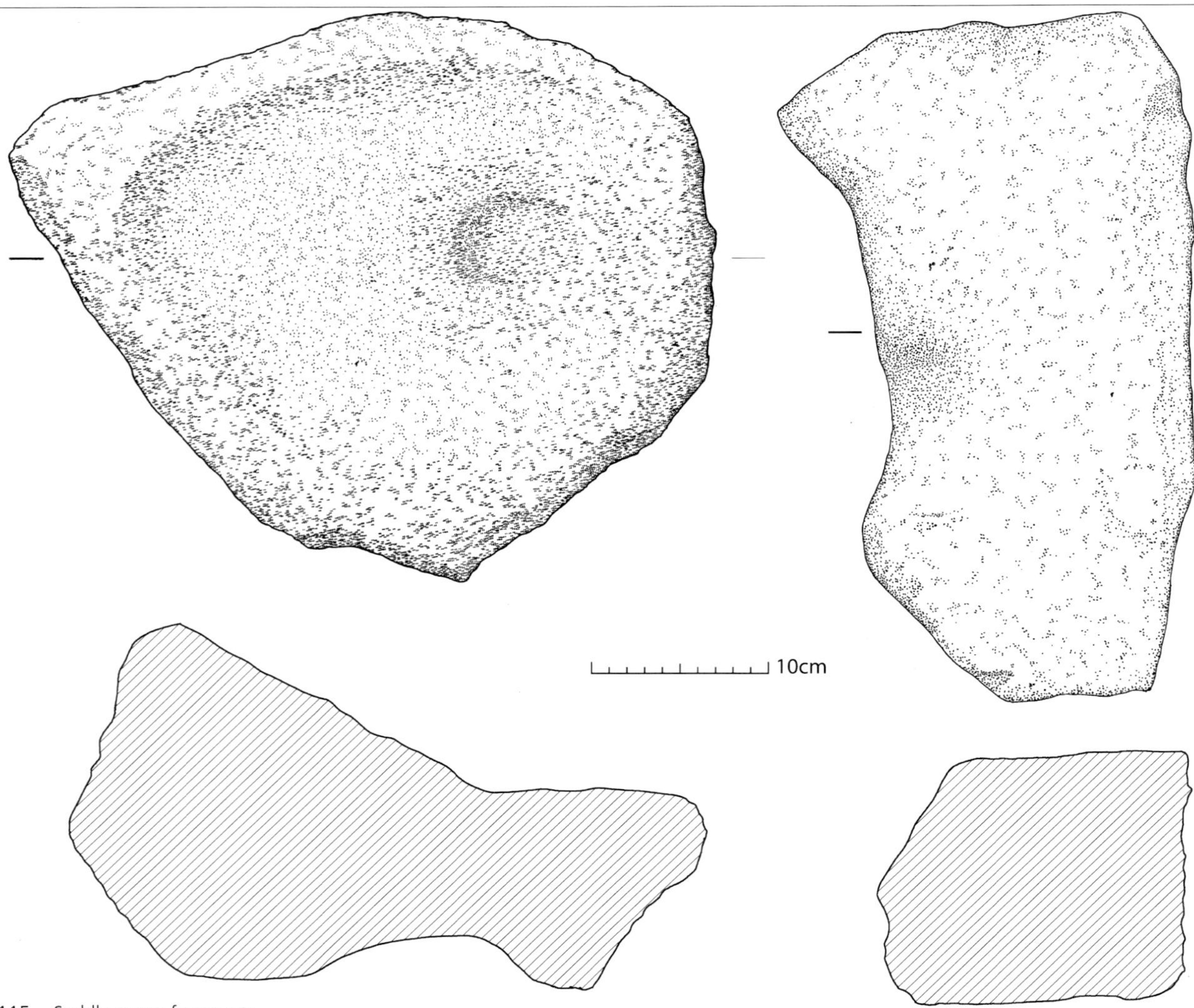

Fig. 3.115—Saddle quern fragments.

E84:5284: Perforated stone object. Circular in plan, rectangular in section. Off-centre perforation wider on one face, stepping down once, rather than tapering, to a narrower diameter of 3.8mm. Number of short, incised grooves along and perpendicular to part of wider edge. Scoring and wear along side of disc and on one face. Mid-grey in colour.

T: 7mm. Diam.: 20.5mm. Diam. of perforation: 5.1mm.

Sq. 64, immediately under sod.

E84:5917: Perforated slate (Fig. 3.109). Irregular, angular, roughly subcircular in plan. Irregular, oblong, subrectangular in section. Possibly originally an angular stone disc, fragmented some three quarters of the way along its width. Both faces are very rough and uneven. The edges are sharp and irregular, as are the sides. The perforation has been drilled from one side and is widest on one side, narrowing to its opening at the other. The maximum diameter of this perforation is 10mm; it is 6mm at its narrowest. There are lines along the interior of the perforation indicating that it has been drilled. Light grey in colour.

L: 45.5mm. W: 38.9mm. T: 3.1mm. Diam. of perforation: 6mm.

Sq. 68.

E84:6544: Perforated disc (Fig. 3.110). Broken through centre; only half of perforation visible. Irregular oblong shape in plan. Slightly S-shaped in section, with tapering ends. Smooth faces. The edge at which there is the perforation is more or less straight in plan, while the rest of the edge is highly irregular. Rough, uneven sides. Interior of perforation is

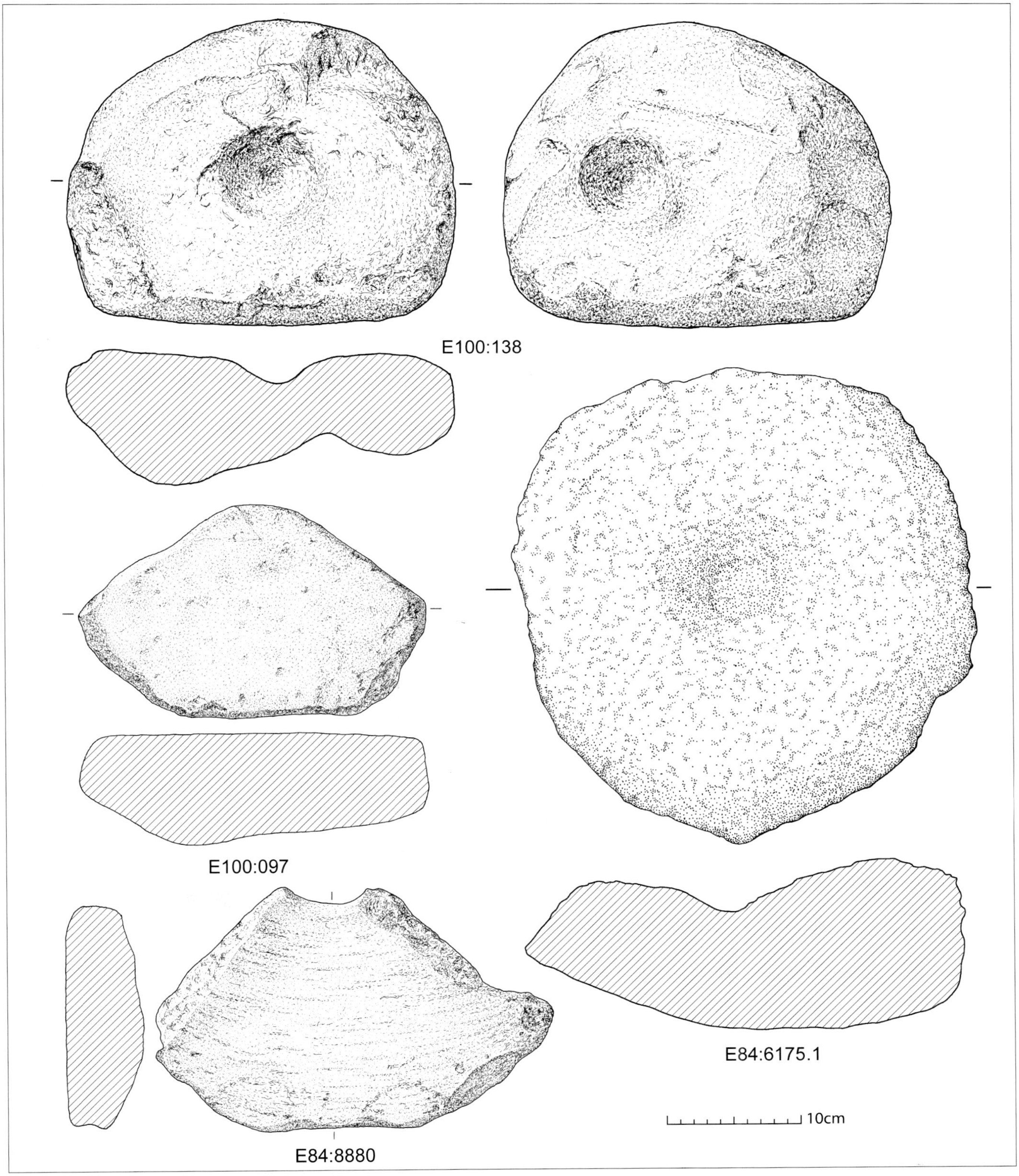

Fig. 3.116—Querns/possible quern fragments.

smooth, in sharp contrast to the rest of that side, where the natural section of the stone is visible. Possibly bored from both sides—subtle hourglass shape visible in the section of the perforation. Light, silvery grey in colour.

L: 47.5mm. W: 31mm. T: 6.5mm. Diam. of perforation: 9mm.

Sq. F2.

E84:6925: Stone disc, worked (Fig. 3.110). Circular in plan, rectangular in section. Both faces, while smooth, are not polished, but are smoother than the circumference, which is comparatively rough. The edges are well defined, though slightly rounded. Some comparatively recent damage as well as more ancient damage on one face, near the edge. On the side there is a possible groove beginning at the edge of one face and moving toward the other at an acute angle; it is unclear whether this is natural or not, but it may be the result of use. Light grey in colour.

T: 12mm. Diam.: 31mm.

Sq. D8.

E84:7715: Perforated stone.

Sq. E/E1.

E84:8003: Perforated slate (Fig. 3.108). Irregular shape in plan; roughly semicircular but with highly irregular 'curved' edge. Oblong in section; very long and thin, with straight longitudinal edges and irregular sides. The stone is broken in half, leaving half of the perforation visible. Both faces have a smooth texture, but one is more even than the other. The more even face has a small number of light incisions near the perforation. The other face is slightly stepped owing to the removal of a layer of slate from one half of the face. Some of the interior of the perforation is polished. The edge of the stone is highly irregular, except for one short length along the opposite longitudinal edge to that where the perforation is. Here the edge is perfectly straight and the side smoothed. This may represent the original edge of this perforated stone object. Light grey in colour.

L: 100mm. W: 64.5mm. T: 6.3mm. Diam. of perforation: 21mm.

Sq. X1 ext.

E84:8277: Stone disc, worked. Circular in plan, rectangular in section. Smooth surface. Light grey in colour.

T: 11.2mm. Diam.: 30.6mm.

Sq. I1, in dark brownish-grey material under 'cobbling' underlying the stone wall.

E84:8404: Stone disc. Worked? Disc-shaped; roughly circular in plan and a flattened oval in section. Polished surface. Brownish-grey in colour.

T: 14mm. Diam.: 53.1mm.

Sq. G1, in grey fill of Pit 32.

E84:8530: Perforated slate.

E84:8944: Fragment of perforated stone object (Fig. 3.110). Slate. Irregular in plan; very roughly suboval. Oblong in section, with straight longitudinal edges and irregular ends. Large, virtually central hourglass perforation. Where original faces are not damaged, circular grooves are visible, oriented around perforation. Broken on one face and along edge. Mid-grey in colour.

L: 106.4mm. W: 88mm. T: 16mm. Diam. of perforation: 30.1mm.

Sq. J5, at a depth of 25cm in black layer of Pit 171, 1m north of loose boulder.

E84:9251: Small, subcircular perforated stone object which has been largely broken and damaged around its circumference (Fig. 3.110). The circular perforation is 3mm in diameter and has been drilled from both sides.

L: 1.85mm. W: 1.6mm. T: 0.4mm.

Sq. K8, in brown at east end.

E84:9352: Spindle-whorl fragment, broken through centre (Fig. 3.110). Semicircular in plan, roughly rectangular in section, but with one sharply tapered end. Half of central hourglass perforation remains. Maximum diameter of perforation is 7mm, narrowing to 4.5mm. No drilling lines visible along inside of boreholes. Surface of both faces smooth. Broken sides are rough and irregular. Edges of disc rounded. Brownish-grey in colour.

T: 8.5mm. Diam.: 41mm. Diam. of perforation: 7mm.

Sq. X11 (Pit 11), Pit 252.

E84:9461: Spindle-whorl fragment, broken through centre (Fig. 3.110). Semicircular in plan, roughly rectangular in section. Half of perforation remains. Smooth exterior curved surface. Both faces flat and smooth. Broken ends of disc rough, irregular. Unbroken edges well defined, slightly rounded and regular. Broken edges sharp, rough and irregular. Grey in colour.

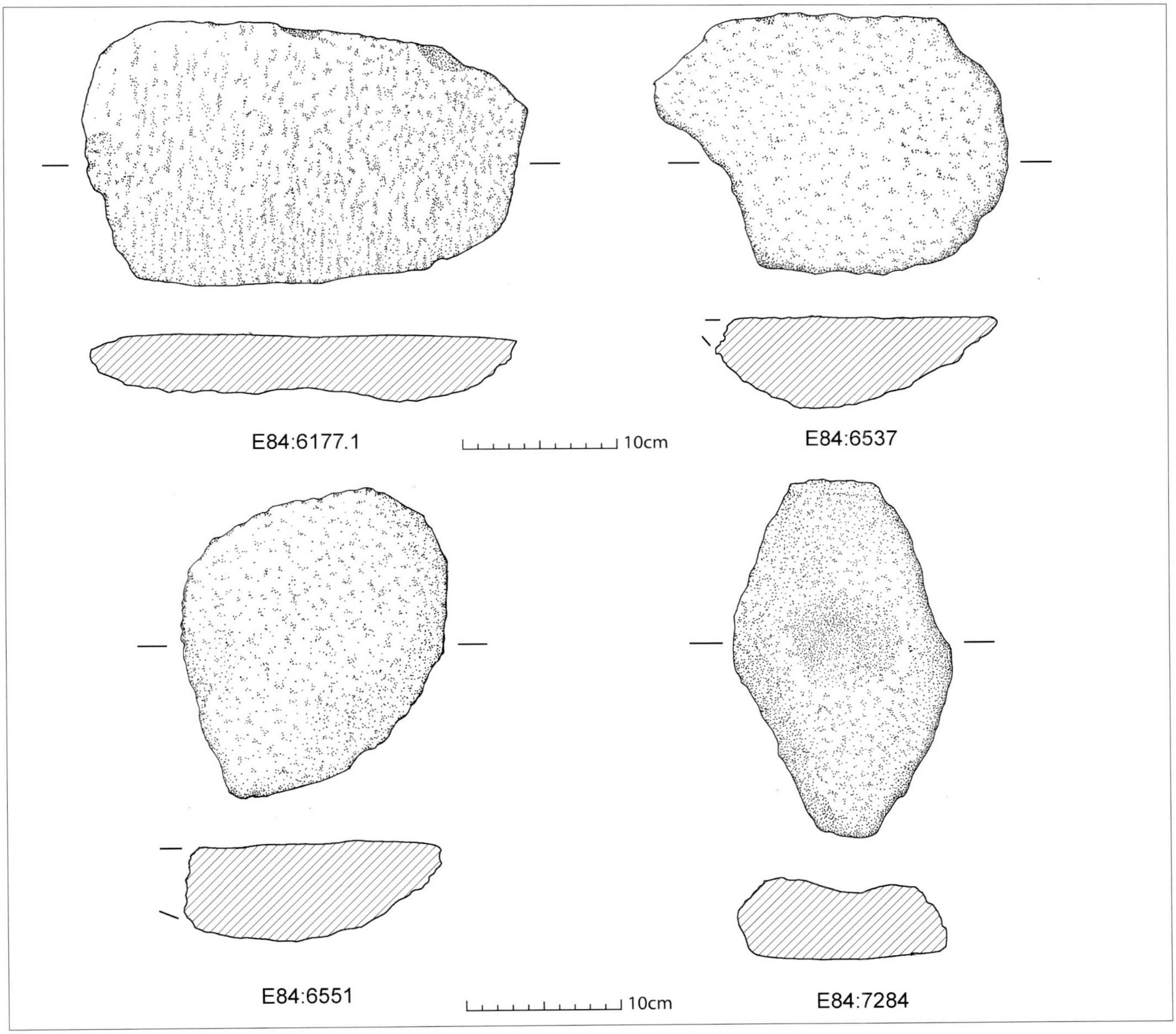

Fig. 3.117—Rubbing stones.

T: 15mm. Diam.: 31mm. Diam. of perforation: 6.9mm.
Sq. G6.

Miscellaneous stone objects

E84:4706: Stone object, possibly a decorating tool (Fig. 3.111). Roughly rectangular in plan, tapered rectangle in section. One longitudinal edge is longer than the other. The shorter has been worked to form a jagged edge of saw-like teeth. Tapers in thickness from longer edge to this saw-like shorter edge.

L: 47mm. W: 28.5mm. T: 4.4mm.

Sq. 38, in grey/mauve gravelly silt near base of ditch (Ring-ditch 1).

E84:9031: Fragment of sandstone ring (Fig. 3.110). Small portion missing. Oval in section. Irregular in width and thickness. Oval perforation. Reddish-brown in colour.

W: 4.6mm. T: 4mm. Diam.: 18mm.

Sq. C3, in brown humus, almost on yellow.

Quern-stones

E100:29: Fragment of saddle quern (Fig. 3.112). Roughly oval in plan with pointed ends. Subrectangular section. Functional surface, worked to edge, is smooth and markedly concave. Longitudinal thickness tapers significantly from one side to the other. Mid-grey colour.

L: 368mm. W: 222mm. T: 99mm.

Sq. Z2:f, in grey fill of Hearth 16, Pit 3B.

E100:62: Fragment of saddle quern. Irregular shape; roughly pentagonal in plan and roughly dome-shaped in section. One face heavily worked, with a polished, concave surface, worked to within 40mm of the original edge, where still visible (edge mostly damaged). The opposite unworked face is rough and very undulating, with a pronounced convexity towards one side, resulting in considerable variation in thickness. Light grey in colour.

L: 245.5mm. W: 235mm. T: 111mm.

Sq. OII:9, stone fill in grey material of Pit 3B, near bottom. This information cannot be confirmed and OII:9 seems to be a misrecording, as Pit 3b, i.e. Hearth 16, is in Sq. OII:6, i.e. Z2:f.

E100:103: Fragment of saddle quern (Fig. 3.112). Subsquare in plan, dome-shaped in section, tapering towards one side. Broken at one corner. Flat face is very smooth, evidently the working surface. The opposite face is quite rough and curves broadly towards the sides, which then flatten out almost vertically and quite regularly, apart from the broken corner. Mid-grey in colour.

L: 185mm. W: 157mm. T: 70mm.

Sq. Z5:d, in brown humus.

E100:130: Fragment of saddle quern, broken across its width (Fig. 3.112). Subtriangular in plan, dome-shaped in section. Flatter face is worked; very slightly concave, almost polished surface. Not worked right to original edges. Rest of surface rough and irregular. Mid-grey in colour.

L: 189mm. W: 215mm. T: 126.5mm.

'Stone circle' (ring-ditch).

E100:195: Fragment of saddle quern. A square parallelogram in plan, dome-shaped in section. Consists of a corner of the original object and thus two original sides remain, the other two broken. The flat face is very smooth, evidently the working surface. The opposite face is rough and curved towards the sides, which flatten out vertically though are still rough. Mid-grey in colour.

L: 150.4mm. W: 107mm. T: 56.9mm.

Sq. Z5:d, among 'cobbling' in south-east of trench.

E84:5084: Fragment of saddle quern, subtriangular in plan, consisting of one original side and two converging broken sides. Subrectangular in section. One worked concave face, worked right to remaining original edge. Opposite face unworked, with a convex irregular surface and smooth finish. Mid-grey in colour.

L: 255mm. W: 154mm. T: 74mm.

Sq. 45. According to Raftery's text, found reused as a packing stone in bedding trench of the 15m structure.

E84:5500: Fragment of saddle quern (Fig. 3.112). Subsquare in plan, concave rectangle in section. Two perpendicular original sides remain. Regular curved sides. Circular area of working on one face; shallow concavity 290mm in diameter. Opposite face very regular, almost flat.

L: 434mm. W: 360mm. T: 114mm.

Sq. 47, in upper levels of ditch, among stones. This is Ring-ditch 1.

E84:5925: Fragment of saddle quern (Fig. 3.113). Almost a quadrant in plan, subrectangular in section. Broken across width at one end. Other sides are original, with only some damage. Worked face acutely concave. Along one longitudinal edge this concavity rises up to a flat, regular 'lip' which is clearly not a working surface. Working continued right to the edge of the other side, however. Also worked to most of original transverse edge except for rise where this edge meets the unworked 'lip'; surface not as smooth here. Opposite unworked face flat, regular but unworked.

L: 287mm. W: 284mm. T: 143mm.

Sq. 51, Pit 127.

E84:5926a–c: Saddle quern in three fragments (Fig. 3.113). Oval in plan, flattened oval in section. Concave, smooth worked face, polished in places around edge, rougher towards centre, and worked almost completely to edge all the way round. Opposite face regular and slightly flattened, stabilising the stone. Light greyish-brown in colour.

L: 457mm. W: 337mm. T: 94mm.

Sq. 51, upper fill of Ring-ditch 1.

E84:6151: Fragment of saddle quern (Fig. 3.113). Subsquare in plan, subrectangular in section. Broken on one side; other three sides are original. One face highly smoothed, evidently the working surface. This surface is slightly concave and in plan quite rounded. The sides are rough but very regular and quite vertical. The unworked face is rough but also very regular, with no major undulation. Mid-grey in colour.

L: 236mm. W: 232mm. T: 89mm.

Found in body of wall of inner ring (*i.e. Rampart 1*) during reconstruction work, near outer edge in the south-west of the enclosure.

E84:6172.1: Fragment of saddle quern (Fig. 3.114). Subtriangular in plan; broken diagonally from one end to the other, and straight across width. Probably originally oval in plan. Curved oval in section. Heavily worked, smooth concave surface in centre of one face, where only one original edge remains. Not worked to this edge; lip left. Original longitudinal side curved and very regular. Opposite face convex. Light grey in colour.

L: 284mm. W: 292mm. T: 122mm.

Found in fill of wall of inner ring (*i.e. Rampart 1)* in south-west, about 20m south of entrance.

E84:6178.1: Fragment of saddle quern, almost complete; broken only along one edge. Suboval in plan, dome-shaped in section. Worked face concave, smooth and worked right to edge. Original sides very regular. Opposite face rough, convex and lichen-covered. Rounded edges on worked surface. Light brownish-grey in colour.

L: 445mm. W: 370mm. T: 165mm.

In wall in north of site.

E84:6186: Fragment of saddle quern (Fig. 3.114). Pentagonal in plan, roughly dome-shaped in section. Of the five sides, four are original. Worked surface of one face slightly concave and very smooth, not worked completely to edges. Original sides quite smooth and regular. Opposite face smooth, regular, broadly convex. On this face is a circular depression beside the broken side. Light brownish-grey in colour.

L: 310mm. W: 282mm. T: 108mm.

From inner stone face of second rampart in east, directly opposite 'workshop' area. This possibly refers to the B/C cuttings.

E84:6187: Fragment of saddle quern (Fig. 3.115). Oval in plan, subrectangular in section. Worked face concave and smooth, rest of surface very rough. On worked face only one original edge remains. In opposite face is a small hollow, possibly worked, roughly 130mm in max. diam., 50mm in min. diam. This hollow has the effect of stabilising the stone when in its working position (smooth face pointing upward). Light brownish-grey in colour.

L: 390mm. W: 310mm. T: 155mm.

From inner stone face of second rampart in south of fort.

E84:6219: Fragment of saddle quern (Fig. 3.115). Subrectangular in plan, subrectangular in section. In plan, one edge of the worked face is broken, resulting in a concave shape on this side. Other three edges appear to be original. Worked face very smooth and slightly concave. Opposite face quite rough and convex.

L: 395mm. W: 211.9mm. T: 130mm.

'Chamber in wall', which is the chamber of uncertain date in the southern part of Rampart 1.

E84:6614: Saddle quern or rubbing stone. Oval in plan, quite pointed at one end. Dome-shaped in section. One face worked all the way to the edges, all of which are original. Particularly smooth in one part of face, almost polished. Opposite face very convex. Rounded, smooth sides. Mid-brownish-grey in colour.

L: 240mm. W: 172mm. T: 92mm.

'Chamber in Wall'.

E84:8233: Fragment of saddle quern (Fig. 3.114). Ovoid in plan, curved oval in section. Concave face worked; surface almost polished. Opposite face rough, regular, convex and unworked. Two perpendicular broken sides. Other side curved and original; surface not worked right to this edge.

L: 240mm. W: 194mm. T: 82mm.

Sq. XI, in north-west corner in grey/brown area.

E84:8477: Sq. J1/J2, on base of Pit 57 in grey material (Fig. 3.114).

No number: Fragment of saddle quern. Roughly oval in plan, pointed at either end. Subrectangular in section, with a tapering concavity on one surface. The worked surface is very smooth and markedly concave, worked right to the very edge, where original edge still visible. The opposite, unworked surface is very rough and heavily undulating, with a prominent roughly circular depression towards the centre of the surface. Tapers considerably in thickness from one longitudinal side to the other. Mid-grey in colour.

L: 368mm. W: 222mm. T: 99mm.

Surface find within stone circle to south-east of Rathgall hillfort. This is likely the saddle quern from the Knockeen hut circle mentioned on p. 351.

E84:1428: Quern-stone. Sq. 2. Found upright in black, burnt, charcoal-like material in ditch (Ring-ditch 1), not far from bottom, 52cm below yellow natural, 82cm below surface.

Possible rotary querns or jamb stones

Some of these may be possible rotary quern fragments, or unfinished examples of such. The possible association of E100:38 with a Bronze Age feature would suggest that another function for this stone is more likely.

E100:202: Fragment of saddle quern? Roughly oval in plan, flattened oval in section. Broken along part of edge and the smooth face, the latter evidently the working surface; surface not smoothed right to edge, however, but to within about 30mm of it. Opposite face is unworked, rougher and curved. Light brownish-grey in colour.

L: 189mm. W: 153mm. T: 63mm.

Sq. Z5:d, stone fill of trench in grey in south-east.

E100:97: Fragment of a possible saddle quern (Fig. 3.116). Roughly oval in plan, subrectangular in section, tapering considerably towards one side. Two original sides remain, joined at an obtuse angle by a gently curving corner. The opposite side appears to be broken. One face is completely flat, evidently the working surface; the other face is more undulating. Mid-grey in colour.

L: 253mm. W: 163mm. T: 78mm.

Sq. Z5:h, in brown humus.

E84:8880: Fragment of rotary quern, a quarter remaining (Fig. 3.116). A quadrant in plan. Subrectangular in section, tapering slightly towards central perforation. Flat, smoothed surface, considerably worked, with striations oriented around central perforation clearly visible. Light grey in colour.

T: 65mm. Diam.: 475mm. Diam. of perforation: 52mm.

Sq. B4, in brown humus at northern end.

E100:138: Possible (unfinished?) rotary quern-stone or jamb stone (Fig. 3.116). Subrectangular in plan but very rounded. Subrectangular in section, varying considerably in thickness from one end to the other. Two distinct corners, with one very regular straight edge. The opposite edge is rounded and irregular, straightening a little at either end to meet the opposite edge almost perpendicularly. Both faces are rough and uneven. In the centre of one face is a circular borehole about 60mm in diameter. The opposite face is also bored, slightly off-centre, the diameter about 55mm. Mid-grey in colour.

L: 298mm. W: 238mm. T: 102mm. Sq.

Z5:e, in brown layer, within putative circle of stones.

E84:6175.1: Quern? Roughly circular in plan, subrectangular in section (Fig. 3.116). One face worked and smooth; circular depression in centre. Opposite face rough and quite irregular, as is side of stone. Mid-brownish grey in colour.

T: 140mm. Diam.: 352mm.

In wall in south of inner ring (of Rampart 1).

E84:9607: Fragment of quern-stone? Roughly oval in plan but angular and irregular. Subtriangular in section, tapering to one side. Two original edges remain, joined at an obtuse angle by a very gently curved corner. Stone tapers towards these edges. Other edge is broken. One face is very flat and smooth, presumably the working surface. Other face is very rough and curving towards smooth face. Light brownish-grey in colour.

L: 166mm. W: 91mm. T: 54mm.

Sq. H7, in middle of square.

No number: Fragment of quern-stone? Subrectangular in plan, roughly dome-shaped in section. One flat, smooth face, evidently the working surface. Appears to have been worked right to the edge, where original edge is still visible (broken along most of it). Opposite, 'domed' surface is rougher, its apex off-centre, so that this face tapers more towards one side than the other. Light grey in colour.

L: 175mm. W: 154mm. T: 81mm.

3.13.6 Stone axeheads

Gabriel Cooney, Stephen Mandal, Emmett O'Keeffe and Chris Coffey

Introduction

Six stone artefacts broadly classed as stone axeheads were discovered during archaeological excavations by Prof. Barry Raftery at Rathgall, Co. Wicklow (licence nos E084 and E100). The assemblage, which represents a range of lithologies, consists of a complete axehead, three central portions of axeheads and two possible butt portions of axeheads.

The stone axeheads
A full analytical report for each axe is included below. The description and analysis follow the Irish Stone Axe Project methodology (Cooney and Mandal 1998). The excavation number is followed by the number of the axehead on the ISAP database.

E84:8996 (ISAP: 21685)
Petrology: Group VI? (Macro ID)
Axe/adze (possible), butt portion. Flaked, ground and polished. Face shape unknown. Sides pointed, with clear facets present on both faces at left side. Surviving portions of faces highly polished, with irregular area on face 2 near right side. Irregular break across lower portion. Butt damaged.
L: 3.3cm. W: 5.3cm. T: 1.4cm.

Fig. 3.118—Burnishing stone E100:161 (photo: John Sunderland).

E100:161 (ISAP 21607)
Petrology: Group VI?
Burnisher/fragment of axe (Figs 3.108 and 3.118). Mid-portion, used as hone. Trapezoidal in plan, rectangular in section. Flat sides and one rounded end. Worn corners, one particularly so, and one damaged. Two longitudinal edges also worn. Green in colour.
L: 62mm. W: 47.5mm. T: 29.9mm.

E84:6122 (ISAP: 21679)
Petrology: Mudstone (Macro ID)
Axe, upper portion (Fig. 3.119). Flaked and ground. Sides rounded to pointed. Clear junction of right side with butt; junction of left side with butt damaged. Faces ground, with light striations visible on face 1. Area close to butt on face 1 may show evidence of re-grinding. Irregular break across the lower portion of the axe, perpendicular to the long axis. Butt irregular, damage extending onto face 2.
L: 3.7cm. W: 3.3cm. T: 1.5cm.

E100:24 (ISAP: 21683)
Petrology: Dolerite
Axe. Pecked, ground and polished. FS03. Sides flattened. Junction between left side and edge, junction of right side and edge obscured owing to damage. Edge gently curved; symmetrical, blunted possibly from reuse. Damage towards junction of right side and edge on face 1. No junction between blade areas and faces. Faces have differential polish, with face 2 being slightly more polished. Striae present on both blade areas and faces. Butt with some damage extending onto adjoining area of face 1. Profile is symmetrical: medium; cross-section is oval with flattened sides.
L: 7.3cm. W: 5.4cm. T: 2.6cm.

E84:6946 (ISAP: 21684)
Petrology: Shale (Macro ID)
Axe/adze, central portion (Fig. 3.119). Flaked and ground. Sides rounded, left side slightly less than right. Large damage scar runs from right side onto face 1. Breaks perpendicular to the long axis of the object define upper and lower extent of faces. Faces gently convex with striae present on both faces. Area of polish on face 2. Cross-section is narrow oval.
L: 4.6cm. W: 7.7cm. T: 2.3cm.

E84:8004 (ISAP: 21681)
Petrology: Dolerite (Macro ID)
Axe/adze, central portion (Fig. 3.119). Flaked, ground and polished. Left side rounded, right side slightly flattened. Faces convex with varied level of polish. Irregular curving breaks perpendicular to the long axis of the object define upper and lower extent of the faces. The character of the breaks may indicate intentional breakage.
L: 6cm. W: 6.4cm. T: 3.2cm.

Production, use and discard
Both flaking and hammering/pecking were used as methods of primary manufacture. The axeheads show variable levels of secondary working (grinding and polishing). It is likely, owing to their morphology, that most of them were manufactured on cobbles from secondary geological sources.

All the axes except one (E100:24) are broken, two central axe portions (E89:6946 and E84:8004; Fig. 3.119) possibly

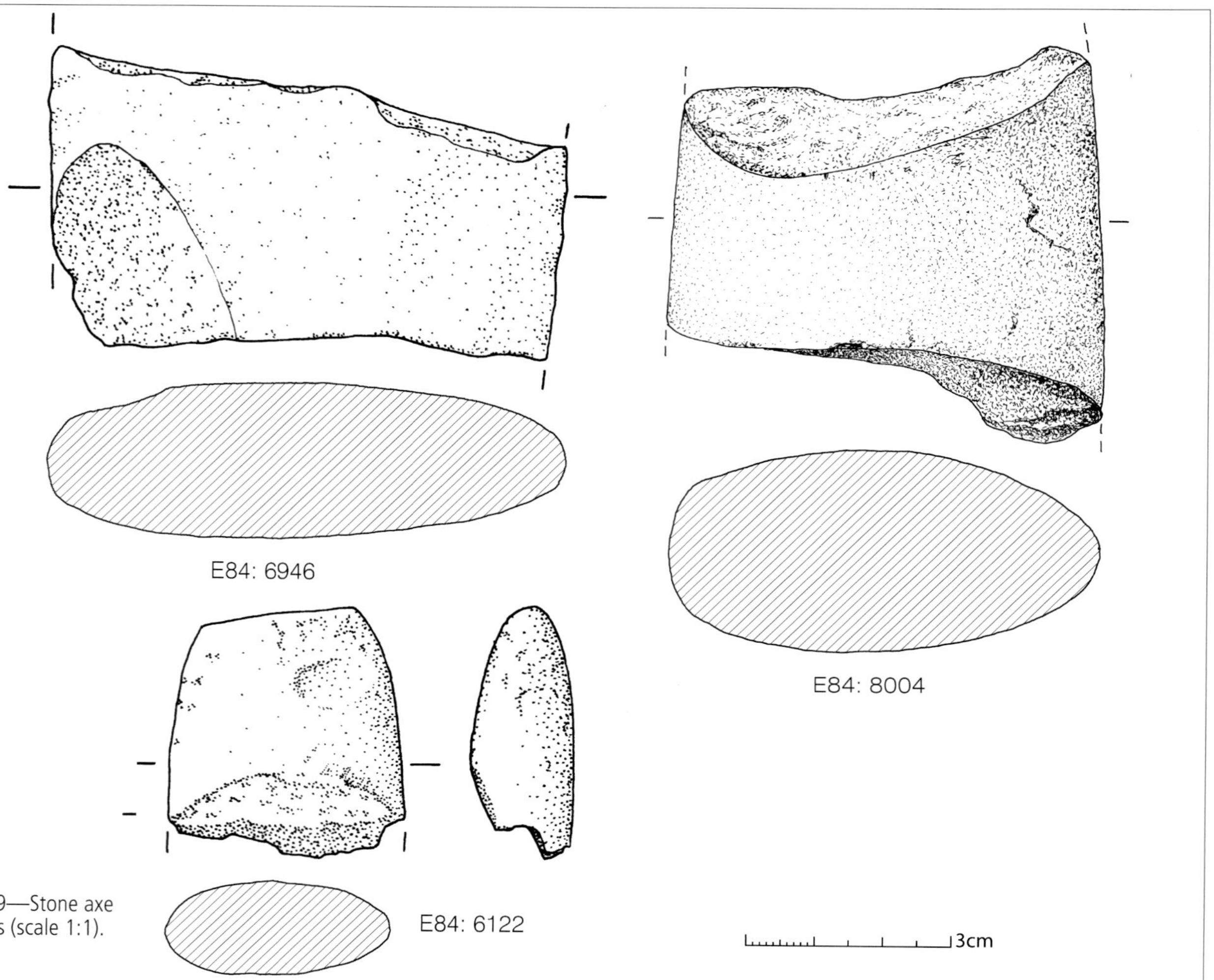

Fig. 3.119—Stone axe fragments (scale 1:1).

intentionally so. The two axe fragments from upper portions of axeheads (E84:8996 and E84:6122) may have broken during use. None of the axes retain their original edge and none have any indications of hafting evidence.

Dating

As with axeheads in general (Cooney 2000), dating is problematic for this small assemblage of axes. Typologically none of these axes are chronologically distinctive. Axes of shale and mudstone are present in the Irish archaeological record from the Early Mesolithic through to the Late Bronze Age, and indeed later (Cooney *et al.* 2011). Irish Group VI tuff axes are known from Early Neolithic contexts, but their use seems to extend across this period. Issues remain as to whether we can regard such axes as definitely imported from the Group VI sources in the Langdale area of Cumbria in north-west England (Bradley and Edmonds 1993) or as indicating the use of similar sources in Ireland (Cooney and Mandal 1998, 146).

Stone axeheads in County Wicklow

A total of 79 stone axes have been recorded from County Wicklow by the Irish Stone Axe Project. The majority of these are morphologically defined as axeheads, with only eight that might be classified as adzes. The dominant lithologies for stone axes in Wicklow are dolerite and porcellanite, of which only dolerite is represented in the Rathgall assemblage. All of the lithologies in the Rathgall assemblage are present in the known lithologies for Wicklow axes. The dominant mode of primary manufacture for axes in County Wicklow is pecking (21 axes) followed by flaking (13 axes).

3.14 PETROGRAPHICAL REPORT ON STONE OBJECTS FOUND DURING ARCHAEOLOGICAL EXCAVATIONS AT RATHGALL, CO. WICKLOW

Stephen Mandal

3.14.1 Introduction

This report is based on the macroscopic (hand specimen) examination of 173 stone objects found during archaeological excavations by Prof. Barry Raftery at Rathgall, Co. Wicklow (licence nos E84 and E100). The purpose of the study was to identify the rock types from which the stone objects were made, to highlight potential sources for them and to comment on their possible function.

3.14.2 Results (Table 3.40)

Stone axeheads

Six axeheads were examined (see Table 3.41). Two (E100:161 and E84:8996) are made from fine-grained banded green tuff, identical in the hand to the Council for British Archaeology Implement Petrology Committee Group VI tuff from sources in Great Langdale in the Lake District of Cumbria. Only a small portion of the original surface of E100:161 is visible at the sides. It has been reused as a whetstone/polishing stone and has been extensively ground and worn smooth. E84:8004 is made from green-blue mottled dolerite. E100:024 is made from medium-grained green dolerite. E84:6122 and E84:6946 are made from secondary sources, modified from water-rolled cobbles; E84:6122 is made from very fine-grained grey, ashy mudstone, while E84:6946 is made from fine-grained, dark grey, parallel-bedded shale.

Hammerstones

The assemblage includes four hammerstones, four possible hammerstones and one hammerstone/decorated stone (see Table 3.42). Sandstone accounts for six of these, dolerite for two and granite for one. The stone types used—sandstone (including quartzite and greywacke), dolerite and granite—are typical of the types of medium- to coarse-grained rocks that are used as hammerstones.

The (possible) hammerstones are all worked natural water-rolled cobbles. Seven (E84:3111, 4146, 4168, 4242, 6197, 7692 and 8898) exhibit evidence of having been pecked at one or both ends, but the level of pecking ranges from clear (e.g. E84:6917) to very subtle (E84:4242). Three (E100:98, E84:7565 and E84:8681) have been pecked around their entire circumference (though the latter has subsequently been worn). E100:98 is particularly interesting, as the level of pecking around the circumference is beyond that of a typical working hammerstone. It is more likely that this stone has been decorated; perhaps it is an unfinished tool of a different type. Finally, it is noteworthy that three of the hammerstones appear to have been burned (E84:3111, 4168 and 6197).

Table 3.40—Summary of results of macroscopic petrographical examination.

	Igneous			Sedimentary						Metamorphic			
Object type	**Granite**	**Dolerite**	**Group VI**	**Sandstone**	**Mudstone**	**Shale**	**Limestone**	**Chert**	**Vein quartz**	**Porcellanite**	**Schist**	**Slate**	**Total**
Axehead		2	2		1	1							6
Hammerstone	1	2		6									9
Grinding stone				1							1		2
Hone				5	2						1		8
Rubbing stone				2									2
Sharpening stone				2									2
Whetstone				1	1		1						3
Quern	11												11
Perforated slate												4	4
Spindle-whorl				2	2								4
Disc		1		6			1				1	2	11
Miscellaneous	1			3							1	2	7
Natural	1	5		52	11	1	6	2	3		2	2	85
Natural, burned	2			15	2								19
Totals	**16**	**9**	**2**	**95**	**19**	**2**	**8**	**2**	**3**		**6**	**10**	**173**

Table 3.41—Petrographical descriptions of stone axeheads.

Excavation no.	Square no.	Context	Petrography	Description	Object type	Note
E100:161	Z5:a	In grey fill of Post-hole 3	Group VI?	Banded fine-grained green tuff, identical in the hand to British Implement Petrology Council Group VI	Axe?/burnisher?	Only a small portion of original surface showing at the sides; it has been reused as a burnisher/polishing stone and has been extensively ground and worn smooth
E100:24	Z3	In brown, 20cm below sod	Dolerite	Medium-grained, green	Axe	See catalogue
E84:6122	20/21	In black layer under wall with mould fragments	Mudstone	Very fine-grained light grey ashy	Axe/adze, possible fragment	See catalogue
E84:6946	D3	In brown	Shale	Fine-grained dark grey parallel-bedded	Axe/adze, possible fragment	See catalogue
E84:8004	B1	In wall	Dolerite	Green/blue, mottled, dolerite	Axe/adze, possible fragment	See catalogue
E84:8996	I6	In brown humus	Group VI?	Fine-grained light green banded volcanic; very similar to Group VI Great Langdale volcanic	Axe/adze, possible fragment	See catalogue

Table 3.42—Petrographical descriptions of hammerstones.

Excavation no.	Square no.	Context	Petrography	Description	Object type	Note
E100:98	Z5:d	In brown humus level	Dolerite		Hammerstone/decorated stone	Water-rolled cobble, hammered around entire circumference
E84:3111	27	In dark brown	Sandstone	Coarse-grained quartz-rich brown	Hammerstone	Water-rolled cobble, lightly hammered both ends, possibly burned
E84:4168	Dump	Dump	Granite	Very fine-grained	Hammerstone	Water-rolled cobble, burned and broken; curved end worn by light pecking
E84:4242	29	In dark brown over ditch	Sandstone	Fine-grained yellow quartz-rich	Hammerstone, possible	Water-rolled cobble, broken, possibly worked by light pecking
E84:6197		In chamber in wall; on 'platform'	Sandstone	Very coarse-grained greywacke	Hammerstone	Water-rolled cobble, extensively hammered at both ends, burned
E84:7565	D/D1	In brown ashy material under black	Sandstone	Coarse-grained quartzite	Hammerstone	Water-rolled cobble, circumference hammered
E84:7692	E1	In black under bank	Sandstone	Fine-grained very dark grey	Hammerstone, possible	Water-rolled cobble; one end pecked
E84:8681	Y2	In black, burnt material along northern extension of square	Sandstone	Coarse-grained yellow quartzite	Hammerstone, possible	Ball-shaped water-rolled cobble; possible hammering of circumference (subsequently worn)
E84:8898	G4	In brown humus, centre	Dolerite		Hammerstone, possible	Water-rolled cobble, broken in half; elongate; one end possibly hammered

Grinding stones (including hones, rubbing stones, sharpening stones and whetstones)

The assemblage includes seventeen stones that have been used to grind, polish or sharpen, grouped together here as it is difficult to confirm their exact function (two grinding stones, eight hones, two rubbing stones, two sharpening stones and three whetstones: see Table 3.43). As is typical of this type of tool, the majority (eleven) are made from sandstone, from fine-grained to very coarse-grained. Two are made from schist, three from mudstone and one from limestone. Schist is also coarse-grained, but both mudstone and limestone are fine-grained (finer-grained than fine-grained sandstone), with fewer abrasive properties.

All the grinding stones have been made from altered water-rolled cobbles or cleaved blocks, with natural erosional planes used for grinding, rubbing or sharpening. As noted above, it is difficult to determine the exact function of these objects.

Spindle-whorls/stone discs

There are four spindle-whorls, two of which are complete (see Table 3.44). Two are made from sandstone and two from mudstone, and all are made from water-rolled pebbles/cobbles. The faces of these objects correspond to natural bedding planes within the sediments, and they have probably been made from natural cleaved pebbles, with perforations in the centre and in some cases minor working

Table 3.43—Petrographical descriptions of grinding stones.

Excavation no.	Square no.	Context	Petrography	Description	Object type	Note
E100:30	Z3	In W end, in brown	Sandstone	Very coarse-grained quartzite	Rubbing stone, possible	Water-rolled cobble, broken; lower face possibly used for rubbing
E100:35	Z2	In brown covering layer	Limestone	Parallel-bedded, dark grey	Whetstone, possible	Very smooth cleaved block, upper and lower faces possibly used for rubbing
E84:1380	2	In black fill of ditch	Sandstone	Fine-grained, parallel-bedded and cleaved	Hone	Worn on all sides
E84:27	24	Lightish brown soil, E	Schist	Fine-grained, low grade	Hone, possible	Smoothed faces consistent with use as hone/rubbing stone
E84:5645	67	Under wall collapse	Mudstone	Dark grey parallel-bedded	Hone	Cleaved and parallel-bedded; upper surface worn with striations
E84:5938	67	Immediately under sod	Sandstone	Fine-grained light grey	Sharpening stone	Water-rolled cleaved block, natural facets exaggerated through use as sharpener
E84:6113	66	Among collapsed wall stones	Mudstone	Fine-grained grey parallel-bedded	Hone, possible	Cleaved and bedded block; upper surface very smooth, may indicate use as hone
E84:6360	G2	In brown	Sandstone	Fine-grained yellow	Hone, possible	Water-rolled cleaved block; one face more worn, possibly owing to use as a hone
E84:64	24	Assoc. with Hearth 3, in dark occupation layer, c. 150cm from S, 185cm from W	Sandstone	Parallel-bedded, dark greywacke	Hone, possible	Water-rolled cobble, worn
E84:6474	G2	In brown, yellow showing, NE	Sandstone	Fine-grained yellow	Whetstone, possible	Water-rolled cobble; striations on two faces consistent with use
E84:6951	D/D1	Black charcoal area	Sandstone	Coarse-grained grey micaceous	Sharpening stone	Water-rolled cobble, large, broken; upper surface has lots of striations consistent with use for sharpening blades
E84:7994	F1	In rabbit burrow	Sandstone	Fine-grained ashy grey	Rubbing stone	Water-rolled cobble; extensively worn to two facets at one end
E84:8302	I1	In brown, almost on yellow, centre	Schist	Very coarse-grained micaceous	Grinding stone, possible	Water-rolled cobble, cleaved; one face appears ground
E84:8866	G4	In brown humus	Mudstone	Ashy grey	Whetstone, possible	Cleaved block; one face smooth
E84:8943	J6	In brown humus immediately below the sod	Sandstone	Fine-grained green greywacke	Grinding stone	Water-rolled cobble, one end ground to two facets
E84:9163	C3	Pit 209	Sandstone	Coarse-grained yellow quartzite	Hone, possible	Water-rolled block, broken, one face flat and smooth
E84:9518	K4	SW corner of Pit 271	Sandstone	Fine-grained, parallel-bedded and cleaved	Hone	Water-rolled cleaved block, one face very smooth

of the circumference to give a disc shape.

There are eleven stone discs, six made from sandstone, two from slate and one each from dolerite, schist and limestone (see Table 3.44). Like the spindle-whorls, all are made from naturally rounded and/or flat-bedded cobbles/pebbles. Seven are perforated, and it is possible that all the discs are simply unfinished spindle-whorls.

Querns

A sample of eleven querns or possible quern-stone fragments was identified. All are made from coarse- to very coarse-grained granite. Granite is a very hard stone, eminently suitable for grinding/milling.

Perforated slate

A sample of four perforated slates was examined, ranging in type from low-grade ashy slate to high-grade slate.

Miscellaneous objects

A further seven stone objects were identified as having been worked.

1) E84:1811 is a highly worked perforated fragment of fine-grained blue/green amphibole schist. Its function is not clear.
2) E84:3330 is a natural water-rolled granite cobble, almost spherical in shape. It has possibly been ground to increase sphericity.

Table 3.44—Petrographical descriptions of spindle-whorls/stone discs.

Excavation no.	Square no.	Context	Petrography	Description	Object type	Notes
E100:150	Z3	In brown under sod	Sandstone	Medium-grained, brown-grey, micaceous	Perforated stone object	
E84:1027	2	Light brown, baulk between Sqs 8 and 2	Sandstone	Breccia, coarse-grained green volcanic	Disc, possible	Naturally disc-shaped stone, possibly roughly shaped
E84:1169	2	Dark brown, W	Sandstone	Green greywacke	Perforated stone disc	Water-rolled pebble
E84:1470	Dump	Found in dump	Sandstone	Fine-grained yellow	Perforated stone object	
E84:5284	64	Immediately under sod	Limestone	Fine-grained dark grey parallel-bedded	Perforated stone object	Water-rolled pebble, perforated
E84:6544			Schist	Micaceous pyrite schist	Disc, perforated	
E84:6925	D8	In brown	Sandstone	Medium-grained dark grey	Disc	Parallel-bedded circular-shaped stone
E84:8277	I1	In dark brownish-grey material under cobbling which underlies the stone wall	Sandstone	Medium-grained green-grey; parallel-bedded/cleaved	Disc	Water-rolled pebble; disc-shaped
E84:8404	G1	In grey fill of Pit 32	Dolerite	Porphyritic; green weathered brown, coarse-grained, phenocryst-rich	Disc	Water-rolled pebble, circular in plan; upper surface very smooth
E84:8944	J5	In black layer of irregular, stone-filled pit, at 25cm depth, 1m N of large boulder	Slate	Grey high-grade	Perforated stone object	Cleaved block; thin perforation
E84:9251	K8	Brown, E end	Slate	Grey	Perforated stone object	Parallel-cleaved pebble, thin, perforated
E84:1493	9	Almost immediately under sod in N of square	Sandstone	Medium-grained green, parallel-bedded	Spindle-whorl	Rounded, perforated
E84:188	33	In brown patch on yellow	Mudstone	Ashy	Spindle-whorl	Water-rolled cobble, perforated
E84:9352	X11	Pit 252	Sandstone	Fine-grained grey	Spindle-whorl, fragment	Water-rolled pebble; perforated, broken
E84:9461	G6	In grey-brown fill of rectilinear trench, NE end of square	Mudstone	Fine-grained light grey	Spindle-whorl, fragment	Water-rolled pebble; flat-sided, perforated, broken

3) E84:4706 appears to be a tool for decorating pottery. It is made from a piece of low-grade black slate, and teeth have been ground into one edge.
4) E84:6075 is a water-rolled flattened cobble of medium-grained grey sandstone. Parts of its circumference are damaged, consistent with striking. Its function is not clear.
5) E84:8142 is a water-rolled pebble of very fine-grained yellow-red quartz-rich sandstone. It has been broken and its broken end is extensively damaged, suggesting striking.
6) E84:8683 is a worked low-grade slate fragment which has possibly been perforated. Its function is not clear.
7) E84:9031 is a ring made from medium-grained quartz-rich sandstone.

Other objects

The remaining objects examined (104 in total) are all natural, unworked stones. The majority of these are water-rolled cobbles and pebbles (89), the remainder being cleaved blocks. Nineteen of the stones appear to have been burnt. Forty are broken, including seventeen of the burned stones.

The majority (92) of the stones are made from sedimentary rock types. Sandstone accounts for 67, mudstone for thirteen, shale for one, limestone for six, chert for two and vein quartz for three. Dolerite accounts for five and granite for three. Finally, there are two each of schist and slate. Interestingly, the burned stones are even more predominantly made from coarse-grained rock types—fifteen of sandstone and two of granite—with only two of fine-grained stone (mudstone). This is consistent with the coarse- to medium-grained rock types associated with *fulachta fiadh* deposits.

3.14.3 Solid geology and soils of the site (see McConnell and Phillcox 1994)

The bedrock around Rathgall consists of Leinster Granite. The Leinster Granite stretches from Dún Laoghaire to New Ross, outcropping over an area of more than 1,500km^2. It consists of five plutons, each representing a separate intrusion. It was intruded during the Caledonian deformation (*c.* 405±2 million years ago; O'Connor *et al.* 1989). The granite is a two-mica peraluminous granite with several mineralogical and textural varieties (Brück and O'Connor 1977). The Leinster Granite contains a number of minor intrusions of dolerite, diorites and grandiorites. Rathgall lies within the Tullow Pluton (fine-grained grandiorite to coarse granite, including porphyritic granite). The Tullow granite is the largest individual pluton in the Leinster Granite but is also the least exposed, outcropping only on isolated hills (McConnell 1994).

To the north-east, east and south-east of Rathgall (closest occurrence *c.* 17km to the south-east) occurs the Ribband Group (Cambrian–Ordovician Age), consisting predominantly of fine-grained sedimentary rocks deposited as muds and silts in deep-water conditions. It may be partly equivalent in time to the Bray Group to the north, representing finer sediment that was carried further into the basin. The Ribband Group rocks in this area belong to the Maulin Formation. This consists of fine-grained metasediments: laminated siltstones and shales, metamorphosed by the Leinster Granite to phyllitic rocks and schists. Close to the contact with the granite occur quartzites (metamorphosed sandstones). In addition, the Group contains minor outcrops of basalt breccia, schist, andesite breccia, andesite and andesitic tuff.

From approximately 6.5km to the west of the site and further west occur younger, Carboniferous rocks of Courceyan to Westphalian age. These include rocks belonging to the Quinagh (lenticular mudstone and coarse siltstone), Ballymartin (limestone and dark grey calc shales), Ballysteen (fossiliferous dark grey muddy limestone), Clay Gall (feldspathic quartzitic sandstone) and Coolbaun (shale and sandstone with thin coals) formations.

Warren (1993) determined that throughout the last glaciation the predominant ice-flow direction in the area was from north-west to south-east. At various stages, the area would have been buried under a substantial thickness of ice. This resulted in the considerable erosion of the underlying bedrock, and accounts for the variety of rock types that occur in the glacial tills of the area. When an ice sheet impinges on a highland area, drainage from both the ice sheet and the highland is impeded. Given that most of the meltwater discharge will occur during a short summer melting season but will be of very large volume, it is not surprising that such situations are characterised by deeply cut drainage channels. The Dublin and Wicklow mountains are surrounded by a virtual chain of such channels.

3.14.4 Potential sources

Igneous

The granite objects are likely to have been derived from glacial material relating to the local Leinster Granite bedrock. Mica occurs as large crystals within the Leinster Granite. Similarly, the vein quartz objects are likely to have been originally derived from veins within the granite of the area and arrived on site in the glacial till or through direct erosion of bedrock. The closest dolerite exposures occur within the Leinster Granite and to the east as part of the Ribband and Bray Groups of Cambrian–Ordovician Age (meta)sediments, in particular occurring as narrow dykes visible in coastal sections.

There is a small number of green tuff outcrops associated with the Ribband Group (McConnell *et al.* 1989). Whilst it is possible that the axehead fragment (E84:8996) and reused axehead (E100:161) were derived from one of these sources, they are most probably not derived from the area. Cooney and Mandal (1998, ch. 5), using thin-section and X-ray diffraction analysis of Irish tuff axes, identified more than 120 axes from find-spots in Ireland that are petrographically and morphologically consistent with the numerically most important British groups of axes, namely Group VI epidotised intermediate tuff, from sources in and around the Scafel Pike and Great Langdale areas of Cumbria (see Clough and Cummins 1988; see also Bradley and Edmonds 1993). Textures such as banding characterise these sources. The petrographical evidence for this hypothesis is supported by the morphology of the axes, which exhibit the same characteristics as many Group VI axes in Britain, most notably faceted sides. These axes are widely distributed throughout Ireland, with notable concentrations in north County Antrim and in the Lough Gur area of County Limerick (see Cooney and Mandal 1998, fig. 5.26). The reused possible axehead (E100:161) is petrographically consistent with typical banded green Great Langdale material.

Discussing potential sources for Group VI axes in Ireland, Cooney and Mandal (1998, 118–19) highlighted the probability that the intermediate volcanic rock sources in and around the Lough Gur area were utilised in axe manufacture in Neolithic Ireland (see also Rees in Grogan and Eogan 1987, 493–5). The discovery of more than 140 flakes and axe fragments at Clogher, Co. Kerry (Kiely 2003), further supports the probability that Irish sources were being utilised to produce axes both petrographically (or, from the perspective of the maker, visually in terms of banding and colour) and morphologically (e.g. with faceted sides) closely resembling British Group VI axes (Cooney and Mandal 2000).

Recent work by Carol Dempsey (pers. comm.) of University College Cork in the Lough Gur region has suggested, however, that the volcanics of this area have a mineralogy and texture distinctly different from Great Langdale material and, importantly, from axeheads found in the area.

Sedimentary

It is likely that the sources for all the objects made from sedimentary rocks are local. As noted above, there are abundant sources for rocks of these types, in particular greywacke sandstone, quartzite and mudstone, within the Ribband Group. It is, however, important to note that these objects are probably not worked from bedrock but from secondary sources, such as water-rolled beach or river cobbles. Chert occurs as bands and nodules within limestone.

Metamorphic

Slate and schist occur in the vicinity of the site at Rathgall, close to the contact between the country rock sediments and the Leinster Granite.

3.14.5 Conclusion

It is not possible to determine a definitive source for these objects based on macroscopic examination alone. Furthermore, with the exception of the tuff axeheads, detailed microscopic analysis would also be unlikely to identify exact sources. A programme of detailed analysis of the tuff axeheads, including thin-section and X-ray fluorescence geochemical analysis, would be very useful in identifying sources for these objects, which are likely to have been imported onto the site from Great Langdale in Cumbria.

Regarding the remaining rock types utilised, it can be stated that the materials from which these objects were manufactured are available locally in outcrop and within the glacial tills. Thus it is probable that these objects were derived from local sources. Furthermore, based on the abundance of water-rolled cobbles and cleaved blocks, it is probably that the secondary sources such as tills and rivers were utilised as opposed to outcrop sources.

3.15 EARTH MATERIALS FROM RATHGALL

Thomas Cummins

Thirty-seven samples of lumps of earth material (as distinct from loose soil) were found in the Rathgall excavation archive, labelled as daub. Detailed descriptions are given in Table 3.45.

Daub is a construction material formed from tempered clay (Sherard 2009), i.e. with added coarse particles such as gravel or ceramic fragments, or, in a more encompassing definition, an earth material formed in a plastic state for construction purposes, typically with fibrous or gravel temper, and most likely to be preserved in deposition context when it has been heated (Parr and Boyd 2002).

Daub recovered from archaeological excavations has been described occasionally rather than consistently, with macroscopic assessments used to discover construction techniques, based especially on plant impressions. Short categorising series have been constructed to organise observed types, generally within a site as here, rather than using a standardised systematic approach applied to sites in general, or an accepted definition of the material (Dolan 2006; Sherard 2009).

3.15.1 Daub from Rathgall

The materials examined in 2012 were principally earthy lumps. These were screened as hand-specimens, and most were examined using low-power microscopy under incident light. Recording conventions are drawn from soil-science norms used to describe earth materials during soil survey (Soil Survey Division 1993; Jahn *et al.* 2006).

Most objects had undergone soil-forming processes, especially colonisation and transformation of their surface by soil fauna into an irregular coating of topsoil-like material. Although described as 'firm', the materials were too soft to wash or brush, and many objects were observed on a freshly broken surface.

Table 3.45—Earth materials recovered from Rathgall (2012).

Label	Description	Interpretation
E84:S70:19 Daub? Sample from Pit A Sq. 35	Three objects. (1) 2.5cm × 1.9cm × 1.6cm; (2) 4.4cm × 3.1cm × 2.3cm. Common quartz inclusions. Fines coating quartz. Many small prominent pores, vughs and packing-voids. Pink 7.5YR 8/4. (3) 1.3cm × 1.5cm × 1.2cm. Softer than fingernail. Reddish-yellow 5R 7/6. Fine matrix.	1 & 2: Type 3, prepared earth. 3: Type 5, ceramic.
E84:S70:21 Baked clay sample From grey silt in ditch Sq. 9/3 28/08/1970	Two earth objects. Micaceous, with sand. Vughy; oriented, elongate irregular planar voids. Slight banding of pedogenic oxidised iron. Intrusions with dark crumb-structured fill. Matrix very pale brown 10YR 7/4.	Type 3, prepared earth.
E84:S70:26 Daub(?) sample Sq. 10 31/08/1970	One earth object. Quartz gravel in a sandy matrix, vughy. Slightly rigid (difficult to break with fingers). Loose fines adhering to sand grains. No coatings. Occasional mica. Pink 7.5YR 8/4 broken.	Type 3, prepared earth.
E84:S70:31 Daub(?) sample From Pit A Sq. 35 31/08/1970	One earth object. Coarse mixture of mostly white mineral materials. Weathering crust or biotic intrusion on one side.	Type 3, possible prepared earth.
E84:S70:34 Daub(?) sample Sq. C1	Three objects, similar. 3cm × 2.2cm × 1.4cm; 3.6cm × 2.8cm × 1.8cm; 4.5cm × 4.2cm × 3cm Vughy, rare channel. Lamination (or foliation?). Broken lumps. Freshly broken surface shows coarse lamination with interlaminar irregular lenticular voids and shrinkage cracks (now four pieces). Fines adhering to quartz grains. Coarse, sandy clay. Yellowish-red 5YR 5/6 to light brown 7.5YR 6/4.	Type 3, prepared earth.
E84:S70:38, 1–2 Daub(?) sample Sq. C1 04/09/1970	Two earth objects. Vughy: irregular, oriented planar pores. Tubular biopore. Pale yellow 2.5Y 8/2 to pink 5YR 8/4, suggestive of localised heating. One object with foliation, pink on one side.	Type 3, prepared earth. Photographed.

Table 3.45 (cont.)—Earth materials recovered from Rathgall (2012).

Label	Description	Interpretation
E84:S70:38, 3–5 Daub(?) sample Sq. C1 04/09/1970	Three earth objects. One object with extensive filled faunal intrusions, with red on one side, suggesting localised heating. One light-coloured object with extensive biopores, including occupants. One object with extensive biopores, and pedogenic iron coatings.	Type 2, low-fired topsoil. Photographed.
E84:S70:38, 6–7 Daub(?) sample Sq. C1 04/09/1970	Two earth objects. One possible weathered stone (no plasticity; thin weathering rind). One natural stone.	Natural rocks.
E84:S70:51 Daub(?) sample Sq. C1 From lower levels of black occupation level	Four earth objects; one piece of bone. 5.4cm × 3cm × 2cm (flattened). Washed under gentle stream of water; no dispersal. Some smearing. Grass impressions. 5.6cm × 4.2cm × 3.5cm (not flattened). 6cm × 6cm × 4cm. Colour banding—fragment of heated earth surface. Micaceous, roots on surface. 2.3cm × 2.5cm × 1.6cm Pinkish-white 7.5YR 8/2. 4.3cm × 1.3cm × 0.5cm. Bone, unburned, characteristic shape	Type 4, daub. Type 4, daub. Earth surface, heated. Possible Type 4, daub. Bone, identifiable.
E84:S72:18 Baked clay sample S72:18 Sq. G2 26/06/1972	One earth object. White N >8/. Involution suggesting plastic lamination (rather than plastic deformation). Surface faunal intrusion. Shrinkage-cracking in a surface coating of fines within pores, possibly from systemic context..	Type 4, daub.
E84:S72:19 Baked clay sample Sq. D[s] 26/06/1972	One earth object. Reddish-yellow 5YR 7/6. Plastic deformation. Porous, small (<1mm) subcircular pores, not biopores. Mica and quartz inclusions in a fine matrix.	Type 5, ceramic.
E84:S72:27, 1–4 Baked clay/daub(?) sample Sq. D 27/06/1972	Four earth objects. Hard. Irregular, with possible faunal intrusions. Coarse gravel inclusions.	Type 3, prepared earth.
E84:S72:27, 5 Baked clay/daub(?) sample Sq. D 27/06/1972	One earth object, pot-formed (body), smooth surface, tapering. Convex surface with distinct fine oriented striations; concave surface with aligned planar surface of gravel inclusions including ceramic fragments. Micaceous. Red inclusions. Matrix very pale brown 10YR 7/4.	Type 5, possible ceramic.

Table 3.45 (cont.)—Earth materials recovered from Rathgall (2012).

Label	Description	Interpretation
E84:S72:38 Baked clay sample Sq. D/D1	Three earth objects + fragments + dust. 1.7cm × 5cm × 2.5cm; embedded red-earthenware ceramic fragment 0.9cm × 0.7cm plus smaller fragments; broad surface impressions to 1.5cm × 2cm; quartz and mica adhering; coarse material; sub-oriented elongate pores, vughs; yellowish-brown.	Type 3f, prepared earth, possible floor.
E84:S72:53 Baked clay sample Sq. D/D1	One earth object. Fines on gravel. Micaceous. Impressions. Red inclusions are possible ceramic fragments. Cavities, possibly remaining from vegetation inclusions. Very pale brown 10YR 7/3.	Type 4, probable daub.
E84:S72:56 Baked clay Sq. E2	One earth object. Hard. Much broken during examination. White surface in part, brown in part, possible gley. Tubular biopores, possibly distorted. Probable foliage impressions (white part). Foliation. Coatings of pedogenic iron on some biopores. Mica, quartz. Possible nodule of pedogenic iron. Diagnosis as gley would rest on iron nodulation, suggesting repeated wetting–drying cycles. Foliation and foliar impressions argue for daub.	Type 4, possible daub.
E84:S72:59, 1–2 Baked clay sample Sq. D/D1	Two earth objects, white. Red ceramic inclusion. Micaceous. Plastic. Larger object 3.7cm × 3.3cm × 2cm, matrix very pale brown 10YR 8/4, with a surface coating white N <8/, possible salt (gypsum?) crust; possible foliage impression. A second possible foliage impression is a cavity containing some faunal granules, perhaps reworking of the foliage contents, or occupation; not interpreted as a faunal intrusion, owing to density of matrix. Faunal occupancy (rather than mechanical intrusion) of a pre-formed triangular hollow.	Type 4, daub.
E84:S72:59, 3–5 Baked clay sample Sq. D/D1	Three earth objects, brown. Micaceous, quartzitic. Faunal colonisation of surface (in storage).	Type 3, prepared earth.
E84:S72:68 Baked clay/daub(?) sample Sq. D/D1 12/07/1972	Two earth objects. Hard. White surface, possible salt (gypsum?) crust. Smaller object 1.8cm × 1.4cm × 1.1cm. Larger object 4.3cm × 2.8cm × 2cm. Pink 7.5YR 7–8/3. Micaceous, quartzitic. Biopores, plastic deformation of. Interpretation of Type 4, rather than possible Type 3, rests on relatively uniform fine material and light colour. Not absolutely clear distinction.	Type 4, daub.
E84:S72:78 Baked clay sample Sq. D/D1	Four objects, rounded. Grass impressions. Black inclusions. Involutions. Root. Pinkish-grey 7.5YR 7/3–4 to very pale brown 10YR 8/3.	Type 4, daub.
E84:S72:87 Sq. D/D1	Six earth objects. Pink 7.5YR 7/4; plastic deformation; gravel inclusions; mica and quartz.	Type 4, daub.
E84:S72:102 Baked clay sample Sq. C1 01/08/1972	Three earth objects. Hard. Separate surfaces white and reddish-yellow 7.5YR 7/6. Striations on one not-freshly-broken surface, possible excavator's brush marks.	Type 4, probable daub.

Table 3.45 (cont.)—Earth materials recovered from Rathgall (2012).

Label	Description	Interpretation
E84:S78:8 Baked clay sample Sq. X12 29/9/[1978]	Two earth objects. Pink 7.5YR 7/4 broken. Occasional surface-connected voids filled with darker material, possible faunal intrusions. Vughy, with orientation of elongate lenticular-section pores. Globular connected sub-tubular pores, possible biopores. Occasional glistening pore linings, reddish-yellow 5YR 6/8. Also granular aggregates. Fines coating globular pores.	Type 2, possible low-fired topsoil.
E84:S78:15	Five earth objects.	Probable metalworking material with diagnostic potential.
	Two natural rocks.	Possible iron-smelting bloom. Recommend view by slag specialist; sample passed on to Katharina Becker, 4 July 2012.
E84:S78:26, 1 Baked clay sample Sq. X5 05/10/1978	One earth object. Fine, light red 2.5YR 6/6, with gravel matrix of multiple-geologies rock fragments, not necessarily local.	Type 5, ceramic. Recommend viewing by ceramic specialist.
E84:S78:26, 2–3 Baked clay sample Sq. X5 05/10/1978	Two earth objects. Circular-section biopores and vughs. Light.	Type 3, prepared earth.
E84:488 Sq. 34	One earth object. 5cm × 2.6cm × 1.8cm, tapering to a broad wedge-end, with a probable finger-impression (but no print). Dispersed in water over sieves to 250µm: earth material; compact, dense and formed, with much gravel; few unpreserved seeds 1–2.3mm and fragments (not identified). Consumed in investigation; earthworm chaetae not sought.	Probable faunal pellet. Possible rook or other crow pellet.
[E84, Pit 118] 1 Holzkohle aus der inneren Füllung [Charcoal from inner wickerwork]	Charcoal.	Charcoal.
[E84, Pit 118] 1 Holzkohle aus der inneren Füllung [Charcoal from inner fill]	Charcoal.	Charcoal
[E84?] 1	Loose soil and earth objects.	Possible heat-working tube, such as tuyère or slag tap.
[No label on or in bag]	Fragment of tubular glaze-finish ceramic set in coarse earthy material; 1cm arc, possibly 1.2cm diameter.	Possible natural redox iron pore-lining.
	Fragments of corroded iron object, forming square-section tube, part within earth object.	Possible hearth.
	Red earth with embedded charcoal.	
[E84 doubtful] 1 [No label on or in bag]	Two organic objects. Peat object, 13cm × 11cm × 6cm, plano-convex; sapric peat. Peat object, 4cm × 3.4cm × 2.4cm, broken irregular sub-hemispherical; fibrous woody objects with sapric matrix. Mineral particles including mica adhering.	Natural peat.

Fig. 3.120—Type 2,low- fired topsoil: the topsoil origin is indicated by tubular biopores and faunal granules in galleries, while heating is evidenced by light colour (since organic matter that makes topsoil dark is not present) and firm consistency. Labelled 'E84:S78:8 Baked Clay Sample SQ. X12 29/9[/1978]'.

Earth lumps were assigned to an expedient categorical system consisting of: Type 1, topsoil; Type 2, low-fired topsoil (Fig. 3.120); Type 3, prepared earth (Fig. 3.123); Type 4, daub (Fig. 3.121); and Type 5, ceramic (Fig. 3.122).

Samples of Type 3 were derived from topsoil, as shown by the presence of distorted but recognisable biopores. This suggests minimal procurement to select this material. Type 4 is derived from a carefully selected material with a fine matrix that can be worked under wet conditions when it is plastic.

Plastic deformation

Type 3 is typified by distinct plastic deformation, while Type 4 has undergone plastic deformation to the extent of fully obliterating any pre-existing internal structure. Plasticised, homogenised earth materials are usually sticky and can be used to adhere to surfaces, to fill irregular space and to join together loose incorporated material; they also provide the opportunity for smearing or burnishing to form a smooth surface.

Addition of gravel and fibrous vegetation

Type 3 may have had additions, while Type 4 and Type 5 (ceramic) (Fig. 3.122) have coarse inclusions that are certainly added—foliage and sand or gravel in the former, gravel in the latter. Both gravel and fibrous inclusions are understood to have the effect of temper in giving dimensional stability, i.e. providing interfaces along which cracks may form, accommodating short-range shrinkage during drying and thus avoiding larger cracks that would lead to structural failure. Gravels observed were consistent with Rathgall site materials, dominated by quartz, mica and granite.

Heating

Heating of earth materials leads sequentially to loss of water, loss of carbon compounds, oxidation of iron, and progressive melting or vitrification of minerals (Pollard and Heron 1996). Loss of carbon compounds, which give topsoils their dark colour, leads to lightening of colour. Red colours in earth materials are attributed to the presence of oxidised forms of iron and are an indication of chemical transformation, such as high temperatures. Type 3 has in general been heated, as indicated by its firmness, light colour and red hue. It is not immediately clear whether Type 4 has been heated: the light colour may derive from a subsoil source originally low in organic matter, and added plant material has not been carbonised. Heating may, however, have oxidised all the organic matter, and the firmness allowing survival may indeed be due to heating, as literature accounts consistently suggest.

Fragmentation and surface forms

These objects are all small lumps, from a few millimetres to perhaps 10cm in maximum dimension. All are fragmentary. Some objects with one extensive relatively flat surface were found, and these may be floors or similar defined earth surfaces (S72:38, S74:27). Figure 3.121 shows an object most closely fitting a concept of 'daub' as a selected, fine-grained earth material which has undergone intensive mechanical manipulation in a wet plastic state and to which materials have been added, especially fresh plant fibres such as grass, leaving clear impressions. Any pores from the original material have been obliterated or re-formed during working, leaving non-oriented star-shaped and concave-polygon pores. Also present are distinctly coarser pieces of gravel, probable deliberate inclusions.

The general absence of defined surfaces on daubs and prepared soils may suggest that most of the earth lumps come from objects of large dimensions, such as structures. Although there is some surface-concentrated destruction of these materials, they have withstood weathering and could have continued in their original form had they not been actively broken. Their current size range would be consistent with persistent breakage during manual cultivation of topsoil for crops, though no direct evidence for this was observed.

Fig. 3.121—Type 4, daub: firm and light-coloured, with intense plastic deformation indicated by non-aligned concave-polygon pores, and fines coating coarse particles, together with sharply defined impressions of incorporated foliar material. Labelled 'E84:S74:26 Baked clay sample S74:26 26/3/74'.

Fig. 3.122—Type 5, ceramic object, broken to reveal its make-up. The fine matrix adheres to the surface of the coarse inclusions. The colour (very pale brown 10YR 7/4) is a little reddish, while faces of inclusions are aligned to the smooth curved surface (out of view). The object is firm but takes a fingernail impression. Scale units are millimetres. While ceramics are abundant on the site, the inclusion of a few ceramics within the 'daub' collection indicates the continuity of characteristics and the difficulty of distinguishing these materials under field conditions. Labelled 'E84:S72:27 Baked clay/Daub(?) Sample SQ. D 27/6/1972'.

Fig. 3.123—Type 3, prepared earth, showing a range of red and lighter colours, along with oriented pores, coarse inclusions, plant impressions, and the surface of the object transformed by faunal channels filled with faecal pellets. The lighter-coloured area at upper right shows transition to characteristics of daub, indicating continuity between Type 3 and Type 4. Labelled 'E84:S74:19 Baked clay sample SQ Y2'.

Spatial distribution

The Rathgall daub samples for which contextual information is available show a distinctly clustered and non-random distribution (Fig. 3.124). A large cluster comes from Sqs D/D1 and the adjacent C1, representing Types 3 and 4, as well as one tentatively identified as floor material (plotted as Type 3f, prepared earth, possible floor). The next cluster is from Sq. Y2, comprising Types 3, 4, the combined type (plotted once as each type) and a piece of tentatively identified floor. There are lesser clusters from Sqs 35 and X5, with two objects of Type 3 from Sqs 9/3 and one from Sq. 10.

It is proposed that Type 4, which is present in a restricted set of locations, is functionally associated with activities carried out at those locations. Type 3 is similarly associated, and has a wider distribution that may be ascribed to a more widely occurring activity. Objects combining Types 3 and 4 only occur where Type 4 occurs, so the composite form appears to be dependent on Type 4, providing evidence that Type 4 is the more specific material.

As regards the spatial distribution of daub samples, locations are specific to 5m grid squares only, not to individual features. Points refer to samples, which each contain 1–25 objects (Fig. 3.124).

Concluding comments

The Rathgall daub collection represents fragments of objects which have been made from the immediate soil surface and from more deliberately sought soil materials, mixed in wet conditions with vegetable fibres and gravel tempers, and plastically formed, presumably into useful shapes for which they now give little evidence, but potentially upstanding structures rather than vessels. These recovered materials had been in many cases strongly heated after shaping. As they would have had stable integrity of form, their entry into a depositional context is suggested to have involved active mechanical destruction. This could mean the tearing and beating of earthen forms or structures with simple hand tools to reduce their size below that which would obstruct cultivation. The soil in which they resided could easily have been cultivated (with continued breakage and rounding likely). Soil fauna, including earthworms, have apparently eroded the surfaces of the fragments, and they were excavated with much topsoil adhering and occupying shallow pits and grooves on the surface.

All plant impressions observed were within the matrix of these objects, and no surface impressions were noted. The absence of impressions consistent with small-dimension woody stems indicates that they were not part of wattle-and-daub structures, but they certainly could have been part of upstanding earthen structures such as kilns, or constructions in a 'clay-walling' material (*clay* here used loosely), including structures of composite materials for which evidence was not found.

The presence of only one sample qualifying as Type 1, topsoil (S73:16), and no lumps of subsoil (with S72:56 rejected as a gleyed subsoil candidate) seems to indicate that the assemblage is largely reliable in terms of initial identification by excavators. This would in turn support interpretations of the spatial distribution in Fig. 3.124 as reflecting the true deposition, rather than being related to any serious bias in recovery. Finally, it can be accepted that the excavators' use of the term 'daub' for the assemblage as a whole is appropriate.

Survival of daub as reported in excavations is typically fragmentary. Wattle-and-daub structures are frequently identified when burned, and survival of daub in general appears to be biased towards burned material, with poor survival of unburned daub. This may limit the potential to regard the present assemblage as specifically associated with active use of fire, and it may better represent end-of-life events in which structures suffered burning. This interpretation could confound the acceptance of the spatial distribution shown in Fig. 3.124, which may therefore only indicate the location of fire-affected daub rather than daub in general.

3.15.2 Rathgall soil samples

Soil samples from Rathgall (Rath East townland, Co. Wicklow, excavation E84) were received from Barry Raftery and described by the author for Margaret Gowen and Co. Ltd in 2003–5. Unpublished internal technical reports were prepared on soil descriptions, charcoal and plant remains (Johnston *et al.* 2003; Cummins 2004; Johnston 2004; O'Donnell 2005). The outcomes of these four reports were consolidated into a single report giving the full data set and results (O'Donnell *et al.* 2005).

A total of 73 dry, bagged and labelled soil samples were received, many of which were very small (<10g). Forty-two soil samples were examined and described in detail, with descriptions reproduced here as Table 3.46. Samples were then processed for retrieval of charred plant material using a simple flotation method. Each sample was soaked in water to suspend the carbonised material; this was poured off and

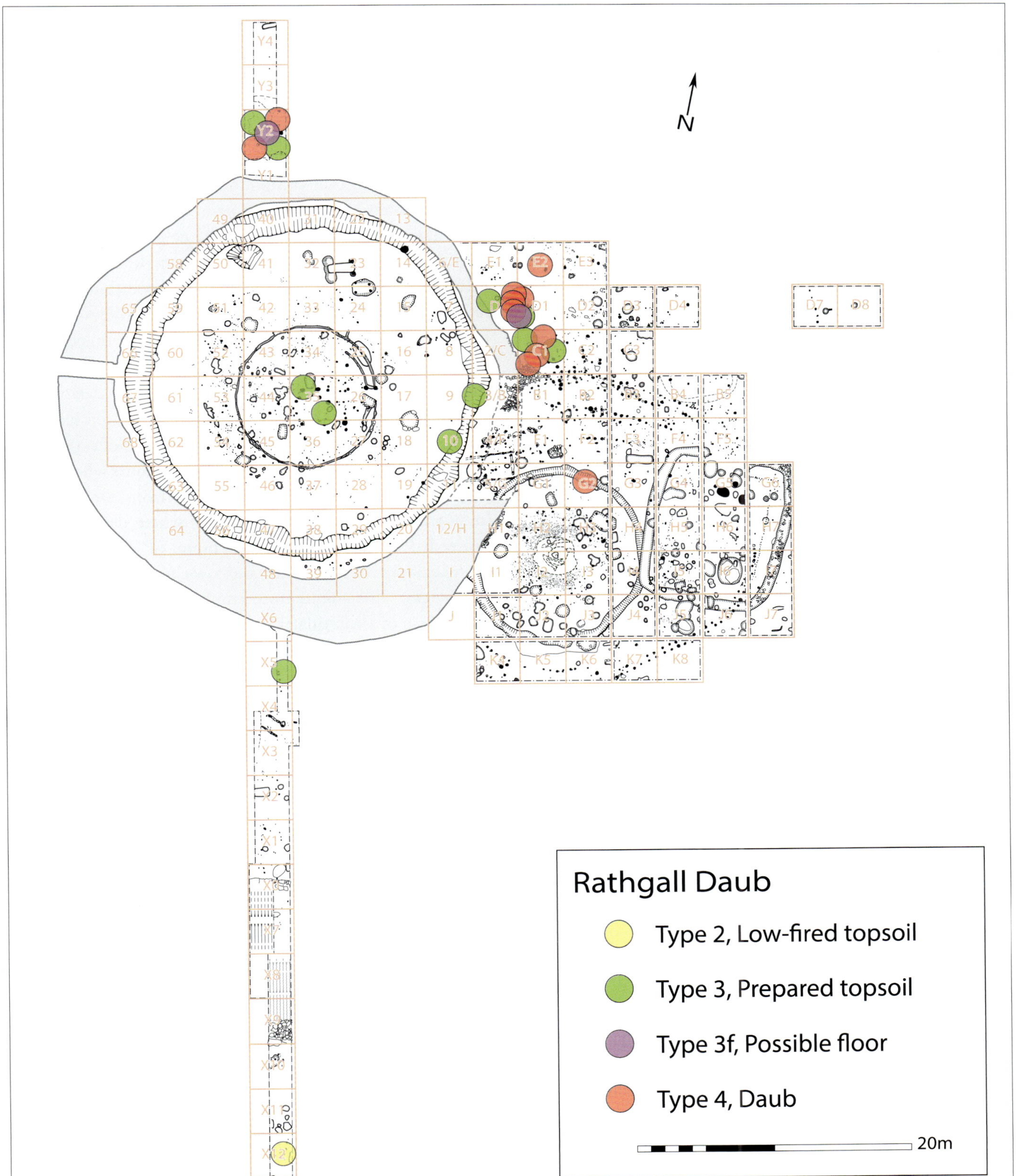

Fig. 3.124—Distribution of daub samples of different types across the site.

trapped in a sieve with a mesh size of 300µm. This 'flot' (i.e. the floated material) was air-dried and stored in sealed plastic bags. Thirteen of the 73 samples yielded seeds and/or tubers. Examination of the flots and identification of the plant material was carried out by Penny Johnston under low-level magnification (×4–×56) using a binocular microscope. Very little identifiable plant material was recovered, with barley the sole identified crop. The report noted a possible association between oat tubers and burnt bone, suggesting a link with cremation ritual. Charcoal was identified by Lorna O'Donnell from fifteen samples, with several taxa identified (*Alnus*, *Quercus*, *Fraxinus*, *Corylus*, *Salix*, Pomoideae and cf. *Prunus*). Amounts recovered were small, and no significant interpretations were offered.

Interpretations of these soil samples focus on identifying soil processes that may be relevant to understanding the site, how deposits may have formed, and how included objects and artefacts may have been transformed during burial. The expectation before assessment was that, being on granite bedrock, the site would produce acid soils and that survival of bone mineral (and shell) would probably be very limited in aerobic deposits. The following general statements were made based on the samples.

Preservation pre- and post-excavation

All the samples appear to have come from dry deposition contexts, with common evidence of active decomposition and with aerobic conditions indicated by the presence of roots. One peat sample ((0.5) 1972 Sq. Z5:a) and one organic sand sample (S84:5911 Sq.) were recorded, though in neither of these was there preservation of macroscopic plant remains.

The soil samples were all in a very dry state. Drying and handling have led to structural breakdown and the loosening of fine material, some of which is lost as dust during further handling. Decomposition of some paper sample labels had occurred in storage.

Soil textures

The soils examined are almost all sands, loamy sands or sandy loams. These coarse-textured soils are expected in materials derived directly from the weathering of granite rock *in situ*, or from the weathering of ice-crushed granite derived from glacial tills. There may have been significant removal of fine particles during soil development. It is plausible that the hilltop location of this site has led to a progressive coarsening of soil textures, owing to rain-wash operating on fresh soil whenever it is exposed at the surface.

Soil colours

Soil colours are described using Munsell terminology, comprising a colour description (e.g. 'light grey'), a hue (10YR, 7.5YR etc.), a value (1–8) representing brightness, and a chroma (1–6) indicating intensity of colour. Samples with very light colours such as 'light grey 10YR 7/2' indicate low levels of the iron compounds that give soils their red-brown colouration and of the organic matter that makes soils dark. These soils therefore show the colours of the mineral grains and are commonly derived from leached horizons below the zone of organic-matter incorporation; they are referred to as E-horizons ('E' from eluvial, indicating leaching). Some soils are light when dry but much darker when moist (e.g. E100:35 Pit 3A Sq. OII:9, probably Z5:a (numbering error)—light grey 10YR 7/2 dry, dark brown 7.5YR 3/2 moist)—the colour that the soil would have had in the field state is closer to the moist colour reported. Several of the soils examined show light colours when moist. These may therefore derive from E-horizons, or may have been produced in cultural situations where decomposition proceeded without the further input of organic matter. Many colours have low value and low chroma, i.e. dark greys and blacks. This colouration, combined with the common appearance of clean quartz grains, indicates a dominance of colouration by organic matter weakly associated with the coarse mineral particles. This latter character would be expected in the surface soils of upland granite-derived lands in Wicklow. Thus the colour evidence is consistent with most of the soils being derived from local, weathered, well-developed surface soils with Leptosol or Podzol character.

Action of soil fauna

Several of the samples had stable biopores in the 2–6mm range, attributable to earthworm activity (E84:6145d Sq. 51; S73:4 Pit 11 (*sic*) H3; S72:79 [1/2] Sq. G2; S73:5 H3 Pit 8; S72:79 [2/2]; E84:5791 Sq. 51; S72:109 Sq. D/D1 Pit 43 Z5:4). These features represent the burrows of large earthworms and imply connection with the surface or with other overlying soil horizons, from where fine particles of up to about 4mm may be transported, along with incorporations of fresh organic matter in the form of plant litter and roots, and ingested organic matter in worm-casts. They suggest locally habitable soil (perhaps just within a pit), with adequate drainage, pH not below about 5.0, and moderate to high nutrient contents. The level of worm activity evidenced by these samples suggests a significantly richer site in nutrient terms than might otherwise be expected on the granite uplands of Wicklow and could potentially be attributed to net nutrient imports to the site by various human activities.

Charcoal

Charcoal amounts are lower than might be expected from the number of label notes indicating hearths; for example, E84:6145c Sq. 51 is described as 'Sample of black material from upper lining of "Hearth"' but recorded only a low level of charcoal during processing (other examples are S164 Sq. 23/32; E84:6145b Sq. 51; E84:6145d Sq. 51; E84:6145c Sq. 51). High levels of charcoal were recorded in three contexts (S72:99; E84:6079 Hearth 10 Sq. 34/35; s73:8 Pit 10 H3), all of which were dominated by charcoal.

Weathered granite

Several of the samples contain coarse granite fragments, with occasional pieces of quartzite. One label suggested that the granite may have been deliberately crushed. The granite found is generally observed to be weathered rather than crushed or broken rock. This is suggested by the ease with which the remaining granite stones can be broken apart, separating the resistant quartz and mica crystals from the softened feldspar matrix. The possibility that the rock has been crushed and has been weathered only during the post-deposition period of a few millennia may be considered: there are difficulties in estimating a weathering rate, it being so dependent on extremely local conditions within the deposit. The most likely interpretation, given the consistent state of the granitic material in so many samples from diverse deposits, must be that the site as a whole is grounded on a weathered-granite substrate.

Reddened stones

Heat-reddened stones were observed in three contexts (PH No. 82 Sq. 25; S73:3 Pit 11 H3 (*sic*); S160 Sq. 23/32). Heat-reddening is ascribed to stones showing strong red colours either with uneven intensity or over only part of their body. (Uniform red colour, by contrast, would be attributed to processes operating at a larger scale in geological contexts.) There may also be heat-fractured stones present, recorded as 'broken' stones (Pit 24 S72:108 Sq. D2). Other red colouration observed is attributed to the deposition of pedogenic iron (i.e. from soil development processes), rather than to heating, on the basis of its distribution as a crust or rind on particles (S72:79 [2/2]).

Broken stones are recorded where coarse-grained stones exhibit very acute angularity or bimodal angularity, such as where a rounded pebble also has a face with angular edges. While not easily diagnostic, such broken stones are consistent with anthropogenic activities such as rock-working, stone-dressing and paving. Where the character of individual stones suggests breakage, this has been recorded (Pit 24 S72:108 Sq. D2).

Preservation of bone

It is likely that acid soil conditions prevail across the site, owing to the granitic parent material. The apparently free-draining conditions would reinforce this tendency. The presence of bone (E84:6090; S73:8; S84:5911; Pit 16 Sq. Z5:d [1/2]; S164 Sq. 23/32; Pit 43 Z5:d; Table 3.47) might reasonably be seen as an indication of formerly more extensive incorporations, with preservation having occurred only under limited local conditions. A single possible lime lump (Pit 19 Sq. Z5:d) may be ultimately derived from bone material. Bones are also recorded as having been present in PH8 Sq. Z5:d.

Surface-oxidised granite

'Surface-oxidised granite' is recorded where there is a distinct rind of red-brown colouration on granite particles. This is not likely to be due to heating (which does not produce a rind and leads to brighter red colours) but is more likely to derive from soil development. Such colours, however, form as coatings in lower soil horizons and not on surface-exposed stones. It is possible, then, that materials exhibiting this phenomenon derive from former subsoil B-horizons of podzols, which may have been truncated *in situ* or which have been disturbed and rearranged to give the deposits as discovered. This was only observed in context S72:79 [2/2].

Conclusions from soil examination

Forty-two soil samples were examined, mostly of very small volume. They were all from free-drained aerobic deposition contexts, with no preservation of uncharred coarse organic matter. Soil textures were sandy. The range of soil colours, with common dark greys and some very light browns, and the fine, weak structures, often single-grain, suggest poor conditions for plant and faunal growth. Thus the presence of frequent indications of worm activity is unexpected and suggests that this site may have been significantly enriched in nutrient terms, which may be explained by the importation onto the site of nutrient-bearing organic materials. Nevertheless, the dominance of granite, the frequency of quartzite, quartz and mica, the sandy textures, the ranges of colours consistent with the most likely regional soil colours,

Table 3.45 (cont.)—Earth materials recovered from Rathgall (2012).

Label	Description	Interpretation
E84:72:113	Nine earth objects. 1. Laminated, alternating fines and aggregates, pink and light greyish-brown; slight pedogenic iron accumulation; mica; quartz to 4mm.	Type 3, prepared earth.
E84:S72:118 Daub(?) sample Sq. C1	Eleven earth objects. 1.3cm × 1.5cm × 0.8cm to 4.1cm × 2.8cm × 1.8cm. Micaceous. Fresh break shows foliation (broad streaking suggestive of heterogeneous materials part-mixed with plastic deformation). Faunal galleries (with 'egg' *in situ*), post-foliation, suggests penetration resistance low in the manufactured material. Colours reddish-yellow 5YR 6/8 close by pinkish-white 5YR(?) 8/2.	Type 4, daub.
E84:S73:1 Sample of black material in Pit 1	Loose black fine material, with coarse charcoal, quartz, mica and granite. Subsample dry-sieved at 500μm revealing fine charcoal.	Charcoal.
E84:S73:16	Earth materials; fragments and powder. Burnt bone, characteristic shapes. Soil material: very pale brown 10YR 7/4 dry; biopores.	Burnt bone. Type 1, topsoil.
E84:S74:14 Baked clay sample	Approx. nineteen earth objects. Group 1, approx. ten objects: red; lamination; quartz; vughs. Group 2, approx. ten objects: fine-grained material between layers of coarser-grained; pedogenic accumulation of iron at interface; gravel inclusions including quartz; white and grey; vughs and elongate sub-parallel planar pores. Iron ring on one object, probable label eye. Groups 1 and 2 rebagged separately within this sample bag.	Group 1: Type 3, prepared earth. Group 2: characteristics of both Type 3 and Type 4—prepared earth–daub combination.
E84:74:16 Baked clay fragments Sq. Y2	Seven earth objects; three examined as representatives. Fibrous inclusions, sub-oriented; light grey and yellowish-brown materials; impressions; pasting of fines on quartz; mica. Strong lamination with curved planar pores; oriented mottles; pedogenic iron accumulation; quartz and mica. Laminated, red and yellowish-brown.	Type 4, daub. Type 4, daub. Type 3, prepared earth.
E84:S74:19 Baked clay sample Sq. Y2	Approx. 24 earth objects. Approx. twenty objects; combined red and grey; impressions in both; faunal intrusions. Four objects. White; laminated; fines; gravel inclusions; circular planar pores.	Combined Type 3–Type 4. Photographed. Type 4, daub.
E84:S74:23	Approx. 40 earth objects; three selected objects examined. Red; quartz with adhering fines; lamination; curved planar pores. Red; impressions; gravel cluster in planar plastic band; slight pedogenic iron accumulation. Faunal intrusion; mica; moderate pedogenic iron.	Type 3, prepared earth.
E84:S74:26 Baked clay sample 26/03/1974	One earth object. Sandy matrix, with mica and quartz, and faunal granules in galleries. Part light red 2.5YR 6/6, including with faunal granules. Broken for photography, revealing abundant foliar impressions.	Type 4, daub.
E84:S74:27 Baked clay sample Sq. Y2 26/03/1974	One earth object, 9.4cm × 7.7cm × 3.3–3.5cm, with nearly parallel faces, one rough and one very flat, with a largely continuous surface. Light brushing of part under water reveals an earthy surface, continuous with the matrix, with light striations, and oriented planar faces of inclusions, suggesting a mechanically finished surface. Brushing is destructive, so not continued, and most of the object remains covered with loose soil. Lower rough surface argues for a floor. Quartz and mica. Foliar? impressions in broken matrix (not on surface).	Type 3f, prepared earth, possible floor.
E84:S78:4 Baked clay sample Pit 78:2 26/09/1972	One earth object. Broken in examination. Many biopores. Herbage impressions, with angular cross-sections, suggesting foliage rather than roots. Fines appressed to stones. Quartz and mica. Reddish-yellow 7.5YR 6/6 broken.	Type 3, prepared earth.

Table 3.46—Soil sample descriptions reported by O'Donnell et al. *(2005).*

Label	Description	Interpretation
E84:6090 Sq. 17/18 Soil [y]le of Black [cin]der fill of large storage pit	Sand; dark greyish-brown 10YR 4/2; very fine, weak, crumb; clean quartz grains; weathered granite to 4cm; ceramic; burned bone.	Clean quartz grains and weak structure suggest that this is an E-horizon, the leached layer of a podzol or a lithosol horizon. It appears to be derived directly from the silica-rich remnants of weathered granite.
E84:6145d Sq. 51 Sample of upper grey fill of 'Hearth' (layer 1) 10/08/1971	[Texture not recorded]; light grey 10YR 7/1; medium, strong, angular blocky; firm; compact peds with one planar surface (with possible striations); common roots; many biopores, stable to 2mm; much clean quartz; fines possibly washed from overlying soil.	A very light-coloured soil. Strong structure, firm, compact consistency and possible surface striations suggest that this is a remnant of a compacted surface or layer. Loose, non-aggregated fines interspersed in the pores are compatible with transport in flowing water from an overlying soil layer. These characteristics would be typical of a soil subjected to (1) compaction, (2) active decomposition, but (3) no input of organic matter. Burial by a large stone or structure could provide these conditions.
S73:8 Pit 10 H3 Sample of black lining of Pit 10	Charcoaly loam; very dark grey 7.5YR 3/1; fine, weak, subangular blocky; few roots; mica flecks; burned bone.	This sample is a mineral soil but has a large content of charcoal. There is some soil structure development.
S73:4 Pit 11 H3 Brownish-grey fill of Pit 11	Loamy sand; light brownish-grey 10YR 6/2; krotovinas dry grey 10YR 5/1, moist very dark greyish-brown 10YR 3/2; coarse, moderate, subangular blocky; common roots, preferentially occupying biopores; stable biopores to 1mm; krotovinas to 1cm.	This is an intensively worm-worked soil. Krotovinas (pores containing material which may be derived from an overlying horizon) permeate the structural bodies. Such burrowing activity could have the effect of concentrating coarse particles, including artefacts, at the base of the burrowed levels.
S73:7 Pit 1 H3 Upper brownish-grey material, Pit 1 19/04/1973	[Texture not recorded]; grey 10YR 5/1; medium, moderate, subangular blocky; and vermigenic crumb; common roots; granite to 2cm; mica; lime lump with crystalline centre.	This soil fabric appears to be derived from weathered granite. An apparent lime lump with crystalline calcite may indicate the former presence of bone which has dissolved in the (presumed) acid conditions to be expected in a granite-derived soil.
S84:5911 Sq. [ ] Blac[k] lining of large storage pit. 10/8/71	Organic sand; dark greyish-brown 10YR 4/2; medium, weak, subangular blocky; mica.	Although having a high organic content, this soil is not expected to exhibit any preservation of coarse organic particles.
PH No. 82 Sq. 25 Fill from large circular post-hole No. 82 in Sq. 25. 8.8.69	Sand; dark grey 10YR 4/1; fine, weak, subangular blocky; and single-grain; common roots; weathered granite to 2cm; one [heat-]reddened fragment; granite; one piece; quartzite to 1cm; mica; quartz.	This soil is derived from weathered granite, as indicated by the ease with which the remaining pieces can be broken, separating the more resistant quartz and mica crystals.
S72:81 Pit 3 Sq. G2 Grey material from Pit 3	Sandy loam; light brownish-grey 10YR 6/2; fine, moderate, subangular blocky; common roots; common subangular (non-granitic) stones to 2cm.	—
S73:3 Pit 11 H3 Black lining, Pit 11	Sandy loam; grey 10YR 5/1; and dark grey N 4/; medium, moderate, subangular blocky; and vermigenic crumb; mixed fabrics, probably krotovinas; common roots; subangular stones to 5cm; few heat-reddened stones to 1cm; granite, quartzite+.	Vermigenic crumb is derived from casting by earthworms. There may be non-granitic stones present. Krotovinas are (in this case) earthworm burrows filled with material transported from another soil deposit (usually an overlying one).
E84:6145 Sq. 51 Sample of black material from upper lining of 'Hearth'. 10/8/71	Sandy loam; dark grey 10YR 4/1; fine, weak, subangular blocky; common roots; some finely mixed fabric and much single-grain material.	Fine, weak structure, mixed fabric and single-grain material suggest disturbance preventing the development of biological activity at the time of deposition.
E84:6145 Sq. 51 Sample of black material forming basal lining of 'Hearth'. 10/8/71	Sandy loam; grey 10YR 5/1; stable biopores to 1mm; weathered granite to 1cm.	Derived from weathered, not apparently deliberately crushed, granite.
E84:6104 Sq. 17/18 Soil sample from yellow filling between wickerworks I + II. Erdprobe von der gelben Fülling zwischen [geflecht] I und II	Sand; very pale brown 10YR 8/3; medium, moderate, subangular blocky; label fragments; fine biopores <1mm; clean quartz.	Seems an unlikely texture of soil to use as a filling within a wicker structure owing to its sandy texture: a sand is not coherent enough to keep its shape when formed.
S72:79 [1/2] Sq. G2 Greyish lower silting of V-shaped trench	[Texture not recorded]; very pale brown 10YR 8/2; medium, weak, subangular blocky; biopores to 2mm; subangular stones to 2cm.	—
S72:99 Sq. D3 Fill of Post-hole 52	[Texture not recorded]; dark brown 10YR 3/3; dry very pale brown 10YR 7/3 and light grey 10YR 7/1; fine, weak, subangular blocky; common subangular stones to 1cm.	This soil material appears to be a mixture of materials, as evidenced by the two colours. It may have been mixed during filling of the post-hole.
Pit 16 Sq. Z5:d [1/2] Black soil	Sandy loam; yellowish-brown 10YR 5/4; slightly thixotropic; burned bone.	The colour of this soil (yellowish-brown 10YR 5/4 dry) does not concur with the label comment 'Black soil', though this is presumably intended to separate this from a second sample with the same context designation and labelled 'Grey-brown soil'.

Table 3.46 (cont.)—Soil sample descriptions reported by O'Donnell et al. *(2005).*

Label	Description	Interpretation
Pit 16 Sq. Z5:d [2/2] Grey-brown soil	[Texture not recorded]; light yellowish-brown 10YR 6/4; slightly thixotropic; few fine roots; subangular stones to 1cm.	This and Pit 16 Sq.Z5:d [1/2] may form a single deposition context, with the colour difference due to soil development. The most plausible arrangement would be with the darker soil [1/2] above, and reflecting the input of organic matter at the surface.
E100:41 Sq. Z2:9 Ext. E Sample of black material lining Pit 3B	Organic sand; dark brown 7.5YR 3/2; very fine, crumb; mica flakes.	Mica flakes indicate a granitic origin, while the sandy texture without gravel suggests that this material is derived from a size-sorted fraction, such as develops in a topsoil derived from worm-casts.
S72:101 Sq. [ ] [2/2] Thin grey layer under black. 27.7.72	Sandy loam; greyish-brown 10YR 5/2; fragments; weathered granite.	The most likely interpretation of a grey layer under black is that these represent the surface horizons of a podzol. The whole is leached, while the upper, black layer has had a significant input of organic matter. Thus these two layers may represent a single deposition context.
Pit 15 [Sq.] Z5:a Black fill. Now grey!	Organic sandy loam; dark greyish-brown 2.5Y 4/2; medium, moderate, subangular blocky; moist soft; common fine roots.	—
Erdprobe vom II Geflecht	Sandy loam; very pale brown 10YR 8/2; fine, moderate, subangular blocky.	A very light-coloured sample.
Pit 13 Sq. Z5:d Grey material; 2	[Texture not recorded]; grey 10YR 6/1; medium, weak, subangular blocky; few roots; common subangular stones to 6mm.	—
Pit 24 S72:108 Sq. D2 Pit 24. Sample of fill of Pit 24	Loamy sand; dark grey 10YR 4/1; very fine, weak, crumb; few roots; broken stone to 4cm, quartz, mica.	—
(0.5) 1972 Sq. Z5:a Sample of black peaty material at centre of circular trench among post-holes	Peat, Von Post H9; black 5YR 2.5/1; medium, weak, subangular blocky and fine crumb; common fine roots to 1mm.	Von Post H9 indicates a highly humified peat in which plant structure is not identifiable.
S160 Sq. 23/32 Hearth No. 2. Sample of burnt powdered granite which immediately underlay the black, charcoal layer of hearth No. 2. 26/8/69	Gravel and coarse sand; brown 7.5YR 4/2; single-grain; few heat-reddened particles; granite weathered.	This granite gravel has a loose, single-grain structure, suggesting weathering rather than recent breakage.
S164 Sq. 23/32 Hearth No. 2. Sample of black, burnt material from east end of hearth No 2. This was the black area which was not covered by yellow fill and was always visible. 28/8/69	Sand; very dark grey 10YR 3/1; fine, weak, subangular blocky; worm burrow to 2mm; common fine roots; common subangular stones to 1cm; mica flakes and granite fragments; and quartz; rare burned bone.	—
S73:5 H3 Pit 8 Grey fill, Pit 8. 19/4/73	Sandy loam; brown 10YR 5/3; coarse, moderate, subangular blocky; biopores to 6mm; common roots; common subangular stones to 2cm; mica flecks.	—
[S 1]00:9 Z1:6 Sample of grey fill from bedding trench of house No 1. 27/8/71	Sandy loam; light brownish-grey 10YR 6/2; medium, moderate, subangular blocky; common fine roots; possible polythene bag fragments; fibrous red-brown material (label fragments?); mica flecks.	—
S72:79 [2/2]	[Texture not recorded]; white 7.5YR 8/1; medium, strong, subangular blocky; abundant biopores <1mm, few stable to 2mm; few roots; stones to 1cm; weathered, surface-oxidised granite to 5mm.	'Surface-oxidised' granite probably represents pedogenic iron deposition, suggesting that this material may be derived from a former spodic B-horizon, a subsoil horizon in a podzol.
Pit 19 Sq. Z5:d Sample of black 'lining' material from Pit 19	Loamy sand; black 7.5YR 2.5/1; fine, weak, subangular blocky; few roots; common subangular stones to 1cm; possible lime lump.	The possible lime lump may be derived from weathered bone. It appears as rhombohedral crystals at the centre of an irregular white mass.
PH 8 Sq. Z5:d Sample of material from Post-hole 8—bones among this. 24/3/1972	Sand; very pale brown 10YR 7/4; possible vermigenic crumb remnants; medium, weak, subangular blocky; few roots; bones not seen.	The label comment 'bones among this' may be taken to mean that bones were found during excavation and were removed, leaving the soil material as described.

Table 3.46 (cont.)—Soil sample descriptions reported by O'Donnell et al. *(2005).*

Label	Description	Interpretation
S72:99	Sandy charcoal; black 7.5YR 2.5/1 (charcoal) and dark brown 7.5YR 3/3 (fines); few roots; few subangular stones to 1cm.	—
E100:35 Pit 3A Sq. Z2:9 Ext. E Sample of grey material from Pit 3A	Sandy loam; light grey 10YR 7/2; common roots to 1mm; burned bone.	—
E84:5791 Sq. 51 Post-hole 231 fill. 27.7.71	Loamy sand; light grey 10YR 7/2; coarse, strong, subangular blocky; stable gravel-lined biopores to 2mm; common roots.	Gravel linings on biopores are due to active transport of particles *c.* 1mm into the burrows by earthworms.
S73:6 Pit 10 H3 Black lining, Pit 10	Loamy sand; black 7.5YR 2.5/1; common roots; weathered granite to 1cm.	—
E84:6079 Hearth 10 Sq. 34/35 Sample of soil from black bottom levels of Hearth No. 10	Slightly sandy charcoal; black N <2.5/ with white flecks; roots not seen; few stones granite and quartzite to 1cm; mica.	—
S72:109 Sq. D/D1 Sample of grey 'floor'	[Texture not recorded]; very pale brown 10YR 7/3; coarse, strong, subangular blocky; common fine roots; biopores to 6mm, stable; label fragments.	The presence of 'biopores to 6mm', which may be attributed to earthworms, means that this soil has been worked by these animals. Fine material from above may be incorporated, though this does not affect the interpretation as a floor.
S72:101 [1/2]	Sandy loam; dark greyish-brown 10YR 4/2; medium, moderate, subangular blocky; common roots; mica flecks.	—
S72:100 Sq. G Sample of black burnt covering material	Sandy loam; very dark grey 2.5Y 3/1; slightly thixotropic; fine, moderate, subangular blocky; granite stone 2cm; mica flakes.	—
E84:6145b Sq. 51 Sample of grey fill (layer 3) between lower black and middle black lining of 'Hearth'	Sand; light grey 10YR 7/2; medium, weak, subangular blocky; few subangular stones to 2cm; common fine roots.	—
Pit 21 Sq. Z5:c 4	Sandy loam; brown 10YR 4/3; medium, weak, subangular blocky; small subangular stones to 5mm.	—
Rathgall (0,5) Pit 20 Sq. Z5:c Black fill	[Texture not recorded]; very dark brown 7.5YR 2.5/2; fine, weak, subangular blocky; possible flint chips.	—
Pit 43 Z5:d Sample of grey material from Pit 43	Sandy loam; light grey 10YR 7/2; coarse, moderate, subangular blocky; common fine roots; biopores to 2mm.	—

and the absence of overtly off-site mineral materials are all consistent with a primarily local origin for the materials from which these soils have formed.

3.16 THE OSTEOLOGY OF THE HUMAN CREMATIONS AT RATHGALL

Laureen Buckley

One of the crucial elements of Rathgall is the great importance of funerary activities (see Chapter 6). In this section Buckley discusses the extant human bone—identified as such during excavation as well as derived from soil samples. Not all samples of human bone that seem to have been recovered have been located in the archive, and thus we have to rely, for example for the bones from Pit 119, on the identification by Erskine. Table 3.47 presents all known instances of recovery of definite or likely human bone from Rathgall, as established by the authors in reconciling the different archival elements.

3.16.1 Methods

Bone consists of an organic and an inorganic part. When it is placed in fire, the organic part undergoes dehydration and an oxidation reaction occurs. Depending on the temperature and how long the bone has been in the fire, the reaction may be complete or incomplete. A complete or efficient burning or deliberate cremation of bone is one in which all the organic content is burnt off and only the inorganic part of the bone remains. The inorganic part generally recrystallises to form a more stable structure, resulting in warping of the bone (Thompson 2005), and this occurs at temperatures above 700°C. The recrystallisation means that fully cremated remains survive for millennia in a well-preserved condition. Efficiently cremated bone is white in colour and usually has a chalky texture. Less well-cremated bone, where the temperature of the pyre was not high enough or where oxygen flow was restricted, or where the body was not burning for long enough, has a blue or a blue/black colour (Holden *et al.* 1995; Walker and Miller 2005). The colour and texture of the bone, which determine the efficiency of the cremation, are recorded. The bone fragments are graded by size to determine the degree of fragmentation. The obvious very large fragments are removed, and the remainder are passed through a series of sieves. The bone from each sieving is stored separately and the fragments weighed. The weight of bone in each sample is used to determine the proportion of the various fragment sizes. The categories of fragment sizes used have been arbitrarily assigned to give the reader an impression of how crushed or not crushed the cremation was. The fragment sizes generally used are: less than 10mm; 10–15mm; 15–25mm; 25–40 mm; and greater than 40mm.The overlap between the groups is deliberate, as it would not be possible to be exact about the size of every fragment.

Although fragmentation of the bone occurs continuously after deposition owing to compression pressures, and also during the disturbance of excavation and processing, it is still possible to assess whether or not the bones were deliberately crushed as part of a cremation ritual. A high proportion of relatively large fragments would suggest that the bones were not deliberately crushed after the cremation, whereas a small deposit of relatively small fragments could indicate a ritually crushed deposit. There are, however, other factors to take into account, such as post-depositional disturbance, how the remains were discovered, and treatment of the remains during the excavation, processing and post-excavation stages. Even storage of the material may affect the fragmentation.

Each fragment of bone is then examined; animal bone is separated from human bone and identified if possible. The degree of identification of fragments is generally dependent on fragment size as well as on the condition of the bone, which may be affected by the cremation process. Larger fragments are usually easier to identify, although phalanges are often found intact among the smaller fragments. Successful identification depends on the number of distinguishing features present on the bone fragments, as well as on expectations of the thickness and cross-section of particular bones.

The minimum number of individuals present can then be determined by the numbers of specific skeletal elements. Bones of the skull—especially the petrous portions of the temporal bones—are easily identifiable and are therefore extremely useful in determining the minimum number of individuals and in distinguishing juveniles from adults. It is possible to distinguish juveniles from adults from the thickness of the bone fragments, the presence or absence of unfused epiphyses and the fragmentation of the teeth. Adult tooth crowns tend to shatter during the cremation process but unerupted juvenile teeth tend to survive intact, as they are protected by the jawbones. It is usually possible to age juveniles if enough teeth are present.

The sex of adult skeletons is determined by examination of morphological features of the skull and pelvis. The criteria for male and female features are those described in Buikstra and Ubelaker 1994. Determining the sex of adult skeletons in cremations is made more difficult by the fragmentation of the bones. In addition, heat exposure may warp and shrink various components to different extents (Fairgrieve 2008, 110–13). The individual features of the skull are the most useful in determining the sex of cremated remains (*ibid.*). Determining the age of adult skeletons in cremations is difficult. The standard methods—including changes in the pubic symphyses (Suchey and Katz 1986; Suchey *et al.* 1988) and the auricular surface of the ilium (Lovejoy *et al.* 1985), as well as the sternal ends of the ribs (Iscan *et al.* 1984; 1985)—depend on the surfaces not being badly affected by heat. As heat fractures frequently occur in these areas (Fairgrieve 2008, 108), they can seldom be used with any degree of reliability. In practice it is normally only possible to identify the young adults who may have some epiphyseal lines visible, and older adults by the presence of severe degenerative joint disease.

3.16.2 Burial 1, Ring-ditch 2 (S73:10)

This cremation weighed a total of 817.3g, an amount close to what would be expected to represent a full adult cremation (Table 3.47). The bone was mainly creamy white in colour, indicating a very efficient cremation, with only 5% (45.3g) still partially blue, indicating that it retained some organic content. The funeral pyre may have been well

Table 3.47—Details of the human cremations at Rathgall (Katharina Becker, Joanne Gaffrey and Laureen Buckley).

	Burial	Sample no.	Year	Square	Context detail	Identification
Area 1	Burial Pit 119	E84:6146, replaced by sample ID S71:120	1971	34/35	From blackened material in hearth 10 (= Pit 119)	Few very small fragments of cremated bone. Text says partial remains of an infant, but this may not be correct.
	Black burnt material	S74:24	1974	Y2	Black burnt material, from charcoal sample	
Area 3	Ring-ditch 2, Burial 1	S73:10	1973	I2	Central burial pit within Ring-ditch 2	Draft text (Raftery): Young adult of indeterminate sex—probably based on Erskine's comments.
	Pyre spread	S74:30, from charcoal sample		H3	'Burnt layer'. Likely from pyre spread around Burial 1	
	Ring-ditch 2, Burial 2	In vessel E84:8484, S74:7	1974	J3		
	Ring-ditch 2, Burial 3	S73:14	1973	H3 (on tag)	Tag says burnt bones from black 'lining' of Pit 10, is Burial 3. Also known as Pit 4 and Pit 54.*	
		S73:08	1973		Pit 10	
	Ring-ditch 2, Burial 4, Pit 32	S72:127	1972	G1	Pit 32	
	Pit 32	S78:65, from a charcoal sample	1978	K6	This pit cannot be identified on the plan for K6	
Z cuttings	Ring-ditch 4, Post-hole 8			Z5:d		
	Ring-ditch 4, Pit 16	No number, 2 bags		Z5:d		
	Ring-ditch 4, Pit 19	No number, from soil sample		Z5:d		This is a likely burial pit outside Ring-ditch 4.
	Isolated cremation pit burial		1971?	Z3	Burial 5	Stone-lined, probable cremation pit. Slivers of bone found in it according to Raftery stratigraphic account. It appears likely that this is E100:15, from Square 3 (probably OV3 is Z3), pit no. 2, as assessed by Erskine as per his report of 29.5.1972, include National Museum of Ireland's file of 8.6.1972
Unknown					Pit O	Three different pit Os known, which were in post-ex re-numbered, but without the square number the pit cannot be identified.
Possible deposits of human bone						
Z cuttings	Pits		1971?	Z1:4	2 pits in a continuous trench containing burnt bone. Pits 1 and 2 are located in the appropriate cutting. However, no 'continuous trench' documented.	

Table 3.47 (cont.) Burnt bone samples from soil retent and charcoal samples

Sample ID	Square no.	Context description	Context interpretation
S74:64			
S70:111	B2	From soil sample	
E84:6090; Soil sample 71:101	17/18	Large storage Pit 118	Pit 118
84:5911	'lining of pit' 17/18	Must be Pit 118	
E84:6145; Soil Sample 71:117	51	Hearth 10	
E84:4771, S71:15 Charcoal sample	2	Ditch fill	
S74:17	Y2	In black burnt material	
S146 or S164	23/32	Hearth 2	Pyre Hearth 2
E100:35	Z3	Pit 3a	Pyre Hearth 16–17 outside Ring-ditch 3
No number	Z5:4	Pit 43	

Erskine	Buckley, this vol.	^{14}C	Other info.	Source of info.	Location	
ine's assessment of 29.5.1972, included in National Museum of Ireland's file .6.1972, only speaks of 'few very small fragments of cremated bones'. A r from J. Raftery (NMI) to Barry Raftery, 8.6.1972, states personal munication Erskine–J. Raftery confirming that these were human.	N/a	Burial dated on charcoal (S71:93, GrN-27101)	Found with gold ring 6070.	Log book, Erskine ID	Missing	
	Human bone, 0.2g					
ine 1973: The collection comprises a large number of small fragments of nated human bones, the majority 1cm up to 4–5cm, probably of one vidual. Fragments of skull: petrous temporal, fragments of vault with ous sinus markings, 9 fragments of tooth roots and 3 crowns. Other bones ntified as segment of head of humerus, a number of fragments of long es and part of middle finger phalanx.	1 adult, older male	SUERC-42578: 1207–1002 cal. BC		Erskine ID and text.	NMI	Additional dates from spreads
	Human bone, 24g		In addition to this sample, also samples S73:12 and S73:19 were associated with the black streaks from this pyre spread. These were identifed by Erskine (7.6.1973, NMI file 17.5.1973) as human, but by Buckley as animal.			
ine 1974: Female ?and infant	1 adult, probably female	GrA-22304: 1041–838 BC	S74:7 bone from pot B2, Sq. J3. Erskine ID, but no mention of female.	Log book, Erskine ID	NMI	
kine 1973: About 100 small fragments 0.5–2cm of cremated human es, possibly of a child under 5 years; small fragments of skull and several ong bones can be recognised.	1 adult	Was dated on charcoal: GrA-23353, GrA-27118		Text, sample label and Erskine ID. Erskine refers to Pit 10, this was Pit 54 in post-ex.	NMI	
	9g human bone, cremated					
	Human bone				NMI	
	Likely human bone, cremated					
fragments of cremated human bones. Rib, long bone and skull can be ognised.		Bone:1260–970 BC: Gr-26533	Text mentions PH 1–3 in Z5:d, Fosse 5. Same post-hole possibly renumbered?	Erskine report 25.4.1972	Missing	
	1 adult	SUERC: 42579: 1195–979 cal. BC			NMI	
	Probably human cremated bone, 0.4g					
v fragments (1–3cm) of cremated bones, probably human according to kine 1972.			No entry in finds logbook.	Text		
	Human bone					
v fragments of cremated bone, probably human.				Logbook, Erskine ID	Missing	

**A pit 10 in E3 is hand-annotated on a plan in the archive as Pit 54 and 'burial S73:14'. This appears to be a misidentification. All evidence speaks to Pit 4/10/ Burial 3 to be located in H3.*

Sample description
uman bone, 2.8g
remated bone, unidentifiable minute fragments
remated bone, unidentified
remated bone, unidentified
remated bone, unidentified
remated bone, possibly human
remated bone, minute unidentifiable fragment
remated bone, unidentifiable
remated bone, unidentified
remated bone, unidentified

tended and the oxygen allowed to flow freely through it. The larger fragments were warped, indicating that the bone had reached a temperature of at least 700°C, causing numerous cracks and fissures of the bone surface and some warping of the larger fragments.

Fragmentation was low, with half the sample consisting of large and very large fragments (Tables 3.48a and 3.48b); the largest fragment was 73mm long. This suggests that there was no deliberate fragmentation of the bone as part of the burial ritual, and fragmentation probably occurred along fissure lines created by the cremation process. As the burial rested on a stone surface, it was protected to some degree from post-depositional fragmentation.

It can be seen that less than a quarter of the weight of the sample consisted of small and very small fragments less than 15mm in length. Most of the fragments were more than 15mm long, with nearly half consisting of large and very large fragments more than 25mm in length.

Identification

It was possible to identify 380.2g (46.5%) of the sample (Table 3.49). In a normal cremation the proportions of the various parts of the skeleton are: skull 18.2%; axial 23.1%; upper limb 20.6%; lower limb 38.1% (McKinley 1989). In this cremation, while all parts of the skeleton are represented, the proportions of the various skeletal regions are not what would be expected. The amount of skull is twice what would be expected, while the proportion of axial skeleton is much reduced. Skull is easier to identify than small slivers of long bone, so in practice the proportion of skull is often higher than it should be. The axial skeleton is very fragile and breaks up easily in the funeral pyre. In addition, there is a high proportion of cancellous bone in the axial skeleton that cannot be identified into individual bone types, so the proportion of identified axial skeleton in cremations is often less than it should be. The percentages of upper and lower limb bones were only slightly less than expected.

Table 3.48a—Fragment size in bone sample S73:10 (1) from Burial 1, Ring-ditch 2.

Fragment size (mm)	Weight (g)
<10	0
10–15	10
15–25	6.9
25–40	19.2
>40	72.3
Total	108.4

Table 3.48b—Fragment size in bone sample S73:10 (2) from Burial 1, Ring-ditch 2.

Fragment size (mm)	Weight (g)
<10	86.9
10–15	86.2
15–25	228.6
25–40	202.3
>40	104.9
Total	708.9

As there was no repetition of skeletal elements, the minimum number of individuals present appears to be one. There are indications that this was a male skeleton, based on the mastoid process of the temporal bone, while the presence of degenerative joint disease and osteoarthritis on several joints indicates an older individual.

Pathology

Degeneration of the synovial joints increases with age owing to repeated stress. Early indications are osteophytic lipping of the margins of the joints, which is an attempt to reduce stress by increasing the surface area. Porosity of the joint surface can follow, and the final stage is eburnation or polishing of the joint surface owing to destruction of the cartilage, resulting in

Table 3.49—Skeletal elements of bone sample S73:10 from Burial 1, Ring-ditch 2.

Bone	Weight (g)	Percentage of identifiable bone
Skull	142.9	37.5
		Skull 37.5%
Vertebrae	41.0	10.8
Rib	15.1	4
		Axial 14.8%
Scapula	9.8	2.6
Humerus	21.2	5.6
Radius	8.4	2.2
Ulna	7.2	1.9
Carpals/MCs/phalanges	1.2	0.3
		Upper limb 12.6%
Femur/patella	110.0	28.9
Tibia	17.9	4.7
Tarsals/MTs/phalanges	5.5	1.5
		Lower limb 35.1%
Total	380.2	100

bone rubbing on bone. Eburnation of the joint surface is diagnostic of osteoarthritis (Rogers and Waldron 1995, 43–5). There was evidence of extensive degenerative joint disease throughout the vertebral column. Osteoarthritis was present on the posterior articular surfaces of the cervical and thoracic region, with eburnation of the joint surfaces. There was also evidence for severe degenerative joint disease (DJD) in the lumbar region, with porosity and marginal lipping of the posterior articular surfaces.

In addition to the osteoarthritis of the posterior synovial joints of the spine, there was also evidence for vertical osteophytes on the sides of the vertical bodies. The joints between the vertebral bodies are not synovial joints, so osteoarthritis cannot occur. These vertical osteophytes have a buttressing effect and can be seen in individuals with collapsed vertebrae. There appeared to be a collapse of at least two cervical bodies and one lumbar vertebra. Fragments of vertical osteophytes were identified, and these may have belonged to thoracic vertebrae. Collapse of the vertebral bodies may be indicative of osteoporosis, which can also occur with age. There are other diseases that are identified by large vertical osteophytes, including diffuse idiopathic skeletal hyperostosis (DISH) (Rogers and Waldron 1995, 47–54), but there are specific features that must be present before a diagnosis of DISH can be made on an inhumation, and this is impossible on a fragmented cremation. On balance, considering the collapse of vertebral bodies, it is more likely that the diagnosis in this case is age-related osteoarthritis with spondylolysis of the vertebral column.

In addition, there were plaques of bone on the internal surface of this individual's frontal bone. This condition is known as hyperostosis frontalis interna. It is also age-related and has traditionally been associated with hormone imbalances in post-menopausal women, although there has been increasing evidence in recent times that it also occurs in older males.

3.16.3 Burial 2 and associated features

Burial 2, Ring-ditch 2 (S74:7)

This cremation weighed a total of 737.6g, which is close to that expected from a full adult cremation. The bone was mainly creamy white in colour, although a significant proportion, 20% (146.1g), was still partially blue or black, indicating that there was still some organic content to the bone and that it was not as efficiently cremated as S73:10. Several fragments had barely been burnt and were black in colour. It is possible that the pyre was not well tended and that oxygen flow was restricted in places, or the fire was allowed to burn out too soon. The larger fragments had cracks and fissures on the bone surface and some of them were warped, indicating that some of the bone had reached a temperature of at least 700°C.

Fragmentation was low, with nearly two thirds of the sample consisting of large and very large fragments over 25mm in length; the largest fragment was 80mm long. As the burial had been in an urn, it may have been protected from post-depositional fragmentation (Tables 3.50a and 3.50b). Again, however, there is an unknown factor: there are no details of the post-excavation processing, and it is possible that small fragments were not included in the sample sent for analysis.

Identification

Owing to the good preservation, it was possible to identify 414.5g (56%) of the sample (Tables 3.47 and 3.51).

Although all parts of the skeleton are represented, the proportion of the various parts is not what would be expected in a normal cremation. Skull fragments represented half of the identified bone. The amount of axial skeleton was much reduced. While the proportion of upper limb was close to what would be expected, the proportion of lower limb was much reduced. The skull appears to have been collected at the expense of the axial skeleton and lower limbs, although the black/blue colour of a significant proportion of the sample meant that many of the fragments of long bone could not be identified.

There was only a tiny amount of skull in the upper layers of the pot; most of it was in the middle and lower layers. This may mean that the skull was collected more carefully and put in the urn first, which would partially explain why there was a high proportion of skull in the identified bone.

Table 3.50a—Fragment size of bone sample recovered from Burial 2, Ring-ditch 2.

Fragment size (mm)	Weight (g)	Percentage by weight
<10	35.8	4.8
10–15	69.9	9.5
15–25	207.3	28.1
25–40	215.3	29.2
>40	209.3	28.4
Total	737.6	100.0

Table 3.50b—Individual bone samples recovered from Burial 2, Ring-ditch 2.

						E84-8484	E84-8484	E84-8484	E84-8484	E84-8484	E84-8484
	First 2in. of fill	Urn, 2–4in. deep	Centre of the fill, 2–4in. deep	E84-8484		Last 3in. of fill, 4–7in.	3in. of fill, 4–7in.	Fragments of bone	Fragments of bone	Fragments of bone	Teeth
Fragment size (mm)	(1)	(2)	(3)	(4)	(5)	(6)	(7)	(8)	(9)	(10	(11)
<10	3.2	11.5	6.5	1.2	8.9	0.5	1.6	0.4	0.7	0.4	0.9
10–15	6.4	16.5	10.2	6.6	15.8	2.8	7.3	0.3	1.6	0.3	2.1
15–25	23.1	17.4	22.2	37.6	61.1	20.6	21	0.6	0.8	0.5	2.4
25–40	28.1	1.4	11.5	59.6	32.9	43.6	38.2				
>40	51.1		12.3	50.7	34.2	38.2	22.8				
Total	111.9	46.8	62.7	155.7	152.9	105.7	90.9	1.3	3.1	1.2	5.4

Table 3.51—Details of bone sample from Burial 2, Ring-ditch 2.

Bone	Weight (g)	Percentage of identifiable bone
Skull	202.7	
		Skull 48.9%
Vertebrae	10.3	2.5
Rib	16.1	3.9
Pelvis	0.9	0.2
		Axial 6.6%
Scapula	11.9	2.9
Humerus	52.5	12.7
Radius	16.9	4.1
Ulna	8.7	2.1
Carpals/MCs/phalanges	3.8	0.9
		Upper limb 22.7%
Femur/patella	54.7	13.2
Tibia	30.8	7.4
Fibula	3.9	0.9
Tarsals/MTs/phalanges	1.3	0.3
		Lower limb 21.8%
Total	414.5	100

It was possible to identify 55% of the bone. As there was no repetition of skeletal elements, the minimum number of individuals was one. This appeared to be a female individual, based on the morphological appearance of the orbits. The diameter of the head of the humerus was also in the female range. There were no obvious indicators of pathological conditions on the bone.

Burial 3: Pit 10 (S73:14): bone from lining of pit

This sample weighed 22.6g. The bone was efficiently cremated and was highly fragmented, with the largest fragment 31mm in length. The sample consisted mainly of small fragments that made identification difficult. It was possible to identify only 4.9g (22%) of the sample, which appears to represent one adult individual (Tables 3.47 and 3.54).

Burial 3, Pit 10, S73:8

This sample consisted of 9g of grey/white human bone. There were heat cracks and fissures evident on the bone, even on some small fragments. The largest fragment was 13mm in length. Most of the sample (7.7g) consisted of fragments less than 10mm in length. Although individual bones could not be identified, most of the sample consisted of fragments of long bone.

Skull, 4.6g

This consisted of fragments of parietal bone, including a fragment from near the squamous suture and another fragment from near the lambdoid suture. There was also a fragment from a single rooted tooth.

Vertebrae, 0.3g

This consisted of a fragment of neural arch from a cervical vertebra and an isolated articular surface.

Pit 32 (S72:127)

This pit contained a small amount (3.6g) of efficiently cremated bone, white in colour with a chalky texture. Most of the fragments were of moderate size, between 15mm and 24mm in length; the largest fragment was 24mm long.

It was not possible to identify the bone fully other than to say that there were slivers of human long bone present.

Table 3.52—Fragment size of bone samples from Pit 16, Ring-ditch 3 (Z5:4).

Fragment size (mm)	Weight (g)	Percentage by weight
<10	4.4	3.1
10–15	23.9	16.9
15–25	53.9	38.0
25–40	42.8	30.2
>40	16.7	11.8
Total	141.7	100.0

Table 3.53a—Details of individual bone samples from Pit 16, Ring-ditch 3 (Z5:4).

Bone	Weight (g)	Percentage of identifiable bone
Skull	14.4	
		Skull 24.2%
Rib	0.5	0.8
		Axial 0.8%
Scapula	4.1	6.9
Humerus	15.8	26.6
		Upper limb 33.5%
Femur/patella	9.6	16.2
Tibia	10.2	17.2
Fibula	4.8	8.1
		Lower limb 41.5%
Total	59.4	100

Table 3.53b—Details of individual bone samples from Pit 16, Ring-ditch 3 (Z5:4).

	(1)	(2)
Fragment size (mm)	Weight (g)	Percentage by weight
<10	0.6	3.8
10–15	5.8	18.1
15–25	28.3	25.6
25–40	39.3	3.5
>40	16.7	
Total	90.7	51.0

Table 3.54—Fragment size of bone samples (S73:14) from lining of Pit 10.

Fragment size (mm)	Weight (g)
<10	6.5
10–15	10.3
15–25	3.8
>25	2
Total	22.6

S74:30, Pyre spread H3, Ring-ditch 2

This sample consisted of 24g of cremated bone, consisting of 116 fragments. The bone was dusty with charcoal but the underlying colour was white, indicating efficient cremation. The largest fragment was 24mm in length. A total of 4.1g (17%) was identified as fragments of skull. The remainder were fragments of long bone, including some fragments of joint ends.

Pit 16, Ring-ditch 4, Z5:d

This sample weighed 141.7g, representing only part of a cremation. The bone was white in colour and efficiently cremated, with only a tiny proportion (2%) consisting of bone that had some organic component remaining. The bone was moderately fragmented, with a low number of small fragments and very large fragments (Tables 3.47 and 3.52); the largest fragment was 44mm long.

It was possible to identify 59.4g (42%) of the sample (Tables 3.53a and 3.53b). Not all bones of the skeleton were present. It seems that most of the bones were long bones and skull, along with a small amount of axial skeleton. There was no repetition of skeletal elements and the size of the bones and the fact that the joint ends had been fused to the shafts of the long bones indicate that one adult individual was present.

3.16.4 Other locations

Pit O

This sample came from the black, sticky, semicircular area at the bottom of Pit O. Only two fragments of bone were present, one 26mm in length and the other 27mm, with a total weight of 2.2g. The bone was white in colour, heavily weathered and difficult to identify, but appeared to represent a long bone fragment and a fragment of the parietal bone from a human skull.

S74:24, Sq. Y

This sample consisted of twelve fragments of white/grey cremated bone with a total weight of 0.2g. The largest fragment was 8mm in length and the remainder were all less than 5mm. The bone was human but was unidentifiable.

S74:64 (no location)

This sample consisted of 2.8g of cremated bone in 23 fragments. The bone was grey in colour and highly fragmented; the largest fragment was 15mm in length. Most of the fragments were fragments of long or short bones, with a few small fragments of skull (0.4g) identified.

3.16.5 Summary

Cremated bone from six contexts was examined. In contrast to most samples, one of the cremations had been buried in an urn; this and another were contained in stone settings. The protected burials were not highly fragmented, so it was possible to acquire more information from them than from the other burials. One was an older male and the other an unaged female. The older male had severe degenerative joint disease in the vertebral column and possibly osteoporosis. It was not possible to age the female.

Other samples were from small pits throughout the site and contained small quantities of human bone. Pit 16, Ring-ditch 4, contained 141.7g of human bone, representing one individual. (See Table 3.47.)

3.16.6 Inventory of Burials 1, 2, Pit 16

Burial 1, Ring-ditch 2, S73:10
This burial is represented by two samples, one on exhibition in the National Museum of Ireland (1), the other in storage (2).

Sample 1 consisted of 108.4g of cremated bone. The bone was white/cream in colour, indicating efficient cremation. There were numerous cracks and fissures on the bone surface. The largest fragment was 70mm in length and the fragmentation of the sample is presented in Table 3.48a. Most of the sample consisted of very large fragments, but these were probably deliberately picked for the museum display.

Owing to the large fragment size, it was possible to identify 54.1g (50%) of the sample. The weight and descriptions of the identified elements are given below.

Skull (22g): fragments of squamous occipital and parietal bones with small areas of sutures visible. There was a fragment of frontal bone with plaques of hyperostosis frontalis interna present. A root of one tooth, probably a premolar, was present.

Vertebrae (7g): a fragment from the superior articular surface of a first cervical vertebra and fragments from other lower cervical and thoracic vertebrae. There were also fragments from the lumbar area. There was severe degenerative joint disease (DJD) and osteoarthritis on the posterior articular surfaces of the cervical and thoracic region, with porosity of the surfaces and eburnation. There was also severe DJD in the lumbar region.

Rib (1.9g): the left first rib and two other rib fragments.

Scapula (0.9g): one fragment of the lateral border of a bone.

Radius (2.1g): one fragment from the proximal third and the proximal surface of a right bone.

Hand phalanges (0.7g): one proximal phalange and the head of a first metacarpal.

Femur (16.3g): fragments of the posterior surface in mid-shaft with the linea aspera visible. There were also fragments from the anterior surface in the distal half of the shaft and some of the medial surface from the proximal end.

Tibia (3.2g): fragments from mid-shaft.

Sample 2 consisted of 708.9g of cremated bone. The bone was mainly white/cream in colour, indicating efficient cremation, although 45.3g (6%) of the sample consisted of fragments that were partially blue in colour, where there was some organic content remaining in the bone. There were numerous cracks and fissures on the bone surface. The largest fragment was 73mm in length and the fragmentation of the sample is given in Table 3.48b. Nearly half of the sample consisted of large and very large fragments, and there was a small proportion of small fragments.

Owing to the large fragment size, it was possible to identify 326.1g (46%) of the sample. The weight and descriptions of the identified elements are given below.

Skull (120.9g):

- *Frontal*: fragments of squamous frontal bone with a fragment of one orbit.
- *Parietal*: the posterior part of the left parietal bone with the foramen and part of the sagittal and lambdoid sutures visible. There was also part of a right parietal bone with the lambdoid suture and several small fragments of parietal bone. The sagittal suture was almost obliterated.
- *Temporal*: the petrous parts of a left and a right temporal bone and a fragment of a mastoid process that was probably from a male individual.
- *Occipital*: the right side of the squamous occipital bone with the lambdoid suture visible, as well as a fragment from the middle of the occipital bone. The right occipital condyle and part of the basilar occipital bone were also present.

- *Zygomatic*: part of the right zygomatic bone and a fragment of the left bone.
- *Maxilla*: the orbital part of the left maxilla.
- *Mandible*: the internal surface of the central part of the mandible with the genial tubercles present. Also another fragment with three sockets present, possibly 32, 33 and 34.
- *Teeth*: these included the root and base of the crown of two mandibular and four maxillary molars, including a second and a third molar. There were eleven single rooted teeth, including two incisors and two partial roots. A crown, possibly from an unerupted third molar, was present and there were other small fragments of crown.

Vertebrae (34g): a minimum of four cervical vertebral bodies, the left side of the arch of T1, other fragments of thoracic bodies, fragments of lumbar bodies, a lumbar spine and the right ala and dorsal surface of the sacrum. At least two of the cervical bodies displayed collapse, with severe marginal and vertical osteophytes forming a buttressing effect to the side of the bodies. In the lumbar vertebral bodies there seemed to be severe porosity of the articular surfaces, mild osteophytes and possible collapse of the centre of the body. The seventh cervical vertebra had severe osteoarthritis on the inferior posterior articular surface, with porosity and eburnation of the surface. The left superior facet on T1 also had severe lipping and porosity, with severe lipping on the inferior facet. There were other fragments of buttressing on the sides of vertebral bodies, possibly thoracic bodies. Degenerative joint disease was also visible on isolated articular surfaces.

Rib (13.2g): there were several rib fragments, representing at least seven left and eight right bones. Most fragments consisted of the medial part of the shaft, with some transverse tubercles and at least two heads present. Degenerative joint disease was evident on a few of the joint surfaces.

Clavicle/scapula (8.9g): the sternal end of the shaft of one clavicle and the sternal facet of another. The joint surface was very porotic. The base of the acromion and the medial part of the acromial spine from a left bone was identified, as well as a fragment from the base of the acromion and the medial part of another acromial spine.

Humerus (21.2g): the head of one humerus and the distal end of a left bone, including part of the trochlea and part of the distal shaft. There was also a fragment from another trochlea and fragments of proximal shaft and from the mid-shaft area with the deltoid tuberosity.

Radius (6.3g): one fragment from a head, a fragment from the distal end of the right bone and fragments from the proximal and mid-shaft areas.

Ulna (7.2g): fragments from the proximal shaft and the distal shaft.

Hand phalanges (0.5g): one proximal phalange.

Femur (92.4g): large fragments of shaft from the posterior surface in the mid-shaft area with the linea aspera visible. There were also fragments from the posterior surface in the distal half of the shaft and some of the anterior and posterior surfaces from the proximal end.

Patella (1.3g): the lateral half of a left patella.

Tibia (14.7g): fragments from the mid-shaft area and the distal shaft.

Tarsals/metatarsals/phalanges (5.5g): fragments from the superior surface of a talus, the head of a talus, the medial and anterior articular surfaces from a calcaneum, the proximal ends of two metatarsals, a first proximal phalange and one other proximal phalange.

Burial 2, Ring-ditch 2

There were several individual samples from E84-8484, which were extracted from the urn in a stratigraphic sequence and are described separately.

(1) Bones from the first 2in. of fill. This sample consisted of 111.9g of cremated bone. The bone was mainly white in colour but 15.9g (14%) of the sample consisted of fragments that were partially blue in colour, indicating that there was still some organic part of the bone remaining. The fragmentation of the sample is given in Table 3.50a. Nearly half of the sample consisted of very large fragments more than 40mm in length, with the largest fragment 70mm long, and there was a very low number of small fragments.

It was possible to identify 65.8g (59%) of the sample. The weights and descriptions of the various identified skeletal elements are given below.

Skull (0.9g): a fragment from the posterior part of the temporal bone.

Vertebrae (3.1g): fragments of vertebral arches.

Ribs (1.8g): fragments of shaft.

Pelvis (0.9g): a fragment of ilium with part of the sciatic notch present.

Humerus (10.8g): a complete head of a humerus (HuHd 42.78mm) as well as fragments of shaft and a fragment from the distal end with part of the trochlea and capitulum present.

Ulna (1.3g): a fragment from the proximal articular surface.

Radius (4.2g): fragments from the mid-shaft and distal shaft areas.

Femur (22.8g): the posterior surface from the distal end of the shaft and fragments of the anterior surface in the mid-shaft area. There was also a fragment from the anterior surface at the proximal end.

Tibia (15.7g): fragments of shaft from the distal and proximal ends of the bone from the anterior and posterior surfaces.

Fibula (3.9g): a few fragments from the mid-shaft area.

Tarsals/metatarsals/phalanges (0.4g): one fragment of calcaneum.

(2) Bones from the centre of the urn, 2–4in. deep. This sample consisted of 46.8g of cremated bone. The bone was mainly white in colour, although a significant amount, 16g (34%), consisted of fragments that were blue or black in colour, indicating that they had barely been burnt and not fully cremated. The fragmentation of the sample is given in Table 3.50b. Over half of the sample consisted of fragments less than 15mm in length; the largest fragment was 39mm long.

As the sample was highly fragmented, it was only possible to identify 7.1g (15%) of the sample.

Skull (4.7g): small fragments of calvarium, a fragment of maxilla with a few partial but unidentifiable sockets, and another fragment with a socket for a molar tooth. There was also a fragment of mandible with sockets for the following teeth:

	43 42 41 31

Vertebrae (0.3g): a few isolated articular surfaces.

Ribs (1.5g): a few fragments of shaft.

Hand bones (0.3g): a shaft of a proximal hand phalange.

Tarsals/metatarsals/phalanges (0.3g): the head of one metatarsal and the distal half of a proximal phalange.

(3) Bones from the centre of the fill, 2–4in. deep. This sample consisted of 62.7g of cremated bone. The bone was mainly white in colour, although a significant amount, 28.7g (46%), consisted of fragments that were blue or black in colour, indicating that they had barely been burnt or not fully cremated. The sample was moderately fragmented (see Table 3.50b), mostly consisting of small to medium-sized fragments, less than 25mm in length; the largest fragment was 51mm long.

It was possible to identify 22.4g (36%) of the sample. The weight and descriptions of the various identified elements are given below.

Skull (9.3g):

- Parietal: a large fragment with the sagittal suture present, as well as another small fragment.
- Teeth: one single rooted tooth root, canine or premolar, and one other premolar root.

Vertebrae (0.9g): fragments of the left side and the right side of a cervical arch.

Ribs (1.4g): small fragments of shaft.

Humerus (2g): fragments of the anterior surface from the distal part of the shaft.

Ulna (3g): the proximal end of the left ulna, with the articular surface and olecranon present. There was also a fragment from the mid-shaft area.

Carpals/metacarpals/phalanges (0.6g): the proximal end of a fifth metacarpal, one other metacarpal fragment and a complete distal hand phalange.

Femur (4.3g): one fragment from mid-shaft.

Tibia (0.9g): one fragment from mid-shaft.

(4) E84-8484: bone from the centre of the urn (sample from Groningen from this bag), 2–4in. deep. This sample consisted of 155.7g of cremated bone. The bone was mainly white in colour but 23.9g (15%) consisted of fragments that were blue or black in colour, indicating that there was still some organic content to the bone. Most of the sample consisted of large and very large fragments, the largest being 54mm long, and there were only a very small number of small fragments (see Table 3.50b).

It was possible to identify 105.4g (68%) of the sample. The weights and descriptions of the identified skeletal elements are given below.

Skull (73.3g):

- *Frontal*: fragments of squamous frontal and an almost complete left orbit, probably from a female individual.
- *Parietal*: a fragment of the posterior part of the left parietal bone with the lambdoid and squamous sutures visible. A large fragment of the right parietal with the lambdoid suture was also present. Other fragments with the sagittal suture were present.
- *Temporal*: the petrous part of the right parietal bone.
- *Occipital*: the right side of the squamous occipital bone.
- *Zygomatic*: the left zygomatic bone was almost

complete.

- *Mandible*: the right mandibular condyle was present; there was also a fragment with the genial tubercles present, as well as another fragment with one socket, possibly for a canine tooth.

Vertebrae (1.1g): the left side of a thoracic arch with the superior and inferior articular surfaces, and part of a first cervical vertebra with the articular area for the dens present.

Ribs (5.2g): various fragments of shaft.

Clavicle/scapula (6.1g): a fragment of clavicle shaft, the almost complete glenoid fossa of a scapula and an acromial spine.

Humerus (10.6g): fragments from the posterior surface near the distal end and fragments from the mid-shaft and proximal shaft areas.

Radius (2.9g): part of a radial head and proximal shaft and fragments from the mid-shaft area.

Ulna (0.6g): the distal end of the shaft with part of the head attached.

Carpals/metacarpals/phalanges (0.6g): the shaft of a metacarpal and one almost complete proximal phalange.

Femur (2.8g): a fragment of shaft.

Tibia (2.2g): a fragment of the posterior surface near the proximal end with the nutrient foramen visible, as well as fragments from mid-shaft.

(5) Sample 5 consisted of 152.9g of cremated bone. The bone was mainly white/cream in colour, indicating efficient cremation, although 19.7g (13%) of the sample consisted of fragments that were partially blue or black in colour, indicating that there was some organic content remaining in the bone. There were numerous cracks and fissures on the bone surface of the larger fragments. The sample consisted of moderate to large fragments, the largest being 80mm in length. Less than a quarter of the sample consisted of small and very small fragments (see Table 3.50b).

Owing to the large fragment size, it was possible to identify 82.6g (54%) of the sample. The weight and descriptions of the identified elements are given below.

Skull (43.9g):

- *Frontal*: small fragments of squamous frontal.
- *Parietal*: fragments from the anterior part of a left and a right bone with the coronal and sagittal sutures visible; the posterior part of the right parietal with part of a sagittal suture; a fragment from the anterior part of a right bone with the squamous suture visible, as well as other small fragments of parietal bone.
- *Temporal*: a fragment of right temporal bone with the mandibular fossa visible; a fragment from the posterior part of a right temporal bone with part of a mastoid area.
- *Occipital*: a large fragment of the left side of the squamous occipital bone, as well as other small fragments.
- *Maxilla*: a fragment from the nasal border of the maxilla.
- *Mandible*: a fragment from the internal surface of a mandible with the genial tubercles visible and fragments from the sockets of three anterior teeth.
- *Teeth*: the root of one maxillary molar and two other root fragments.

Vertebrae (4.3g): the right half of a second cervical vertebra; the odontoid process of a second cervical vertebra; a fragment of lower cervical body and fragments of cervical arches. A few articular surfaces from lumbar vertebrae were present.

Ribs (3.6g): fragments of shaft representing a minimum of two right ribs.

Humerus (5.9g): small fragments of shaft.

Radius (4g): fragments of shaft and distal articular surface.

Ulna (0.9g): fragments from the distal area of shaft.

Carpals/metacarpals/phalanges (0.9g): a scaphoid, a right lunate and the head of a first metacarpal.

Femur (10g): fragments of the posterior surface from the middle and distal areas of the shaft.

Tibia (8.6g): fragments of shaft, including fragments from the posterior and anterior surface from the proximal end and some fragments from the distal end.

Tarsals/metatarsals/phalanges (0.5g): fragments of talus as well as a proximal phalange.

(6) E84:8484: Bags 6 and 7: bones from last 3in. of fill 4–7in. This sample consisted of 105.7g of cremated bone. The bone was mainly white in colour, indicating efficient cremation, but 19g (18%) were blue, indicating organic content to the bone. Most of the sample consisted of large and very large fragments, the largest 77mm long, with only a very small number of small fragments present (see Table 3.50b).

It was possible to identify 79.4g (75%) of the sample. The weights and descriptions of the identified bone are given below.

Skull (45g):

- *Frontal*: the right side of the frontal bone with the orbit. Also fragments of squamous frontal, some with the crista interna present.
- *Parietal*: the anterior part of the left parietal bone with the coronal suture.
- *Temporal*: a mandibular fossa.
- *Maxilla*: a fragment from the right side of the maxilla with the following sockets: 14 13 12 11 – . A fragment from the posterior part of the maxilla was also present.
- *Mandible*: the right ramus of the mandible with the coronoid process and the internal angle visible, with part of a socket for a molar tooth. Also a small fragment of mandible with a few tooth sockets.

Vertebrae (0.6g): a few fragments of articular surface.

Ribs (1g): fragments of shaft.

Scapula (5.8g): a large fragment with the base of the acromion from a right bone as well as the lateral border. The glenoid surface had broken off.

Humerus (15.8g): the distal end of a right bone with the trochlea and capitulum present; the distal half of the shaft of a right bone with the lateral border visible, as well as smaller fragments from the mid-shaft area.

Radius (1.4g): part of a head and the neck and part of the proximal shaft from one bone.

Ulna (1.3g): one fragment from mid-shaft.

Femur (5.1g): fragments from the proximal shaft.

Tibia (3.4g): small fragments from the mid-shaft area.

(7) E84:8484: Bags 6 and 7: bones from last 3in. of fill 4–7in. This sample consisted of 90.9g of cremated bone. The bone was mainly white in colour, indicating efficient cremation, but 22g (24%) of the sample consisted of fragments that were blue or partially blue, indicating that there was still some organic content to the bone. Most of the sample consisted of large and very large fragments, the largest being 62mm long, with only a very small number of small fragments present (see Table 3.50b).

It was possible to identify 46.1g (51%) of the sample. The weights and descriptions of the identified bone are given below.

Skull (20.2g):

- *Parietal*: only a few small fragments were present.
- *Temporal*: the left petrous temporal bone was identified.
- *Sphenoid*: a greater wing of sphenoid was present.

Ribs (1.3g): fragments of shaft.

Humerus (7.4g): the distal end of a left humerus above the articular surface and with the lateral border visible, as well as smaller fragments from the distal end of a left bone.

Radius (4.4g): two fragments of shaft.

Ulna (1.6g): two fragments from mid-shaft.

Carpals/metacarpals/phalanges (1.4g): the head of a metacarpal and part of the shaft, another metacarpal shaft, one proximal and one middle hand phalange.

Femur (9.7g): fragments from the posterior and anterior surface of the proximal shaft.

Tarsals/metatarsals/phalanges (0.1g): a fragment of proximal phalange.

(8) E84:8484: Fragments of bone. This sample consisted of 1.3g of cremated bone. The bone was stained with charcoal, so colour was difficult to determine, but 0.3g (23%) of the sample was blue, indicating that there was still some organic content in the bone. Most of the sample consisted of small fragments of cancellous bone, which cannot be identified fully; the largest fragment was 17mm long (see Table 3.50b).

(9) E84:8484: Fragments of bone, clay, charcoal. This sample consisted of 3.1g of cremated bone. The bone was stained with charcoal but 0.6g (19%) of the sample consisted of fragments that were blue in colour, indicating organic content. Most of the sample consisted of small and very small fragments, the largest being 19mm long (see Table 3.50b). This made identification difficult, but it was possible to identify a fragment of rib (0.3g).

(10) E84:8484: Fragments of bone, clay, charcoal. This sample consisted of 1.2g of cremated bone. The largest fragment was 23mm in length (see Table 3.50b). It was not possible to identify the bone.

(11) E84:8484: Teeth. This sample contained all the teeth fragments from all the previous samples. The largest fragment was 17mm in length (see Table 3.50b). Teeth present included the roots of a maxillary and two mandibular molars, small fragments of molar roots, roots of at least three premolars and two canines, roots and crowns of a mandibular premolar and a central incisor, as well as smaller fragments of roots and tooth crowns.

Individual samples from Pit 16

(1) Pit 16, Ring-ditch 3, Z5:4. This sample consisted of

90.7g of cremated bone. The bone was mainly white in colour, indicating efficient cremation, with only a tiny amount, 1g (1%), consisting of fragments that were blue or partially blue, indicating some organic content. Most of the sample consisted of large and very large fragments, the largest being 44mm long, with only a very small number of small fragments present (see Table 3.53b).

It was possible to identify 53.9g (59%) of the sample. The weights and descriptions of the identified bone are given below.

Skull (9.6g):

- *Occipital*: a small fragment from the left side of the squamous part near the lambdoid suture and other small fragments of squamous occipital.
- *Parietal:* only a few small fragments.
- *Frontal*: one fragment of squamous frontal.

Rib (0.5g): one fragment from a left rib.

Scapula (4.1g): the base of the acromion and part of the acromial spine from a right bone.

Humerus (15.8g): the distal half of the shaft of a left bone with the lateral border visible, as well as smaller fragments from the middle and proximal areas of shaft.

Femur (9.6g): fragments from the anterior surface of the mid-shaft area.

Tibia (9.5g): a fragment from near the proximal end of a right bone with the medial surface visible, and a fragment from the distal end of the shaft.

Fibula (4.8g): two fragments from mid-shaft.

(2) Pit 16, Ring-ditch 3, Z5:4. This sample consisted of 51g of cremated bone. The bone was mainly white in colour, although 2.3g (4.5%) of the sample was blue, indicating some organic content. Most of the sample consisted of small and moderate-sized fragments, the largest being 30mm long, with only a few large fragments present (see Table 3.53b).

It was possible to identify 5.5g (11%) of the sample. The weights and descriptions of the identified bone are given below.

Skull (4.8g):

- *Parietal*: only a few small fragments were present.
- *Temporal*: a fragment of mastoid was identified.

Tibia (0.7g): a fragment of the proximal joint surface.

3.17 THE ANIMAL BONES FROM RATHGALL HILLFORT

Finbar McCormick

The animal bones survived very badly owing to the acidic nature of the soils (Table 3.55). About 700 fragments were collected, most of which were only between 1cm and 2cm in size. Of these only about 120 were identifiable. The vast majority were teeth, as enamel survives much better than ordinary bone in acidic conditions. As many of the teeth, especially those of cattle, were broken into small fragments, only their approximate number could be estimated. In many cases several teeth were found together, and this would indicate that originally the mandible or maxilla had been present but that the bone had rotted away. Many burnt fragments were present but in most cases these were unidentifiable. The sample of bones is too small to give any definite information on the food economy of the period except that cattle were the dominant animal present. Material from other Late Bronze Age sites in Ireland shows considerable variation in the livestock economy (McCormick and Murray 2007, 144). The low incidence of sheep/goat and pig at Rathgall is unusual but it is likely to be due to taphonomic factors, given the poor preservation of bone on the site.

Table 3.55—Animal bone analysed from the Rathgall excavations.

	Cattle	Pig	Sheep/goat
Skull frag.	1		
Teeth (approx.)	120	6	15
Humerus			1
Radius		1	2
Tibia		1	1
Astragalus		1	
Calcaneus			1
Metatarsal	1	4	
Metapodia		2	
Metacarpal			1
Phalanx	1		
Mandible			1
Total	93	12	19

3.18 A PRELIMINARY PALYNOLOGICAL INVESTIGATION AT RATHGALL HILLFORT, CO. WICKLOW

Gill Plunkett

3.18.1 Introduction

Palynological studies in the vicinity of Irish Late Bronze Age hillforts such as Haughey's Fort, Co. Armagh, Mooghaun, Co. Limerick, and Rahally, Co. Galway, have greatly complemented the archaeological record through their demonstration of extensive landscape exploitation at the time of hillfort occupation (Weir 1993; Molloy 2005; Molloy and O'Connell 2016). No such work had previously been undertaken in the vicinity of Rathgall, possibly owing to the absence there of an obvious classic coring site, such as a lake or a bog. In July 2006 a field visit was made to Rathgall hillfort to assess the potential for obtaining a palaeoenvironmental sequence that would enable a reconstruction of the environmental history of the area. Following the identification of marshy ground to the north of the hillfort, a core was collected and formed the basis for an outline pollen diagram, the results of which are presented here.

3.18.2 Methodology

Following an inspection of the landscape surrounding the hillfort, a small area of marsh (~50m in diameter) was identified in a field less than 1km (IGR S89802 73970) to the north of, and downhill from, the site (Figs 3.125 and 3.126). At the time, the field was being used for cattle grazing and the surrounding fields were under pasture. Permission was sought from the landowner to access the land and take a series of cores from the marsh.

Cores were extracted from alternating boreholes in the centre of the marsh using a Russian corer with a barrel diameter of 5cm and a length of 50cm. A total peat depth of 160cm was collected, below which dark grey silts were recorded. The cores were wrapped and sealed in polythene and brought back to the Palaeoecology Centre, Queen's University Belfast, for analysis and cold storage.

At the Palaeoecology Centre, the cores were opened and cleaned and the peat stratigraphy was recorded. Bulk peat samples of 1cm thickness were extracted from 140–141cm and 36–37cm for AMS ^{14}C dating. The samples were submitted to the Radiocarbon Laboratory, Queen's University Belfast, for pre-treatment, and were analysed at the Oxford Radiocarbon Accelerator Unit. Results were calibrated using OxCal 4.4.4 (Bronk Ramsey 1995; 2009) and the INTCAL2020 calibration curve (Reimer *et al.* 2020).

To assess the quality of pollen preservation through the core, samples of 0.5cm thickness were extracted at 8cm intervals between the depths of 28cm and 156cm. Samples were prepared using alkali digestion, acetolysis and sieving, and were washed in alcohol prior to mounting in silicon oil (Fægri and Iversen 1989). Pollen grains and palynomorphs were counted at x400 magnification on a Leitz Wetzlar light microscope. Cerealia-type pollen is distinguished from Gramineae on the basis of a minimum grain diameter of 37μm and minimum annulus diameter of 8μm (cf. Andersen 1979). As the purpose of this exercise was for assessment only, a minimum pollen sum of 200 terrestrial grains was chosen. When ^{14}C results became available, four additional pollen samples were subsequently extracted, prepared and counted from between 32cm and 40cm to provide a more detailed record (2cm resolution) of the later prehistoric landscape. Pollen counts for these levels were increased to a minimum of 300 terrestrial pollen grains. A pollen diagram was drawn up using Tilia (Grimm 1992; 2004; 2011). Percentages are based on total terrestrial pollen. An age model for the profile was obtained using the deposition model in OxCal (Bronk Ramsey 2008; 2009b; Bronk Ramsay and Lee 2013). The cores were re-examined in 2011 with a view to obtaining additional ^{14}C dates and increasing the pollen sampling resolution, but despite cold storage the condition of the uppermost (and most critical) core had deteriorated substantially and further analyses were not pursued.

3.18.3 Results

The peat profile consisted mainly of a dark, very well-humified amorphous peat, with occasional fine detritus. Below 148cm the peat was increasingly silty, representing the transition from the underlying silts to peat accumulation. The upper 36cm of the profile contained a high clay content and were penetrated by roots from surface vegetation.

Table 3.56—Radiocarbon dates from pollen recovered from Rathgall.

Depth (cm)	Lab. no.	^{14}C date	δ^{13}C	Calibrated range
36–37	UB-7129	2822±38 BP	-30	1120–850 cal. BC
140–141	UB-7130	12,294±61 BP	-29	12,870–12,110 cal. BC

Fig. 3.125—Location of the pollen core sampling site in relation to Rathgall and Knockeen hillforts (image from Google Earth).

Fig. 3.126—View of pollen core sampling site from east.

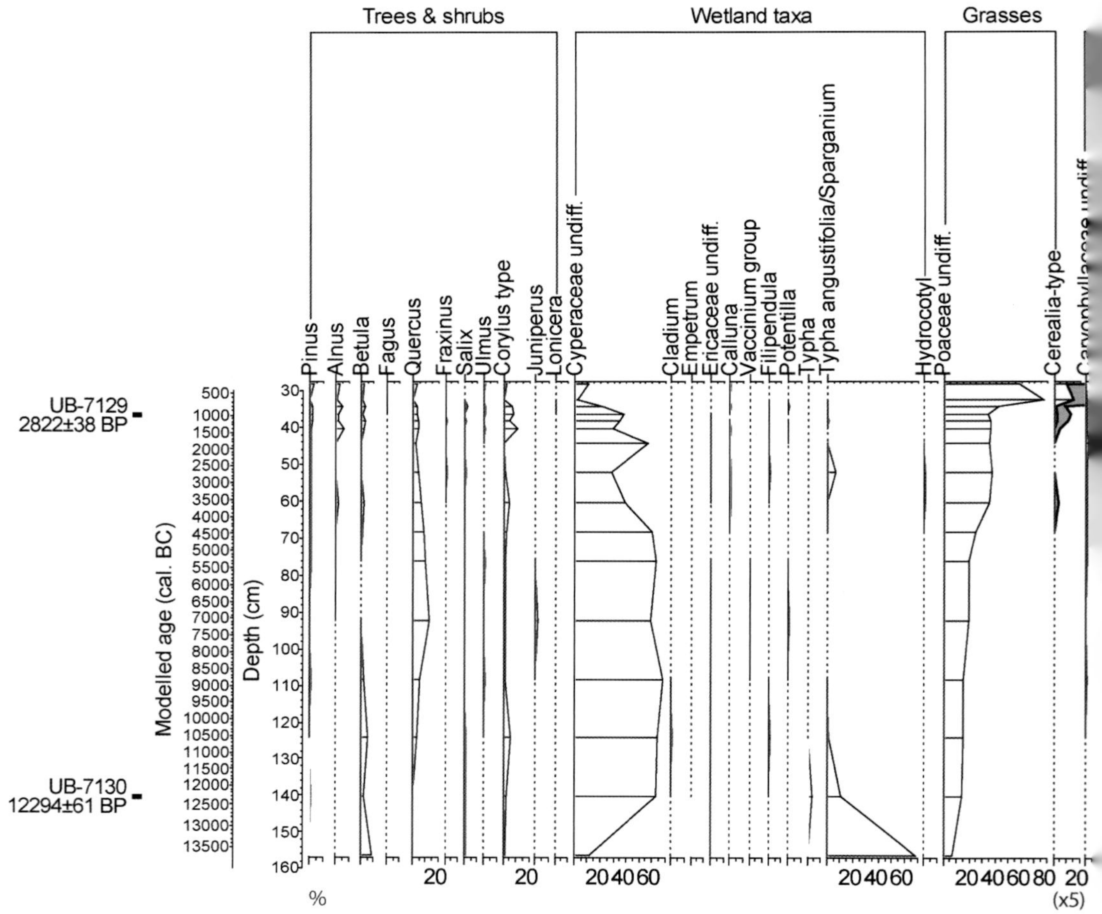

Fig. 3.127—Percentage pollen diagram from vicinity of Rathgall. Percentages are based on total terrestrial pollen. The period corresponding to the Middle and Late Bronze Age is highlighted by a grey band.

The ^{14}C results (Table 3.56) demonstrate that the peat at this site accumulated between at least *c.* 12,350 cal. BC and *c.* 1000 cal. BC, therefore apparently spanning the end of the Late Glacial and most of the Postglacial period. The available data suggest an average peat accumulation rate of 101yr cm^{-1}. Extrapolation of age estimates to 28–29cm, corresponding to the uppermost pollen sample examined, suggests a date of *c.* 300 cal. BC for the top of the profile. Although this should be considered a very rough estimate only, it nevertheless indicates that the sequence spans the period of interest, namely the Late Bronze Age (*c.* 1200–700 cal. BC). The pollen record (Fig. 3.127) reflects the change from a Late Glacial to Postglacial environment. Perhaps not surprisingly in view of the small size of the sampling basin, the record is strongly dominated throughout the profile by pollen derived from local taxa (i.e. plants growing in and around the marsh, probably within tens of metres of the sampling site), but there is nevertheless evidence for vegetation changes in the wider landscape (encompassing probably several hundreds of metres). The results are discussed below in terms of local environment, regional vegetation and human activity.

Local environment

At the base of the diagram, the aquatic *Myriophyllum* spp (water milfoils) and *Potamogeton* (pondweeds) and the semi-aquatic *Typha angustifolia*/*Sparganium* (lesser bulrush/bur-reeds) indicate that a small lake or pond was present in the Late Glacial period. As peat accumulated, the pollen record suggests the development of a rich fen community, dominated by Cyperaceae (sedge family) and Poaceae (grass family), which could include species such as *Phragmites australis* (common reed); other fen taxa include tall herbs such as *Filipendula* (meadowsweets) and *Potentilla* (cinquefoils), the semi-aquatic *Hydrocotyle* (pennyworts), *Equisetum* (horsetails) and possibly *Galium*-type (bedstraws). Although aquatic taxa decline during the Postglacial period, the continuing presence of small pools is demonstrated by a variety of algae that signify standing water. Aquatic plants are again evident in the uppermost levels as Cyperaceae declines,

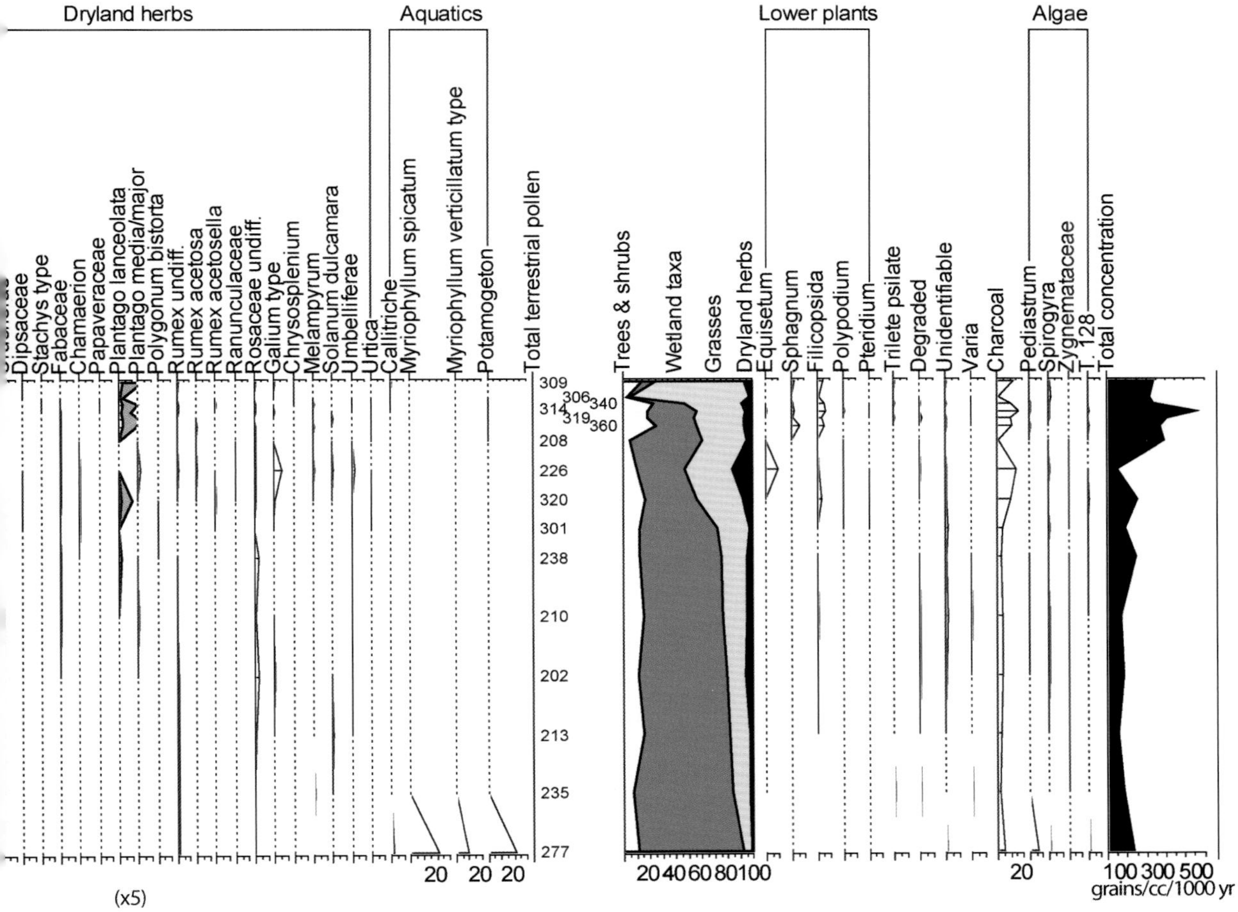

hinting that water-levels may have risen at the site.

Regional vegetation

The dominance of pollen derived from the local vegetation suppresses the representation of extra-local vegetation, but some comment regarding woodland development in the surrounding catchment is nevertheless possible. At the base of the profile, a Late Glacial landscape is characterised by scrub taxa *Betula* (birch) and *Salix* (willow), and *Empetrum* (crowberries), accompanied by *Artemisia* (mugworts) and *Rumex* spp (docks). *Corylus*-type (hazel) is relatively well represented by *c.* 10,500 cal. BC. *Quercus* (oak) is also evident at this time, somewhat earlier than expected, but the development of climax woodland is more certainly seen from at least *c.* 9000 cal. BC with the expansion of *Quercus*, the arrival of *Ulmus* (elm) and a corresponding decline of *Betula* and *Salix*. *Pinus* (pine) is unusually inconspicuous through the diagram but increases slightly *c.* 5500 cal. BC, when *Alnus* (alder) also makes its first appearance in this record. *Pinus* continues to be represented throughout the profile and, unlike in more northerly areas of Ireland, does not decline in the mid-Postglacial period. *Fraxinus* (ash) is evident in the upper part of the diagram and probably expanded as secondary woodland in the Neolithic period following anthropogenic disturbance of the forest.

Human activity

The mainly local nature of the pollen record hinders the recognition of small-scale human impact on the vegetation prior to the onset of farming. The first instance of Cerealia-type (grains referable to cereals) occurs at *c.* 3500 cal. BC, coinciding with a rise in Poaceae and *Plantago lanceolata* (ribwort plantain), and suggests farming activity in the vicinity of the sampling site during the Neolithic period. Microscopic charcoal values also increase from this time. Although Poaceae values remain high thereafter, farming appears to have declined by the late Neolithic, and Cerealia-type and *P. lanceolata* are not continuously represented until after *c.* 1400 cal. BC, after which time evidence for agriculture, represented mainly by these two taxa, is pronounced. Some woodland disturbance is suggested by declines in *Corylus*-type, *Alnus* and *Ulmus*. The ^{14}C determination at 36–37cm provides a calibrated date range of 1120–850 cal. BC and demonstrates that this increased activity also spans the period in which Rathgall hillfort was occupied, but the resolution of the samples is too low to determine whether there were declines or intensifications of activity between or within the Middle to Late Bronze Age. An intensification of arable agriculture in the immediate locality can be seen from *c.* 640 cal. BC, with Cerealia-type exceeding 14% of the total terrestrial pollen count. Poaceae values also rise substantially at these levels, suppressing all other taxa.

3.18.4 Discussion and conclusions

A peat sequence spanning the Postglacial period has been obtained from the vicinity of Rathgall hillfort. The sequence contains well-preserved pollen in sufficient concentrations to enable a reconstruction of the vegetation history of the area. The small size of the basin necessarily means that its pollen catchment will also be limited, but the site is located sufficiently close to Rathgall to allow land-use activities adjacent to the hillfort to be examined. The nearby presence of Knockeen hillfort should also be noted, however, and the Bronze Age activity identified in this record may well reflect farming associated with the occupation there. The dominance of local flora in the pollen record means that a substantial pollen count (>1,000–1,500 terrestrial taxa) is needed to obtain a better representation of the extra-local vegetation.

The significant dominance of local taxa results in a pollen diagram that does not reveal the typical Late Glacial to Postglacial transition from shrubland to climax forest, as seen further north in the Wicklow Mountains (Haslett *et al.* 2006; Leira *et al.* 2007). Nevertheless, it is evident that *Corylus* was a much less significant component of the woodland in this area, and that *Quercus* was the dominant tree taxon during the mid-Postglacial. Human activity is first recorded in the Rathgall sequence during the Neolithic period. Expansions in Poaceae at Kelly's Lough and Glendalough indicate a more general woodland clearance from this time (Bradshaw and McGee 1988; Haslett *et al.* 2006; Leira *et al.* 2007), although evidence for farming *per se* at these sites is lacking. A more substantial and sustained impact on the vegetation is seen from the Middle Bronze Age. The pollen record suggests that farming activity, including crop cultivation, took place from this time through to the Early Iron Age. A continuous cereal record is similarly found at Arts Lough, 25km to the north-east in the Wicklow Mountains (Bradshaw and McGee 1988). In view of the apparently slow accumulation rate of the peat near Rathgall, however, the current sampling resolution is rather coarse, with intervals of as much as 200 years possibly represented between samples. It is therefore not possible to ascertain whether human activity was continuous or intermittent across this period. In pollen diagrams from elsewhere in Ireland, an expansion of farming is evident during the Middle Bronze Age but declines briefly before a more considerable period of clearance and mixed agriculture from around 1000 cal. BC (Plunkett 2009a; Plunkett *et al.* 2009). Additional ^{14}C determinations would also have been required to establish the timing of events with more precision.

The results demonstrate that, as at other Late Bronze Age hillforts, some level of land exploitation, including arable farming, was taking place in the surrounding area during the period in which Rathgall was occupied. A more significant impact on the vegetation can be seen at a later date, perhaps towards the beginning of the Early Iron Age, when crop cultivation was almost certainly taking place on the land surrounding the marsh. Given the proximity of these samples to the surface of the field, it is possible that the upper levels have been directly affected by cultivation in the recent past.

3.19 THE ROLE OF WOOD IN LIFE AND DEATH AT RATHGALL: THE ANTHRACOLOGICAL RESULTS

Ingelise Stuijts

3.19.1 Introduction

The analysis of archaeological charcoal was part of Raftery's strategy for his excavations at Rathgall hillfort from the very start. The initial aim was to obtain dating evidence, but over time Raftery became aware of the environmental evidence that could be gleaned, recognising the potential of anthracological research over 50 years ago at Rathgall.

In prehistoric times, wood was one of the most utilised natural resources, for everything from the building of structures and means of transport to the crafting of domestic and artistic objects. Much wood ended its life in domestic fires, or was used as fuel in craft processes or funerary fires, leaving behind charcoal and ashes.

Deliberately made charcoal is also a useful resource, especially for obtaining high temperatures for the smelting of metal ores. On archaeological sites charcoal is one of the most common ecofacts, as it is chemically and physically inert and thus can be preserved on the dry-land site of Rathgall, where conditions preclude the preservation of wood.

The charcoal from the excavations is one of the few (plant) ecofacts that provides information on site conditions, fuel selection, and the features and nature of woods.

3.19.2 Methodology

Each piece of charcoal was examined under low magnification (4–40x), using a binocular microscope (Euromex). The individual lumps were then broken along the three major axes (cross-section, radial and tangential) to expose a clear surface. After temporary mounting in plasticine, the surfaces were studied under indirect light under a metallurgical microscope (Olympus) with higher magnification (100–400x). For species such as oak (*Quercus*) and ash (*Fraxinus*) the cross-section is often sufficient for a reliable identification. More characteristics are needed to identify other wood species, especially diffuse-porous species such as alder (*Alnus*) and willow (*Salix*). The identification followed the keys provided by Schweingruber (1978), Hather (2000) and Wheeler *et al.* (1989), and the author's reference collection.

Maloideae (formerly called Pomoideae, pomaceous fruitwood or apple-type) is included in the subfamily Spiraeoideae (Evans and Campbell 2002; Potter *et al.* 2007). This group includes wood species such as crab-apple (*Malus* sp.), wild pear (*Pyrus* sp.), hawthorn (*Crataegus* sp.) and whitebeam (*Sorbus* sp.). They are mentioned in the text and figures as apple-type and Maloideae respectively unless otherwise specified. The various genera from the Maloideae cannot be distinguished from each other on the basis of wood anatomy characteristics. Identification to genus level was therefore 'cf.' (Latin *confer* = 'compare'; the wood resembles a specific known taxon but they differ in detail). In two cases, however, a charcoal piece included fragments of a thorn, pointing to the presence of hawthorn (*Crataegus* sp.).

Microscopic and macroscopic details may inform on the *quality* of the wood that was burnt. The presence or absence of *bark*, *fungal hyphae* (especially in the radial sections) and *beetle channels*, for example, will all indicate whether the wood was fresh or derived from deadwood. *Frass*, or excrements, from beetles and other burrowing insects in channels can indicate that wood is not from recently felled trees but may derive from deadwood, stockpiles or rotten structures.

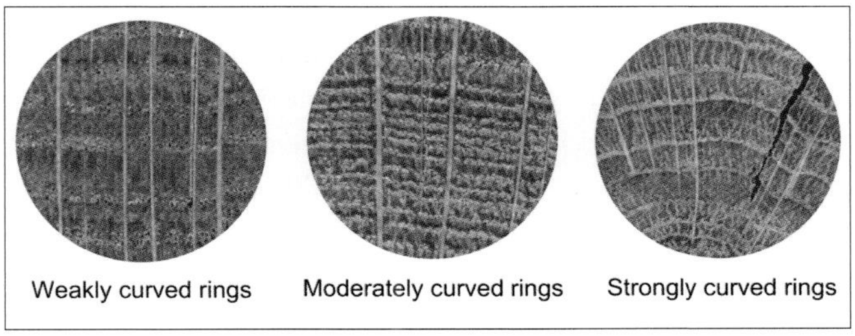

Fig. 3.128—Test card for evaluation of tree-ring curvature (after Marguerie and Hunot 2007).

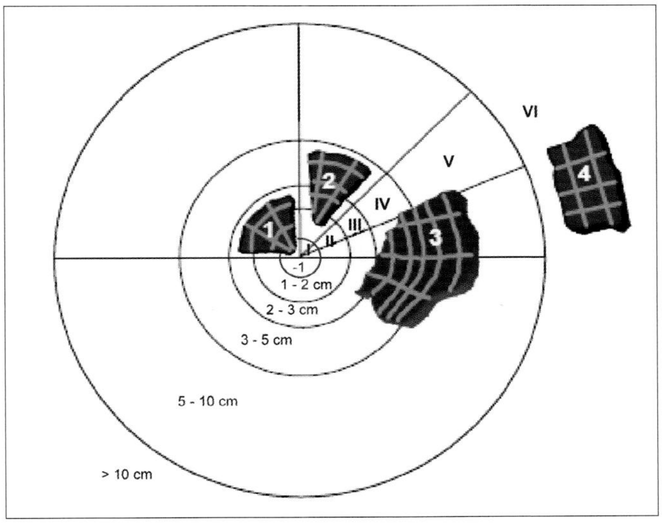

Fig. 3.129—Diameter template and examples of charcoal fragments to be sized (1–4) (after Ludemann 2006).

Distinct patterns and galleries located between bark and wood may be caused in living and/or dead wood, often in weak specimens, by bark beetles of the subfamily Scolytinae.

Large numbers of *tyloses* in vessels within the wood in species such as oak can denote the presence of heartwood. In sapwood tyloses are only found in small quantities (Dufraisse *et al.* 2017). The process of heartwood formation starts when deciduous oak is about 25 years old. The presence of many tyloses may therefore indicate that wood of some age with heartwood was burnt and thus provide supplemental information that wood from larger and older trees was burnt.

Growth patterns (fast, slow or medium, regular or variable) reflect the growing conditions and form of tree growth (e.g. Schweingruber 2001, 120). Fast-grown, uniformly rod-shaped brushwood may result from coppicing processes, but this is difficult to prove.

Gnarly wood has various origins, from scrub, roots, diseased and damaged trees, and is in general not suitable for use in construction.

Size matters. The distinction between twigs, brushwood, larger roundwood or trunk fragments may allow conclusions to be drawn regarding the activity providing the charcoal.

When bark and pith are present, the counting of annual rings will give the *age* of the tree that was burnt. Counting of the number of rings on any given charcoal piece reveals the minimum age and speed of growth, allowing comparison to other fragments in the same sample.

It is possible to estimate the former diameter of wood based on the curvature of its annual rings by using templates (Figs 3.128 and 3.129) (Marguerie and Hunot 2007; Ludemann 2006, fig. 5; Ludemann and Nelle 2002, fig. 13). Such estimates cannot be considered to give precise dimensions (Dufraisse and García-Martínez 2011; Dufraisse *et al.* 2018; Paradis-Grenouillet *et al.* 2013). In combination, however, the two templates offer a good estimation and help to distinguish between *twigs* (less than 10mm in diameter), *small brushwood* (up to 20mm), *brushwood* (between 20–30mm and 30–50mm), *roundwood* (between 50mm and 100mm) and *larger* material. It was occasionally possible to measure the diameter more accurately when the lumps included the actual outer limit.

Sometimes evidence of *woodworking* is preserved by form, facets or wood-waste chips.

3.19.3 The analysis programme

The Rathgall excavations commenced at a time when it was not customary to collect soil samples in bulk for comprehensive environmental analysis. Rather, areas that seemed rich in charcoal were sampled by hand-picking larger charcoal fragments. When bulk soil samples were taken, the quantities were relatively small, generally around 0.5l or less, compared to the modern preferences of from 10l up to 40–60l (English Heritage 2002; Institute of Archaeologists of Ireland 2007). Some samples therefore contained very little charcoal, whereas a few were so rich that they were divided into several bags. Sometimes multiple samples with different sample numbers were taken from larger features. The results are thus predictably skewed in favour of these.

Of the overall 146 samples (162 bags), an initial 46 sample bags were selected for analysis by Raftery in 2002. Later, thirteen sample bags were analysed in 2012 and 103 in 2021. In 2012 and 2021 the WODAN methodology (Stuijts *et al.* 2012) was applied and the characteristics of each individual charcoal fragment recorded, whereas analysis in 2002 presented lumped information only. As no overall sample register survived, identification of contexts relies mostly on sometimes varying descriptions on sample labels. Hence in Appendices 1 and 2 (dri.ie) results are presented per sample bag, even if they carry the same sample number. Growth patterns are also listed in these appendices, unless they inform the interpretation of the assemblage from a given context.

The recorded characteristics of the charcoal assemblages were evaluated in relation to the archaeological interpretation of the features, considering also taphonomic factors and especially drawing on information on the primary or secondary deposition of charcoal. Contexts are assigned to chronological stages adapted from the chronological model developed in Chapter 4, with BA1 referring to the rectangular structure in G, BA2 referring to all contexts dated to the main phase of Bronze Age activity, and BA3 representing the latest Bronze Age or Early Iron Age stage of the site (15m structure and related material). BA refers to likely Bronze Age phase, without any differentiation possible. In many instances the dating of samples is ambiguous.

3.19.4 Charcoal sample condition and quality

The charcoal from Rathgall is variable in quality. Many samples include lumps that are fragile, dirty, covered with minerals or a limy layer, and with beetle channels and/or modern roots. Some pieces are on the point of turning into soil, with many small voids, grainy and in colour more brown than black—the last step in a degradation process which is quite unusual for charcoal from an archaeological site (e.g. S78:024, Sq. H7; S78:062, Sq. K6). Possibly mechanical destruction by, for example, ploughing is a factor. In some samples the charcoal is somewhat rounded, a bit grey in colour and almost stone-like on the inside, but still so degraded, especially on the outside, that it falls apart when breakage is attempted (E84:138, Sq. 33; S70:012, Sq. 27; S72:100, Sq. G2). The rounded form in particular appears suggestive of water or waterlogged conditions possibly having played a role, but there is no indication of such having prevailed on the site. In contrast, other charcoal lumps are almost unbreakable, and when eventually broken do not show the clear surfaces one would expect (S70:012, Sq. 27, birch; S71:104, hazel).

Some samples were sieved in 2004 for soil analysis, possibly resulting in some cases in breakage and reduction in size, especially turning larger fragile oak lumps into radial slivers and reducing others to charcoal dust (S72:099, Sq.

D3). Because of such fragility, the remaining samples were not washed, sieved or prepared in any way before the extraction of identifiable charcoal.

The almost dirty appearance of charcoal lumps did cause some problems in identifying the presence of tyloses, but radial cracks could be observed without problems. The latter, especially in oak, have been discussed—but not securely established—as the results of the carbonisation of waterlogged, or green, wood (Prior and Alvin 1986; Théry-Parisot and Henry 2012). Temperature also plays a role (Théry-Parisot 2002). Because of their uncertain meaning, radial cracks are noted in Appendix 2 but not further discussed.

3.19.5 Results of charcoal analysis

The charcoal assemblage from Rathgall consists of a total of 146 samples (162 bags), representing 3,773 fragments weighing 1,170g, deriving from all areas of the excavation but primarily from Areas 1–3 (Table 3.57; Figs 3.130–3.132). The total results include identification of fourteen charcoal lumps by O'Donnell (Cummins *et al.* 2005) with some modifications. Wood usage in the main areas and the most noteworthy features is discussed here (with a general overview of the areas in Figs 3.133 and 3.134; Tables 3.58 and 3.59). Detailed description of all samples can be found in the online archive (Stuijts 2021, Rathgall charcoal report and Appendices 1 and 2). Except for the large samples from Area 3, only frequencies are mentioned in the text.

The charcoal assemblage represents a total of seventeen wood species: alder (*Alnus glutinosa*), birch (*Betula* sp.), hazel

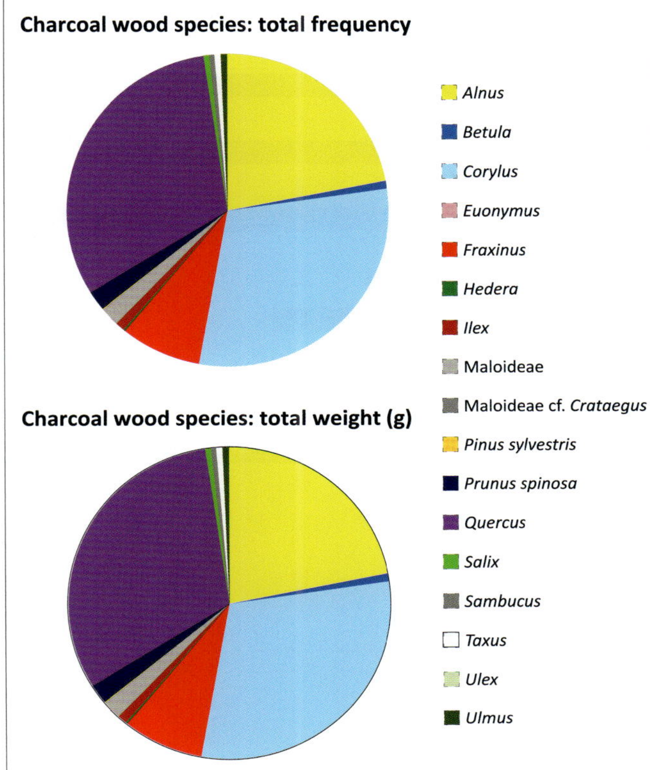

Fig. 3.130—Total results: frequency and weight (g).

Wood species	Frequency	Weight (g)	Sample score	English names
Alnus glutinosa	828	286.37	71	Alder
Betula sp.	31	22.49	10	Birch
Corylus avellana	1136	349.17	112	Hazel
Euonymus europaeus	1	0.24	1	Spindle
Fraxinus excelsior	307	135.82	62	Ash
Hedera helix	7	1.12	5	Ivy
Ilex aquifolium	35	4.21	13	Holly
Maloideae	72	18.33	26	Apple-type
Maloideae cf. *Crataegus* sp.	2	1.84	2	Hawthorn
Pinus sylvestris	4	4.35	4	Scots pine
Prunus spinosa	77	12.01	18	Sloe
Quercus sp.	1184	312.74	86	Oak
Salix spp	22	2.21	11	Willow
Sambucus nigra	19	1.23	4	Elder
Taxus baccata	23	11.3	2	Yew
Ulex europaeus	1	0.56	1	Gorse/furze
Ulmus glabra	24	6.15	10	Elm
	3773	1170.14	(162 is max.)	

Table 3.57—Charcoal identifications: total results.

Fig. 3.131—Total results: sample score (162 is maximum).

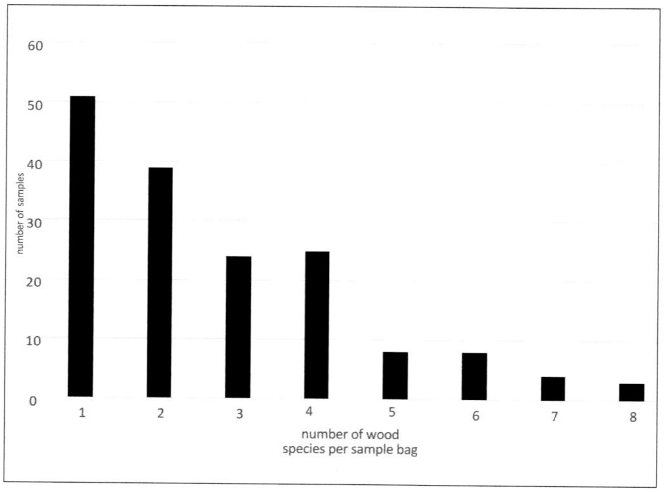

Fig. 3.132—Number of different wood species per sample bag.

(*Corylus avellana*), spindle (*Euonymus europaeus*), ash (*Fraxinus excelsior*), ivy (*Hedera helix*), holly (*Ilex aquifolium*), Scots pine (*Pinus sylvestris*), apple-type including hawthorn (Maloideae and Maloideae cf. *Crataegus* sp.), sloe (*Prunus spinosa*), oak (*Quercus* sp.), willow (*Salix* spp), elder (*Sambucus nigra*), yew (*Taxus baccata*), elm (*Ulmus glabra*) and gorse/furze (*Ulex europaeus*). These are all native species belonging to the natural flora of Ireland (Hickie 2002; Webb *et al.* 1996). In the following text, English names will be used for the various wood species. In the figures, however, only Latin names are used.

Across the site the dominant wood species in terms of fragment frequency numbers are hazel and oak, followed by alder (Fig. 3.130). By weight, hazel is slightly more common than oak (30% and 27% respectively), in contrast to the number of fragments identified (31% oak, 30% hazel), which may possibly be due to the aforementioned higher fragmentation in the post-excavation processing. It appears that both hazel and oak were equally important at Rathgall, though it must be kept in mind that a few very large samples provided most of the charcoal. Alder (24% weight, 22% frequency) and ash (12% weight, 8% frequency) are also common, but all other species are unimportant, with maximum values of 2%. In comparison with many investigated Irish sites (Stuijts 2007), the proportion of apple-type in particular is remarkably low.

In respect of the number of sample bags in which species occur, hazel is by far the most common wood species in Rathgall, occurring in 112 of the 162 sample bags (Fig. 3.131). Oak occurs in 86 sample bags, followed by alder in 71 bags and ash in 62 bags. Many samples contain only one wood species (51 of the 162 sample bags) or two wood species (39 sample bags) (Fig. 3.132). This could suggest selection of a wood species with little residual component, though small, hand-picked samples may skew the picture. Few samples include more than six wood species.

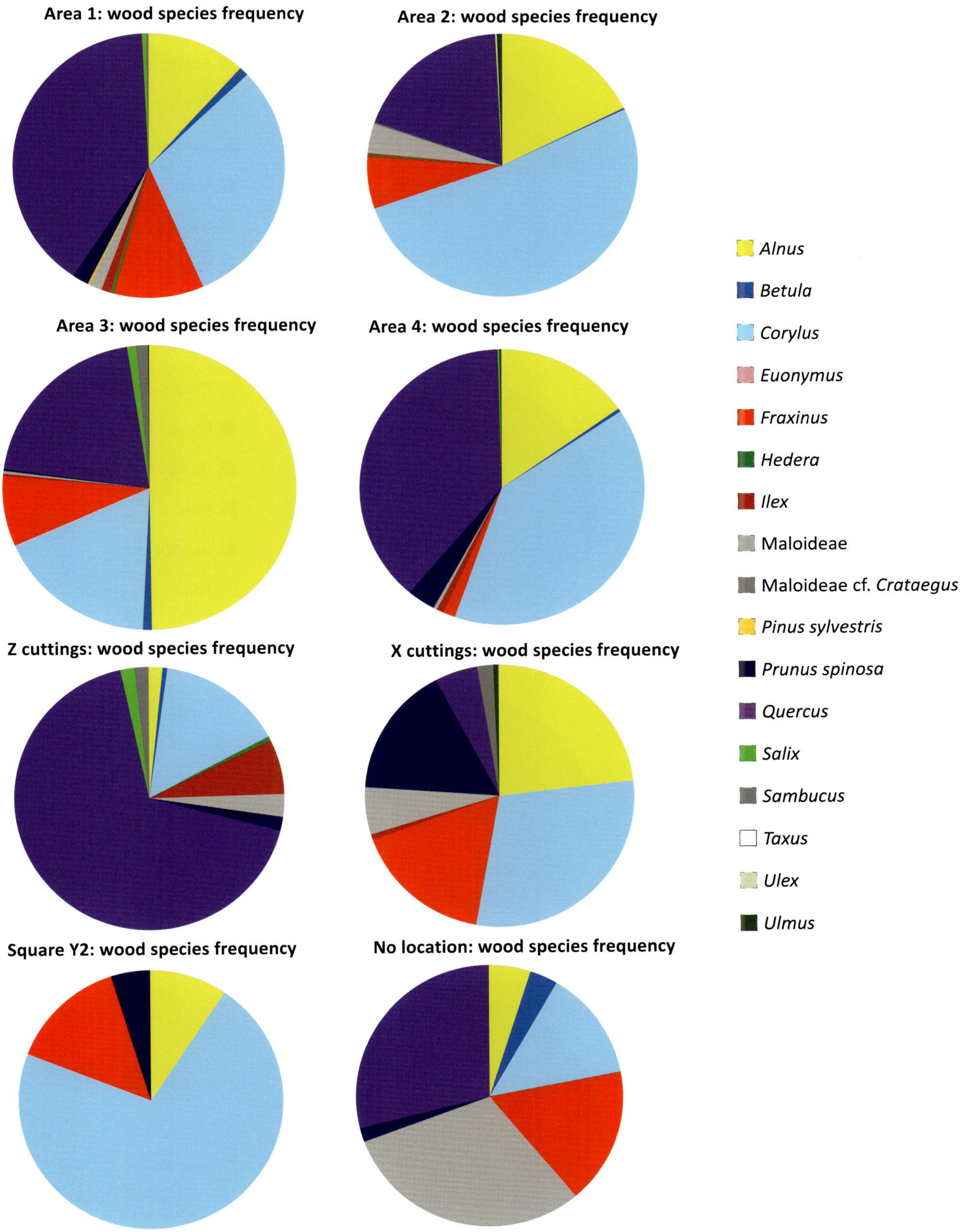

Fig. 3.133—Species frequency in all areas.

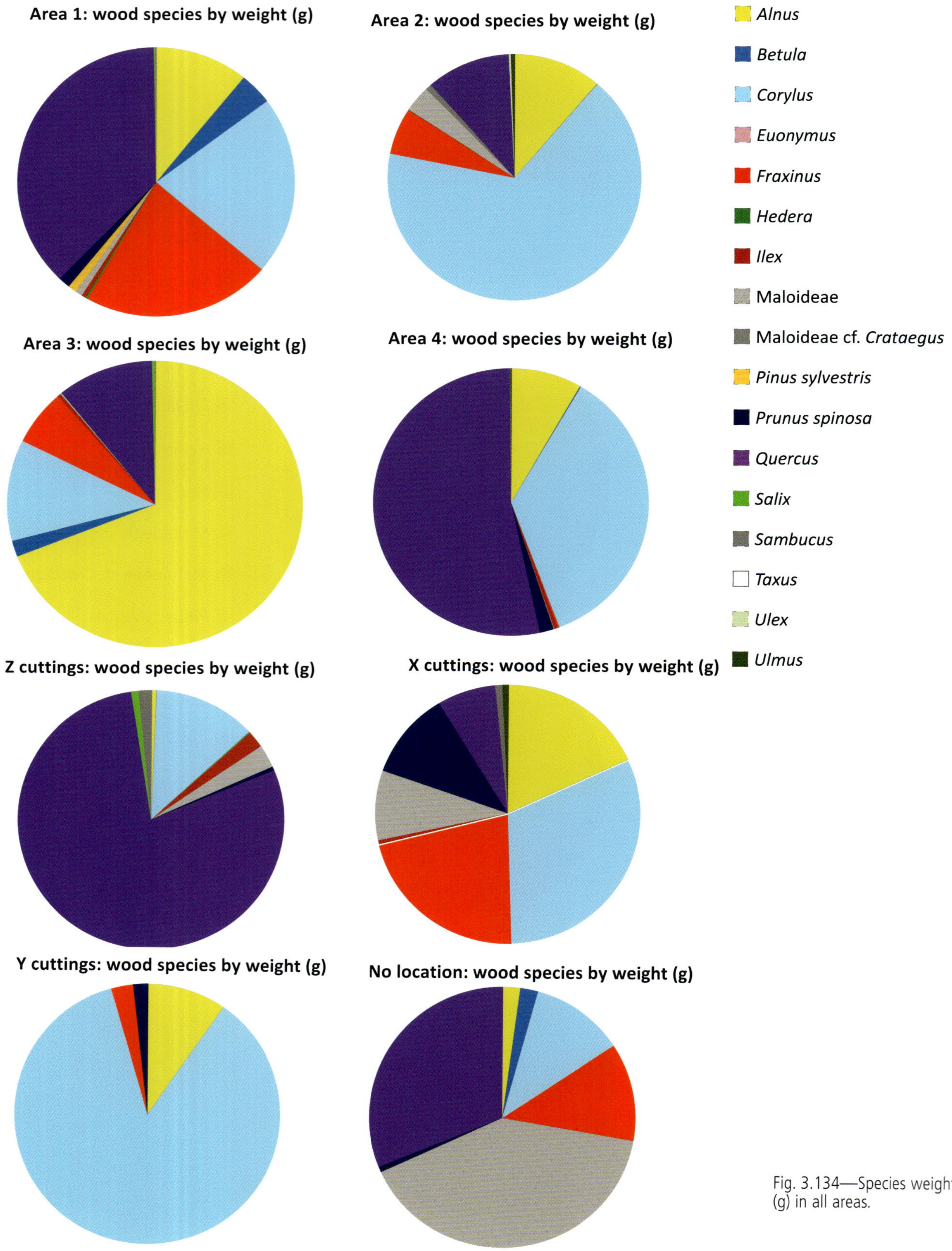

Fig. 3.134—Species weight (g) in all areas.

3.19.6 Area 1

Pit 119 (nine bags, six samples), BA2

The charcoal was sampled from the black 'lining' of the pit (S71:090A/B, 093A/B, 094A/B), also called the 'black bottom layer' (S71:092 and probably E84:6072), and one sample from black humus mixed with charcoal that may represent the top level of this black layer (E84:6071).

Only oak and ash are of importance (Fig. 3.135). Many fragments are from roundwood, not larger than 100mm in maximum dimension and mostly from immature trees, although a few pieces from mature, larger-sized oak of gnarly quality are present in samples S71:094A/B. A number of fragments, especially of oak, which dominates samples S71:090A/B and S71:093A/B, are gnarly wood of bad quality, most likely from tree roots, given the lack of beetle channels. Samples S71:094A/B are dominated by ash, which is from roundwood of rotten quality, with large channels. A few ash roundwood fragments from these and sample E84:6071 had been modified.

While Raftery used the term 'lining' to describe the black fill, considering the sizes of the wood and the virtual absence of hazel it is unlikely that the charcoal represents the remains of wickerwork. The presence of gnarly oak and rotten ash roundwood, which may represent rotten structural timbers, suggests the burning of otherwise unusable material. The burning of oak would be characteristic of pyre remains, as often evidenced in burials. The considerable amount of ashy

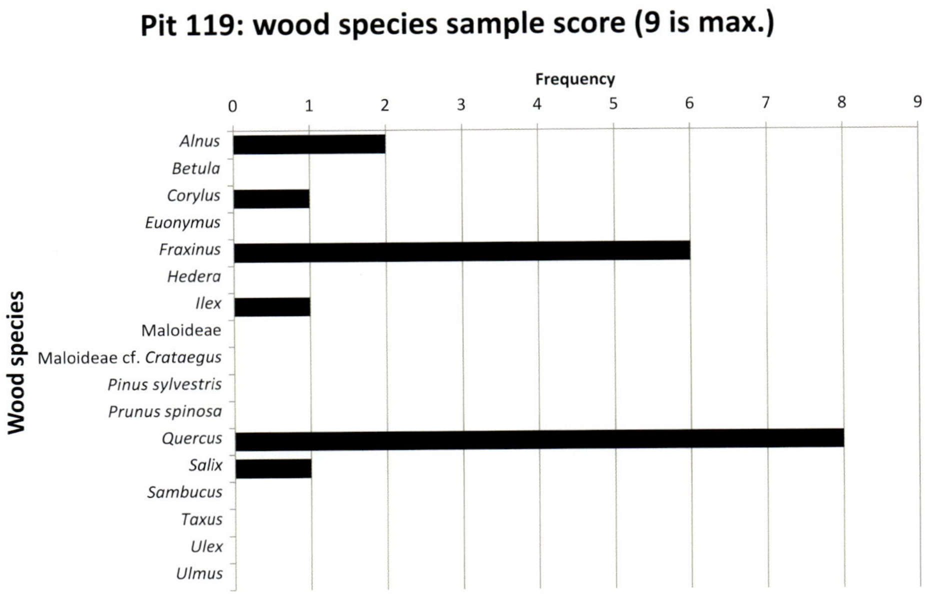

Fig. 3.135—Area 1, Pit 119: wood species frequency, weight (g) and sample score.

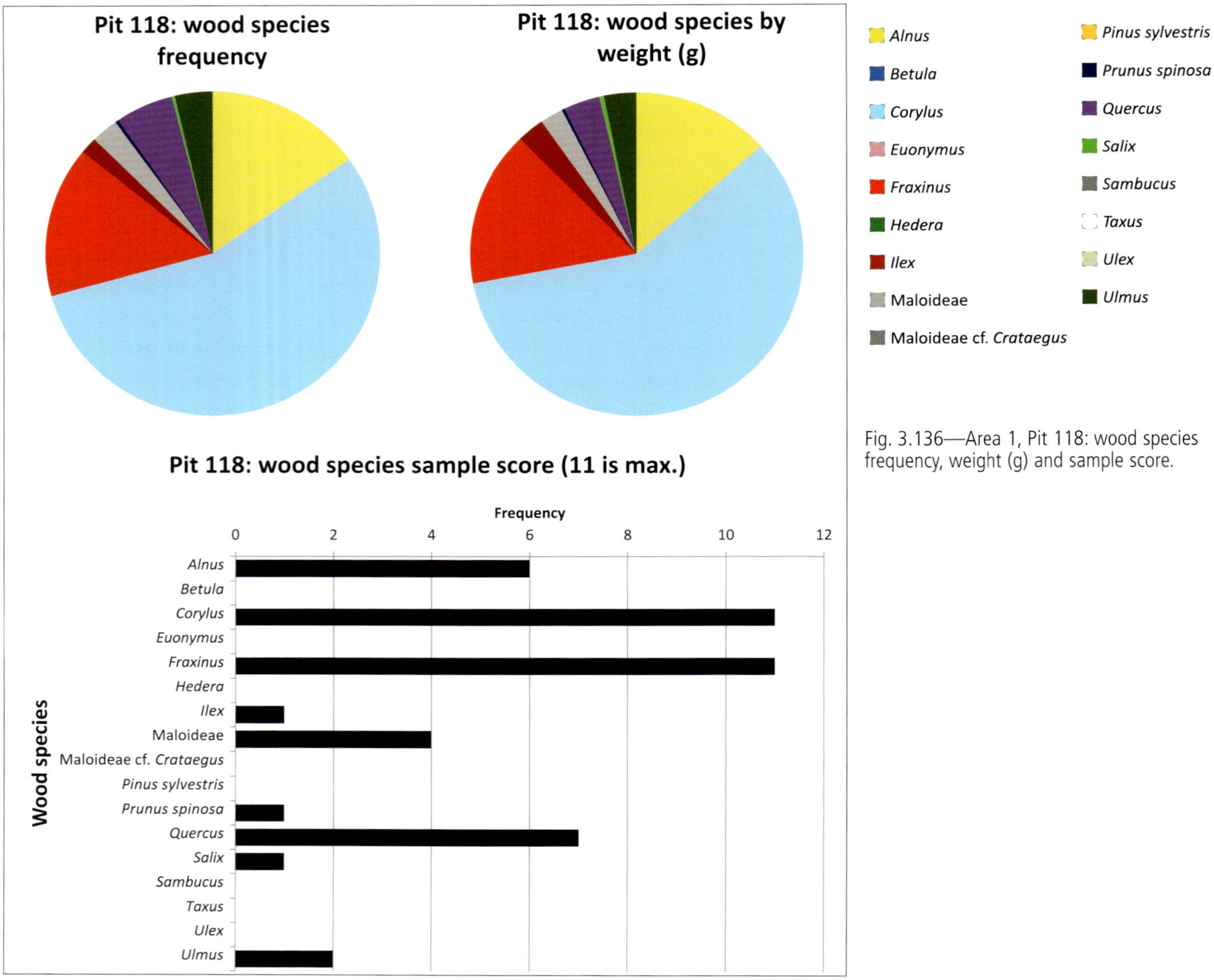

Fig. 3.136—Area 1, Pit 118: wood species frequency, weight (g) and sample score.

residue (especially in E84:6071, and further in S71:092 and S71:093B) would support the interpretation of *in situ* burning in a pyre.

Pit 118, Sq. 17/18 (eleven bags, ten samples), BA2

Hazel is the most important species in almost all samples, with almost 60% (Fig. 3.136), followed by alder and ash (15%) and oak (5%). Except for sample S71:096A from the black outer level, samples are small. The occurrence of small quantities of elm in two samples from wickerwork 2 is noteworthy (S71:099 and S71:105), as it is rare at the site.

Samples S71:096A/B and E84:5911 from the black outer level are dominated by hazel (34x), with some ash, alder, oak, some apple-type and one sloe. Most are twigs, small and larger brushwood. Some larger hazel and ash (50–100mm) and some apple-type (over 100mm) roundwood pieces are also present. Hazel and alder have frequent beetle channels, and a modified fragment of hazel suggests secondary use. Some bark is noted in the samples.

Two thin layers of black burnt material were interpreted by Raftery as basket inserts, separated by a sterile yellow clay layer. For wicker, usually thin twigs or rods, 10mm or less in diameter, are used. A small sample (S71:109) representing the first, outer layer of possible basketwork includes alder (11x), holly (5x), hazel (7x), ash (3x), oak (4x) and apple-type (1x). Beetle channels are noted in alder (many including frass), holly (medium), ash (few) and apple-type (many), indicating that these represent rotten wood fragments. Only the hazel is not rotten, but its diameter was not recorded in 2002.

Table 3.58a—Charcoal table: detailed results (frequency, weight) per area.

	Area 1	Area 1	Area 2	Area 2	Area 3	Area 3	Area 4	Area 4
Wood species	Frequency	Weight (g)	Frequency	Weight (g)	Frequency	Weight (g)	Frequency	Weight (g)
Alnus glutinosa	168	46.78	88	25.54	452	196.96	76	9.03
Betula sp.	16	16.8	1	0.09	9	5.25	2	0.15
Corylus avellana	435	92.96	286	173.82	162	32.37	197	39.15
Euonymus europaeus					1	0.24		
Fraxinus excelsior	152	95.18	38	14.66	74	17.94	7	0.21
Hedera helix	6	1.05	1	0.07				
Ilex aquifolium	16	2.34	1	0.05	2	1.05	4	0.48
Maloideae	21	3.51	18	7.98	3	0.48	2	0.08
Maloideae cf. *Crataegus* sp.			1	1.82				
Pinus sylvestris	4	4.35						
Prunus spinosa	28	6.01	2	0.42	2	0.09	16	1.8
Quercus sp.	567	162.34	93	24.84	188	29.99	190	58.2
Salix spp	7	0.69			9	0.9	1	0.04
Sambucus nigra	4	0.72			12	0.25		
Taxus baccata								
Ulex europaeus			1	0.56				
Ulmus glabra			3	1.23	1	0.04	1	0.2
Total	1424	432.73	533	251.08	927	290.72	496	109.34
	64 bags		37 bags		23 bags		22 bags	
	52 samples		35 samples		21 samples		22 samples	

Table 3.58b—Charcoal table: detailed results (frequency, weight) per area.

	Z cuttings	Z cuttings	X cuttings	X cuttings	Y cuttings	Y cuttings	No location	No location
Wood species	Frequency	Weight (g)	Frequency	Weight (g)	Frequency	Weight (g)	Frequency	Weight (g)
Alnus glutinosa	1	0.01	36	5.66	4	2.21	3	0.18
Betula sp.	1	0.01					2	0.19
Corylus avellana	2	0.02	46	9.85	30	19.77	8	1
Euonymus europaeus								
Fraxinus excelsior			26	6.77	6	0.62	10	1.06
Hedera helix								
Ilex aquifolium	7	0.13	1	0.16				
Maloideae	2	0.02	9	2.74			18	3.54
Maloideae cf. *Crataegus* sp.								
Pinus sylvestris								
Prunus spinosa	3	0.21	25	3.42	2	0.42	1	0.06
Quercus sp.	120	32.37	8	2.26			17	2.74
Salix spp	3	0.36						
Sambucus nigra			3	0.26				
Taxus baccata								
Ulex europaeus								
Ulmus glabra			1	0.25				
Total	139	33.13	155	31.37	42	23.02	59	8.77
	5 bags		9 bags		1 bag		1 bag	
	5 samples		9 samples		1 sample		1 sample	

Table 3.59a—Charcoal table: detailed results (frequency, weight) per period.

	BA	BA	BA1	BA1	BA2	BA2	BA2/3	BA2/3
Wood species	Frequency	Weight (g)	Frequency	Weight (g)	Frequency	Weight (g)	Frequency	Weight (g)
Alnus glutinosa	15	2.17	6	0.52	387	222.13	3	0.77
Betula sp.	1	0.01			9	5.33		
Corylus avellana	39	8.12	7	1.02	538	226.24	3	2.63
Euonymus europaeus								
Fraxinus excelsior	11	1.45	2	0.53	192	119.14	1	0.24
Hedera helix					4	0.76		
Ilex aquifolium	8	0.29			9	1.64		
Maloideae	7	2.14			32	10.41		
Maloideae cf. *Crataegus* sp.					1	1.82		
Pinus sylvestris								
Prunus spinosa	8	1.16			23	5.11		
Quercus sp.	134	34.39			287	101.42	20	4.84
Salix spp	3	0.36			3	0.41		
Sambucus nigra								
Taxus baccata								
Ulex europaeus					1	0.56		
Ulmus glabra	2	0.29			15	4.6		
Total bags	9		1		67		4	
Total samples	9		1		60		2	

Table 3.59b—Charcoal table: detailed results (frequency, weight) per period.

	BA3	BA3	IA	IA	Med.	Med.	Poss. BA	Poss. BA
Wood species	Frequency	Weight (g)	Frequency	Weight (g)	Frequency	Weight (g)	Frequency	Weight (g)
Alnus glutinosa	90	8.38			12	1.98	74	11.02
Betula sp.			1	0.05			1	0.01
Corylus avellana	50	4.6	47	19.08	15	1.42	62	12.16
Euonymus europaeus								
Fraxinus excelsior	21	1.1					24	5.67
Hedera helix			2	0.3				
Ilex aquifolium	7	1.06						
Maloideae							4	0.62
Maloideae cf. *Crataegus* sp.								
Pinus sylvestris								
Prunus spinosa	1	0.01	1	0.2	21	2.44	1	0.12
Quercus sp.	225	31.7	10	2.82	95	22.92	60	25.41
Salix spp	1	0.01					14	0.47
Sambucus nigra	1	0.04			3	0.26		
Taxus baccata			23	11.3				
Ulex europaeus								
Ulmus glabra								
Total bags	10		2		6		12	
Total samples	8		1		4		11	

Table 3.59c—Charcoal table: detailed results (frequency, weight) per period.

	Med.?	Med.?	BA or Med.	BA or Med.	Unknown	Unknown
Wood species	Frequency	Weight (g)	Frequency	Weight (g)	Frequency	Weight (g)
Alnus glutinosa			180	33.19	61	6.21
Betula sp.					19	17.09
Corylus avellana	42	8.71	118	32.22	215	32.97
Euonymus europaeus			1	0.24		
Fraxinus excelsior			28	4.17	28	3.52
Hedera helix					1	0.06
Ilex aquifolium					11	1.22
Maloideae			2	0.2	27	4.96
Maloideae cf. *Crataegus* sp.					1	0.02
Pinus sylvestris					4	4.35
Prunus spinosa					22	2.97
Quercus sp.	38	11.17	167	36.68	148	41.39
Salix spp			9	0.9	4	0.31
Sambucus nigra					3	0.68
Taxus baccata						
Ulex europaeus						
Ulmus glabra					7	1.26
Total bags	4		15		32	
Total samples	4		15		31	

The samples from the second layer of possible wickerwork are small and many of them fragile and disintegrating with voids. Hazel twigs or brushwood dominate in S71:099 (0–10mm, 10–20mm and some 20–30mm) and S71:105 (no size recorded in 2002). Sample *'II Geflecht Erdprobe'* and E84:6103 contain rods of 0–10mm, and small brushwood between 10mm and 20mm. The strong curvature of many of these suggests a small diameter. In both S71:105 and the small sample S71:122 the wood is affected by beetle channels, which also affect the hazel in S71:105. Other species such as elm, ash and willow are mostly represented by small brushwood and brushwood.

The small size of the hazel fragments could support Raftery's basketry interpretation. The presence of channels in some of the potential basketry samples is curious, as it suggests the presence of partially rotten baskets. Interestingly, thin, rod-sized, fast-grown hazel, as well as ash, was also found in the infill of the pit (E84:6103), and not just in the 'basket' layers. Most samples suggest the use of fast-grown brushwood.

The fact that a few fragments are most likely from modified pieces, from the basal black layer (S71:096B), wickerwork sample 2 (S71:105) and the innermost last brown infill (S71:110), suggests that this is not high-quality material. Furthermore, it is suggested that the material deposited in the pit represents a fairly brief period of activity, because of the limited variations in wood species and their qualities.

Hearth 1, Sq. 25 (one bag/sample), BA2

This hearth produced evidence for *in situ* burning and a sequence of charcoal-rich deposits. It is not clear from which of these layers the sample S69:012 derives. It is dominated by hazel brushwood (20x), followed by apple-type (5x) and ivy (3x). The apple-type is rotten with many beetle channels. The hazel is of very fast growth, with brushwood up to seven years old, which may have been rods or sails, or alternatively brushwood from coppice, based on fast growth and the presence of bark.

Hearth 10, Sq. 51 (two bags/samples), BA3[13]

Hearth 10 (north-west of the 15m structure) is located in a concentration of bronze-casting moulds (Metalworking Zone 1) and also contained some of these in its fill. E84:6145 from the basal black layer contained some burnt bone and E84:6145C from an upper black layer of the hearth some undetermined cereals, both separated by a grey fill. The charcoal is small and fragmented, and the lumps fairly rounded.

The basal layer is dominated by alder charcoal (22x).

Hazel (6x) and one piece each of elder and holly are also represented. The upper layer is dominated by hazel (17x); additional wood species are alder (2x), sloe (1x) and oak (1x).

Alder in the basal layer is of mixed origin: twigs, small brushwood, brushwood and roundwood (100mm). Beetle channels are present, sometimes in abundance, and large channel size is noted (2mm). Bark is attached to some brushwood (30–50mm).

Hazel in the basal layer is brushwood (20–50mm), often with beetle channels including frass and of large size (2mm). Elder and a small holly brushwood are probably admixtures.

In the upper layer, seventeen hazel fragments derive from fast-grown twigs and brushwood (20–30mm) with few beetle channels. Two pieces of alder brushwood of 30mm are also identified, without beetle channels. A tiny piece of sloe and an oak twig complete the assemblage.

The two samples may represent different episodes of burning, as also indicated by the stratigraphy, with the basal layer (with burnt bones and rotten alder) and the upper layer, with mainly fast-grown thin hazel and few beetle channels, possibly relating to more domestic purposes.

The charcoal is not suggestive of metalworking. It is likely that the hearth was used on more than one occasion for a variety of purposes, using rotten or degraded alder in the primary fill, and hazel possibly from rods (based on the general small size) in the upper fill. The latter may suggest—using comparison with storage Pit 118, for example—the use or presence of some form of woven structure or the burning of the remains thereof inside the hearth.

Outer bedding trench of 15m structure, Sq. 27 (one bag/sample), BA3

S70:037 is taken from burnt patches in the outer bedding trench of the 15m structure. Three wood species are found in the sample: hazel (11x), oak (6x) and ash (3x). Hazel is primarily small, fast-grown young brushwood (10–20mm) and also brushwood (20–30mm), with pith present. Oak is from roundwood with a diameter of 50–100mm, with tyloses. Ash brushwood is 30mm; one fragment has beetle channels. Both oak and ash may derive from mature trees which may well represent the posts, whereas the hazel may represent burnt rods/sails of the structure.

Pit 117 (formerly called Pit O), Sq. 17/26 (one bag/sample), poss. Bronze Age

Only fragile and slightly degraded hazel charcoal (12x) is found in the sample (no number), including two twigs and eight pieces of brushwood, most with beetle channels. The template of Ludemann and Nelle (2002) suggests the presence of brushwood (30mm and 50mm). The sample is from a black, sticky, semicircular area in the base of the pit, which suggests an *in situ* deposit, supported by the exclusive presence of hazel. It is not clear whether (as in Pit 118) it represents a woven structure lining the base of the pit, but the connection between small-sized hazel and dense charcoal-rich layers that were described as possible linings is interesting.

Ring-ditch 1 (ten bags, eight samples), BA2 and later

A number of samples derive from the black, finds-rich fills on the eastern side of Ring-ditch 1 which were postulated by Raftery to derive from Area 2.

S148 (Sq. 2) contains equal amounts of oak and sloe, though in weight oak is more important (oak 20x, sloe 19x). One fragment of alder is also present. The sloe is not a useful material in the context of Rathgall.

In S69:147 (north end of Sq. 7) the main wood species is oak brushwood (17x) with a maximum of 35 rings and some bark. Hazel brushwood (4x) and ash (1x), both with bark, are also present. The high values for oak do not compare well to the general wood identifications from Area 2.

S70:008 (Sq. 9) is a small sample which also contains burnt human bone. The charcoal is fragile, with some fairly rounded pieces. Wood species include alder (7x), hazel (4x) and oak (1x). The alder is roundwood (50–100mm); almost all wood includes few to medium beetle channels, some with frass, and one fragment has 63 rings on 21mm, deriving from a mature tree. The oak is small brushwood. The hazel is from brushwood (20–30mm) and roundwood (50–100mm). A few beetle channels are included.

S70:013 (Sq. 9/3) is dominated by alder (9x). One piece of gnarly elm brushwood (30–50mm) of slow growth and no great value is also identified. The alder is mostly roundwood (50–100mm), with one piece of brushwood (30–50mm). Many fragments have insect channels to varying degrees. The alder lumps are fragile and from rotten wood.

S70:032 (south-east corner of Sq. 10) is dominated by alder (18x). Two fragments of hazel are also included. The alder is roundwood (50–100mm) and channels occur in seven fragments. The hazel is small brushwood (less than 20mm) with pith.

As most samples from Area 2 (see below) are conspicuously devoid of oak, it may be possible to consider that S69:147, and perhaps also S148, relate to Area 1, where oak occurs (Figs 3.133 and 3.134). In contrast, a number of samples from the fill of Ring-ditch 1 in Sqs 9 and 10 are comparable to samples from Area 2 dominated by alder, often rotten but of roundwood size, suggesting a possible structural background.

There are a number of samples from other areas of Ring-ditch 1. Four samples derive from Sq. 29, in which Raftery locates one of his metalworking zones. These deposits described here can be interpreted as a dump of materials similar to those observed in Area 2, containing charcoal-rich soil and mould fragments, and may derive from the immediate surroundings.

S71:007A/B (Sq. 29) includes hazel (3x), with beetle channels. S71:008A/B (Sq. 29) consists of a large quantity of residue (almost 135g). Oak is the only wood species present (20x). Most is brushwood (30–50mm), but two pieces of roundwood (100–120mm) with few tyloses are also present.

Small samples S71:008A/B (Sq. 29), 'from a black organic layer', contained alder with some beetle channels (2x) and ash (1x, S71:008A, and one fragment of alder, S71:008B).

The quite different composition, especially of samples 007A and 007B, suggest that these represent different sampling locations within a charcoal-rich deposit. An association between oak and casting activities can be expected, and the degraded hazel and alder may represent residual material.

S71:034 (Sq. 56) is from 'a grey fill under stones', in an area of possible gradual infilling of the ring-ditch, which is supported by the presence of only one hand-picked piece of modified hazel.

Pit 120, Sq. 29 (two bags, one sample), BA3

The samples (S71:no number A/B) likely derived from a dense lens at the bottom of the pit completely filled with a 'black organic fill, including charcoal'. The fragile charcoal is dominated by oak (117x), followed by alder and some hazel. The hazel (7x) is from four twigs and one small piece of brushwood, mostly with bark and pith, less than 20mm in size. One piece of rotten roundwood is indicated in sample A. Most fragments show few to a medium number of beetle channels. Hazel is of fast growth, and at least some pieces are seven years old. Alder (12x) is mostly from twigs including bark and pith, but brushwood and one roundwood are also present, with frass.

Oak charcoal fragments vary from brushwood (20–50mm) to roundwood (50–100mm), and most are of moderate to weakly curved wood. Beetle channels are only found in two fragments. Most pieces are of fast growth. Tyloses are observed in a third of the fragments of bag B, suggesting that these are from mature wood.

Perhaps this pit bears some relation to charcoal production, based on the dominance of medium-sized, probably mature oak. The alder and hazel from rotten roundwood and twigs may be a secondary deposit, not related to the original function of the pit.

Iron-working hearth, Sq. 65 (two bags, one sample), Iron Age

The assemblage from sample S71:104A/B is dominated by hazel (47x), followed by yew (23x). Oak is also found (10x) and ivy is present once in both bags, while sloe and birch only occur once in S71:104B.

The template measurements indicate that most material is small to medium-sized brushwood. Only six pieces suggest roundwood between 50mm and 100mm (yew 4x and oak 2x), and the presence of tyloses in one of these oak fragments may indicate use of a mature tree. Two yew fragments have 50 and 59 rings respectively, the latter on 29mm, suggesting the use of a mature tree.

Hazel is from brushwood, sometimes with bark, of various ages: seven, thirteen and fourteen years. The outer rings indicate that many of these were felled after the growing season, i.e. most likely in winter. The fragments are partly eaten, with some large channels in evidence. Some variation in growth patterns may suggest an origin from coppice. Growth is generally fast, with some exceptions. The hazel fragments are difficult to break.

Át least seven pieces of hazel and six of yew (of mixed age and size) have been modified with radial and trapezium cuts, but not extensively worked. High temperatures are required to smelt iron, and traditionally oak charcoal rather than wood was used to reach these temperatures. This cannot be confirmed in this sample, with only small amounts of oak present. The yew may instead have provided the fuel, possibly reusing material previously used elsewhere.

Summary of Area 1

While Area 1 is dominated by oak, followed by hazel and a relatively low proportion of alder, the functionally diverse range of contexts show distinct patterns of wood use. Oak and ash dominate funerary Pit 119, and hazel dominates Pit 118, but ash also plays a role in the redeposited material within the pit.

The redeposited fills of the ring-ditch show on the eastern side a composition dominated by material resembling that in Area 2, with rotten alder and brushwood most prominent. While based on small sample numbers, the fills of Ring-ditch

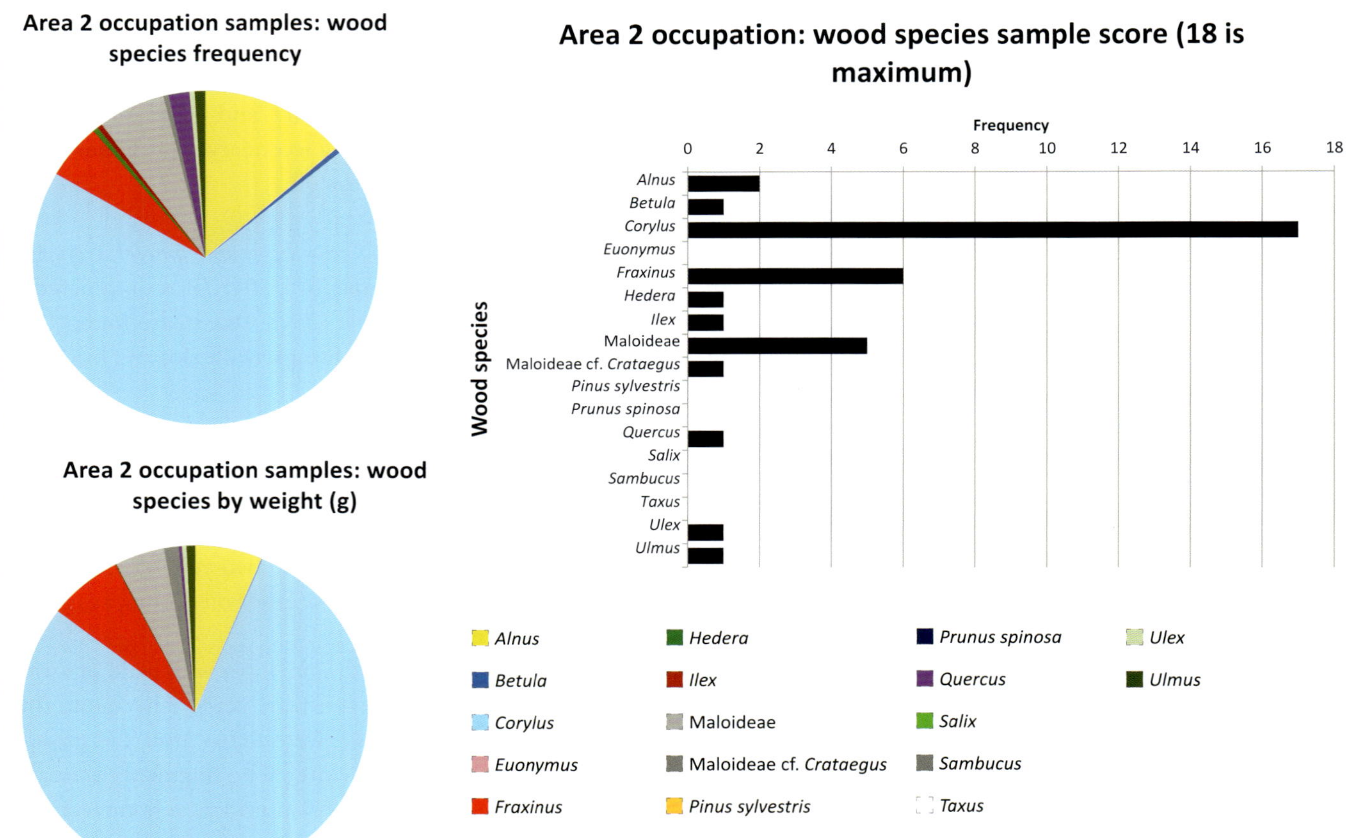

Fig. 3.137—Area 2 occupation deposit samples by frequency, weight (g) and sample score.

1 in its northern-eastern part may be due to the presence of oak derived from the west. The nature of the charcoal from this fill or that of Hearth 10 does not clearly suggest metalworking, where higher calorific fuels would be expected. Instead, here, as in Area 2, rotten alder is characteristic. In addition, the late Iron Age metalworking hearth did not show the expected dominance of oak but may indicate the use of yew instead. Oak is present, however, in the dump of casting-related material in Sq. 29. The 15m structure was likely constructed of oak or ash posts, with hazel.

Interesting is the occurrence of pine in Sqs 23, 24 and 33, one of the pieces partially wood. The date of these is unclear, as they derive from surface deposits within the heavily disturbed Area 1. Their composition is largely indistinct but includes pine charcoal, which is otherwise not found at Rathgall and is rare on archaeological sites in general. While samples S040 (Sq. 23), S69:034 (Sq. 23) and S69:014 (Sq. 24) contain small pieces of pine twig, brushwood and possibly roundwood, E84:172 (Sq. 33) contains an interesting dried brushwood of modified pine, 67mm long and charred on the walls of its hollow centre. This piece of pine is 20mm in diameter and of fast, irregular growth—the only (partly) wooden remains from Rathgall.

3.19.7 Area 2

Samples are small and were probably hand-picked from the so-called occupation deposits in Area 2, in which the samples focused on the cobbling in the C squares (Raftery's Metalworking Zone 2) were also included (Fig. 3.137). The deposits in this area were up to 0.5m deep. They were characterised by large amounts of charcoal, as well as a high density of prehistoric finds, especially bronze-casting moulds. While some disturbance of the area is assumed, it has a set of largely coherent Bronze Age dates (BA2).

In total, 37 bags (35 samples) were analysed from an area of cobbling where a possible workshop (Metalworking Zone 2) was located (six bags), occupational charcoal-rich material east and north of this area (eighteen bags from seventeen samples), and deposits from the northernmost part of the area (seven bags). For two bags (S70:041A and B) the provenance is unknown; S72:108 is from Pit 44 (Sq. D2), S72:099 from Post-hole 52 (Sq. D3), S72:028 from habitation material (Sq. F2) north of Ring-ditch 2, and S72:042 from the ring-ditch in Area 2 (Sq. G2).

Especially important are the samples associated with the possible workshop area/stone cobbling in Sqs C1 and 3 (in Metalworking Zone 2) (unnumbered sample 1, S70:002 and S70:045; six bags/samples). Hazel is the dominant wood species in Sq. C1, followed by ash and alder. Most wood is of brushwood size and represents rotten wood. Two samples (no number) from the 'square post-hole', i.e. the centre of the cobbling (Sq. C1), is dominated by hazel brushwood (34x), more than half of which includes beetle channels suggestive of the burning of rotten or dead wood. Some apple-type (6x), alder and elm brushwood (1x each) and ash (2x) and apple-type with one roundwood (50–100mm) also occur. Whereas hazel is dominant in C1, alder is more common in the small samples from Sq. 3. They contain rotten alder of medium brushwood and roundwood (50–100mm) and rotten ash roundwood (50–100mm).

These reflect the patterns observed in most of the samples from the occupation deposits in Area 2 (Figs 3.137 and 3.138), which show clear dominance of hazel and a small role for oak. The samples are few, small and hand-picked yet they are quite variable, with a mixture of sizes, ages and growth patterns, including gnarly wood, dead wood and well-grown brushwood along with both unworked and slightly modified material, possibly representing small structural wood and maybe also fuel. Noteworthy is the fact that a number of samples include modified wood, mainly of hazel, alder, ash and elm. In all, this is a very mixed assemblage in which most of the charcoal is rotten and of medium age. It is possible that some of the rare species also reflect dead wood collected for fires, considering their mostly small size, and/or suggesting shortage of wood availability. There is a good range of species, including rare species that only occur once (birch, furze, hawthorn, holly, ivy) or twice (elm) in the samples. In fact, gorse/furze and hawthorn, minor trees/shrubs from fringe vegetation, are only found in this part of the excavations. This fits well with the interpretation as occupation-related material, not underpinned by particular selection strategies, but does not tally with the interpretation of deposits as related to metalworking activity.

3.19.8 Area 3

A total of 23 bags representing 21 samples were analysed from Area 3, relating mostly to Bronze Age and undated features. Twelve wood species occur in Area 3. The total results (Figs 3.133 and 3.134) show a clear dominance of alder, followed by hazel and oak, and then ash (Fig. 3.138; sample score 20 of 24 bags).

Slot-trench structure, Sq. G, BA1

Small sample S72:115 derives from the southern bedding trench of a rectangular structure. It contains hazel, followed by alder and ash, all of rotten quality with many channels. The hazel is of brushwood size.

Ring-ditch 2, BA2 and possibly later

Two samples are from the fill of Ring-ditch 2: S72:082 from Sq. G2 to the north, and S78:053 from Sq. K5 to the south. The low quantities of mixed material, dominated by hazel and oak, appear residual.

The area inside Ring-ditch 2 is represented by ten samples (twelve bags). Three samples derive from 'black layer in pit 10' (Pit 4/Burial 3), which also produced cremated human bone, of which those in S73:008 were identified as human (see section 3.16). While S73:006 is dominated by almost equal amounts of alder and ash and only included one fragment of oak, S73:008 and S74:028 in contrast consist almost exclusively of oak (40 and 55 fragments respectively), represented mainly by brushwood of varying sizes up to a diameter of 50mm; one lump is ten years old. Both the diameter and the lack of tyloses in fragments point to the presence of rather young wood.

The Marguerie and Hunot (2007) template indicates moderate and weak curvature for alder, suggesting larger brushwood or roundwood size, and for the ash charcoal both small brushwood, brushwood and roundwood of 100mm. Some beetle channels are present in alder. A few fragments of holly and hazel brushwood occur in samples S78:006 and S74:028.

While there is no evidence for a stratigraphic differentiation within this fill on archaeological grounds, the presence of only oak charcoal and some burnt bone in one sample and alder and ash but virtually no oak in other samples may suggest different infill episodes.

Two charcoal samples derive from Pit 7, immediately to the east of Burial 3 (S73:003 and small sample S73:017). Both are dominated by alder: those fragments (31x) from S73:003, the black primary fill of Pit 7, derive from twig, brushwood and roundwood of 50–100mm. Three fragments are gnarly, and beetle channels are noted in ten pieces. Four alder roundwood fragments of 100mm and over, with few beetle channels, are present in S73:017, the grey fill of the pit. One lump has a square format and may have been modified. Other species (oak, hazel and ash) are represented by small amounts of mostly medium-sized brushwood.

The largest samples from Rathgall (five substantial bags, three samples) derive from the heavily burnt area within the horseshoe-shaped post-hole arrangement (S72:093A, 093B, 094, 095A, 095B) in Sqs H2/H3/I2/I3 around Burial 1 in the centre of Ring-ditch 2 from which human cremated bone was also recovered. There are considerable quantities of virtually pure charcoal dust in most of the bags (S72:093B, 145.87g; S72:094, 191.39g; and S72:095B, 340g). It is not clear from where exactly the samples were taken, but they appear similar and it may be that they relate to the three black streaks in the area of burning around Burial 1.

The samples are consistently dominated by alder (S72:093A/093B, x65; S72:094, x87; S72:095A/095B, x42), with few fragments of ash, birch and one hazel. While some brushwood is present in samples S72:093B and S72:094, they mostly contain roundwood of 50–100mm, 100mm and larger sizes, including a fragment of a mature tree with 70 rings on 26mm in S72:094. Other samples suggest medium-aged trees, with 35 rings counted in S72:093B, 32–37 rings in S72:095A and 40 rings in S72:095B. In S72:095B, 49 of the 57 alder fragments were 80mm, 90mm and 100mm roundwood and more (using the Ludemann and Nelle (2002) template and in part representing the actual size).

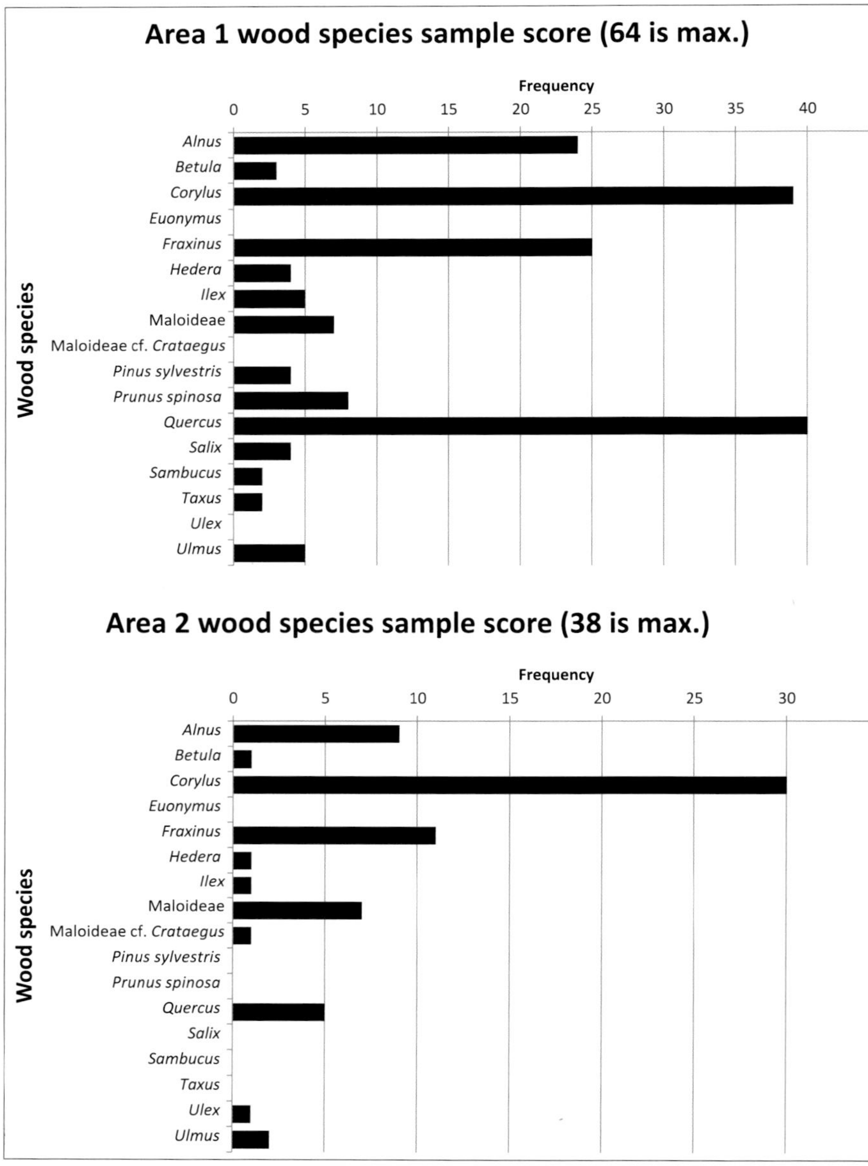

Fig. 3.138 (above and right)—Comparison of the four main activity areas (sample score).

Most alder is of very fast or fast growth (88 fragments from three samples with this information), much less of medium (ten) or slow growth (eighteen). The maximum number of rings is 40 on 20mm in these latter samples. Two samples have detailed information (S72:094 and S72:095B), with fifteen gnarly fragments. In fourteen pieces the growth is slower in the outer rings, suggesting wood from a dense position, but one fragment includes fast growth in its last rings and two had a slow start in life.

Among the other species, mostly represented as fast-growing brushwood, a few birch and ash fragments in S72:093B and S72:094 derive from roundwood of 100mm or larger.

Beetle channels are prominently present in alder, some of them of large size (6–7mm) and filled with frass. The quantity varies but compared to other samples it represents quite a lot and indicates that virtually all the alder was rotten when burnt. To be specific, 44 of 51 lumps from S72:093B are affected by channels, 38 of 42 in S72:094 and 49 of 57 in S72:095B. There are indications that at least some lumps with beetle channels derive from just under the bark. This could suggest that the

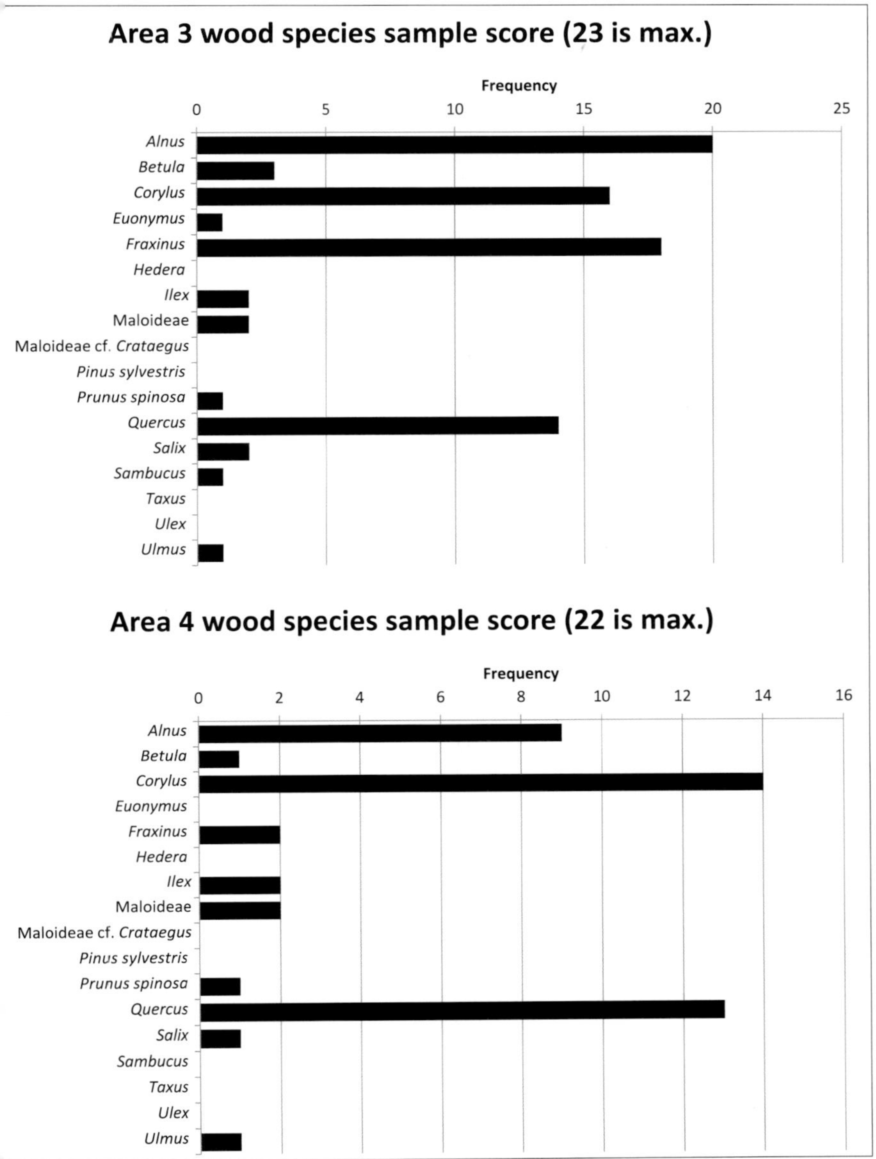

responsible beetles could be bark beetles. Only a few channels were observed in ash charcoal (S72:094) but almost all birch fragments include various numbers of channels, suggesting that birch, like alder, was rotten when burnt.

Given that these deposits are all clearly related to funerary pyres, the lack of oak and the high proportion of alder, especially rotten alder, is notable. The samples from within the horseshoe-shaped stake arrangement as well as Burial Pit 10 and possibly related Pit 7 represent burnt fragments of mainly rotten alder roundwood, along with a few larger pieces of roundwood of birch (also rotten) and ash. The alder includes some gnarly pieces, certainly not the best of materials but of course good enough for firing purposes. At least some fragments were not debarked. Some modification is noted (some alder fragments from S72:095B are from slightly modified wood, of possibly rectangular format), and it is here suggested that the alder derives from a stockpile of rotten wood (from a structure, shed, house?) of fairly uniform quality and size that was conveniently used for firing purposes in a funeral pyre. One may wonder whether the three longitudinal black streaks in fact represent a collapsed burnt structure *in situ*.

Pit 272, Sq. K4, south of Ring-ditch 2 (five samples)

The samples from this pit (S78:047, 048, 061, 062, 063) are dominated by alder, which makes up more than 60% of the assemblage (Fig. 3.139). This is followed by hazel, which comprises between 17% and 20% (by frequency and weight respectively). Ash is common with values around 10%, followed by oak with values less than 10%. Noteworthy is the occurrence of willow brushwood in two samples. Rare species are one brushwood fragment of apple-type and spindle (the only occurrence at Rathgall).

The alder is mostly rotten, of equal brushwood and roundwood size. Two fragments are from roundwood larger than 100mm, possibly representing the dumping of structural wood. The curvature template from Marguerie and Hunot (2007) suggests the presence of more fragments of substantial size. Some bark from roundwood is present. The ring numbers suggest medium-aged wood but not from old, mature trees.

Hazel is mainly represented as brushwood, along with some small brushwood and roundwood (50–100mm). Oak is from twigs and brushwood, one a gnarly piece. Ash is of mixed size, from twigs and brushwood to larger roundwood. One piece of brushwood is a gnarl.

Pit 272 seems to have been a dump for a variety of material of mixed origin, and possibly with some later disturbance that accounts for finds of willow, spindle and apple-type. The rotten alder may previously have had a structural function.

Pit 13, Sq. K4

This sample, S78:046, is dominated by both alder and hazel; some oak and ash are also present. Included are some

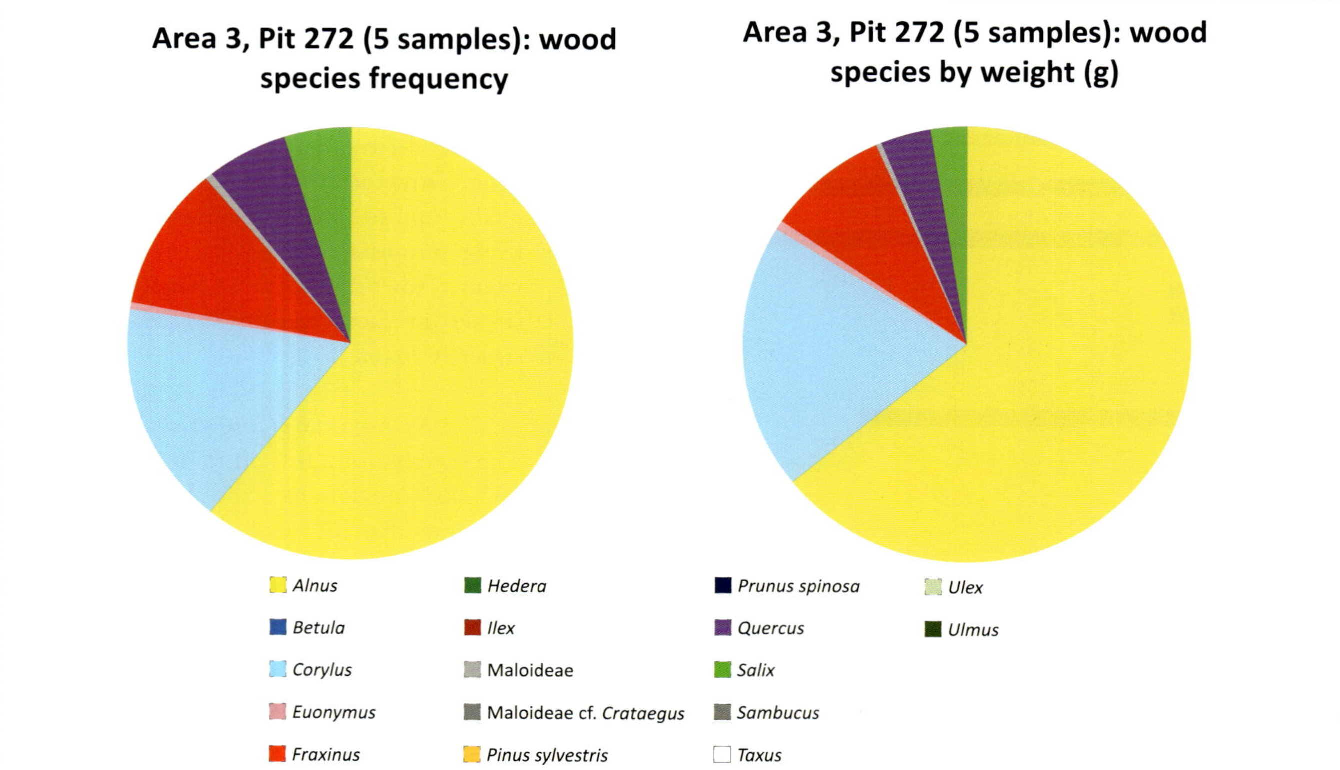

Fig. 3.139—Area 3, Pit 272: frequency and weight (g).

modified fragments, of mostly brushwood size. Alder, however, represents mostly larger material of 50mm and 50–100mm of rotten quality. The hazel is mostly twig and small brushwood, with one roundwood and few beetle channels.

Pit 273, Sq. K6

Sample S78:065 from Pit 273, with some burnt bone, includes equal amounts of rotten alder and hazel, also with channels. Present, too, is some ash, apple-type and oak. The apple-type and one ash fragment may be residual, as they are from twigs. Based on the low values for oak and ash, it is suggested that the fill of this pit has a domestic background, with no evidence for *in situ* burning, and that the burnt bone may be of animal origin.

Summary of Area 3

In summary, the charcoal assemblage from Area 3 derives in the main from the burial-related features associated with Bronze Age Ring-ditch 2. The presence of rotten alder in two of the undated pits outside the ring-ditch may suggest that they include material of a similar origin. The rectangular structure may have been constructed from alder or ash and hazel. The samples from outside Ring-ditch 2 differ from those inside (Fig. 3.140), with alder the most important species inside and hazel more common outside the ditch.

3.19.9 Area 4 with medieval house

From this area 22 samples were analysed, of which eight are directly associated with medieval features of the house (Sqs G6 and H7, the eastern aspect of the house, four post-holes and one rectangular trough; Sq. I5, the south-western aspect of the house, Pits 235 and 236, and a pit with a medieval pot base).

The other samples mostly derive from within the footprint of the house, but it is unclear whether they are of medieval date or are associated with earlier, Bronze Age, activities (Sqs G4, H5 and I5 on the western side of the house, and K8 south of the house on its western side). One small sample is from Post-hole 3 in Sq. I6, in the south-east of the house. The exact provenance of five other samples from Area 4 is unknown.

The main wood species in Area 4 (Figs 3.133 and 3.134) are hazel and oak, followed by alder, which is less common. Together these species form more than 90% of the assemblage

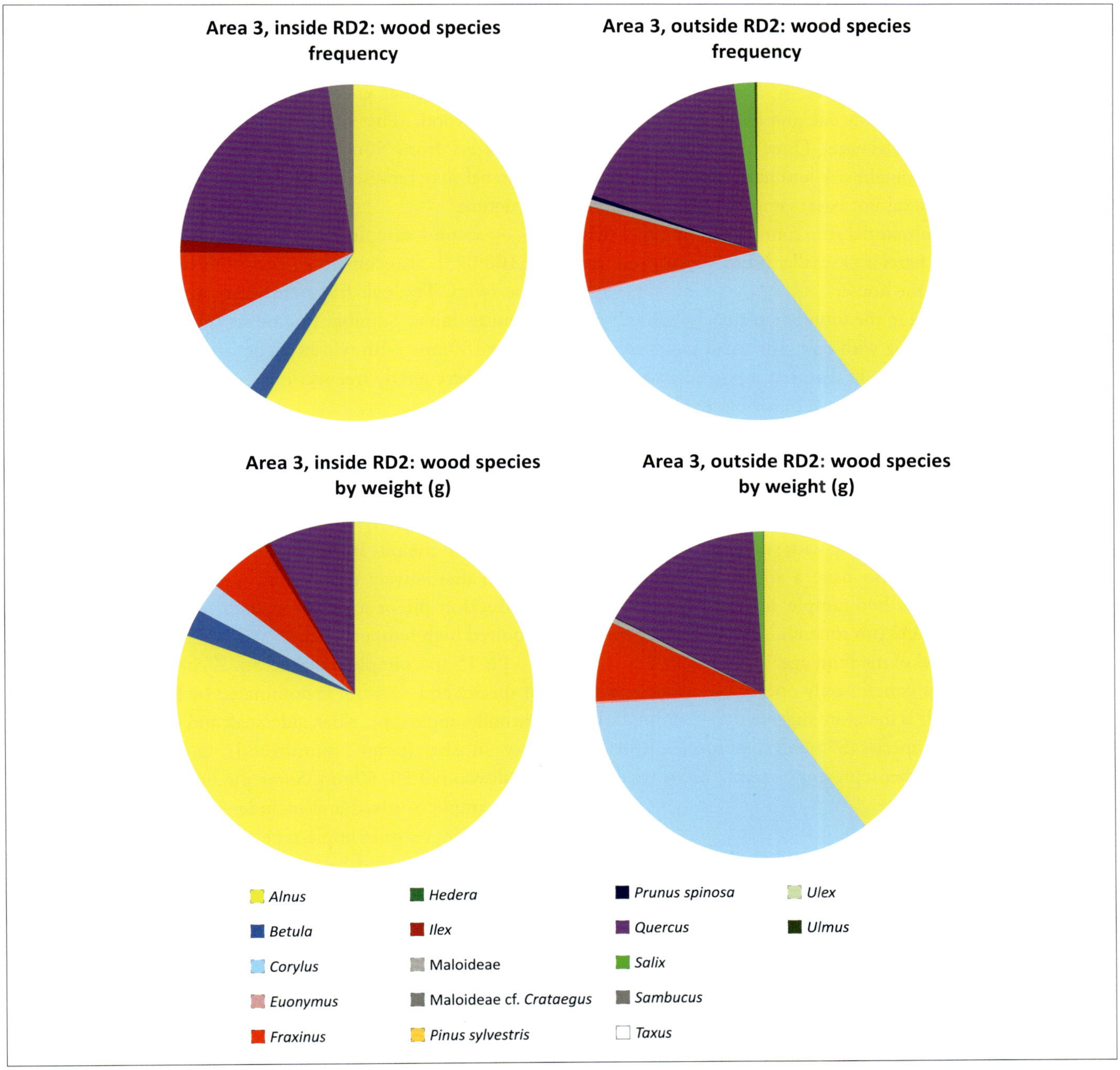

Fig. 3.140—Area 3: comparison between areas inside and outside Ring-ditch 2 (by frequency and weight).

(93% by frequency, 97% by weight). Sloe occurs regularly (3%) but ash is infrequent (1%). Rare species include holly, birch, apple-type, willow and elm.

The samples from the medieval house (eight samples: S78:029, Sq. H6, trough/foundation trench; S78:035, Sq. H7, Post-hole 19; S78:036, Sq. G6, Post-hole 17; S78:038, Sq. H7, Post-hole 18; S78:044, Sq. H7, Post-hole 17; S78:050, Sq. I5, Pit 236; S78:051, Sq. 15, pit; S78:052, Sq. 15, Pit 235) are rather similar, with mostly larger-sized oak with diameters of 100mm or more, and twig or rod-sized hazel of young age that is sometimes eaten by beetles and possibly slightly modified. The hazel pieces are often quite uniform, and it can be suggested that they represent rods which mostly would appear to have had a horizontal position, although some, based on the erosion on one end, may have been in a vertical position. The uniformity may suggest an origin in coppice wood. The number of species is small, which suggests that the samples are not collections of residual material.

In the medieval house only oak and hazel play a role, with almost twice as much oak as hazel. Three pits in the south-west of the house (Sq. I5) contain oak and hazel (Pit 235, Pit 236 and a pit with a medieval pot base; samples 78:050, 052 and 051). The oak is of substantial size, roundwood or larger than 100mm, whereas the hazel is of smaller brushwood or rod size, relating to pits inside the house.

Alder is found once in the foundation trench (S78:029) of the medieval house, along with oak. The small pieces of alder brushwood of up to 30mm in diameter are so consistent that that they may derive from a single burnt piece of wood. The oak is mainly of roundwood.

A number of other samples from Area 4 are very similar to those from the medieval house, dominated by oak roundwood and rod-sized hazel. One undated sample (no number, Sq. G4) includes alder roundwood, along with young hazel of twig/rod size. This sample may also have a structural background, though there is no further sample information available. Another sample, S75:032 (no square), is dominated by rotten mature alder and hazel of medium age.

Most sample bags contain only one or two wood species with few exceptions. It is therefore suggested that samples with more than three wood species (S75:042 eight species, K78:017 six species) probably either represent clearance or are residual.

3.19.10 Z cuttings

Samples from the Bronze Age 'outside cemetery' in the Z cuttings are associated with Ring-ditch 3 (four samples) and Ring-ditch 4 (one sample). One additional sample is from Pit 15 (Figs 3.133 and 3.134).

Ring-ditch 3 (four samples)
Two adjoining hearths (16 and 17), interpreted as pyre pits, produced two small samples (E100:035, E100:041) of fragile charcoal, with minimal burnt bone in E100:035. The composition in both is similar—dominated by oak (22x) of fast growth with few tyloses, thus immature trees. The oak fragments are too small for size measurements. Other species include holly (7x), followed by one fragment of apple-type, hazel and willow in each sample, and an additional piece of alder, birch and sloe in E100:041—thus minimal numbers and mostly of twig or small brushwood size suggestive of admixture.

Another pyre sample from Sq. Z2 (no number, OII:8, probably Z5:a) consists of only oak. The material is uniform, with fast, regular growth and no tyloses indicating use of young wood. The majority represents roundwood with diameters from 50mm to 50–100mm and 100mm. The charcoal may represent either the remains of fuel or a burnt structure.

A second sample from Sq. Z2, west of Ring-ditch 3 (E100:023), also consists of oak, with two additional gnarly sloe twigs. The oak fragments, too, are mostly gnarly and unmeasurable. Suitable fragments indicated a diameter of about 100mm, with tyloses suggesting the burning of an oak root or very gnarly tree section.

Ring-ditch 4 (one sample)
The sample from possible pyre Pit 25, south of Ring-ditch 4, consists of 100% oak. Part of the material is gnarly (almost 10%), with some tyloses. The results suggest the burning of oak root in the pit. It may be that roots were used as fuel for a pyre; alternatively, the pit may have been used as a charcoal production pit or a hearth related to other activities that required high temperatures.

Pit 15 (no sample number, Sq. Z5:a) contains a mixture of species and sizes but is dominated by hazel. Other species are holly, apple-type, elder, alder, oak and ivy. Hazel fragments vary in size (twigs, roundwood), but are mostly from brushwood of 30–50mm. Some pieces have beetle channels. This sample is mixed and includes species such as climbing ivy and fringe shrubs apple-type and elder. It is not usual that ivy and elder would be selected for fuel, hence it may be suggested that this sample represents the clearance and burning of shrub-like material.

The total assemblage from this area is dominated by oak, even given that it is distorted by the results from Pit 15, which is dominated by hazel and only one fragment of oak and does not compare with the other samples, which consist exclusively of oak. This can be taken as an argument for the proposition that Pit 15 is not associated with the other, mainly pyre-related samples.

Y cuttings (one sample)
One sample taken from Sq. Y2, north of Ring-ditch 1, is dominated by hazel brushwood, with a few alder and ash lumps from rotten wood and sloe brushwood. The sample resembles habitation/workshop material as found in Area 2 (where hazel is common).

3.19.11 The X cuttings (nine samples)

The X cuttings, excavated by Raftery in 1978, produced two samples dated to the Bronze Age (S72:128, Pit 166; S78:028, pre-Rampart 3), two medieval samples (S78:030 and S78:031, Rampart 2 ditch) and five samples probably of Bronze Age date (S78:001, pit; 002, pit; 013, 040 and 042). The number of fragments in the samples is small.

The lumped results from the X cuttings are presented in Fig. 3.141 (frequency only, as the weight is small). They show a mixed picture, with hazel dominant, followed closely by alder and ash. Noteworthy is the regular occurrence of sloe.

When the results are sorted to medieval and Bronze Age periods there is no great difference in the importance of hazel, but the Bronze Age samples are much more varied. Ash, holly, apple-type and elm are absent from the medieval samples, whereas sloe is much less important in the Bronze Age.

Much of the Bronze Age material is very rotten, with many beetle channels, and consists of slightly larger alder roundwood, but almost all wood was rotten when burnt. The two medieval samples (S78:030 and S78:031) are suggestive of clearance, with mainly sloe and elder twigs and some alder and hazel brushwood, suggestive of open growth conditions.

The X cuttings were partly re-excavated in 2011 (Seaver 2012), when the charcoal identifications were also low (108 identifications in total). A few charcoal samples from 1978 overlap with those from excavations of 2011, especially in Cuttings X7 and X8 (S78:028, 030 and 031). Generally, the Bronze Age samples from 1978 (72:128, Pit 166; S78:028) are comparable to those of the 2011 excavation (O'Donnell 2012, samples 5, 7 and 11 from Feature 1 and sample 6 from Feature 3), assuming that *Prunus* spp is most likely sloe, with the exception of ash, which is absent from the 2011 excavation.

The medieval results, however, are very different. Alder, elder and sloe are absent from the 2011 samples (sample 8 from Feature 6, samples 9 and 10 from Feature 7 and sample 12 from Feature 8), whereas yew and oak are common. The 1978 samples (S78:030 and S78:031) are dominated by sloe and hazel. In short, the identifications do not agree at all. This is most likely a result of the small number of identifications (41 medieval lumps and 34 Bronze Age lumps from 1978; 50 medieval lumps and 39 Bronze Age lumps from 2011), and possibly clearance, considering the importance of sloe.

Bronze Age rectangular Pit 166 (X cuttings), with many finds, included a variety of seven wood species without a clear dominant species. The oak is in part gnarly, and the alder is rotten. The mixture of everything is suggestive of a domestic dump.

A sample (S78:001) from a pit in the north-eastern corner of the X cuttings contains charcoal from mainly rotten alder of various sizes, from brushwood to large roundwood (100mm), and some apple-type, hazel and willow.

3.19.12 Discussion

While bearing in mind the often selective recovery of samples, a number of conclusions can be drawn on the use of wood at Rathgall in the excavated areas. The main activity areas in Rathgall differ in their wood usage, largely according to the features and types of activities represented and sampled. Alder forms half or more of the assemblage in Area 3, especially those contexts related to funerary activities. In contrast, oak dominates the outside cemetery, with virtually no other wood species used in the funerary activities here. Area 2 stands out for the dominance of hazel in the occupation deposits, whereas oak is more common in Area 1. In Area 4, mainly represented by the samples from the medieval building, hazel and oak are the two most important wood species. The X cuttings show a mixed picture, suggesting that this area was disturbed in the past, and the prominence of sloe may suggest clearance. There is no detailed information for a large number of samples from Area 1, but the limited occurrence of Scots pine in Sqs 23, 24 and 33 is noteworthy.

The total Bronze Age assemblage (Figs 3.142 and 3.143) has almost equal hazel and oak, both about a third of the total assemblage, though in weight oak is less well represented (21%). As most of the functionally diverse range of features date from the Bronze Age, comparison with the small number of later features is difficult. Notable is the presence of yew in the Iron Age samples from the iron-working furnace, as well as from the ditch fill in the X cuttings (Fig. 3.141, yew only present in samples analysed by O'Donnell in 2012).

The relative importance of alder in Rathgall is surprising, considering its raised dryland location with few obvious locations for alder trees. The pollen diagram obtained from a wetland location some 900m from the hillfort (Plunkett, this volume) is dominated by local plant taxa growing close to the sampling site. Low values for tree pollen, including oak, hazel, ash, elm, willow and alder, indicate at best their occurrence in the wider landscape. Lower values for elm and oak suggest clearance at a time broadly corresponding to the main Bronze Age activity in Rathgall, but the alder curve does not give much information. The source of alder must thus lie elsewhere, away from the coring location and from Rathgall, in an as-yet-unidentified wetland location or along a stream or river.

Interestingly, woodland clearance during the Bronze Age could suggest that wood was a scarce commodity at the time. Maybe this was an incentive for use of rotten or lower-quality wood—or even 'recycled' wood—at Rathgall.

In the medieval period only two species are of importance: oak and hazel (Figs 3.142 and 3.143). Other wood species include sloe, alder and elder, and the absence of ash is noteworthy. An interesting point is the fact that oak was so commonly used in medieval times in Rathgall. The majority is of medium rather than mature age, based on the presence of few tyloses and (very) fast to medium growth (98 versus five slow-grown pieces).

Post-holes, buildings and occupation deposits

The charcoal samples suggest the use of oak and hazel as the predominant building materials for the 15m structure and the medieval house at Rathgall.

No samples from post-holes are available for Area 2. Instead, the deposits from this area are dominated by hazel and other wood of small size, unlikely to represent either fuel for metalworking or building material for substantive buildings (but note further below). Of interest is the fact that a number of samples from Area 2 include modified wood, mainly of hazel, alder, ash and elm (not oak) of rotten quality and medium age. The sample from the bedding trench of the rectangular slot-trench building in Sq. G in Area 3 consisted of hazel, alder and ash. Post-hole 52 in the X cuttings produced sample S72:040, consisting of ash of post-sized fast growth, and alder in S78:018.

Pyres, pyre pits and possible burial-related pits (35 samples, 29 bags)

Possible pyres or pits containing redeposited pyre material are found in Area 1 (Pit 119 in Sq. 34/35 in the centre of Ring-ditch 1, and Hearth 1 in Sq. 25 underneath the 15m structure), Area 3 (Burial 3-related deposits in Sq. H3, and a pyre area inside the circle formed by the 'horseshoe-shaped' post-hole arrangement) and the 'outside cemetery' (pyre Pits/Hearths 16/17 (E100:035 and E100:041), a pyre in Ring-ditch 3, Sq. Z2 (no sample number), and Pit 25 in the area of Ring-ditch 4, Sq. Z5:d (no sample number)).

Burial or pyre deposits in Area 1 and the outside cemetery of the Z cuttings are dominated by sometimes gnarly oak, whereas the pyre and associated features within Ring-ditch 2 are dominated overall by the burning of oak, although rotten alder dominates in Pit 7. The use of gnarly oak suggests that these fragments relate to fuel in the pyre rather than an associated funerary structure. For alder in Pit 7, which is similarly partly gnarly, this seems less certain.

The possible pyre Pit 119 in Area 1 has a charcoal profile dominated by oak and ash. The occurrence of gnarly oak combined with a lack of insect channels suggests the usage of oak root or otherwise unusable oak wood as fuel. Maybe the ash, represented by fragments of structural size, formed part of a pyre construction, though beetle channels may here, too, indicate reuse of old wood for fuel.

Hearth 1 in Area 1, which is discussed in Chapter 6 as a possible pyre pit, shows a charcoal profile more typical of a domestic hearth. Likewise, the charcoal from Pit 118, Area 1, has a more domestic appearance, with the dominance of hazel followed by ash. Although metalworking-related finds and some unidentified cremated bone are associated with this pit, the charcoal identifications do not suggest its origin in metalworking or funerary processes.

One remarkable pyre deposit is formed by the charcoal surrounding the heavily burnt area with Burial 1 inside the horseshoe-shaped stake arrangement in Ring-ditch 2. This location, which has the best-quality charcoal from Rathgall, is surprisingly undisturbed, and three longitudinal charcoal concentrations indicated on the plans may be suggestive of a collapsed structure above the burial. The deposits are dominated by alder of degraded quality, with many beetle channels including frass, and substantial size. Some birch, ash and one piece of hazel are also present. It is possible that birch and ash had a structural role, while for alder this seems clear. As cremated human bone was found in these charcoal samples, it is clear that they must derive from the pyre.

Whether the alder was really burnt for fuel or derived from an erected pyre structure is open for discussion. Based on the fact that degraded alder is a common feature in many samples from Rathgall, it may simply have been conveniently available. Generally oak appears to be a more common fuel in a funerary context, as demonstrated, for example, at Templenoe, Co. Tipperary, dating from the Early Bronze Age to the Middle Bronze Age (O'Donnell 2016). Here oak, apple-type wood and ash could be shown to have been used for cremation, in contrast to contemporary post-holes and domestic pits, which were dominated by oak and hazel respectively. The use of alder in a funerary context can be

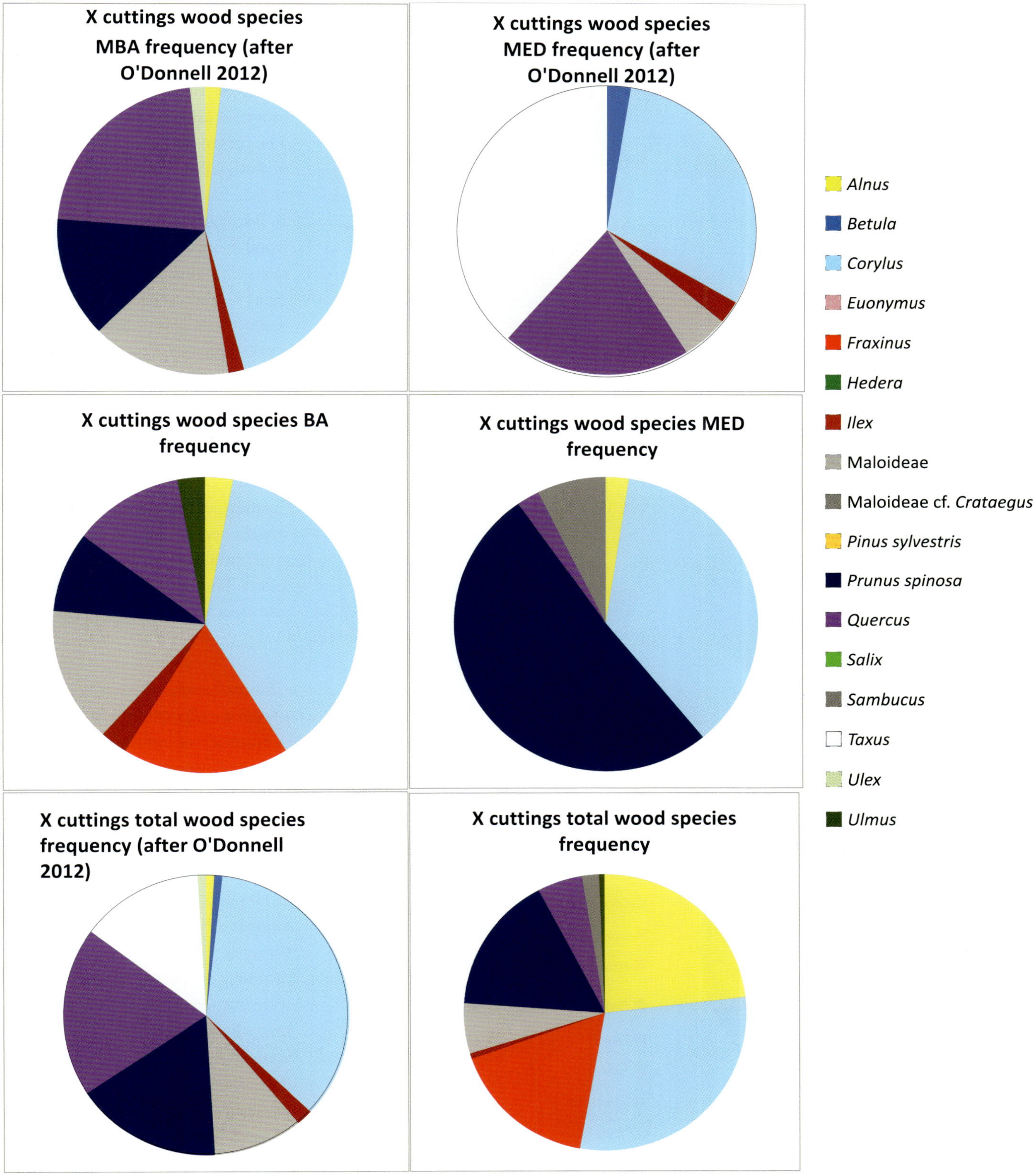

Fig. 3.141—Compiled results from the X cuttings (inclusive of O'Donnell's 2012 identifications of the samples obtained on the 2011 excavation of the rampart cutting (Chapter 2, section 2.8, Appendix 2). BA = Bronze Age; MBA = Middle Bronze Age; MED = medieval.

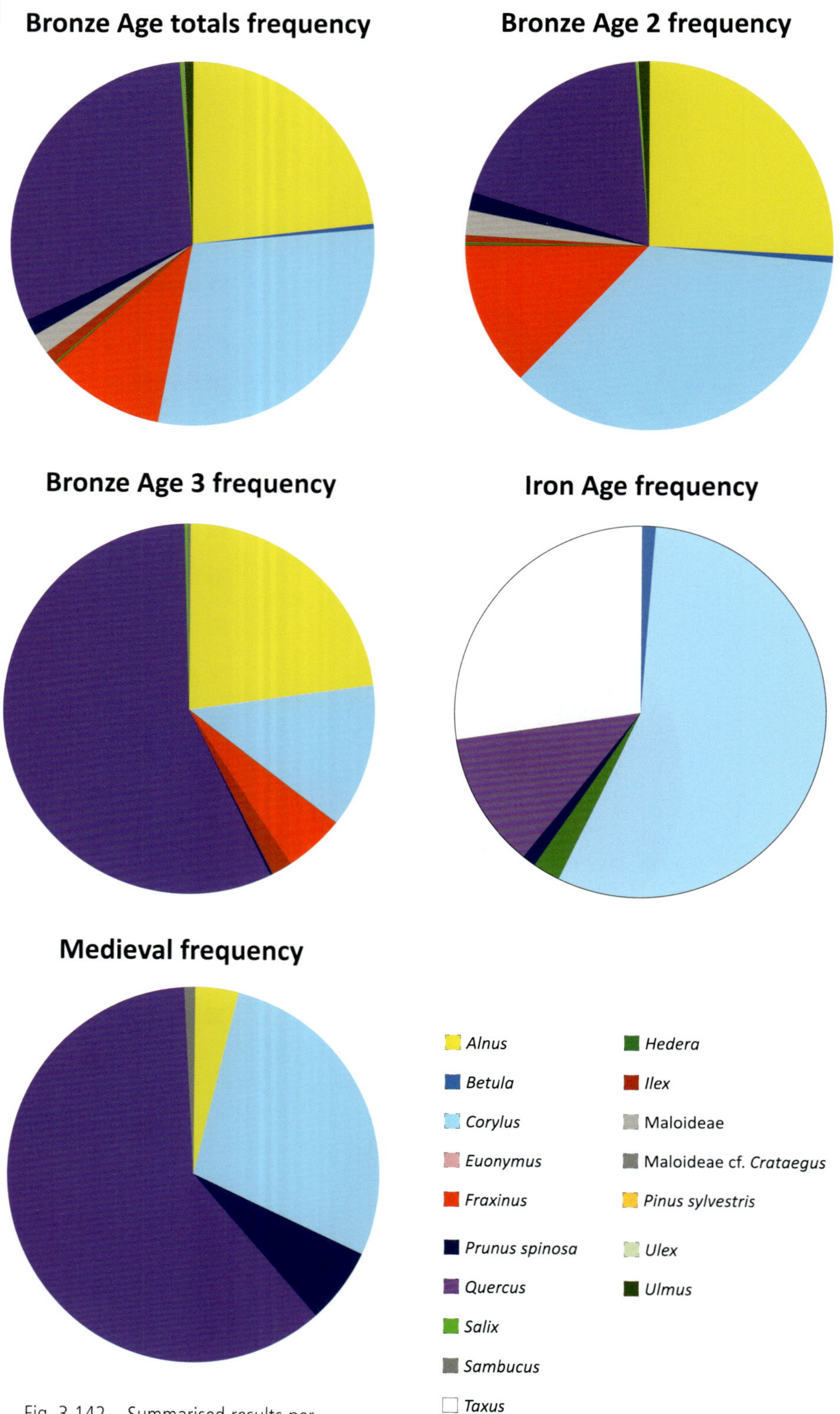

Fig. 3.142—Summarised results per period (frequency).

paralleled at Killoran 10, Co. Tipperary (Stuijts 2005), a site located on dry land close to bog marginal wood which may have provided an ample supply of alder. The presence of alder in the vicinity of Rathgall is clearly implied in the charcoal assemblage. Was it a choice at Rathgall to recycle rotten alder wood from structures as fuel or as pyre elements to support funeral pyres—in effect recycling degraded wood from buildings such as workshops etc.—or did people use specific stockpiles of otherwise unusable wood for funeral firing purposes? And was there a shortage of more suitable wood species that would provide higher caloric burning values, such as oak or ash, which necessitated the use of less appropriate wood species such as alder? The use of gnarly oak may also be relevant in this regard.

Charcoal production pits or stockpiles of poor-quality wood at Rathgall?

A number of samples from non-funerary contexts also include material that contains almost exclusively gnarly, barely recognisable oak, reflecting contorted or stunted growth (E100:023, Pit 120, Pit 25, Pit 96, deposit S78:049). At first it was thought that this material represented roots from trees that were burned *in situ* to clear the area, but their frequent presence in archaeological contexts may suggest that roots were used as fuel at Rathgall. The use of tree roots and *Krüppelholz* (wood from stunted trees) as fuel has been discussed in the context of charcoal production pits (Ludemann and Nelle 2002)

(Fig. 3.144). These pits were of various depths (about 3–4ft), and after initial firing were filled with more wood and then covered with grass, leaves and soil to exclude oxygen. The process would take about a week, during which the fires needed to be tended (Kenny 2010).

Charcoal production is dirty work, hence it would not be a good idea to have these pits close to a settlement. The process requires a large amount of wood, and therefore charcoal production sites are mostly located close to woodland. For Rathgall this would mean that woods with oak (possibly managed to some extent to ensure continuous supply) must have been present close to the hillfort, to avoid transport over long distances.

According to literature, charcoal-burning mostly occurred during the summer period, when there was little rain. Wood had to be dried for some months before burning, so it can be assumed that stockpiles were located somewhere in the area. Charcoal production pits, in contrast to the charcoal production mounds or platforms of later times, could be indicative of a small-scale rural enterprise, undertaken mainly to meet individual and/or local needs (O'Sullivan and Downey 2009). As gnarled oak is also sometimes found in pyre deposits (such as E100:023, Pit 25 and Pit 119), one may wonder whether this material was chosen for cremation activities as well, using otherwise unusable oak roots and other scrub material.

Notable, too, is the great proportion of rotten wood both in wood that was possibly used as fuel and in some apparently primary contexts, such as the rectangular structure in Area 3, possibly implying the rotting of buildings and structures *in situ*.

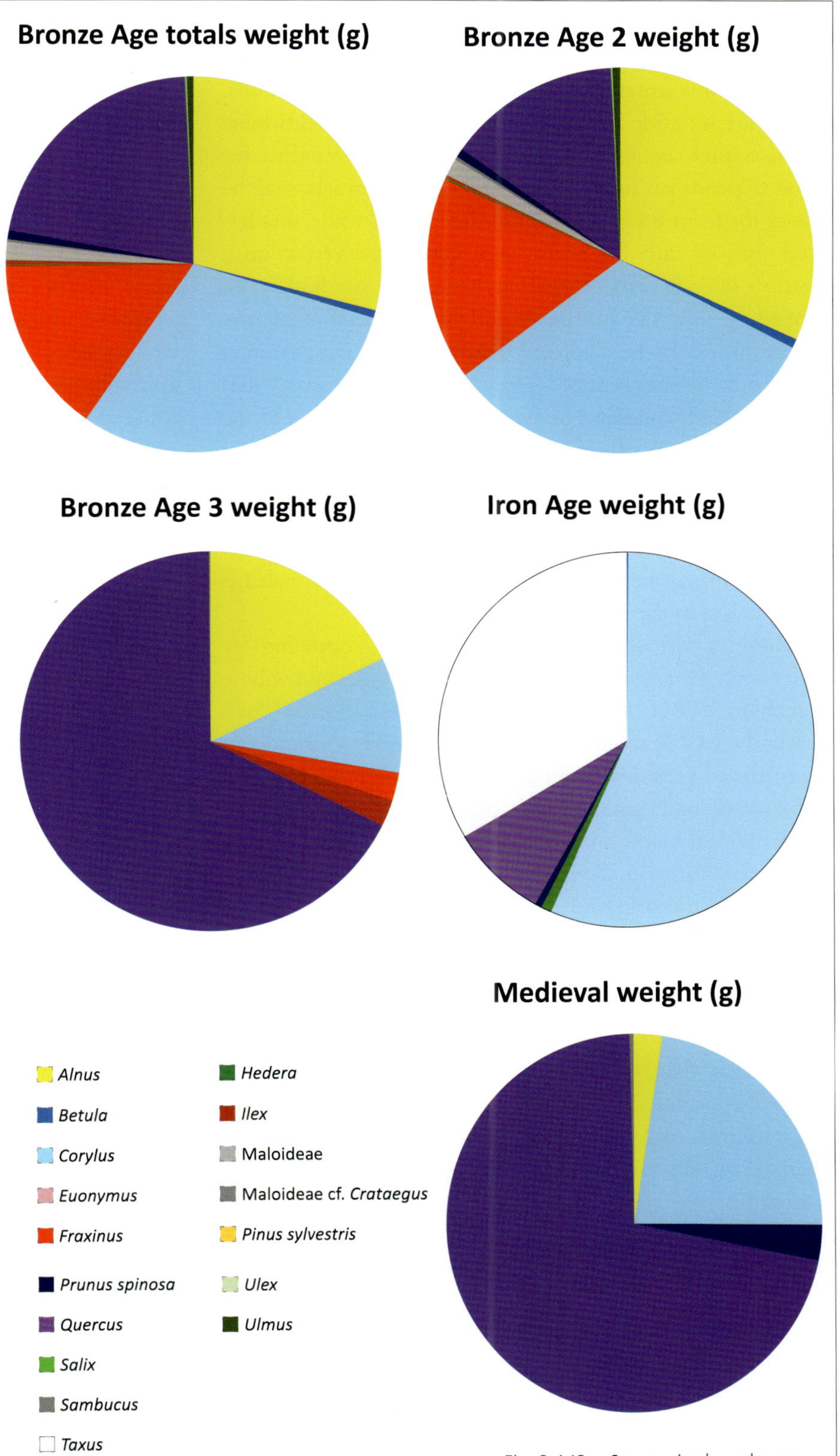

Fig. 3.143—Summarised results per period (weight).

Are there indications of woodland management at Rathgall? Managing woodland for underwood and timber represents a long-term investment by a community over generations. Woods are set aside for production reasons, with additional purposes such as mast for pigs, etc. The turnover time for wood depends on its purpose: larger-sized timbers may be grown for from 25 to several hundred years, while smaller-sized rods or sails for households can be harvested on a rotation of 3–8 years or so. The harvesting methods vary, depending on the purpose and the expertise of the communities. Early medieval, medieval and later sources describe a well-organised legal system, suggesting that coppicing and woodland management were common at the time (Kelly 2000; Murphy and Potterton 2010; O'Sullivan 1998b), and archaeological finds of woven structures such as hurdles or Bronze Age round houses using posts and wattle (also used in *fulachta fiadh*, as at Lisheen, Co. Tipperary; Stuijts 2005) tell tales of woodland management knowledge and practices in the past.

Many wood species are suitable for coppicing or underwood management, such as hazel, ash, alder and willow (Rackham 1980; 1982; 1994). A combination of oak standards with hazel underwood was the most common in the medieval period (O'Sullivan 1998b). It is challenging to prove woodland management practices on the basis of archaeological wood and charcoal, apart from the fact that woven structures in themselves do suggest a selection for material of a uniform size. Recent research (Out *et al.* 2017) suggests, however, that even woven structures are not necessarily evidence for wood management or coppicing, since many species coppice naturally when cut and such new growth is fast, with even, long rods and poles.

It is clear that most charcoal from Rathgall derives from unmodified, small and medium-sized wood, sometimes with bark attached. Any modification is minimal. Hazel is mostly of mixed quality and not necessarily of uniform fast growth, as would be expected. In Area 2, for example, interpreted as a domestic/industrial activity area with workshops, hazel is of intermediate age more than twenty years old, which does not argue in favour of coppicing practices. Evidence for coppicing may, however, be seen in the association of very thin hazel rods with the features interpreted as possible basketry Pit 118. The only possible secure evidence for managed hazel can be postulated for the medieval house, where the small number of analysed hazel fragments are of similar small size and young age, between three and nine years old.

Oak at Rathgall is of mixed quality and size, from gnarly scrub and roots to natural twigs. In some cases the absence of vessels, combined with the gnarly nature, suggests the use of roots and/or brush, mostly immature or of medium age, though in some cases more than 50 years old. Gnarly wood is not managed wood, while some examples of roundwood of structural size and quality, of young age and fast growth, such as in the medieval house (S78:044/050/051) and the Z cuttings (Sq. Z2, unnumbered sample), may be indicative of managed woodlands.

Alder, which plays an important role at Rathgall, is not a wood species usually associated with coppice management, although it regenerates easily and can produce many shoots. Most alder at Rathgall is of medium age. There are a few exceptions, such as S70:008 (63 rings from Ring-ditch 1 fill) and S72:094 (70 rings from Area 3, 'horseshoe-shaped' area). The quality of the lumps, often with bark attached, sometimes of weak quality, considering the presence of bark beetle galleries, and sometimes gnarly, is not indicative of management.

Ash is common at Rathgall, but usually plays a subordinate though interesting role. The most rings were counted in brushwood in S70:037 (48 rings in Area 1, BA3) and S72:082 (38 rings in Area 3, BA2). In Area 1, Pit 119 is interesting, with some samples including uniform brushwood and roundwood of fast growth, with up to 35 rings, that includes possibly modified material (S71:094B and E84:6071). In Area 2, ash seems to have been regularly modified but there is little information on age. Though anthracological observations do not suggest a coppice background, the regular modification, the relatively young age and the consistent choice of ash are noteworthy and may relate to young woods.

There is thus little evidence for management or coppicing at Rathgall. Rather, the anthracology suggests the use of mostly relatively young—at most medium-aged—wood, of which a large part is not the best of cuts. In part, the slow growth and gnarly nature of the material may indicate that local woods at times may have been closed and not routinely felled. These may have complemented managed wood, the yields of which were most likely used for structural purposes, as is also occasionally indicated at Rathgall.

3.19.13 Conclusions

Anthracological analysis from Rathgall indicates a complex use of the hilltop area for a variety of specialised activities, but with few indications of habitation. The occupation deposits may represent a variety of different activities. All wood species are indigenous, with hazel, alder, oak and ash the most important species. Compared to other sites, apple-type wood is relatively unimportant. Willow plays hardly any role.

Most material is from roundwood, brushwood and smaller round material but not from heavily modified wood, and bark is regularly present. Any indications of modification are usually limited to barely visible quick adjustments to create stake points or the like.

There is little evidence for the use of mature trees, partly owing to the size of the charcoal fragments. Indirect evidence comes from some single lumps in samples, such as oak with tyloses, and fragments with large numbers of rings, such as alder and yew. These fragments are often of slow or gnarly growth, which could indicate a closed growing location. Most fragments, however, suggest the use of wood of medium or young age, and not the best cuts.

The Bronze Age pyres and related features are dominated overall by oak in Area 1 and in the outside cemetery. In Area 3, however, rotten alder is by far the most important wood species, especially in the horseshoe-shaped post-hole arrangement but also in Pits 4 and 7. Ash, equally degraded, plays a subsidiary but consistent role in the funerary-related features of Area 3.

The Iron Age smelting pit includes a mixed assemblage in which yew plays an important role, something that is not apparent in other samples.

The medieval assemblage, with most remains deriving from a house, indicates that hazel and oak are the main wood species, with few other species represented. Hazel and oak mostly reflect burnt structural remains.

The material gives the overall impression that the hillfort area was cleared of trees and that smaller-sized wood was used for firing purposes, whereas larger-sized wood was used for construction (as posts, etc.).

The relative importance of alder is somewhat surprising and could suggest the local availability of this tree, which would indicate relatively wet conditions locally. An important aspect is the repeated use of degraded material, especially alder, as expressed by the presence of beetle channels and frass in samples from many Bronze Age features. Whether degraded material, deadwood or the structural remains of, for example, houses that had outlived their usefulness were burnt is unclear.

Another important aspect is the repeated finding of gnarly wood, especially from oak. On the one hand, this may relate to the specific use of oak roots or unusable brush oak, both in possibly a simple charcoal production pit methodology and as fuel in funerary contexts. On the other hand, the use of gnarly and rotten wood suggests the limited availability of wood during the Bronze Age phase at Rathgall. Maybe better-quality wood was reserved for domestic and house-building purposes elsewhere, away from Rathgall (at Knockeen hillfort, for example). Indeed, the presence of oak in samples relating to the few definite structures would support this model.

All the same, the anthracological results suggest a general shortage of wood, with the use of every bit that was available, indirectly suggesting management of the surrounding landscape. Maybe the wider landscape around Rathgall was in use by a community that had organised it into functional units, with agricultural fields and wooded areas to provide the supplies needed for the working and funerary areas of Rathgall, and the living areas elsewhere. The author is not aware of comparable evidence for such a proposition at this moment in time.

A number of samples, spread over all areas, include a small number of fringe trees, such as elder, apple-tree group and/or hawthorn, ivy, sloe and single finds of furze/gorse and spindle, which are not suitable for general building purposes. It is suggested that these may be admixtures from either clearance of an area or later agricultural practices. Maybe there was little fringe vegetation around Rathgall, which would imply that the area was kept free of shrubs and trees. The apple-type is notably of little importance at Rathgall compared to other sites such as burnt mounds, for example.

The quality of the charcoal indicates that many deposits were disturbed in the past—not surprising, considering the long time during which Rathgall was in use. In part it explains why some samples are of mixed content. It is a surprise, however, that some samples include charcoal of pristine quality and that the layers of pits were sometimes so clearly defined. In this respect, the fact that in Area 3 the three black streaks with immaculate charcoal have been preserved in such integrity seems almost miraculous and may suggest that this area, which includes Burial 1, was avoided over time or covered by a mound.

The medieval structure and the concentration of oak in its vicinity suggest a wider availability of oak during this phase. Hazel brushwood, sometimes with bark, of young age (seven, thirteen and fourteen years) was felled after the growing season, i.e. most likely in winter. The fragments are partly eaten, with some large channels in evidence. Some variation in growth patterns may suggest an origin from coppice.

Fig. 3.144—A simple manner of charcoal-burning in small hollows in the ground (Biringuccio 1540) (after Ludemann and Nelle 2002, 17, fig. 3).

Ideally, large undisturbed samples would have formed the basis for anthracological research, with hand-picked lumps only collected for specific dating purposes. The sieving and/or floating of fragile material, such as that from Rathgall, is not to be recommended, as it results in fragmentation (especially of oak) or complete disappearance of species, and the loss of important indirect information such as for burning *in situ* and the presence of ash.

DEDICATION

The author would like to dedicate this contribution to Barry Raftery, his good friend Wil Casparie and Mags Gowen Larsen, who all introduced me to Ireland and its wonderful archaeology (Fig. 3.145).

Fig. 3.145—Wil Casparie, Mags Gowen Larsen and Barry Raftery, in Derryville Bog, 31 July 1996 (photo: Anneke Casparie).

APPENDICES

Appendix 1—Charcoal lumped results per sample bag (dri.ie).

Appendix 2—Charcoal detailed results per species per sample bag (dri.ie).

NOTES

1 Two beads came from the 'grey floor'; the bronze gouge is from Sq. C2.
2 These analyses were carried out by the National Museum of Ireland in Dublin. For a fuller description of the methodology and instrumentation see Warner and Cahill 2012, note 7.
3 The finds catalogue lists a further four beads which appear to be non-voided entries.
4 E84:838 and 6562 published in Raftery and Henderson 1987, 42–6, as 1815\16 and 6462.
5 The description of the find contexts of these locates them all in brown material in the west of D2 but does not name the depression.
6 Raftery and Henderson (1987, 47) locate this in the primary silting of Ring-ditch 2.
7 Logbook just says 'beside stone in middle of square'.
8 These, however, expand close to the collar, whereas the piece from Rathgall continues in the form of a bar with a cross-section similar in shape and dimension, but rotated along its axis.
9 Logbook has changed this to Sq. 7 but also notes Baulk 14/6 W.
10 Apparently contrasting information was provided by the finds records, which attribute the ring to the first visible extent of the ring-ditch, 'dark brown'. Raftery's account of the stratigraphy here, and recorded in section, calls the upper fill grey-brown or grey-brown spongy. Moreover, an upper deposit in the ring-ditch should probably not be called silt.
11 This could not be identified.
12 There is no record of this quern-stone.
13 Please note that this features in the chronological models as part of the main Bronze Age phase (see Chapter 4).

4. THE RATHGALL SEQUENCE AND DATING

4.1 THE DATING OF RATHGALL—INTRODUCTION

Katharina Becker

Artefactual, stratigraphic and radiocarbon evidence combines to allow the reconstruction of human activity at Rathgall from the Neolithic onwards into the modern period. Rathgall was one of the first sites in Ireland from which radiocarbon dates were obtained (Smithsonian lab, courtesy of Bernard Wailes), and Raftery's sampling strategy allowed him to obtain further dates in the following decades of post-excavation work. In the most recent phase of work on Rathgall a further set of dates was obtained from critical contexts to target particular problems or issues, some of which the older radiocarbon dates had brought to light. With the digitisation of especially the finds records in the last phase of the project the artefactual evidence became far more accessible and easier to interrogate in a systematic fashion.

This chapter presents a discussion and analysis of associations, radiocarbon dates and stratigraphy, which are put side by side with the account and interpretation of the stratigraphic sequence as written by Raftery prior to the availability of the bulk of the radiocarbon dates and additional stratigraphic information provided by the re-examination of the site archive.

Raftery's stratigraphic account (section 4.2) is followed by an assessment of the stratigraphy and related evidence. Both Raftery's and an alternative preferred relative chronological scenario are presented. Both scenarios must, however, remain tentative owing to a lack of direct and unambiguous stratigraphic relationships. The Bayesian assessment of the radiocarbon-dated samples and the dates themselves thus does not attempt to model those scenarios but instead presents two models (1 and 2) that are not reliant on ambiguous evidence (see section 4.4). The implications of this for the preferred scenario, developed in section 4.3, are further explored in Chapter 6.

4.2 THE STRATIGRAPHIC SEQUENCE OF BRONZE AGE RATHGALL

Barry Raftery

It seems evident that the Bronze Age phases at Rathgall represent a tight continuum, with one period of activity giving way to the next with no significant time-lag. As has already become apparent in the account of the excavation, numerous local developments can be clearly recognised where one pit gives way to another to be cut into by a third, or a trench was sunk into the fill of an abandoned hearth. Such phases of activity, evident all over the site, reflect the intensity of the activity on the site over the period of its occupation. The time-span of these various activities, however, need not necessarily have been great.

As has already become evident, the extensive destruction of the prehistoric levels through ploughing activities over much of the excavated area has made the proper elucidation of the Bronze Age occupation sequence extremely difficult. A number of important stratigraphical overlaps were, however, clearly recognisable and these are of major significance in attempting to establish an overall sequence of activity on the site.

The excavation initially focused on the area within Fosse 1 (Ring-ditch 1), but it was already apparent from the first season's work in 1969 that in the zone to its immediate east intensive and prolonged activity had taken place which undoubtedly overlapped chronologically with that associated with the ditched enclosure. As already outlined above, two zones of activity could be recognised there: a northern sector (extending from the northern portion of B as far as the end of the excavated zone in E—Area 2) where intensive industrial and domestic activity occurred, and a southern zone (Cuttings F to K—Areas 3 and 4) where evidence for domestic activity was limited, far fewer finds came to light and the dominant recognisable feature was a burial enclosure. The large number of post-holes in this southern zone seemed not to be related to any obvious domestic activity.

A key element in attempting to elucidate the complex Rathgall stratigraphy is the stratigraphical position of Ring-ditch 1 in relation to the other features uncovered. In this regard it may be taken as certain that the low yellow bank that was exposed outside Ring-ditch 1 in Sqs E, G and Y can hardly be other than upcast from digging the fosse. Obviously, therefore, material underlying this bank must be earlier than Ring-ditch 1 and must thus be earlier than all the features related to it.

In the east, however, where the most intensive activity took place, the bank was absent for a length of 17.5m from F to E, raising several possibilities. Was an already existing bank removed to make space for later occupation activity, or did the diggers deliberately avoid an already existing occupation zone when digging the ditch? In other words, was the eastern activity earlier or later than the digging of the ditch? The latter hypothesis seems implausible, so the probability is that the absence of the bank around the east is a secondary feature (i.e. an existing bank removed later on) (see below).

The most intensive industrial and habitational[1] activity on the site took place from the northern edge of B/B1 to the north of Cutting D. While there was a spread of artefacts across this entire zone, two main areas of activity could be recognised, a northern zone (mainly in Cutting D) and a southern zone (in the northern part of B and the adjoining, southern part of C). These contained significant quantities of material, including in each instance metalworking debris (Metalworking Zones 2 and 3). In D/D1, a few metres east of the main metalworking focus, a further though less intensive concentration of material occurred, including once more a discrete spread of clay mould fragments (Metalworking Zone 4). In Metalworking Zones 3 and 4 the material came from pits or hollows or lay directly on the grey subsoil, or at times sunk slightly into it. It thus seems that there is little chronological discrepancy between them.

Immediately inside Ring-ditch 1, opposite the main zones of activity referred to in Cuttings B–D, a significant concentration of potsherds and other material occurred (including glass beads). In addition, three large sunken hearths (nos 4–6) were uncovered in Sqs 7, 8 and 8/16, all of which, perhaps significantly, contained fragments of clay moulds in their fill.

It is scarcely reasonable not to assume that this significant concentration is not directly related to the activity discovered on the immediate outside of the ditch. If this is accepted, it follows either that the ditch was dug through a discrete occupation zone (including metalworking) after the abandonment of the latter or that the ditch pre-dates this phase of intensive activity.

The stratigraphy of the ditch fill in the zone between the outer and inner layers of activity referred to above is crucial in shedding light on the Bronze Age sequence at Rathgall. In the first instance, it is important to bear in mind that a concentration of mould fragments came from the outer edge of the ditch in Sqs 3/9 immediately adjacent to the Metalworking Zone 2 mould concentration (B/C).

The moulds occurred in several parts of the fill, including those which occurred close to primary silting,[2] a situation not reciprocated in the ditch opposite the Metalworking Zone 3 (D/D1) activity. Similarly, while potsherds occurred in the fill of the ditch adjacent to the latter, their quantity was nowhere near as extensive as was the case adjacent to Metalworking Zone 2.[3]

As noted earlier, it was evident in this area that black occupation material from Metalworking Zone 2 (Fig. 2.54) had filtered directly into the ditch, resting on a thick layer of silted material. This indicates that the ditch at this point was only partly silted. In addition, in the northern two thirds of Sq. 3/9, the layer of so-called 'cobbling' occurred (above, p. 95) in the upper layers, and most of the mould fragments came from among the stones and in the immediately underlying black material.

This 'cobbled' fill is important, for it occurred in the upper levels of the ditch around much of its circumference, especially in the east and south. There can be no doubt that it represents a single, deliberate act of filling. The extent of the ditch fill obviously differed from one section to another, so that the extent of the upper fill also varied. It seems that in the east, however, the ditch was still relatively open when metalworking and related activity commenced in Metalworking Zone 2. After some time, the ditch-filling was completed at the same time as the rest of the ditch was filled, and in the course of continuing metalworking activity moulds and other items were deposited amongst the stones of the 'cobbled' layer.

The presence of the moulds in Sq. 7 opposite the major D/D1 focus is significant. The small group of 21 fragments in upper levels may be random scatters or might come (though less likely) from the activity associated with Hearths 4–6 rather than from the D/D1 activity. Nonetheless, considering the large number of mould fragments in Sqs D/D1 and further east, the low number of mould fragments from this section of the ditch, in contrast to the heavy concentration in the neighbouring Sqs 9/3, is striking. It is possible to suggest that here (in possible contrast to the metalworking in B/C) some sort of structure existed which was closed to the west and open eastwards. Thus the spread of discarded fragments would only be to the east. Indeed, if the Zone 2 metalworking was carried out in the open air, in contrast to a hypothetical enclosed workshop suggested for Zone 3, deposition in the silted-up ditch to the west in 9/3 would, perhaps, have been most likely.[4]

The probability is, however, that the D/D1 zone of metalworking pre-dates the digging of Fosse 1. This would not only explain the almost total absence of mould fragments in the ditch fill in Sq. 7 but also be well in keeping with several other features which have already been noted. Most obvious and important is the fact that the southern end of the low bank slightly, but nonetheless significantly, overlies the northern edge of the D/D1 deposits. Similarly, a concentration of post-holes in Sq. E, completely sealed by the low bank, is probably part of a post-hole zone which to a noticeable extent bounds the D/D1 occupation/industrial zone. The many glass beads heavily concentrated in the D/D1 complex but also occurring in substantial numbers immediately inside the ditch (with only three coming from the silting[5] of the ditch itself) could also support the suggestion put forward above that the D/D1 concentration pre-dates the ditch. In this regard, finally, it is noticeable that the potsherd density in the silted fill of Fosse 1 opposite the D/D1 concentration is significantly less marked than is the case in the ditch directly opposite the B/C metalworking zone. This could support the argument of the chronological primacy of the D/D1 activity, the sherds in the ditch in that area thus coming from B/C activity and not from D.

The large, sunken hearths may also be significant in this regard. In the first instance, Hearth 1 in Sq. 25 is, as already noted, certainly earlier than the central palisaded enclosure (15m structure). The other large and unusual hearths may well be contemporary with Hearth 1. In particular, Hearths 4, 5 and 6, close to the ditch directly opposite the D/D1 complex, in Sqs 7 and 8, may also belong to this suggested pre-ditch group of hearths. The presence of mould fragments in the latter three hearths again supports the argument that they belong to a pre-ditch phase, one related to the D/D1 activity.

This scenario thus envisages a primary, Bronze Age phase of activity with heavy emphasis on metalworking, including the zone of occupation in the D/D1 area, the zone of large hearths as far west as Sq. 25 and an unspecified distance north-east, including the activity in Sq. Y1. No clear boundaries for this suggested primary zone of activity can be suggested, so that it is open to question, for instance, whether the concentration of bronze-casting in Sqs 53/54 or the complex Pit 118 in Sqs 17/18 are part of this early complex. Nevertheless, since almost all the available radiocarbon dates for relevant features are broadly comparable, clearly concentrated in the last centuries of the second millennium BC, it seems evident that, no matter what the detailed stratigraphy, all these features belong to the same broad Middle Bronze Age cultural horizon.[6]

The implication, if the suggestions put forward above are correct, is that the B/C bronze-working zone post-dates this primary phase. The moulds from the latter phase of activity, as noted above, include fragments from well down in the ditch, which was thus open when the casting was in train. By this time, however, a considerable amount of silting had occurred, for the depth of sterile silted material in the base of the ditch in places reached as much as 18cm. There was thus a gap of some time between the ditch excavation and the B/C casting. Because of the depth of the moulds in the ditch, however, the gap cannot have been great. As well as this, it seems clear that no significant stratigraphical division between the activity in B/C and that in D/D1 was recognisable. The three phases of activity suggested here are thus seen as succeeding each other with no great chronological intervals dividing them, and this fully agrees with the spread of the relevant radiocarbon dates in this area. This scenario seems to imply, however, that the exceptional intensity of the first phase of activity diminished, though the casting of bronze continued on a considerable scale.

From the above, therefore, a number of tentative conclusions seem possible. First, it is evident that the metalworking represented by the moulds in Zone 2 took place at a time when the ditch was open. Second, it seems that the metalworking of Zone 3 took place at a time when the ditch was either silted up or had not yet been dug. It is decidedly possible that the Zone 3 metalworking took place before the ditch was dug and so pre-dates that of Zone 2.

There are indications to support this latter possibility. All the large hearths are in the north-east (of Area 1) and are absent elsewhere.[7] Three—Hearths 4, 5 and 6—occur close to the ditch opposite Metalworking Zone 3, and all three contained mould fragments. In the case of Hearth 4, that closest to the ditch, no fewer than 34 mould fragments occurred in the hearth itself and 24 in an associated post-hole. Hearth 3 (Figs 4.1 and 2.46) produced two crucible fragments but, perhaps most significantly, Hearth 1 was cut through by the bedding trench of the 15m structure at a time when the latter had silted up. In addition, it should be noted that in Cutting E the occupation layer was overlain by the yellow bank, which, it is assumed, was created from soil excavated from the circular ditch and which also extended slightly onto

Metalworking Zone 3. A key question is whether this bank originally extended around the eastern perimeter of the ditch.

It is therefore possible to suggest that the main occupation in Cutting D with the associated metalworking belongs to a phase contemporary with the large sunken hearths and that these pre-dated the ditched enclosure. The Zone 2 metalworking in B and C, material from which filled the ditch, belonged to a phase when the ditch had been dug but was largely without silting. This scenario envisages an initial phase of dense occupation related to the large fire-pits (hearths), the occupation zone in Sq. D including the Zone 3 metalworking. This was followed by the digging of Fosse 1 with the central bedding trench, the pits and post-holes—or some of them at least—outside and inside the bedding trench and, above all, Pit 119 with the cremation and the small gold ring. The second phase of metalworking in B/C took place outside Fosse 1 when the latter was still substantially open. Thus it can be argued that the initial Bronze Age activity is represented by the larger hearths and the settlement zone, including pottery, five glass beads and the blade fragment, uncovered beneath the yellow bank in X/X1 in the north. At a period not long after this, Fosse 1 was dug through the zone of this primary activity, initially covering the latter with the yellow upcast from the ditch. There then followed the removal of a lengthy stretch of the bank in the east, allowing for extensive occupational and industrial activity in the B–E zone, at a time when the ditch was by now to a large extent silted up, apart from a few areas which were still substantially open. It is very possible that the 15m enclosure, its entrance facing the B–E zone, was built at this time. The further metalworking to the north and west of the enclosure may also belong to this phase.

As has been noted earlier, the east–west zone of gravelly material in Sqs B1/B2 marks a clear division between the dense occupation/industrial activity to the north and the burial complex to the south with occupation material significantly reduced. This was especially noteworthy under the recent wall in Sq. 5/G, where the yellow bank lay directly on a brownish-black layer containing thin, darker bands extending longitudinally along its length. This layer was only preserved under the wall and, significantly, it was virtually devoid of prehistoric artefacts. This, therefore, was clearly not an occupation horizon. The total absence of this layer outside the zone covered by the recent stone wall (which also exactly covered the yellow material of the low bank), its extent immediately under the yellow bank and the thin, overlapping zones of darker material may suggest that the bank was initially marked by layers of sods, dug from the upper levels of the contemporary ground surface, before the yellow soil from the fosse was piled on top. This hypothesis is, of course, weakened by the absence of such a suggested sod layer in the two other excavated zones. The frequent and often quite inexplicable inconsistencies in so many aspects of prehistoric activity remind us, however, that 21st-century considerations need not necessarily be relevant in our attempts to explain the activities of prehistoric people.

The layer just referred to and the yellow bank were clearly cut through by the ditch of the Ring-ditch 2 enclosure. The latter also cut through the main occupation in G, where it was preserved under the late wall. Its upper silt, however, is sealed by the 'cobbling'.

4.3 THE LATER PREHISTORIC SITE SEQUENCE

Katharina Becker, Joanne Gaffrey and Derek Hamilton

Human activity at Rathgall can be traced from the Neolithic to the late medieval period. The period of the greatest archaeological complexity is the Late Bronze Age, which appears to be represented by the bulk of the excavated archaeology, in spite of the evidence for frequent disturbance and probably truncation of deposits relating to this phase.

The key stratigraphic relationships between some of the main elements of the site are discussed by Raftery in the stratigraphic account (Chapter 2), and he develops his thoughts on the relative chronological sequence in section 4.2 above. The post-excavation analysis provided additional evidence that contributes to the discussion of both the complex relative chronology and the absolute dating of the later prehistoric sequence—some of it contradicting aspects of the evidence available to Raftery at the time but not necessarily making his model unviable. The problems inherent to an examination of a site archive without having first-hand experience of the site are obvious, and thus the excavator's voice must take a central place in the account of the site. While juxtaposed with observations based on the post-excavation process, we chose not to tamper with Raftery's observations in the stratigraphic account and in section 4.2 where apparently contradicted by the new evidence. Instead, we highlight these contradictions throughout the volume, and in this section we develop and discuss the evidence from a different perspective, without affecting the narrative in the main stratigraphic report and Raftery's discussion of the site sequence in section 4.2.

4.3.1 Taphonomy—survival and disturbance of archaeological evidence

A lack of vertical stratigraphic relationships, likely caused by truncation by later activity, especially within the cashel (Rampart 1), makes it difficult to tie the different parts of the site or features into a relative chronological sequence. A substantial degree of disturbance, in the main caused by ploughing, lazy-bed cultivation and rabbit activity, is noted by Raftery to have created an undifferentiated layer of brown humus, varying in thickness from about 15cm to a maximum of about 30cm, on top of the archaeology observed, which often only consists of the base of features cut into the natural (see Chapter 1). In some areas plough furrows consistently went down onto the natural. This appears to have been particularly the case in Area 1, the area enclosed by the later cashel (Rampart 1), and is evidenced by the finding of medieval and post-medieval objects right beside, or in, the upper fills of many prehistoric features—for example, medieval finds were documented directly on top of the heavily truncated bedding trench of the 15m structure or associated with hearths. The degree of truncation of these features and the corresponding dispersal of finds into the disturbed topsoil becomes apparent when considering how sherds from individual vessels are found within features and in the 'brown soil' overlying them (Table 4.1[8]). It is also likely that in cases where finds are attributed to features with phrasing such as 'black of hearth X' this can refer to areas of disturbance of such features, cautioning against over-reliance on such associations. Sections show how the disturbed topsoil 'brown humus' sits directly on top of the cuts of prehistoric features. While the level of disturbance can be gauged to a degree by establishing the depths at which typologically later finds occur, the additional disturbance caused by the apparently extensive rabbit activity can rarely be accounted for, although it is documented in some of the long sections and in the finds records, e.g. for strap-tag E84:1153. In some cases the question of whether later finds are intrusive or the result of disturbance is unclear, as is the question of at which point in the site's history disturbances occurred.

Area 1 (Figs 2.3 and 2.5)
Area 1, under and within the area enclosed by the medieval stone cashel, was significantly disturbed, probably not only by agricultural use but also by the construction of the cashel itself. Deposits under the cashel wall produced Leinster Cooking Ware, other medieval wares and finds, and a 1948 penny—further evidence of later disturbance as well as of modification of the cashel. This is also apparent in the visible distinction between the upper level of the deposits directly under the wall and the underlying black deposits (see below). Lower courses of the wall appear to consist of smaller stones, whereas the upper parts consist of a more loosely piled mass of large stones, also possibly reflecting later modifications of the wall.

Disturbance demonstrably affected the upper levels of the Ring-ditch 1 fill, from which medieval artefacts were frequently recorded. In contrast, the lower levels of the ditch fill contained mainly Bronze Age material, although accompanied in some areas by later material culture and radiocarbon dates. Whether these are the result of localised disturbance or are contemporary with the infilling of the ditch is open to debate and will be further explored below.

There is some suggestion that undisturbed prehistoric deposits may have survived in some locations within Area 1. This is indicated by the distinct spatial distribution of moulds in the north-western part of the enclosure (Raftery's Metalworking Zone 1), focused on Sq. 51 (Hearth 10), or by a section (Fig. 4.1) that illustrates how Hearth 3 in Sq. 23/24

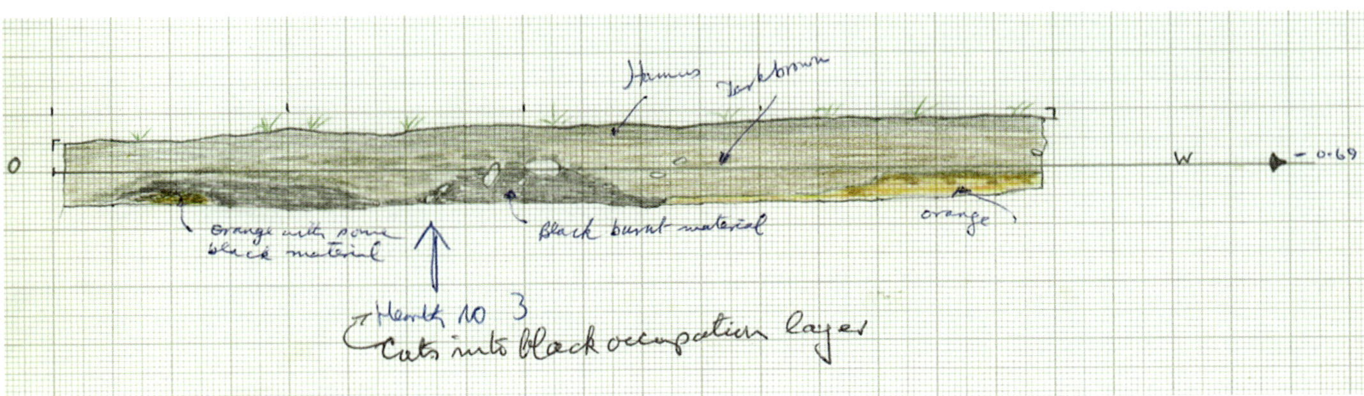

Fig. 4.1—Squares 23/24 and Hearth 3, which cuts into a black occupation layer in this zone (original site drawing).

cuts into a black 'occupation layer' in this zone. It has to be assumed that small patches of such *in situ* strata remained in some locations, though Raftery states:

> 'Apart from these sometimes enigmatic fire-pits [*hearths—Ed.*] there were no other significant features within the central enclosure. A number of shallow depressions were examined in differing parts of the excavated area but these were of no obvious significance. It is impossible to say how many, if any, of these had been deliberately dug. They were almost always revealed as patches of grey in the yellow subsoil and in every case they emerged, upon examination, as shallow, irregular depressions. Usually such features contained a few scraps of coarse pottery, but a few contained miscellaneous clay mould fragments and occasionally other items. These are all objects which had been scattered randomly across the surface.'

It appears that truncation was especially strong within the cashel, whereas 'occupation deposits' survived *in situ* in Area 2 and under the cashel wall in Area 3.

Area 2 (Figs 2.3 and 2.53)

Area 2 is one of the two areas of the site where apparently stratified deposits were encountered, and it produced most of the finds. The taphonomy of the Area 2 'occupation' deposits is of central importance for the understanding of the sequence as well as the function of Rathgall. Without the possibility of examining the deposits *in situ*, or even *ex situ*, we rely on the description of the deposits that contained the bulk of the Bronze Age artefactual material. Moulds, glass beads and some metal artefacts were concentrated in this area, and the presence of some burnt but unidentified bone has been noted. Tantalising records in the finds logs and in Raftery's notes speak also of the finding of a 'wooden vessel' and an agglomerate of grain (cf. Monk 1985–6).

The lack of exact recording of finds hinders a detailed analysis of the make-up of the occupation deposits, with finds mostly localised to 5m grid square and an approximate depth range. The description of the contexts with which they were associated is often ambiguous, as fills and strata were not recorded by context. The finds were embedded in a matrix that was generally described as charcoal-rich, particularly in its upper layers. As outlined in Chapter 2, Raftery describes a sequence of spreads in this area (section 2.3.1). While this sequence seems securely evidenced and can be tallied with the deposits visible in the long sections in this area, it is possible that they are themselves reflective of a sequence of small-scale redeposition events or processes. Evidence for this may be that the sherds of Vessel 209 (Table 4.1), spread across Sqs D/D1, were found in the top 'lumpy' layer but also in the black, charcoal-rich material of the underlying deposit at depths of between 20–28cm and 40–60cm. The same is true for Vessels 207 and 203. This may suggest that the uppermost layer and the main black charcoal-rich material do not necessarily represent different phases of deposition but may have been generated in close temporality. Post-depositional disturbance, on the other hand, may also play a role in this, though not possible to reconcile with the apparently clear stratigraphic make-up of the layers, unless these are post-depositional as well. The underlying brown layer has not produced material that would help to clarify its relationship to the 'black' and 'lumpy' deposits. The lowest layer, described as a hard grey floor, is possibly a layer of leaching into the natural, which finds support in the lack of recorded finds from this layer in Area 2 (but see the area of cobbling and Area 3). In general, the relatively large number of sherds assigned to vessels in this area, such as Vessels 204 and 205, suggests that they were still substantially complete when deposited.

Both the ubiquitous material culture from these deposits and the large and coherent range of radiocarbon dates obtained on charcoal samples date them to the Late Bronze Age. Raftery suggested that different metalworking foci can be distinguished in Area 2 (i.e. Metalworking Zones 2–4; see above). Indeed, there are concentrations of moulds in the B/C (Metalworking Zone 2) and D cuttings (Metalworking Zones 3 and 4). A concentration of fragments of moulds for the casting of implements with socket moulding in Metalworking Zones 3 and 4 and one of moulds for the casting of an implement with midrib in Metalworking Zone 2 may indicate that these are *in situ* deposits, although the fragmentation of a single valve or mould could also produce similar patterns. Moreover, contrasting evidence for links *between* mould fragments in different zones suggests a degree of dispersal between the 'metalworking zones', specifically northwards from Metalworking Zone 2 into Metalworking Zones 3 and 4. Likewise, sherds of pottery Vessel 35 were found in Sqs E1 and D2, indicating a close relationship between the deposits of Metalworking Zones 3–4. As noted in Chapter 3, section 3.9, it is striking that the condition of the moulds varies significantly, probably owing to processes of displacement during which some fragments were exposed

Metalworking Zone 2						
3/B	**3/B disturbance**	**B1**	**B1 disturbance**	**C1**	**C1 disturbance**	**Depth**
Various	Medieval artefacts to 20cm	Black 15–20cm	Iron fragments and medieval pottery down to 30cm	Brown/black areas 15–25cm	Medieval pottery down to 30cm in SW of C1 near cashel wall in dark brown/black AND amber bead 4246 In black occupation level, almost on grey 'floor'	15–25cm
	Iron nails 20–35cm	Dark black concentration 20–25cm		Brown and dark black ocupation levels 20–35cm		20–35cm
				Cobbling		30cm
Grey floor						

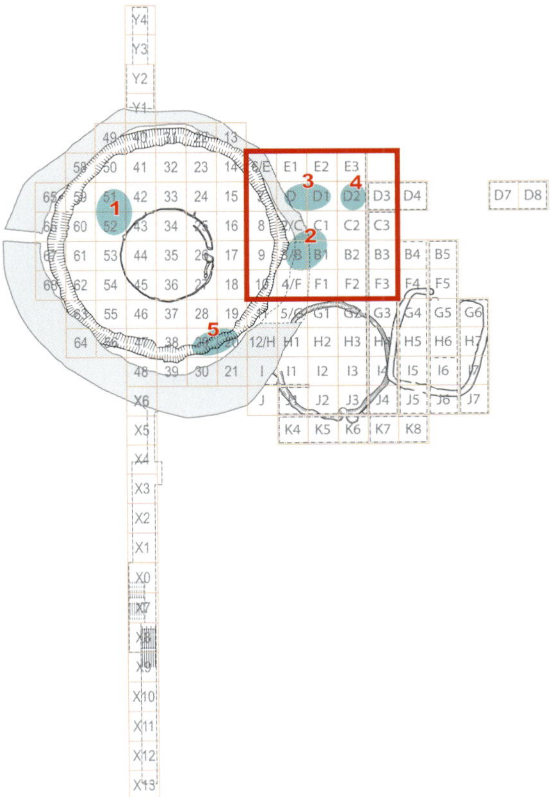

Metalworking zone 3			
D	**D1**	**D & D1 disturbance**	**Depth**
'Lumpy' layer		Medieval pottery to 21cm	15–32cm
Thick black charcoal layer immediately below lumpy material			27–65cm
Lowest level of black		Iron object 7430, in black habitation material 40–60cm depth	40–60cm
Brown ashy material (under black)			35–65cm

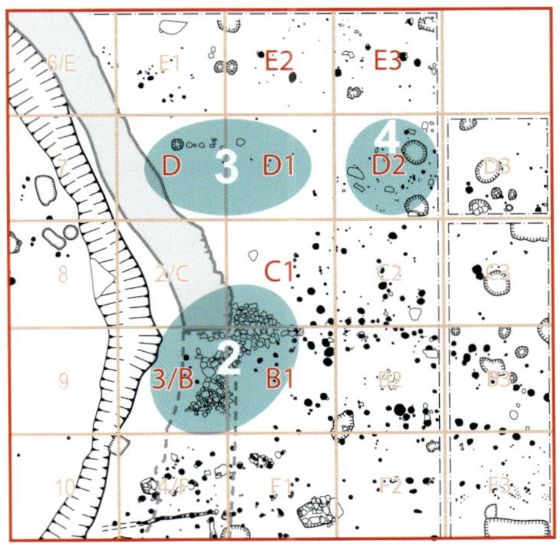

Metalworking zone 4					
E2	**E3**	**E2 & E3 disturbance**	**D2**	**D2 disturbance**	**Depth**
Brown-black		Medieval pottery E3: 20cm; E2: 26cm	Brown-black Contained mercury-gilt mount at a depth of 27-30cm in the fill of depression D84	Medieval pottery and iron fragment 6597 down to 30cm	10–35cm
			Brown and ashy brown		35–40cm

Fig. 4.2—Stratigraphy and level of disturbance in Area 2 metalworking concentrations.

Fig. 4.3—Area 2 under excavation (Sqs C1/C2, looking west).

on the surface and subject to abrasion whereas others were protected within soil deposits or cut features. The examination of the moulds, however, did not produce any correlations between contexts and condition.

The timing and extent of this disturbance and movement of objects or deposits are difficult to date. While there is much to suggest that the dispersal of the moulds took place not long after their deposition, other—possibly much later—intrusions into these levels are also evident. Highlighting the occurrence of disturbances, the distribution of medieval finds in the uppermost layers (Fig. 4.2) suggests that these were probably dragged in by ploughing—indeed, agricultural marks on the surface of these deposits were regularly observed (Fig. 4.3). While an iron object found at a depth of 40–60cm in Sq. D/D1 could be speculated to be an example of early iron use, the typologically unambiguous assignation of an early medieval date to amber bead E84:4246, found within the lowest levels of the black occupation deposits in C1, 'almost on the grey floor', provides clear evidence of disturbance to this depth.

Area 3 (Figs 2.3 and 2.87)

With the exception of the areas under the rampart in Sqs 11/5/G, no *in situ* deposits seem to have been present in this area, beyond the fill of features cut into the subsoil, such as Ring-ditch 2 or pits. This is evident from the description of rather homogeneous brown deposits across the area, which are also depicted in various long sections that record these on top of the cut features. Finds records further demonstrate the presence of medieval pottery to significant depths, including to just above the natural. Medieval pottery was found in Sq. 4, in a 'black soil' near the wall and in 'light brown material' at a depth of between 25cm and 28cm. In this 'black area near wall' Dublin-type coarseware, too, was found at a depth of 15–20cm. In addition, in F1 medieval and post-medieval pottery sherds (Dublin ware and pearlware) were found at a depth of between 20cm and 40cm in 'the brown'. In F2/G1/G2 significant amounts of various medieval wares are

Table 4.1—Table of vessel units and their contexts.

Vessel no.	Artefact type	Area	Sq. no.	Feature/area	Artefact	Context	Depth (cm)
40	Coarse pottery	1	29	Pit 121	E84:6020, 6021, 6023	Fill of Pit 121	
			38	Ring-ditch 1	E84:4326	Grey fill in upper levels of ditch	20
		2	D/D1		E84:7549	In brown ashy material under black	50–60
35	Middle Bronze Age domestic urn-type	2	D2		E84:6457	In very dark brown; some lumpy material in S of square	27–30
			D4		E84:7024	In brown, black patches showing	17–20
			E1		E84:6705	In brown, yellow showing (bank)	20–29
					E84:7252, 7383, 7396, 7397, 7298	In black area outside bank	35–40
			E2		E84:6477, 6419	In brown	15–19
					E84:6586	In brown	20–22
					E84:6650, 6651	In brown	24–26
					E84:7158, 7196	Extreme W of square, in dark material outside 'bank'	30–35
			E3	Pit 55	E84:7653	Pit 55	
42	Coarse pottery	1	67		E84:5950	In section strip, under sod over 'cobbling'	
			41	Ring-ditch 1	E84:5327	In upper level, grey fill of ditch	
44	Coarse pottery	1	2		E84:1100	Black near wall, SE	35 below lower wall stones
				Ring-ditch 1	E84:1417	In black fill of ditch, S	20–29 below yellow
45	Coarse pottery	1	6		E84:1231	Dark brown, SW	23
			7		E84:937, 1401, 1336, 855	Dark brown, W	26
47	Coarse pottery	1	7	Ring-ditch 1	E84:1227	Black, N	40 below lowest wall stones
					E84:1188	Dark brown, near middle of square	40
					E84:759	Darkish brown near middle of square	15–20
					E84:1338	In black fill of ditch, upper levels	
					E84:665	Light brown, SE	12
59	Coarse pottery	1	17/18	Pit 118	E84:6167, 6176b, 6152a–c, 5999a,c–i	In large storage pit in dense black 'ring'; Pit 118	
60	Coarse pottery	1	17/18	Pit 118	E84:6058, 6172, 6174, 6176a, 6161, 4494	In black outer ring of large storage pit; Pit 118	
			20	Ring-ditch 1	E84:4518	In black fill of ditch	
61	Coarse pottery	1	17/18	Pit 118	E84:4492, 4484, 4485, 5929, 5928, 5935, 6169a–e	In black sticky 'semicircle' around the bottom edge of Pit 118	10
			38	Ring-ditch 1	E84:4509a	In grey fill on outer edge of ditch	
62	Coarse pottery	1	17/18	Pit 118	E84:6144a–c	From main yellow fill touching outer black of large storage pit; Pit 118	
					E84:6000	From outer black layer in storage pit, Pit 118	
					E84:6156	Large storage Pit 118 in dense black 'ring'	
80	Coarse pottery	1	40	Ring-ditch 1	E84:5209	In fill of ditch, greyish material 35cm deep	70 below sod
			66		E84:5652	In section strip	25–30
81	Coarse pottery	1	29	Ring-ditch 1	E84:4898	Grey fill of ditch, W	30 in ditch
			29		E84:3800	In brown, centre	25
131	Coarse pottery	1	7/8	Ring-ditch 1	E84:1482i	Almost on base of ditch under baulk	50 below yellow
			2		E84:1086	Black near wall, N	20 below lower wall stones

Table 4.1 (cont.)—Table of vessel units and their contexts.

Vessel no.	Artefact type	Area	Sq. no.	Feature/area	Artefact	Context	Depth (cm)
134	Coarse pottery	1	6	Ring-ditch 1	E84:1446	At base of black fill on bottom of ditch	55 below yellow
					E84:1498.1	First layer under sod	10
147	Coarse pottery	1	7	Ring-ditch 1	E84:1361	Brown/black fill of ditch, E	30–35 below yellow
		1	8/16	Hearth 6	E84:2126	Hearth 6, grey level at bottom	
153	Coarse pottery	1	8		E84:892	Black, E	30
				Ring-ditch 1	E84:1435	In black fill of ditch, close to bottom, NE	40–50 below yellow
				Ring-ditch 1	E84:1437	In black fill of ditch, close to bottom, NE	40–50 below yellow
		1	7	Hearth 5?	E84:809	Very dark material in parts almost black; heavy occupation in this area; Hearth 5	21
154	Coarse pottery	1	7	Ring-ditch 1	E84:1404	In black fill of ditch	30–37 below yellow
					E84:1010	In dark, black occupation near wall, E	35
155	Coarse pottery	1	7	Ring-ditch 1	E84:1357	Brown/black fill of ditch	30–35 below yellow
166	Coarse pottery	1	27		E84:2161	In light brown soil	20–25
			45/36		E84:6036	In section strip	
			28		E84:3343	On orange	
			44	Pit 143	E84:5020	Pit H = Pit 143	
168	Coarse pottery	1	17		E84:1805	Dark patch in NW of square	30
			20	Ring-ditch 1	E84:4513	In black fill of ditch	
			29		E84:3619	In dark brown soil, NE	20
			27/28		E84:5894	In section strip	
172	Coarse pottery	1	29	Ring-ditch 1	E84:4267	Black spongy fill of ditch	20–25 in ditch
			28		E84:2736	Brown soil	15–20
			37		E84:2791	In brown soil, centre	20–25
173	Coarse pottery	1	37		E84:2634	In brown soil	15–20
			45/36		E84:6038.1	In section strip	
			33		E84:1092	No context information	
			45	Pit 149	E84:5093	Pit 149 encroaching on circular bedding trench in SW of square	
209	Coarse pottery	1	27		E84:2071	In light brown soil	15–20
		2	D	Metalworking Zone 3	E84:6522	In thick black charcoal area; lumpy habitation refuse removed; SE	29–32
					E84:6408	In black, among lumpy areas; small amounts of charcoal and burnt bone; small amounts of baked clay	24–28
					E84:6522	In thick black charcoal area; lumpy habitation refuse removed; SE	29–32
			D1		E84:6377	In dark brown/black among ferrous lumpy material	22–24
			D/D1		E84:6582	In black charcoal material, under lumpy black occupation material	30
					E84:7180	In black charcoal habitation area	40–60
					E84:7321	In brown	40–60
241	Coarse pottery	2	B1		E84:1764.1		
			F1		E84:6941	In brown, on edge of black stone-filled area	
			F1	Pit 38	E84:7656	Pit 38	20
243	Coarse pottery	1	14		E84:248	In light brown sandy-coloured material, NE	14–17
			G2	Pit 23	E84:7522	Pit 23	
250	Coarse pottery		J2	Ring-ditch 2	E84:8383	Grey fill of ditch 10–15cm from base	
			J2		E84:8364	Grey on yellow, W part of square	35–40
			J4		E84:8402	In brown humus at W end of square	40

Table 4.1 (cont.)—Table of vessel units and their contexts.

Vessel no.	Artefact type	Area	Sq. no.	Feature/area	Artefact	Context	Depth (cm)
266	Coarse pottery	2	X3		E84:7736	From black patches in brown	20–25
			D/D1		E84:7464	In black material	40–60
			X1		E84:7502	In brown	15–20
			X3		E84:7664	In brown	20
			X3		E84:7665	In brown	20
			X3		E84:7700	In brown	20
			X3		E84:7705	In brown	20
			X3		E84:7777	In brown	20–25
			X3		E84:7778	In brown	20–25
			X3		E84:7824	In brown	20–25
			X3		E84:7825	In brown	25
			X3		E84:7831	In brown	20–25
			X3		E84:7840	In brown	20-25
		1	29	RD1?	E84:4325	In brown area between stones on N edge of ditch	20
274	Coarse pottery	2	B3	Pit 204	E84:9110	Black fill of Pit 204	30
			C1	Metalworking Zone 2	E84:7892	In black under wall	
			C2		E84:2928	In dark brown soil	30
299	Coarse pottery	2	E1		E84:7688.1		35
			E1	Top of 'bank'	E84:7674	In black on top of 'bank'	35
			E1		E84:6638	In dark brown, 20cm bank? Yellow	20–29
325	Coarse pottery		K6	Pit 273	E84:9619	Grey and black layers, Pit 273	
			K6		E84:9620	Grey and black layers, Pit 273	
			K4	Pit 272	E84:9554	Pit 272	
326	Coarse pottery		X1		E84:7770	In brown	20–25
327	Coarse pottery		X1ext.		E84:7945	In brown	25
355	Coarse pottery	2	B/C	Metalworking Zone 2	E84:8082, 8084, 8086	In black under wall; lower levels	
					E84:8210	In section in brown humus	
			B1/C1		E84:8122, 8123	In black under wall; lower levels	
			B5		E84:9096b	In brown humus	30
			C1		E84:3999	In dark black occupation layer	25–35
			D1/C1		E84:8090	In black under wall; lower levels	
363	Coarse pottery	1	20/21		E84:6128, 6129	In black layer under wall	25–30
			61		E84:5502	In brown	20–25
403	Coarse pottery	Z	Z5:d	Pit 16	E100:119, 120, 121, 142, 143, 156	Black fill, Pit 16	
				Ring-ditch 5	E100:158	In grey-brown fill of circular trench	
404	Coarse pottery	Z	Z5:d		E100:166, 167, 168, 169, 170, 171	In black fill of Pit 16	
					E100:152, 153	In grey silty fill of curvilinear trench; all concentrated towards SE end	
410	Coarse pottery	Z	Z5:d		E100:95	In black charcoal area at W end of square	
					E100:96	In black charcoal area at W end of square	
					E100:172	In Black fill of Pit 16	

Table 4.1 (cont.)—Table of vessel units and their contexts.

Vessel no.	Artefact type	Area	Sq. no.	Feature/area	Artefact	Context	Depth (cm)
411	Coarse pottery	Z	Z5:h		E100:111, 112, 113, 114, 115, 116	In dark brown fill of Pit 15	
					E100:101	In grey-black charcoal area in SW part of sq.	
425	Coarse pottery	4	B5	Hearth 14	E84:9107	In black area in SE corner of square; Hearth 14	30
			G4		E84:8505	In mottled grey-brown almost on yellow, E extension of initial cutting	25
431	Beaker	1	2		E84:1104a,b	Dark brown, baulk 2/8, W	25
			66	Ring-ditch 1	E84:5912a,b	In grey upper fill of ditch	30–35
			45		E84:4648	Yellow starting to show in brown	18–22

recorded to have been found to depths of 35cm in brown, 'immediately over natural', and in G2 a clay pipe is recorded as having been found on top of the natural. A comparable situation is documented in Sqs H1, H2 and I1, but also in the northern extent of 5/G and 4/F, under the former rampart. Here the amorphous nature of the overlying fills is apparent (see Chapter 2, section 2.4.1). Deposits under the rampart produced Leinster Cooking Ware, other medieval wares and finds, and a 1948 penny. (This is documented in the upper level of the deposits directly under the wall.) An apparently *in situ* prehistoric but sterile layer is cut by Ring-ditch 2.

4.3.2 The stratigraphic evidence

Area 1 stratigraphy

Area 1 is defined broadly by the extent of Ring-ditch 1. A variety of cut features—pits, post-holes and hearths—occur within it, along with the overlying stone-built stone cashel Rampart 1 and the various cut features within the enclosed area. Apart from the unambiguous relationship of the stone cashel and the Iron Age iron furnace to the underlying prehistoric archaeology, a great number of cut features, including Ring-ditch 1, are dated primarily on the basis of associated artefacts or radiocarbon dates, and only a few stratigraphic relationships can be observed.

Clearly observable stratigraphic relationships in the area are listed here.

1 –The medieval stone cashel overlies Ring-ditch 1 in some grid squares.

2 –An iron-working furnace was cut into the fill of Ring-ditch 1 when it had completely silted up.

3 –The bedding trench of the 15m structure at the centre of the area enclosed by Ring-ditch 1 cuts through Hearth 1.

4 –A number of pits cut or are cut by Ring-ditch 1.

5 –A number of pits cut or are cut by the 15m structure.

6 –The fill of Ring-ditch 1 contains in its eastern extent thick, intrusive 'occupation material' deposits, which create a link between Areas 1 and 2 in Sqs 7–9 and also 2/C and 3/B. There also seem to be some dumps of similarly finds- and charcoal-rich material within the ring-ditch fill in Sqs 20 and 29 (Metalworking Zone 5). Moulds and coarseware pottery are found throughout the fill of Ring-ditch 1 around its circumference, including the grey silt at the bottom of the ditch. Medieval pottery and artefacts were found in some areas of the ring-ditch on its western side.

7 –Yellow redeposited soil that Raftery considered to be the upcast from the digging of Ring-ditch 1 sits on top of occupation material of apparent Bronze Age date in Sqs Y1 and E1. Black 'occupation material' was found on top of the yellow material in Sq. E1.

8 –The occupation deposits in the E cuttings were overlain by yellow soils that Raftery interpreted as upcast from the creation of Ring-ditch 1, representing an external bank (see below). He considered the lack of such deposits in the central, eastern zone and the corresponding intrusive deposits from Area 2 into Ring-ditch 1 to be evidence for the absence of a bank at this point.

Area 2 stratigraphy

Area 2 is defined by the presence of charcoal- and finds-rich deposits (Raftery's occupation layers), which seem to be bounded on the south by an arc of post-holes running in an east–west direction in the B (B1–B4) cuttings, emanating from 'the cobbling' in Sq. 3/B. As individual strata and deposits were not uniquely identified by context numbers, there is some ambiguity regarding their sequence. Based on the recorded depths of finds and their attribution to distinctly described deposits, a broad stratigraphic sequence can be identified (see section 2.3.1, and above). The natural in Area 2 is overlain by the 'grey hard floor' (probably a zone of leaching), which in turn is overlain by the actual 'occupation deposits'. The differentiation of different strata within this occupation material may not, however, represent a chronological sequence as such, as indicated by the distribution of vessel units through these layers (see Chapter 3, section 3.9.1). Likewise, the mould links between Areas 1 and 2 suggest that both derive from the same activity, with Metalworking Zones 3 and 4 showing clear links to Metalworking Zone 2.

Raftery attempts further—horizontal—chronological differentiation of the activity in Area 2 into that pre-dating and that post-dating the digging of Ring-ditch 1. He postulates that, in the northern part of Area 2, Metalworking Zone 3 (grid squares D) can be differentiated from Metalworking Zone 2 (B and C grid squares). He argues that, based on the low frequency of mould finds in the fill of Ring-ditch 1 adjacent to Metalworking Zone 3, the metalworking activity must have pre-dated the digging of the ditch. He contrasts the low number of moulds in the ditch adjacent to Metalworking Zone 3 with the high numbers adjacent to Metalworking Zone 2 and concludes that these must represent metalworking respectively before and after the digging of the ditch. The impression of an apparent lack of moulds from the initial phase of sterile silt accumulation within the ditch further adds to an argument about the relationship of these processes with a putative bank creation and removal. The reanalysis of the distribution of finds, however, demonstrates the presence of significant numbers of moulds in the ditch adjacent to Metalworking Zone 3 and of other finds in the silt at the base of the ditch in Sq. 7, adjacent to Metalworking Zone 2.

Based on the available evidence, no chronological differentiation—horizontal or vertical—within Area 2 can be clearly demonstrated (see Chapter 3, section 3.9). Instead, a largely coherent sequence of deposition over time is indicated, focusing on or emanating from the area of Metalworking Zone 2, with metalworking debris and pottery disposed of in this zone and towards the north and east. Notably the majority of the heat-affected daub also comes from here, possibly representing kilns or other structures or floors.

Area 3 stratigraphy

A number of stratigraphic links between Ring-ditch 2 in Area 3 and other features can be observed.

1 – Ring-ditch 2 appears to cut the north-western corner of a rectangular structure in the F/G squares. Photographic evidence of the intersection of Ring-ditch 2 and the rectangular structure documents both features after excavation, after the cuts had been emptied of their fills, as does the section drawing. This makes it difficult to suggest which of the two is earlier, but Raftery clearly asserts that Ring-ditch 2 had cut the rectangular structure.

2 – The primary focus of Ring-ditch 2 is the central zone of burning surrounded by a 'forest' of stake-holes, which is evidently a pyre into which Burial 1 had been inserted. The second pyre (Chapter 6, section 6.3, Hearth 15) may, like Burial 2 and other burial deposits within the enclosure, represent a second phase of use.

3 – A layer of cobbling under the cashel in grid square 5/G overlies possible bank deposits of Ring-ditch 1 and overlies Ring-ditch 2. It is probably part of the base construction of the cashel and has produced no prehistoric material. A coin from 1948 from the same layer may be intrusive and it is most likely that the medieval pottery creates a secure *terminus post quem* for the creation of this layer, though later modifications of the walls are probably also to be expected.

4 – Ring-ditch 2 cuts prehistoric possible sod and layers under the cashel that Raftery identified as part of the yellow bank of Ring-ditch 1.

5 – Ring-ditch 2 is cut by the enclosure ditch of the medieval house in Sqs H4/I4.

6 – The stockade or palisade enclosure that encircles most of Areas 3 and 4 appears focused on Ring-ditch 2. Raftery considered the post alignment or enclosure to be broadly contemporary with Ring-ditch 2 and to have functioned as either an enclosure or the delineation of an access route to Ring-ditch 1. If completed to a full circle, this post alignment would intersect with the line of Ring-ditch 1, which appears an unlikely design. The cutting of Ring-ditch 1 through an existing or derelict palisade appears more likely, with evidence for its missing portion having been removed by the truncation within Area 1. Thus it appears likely that Ring-ditch 2 pre-dates Ring-ditch 1.

Area 4 stratigraphy

In Area 4 there is only limited evidence for Bronze Age activity, mostly in the form of pits, and the medieval deposits appear to rest more or less directly on subsoil. The medieval enclosure around the rectangular house (see Chapter 2, section 2.5) cuts into the upper levels of Ring-ditch 2. Its later dating to the medieval period is further confirmed by the artefactual associations.

Rampart 2

Rampart 2, within which at least two phases of construction are clearly identifiable, rests on a horizon of ploughsoil or other agricultural surface, which also contained cut features that yielded Bronze Age artefacts, as exposed by the 1970s excavation. No date is available for the actual rampart construction, but radiocarbon dates obtained from the initial silting of the ditch suggest that it filled up in the early medieval period, suggesting the creation or recutting of the ditch at this time (Chapter 2, section 2.8).

Cutting X

Various features within this cutting contained Bronze Age material culture. There are no stratigraphic relationships with the other areas of excavation.

Z cuttings ('outside cemetery')

The 'outside cemetery' produced ample evidence for funerary activity, as well as a possibly contemporary small circular building. The dating available for features associated with the burial activity places it broadly in the same horizon as the main activity on the site. There are no stratigraphic relationships with the other areas of excavation.

4.3.3 Stratigraphic sequence

The three main elements of activity at Rathgall—metalworking, burial activity and Ring-ditch 1, with the 15m structure at its centre—are intertwined spatially and temporally. Untangling them to sort them into a relative chronological sequence relies on assumptions about the functions of features, as well as about the taphonomic processes that led to the creation of deposits.

Scenario 1 (Raftery's scenario)

This scenario derives from and summarises the central aspects of Raftery's hypothesis of site development (section 4.2), which sees Ring-ditches 1 and 2 as well as the metalworking activity as part of a chronologically tight sequence, linked through the yellow bank of Ring-ditch 1, the redeposition of Area 2 material into Ring-ditch 1 and the intercutting of Ring-ditch 2 and the bank of Ring-ditch 1. Scenario 1 sees hearths—in particular Hearths 4–6—as contemporary with or integral to the Area 2 metalworking activity in its initial phase, contemporary with activity in the D cuttings. Pit burial 119 is seen as the focus of Ring-ditch 1, though Raftery also sees the 15m structure as contemporary with it—if, however, at a later stage that is contemporary with the moving of the deposits from the east after removal of the bank.

Central to Raftery's arguments about the relative position of the occupation deposits and Ring-ditch 1 are three deposits of sterile 'yellow soil', which he interpreted as the remains of an external bank of Ring-ditch 1. These, observed in Sqs Y1, E1 and 5/G (see below), rested on top of the occupation layer of Bronze Age date and thus had to post-date the main phase of bronze-casting activity. As in Sq. E small accumulations of 'occupation deposits' were also observed on top of this possible bank, the digging of the ring-ditch itself was tied into the Bronze Age sequence. This yellow bank (see Chapter 2, section 2.2.1) is therefore the crucial element that creates the *terminus ante quem* that for Raftery anchored Ring-ditch 1 in the Bronze Age sequence of the site, followed by the digging of Ring-ditch 2 (see below). The evidence provided for Raftery's scenario in the form of the yellow bank is crucial, as it links Ring-ditch 1, Ring-ditch 2 and the Bronze Age activity in Area 2. If the yellow deposits in Y and E, sitting on top of Bronze Age deposits, are indeed the upcast from the digging of Ring-ditch 1, this would link it directly into the Bronze Age sequence of the site. In addition, small patches of dark soil on top of the supposed yellow bank in E were also dated to the Bronze Age and are thought to bracket the bank within the sequence of activity in Area 2.

The main events of Scenario 1 may be summarised as follows.

1 – Metalworking activity takes place in the D cuttings (Metalworking Zone 3) in Area 2 with contemporary 'deep hearths', e.g. Hearths 1–6.
2 – Ring-ditch 1 is cut and burial Pit 119 created.
3 – Metalworking activity commences in the B and C cuttings in Area 2.
4 – Bank removal and Ring-ditch 1 infilled with material emanating from Area 2.
5 – The 15m structure is created; Hearth 7 is contemporary.
6 – Ring-ditch 2 is cut to enclose a series of burials.
7 – The iron-working hearth is inserted into the silted-up Ring-ditch 1.

Scenario 2—-untangling Ring-ditch 1, 2 and the 'yellow bank'
Ring-ditch 1 plays a central role in the site sequence owing to its entanglement with the Area 2 metalworking deposits, along with the burial evidence and the enclosed 15m structure. The taphonomy of the fill of Ring-ditch 1, as well as of other deposits, is of crucial importance for understanding the relative sequence of events, as well as the absolute dates that can be attached to them. Some fundamental differences in interpretation of the function of some features are, however, also at the heart of Scenario 2, among them the understanding of the large hearths as pyre pits. Their distribution extends across Areas 1 and 3 and includes Burial Pit 119, which because of its central position is seen as the focus of Ring-ditch 1 in Scenario 1. Grouping Pit 119 with the other pyres and burial features allows it to be detached from the ring-ditch and instead seen as part of a spread of funerary activity across Areas 1 and 3.

An important piece of evidence for this is that Ring-ditch 1 can be shown to cut through this zone, and it is here hypothesised that a former internal bank would have overlain the pyre hearths within Area 1. Instead of an external bank, as postulated by Raftery, evidence for the former existence of an internal bank is provided by the differential patterning of features in the area enclosed by Ring-ditch 1. A zone of intense activity extends in a halo-like shape around the 15m structure, with the exception of the entrance area on the east. This patterning suggests that the various pits and occasional post-holes in this zone represent activity associated with the structure. The possibility that they might represent an earlier phase of construction was considered, but no meaningful patterns of features could be identified. Rather, the clear and sharply delineated shape of this otherwise random assortment of features is likely to reflect activity within the former extent of an internal bank (Fig. 4.6). Projecting the extent of the halo, which is clearest to the west of the structure, the resulting enclosure is slightly off-centre to the ditch but creates a perfect central position for the 15m structure. While most of the area of the projected bank is empty of features, the hearth pyres and probably Pit 118 lie within its extent, reflecting their earlier, pre-bank date. These particularly deep features were protected here, while shallower features that may have existed in this earlier phase across the entirety of the enclosure interior would have been removed in the process of bank and ditch construction.

Further strong evidence for an internal bank is provided by the cobbling that Raftery observed within the fill of Ring-ditch 1. It formed part of the uppermost layer of fill in many zones and was likely derived from the dismantling of a former inner wall or rampart. Tip lines visible in a number of sections clearly indicate the infilling of the ditch from the inside, probably including the positioning of the large boulder in Sq. 10, resting on the inner face of Ring-ditch 1. Raftery highlights some instances where the available directional evidence suggests that the infilling took place from the inside, e.g. grid square 22, section V (Figs 2.23 and 2.26). In addition to his examples, it can be noted that photographs show stones lying on top of the black 'occupation' fill in Sqs 3/9, F1 and 62 (Figs 2.27, 2.28 and 4.7), slumping from the inside on top of the ditch fill and into the ditch. Stone and boulder spreads are often seen to extend around the inside of the interior of the ring-ditch (e.g. Figs 2.26 and 2.14).

Additional evidence for the former existence of an internal bank is provided by the joins that have been shown to link mould fragments in Areas 1 and 2. While some links exist between moulds in Area 2 and in the fill of Ring-ditch 1, fragments of a number of moulds were found in Area 2 and in the pyre hearths in Area 1, the links they create thus 'crossing' Ring-ditch 1. They thus clearly pre-date the existence of ditch and bank. A second group of mould joins can be shown to create links with the fill of Ring-ditch 1 from *both* sides, from directly adjoining squares (see Chapter 3, section 3.9), and not only from the east. This means that some moulds had been distributed across the site before the ring-ditch (and its accompanying bank) was built, some remaining *in situ* in cut features and others being incorporated into the fill of the ring-ditch through secondary deposition processes. Importantly, the existence of an internal bank resolves many of the problems inherent in the existence of an external bank with regard to explaining the movement of the finds-rich deposits from the east into the ditch across or over it that Raftery pondered in his accounts.

Furthermore, evidence for the yellow external bank postulated by Raftery is tentative. While it is indisputable that stoneless yellow soil deposits existed in Sqs Y and E, closer scrutiny introduces doubt concerning their function as the bank of the ditch, owing to their intermittent nature and the almost total lack of stones within them—difficult to envisage if they represent the upcast from the digging of the ditch on this stone-rich site. In addition, the northern (north-eastern?) stretches of possible bank are positioned at a quite significant distance from the edge of Ring-ditch 1. Moreover, the exact relationship between the yellow bank deposits and the ditch cannot be securely established, as the stone cashel was not removed in those areas where a bank had been documented on its outside in the Y1 and E1 squares. Thus no possible stratigraphic link between the two could be documented.

The apparent bank evidence in Sq. 5/G is the most problematic, given its interrelationship with Ring-ditch 2 (see below). After removal of a stretch of the cashel wall in the F/G cuttings, possible yellow bank deposits were identified that were cut by the Bronze Age Ring-ditch 2, establishing that this post-dated Ring-ditch 1. These supposed bank deposits rest on a prehistoric sod layer that is likewise cut by Ring-ditch 2 and is described as sterile:

> 'This was a brownish-black layer containing thin, longitudinal bands of brownish and blackish organic material. Significantly, this layer was almost completely devoid of prehistoric artefacts and was thus clearly not an occupation horizon. Its purpose is uncertain but it is conceivable that the fact that (at least in its present state) it was almost exactly covered by the yellow material of the bank it might be taken as representing layers of sods, dug from the upper levels of the contemporary ground surface, before the yellow soil from the fosse had been piled on top. In this regard the thin, discontinuous lines of black material extending irregularly along the length of the soil could represent the original upper levels of the sods. The suggestion is plausible, but is weakened by the absence of such a layer elsewhere where the yellow bank was exposed. It must thus be admitted that this layer could, in fact, pre-date the yellow bank, in which case its original function is unclear. The most important point to stress, however, is that this was, effectively, a completely sterile layer and thus had nothing to do with any occupation activity.'

Section 13 shows that these marled layers and an underlying grey layer are cut by Ring-ditch 2 (Figs 4.4 and 4.5). Nevertheless, accepting the prehistoric nature of those deposits that are cut by the ring-ditch, it is still unclear whether they are part of the yellow deposits that represent the possible bank in the western part of section 13 and that are clearly visible on top of substantial black deposits in sections 11 and 12 (cf. Chapter 2, section 2.4.1). It is notable in this regard that the annotation of the original drawing of these deposits as 'bank' is marked with a query (Fig. 2.79, section 13). Raftery, however, affirmed this interpretation, and therefore it must be highlighted as a possible argument against Scenario 2.

Opposite page

Fig. 4.4 (top)—Area 3 under excavation in Sqs B/3 and B1 (right), with section 13 below Rampart 1 in Sqs 11 and 5/G (top) and the northern part of Ring-ditch 2 (left), looking south-west.

Fig. 4.5 (bottom)—Section 13 below Rampart 1 (stone cashel) in Sqs 11 and 5/G (top), and the rectangular structure and Hearth 7 in Sqs 5/G and 4/F (centre), looking south.

How and when was the ditch dug and filled?

The above evidence suggests a broad sequence of metalworking/funerary activity followed by the creation of Ring-ditch 1 and the centrally enclosed 15m structure. The question remains as to when the ditch was dug, and when it was filled in.

The re-examination of the finds archive has demonstrated that the initial layer of grey silt included both pottery and mould fragments, thus providing a *terminus post quem* for the silting. No black soil, so characteristic of the later infill in the east, found its way to the bottom of the ditch in this area. All section drawings are unambiguous in this regard.

The 'grey' fill thus represents silting, incorporating pottery and mould fragments that were on the adjacent ground surface and entered the ditch through erosion.

This in turn suggests that the black deposits on the immediate edge of the ditch on the east were not yet *in situ* when the ditch was cut, as they should otherwise have silted into the ditch. The possibility of a revetment that held back the material for the initial phase of the ditch's existence, as proposed by Raftery (see section 4.3.1), could explain this lag. However, the illustration of the fill of the ring-ditch as well as the photographs of the sections in Sqs 22, 8/2, 10/4 and 11 5/G indicate homogeneous fills that are best explained by large-scale soil movement. The black fills illustrated and photographed in sections 6, VI and VII, for example, do not show any differentiation of episodic silting and infilling. This may include Sq. 10, where section IX seems to suggest that it was also filled in from the outside, as large stones sit on the edge of the silting on the inside of the ditch. (It should also be noted that the grey silt depicted in section 7 includes relatively large stones.)

In these instances, and more broadly in the entire eastern

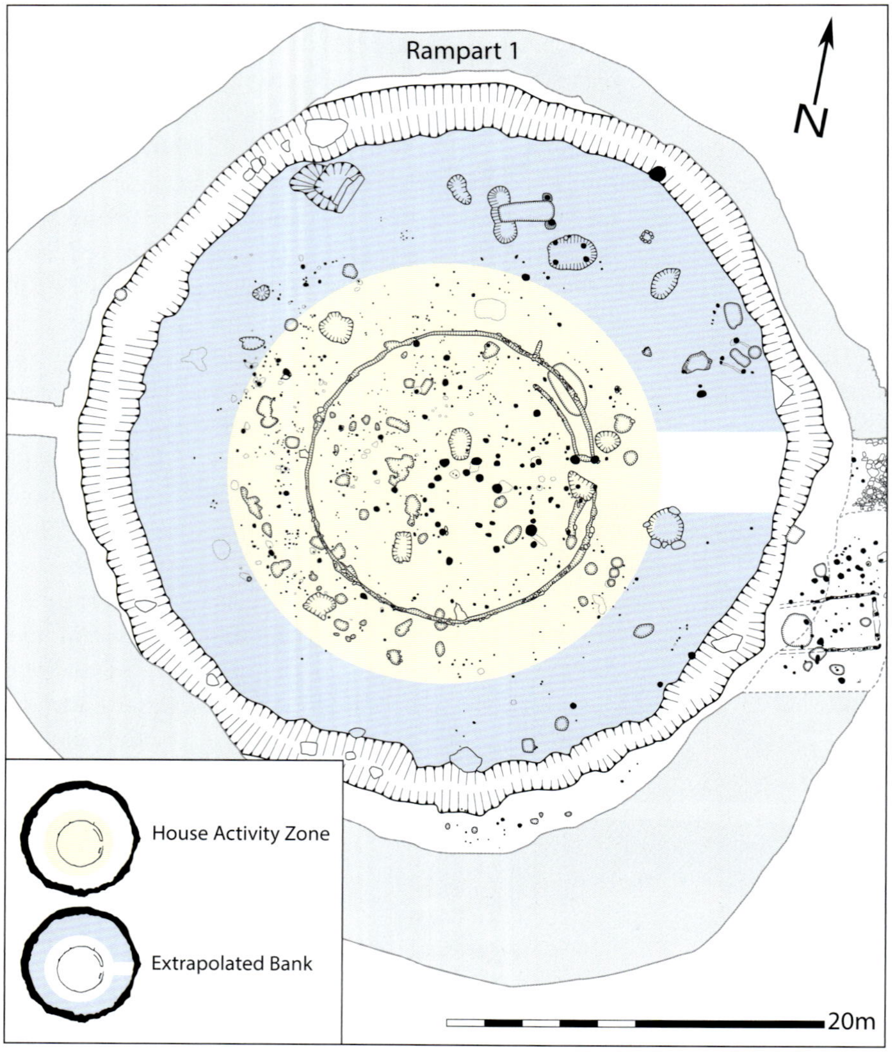

Fig. 4.6—Conjectural reconstruction of the extent of the bank of Ring-ditch 1 and the house activity zone.

half of the ditch, it would seem that the fills are the result of large-scale redeposition. All sections from section IV in Sq. 31 to section IX in Sq. 10/11 and an unnamed section in Sq. 5/G show evidence for what appears to be the deposition of one homogeneous, very stone-rich fill after an initial layer of silt.

In contrast, the remainder of the ring-ditch—largely its western portion—is described as having filled in naturally over time. For example, in Sqs 40 and 50, and, indeed, Sq. 56, bands of silting alternate with other fills, similar to squares in the north and documented in sections I and III in Sqs 58 and 40. A Hiberno-Norse ingot—possibly intrusive—found its way into the ditch fill rather low down in Sq. 56, and medieval pottery has been noted in a number of locations in what appear to be the upper fills of this ditch

Raftery noted that the fill in Sq. 10 appeared to show evidence for the ditch having been open for a relatively long time, with what was interpreted as natural turf growth representing vegetation growth after an initial phase of silting.

In the north and east, infilling events that include large amounts of stone, reminiscent of deliberate operations (cf. Chapter 2, section 2.2.2), are notable.

This suggests that the eastern part of the ditch filled up in a different manner than on the west, where natural infilling processes seem to have been at play for a longer time.

As is the case for the initial silting, any datable material in the ditch fill—such as pottery, moulds or radiocarbon-dated charcoal fragments—only provide a *terminus post quem* for the filling of the ditch, unless we can demonstrate that the material was generated close in time to its integration into the ditch fill. Processes of residuality, redeposition and intrusion may affect the relationship between the datable material and its depositional context.

Datable materials within the ditch fill comprise, as discussed by Raftery, the substantial quantities of Bronze Age moulds and pottery and other chronologically diagnostic artefacts, as well as radiocarbon-dated samples. Such materials occur throughout the ring-ditch but are especially notable in the eastern portion of Ring-ditch 1 and in Sq. 29, where there are deposits that are particularly rich in artefacts and charcoal. These deposits were suggested by Raftery to be the result of primary or near-primary deposition into an open ring-ditch (cf. Chapter 2, section 2.2.2, and section 4.2 above), as discussed above, and thus thought to date the infilling as well as the use of the ring-ditch (i.e. when it was open).

Scenario 2 instead sees the large-scale movement of materials into the eastern portion of the ditch as a later event and draws on radiocarbon evidence that suggests that this happened at a significantly later time. As outlined above, a significant degree of disturbance can be observed throughout the upper levels of features recorded within Ring-ditch 1. Such disturbance is mostly restricted to the upper levels of ditch fills, but later or potentially later material has also been identified within ditch fills that seem to be low within the cut. This later material includes some medieval finds (see Chapter 2, section 2.2.2, or Table 4.1 for convenience) in Sqs 58–67, where Leinster Cooking Ware and iron objects were found in a 'grey brown fill' at unspecified depths, down to 20cm and 25–40cm, the latter possibly related to the Iron Age furnace in Sq. 65. In Sq. 56 in the south-west a Viking silver ingot was found at a significant depth, and in the northern Sqs 22 and 31 two iron objects were found at unspecified depths. These could all be explained as localised disturbances, intrusive material or unrecognised later recuts, or, as in the case of the ingot, as the migration of small, heavy objects through the matrix. Notably, however, no medieval finds were identified anywhere in the ring-ditch except for its western extent. This seems to be a result of different infilling processes. The western portion of the ring-ditch, as discussed above and evidenced in the more complex fills, filled up more slowly. This may, in some areas such as Sqs 58–67 where a lot of medieval finds were retrieved, indicate that it was still largely open at this time.

Later material was also, however, recorded as having come from the fill in the eastern part of the ditch, where it was specifically noted as having been associated with the black, charcoal-rich deposits of Bronze Age material here. An iron object (E84:1478) was documented at a depth of 30–50cm below yellow in Sq. 6/7, which possibly refers to the yellow natural representing the edge of the ditch.[9] While this again could be the result of localised disturbances, or, indeed, a very early example of iron use (so far unprecedented in a Late Bronze Age context in Ireland but not elsewhere), it complements the radiocarbon evidence from the black deposits that raise questions about the date of deposition of the black material into Ring-ditch 1. The dates in question (SI-1483, 430–50 cal. BC; SI-1484, 780–400 BC; GrN-27099, 760–450 BC; D-135, 880–290 BC) were obtained by Raftery on material that he identified as 'black fill' or 'black occupation deposits', i.e. the intrusive material from the east, which would have been the focus of his enquiries into the dating of Ring-ditch 1. Some of these dates may be considered problematic, as they are on unidentified bulk charcoal or belong to the early series of Smithsonian dates that must be considered with caution (see section 4.4). Nevertheless, in their sum and their definite association with the ditch fill (D-135: Sq. 13, upper fill) and black fill (SI-1483: Sq. 10, black fill of Ditch 1, organic build-up?; SI-1484: black fill in lower portion of Ditch 1, no square no.; GrN-27099: Sq.7, organic material, 30–40cm below ditch rim)—and, in the case of GrN-27099 and SI-1484, explicitly from the lower part of the ditch—they open up the possibility that the Bronze Age material may have been redeposited in the ditch at a later date, post-dating the creation of the black, finds-rich 'occupation material' itself.

It could, of course, also be argued here that localised disturbances may explain the Iron Age dates. Particularly in the eastern portion of the ring-ditch, filled with dark, charcoal-rich soils, it may have been virtually impossible to recognise pit cuts, for example. Another possible explanation may be significant disturbance by rabbit burrows. There is evidence from the finds logbooks for rabbit burrowing/disturbance in Sqs 6 and 7 of Area 1. Finds 1151 (bronze tweezers), 1153 (strap-tag) and 1154a,b (coarse pottery) are all described as coming from 'disturbed zone—rabbit burrows'. The depths recorded for these finds are from 30cm to 50cm 'below the lowest stones of the cashel wall' in squares adjacent to it. It is likely, however, that this disturbance was restricted to the general humus layer in this area—variously 30–50cm thick and visible on sections 6 and 7 as level with or below the lowest part of the rampart. Thus these possibly later finds and definitely later radiocarbon dates suggest that the black deposits, rich in charcoal, only entered the ditch at a rather later date than expected, and later than they themselves were generated (as indicated by associated radiocarbon dates). As the radiocarbon dates only provide a *terminus post quem* for this, it could also have taken place much later. The possibly slightly later date SI-1483 comes from Sq. 10, for which Raftery describes gradual infilling with vegetation growth after initial silting.

A possibly different situation presents itself in Sqs 31 and 68, where such large portions of pots 41 and 343 respectively were found that the assumption may be that these vessels were substantially complete when they went into the ditch fill and thus not far removed from their use on the site. They are coarseware pots of Late Bronze Age type and were part of the fill of the ditch post-dating the initial silting phase. The mould deposits in the eastern portion of the ring-ditch only provide a *terminus post quem* for the infilling of the ditch, as they appear to represent redeposition. The nearly complete vessels in the ring-ditch fill in Sqs 31 and 68 provide a better approximation of the date of the infilling of the ditch, as they may in contrast have been complete not long before their deposition. However, it is important that we remember that the ditch may have had a complex history prior to the infill encountered in the excavation, being likely subjected to regular maintenance and clearing out. In fact, the probably short period of silting suggests that it had been maintained until not long before its infilling on the east. The deposition of the coarseware pots thus may provide a *terminus ante quem* for the digging of the ditch of 800 or 700 BC, the conventional end date for coarseware pottery in Ireland. This falls onto a 'flat' area on the calibration curve *c.* 800–400 cal. BC that closely corresponds to the Hallstatt period in Central Europe and is often referred to as the Hallstatt Plateau. The flatness of the curve leads to blurring of chronologies in the earlier Iron Age period (Hamilton *et al.* 2015).

The radiocarbon date obtained for one of the posts of the 15m structure in the interior of the ditch is indicative of a plateau date for its construction. If we assume that the ditch was dug to surround the structure, this likewise points to a date around 800 BC.

While a broad sequence of events thus becomes apparent, its details present further questions. The radiocarbon date of the internal structure and the eastern deposits may be broadly contemporary and definitely post-date the main Bronze Age phase of activity, but it is not clear whether the enclosure was built to enclose the 15m structure or whether the infilling of the ditch on the east is contemporary with the building of the structure. As noted above, the entirety of Ring-ditch 1 was not filled in but only its eastern half, from section VII (north of Sq. 8) to Section IX (Sq. 10, southern baulk). This may have been an attempt to provide a wide entrance area (15m wide) across the ditch, which is difficult to imagine having happened soon after the digging of the ditch itself. We may consider the plateau dates as *termini post quos* for the infilling of the ditch, thus allowing for a later date for this event. The hypothetical clearing of the F and B zone, which Raftery suggested to have been intended to create an access towards this eastern entrance, may have gone hand in hand with the infilling of the ditch.

Metalworking and burial in the site sequence

As outlined above, both metalworking and burial activities represented by the various pyre hearths seem to pre-date Ring-ditch 1 in the northern part of the site. There is also evidence that the burial activity represented in Area 3—Ring-ditch 2—pre-dates Ring-ditch 1: the stockade or palisade enclosure that encircles most of Areas 3 and 4 is focused on Ring-ditch 2 and was considered by Raftery as broadly contemporary with Ring-ditch 2, either functioning as an enclosure or delineating an access route to the later 15m structure. If completed to a full circle, this post alignment would intersect with the line of Ring-ditch 1 and is thus likely to pre-date the creation of Ring-ditch 1. It is not visible here, however, probably owing to the heavy truncation in this area. This point contrasts most strongly with Raftery's Scenario 1, as he saw Ring-ditch 2 as cutting the yellow bank of Ring-ditch 1 (see above).

No direct stratigraphic links exist between Areas 2 and 3. The dark, finds-rich deposits found in Area 2 are notably not found in Area 3, where a greater level of disturbance seems to have created largely homogeneous brown deposits overlying the cut features. This difference in deposits is also mirrored in the distribution of finds in both areas. It is striking that virtually no moulds have been recorded from the disturbed deposits that overlay Area 3—or, for that matter, from Area 4—and hardly any from within the cut features in this zone, such as Ring-ditch 2. The lack of mould fragments (with the exception of possible mould fragment 8583) within the ditch fill of Ring-ditch 2 is curious, particularly considering that the few examples of mould and crucible fragments in this area were concentrated on Pyre Hearth 15 and a number of associated pits, in particular Pit 20 (see below). This stands in contrast to the 64 coarseware sherds, two amber beads and one glass bead found in its fill.

The lack of links created by sherds from vessel units across Areas 2 and 3 (Table 4.1) further supports the impression that no material from Area 2 was redeposited in Area 3, which may indeed support the notion that the northernmost part of the post enclosure represents a physical boundary that separated both zones—as Raftery outlined, the deposits of occupation material as well as the underlying grey appeared to be bounded by the line of post-holes in the B/C squares. On the other hand, chronological rather than spatial differences may be implied. Pyre 15 appears to belong to a secondary phase of funerary activity following that represented by the pyre and Burial 1 at the centre within Ring-ditch 2, and the mould fragments within this feature and other pits within its extent may thus be evidence for moulds having a wider distribution at this point, in contrast to the initial phase of the digging of Ring-ditch 1. Only one mould fragment was attributed to the 'black area immediately south of the burial pit' in I3, and thus possibly associated with the central pyre. This may support this admittedly rather tenuous hypothesis.

It is thus still unclear whether the moulds and crucibles are contemporary with the funerary activity or whether the metalworking material is residual within these contexts. The presence of almost all fragments of a crucible in Area 3 in Pit 20 is suggestive of near-contemporary use, definitely underpinning the intertwining of both activities. Their contemporaneity is also suggested by the broad spatial division of the site, with burial only found in Areas 1 and 3, and metalworking but no burial in Area 2 (Fig. 6.2).

Summary of the main events of Scenario 2

- Area 2 material is being produced—metalworking activity. It is unclear whether this is contemporary with the burial activity in adjacent areas.
- Pyres (hearths) 1–6 and Pit 119 are created and filled, some integrating Area 2 material. Importantly, this sees Pit 119 as one of the pyres.
- Ring-ditch 2 in Area 3 is created to focus on the central pyre and Burial 1. It post-dates (cuts) the rectangular structure.
- A second phase of burial activity in Area 3 consists of Pyre Hearth 15 (incorporating material from Area 2) and further burials (i.e. Burial 2). This is possibly also the period of hoard deposition.
- Ring-ditch 1 is cut and the bank cast up on its inside. The 15m structure is built, followed by pit-digging around the building, including Hearth 7. There is a narrow access across the ditch in Sq. 10. All this takes place around 800 BC, as the structure seems to date from this time.
- Silting into the ditch occurs, including some moulds from the outside (Area 2). There are perhaps repeated episodes of clearing and silting, but it is unclear for how long this continued and whether it occurred everywhere or just in the east.
- There is slow infilling in the west through silting episodes. This phase also includes the deposition of large portions of coarseware pots.
- Area 2 material is redeposited into Ring-ditch 1. This entails a large-scale shifting of materials (between 800 and 400 BC). In the northern part of the ditch there are also infilling episodes, e.g. section 5 in Sq. 22. Infilling occurs from the inside, too, as demonstrated by tip lines, stones and boulders (Fig. 4.7). In the south there are occasional dumps of redeposited material. This means that the ditch appears to be infilled through redeposition primarily on its eastern half (Fig. 4.8, b–c).
- The iron-working hearth is inserted into the silted-up Ring-ditch 1.

Fig. 4.7—Tip line of bank material into Ring-ditch 1 in unknown grid squares.

- Infilling of the ditch continues into the medieval period, according to finds in the western half of the ditch and the complex ditch fills here.

4.4 RADIOCARBON DATING AND BAYESIAN MODELLING

Derek Hamilton and Katharina Becker

A total of 72 samples of charcoal, charred macrobotanical remains, carbonised food residues on pottery and cremated human bone have been radiocarbon-dated since the Rathgall site was first excavated by Barry Raftery in 1969–75 and 1978, with further excavations undertaken in 2011 by Matt Seaver for UCD. Five different labs have been used for the radiocarbon dating over the past four decades: the Smithsonian Institution (SI); Trinity College Dublin (D); the University of Groningen, the Netherlands (GrN and GrA); Queen's University Belfast (UB and UBA); and the Scottish Universities Environmental Research Centre, East Kilbride (SUERC). Furthermore, the radiocarbon measurements have been made through both conventional ^{14}C dating techniques and the use of accelerator mass spectrometry (AMS).

The longevity of the dating programme has meant that samples dated at the beginning of the project were subject to a completely different set of selection criteria than those selected at the end. The shift from conventional to AMS dating resulted in a dramatic reduction in required sample size—from as much as 20g to approximately 0.1g in the case of charcoal. Furthermore, despite Waterbolk's (1971) warning of the effect that old wood can have on the date of a mixed sample, bulk samples of charcoal did not routinely undergo species identification analysis prior to the advice of Ashmore (1999) for single-entity dating, which most often now includes the identification of short-lived species or samples (e.g. roundwood charcoal). The end result for the suite of dates from Rathgall is that, of the 61 measurements made on charcoal, 43 are on bulked samples, and 21 of those samples were completely unidentified.

There are two main cases, based solely on the material dated, in which the sample dated may not accurately date the context. First, in a few instances it was clear from the descriptions that the bulk charcoal sample was derived from a considerable amount of ditch fill. These large samples could have been forming over a long period of time. Since the material is not necessarily functionally related to the context, such as a discrete dump of hearth ash, the best that can be said is that the ^{14}C age pre-dates the formation of the context, although there is the possibility that it represents an accurate date for context formation. Second, it is possible that there was old wood in unidentified samples in the form of oak or elements of other longer-living species (i.e. ash or alder trunk wood). Oak trees can live for centuries, and without any further indication that the material is short-lived (e.g. identification of the oak charcoal as sapwood or roundwood) we must assume that the results on samples that are known to contain oak, or that are completely unidentified and could contain long-lived wood, are representative of the earliest possible date for a context. In both cases, therefore, the dates are included as *terminus post quem* (TPQ) results, which in the coding of OxCal is represented by the 'After' parameter.

The aim of Raftery's initial programme of radiocarbon dating was to establish the broad 'absolute' date of the site. Rathgall was one of the first sites in Ireland to obtain radiocarbon dates (from the Smithsonian lab), and the advances in the development of the method, as well as the desire to clarify particular chronological issues, triggered the submission of further suites of samples in following years to the Dublin, Belfast and Groningen laboratories. Judging by the dates obtained, one of Raftery's main concerns was the dating of the material within Ring-ditch 1, in order to date the cutting and infilling of this particular feature and relate it to the dating of the Rampart 2 ditch. The characteristic problems associated with the dating of ditch fills affect these two major components of the site to this day (see below). Although Warner (2015) has recently presented an attempt at developing a chronological model for Rathgall, we opt to apply the cutting-edge methodology of the Bayesian approach, which takes into account sample information, taphonomy, site processes and, most importantly, the site stratigraphy in order to create robust chronological models in which we use the most up-to-date statistical methods.

As part of the most recent post-excavation phase, an attempt has been made to clarify a number of questions that arose out of the re-examination of the stratigraphy and the available dating evidence. This included further attempts to refine the dating of coarseware pottery found on the site, as conventional typological dating places it late in the Late Bronze Age (see Roche, this volume) while associated radiocarbon dates indicate a date in its earlier part. Carbonised food residues on some vessels were therefore dated. These served, in combination with dates obtained on samples that had survived from the original excavation, to further examine the date of the infilling of Ring-ditch 1, also in squares outside the main zone of deposition of Bronze Age material (i.e. Sqs 10 and 29). They also added to the dating of Pit 118 in Area 1 and Ring-ditch 4 in the outside zone of the Z cuttings.

Another concern was the dating of previously undated important features—Hearth 6 in Area 1, Burial 1 at the centre of Ring-ditch 2 in Area 3, and Ring-ditch 4 and associated Pit 16 in the Z cuttings.

The re-excavation of the Rampart 2 ditch served to further clarify the problematic sequence of dates produced by the initial dating campaign. It was possible to obtain suitable material for dating from a layer of primary silting, which helps to start addressing the history of this line of enclosure of Rathgall.

4.4.1 The laboratory methods

Four samples of bulked unidentified charcoal were submitted in the 1970s to the radiocarbon laboratory at Trinity College Dublin (D-). While the exact method of pre-treatment used is unclear, the standard pre-treatment at the time for charcoal samples would have been similar to that of Stenhouse and Baxter (1983) and would have followed an acid/alkali/acid protocol of Mook and Waterbolk (1985). The samples were then processed as described by Dresser and McAulay (1974) for liquid scintillation counting. The four results are reported in Dresser 1980.

Ten samples, all of bulk unidentified charcoal, were submitted to the radiocarbon laboratory at the Smithsonian Institution, USA (SI-). Like the Dublin samples, it is unclear exactly what method of pre-treatment was used; from previously published date lists, it would appear that the pre-treatment methodology in use had been changing annually. While it is thus difficult to be sure what pre-treatment protocol was used, at the time of these measurements the Smithsonian Institution was only undertaking radiocarbon dating by gas-proportional counting.

Seven samples of unidentified bulk charcoal were submitted in 1978 to Queen's University Belfast (UB-) from beneath Rampart 2 and the fills of the associated ditch. The sample pre-treatment involved placing the sample in a clean 100ml beaker and immersing it in hydrochloric acid (HCl, 4%, 30–50ml). The contents of the beaker were then heated on a hotplate (80°C for 2–3 hours), and subsequently washed with deionised water until neutral. A second step involved the addition of sodium hydroxide (2%, at 80°C for 2hrs) to remove humic acids, followed by further rinsing with deionised water until neutral. After this the initial step with hydrochloric acid was repeated (S. Hoper, pers. comm.).

A further seven samples were submitted more recently for AMS dating at Queen's University (UBA-). These were processed using an acid/alkali/acid pre-treatment first described by de Vries and Barendsen (1952). The pre-treated and dried samples were placed in quartz tubes with a strip of silver ribbon to remove nitrates, chlorides and CuO. The samples were then sealed under vacuum and combusted to CO_2 overnight at 850°C. The samples of CO_2 were converted to graphite on an iron catalyst using the zinc reduction method (Vogel *et al.* 1984). The graphite samples were analysed with an 0.5MeV NEC pelletron compact accelerator, with the $^{14}C/^{12}C$ ratios corrected for fractionation using the on-line measured $^{13}C/^{12}C$ ratio and in accordance with Stuiver and Polach 1977.

A total of 34 samples were submitted to the radiocarbon laboratory at the University of Groningen, the Netherlands. Twenty-two of the samples (GrN-) were of bulk charcoal; they were pre-treated following Mook and Waterbolk 1985 and converted to carbon dioxide for measurement by gas-proportional counting (Mook and Streurman 1983). The remaining samples were measured by AMS (GrA-). The sample of unburnt bone was prepared as described by Longin (1971), and the charcoal samples were prepared with the acid/alkali/acid protocol of Mook and Waterbolk (1985). The samples were then combusted to carbon dioxide and graphitised as described by Aerts-Bijma *et al.* (1997; 2001) and dated by AMS (van der Plicht *et al.* 2000).

Ten samples were submitted to the Scottish Universities Environmental Research Centre (SUERC-). These included two individual charcoal fragments, six carbonised food residues on pottery sherds, and one each of human bone and cremated human bone. The samples were pre-treated and measured by AMS following the methods set out by Dunbar *et al.* (2016).

The radiocarbon results given in Table 4.2 and discussed below are quoted in accordance with the international standard known as the Trondheim convention (Stuiver and Kra 1986). They are conventional radiocarbon ages (Stuiver and Polach 1977).

The calibrations of the results, relating the radiocarbon measurements directly to calendar dates, are also given in Table 4.2. All have been calculated using the calibration

Table 4.2—Radiocarbon dates from Rathgall.

Lab ID	Sample ID	Area	Grid square	Feature	Context details from sample records and other sources
Ring-ditch 1					
D-135	S140	Area 1	31	Ring-ditch 1 ditch fill	Charcoal from upper levels of ditch surrounding circular house (15m structure)
GrA-23350	S71:007, E84:4771	Area 1	29	Ring-ditch 1 ditch fill	In black organic material, Ditch 1, 55cm below yellow natural. Also described as de part of ditch. Black silting
SUERC-42586	E84:4622	Area 1	29	Ring-ditch 1 ditch fill	In black fill of ditch, SE corner among stones
SUERC-42585	E84:1441	Area 1	8	Ring-ditch 1 ditch fill	In black fill of ditch near bottom, NE
GrA-23351	S69:147	Area 1	7	Ring-ditch 1 ditch fill	Ditch 1, northern end of square. In blackish, organic material, 30–40cm below ditch edge
GrN-27099	S69:147	Area 1	7	Ring-ditch 1 ditch fill	Ditch 1, northern end of square. In blackish, organic material, 30–40cm below ditch edge
GrN-27098	S69:097	Area 1	2	Ring-ditch 1 ditch fill	Thick black occupation level of ditch, 50cm west of wall. Depth 25cm
SI-1484	S159	Area 1		Ring-ditch 1 ditch fill	Black fill in lower portion of Ditch 1
SI-1485	?	Area 1	8?	Ring-ditch 1 ditch fill	Fill at base of ditch
SI-1483	S70:35	Area 1	10	Ring-ditch 1 ditch fill	Black fill of Ditch 1
SUERC-42580	S70:32	Area 1	10	Ring-ditch 1 ditch fill	From black fill of ditch in SE corner of 10
GrA-23341	S71:034	Area 1	56	Ring-ditch 1 ditch fill	In grey fill of Ditch 1, under stones
Inside Ring-ditch 1					
GrA-23344	S71:109, E84:4771	Area 1	17/18	Pit 118	From basketry lining, phase 1. Large Storage Pit 118. Also described as charcoal fro wickerwork 2
GrA-23345	S71:110, E84:6102	Area 1	17/18	Pit 118	From innermost brown filling. Large Storage Pit 118
GrN-27104	S71:105	Area 1	17/18	Pit 118	Storage Pit 118, basketwork 2
GrN-27102	S71:096	Area 1	17/18	Pit 118	From black outer level of large storage pit, Pit 118
SUERC-42589	S2011.E84:5927b	Area 1	17/18	Pit 118	Coarseware potsherds in black outer layer, i.e. primary fill of pit
SUERC-43732	S71:99	Area 1	17/18	Pit 118	Wickerwork lining
D-132			17/18		Upper level fills of the basket-lined storage pit outside of the central structure in Fosse 1
GrA-23355	S71:?	Area 1	29	Pit 120	Pit 120
GrN-27100	S69:163	Area 1	14	Pit 96	Fill of small, stone-lined Pit 96
GrN-27101	S71:093, E84:6080	Area 1	35	Pit 119	Charcoal from black lining of Pit 119, associated with human bones and gold ring
SI-1481	S70:37	Area 1	36	Pit G (??) = Pit 110?	Upper level of Pit G
SUERC-42581	S70:37	Area 1	27	15m structure	Ring-ditch 1 charcoal patches (burnt posts) in outer bedding trench of 15m structure
Iron furnace					
GrN-27103	S71:104, E84:6093	Area 1	65	Iron-smelting pit	Charcoal from iron-smelting pit
SI-1480	?	Area 1	65	Iron-smelting pit	Smelting pit
Hearths					
D-134	S113=S69:12?	Areas 1–4	25	Hearth 1	Charcoal from Hearth 1, Phase II
SI-1476	S157	Areas 1–4	23/32	Hearth 2	Hearth 2 in burnt layer
D-133	S151	Areas 1–4	32	Hearth 2	Charcoal from pit at SW corner of Hearth 2

omments	Material dated	Radiocarbon age (BP)	$\delta^{13}C$ (‰)	Calibrated date (95% probability)
ondescript part of RD. The material that was actually dated was the charred morphous lumps containing whole cereal grains, and any charcoal was excluded.	Charcoal: Unidentified	2490 ±120		880–290 cal. BC
ump. The black fill here contained plenty of finds — only concentration of such utside the area of intrusive material.	Charcoal: *Corylus* sp.	2900 ±45	−26.45	1230–940 cal. BC
ump. The black fill here contained plenty of finds — only concentration of such utside the area of intrusive material.	Carbonised residue	2929 ±29	−27.3	1230–1020 cal. BC
ntrusive deposits from the east — Area 2	Carbonised residue	2915 ±29	−25.5	1210–1010 cal. BC
ossibly intrusive deposits from the east — Area 2	Charcoal: *Corylus* sp.	2975 ±45	−6.31	1370–1040 cal. BC
ossibly intrusive deposits from the east — Area 2	Charcoal: *Quercus* sp. branch wood	2475 ±25	−24.48	760–450 cal. BC
ossibly intrusive deposits from the east — Area 2	Charcoal: *Corylus* sp. branch wood	2945 ±40	−25.66	1280–1020 cal. BC
ot clear which deposit, possibly intrusive Area 2	Charcoal: Unidentified	2450 ±75		780–400 cal. BC
ot clear which deposit, probably intrusive Area 2	Charcoal: Unidentified	2930 ±75		1380–930 cal. BC
rganic black build-up	Charcoal: Unidentified	2215 ±80		430–50 cal. BC
ossibly intrusive material from Area 3	Charcoal: *Corylus* sp.	2914 ±29	−26.5	1210–1010 cal. BC
ondescript part of RD, possibly under cobbling	Charcoal: *Corylus* sp.	2915 ±45	−26.91	1260–960 cal. BC
	Charcoal: *Corylus* sp.	2985 ±45	−25.88	1380–1050 cal. BC
	Charcoal: *Corylus* sp.	2920 ±45	−26.1	1260–970 cal. BC
	Charcoal: Bulk sample of *Alnus* sp., *Corylus* sp., *Fraxinus* sp., *Quercus* sp. and *Ulmus* sp.	2965 ±45	−25.74	1370–1030 cal. BC
	Charcoal: *Corylus* sp. branch wood	2880 ±30	−25.46	1190–940 cal. BC
	Carbonised residue	2869 ±29	−26.4	1180–930 cal. BC
	Charcoal: *Corylus* sp.	2945 ±29	−24.7	1260–1040 cal. BC
	Charcoal: Unidentified bulk sample	2960 ±110	−25.8	1440–890 cal. BC
	Charcoal: *Corylus* sp.	2585 ±45	−27.28	820–550 cal. BC
	Charcoal: *Quercus* sp. branch wood	1410 ±40	−25.44	cal. AD 570–680
	Charcoal: *Quercus* sp. branch wood	2950 ±30	−25.62	1260–1040 cal. BC
	Charcoal: Unidentified	7525 ±115		6600–6100 cal. BC
	Charcoal: *Corylus* sp.	2465 ±29	−24.6	760–420 cal. BC
	Charcoal: *Corylus* sp. branch wood	1645 ±35	−25.6	cal. AD 270–540
	Charcoal: Unidentified	1685 ±70		cal. AD 230–540
Pre-dates 15m structure	Charcoal: Unidentified	2855 ±105		1360–820 cal. BC
Complex hearth	Charcoal: Unidentified	2470 ±80		790–400 cal. BC
	Charcoal: Unidentified	2810 ±105		1290–800 cal. BC

Table 4.2 (cont.)—Radiocarbon dates from Rathgall.

Lab ID	Sample ID	Area	Grid square	Feature	Context details from sample records and other sources
GrN-27097	S69:012	Areas 1–4	Sq. 24; Groningen list: 25	Hearth 1 or 3?	*Circa* 20cm below surface. In dark occupation level, 1.25cm from E, 1.55cm from W. This is black spread from Hearth 3. Groningen list: Hearth 1. Lower black organic layer containing charcoal. As Hearth 1 did not really have a spread around it but Hearth 3 does, the latter seems the likely candidate.
SUERC-42588	S2011.E84:941_942	Areas 1–4	16/8	Hearth 6	In black burnt area, NW. Hearth 6
SUERC-43325	S2011.E84:2117	Areas 1–4	16/8	Hearth 6	Hearth 6. Grey level at bottom. Coarseware sherd E84:2117
SI-1477	S70:5	Areas 1–4	5/G	Hearth 7	
SI-1478	S70:35	Areas 1–4	51	Hearth 10	Burnt fill of Hearth 10
Ring-ditch 2 and enclosed features					
GrN-27112	S72:082	Area 3	G2	Ring-ditch 2	From V-shaped trench
GrA-22304	E84:8484	Area 3	J3	Burial 2	Cremation in coarseware vessel
GrN-27114	S72:093	Area 3	G/G1	Pyre spread Burial 1	Black, heavily burnt horseshoe-shaped area. This is material of Fosse 2 (burial enclosure)
SI-1479	S72:1	Area 3	G1	Pit 25	Black lining of Pit 25
GrN-27118	S74:028	Area 3	H3	Burial 3 (Pit 4)	Black fill of Pit 4
GrA-23353	S74:028	Area 3	H3	Burial 3 (Pit 4)	From black fill of Pit 4
SUERC-42578	S73:10	Area 3	I2	Burial 1	
Rectangular structure					
GrA-23347	S72:115	Area 3	G	Rectangular structure	From bedding trench of subrectangular structure
Occupation layers in Area 2					
GrN-27113	S72:088	Area 2	E1	Occupation material on top of yellow	Black material overlying bank
GrA-23346	S72:057	Area 2	E2	Occupation layer	In darkish brown material immediately east of bank. Probably earlier than the latter. Also described as brown outside black bank in E2
GrN-27108	S72:034	Area 2	D	Occupation layer?	Charcoal from suspected wooden feature. Organic concentration in east of square
GrN-27106	S72:013	Area 2	D	Black layer North, wall break	From among charcoal patches and ferrous lumps. This is the upper zone of black occupation layer
GrN-27109	S72:036	Area 2	D/D1	Black layer	Heavy black charcoal-filled layer
GrN-27110	S72:043	Area 2	D/D1	Black layer	Heavy black charcoal-filled layer
GrN-27111	S72:075	Area 2	D/D1	Occupation layer?	In light, mottled ashy brown material immediately south of black concentration
GrN-27105	S71:113, E84:6114	Area 2	3/4	Black layer, wall break	(Recte 2/3) Thick black layer under wall, 26–30cm deep, associated with pottery and mould fragments
GrN-27115	S72:110	Area 2	B1/C1		Black material in section-strip. Black burnt area
SI-1482	S70:30	Area 1		Concentration in F1?	Heavily burnt area on NE side of ditch 40cm below humus
Area 3					
GrN-27107	S72:028	Area3	F2	Occupation layer?	In brown material
Y cutting					
GrN-27117	S74:022	Y cutting	Y2	Occupation material on top of yellow	Black occupation layer covering square
X cutting					
GrA-23349	S72:128	X cutting	X2	Pit 166	Black fill of Pit 166. Numerous finds
GrN-27116	S72:128		X2	Pit 166	Black fill of Pit 166. Numerous finds

omments	Material dated	Radiocarbon age (BP)	$\delta^{13}C$ (‰)	Calibrated date (95% probability)
ts in spread of material that seems to be old occupation horizon. This is what seems . be dated, rather than the hearth.	Charcoal: *Corylus* sp. branch wood	2950 ±45	−24.99	1380–1070 cal. BC
mple hearth	Carbonised residue	2934 ±26	−26.2	1230–1030 cal. BC
	Carbonised residue	2924 ±27	−25.8	1220–1020 cal. BC
obably simple hearth	Charcoal: Unidentified	2475 ±80		790–400 cal. BC
mple hearth not pyre	Charcoal: Unidentified	2560 ±105		920–410 cal. BC
	Charcoal: *Corylus* sp.	2990 ±40	−26.58	1380–1070 cal. BC
	Cremated human bone	2805 ±35	−27.5	1070–840 cal. BC
	Charcoal: *Alnus* sp.	2940 ±30	−26.66	1250–1030 cal. BC
	Charcoal: Unidentified	1330 ±70		cal. AD 590–880
	Charcoal: *Quercus* sp.	3175 ±35	−25.53	1510–1330 cal. BC
	Charcoal: *Corylus* sp.	2955 ±45	−28.84	1360–1020 cal. BC
	Cremated human bone	2896 ±26	−27.3	1200–1000 cal. BC
	Charcoal: *Corylus* sp.	2965 ±45	−27.41	1370–1030 cal. BC
	Charcoal: *Corylus* sp. branch wood	2970 ±30	−25.68	1300–1060 cal. BC
	Charcoal: Corylus sp.	2940 ±50	−25.92	1340–990 cal. BC
	Charcoal: *Corylus* sp. branch wood	2890 ±30	−24.79	1200–960 cal. BC
	Charcoal: *Corylus* sp. roundwood	2910 ±25	−24.12	1210–1010 cal. BC
	Charcoal: Bulk sample of *Corylus* sp., *Fraxinus* sp. and Pomoideae	2910 ±35	−24.91	1220–990 cal. BC
	Charcoal: *Corylus* sp.	3000 ±30	−25.56	1380–1120 cal. BC
	Charcoal: *Corylus* sp.	2880 ±35	−25.21	1200–930 cal. BC
hould be broadly the same material, but spatially separated	Charcoal: *Alnus* sp.	2910 ±40	−26.76	1230–970 cal. BC
	Charcoal: *Fraxinus* sp.	2910 ±30	−26.25	1210–1010 cal. BC
	Charcoal: Unidentified	1055 ±60		cal. AD 820–1150
	Charcoal: *Alnus* sp.	2870 ±35	−27.37	1190–930 cal. BC
	Charcoal: *Corylus* sp. branch wood	2930 ±30	−25	1230–1020 cal. BC
	Charcoal: *Alnus* sp.	2930 ±45	−26.79	1270–990 cal. BC
	Charcoal: Bulk sample of *Corylus* sp., *Fraxinus* sp. and Pomoideae	3100 ±40	−25.23	1460–1240 cal. BC

Table 4.2 (cont.)—Radiocarbon dates from Rathgall.

Lab ID	Sample ID	Area	Grid square	Feature	Context details from sample records and other sources
Rampart 2 and its ditch					
UB-2343	S78:016	X cutting		Under Rampart 2	From greyish material under main rampart
UB-2344	S78:020	X cutting		Under Rampart 2	From greyish, mottled area at southern end, under main rampart near 'kerbstones'
UB-2345	S78:021	X cutting		Rampart 2, ditch fill	Upper level of ditch. In greyish, mottled material among and above stones
UB-2346	S78:022	X cutting		Rampart 2, ditch fill	From upper, brownish fill of ditch, 25–50cm deep
UB-2347	S78:025	X cutting		Rampart 2, ditch fill	From upper, brownish fill of ditch
UB-2348	S78:033	X cutting		Rampart 2, ditch fill	Scattered charcoal at various levels in upper metre of ditch fill
UB-2350	S78:041	X cutting		Rampart 2, ditch fill	Charcoal from upper metre of ditch fill
UBA-19277	[E4394:S12:F8]	X cutting		Rampart 2, ditch fill	Primary fill of Ditch 2
UBA-19279	[E4394:S12:F8]	X cutting		Under Rampart 2	Grey deposit beneath rampart of Ditch 2
UBA-19280	[E4394:S6:F3]	X cutting		Under Rampart 2	Reddish silt under F1 beneath Ditch 2 rampart
UBA-19281	[E4394:S8:F6]	X cutting		Rampart 2, ditch fill	Primary fill of Ditch 2
UBA-19282	[E4394:S9:F7]	X cutting		Rampart 2, ditch fill	Primary fill of Ditch 2
UBA-19278	[E4394:S11:F1]	X cutting		Under Rampart 2	Grey deposit beneath rampart of Ditch 2
UBA-19283	[E4394:S10:F7]	X cutting		Rampart 2, ditch fill	Primary fill of Ditch 2
Z cuttings					
GrA-26533	?	Z cuttings	Z5:4	Ring-ditch 4	Post-hole 2 (8?)
SUERC-42587	E100:183	Z cuttings	Z5:5	Ring-ditch 4	In grey fill of circular trench, upper levels, SW
SUERC-42579	E100:Pit16	Z cuttings	Z5:4	Ring-ditch 4	Pit 16

curve of Reimer *et al.* (2020) and the computer program OxCal v4.4 (Bronk Ramsey 1995; 1998; 2001; 2009). The calibrated date ranges cited in the text are those for 95% confidence. They are quoted with the end points rounded outwards to ten years if the error term is greater than or equal to 25 radiocarbon years or to five years if it is less. The ranges quoted in italics are posterior density estimates derived from mathematical modelling and are rounded off to five years. The ranges in plain type in the table have been calculated according to the maximum intercept method (Stuiver and Reimer 1986). All other ranges are derived from the probability method (Stuiver and Reimer 1993).

Although the Dublin and Smithsonian laboratories were operating prior to international inter-comparison studies, the Groningen, Belfast and SUERC laboratories do maintain rigorous internal quality assurance procedures that include participation in international inter-comparisons (Scott *et al.* 1998; Scott 2003). These inter-comparisons indicate no laboratory offsets, thus validating the measurement precision quoted for the radiocarbon ages.

4.4.2 The analysis

Traditionally, suites of radiocarbon dates have been analysed using classical statistical methods (e.g. chi-square tests, cluster analyses) and subjective reasoning, combined and presented with logical arguments that incorporate the site stratigraphy and phasing. While this approach was the best methodology available for many years, with the increasing power and lower cost of personal computers a new revolution in radiocarbon dating has been ushered in by the implementation of Bayesian statistical analysis, an explicitly probabilistic analytical methodology, for the interpretation of the chronology from archaeological sites (Bayliss 2009).

The Bayesian approach (Buck *et al.* 1996) has been used

mments	Material dated	Radiocarbon age (BP)	$\delta^{13}C$ (‰)	Calibrated date (95% probability)
	Charcoal: Unidentified	3440 ±120	−23.9	2100–1480 cal. BC
	Charcoal: Unidentified	3780 ±140	−25.0*	2630–1820 cal. BC
	Charcoal: Unidentified	1800 ±155	−21.4	170 cal. BC–cal. AD 560
	Charcoal: Unidentified	1365 ±220	−24.1	cal. AD 200–1130
	Charcoal: Unidentified	1805 ±75	−21.8	cal. AD 50–410
	Charcoal: Unidentified	2915 ±75	−24.7	1370–910 cal. BC
	Charcoal: Unidentified	1465 ±65	−25.0	cal. AD 440–670
	Charcoal: *Corylus* sp.	1388 ±29	−23.8	cal. AD 600–680
	Charcoal: Wild cherry	3054 ±27	−18.3	1410–1220 cal. BC
	Charcoal: *Corylus* sp.	3018 ±26	−25.6	1380–1140 cal. BC
	Charcoal: *Corylus* sp.	3339 ±33	−25.2	1730–1520 cal. BC
	Charcoal: *Corylus* sp.	1387 ±24	−25.1	cal. AD 600–670
	Charcoal: *Corylus* sp.	3072 ±28	−27.3	1420–1240 cal. BC
	Charred vetch	7265 ±34	−25.9	6220–6040 cal. BC
	Cremated bone	2905 ±35	−22.55	1220–980 cal. BC
's layer is in the text described as silted, but about 25 sherds and 15 mould gments were clustered in a particular part of the trench. All finds under or in liberate stone cobbling that apparently extended all around the ditch	Carbonised residue	2761 ±28	−30.3	1000–830 cal. BC
	Cremated human bone	2890 ±29	−25.5	1200–970 cal. BC

*** = assumed value**

to analyse the dating evidence from Rathgall. Although the simple calibrated dates are accurate estimates of the dates of the samples, this is usually not what archaeologists really wish to know. It is the dates of the archaeological events represented by those samples that are of interest. In the case of Rathgall, it is the overall Bronze Age chronology of the site and its various elements—when activity began, when it ended and its duration—that is under consideration, not necessarily the dates of any individual samples. The dates of this activity can be estimated not only by using the absolute dating information from the radiocarbon measurements on the samples but also by using the stratigraphic relationships between samples.

While traditional approaches to radiocarbon dating analysis will often look at the dating along with the archaeological phasing and stratigraphy, the Bayesian methodology allows the combination of these different types of information explicitly, to produce realistic estimates of the dates of archaeological interest. By combining the archaeological data with the radiocarbon dates we often increase the precision of the results while also developing more robust site chronologies. For Rathgall, the archaeological information used in the model consisted primarily of the main spatial groupings of activity that are thought to represent relatively continuous periods of activity. These were then supplemented by any direct stratigraphic associations that were either clearly documented in or strongly inferred from the site records.

It should be emphasised that the posterior density estimates produced by this modelling are not absolute. They are interpretative estimates, which can and will change as further data become available and as other researchers choose to model the existing data from different perspectives. The technique used is a form of Markov Chain Monte Carlo sampling and has been applied using the program OxCal v4.4. Details of the algorithms employed by this program are available from the on-line manual (or see Bronk Ramsey 1995; 1998; 2001; 2009). The algorithm used in the model described below can be derived directly from the model structure shown in Fig. 4.9.

4.4.3 The models of site development

The primary focus of the modelling exercise has been to establish the dating of the Bronze Age and Iron Age phases of activity on the site, with the former providing the bulk of the dates and archaeological data. The modelling began by attempting to use Raftery's sequence of events from across the site (Scenario 1), but as the process moved forward and this model showed low agreement it became clear that a different approach was needed. The alternative scenario (Scenario 2) developed in section 4.3 depends to a great extent on radiocarbon dating evidence and, like Raftery's scenario, on implied rather than explicit stratigraphic relationships between different site elements. To avoid circularity of arguments and in order not to model tentative stratigraphic links, it was decided to model activity associated with specific areas independently (Model 1) and in conjunction with an ongoing dialogue between the dating results and Raftery's stratigraphic account and what it suggests about taphonomic processes on site (see section 4.3). The net result is that many, though not all, of the stratigraphic relationships suggested by Raftery have been removed in favour of modelling spatially related groups as 'activity' areas, and only a few definite stratigraphic links form part of these activity area models.

As outlined below, a small number of Iron Age dates have been excluded from the modelling, as they are much later than the main phase of activity under primary consideration here. While they are still depicted in the models, they are not actually included in the mathematical modelling *per se*. A second model (Model 2) was created that grouped the results into broad periods of activity in the Bronze Age and Iron Age for the overall site. This was done as a form of sensitivity analysis that allows for all the results to come from samples that were reworked and residual in the contexts from which they were recovered but which reflect the overall activity at Rathgall in a specific period.

4.4.4 The samples

This section is designed to provide detailed contextual information about each radiocarbon-dated sample, and to show how the individual dates have been put together into a chronological model. It is here where the validity of a measurement to date its context, the functional relationship and its strength is presented, while also providing scientific and taphonomic explanations for seemingly aberrant results. To preface this section, it is important to highlight that recent comparative radiocarbon data obtained on the same samples as older Smithsonian-dated samples and contexts from numerous Irish sites suggest that there are likely to be errors that are not necessarily systematic, and thus not correctable, in these dates (G. Warren, pers. comm.). The Smithsonian dates are included in the tables for completeness of the record, but a decision was made early on to exclude them all from the actual chronological modelling of the site, as there was not enough information to make informed evaluations of individual results and that was leading to clear instances of circularity (i.e. it looks similar to other dates so it might be okay, whereas the other date looks rather different and must be incorrect), which we found to be unacceptable.

Area 2 and the black occupation deposits

The model contains thirteen radiocarbon dates from the Bronze Age deposits in Area 2, as well as from material in Ring-ditch 1 (Ditch 1) adjacent to Area 2, which is interpreted as deriving from Area 2.

There are four results from black occupation material found in the eastern part of Ring-ditch 1: GrN-27098 and GrN-27099 on bulk hazel and oak branch wood respectively, GrA-23351 from a fragment of hazel charcoal, and SUERC-42585 from charred food residue on a sherd of pottery recovered from near the base of the ditch.

The remaining results from Area 2 itself (GrN-27105–6, GrN-27108–11, GrN-27113, GrN-27115 and GrA-23346) are from samples of charcoal that only include short-lived material. All the material comes from a sequence of discrete spreads, which seem to follow each other stratigraphically (see Chapter 2, section 2.3.1). Firstly, GrA-23346 comes from a spread that underlies all deposits in E2, and GrN-27113 comes from the top of the bank in the adjacent E1. Also, while it is not possible to relate GrN-27109–11 to one another through vertical stratigraphy, all three underlie the spread from which the sample that produced GrN-27106 was recovered. The remaining results are unordered, with all the results modelled as being indicative of the overall chronological use of this area of high activity. The evidence for disturbance of or intrusive mechanisms in this area implied by later material found within these Bronze Age deposits should be noted (see section 4.3).

While most dates derived from the Area 2 deposits found in Ring-ditch 1 were included in the model for Area 2, one of them (GrN-27099) is substantially later than all other dated material from the black deposits associated with the Bronze Age activity in Area 2 and has been excluded from the modelling of the Area 2 activity and Ring-ditch 1. It was recovered from within Ring-ditch 1, 30–40cm beneath the ditch edge and, as originally thought, from the black deposits that had slumped into the open ditch at the time they were being formed. Had this result been on a single fragment of charcoal we might conclude that it was intrusive in the context from which it was recovered, but since it came from a bulk sample of charcoal from a well-sealed context it has raised questions concerning the traditional view of site development at Rathgall that sees the formation of these deposits and the ditch being open as contemporary (see sections 4.1 and 4.2). Instead, it appears likely that earlier material was redeposited into the ditch much later, during the Iron Age occupation of the site, as implied by sample GrN-27099 as well as by the make-up of these deposits (section 4.3). If this is the case, then all the material within the ditch should be considered residual in nature and these deposits are therefore modelled with Area 2, from where they are likely to have derived.

For the dating of the Area 2 deposits, both from within Ring-ditch 1 and from Area 2, this means that all the dates from these deposits with the exception of GrN-27099 are included in the model to estimate the date of the formation of the Area 2 deposits but similarly can also provide an estimate for the date of Ring-ditch 1, if it was dug in the Bronze Age. If the ditch is an Iron Age creation, the calibrated date from GrN-27099 provides the best estimate for that scenario.

There is a fourteenth result (SI-1482) on an unidentified bulk sample of charcoal from Area 2 that is problematic as it is (1) not located by square number and (2) unclear from descriptions whether the sample derives from fills in Ring-ditch 1 or from an area immediately adjacent to the ditch (more likely). While this result is already excluded on the grounds that it is from the Smithsonian laboratory (see above), it would have been excluded on these grounds as well.

Ring-ditch 1 and its interior

There are seven results (D-132, GrN-27102/4, GrA-23344/5 and SUERC-42589/43732) on charcoal and carbonised residues on a pottery sherd from fills of the large storage pit, Pit 118, which is within the interior of Ring-ditch 1, east of the central structure. D-132 is an unidentified bulk sample of charcoal and GrN-27104 had oak identified in the sample. Despite the fact that all seven measurements are statistically consistent (T =8.8; v=6; T (5%)=12.6; Ward and Wilson 1978), D-132 and GrN-27104 have been included as TPQs for the pit. GrN-27104 and GrA-23344 come from what was interpreted as a burnt wickerwork/basketry lining of the pit that is cut into the fill from which GrN-27102 was collected. Although the remaining dates are from the fills within the wicker basketwork, it is not clear from the site records whether this represents discrete episodes of infilling or whether some deposits may be reworked, which could result in inverted stratigraphy. The remaining radiocarbon results remain unordered in relation to the identified stratigraphic sequence. When there are two dates from a feature, it is common best practice to use the latest result as providing the best estimate for the date of the context/feature. With the number of dates here, the 'Last' function in OxCal was used to produce a probability for the date of the latest event associated with this pit, based on the radiocarbon dating results.

There are results from four other pits within the area delimited by Ring-ditch 1. These include GrA-23355, on a fragment of hazel charcoal from Pit 120; GrN-27100, on a bulk sample of oak branch wood from Pit 96; GrN-27101, on a bulk sample of oak branch wood from Pit 119; and SI-1481, on an unidentified bulk sample of charcoal from Pit 110. Although the Smithsonian dates have all been excluded from modelling, SI-1481 would normally have provided a TPQ for the infilling of Pit 110. Furthermore, the date from Pit 96 (GrN-27100) is early medieval and so this result is excluded from the modelling of the Bronze Age activity on the site.

A result (SUERC-42581) was obtained on a fragment of hazel charcoal recovered from one of the discrete patches of charcoal in the outer bedding trench of the 15m structure at the centre of Area 1. The patches were interpreted on site as potential areas where burnt posts were located, though no post-holes were identified, and the dated piece of charcoal could potentially have formed part of a post (Ingelise Stuijts, pers. comm.). When initially included within the Bronze Age dating of the site, this result has very low agreement, with only an 11% probability of being part of this phase. Since part of the 15m structure cuts a Bronze Age feature (Hearth 1) it has been placed into the Iron Age phase of activity; the date is excluded here when considering the Bronze Age activity within the enclosed area but is discussed below in the results with regard to the Iron Age activity at Rathgall.

In addition, there are eight results from six 'hearth' areas that were excavated within the Ring-ditch 1 interior. Activity at Hearths 1 (D-134), 2 (D-133 and SI-1476), 7 (SI-1477) and 10 (SI-1478) was dated by samples of unidentified bulk charcoal, which only provide a TPQ for the features, and the Smithsonian dates are all excluded for reasons given above. Hearth 3 was dated (GrN-27097) with a bulk sample of hazel branch wood, which should provide a date for the latest use of the feature. Hearth 6 (SUERC-42588/-43325) was dated by carbonised residues on pottery sherds, which directly dates the use of the pots and should provide a reliable date estimate for the activity associated with the hearth.

A total of twelve results are available from various sections and fills of Ring-ditch 1. These are poorly contextualised and so, while it is possible in nearly every case to locate a sample to its grid square, when there are multiple samples from a square it is not always clear what, if any, stratigraphic order might have existed. To add a layer of complication, in the eastern portion of Ring-ditch 1 there is a black charcoal- and finds-rich fill that appears to be a continuation of an area of high activity outside Ring-ditch 1 in Area 2 that made its way into the ditch through either natural or anthropogenic means (see Chapter 2, section 2.2.2, and sections 4.2 and 4.3 above). The material forming this layer could have originally formed either prior to the cutting of the ditch, and then been redeposited into it, or formed after its creation.

GrA-23351 and GrN-27098/9, from charcoal samples in these black deposits thought to derive from Area 2, are included here as TPQs, since they are likely to be related to the redeposition of this material into the ditch. There is one date (GrA-23341) on hazel charcoal from a grey fill in Ring-ditch 1 to the south-west and sealed beneath stones. D-135 was obtained from a bulk sample of grain from an upper level of fill on the north side of the ditch.

There were Smithsonian dates from a number of contexts—SI-1483 from a black fill in Sq. 10 on the east, SI-1484 from a lower black fill in an unlocated excavation square and SI-1485 from a fill in the base of the ditch in Sq. 8 to the north-east—but they are excluded from the actual modelling. Since a better understanding of the chronology of the ditch has been an important element of the dating programme for Rathgall, new samples were submitted from some previously Smithsonian-dated contexts. SUERC-42580 is on a fragment of hazel charcoal from a layer of black fill of Ring-ditch 1 in Sq. 10, and SUERC-42585 is on carbonised residue from the surface of a potsherd in a black fill near the bottom of Ring-ditch 1 in Sq. 8. Another result (GrA-23350) on a fragment of hazel charcoal from a black organic deposit in Sq. 29, in the south-east of Ditch 1, is stratigraphically earlier than the final result (SUERC-42586) on a carbonised residue from a sherd of pottery from the same square.

Our initial model (Model 1) considers the Bronze Age dates in Ring-ditch 1 as representing primary deposition, i.e. assumed to have formed after the ditch had been dug. If, however, we accept that Ring-ditch 1 is not a Bronze Age feature but filled with redeposited Bronze Age material, then the later dates, GrN-27099 and D-135, which are not included in the mathematical modelling of these ditch dates, provide the best date estimate for when the ditch was open in the Iron Age. GrN-27099 should be considered the preferred date of the two, since the sample was located 30–40cm below the ditch edge, while D-135 appears, from the site records, to have come from nearer the surface.

Ring-ditch 2 and subrectangular structure

Ring-ditch 2 lies to the south and east of Ring-ditch 1 and runs under the later cashel wall, although the relationship between the suggested yellow bank deposits and the ditch in this zone is unclear. Raftery states—and this is corroborated in the section drawing of this zone—that Ring-ditch 2 cuts through the deposit that he interpreted as a bank. Its relationship to Ring-ditch 1 is not clear, however, and the dating of the deposits underlying the rampart in this zone is highly ambiguous (see section 4.3), and for this reason we model the ring-ditch and the rectangular structure as one activity area only.

Seven dates are available from material associated with pits and cremation burials in the area of Ring-ditch 2.

There is a result (GrA-23347) on a fragment of hazel charcoal from the bedding trench of the subrectangular structure. This structure is cut by Ring-ditch 2, from which there is a result (GrN-27112) on a bulk sample of hazel charcoal from the fill of the ditch. The dates have been modelled following this identified stratigraphic sequence.

Three of the burials in this area were dated. The first, Burial 1, yielded a result (SUERC-42578) on a fragment of cremated human bone. A date (GrA-22304) is available on cremated human bone from Burial 2, which was contained in a coarseware urn. In the north-east quadrant of the ring-ditch interior there is Burial 3 (Pit 4), from which there is a result (GrA-23353) on a fragment of hazel charcoal and another (GrN-27118) on a bulk sample of oak charcoal. The latter result is only included as a TPQ.

In the centre of the ring-ditch were the spread remains of what was interpreted as a pyre into which Burial 1 was cut. A result (GrN-27114) was obtained from a bulk sample of alder from this spread. While the stratigraphic relationship would suggest that the result from this spread and that from Burial 1 could be placed in a sequence, the taphonomy of the associated activity is such that the material in the burial and the remains of the pyre could represent the same temporal activity, so the physical relationship between the contexts has not been included in the model.

Finally, there is a result (SI-1479) on a bulk unidentified sample of charcoal from Pit 25, which cuts Ring-ditch 2. While the nature of the sample would make this result only provide a TPQ for the filling of the pit, it is a Smithsonian result and has been excluded from the chronological modelling for reasons given above.

Rampart 2

Rampart 2, the innermost line of the multivallate enclosure of the site, was excavated in both the original excavations and the most recent work in 2011 (Chapter 2, sections 2.7 and 2.8). There are a total of fourteen radiocarbon results from immediately beneath the rampart and from the ditch fills. Seven of the results were from bulk unidentified charcoal samples and are included as TPQs, while the newer results are from single charcoal fragments from just beneath the rampart or the primary ditch silting fills. UB-2343/4 provide TPQs for the overlying rampart, while UBA-19278–80 come from single fragments of charcoal from short-lived species. UB-2345–8 and UB-2350, from fills that are generally described as being from upper levels in the associated ditch, are on unidentified charcoal and so only provide TPQ dating. UBA-19277 and UBA-19281–3 are from single fragments of charcoal from short-lived species that were recovered from the primary ditch fills and are related to material entering the ditch during the initial silting. The chronological model considers the dates from under the rampart and within the ditch fills as providing the time-frame for the digging of the Rampart 2 ditch.

4.4.5 Non-modelled results

There are a number of areas that had too few dates to construct viable activity area models, and so the results from the associated features are discussed here in brief and shown as calibrated results in Fig. 4.11.

Area 3

A single result (GrN-27017) was obtained on alder charcoal from a presumed occupation deposit in Area 3, which lies on the exterior of the south-eastern edge of Ring-ditch 1. While this area was not modelled independently of the others in the initial model, Area 3 conjoins Areas 1, 2 and 4 and so this date has been included in the secondary model that considers all of the Bronze Age activity in the central core area of Rathgall.

Iron furnace

There are two results (GrN-27103 and SI-1480) from bulk charcoal samples recovered from an iron-smelting pit that was cut into the fills of Ring-ditch 1 in the north-west (Sq. 65). While the two results are statistically consistent (T′=0.3; v=1; T′ (5%)=3.8) and could be the same actual age, the Smithsonian dates have all been excluded and GrN-27103, which is on a bulk sample of hazel branch wood, provides the best estimate for the date of the late Iron Age activity associated with this pit.

Cutting X: Pit 166

Pit 166 lay just north of Rampart 2, and there are two results from black fills that contained numerous finds. The first result (GrN-27116) is on a bulk sample of non-oak charcoal, while the second (GrA-23349) is on a single fragment of hazel charcoal. The two results are not statistically consistent (T′=8.0; v=1; T′(5%)=3.8). While it is plausible that either the non-oak bulk sample contained old-growth wood or the hazel charcoal sample is intrusive, the later date, GrA-23349, has been used to provide the best date estimate for this feature.

Cutting Y

To the north of Ring-ditch 1 there was a spread of black occupation material that was dated. The result (GrN-27117) from a bulk sample of hazel branch wood provides an estimated date for this activity.

Cutting Z
A result (GrA-26533) was obtained on a fragment of cremated human bone that was recovered from the fill of a post-hole associated with Ring-ditch 4, outside the main occupation zone and downslope to the south. As the fragment of bone is likely to be redeposited, it only provides a TPQ for the feature. Two recent results (SUERC-42579/42587) were obtained on a fragment of human bone in Pit 16 and a residue on a pottery sherd in the upper fills of the circular trench, recovered with some 25 sherds and fifteen mould fragments that were clustered under and within a deliberate stone cobbling that apparently extended all the way around the ditch.

4.4.6 Results

The samples, described in section 4.4.4. were modelled by area (Model 1). This chronological model depicted in Fig. 4.8 demonstrates good agreement between the radiocarbon dates and the archaeological information as described above (Amodel=82).

Ditch 1, Ring-ditch 2 and Area 2 deposits
The modelling suggests that Area 2 activity began in *1275–1110 cal. BC* (*95% probability*; Fig. 4.8, AREA2; *start: Occupation layers in Area 2*), and probably in *1210–1125 cal. BC* (*68% probability*). The dated activity in this area lasted for *1–215 years* (*95% probability*; Fig. 4.10, SPANS; *use: Occupation layers in Area 2*), and probably for *1–125 years* (*68% probability*); the activity ended in *1185–1005 cal. BC* (*95% probability*; Fig. 4.8, AREA2; *end: Occupation layers in Area 2*), and probably in *1120–1045 cal. BC* (*68% probability*).

The Bronze Age activity in the space bounded by Ring-ditch 1 began in *1385–1135 cal. BC* (*95% probability*; Fig. 4.8, INTRD1; *start: Interior Ditch 1*), and probably in *1280–1175 cal. BC* (*68% probability*). The activity lasted for *290–725 years* (*95% probability*; Fig. 4.10, SPANS; *use: Bronze Age activity, Ditch 1 interior*), and probably for *385–565 years* (*68% probability*); the activity ended in *895–595 cal. BC* (*95% probability*; Fig. 4.8, INTRD1; *end: Interior Ditch 1*), and probably in *805–705 cal. BC* (*68% probability*).

This model has allowed for nearly all the dated material within Ring-ditch 1 to have been recovered from its primary depositional context. With that in mind, it suggests that Ring-ditch 1 might have been dug in *1275–1060 cal. BC* (*95% probability*; Fig. 4.8, RD1; *start: Ditch 1*), and probably in *1200–1100 cal. BC* (*68% probability*). The dated material in the ditch potentially spans a long period of time, with Bronze Age deposition ceasing perhaps at some time in *1180–950 cal. BC* (*95% probability*; Fig. 4.8, RD1; *end: Ditch 1*), and probably in *1120–1035 cal. BC* (*68% probability*). We have made the argument, however, that there is a higher likelihood that the Bronze Age material was reworked into the ditch from the adjoining Area 2 deposits and that the later dates in the ditch more accurately reflect the period when the ditch was open and filling up. Since GrN-27099 was from 30–40cm below the ditch edge and D-135 was recorded as coming from near the surface, the former gives a better estimate of when the ditch was actively filling up in the period 770–480 cal. BC (95% confidence; Fig. 4.8, RD1; GrN-27099: ditch).

The dating results from the Ring-ditch 2 area, Area 3, are similar to the results for the Bronze Age activity in the Ring-ditch 1 interior and Area 2. The model suggests that the earliest activity in this area occurred in *1390–1060 cal. BC* (*95% probability*; Fig. 4.8, RD2; *start: Ring-ditch 2 area*), and probably in *1275–1130 cal. BC* (*68% probability*). Ring-ditch 2, which cut the rectangular structure, was dug in *1255–1050 cal. BC* (*95% probability*; Fig. 4.8, RD2; *build: Ring-ditch 2*), and probably in *1195–1085 cal. BC* (*68% probability*). The dated activity in this area ended in *1180–820 cal. BC* (*95% probability*; Fig. 4.8, RD2; *end: Ring-ditch 2 area*), and probably in *1100–950 cal. BC* (*68% probability*). The area around Ring-ditch 2 was used for up to *490 years* (*95% probability*; Fig. 4.10, SPANS; *use: Ring-ditch 2 area*), but probably for *1–300 years* (*68% probability*).

Rampart 2
The initial interpretation of the chronology of Rampart 2 was that it was Bronze Age in origin. Not only are the original Belfast results (UB-2343/4) from the ground surface beneath the rampart, as well as pottery and mould finds from these levels, of Bronze Age date, but one of the results (UB-2348) from within the ditch fills was Bronze Age as well. The remaining original dates from within the ditch fills were medieval.

The seven new samples taken for radiocarbon dating during the most recent excavations in advance of stabilising the ditch prior to opening the site to visitors have shed some light on the chronology. The three samples taken from beneath the rampart (UBA-19278–80) are all Bronze Age and very similar in date to all the other dated Bronze Age activity at Rathgall. Of interesting note are the results from the primary silting fills of Ring-ditch 2. While one of the results is Bronze Age (UBA-19281) and a second is Mesolithic (UBA-19283), the remaining two results are medieval (UBA-19277/83).

The latest dating from beneath the rampart suggests that the ditch was dug after *1390–1190 cal. BC* (*95% probability;* Fig. 4.8, RAMPART2; UBA-19280). The latest dating from the secure basal fills in the Rampart 2 ditch suggests that the ditch began filling up in or very shortly after *cal. AD 600–675* (*95% probability;* Fig. 4.8, RAMPART2; UBA-19277).

The dating allows for two likely scenarios: (1) Rampart 2 and its ditch originally date from the Bronze Age and the ditch was later cleaned/redug and reused in the medieval period; or (2) there had been intensive Bronze Age activity in the area excavated, but Rampart 2 and the ditch were a medieval construction, and there had been very little activity in the area in the intervening period.

4.4.7 Alternative model—Model 2

The alternative model views the radiocarbon dates as only being indicative of the relatively continuous activity on the site during specific periods, such that all the Bronze Age dates are grouped into a general phase of Bronze Age activity. This model allows the dates on material deposited in Ring-ditch 1 to be combined with those from the Ring-ditch 1 interior, Area 2 and the Ring-ditch 2 area into a unified phase of activity, so that the statistical scatter from all the radiocarbon dates is accounted for fully. This alternative model still includes some samples as TPQs, as stated above, but strips away any stratigraphic relationships, making it much less constrained in many ways than the previous model. Most radiocarbon results are from features associated with the Bronze Age activity. While four results ultimately have been considered as coming from Iron Age activity (SUERC-42581 from the 15m structure, GrA-23355 from Pit 120, and D-135 and GrN-27099 from the fills of Ring-ditch 1), initially the result from Pit 120 was included in the Bronze Age activity for archaeological reasons associated with that feature and discussed in section 4.2. The result had very low individual agreement when combined with the other Bronze Age dates (A=3.8), however, raising questions about the validity of the previously made inference. Therefore it was felt that the assumption that the pit was probably sealed by a now non-extant bank is incorrect, or that the pit formed part of a phase of earliest Iron Age activity in that area before being sealed by the bank, thus placing the feature and its radiocarbon result into the Iron Age phase of activity at Rathgall.

The alternative model (Fig. 4.12, ALT) has good agreement between the radiocarbon results and the assumption that the samples belong to these two uniform phases of activity (Amodel=75).

This model estimates that Bronze Age activity at Rathgall commenced in *1335–1230 cal. BC* (*95% probability*; Fig. 4.12, ALT; *start: Bronze Age Rathgall (alt)*), and probably in *1315–1245 cal. BC* (*68% probability*). This activity lasted for *215–385 years* (*95% probability*; *use: Bronze Age Rathgall (alt)*), and probably for *260–340 years* (*68% probability*). Bronze Age activity ended in *1040–935 cal. BC* (*95% probability*; Fig. 4.12, ALT; *end: Bronze Age Rathgall (alt)*), and probably in *1010–960 cal. BC* (*68% probability*). The dating of the Bronze Age activity in this alternative model is very similar to the results from Model 1, especially those from the activity within the interior of Ring-ditch 1, thus demonstrating the robustness of the model to the prior assumptions.

While the alternative model is also capable of providing an extremely crude chronological model for the dated Iron Age activity at the site, the facts that there are only four Iron Age results and that they all calibrate to the period associated with the Hallstatt plateau make this chronology particularly imprecise (see Steier and Rom 2000 for further discussions regarding this technical matter). Despite this, all four results, when subjected to a basic chronological model (detailed in Hamilton and Kenney 2015), have posterior probabilities that span from approximately 800 cal. BC to 550 cal. BC (in their 95% probability ranges), firmly placing this activity in what might be considered the earliest Iron Age period, and taking place a century or two later than the dated Bronze Age activity.

The dates from the Late Iron Age iron furnace and features in Cuttings X, Y and Z remain unmodelled, and the calibrations in Table 4.2 provide the best estimate for the activity associated with those features.

4.4.8 Carbonised residues on pottery sherds

Given the importance of the pottery assemblage from the site, both for its dating and for its integration into wider typologies, a sub-programme was developed in the latest dating round to select pottery sherds with carbonised food residues adhering to the surface. In total, six radiocarbon dates are available from these residues in addition to the result from the urned burial. Where these are direct dates on the pots, they represent the last or almost last use of the pot. These seven results are considered to securely date the specific pottery type, regardless of where the sherd was recovered, but they also provide dating evidence in general for the Bronze Age activity at Rathgall.

The modelled dating results for these pottery sherds, for both the model based on Model 1 and the more generic 'Bronze Age activity' model, are given in Table 4.3.

4.4.9 Discussion

The high number of dates that could only be included as TPQs in some areas has resulted in a lower level of overall model precision than might otherwise have been expected (Steier and Rom 2000). The decreased precision should not be misinterpreted as a decrease in accuracy. The result is that the 95% probability for the date of a modelled event has an especially long tail (i.e. start and end dates for Ring-ditch 1 and Rampart 2), but in many instances the 68% probability is likely to provide a more realistic estimate for the date of the event.

A comparison of the modelled dates for the pottery sherds in the primary and alternative chronological models demonstrates the robustness of the data and the assumptions. However, SUERC-42587, which is substantially younger than the other dates from carbonised food residues, has a very low agreement when combined with the other dated Bronze Age features (A=7) and suggests that either the pottery is early first-millennium cal. BC in date or the radiocarbon date is in error and the pot actually dates from the end of the second millennium cal. BC.

The site models indicate a narrow horizon of activity at the site in the twelfth and eleventh centuries cal. BC in which the metalworking and burial activity took place. The dating of those materials that are suggested to have been redeposited into Ring-ditch 1 is virtually identical to that of those from Area 2, supporting this hypothesis.

Both Area 1 and Area 3 show a slightly earlier start of activity. In Area 3 this is due to the dating of the rectilinear

Fig. 4.8—Bayesian models.

AREA2

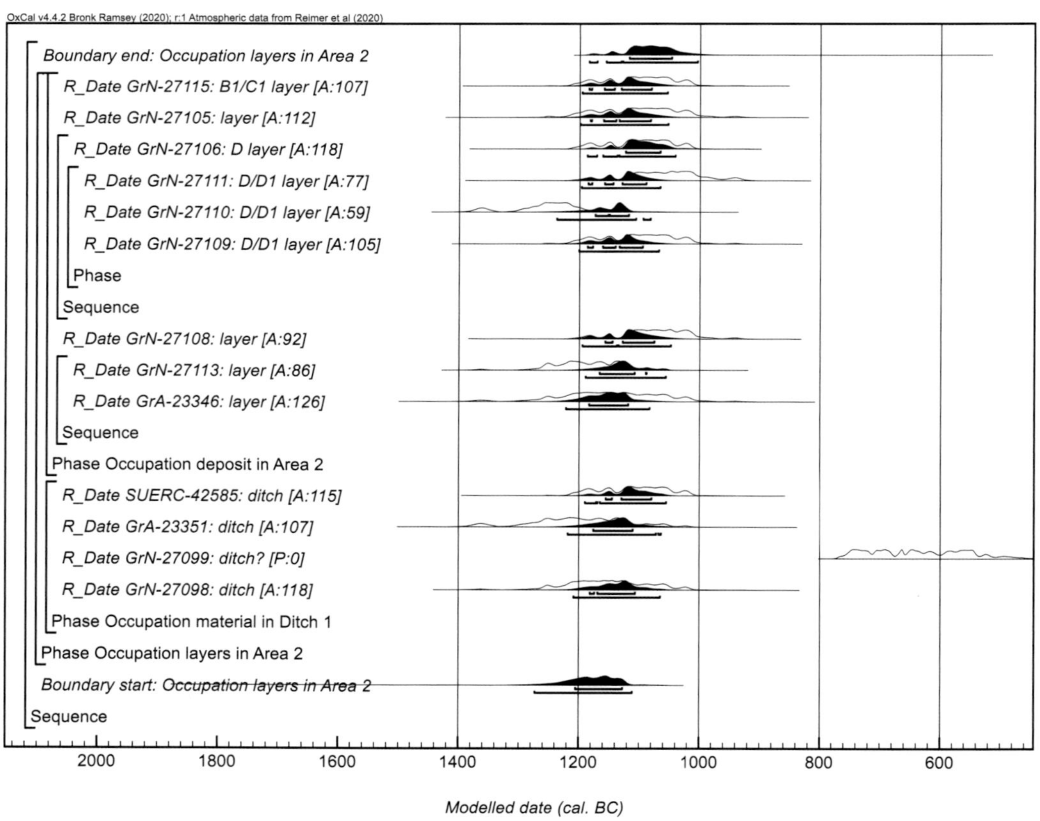

Fig. 4.8 (cont.)—Bayesian models.

INTRD1

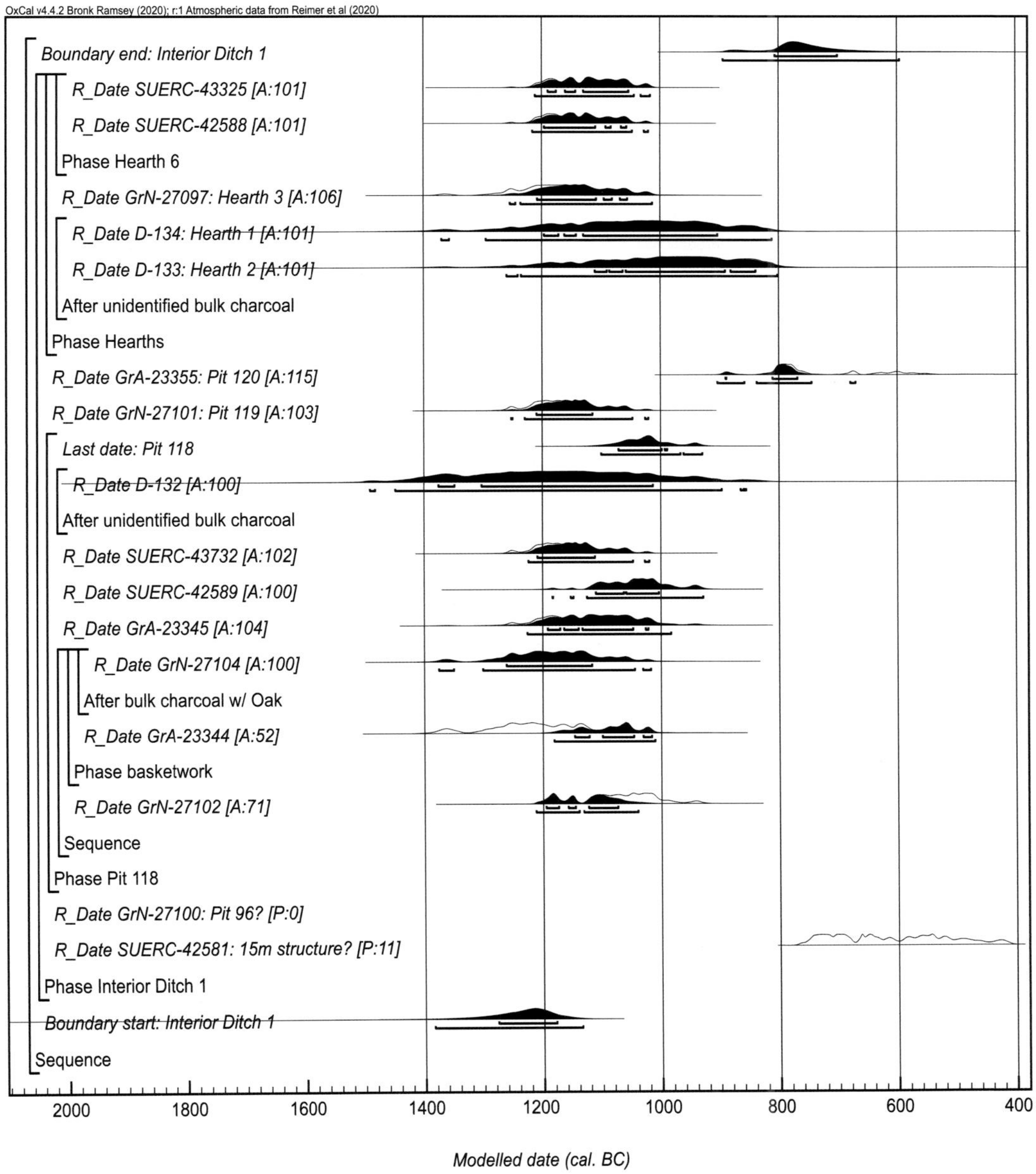

structure, cut by Ring-ditch 2, which preceded the main phase of Bronze Age activity. The digging of Ring-ditch 2 and the ensuing activity in its interior are similar in date to the activity in Area 2, with both dated to the twelfth and eleventh centuries cal. BC.

The slightly later date obtained on the bone accompanying the urn in Burial 2 in Ring-ditch 2 (GrA-23304) may suggest a marginally longer duration of the activity in this area beyond the eleventh century cal. BC, which is similarly suggested by the late date (SUERC-42587) on a carbonised residue sample from the Z cuttings.

Most dates obtained on pottery fragments from the site fall into the twelfth or eleventh century cal. BC. If, as discussed above, the later date SUERC-42587 is not an error, another explanation for this later date could be that, since it was found in the upper layer of infill of Ring-ditch 3, it represents a later phase of activity in this area.

Overwhelmingly, however, the dates for the main areas are restricted to the 200-year period between *c.* 1200 and 1000 cal. BC. The activity within Ring-ditch 1 continues into the first half of the first millennium BC if Pit 120 is modelled as part of the Bronze Age activity in this area, but

Fig. 4.8 (cont.)—Bayesian models.

RD1

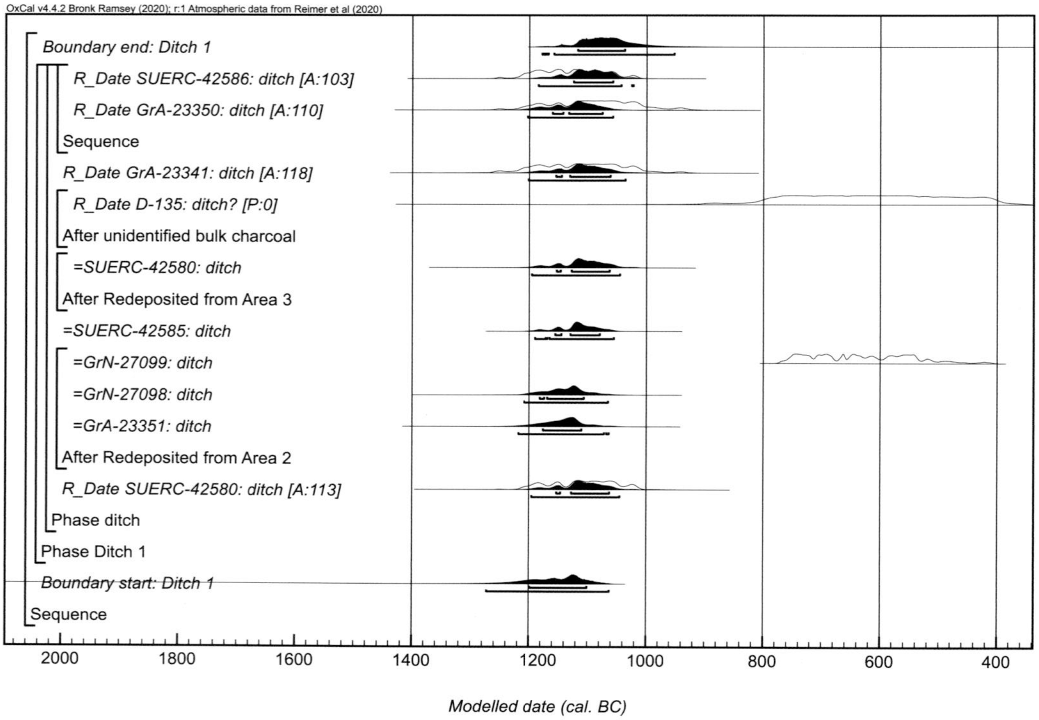

Fig. 4.8 (cont.)—Bayesian models.

RD2

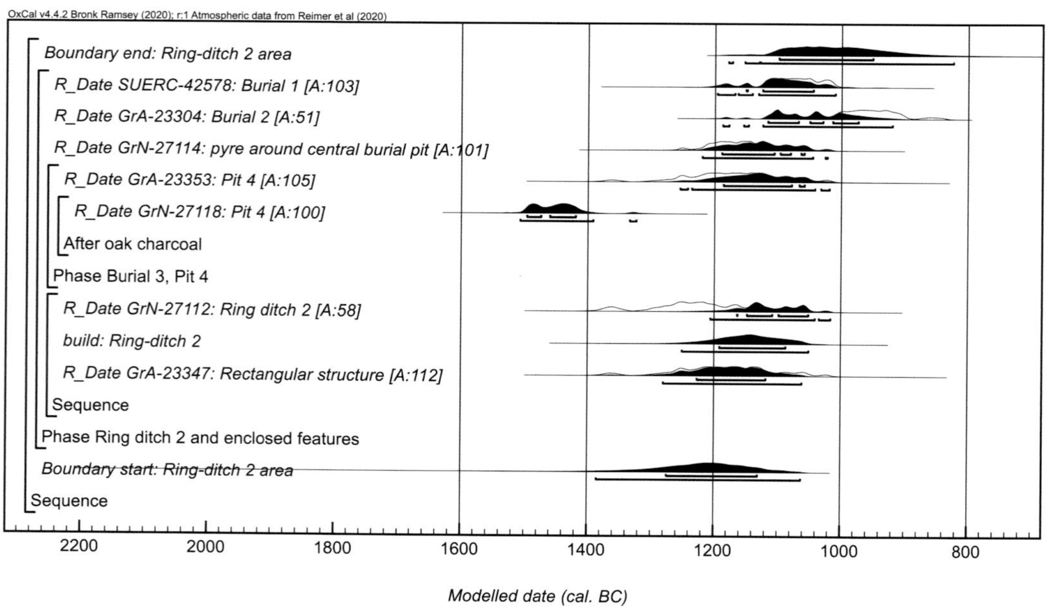

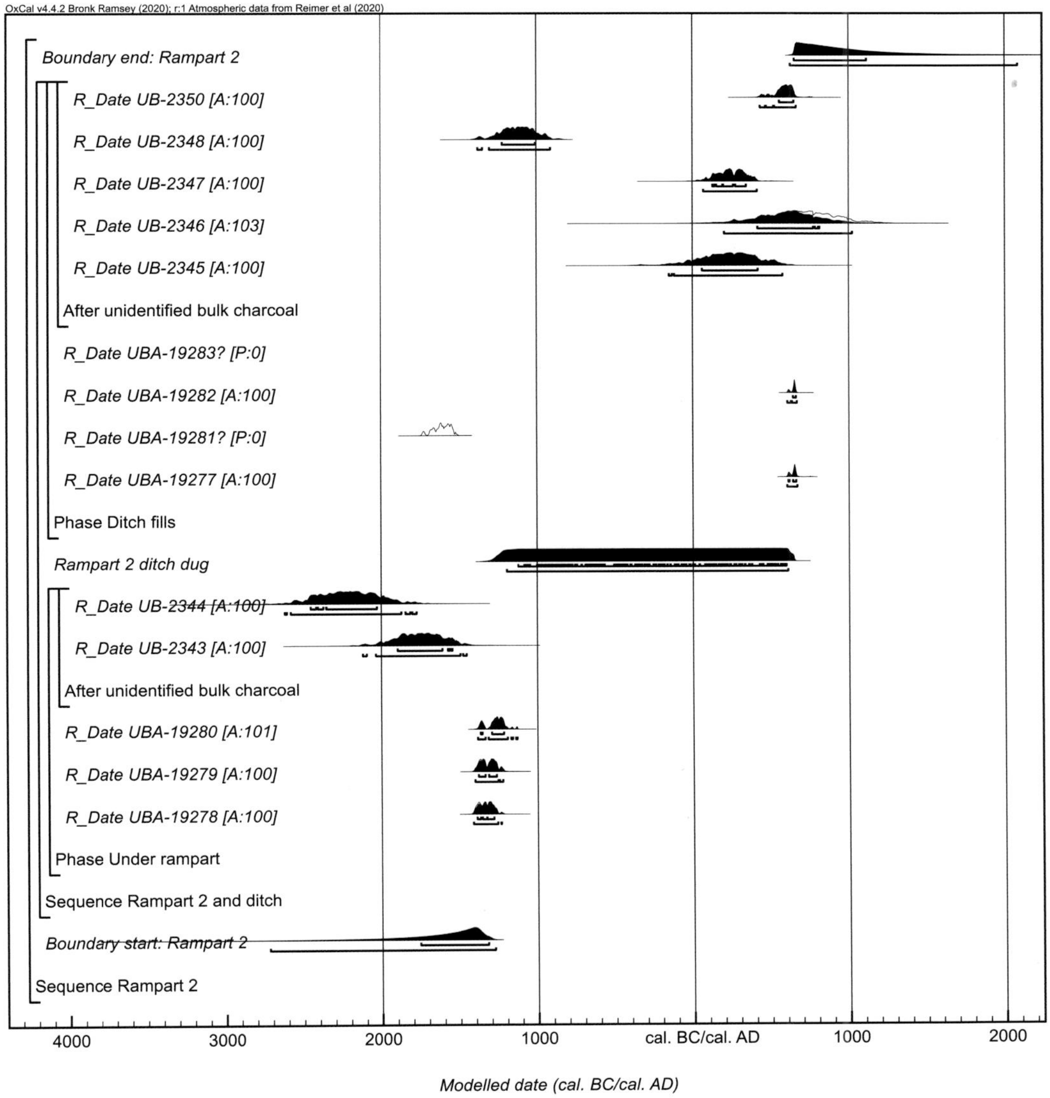

Fig. 4.8 (cont.)—Bayesian models.

RAMPART2

if it is excluded from the Bronze Age phase, as in the alternative model (Model 2), the Bronze Age activity within the area ends only slightly later than the main phase of Bronze Age activity.

Rather than a protracted period of activity from the Bronze Age through to the Early Iron Age, which might be suggested from a visual inspection of the entire corpus of dates, a second phase of activity is inferred. This Iron Age activity is specifically examined using the alternative model and dates from between 800 and 550 cal. BC, with the primary locus of activity represented by activity within Area 1.

The dating of Rampart 2 in its current form can be placed in the medieval period, post-dating, but not directly following, a Bronze Age horizon in this area dating from between 1400 and 1200 cal. BC.

NOTES

1 For Raftery's interpretation of Area 2 as the place of habitational structures see Chapter 6.

2 The finds records note that in Sq. 9/3 finds came from the 'grey silting near the base'; similarly, in Sq. 3 finds are recorded from an unspecified grey fill (see Table 2.3b).

3 This cannot be verified through the finds records for Sq. 7, where

Fig. 4.9—
Bayesian
models.

SUMMARY

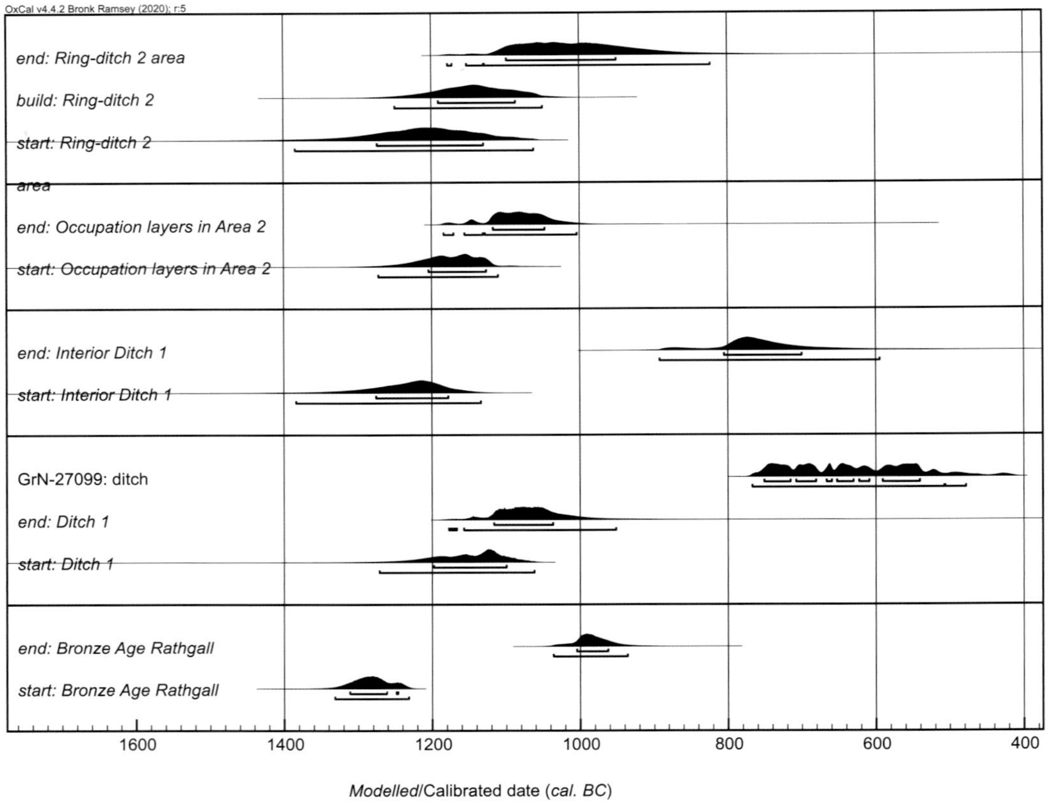

Fig. 410—
Bayesian
models.

SPANS

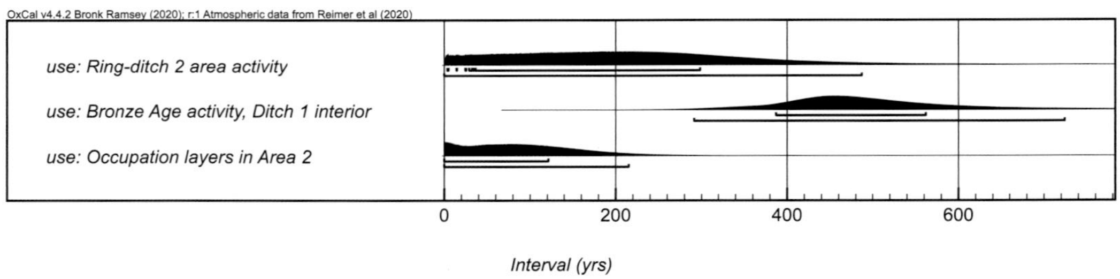

Fig. 4.11—
Bayesian models.

UNMODELLED

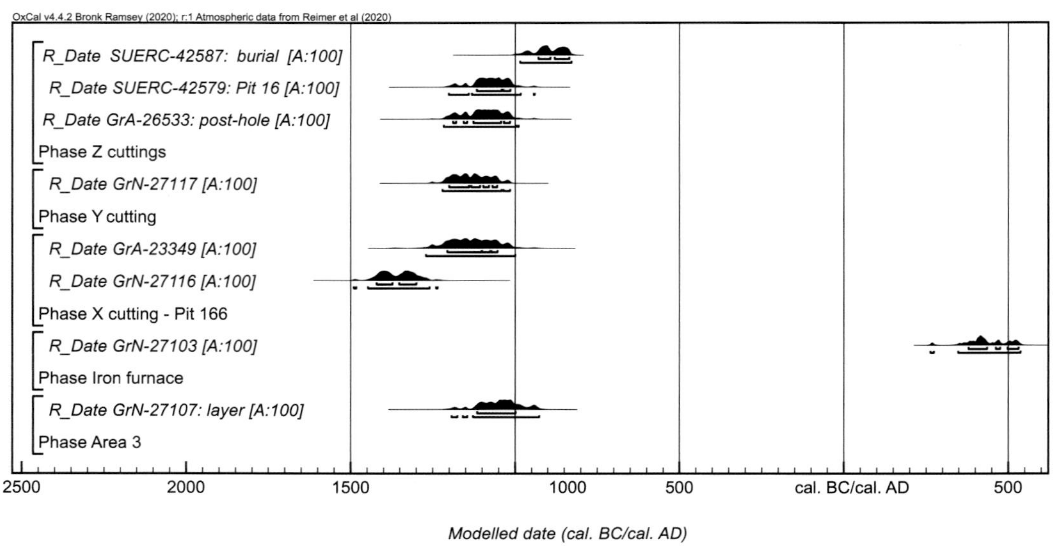

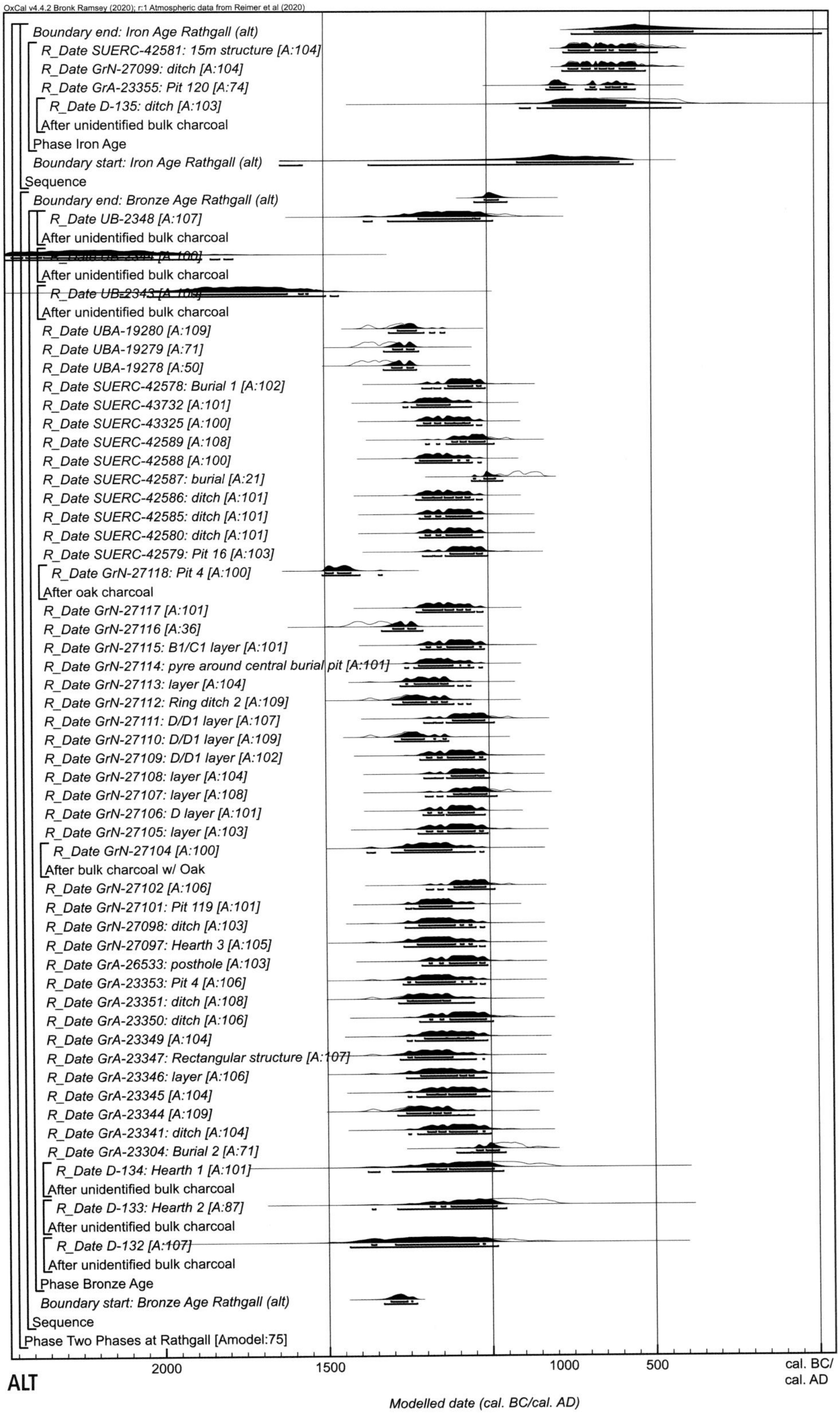

Fig. 4.12—Bayesian models.

the finds records do not allow differentiation. However, pottery and moulds are recorded to have been found in lower levels in the fill of the ditch in Sq. 7 and in Sq. 8 (Table 2.3b). It appears that this information was not available to Raftery at the time of writing. Also, adding all finds per square (cf. Table 2.3a), relatively equal numbers of pottery and moulds are found in the squares opposite both metalworking zones. This removes some differences between Metalworking Zones 2 and 3 and allows for a similar history for the deposits that were incorporated into the ditch fill in both areas.

4 See note 3 and Table 2.3b.

5 It appears that the term 'silting' can apply to a variety of different fills.

6 The overall set of available radiocarbon dates today suggests a Middle/Late Bronze Age date for this; see section 4.4.

7 Raftery saw the large, elaborate hearths as related to the metalworking activity, but see Chapter 6.

8 As agricultural furrows were initially recorded as trenches, the description of some finds as having been found in a 'trench' in the finds records can refer to plough furrows.

9 A further problematic find is E84:1298a, a medieval sherd with a green glaze in Sq. 6. It has a recorded depth of 54cm (from the top of the humus), which probably indicates a depth of 25cm below the upper edge of the ditch cut. It was recorded as having been found in the 'upper level' of the dark fill of the ditch, but this may be a recording error.

Table 4.3—Modelled dates for coarseware pottery.

	Find no./ context no.	Pottery type	Activity area model (Model 1)		Alternative 'Bronze Age activity' model	
Lab ID			*68% probability*	*95% probability*	*68% probability*	*95% probability*
SUERC-42585	Ring-ditch 1 fill, Sq. 8	E84:1441. Medium fabric base angle sherd of Late Bronze Age pottery not assigned to a particular vessel.	*1160–1145 cal. BC (8%) or 1130–1080 cal. BC (60%)*	*1190–1055 cal. BC*	*1190–1175 cal. BC (8%) or 1160–1145 cal. BC (8%) or 1130–1045 cal. BC (52%)*	*1210–1015 cal. BC*
SUERC-42586	Ring-ditch 1 fill, Sq. 29	E84:4622. Barrel-shaped vessel with internally bevelled rim. Poor-quality hard gritty fabric with a high content of inclusions (≤4.2mm). The surfaces are uneven but an effort has been made to smooth over the protruding inclusions on the exterior surface. A thick deposit of carbonised residue is present on the exterior surface and traces are present on the interior surface and the surface of the bevel. C: black/black/black-orange. Estd rim diameter 23.4cm. T: 12.2mm.	*1125–1055 cal. BC*	*1185–1020 cal. BC*	*1200–1055 cal. BC*	*1220–1015 cal. BC*
SUERC-42587	Ring-ditch 4 Upper levels	Vessel 402. Rim. Barrel-shaped vessel with rounded rim. Hard, compact, good-quality fabric with a moderate to high content of inclusions (≤5.4mm). The surfaces are smooth. Heavy carbonised residue is present on the interior and exterior surfaces and on the rim surface. Estd rim diameter c. 20cm. C: black-orange/black/black. T: 11mm.	*930–835 cal. BC*	*990–825 cal. BC*	*1045–1035 (6%) or 1015–975 cal. BC (62%)*	*1050–950 cal. BC*
SUERC-42588	Hearth 6	Base angle fragment 941/942. Barrel-shaped vessel with flat, inwardly expanded rim. Poor-quality gritty fabric with a high content of inclusions (≤5.3mm). The surfaces are uneven but an effort has been made to smooth the protruding inclusions on the exterior surface. Thick deposit of carbonised residue is present on the interior surface near the base. Carbonised residue on the surface of the rim forms a distinct black demarcation on the interior area of the surface of the rim. A perforation is present on sherd 940a, 13.3mm below the rim. C: orange/brown/brown-orange. T: 9.8–10.9mm.	*1200–1055 cal. BC*	*1220–1045 cal. BC (94%) or 1030–1020 cal. BC (1%)*	*1210–1110 cal. BC (63%) or 1095–1085 cal. BC (2%) or 1065–1055 cal. BC (3%)*	*1225–1045 cal. BC (94%) or 1030–1020 cal. BC (1%)*
SUERC-42589	Pit 118, black outer layer	S2011. E84:5927b. Barrel-shaped vessel with flat rim. Good-quality, hard gritty fabric with a high content of inclusions (≤8.6mm).	*1110–1000 cal. BC*	*1125–925 cal. BC*	*1110–1005 cal. BC*	*1190–1175 cal. BC (1%) or 1160–1145 cal. BC (1%) or 1130–980 cal. BC (93%)*
SUERC-43325	Hearth 6	S2011. E84:2117. Medium fabric body sherd of Late Bronze Age pottery not assigned to a particular vessel. Carbonised food residue visible on inner surface.	*1190–1050 cal. BC*	*1215–1015 cal. BC*	*1195–1050 cal. BC*	*1215–1015 cal. BC*
GrA-23340	Burial 2, Ring-ditch 2	Coarseware urn	*1120–1030 cal. BC (46%) or 1015–975 cal. BC (22%)*	*1190–1175 cal. BC (1%) or 1155–1145 cal. BC (1%) or 1125–920 cal. BC (93%)*	*1050–975 cal. BC*	*1110–955 cal. BC*

5. EARLY PREHISTORIC RATHGALL

Barry Raftery and Katharina Becker

5.1 NEOLITHIC

The evidence from Rathgall, outlined and discussed in previous chapters, provides a record of occupation of the site from the Neolithic to modern times. While there are periods in which lower levels of activity are evident, these nevertheless can serve to create a picture of perhaps intermittent but long-lived use of the site over time.

Activity at Rathgall is possibly evidenced from the Mesolithic onwards in the form of two radiocarbon dates. These may represent early use of the site, obliterated through later disturbance, although they may also represent the inclusion of older, non-anthropogenic charcoal in later pit contexts. While some of the excavated features may be datable to the Neolithic or the Early Bronze Age, the more substantial evidence for archaeological activity could in almost all cases be dated to the later Bronze Age, the Iron Age or the medieval period.

In the course of the excavation pottery, flint, chert and stone artefacts of probable Neolithic date were recovered. None of the many features exposed, however, could be dated with confidence to this period. It is, of course, entirely possible that at least some of the many pits and depressions revealed belonged to this early phase of activity but in no instance could this be objectively demonstrated, even though a number contained early material.

The most clearly recognisable early material consisted of sherds from a minimum of 22 Early Neolithic and a minimum of five Middle Neolithic pottery vessels which can be isolated from the great mass of Bronze Age pottery, as well as fragments of one Middle Neolithic globular stone bowl (see Chapter 3, section 3.11.1). These indicate initial occupation in the area from early in the fourth millennium BC, with activity continuing, presumably sporadically, over the succeeding millennium. The sherds were randomly scattered across the excavated area. Several came from occupation layers but, as the latter are in every instance clearly of Bronze Age date, the Neolithic fragments must be seen as in secondary positions. This is particularly evident in the examples of Early Neolithic carinated bowl fragments of Vessels 16–18, which derived from Pit 22 associated with Ring-ditch 4 in the Z cuttings, where they were associated with later Bronze Age coarseware sherds, and from other secondary contexts primarily in Areas 1 and 2, or Middle Neolithic sherds E84:9441, Vessel 28, from Pit 247 in Cutting X in association with coarseware sherds.

Pit 231 in Sq. G5, however, may represent an actual Neolithic feature. The pit was regularly oval, with internal dimensions of 1.5m by about 2.2m. It had a shallow, concave profile, with the sides sloping gently and regularly to a maximum depth of no more than 20cm. It was filled with a uniform layer of greyish-brown, silt-like material completely without charcoal and was entirely unexceptional but for the fact that it contained three sherds of a finely decorated Bipartite Bowl of Middle Neolithic date (E84: 9224a, b, 9225). It is therefore possible that the pit was dug in the Neolithic period, and it might thus be speculated that at least some of the other pits found in the area could be of the same date.

A small assemblage of flakes, nodules and finished items of flint and chert, totalling 299 in all, were recovered, some or all of which are likely to belong to the Neolithic horizon. Like the pottery, the Neolithic flint component of the site suggests possibly either or both Early and Middle Neolithic activity (see Chapter 3, section 3.12). Though they were scattered across the excavated area, generally in secondary contexts, there was a noticeable paucity of flints in the area enclosed by Ring-ditch 2, in contrast to a more concentrated spread around its eastern and northern perimeters. It is possible that some of these artefacts might date from the phase of Bronze Age activity, though most of the finds must be considered residual. It is striking that most of the raw materials appear to have been imported from beach sources—over a distance of at least 30km—whereas the Early Bronze Age use of chert may suggest the use of a less than ideal but locally available material.

At least five fragmentary polished stone axeheads scattered across the site may, with reasonable confidence, be regarded as of Neolithic date (E100:24, E84:6122, 6946, 8004, 8996; see Chapter 3, section 3.13.3). One of these consists of non-local materials. E84:8996 may possibly have been imported from Britain, as it is petrographically consistent with typical banded green Great Langdale material—a material that may, however, also have originated from Irish sources. In any case, the stone is not local to Rathgall.

The scattered and fragmentary potsherds are scarcely indicative of any significant occupation, but the spread of waste flakes, including cores and other indications of flint-knapping, must be evidence for some degree of activity. It would thus appear that there was small-scale intermittent use of the hilltop over a considerable period during the many centuries of the Neolithic, though individual phases could have been extremely short. The intensive later Bronze Age activity which succeeded this on the site (quite apart from the modern ploughing) has obviously obliterated whatever Neolithic levels had existed at Rathgall.

It is possible, however, that some of the features revealed in the geophysical survey may be of earlier date: for example, as Raftery suggested, the almost completely obliterated enclosure between Ramparts 1 and 2 may also conceivably be of Neolithic date. Both the residual artefacts and the pollen record (see Chapter 3, section 3.18) indicate human activity on and in the vicinity of the site. The lack of identifiable features within the excavated zone is probably due to obliteration and truncation by later prehistoric, historical and modern activity.

The Middle Neolithic assemblage includes a bipartite bowl and a stone globular vessel, which can be paralleled in funerary contexts. As such, they appear unusual for a domestic assemblage and may hint at possible funerary activity at Rathgall at this time also.

5.2 BEAKER PERIOD, EARLY AND MIDDLE BRONZE AGE

It is striking that there is little evidence after the Middle Neolithic, coinciding with a lack of evidence in the pollen record for human activity in the area until about 1500 BC (Chapter 3, section 3.18). At any rate, it does appear that this Neolithic activity was followed by an extended period during which the hilltop was abandoned or saw only very limited use. A small number of Beaker sherds were found in what are probably secondary contexts, with two sherds in association with coarseware (e.g. E84:9359 and E84:9296 from Pit 242 in Cutting X), E84:2004 from Hearth 4, two from Ring-ditch 1 and the remainder from topsoil contexts within the main area of excavation, as well as one from the Z cuttings.Two chert barbed and tanged arrowheads (see Chapter 3, section 3.12) are both unstratified finds from the upper ploughsoil. Some dome-shaped scrapers may possibly also belong to an Early Bronze Age horizon.

The earliest phase of Bronze Age activity is dated by two Early–Middle Bronze Age radiocarbon dates from the pre-Rampart 2 ploughsoil horizon, suggesting possible Early Bronze Age agricultural activity here on the site. The artefacts of later Bronze Age type apparently associated with this level were explained by Raftery as a later addition, trodden in from above. The finding of one of the barbed and tanged arrowheads not far from this area in Sq. X11 adds to the picture of Early Bronze Age activity in this zone. It is, of course, possible that residual charcoal was dated that reflects earlier activity, not necessarily related to the pre-rampart horizon. Similarly, an earlier, residual date from Pit 166, in combination with a later date obtained from the same context, demonstrates a phase of Early Bronze Age activity on the site.

The Middle Bronze Age is represented by some Middle Bronze Age coarsewares, which offer little information on their functional context though a primarily domestic function can perhaps be assumed. The sherds represent 30 vessels, with Vessel 35 particularly well represented. The fragments of this vessel were dispersed through a number of contexts in the E and D squares, including Pit 55, where it was associated with Late Bronze Age artefacts (see Chapter 3, sections 3.11.4 and 3.11.5).

6. LATER PREHISTORIC RATHGALL

Katharina Becker

Rathgall has produced ample evidence for Late Bronze Age life, contributing information and new insights on a range of themes that are central to our understanding of later prehistoric Ireland. The excavations have provided a wealth of Bronze Age material and exceptionally good dating evidence, in spite of the problems inherent in a legacy data set (see Chapter 4, section 4.4). The majority of the archaeological remains date from the Bronze Age, and the large suite of ^{14}C dates allows the determination of the chronological parameters of this phase with some certainty. While there are some discrepancies between Raftery's and the preferred reading of the site stratigraphy as explored in Chapter 4, sections 4.2 and 4.3, the dating of the main phases of Bronze Age activity lies unequivocally in the twelfth and eleventh centuries BC (section 4.4). This is the phase during which there were intensive levels of bronze-casting activity, unparalleled on any Irish site, as well as the probably broadly contemporary use of the site for funerary activity. As discussed in sections 4.2 and 4.3, these activities are difficult to untangle stratigraphically and their closeness in absolute chronological terms—as established via the modelling of the ^{14}C dates—does not allow for temporal differentiation. Nevertheless, enough circumstantial evidence presents itself to support the notion of their contemporaneity (cf. sections 3.9 and 4.3).

Both activities, which may also have had close technological and conceptual links, appear to have taken place in different areas of the main site, with burial exclusively taking place in Areas 1 and 3, possibly separated from the metalworking activity by the stockade or revetting posts that run in a west–east direction between Areas 2 and 3 and also demarcate the main area of the artefact-rich deposits (Figs 2.2, 2.54, 6.1, a; cf. pp 456–7).

While the lack of stratigraphic relationships between the features of the Bronze Age phase in Areas 1–3 and those in other areas makes it impossible to tie the latter securely into the dating models, their radiocarbon dates as well as associated material culture and similarity of features suggest a broadly contemporary date. This is especially true for the Z cuttings, where burial-related features that produced radiocarbon dates in the second half of the second millennium BC were also accompanied by metalworking evidence (see section 4.4).

Fundamental change in site use at some point between 800 and 550 cal. BC saw the creation of Ring-ditch 1 and the 15m structure or house (Fig. 6.1, b; cf. pp 457 and 471). While the wide probability margins of the Hallstatt plateau dates (see Chapter 4) do not help to demonstrate the two features' contemporaneity, on stratigraphic grounds Ring-ditch 1 and the 15m structure are interpreted as representing a coherent phase of activity. Their creation was quickly followed by the infilling of Ring-ditch 1 on its eastern side with material from Area 2 (Fig. 6.1; cf. Chapter 4, section 4.4.9). This may have followed an initial phase in which access was provided across the shallow eastern part of the ditch, possibly directly across from the entrance to the 15m structure. Possibly soon after, however, a wider access was created by the infilling of the ditch with external material, primarily from Area 2 (see p. 457). This took place after a brief period of silting of the ditch, which, however, may have been previously cleared out a number of times—archaeologically impossible to prove or disprove. It is thus difficult to say after what length of time the infilling of the eastern ditch segment took place. What we do know, however, is that the silt included clay mould fragments that had been present on the ground surface, both inside and outside the ditch.

While broadly contemporary, as indicated both by their spatial relationship and by the radiocarbon dating evidence, the exact chronological relationship between the 15m structure and Ring-ditch 1 remains unclear. A pointer to the possibility that the house was created first may be the date derived from Pit 120, which can be positioned below the projected internal bank of Ring-ditch 1 but has produced a date that belongs to the group of Iron Age dates.

We have to imagine that some of the large hearths, as well as the remains of Ring-ditch 2 and its enclosing stockade, may still have been visible on the site (Fig. 6.1, b and c). The concentration of pits around the 15m structure suggests the digging of a significant proportion of the features in this area in the context of the use of the 15m structure.

Precisely when within the period encapsulated by the

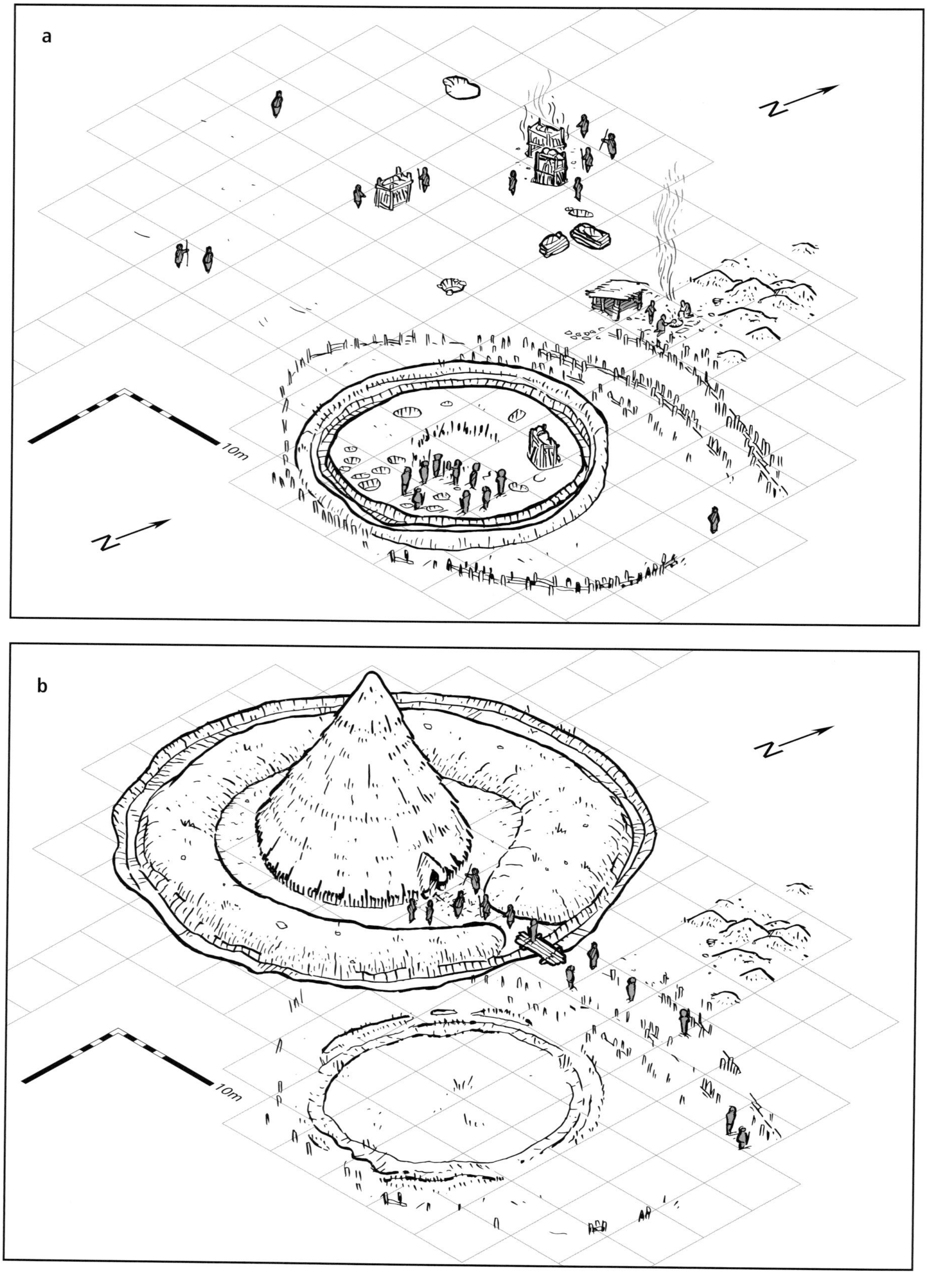

Fig. 6.1—Site reconstruction, phased.

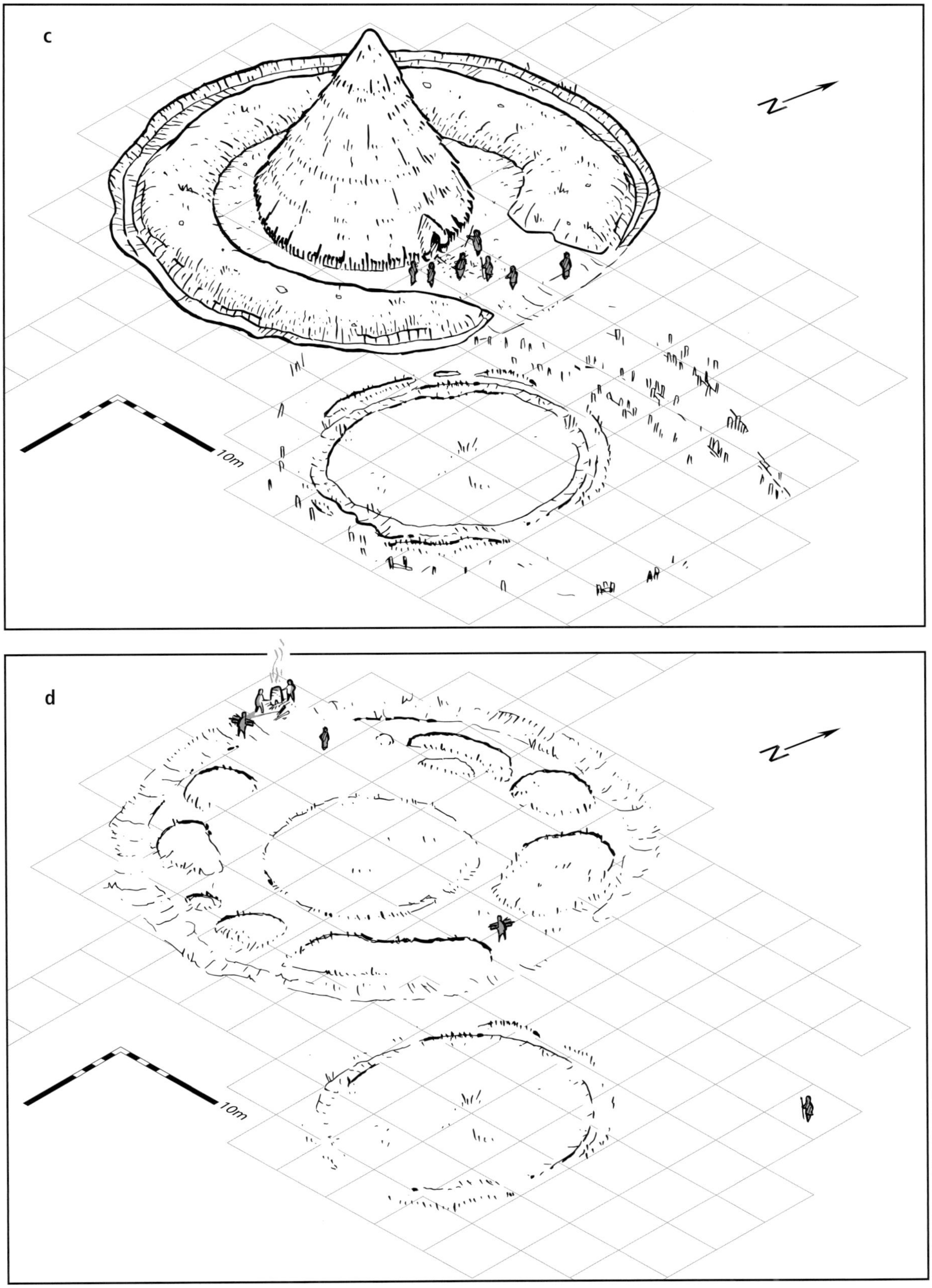

Fig. 6.1—Site reconstruction, phased.

Hallstatt plateau these activities occurred is not entirely clear. The fragments representing large portions of two coarseware pots that were found in the fill of Ring-ditch 1 (Vessel 41 in Sq. 31 in grey fill, deep; Vessel 343 in Sq. 68, grey fill) may, however, indicate *in situ* breakage. Given the current understanding of coarseware pottery in Ireland as not post-dating 700 BC or so, this would indicate a date for the ring-ditch at the very beginning of the Hallstatt plateau, e.g. in the eighth century BC. The bronze bar toggle and the possible cauldron rivets (Chapter 3, section 3.6) are also dated to this period on typological grounds. On the other hand, these pot portions may also derive from redeposition on a large scale, as argued for the deposits on the eastern side of the ditch.

After the first phase of Iron Age activity, it was only in the first half of the first millennium AD that Rathgall saw renewed activity in the form of an iron-smithing workshop, belt fittings, two bronze studs and possibly glass beads (Fig. 6.1, d), reflecting low-level activity, possibly on a seasonal basis, as indicated by the winter felling dates for the hazel from the iron-smithing hearth (section 3.19).

The question of whether the congruent gaps in the radiocarbon and artefactual data sets are due to an actual hiatus in archaeological activity at Rathgall is impossible to answer. Taphonomic and research-related filters are clearly at work. The intensive levels of wood consumption in the metalworking and funerary activity on the site and the debris-rich activities of metalworking and pottery consumption clearly provided extensive quantities of available material for sampling and dating. The spectacular nature of the finds associated with these charcoal-rich layers furthermore attracted particular efforts to establish their dating.

The severe truncation that the site must have seen in the medieval period during the construction of the cashel/Rampart 1, as well as the significant activity indicated by the medieval structure in Area 4 (Chapter 7), the large quantities of post-medieval pottery and the agricultural activities of more recent times, will have contributed to the obliteration of later phases and of more ephemeral features.

6.1 LATE BRONZE AGE TYPOLOGIES AND PHASING

Rathgall makes a particularly significant contribution to our understanding of the typo-chronology and metalworking traditions at the transition between the Middle Bronze Age and the Late Bronze Age. This is a period with few hoard or settlement assemblages to provide any helpful associations that would allow contextualisation of those artefacts that can be identified on the basis of their typological links, especially to Britain. Rathgall offers an exceptionally rich and well-dated assemblage, dating from about 1200 to 1000 BC, that to a great extent appears to have been manufactured here on site. Typo-chronologically, the material culture agrees well with this radiocarbon-dated horizon, with most artefacts having their best parallels in either late Middle Bronze Age or early Late Bronze Age assemblages (see Chapter 3, sections 3.1–3.9).

Eogan (1964, 268) devised the still-used framework of Middle and Late Bronze Age metalworking phasing and defined the Bishopsland, Roscommon and Dowris metalworking stages as equivalent to the British Ornament Horizon/Penard, Wilburton and Ewart Park stages. These stages were defined on the basis of the typo-chronological parallels of a range of objects with British materials. Find associations are rare for the earlier of these horizons, especially as far as the association between gold and bronze artefacts is concerned. Only few hoards can be attributed on typological grounds to the Bishopsland phase and only one hoard to the Roscommon phase. It was only for the latest part of the Dowris phase of the Bronze Age that a horizon of hoard assemblages can be identified in Ireland (see Eogan 1983). This left many of the bronze and gold typo-chronologies—as, for example, developed by Ramsey (1995; 1989) for the Middle Bronze Age corpus of spearheads, dirks and rapiers, and palstaves—free-floating (see also Becker 2013a; 2013b).

Eogan's Bishopsland phase, named after the eponymous hoard, corresponds to the Taunton/Ornament Horizon and Penard phases of the British Middle Bronze Age (Eogan 1964; 1994, 74). The dating of the Bishopsland, Co. Kildare, hoard, which Eogan (1964, 277) assigned to the Taunton/Ornament horizon, has itself been criticised and a date in the Penard phase suggested (Burgess 1968b, 4–5). Unfortunately, the few bronze hoards of the Middle Bronze Age contained only some of the types of the range of Middle Bronze Age weaponry found mainly singly. The Bishopsland hoard, for example, contained many object types that are unknown in the single-find record and only one palstave. Ten gold hoards from Ireland that had also been classified as belonging chronologically to the Bishopsland phase on the basis of their parallels to the Taunton/Ornament Horizon material (Eogan 1983, 2) may now, however, find better parallels in Penard phase associations. Owing to the lack of association, the continued use of Middle Bronze Age weapon types during the Bishopsland phase had merely to be assumed. Thus, while Eogan (1983) defined a small group of bronze hoards containing palstaves and spearheads as 'non-Bishopsland Middle Bronze Age', it was not clear how they related to the material of the Bishopsland complex (Ramsey 1989, 78–9).

The succeeding Late Bronze Age material was attributed to the Roscommon and Dowris phases. The Roscommon phase was named after the eponymous hoard from County Roscommon, which, on the basis of its artefact types and character (scrapped material), could be paralleled in the Wilburton material of southern Britain. On typological grounds, Eogan (1964, 288) argued that singly found tubular spear ferrules, the earliest pegged spearheads, spearheads with lunate openings in the blade, Class 1 socketed axes, Class 2 and 3 swords and large tongue-shaped chapes should be grouped with the material from the Roscommon hoard and considered as a local representation of the British Wilburton phase, which has since been dated to between *c.* 1140 and 1020 BC (Needham *et al.* 1997, 90–1, illus. 15). Subsequent changes, including the introduction of types that can be paralleled in the material of the British Ewart Park/Carp's-tongue complex, define Eogan's Dowris phase and are often considered as indicating the beginning of the Irish Late Bronze Age proper. Recent evidence dates the Blackmoor/Ewart Park assemblage to around 1020–750 BC, Needham's period 7 (*ibid.*, 93; Needham 1996, 136).

The existence of a metalworking stage preceding that of the Dowris phase but post-dating the Bishopsland phase in the form of the Roscommon phase has been a contentious issue owing to the rarity of finds, making the notion of a local metalworking industry at this time producing 'Roscommon' types difficult to demonstrate. Only two hoards (County Roscommon and 'North of Ireland') contained material of this group, with the County Roscommon hoard itself discussed as a modern import[1] (e.g. Megaw and Simpson 1979, 310). Eogan (1983, 7) himself pondered whether the small number of Roscommon types might possibly have been superimposed on a Bishopsland substratum, to which some of the non-diagnostic Middle Bronze Age hoards may also belong. In a more optimistic vein were his attempts to differentiate between an early and a late Roscommon phase (Eogan 1994, 82, table on p. x): the first was now seen to mirror the British Penard phase and to include Class 1 swords (Ballintober); the second, corresponding to the typical Wilburton assemblage, included flange-hilted swords with leaf-shaped blades (Classes 2 and 3), long, tongue-shaped chapes, tubular ferrules, and spearheads with lunate-shaped openings in the wings. Eogan noted that the Roscommon material appeared to be a regional phenomenon; the distribution of socketed axes of Classes 2–4, for example, is mainly restricted to the northern part of the country.

A similar debate took place in Britain about the Wilburton phase. This material also appears to represent a regional phenomenon, even more so after the backdating of the Wallington material (which had previously been seen as being contemporary with the Wilburton complex[2]) to the Penard phase. Needham (1990, 265–7) considered whether Wilburton material was indeed in use all over England and Wales but simply did not survive owing to differing recycling and deposition strategies. The representation of otherwise unknown types on moulds at Rathgall hints strongly at this, as does the finding of moulds in areas lacking in Wilburton metalwork in Britain. Alternatively, it could be seen as relating to a specific 'social or industrial phenomenon, holding sway in certain centres only and running parallel to the metalwork assemblages' (*ibid.*, 265–6) of the Middle Bronze Age or Late Bronze Age. In this scenario, the continuation of the preceding Bishopsland phase or the earlier onset of the Dowris phase metalworking tradition could be assumed, with the Roscommon material, to represent a contemporary but regionally or socially restricted fashion.

No goldwork appeared to fill the gap between the 'flourishing gold industries of the Bishopsland and the Dowris phases', possibly indicating that not only the deposition of gold objects but also gold-working itself might have ceased in this period (Eogan 1994, 81). Gold ornaments, however, are frequently found in Penard and Wilburton phase hoards (Needham 1990, 260; 2017). In the Thirsk, North Yorkshire, Wilburton phase hoard, a pegged leaf-shaped spearhead, a spearhead with lunate openings, a tubular ferrule and a tanged knife were associated with a sheet-gold ring and a corrugated sheet-gold bracelet with hooked terminals (Needham 1990, 257–60, 263). The associated gold artefact types demonstrate the continuation of goldwork throughout the period, and to conclude from the lack of gold deposition that gold was no longer used and 'a period of wealth and innovation diminished' (Eogan 1994, 81) would appear to overestimate the importance of the deposited evidence as a reflection of actual availability and use.

This very general point is demonstrated by the Rathgall assemblage, in which the moulds in particular present evidence for a range of types of objects at a time when otherwise little artefactual material can be securely identified. It provides a well-dated corpus of Bronze Age metalwork and pottery that can be demonstrated to centre on the transition from the Middle Bronze Age to the Late Bronze Age or the earliest Late Bronze Age, *c.* 1200–1000 BC, if related to the classic subdivisions of the period. The range of artefacts—both those represented on the moulds and actual finds—incorporates elements that we know to exist already in the late Middle Bronze Age and later in the Late Bronze Age. The majority of the artefacts come from Area 2, and here the chronological modelling indicates a minimum duration of twenty years and a maximum of 160 years. There is no evidence for significant periods of abandonment within Area 2 and it appears most likely that the material accumulated over a relatively short period of time, as also suggested by the striking consistency of the radiocarbon dates associated with the deposits that produced the Bronze Age moulds and metal artefacts.

The Rathgall assemblage contains forms deriving from a Middle Bronze Age tradition with distinct parallels in Penard assemblages, such as a biconical gold bead, gold bar-twisted wire, the possible rapiers and the protected looped spearheads, palstaves, rope moulding and ribbed collars around socketed tools, including axes (Chapter 3, section 3.8). Conversely, the hair-rings, the large, tongue-shaped chapes with curved mouth openings and socketed gouges have better parallels in Roscommon or Wilburton phase contexts (section 3.8.2). Moulds for different forms of axes, with bodies of subrectangular cross-section as well as bag-shaped axes, are represented. The earliest bag-shaped axes, Class 2 axes, may be an Irish type (Eogan 2000, 30–1). The only known association of a Class 2a axe in Ireland is in the County Roscommon hoard, and the fragments of moulds for such axes from Rathgall add to the early evidence for this form. The moulds from Rathgall show the contemporaneity of small disc-headed pins, usually assigned to the Dowris phase, and ribbed bracelets, considered to be earlier Middle Bronze Age.

There are also mould fragments for the casting of a sword. The lack of typological detail on the sword moulds makes it impossible to date them closely, though it appears that they lack the midrib of the earliest, Ballintober, swords and are thus more likely to represent any form of leaf-shaped sword which elsewhere is attributed to the Penard phase onwards. A possible, but only tentatively identified, sword hilt mould shows a row of centrally placed rivet holes, as found on flange-hilted Bronze Age swords, but the mould does not show evidence for a flange.

Socketed tools, particularly socketed gouges, are usually considered a Dowris phase type and occur in hoards of this period (Eogan 1964, 296; Hodges 1956, 41). The Rathgall example, however, indicates the earlier presence of such forms. Socketed tools in the Bishopsland hoard show the production of such items in the Middle Bronze Age, albeit decorated with rope moulding and of subrectangular cross-section, as opposed to those of the Dowris period with a round cross-section. Likewise, gouges are present in Wilburton hoards (e.g. O'Connor 1980, 137). Some of the small, socketed tools represented in a range of moulds at Rathgall may have been small gouges, chisels or small axes. The chisel from the hoard (Pit 31) within the area enclosed by Ring-ditch 2 is an unparalleled type. It was associated with a fragment of a sword blade and a small socketed and pegged spearhead. Raftery suggested that the sword blade represents a sword of Eogan's Class 4, of Dowris phase date; while this is possible, the small fragment may also have formed part of an earlier Class 2 sword. These swords, while not securely dated, appear to be the Roscommon phase equivalent of the British Wilburton horizon (Eogan 1965, 10). The Youghal, Co. Cork, hoard is the only known association of Class 3 swords where they were found together with two plain leaf-shaped spearheads with peg holes. In England a similar type also occurs in hoards of the Wilburton and Ewart Park complexes (*ibid.*). Spearheads with peg holes are known from Wilburton and Blackmoor (Coles 1959–60; Burgess 1968b) and Middle Bronze Age Penard phase assemblages (Burgess 1968b, 34, note 6). An early Middle Bronze Age date for haft wood from a pegged spearhead was also obtained from a radiocarbon-dated example (Needham *et al.* 1997, 87), supporting the typo-chronologically obtained dates. In Ireland the earliest examples of pegged spearheads, although of Middle Bronze Age blade morphology and size, can similarly be dated to between the fourteenth and eleventh centuries cal. BC (Becker 2013a). Two different morphologies of spearheads are also represented in the moulds from Rathgall, with both a protected looped and a pegged spearhead.

The mercury-gilded mount from the site had been discussed as a possible Bronze Age artefact (Chapter 3, sections 3.1.5 and 3.3). There are no known morphological or contemporary technological parallels (see sections 3.1 and

3.2) and it is best attributed to disturbance which occurred in Area 2 to significant depths, as indicated, for example, by a medieval amber bead found 'just above the grey' (cf. p. 444). An iron object found 40–60cm down in the lowest level of black soil may likewise have been introduced through such disturbance. While the earliest use of iron in Ireland is currently understood to date from the eighth or seventh century BC (Becker 2012), it is not inconceivable that iron may have been in use earlier, as indicated as a possibility on British sites such as Hartshill (Collard *et al.* 2006). Similarly, iron found within fills of the northern section of Ring-ditch 1 may also be evidence for early iron use rather than disturbance, but this is impossible to clarify given the condition of the objects.

Besides gold and bronze objects, pottery and glass items also comprise part of the range of artefacts produced and consumed at Rathgall. While the parallels for annular glass beads found at Rathgall have quite a wide date range of about 1200–800 BC, the eye beads are a more distinct form; on other sites where the beads have the same composition of early European glass (LMHK) they date from early in the Late Bronze Age (see Chapter 3, section 3.4.3). Similar beads found at Lough Gur (e.g. Henderson 1987) and Freestone Hill (Raftery 1969) underpin the fact that Rathgall is not isolated in Ireland as a place with far-reaching connections. While mainly found in the Area 2 deposits, the glass beads also spread across Area 3 and, to an extent, Area 1, and were even found in small numbers in the Z cuttings. This is only explicable through processes of redeposition in prehistory, and the primary phase of deposition for these items is to be seen in the twelfth or eleventh century BC, as part of the Area 2 activity.

By far the largest group of material culture is coarseware pottery (Chapter 3, section 3.11). As is characteristic of this period, this is largely plain tub- or barrel-shaped, of Class II after Ó Ríordáin 1954. Where decoration occurs, it is confined to the rim and neck areas and is mostly incised, with the exception of one vessel (No. 266) which has an applied cordon. The Rathgall pottery was largely derived from contexts securely dated to 1200–1000 cal. BC, and this dating is supported by direct radiocarbon dating of residues on some of the sherds (p. 472 and Table 4.3). A possible later phase of coarseware pottery use on the site is indicated by the two radiocarbon dates discussed for the urn accompanying Burial 2 in Ring-ditch 2 (GrA-23304; 1050–845 cal. BC; modelled) and for a sherd from the upper fill of Ring-ditch 4 (SUERC-42587; 994–832 cal. BC) (Chapter 4, section 4.4), as well as possibly by the substantial portions of two vessels likely broken *in situ* in Ring-ditch 1 and on the basis of stratigraphic considerations late in the Bronze Age (see p. 456).

While traditionally considered to be restricted to the Late Bronze Age, the recognition of coarseware pottery at Middle Bronze Age sites has pushed back the earliest dating of tub- or barrel-shaped coarseware vessels. Sites such as Chancellorsland, Co. Tipperary, show the existence of this form of pottery already at some point between 1600 and 1400 BC (Cleary 2008). The pottery style continued throughout the later parts of the Bronze Age at Corrstown, Co. Antrim (Roche and Grogan 2011), and Lough Gur, Co. Limerick (Cleary 1995; 2003; 2018), with date ranges of 1493–811 BC and 1500–800 BC respectively, and at Dún Aonghasa, Aran Islands, which dates from 1000–800 BC (Cleary 2012).

These sites demonstrate a great consistency between earlier and later coarseware forms, with plain and decorated vessels found throughout. Roche (see Chapter 3, section 3.11) differentiates a small group of Middle Bronze Age forms within the corpus from the bulk of Late Bronze Age coarsewares from Rathgall. A small amount of the Rathgall assemblage includes decorated wares, some with applied cordons, incised lines or cord-impressed decoration, while others are undecorated. Roche (this volume; Grogan and Roche 2009b) introduced the term 'domestic cordoned urns' for vessels that they attributed to the Middle Bronze Age in order to acknowledge the earlier origin of these decorative motifs and vessel forms, found on funerary ceramics (cordoned urns) of the earlier Bronze Age (cf. Brindley 2007).

Chronological differentiation of the Late Bronze Age undecorated coarsewares, and also of decorated vessels, often seems to depend only on changes in fabric texture: Roche and Grogan (2011, 185) identify the flat-based, barrel-shaped coarseware at Corrstown as early in the Later Bronze Age on the basis of its loose-textured matrix and chalky-textured surfaces. Similarly, a change to coarser fabrics and better firing appears to distinguish Late Bronze Age from Middle Bronze Age forms (Cleary 2000; Grogan and Roche 2010a; 2009b, 134). Such changes, however, may be affected by raw materials, batches and potters' skills as much as by the differences in firing, which makes it unlikely that such subtle changes can be used as absolute dating evidence.

The typological overlap between hypothesised earlier and later coarseware, with regard to the overwhelmingly consistent vessel shapes, similar decoration and presence of perforations noted, underpins the impression that a broadly consistent chronological horizon is represented in the pottery assemblage. The bulk of the Rathgall pottery derives from the deposits in Area 2 in their primary or secondary position, as well as from Pit 118 and various burial contexts. In order to verify the dating of the pottery, which appeared early for many of the vessels, a number of dates were also obtained on carbonised food residues on the pottery. The increasing number of dates directly obtained on vessels in Ireland in general allows refinement of the dating of coarseware pottery and, here at Rathgall, the identification of an early Late Bronze Age assemblage that includes both plain and decorated coarseware. The bulk of the Late Bronze Age pottery appears to be in primary depositional contexts, such as Pit 118 and the various deposits that form the 'occupation material' in Area 2 and which date from between 1200 and 1000 cal. BC (Chapter 4, section 4.4). As noted by Roche (p. 303), the frequently good condition of the sherds suggests that they were not exposed to much dispersal or trampling, implying that they were in their primary depositional position.

A context with particular importance in the consideration of the dating of coarseware pottery at Rathgall is Pit 118. The bottom layer contained a large deposit of charcoal-rich material and seventeen vessel units. These are barrel-shaped with round or flat rims. Seven of these had a row of perforations below their rims—a motif that was also found on some of the 'Middle Bronze Age' wares on the site, such as Vessel 179. The sequence of radiocarbon dates obtained on samples from this context from the twelfth or eleventh century BC (section 4.4) is supported by the dating of a carbonised food accretion on sherd SUERC-42589—1130–980 cal. BC (93%) if modelled as part of the overall Bronze Age activity (section 4.4). This confirms a date for the use of these vessels and their deposition between *c.* 1200 and 1000 cal. BC (section 4.4). While a general Late Bronze Age date is indicated by the finding of pottery with such perforations at a number of sites in Late Bronze Age contexts—e.g. Site D, House 1, at Lough Gur (Ó Ríordáin 1954, 392–4), Freestone Hill, Co. Wicklow (Raftery 1969, 91), and Navan Fort, Co. Armagh (McCorry 1997)—the contextual and directly obtained dates for the pottery from Rathgall, and especially from Pit 118, allow the refining of the date of this pottery form to early within the period, i.e. between 1200 and 1000 BC.

The Rathgall dates find confirmation in similarly early dates directly obtained on other vessels of this form, such as a vessel with perforation at Tinoran, Co. Wicklow (Cleary 2017a; 2017b). Carbonised food accretions on an *in situ* broken coarseware vessel with perforations below its rim were dated to 1220–990 cal. BC (GrA-64440; 2905±35 BP; 95% confidence). Vessels with perforations at Lough Gur (Class II vessels) have been dated to 1400–1100 BC on stratigraphic grounds (Cleary 2003, 144–6), and a vessel with the same decoration from Site C to *c.* 1400–1150 BC on the basis of carbonised food accretions (UBA-38828; 2922±32 BP; 1220–1010 cal. BC; 95% confidence; Rose Cleary, pers. comm.). Food accretions on a vessel with perforations from Lough Gur Site C produced a Hallstatt plateau date (UBA-38826; 2580±38 BP; 820–550 cal. BC; 95% confidence; Rose Cleary, pers. comm.), suggesting that this motif may have an altogether longer currency than the other dates suggest, but it is equally plausible that this date is an anomalous outlier.

Rilling or horizontal bands of grooves or incisions below the rim can be paralleled at Site C, Lough Gur, and a vessel from the same site decorated with cord impressions—a decoration also found at Rathgall—provides the second early date on decorated Class II ware also from Lough Gur on carbonised food accretions (UBA-38828; 2922±32 BP; 1220–1010 cal. BC; 95% confidence; Rose Cleary, pers. comm.). In fact, the Lough Gur Site C assemblage shares a wide range of characteristics with the Rathgall assemblage not only in pottery but also in comparable forms of metalwork, including LMHK glass beads, a tanged narrow blade and a rope-moulded socketed axehead (Cleary 2003; 2018; Ó Ríordáin 1954), as well as pottery showing the closest typological parallels to the assemblage from Chancellorsland (Cleary 2018, 178). This assemblage has been radiocarbon-dated to between *c.*1600 and *c.* 1400 BC (Cleary 2008). The artefactual material from the Bronze Age house at Knockadoon included parts of a stone mould for the casting of a palstave and a clay mould for the casting of a looped spearhead—possibly earlier typologically than those from Rathgall. Decoration on the Chancellorsland pottery included parallel lines below the rim, either executed by incision or by cord impressions, and these in fact represent the most common motif (Cleary 2008, 269).

The small vessel V321 from Rathgall (p. 316) can be compared to a shallow bowl with a height of 7.4cm and a rim diameter of about 10.5cm found at Kilgreany Cave (Roche 2016, 93, fig. 4.9) and a small vessel with a height of 14cm dated to the Middle Bronze Age (on food accretion: GrA-63008; 3170±35 BP; 1500–1410 cal. BC; 95% confidence; O'Brien and O'Driscoll 2017, 270) at Rathnagree, Co. Wicklow (Cleary 2017a, 262–3). Cleary also drew attention to small 'tableware' vessels from Middle to Late Bronze Age contexts at Lough Gur and Chancellorsland, and also at later Late Bronze Age sites (*ibid.*, 263–4).

6.2 RATHGALL AS A PLACE OF PRODUCTION

'The intensity of metalworking begs the question as to whether the site was primarily a focus for bronze-working. Could it have been an industrial centre with a succession of smelting and casting sites spreading across the site? Thus might it be that the intensity of the casting activities, and the dispersal of the finished products, formed the basis for the obvious wealth of the Rathgall occupants' (Raftery, draft text).

The overwhelming evidence for Rathgall as a craft centre is indeed striking and over the past 50 years since its discovery has not been surpassed in an Irish context. Alongside bronze, the working of shale, possibly gold and (less likely) glass may have taken place on the site, alongside most likely the production of the moulds and possibly pottery that were used there.

In spite of the wide distribution of the mould fragments across the site, extending down into the Z cuttings and probably here also representing a place of production, a distinct focus of this activity is in Area 2. The concentration of the material here represents a high degree of metalworking activity in particular, and the association of the different materials may suggest that they were all integral to the production or craft activities taking place in Area 2.

The large number of mould fragments, representing a wide range of artefacts, confirms that the main industrial activity was bronze-casting. Some metalworking tools include a possible graving tool from the hoard in Pit 31 (E84:8344), the fine gouge (E84:3300) and fragmentary remains of other tools such as E84:8080. Two burnishing stones (e.g. E100:161; Fig. 3.118) found in the Z cuttings of the site would have been used in the finishing of bronze or gold objects, but they remain undated. A possible bronze ingot (E84:2010) and scrap metal were also recovered. The date of these finds is unclear and some, along with other fragments of bronze objects, may belong to later periods of metal production and use on the site. Casting jets, wasters and any other forms of either raw or waste products of the bronze-working were absent from the excavated Bronze Age levels.

The clay crucibles are in the main characteristic bronze-casting crucibles, demonstrating several episodes of use in most instances. The three or four Bronze Age crucibles represent one of the largest assemblages of objects of this type from Ireland and again reflect the extraordinary level of metalworking activity. The majority of identifiable pieces adhere to conventional Late Bronze Age types, but the small crucible (E84:9000) raises questions and there is a possibility that it belongs to the medieval phase of the site's use.

The dating of the deposits in which it was found in Area 2, as well as the fact that it is composed of LMHK glass, places the glass from Rathgall in the earliest horizon of European glass production and use. Glass-working—and especially glass manufacture—is difficult to demonstrate; while there may be some grounds for speculation about Insular glass-working (as opposed to glass-making; see Chapter 3, section 3.4), it cannot be assumed. Nevertheless, the association of glass- and bronze-working would not be unusual (Henderson 1988a, 438), as copper ores or copper alloys were added as colorants. In the case of the Rathgall glass, the addition of cupric oxide was indeed suggested as intentional by Henderson (1988b) and may have taken the form of a copper–bronze alloy. The association of these two technologies is also evidenced at Frattesina, where other raw materials such as amber have also been found, as at Rathgall (Henderson 1998a, 440). The subtriangular-shaped beads with eye decoration clearly set the Rathgall glass in an international context, as do the rather ubiquitous but undiagnostic ring-beads. The eye beads, however, are not identical in shape and decoration to those from any of the other known early European sites, supporting the idea of varying, locally produced forms.

Whether the glass was imported as raw material or as finished beads, the extent of the connections of the Rathgall community is clear and particularly striking, perhaps suggesting direct links between Ireland and the Continent, though the recently identified individual LMHK beads at three sites in Britain open up the possibility of a wider distribution of this glass than previously thought. The fashion and method of mounting of one of the glass beads in gold are comparable to an example from Milmorane, Co. Cork (see Chapter 3, section 3.4), and may add credence to the suggestion that at the very least the setting of the glass in its mount may have taken place in Ireland (see below).

The small collection of gold artefacts is significant in several respects, providing one of the rare instances in which gold objects are found within archaeological contexts in Ireland, where otherwise burials and settlements are largely devoid of metal finds and gold is exceedingly rare. Ireland's wealth of Bronze Age gold was instead deposited primarily in the form of hoards or single finds outside settlement or burial areas. The gold penannular 'hair-ring' in pyre Pit 119 clearly links this type of ornament as well as the burial practices on this site into international patterns. Many of the French and Dutch finds have also been found in burial contexts and suggest that these items were body ornamentation, worn individually (see Chapter 3, section 3.3, for speculation about the mode of wear).

The fragment of bar-twisted gold wire is likely a piece of scrap (cf. Cahill 2009, 96–7) and may point to gold-working having taken place on site. It may also, however, have been deposited on site in the context of funerary rituals. The singularity of the gold-mounted glass bead may be simply due to the fact that, as Raftery suggested, it was perhaps imported together with the other beads as part of a necklace. There is clear evidence for gold-working at contemporary sites such as Lough Gur, Co. Limerick (in the form of a piece of sheet bronze and a small gold ingot found within the same structure; Cleary 2018, 160; Cahill 2003), and at Haughey's Fort (Mallory 1995; Warner 2014). However, the evidence from Rathgall is ambiguous.

6.2.1 The organisation of production at Bronze Age Rathgall

The primary focus of the industrial activity was Area 2 (Fig. 6.2), which produced the main concentration of finds, particularly of metalworking-related material and specifically the moulds. A second area of activity was located in Area 1 around Hearth 10, and a further concentration of mould fragments indicates that bronze-casting also took place in the Z cuttings (associated especially with Ring-ditch 3). A distinct concentration of moulds in Ring-ditch 1 in Sq. 29 may likewise represent another focus of metalworking in that part of the site (cf. Chapter 3, section 3.9).

As explored in Chapter 4, section 4.3, unless the *in situ* breakage of a mould or vessel can be demonstrated, the presence of fragments cannot be demonstrated to represent primary deposits. Instead, secondary deposition, as the result either of taphonomic processes, including residuality, or of deliberate deposition, has to be assumed. In both instances, it is possible that the sherds were already present, possibly for a substantial period of time. Likewise their inclusion in the hearths and pyres can thus only be understood as a *terminus ante quem* for their creation, use and breakage.

Crucibles (Chapter 3, section 3.7) are concentrated in Area 2—as is to be expected, given the concentration of moulds in this area—but also in Areas 3 and 4. As discussed in section 3.9, it appears that the deposition of crucibles can be contrasted with that of mould fragments—the latter being dumped in discrete areas, while crucibles outside of Area 2 were deposited in special contexts. Strikingly, in Area 4 the small, complete crucible (E84:9000) was found in Pit 215, which also produced a glass bead, some coarse pottery and flint debitage in a black layer, sealed with a large boulder. Pit 20 in G2 produced several fragments which may or may not have formerly represented part of the same crucible. The fill of this pit is an unusual deposit and one of the substantial mould deposits outside Area 2, containing five fragments of coarse pottery, three crucible fragments and sixteen mould fragments. Nevertheless, the association of prehistoric artefacts with medieval pottery, such as in Pit 76 in H3 and apparently in Pit 244 in X11, calls for caution in interpreting these contexts as primary deposits of the Bronze Age items. Thus the small crucible (E84:9000) found in a deposit with Bronze Age artefacts but within the area of the medieval house may have been deposited here at a later time, possibly explaining its unusual form for the Bronze Age (cf. p. 253). Medieval construction or pit-digging activity must have been accompanied by the constant encounter with the remains of the past, given the concentration of prehistoric finds.

In contrast to the crucibles, moulds have a wider distribution, beyond Area 2 and the adjacent fill of Ring-ditch 1. They are present in a number of undiagnostic pit features which may or may not represent prehistoric activity (e.g. Pits 128 and 95 and a post-hole of Hearth 4 in Area 1, but also in Pits 53 and 54 in the E cuttings). Their deposition in Hearth 10 and in Hearths/Pyres 3 and 15, within the black lining of the latter, may suggest contemporaneity with the use of these features. The charcoal-rich layers and mould fragments in pits such as, for example, Pit 244 in X11 may reflect metalworking activity in the immediate vicinity, outside the main focus of the site. The finding of moulds in the Z cuttings further underpins this and suggests metalworking at these loci.

It thus appears likely that the main focus of bronze-working activity was in Area 2, extending into Area 1, with secondary deposits in Area 4. As outlined by Raftery (Chapter 2, section 2.3.1 especially), the primary deposits and places of production appear to have been Metalworking Zones 2 and (possibly) 3. Raftery commented on the flat, homogeneous, stoneless character of the deposits in Area 2.

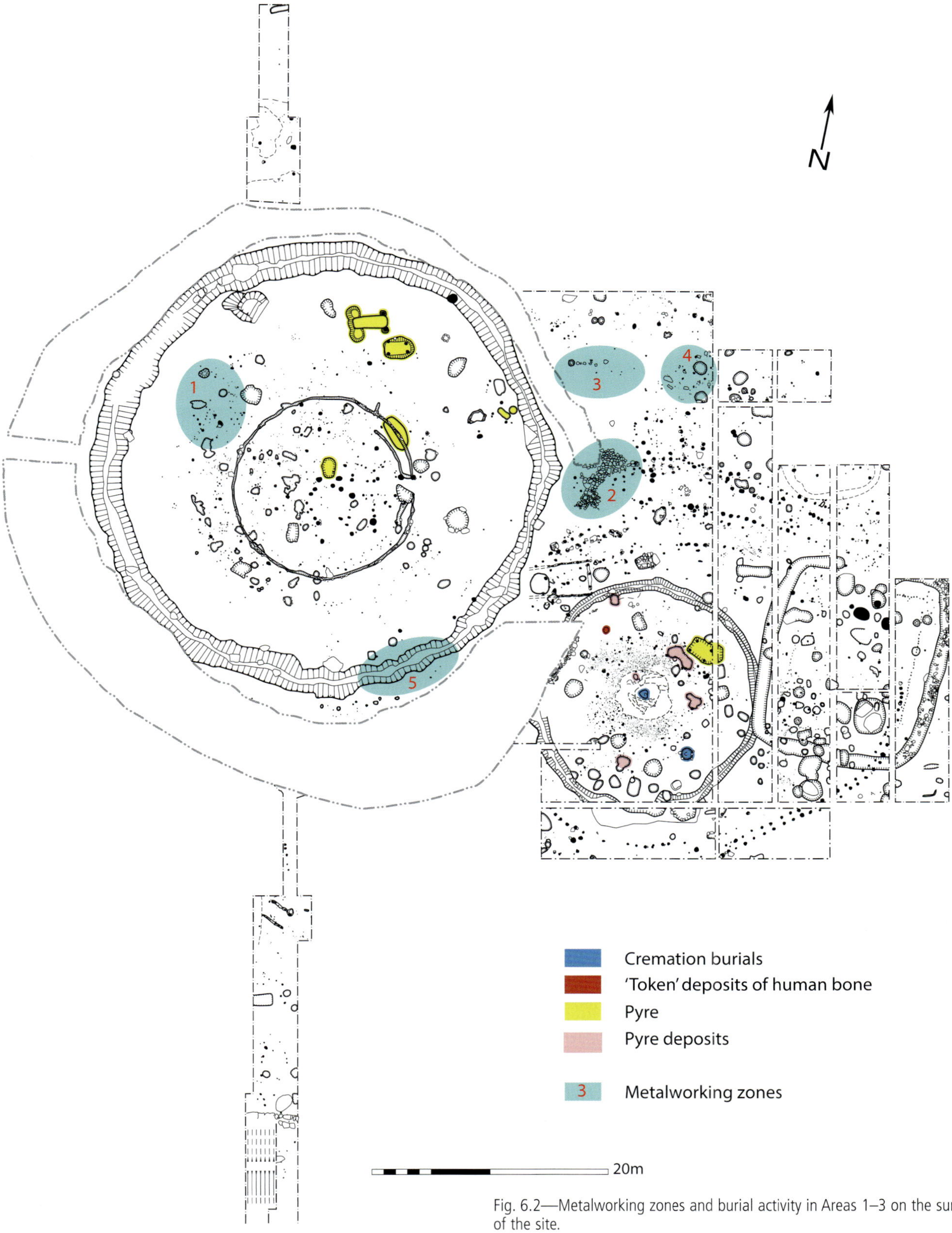

Fig. 6.2—Metalworking zones and burial activity in Areas 1–3 on the summit of the site.

These may represent the accumulation of workshop-related debris, as well as the dumping of pottery, with rather tentative evidence for a hearth and work surface (see Chapter 3, section 3.15). Concentrations of particular mould types or fragments of particular moulds, such as those of rope-moulded objects in and to the west of Metalworking Zone 2, may support this.

Besides metal, other craft activities also appear to have been part and parcel of the range of crafts practised on the site: half-finished shale bracelets are likely to belong to the later prehistoric horizon (section 3.12) and were with few exceptions found also in the B–E cuttings and thus closely associated with the Bronze Age metalworking activity. Repair attempts are also represented in the corpus.

While the technological association of metal- and glass-working is in principle obvious (e.g. Fenn 2015; see also Chapter 3, section 3.4), the evidence for glass-working at Rathgall is tentative and it appears more likely that the glass beads were only deposited on the site. The bead decorated with gold wire and other gold in the black deposits of Area 2 suggest that both metalworking debris and items of personal ornament were deposited here. Perhaps these deposits comprised not only metalworking debris but also objects that belonged to the dead. It is tempting to speculate that the deposits included pyre remains and metalworking debris, which might go some way towards explaining the curious mixture of finished precious artefacts and metalworking debris, as well as the large-scale consumption of foodstuffs indicated by the vast number of pottery vessels deposited here. Cremated human bone remains were not identified in this zone at the time of excavation, however, and no relevant samples survive in the archive, while the predominance of brushwood and hazel in the samples from this area does not lend itself easily to such interpretation.

Metalworking took place in or beside Area 2, taking into account the significant dispersal and disturbance, and the substantial deposits including pottery and food consumption evidenced by carbonised food accretions. Owing to poor bone preservation, it is unclear whether meat consumption was associated with this activity. The possibility of the existence of a workshop structure, either in the area of the cobbling or in the form of the rectangular slot-trench structure in Sq. G, would allow for year-round metal production, providing the sheltered conditions necessary for the drying of moulds during the cooler and wetter seasons (Ó Faoláin 2004, 109).

6.2.2 Pottery production and consumption

It appears likely that the moulds were manufactured on site, having been tempered with locally available granite. Likewise, on-site production of pottery, which also used locally available granite and quartzite as temper (Chapter 3, section 3.11), is not inconceivable, although pottery may have been imported from the near vicinity. In comparison with that found on other sites the pottery is well fired (H. Roche, pers. comm.), which also argues for production in a single workshop.

The minimum number of 400 vessels (section 3.11), accumulated mainly in Area 2 over a rather short period of time, as is evident in the rather consistent nature of the 'occupation layers', suggests a high incidence of cooking, transportation of foodstuffs to the site and possibly on-site pottery manufacture. Of the 385 Late Bronze Age vessel units, 328 (65%) showed evidence for carbonised food residues. This suggests that the vast majority of vessels were used for cooking, and those without manifest accretions may have been used in food preparation or for storage. This in turn provides important evidence for the activities that took place at Rathgall, in which food consumption, possibly in the form of feasting, accompanied metalworking and funerary activity.

The size of the pottery assemblage is an indication of the intensity of Late Bronze Age activity. The largest concentrations of vessels are found in the occupation layers in Area 2, in the materials probably redeposited from there into Ring-ditch 1 and in Pit 118, whereas few sherds can be shown to be associated with the hearths or pyres.

The presence of the pottery was in itself considered by Raftery as possible evidence for the presence of a house in the area of the greatest concentration of finds in Metalworking Zone 2. The single largest concentration of vessels occurred in the occupation layers in Area 2, where *c.* 145 (38%) were found. The residues(?) of both metalworking and food consumption were found here and, while the consumption of food in a workshop context is conceivable, they were discarded in such large numbers—building up to a depth of almost 0.5m—as to suggest that this was not a random process but rather deliberate dumping in a designated area of the site, particularly the deposits in industrial activity Area 2.

Food preparation and consumption appear to have been intrinsic to metalworking as well as to the funerary activities. The reuse of coarseware cooking vessels for the interment of cremated remains has been noted (see Chapter 3, section

3.11), but rather than the reuse of domestic vessels it could be speculated that vessels were used in a funerary feast. Where larger groups of mourners took part in funeral rites, surplus vessels may have been deposited and abandoned on site. In any case, given the lack of long-term settlement evidence at Rathgall and the large quantity of vessels, the deliberate breaking of the vessels after use may indeed be implied—it may not have been practical, feasible or, indeed, appropriate to use them in a domestic setting after their use at Rathgall.

6.3 THE BRONZE AGE NECROPOLIS

The extensive evidence for burial makes this aspect of Bronze Age life a particular focus at Rathgall. At least ten deposits of human remains (Chapter 3, section 3.16) can be securely identified, in addition to features that can be interpreted as pyres, adding to our understanding of the processes and rituals of burial in Late Bronze Age Ireland.

Until recently, evidence for burial after the end of the Cordoned Urn tradition had been scarce. Besides Mullaghmore, Co. Down (Mogey *et al.* 1956), it was indeed Rathgall that was highlighted by Raftery in his 1973 *Antiquity* paper as providing rare and, at the time, unique evidence for burials accompanied by coarseware vessels. While in recent decades more sites with absolute dating where the burials were accompanied by coarseware pottery or radiocarbon-dated to the period after about 1500 BC have come to light, Rathgall still stands out as important for the understanding of burial practices in this period, if, however, unusual when considered against the wider corpus.

Within the extent of the excavations at Rathgall there are two distinct zones of funerary and burial activity. The best-preserved and most extensive one is in the central part of the site (Fig. 6.2), centred in and around burial in Ring-ditch 2 and Area 1. A second zone is located in the Z cuttings.

Ring-ditch 2 in Area 2 enclosed a central cremation Burial 1 in a stone-lined pit. This mode of burial is mirrored in urn Burial 2, also within Ring-ditch 2, and Burial 5 in Z3, (see Table 3.47). Three small deposits of cremated bone were found in two further pits within the area enclosed by Ring-ditch 2—a cremation deposit in Pit 32 and 'Burial 3' in Pit 4 (Chapter 2, sections 2.4.4. and 2.9.2–2.9.4).

Pit 119 was in Raftery's scenario the focus of Ring-ditch 1; in the preferred scenario, however, it is seen as only co-incidentially located at its centre. It contained a small amount of cremated human bone. A number of samples of cremated but unidentifiable bone were derived from features in Area 1, and a sample of cremated human bone was recovered from a deposit of soil in the Y cuttings, likely in a secondary position (section 3.16; Table 3.47). None of the many soil samples examined from Area 2 (see section 3.19) contained cremated bone, although it should be noted that most samples from this area had been hand-picked.

Two ring-ditches were excavated within the Z cuttings, one of which, Ring-ditch 3, produced cremated human bone (Chapter 2, section 2.9.2). A stone-lined burial (Burial 5) in Z3 contained slivers of human bone. Raftery suggested that further burials may remain unexcavated in this zone and (Chapter 2.10) has produced evidence for possible burial enclosures in this area, extending the burial zone further to the south-west. Annular or penannular structures recorded in the survey may not, however, in all cases represent ring-ditches, and only excavation can differentiate these from house or hut sites. A small hut had indeed been excavated in the Z cuttings (section 2.9.1) and may be considered part of the funerary activity in this area. Likewise, a number of Raftery's hearth features, found across all areas of burial activity, will be suggested below also to form part of the funerary activity, representing pyres.

6.3.1 Human bone

Some of the human bone deposits were substantial enough to be identified to age (Table 3.47; section 3.16). Four of these are of adults, two represented only by smaller amounts of bone. The most substantial quantities of human cremated bone are Burials 1 (over 800g) and 2 (over 700g) within Ring-ditch 2 (see Chapter 3, section 3.16). The central burial within Ring-ditch 1 is that of an older male with osteoarthritis, and the second burial, possibly inserted at a later stage than Burial 1, is that of a female (section 4.3.2). Burial 2, contained in an urn, was surrounded by charcoal-rich material, including human bone (S74:5), packed around the urn. Likewise, the charcoal spread into which Burial 1 was inserted produced both animal and human bone. The evidence for burning and the presence of human bone clearly indicate the function of this area as a pyre, surrounded by the enigmatic horseshoe-shaped setting of stake-holes (see discussion below). As indicated by comparable radiocarbon dates, this may relate to the burial inserted into its centre, adding further bone to the count of the primary cremation. They may also, however, relate to another episode of burial.

All other deposits, as far as they survive within the archive (Table 3.47), are of smaller, sometimes minute amounts (see below). Among these is the bone found in Pit 119, central to Area 1 at the centre of Ring-ditch 1. This was published as a burial (Raftery 2004) and, according to Erskine, the cremated bones represented an infant. Infant bones were apparently also noticed within the cremation in the urn in Burial 2 within Ring-ditch 2, in addition to the burial of an adult female. The sample from Pit 119 does not survive, however, and the re-examination of the remains from Burial 2 in Ring-ditch 2 did not produce evidence for an infant (Chapter 3, section 3.16).

The extant samples of human bone from the outer burial zone in the Z cuttings did not survive to a sufficient extent to identify sex or age but demonstrate the deposition of human bone in Burial 5 in Z3 inside as well as outside Ring-ditch 4 (Post-hole 8 and Pits 16 and 19). Unidentifiable cremated bone was also found in Pit 43 inside Ring-ditch 4. While no identifiable human bones were found associated with Ring-ditch 3, the monument form suggests a funerary function, and the double hearth 16/17 produced some samples of unidentifiable cremated bone.

6.3.2 Burial monuments

Two forms of ring-ditch are present at Rathgall. Ring-ditch 2 (Chapter 2, section 2.4.4.) and Ring-ditch 4 are annular, with no apparent causeway or entrance, whereas Ring-ditch 3 is penannular (section 2.9). A variety of different burial monuments have been documented in Irish prehistory, such as ring-ditches, ring-barrows and other circular monuments, which are differentiated mainly on the basis of the presence or absence of banks and mounds (Newman 1997b, 153–60; McGarry 2009). The chronological sequence of these monuments and their function are not well understood, mostly owing to issues of truncation and the lack of the dating evidence that would allow an accurate classification. Among different forms of ring monument emerging within the record, a small group of annular ring-ditches with a concentrically placed primary burial pit stand out, such as those at Ballintaggart, Co. Down (Ring-ditches 1, 4–8; Chapple *et al.* 2009), which show similarities to the arrangement of Ring-ditch 2 and the central pit at Rathgall.

Such annular ditches with central burials appear to suggest the former presence of a mound. The survival of a number of burial deposits and, most importantly, the complex horseshoe arrangement around the central Burial 1 at Rathgall suggest that at least in this phase such a covering may have indeed provided protection. The substantially later addition of the hoard in Pit 31 and Burial 2 as well as other features at what appears to be a comparable level in the stratigraphy does not, however, allow for any substantial mound. Likewise, at Ring-ditch 3 and Ring-ditch 4 no evidence for bank or mound survives.

A great number of pits and post-holes were recorded within the penannular Ring-ditch 3 (Fig. 2.137). It appears to have been surrounded by a light stockade with a south-western entrance, and a possible porch, orientated broadly towards the entrance gap of the ring-ditch. This arrangement may mirror that of Ring-ditch 2, which had possibly been enclosed by a now-incomplete stockade (Chapter 2, section 2.4.5, Figs 2.106–2.107). The absence of datable material from the post-holes of either enclosure makes it difficult to determine whether the stockade was intended to accompany this structure or whether its location was fortuitous.

A striking feature of Ring-ditch 4 is the pebbling or cobbling within its ditch fill, a feature that has frequently been observed on other sites, such as Parknahown 2, Co. Laois (T. O'Neill 2009), and Grange 3, Co. Meath (Kelly 2010). The cobbling within the ditch at Rathgall may represent the creation of a surface for particular activities or, indeed, the infilling of the ditch with bank remains (Raftery, archival notes), as similarly observed in Ring-ditch 1.

6.3.3 Burial ritual

Cremation was the predominant burial rite in Ireland from the Middle Bronze Age well into the first millennium AD. This cultural tradition is one of the prevailing traits of the Irish Bronze Age and Iron Age, stressing a great degree of continuity that accompanied all cultural changes throughout later prehistory. Cremation burial was also practised at Rathgall, and the site provides an unusual insight into a variety of aspects of burial practices and the accompanying rituals, including evidence for on-site cremation.

About sixteen features were identified by Raftery and recorded in the field as hearths or possible hearths (Fig. 2.87; Chapter 2, sections 2.2.4, 2.3.5 and 2.9.2 for Hearths 16/17). These are defined by different forms of pits with evidence for burning and charcoal-rich fills. Vitrification of the surrounding soils is visible in many images. Some of these hearths had either round or subcircular profiles, with a mostly uniform fill consisting of a mix of charcoal-rich material.

Some of these hearths, however, were subrectangular and accompanied by two or four post-holes (Hearths 2, 3 and 15 in Ring-ditch 2, and Hearths 16 and 17 within the enclosure around Ring-ditch 3; also possibly the pit arrangement in Sqs F3/G3). The post settings are positioned within the subrectangular hearth pit where the burning took place. The rather substantial posts at the western end of Hearth 3 were positioned within separate post-pits. The fills of the four-poster hearth features differ significantly from those consisting of simple pits. Hearth 16 showed evidence for *in situ* burning and the fill was full of tightly packed stones in some areas, many of them heat-affected. Hearths 2 and 3 show a sequence of fills which are the product of several burning episodes, some possibly separated or completed by a layer of cobbling. A very similar sequence can be observed in the case of Hearth 1, which, however, lacks evidence for post-holes.

The 'lining' of Hearth 16 (pp 174–6; Figs 2.143–2.146) consisted almost entirely of carbonised wood, which Raftery suggested may have represented basket lining, a feature that he had encountered in the excavation of Pit 118. This carbonised material, however, also filled the post-holes, representing clearly *in situ* charcoal deposits. Raftery had suggested (1976, 343) that the posts around these hearths may have supported a superstructure, screen or canopy related to a presumed metalworking function for these features. This assumption was based on the fact that six of the nine possible hearths contained pottery, moulds and crucible fragments. While this interpretation may be valid for Hearth 4, it clearly cannot have been the case for the large four-poster hearths, where the posts would, as clearly indicated by the black fill within them, have been subjected to high temperatures in the course of the use of the hearths. The use of substantial posts further suggests that they had to support or withstand some significant weight or pressure. These posts must have played an integral part in whatever heat-based process took place within these large pits, and their burning was an expected and tolerated part of the proceedings.

A strikingly similar feature to the four-poster pits at Rathgall has been recently documented at Newford, Co. Galway, where a significant quantity (700g) of human bone was retrieved from a large subrectangular pit with evidence for burning and with posts in each of the four corners. Cremated bone from two separate deposits within the fill of the pyre produced radiocarbon dates comparable to those from Rathgall (Wilkins 2008, 8). The excavator's reconstruction interpreted the four posts as retaining the pyre in place, with the body supported on the top and the pit serving as a draughting pit (Fig. 6.3; Wilkins 2011, 103–5, illus. 5). Alternatively, the posts may have supported a canopy on which the body was placed for cremation. Either scenario would also explain the substantial nature of the supporting posts at Rathgall. The location of Hearth 15 inside the enclosed burial complex in Area 2 and that of Hearths 16 and 17 just beside the burial in Ring-ditch 3 can thus be explained as pyres. The stone packing observed in some of these possible pyres, which Raftery describes as having been destroyed by heat, either may have served as draught pits to facilitate ventilation or may have been intended to close—literally and possibly symbolically—discrete episodes of burning. The repeated and episodic nature of the use of the Rathgall pyres is one of the conspicuous aspects of these features, adding to the complexity and density of burial evidence at the site.

Pit 119 at the centre of Ring-ditch 1, which had contained some identifiable human bone and a gold hair-ring, may represent a related feature and offer support for the interpretation put forward here. Raftery was reluctant to consider this deposit a burial and continued to interpret the feature as a pit rather than integrating it into his burial numbering system (cf. Raftery 2004). This was due to the small quantity of human bone recovered, as well as, for a burial, the unusual shape of the pit. Posts adjacent to the pit appeared to fit into the reconstructions of internal supports of the large 15m structure or a small post setting around the pit. As reconsideration of some of the site photographs demonstrates, however, there appear to be additional posts present on both sides of the pit (Fig. 2.43), suggesting the former presence here of two sets of posts on either end of the long pit. The black lining of the pit can, as in the case of the hearths, be seen as the remains of a burning event within the pit; indeed, the site photographs show evidence for *in situ* burning, with the characteristic hollowed-out pit profile as a result of the destabilisation of the pit edges through heat (Fig. 2.40). The minute amounts of human bone in the black fill may have remained *in situ* after the removal of most of the cremated remains. The pit was closed with a large boulder (Chapter 2, section 2.2.3) and this, together with the presence—possibly deliberate—of the gold hair-ring found on top of the charcoal, may be evidence that this was considered a special deposit.

Fig. 6.3—Pyre reconstruction (Headland Archaeology).

The large and irregular Pit 43 within Ring-ditch 3 and the external Pit 25 also showed evidence for burning, and the fill of Pit 43 contained mould fragments, pottery and burnt, unidentifiable bone, which may all be considered the truncated remains of the site of the actual cremation pyre.

Pyres have until recently been a rather elusive part of the funerary record. Pits containing little charcoal and no bone were interpreted as possible pyres in the context of a flat cemetery at Templenoe, Co. Tipperary (Geber 2009, 222–4; O'Donnell 2016), while at the cemetery of Cloghskelt, Co. Down, a thick spread of charcoal across an area of 9m by 6m containing minute amounts of burnt bone has been seen as a pyre (Waddell 2010, 156). A specific pyre construction with draught-enhancing features has been suggested for a cruciform flue arrangement in a pit at Rockfield, Co. Kerry (Collins 2003). Simple linear burnt pits with human bone in the fills were interpreted as possible pyre remains or pyre draught pits at Busherstown, Co. Carlow, where the suspected pyre was positioned close to a burial ring-ditch (H. O'Neill 2009), and the Rathgall and Newford features add significantly to this range of likely pyre features.

When reconsidering some of the well-known burial sites, it appears that there is more evidence for the existence of pyres than was previously thought. The use of subrectangular or oval pits with three or (mostly) four supporting posts or stakes can be identified at a number of sites. At Shanaclogh, Co. Limerick (Gowen 1988, 68–72, fig. 70, pl. 20), and at Adamstown, Co. Limerick (*ibid.*, 94–8, fig. 46), heavily truncated arrangements of this type can be identified, which also contained human bone and charcoal-rich deposits in the fills. In addition to the main firing pit at Shanaclogh, each of the four corner post-holes contained small amounts of human bone. This led to the identification of the site as a cluster of token cremation pits. At Adamstown an unburnt human mandible was present in addition to charcoal, burnt animal bone, the remains of a coarseware vessel and a chip of flint (*ibid.*, 96). Four stake-holes flanked the pit. A third site with a possible pyre is Duntryleague, Co. Limerick, where a subrectangular pit with burning at its base contained charcoal, flecks of cremated bone and sheep/goat enamel (*ibid.*, 76, fig. 29). Only one stake-hole provided possible evidence for a formerly existing pyre support. In all three cases the pyres were surrounded by a penannular ditch, most clearly in the case of Shanaclogh, framing and containing the pyre site. In the case of Duntryleague, a round barrow was located immediately beside it and it is tempting to assume that the associated burial took place there.

The occurrence of two rectangular pits with four post-holes in each case at Kilcarrig, Co. Carlow (Clark and Kozlowska 2009, 17–19, figs 9 and 11), not far from Rathgall, should be noted. Only Pit 045 at Kilcarrig had evidence for heat-affected stones and, although *in situ* burning within the pits was not noted, there are parallels to the pyres at Rathgall. Four-posters are a simple form of structure also frequently observed in the context of *fulachtaí fia* and may have served a variety of functions. The recurring association of four-poster structures with burial evidence has in the past led to their interpretation as supports for canopies, excarnation platforms or mortuary houses, and can in some further cases be suggested to be related also to pyres. At Ballintaggart, Co. Down (Dunlop 2015), two such arrangements were uncovered in the context of a cremation cemetery of Late Bronze Age date. While one of the four-posters is located between two burial ring-ditches (Ring-ditches 6 and 7), another is located within the area enclosed by Ring-ditch 2. Seeing such arrangements as part of funerary practices opens up interesting avenues of thinking about the function of ring-ditches. These may have served to enclose and delineate a place of cremation rather than being places of burial deposition, as similarly argued by McGarry (2009).

Besides the pit features at Rathgall, the area around Burial 1 at the centre of Ring-ditch 2 seems also to represent the remains of a cremation event. The charcoal spread (Fig. 2.43, b) contained possibly human bone and cremated animal bones (S73:12 and S73:19), supporting this theory. The largely undisturbed pyre deposits appear to have consisted of almost pure charcoal and large amounts of ash, suggesting little disturbance after their deposition (Chapter 3, section 3.19). The central area of Ring-ditch 2 was surrounded by a horseshoe-shaped arrangement of more than 1,500 stake-holes. The radiocarbon dates from the human bone fragments in the spread and in Burial 1 allow for both being from the same interment.

Hearth 15, interpreted here as a pyre, located off-centre but also within Ring-ditch 2, may represent a further episode of cremation within this enclosure, following the presumably primary pyre at its centre. Accordingly, any of the various other deposits of human remains within the enclosure may relate to the use of Hearth 15. This, together with its associated animal bones, may represent part of the burial ceremony that took place within the area enclosed by the 1,500 stake-holes. Nevertheless, the charcoal layer representing this burning or cremation event, while delineated by the 1,500 stake-holes, does not extend into the stake-hole arrangement, whose function remains unclear (Fig. 2.95; Chapter 2, section 2.4.4.9).

The morphology of Hearth 1, with several layers of charcoal interspersed with heat-affected stones, within the Ring-ditch 1 enclosure and truncated by the later 15m structure may suggest that it also functioned as a pyre. The charcoal assemblage from this feature differs strongly, however, from that of those features that have been interpreted as funerary in nature (Chapter 3, section 3.19).

The lack of grave-goods—apart from pottery vessels—is one of the characteristics of burial in Ireland after about 1500 BC (cf. Cahill and Sikora 2011; Waddell 2010; 1998). The little gold ring within the pyre Pit 119 is thus highly unusual and may indicate that burial goods were instead included on, or in, the pyre. The position of the ring, described by Raftery as on top of the charcoal layer and directly under the boulder, and its good condition (Fig. 3.1) may indicate deliberate placement just before the formal closing of the pyre pit by sealing it with the large boulder. The use of stones or large boulders as possible closing deposits can also be observed in other parts of the site. Pit 118, Area 1, was covered with a layer of large stones, and at least two of the large pits in Area 4 that contained a great number of Bronze Age artefacts were also 'closed' and possibly marked at the same time by exceptionally large boulders.[3] Penannular rings have been found primarily in burial contexts on the Continent, suggesting that their function as personal ornaments should be noted (Chapter 3, section 3.3).

Pit 118 is one of the most enigmatic features at Rathgall. This large, funnel-shaped pit contained several fills, separated by what were convincingly interpreted at the time of excavation as wooden baskets inserted into the pit on consecutive occasions. As Raftery noted, baskets have been recorded at some crannog sites in waterlogged conditions. 'Crannog 61 in Lough Gara, Co. Sligo, yielded basketry hearths which had been created with great skill and the small basket-lined pits from Ballinderry, Co. Offaly/Westmeath, the purpose of which is uncertain, would, if decayed, have produced pits with black organic lining such as those found at Rathgall' (Raftery, archival notes). The basket inserts are represented by layers of irregularly carbonised material. This suggests that they were subjected to reducing conditions *in situ*, i.e. the application of heat to the pit, before infilling with another layer of soil and the insertion of a further basket.[4] The primary fill of the pit contained a great quantity of pottery sherds, moulds and fragments of an almost complete crucible. While some sort of storage function for such a pit is conceivable, the sequence of basket insertions raises questions, as does the charred condition of the basketry that led to its preservation. A possible scenario is suggested by a basket burial recovered at Derrycraw, Co. Derry (Dunlop 2015). This was dated on charcoal to the Middle Bronze Age and had been placed 'within a small pit on the southern edge of the cairn. The "basket" primarily consisted of thin strands (5–10mm wide) of interwoven alder. There were some larger concave pieces of possible bark towards the base. This bark may have lined or been woven into the "basket" to provide a more secure container. Two strands of curved wicker found on the side of the basket may have been the remains of "basket handles". The basket was carbonised *in situ*, possibly from the cremation still being hot when it was placed in the pit. The identifiable wood was alder, which is not normally a basketry wood. The basket was straight sided, 0.35m in diameter and 0.3m deep. The cremation within this basket was of a young adult aged between 13 and 17 (Dunlop 2015, 81). The description of this feature at Derrycraw is cited here as it is so similar to Pit 118 at Rathgall, though no definite human remains were documented from the latter; cremated bone was, however, present in soil samples from this context (see Table 3.47).

Pyre remain deposits

Burials 3 (Pit 10) and 4 (Pit 32) and Post-hole/Pit 8/19 associated with Ring-ditch 4 contained only minute amounts of human bone (Chapter 3, section 3.16; Table 3.47). Such deposits would conventionally be interpreted as token burials representing the *pars pro toto* deposition of the human body after cremation. This is based on the fact that cremation deposits frequently contain less bone than expected according to values generated by modern cremations, and a careful selection of the bones from the pyre and their inclusion in these pits is assumed (cf. Lynch and O'Donnell 2007, 109–10; Chapter 3, section 3.16). The difference in treatment between these burials, deposited in unmarked and unfurnished pits, and the clearly defined, formal Burials 1 and 2 is marked. A rather different depositional purpose seems to be reflected by the differing mode of deposition.

Pit 119, which above has been argued to represent the base of a pyre pit, contained human bone in a layer of what Raftery describes as 'sticky, black lining'.[5] At least five of the minor deposits of cremated bone on the site have been recorded as having been contained in such a black so-called 'lining', and a much greater number of pits were 'lined' but did not necessarily produce evidence for human bone (Chapter 2, section 2.4.4.2). Rather than representing token burials, perhaps these deposits should thus be understood as deposits of pyre material that in some cases, as in the *in situ* deposits in pyre/Pit 119, still contained some amount of human bone (cf. Becker 2014).

Similarly, Pit 16 near Ring-ditch 4, in contrast to the normal burial practice, contained artefacts in association with a substantial amount of human bone. While not representing a complete cremation (see Chapter 3, section 3.16), the amount of 104.7g appears to have been deposited as an entity within the black layer that also contained pottery sherds representing at least three vessels (Vessels 403, 404, 410) and a flint blade (E100:110). Rather than being residual inclusions, their direct association in a regularly circular pit may suggest that fragments of the vessels were used in the burial ritual and deposited with pyre remains. Some probable cremated human bone was recovered from a sample derived from the 'black lining' of Pit 19, at a distance of about 3m from Pit 16. A number of similar circular pits clustered around Pit 16 show the typical morphology of a black lining. These may have held minute amounts of human bone not recognised during excavation or, as argued for comparable deposits in Area 2, may constitute deposits of pyre remains which did not include human remains.

Raftery described the black basal layers in these pits as 'lining', often additionally qualified by 'sticky', in deposits interpreted here as pyre debris and *in situ* pyre remains, as in the case of Pit 119. The thin black layers in Pit 118 were probably basketwork (see above), and the layers in the pits discussed here—including Pit 16—appear in contrast to be rather substantial charcoal-rich deposits. Raftery interpreted the charcoal layers as lining rather than as fill owing to the rather unusual positioning of this layer within the pits. An example of this is recorded in 'Burial' 4 within Ring-ditch 2, where the black material apparently lined the sides of the pit and was visible in plan as a dark circle along the outer edge of the pit. This is best explained as the result of settling processes of very loose, charcoal-rich pyre material, which was compressed by overlying strata. Such processes can be observed especially well on sites with pits underlying later strata, where the subsidence of the overlying material and compression within the earlier pit become very clear.

The deposition of pyre material that presents itself as

'lining' has been noted at a number of sites. Examples include Killoran 10, Co. Tipperary, where a charcoal-rich silty matrix may also have represented pyre debris (Stevens 2005). The excavator differentiated between burials with pyre material and deposits solely of pyre material. These 'empty' pits, which were clearly not burials, were nevertheless afforded a special treatment (Lynch and O'Donnell 2007). It appears that of 26 clay-capped (i.e. sealed) pits only twenty produced cremated bone. While it is not possible to correlate those deposits that contained human bone with those that are recorded as having contained a charcoal-rich silty matrix that may represent pyre material, it appears that some of the capped examples without human bone also contained pyre material (*ibid.*, 118). The evidence from Rathgall concurs with Lynch and O'Donnell's conclusion that pyre remains received special treatment. Rather, however, than stressing the difference between the deposits containing human bone and those that contained only pyre debris as a special treatment of a by-product of the bone selection process (*ibid.*), the evidence from Rathgall suggests a lack of differentiation between these groups of pits. Pits containing minute quantities of bones and pits only containing bone-free pyre remains are in fact the same, and the lack of differentiation in their deposition at Killoran 10 and at Rathgall provides evidence for this. Rather than burials without grave-goods, 'cenotaphs' (*ibid.*; Grogan 2004d, 67) or token burials, such deposits should be considered as deposits of pyre material that required a particular treatment, just as did the remains of the human body itself (Becker 2014).

As becomes clear both in the formal closing of pyre Pit 119 and in the deposition of portions of pyre material in these pits, the disposal of the remains of the cremation was a significant and important aspect of the overall burial ritual. The evidence for episodic use of some of the pyres may imply the need for disposal to facilitate the reuse of the pyre pit for the next act of cremation. This very functional concern may have been accompanied by the need to legitimise this action symbolically. The remains of the pyre could not simply have been discarded but needed to be dealt with in a particular manner, within the sacred or special area delineated by the ring-ditch and—possibly—the outer stockade. The evidence from within and around Ring-ditch 2 thus provides unparalleled insight into the otherwise rather invisible steps before the final interment of the remains of the human body.

The function of a large number of closely spaced stake-holes around the possible pyre site at the centre of Ring-ditch 2 remains an enigma. Raftery explored the possibility of a symbolic significance of this 'forest' of stake-holes. While describing an overall horseshoe shape, the arrangement of the posts is otherwise irregular and could possibly represent multi-phase activity. It is not recorded whether the stake-holes contained charcoal or whether they rotted *in situ*. After the removal of the top layer of ash and heat-affected soil in the central area, pits and post-holes underlying this may suggest an earlier phase of activity.

A comparable cluster of stake-holes around a burial in the interior of a Bronze Age ring-ditch at Bay Farm, Co. Antrim, is notable (Jim Mallory, pers. comm.) and may be tentatively paralleled by other posts associated with Ring-ditch 3 at Rathgall. The predominance of alder in the Rathgall samples associated with the pyre, in contrast to all other burial deposits on the site, is notable. The alder is from wood that clearly did not derive from the stake-holes but from larger branches. Stuijts (this volume) suggests that the wood may have been structural and notes the presence of rot and insect channels on the alder. Could it be suggested that a structure that had decayed *in situ* had been reused as pyre firewood?

The charcoal from the burial features within Ring-ditch 2 is indeed dominated by alder, whereas the expected highly calorific oak wood only features in the Z cuttings, where it is used exclusively. The use of alder, although unexpected, can be shown, however, to be also found at other sites (see Chapter 3, section 3.19).

Six rim sherds (Vessels 404 and 403) with food accretions in Pit 16 at Ring-ditch 4, as well as animal bones within the spread of the central pyre within Ring-ditch 2, may provide a tantalising glimpse of food consumption in association with the burial ceremonies at the site.

6.3.4 Continuity of practice

The probable succession of burials within Ring-ditch 2 is a conspicuous expression of the continued use not of Rathgall hill in general but of Ring-ditch 2 in particular for burial over a long period of time, possibly indicating the maintenance of the site over generations. Burials 1 and 2 in and on rather similar stone settings may underline continuity in burial practices and also distinguish them as formal burials from other deposits of human bone on the site.

Stones and charcoal layers observed in some of the pyres suggest successive episodes of use. In addition, the superimposed possible pyre pits in the outside zone of the site demonstrate in a rather impressive way continuity of practice and the use of the same ring-ditch for burial on at least two successive occasions. It is suggested here that pits were emptied of pyre detritus and reused for multiple firings. A shallow, oval pit (1m by 1.25m), *c.* 5m east of the enclosure of Ring-ditch 4, showed evidence and residues of intense burning, possibly providing additional evidence of a cremation episode.

Charred food accretions on the internal face of a heavily sooted vessel from the upper layer of fill in Ring-ditch 4 produced a later date in the Late Bronze Age that may indicate continued use or reuse of the monument, but the lack of dates from this area of the site makes it impossible to subject it to statistical modelling or to tie it into the overall site model (Chapter 4, section 4.4). This vessel fragment is part of a larger group of objects that were all found in the upper parts of the ring-ditch, whereas the lower fill consisted largely of sterile silt rather than deliberate infill. Ring-ditch 3 silted up rather rapidly and yielded a small number of probably residual pieces of pottery and a mould fragment. This ring-ditch itself cut a pit and post-holes, some of which also contained Bronze Age pottery, suggesting again a continuity of activity at this location. The character of the earlier phase is, however, unclear.

The repeated use of the site is also evidenced by the multiple burials in the area enclosed by Ring-ditch 2 (see above). Assuming that the central Burial 1 was the primary burial on the site, it was followed or accompanied by the deposition of pyre material in Pit 4 (Burial 3). On the basis of its position and given the slightly later radiocarbon dates (see Table 4.2), Burial 2, off-centre within the ring-ditch and interred in an urn, appears possibly to have been a later episode than Burial 1. Similarly late may be the hoard of three metal objects deposited likewise in the area enclosed by Ring-ditch 2. The deposition of this collection of three bronzes in a small, circular pit is a unique example of the deposition of objects in a funerary context, and rare as an example of a hoard within any archaeological setting.

6.4 HIGH-TEMPERATURE TECHNOLOGIES AT RATHGALL

An aspect crucial to the understanding of Late Bronze Age Rathgall is the association and context of the metallurgical activity and the contemporaneous closely relatable burial activity. A characteristic shared by all these materials and activities is that they are based on and require high temperatures. In very practical and functional terms, therefore, the association of different technologies is not surprising, as they required a very similar skill set and resources.

The association of metalworking with death and burial has frequently been observed in the Iron Age (e.g. Giles 2007; Reid and MacLean 1995). In Bronze Age research the connection between the two technologies of cremation and metalworking has often been stressed and extensively explored in the context of bronze hoards and issues of fragmentation of objects within them (e.g. Becker 2013b; Bradley 2005; Brück 1999; 2001; 2006; Turner 1998). Fragmentation of objects and other references to metalworking in hoards have been interpreted primarily in terms of their potential symbolic potency, linked to concepts of death, rebirth, regeneration and fertility, though the functional aspects of the rituals that cite these links have been pointed out (Becker 2012). Similarly, the close link between metalworking and cremation at Rathgall may have had a functional aspect. Raftery interpreted some of the pyres on the site as large hearths, perhaps highlighting in retrospect how cremation and metalworking were inextricably linked in terms of high-temperature technology. Both activities require heat, consume a lot of fuel and require the skilful maintenance and control of temperature. The idea of metalworkers being in control of both technologies is feasible, and a direct functional connection has also been suggested in order to explain the occurrence of human remains in furnaces (Goldhahn and Oestigaard 2008).

The contemporaneity of both activities at Rathgall depends on circumstantial evidence (see Chapter 4), such as the fact that the location of pyres and burials and the deposition of the moulds and crucibles representing metalworking industrial activity appear to be mutually exclusive (Area 2). The only overlap between these activities is the inclusion of mould fragments in the fill of some pyre hearths (Chapter 3, section 3.9). The inclusion of a near-complete crucible in Pit 118 may likewise, if this is interpreted as having a funerary function, underpin the association of metallurgy and cremation. Evidence for the possible association is also provided in the Z cuttings, where pits associated with Ring-ditch 4 (Pit 16) contained both moulds and human bone, while in Pit 43, within the ring-ditch, moulds, pottery and burnt unidentifiable bone were recovered from the fill. Pit 11, associated with Ring-ditch 3 and the likely pyre Hearth 15, also included mould fragments.

While the majority of the known sites in Ireland that have produced moulds are settlement sites, Rathgall, with its close association of burial and metalworking, forms part of a range of sites that appear to represent similar funerary associations. At Johnstown South, Co. Wicklow (Fitzpatrick 1998), an enclosure consisted of an intermittent spread of stones, C4, faced on the outside with larger boulders, and with indications of such also having been present along its interior edge in some parts. The stone layer was in some areas found to have sat on top of/formed part of a bank.The removal of the stone bank in the eastern half showed it to sit on top of layer C304, a charcoal-rich layer which contained burnt bone, flint, pottery and the bulk of the moulds and produced a radiocarbon date in the twelfth–tenth centuries BC (Fitzpatrick 1998). Crucible fragments were also found on the site. A cremation pit (C154–155) in the interior of the enclosure produced a radiocarbon date in the fifteenth–twelfth centuries BC, and a stone-lined cremation pit (C26–27) had been inserted into the bank. A cluster of seventeen pits within the enclosure produced evidence for burning and metal slag. The pits may be related to the metalworking or, indeed, to burial activity. Both earlier and later burial activity as well as the metalworking seem to be of Late Bronze Age date, with the burial activity possibly pre-dating or, if affected by the old wood effect, being contemporary with the metalworking (Martin Fitzpatrick, pers. comm.). Fragments of perhaps seven crucibles, including a possibly footed one, were recovered at Darcystown 2, Co. Dublin, from the fill of a burial ring-ditch within which several cremation deposits, as well as pottery vessels, had been reported (Grogan and Roche 2008c, 98, 99). A shallow pit at Ballynakelly/ Rathcreedon, Co. Dublin, contained a fill of charcoal-rich soil that included fragments of a mould and a crucible besides some Late Bronze Age coarseware and some unidentifiable cremated bone. While the casting materials may be residual, the association with cremated bone on a funerary site with Late Bronze Age and Iron Age funerary activity appears significant (McCarthy 2010, 37–8). The pottery, mould and crucible fragments found in the fill of a palisaded enclosure at Clonard, Balbriggan, Co. Dublin, are not clearly associated with the unidentified cremated bone also found in contexts associated with the palisade (McGlade 2019, 35–8). Indeed, Ó Faoláin (2004, 70) had previously drawn attention to a number of sites where metalworking evidence was found in a funerary context or focused on funerary sites. These include a ring-barrow/burial monument at Old Connaught, and crucibles and stone moulds from the wedge tombs at Lough Gur, Co. Limerick, Moylisha, Co. Wicklow, and Loughash, Co. Tyrone. The association of mould deposits alongside skulls within the King's Stables, Co. Armagh, may further support the connection between death and metalwork in the Late Bronze Age (Lynn 1977).

These examples thus provide a context of sorts for the association of the two activities at Rathgall, which may have had practical as well as conceptual causes. Importantly, at Rathgall, as well as at the above sites, they were apparently conducted at a remove from contemporary settlement.

6.5 STRUCTURES AND SETTLEMENT AT RATHGALL

The question of whether Rathgall was occupied was, for Raftery, synonymous with the question of whether there were houses at Rathgall. Having set out to excavate a hillfort and encountering an exceptionally rich artefactual record, especially vast amounts of pottery, the lack of positive evidence for structures and occupation presented interpretational difficulties. While there is some limited evidence for Bronze Age structures, the possibility of others that are not visible in the archaeological record has to be considered. While Raftery also saw agriculturally related artefacts, particularly the rotary and saddle querns but primarily the pottery, as evidence for intensive activity and occupation of the area (Raftery, archival notes), he had serious doubts about the interpretation of Rathgall as a conventional settlement site. He particularly questioned whether the association of both secular and ritual activity in the same location was conceivable. Rather than a juxtaposition of a burial-ground with a settlement site, the apparent intertwining of both activities at Rathgall within the same space and the same chronological horizon concerned him. Indeed, while the deposition of human remains in settlement contexts is frequently observed throughout Irish prehistory, the direct association of contemporary formal burial and settlement is not documented elsewhere. While Ginn (2016, 137) pointed to the frequent presence of burial sites in the vicinity of settlements within a 3km buffer zone, direct association on the same site is not known. Instead, the Rathgall model suggests a distinct separation, while still spatially not that far away; even if, as in twelve of Ginn's case-studies, only 100m away, and similarly close at Rathgall, the clear separation is still evident.

Raftery drew attention to the zone of particularly dense charcoal-rich material of what he describes as a rectangular area in Metalworking Zone 3. If a structure can be assumed here, it was not supported by stakes or post-holes (see Chapter 7). Raftery explores the very problematic issue of recognising structures that are not post-built. They are potentially invisible in the archaeological record, and the existence of turf-built houses, which are well known from vernacular Irish architecture, has also to be considered a realistic possibility for the construction of houses in the prehistoric past. Buildings with stone walls or stone wall footings have repeatedly been observed in the Irish Bronze Age, for example at Ballyhackett, Co. Antrim (Phil MacDonald, pers. comm.), and Corrstown, Co. Derry (Ginn and Rathbone 2011), and are thought to have been topped by turf walling. The use of both stone- and clay-footed structures, where the roof is supported on the walls rather than on the ring-beam of the classic roundhouse reconstruction, was noted by Ó Néill (2009, 19, Ground Plan 4). Structures with an inner slot-trench alongside a solid wall were also captured in his GP 6—here, however, on the basis of the type site at Ballyutoag, Co. Antrim, with an external ditch rather than a second slot-trench (*ibid.*, 16). Turf construction is indeed a viable option; turf-walled houses have until very recently been in use in Ireland and may not leave any traces in the archaeological record (cf. Loveday 2006; Romankievicz 2023).

Similarly, as Raftery points out, simple horizontal beam (*Blockbau*) constructions potentially leave no traces in the ground. Examples of such buildings laid directly on the ground or slightly elevated, resting on stone foundations or individual boulders, are well known from the Lausitz region of Germany. Here occasionally rather ephemeral stone foundations survive to indicate the outline of the rectangular houses, whereas at other sites only the *absence* of features in rectangular zones between clusters of pits indicates the former location of houses, e.g. Wolkenberg 13 in the Lausitz (Eilbracht 2005). Indirect evidence sometimes survives in the form of clay fragments with the imprints of beams and of triangular cross-section, such as at the *Fugenverstriche* of the *Bohlenhaus* (Bönisch 1996; 2007). Sill-beam constructions, which can be applied to the construction both of rectangular houses and of roundhouses, will leave no trace on a dryland site and have been recorded both in Britain (Harding 2009, 49) and in Ireland at Ballinderry II (Newman 1997a).

Associated hearths, pit formations, refuse accumulations or voids in the distribution patterns of other features may then remain as the only means of identifying these sites. At Rathgall, the accumulation of substantial deposits in Area 2 forms one of the problematic complex zones, and the spatial distribution of charcoal-rich deposits and finds in this area suggests localised craft activities which could well be envisaged as having taken place in a structure—as thought by Raftery during phases of his work on the site, and apparently supported by a stretch of clay that he observed along the D squares. The daub samples from this area were not suitable for a wattle-and-daub construction (see Chapter 3, section 3.15) but more likely were part of a kiln or similar construction with clay walling. The samples had in many cases been subject to high temperatures after shaping, suggesting their use in a heat-based technology. A fragment of daub identified as a possible floor surface adds to the concentration here in the area of Metalworking Zone 3 and, indeed, in the Y cutting further north. These materials provide evidence for the existence here of some form of structure, possibly a kiln or hearth, and a possibly associated work surface or floor.

No daub that was evidently used in wattle-and-daub constructions or plank walling could be identified among the daub samples from Rathgall. This in itself does not contradict the assumption of the use of daub, as experimental destruction of houses in the Butser Farm project has demonstrated that virtually no daub necessarily remains after the burning of a house (Reynolds 2000, 97). The rectangular structures that are clearly evidenced in the F/G and X cuttings at Rathgall are also likely to have produced daub fragments upon their destruction. There is, however, no evidence to suggest that a lack of surviving daub means that it was not in use in prehistory, particularly on severely truncated sites such as Rathgall.

Nevertheless, the evidence for daub and floor materials in combination with the evidence for metalworking in Metalworking Zone 3 may at best suggest the possible presence of a small workshop rather than an actual domestic structure. These remains were found precisely in the substantial stratified deposits of Zone 3 rather than in Metalworking Zone 4, which was an accumulation of metallurgical waste in shallow depressions (cf. Chapter 2, section 2.3.1). The archaeological evidence thus appears to identify Zone 3 as the actual location of metalworking. Alternatively, this accumulation may represent the by-products of metalworking processes taking place in the hearth and area of paving/cobbling in Metalworking Zone 2. The character of the build-up of deposits with their rather extensive horizontal spreads in Metalworking Zone 3 contradicts, however, the interpretation of Metalworking Zone 2 as a midden, as does the evidence for a kiln and floor surface. Burnt stones in the upper deposits in Metalworking Zone 2 further support this. Interestingly, the second occurrence of both daub and a possible floor surface is in the Y cuttings, where very similar deposits to those in Area 2 were observed. Thus the presence of a workshop in this location can be suggested, although the morphology of the structure, such as a roofed building or a shelter, cannot be demonstrated.

A nearby subcircular feature in B4/B5 may also be the remains of a building, representing, as Raftery suggested, a turf-built or earthen basket-shaped structure. Basket-shaped structures are well known from the early medieval period and, indeed, may have their roots in earlier periods (Lynn and McDowell 2011).

The only clearly recognisable structures datable to the Bronze Age phase at Rathgall are two rectangular structures in the F/G and X cuttings. A small rectangular building survives in the form of two parallel rows of small posts in slot-trenches in the northern part of Area 3 in the F/G cuttings. Radiocarbon dates and stratigraphy suggest an earlier Late Bronze Age date and the structure could be part of the Area 2 activity with its possible workshop floor remains, described above (see Chapter 4, section 4.4). The second rectangular structure was found in the X cuttings and, like that observed in the F/G cutting in Area 3, presents itself as a building of moderate size with extant remains indicating only two parallel walls. Rectangular structures occur repeatedly within the range of Bronze Age structures in Ireland. Doody (2000, 139–41) recorded eleven rectangular timber houses, often set in a footing trench similar to the examples from Rathgall, though mostly larger in size. Elsewhere 8% of all structures of Bronze Age date were found to be rectangular (Ó Néill 2009, 55). Some of them, such as Structure 1 at Chancellorsland, were only 2.4m wide (Doody 2008, 88), similar to those at Rathgall. Their small size suggests that they may have provided shelter for activities rather than being living spaces. A fitting comparison for the Rathgall structures is the Iron Age workshop found at Tara, which was closely associated with a hearth in which iron-, bronze- and possibly glass-working took place (Crew and Rehren 2002). Rectangular house plans represent 9% of buildings in Ginn's study (2016, 97), and Ó Néill (2009, 55) notes that some may be non-domestic, and clearly the structures represented here at Rathgall are of a fundamentally different nature than the large structures as found, for example, at Ballinderry.

The 15m structure or house (see below) and two rectangular buildings in the F/G and X cuttings are the only positive evidence for structures on or immediately off the summit of the hill which are probably—or, in the case of the oval structure, possibly—datable to the later prehistoric phase of the site. A very small round structure with an elaborate entrance was documented in the Z cuttings and may be related to the burial activity in the same area (Chapter 2, section 2.9.2).

In essence, as it currently stands, only tentative evidence for larger structures can be identified at Rathgall. The geophysical survey has, however, identified evidence for further circular and rectangular—and at times rather large—possible structures (Chapter 2, section 2.10).

6.6 BRONZE AGE RATHGALL IN ITS CONTEXT

'The metalworking seems more than merely an adjunct to everyday agricultural practice. The intensity of metalworking, its dispersed nature across the site and, indeed, the variety of objects which were cast point strongly to specialist activity. Thus it might be argued that the obvious importance of Rathgall and the clear prosperity of its inhabitants suggest that this was the focus for metalworking on a scale of industrial intensity. A focus of exchange and distribution, Rathgall would have had widespread contacts abroad and thus the exotic produce, and, indeed, the extent of such material, present on the site is readily explained' (Raftery, draft text).

Throughout prehistory people returned to Rathgall but, based on the archaeology encountered during the excavations, the peak of activity seems to have taken place during a relatively brief phase between the twelfth and tenth centuries BC. This period, while generally underrepresented in the Irish artefactual record if compared to the ninth-century Dowris phase, sees high levels of activity in the site record (e.g. Armit *et al.* 2013; Ginn 2016, esp. pp 47–8). Rathgall, with its extensive mould assemblage, especially serves to make aspects of this period visible that are otherwise for cultural and taphonomic reasons invisible. A central question is why Rathgall saw this surge of activity at this time and how it functioned within contemporary society, and, especially, how the metalworking activity can be situated in our models of Bronze Age society.

Bronze Age Rathgall was located in a probably very lively contemporary landscape. From the pollen record, we can glean an image of a landscape that from about 1500 BC saw a rise in agricultural activity, which may have been at its peak during Rathgall's Late Bronze Age phase (Chapter 3, section 3.18). Owing to the lack of animal bone, our understanding of this important aspect of subsistence patterns is limited, but the expected range of species seems to be indicated (section 3.17). An agricultural basis for, and an indication of an increase in, population numbers in this area may be suggested by the pollen record, and the recently excavated sites on the N9/N10 Kilcullen to Waterford road scheme west of Rathgall also demonstrate an intensely settled landscape (Fig. 6.4). Within the closer vicinity of Rathgall, the possible enclosure and cemetery at Knockloe and a recently recognised enclosure at Tullow may represent contemporary sites in close proximity, as do the nearby hillfort of Knockeen and the Rathgall hut circle (Fig. 1.2). The pressure on a mostly open landscape may also be indicated by the use of gnarly, low-quality woods, including rotten material, for the firing of pyres at Rathgall and possibly for charcoal production (see section 3.19). The geophysical survey of Rathgall itself suggests that the excavations captured part of a larger zone of activity on the hill which, if of Bronze Age date, would have represented an even greater burden on resources than already suggested by the many and substantial charcoal-rich deposits documented. The limited evidence for wood management by coppicing and the use of mostly young wood at the site do not indicate the existence of long-term managed wood for specialised use at Rathgall. This, however, does not suggest that such did not exist but rather that selection of wood was specific to its intended use, with better material reserved for structural purposes, for example in a settlement context, such as at the adjacent site of Knockeen hillfort.

This hillfort, very closely located on the same ridge as Rathgall, provides a highly important context. The large number of possible house footprints revealed in the geophysical record (see Chapter 2, section 2.10) contrast with the evidence from Rathgall, which is characterised by funerary and industrial activity. While Knockeen remains currently undated, it seems likely that both sites have to be considered in tandem, forming a settlement unit that may have been further enclosed, as suggested in Chapter 1 (see also O'Driscoll and Becker 2022). Such a model of a larger settlement unit consisting of functionally complementary sites, not unlike what was proposed by Condit (1998) for paired hillforts, would also go a long way towards explaining the peculiar patterns of wood selection at Rathgall itself. Rathgall speaks to a strict separation between the sphere of the living and activities to do with death and metalworking, which were differently constituted from domestic life both physically and existentially. Such separation has also been noted within Britain and Ireland by Johnston (2021, 355), who suggests that Dún Aonghasa and places of this type, like Rathgall, stand outside the regular settlement sphere. Johnston sees these as places for the communication with other worlds through performance and gatherings, from which people would emerge bound into new, transformed kin-relations (*ibid.*, 229). Transformative processes are indeed at the heart of the 'segregated' Rathgall. Whether the site was constituted by the communities of the wider landscape or existed in tandem with the possible settlement at Knockeen is, however, unclear.

The presence of precious and imported materials convinced Raftery that people at Rathgall were engaged in wider trade networks, which would have been facilitated by its location near rivers creating a route—if, however, not uninterrupted—towards the Irish Sea in the east and the south. The range and quality of objects, including imported materials such as the amber and glass, highlight the site's affluent and special position.

The resources needed for the industrial activity on the one hand and for the funerary activity on the other must have been significant, with wood, charcoal and clay being used in great quantities. While charcoal appears to have been locally produced, and regionally available clay for the production of moulds and pottery is assumed, the source of both gold and the raw materials used for the production of copper-alloy objects is unknown. The fact that there is a cluster of metalworking sites in the greater south Dublin/Wicklow area, including Rathgall, is striking (Ó Faoláin 2004, 105–6, fig. 6.2), perhaps suggesting the use of local deposits. The use, however, of local copper supplies in Ireland after the Early Bronze Age appears to have been limited (O'Brien 2019; 2016; 2015) and instead, as for Britain, the use of imported raw material is assumed (Northover 1982; O'Brien 2015, 299–300). While the origin of Early Bronze Age gold from Irish sources had been considered possible (e.g. Warner *et al.* 2010), isotopic analysis suggested a south-west English origin (Standish *et al.* 2015). No comparable data exist, however, for the later parts of the Bronze Age with its vast amounts of gold consumption in Ireland.

In any case, the presence of gold, glass and amber reflects

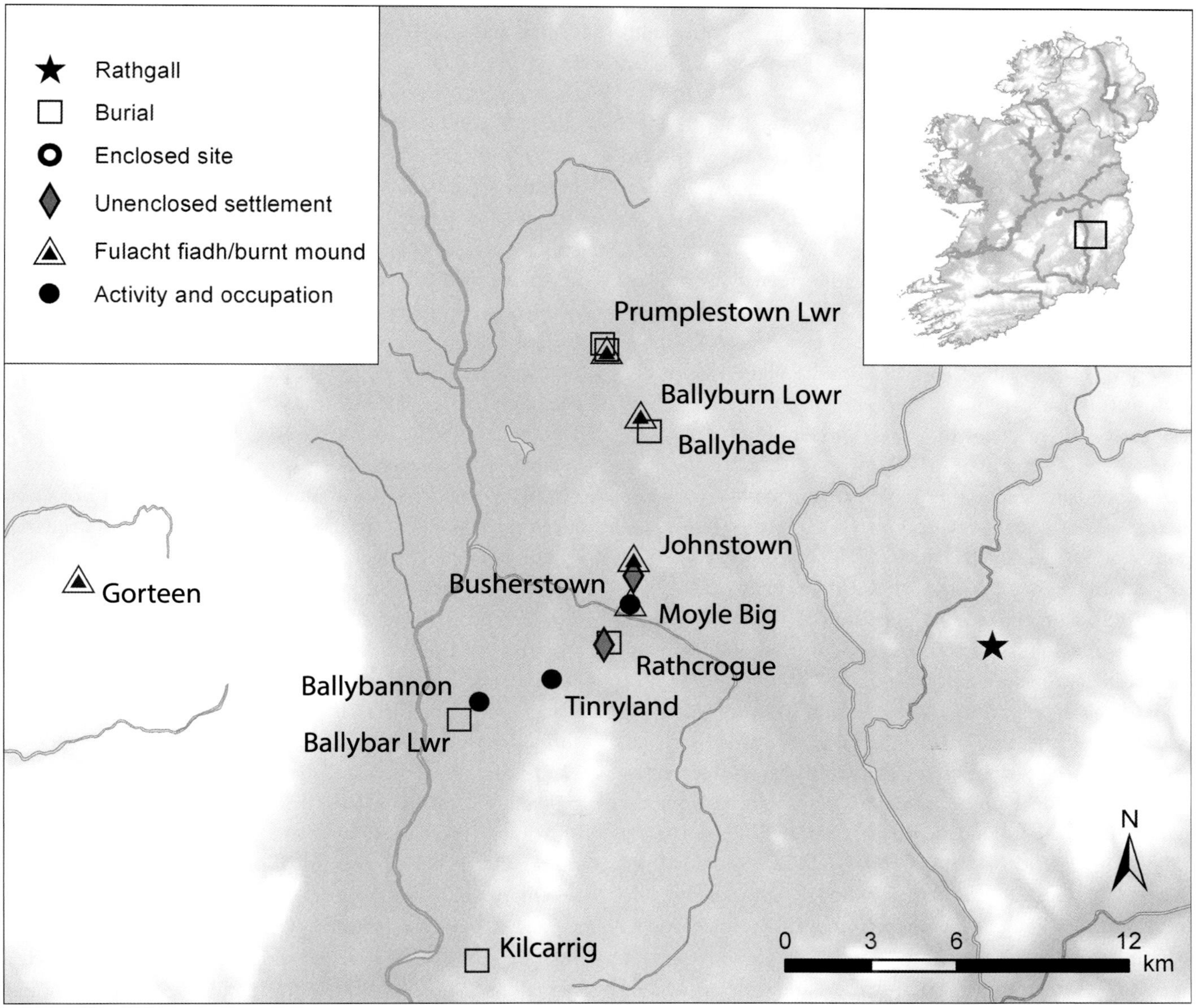

Fig. 6.4—Bronze Age sites excavated in County Carlow. [6]

a society well connected within Ireland and the wider Bronze Age world. What Rathgall's wealth was based on is unclear; its advantageous location may have provided the area with access to wider trade networks, perhaps playing an intermediary role between the coastal region and the interior of the island. Perhaps there is also an underestimation of the amount of material wealth in circulation at the time and especially expended in a funerary context, and the evidence for both bronze- and gold-working at Lough Gur, Co. Limerick (Cleary 2003; 2018, 160; Ó Ríordáin 1954; Cahill 2003), as well as the presence of imported LMHK glass at this site and at Freestone Hill, Co. Kilkenny, should be highlighted.

The levels of metalworking activity, as well as the expansive range of objects cast and the complex metalworking technologies employed, may indeed suggest Rathgall's role as a technological centre, with access to knowledge, skills and resources that set it apart from all other recorded Irish sites.

Within Ireland and Britain, Rathgall stands out in terms of the sheer volume of evidence for metalworking activity. The well over 1,000 mould fragments are a problematic representation of activity, as they are highly fragmented and can not be easily read as indicating the number of moulds they formerly constituted; likewise, the *c.* 40–50 individual moulds that have been reconstructed are clearly an underrepresentation of the former corpus, making Rathgall exceed by far the size of assemblages that have been reported from other Bronze Age sites in Britain and Ireland, most of which have not produced more than fragments of up to twenty moulds (Webley *et al.* 2020, 111). Ó Faoláin (2004, 31ff) examined sixteen Irish sites with evidence for bronze-casting in the form of clay moulds. Only four yielded more than 100 fragments. Two of these, however, Lough Gur, Co. Limerick (Ó Ríordáin 1954, 400), and Dalkey Island, Co. Dublin (Liversage 1967–8, 89–91, figs 20 and 21), yielded less than 200 pieces, while the third, at Dún Aonghasa, produced 460 fragments (O'Carroll 2012a, 28). Small numbers of sites containing mould fragments have come to light in recent years—at Corrstown, Co. Antrim (Ginn and Rathbone 2011), Ballylegan, Co. Tipperary (Becker 2009, 336–8), Johnstown South, Co. Wicklow (Fitzpatrick 1998; n.d.; Ó Faoláin, n.d.), and Harristown Big, Co. Wexford (Tierney and Johnston 2009), among others—but Rathgall still stands out in several respects.

Rathgall is one of the earliest sites in Ireland to produce evidence for the use of clay moulds. Outside Rathgall, evidence for the earliest use of clay moulds is represented by the rope moulding on an axe and a hammerhead from the eponymous Bishopsland hoard in County Kildare (Eogan 1983, nos 2, 3, 16; Ó Faoláin 2004, 9). Clay moulds from Lough Gur, Co. Limerick (sites D and F, and possibly also site K and the Lough Gur wedge tomb; Ó Ríordáin and Ó h-Iceadha 1955; Ó Ríordáin 1954), were found that are likely to be similarly early. Among these and other associated fragments at Site F are the remains of spearheads and Group 4 rapiers with notched butts (Burgess and Gerloff 1981), which may date from between *c.* 1300 and *c.* 1000 BC.

Similarly dated metalworking may be represented at Harristown Big, Co. Wexford, where possibly three crucibles were represented and where a radiocarbon date placed activity roughly into the twelfth to tenth centuries BC but was not associated directly with the crucibles. Hearths with evidence for episodes of burning were also recorded at the site and may have been linked to the use of the separately found crucible fragments (Tierney and Johnston 2009). Possible evidence for polypod crucibles was found at Harristown Big and Johnstown South, similar to finds from Dainton, Devon (Needham 1980), and from a second important Wilburton period metalworking site at Holborough Quarry (Peter Clarke, pers. comm.). Harristown and Johnstown South may thus add to the Roscommon metalworking phase in Ireland if these crucibles could indeed be shown to be specific to this chronological horizon.

This, of course, raises the issue of what system of metal production was in place at Rathgall. A central question, discussed in previous research with regard to metalworking and its organisation, is whether metalworking was a widely accessible skill set or was left in the hands of specialised craftsmen, as suggested above (p. 503) by Raftery. That bronze-working was a specialist activity is probably indicated by the skill implied by the moulds and our understanding of the complexities of metalworking (cf. Ó Faoláin 2004, 107; Rowlands 1976, 116). Part- or full-time activity and both mobile and sedentary models have been put forward. Childe's (1930) model of the itinerant smith has fallen out of favour, given the regional characteristics of object forms and the lack of ethnographic analogies (Rowlands 1976; Ó Faoláin 2004, 107). While presenting a welcome degree of variety, which has the potential to reflect reality more than rigid models, Howard's (1983) model of clay mould assemblages representing sedentary smiths in contrast to mobile smiths using stone moulds, each producing different sets of object forms, does not map onto the Irish record. Especially at Rathgall, where all categories of artefact imaginable are represented (weapons, axes, ornaments, tools)—and, indeed, at many of its contemporary Irish sites—multiple categories of objects were being cast (Ó Faoláin 2004, table 3.7). A sedentary model for the metalworkers at Rathgall is preferred here also, however, following Ó Faoláin in his argument for Irish Late Bronze Age metalworking in general, based on the notable lack of Late Bronze Age stone and bronze moulds, which can be contrasted with their relative frequency in, for example, Britain.

The possible evidence for other craft activities going hand in hand at Rathgall (e.g. shale-working, pottery production, and the less likely glass- and gold-working) further suggests that, not unlike what is implied at Iron Age Tara, other craft activities were also being conducted by the same specialists. Part of the range of their skill set seems to have been the control of funerary activities, as argued above, as specialists in charge of a variety of transformative processes. Envisaging metalworkers as also instrumental in other activities, such as cremation burial, would further reinforce the likelihood that they were part of a settled community.

Whether they were full-time or part-time is impossible to discern on the basis of the given evidence. Models that see the sustaining of full-time specialists assume a degree of societal prosperity and centralisation to provide the appropriate setting for the maintenance of full-time smiths and, in turn, the achieving of high levels of skill in conjunction with patronage from an élite group (Ó Faoláin 2004, 108–9). Such conditions may be indicated for Bronze Age Rathgall by the evidence for a high density of settlement and agricultural activity in the surrounding landscape. If, as suggested above, Rathgall and Knockeen have to be understood as a paired settlement, such an élite could be envisaged to have been located here, although both the concept of full-time metalworkers and the necessity of an élite being the required context for these may be anachronistic for the society represented at Rathgall.

The interpretation of hillforts and related enclosed sites, such as ringworks or hengiform enclosures in particular, is a divisive topic. Some see them as the apex of a settlement hierarchy, representing the residences of the élite, with storage of material wealth and specialised craftworking (e.g. O'Brien 2017a, 401; O'Brien 2017c, 442; Grogan 2005b; 2005c, 401) at a time when society was becoming increasingly complex, with social tensions and growing militarism (O'Brien 2017a, 414). O'Brien (*ibid.*, 446) proposes a ranked society of chiefdoms in which a warlord's power was based on control of the distribution of exotic goods (e.g. O'Brien 2017b, 440; O'Brien 2017c, 442–3; O'Driscoll 2017b, 421; 2016, 440), as reflected in the visibility of a 'warrior culture' in Atlantic Europe. He sees hillforts as a central component of competitive and militarised societies, where territories were controlled by those in strategically located hillforts, which may have functioned as nodes in increasingly centralised landscapes (e.g. O'Driscoll 2016, 421). An increased centralisation alongside the expansion of supra-regional networks is also envisaged by Ginn (2016, 215). Such models contrast with those that emphasise kinship and kin work as major factors in the formation of society. While the latter envisage degrees of specialisation that contributed to the constitution of different categories of kinship and social roles, they do not envisage an élite level of authority in control (Johnston 2021, 355). Relational frameworks such as Johnston's or Brück's see the traditional chiefdom model as conceptually problematic in its application to the Bronze Age (e.g. Brück 2019, 4–5; Brück and Fontijn 2013), and therefore hillforts and other special enclosures are not regarded as élite residences but as special places, deliberately marked off as distinct from the lived-in landscape (Johnston 2021, 229). Conceptualising hillforts and related sites as gathering places for dispersed communities and as an important component of identity creation (Brück 2019, 157), possibly marking out and monumentalising natural places of long-standing importance, opens up other ways of thinking about the role of sites such as Rathgall within contemporary Late Bronze Age Ireland.

Indeed, given our lack of understanding of the contemporary landscape, it is difficult to judge what relationship the site may have had—on its own or in tandem with Knockeen—to its surrounding landscape. To place Rathgall at the top of a hierarchical model of settlement and society appears problematic in view of the conceptual issues that are inherent in the projection of such chiefdom models, which assume centralised, stratified societies, onto Bronze Age society (e.g. Brück and Fontijn 2013). It is also problematic in that we have indications that Rathgall, or the Rathgall/Knockeen complex, was situated in a likely very densely settled landscape (see above) with further hilltop enclosures, including a possible multivallate hillfort at nearby Tullow, Co. Carlow. If these are contemporary—and the pollen and charcoal macro-records certainly imply a densely settled landscape—it would be difficult to picture competitive chiefdoms operating at such density. Instead, groups operating cooperatively, with sites such as Rathgall fulfilling a particular function for the wider community, may have to be envisaged.

Moreover, the great volume of metalworking evidence and the intensity of burial activity raise the question of whether the site may have served a wider landscape. Rathgall sits alongside a number of small settlement sites in Ireland that have produced smaller quantities of metalworking evidence. Rather than any qualitative technological difference between the assemblages, or even between the categories of objects, it seems to be the high level of activity and the range of forms that distinguish Rathgall, suggesting that the workshops of the smaller sites may have catered only for the needs of the immediate community while Rathgall was possibly a funerary and metallurgical centre for the wider community.

The volume of metalworking evidence also raises the question of whether objects were produced for consumption only in the immediate community or whether they were traded.

In a wider European context, Rathgall fits into a group of

sites that have produced evidence for metalworking of high intensity. Examples include Hauterive-Champréveyres (Rychner-Faraggi 1993) and the recently excavated site of Aubervilliers in France (Melin 2016), Frattesina in Italy and, in a league of its own, the hillfort of Le Fort-Harrouard at Sorel-Moussel (Eure-et-Loir) in northern France (Mohen and Bailloud 1987; Mohen *et al.* 1989; Mohen and Walter 1998), which Raftery considered a highly relevant comparison. This and the twelfth–ninth-century BC site of Frattesina in the Po Valley (e.g. Bietti Sestieri *et al.* 2015), which has been discussed as the possible origin of the glass beads of LMHK glass (see p. 219), are considered centres of production and redistribution, drawing in raw materials and transforming them into products for export (see Pearce *et al.* 2020, 67, for an overview of the literature). At Frattesina were found not only about 100 moulds (Le Fèvre-Lehöerff 1994) but also founders' hoards and evidence for the working of amber, ivory, ostrich shell, antler and, of course, glass. The best parallel for the range of artefacts produced at Rathgall, however, may be Aubervilliers, with a similar extensive range of objects, high levels of metalworking activity and the presence of LMHK glass.

While the relationship of Rathgall to these sites in the twelfth–tenth-century horizon—and the differences between them—requires further investigation, it shares with them not only evidence for high-intensity metalworking but also a high degree of connectivity with the outside world in the earliest part of the Late Bronze Age, contributing to the emerging picture of this as a phase of prosperity before the obvious peak of hoard deposition in the Dowris phase Bronze Age.

6.7 EARLY IRON AGE RATHGALL

The next phase of activity in the latest stage of the Bronze Age—or, indeed, the Earliest Iron Age (Chapter 4, section 4.4.)—is characterised by the creation of a ditched enclosure with a large roundhouse structure at its centre dating from possibly the eighth century BC or thereafter during the Hallstatt plateau. While the earlier Late Bronze Age phase is characterised by metalworking and funerary activity, the next phase of use seems to be focused on fundamentally different activities and would appear to have been accompanied also by the cessation of burial activity on this very location.

The 15m structure or house at Rathgall is one of the central features of the site and was discussed by Raftery in previous publications (e.g. Raftery 1970a; 1971) in terms of both the structural interpretation and its role within the Bronze Age horizon at the site. Raftery interpreted the structure as belonging to a different phase from Pit 119, which is located within its footprint; nevertheless, he saw the house, or enclosure, as belonging to the Bronze Age phase, as seemingly indicated by the association of Bronze Age pottery sherds within the footing trench (Chapter 4, section 4.2).

It now appears likely that the 15m structure is contemporary with the enclosing Ring-ditch 1 (section 4.3). This re-phasing and dating of Ring-ditch 1 to the latest part of the Bronze Age or Early Iron Age represents one of the most significant changes in the interpretation of the site, contrasting with Raftery's preferred model, as set out in Chapter 4, section 4.1. In particular, the position of Pit 119 central to Ring-ditch 1 had tied these two features together, and thus the dating of the ring-ditch to the earlier part of the Late Bronze Age. The reinterpretation of the ring-ditch as being focused on the 15m structure sees the central position of Pit 119 as a red herring that is negated by a number of other pieces of evidence for the dating of Ring-ditch 1. The radiocarbon dates obtained on a probable post of the structure, as well as stratigraphic indicators provided by the enclosing Ring-ditch 1, place both features into the period 800–550 cal. BC. Both may date from any point in time during the Hallstatt plateau, and it is only the tentative evidence provided by the large portions of coarseware pottery in Ring-ditch 1 that would suggest an earlier date within this span. Raftery had compared the structure in terms of its large size and the evidence for plank walling to the Navan 40m Structure and hence had drawn attention to Iron Age parallels. What he considered just an analogy at the time takes on now, after the revision of the dating of this structure, a different significance. The construction method and the morphological details of the 15m structure find very close parallels in the corpus of Irish Iron Age structures.

The group consists of slot-trench- or footing trench-built structures with double walling. In all cases, large post-holes flank the entrances on either side of the entrance gap. These large houses are all more than 10m in diameter; not only do they share their construction method and overall design but also they consistently date from the Iron Age, between 800 BC and the centuries around the turn of the millennium. This seems to further support the independently derived date for the Rathgall building and requires a consideration of the group as a whole (Fig. 6.5) (see also Becker 2019).

The earliest example of such a structure is Building A at

Raffin, Co. Meath, which produced a radiocarbon date of 810–590 cal. BC (UB-3712; 2565±22 BP; 95% confidence; Newman 1995a, 62; pers. comm.) on a carbonised timber post from the foundation trench. This building, with a diameter of 12.5m, is slightly smaller than the Rathgall example but is also of slot-trench construction, with posts or planks forming the outer wall (Newman 1995a, 61–2). There is, however, a complete inner footing ring, which is consistently 70cm distant from the outer ring from midpoint to midpoint. The trenches are 20–30cm wide and their depths vary from 30cm to 50cm (*ibid.*). As at Rathgall, frequently flat bracing or packing stones occur at different points, and there is a possible indication that the posts were placed at 20cm intervals—perhaps suggesting wattling rather than plank walling (*ibid.*). In addition to the charred posts, the oxidisation of the ground indicates the burning of the building (*ibid.*). The former presence of an inner circle of post-holes at Rathgall is clearly evident in the initial southern extent of the building, and the continuation of this for most of the circumference of the structure is suggested in Fig. 6.5. It is, however, less clear-cut: while post-holes were positioned in relatively appropriate positions in relation to the wall slot, their selection for this drawing from a larger spread of features throughout the interior of the structure has to be noted. Regardless, the constructional and dimensional similarity of the two structures is striking. In addition to the footing trench and the double-ring construction (complete or otherwise), clear comparisons can be seen in the joining of the two rings at the entrance with a short stretch of foundation trench, housing two larger posts flanking the entrance on either side in some.

Similar ground-plans with double walling are recorded at Sites A and B at Navan Fort and Dún Ailinne. Similar foundation trench constructions have, in the past, been interpreted at Navan Fort as single-walled buildings. The triple foundation trenches were interpreted as a complex series of wall replacements, and at Dún Ailinne as supports for viewing platforms. The building from Navan Site A belongs to the undated Phase B of that site. It consists of two concentric ring-slots with diameters of between 12m and 16m (Waterman 1997, 133). The entrance was also flanked by two sets of post-holes. There is, however, no evidence for a connecting slot-trench between both rings. This is not a constructional difference but represents merely the digging of two separate post-holes rather than a trench to house both entrance posts. These slot-trenches were interpreted by Waterman as a double-ring building, which may be of early medieval date and possibly contemporary with the surrounding ring-ditch (*ibid.*, 140). While no dating evidence is available to clarify whether this structure was of Iron Age or early medieval date, Lynn (*ibid.*, 142–4) argued that parallels for similar plans were not to be found in the medieval corpus, suggesting a prehistoric date. He also drew attention to the 15m house at Rathgall but considered the slot-trenches A1–A2–A3 at Navan Site A to be a better parallel (*ibid.*, 143). The Site A trenches are also concentric and have a similarly large size (12m and 16m). Lynn thus essentially argued that the footprint at Site A did not represent a double-walled house but rather reflected a sequence of wall construction. He suggested that a missing third bedding trench would make it essentially the same as Site A slot-trenches A1–3, which he interpreted, like all the multiple pre-mound multi-slot-trench structures, as sequences of wall replacements of single-walled buildings (*ibid.*, 150). While the sequence of construction of the individual trenches appears correct, it is difficult to concur with the interpretation as sequential post replacement. While the outer ring, for example, of the slot-trench Structure E clearly cuts the middle bedding trench of Structure E, it is not clear why the two outer slot-trenches (E2 and E3) cannot be contemporary. Rather, it appears that double-walled structures are represented here which saw replacement of either their inner or outer walls. The connective trenches between both sets of doorposts, which Lynn (*ibid.*, 156) suggests as representing traces of the *in situ* moving of the door-frame, seem more likely to represent slot-trenches connecting contemporary posts.

The comparable structures at Dún Ailinne were contemporary, as they consisted of two unambiguously conjoined footing trenches (Wailes 2007, 13–15 and fig. 2.12). Charred planking or posts were also located in these and appear to have been rather substantial in size (Johnston and Wailes 2007, pl. 2.6). In all these cases it appears very possible, considering the ground-plans, to argue that double-walled structures, comparable to those at Raffin and Rathgall, are represented (see also Becker 2019).

Very contrasting reconstructions have been suggested for these sites, including roofed roundhouses (in the case of the Navan Site B structures), enclosures (Rathgall) or an open-air seating platform (Dún Ailinne). Owing to the presence of hearths at the centre of the smaller parts of the figure-of-eight structures at Navan they were considered roofed, though the construction and the issue of roof supports remained unclear. While some considered the equivalent

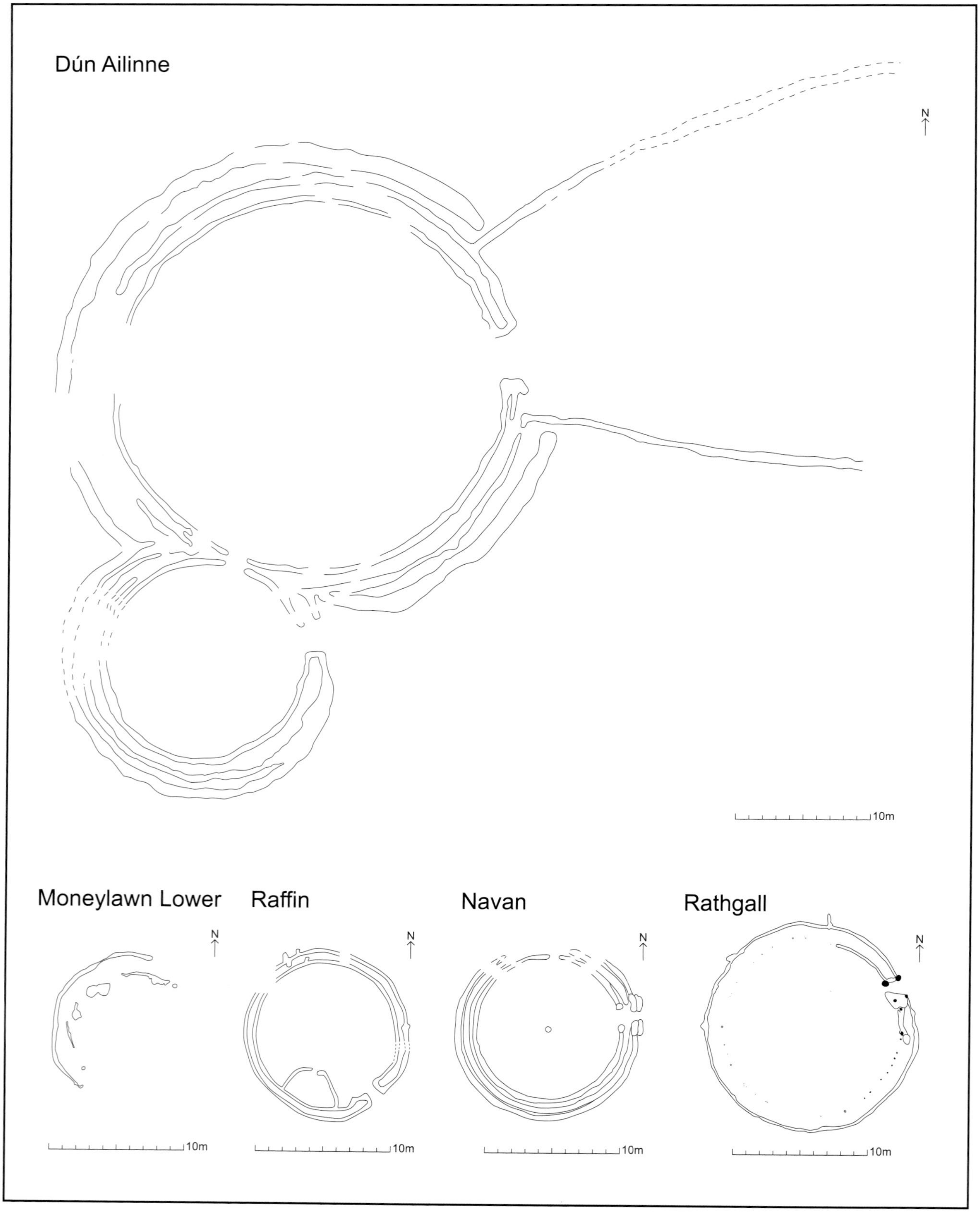

Fig. 6.5—Comparative forms of double-slot-trench round buildings from Ireland.

part of the Dún Ailinne figure-of-eight structure, with its diameter of 21m, to have been roofed (cf. Harding 2009, 237), the excavator reconstructed it as an open-air arena-like structure (Wailes 2007, 16, fig. 2.13).

Raftery (1971, 296; 1976, 341) originally considered that the internal arrangement of post-holes within the 15m structure at Rathgall provided roof support for this rather large building. In his reconsiderations of this issue (archival notes) he again explored the possibility that the 15m structure was roofed and came to a more negative conclusion than in his previous publications. Indeed, the internal post-holes at Rathgall do not form an arrangement that can be interpreted as roof supports. Raftery speculated that the external clustering of post-holes and pits might be related to the 15m structure but there is no identifiable arrangement. While truncation may account for the lack of many features at Rathgall and on other sites, the evidence from Navan, with central hearths in each of the structures, militates against central posts, and the good survival of stratigraphy led Lynn (Waterman 1997, 150) to disregard even the possibility of pads that may have supported posts. A single post that was initially considered to be a possible central roof support at Raffin (Newman 1993, 23), is now considered part of a preceding, Neolithic, post circle (Newman, pers. comm.). Raftery (archival notes) pointed to the (as he thought) flimsy nature of the bedding trench at Rathgall and the posts it contained, suggesting that it may not have supported a large roof, spanning the entire 15m. The post-holes that form the entrance are, however, of considerable size and suggest a substantial construction; indeed, the size of the bedding trench and posts is also relatively large. Apart from a wider zone near the entrance, the measurements of the bedding trench at Rathgall, with a width of about 20cm and a depth of 20–25cm and occasionally 30cm, and factoring in its truncated state upon excavation, suggest the use of supports of significant size. Raftery describes some of these as remaining *in situ* in the form of burnt 'D'-shapes, suggesting split or halved posts rather than flat planks. The consistency across the corpus of structures in the lack of evidence for internal supports and the evidence from the houses at Navan suggest that we underestimate the capacity of such structures to carry a roof which spanned quite significant diameters. The roofing of the smaller parts of the annexes at Navan Site B has never been in doubt, probably owing to the presence of hearths. In their previous reconstruction as single-walled buildings, and even more so as double-walled structures, as suggested here, the roofs would have spanned widths of between 10m and 14m (see also Becker 2019).

The large size of these structures does indeed set them apart from both Bronze Age and Iron Age roundhouses of any construction type. Bronze Age roundhouses in Ireland are documented with diameters of about 5–9m, with four examples over 10m (Doody 2008, 88). Upper sizes listed by Ginn (2016) range around 10m x 11m or 13m x 12m (see Fig. 6.5), with reconstructions of buildings without an inner post ring appearing feasible (Pope 2003, 10; Romankiewicz 2011). The northern British Iron Age ring-groove houses (Harding 2009, 71–6) are closely comparable; there, however, the ring-groove seems to retain the wattle or other continuous wall, whereas the weight-bearing timbers were contained in an inner circle of individual post-holes (*ibid.*, 73). A structure with two bedding trenches or slot-grooves from Scotstarvit, Fife, had a further, internal ring of weight-bearing timbers supporting the 18m-diameter structure (Bersu 1948; Harding 2009, 71–2). There are also examples of rather large structures, such as the ring-ditch house with surrounding ring-groove from High Knowes A, Alnham, but there was also an internal circle of quite substantial post-holes supporting the roof (Jobey and Tait 1966).

The exact character of the walling that was set in these Irish footing trenches is unclear. Planks or split posts (Rathgall) and posts (at Dún Ailinne) have been suggested, while at Raffin there is tentative evidence for spaced posts in the outer trench. The innermost circles of the structures at Navan also held spaced posts, similar to the internal circle at Rathgall.

A comparable form of building, with a doubled wall and no internal supports, may be represented by the stone brochs of the Atlantic Iron Age. Like the Irish houses under discussion, these can be of significant size, with examples among Orkney sites measuring well over 10m (internal diameters ranging from 7m to nearly 14m, and external diameters from 12m to 23m; Armit 2004, 57). It is argued (*ibid.*) that the double wall supported the roof, with the rafters resting on the internal wall and against the outer wall, and possibly a similar construction could be envisaged for the Irish structures. The solid stone walling of the brochs provided a different type of support from the double plank walling on the Irish sites. Perhaps the space between the closely set walls served to contain turf sods, which have in other contexts been argued to form the walls of prehistoric houses in Ireland (Becker 2019) as well as in Britain, where facing with stone slabs has, for example, been suggested in order to explain the thin walls of some Orkney wheelhouses (Harding 2009, 50–1).

Recent research has indicated that the load-bearing capacity of single-ring structures has indeed been vastly underestimated, influenced by the southern examples of Wessex houses with multiple post-rings of support. In the north of England and Scotland a number of sites show very limited internal supports (e.g. Broxmouth; Armit and McKenzie 2013), and even for the south it has been suggested that double post-rings were not necessarily needed to support the roofs of larger houses but probably provided for upper floor space (Pope 2007, 220). A number of houses at Broxmouth have either no internal supports or two rather closely spaced slot-trench wall footings (Armit and McKenzie 2013). As discussed elsewhere, the basic construction of the prehistoric roundhouse gets its stability from the tension created by the round beam inside the conical roof. It would not even require earthfast foundations to stand on but could merely rest on its cylinder-shaped base. Harding (2009, 56) suggested that making posts earthfast was part of the construction process in order to provide stability to the structure. The diameter limits within which this principle can work are not quite clear. The diameter of some of the larger Wessex roundhouses with two wall rings, one of which was so insubstantial that it cannot be considered load-bearing, suggests, however, that it is possible to roof what are in essence single-ring buildings well beyond 10m in diameter (e.g. with a diameter of about 11m at Crickley Hill, or over 12m in the main enclosure at Longbridge Deverill Cow Down).

The significant size of the 15m structure at Rathgall and its substantial entrance posts suggest a building of impressive proportions. Its position within a ditched enclosure, on a site that must have held great significance for the wider community owing to its association with burial ritual as well as metalworking, may not be coincidental but intended to draw on this very association. Every instance of soil-moving would have produced evidence for its past, especially in the form of mould and pottery fragments. To literally position oneself among and within the remains of the past would have made a strong statement about what may have represented a new social order (Becker 2019).

In its association with metalworking and possibly feasting evidence in the form of the vast amounts of pottery the enclosure resembles ringwork sites as found in south-eastern Britain and Wales (cf. Parker Pearson *et al.* 2018; Bradley 2007, 206–12; Brück 2007). These sites are characterised by an internally ditched enclosure that can be between 40m and 120m in diameter (Manby 2007, 405–17; Parker Pearson *et al.* 2018, 137) and can contain, like that at Thwing, a large central roundhouse. The ringworks at Mucking and Springfield Lyons are also notable for having produced Late Bronze Age mould assemblages, as well as, in the case of Mucking, a hair-ring like those found at Rathgall (Bond 1988).

Furthermore, while evidently founded in some cases in the Late Bronze Age, some of these sites have produced evidence for later phases of activity that places their use, especially that connected with metallurgy and craftworking and associated midden-like debris, in around the eighth century BC (Needham 2007, 48–9). For example, Springfield Lyons was occupied *c.* 1210–980 cal. BC and abandoned *c.* 840–690 cal. BC (both at 95.4% probability; Brown and Medlycott 2013, 147). While such comparisons may at first sight tie Rathgall into this broader group of monuments (cf. Bradley 2007, 217), differences also exist, with the bulk of the metalworking evidence pre-dating the enclosure phase and likely an internal bank having accompanied Ring-ditch 1, as proposed on pp 452–6.

If the building—which, with its 15m external diameter, is a substantial structure—was used as a habitation space, it would clearly have functioned in a different way than the smaller roundhouses generally observed in the Irish Late Bronze Age record. While in some respects, including the choice of location and the possible continued use of coarseware pottery, standing in a strong Bronze Age tradition, the emergence of large roundhouses here and at other sites suggests a shift in the underlying societal structure (cf. Becker 2019). This may go hand in hand with a decline in activity that is also observable in the general archaeological record from about 1000–900 BC, leading into the 'collapse' that appears to follow from about 700 cal. BC (Armit *et al.* 2013; 2014; based on aggregated ^{14}C-dated sites). The contraction of perhaps more dispersed settlement patterns to such sites may have been part of these changes. It is striking that, at least within the excavated areas at Rathgall, as also observed in the national record, there are few grounds for belief that it was a continuous activity throughout the Hallstatt plateau. However, while settlement activity elsewhere re-emerges in the second half of the first millennium BC, at Rathgall there is so far a conspicuous absence of evidence for activity until the first centuries AD. The possibility of a strong increase in the growing of Cerealia at the beginning of the second half of the first millennium

BC (see Chapter 3, section 3.18) suggests that we are still missing the relevant evidence. Far too little is known as yet about the areas of Rathgall outside the excavation cuttings, and further clarification in particular of the presence of monuments associated with the barrow cemetery at Knockloe may provide missing evidence.

6.8 LATER IRON AGE RATHGALL

'We cannot, of course, be certain that the wearer of this belt was one of the iron-smiths at Rathgall, or was related to them. Or, indeed, he could have been a customer. The radiocarbon dates, at any rate, are entirely in keeping with the archaeological dating of the bronzes, leaving little room to doubt the probability that the metalwork and the smelting were related. Furthermore, dating in the second or third century AD seems clear.

There was nothing else found on the site which could be dated to the same period as the bronzes and the iron-smelting. It is thus unclear to what extent these Iron Age remains represent an occupation of any permanence. There are no structures which might be contemporary with this phase of activity, and the presence of coarse pottery (and other Bronze Age items) in so many of the pits dotting the site strongly suggests that most, if not, indeed, all, belong to the Bronze Age horizon long pre-dating the iron-working.

The likelihood thus seems to be that the site in the second or third century AD was not a secular settlement but was rather a small, isolated forge which was occupied for a brief period before the smith and his assistants moved on' (Raftery, publication draft).

Raftery discusses here the strongest evidence for activity that we can securely assign to the first few centuries AD, after what appears to be a possible hiatus of perhaps a few hundred years following the construction of the 15m structure and the enclosing ring-ditch, though the usual caveats regarding archaeological visibility and survival should be applied here, too.

The iron-smithing hearth, which also produced evidence for bronze-casting in the form of some crucible fragments (Chapter 3, section 3.10), as well as the *Kerbschnitt*-decorated strap-tag and the two mounts or buttons (section 3.6), may be added to the tubular glass beads in the assemblage as evidence for a range of late Iron Age activities. The belt strap, discussed by Raftery in this volume and in one of his earliest publications on Rathgall (Raftery 1970b), presents a mixture of Roman form and La Tène ornamentation that Raftery identified as provincial Roman in character. In strong contrast to the kinds of scenarios that Bateson (1973) proposed for the origin of 'Roman' material in this country, he considered the possibility that it might have been manufactured in Ireland, pointing to a similarly decorated mount from Freestone Hill. Indeed, Raftery proposed that it represented, in context, the fusion of foreign and local ideas and the 'emergence of a distinct cultural complex' spanning the period between the earliest phase of the Iron Age in this country and its development into the new and complicated forms of the Early Christian centuries (*ibid.*, 211). While the rigid nature and clearly provincial Roman character of the decoration of the mount jars significantly with the style of other La Tène metalwork of the first two centuries AD, such as the Petrie Crown or late ring-headed pins (Newman 1995b), complexity and variation in styles on the margins and outside the Roman Empire are to be expected (Davis and Gwilt 2008).

But what brought the person wearing the belt to Rathgall? Orpen (1913) suggested that Rathgall was possibly the *Dunum* that Ptolemy located in what may be south Wicklow. Raftery was not alone in being sceptical about this; indeed, the low levels of activity indicated by the available evidence—no matter how filtered by taphonomic processes—do not suggest that Rathgall was a significant centre at this time.

'It may be entirely coincidental that iron-working took place on the same site which a millennium earlier was a significant centre of bronze-working. It could be speculated, however, that Rathgall had been imbued with a special status as a metalworking place, appropriate for the mysteries of a sacred skill and preserving a status which persisted over the centuries. Such fantasy, however, regrettably widespread in so much of the modern archaeological literature, should not be given too much weight' (Raftery, draft text).

6.9 RING-DITCH, HILLFORT AND CASHEL—ENCLOSING RATHGALL

'It was hoped to shed light on the nature of a hillfort: was it a settlement, a place of refuge, a ritual enclosure or even an enclosure for animals, all of which had by then been postulated, at various times, in hillfort studies abroad? What could be learned about the material culture of those who used the site? What was its date and to what extent, if at all, could the hillfort

be recognised as an index of foreign intrusion?' (Raftery, this volume, Chapter 1, section 1.1).

The story of Rathgall is also the story of Irish hillfort research. Rathgall was selected as the target of a campaign that sought to excavate and understand an Iron Age defensive hilltop enclosure, but it soon became clear that the main phases of activity on this and other sites dated from the Late Bronze Age. This change in interpretation was in the main due to advances in the understanding of the dating of coarseware pottery (see section 1.1). The paradigm of hillforts dating from the Iron Age changed quickly over the next couple of decades to one that sees them as of Late Bronze Age construction. The significant advance in archaeological sciences in the form of radiocarbon dating helped to confirm this interpretation but, ironically, in the case of Rathgall (and other sites) also reintroduced the Iron Age—and, indeed, the medieval period—into the history of the site as a phase of significant activity and modification. Most importantly, as with any advance in archaeological method, the increase in precision and detail, particularly provided by refinement of radiocarbon dating and analysis, started to reveal a much more complex and complicated scenario. The excavation of Irish hilltop sites has revealed a great range of forms and functions, to which Rathgall adds an important variant, complementing and further complicating the story of Irish hilltop enclosures.

Rathgall occupies a strategically advantageous position, rising above the surrounding landscape. As outlined by Raftery (Chapter 1, section 1.2), the gentle rise of the ridge on which the site is located provides far-reaching views, but access is not difficult. In fact, its accessibility was, as Raftery also outlines, a reason for the selection of the site for excavation. The slightly elevated position creates the impression not so much of a site that provides protection and dominates but rather of one that is a focal point for, and embedded in, its surrounding landscape. The classification of the site as a hillfort is based on the substantial ramparts that surround it. The multivallation of this Class II hillfort, in its current form, was at least significantly augmented in the medieval period and can be assumed to have had prehistoric predecessors. The first phase of Rampart 2 and the enclosure between Ramparts 3 and 4 that was mapped in the topographical and geophysical surveys are likely contenders for an earlier enclosure, but not necessarily of Bronze Age date. Raftery considered that the ephemeral nature of this earlier enclosure suggested a Neolithic date. The initial phase of Rampart 2 rests on a horizon that also produced later Bronze Age artefacts, as well as radiocarbon dates on charcoal from the same period. Burial and metalworking activity on the summit as well as in the outside Z cutting is not only contemporaneous but also similar in character. A contemporary date for the ramparts, cutting through this overall zone of Bronze Age activity, seems unlikely; on the other hand, extramural activity may complement the focus of the site on the top of the hill.

The initial phase of the construction of Rampart 2 may thus be of Late Bronze Age date, post-dating a phase of distribution of Late Bronze Age material culture such as moulds and pottery and a single glass bead (9400) outside the rampart in the X cuttings. Rampart 2 may, however, equally date from the Iron Age or, indeed, the early medieval period. The fact that the bank appears to immediately overlie Bronze Age features but no notable remains of later periods is not necessarily problematic, as any such may have been truncated by the construction of the rampart.

It was during the medieval phase that the enclosing aspects of the site were at least significantly elaborated (if not, indeed, created), so that, in essence, the *hillfort* comprised of Ramparts 1–3 and possibly 4 is of medieval date. Medieval reuse or reoccupation of pre-existing hilltop monuments can frequently be observed on prehistoric sites, including hilltop enclosures at Mooghaun, Co. Clare, Rahally, Co. Galway, and Clogher, Co. Tyrone—often, as at Rathgall, in the form of small cashels (see Chapter 7). Recognising the role that their advantageous position in the landscape would have played in these choices, the medieval use of these sites also, however, reflects a deliberate engagement with the known or perceived history of the location (see also section 6.1). In addition to the medieval creation or elaboration of an earlier monument, other aspects of the medieval use of the site demonstrate awareness of the earlier phases.

The south-western bulge of the line of Rampart 4, which was inexplicable until recently, appears to have been designed to include a circular structure recorded in the geophysical survey. A later prehistoric date for this circular structure may be postulated, however; if the ramparts are of medieval date, the integration of a pre-existing monument into their course appears possible. The integration of older, pre-existing monuments in a very similar manner can be observed on medieval sites such as Parknahown 2, Co. Laois (T. O'Neill 2009), where a small annexe to a Late Iron Age or early medieval ringfort was created to enclose an Early Iron Age ring-ditch or barrow, while at Cappydonnell Big 1,

Co. Westmeath, a subrectangular medieval ditch encloses a palimpsest of prehistoric burials, including a later prehistoric ring-ditch (Coughlan 2010).

The almost exact positioning of Rampart 1 on top of Ring-ditch 1 may also indicate deliberate continuity. It may suggest awareness of pre-existing monuments and a desire to connect with the history of this place, as well as the possibility that the footprint of the ring-ditch was still visible. The placement of the iron-working hearth on the ring-ditch within the first few centuries AD may also not be entirely fortuitous.

The ramparts are of substantial size, reflecting a significant investment in labour, albeit the unlikelihood of their defensive nature has to be considered. Some of the entrance gaps along their length were stone-lined, providing access to the site at various points. These entrance linings appear contemporary with the internal stone façade of Rampart 2. This façade, however, was only added to the pre-existing rampart on its *inside*, underlining (at least for this phase) that the rampart was not about external display but about the creation and framing of space *within* the enclosure. It is not clear whether the entrance gaps were already part of the initial phase of the rampart-building. It is striking, however, that Rampart 3 has corresponding entrance gaps, suggesting the contemporary alteration, if not creation, of both Ramparts 2 and 3.

Unlike in Britain and continental Europe, in Ireland evidence such as coarseware pottery, moulds and radiocarbon dates from Freestone Hill and Rathgall (see also Raftery in Chapter 1) contradicted the assumption that hillfort construction dated from the Iron Age. Later campaigns at Dún Aonghasa, Mooghaun and Haughey's Fort seemed to confirm this new paradigm that Irish hillforts are primarily of Bronze Age construction. Recent excavations of a number of sites, including Rathnagree, not far from Rathgall in County Wicklow, indicate the emergence of hillfort enclosure in the Middle Bronze Age from the fourteenth century BC (O'Brien and O'Driscoll 2017, 340). A burnt timber rampart at the hillfort at Clashanimud, Co. Cork, suggests a date in the twelfth or eleventh century BC for the enclosing of the site (O'Brien 2016, 5). Haughey's Fort also belongs to the earlier part of the Late Bronze Age, between 1200 and 1000 BC (Mallory 1991a; 1991b; 1995, 85).

It is striking that at several sites excavated by O'Brien and O'Driscoll the early Late Bronze Age enclosures consisted of ditches and banks with palisades, which in a later phase were replaced by a stone-faced bank at Rathnagree, Co. Wicklow (O'Brien 2016, 21). The banks and ditches excavated at Rathgall have not produced evidence for a palisade or stone facing, except for the innermost Rampart 2, with its various stone-faced entrances of presumably medieval date.

NOTES

1 While the number of objects that can be ascribed to the Roscommon complex is still small today, two more finds of contemporary date are now known, the hoards from Tamlaght, Co. Antrim (Ó Néill and McDonald 2009), and no provenance, Co. Offaly (Harbison 2004).

2 Parallels between some of the Roscommon material and the contemporary Wallington complex in northern Britain have been suggested elsewhere (e.g. Burgess 1968a, 36).

3 A number of other pits on the site are also filled with stones (e.g. nos 95, 97, 111, 117, 144), but neither their function nor their date is clear and, as stone-filled Pit 96 demonstrates, they could also be of later, possibly medieval date.

4 A white film was found deposited on *Ulmus* (elm) and *Fraxinus* (ash) samples derived from the basketry layer. There is a small possibility that this may be due to post-excavation treatment to stabilise the material, but this appears unlikely. The examination of the micromorphology (SEM) suggested a mineral origin but attempts to examine the microchemistry (RAMAN) did not produce any results (Schotsmans *et al.* 2019).

5 A number of pits with black lining could be identified on the basis of their sections or their mention as having had black lining in Raftery's text—which, however, sometimes contradicts the evidence from the section drawings. This may have to do with the renumbering of pits that occurred in the post-excavation process.

6 Ballybannon: O'Connell 2009; Ballyburn Lwr and Ballyhade E2566: Hackett 2009; Ballyhade E2573: O'Connell and Hegarty 2009; Busherstown E2580: O'Neill 2009; Gorteen 05E1319: Hackett 2007; Johnstown E2586: Breen and Clark 2009; Johnstown E3041: Elder and Ginn 2009a; Johnstown E3052: Elder and Ginn 2009b; Rathcrogue/Moyle Big E2596: Doyle 2009a; Rathcrogue E2591: Doyle 2009c; Tinryland E2590: Doyle 2009b; Kilcarrig 07E0962: Clark and Kozlowska 2009.

7. MEDIEVAL RATHGALL

7.1 INTRODUCTION

Katharina Becker

Excavations at Rathgall provide clear evidence of extensive medieval use of the site. Some of this evidence, such as a rectangular later medieval house (Chapter 2, section 2.5) and spreads of medieval pottery (Chapter 3, section 3.11.7), was recognised during the original excavations. Subsequent programmes of fieldwork, radiocarbon dating and artefact analysis have revealed that there was an extensive period of early medieval settlement which redefined the prehistoric structures on the hilltop. This can be considered in the context of the early medieval reuse of prehistoric monuments elsewhere in Ireland and of later medieval settlement patterns.

7.2 EARLY MEDIEVAL RATHGALL

Matthew Seaver

The fieldwork at Rathgall in 2011 provided new secure and close dates for the Bronze Age activity that pre-dated Rampart 2. It identified four stages in the construction of that rampart. Significant questions remain about the dating of these phases, but secure dates helped to put the original radiocarbon dates from the ditch into context. If we can take it that Ditch 2 and at least part of Rampart 2, including the stone facing on its inner face, the latest phase in the sequence in the rampart construction, date from the seventh century AD, what does this say about the early medieval use of Rathgall and how does it fit into our wider understanding of hillforts in this period?

Rathgall in the early medieval period is poorly understood. It lay within the historic kingdom of Leinster, which was split into numerous sub-kingdoms. There are no known explicit medieval references to Rathgall, although attempts were made to link it with a number of proto-historical and historical sites and groups (Orpen 1911; 1913). Orpen (1911) argues that in the earliest historic period Rathgall was part of the extensive lands controlled by the Dál Messin Corb, who were ascendant in the province of Laigin (Leinster) in the sixth century. He sketched out the importance of the landscape around Rathgall, emphasising early battles in the *Boroma* saga which took place in the area of Tullow, its proximity to an *óenach* or assembly site, which he places at the prehistoric cemetery at Ballon, Co. Carlow (8km from Rathgall), and its proximity to the early church site at Aghowle, Co. Wicklow. He proposed that Rathgall could be *Bolg-luatha*, the seat of an Uí Chennselaig king that may be equated with *Dún-bolg*, a site mentioned in the saga, which describes a monumental battle in AD 597 in a glen near Donard, Co. Wicklow. In a further article Orpen attempts to link Rathgall and *Dún nGalion*, a place of battle in the Book of Leinster associated with the Dál Messin Corb. He further suggests that Rathgall is represented by the place-name *Dunum* on Ptolemy's map. This was challenged by O'Rahilly, who suggested that *Dunum* was likely to be *Dind Rig*, possibly sited near Leighlinbridge, Co. Carlow (Stout 1994, 21).

There are very significant difficulties in discussing the pre-eighth-century geopolitics of Leinster: there are no contemporary sources, and those compiled later are biased by the aspirations of the dynasts who commissioned them (Mac Shamhráin 1996, 44–6). Rathgall belongs within the barony of Shillelagh, which derives from the Síl nÉlóthaig, an early medieval people who took their name from an eighth-century king of the Uí Chennselaig, an extensive kingdom which ran into modern County Wexford (MacCotter 2008, 254–5). The church at Aghowle had an abbot of the Uí Chennselaig family, suggesting a political presence near Rathgall from an early stage (Price 1956, 83). The associated sept of Uí Felmeda Tuaid controlled the nearby area close to Tullow throughout the early medieval period from a centre at Rathvilly and provided early kings of the Uí Chennselaig (Smyth 1994, 41, 72; MacCotter 2008, 131). This area contained part of the later barony of Shillelagh, including the area around Rathgall. There are no indications of the antiquity of the name Rathgall beyond the nineteenth century—*an Rátha Ghil*, which could mean 'the white fort' or 'the fort of the foreigners' (http://www.logainm.ie/1390492.aspx, Official Irish Placenames record, accessed 1 May 2012). In reality, archaeology is the main tool for interpreting the site in this period.

The paradox with the new radiocarbon dating information suggesting a seventh-century AD date for the digging of or recutting of Ditch 2 and the construction of

Rampart 2 is that archaeological evidence for early medieval use is quite poor. The only archaeological features at Rathgall that produced radiocarbon dates of the early historic period other than the rampart ditch were a stone-lined pit to the north-west in Area 1, a burnt area probably in F1 and a pit in Area 2, two of these being problematic Smithsonian dates' (GrN-27100; SI-1482; SI-1479; see Chapter 4, section 4.4). While both the inner face of Rampart 2 and the inner stone enclosure referred to as Rampart 1 have been thought to be medieval (Raftery 1970), their dating remains unclear. The former clearly post-dates the rampart and therefore is likely to be seventh-century or later. It has been suggested recently, in an article outlining the evidence for extending the occupation date and construction of Irish native settlement enclosures, that Rampart 1 could be of high medieval construction based on the significant quantity of medieval pottery and the smaller number of coins found in its vicinity (Fitzpatrick 2009, 281; see Chapter 3, section 3.11.7). In the wider area there are a group of ringforts and other unclassified enclosures around the base of the hill on which the Rathgall and Knockeen enclosures sit, something which is a feature of other hillforts (see below).

Although there are no other cashels within hillforts in Wicklow, the construction of cashels in the Wicklow upland area can be compared to the structure at Rathgall. Cashel-building in Wicklow/Carlow/north Wexford is attested by 23 records. Many of these are no longer extant or do not survive sufficiently to allow examination of their structural remains. A further number have earthen banks faced with stone and are not of the same character as Rathgall. Examples of cashels close to Rathgall such as Aghowle (WI-042-027) are characterised by inner and outer kerbs of granite boulders with internal rubble walls. These cashel walls have widths of 1.2–3m but none match the scale of the Rathgall ramparts, whose width would correspond to that of larger Western Stone Forts such as Cahergal, Co. Kerry (5–5.5m), and Grianán an Aileach, Co. Donegal (5m), all of which have considerably higher surviving ramparts and are more regular in plan than Rathgall. The origin and dating of the Rathgall Rampart 1 are uncertain, and it lacks the terracing or stairways which are common features of these Western forts.

There is a rectangular wall chamber in the thickness of Rampart 1 at Rathgall. Such chambers are a feature of Western Stone Forts but are usually accessed from the interior of the enclosure through a restricted entrance—for example at Cahergal, Grianán an Aileach and Dún Aonghasa—even in examples where there are further outer enclosures. Evidence from Rathgall from earlier surveys does not indicate wall passages or chambers and it is not certain when the current rectangular room was mapped. Orpen (1911, 142) in his survey of Rathgall specifically states that 'nor could I discover any chambers or passages in the thickness of the walls'. The rectangular chamber at Rathgall is situated within the thickest part of the Rampart 1 wall. The earliest editions of the Ordnance Survey maps do not map Rampart 1 in sufficient detail to indicate its presence. The Rathgall feature is thus unlikely to be of early medieval date.

Therefore, while the most obvious parallels for Rampart 1 are of early medieval date, such as Cahergal, Co. Kerry, which is firmly dated to the seventh–ninth century (Manning 2016, 121), the absence of specific comparative features typical of such sites and the lack of precisely dated features make its dating a difficult task.

Artefact evidence for early medieval use of Rathgall is relatively sparse and comprises objects which are many hundreds of years apart in date. A globular polychrome glass bead is likely to have been imported from the Anglo-Saxon world or from north-western Europe in the sixth century (Chapter 3, section 3.4). The presence of a silver ingot of Viking age is a relatively unusual find for the Leinster region (section 3.5) and suggests ninth- to tenth-century occupation. An amber bead from the dark deposits in Area 2 is likely to be of early medieval date, and parallels with objects from Hiberno-Norse Dublin could indicate that it is ninth- to eleventh-century in date (section 3.1). A rotary quern fragment (E84:8880) was recorded during the original excavation and is likely to be early medieval. Two stick-pins found at Rathgall are probably more likely to belong to the later medieval period. Analysis of the crucible assemblage (section 3.7) shows cupellation vessels and crucibles which are best compared to early medieval examples. These results suggest periods of early medieval casting with non-ferrous metals. The absence of moulds for definitive early medieval objects makes it difficult to expand on the nature and dating of this activity; given the friable nature of clay moulds, however, these may simply not have survived.

The nature of the soils at Rathgall are not conducive to the survival of unburnt animal bone and it is therefore difficult to assess whether substantial features like the early medieval ditch of Rampart 2 contained this key indicator of settlement and ritual. Likewise, the many iron objects recovered did not survive to the extent where they could be readily identified to a specific period. This relatively sparse artefact record stands in contrast to the resources and energy

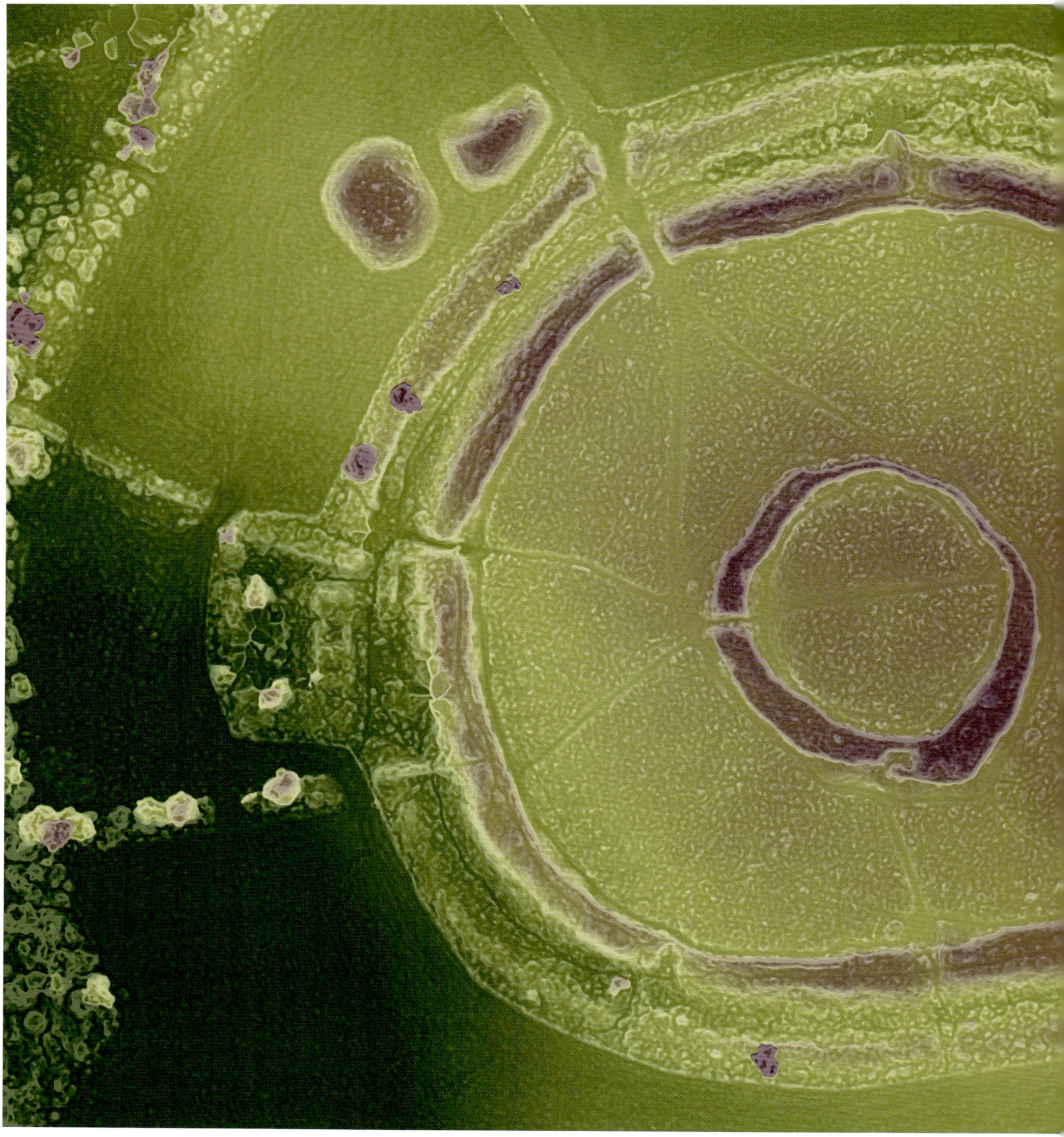

Fig. 7.1—Hill-shaded model of Rathgall hillfort, showing Ramparts1–3 (James O'Driscoll).

required to construct the ditched enclosure, Rampart 2 and possibly Ramparts 3–4 and to build the internal cashel. The absence of artefacts at some of the large stone forts has been taken to mean that the occupants were of low status. In contrast, Manning (2016, 182), discussing the excavation of the substantial cashel at Cahergal, suggests that the absence of significant artefacts may indicate that it was used for ceremonial high-status events.

Can we find comparative reuse of hillforts in the early medieval period? The relatively small numbers of hillforts partially excavated in Ireland have revealed different patterns of early medieval reuse. Radiocarbon dates from excavated hearths within the hillfort at Knockanacuig/Lohercannon, Co. Kerry, indicate activity in the Late Iron Age/early medieval period, cal. AD 398–544—a very similar range to samples from the upper ditch of the hilltop enclosure at Clenagh, Co. Clare, indicating that the ditch no longer had significance (Dunne and Bartlett 2009; Grogan and Daly 2005). Dating and stratigraphy at both sites indicate that they were enclosed at a considerably earlier date.

More substantial reuse is indicated by the presence of ringforts and stone cashels at the heart of many hillforts; these have been recognised through fieldwork and survey but the date of their construction is often unclear. As at Rathgall, these enclosures vary considerably in size and construction. For example, the spectacular cashel at Grianán an Aileach, a historically attested early medieval strategic and political centre, clearly stands within a larger hillfort of likely prehistoric date, although we know little about the dating of the outer enclosures (Moore *et al.* 2010). The hillfort at Knockacarrigeen, Co. Galway, had an off-centre cashel and at least three ringforts around its outer enclosures. Excavations here confirmed Bronze Age occupation levels both within and beneath the inner rampart but the impact of a pipeline did not allow examination of early medieval structures (Carey 2002). Excavations at Mooghaun, Co. Clare, indicated that the series of cashel enclosures on the summit and within the outer ramparts contained early medieval evidence (Grogan 2005c). A series of circular houses were radiocarbon-dated to the eighth–thirteenth century AD (O'Sullivan 2005), although it has been argued that these could represent secondary use and that the buildings could still have been constructed in the Bronze Age (Henderson 2007, 183). The inner cashel enclosure at the same site contained the shank of a ringed pin or stick-pin, a rotary quern and a burnt hog-backed bone comb, suggesting its use within the earlier part of the first millennium AD. Clogher hillfort contained extensive Later Iron Age and early medieval evidence, with artefacts and structures on a scale vastly greater than much of the evidence from other hillfort sites (Kerr *et al.* 2010, 649–51). Much closer to Rathgall, survey evidence from Tinoran and Hughstown hillforts, Co. Wicklow, suggests that 'ringfort' enclosures, probably of early medieval date, exist at their centre (O'Driscoll 2017a).

At Rahally, Co. Galway, the annexe attached to a bivallate ringfort was uncovered within the excavated area on the summit of a trivallate hillfort. Two further ringforts were found within the outer enclosure, with occupation from the seventh to the twelfth century AD (Mullins 2009). Two burials were placed in the annexe and its ditch; a further example within the ringfort ditch at the base of the hill was dated to the eleventh century, and a further undated human mandible was found in the upper fill of the outer hillfort ditch (*ibid.*; Seaver 2011). These acts would seem to tie together the hillfort, the ringforts and the group who lived there. The contemporaneity of these sites could be interpreted to suggest that the hilltop formed the focus of a particular kin group. There was no evidence at any of these sites that the enclosing ditches and ramparts were anything but later Bronze Age in date. At Dún Aonghasa on Inis Mór, Co. Galway, the cliff-top stone enclosure which contained extensive Bronze Age habitation and metalworking evidence was reworked during the early medieval period. A series of circular houses were built within the inner enclosures, and their position and associated artefacts suggest that they were early medieval in date (Cotter 2012). During this period the outer enclosure was heavily rebuilt and two burials were placed at a blocked entrance. The refurbished inner wall contained a mural chamber with internal deposits dated to between the seventh and ninth centuries AD. As at Rathgall, there was little artefactual evidence for occupation.

The key question, therefore, is the role of Rathgall in the early medieval period. Was activity at hillforts simply utilitarian—the reuse of ready-made enclosures to contain settlements? A deep concern with reusing past burial monuments or investing them with narratives that mythologised the dead to continue their use as legal boundary-markers was a key part of the beginning of the early medieval period in Ireland (O'Brien 1999; O'Brien and Bhreathnach 2011; Huckins 2012). Prehistoric burial mounds and enclosures became important in the geography of kingship as places of inauguration, assembly and justice, and the sites of many of these places are often unknown for the earlier part of the period (Fitzpatrick 2004). *Óenach Carmain*, burial mounds on the plain of the Curragh, was the assembly site for the historic kingdom of Leinster. The idea of past artefacts and discoveries in the consciousness of early medieval people has been discussed in relation to crannogs and houses (Fredengren 2002, 241–2; O'Sullivan and Nicholl 2010, 74–5), but it could be said that the conscious reuse of the monumental past on other settlement sites has not received the same attention and is perhaps seen as more pragmatic. The role of the past in kingship has been the subject of considerably more research. Excavations at Knowth have demonstrated the conscious reuse of the passage tomb for burial and settlement as a royal residence (Eogan 2012). The great ceremonial centres of early medieval Ireland such as Tara and Rathcroghan drew their power from a constructed past during the period (Waddell 2011). The substantial ditch at Rathgall was larger than the 85m-diameter enclosure that carefully enclosed the passage tomb at Knowth. Enclosures on the scale of that at Rathgall are frequently seen at ecclesiastical sites such as that around Cathedral Hill, Downpatrick, Co. Down, which itself was thought to be a potential Bronze Age hillfort prior to excavation (Proudfoot 1954). It would seem that the importance of different types of prehistoric hilltop enclosures in local narratives could be utilised in different ways in the early medieval period by groups with different objectives, whether local (such as at Mooghaun, Rahally or Dún Aonghasa) or regional (such as at Clogher or Grianán an Aileach). While there are still many questions about the character of early medieval settlement at Rathgall, the construction of the ditch clearly demonstrates the resources required to achieve this redefinition and the equivalent power needed to make such a statement.

7.3 LATER MEDIEVAL RATHGALL

Caroline Sandes, Matthew Seaver and Clare McCutcheon

Until the beginning of the seventeenth century County Wicklow was part of what are now the counties of Dublin, Kildare, Wexford and Carlow. The area around Tullow was from the seventh century the centre of the kingdom of Uí Felmeda Tuaid (Murphy 2008, 237). In the later twelfth century Diarmait MacMurrough installed Dalbach, ancestor of the MeicDalbaig, as king of this territory in order to weaken his enemies, the O'Donnells, who dominated this area (O'Byrne 2001, I, 66). The king of Uí Felmeda Tuaid may have continued to hold the kingdom after submission to Henry II (*ibid.*). The Anglo-Normans inhabited the south-eastern coastal strip and all the land below 200m OD to the west and south-west of the county (Long 1994). The central upland region remained under Gaelic control, and the three main families in this region were the Mac Murchadas (MacMurroughs), the Ó Tuathails (O'Tooles) and the Ó Broins (O'Byrnes). Theobald Walter was granted the manor of Tullach Ua Felmeda along with Arklow in 1189–92 (Murphy 2008, 238). This territory included the barony of Rathvilly and the north-west of Shillelagh, which contained Rathgall. In the mid-thirteenth century the political unrest in England resulted in upheaval in Ireland. From this time, and throughout the fourteenth century, there were continual disturbances and wars in Leinster. By 1360 the Earl of Ormond appears to have been successful in subduing the Mac Murchadas, the Ó Broins and the various other Irish septs involved. Sporadic warfare continued, however, in the vicinity of Carlow and Tullow, and therefore Rathgall, throughout the rest of the century. Finally, in 1449 Richard, Duke of York, succeeded in subduing the Ó Broins of north Wicklow, and the other Irish of the south-east submitted, led by Mac Murchada (Otway-Ruthven 1980, 380).

The main concern underlying the need to keep the Irish under control was to protect two important routeways. There was the royal road south from Dublin to Arklow, via Bray and Wicklow along the coast, on which Newcastle McKynegan (Newcastle, Co. Wicklow) was the vital point of defence. The other was the Barrow route between Dublin and Waterford. It appears that during this period Dublin was considered difficult to reach by most royal ministers and lords of liberties. This is reflected, for instance, in discussions held in 1379 with Mac Murchada, Ó Broin and other Irish leaders at Baltinglass, where Art Mac Murchada, as 'captain of his nation', swore to keep the ways between Carlow and Kilkenny safe (*ibid.*, 313). The closure of these routes led to the loss of revenue for the Dublin administration and is one of the reasons why Carlow became the seat of the exchequer for a time in the second half of the fourteenth century (Frame 1973, 20–1).

One of the important Irish families in this region were the Ó Broins, sub-chiefs of Mac Murchada. Their original homeland was Ui Fáelain in Kildare. From here they either fled or were transferred by the Anglo-Normans to the upland areas of south Leinster (Nicholls 1982, 374). By the early fourteenth century, however, they were recognised as tenants in the barony of Wicklow. In 1308 they also gained lands in east Wicklow. In that year some of the Ó Tuathails were accused of being rebels and felons; as a result, the lands that they held in freehold from the archbishop of Dublin were confiscated and deliberately granted to Murchadh Ó Broin 'to promote dissension between the kindreds' (*ibid.*, 376).

Research has suggested that it was the Ó Broins who owned Rathgall (Long 1994). From the 1270s onwards, poor harvests and constant war with various Irish septs of this part of Leinster resulted in a decline in Anglo-Irish settlement, and many manors became 'waste'. By 1303 two Ó Broins and Tothil Oconil appear to have held lands of the Earl of Ormond in the manor of Liscolman, in the immediate vicinity of Rathgall (*ibid.*). The latter held half a carucate in *Derathmaure*, which had previously been owned by the betaghs and cottiers of the old grange, and Liscolman (Murphy 2008, 249). Although there appears to be no direct reference to Rathgall in the documents, the fact that land was leased suggests that the site was reoccupied. A reference of 1277 mentions that when the Irish were driven out of Glenmalure they fled to 'another strong place', an apt description for Rathgall, with its prominent position and extensive views of the surrounding countryside (Sweetman 1877, no. 1400). The documentary evidence, then, points to occupation by the native Irish family of Ó Broin from at least the beginning of the fourteenth century, and possibly from the end of the thirteenth.

The history of the region for the period from the late twelfth century to the mid-fifteenth century gives a picture of almost continuous unrest and warfare. The location of Rathgall within an Irish-held area (Long 1994) near Anglo-Norman territory suggests that it may have played some part in the offensives of the Irish. The incursions by the Anglo-Normans may have made the continued occupation of Rathgall by the Irish during the fourteenth century a case of necessity rather than choice. We know that Rathgall was extensively modified in the early medieval period with the construction of Rampart 2 or the redigging of its ditch (Chapter 2, section 2.8). The augmentation of the stone rampart and the construction of Rampart 1 at the heart of the monument are likely to be early or later medieval in date (Raftery 2007, 98–9). Even today the second rampart is as much as 6m above external ground level. Furthermore, the commanding position afforded by the site would have remained important.

7.3.1 The house enclosure

When the first account of the thirteenth- to fourteenth-century structure, dated by the presence of Leinster Cooking Ware and Dublin Ware, at Rathgall was published, it was only one of a handful of such rural buildings excavated in Ireland (Raftery 2007; O'Conor 1998, 95–7; 2002). Since that time substantial numbers of such structures have been excavated (for multiple examples see Potterton and Corlett 2009). Despite this, the later medieval Rathgall structure has considerable significance in discussing the question of what these buildings looked like. One of the main questions about its construction is whether the subrectangular trench around the Rathgall structure functioned as a foundation trench or as a drip-gully under the eaves of the building. Based on interpretations of similar twelfth- to fourteenth-century houses at Lough Gur, Co. Limerick (Cleary 1982; 1983), Raftery suggested that the trenches acted as foundation trenches, with the internal stake line working as an internal wall support. This would mean that the structures had larger internal dimensions than if the trench was interpreted as a gully. This remained the prevailing view up to recent times. Reconstructions of a thirteenth-century structure at Ballinvinny South, Co. Cork, interpreted the trenches as foundations with a chimney set within the walls (Hanley 2009, 130–1). Gardiner and O'Conor (2017, 145–6) argue, to the contrary, that the chimney and post-holes inside the trench (Cotter 2013) indicate internal timber walls abutting the chimney and that these stone-filled trenches were 'French drains', i.e. drip-gullies filled with stones to prevent them from silting up. The same authors argue that a clay floor delineated by post-holes set back from external trenches at Mondaniel, Co. Cork (Quinn 2013), represents a thick cob wall set back from the edge of the drip-trench. Rathgall is of considerable importance in this debate because it has a line of stake-holes on the interior of the external trenches, adding weight to the latter interpretation of the structure's design, i.e. that they functioned as drip-gullies.

If the function of the trench as a drip-gully is accepted, there are different possibilities for the construction of the house walls and superstructure at Rathgall: cob walls with an internal wattle screen or lining, a timber-framed building with sod walls and an inner lining of wattle, or a structure with purely wattle-built walls. The gap between the internal line of stake-holes and the enclosure trench could have accommodated a cob or sod wall. Cob-walled buildings are difficult to identify from excavated remains and to date the only excavated example in Ireland is at Monadreela, Co. Tipperary, where the excavators noted walls up to 1.5m thick (Hughes and O'Droma 2011). Typically, when excavated in England these mud walls are up to 1m thick. The line of stake-holes at the Rathgall structure would not have been functionally necessary for a mud-walled building but could have served an aesthetic purpose, such as for wainscoting.

Sod walling is a possibility, with some upstanding examples having internal wattle wainscoting. There are no examples known from medieval Ireland, but examples are known from Iceland, Greenland (Sigurðardóttir 2008) and nineteenth- and twentieth-century Ireland (Evans 1969). Unlike cob-built walls, this type of construction with an internal timber structure provides the additional strength to carry the weight of the roof. Neither of these construction types would require large posts for supporting the roof, the lack of which were a concern in initial considerations of the Rathgall building (Raftery 2007, 102–3).

Either of these techniques could have used crucks to support the roof. Crucks—curving timber supports for roofs, resting on padstones on the ground—were used in medieval Ireland and are referred to in documentary sources (Murphy and Potterton 2010, 179). If they were used at Rathgall they would have to have been located inside the line of stake-holes that formed the walling. End crucks cannot have been used because they would have blocked the doorway. The problem with identifying this as either a cruck or a post-and-truss building is the distance between the walls and the eaves drip-trench. The thickness of the thatch would have ensured that rainwater was shed well away from the walls, but the distance of 1.25m between the walls and the inner edge of the trench is towards or beyond the likely upper limit for projecting thatch.

Wattle buildings are known from medieval Irish architecture, particularly from Deer Park Farms (Lynn and McDowell 2011), Co. Antrim. Such a construction technique may have been a possibility at Rathgall.

It is unclear which of these structural possibilities might have been employed for the building at Rathgall. Other aspects of the building's construction may hint at the cultural tradition from which it comes. The Rathgall structure is unusual in having an entrance in the end wall. Houses in the Anglo-Norman and north-western European hall tradition typically have entrances in their side walls and are open to the rafters. The closest parallels for the location of the entrance at Rathgall and other Irish medieval buildings are the tenth- and eleventh-century structures of Hiberno-Norse Dublin (Boyd 2015). These buildings share distinct similarities with those excavated at Knowth, Co. Meath, such as an end entrance and a low width to length ratio. Wallace (2012) has argued that these buildings are closer in design to houses at Ballywee, a settlement site with a series of rectangular houses and a souterrain with an enclosing bank. One of the rectangular houses at Ballywee had an entrance in one of the end walls. Rathgall may therefore belong to a tradition of buildings which looked back to a hybrid early medieval building tradition.

The location of a rectangular thirteenth-century building within the outer enclosure of a cashel, which itself probably lay within an earlier hillfort, is significant. A range of rectangular structures and artefacts including thirteenth–fourteenth-century coins have been found at a significant number of cashel and rath sites, and Fitzpatrick (2009) argues that many native enclosed settlements were not abandoned by AD 1000 as argued previously. Other sites in County Wicklow, such as the circular enclosure at Charlesland, were occupied in the early medieval period and continued to be modified and used in the thirteenth to fourteenth century (Molloy 2009b, 155). Rathgall is likely to be an example of a place of considerable significance and strength in the wider landscape which continued to be occupied.

7.3.2 Conclusions

The house remains are those of a substantial structure, irrespective of the construction technique of the walls. Such a house was almost certainly a permanent structure. It is unclear whether it was isolated within the enclosed area of Rathgall or whether there were a series of such structures within the unexcavated area. Similarities with the plan of earlier Irish medieval buildings combined with its position within the mountains suggest a strong possibility that it was built and controlled by the Gaelic Irish. The spread of medieval pottery around the structures and in the vicinity of Rampart 1 in Areas 1–4 shows that this occupation area was extensive.

The relative proximity of Rathgall to the River Barrow, the artery of the south-east, must have been a prominent factor in local trade contacts. The Barrow, apart from being the main routeway between Dublin and the south, connected with the port of New Ross, one of the principal ports of foreign trade throughout the medieval period (Barry 1987, 127). In the medieval period cattle hides were one of the main exports produced by Ireland. The wealth of the Gaelic Irish was generally measured by the size of their herds of cattle (O'Neill 1987, 77, 80), and cattle may have provided a source of revenue for the inhabitants of Rathgall. Goods imported included wine, salt, olives and iron, all of which Ireland lacked. There are records of trade with Spain and Portugal from at least the late fourteenth century (Bradley 1978, 121), and there is a reference to a safe conduct that was granted to one Robert Rusel in 1315–16 to bring wines, salt and other merchandise from Spain to New Ross (O'Neill 1987, 86). Salt was important for the preservation of fish and meat, and cattle hides were the second most important export from Ireland after fish during the medieval period. The Irish were well aware of the value of hides. This would have bought them into direct contact with traders, as, for instance, in the case of the merchant John Beek, who visited Diarmuid MacMurrough Láimhdherg in 1379 because the latter owed him money for various items, including '31s for one basin broke' (*ibid.*, 76), although this refers to a metal rather than a ceramic basin.

The date range of the medieval pottery from Rathgall could extend from the later twelfth to the beginning of the fifteenth century, but the fact that the pottery had been subjected to weathering and was from disturbed contexts makes it difficult to refine the date. In view of the evidence from extensive rural and urban excavations around Ireland, the presence of primarily wheel-thrown glazed ware, much of it in a clean, low-fired clay, suggests a later thirteenth- to early fourteenth-century date. The coins of Edward I (1272–1307) and Edward III (1327–77) found at Rathgall also suggest that this is the most likely date of occupation. The evidence for other medieval artefacts is slight, with two stick-pins likely to have been dress-fasteners during this period.

Rathgall was initially reoccupied owing to pressure from the Anglo-Norman attacks and was probably deserted as the declining fortunes of the latter led them to retreat to Dublin. By 1416 Wicklow was completely under the control of the Ó Broins, and by 1435 Carlow was also under Irish control (Cosgrove 1987b, 536). Many of the later Irish centres of power in Wicklow included stone tower-houses or circular enclosures containing rectangular buildings (Shannahan 2005, 147–8). There is, however, no artefactual or structural evidence of fifteenth- and sixteenth-century date at Rathgall. It would seem likely that Rathgall was abandoned at this stage when better land became available to the Irish.

BIBLIOGRAPHY

Aerts-Bijma, A.T., Meijer, H.A.J. and van der Plicht, J. 1997 AMS sample handling in Groningen. *Nuclear Instruments and Methods in Physics Research B* **123**, 221–5.

Aerts-Bijma, A.T., van der Plicht, J. and Meijer, H.A.J. 2001 Automatic AMS sample combustion and CO_2 collection. *Radiocarbon* **43**, 293–8.

Andersen, S.T. 1979 Identification of wild grass and cereal pollen. *Danmarks Geologiske Undersøgelse årbog 1978*, 69–92.

Anderson, J. 1911 Notice of a hoard of bronze implements recently found in Lewis. *Proceedings of the Society of Antiquaries of Scotland* **45**, 27–46.

Angelini, I., Artioli, G., Bellintani, P., Diella, V., Gemmi, M., Polls, A. and Rossi, A. 2004 Chemical analysis of Bronze Age glasses from Frattesina di Rovigo, northern Italy. *Journal of Archaeological Sciences* **31**, 1175–84.

Angelini, I., Artioli, G., Bellintani, P. and Polla, A. 2005 Protohistoric vitreous materials of Italy: from early faience to final Bronze Age glasses. In *Proceedings of the 16th Congress of the International Association of the History of Glass, London 2003*, 32–6. AIHV, Nottingham.

Angelini, I., Polla, A., Giussani, B., Bellintani, P. and Artioli, G. 2009 Final Bronze-Age glass in northern and central Italy: is Frattesina the only glass production centre? In J.-F. Moreau, R. Auger, J. Chabot and A. Herzog (eds), *Proceedings: ISA 2006: 36th International Symposium on Archaeometry*, 329–37. Université Laval, Quebec.

Anheuser, K. 1999 *Im Feuer vergoldet: Geschichte der Feuervergoldung und Amalgamversilberung*. AdR-Schriftenreihe zur Restaurierung und Grabungstechnik 4. Stuttgart.

Arkush, E. 2011 *Hillforts of the ancient Andes: Colla warfare, society, and landscape.* University Press of Florida, Gainesville.

Armbruster, B. 2001 Zu bronzezeitlichen Werkzeugen der plastischen Verformung im nördlichen und westlichen Europa. In W.H. Metz, B.L. van Beek and H. Steegstra (eds), *Patina: essays presented to Jay Jordan Butler on the occasion of his 80th birthday*, 7–26. Van Beek and Steegstra, Metz.

Armbruster, B. 2010 Lithic technology for Bronze Age metalworking. In B.V. Eriksen (ed.), *Lithic technology in metal using societies. Proceedings of a UISPP Workshop*, 9–22. Jutland Archaeological Society, Lisbon.

Armit, I. 2004 *Towers in the north: the brochs of Scotland.* Tempus, Stroud.

Armit, I. 2007 Hillforts at war: from Maiden Castle to Taniwaha Pa. *Proceedings of the Prehistoric Society* **73**, 25–37.

Armit, I. and McKenzie, J. 2013 *An inherited place: Broxmouth Hillfort and the south-east Scottish Iron Age.* Society of Antiquaries of Scotland, Edinburgh.

Armit, I., Becker, K. and Swindles, G. (in prep.) *Mobility, climate and culture: re-modelling the Irish Iron Age.*

Armit, I., Swindles, G. and Becker, K. 2013 From dates to demography in later prehistoric Ireland? Experimental approaches to the meta-analysis of large 14C data-sets. *Journal of Archaeological Science* **40** (1), 433–8.

Armit, I., Swindles, G., Becker, K., Plunkett, G. and Blaauw, M. 2014 Rapid climate change did not cause population collapse at the end of the European Bronze Age. *Proceedings of the National Academy of Sciences* **111** (48), 17045–9.

Armstrong, E.C.R. 1933 *Guide to the collection of Irish antiquities: catalogue of Irish gold ornaments in the collection of the Royal Irish Academy*. Stationery Office, Dublin.

Ashmore, P.J. 1999 Radiocarbon dating: avoiding errors by avoiding mixed samples. *Antiquity* **73** (279), 124–30.

Ashmore, P. 2001 Settlement in Scotland during the second millennium BC. In J. Brück (ed.), *Bronze Age landscapes: tradition and transformation*, 1–9. Oxbow, Oxford.

Austellung [Exhibition] 1981 *Gold aus Irland: Gold-, Silber- und Bronzeschmuck dreier Jahrtausende.* Museum für Vor- und Frühgeschichte, Frankfurt am Main.

Barry, T. 1987 *The archaeology of medieval Ireland.* Methuen, London.

Bateson, J.D. 1973 Roman material from Ireland: a reconsideration. *Proceedings of the Royal Irish Academy* **73C**, 21–97.

Baudou, E. 1960 *Die regionale und chronologische Einteilung der jüngeren Bronzezeit im Nordischen Kreis.* Studies in North-European Archaeology 1. Stockholm.

Bayley, J. 1991 Archaeological evidence for parting. In E. Pernika and G.A. Wagner (eds), *Archaeometry '90*, 19–28. Birkhäuser Verlag, Basel.

Bayley, J.C. 1992 Non-ferrous metalworking in England: Late Iron Age to early medieval. Unpublished Ph.D thesis, University of London.

Bayley, J. 2008 Medieval precious metal refining: archaeology and contemporary texts compared. In M. Martinón-Torres and Th. Rehren (eds), *Archaeology, history and science: integrating approaches to ancient materials*, 131–50. University College London Institute of Archaeology Publications. Left Coast Press, Walnut Creek, CA.

Bayliss, A. 2009 Rolling out revolution: using radiocarbon dating in archaeology. *Radiocarbon* **51** (1), 123–47.

Beck, C. and Shennan, S. 1991 *Amber in prehistoric Britain*. Oxbow, Oxford.

Beck, F., Monthel, G. and Rabeisen, E. 1982–3 Note sur un moule à fibules de Bibracte. *Antiquités Nationales* **14–15**, 78–85.

Becker, K. 2009 Metalworking moulds. In M. McQuade, B. Molloy and C. Moriarty (eds), *In the shadow of the Galtees: archaeological excavations along the N8 Cashel to Mitchelstown Road Scheme*, 336–87. National Roads Authority Monograph 4. National Roads Authority, Dublin.

Becker, K. 2010 *Rathgall, Co. Wicklow. Archaeology Ireland* Heritage Guide 51. Wordwell, Dublin.

Becker, K. 2012 The introduction of iron working to Ireland. In A. Kern and J. Koch (eds), *Technologieentwicklung und -transfer in der Eisenzeit. Tagungsbericht der AG Eisenzeit, Hallstatt 2009*, 173–80. Beiträge zur Ur- und Frühgeschichte Mitteleuropas, Langenweissenbach.

Becker, K. 2013a The dating of Late Bronze Age Dowris metalwork—a pilot study. *Journal of Irish Archaeology* **21**, 7–15.

Becker, K. 2013b Transforming identities: deposition in Bronze Age Ireland. *Proceedings of the Prehistoric Society* **79**, 225–63.

Becker, K. 2014 Token explanations—Rathgall and the interpretation of cremation deposits in later prehistoric Ireland. *Archaeology Ireland* **28** (1), 13–15.

Becker, K. 2019 Irish Iron Age settlement and society: reframing royal sites. *Proceedings of the Prehistoric Society* **85**, 273–306.

Becker, K. 2021 Copper alloy artefacts. In M. Connolly (ed.), *Stone, bone and belonging*, 272–4. Kerry County Council, Tralee.

Becker, K., Armit, I. and Swindles, G. 2010 From data to knowledge—the new Irish Iron Age. *Archaeology Ireland* **24** (3), 13.

Becker, K., Cowie, T., Troalen, L. and Tate, J. 2020 The Late Bronze Age objects. In I. Armit and L. Büster (eds), *Darkness visible: the Sculptor's Cave, Covesea, from the Bronze Age to the Picts*, 117–29. Society of Antiquaries of Scotland, Edinburgh.

Bellintani, P. and Stefan, L. 2009 Nuovi dati sul primo vetro europeo: il caso di Frattesina. In *Atti del primo convegno interdisciplinare sul vetro nei beni culturali e nell'arte di ieri e di oggi (Parma, 27–28 novembre 2008)*, 71–86. Università degli studi di Parma, Parma.

Berger, A. 1984 *Die Bronzezeit in Ober- und Mittelfranken.* Bayerisches Landesamt für Denkmalpflege, Band 52. Kalmunz/Opf, Munich.

Bergh, S. 2009 Black is the colour ... Chert, concave scrapers and passage tombs. In B. O'Connor, G. Cooney and J. Chapman (eds), *Materialitas: working stone, carving identity*, 105–12. Prehistoric Society Research Paper No. 3. Oxbow, Oxford.

Bergh, S. 2015 Where worlds meet: two Irish prehistoric mountain-top 'villages'. *Il Capitale Culturale: Studies on the Value of Cultural Heritage* **12**, 21–44.

Bernatzky-Goetze, M. 1987 *Morigen, die spatbronzezeitlichen Funde.* Antiqua 16. Schweizerische Gesellschaft für Ur- und Frühgeschichte, Basel.

Bersu, G. 1948 'Fort' at Scotstarvit Covert, Fife. *Proceedings of the Society of Antiquaries of Scotland* **82**, 241–63.

Bersu, G. 1951 Freestone Hill: a preliminary report on the excavations. *Old Kilkenny Review* 4, 5–10.

Bietti Sestieri, A.M., Bellintani, P, Salzani, L. *et al.* 2015 Frattesina: un centro internazionale di produzione e di scambio nell'Età del bronzo del Veneto. In G. Leonardi and V. Tinè (eds), *Preistoria e protostoria del Veneto*, 427–36. Studi di Preistoria e Protostoria 2. Istituto Italiano di Preistoria e Protostoria, Firenze.

Billand, G. and Talon, M. 2007 Apport du Bronze Age study group au vieillissement des 'hair-rings' dans le Nord de la France. In C. Burgess, P. Topping and F. Lynch (eds), *Beyond Stonehenge: essays on the Bronze Age in honour of Colin Burgess*, 345–53. Oxbow, Oxford.

Biringuccio, V. 1540 *De la pirotechnia*. Libri rari I (1977 reprint of the 1540 edition published by V. Roffinello, Venice). Il Polifilo, Milan.

Blake, H. and Davey, P. (eds) 1983 *Guidelines for the processing and publication of medieval pottery from excavations*. Directorate of Ancient Monuments and Historic Buildings Occasional Paper 5. Department of the Environment, London.

Blankenfeldt, R. 2015 *Das Thorsberger Moor, 2. Die persönlichen Ausrüstungen*. Verein zur Förderung des Archäologischen Landesmuseums e.V. Schloss Gottorf, Schleswig.

Bleuer, E., Hochuli, S., Nielsen, E. and Spycher, H. 2004 La Suisse centrale au Néolithique et à l'âge du Bronze: les sites palafittiques. *Archäologie der Schweiz* **27**, 30–41.

Bøe, J. 1940 *Viking antiquities in Great Britain and Ireland, part 3: Norse antiquities in Ireland*. Aschehoug, Oslo.

Bond, D. 1988 *Excavation at the North Ring, Mucking, Essex: a Late Bronze Age enclosure*. East Anglian Archaeology 43. Essex County Council, Chelmsford.

Bönisch, E. 1996 Bronzezeitlicher Schwellrahmenbau in der Niederlausitz. *Archäologie in Deutschland* (1996) (3), 43.

Bönisch, E. 2007 Bronzezeitliche Siedlungen in der Niederlausitz. In F. Koch (ed.), *Bronzezeit. Die Lausitz Vor 3000 Jahren*, 30–2. Museum der Westlausitz, Kamenz.

Boyd, R. 2015 Where are the longhouses? Reviewing Ireland's Viking-age buildings. In H.B. Clarke and R. Johnson (eds), *The Vikings in Ireland and beyond: before and after the Battle of Clontarf*, 325–45. Four Courts Press, Dublin.

Bradley, J. 1978 The topography and layout of medieval Drogheda. *Journal of the County Louth Archaeological and Historical Society* **19**, 98–127.

Bradley, J. 2004 Moynagh Lough, Co. Meath, in the Late Bronze Age. In H. Roche, E. Grogan, J. Bradley, J. Coles and B. Raftery (eds), *From megaliths to metals: essays in honour of George Eogan*, 91–8. Oxbow, Oxford.

Bradley, R. 1987 Time regained: the creation of continuity. *Journal of the British Archaeological Association* **140** (1), 1–17.

Bradley, R. 2005 *Ritual and domestic life in prehistoric Europe*. Routledge, London and New York.

Bradley, R. 2007 *The prehistory of Britain and Ireland*. Cambridge University Press, Cambridge.

Bradley, R. and Edmonds, M. 1993 *Interpreting the axe trade*. Cambridge University Press, Cambridge.

Bradshaw, R. and McGee, E. 1988 The extent and time course of mountain blanket peat erosion in Ireland. *New Phytologist* **108**, 219–24.

Brandherm, D. 2014 Late Bronze Age casting debris and other base metal finds from Haughey's Fort. *Emania* **22**, 59–68.

Brandherm, D., McSparron, C., Kahlert, T., Bonsall, J., Wilkinson, A. and Kytmannow, T. 2018 The hill of the fairies. *Archaeology Ireland* **32** (3), 30–3.

Breen, G. and Clark, L. 2009 N9/N10 Kilcullen to Waterford Scheme: Kilcullen to Powerstown. Archaeological Services Contract No. 4. Resolution, Prumplestown to Powerstown. Final report on archaeological investigations at Site E2586, in the townland of Johnstown, Co. Carlow. Unpublished report for Headland Archaeology Ltd.

Brewster, T.C.M. 1963 *The excavation of Staple Howe*. East Riding Archaeological Research Committee, Scarborough.

Briard, J., Eluère, C., Mohen, J.P. and Verron, G. 1982–3 Missions au British Museum: objets de l'âge du bronze trouvés en France. I—Les ensembles. *Antiquités Nationales* **14–15**, 34–58.

Briggs, C.S. 1997 The discovery and origins of some Bronze Age amber beads from Ballycurrin Demesne, Co. Mayo. *Journal of the Galway Archaeological and Historical Society* **49**, 104–21.

Brill, R.H. 1992 Chemical analysis of some glasses from Frattesina. *Journal of Glass Studies* **34**, 11–22.

Brindley, A. 2001 Tomorrow is another day: some radiocarbon dates for Irish bronze artefacts. In W.H. Metz, B.L. Van Beek and H. Steegstra (eds), *Patina: essays presented to Jay Jordan Butler on the occasion of his 80th birthday*, 145–60. Van Beek and Steegstra, Metz.

Brindley, A.L. 2007 *The dating of food vessels and urns in Ireland*. Bronze Age Studies 7. National University of Ireland, Galway.

Brindley, A.L. and Lanting, J.N. 1989–90 Radiocarbon dates for Neolithic burials. *Journal of Irish Archaeology* **5**, 1–7.

Brindley, A., Lanting, J.N. and Mook, W.G. 1990 Radiocarbon dates from Irish *fulachta fiadh* and other burnt mounds. *Journal of Irish Archaeology* **5**, 25–33.

Britton, D. 1968 *Late Bronze Age finds in the Heathery Burn Cave, Co. Durham*. British Museum, London.

Britton, D. 1971 The Heathery Burn Cave revisited. In

D. Britton and I. Heaps (eds), *Prehistoric and Roman studies*, 20–38. British Museum, London.

Bronk Ramsey, C. 1995 Radiocarbon calibration and analysis of stratigraphy: the OxCal program. *Radiocarbon* 37, 425–30.

Bronk Ramsey, C. 1998 Probability and dating. *Radiocarbon* **40** (1), 461–74.

Bronk Ramsey, C. 2001 Development of the radiocarbon calibration program. *Radiocarbon* **43**, 355–63.

Bronk Ramsey, C. 2008 Deposition models for chronological records. *Quaternary Science Reviews* **27**, 42–60.

Bronk Ramsey, C. 2009a Bayesian analysis of radiocarbon dates. *Radiocarbon* **51** (1), 337–60.

Bronk Ramsey, C. 2009b Dealing with outliers and offsets in radiocarbon dating. *Radiocarbon* **51**, 1023–45

Bronk Ramsey, C. and Lee, S. 2013 Recent and planned developments of the program OxCal. *Radiocarbon* **55**, 720–30.

Brooks, C.M. 1987 *Medieval and later pottery from Aldwark and other sites.* The Archaeology of York: The pottery, 16/3. Council for British Archaeology, London.

Brown, I. 2009 *Beacons in the landscape: the hillforts of England and Wales.* Oxbow, Oxford.

Brown, N. and Medlycott, M. 2013 *The Neolithic and Bronze Age enclosures at Springfield Lyons, Essex: excavations 1981–1991.* East Anglian Archaeology 149. Essex County Council, Chelmsford.

Brück, J. 1999 Ritual and rationality: some problems of interpretation in European archaeology. *European Journal of Archaeology* **2–3**, 313–44.

Brück, J. 2001 Body metaphors and technologies of transformation in the English Middle and Late Bronze Age. In J. Brück (ed.), *Bronze Age landscapes: tradition and transformation*, 149–60. Oxbow, Oxford.

Brück, J. 2002 Settlement, landscape and social identity: the Early–Middle Bronze Age transition in Wessex, Sussex and the Thames Valley. *Oxford Journal of Archaeology* **19** (3), 273–300.

Brück, J. 2006 Fragmentation, personhood and the social construction of technology in middle and late Bronze Age Britain. *Cambridge Archaeological Journal* **16**, 297–315.

Brück, J. 2007 The character of Late Bronze Age settlement in southern Britain. In C. Haselgrove and R. Pope (eds), *The earlier Iron Age in Britain and the near Continent*, 24–38. Oxbow, Oxford.

Brück, J. 2019 *Personifying prehistory: relational ontologies in Bronze Age Britain and Ireland.* Oxford University Press, Oxford.

Brück, J. and Fokkens, H. 2013 Bronze Age settlements. In H. Fokkens and A. Harding (eds), *The Oxford handbook of the European Bronze Age*, 82–101. Oxford University Press, Oxford.

Brück, J. and Fontijn, D. 2013 The myth of the chief: prestige goods, power and personhood in the European Bronze Age. In H. Fokkens and A. Harding (eds), *The Oxford handbook of the European Bronze Age,* 197. Oxford University Press, Oxford.

Brück, P.M. and O'Connor, P.J. 1977 The Leinster Batholith: geology and geochemistry of the northern units. *Geological Survey of Ireland Bulletin* **2**, 107–41.

Brugmann, B. 2004 *Glass beads from early Anglo-Saxon graves: a study of the provenance and chronology of glass beads from early Anglo-Saxon graves, based on visual examination.* Oxbow, Oxford.

Buck, C.E., Cavanagh, W.G. and Litton, C.D. 1996 *Bayesian approach to interpreting archaeological data.* Wiley, Chichester.

Buikstra, J.E. and Ubelaker, D.H. 1994 *Standards for data collection from human skeletal remains.* Arkansas Archaeological Survey Research Series No. 44. Arkansas Archaeological Survey, Fayetteville.

Burenhult, G. 1984 *The archaeology of Carrowmore: environmental archaeology and the megalithic tradition at Carrowmore, Co. Sligo, Ireland.* Institute of Archaeology, University of Stockholm, Stockholm.

Burgess, C. 1968a *Bronze Age metalwork in northern England,* c. *1000 to 700 BC.* Oriel Press, Newcastle upon Tyne.

Burgess, C. 1968b The later Bronze Age in the British Isles and north-western France. *Antiquaries Journal* **125**, 1–45.

Burgess, C. 1995 Bronze Age settlements and domestic pottery in northern Britain: some suggestions. In I. Kinnes and G. Varndell (eds), *'Unbaked urns of rudely shape': essays on British and Irish pottery*, 145–58. Oxbow, Oxford.

Burgess, C. 2012 Alignments: revising the Atlantic Late Bronze Age sequence. *Archaeological Journal* **169**, 127–58.

Burgess, C.B. and Colquhoun, I. 1988 *The swords of Britain.* Prähistorische Bronzefunde IX/5. C.H. Beck, Munich.

Burgess, C.B. and Gerloff, S. 1981 *The dirks and rapiers of Great Britain and Ireland.* Prähistorische Bronzefunde

IV/7. C.H. Beck, Munich.

Burgess, C., Coombs, D. and Davies, D.G. 1972 The Broadward Complex and barbed spearheads. In F. Lynch and C. Burgess (eds), *Prehistoric man in Wales and the West*, 211–83. Adams and Dart, Bath.

Byrnes, E. 1999 Recent excavations at Richardstown, Co. Louth. *Archaeology Ireland* **13** (4), 33.

Byrnes, E. 2004 Flemington, Co. Dublin. Curvilinear ditch. In I. Bennett (ed.), *Excavations 2002*, 160. Wordwell, Dublin.

Cahill, M. 2003 Appendix V: Two fragments of scrap gold. In R. Cleary, 'Enclosed Late Bronze Age habitation site and boundary wall at Lough Gur, Co. Limerick', 173–5. *Proceedings of the Royal Irish Academy* **103**C, 97–189.

Cahill, M. 2009 Working with wire—the function and decorative uses of gold wire in Bronze Age Ireland, 2200–700 BC. In G. Cooney, K. Becker, J. Coles, M. Ryan and S. Sievers (eds), *Relics of old decency: archaeological studies in later prehistory*, 91–105. Wordwell, Bray.

Cahill, M. and Mullarkey, P. 2010 Appendix VII. A tin bead from Sonnagh. In R.F. Gillespie and A. Kerrigan (eds), *Of troughs and tuyères—the archaeology of the N5 Charlestown bypass*, 89–91. NRA Scheme Monographs 6. National Roads Authority, Dublin.

Cahill, M. and Sikora, M. (eds) 2011 *Breaking ground, finding graves: reports on the excavations of burials by the National Museum of Ireland, 1927–2006*. National Museum of Ireland Monograph Series 4. Wordwell, Bray.

Carey, A. 2002 Excavations at Knockacarrigeen Hill, Tuam, County Galway. *Journal of the Galway Archaeological and Historical Society* **54**, 55–71.

Case, H.J. 1961 Irish Neolithic pottery: distribution and sequence. *Proceedings of the Prehistoric Society* **27**, 174–233.

Chapple, R.M., Dunlop, C., Gilmore, S. and Heaney, L. 2009 *Archaeological investigations along the A1 dualling scheme, Loughbrickland to Beech Hill, Co. Down, N. Ireland*. British Archaeological Reports, British Series 479. Archaeopress, Oxford.

Cherel, A.F. and Gratuze, B. 2018 Les perles en faïence et en verre de l'âge du Bronze découvertes en Bretagne: nouvelles données, nouvelles approches. Étude typo-chronologique, composition, provenance. *Bulletin de la Société Préhistorique Française* **115** (2), 327–60.

Childe, V.G. 1930 *The Bronze Age*. Cambridge University Press, Cambridge.

Church, C. 2003 Radiocarbon dating. In I. Suddaby (ed.), 'The excavation of two Late Bronze Age roundhouses at Ballyprior Beg, Island Magee, County Antrim'. *Ulster Journal of Archaeology* **62**, 78–9.

Chytrácek, M. 2007 Die Höhensiedlungen der Bronze- und Urnenfelderzeit an der oberen Radbuza in Westböhmen. *Bericht der bayerischen Bodenkmalpflege* **47** (38), 15–31.

Clark, A.J. 1996 *Seeing beneath the soil* (revised edn). Batsford, London.

Clark, L. and Kozlowska, D. 2009 Kilcarrig quarry scheme: final report on the archaeological investigations in the townland of Kilcarrig, Bagenalstown, Co. Carlow. Unpublished report for Headland Archaeology Ltd.

Cleary, R.M. 1982 Excavations at Lough Gur, Co. Limerick, 1977–1978: Part II. *Journal of the Cork Historical and Archaeological Society* **87**, 77–106.

Cleary, R.M. 1983 Excavations at Lough Gur, Co. Limerick, 1977–1978: Part III. *Journal of the Cork Historical and Archaeological Society* **88**, 51–80.

Cleary, R.M. 1987 Drumlummin, Co. Tipperary. In R.M. Cleary, M.F. Hurley and E.A. Twohig (eds), *Archaeological excavations on the Cork–Dublin gas pipeline*, 116–45. University College Cork, Cork.

Cleary, R.M. 1995 Later Bronze Age settlement and prehistoric burials, Lough Gur, Co. Limerick. *Proceedings of the Royal Irish Academy* **95**C, 1–92.

Cleary, R. 2000 The potter's craft in prehistoric Ireland. In A. Desmond, G. Johnson, M. McCarthy, J. Sheehan and E. Shee Twohig (eds), *New agendas in Irish prehistory: papers in commemoration of Liz Anderson*, 119–34. Wordwell, Dublin.

Cleary, R. 2003 Enclosed Late Bronze Age habitation site and boundary wall at Lough Gur, Co. Limerick. *Proceedings of the Royal Irish Academy* **103**C, 97–189.

Cleary, R. 2008 The pottery from Site A. In M. Doody (ed.), *The Ballyhoura Hills Project*, 259–303. Discovery Programme Monograph No. 7. Wordwell, Bray.

Cleary, R. 2012 Dún Aonghasa. In C. Cotter, *The Western Stone Forts Project: excavations at Dún Aonghasa and Dún Eoghanachta*, Vol. 2, 8–27. Discovery Programme Monograph. Wordwell, Dublin.

Cleary, R. 2017a Rathnagree pottery. In W. O'Brien and J. O'Driscoll (eds), *Hillforts, warfare and society in Bronze Age Ireland*, 262–4. Archaeopress, Oxford.

Cleary, R. 2017b Tinoran pottery. In W. O'Brien and J.

O'Driscoll (eds), *Hillforts, warfare and society in Bronze Age Ireland*, 296–7. Archaeopress, Oxford.

Cleary, R. 2018 *The archaeology of Lough Gur*. Wordwell, Dublin.

Cleary, R.M., McKeown, S.A., Tierney, J., Hannon, M., Anderson, E., Cahill, M. and O'Shaughnessy, J. 2003 Enclosed Late Bronze Age habitation site and boundary wall at Lough Gur, Co. Limerick. *Proceedings of the Royal Irish Academy* **103**C, 97–189.

Clough, T.H. McK. and Cummins, W.A. 1988 *Stone Axe Studies Volume 2: The petrology of prehistoric stone implements from the British Isles*. CBA Research Report 67. Council for British Archaeology, London.

Coghlan, H.H. and Raftery, J. 1961 Irish prehistoric casting moulds. *Sibrium* **6**, 223–44.

Coles, J. 1959–60 Scottish Late Bronze Age metalwork: typology, distributions and chronology. *Proceedings of the Society of Antiquaries of Scotland* **28**, 16–134.

Coles, J.M. 1962 European Bronze Age shields. *Proceedings of the Prehistoric Society* **28**, 156–90.

Coles, J.M. 1963 Irish Bronze Age horns and their relations with northern Europe. *Proceedings of the Prehistoric Society* **29**, 326–56.

Collard, M., Darvill, T. and Watts, M. 2006 Ironworking in the Bronze Age? Evidence from a 10th-century BC settlement at Hartshill Copse, Upper Bucklebery, West Berkshire. *Proceedings of the Prehistoric Society* **72**, 367–421.

Collins, A.E.P. 1959 Further investigations in the Dundrum sandhills. *Ulster Journal of Archaeology* **22**, 5–20.

Collins, A.E.P. 1965 Ballykeel dolmen and cairn, Co. Armagh. *Ulster Journal of Archaeology* **28**, 47–70.

Collins, A.E.P. 1970 Bronze Age moulds in Ulster. *Ulster Journal of Archaeology* **33**, 23–36.

Collins, A.E.P. and Seaby, W.A. 1960 Structures and small finds discovered at Lough Eskragh, Co. Tyrone. *Ulster Journal of Archaeology* **23**, 25–37.

Collins, T. 2003 An excavation of a crematorium at Rockfield, County Kerry. *Journal of the Kerry Archaeological and Historical Society* **36**, 43–54.

Comber, M. 2004 *Native evidence of non-ferrous metalworking in early historic Ireland*. British Archaeological Reports, International Series 1296. Archaeopress, Oxford.

Comber, M. 2019 Caherconnell Cashel, Co. Clare. Preliminary archaeological excavation report for 2019 season, 10E0087. Unpublished report for statutory authorities (available at www.caherconnell.com; accessed 21 May 2020).

Condit, T. 1992 Ireland's hillfort capital—Baltinglass, Co. Wicklow. *Archaeology Ireland* **6** (3), 16–20.

Condit, T. 1998 Observations on aspects of the Baltinglass hillfort complex. *Wicklow Archaeology and Discovery* **1**, 9–25.

Connolly, M., Coyne, F. and Lynch, L.G. 2005 *Underworld: death and burial in Cloghermore Cave, Co. Kerry*. Wordwell, Bray.

Conway, M., Gahan, A. and Rathbone, S. 2004–5 Corrstown: a large Middle Bronze Age village. *Current Archaeology* **195**, 120–3.

Cooney, C. 2000 *Landscapes of Neolithic Ireland*. Routledge, London and New York.

Cooney, G. 2009 Tracing lines across landscapes: corporality and history in later prehistoric Ireland. In G. Cooney, K. Becker, J. Coles, M. Ryan and S. Sievers (eds), *Relics of old decency: archaeological studies in later prehistory*, 375–88. Wordwell, Bray.

Cooney, G. and Mandal, S. 1998 *The Irish Stone Axe Project, Monograph I*. Wordwell, Bray.

Cooney, G. and Mandal, S. 2000 The Irish Stone Axe Project: sources for stone axes in Ireland. *Krystalinikum* **26**, 45–55.

Cooney, G., Mandal, S. and O'Keeffe, E. 2011 The Irish Stone Axe Project: reviewing progress, future prospects. In V. Davis and M. Edmonds (eds), *Stone Axe Studies III*, 427–42. Oxbow, Oxford.

Cosgrove, A. 1987 The emergence of the Pale, 1399–1447. In A. Cosgrove (ed.), *A New History of Ireland, Vol. II. Medieval Ireland 1169–1534*, 533–56. Clarendon Press, Oxford.

Cotter, C. 2012 *The Western Stone Forts Project: excavations at Dún Aonghasa and Dún Eoghanachta* (2 vols). Discovery Programme Monograph. Wordwell, Dublin.

Cotter, C. 2013 Ballinvinny South AR16—moated settlement. In K. Hanley and M.F. Hurley (eds), *Generations: the archaeology of five national road schemes in County Cork*, Vol. II, 258–64. Wordwell, Bray.

Coughlan, T. 2010 N6 Kinnegad–Athlone Road Scheme Phase 2: Kilbeggan to Athlone dual carriageway. Cappydonnell Big 1: final report. Unpublished report by Irish Archaeological Consultancy for Westmeath County Council.

Cowie, T., O'Connor, B. and Proudfoot, E. 1991 A Late Bronze Age hoard from St Andrews, Fife, Scotland: a preliminary report. In C. Chevillot and A. Coffyn (eds), *L'âge du bronze atlantique: ses faciès, de l'Écosse à l'Andalousie et leurs relations avec le bronze continental et la méditerranée*, 49–58. Actes du 1er Colloque du Parc Archéologique de Beynac. Association des Musées du Sarladais, Beynac-et-Cazenac.

Craddock, P.T. 1977 The composition of copper alloys used by the Greek, Etruscan and Roman civilizations, 2: the Archaic Greeks. *Journal of Archaeological Science* **4**, 103–24.

Craddock, P.T. 2001 Conservative metal alloying traditions in the Migration Period. In B. Plešingerova (ed.), *Archaeometallurgy in Central Europe III*, 175–85. *Acta Metallurgica Slovaca* 7 (special issue).

Craddock, P.T., Wallis, J.M. and Merkel, J.F. 2001 The rapid qualitative analysis of groups of metalwork: making a dream come true. In M. Redknap, N. Edwards, S. Youngs, A. Lane and J. Knight (eds), *Pattern and purpose in Insular art*, 117–24. Oxbow, Oxford.

Crew, P. and Rehren, Th. 2002 Appendix 1. High-temperature workshop residues from Tara: iron, bronze and glass. *Discovery Programme Reports* **6**, 83–102.

Cummins, T. 2004 Analysis of further soil samples from Rathgall, Rath East, Co. Wicklow. Unpublished report for Margaret Gowen and Co. Ltd.

Cummins, T., O'Donnell, L. and Johnston, P. 2005 Assessment of environmental samples from Rathgall, Rath East, Co. Wicklow, report no. 04187-R1. Unpublished report for Margaret Gowen and Co. Ltd.

Cunliffe, B. 1991 *Iron Age communities in Britain* (3rd edn). Routledge, London and New York.

Cunliffe, B. 2001 *Facing the ocean: the Atlantic and its peoples, 8000 BC–AD 1500*. Oxford University Press, Oxford.

David, A. 2008 *Geophysical survey in archaeological field evaluation* (2nd edn). English Heritage Publishing, Swindon.

Davies, O. 1950 *Excavations at Island MacHugh*. Supplement to the *Proceedings and Reports of the Belfast Natural History and Philosophical Society*. The Northern Whig, Belfast.

Davis, M. 1993 The identification of various jet and jet-like materials used in the Early Bronze Age in Scotland. *The Conservator* 17, 11–18.

Davis, M. and Gwilt, A. 2008 Material, style and identity in first century AD metalwork, with particular reference to the Seven Sisters hoard. In D. Garrow, C. Gosden and J.D. Hill (eds), *Rethinking Celtic art*, 146–84. Oxbow, Oxford.

Davis, R. 2015 *The Late Bronze Age spearheads of Britain*. Prähistorische Bronzefunde V/7. Franz Steiner, Stuttgart.

de Paor, L. 1962 Ballyloughan Castle, Co. Carlow. *Journal of the Royal Society of Antiquaries of Ireland* **92**, 1–14.

de Vries, H. and Barendsen, G.W. 1952 A new technique for the measurement of age by radiocarbon. *Physica* **18**, 652.

Dehaene, G. 2004 Skidoo, Co. Dublin: Bronze Age. In I. Bennett (ed.), *Excavations 2002*, 187–8. Wordwell, Dublin.

Dobiat, C. 1987 Perlen mit konzentrischen Ringen. In C. Dobiat, H. Matthäus, B. Raftery and J. Henderson, *Glasperlen der Vorrömischen Eisenzeit II nach Unterlagen von Th.E. Haevernick*, 15–35. Marburger Studien zur Vor- und Frühgeschichte 9. Philip von Zabern, Mainz.

Dolan, J.B. 2006 Frontier impressions: the role of daub at the Beaver Creek Trail Crossing Site. *Nebraska Anthropologist* **21** (http://digitalcommons.unl.edu/nebanthro/16).

Doody, M. 2000 Bronze Age houses in Ireland. In A. Desmond, G. Johnson, M. McCarthy, J. Sheehan and E. Shee Twohig (eds), *New agendas in Irish prehistory: papers in commemoration of Liz Anderson*, 93–100. Wordwell, Dublin.

Doody, M. 2008 *The Ballyhoura Hills Project*. Discovery Programme Monograph 7. Wordwell, Dublin.

Doyle, M. 2015 Early medieval crafts and the manufacture and use of dress ornament. In T. Kerr, M. Doyle, M. Seaver, F. McCormick and A. O'Sullivan (eds), *Early medieval crafts and production in Ireland, AD 400–1100: the evidence from rural settlements*, 88–102. British Archaeological Reports, International Series 2707. Archaeopress, Oxford.

Doyle, T. 2009a N9/N10 Kilcullen to Waterford Scheme: Kilcullen to Powerstown. Archaeological Services Contract No. 4. Resolution, Prumplestown to Powerstown. Final report on archaeological investigations at Site E2596, in the townland of Rathcrogue, Co. Carlow. Unpublished report for Headland Archaeology Ltd.

Doyle, T. 2009b N9/N10 Kilcullen to Waterford Scheme: Kilcullen to Powerstown. Archaeological Services Contract No. 4. Resolution, Prumplestown to Powerstown. Final report on archaeological investigations at Site E2590, in the townland of

Tinryland, Co. Carlow. Unpublished report for Headland Archaeology Ltd.

Doyle, T. 2009c N9/N10 Kilcullen to Waterford Scheme: Kilcullen to Powerstown. Archaeological Services Contract No. 4. Resolution, Prumplestown to Powerstown. Final report on archaeological investigations at Site E2591, in the townland of Rathcrogue, Co. Carlow. Unpublished report for Headland Archaeology Ltd.

Dresser, P.Q. 1980 Dublin radiocarbon dates III. *Radiocarbon* **22** (4), 1028–30.

Dresser, P.Q. and McAulay, I.R. 1974 Dublin radiocarbon dates II. *Radiocarbon* **16** (1), 6–9.

Drewett, P. 1979 New evidence for the structure and function of Middle Bronze Age roundhouses in Sussex. *Archaeological Journal* **136**, 3–11.

Driehaus, J. 1968 Ein bronzezeitliches Vollgriffschwert aus der Niers. *Bonner Jahrbücher* **168**, 319–69.

Driscoll, K. 2011 Lithics. In S. Caulfield, G. Byrne, N. Dunne and G.M. Warren (eds), *Excavations on Céide Hill, Behy and Glenulra, North Co. Mayo, 1963–1994*, 28–38, 61–6, 100–23. UCD School of Archaeology/INSTAR.

Driver, T. 2013 *Architecture, regional identity and power in the Iron Age landscapes of mid Wales: the hillforts of north Ceredigion.* British Archaeological Reports, British Series 583. Archaeopress, Oxford.

Dufraisse, A. and García-Martínez, M.S. 2011 Mesurer les diamètres du bois de feu en anthracologie. Outils dendrométriques et interprétation des données. *Anthropobotanica* **2**, 1–18.

Dufraisse, A., Coubray, S., Girardclos, O., Dupin, A. and Lemoine, M. 2017 Contribution of tyloses quantification in earlywood oak vessels to archaeological charcoal analyses: estimation of a minimum age and influences of physiological and environmental factors. *Quaternary International* **463**, Part B, 250–7.

Dufraisse, A., Coubray, S., Girardclos, O., Nocus, N., Lemoine, M., Dupouey, J. and Marguerie, D. 2018 Anthraco-typology as a key approach to past firewood exploitation and woodland management reconstructions. Dendrological reference dataset modelling with dendro-anthracological tools. *Quaternary International* **463**, Part B, 232–49.

Dunbar, E., Cook, G.T., Naysmith, P., Tripney, B.G. and Xu, S. 2016 AMS ^{14}C dating at the Scottish Universities Environmental Research Centre (SUERC) Radiocarbon Dating Laboratory. *Radiocarbon* **58**, 9–23.

Dungworth, D. 2000 A note on the analysis of crucibles and moulds. *Historical Metallurgy* **34**, 83–6.

Dunlop, C. 2015 *Down the road: the archaeology of the A1 road schemes between Lisburn and Newry.* A Road to the Past 1. Northern Archaeological Consultancy Ltd, Belfast.

Dunne, C.M. 2003 The hair-ring. In I. Suddaby, 'The excavation of two Late Bronze Age roundhouses at Ballyprior Beg, Island Magee, County Antrim', 78–9. *Ulster Journal of Archaeology* **62**, 45–91.

Dunne, L. and Bartlett, T. 2009 Excavations at Knockanacuig/Lohercannan, Co. Kerry. In I. Bennett (ed.), *Excavations 2006*,. 226–7. Wordwell, Dublin.

Edwards, N. 1990 *The archaeology of early medieval Ireland.* Batsford, London.

Eilbracht, H. 2005 Der jüngstbronzezeitliche Siedlungsplatz Wolkenberg 13 auf dem Niederlausitzer Landrücken. In F. Schopper (ed.), *Veröffentlichungen zur brandenburgischen Landesarchäologie*, Band 36/37, 63–88. Brandenburgisches Landesamt für Denkmalpflege und Archäologisches Landesmuseum, Wünsdorf.

Eiroa, J.J. 1981 Moldes de arcilla para fundir metales procedentes del Castro Hallstáttico de El Royo (Soria). *Zephyrus* **32–3**, 181–93.

Elder, S. and Ginn, V. 2009a Report on the archaeological excavation of Johnstown 1, Co. Meath, E3041. Unpublished report for Archaeological Consultancy Services.

Elder, S. and Ginn, V. 2009b Report on the archaeological excavation of Johnstown 4, Co. Meath, E3052. Unpublished report for Archaeological Consultancy Services.

English Heritage 2002 *Environmental archaeology: a guide to the theory and practice of methods, from sampling and recovery to post-excavation.* English Heritage, Swindon.

Eogan, G. 1964 The Later Bronze Age in Ireland in the light of recent research. *Proceedings of the Prehistoric Society* **30**, 268–351.

Eogan, G. 1965 *Catalogue of Irish bronze swords.* Stationery Office, Dublin.

Eogan, G. 1966 Some notes on the origin and diffusion of the bronze socketed gouge. *Ulster Journal of Archaeology* **29**, 97–102.

Eogan, G. 1967 The associated finds of gold bar torcs. *Journal of the Royal Society of Antiquaries of Ireland* **97**, 129–75.

Eogan, G. 1972 'Sleeve-fasteners' of the Late Bronze Age. In F. Lynch and C. Burgess (eds), *Prehistoric man in*

Wales and the West, 189–209. Adams and Dart, Bath.

Eogan, G. 1974 Pins of the Irish Late Bronze Age. *Journal of the Royal Society of Antiquaries of Ireland* **104**, 74–119.

Eogan, G. 1983 *The hoards of the Irish Later Bronze Age*. University College Dublin, Dublin.

Eogan, G. 1984 *Excavations at Knowth 1*. Royal Irish Academy, Dublin.

Eogan, G. 1994 *The accomplished art: gold and gold-working in Britain and Ireland during the Bronze Age*. Oxbow, Oxford.

Eogan, G. 1997 Hair-rings and European Late Bronze Age society. *Antiquity* **71**, 308–20.

Eogan, G. 1999 From Skane to Scotstown: some notes on amber in Bronze Age Ireland. In A.F. Harding (ed.), *Experiment and design: archaeological studies in honour of John Coles*, 75–86. Oxbow, Oxford.

Eogan, G. 2000 *The socketed bronze axes in Ireland.* Prähistorische Bronzefunde IX/22. Franz Steiner Verlag, Stuttgart.

Eogan, G. 2012 *Excavations at Knowth 5. The archaeology of Knowth in the first and second millennia AD*. Royal Irish Academy, Dublin.

Eogan, G. and Roche, H. 1997 *Excavations at Knowth 2*. Royal Irish Academy, Dublin.

Eogan, J. 2012 An Iron Age penannular ring-ditch at Ballybronoge south, Co. Limerick. In C. Corlett and M. Potterton (eds), *Life and death in Iron Age Ireland in the light of recent archaeological excavations*, 105–20. Wordwell, Dublin.

Evans, E.E. 1953 *Lyles Hill: a Late Neolithic site in County Antrim*. Archaeological Research Publications 2. HMSO, Belfast.

Evans, E.E. 1966 *Prehistoric and Early Christian Ireland: a guide*. Batsford, London.

Evans, E.E. 1969 Sod and turf houses in Ireland. In G. Jenkins (ed.), *Studies in folk-life: essays in honour of Iowerth Peate*, 9–90. Routledge, London.

Evans, R.C. and Campbell, C.S. 2002 The origin of the apple-type (Maloideae; Rosaceae) is clarified by DNA sequence data from duplicated GBSSI genes. *American Journal of Botany* **89** (9), 1478–84.

Fægri, K. and Iversen, J. 1989 *Textbook of pollen analysis* (4th edn). John Wiley and Sons, Chichester.

Fairgrieve, S.I. 2008 *Forensic cremation: recovery and analysis*. CRC Press, Boca Raton, FL.

Fenn, T.R. 2015 A review of cross-craft interactions between the development of glass production and the pyrotechnologies of metallurgy and other vitreous materials. *Cambridge Archaeological Journal* **25**, 391–8.

FitzGerald, M. and Warner, R. 2012 Blue glass beads. In C. Cotter, *The Western Stone Forts Project: excavations at Dún Aonghasa and Dún Eoghanachta*, Vol. 2, 98–102. Wordwell, Dublin.

Fitzpatrick, E. 2004 *Royal inauguration in Gaelic Ireland* c. *1100–1600: a cultural landscape study*. Boydell Press, Woodbridge.

Fitzpatrick, E. 2009 Native Irish enclosed settlement and the problem of the Irish 'ringfort'. *Medieval Archaeology* **53**, 271–307.

Fitzpatrick, M. 1998 Johnstown South enclosure, Co. Wicklow. In I. Bennett (ed.), *Excavations 1997*, 199–200. Wordwell, Dublin.

Fitzpatrick, M. (n.d.) Excavation at Johnstown South, Co. Wicklow. Unpublished excavation report for Valerie J. Keeley.

Foley, C. 1989 Jerpointchurch townland, Co. Kilkenny. *Proceedings of the Royal Irish Academy* **89**C, 71–126.

Fox, C. 1939 The socketed bronze sickles of the British Isles with special reference to an unpublished specimen from Norwich. *Proceedings of the Prehistoric Society* **11**, 222–48.

Frame, R. 1973 The justiciarship of Ralph Ufford: warfare and politics in fourteenth century Ireland. *Studia Hibernica* **13**, 7–47.

Fredengren, C. 2002 *Crannogs: a study of people's interaction with lakes, with particular reference to Lough Gara in the north-west of Ireland*. Wordwell, Bray.

Fredengren, C., Kilfeather, A. and Stuijts, I. 2010 *Lough Kinale: studies of an Irish lake*. Wordwell, Dublin.

Freestone, I., Meeks, N. and Middleton, A. 1985 Retention of phosphate in buried ceramics: an electron microbeam approach. *Archaeometry* **27**, 161–77.

Freudenberg, M. 2009 Steingeräte zur Metallbearbeitung. *Archäologisches Korrespondenzblatt* **39**, 1–20.

Gahan, A. 2004 Ballynabarny, Sites 8 and 9, Co. Wicklow. Prehistoric landscape. In I. Bennett (ed.), *Excavations 2002*, 531–2. Wordwell, Dublin.

Gahan, A. and McCutcheon, C. 1997 The pottery. In M.F. Hurley and O.M.B. Scully (eds), *Late Viking Age and medieval Waterford: excavations 1986–1992*, 285–336. Waterford Corporation, Waterford.

Gale, R. 2003 Wood based industrial fuels and their environmental impact in lowland Britain. In P. Murphy and P.E.J. Wiltshire (eds), *The environmental archaeology of industry*, 30–47. Oxbow, Oxford.

Gardiner, M.F. 2013 The sophistication of Late Anglo-Saxon timber buildings. In M.D.J. Bintley and M.G. Shapland (eds), *Timber, trees and woodland in Anglo-Saxon England*, 45–77. Oxford University Press, Oxford.

Gardiner, M. and O'Conor, K. 2017 The later medieval countryside lying beneath. In M. Stanley, R. Swan and A. O'Sullivan (eds), *Stories of Ireland's past*, 133–52. Wordwell, Dublin.

Geber, J. 2009 The human remains. In M. McQuade, B. Molloy and C. Moriarty (eds), *In the shadow of the Galtees: archaeological excavations along the N8 Cashel to Mitchelstown Road Scheme*, 209–40. National Roads Authority Monograph 4. National Roads Authority, Dublin.

Gerloff, S. 2007 Reinecke's ABC and the chronology of the British Bronze Age. In C. Burgess, P. Topping and F. Lynch (eds), *Beyond Stonehenge: essays on the Bronze Age in honour of Colin Burgess*, 117–61. Oxbow, Oxford.

Gerloff, S. 2010 *Atlantic cauldrons and buckets of the late Bronze and early Iron Age in Western Europe: with a review of comparable vessels from Central Europe and Italy*. Prähistorische Bronzefunde, Abteilung II/18. Franz Steiner Verlag, Stuttgart.

Giles, M. 2007 Making metal and forging relations: ironworking in the British Iron Age. *Oxford Journal of Archaeology* **26** (4), 395–413.

Ginn, V. 2013 Power to the people: re-interpreting Bronze Age society. *Emania* **21**, 47–58.

Ginn, V. 2016 *Mapping society: settlement structures in Later Bronze Age Ireland*. Archaeopress, Oxford.

Ginn, V. and Rathbone, S. (eds) 2011 *Corrstown: a coastal community—excavations of a Bronze Age village in Northern Ireland*. Oxbow, Oxford.

Giumlia-Mair, A. 2020 Plating and surface treatments on ancient metalwork. *Advances in Archaeomaterials* **1** (1), 1–26.

Goldhahn, J. and Oestigaard, T. 2008 Smith and death—cremations in furnaces in Bronze and Iron Age Scandinavia. In K. Childis, J. Lund and C. Prescott (eds), *Facets of archaeology: essays in honour of Lotte Hedeager on her 60th birthday*, 215–42. Oslo Arkeologiske Series 10. Oslo Academic Press, Oslo.

Good, C.L. and Russet, V.E.J. 1987 Common types of earthenware found in the Bristol area. *Bristol and Avon Archaeology* **6**, 35–43.

Gowen, M. 1978 Dunboy Castle, Co. Cork. *Journal of the Cork Historical and Archaeological Society* **83**, 1–49.

Gowen, M. 1988 *Three Irish gas pipelines: new archaeological evidence in Munster*. Wordwell, Dublin.

Gowen, M. and Halpin, E. 1992 A Neolithic house at Newtown. *Archaeology Ireland* **20**, 25–7.

Gowen, M. and Tarbett, C. 1988 A third season at Tankardstown. *Archaeology Ireland* **8**, 156.

Graham-Campbell, J. 1975 Bossed penannular brooches: a review of recent research. *Medieval Archaeology* **19**, 33–47.

Graham-Campbell, J. 1987 Some archaeological reflections on the Cuerdale hoard. In D.M. Metcalf (ed.), *Coinage in ninth-century Northumbria: the tenth Oxford Symposium on Coinage and Monetary History*, 320–44. British Archaeological Reports, British Series 180. BAR, Oxford.

Graham-Campbell, J. 2011 *The Cuerdale hoard and related Viking-age silver and gold, from Britain and Ireland, in the British Museum*. British Museum, London.

Graham-Campbell, J. and Sheehan, J. 2009 Viking-age gold and silver from Irish crannogs and other watery places. *Journal of Irish Archaeology* **18**, 77–93.

Grant, A. 1983 *North Devon pottery: the seventeenth century*. University of Exeter, Exeter.

Green, H.S. 1980 *The flint arrowheads of the British Isles: a detailed study of material from England and Wales with comparanda from Scotland and Ireland*. British Archaeological Reports, British Series 75 (i). BAR, Oxford.

Grimm, E. 1992 *TILIA/TILIA.GRAPH*. Illinois State Museum, Springfield.

Grimm, E. 2004 *TGView*. Illinois State Museum, Springfield.

Grimm, E. 2011 *TILIA 1.7.16*. Illinois State Museum, Springfield.

Grogan, E. 1990 Bronze Age cemetery at Carrig, Co. Wicklow. *Archaeology Ireland* **16**, 12–14.

Grogan, E. 2004a The prehistoric pottery assemblage from Kilgobbin, Co. Dublin. Unpublished report for Margaret Gowen and Co.

Grogan, E. 2004b The prehistoric pottery assemblage from Beaverstown, Co. Dublin. Unpublished report for Margaret Gowen and Co.

Grogan E. 2004c The prehistoric pottery assemblage from Charlesland, Greystones, Co. Wicklow. Unpublished report for Margaret Gowen and Co.

Grogan, E. 2004d Middle Bronze Age burial traditions in Ireland. In H. Roche, E. Grogan, J. Bradley, J. Coles and B. Raftery (eds), *From megaliths to metals: essays in honour of George Eogan*, 61–71. Oxbow, Oxford.

Grogan, E. 2005a *The North Munster Project, Vol. 1. The later prehistoric landscape of south-east Clare*. Discovery Programme Monograph 6. Wordwell, Bray.

Grogan, E. 2005b *The North Munster Project, Vol. 2. The prehistoric landscape of north Munster*. Discovery Programme Monograph 6. Wordwell, Bray.

Grogan, E. 2005c The excavation. In E. Grogan, *The North Munster Project, Vol. 1. The later prehistoric landscape of south-east Clare*, 131–216. Discovery Programme Monograph 6. Wordwell, Bray.

Grogan, E. and Daly, A. 2005 Excavations at Clenagh, Co. Clare. In E. Grogan (ed.), *The North Munster Project, Vol. 1. The later prehistoric landscape of south-east Clare*, 247–63. Wordwell, Bray.

Grogan, E. and Eogan, G. 1987 Lough Gur excavations by Seán P. Ó Ríordáin: further Neolithic and Beaker habitations on Knockadoon. *Proceedings of the Royal Irish Academy* **87**C, 299–506.

Grogan, E. and Kilfeather, A. 1997 *Archaeological inventory of County Wicklow*. Stationery Office, Dublin.

Grogan, E. and Roche, H. 2004 The prehistoric pottery from Site 6B, Priestsnewtown, Greystones, Co. Wicklow. In S. Tobin, D. Swift and K. Wiggins, 'Greystones Southern Access Route (GSAR), Co. Wicklow. Sites 6/6a–g, Priestsnewtown. Excavation report 04E0401'. Unpublished report for the National Roads Authority.

Grogan, E. and Roche, H. 2007 Preliminary report on the prehistoric pottery from the N8, Co. Cork. Unpublished report for Eachtra Archaeology Ltd.

Grogan, E. and Roche, H. 2008a The prehistoric pottery assemblage from Darcystown 1, Balrothery, Co. Dublin (03E0067/03E0067 extension). In J. Carroll, F. Ryan and K. Wiggins, *Archaeological excavations at Glebe South and Darcystown, Balrothery, Co. Dublin*, 48–69. Judith Carroll and Co., Dublin.

Grogan, E. and Roche, H. 2008b The prehistoric pottery from Kilbane, Castletroy, Co. Limerick. In N. O'Callaghan, 'Archaeological excavation report, Kilbane, Castletroy, Co. Limerick, 03E1717'. Unpublished report for Eachtra Archaeological Projects.

Grogan, E. and Roche, H. 2008c The prehistoric pottery assemblage from Darcystown 2, Balrothery, Co. Dublin (04E0741). In J. Carroll, F. Ryan and K. Wiggins, *Archaeological excavations at Glebe South and Darcystown, Balrothery, Co. Dublin*, 85–101. Judith Carroll and Co., Dublin.

Grogan, E. and Roche, H. 2009a The prehistoric pottery assemblages from the M3 Clonee–North of Kells, Co. Meath, Lismullin 1 (E3074). In A. O'Connell, 'Report on the archaeological excavation of Lismullin 1, Co. Meath, E3074'. Unpublished report for Archaeological Consultancy Services.

Grogan, E. and Roche, H. 2009b An assessment of Middle Bronze Age domestic pottery in Ireland. In G. Cooney, K. Becker, J. Coles, M. Ryan and S. Sievers (eds), *Relics of old decency: archaeological studies in later prehistory*, 127–36. Wordwell, Bray.

Grogan, E. and Roche, H. 2010a Clay and fire: the development and distribution of pottery traditions in prehistoric Ireland. In M. Stanley, E. Danaher and J. Eogan (eds), *Creative minds: production, manufacturing and invention in ancient Ireland*, 27–46. National Roads Authority, Dublin.

Grogan, E. and Roche, R. 2010b Appendix 1: The prehistoric pottery from Burton Little, Co. Kildare (E2989). In C. Moloney (ed.), 'N9/N10 Kilcullen to Waterford Scheme: Phase 3, Kilcullen to Carlow. Archaeological Services Contract No. 5. Final Report.' Unpublished report for Headland Archaeology (Ireland) Ltd.

Grogan, E., O'Sullivan, A., O'Carroll, F. and Hagen, I. 1999 Knocknalappa, Co. Clare: a reappraisal. *Discovery Programme Reports* **6**, 111–23.

Guido, M. 1978 *The glass beads of the prehistoric and Roman periods in Britain and Ireland.* Reports of the Research Committee of the Society of Antiquaries of London No. 35. Thames and Hudson, London.

Gutiérrez, A. 2007 Portuguese coarsewares in early modern England: reflections on an exceptional pottery assemblage from Southampton. *Post-Medieval Archaeology* **41** (1), 64–79.

Gwilt, A. 2009. NMGW-99E8C7: A Bronze Age Bead, (https://finds.org.uk/database/artefacts/record/id/244776; accessed:13 May 20140.

Gwilt, A., Lodwick, M. and Davis, M. 2007 Entry 485. Burton, Wrexham: Middle Bronze Age hoard of gold adornments and bronze tools with a pot (04.2). *Treasure Annual Report 2004*, 198–9 and figs 485.1–3. Department for Culture, Media and Sport, London.

Hackett, L. 2007 Final report on an archaeological excavation of a Late Bronze Age burnt spread at Gorteen Quarry, Co. Kilkenny. Unpublished report for Headland Archaeology Ltd.

Hackett, L. 2009 N9/N10 Kilcullen to Waterford Scheme: Kilcullen to Powerstown. Archaeological Services Contract No. 4. Resolution, Prumplestown to Powerstown. Final report on archaeological investigations at Site E2566, in the townland of Ballyburn Lower and Ballyhade, Co. Carlow. Unpublished report for Headland Archaeology Ltd.

Haevernick, T.E. 1978 Urnenfelderzeitliche Glasperlen. *Zeitschrift für Schweizerische Archäologie und Kunstgeschichte* **35**, 145–57.

Hall, V. 2011 *The making of Ireland's landscapes since the Ice Age*. The Collins Press, Cork.

Hamilton, D. and Kenney, J. 2015 Multiple Bayesian modelling approaches to a suite of radiocarbon dates from ovens excavated at Ysgol yr Hendre, Caernarfon, North Wales. *Quaternary Geochronology* **25**, 72–82.

Hamilton, D., Haselgrove, C. and Gosden, C. 2015 The impact of Bayesian chronologies on the British Iron Age. *World Archaeology* 47 (4), 642–60.

Hanley, K. 2009 Reconstructing prehistoric and historic settlement in County Cork. In M. Stanley, E. Danaher and J. Eogan (eds), *Dining and dwelling: proceedings of a public seminar on archaeological discoveries on national road schemes, August 2008*, 121–32. National Roads Authority, Dublin.

Harbison, P. 2004 Three midland megaliths as drawn and described in 1786 by J. Brownrigg, Surveyor. In H. Roche, E. Grogan, J. Bradley, J. Coles and B. Raftery (eds), *From megaliths to metals: essays in honour of George Eogan*, 247–53. Oxbow, Oxford.

Harding, D.W. 2009 *The Iron Age round-house: later prehistoric building in Britain and beyond.* Oxford University Press, Oxford.

Harper, A.E.T. 1973–4 The excavation of a rath in Crossnacreevy townland, County Down. *Ulster Journal of Archaeology* **36–7**, 32–41.

Hartmann, A. 1970 *Prähistorische Goldfunde aus Europa.* Studien zu den Anfänge der Metallurgie 3. Römisch-Germanisches Zentralmusem, Stuttgart.

Hartmann, A. 1982 *Prähistorische Goldfunde aus Europa II.* Römisch-Germanisches Zentralmusem, Stuttgart.

Hartmann, G., Kappel, I., Grote, K. and Arndt, B. 1997 Chemistry and technology of prehistoric glass from Lower Saxony and Hesse. *Journal of Archaeological Science* **24**, 547–59.

Harvey, P. (forthcoming) *Amber working in Viking Dublin.* National Museum of Ireland, Dublin.

Haslett, J., Whiley, M., Bhattacharya, S. *et al.* 2006 Bayesian palaeoclimate reconstruction. *Journal of the Royal Statistical Society Series A—Statistics in Society* **169**, 395–430.

Hather, J.G. 2000 *The identification of the northern European woods: a guide for archaeologists and conservators.* Archetype, London.

Hawkes, C.F.C. 1961 Gold ear-rings of the Bronze Age, east and west. *Folklore* 72, 438–74.

Hawkes, C.F.C. and Smith, M.A. 1957 On some buckets and cauldrons of the Bronze and Early Iron Ages: the Nannau, Whigsborough and Heathery Burn bronze buckets and the Colchester and London cauldrons. *Antiquaries Journal* **37**, 131–98.

Hencken, H.O'N. 1942 Ballinderry Crannog No. 2. *Proceedings of the Royal Irish academy* **47**C. 1–76

Henderson, J. 1985 The raw materials of early glass production. *Oxford Journal of Archaeology* 4 (3), 267–91.

Henderson, J. 1987 Appendix D: The chemical analysis of glass from Lough Gur and its archaeological interpretation. In E. Grogan and G. Eogan, 'Lough Gur excavations by Seán P. Ó Ríordáin: further Neolithic and Beaker habitations on Knockadoon'. *Proceedings of the Royal Irish Academy* **87**C, 299–506, at pp 502–6.

Henderson, J. 1988a Glass production and Bronze Age Europe. *Antiquity* **62**, 435–51.

Henderson, J. 1988b Electron probe microanalysis of mixed-alkali glasses. *Archaeometry* **30** (1), 77–91.

Henderson, J. 1989a The scientific analysis of ancient glass and its archaeological interpretation. In J. Henderson (ed.), *Scientific analysis in archaeology and its interpretation*, 30–62. Oxford University Committee for Archaeology, Oxford.

Henderson, J. 1989b The earliest glass in Britain and Ireland. In M. Feugère (ed.), *Le verre préromain en Europe occidentale*, 19–28. Editions Monique Mergoil, Montagnac.

Henderson, J. 1993 Chemical analysis of the glass and faience from Hauterive-Champréveyres, Switzerland. In A.-M. Rychner-Faraggi (ed.), *Hauterive-Champréveyres 9. Métal et parure au Bronze final*, 111–17. Archéologie neuchâteloise 17. Musée cantonal d'archéologie, Neuchâtel.

Henderson, J. 1997 The glass objects from Navan Site B: composition and archaeological implications. In D.M. Waterman, *Excavations at Navan Fort 1961–1971* (ed. C.J. Lynn), 95–100. Stationery Office, Belfast.

Henderson, J. 2013 *Ancient glass: an interdisciplinary*

exploration. Cambridge University Press, Cambridge.

Henderson, J., Bellintani, P. and Evans, J. 2015 Production, mixing and provenance of Late Bronze Age mixed alkali glasses from northern Italy: an isotopic approach. *Journal of Archaeological Science* **55**, 1–8.

Henderson, J.C. 2007 *The Atlantic Iron Age: settlement and identity in the first millennium BC*. Routledge, London.

Henry, S. 1934 A find of prehistoric pottery at Knockaholet, parish of Loughguile, Co. Antrim. *Journal of the Royal Society of Antiquaries of Ireland* **64**, 264–5.

Herity, M. 1982 Irish decorated Neolithic pottery. *Proceedings of the Royal Irish Academy* **82**C, 247–404.

Herity, M. and Eogan, G. 1977 *Ireland in prehistory.* Routledge, London.

Hickie, D. 2002 *Native trees and forests of Ireland*. Gill and Macmillan, Dublin.

Hodges, H.W.M. 1954 Studies in the Late Bronze Age in Ireland 1. Stone and clay moulds and wooden models for bronze implements. *Ulster Journal of Archaeology* **17**, 62–80.

Hodges, H. 1956 Studies in the Late Bronze Age in Ireland 2. The typology and distribution of bronze implements. *Ulster Journal of Archaeology* **19**, 29–56.

Holden, J.L., Phaky, P.P. and Clement, J.G. 1995 Scanning electron microscopic observations of incinerated femoral bone: a case study. *Forensic Science International* **74**, 17–28.

Hook, D. and Needham, S. 1989 A comparison of recent analyses of British Late Bronze Age goldwork with Irish parallels. *Jewellery Studies* **3**, 15–24.

Houghton, J. (ed.) 1979 *Atlas of Ireland—prepared under the direction of the Irish National Committee for Geography*. Royal Irish Academy, Dublin.

Howard, H. 1983 The bronze casting industry in later prehistoric Britain. Unpublished Ph.D thesis, Southampton University.

Huckins, J. 2012 Landscape and lamentation: constructing commemorated space in three middle Irish texts. *Proceedings of the Royal Irish Academy* **112**C, 189–217.

Hughes, J. and Ó Droma, M. 2011 Finding the plot: urban and rural settlement in 13th century Cashel. In S. Conran, E. Danaher and M. Stanley (eds), *Past times, changing fortunes: proceedings of a public seminar on archaeological discoveries on national road schemes, August 2010*, 17–30. Archaeology and the National Roads Authority Monograph Series No. 8. Wordwell, Bray.

Hundt, H.-J. 1958 Spätbronzezeitliches Doppelgrab in Frankfurt-Berkersheim. *Germania* **36**, 344–61.

Hunter, F. 2006. New light on Iron Age massive armlets. *Proceedings of Society of Antiquaries of Scotland* **136**, 135–60.

Hunter, F. 2008 Jet and related materials in Viking Scotland. *Medieval Archaeology* **52**, 103–18.

Hunter, F. 2016 Coal money from Portpatrick (south-west Scotland): reconstructing an early medieval craft centre from antiquarian finds. In F. Hunter and A. Sheridan (eds), *Ancient lives: object, people and place in early Scotland. Essays for David V. Clarke on his 70th birthday*, 281–302. Sidestone Press, Leiden.

Hunter, F. and Davis, M. 2020 The glass objects. In I. Armit and L. Büster, *Darkness visible: the Sculptor's Cave, Covesea, from the Bronze Age to the Picts*, 161–4. Society of Antiquaries of Scotland, Edinburgh.

Hunter, F. and Sheridan, A. 2009 Appendix 11. Bangle fragment from Adamstown 2, Co. Waterford. In I. Russell and V. Ginn, 'Final report: Adamstown 2 and 2ex. 03E1216'. Unpublished report by Archaeology Consultancy Services Ltd.

Hunter, F. and Sheridan, A. 2014 Lignite, cannel coal and oil shale jewellery. In I. Russell, M.F. Hurley and J. Eogan (eds), *Woodstown: a Viking-age settlement in Co. Waterford*, 320–3. Four Courts Press, Dublin.

Hurl, D., Nelis, E. and Murray, B. 1995 *Data structure report no. 037. Excavations at Killymoon, Co. Tyrone, 1995*. Centre for Archaeological Fieldwork, Queen's University, Belfast.

Hurley, M.F. 1987a Kilferagh, Co. Kilkenny. In R.M. Cleary, M.F. Hurley and E.A. Twohig (eds), *Archaeological excavations on the Cork–Dublin gas pipeline*, 88–100. University College Cork, Cork.

Hurley, M.F. 1987b The finds. In M.J. Sleeman and M.F. Hurley, 'Blackcastle, Co. Kildare', in R.M. Cleary, M.F. Hurley and E.A. Twohig (eds), *Archaeological excavations on the Cork–Dublin gas pipeline*, 101–5. University College Cork, Cork.

Hurley, M.F. 1989 Excavations at Grand Parade, Cork, II. *Journal of the Cork Historical and Archaeological Society* **94**, 27–45.

Hurley, M.F. and McCutcheon, S.W.J. 1997 Wooden artefacts. In M.F. Hurley and O.M.B. Scully (eds), *Late Viking Age and medieval Waterford: excavations 1986–1992*, 553–634. Waterford Corporation, Waterford.

Hurst, J.G., Neal, D.S. and van Beuningen, H.J.E. 1986 *Pottery produced and traded in north-west Europe 1350–*

1650. Museum Boymans-van Beuningen, Rotterdam.
Ilkjær, J. 1993 *Illerup Ådal 3. Die Gürtel Bestandteile und Zubehör*. Jutland Archaeological Society Publications XXV:3. Aarhus University Press.
Institute of Archaeologists of Ireland 2007 *Environmental sampling: guidelines for archaeologists*. Online document obtainable from http://www.iai.ie.
Iscan, M.Y., Loth, S.R. and Wright, R.K. 1984 Metamorphosis of the sternal rib end: a new method to estimate age at death in white males. *American Journal of Physical Anthropology* **65**, 147–56.
Iscan, M.Y., Loth, S.R. and Wright, R.K. 1985 Age estimation from the rib by phase analysis: white females. *Journal of Forensic Sciences* **30**, 853–63.
Jahn, R., Blume, H.P., Asio, V.B., Spaargaren, O. and Schad, P. 2006 *Guidelines for soil description*. FAO, Rome.
Jennings, S. 1981 *Eighteen centuries of pottery from Norwich*. East Anglian Archaeology 13. Norwich Survey and Norfolk Museums Service, Norwich.
Jett, P. and Chase, W.T. 2000 The gilding of metals in China. In T. Drayman-Wesisser (ed.), *Gilded metals: history, technology and conservation*, 145–56. Archetype, London.
Joachim, H.E. and Willer, F. 2013 Alte Waffe mit neuem Griff. Das vermeintlich mittelbronzezeitliche Schwert von Oedt. *Bonner Jahrbücher* **213**, 9–16.
Jobey, G. and Tait, J. 1966 Excavations on palisaded settlements and cairnfields at Alnham, Northumberland. *Archaeologia Aeliana* **44**, 5–48.
Johansen, O.S. 1973 Bossed penannular brooches. *Acta Archaeologica* **44**, 63–124.
Johnston, P. 2004 Plant remains from soil samples, Rathgall, Rath East, Co. Wicklow. Unpublished report for Margaret Gowen and Co. Ltd.
Johnston, P., Cummins, T. and Daly, C. 2003 Analysis of soil samples from Rathgall, Rath East, Co. Wicklow. Unpublished report for Margaret Gowen and Co. Ltd.
Johnston, R. 2021 *Bronze Age worlds: a social prehistory of Britain and Ireland*. Routledge, London.
Johnston, S.A. and Wailes, B. 2007 *Dún Ailinne: excavations at an Irish royal site, 1968–1975*. University Museum Monograph 129. University of Pennsylvania Museum of Archaeology and Anthropology, Philadelphia.
Johnston, S.A. 2007 Chronology—absolute dates. In S.A. Johnston and B. Wailes, *Dún Ailinne: excavations at an Irish royal site, 1968–1975*, 178–82. University Museum Monograph 129. University of Pennsylvania Museum of Archaeology and Anthropology, Philadelphia.
Kaenel, G. and Klausener, M. 1990 Quelques tombes à incineration du Bronze final (Xe siècle av. J.-C.) & Vady (Lausanne VD). *Jahrbuch der Schweizerischen Gesellschaft für Ur- und Frühgeschichte* **73**, 51–79.
Kalliefe, H. 1918 Drei tönerne Gussformen in der Kieler Samlung. *Prähistorische Zeitschrift* **10**, 176–8.
Kars, M. 2011 A cultural perspective on Merovingian burial chronology and the grave goods from the Vrijthof and Pandhof cemeteries in Maastricht. Unpublished Ph.D thesis, Vrije Universiteit Amsterdam (https://research.vu.nl/en/publications; accessed 21 May 2020).
Kasseroler, A. 1959 Das Urnenfeld von Volders. *Schlern-Schriften* **204**, 7–246.
Kearns, T., Martinón-Torres, M. and Rehren, Th. 2010 Metal to mould: alloy identification in experimental casting moulds using XRF. *Historical Metallurgy* **44**, 48–58.
Kelly, A. 2010 M3 Clonee–North of Kells motorway scheme, Archaeological Services Contract 4, Navan to Kells and Kells bypass: Grange 3 final report. Unpublished report for Irish Archaeological Consultancy.
Kelly, E. 1978 A reassessment of the dating evidence for Knockadoon Class II pottery. *Irish Archaeological Research Forum* **5**, 23–6.
Kelly, E.P. 2006 Security and sanctity: the ecclesiastical metalwork of Lough Kinale. *Irish Arts Review* **23** (1), 106–9.
Kelly, F. 1976 The old Irish tree-list. *Celtica* **11**, 107–24.
Kelly, F. 2000 *Early Irish farming*. Dublin Institute for Advanced Studies, Dublin.
Kenny, N. 2010 Charcoal production in medieval Ireland. In M. Stanley, E. Danaher and J. Eogan (eds), *Creative minds: production, manufacturing and invention in ancient Ireland*, 99–116. National Roads Authority, Dublin.
Kerr, T., Harney, L., Kinsella, T., O'Sullivan, A. and McCormick, F. 2010 *Early medieval dwellings and settlements in Ireland, AD 400–1100*, Vol. 2. Early Medieval Archaeology Project Report 4.2. University College Dublin and Queen's University Belfast.
Kerr, T.R., McCormick, F. and O'Sullivan, A. 2013 The economy of early medieval Ireland (Early Medieval Archaeology Project Report 7:1). Unpublished report

submitted for INSTAR programme 2013 (www.emap.ie).

Kerrigan, A. and Gillespie, R. 2010 Fulachta fiadh. In R.F. Gillespie and A. Kerrigan (eds), *Of troughs and tuyères—the archaeology of the N5 Charlestown bypass*, 45–143. NRA Scheme Monographs 6. National Roads Authority, Dublin.

Kiely, J. 2003 A Neolithic house at Cloghers, Co. Kerry. In I. Armit, E. Murphy, E. Nelis and D. Simpson (eds), *Neolithic settlement in Ireland and western Britain*, 182–7. Oxbow Books, Oxford.

Kilbride-Jones, H. 1950 The excavation of a composite Early Iron Age monument with 'henge' features at Lugg, Co. Dublin. *Proceedings of the Royal Irish Academy* **53**C, 311–32.

Koch, U. 2001 *Das alamannisch-fränkische Gräberfeld bei Pleidelsheim*. Forschungen und Berichte zur Vor und Frühgeschichte in Baden-Württemberg 60. Theiss, Stuttgart.

Kristiansen, K. 2018 Warfare and the political economy: Europe 1500–1100 BC. In C. Horn and K. Kristiansen (eds), *Warfare in Bronze Age society*, 23–46. Cambridge University Press, Cambridge.

Kruse, S.E. 1993 Silver storage and circulation in Viking-age Scotland. In C.E. Batey, J. Jesch and C.D. Morris (eds), *The Viking Age in Caithness, Orkney and the North Atlantic: select papers from the proceedings of the Eleventh Viking Congress, Thurso and Kirkwall, 1989*, 187–203. Edinburgh University Press, Edinburgh.

Kruse, S.E. and Graham-Campbell, J.A. 2011 Classification and discussion of the Cuerdale objects, Part 1: ingots. In J.A. Graham-Campbell (ed.), *The Cuerdale hoard and related Viking-age silver and gold, from Britain and Ireland, in the British Museum*, 73–86. British Museum Press, London.

Kruse, S.E. and Tate, J. 1995 XRF analysis of Viking-age silver from Scotland. In J. Graham-Campbell (ed.), *The Viking-age gold and silver of Scotland, AD 850–1100*, 73–9. National Museum of Scotland, Edinburgh.

Kruse, S.E., Smith, R.D. and Starling, K. 1988 Experimental casting of silver ingots. *Historic Metallurgy* **22** (2), 87–92.

Le Fèvre-Lehöerff, A. 1994 Les moules de l'Âge du bronze dans la plaine orientale du Pô: vestiges de mise en forme des alliages base cuivre. *Padusa* **28** (1992), 131–243.

Le Patourel, H.E.J. 1968 Documentary evidence and the medieval pottery industry. *Medieval Archaeology* **12**, 101–26.

Leeds, E.T. 1930 A bronze cauldron from the River Cherwell, Oxfordshire, with notes on cauldrons and other bronze vessels of allied types. *Archaeologia* **80**, 1–36.

Leira, M., Cole, E.E. and Mitchell, F.J.G. 2007 Long-term impacts of atmospheric deposition and peat erosion on an oligotrophic lake in eastern Ireland. *Journal of Paleolimnology* **38**, 49–71.

Lins, P.A. and Oddy, W.A. 1975 The origins of mercury gilding. *Journal of Archaeological Science* **2** (4), 365–73.

Liversage, G.D. 1967–8 Excavations at Dalkey Island, Co. Dublin, 1956–1959. *Proceedings of the Royal Irish Academy* **66**C, 53–233.

Lock, G. 2011 Hillforts, emotional metaphors, and the good life: a response to Armit. *Proceedings of the Prehistoric Society* 77, 355–62.

Loewe, G. 1971 *Kreis Kempen-Krefeld*. Archaeologische Funde und Denkmaler des Rheinlandes, Band 3. Rheinland-Verlag, Düsseldorf.

Long, H. 1994 Three settlements of Gaelic Wicklow 1169–1600: Rathgall, Ballinacor and Glendalough. In W. Nolan and K. Hannigan (eds), *Wicklow: history and society*, 237–66. Geography Publications, Dublin.

Longin, R. 1971 New method of collagen extraction for radiocarbon dating. *Nature* **230**, 241–2.

Lourdaux, S. and Gomez de Soto, J. 1998 La parure de la nécropole de l'âge du Bronze final des Ouches à Auzay (Vendée). In C. Mordant, M. Pernot and V. Rychner (eds), *L'atelier du bronzier en Europe du XXe au VIIIe siècle avant notre ère*, 115–28. Comité des travaux historiques et scièntifiques, Paris.

Loveday, R. 2006 Where have all the Neolithic houses gone? Turf—an invisible component. *Scottish Archaeological Journal* **28** (2), 81–104 (DOI 10.3366/E1471576707000046, ISSN 1471-5767).

Lovejoy, C., Meindl, R., Pryzbeck, T. and Mensforth, R. 1985 Chronological metamorphosis of the auricular surface of the ilium: a new method for the determination of adult skeletal age at death. *American Journal of Physical Anthropology* **68**, 15–28.

Lucas, A.T. 1970 National Museum of Ireland: archaeological acquisitions in the year 1967. *Journal of the Royal Society of Antiquaries of Ireland* **100**, 145–66.

Ludemann, T. 2006 Anthracological analysis of recent charcoal-burning in the Black Forest, SW Germany. In A. Dufraisse (ed.), *Charcoal analysis: new analytical tools and methods for archaeology*, 61–70. British

Archaeological Reports, International Series 1483. Archaeopress, Oxford.

Ludemann, T. and Nelle, O. 2002 *Die Wälder am Schauinsland und ihre Nutzung durch Bergbau und Köhlerei*. Schriftenreihe Freiburger förstliche Forschung Bd. 15. Freiburg Förstliche Versuchs- und Forschungsanstalt, Baden-Württemberg.

Lynch, A. 1984 Excavations of the medieval town defences at Charlotte's Quay, Limerick. *Proceedings of the Royal Irish Academy* **84**C, 281–321.

Lynch, G.L. and O'Donnell, L. 2007 Cremation in the Bronze Age: practice, process and belief. In E. Grogan, L. O'Donnell and P. Johnston (eds), *The Bronze Age landscapes of the Gas Pipeline to the West: an integrated archaeological and environmental assessment*, 105–24. Wordwell, Bray.

Lynn, C.J. 1977 Trial excavations at the King's Stables, Tray townland, Co. Armagh. *Ulster Journal of Archaeology* **40**, 42–62.

Lynn, C.J. 1981–2 The excavation of Rathmullan, a raised rath and motte in County Down. *Ulster Journal of Archaeology* **44–5**, 65–171.

Lynn, C.J. and McDowell, J.A. 2011 *Deer Park Farms: the excavation of a raised rath in the Glenarm Valley, Co. Antrim*. Northern Ireland Archaeological Monographs No. 9. Stationery Office, London.

McCarthy, C. 2010 Final archaeological report. Hotel development, Ballynakelly and Rathcreedan, Newcastle, Co. Dublin. Unpublished report for Arch-Tech.

McConnell, B. 1994 *Geology of Carlow–Wexford*. Geological Survey of Ireland, Sligo.

McConnell, B. and Phillcox, M.E. 1994 *Geology of Kildare–Wicklow*. Geological Survey of Ireland, Sligo.

McConnell, B., Aftalion, M. and Kennan, P.S. 1989 Isotopic UU-Pb ages of zircon and monzanite from the Leinster Granite, southeast Ireland. *Geological Magazine* **126**, 725–8.

McCormick, F. and Murray, E.V. 2007 *Knowth and the zooarchaeology of Early Christian Ireland*. Royal Irish Academy, Dublin.

McCorry, M. 1997 Coarseware pottery from phase 3. In D.M. Waterman, *Excavations at Navan Fort 1961–71* (ed. C.J. Lynn), 72–9. Stationery Office, Belfast.

McCorry, M. 2007 Petrological analysis of medieval pottery. In M. Clyne (ed.), *Kells Priory, County Kilkenny: archaeological excavations by T. Fanning and M. Clyne*, 339–42. Stationery Office, Dublin.

MacCotter, P. 2008 *Medieval Ireland: territorial, political and economic divisions*. Four Courts Press, Dublin.

McCutcheon, C. 2000 Medieval pottery in Dublin: some dates and new names. In S. Duffy (ed.), *Medieval Dublin I*, 117–25. Four Courts Press, Dublin.

McCutcheon, C. 2003 Pottery. In R.M. Cleary and M.F. Hurley (eds), *Excavations in Cork City 1984–2000*, 197—235. Cork City Council, Cork.

McCutcheon, C. 2006 *Medieval pottery from Wood Quay, Dublin: the 1974–6 waterfront excavations*. Royal Irish Academy, Dublin.

McCutcheon, C. 2007 The medieval pottery. In M. Clyne (ed.), *Kells Priory, County Kilkenny: archaeological excavations by T. Fanning and M. Clyne*, 316–38. Stationery Office, Dublin.

McCutcheon, C. 2012 The medieval pottery. In T. Breen, 'South-Eastern Motorway Scheme: archaeological resolution. Final report: 00E0525, 02E1532—Carrickmines Great, County Dublin'. Unpublished report for Valerie J. Keeley.

McGarry, T. 2009 Irish late prehistoric ring-ditches. In G. Cooney, K. Becker, J. Coles, M. Ryan and S. Sievers (eds), *Relics of old decency: archaeological studies in later prehistory*, 413–23. Wordwell, Bray.

McGlade, S. 2019 Final report. Excavations at Clonard, Balbriggan, 15E0586. Unpublished excavation report for Archaeology Plan.

McKinley, J. 1989 Cremations: expectations, methodologies and realities. In C.A. Roberts, F. Lee and J. Bintliff (eds), *Burial archaeology: current research, methods and developments*, 65–76. British Archaeological Reports, British Series 211. BAR, Oxford.

McKinley, J.I., Leivers, M., Schuster, J., Marshall, P., Barclay, A. and Stoodley, N. 2015 *Cliffs End Farm, Isle of Thanet, Kent: a mortuary and ritual site of the Bronze Age, Iron Age and Anglo-Saxon period with evidence for long-distance maritime mobility*. Wessex Archaeology, Salisbury.

McLoughlin, C. 2001 Rathmore, Co. Wicklow. In I. Bennett (ed.), *Excavations 2001*, no. 1380. Wordwell, Bray.

McLoughlin, C. 2004 Rathmore, Co. Wicklow: prehistoric. In I. Bennett (ed.), *Excavations 2002*, 187–8. Wordwell, Dublin.

McMahon, M. 1988 Archaeological excavations at the site of the Four Courts extension, Inns Quay, Dublin. *Proceedings of the Royal Irish Academy* **88**C, 271–319.

McNeill, T.E. and Baillie, M.G.L. 1988 An early eighteenth-century pottery assemblage from Dunbar

Street, Belfast. In G. MacNiocaill and P.F. Wallace (eds), *Keimelia—studies in medieval archaeology and history in memory of Tom Delaney*, 349–64. Galway University Press, Galway.

Mac Shamhráin, A. 1996 *Church and polity in pre-Norman Ireland: the case of Glendalough*. Maynooth Monographs 7. An Sagart, Maynooth.

MacWhite, E. 1944a Amber in the Irish Bronze Age. *Journal of the Cork Historical and Archaeological Society* **49**, 122–7.

MacWhite, E. 1944b The bronze socketed gouge in Ireland. *Journal of the Royal Society of Antiquaries of Ireland* **74**, 160–5.

Mahr, A. 1937 New aspects and problems in Irish prehistory. Presidential address for 1937. *Proceedings of the Prehistoric Society* **3**, 261–436.

Malcolmson, R. 1864–6 Proceedings and papers: Ardnehue, Carlow. *Journal of the Royal Society of Antiquaries of Ireland* **5**, 117–21.

Mallía-Guest, M.S. 2011 Make me, use me, leave me. A life-history approach to the flint assemblages from Early Neolithic houses at Corbally, Co. Kildare. Unpublished MA thesis, UCD School of Archaeology.

Mallory, J.P. 1991a Excavations at Haughey's Fort: 1989–1990. *Emania* **8**, 10–26.

Mallory, J.P. 1991b Further dates from Haughey's Fort. *Emania* **9**, 64–5.

Mallory, J.P. 1995 Haughey's Fort and the Navan Complex in the Late Bronze Age. In J. Waddell and E. Shee Twohig (eds), *Ireland in the Bronze Age*, 73–86. Stationery Office, Dublin.

Mallory, J. and Baban, G. 2014 Excavations in Haughey's Fort East. *Emania* **22**, 13–32.

Manby, T.G. 2007 Continuity of monumental traditions into the Late Bronze Age? Henges to ring-forts, and shrines. In C. Burgess, P. Topping and F. Lynch (eds), *Beyond Stonehenge: essays on the Bronze Age in honour of Colin Burgess*, 403–24. Oxbow, Oxford.

Manning, C. 2016 Excavations at Cahergal, Co. Kerry: a venue for royal ceremony in early medieval Corcu Duibne. *Proceedings of the Royal Irish Academy* **116**C, 121–88.

Mannion, M. 2013 An examination of glass beads from early medieval Ireland (2 vols). Unpublished Ph.D thesis, NUI Galway.

Marguerie, D. and Hunot, J.Y. 2007 Charcoal analysis and dendrology: data from archaeological sites in north-western France. *Journal of Archaeological Science* **34**, 1417–33.

Martinón-Torres, M. and Ladra, L. 2011 On the origin of mercury gilding: contributions from the protohistoric goldwork of northwest Iberia. *Trabajos de Prehistoria* **68**, 187–98.

Matešić, S. 2017 Germanen am Limes. Riemenendbeschläge als Indikatoren für germanische Präsenz in römischen Militärlagern. In B.V. Eriksen, A. Abegg-Wigg, R. Bleile and U. Ickerodt (eds), *Interaction without borders. Exemplary archaeological research at the beginning of the 21st century*, I, 347–56. Stiftung Schleswig-Holsteinische Landesmuseen, Schleswig.

Mecking, O. and Walter, D. 2004 Gussformen und Tiegel aus zwei Siedlungen der Urnenfelderzeit im nördlichen Thüringen. *Alt-Thüringen* **37**, 53–67.

Meeks, N., Craddock, P.T. and Needham, S.P. 2008 Bronze Age penannular gold rings from the British Isles: technology and composition. *Jewellery Studies* **11**, 13–30.

Meenan, R. 1997 Post-medieval pottery. In M.F. Hurley and O.M.B. Scully (eds), *Late Viking Age and medieval Waterford: excavations 1986–1992*, 338–55. Waterford Corporation, Waterford.

Megaw, J.V.S. and Simpson, D.D.A. 1979 *Introduction to British prehistory*. Leicester University Press, Leicester.

Melin, M. 2016 *Aubervilliers (Seine-Saint-Denis). Rue Saint-Denis, Rue du Port, Rue du Chemin Vert. Un atelier de bronzier du Bronze final IIb–IIIa. Rapport final d'opération* (2 vols). Arkemine, Service regional d'Archéologie d'Île-de-France, St-Denis.

Melin, M., Arles, A., Roguet, G. and Flament, J. 2017 Un important atelier de fonte du Bronze final IIb–IIIa à Aubervilliers, la Rue du Port (Seine-Saint-Denis). *Bulletin de l'Association pour la Promotion des Recherches sur l'Age du Bronze* **15**, 43–5.

Meyerdirks, U., Rehren, Th. and Harvey, A. 2005 Appendix 8: Reconstructing the early medieval copper smelting at Ross Island. In W. O'Brien (ed.), *Ross Island: mining, metal and society in early Ireland*, 651–64. Bronze Age Studies 6. Department of Archaeology, NUI Galway.

Mildner, S., Schüssler, U., Falkenstein, F. and Brätz, H. 2014 Bronzezeitliches Glas im westlichen Mitteleuropa—Funde, Zusammensetzung und die Frage nach seiner Herkunft. In B. Nessel, I. Heske and D. Brandherm (eds), *Ressourcen und Rohstoffe in der Bronzezeit: Nutzung—Distribution—Kontrolle*, 100–8. Arbeitsberichte zur Bodendenkmalpflege in

Brandenburg 26. Brandenburgisches Landesamt für Denkmalpflege und Archäologisches Landesmuseum, Wünsdorf.

Mitchell, G.F. 1948 The related ages of archaeological objects found in bogs in Ireland. *Proceedings of the Royal Irish Academy* **50**C, 1–19.

Mitchell, G.F. 1951 Studies in Irish Quaternary deposits, no. 7. *Proceedings of the Royal Irish Academy* **53**B, 111–206.

Mitchell, G.F. 1976 *The Irish landscape*. Collins, London.

Mogey, J.M. 1949 Preliminary report on excavations in Mullaghmore td, Co. Down. *Ulster Journal of Archaeology* **12**, 82–8.

Mogey, J.M., Thompson, G.B. and Proudfoot, V.B. 1956 Excavations of two ring-barrows in Mullaghmore townland, Co. Down. *Ulster Journal of Archaeology* **19**, 11–28.

Mohen, J.-P. 1973 Les moules en terre cuite des bronziers protohistoriques. *Antiquités Nationales* **5**, 33–44.

Mohen, J.-P. and Bailloud, G. 1987 *L'âge du bronze en France—4. La vie quotidienne: les fouilles du Fort-Harrouard*. Picard, Paris.

Mohen, J.-P. and Walter, P. 1998 La métallurgie de l'Âge du Bronze sur le Fort-Harrouard (Sorel-Moussel, Eure-et-Loir, France). In C. Mordant, M. Pernot and V. Rychner (eds), *L'atelier du bronzier en Europe du XXe au VIIIe siècle avant notre ère*, 117–22. Comité des travaux historiques et scièntifiques, Paris.

Mohen, J.-P., Aufaure, C., Bouet, B. *et al.* 1989 Ateliers métallurgiques dans l'habitat protohistorique du Fort-Harrouard. *Bulletin de la Société Préhistorique Française* **86** (10/12), 404–8.

Molloy, B. 2009a N8 Cashel to Mitchelstown Road Improvement Scheme final archaeological excavation report: (E2341) Knockcommane. In M. McQuade, B. Molloy and C. Moriarty (eds), *In the shadow of the Galtees: archaeological excavations along the N8 Cashel to Mitchelstown Road Scheme: final excavation reports* (on disc). National Roads Authority, Dublin.

Molloy, B. 2009b The excavation of a medieval enclosure at Charlesland, Co. Wicklow. In M. Potterton and C. Corlett (eds), *Rural settlement in medieval Ireland in the light of recent archaeological excavations*, 149–56. Wordwell, Bray.

Molloy, K. 2005 Holocene vegetation and land-use history at Mooghaun, south-east Clare, with particular reference to the Bronze Age. In E. Grogan, *The North Munster Project, Vol. 1. The later prehistoric landscape of south-east Clare*, 255–301. Discovery Programme Monograph 6. Wordwell, Bray.

Molloy, K. and O'Connell, M. 2016 Farming impact on Ireland from the Neolithic to recent times with particular reference to a detailed pollen record from east Galway. In M.O'Connell, F.Kelly and J.H. Adam (eds), *Cattle in ancient and modern Ireland: farming practices, environment and economy*, 27–43. Cambridge Scholars Publishing, Newcastle-upon-Tyne.

Molloy, K., Feeser, I. and O'Connell, M. 2014 Pollen investigations at Ballinphuill, east Galway: towards reconstruction of vegetation and land-use history on the route of the M6 Galway to Ballinasloe national route. In J. McKeon and J. O'Sullivan (eds), *The quiet landscape: archaeological investigations on the M6 Galway to Ballinasloe national road scheme*, 116–18. NRA Scheme Monographs 15. National Roads Authority, Dublin.

Moloney, C. 2010 N9/N10 Kilcullen to Waterford Scheme: Phase 3, Kilcullen to Carlow. Archaeological Services Contract No. 5—Resolution, Kilcullen to Moone and Athy Link. Final report on archaeological investigations at Site E2989, in the townland of Burtown Little, Co. Kildare. Unpublished report for Headland Archaeology Ireland.

Monk, M.A. 1985–6 Evidence from macroscopic plant remains for crop husbandry in prehistoric and early historic Ireland—a review. *Journal of Irish Archaeology* **3**, 31–6.

Mook, W.G. and Streurman, H.J. 1983 Physical and chemical aspects of radiocarbon dating. In W.G. Mook and H.T. Waterbolk (eds), *Proceedings of the First International Symposium ^{14}C and Archaeology, Groningen*, 31–55. PACT 8. Council of Europe, Strasbourg.

Mook, W.G. and Waterbolk, H.T. 1985 *Radiocarbon dating: a publication of the Sub-committee for Archaeology of the Standing Committee for the Humanities*. European Science Foundation, Strasbourg.

Moore, D.G. 2004 Hostilities in Early Neolithic Ireland: trouble with the new neighbours—the evidence from Ballyharry, County Antrim. In A. Gibson and A. Sheridan (eds), *From sickles to circles: Britain and Ireland at the time of Stonehenge*, 142–54. Tempus, Dublin.

Moore, F., McMahon, P. and Moore, D. 2010 *The Grianán of Aileach. Archaeology Ireland* Heritage Guide No. 48. Wordwell, Bray.

Mullins, G. 2008 Three thousand years of human activity

at Rahally, Co. Galway. In J. O'Sullivan and M. Stanley (eds), *Roads, rediscovery and research: proceedings of a public seminar on archaeological discoveries on national road schemes, August 2007*, 25–35. National Roads Authority, Dublin.

Mullins, G. 2009 Final report on excavations at Rahally, County Galway, A041. Unpublished report by CRDS Ltd for Galway County Council.

Murphy, M. 2008 Tullow—from medieval manor to market town. In T. McGrath (ed.) *Carlow: history and society*, 235–57. Geography Publications, Dublin.

Murphy, M. and Potterton, M. 2010 *The Dublin region in the Middle Ages: settlement, land-use and economy*. Four Courts Press, Dublin.

Musson, C. 1970 House-plans and prehistory. *Current Archaeology* **10**, 267–75.

National Soil Survey 1980 *General soil map of Ireland* (2nd edn). An Foras Talúntais, Dublin.

Needham, S. 1980 An assemblage of Late Bronze Age metalworking debris from Dainton, Devon. *Proceedings of the Prehistoric Society* **46**, 177–215.

Needham, S. 1990 The Penard–Wilburton succession: new metalwork finds from Croxton (Norfolk) and Thirsk (Yorkshire). *Antiquaries Journal* **70** (2), 253–70.

Needham, S. 1991 *Excavation and salvage at Runnymede Bridge, 1978: the Late Bronze Age waterfront site*. British Museum Press/English Heritage, London.

Needham, S. 1996 Chronology and periodisation in the British Bronze Age. In K. Randsborg (ed.), *Absolute chronology: archaeological Europe, 2500–500 BC*, 121–40. Acta Archaeologica 67. Munksgaard, Copenhagen.

Needham, S. 2007 800 BC, the great divide. In C. Haselgrove and R. Pope (eds), *The Early Iron Age in Britain and the near Continent*, 39–63. Oxbow, Oxford.

Needham, S. 2017 Assemblage, structure and meaning in bronze metalwork studies: an analysis of the British Penard assemblage. *Oxford Journal of Archaeology* **36** (2), 111–56.

Needham, S. and Bridgford, S. 2013 Deposits of clay refractories for casting bronze swords. In N. Brown and M. Medlycott (eds), *The Neolithic and Bronze Age enclosures at Springfield Lyons, Essex: excavations 1981–1991*, 47–74. East Anglian Archaeology 149. Essex County Council, Chelmsford.

Needham, S.P., Bronk Ramsey, C., Cartwright, C. and Pettitt, P. 1997 An independent chronology for British Bronze Age metalwork: the results of the Oxford radiocarbon Accelerator Programme. *Archaeological Journal* **154**, 55–107.

Neuburg, F. 1949 *Glass in antiquity*. Rankin Brothers, London.

Neuninger, H. and Pittioni, R. 1959 Woher stammen die blauen Glasperlen der Urnenfelderkultur? *Archaeologia Austriaca* **6**, 52–6.

Newman, C. 1993 Sleeping in Elysium. *Archaeology Ireland* 7 (3), 20–3.

Newman, C. 1995a Raffin Fort, Co. Meath: Neolithic and Bronze Age activity. In E. Grogan and C. Mount (eds), *Annus Archaeologiae: proceedings of the OIA Winter Conference 1993*, 55–66. Organisation of Irish Archaeologists, Dublin.

Newman, C. 1995b The Iron Age to Early Christian transition: the evidence from dress fasteners. In C. Bourke (ed.), *From the isles of the north: early medieval art in Ireland and Britain*, 17–25. HMSO, Belfast.

Newman, C. 1997a Ballinderry crannog no. 2, Co. Offaly: the Later Bronze Age. *Journal of Irish Archaeology* **8**, 91–100.

Newman, C. 1997b *Tara: an archaeological survey*. Discovery Programme Monograph 2. Royal Irish Academy, Dublin.

Newstead, S. 2013 Merida no more: Portuguese redware in Newfoundland. In P.E. Pope (ed.), *Exploring Atlantic transitions: archaeologies of transience and permanence in new found lands*, 140–51. Boydell and Brewer, Woodbridge.

Nicholls, K.W. 1982 Anglo-French Ireland and after. *Peritia* **1**, 370–402.

Nicholson, R. and Hillam, J. 1987 A dendrochronological analysis of oak timbers from the early medieval site at Dundas Wharf, Bristol. *Transactions of the Bristol and Gloucestershire Archaeological Society* **105**, 133–45.

Northover, J.P. 1982 The exploration of long-distance movement of bronze in Bronze and Early Iron Age Europe. *Bulletin of the Institute of Archaeology* **19**, 45–71.

Northover, P. 2000 Ring money: the problem child of Bronze Age gold. *Beiträge aus der Mineralogie, Geochemie, Lagerstättenforschung, Archäometrie, Archäologie und Denkmalpflege Munchner Geologische Hefte* **28**, 299–304.

Northover, P. and Anheuser, K. 2000 Gilding in Britain: Celtic, Roman and Saxon. In T. Drayman-Weisser (ed.), *Gilded metals: history, technology and conservation*, 109–21. Archetype, London.

O'Brien, E. 1999 *Post-Roman Britain to Anglo-Saxon England: burial practices reviewed.* British Archaeological Reports, British Series 289. Archaeopress, Oxford.

O'Brien, E. and Bhreathnach, E. 2011 Irish boundary ferta, their physical manifestation and historical context. In F. Edmonds and P. Russell (eds), *Tome: studies in medieval Celtic history and law in honour of Thomas Charles-Edwards*, 53–64. Boydell and Brewer, Woodbridge.

O'Brien, W. 2015 *Prehistoric copper mining in Europe: 5500–500 BC.* Oxford University Press, Oxford.

O'Brien, W. 2016 Clashanimud and the Bronze Age hillforts of Munster. *Emania* **23**, 5–18.

O'Brien, W. 2017a Hillforts and warfare in Bronze Age Ireland. In W. O'Brien and J. O'Driscoll, *Hillforts, warfare and society in Bronze Age Ireland*, 393–414. Archaeopress, Oxford.

O'Brien, W. 2017b Hillforts and social hierarchies. In W. O'Brien and J. O'Driscoll, *Hillforts, warfare and society in Bronze Age Ireland*, 439–42. Archaeopress, Oxford.

O'Brien, W. 2017c A time of trouble. In W. O'Brien and J. O'Driscoll, *Hillforts, warfare and society in Bronze Age Ireland*, 443–6. Archaeopress, Oxford.

O'Brien, W. 2019 Derrycarhoon mine and the supply of copper in later Bronze Age Ireland. In D. Brandherm (ed.), *Aspects of the Bronze Age in the Atlantic archipelago and beyond: proceedings from the Belfast Bronze Age Forum, 9–10 November 2013*, 121–43. Curach Bhán Publications, Hagen.

O'Brien, W. and O'Driscoll, J. 2017 *Hillforts, warfare and society in Bronze Age Ireland.* Archaeopress, Oxford.

O'Byrne, E. 2001 War, politics and the Irish of Leinster 1156–1606. Unpublished Ph.D thesis, Trinity College Dublin (http://hdl.handle.net/2262/77229; accessed May 2017).

O'Carroll, F. 2012a Clay moulds. In C. Cotter, *The Western Stone Forts Project: excavations at Dún Aonghasa and Dún Eoghanachta*, Vol. 2, 28–42. Discovery Programme Monograph. Wordwell, Dublin.

O'Carroll, F. 2012b The crucible assemblage. In C. Cotter, *The Western Stone Forts Project: excavations at Dún Aonghasa and Dún Eoghanachta*, Vol. 2, 42–4. Discovery Programme Monograph. Wordwell, Dublin.

O'Connell, T.J. 2009 N9/N10 Kilcullen to Waterford Scheme: Kilcullen to Powerstown. Archaeological Services Contract No. 4. Resolution, Prumplestown to Powerstown. Final report on archaeological investigations at Site E2610, in the townland of Ballybannon, Co. Carlow. Unpublished report for Headland Archaeology Ltd.

O'Connell, T.J. and Hegarty, L. 2009 N9/N10 Kilcullen to Waterford Scheme: Kilcullen to Powerstown. Archaeological Services Contract No. 4. Resolution, Prumplestown to Powerstown. Final report on archaeological investigations at Site E2573, in the townland of Ballyhade, Co. Kildare. Unpublished report for Headland Archaeology Ltd.

O'Connor, B. 1980 *Cross-channel relations in the Later Bronze Age.* British Archaeological Reports, International Series 91. Archaeopress, Oxford.

O'Connor, B., Roberts, B. and Wilkinson, N. 2017 The Ornament Horizon revisited: new and old finds of Middle Bronze Age ornaments in southern England. In T. Lachenal, C. Mordant, T. Nicolas and C. Veber (eds), *Le Bronze moyen et l'origine du Bronze final en Europe occidentale, de la Mer du Nord à la Méditerranée (XVIIe–XIIIe siècle avant notre ère)*, 269–81. Mémoires d'Archéologie du Grand-Est, Strasbourg.

O'Connor, P.J., Aftalion, M. and Kennan, P.S. 1989 Isotopic UU-Pb ages of zircon and monzanite from the Leinster Granite, southeast Ireland. *Geological Magazine* **126**, 725–8.

O'Conor, K. 1998 *The archaeology of medieval rural settlement in Ireland.* Discovery Programme Monograph 3. Royal Irish Academy, Dublin.

O'Conor, K. 2002 Housing in later medieval Gaelic Ireland. In J. Klašptě (ed.), *The rural house from the Migration Period to the oldest still standing buildings*, 197–206. Ruralia 4. Brepols, Prague.

O'Donnell, L. 2004a Charcoal analysis from Charlesland, Co. Wicklow (licence no. 03E0146). Unpublished report for Margaret Gowen and Co. Ltd.

O'Donnell, L. 2004b Charcoal analysis from Charlesland, Co. Wicklow (licence no. 04E0774). Unpublished report for Margaret Gowen and Co. Ltd.

O'Donnell, L. 2005 Assessment of soil samples, Rathgall, Rath East, Co. Wicklow. Unpublished report for Margaret Gowen and Co. Ltd.

O'Donnell, L. 2006 Charcoal analysis from Ballynagran, Co. Wicklow (licence no. 06E0552). Unpublished report for Margaret Gowen and Co. Ltd.

O'Donnell, L. 2007 The wood and charcoal. In E. Grogan, L. O'Donnell and P. Johnston (eds), *The Bronze Age landscapes of the Gas Pipeline to the West: an integrated archaeological and environmental assessment*, 27–69. Wordwell, Bray.

O'Donnell, L. 2011 People and woodlands: an investigation of charcoal remains as indicators of cultural selection and local environment in Bronze Age Ireland. Unpublished Ph.D thesis, University College Dublin.

O'Donnell, L. 2012 Charcoal analysis from Rathgall, Co. Wicklow (E4394). In M. Seaver, 'Final report on the archaeological assessment of Trench X, Area 9, prior to reinstatement at Rathgall, Rath East, County Wicklow. Ministerial Consent C495/ E4394', 24–39. Unpublished report for the School of Archaeology, University College Dublin.

O'Donnell, L. 2016 The power of the pyre—a holistic study of cremation focusing on charcoal remains. *Journal of Archaeological Science* **65**, 161–71.

O'Donnell, L., Johnston, P. and Cummins, T. 2005 Analysis of further soil samples, charcoal, and charred plant remains from Rathgall, Rath East, Co. Wicklow. Unpublished report for Margaret Gowen and Co. Ltd.

O'Donovan, E. 1998 Cherrywood/Laughanstown, Co. Dublin. Prehistoric/post-medieval. In I. Bennett (ed.), *Excavations 1997*, 128. Wordwell, Dublin.

Ó Drisceoil, C. 2003 Archaeological excavations of a Neolithic settlement at Coolfore, Co. Louth. In I. Armit, E. Murphy, E. Nelis and D. Simpson (eds), *Neolithic settlement in Ireland and western Britain*, 176–81. Oxbow, Oxford.

Ó Drisceoil, C., McCutcheon, C. and Wren, J. 2022 The products of the Highhays pottery. In E. Devine and C. Ó Drisceoil, *Highhays, Kilkenny: a medieval pottery production centre in south-east Ireland*, 80–138. Oxbow, Oxford.

O'Driscoll, J. 2016 The Baltinglass landscape and the hillforts of Bronze Age Ireland. Unpublished Ph.D thesis, University College Cork.

O'Driscoll, J. 2017a Ireland's hillfort capital revisited. *Archaeology Ireland* **31** (4), 30–4.

O'Driscoll, J. 2017b Hillforts, trade and routeways. In W. O'Brien and J. O'Driscoll, *Hillforts, warfare and society in Bronze Age Ireland*, 420–38. Archaeopress, Oxford.

O'Driscoll, J. 2019a Picture perfect: using drone technology and photogrammetry techniques to map the Western Stone Forts of Ireland. *Journal of Field Archaeology* **44** (2), 126–46.

O'Driscoll, J. 2019b A case study for landscape applications of drone and photogrammetry techniques: Faha and Caherconree hillforts, Co. Kerry. *Journal of the Kerry Archaeological and Historical Society* (2019), 1–28.

O'Driscoll, J. (forthcoming) High society: settlement conglomerations at Bronze Age hillforts in Ireland. In M. Murphy and R. Tracey (eds), *Irish settlement studies*. Four Courts Press, Dublin.

O'Driscoll, J. and Becker, K. 2022 Piecing together the mosaic of the Rathgall landscape. *Archaeology Ireland* **36** (4), 30–6.

O'Driscoll, J. and Gleeson, P. 2021 Locating historical Dún Bolg and the early medieval landscape of Baltinglass, Co. Wicklow. *Proceedings of the Royal Irish Academy* **121** C, 1–34.

Ó Faoláin, S. 2004 *Bronze Age artefact production in Late Bronze Age Ireland: a survey*. British Archaeological Reports, British Series 382. Archaeopress, Oxford.

Ó Faoláin, S. (n.d.) The Johnstown South refractory ceramics. In M. Fitzpatrick, 'Excavation at Johnstown South, Co. Wicklow'. Unpublished excavation report for Valerie J. Keeley.

Ó Floinn, R. 1976 Medieval cooking pottery in Leinster, thirteenth to fourteenth century. Unpublished MA thesis, NUI.

Ó Floinn, R. 1988 Handmade medieval pottery—Leinster Cooking Ware. In G. Mac Niocaill and P.F. Wallace (eds), *Keimelia—studies in medieval archaeology and history in memory of Tom Delaney*, 325–48. Galway University Press, Galway.

Ó h-Iceadha, G. 1946 The Moylisha megalith, Co. Wicklow. *Journal of the Royal Society of Antiquaries of Ireland* **76**, 119–28.

O'Kelly, M.J. 1952–3 Three promontory forts in Co. Cork. *Proceedings of the Royal Irish Academy* **55**C, 25–60.

O'Kelly, M.J. 1982 *Newgrange: archaeology, art and legend*. Thames and Hudson, London.

O'Kelly, M.J. 1989 *Early Ireland: an introduction to Irish prehistory*. Cambridge University Press, Cambridge.

O'Neill, H. 2009 N9/N10 Kilcullen to Waterford Scheme: Kilcullen to Powerstown. Archaeological Services Contract No. 4. Resolution, Prumplestown to Powerstown. Final report on archaeological investigations at Site E2580, in the townland of Busherstown, Co. Carlow. Unpublished report for Headland Archaeology Ltd.

Ó Néill, J. 2004 Data Structure Report 38. Excavations at Ballyarnet, Co. Londonderry. Unpublished report for the Centre for Archaeological Fieldwork, QUB.

Ó Néill, J. 2009 Inventory of Bronze Age structures. Unpublished report for the Heritage Council.

Ó Néill, J. and Macdonald, P. 2009 Investigation of the

find-spot of the Tamlaght hoard, Co. Armagh. In G. Cooney, K. Becker, J. Coles, M. Ryan and S. Sievers (eds), *Relics of old decency: archaeological studies in later prehistory*, 167–80. Wordwell, Bray.

Ó Néill, J., Schulting, R., Whitehouse, N., Adams, K. and Kerr, T. 2002 Data Structure Report 5. Excavations at Ballyarnet, County Londonderry. Unpublished report for the Centre for Archaeological Fieldwork, QUB.

O'Neill, T. 1987 *Merchants and mariners in medieval Ireland*. Irish Academic Press, Dublin.

O'Neill, T. 2009 M7 Portlaoise–Callahill motorway scheme. Contract 1, Gortnaclea–Oldtown, Phase 2—excavation: report on the archaeological excavation of Parknahown 2, Co. Laois. Unpublished report for Archaeological Consultancy Services Ltd.

O'Rahilly, C. 1998 A classification of bronze stick-pins from the Dublin excavations 1962–72. In C. Manning (ed.), *Dublin and beyond the Pale: studies in honour of Patrick Healy*, 23–34. Wordwell, Bray.

Ó Ríordáin, B. and Waddell, J. 1993 *The funerary bowls and vases of the Irish Bronze Age*. Galway University Press, Galway.

Ó Ríordáin, S.P. 1942a *Antiquities of the Irish countryside.* Cork University Press, Cork.

Ó Ríordáin, S.P. 1942b The excavation of a large earthen ringfort at Garranes, Co. Cork. *Proceedings of the Royal Irish Academy* 47C, 77–150.

Ó Ríordáin, S.P. 1949 Lough Gur excavations: Carraig Aille and the 'Spectacles'. *Proceedings of the Royal Irish Academy* **52**C, 39–111.

Ó Ríordáin, S.P. 1951 Lough Gur excavations: the Great Stone Circle (B) in Grange townland. *Proceedings of the Royal Irish Academy* **54**C, 37–74.

Ó Ríordáin, S.P. 1954 Lough Gur excavations: Neolithic and Bronze Age houses on Knockadoon. *Proceedings of the Royal Irish Academy* **56**C, 297–459.

Ó Ríordáin, S.P. 1979 *Antiquities of the Irish countryside* (5th edn, revised by Ruaidhri de Valera). Methuen, London and New York.

Ó Ríordáin, S.P. and Ó h-Iceadha, G. 1955 Lough Gur excavations: the megalithic tomb. *Journal of the Royal Society of Antiquaries of Ireland* **85**, 34–50.

O'Sullivan, A. 1998a Woodland management and the supply of timber and underwood to Anglo-Norman Dublin. In G. De Boe and F. Verhaeghe (eds), *Environment and subsistence in medieval Europe*, 135–41. Scientific Institution of the Flemish Community, Doornveld.

O'Sullivan, A. 1998b Woodmanship and the supply of underwood and timber to Anglo-Norman Dublin. In C. Manning (ed.), *Dublin and beyond the Pale*, 59–70. Wordwell, Bray.

O'Sullivan, A. 2005 The middle enclosure. In E. Grogan, *The North Munster Project, Vol. 1. The later prehistoric landscape of south-east Clare*, 153–62. Wordwell, Bray.

O'Sullivan, A. and Nicholl, T. 2010 Early medieval settlement enclosures in Ireland: dwellings, daily life and social identity. *Proceedings of the Royal Irish Academy* **111**C, 59–90.

O'Sullivan, A., McCormick, F., Kerr, T. and Harney, L. 2008 *Early medieval Ireland: archaeological excavations 1930–2004*. Early Medieval Archaeology Project (EMAP) Report 2.1. UCD/ QUB/Heritage Council, Dublin.

O'Sullivan, M. and Downey, L. 2009 Charcoal production sites. *Archaeology Ireland* **23** (4), 22–5.

Oddy, A. 1993 The gilding of metals in the Old World. In S. La Niece and P.T. Craddock (eds), *Metal plating and patination*, 161–70. Butterworth Heineman, Oxford.

Oldeberg, A. 1943 *Metallteknik under Förhistorisk Tid*, Del II. Otto Harrasowitz, Lund.

Orpen, G.H. 1911 Rathgall, County Wicklow. *Journal of the Royal Society of Antiquaries of Ireland* **1** (2), 138–50.

Orpen, G.H. 1913 Rathgall, County Wicklow, Dún Gallion and the 'Dunum' of Ptolemy. *Proceedings of the Royal Irish Academy* **32**C, 41–57.

Orpen, G.H. 1931 Rathgall: the rath of the foreigners. *Journal of the Kildare Archaeological Society* **11**, 31–5.

Otway-Ruthven, A.J. 1980 *A history of medieval Ireland.* E. Benn, London.

Out, W., Hänninen, K. and Vermeeren, C. 2017 Using branch age and diameter to identify woodland management: new developments. *Environmental Archaeology* **23** (3), 254–66.

Panter, I. 2000 Jet and amber. In A.J. Mainham and N.S.H. Rogers, *Craft, industry and everyday life: finds from Anglo-Scandinavian York*, 2469–74 and 2500–17. The Archaeology of York 17/14. Council for British Archaeology, York.

Paradis-Grenouillet, S., Dufraisse, A. and Allee, P. 2013 Radius of curvature measurements and wood diameter: a comparison of different image analysis techniques. In F. Damblon (ed.), *Proceedings of the Fourth International Meeting of Anthracology*, 173–82. British Archaeological Reports, International Series 2486. Archaeopress,

Oxford.

Parker Pearson, M., Casswell, C. and Welham, K. 2018 A Late Bronze Age ring-fort at Bayvil Farm, Pembrokeshire. *Archaeologia Cambrensis* **167**, 113–41.

Parr, J.F. and Boyd, W.E. 2002 The probable industrial origin of archaeological daub at an Iron Age site in northeast Thailand. *Geoarchaeology: An International Journal* 17 (3), 285–303 (https://doi.org/10.1002/gea.10013).

Paynter, S. 2014 Late Bronze Age glass beads. *Glass News* **35**, 8–9.

Peake, J. and Freestone, I. 2012 Cross-craft interactions between metal and glass working: slag additions to early Anglo-Saxon red glass. *Proceedings of SPIE 8422: Integrated Approaches to the Study of Historical Glass* (https://doi.org/10.1117/12.973765). Society of Photo-Optical Instrumentation Engineers, Brussels.

Pearce, J.E., Vince, A.G. and Jenner, M.A. 1985 *A dated type-series of London medieval pottery, part 2: London-type ware*. London and Middlesex Archaeological Society, London.

Pearce, M., Bellintani, P. and Nicolis, F. 2020 Frattesina and the later Bronze Age–Early Iron Age metals trade: the absolute chronology of smelting sites in the Trentino–Alto Adige/Südtirol. *Padusa* **55**, 67–86.

Perea, A., Montero, I., Gutiérrez, P.C. and Climent-Font, A. 2008 Origen y trayectoria de una técnia esquiva: el dorado sobre metal. *Trabajos de Prehistoria* **65** (2), 117–30.

Plunkett, G. 2009 Land-use patterns and cultural change in the Middle to Late Bronze Age in Ireland: inferences from the pollen record. *Vegetation History and Archaeobotany* **18**, 273–95.

Plunkett, G., Whitehouse, N.J., Hall, V.A., Charman, D.J., Blaauw, M., Kelly, E. and Mulhall, I. 2009 A multi-proxy palaeoenvironmental investigation of the findspot of an Iron Age bog body from Oldcroghan, Co. Offaly, Ireland. *Journal of Archaeological Science* **36**, 265–77.

Pollard, A.M. and Heron, C. 1996 *Archaeological chemistry*. Royal Society of Chemistry, Cambridge.

Pollock, A.J. and Waterman, D.M. 1963 A medieval pottery kiln at Downpatrick. *Ulster Journal of Archaeology* **26**, 79–104.

Ponsford, M. 1991 Dendrochronological dates from Dundas Wharf, Bristol, and the dating of Ham Green and other medieval pottery. In E. Lewis (ed.), *Custom and ceramics: essays presented to Kenneth Barton*, 81–103. APE, Wickham.

Pope, R. 2003 Prehistoric dwelling. Circular structures in north and central Britain *c.* 2500 BC–AD 500. Unpublished Ph.D thesis, University of Durham.

Pope, R. 2007 Ritual and the roundhouse: a critique of recent ideas on the use of domestic space in later British prehistory. In C. Haselgrove and R. Pope (eds), *The earlier Iron Age in Britain and the near continent*, 204–28. Oxbow, Oxford.

Potter, D., Eriksson, T., Evans, R.C. *et al.* 2007 Phylogeny and classification of Rosaceae. *Plant Systematics and Evolution* **266** (1–2), 5–43.

Potterton, M. and Corlett, C. 2009 *Rural settlement in medieval Ireland in the light of recent archaeological excavations*. Wordwell, Bray.

Powell, T.G.E. 1938 Excavation of a megalithic tomb at Ballynamona Lower, County Waterford. *Journal of the Royal Society of Antiquaries of Ireland* **68**, 260–71.

Price, L. 1956 The barony of Shillelagh. *Journal of the Royal Society of Antiquaries of Ireland* **86** (1), 77–83.

Prior, J. and Alvin, K.L. 1986 Structural changes on charring woods of *Dichrostachys* and *Salix* from Southern Africa: the effect of moisture content. *IAWA Bulletin* 7 (3), 243–9.

Proudfoot, B. 1954 Excavations at Cathedral Hill, Downpatrick, Co. Down: preliminary report on excavations in 1953. *Ulster Journal of Archaeology* (3rd ser.) 17, 97–102.

Pryor, F. 2001 *The Flag Fen Basin: archaeology and environment of a fenland landscape*. English Heritage, London.

Purcell, A. 1998 Brownstown, Corbally and Silliot Hill, Co. Kildare. In I. Bennett (ed.), *Excavations 1997*, 91. Wordwell, Dublin.

Purcell, A. 1999 Neolithic houses at Corbally, Kilcullen, Co. Kildare. *Archaeology Ireland* **47**, 15.

Quinn, A. 2013 Mondaniel 3—undefended rural farmstead. In K. Hanley and M.F. Hurley (eds), *Generations: the archaeology of five national road schemes in County Cork*, Vol. 2, 252–7. National Roads Authority Monograph 13. Wordwell, Bray.

Rackham, O. 1980 *Ancient woodland: its history, vegetation and uses in England*. Edward Arnold, London.

Rackham, O. 1982 The growing and transport of timber and underwood. In S. McGrail (ed.), *Woodworking techniques before AD 1500*, 199–218. British Archaeological Reports, International Series 129. Oxford.

Rackham, O. 1994 Woodmanship. *Botanical Journal of*

Scotland **46**, 651–7.

Raddatz, K. 1957 *Der Thorsberger Moorfund. Gürtelteile und Körperschmuck*. Offa-Bücher 13. Karl Wachholtz, Neumünster.

Raftery, B. 1969 Freestone Hill, Co. Kilkenny: an Iron Age hillfort and Bronze Age cairn. *Proceedings of the Royal Irish Academy* **68**C, 1–108.

Raftery, B. 1970a The Rathgall hillfort, County Wicklow. *Antiquity* **44**, 51–4.

Raftery, B. 1970b A decorated strap-end from Rathgall, Co. Wicklow. *Journal of the Royal Society of Antiquaries of Ireland* **100**, 200–11.

Raftery, B. 1970c Rathgall, Co. Wicklow (S902731). *Bulletin of the Group for the Study of Irish Historic Settlement* **1**, 17–18.

Raftery, B. 1970d No. 35. Rathgall, Rath East td. *Excavations 1970*, 21–3. Association of Young Irish Archaeologists, Belfast.

Raftery, B. 1971a Rathgall, Co. Wicklow: 1970 excavations. *Antiquity* **45**, 296–8.

Raftery, B. 1971b No. 34. Rathgall (td. Rath East). S902 731. *Excavations 1971*, 26–8. Association of Young Irish Archaeologists, Belfast.

Raftery, B. 1972a Irish hill-forts. In C. Thomas (ed.), *The Iron Age in the Irish Sea province*, 37–58. CBA Research Report 9. Council for British Archaeology, London.

Raftery, B. 1972b No. 36. Rathgall (td. Rath East). S902 731. In T.G. Delaney (ed.), *Excavations 1972: summary accounts of archaeological work in Ireland*, 30. Association of Young Irish Archaeologists, Belfast.

Raftery, B. 1973a Rathgall: a Late Bronze Age burial in Ireland. *Antiquity* **47**, 293–5.

Raftery, B. 1973b Rathgall (td. Rath East). S902 731. In T.G. Delaney (ed.), *Excavations 1973: summary accounts of archaeological work in Ireland*, 28–9. Association of Young Irish Archaeologists, Belfast.

Raftery, B. 1974 A prehistoric burial mound at Baunogenasraid, Co. Carlow. *Proceedings of the Royal Irish Academy* 74C, 277–312.

Raftery, B. 1975 A Late Bronze Age bar toggle from Ireland. *Archaeologia Atlantica* **1** (1), 83–9.

Raftery, B. 1976 Rathgall and Irish hillfort problems. In D.W. Harding (ed.), *Hillforts: later prehistoric earthworks in Britain and Ireland*, 339–57. Academic Press, London.

Raftery, B. 1983 *A catalogue of Irish Iron Age antiquities*. Veröffentlichung des Vorgeschichtlichen Seminars Marburg, Sonderband 1. Kempkes, Marburg.

Raftery, B. 1994 *Pagan Celtic Ireland: the enigma of the Irish Iron Age*. Thames and Hudson, London and New York.

Raftery, B. 1995 The conundrum of Irish Iron Age pottery. In B. Raftery, V. Megaw and V. Rigby (eds), *Sites and sights of the Iron Age: essays on fieldwork and museum research presented to Ian Mathieson Stead*, 149–56. Oxbow Monograph 56. Oxbow, Oxford.

Raftery, B. 1997a *Trackway excavations in the Mountdillon Bogs, Co. Longford, 1985–1991*. Irish Archaeological Wetland Unit Transactions 3. Crannóg Publications, Dublin.

Raftery, B. 1997b Discussion of diagnostic finds. In D.M. Waterman, *Excavations at Navan Fort 1961–1971* (ed. C.J. Lynn), 90–5. Stationery Office, Belfast.

Raftery, B. 2004 Pit 119: Rathgall, Co. Wicklow. In H. Roche, E. Grogan, J. Bradley, J. Coles and B. Raftery (eds), *From megaliths to metals: essays in honour of George Eogan*, 83–90. Oxbow, Oxford.

Raftery, B. 2007 The medieval settlement at Rathgall, County Wicklow. In C. Manning (ed.), *From ringforts to fortified houses: studies on castles and other monuments in honour of David Sweetman*, 95–206. Wordwell, Bray.

Raftery, B. and Henderson, J. 1987 Some glass beads of the later Bronze Age in Ireland. In C. Dobiat, H. Matthäus, B. Raftery and J. Henderson, *Glasperlen der Vorrömischen Eisenzeit II nach Unterlagen von Th.E. Haevernick*, 39–48. Marburger Studien zur Vor- und Frühgeschichte 9. Philip von Zabern, Mainz.

Raftery, J. 1942 Knocknalappa crannog, Co. Clare. *North Munster Antiquarian Journal* **3**, 53–72.

Raftery, J. 1944 A Neolithic burial in County Carlow. *Journal of the Royal Society of Antiquaries of Ireland* **74**, 61–2.

Raftery, J. 1951 *Prehistoric Ireland*. Batsford, Dublin.

Ralston, I. 2006 *Celtic fortifications*. Tempus, Stroud.

Ramsayer, D. and Stöckli, L. 2001 L'habitat de l'âge du bronze final d'Ursy, FR-En la Douchière. *Jahrbuch der Schweizerischen Gesellschaft für Ur- und Frühgeschichte* **84**, 158–70.

Ramsey, G. 1989 Middle Bronze Age weapons in Ireland. Unpublished Ph.D thesis, Queen's University, Belfast.

Ramsey, G. 1995 Middle Bronze Age metalwork: are artefact studies dead and buried? In J. Waddell and E. Shee Twohig (eds), *Ireland in the Bronze Age*, 49–63. Stationery Office, Dublin.

Rathbone, S. 2006 Berrilstown 1, E3062: final excavation report. Unpublished report for ACS Ltd.

Rathbone, S. 2013 A consideration of villages in Neolithic and Bronze Age Britain and Ireland. *Proceedings of the Prehistoric Society* **79**, 39–60.

Reid, A. and Maclean, R. 1995 Symbolism and the social contexts of iron production in Karagwe. *World Archaeology* **27** (1), 144–61.

Reimer, P.J., Austin, W.E.N., Bard, E. *et al.* 2020 The IntCal20 Northern Hemisphere radiocarbon age calibration curve (0–55 cal kBP). *Radiocarbon* **62**, 725–57.

Reimer, P.J., Baillie, M.G.L., Bard, E. *et al.* 2004 IntCal04 terrestrial radiocarbon age calibration, 0–26 cal kyr BP. *Radiocarbon* **46**, 1029–58.

Reynolds, P.J. 1979 *Iron Age farm: the Butser experiment*. British Museum Publications and Colonade Books, London.

Reynolds, P. 2000 Butser Ancient Farm: the burning house experiment. *Current Archaeology* **171**, 92–7.

Rice, K. 2006 The prehistory of Piperstown: a reassessment of an upland landscape. Unpublished MA thesis, National University of Ireland.

Roberts, B. 2007 Adorning the living but not the dead: a reassessment of Middle Bronze Age ornaments in Britain. *Proceedings of the Prehistoric Society* **73**, 135–67.

Roche, H. 2004a The prehistoric pottery assemblage from Skidoo, Co. Dublin. Unpublished report for Arch-Tech Ltd.

Roche, H. 2004b The prehistoric pottery assemblage from Lusk, Co. Dublin. Unpublished report for Arch-Tech Ltd.

Roche, H. 2004c The dating of the embanked stone circle at Grange, Co. Limerick. In H. Roche, E. Grogan, J. Bradley, J. Coles and B. Raftery (eds), *From megaliths to metals: essays in honour of George Eogan*, 109–16. Oxbow, Oxford.

Roche, H. 2016 Neolithic and Bronze Age pottery from Irish caves. In M. Dowd (ed.), *Underground archaeology*, 79–104. Oxbow, Oxford.

Roche, H. and Eogan, G. 2007 A re-assessment of the enclosure at Lugg, County Dublin, Ireland. In C. Gosden, H. Hamerow, P. de Jersey and G. Lock (eds), *Communities and connections: essays in honour of Barry Cunliffe*, 154–68. Oxford University Press, Oxford.

Roche, H. and Grogan, E. 2005 The prehistoric pottery from Ward Upper, Co. Dublin. Unpublished report for CRDS Ltd.

Roche, H. and Grogan, E. 2011 Pottery. In V. Ginn and S. Rathbone (eds), *Corrstown: a coastal community—excavations of a Bronze Age village in Northern Ireland*, 167–85. Oxbow, Oxford.

Rogers, J. and Waldron, T. 1995 *A field guide to joint disease in archaeology*. Wiley and Sons, Chichester.

Romankiewicz, T. 2011 *The complex roundhouses of the Scottish Iron Age*, Vol. 1. British Archaeological Reports, British Series 550. Archaeopress, Oxford.

Romankiewicz, T. 2023 The building blocks of circular economies: rethinking prehistoric turf architecture through archaeological and architectural analysis. *Open Archaeology* **9** (https://doi.org/10.1515/opar-2022-0331).

Roth, H. 1974 Ein Ledermesser der Atlantischen Bronzezeit aus Mittelfranken. *Archäologisches Korrespondenzblatt* **4**, 37–47.

Rowlands, M. 1976 *The production and distribution of metalwork in the Middle Bronze Age in southern Britain*. British Archaeological Reports, British Series 31. BAR, Oxford.

Ryan, M. 1973 The excavation of a Neolithic burial mound at Jerpoint West, Co. Kilkenny. *Proceedings of the Royal Irish Academy* **73C**, 107–27.

Ryan, M., Ó Floinn, R., Lowick, N., Kenny, M. and Cazalet, P. 1984 Six silver finds of the Viking period from the vicinity of Lough Ennell, Co. Westmeath. *Peritia* **3**, 334–81.

Rychner-Faraggi, A.-M. 1993 *Hauterive-Champréveyres 9. Métal et parure au Bronze final*. Archéologie neuchâteloise 17. Musée cantonal d'archéologie, Neuchâtel.

Sandes, C. 1993 Rathgall, Co. Wicklow: the medieval pottery, and its wider context. Unpublished MA thesis, National University of Ireland.

Sandes, C.A. with McCutcheon, C. 2012 Medieval and post-medieval pottery. In G. Eogan, *Excavations at Knowth 5: The archaeology of Knowth in the first and second millennia AD*, 444–501. Royal Irish Academy, Dublin.

Savage, G. and Newman, H. 1985 [2000] *An illustrated dictionary of ceramics* [reprint]. Thames and Hudson, London.

Schotsmans, E., Toksoy Köksal, F., Brettell, R.C. *et al.* 2019 Not all that is white is lime. White substances from archaeological burial contexts. *Archaeometry* **61** (4), 809–27.

Schwab, R., Willer, F., Meinel, D., Schmauder, E. and Pernicka, E. 2010 The Oedt sword: a note on brass and fire-gilding in the European Bronze Age. *Journal of the Historical Metallurgy Society* **44** (1), 1–9.

Schweingruber, F.H. 1978 *Microscopic wood anatomy.* Swiss Federal Institute for Forest, Snow and Landscape Research, Birmensdorf.

Schweingruber, F.H. 2001 *Dendroökologische Holzanatomie. Anatomische Grundlagen der Dendrochronologie.* Haupt, Bern.

Scott, E.M. 2003 The Third International Radiocarbon Intercomparison (TIRI) and the Fourth International Radiocarbon Intercomparison (FIRI) 1990–2002: results, analysis, and conclusions. *Radiocarbon* **45** (2), 135–408.

Scott, E.M., Harkness, D.D. and Cook, G.T. 1998 Interlaboratory comparisons: lessons learned. *Radiocarbon* **40**, 331–40.

Scully, O. 1997 Section 15: Metal artefacts. In M.F. Hurley and O.M.B. Scully (eds), *Late Viking Age and medieval Waterford: excavations 1986–1992*, 438–48. Waterford Corporation, Waterford.

Seaver, M. 2011 Back to basics: contexts of human burial on Irish early medieval enclosed settlements. In S. Conran, E. Danaher and M. Stanley (eds), *Past times, changing fortunes: proceedings of a public seminar on archaeological discoveries on national road schemes, August 2010*, 113–29. National Roads Authority, Dublin.

Seaver, M. 2012 Final report on the archaeological assessment of Trench X, Area 9, prior to reinstatement at Rathgall, Rath East, County Wicklow. Ministerial Consent C495/ E4394. Unpublished report for the School of Archaeology, University College Dublin.

Shannahan, B. 2005 The manor in east County Wicklow. In J. Lyttleton and T. O'Keeffe (eds), *The manor in medieval and early modern Ireland*, 132–59. Four Courts Press, Dublin.

Sheehan, J. 1998 Early Viking-age silver hoards from Ireland and their Scandinavian elements. In H.B. Clarke, M. Ní Mhaonaigh and R. Ó Floinn (eds), *Ireland and Scandinavia in the early Viking Age*, 166–202. Taylor and Francis, Dublin.

Sheehan, J. 2011 Hiberno-Scandinavian broad-band armrings. In J. Graham-Campbell (ed.), *The Cuerdale hoard and related Viking-age silver and gold, from Britain and Ireland, in the British Museum*, 94–100. British Museum Press, London.

Sheehan, J. 2014 Silver. In M. Hurley and I. Russell (eds), *Woodstown: a Scandinavian settlement in context*, 194–222. Four Courts Press, Dublin.

Sherard, J.L. 2009 Analysis of daub from Mound V, Moundville: its role as an architectural indicator. *Bulletin of the Alabama Museum of Natural History* (2009), 27–42.

Sheridan, A. 1995 Irish Neolithic pottery: the story in 1995. In I. Kinnes and G. Varndell (eds), '*Unbaked urns of rudely shape*': *essays on British and Irish pottery*, 3–21. Oxbow, Oxford.

Sheridan, A. 2010 Irish Neolithic pottery: the story in 1995. In I. Kinnes and G,. Varndell (eds), *'Unbaked urns of rudely shape': essays on British and Irish pottery*, 3–21. Oxbow, Oxford.

Siegmund, F. 1995 Merovingian beads on the Lower Rhine. *Journal of the Society of Bead Researchers* **7**, 37–53.

Sigurðardóttir, S. 2008 *Building with turf.* Smárit Byggðasafns Skagfirðinga X. Skagafjörður Historic Museum, Langholt, Iceland.

Sikora, M. and Reilly, F. 2011 Tomfarney. In M. Cahill and M. Sikora (eds), *Breaking ground, finding graves: reports on the excavations of burials by the National Museum of Ireland, 1927–2006*, 598–645. National Museum of Ireland Monograph Series 4. Wordwell, Bray.

Smith, M.A. 1959 Some Somerset hoards and their place in the Bronze Age of southern Britain. *Proceedings of the Prehistoric Society* **25**, 144–87.

Smyth, A.P. 1994 Kings, saints and sagas. In K. Hannigan and W. Nolan (eds), *Wicklow: history and society*, 41–111. Geography Publications, Dublin.

Smyth, A.P. (ed.) 2000 *Seanchas: studies in early and medieval Irish archaeology, history and literature in honour of Francis J. Byrne.* Four Courts Press, Dublin.

Soil Survey Division 1993 *Soil survey manual.* Department of Agriculture Handbook 18. Department of Agriculture, Washington, DC.

Standish, C.D., Dhuime, B., Hawkesworth, C.J. and Pike, A.W.G. 2015 A non-local source of Irish Chalcolithic and Early Bronze Age gold. *Proceedings of the Prehistoric Society* **81**, 149–77 (doi:10.1017/ppr.2015.4).

Steier, P. and Rom, W. 2000 The use of Bayesian statistics for ^{14}C dates of chronologically ordered samples: a critical analysis. *Radiocarbon* **42**, 183–98.

Stenhouse, M.J. and Baxter, M.S. 1983 ^{14}C reproducibility: evidence from routine dating of archaeological samples. *PACT* **8**, 147–61.

Sternke, F. 2010 From boy to man: 'rights' of passage and the lithic assemblage from a Neolithic mount in Tullahedy, Co. Tipperary. In M. Stanley, E. Danaher and J. Eogan (eds), *Creative minds: production, manufacturing and invention in ancient Ireland. Proceedings of a public seminar on archaeological discoveries on national road schemes, August 2009*, 1–14. National Roads Authority Monograph Series No. 7. National Roads Authority, Dublin.

Sternke, F. 2011 The stone tools. In R.M. Cleary and H. Kelleher (eds), *Archaeological excavations at Tullaheedy, County Tipperary: Neolithic settlement in north Munster*, 216–321. Collins Press, Cork.

Stevens, P. 2005 Killoran 6. In M.J. Gowen, J. Ó Néill and M. Phillips (eds), *The Lisheen Mine archaeological project 1996–8*, 292–4. Wordwell, Bray.

Stout, G. 1994 Wicklow's prehistoric landscape. In K. Hannigan and W. Nolan (eds), *Wicklow: history and society*, 1–40. Geography Publications, Dublin.

Stout, G. 2000 Wicklow's prehistoric landscape. In A.P. Smyth (ed.), *Seanchas: studies in early and medieval Irish archaeology, history and literature in honour of Francis J. Byrne*, 1–40. Four Courts Press, Dublin.

Stuijts, I. 2005 Wood and charcoal identification. In M. Gowen, J. Ó Néill and M. Phillips (eds), *The Lisheen Mine Archaeological Project 1996–8*, 137–86 and appendix. Wordwell, Dublin.

Stuijts, I. 2007 Wood and charcoal research in Ireland. In E.M. Murphy and N.J. Whitehouse (eds), *Environmental archaeology in Ireland*, 179–93. Oxbow, Oxford.

Stuijts, I. 2021 Charcoal identifications from Rathgall, Rath East, County Wicklow, with detailed sample description. Unpublished report, available on dri.ie.

Stuijts, I., O'Donnell, L. and Lyons, S. 2012 Cloud-computing in anthracology—experiences with the WODAN online database in Ireland. In E. Badal, Y. Carrión, M. Macías *et al.* (eds), *Wood and charcoal: evidence for human and natural history*, 291–9. *Saguntum* Special Issue 13. Departament de Prehistòria i Arqueologia, Universitat de València.

Stuiver, M. and Kra, R.S. 1986 Editorial comment. *Radiocarbon* **28**, ii.

Stuiver, M. and Polach, H.A. 1977 Reporting of ^{14}C data. *Radiocarbon* **19** (3), 355–63.

Stuiver, M. and Reimer, P.J. 1986 A computer program for radiocarbon age calibration. *Radiocarbon* **28** (2B), 1022–30.

Stuiver, M. and Reimer, P.J. 1993 Extended ^{14}C data base and revised CALIB 3.0 ^{14}C calibration program. *Radiocarbon* **35** (1), 215–30.

Suchey, J.M. and Katz, D. 1986 Age determination from the male *os pubis*. *American Journal of Physical Anthropology* **69**, 427–35.

Suchey, J.M., Brooks, S.T. and Katz, D. 1988 *Instructional materials accompanying female pubic symphyseal models of the Suchey Brooks system.* Distributed by France Casting, Colorado.

Suddaby, I. 2003 The excavation of two Late Bronze Age roundhouses at Ballyprior Beg, Island Magee, County Antrim. *Ulster Journal of Archaeology* **62**, 45–91.

Sweetman, H.S. 1877 *Calendar of documents relating to Ireland preserved in Her Majesty's Public Record Office, London. Vol. 2: 1252–1284*. Longman, London.

Sweetman, P.D. 1978 Archaeological excavations at Trim Castle, Co. Meath, 1971–4. *Proceedings of the Royal Irish Academy* **78**C, 127–98.

Sweetman, P.D. 1979 Archaeological excavations at Ferns Castle, County Wexford. *Proceedings of the Royal Irish Academy* **79C**, 217–45.

Sweetman, P.D. 1980 Archaeological excavations at King John's Castle, Limerick. *Proceedings of the Royal Irish Academy* **80**C, 207–29.

Sweetman, P.D. 1984 Archaeological excavations at Shop Street, Drogheda, Co. Louth. *Proceedings of the Royal Irish Academy* **84**C, 171–224.

Tait, H. 1976 *Jewellery through 7,000 years*. British Museum Press, London.

Taylor, J.J. 1980 *Bronze Age goldwork of the British Isles.* Cambridge University Press, Cambridge.

Telford, W.M., Geldart, L.P. and Sheriff, R.E. 1990 *Applied geophysics* (2nd edn). Cambridge University Press, Cambridge.

Tempelmann-Maczyńska, M. 1985 *Die Perlen der römischen Kaiserzeit und der frühen Phase der Völkerwanderungszeit im mitteleuropäischen Barbaricum.* Römisch-germanische Forschungen, Bd. 43. Von Zabern, Mainz am Rhein.

Théry-Parisot, I. 2002 Gathering of firewood during the Palaeolithic. In S. Thiébault (ed.), *Charcoal analysis: methodological approaches, palaeoecological results and wood uses*, 243–9. British Archaeological Reports, International Series 1063. Archaeopress, Oxford.

Théry-Parisot, I. and Henry, A. 2012 Seasoned or green? Radial cracks analysis as a method for identifying the use of green wood as fuel in archaeological charcoal. *Journal of Archaeological Science* **39** (2), 381–8.

Thevenot, J.P. 1998 Un outillage de bronzier: le dépot de la Petite Laugère, à Génelard (Saône-et-Loire, France).

In C. Mordant, M. Pernot and M. Rychner (eds), *L'atelier du bronzier en Europe du XXe au VIIIe siècle avant notre ère*, 123–44. Comité des travaux historiques et sciêntifiques, Paris.

Thomas, J. 2007 *Place and memory: excavations at the Pict's Knowe, Holywood and Holm Farm, Dumfries and Galloway, 1994–8*. Oxbow, Oxford.

Thompson, T.J.U. 2005 Heat-induced dimensional changes in bone and their consequences for forensic anthropology. *Journal of Forensic Sciences* **50** (5), 1008–15.

Tierney, J. 1998 Woods and woodlands in early medieval Munster. In M. Monk and J. Sheehan (eds), *Early medieval Munster: archaeology, history and society*, 53–8. Cork University Press, Cork.

Tierney, M. and Johnston, P. 2009 Archaeological excavation report E0425—Harristown Big, Co. Wexford, Ireland. Unpublished report for Eachtra Archaeological Projects Ltd.

Towle, A.C. 2002 A scientific and archaeological investigation of prehistoric glasses from Italy. Unpublished Ph.D thesis, University of Nottingham.

Turner, C.E.L. 1998 A re-interpretation of the Late Bronze Age metalwork hoards of Essex and Kent. Unpublished Ph.D thesis, Glasgow University.

Tylecote, R.F. 1978 Early tin ingots and tinstone from western Europe and the Mediterranean. In A.D. Franklin, J.J. Olin and T.A. Wertime (eds), *The search for ancient tin*, 49–52. Smithsonian Institution, Washington, DC.

Tylecote, R.F. 1986 *The prehistory of metallurgy in the British Isles*. Institute of Metals, London.

van der Plicht, J., Wijma, S., Aerts, A.T., Pertuisot, M.H. and Meijer, H.A.J. 2000 Status report: the Groningen AMS facility. *Nuclear Instruments and Methods in Physics Research B* **172**, 58–65.

Varbert, J., Gratuze, B. and Kaul, F. 2015 Between Egypt, Mesopotamia and Scandinavia: Late Bronze Age glass beads found in Denmark. *Journal of Archaeological Science* **54**, 168–81.

Varbert, J., Gratuze, B., Kaul, F., Haslund Hansen, A., Rotea, M. and Wittenberger, M. 2016 Mesopotamian glass from Late Bronze Age Egypt, Romania, Germany, and Denmark. *Journal of Archaeological Science* 74, 184–94.

Varndell, G. 2001 Ringing the changes: when terminology matters. *Antiquity* **75**, 515–16.

Veldhuijzen, H.A. 2003 'Slag fun'—a new tool for archaeometallurgy: development of an analytical (P)EDX-XRF method for iron-rich materials. *Papers of the Institute of Archaeology* **14**, 102–18.

Venclová, N., Chenery, S., Henderson, J., Hložek, J., Hulínský, V. and Šulová, L. 2011 Late Bronze Age mixed-alkali glasses from Bohemia. *Archeologicke Rozhledy* **63B**, 559–85.

Vogel, J.S., Southon, J.R., Nelson, D.E. and Brown, T.A. 1984 Performance of catalytically condensed carbon for use in accelerator mass-spectrometry. *Nuclear Instruments and Methods in Physics Research* B **233**, 289–93.

Waddell, J. 1995 Celts, Celticisation and the Irish Bronze Age. In J. Waddell and E. Shee Twohig (eds), *Ireland in the Bronze Age*, 158–69. Stationery Office, Dublin.

Waddell, J. 1998 *The prehistoric archaeology of Ireland*. Galway University Press, Galway.

Waddell, J. 2010 and 2022 *The prehistoric archaeology of Ireland*. Wordwell, Bray.

Waddell, J. 2011 Continuity, cult and contest. In R. Schot, C. Newman and E. Bhreathnach (eds), *Landscapes of cult and kingship*, 192–211. Four Courts Press, Dublin.

Wailes, B. 2007 Excavation of the Summit Area. In S.A. Johnston and B. Wailes, *Dún Ailinne: excavations at an Irish royal site, 1968–1975*, 9–27. University Museum Monograph 129. University of Pennsylvania Museum of Archaeology and Anthropology, Philadelphia.

Wakeman, W.F. 1894 *Catalogue of antiquities belonging to the Royal Irish Academy now in the Science and Art Museum, Dublin*. National Museum of Science and Art, Dublin.

Walker, P.L. and Miller, K.P. 2005 Time, temperature and oxygen availability: an experimental study of the effects of environmental conditions on the colour and organic content of cremated bones. *American Journal of Physical Anthropology Supplement* **40**, 216–17.

Wallace, P.F. 2012 Knowth and Dublin: a comparison of early medieval archaeologies. In G. Eogan (ed.), *The archaeology of Knowth in the first and second millennia AD*, 708–45. Royal Irish Academy, Dublin.

Ward, G.K. and Wilson, S.R. 1978 Procedures for comparing and combining radiocarbon age determinations: a critique. *Archaeometry* **20**, 19–32.

Warmenbol, E. 1999 Le soleil des morts. Les ors protohistoriques de Han-sur-Lesse (Namur, Belgique). *Germania* 77, 39-69.

Warmenbol, E. 2004 Gold pickings and PIXE analysis.

More about the Bronze Age gold found in the cave of Han-sur-Lesse (Namur, Belgium). *Nuclear Instruments and Methods in Physics Research B* **226**, 208–21.

Warmenbol, E. 2017 Un anneau pénannulaire plaqué d'or (dit 'hair-ring') du Bronze final découvert à Thieusies (prov. de Hainaut, Belgique). *Lunula* **25**, 69–72.

Warner, R. 2004 Irish gold artefacts: observations from Hartmann's analytical data. In H. Roche, E. Grogan, J. Bradley, J. Coles and B. Raftery (eds), *From megaliths to metals: essays in honour of George Eogan*, 72–82. Oxbow, Oxford.

Warner, R. 2014 The gold fragments from Haughey's Fort, Co. Armagh: description and XRF analysis. *Emania* **22**, 69–76.

Warner, R. 2015 The gold ornaments from Rathgall: the analytical evidence for their date and the sources of their gold. *Journal of Irish Archaeology* **23**, 143–55.

Warner, R. and Cahill, M. 2012 Analysing ancient Irish gold: an assessment of the Hartmann database. *Journal of Irish Archaeology* **20**, 45–52.

Warner, R., Moles, N. and Chapman, R. 2010 Evidence for Early Bronze Age tin and gold extraction in the Mourne Mountains, Co. Down. *Journal of the Mining Heritage Trust of Ireland* **10**, 29–36.

Warren, G.M. and Little, A. 2017 The stone tool assemblage. In K. Cleary, A. Little and G.M. Warren, 'Material culture', in G. Eogan and K. Cleary (eds), *Excavations at Knowth 6: The Neolithic archaeology of the large passage tomb at Knowth, Co. Meath*, 471–85. Royal Irish Academy, Dublin.

Warren, W.P. 1993 *Wicklow in the Ice Age: introduction and guide to the glacial geology of the Wicklow district.* Geological Survey of Ireland, Dublin.

Waterbolk, H.T. 1971 Working with radiocarbon dates. *Proceedings of the Prehistoric Society* **37**, 15–33.

Waterman, D.M. 1952 Excavations at the entrance to Carrickfergus Castle, 1950. *Ulster Journal of Archaeology* **15**, 103–18.

Waterman, D.M. 1954 Excavations at Clough Castle, Co. Down. *Ulster Journal of Archaeology* **17**, 103–57.

Waterman, D. 1965 The court cairn at Annaghmare, Co. Armagh. *Ulster Journal of Archaeology* **28**, 3–46.

Waterman, D.M. 1967–8 Medieval pottery from Dalkey Island. In C.D. Liversage (ed.), 'Excavations at Dalkey Island, Co. Dublin, 1956–59'. *Proceedings of the Royal Irish Academy* **66**C, 186–91.

Waterman, D.M. 1997 *Excavations at Navan Fort 1961–1971* (ed. C.J. Lynn). Stationery Office, Belfast.

Webb, D.A., Parnell, J. and Doogue, D. 1996 *An Irish Flora*. Dundalgan Press, Dundalk.

Webley, L., Adams, S. and Brück, J. 2020 *The social context of technology. Non-ferrous metalworking in later prehistoric Britain and Ireland.* Prehistoric Society Research Paper 11. Oxbow, Oxford.

Weir, D.A. 1993 An environmental history of the Navan area, Co. Armagh. Unpublished Ph.D thesis, Queen's University, Belfast.

Westropp, T.J. 1902 The ancient forts of Ireland: being a contribution towards our knowledge of their types, affinities, and structural features. *Transactions of the Royal Irish Academy* **31** (XIV), 579–730.

Wheeler, E.A., Baas, P. and Gasson, P. (eds) 1989 IAWA list of microscopic features for hardwood identification. *IAWA Bulletin* **10**, 219–332.

Whitehead, R. 1996 *Buckles, 1250–1800.* Greenlight Publishing, Chelmsford.

Wilde, W.R. 1861 *A descriptive catalogue of the antiquities of animal materials and bronze in the museum of the Royal Irish Academy,* Vol. 2. Hodges, Smith and Co., Dublin.

Wilkins, B. 2008 N6 Galway to Ballinasloe Scheme, Contract 2. Final report on archaeological investigations at Site E2437, a Bronze Age cremation pyre and burnt mound in the townland of Newford, Co. Galway. Unpublished report for Headland Archaeology.

Wilkins, B. 2011 Excavating death on the M6: 3500 BC to AD 1500. In S. Conran, E. Danaher and M. Stanley (eds), *Past times, changing fortunes*, 99–112. Archaeology and the National Roads Authority Monograph 8. National Roads Authority, Dublin.

Williams, B.B. 1978 Excavations at Lough Eskragh, Co. Tyrone. *Ulster Journal of Archaeology* **41**, 37–48.

Williams, C.E. and McArdie, P. 1978 Ireland. In H.U. Bowies, A. Kvalheim and H.W. Haslam (eds), *Mineral deposits of Europe I. Northwest Europe*, 319–45. Institution of Mining and Metallurgy/Mineralogical Society, London.

Williams, G. and Mytum, H. 1998 *Llawhaden, Dyfed: excavations on a group of small defended enclosures, 1980–4.* British Archaeological Reports, British Series 275. Archaeopress, Oxford.

Woodman, P.C. and Scannell, M. 1993 A context for the Lough Gur lithics. In E. Shee Twohig and M. Ronayne (eds), *Past perceptions: the prehistoric archaeology of south-west Ireland*, 53–62. Cork University Press, Cork.

Woodman, P.C., Finlay, N. and Anderson, E. 2006 *The*

archaeology of a collection: the Keiller–Knowles collection of the National Museum of Ireland. Wordwell, Dublin.

Wyss, R. 1971 Siedlungswesen und Verkehrswege. In W. Drack (ed.), *Ur- und frühgeschichtliche Archäologie der Schweiz III: Bronzezeit*, 103–22. Schweizerische Gesellschaft für Ur- und Frühgeschichte, Basel.

Wyss, R. 1974 Technik, Wirtschaft, Handel und Kriegswesen der Eisenzeit. In W. Drack (ed.), *Ur- und frühgeschichtliche Archäologie der Schweiz IV: Eisenzeit*, 104–38. Schweizerische Gesellschaft für Ur- und Frühgeschichte, Basel.

Xu, S., Anderson, R., Bryant, C. *et al.* 2004 Capabilities of the new SUERC 5MV AMS facility for ^{14}C dating. *Radiocarbon* **46**, 59–64.

INDEX

Note: Page locators in bold refer to photographs, illustrations and diagrams.